Contents

KT-164-178

Introduction to
Kenya

Lapped by the Indian Ocean, straddling the equator, and with Mount Kenya rising above a magnificent landscape of forested hills, patchwork farms and wooded savanna, Kenya is a richly rewarding place to travel. The country's dramatic geography has resulted in a great range of natural habitats, harbouring a huge variety of wildlife, while its history of migration and conquest has brought about a fascinating social panorama, which includes the Swahili city-states of the coast and the Maasai of the Rift Valley.

Kenya's world-famous national parks, tribal peoples and superb beaches lend the country an exotic image with magnetic appeal. Treating it as a succession of tourist sights, however, is not the most stimulating way to experience Kenya. If you get off the beaten track, you can enter the world inhabited by most Kenyans: a ceaselessly active scene of muddy farm tracks, corrugated-iron huts, tea shops and lodging houses, crammed buses and streets wandered by goats and children. Both on and off the tourist routes, you'll find warmth and openness, and an abundance of superb scenery – rolling savanna dotted with Maasai herds and wild animals, high Kikuyu moorlands grazed by cattle and sheep, and dense forests full of monkeys and birdsong. Of course the country is not all postcard-perfect: Kenya's role in fighting Al-Shabaab terrorists in Somalia has resulted in reprisal attacks, while if you start a conversation with any local you'll soon find out about the country's deep economic and social tensions.

Where to go

The **coast** and major **game parks** are the most obvious targets. If you come to Kenya on an organized tour, you're likely to have your time divided between these two attractions. Despite the impact of human population pressures, Kenya's **wildlife spectacle** remains a compelling experience. The million-odd annual visitors are easily absorbed in such a large

ABOVE AGAMA LIZARD **OPPOSITE** NAIROBI AT DUSK

country, and there's nothing to prevent you escaping the predictable tourist bottlenecks: even on an organized trip, you should not feel tied down.

The major **national parks and reserves**, watered by seasonal streams, are mostly located in savanna on the fringes of the **highlands** that take up much of the southwest quarter of the country. The vast majority of Kenyans live in these rugged hills, where the ridges are a mix of smallholdings and plantations. Through the heart of the highlands sprawls the **Great Rift Valley**, an archetypal East African scene of dry, thorn-tree savanna, splashed with lakes and studded by volcanoes.

The hills and grasslands on either side of the valley – **Laikipia** and the **Mara conservancies**, for example – are great walking country, as are the high forests and moors of the **Central Highlands** and **Mount Kenya** itself – a major target and a feasible climb if you're reasonably fit and take your time.

Nairobi, at the southern edge of the highlands, is most often used just as a gateway, but the capital has plenty of diversions to occupy your time while arranging your travels and some very worthwhile natural and cultural attractions in its own right.

In the far west, towards **Lake Victoria**, lies gentler countryside, where you can travel for days without seeing another foreign visitor and immerse yourself in Kenyan life and culture. Beyond the rolling **tea plantations** of Kericho and the hot plains around the port of Kisumu lies the steep volcanic massif of **Mount Elgon**, astride the Ugandan

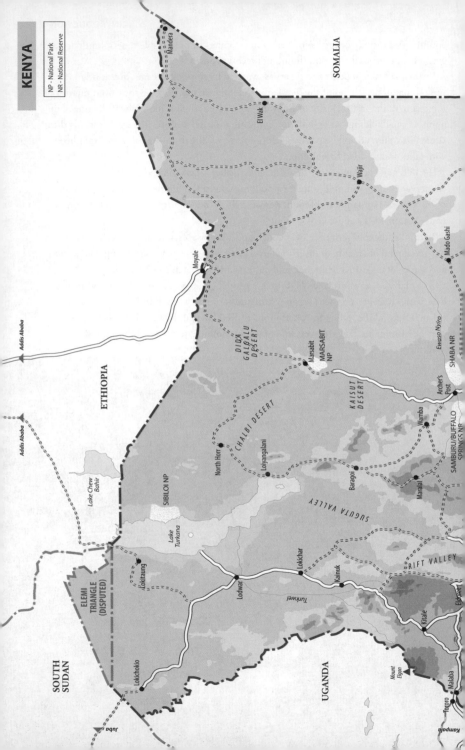

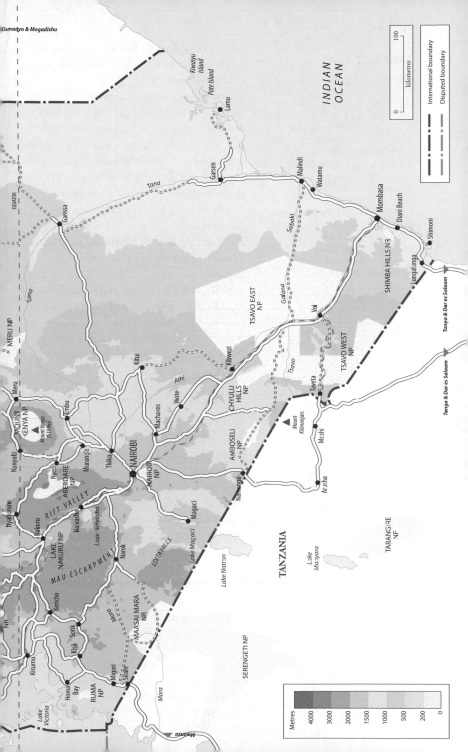

border. The **Kakamega Forest**, with its unique wildlife, is nearby, and more than enough reason to strike out west.

In the north, the land is **desert** or semi-desert, broken only by the highlight of gigantic **Lake Turkana** in the northwest, almost unnaturally blue in the brown wilderness and one of the most spectacular and memorable of all African regions.

Kenya's "upcountry" interior is separated from the **Indian Ocean** by the arid plains around Tsavo East National Park. Historically, these have formed a barrier that accounts in part for the distinctive culture around **Mombasa** and the coastal region. Here, the historical record, preserved in mosques, tombs and the ruins of ancient towns cut from the jungle, marks out the area's **Swahili civilization**. An almost continuous **coral reef** runs along the length of the coast, beyond the white-sand beaches, protecting a shallow, safe lagoon from the Indian Ocean.

When to go

Kenya has complicated and rather unpredictable weather patterns, and the impact of **climate change** is striking hard. Broadly, the seasons are: hot and dry from January to March; hot and wet from April to June (the "long rains"); warm and dry from July to October; and warm and wet for a few weeks in November and early December – a period called the "short rains". At high altitudes, it may rain at almost any time. Western Kenya, including the Maasai Mara, has a scattered rainfall pattern influenced by Lake Victoria, while the eastern half of the country, and especially the coast itself, are largely controlled by the Indian Ocean's **monsoon winds** – the dry northeast monsoon (*kaskazi*) blowing in from November to March or April and the moist southeast monsoon (*kusi*) blowing in from May to October. The *kusi* normally brings the heaviest rains to the coast in May and June.

KENYA'S PEOPLES

For Kenya's forty-plus ethnic groups, the most important social marker is language and the best definition of a tribe (a term with no pejorative connotation) is people sharing a common first language. It's not uncommon for people to speak three languages – their own, Swahili and English – or even four if they have mixed parentage.

The largest tribe, the **Kikuyu**, based in the Central Highlands, make up about 20 percent of the population; the **Kalenjin** from the Rift Valley 15 percent; the **Luhya** of western Kenya 14 percent; the **Luo** from the Nyanza region around Kisumu 12 percent; and the **Kamba** from east of Nairobi 11 percent. Many people from these big ethnic groups have had a largely Westernized orientation for two or three generations and their economic and political influence is considerable. Which isn't to say you won't come across highly educated and articulate people from every tribal background. "Tribes" have never been closed units and families often include members of different ethnic background, nowadays more than ever. Politics still tends to have an ethnic dimension, however: people retain a strong sense of whether they are locals or newcomers. Inter-tribal prejudice, although often regarded as taboo, or at best an excuse for humour, is still quite commonplace and occasionally becomes violent.

Smaller ethnic groups include the closely related **Maasai** and **Samburu** peoples, who make up little more than two percent of the population. Well known for their distinctive and still commonly worn traditional dress and associated with the national reserves named after them, they herd their animals across vast reaches of savanna and, when access to water demands it, drive them onto private land and even into the big towns. Many **Turkana** and some of the other remote northern groups also retain their traditional garb and rather tooled-up appearance, with spears and other weapons much in evidence.

Kenya has a large and diverse **Asian** population (perhaps more than 100,000 people), predominantly Punjabi- and Gujarati-speakers from northwest India and Pakistan, mostly based in the cities and larger towns. Descendants in part of the labourers who came to build the Uganda railway, they also include many whose ancestors arrived in its wake, to trade and set up businesses. There's also a dispersed Christian Goan community, identified by their Portuguese surnames, and a diminishing **Arabic** community, largely on the coast.

Lastly, there are still an estimated 30,000 **European** residents – from British ex-servicemen to Italian aristocrats – and another 30,000 temporary expats. Some European Kenyans maintain a scaled-down version of the old farming and ranching life, and a few still hold senior civil service positions. Increasingly, however, the community is turning to the tourist industry for a more secure future.

AVERAGE DAILY TEMPERATURES AND RAINFALL

	Jan	Feb	Mar	Apr	May	Jun	Jul	Aug	Sep	Oct	Nov	Dec
NAIROBI (ALT 1660M)												
Max/min (°C)	25/12	26/13	25/14	24/14	22/13	21/12	21/11	21/11	24/11	24/13	23/13	23/13
Rainfall (mm)	38	64	125	211	158	46	15	23	31	53	109	86
Days with rainfall	5	6	11	16	17	9	6	7	6	8	15	11
MOMBASA (SEA LEVEL)												
Max/min (°C)	31/24	31/24	31/25	30/24	28/24	28/23	27/22	27/22	28/22	29/23	29/24	30/24
Rainfall (mm)	25	18	64	196	320	119	89	66	63	86	97	61
Days with rainfall	6	3	7	15	20	15	14	16	14	10	10	9
KISUMU (ALT 1135M)												
Max/min (°C)	29/18	29/19	28/19	28/18	27/18	27/17	27/17	27/17	28/17	29/18	29/18	29/18
Rainfall (mm)	48	81	140	191	155	84	58	76	64	56	86	102
Days with rainfall	6	8	12	14	14	9	8	10	8	7	9	8

Temperatures are determined largely by altitude: you can reckon on a drop of 0.6°C for every 100m you climb from sea level. While the temperature at sea level in Mombasa rarely ever drops below 20°C, even just before dawn, Nairobi, up at 1660m, has a moderate climate, and in the cool season in July and August can drop to 5°C at night, even though daytime highs in the shade at that time of year easily exceed 21°C and the sun is scorching hot. Swimming pools around the country are rarely heated, and only those on the coast are guaranteed to be warm.

The main **tourist seasons** tie in with the rainfall patterns: the biggest influxes of visitors are in December–January and July–August. Dry-season travel has a number of advantages, not least of which is the greater visibility of wildlife as animals are concentrated along the diminishing watercourses. July to September is probably the best period, overall, for game-viewing, with early September almost certain to coincide with the annual wildebeest migration in the Maasai Mara. October, November and March are the months with the clearest seas for snorkelling and diving. In the long rains, the mountain parks are occasionally closed, as the muddy tracks are undriveable. But the rainy seasons shouldn't deter travel unduly: the rains usually come only in short afternoon or evening cloudbursts, and the landscape is strikingly green and fresh even if the skies may be cloudy. There are bonuses, too: fewer other tourists, reduced prices and often perfect light for photography.

Author picks

Our authors have travelled the length and breadth of Kenya, squashing into countless matatus and buses in the preparation of this new edition. Here are some of their favourite experiences and encounters.

Exploring the mountains of the north Climbing from northern Kenya's arid plains into lush highland forests delivers you into a world of gushing streams and cool shade (p.530).

Nairobi nightlife Once a virtual no-go zone after dark, Nairobi's Central Business District has reignited at weekends, with dozens of clubs, bars and restaurants (p.136) shaking until the early hours.

Umani Springs Relax at this affordable and beautifully designed self-catering lodge in the idyllic Kibwezi Forest, just minutes from the rush of the Nairobi–Mombasa highway (p.324).

Kaya Kinondo The Mijikenda sacred groves (box, p.434) are ancient sites in the coastal forest, preserving wildlife as well as cultural traditions. This is the first to open its secrets to visitors.

Maralal International Camel Derby This fun and unique event, a celebration for the local Samburu people, brings colour to this usually arid and dusty northern town over a weekend in August (box, p.525).

Nyama choma Tuck into a traditional Kenya meatfest, where scrumptious grilled goat is paired with piping hot *ugali* (solid cornmeal porridge), chopped *kachumbari* (tomato and onion relish) and a bottle or two of local brew (p.62).

Kitengela Glass The sheer creative energy that emerges from this community of artisans and an endless supply of old bottles has to be seen to be believed (p.141).

Karura Forest An astonishingly large sanctuary of highland forest, close to the heart of Nairobi, Karura's stands of giant trees, caves and waterfall – recently opened to visitors – are just a short walk from the busy traffic (p.115).

> Our author recommendations don't end here. We've flagged up our favourite places – a perfectly sited hotel, an atmospheric café, a special restaurant – throughout the guide, highlighted with the ★ symbol.

FROM TOP NYAMA CHOMA, NAIROBI; MOUNT NYIRU AND THE EWASO RONGAI VALLEY; KITENGELA GLASS

19

things not to miss

It's not possible to see everything that Kenya has to offer in one trip – and we don't suggest you try. What follows is a selective and subjective taste of some of the country's highlights, including standout experiences, spectacular sights and unexpected wildlife. All entries have a page reference taking you straight to the relevant place in the book, where you can find out more.

1

1 MOUNT KENYA
Page 169
Many climbers consider Africa's second-highest peak a tougher test than Kilimanjaro: it's certainly less of a highway to the top. You'll be glad of its *via ferrata* on the last morning.

2 MARA NABOISHO CONSERVANCY
Page 373
This conservancy in the greater Mara region combines wildlife conservation with community involvement and offers outstanding viewing of big cats, elephants and giraffes.

3 THIMLICH OHINGA
Page 267
Even most Kenyans have never heard of their most impressive upcountry ancient site – huge stone circles in a remote part of western Kenya.

4 GRACEFUL HIPPOS
Page 347
The chain of lakes at Mzima Springs, fed by subterranean meltwater from Kilimanjaro, is a magical location in an exceptionally beautiful park – Tsavo West.

4

5

6

7

8

9

13

10 WARRIOR TRAINING
Page 372

Head to a Maasai-run eco-camp and learn the ways of warriorhood – which you'll soon discover involves playfighting with sticks and much singing and jumping.

11 LAKE NAIVASHA
Page 205

The perfect getaway from Nairobi: excellent backpackers hostels, boating, a music festival, hippos , a rich array of birdlife and the secluded Crater Lake Game Sanctuary.

12 LOLLING IN THE LAGOON
Box, page 419

The Indian Ocean coast is sheltered by a coral reef for nearly its entire length: you can drift among shoals of fish or skim around on a kite- or surfboard.

13 NAIROBI NATIONAL PARK
Page 144

On the city's doorstep, the park is home to nearly all Kenya's big mammals, including the largest of Kenya's antelopes, the eland.

14 DESERT LAKE
Page 515

Venture to the shores of Lake Turkana in the barren lands close to the Ethiopian border where the climate is harsh, life precarious and the landscapes searingly beautiful.

14

15

16

Itineraries

The following itineraries include the most important parks, lakes, highlands, deserts, beaches and towns; and the top spots for birdwatching, megafauna, rare mammals and appreciating Kenya's ethnic diversity. Join the itineraries together and you'd have an unforgettable three-month tour of the country. NP: National Park; NR: National Reserve.

NORTHERN FRONTIERS

From the capital's contrasts to the highs and lows of the highlands, this route is about extremes – nowhere more so than where the Jade Sea cuts through the desert. Allow two to four weeks for some or all of this loop.

❶ Nairobi Wildlife, parks and forests bring balance to East Africa's biggest city, where urban life – from museums and crafts workshops to cutting-edge restaurants and clubs – sets the agenda. **See p.98**

❷ Mount Kenya NP Scale Africa's second-highest peak on one of four different routes, but take time to enjoy the wildlife-rich forests and frenetically active towns on the lower slopes. **See p.169**

❸ Laikipia Challenging the Maasai Mara as Kenya's best wildlife destination, Laikipia offers rare rhinos and opulent conservancy stays as well as wild dog-tracking and budget camping. **See p.505**

❹ Maralal This semi-desert, alternately dusty and muddy cowboy outpost, the unofficial capital of the Samburu people, hosts an annual camel derby. **See p.524**

❺ Samburu NR Watered by the forest-fringed Ewaso Nyiro, this is a relaxing area to encounter northern wildlife – from reticulated giraffe to Somali ostrich. **See p.377**

❻ Marsabit NP A true desert oasis, this mountainous outburst of volcanic craters and rich soil stands thick with misty, creeper-swathed forest. **See p.548**

❼ Lake Turkana Getting to the fabled Jade Sea is half the fun, but the annual Lake Turkana Festival is a huge incentive. And at any time of year, expect colourful cultural adventures. **See p.515**

WESTERN LAKES, SAVANNAS AND FORESTS

Strike out across the Great Rift Valley to freshwater and soda lakes, then climb to the Mara basin's rolling grasslands, one of the last rainforests in Kenya, and giant Lake Victoria. Some of this journey could be done in a fortnight, but allow three weeks to do it all.

❶ Lake Naivasha Head into the Rift Valley for a breezy escape from Nairobi, with country retreats and backpackers camps and walks in Hell's Gate and austere Mount Longonot. **See p.205**

❷ Maasai Mara NR Only in the Mara can you experience a wildlife panorama stretching from horizon to horizon. Stay on a community wildlife conservancy and see the herds without the crowds. **See p.356**

❸ Lake Victoria Spend a day or two in characterful Kisumu and catch musicians and markets. Then head for one of the islands to see rock paintings and watch fishermen. **See p.253**

ABOVE FROM LEFT FORT JESUS, MOMBASA; RETICULATED GIRAFFES, SAMBURU NR; FISHING BOATS ON LAKE VICTORIA

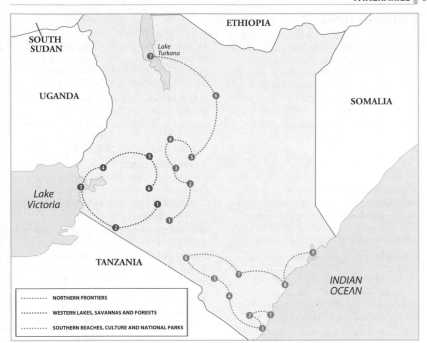

④ Kakamega Forest NP The bird and reptile hotspot of western Kenya, this stranded piece of central African rainforest is a joy for independent travellers. **See p.306**

⑤ Lake Baringo On one side the changing lake colours, crocs and hippos and Njemps fishermen of the lake; on the other the green lawns, backpacker haunts and safari camps of the shores and islands. **See p.237**

⑥ Lake Nakuru NP This Rift Valley soda lake is famous for black and white rhinos, leopards and (sometimes vast) flocks of flamingos. **See p.224**

SOUTHERN BEACHES, CULTURE AND NATIONAL PARKS

Historic sites dot Kenya's coast behind the coral beaches, while inland, vast national parks offer the classic safari experience. Allow three weeks for this loop, and don't stint on days in Lamu.

① Mombasa This island city, dating back more than a thousand years, is best explored on foot. Don't miss Fort Jesus Museum and the narrow streets of the Old Town. **See p.392**

② Shimba Hills A park of forested hills – Shimba is the only place to see sable antelope in Kenya – is less than an hour's drive from shimmering Diani Beach. **See p.428**

③ Kaya Kinondo The first Mijikenda sacred forest to be opened to visitors, this hidden jungle treat is packed with buttress-rooted trees and woodland wildlife. **See box, p.434**

④ Taita Hills Off the tourist routes, the people of these fertile peaks have preserved some of their culture – including fascinating caves of ancestors' skulls. **See p.331**

⑤ Tsavo West NP Prepare to be enchanted by Tsavo's landscapes, including lava flows and the magical Mzima Springs. **See p.346**

⑥ Amboseli NP Magnificent Kilimanjaro rises behind plains and marshes roamed by huge herds of elephants and other wildlife. **See p.337**

⑦ Tsavo East NP Kenya's biggest national park is home to brick-red elephants, lions and cheetahs, crocs, hippos and superb birdlife. **See p.351**

⑧ Malindi Diving, kitesurfing, eating out and nightlife are all big here, and it's close to the small resort of Watamu and fascinating Gedi ruins. **See p.464**

⑨ Lamu A cultural as well as a physical island, Lamu's unmissable combination of historic town and laidback beaches is the best place to finish a Kenya trip. **See p.478**

BIRDWATCHING

Kenya has the second highest bird count in Africa after the Democratic Republic of Congo. From October to February native species are boosted by migrants from Europe and Russia. This itinerary of important bird areas could be covered in three weeks and might allow you to see more than half of Kenya's 1100 species.

❶ African crowned eagles Along the Langata Road in suburban Nairobi, look out for the wheeling shapes of this huge raptor – and sometimes their nests in the Ngong Road Forest Sanctuary. **See p.116**

❷ Hinde's babbler One of Kenya's rarest endemics, this species can be seen at Wajee Nature Park in Mount Kenya's southwestern foothills – also home to common and pretty white-eyed slaty flycatchers. **See p.166**

❸ Sunbirds The forests of Kenya's Central Highlands – the Aberdare Range and Mount Kenya – harbour nine species of sunbird. The mountains are crowned by Afro-alpine moorlands where you'll see the striking scarlet-tufted sunbird. **See p.174**

❹ Goliath herons Freshwater Lake Baringo is an oasis in the dry northern Rift. The new Ruko Conservancy includes a Ramsar wetlands area

where you punt through a water-bird wonderland. **See p.238**

❺ Lesser flamingos Finding the iconic scene of vast pink flocks can be tricky: the classic site of Lake Nakuru has ceded to lakes Bogoria, Oloiden, Magadi and Elmenteita. **See p.235**

❻ Fish eagles Lake Naivasha has been transformed by horticulture, but there are still wooded spots around the shores where the thrilling sight – and cry – of fish eagles lends a haunting atmosphere. **See p.208**

❼ Great blue turacos The Kakamega Forest bursts with birdlife. These handsome, noisy fruit-eaters are the stars of a canopy that is also the unique home in Kenya of the blue-headed bee-eater. **See box, p.307**

❽ Ground hornbills and secretary birds In addition to these distinctive walking birds, the Maasai Mara ecosystem – the national reserve and neighbouring conservancies – is home to more than 400 other species. **See p.356**

❾ Sokoke scops owl As well as this miniature owl, there are five other endangered and localized species in the sprawling coastal woods of the Arabuko Sokoke forest, plus the red-capped robin chat, companion of the golden-rumped elephant shrew. **See box, p.455**

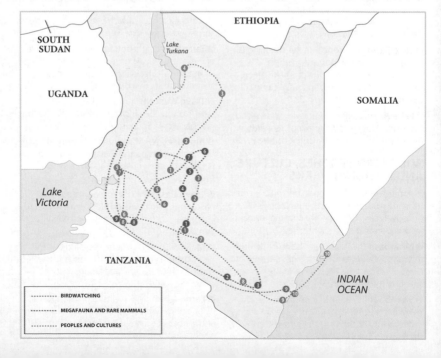

⑩ Crab plovers Just a short way from the resorts of Watamu and Malindi, these unusual visitors from Somalia can often be seen from the community bird hide at Mida Creek. See p.456

MEGAFAUNA AND RARE MAMMALS

Kenya's parks, reserves and conservancies are home to some of the densest concentrations of the earth's remaining megafauna, including a number of species that are highly endangered. An itinerary like this could be done in a couple of weeks.

❶ Black rhinos in Nairobi The city's sizeable national park is a surprising sanctuary for rare black rhinos as well as their less threatened white cousins. See p.147

❷ Eyeballing hippos Enter the underwater hide at Mzima Springs, and watch graceful hippos tip-toeing over the lake bed. See p.347

❸ Big tuskers in Tsavo East Strike out into the eastern parts of the park and track some of Africa's biggest remaining big tuskers. See p.351

❹ Mountain bongos Drive or track on foot through the dense forests of the Aberdare range in search of this handsome giant antelope. See p.192

❺ Northern white rhinos At Ol Pejeta Conservancy, the last of the world's rarest rhinos are easy to meet in their sanctuary within a sanctuary. See p.507

❻ Reticulated giraffes Kenya's handsomest giraffes are abundant in the Samburu National Reserve and neighbouring conservancies. See p.378

❼ Wild dogs on the run Watch a pack of multi-hued hunting dogs playing, hunting or lounging at Sosian Ranch – particularly entertaining when the pups are newly out of the den. See p.514

❽ Big cats in the Mara As felines move out of the busy Maasai Mara reserve the neighbouring conservancies are getting a reputation for some of the best lion-, leopard- and cheetah-watching in Africa. See p.359

❾ Wildebeest on the move Join many others witnessing thousands of wildebeest surging across the Mara River during migration time, or retreat to the quieter conservancy areas to see them massing on the plains. See box, p.363

⑩ Sitatunga One of Kenya's rarest and strangest antelopes can be easily spotted at the tiny Saiwa Swamp National Park. See p.292

PEOPLES AND CULTURES

Kenya's mix of peoples is one of its greatest assets, but the tension between diversity and tribalism needs constant rebalancing. To fully experience this ethnic and linguistic variety, you should follow this three-week itinerary in a spirit of reaching out and one-to-one interaction.

❶ Kikuyu You'll meet Kikuyu people everywhere, but their homeland is the Central Highlands. At the pretty Thomson's Falls, outside Nyahururu, traditionally dressed Kikuyu models pose for photos. See box, p.161

❷ Samburu herders Maralal is one of the best places to meet Samburu people – close ethno-linguistic cousins of the Maasai – especially at the annual camel derby in August. See p.524

❸ Rendille You may meet Rendille people in Marsabit, but you're more likely to encounter these traditional camel herders out in the desert when doing a camel trek yourself. See p.547

❹ Turkana Travelling through the far northwest, you're always aware of the local Turkana, and their fearsome (happily exaggerated) reputation. Make for Loiyangalani, especially for the annual cultural festival. See box, pp.520–521

❺ Luo-land The shores of Lake Victoria are the homeland of one of Kenya's largest and most cohesive peoples, the Luo – fishing and farming people who invented the fast-paced *benga* guitar music. See box, p.255

❻ Meeting the Maasai You'll run into Maasai all over southern Kenya, often as driver-guides and safari camp staff, but Maji Moto Group Ranch provides some of the most rewarding encounters. See p.372

❼ Kamba Security guards, soldiers, wood carvers and traditional poison-arrow hunters par excellence, Kamba folk these days are more likely to be running tech start-ups or coffee shops. Machakos is their buzzing capital. See box, p.315

❽ Taita The people of the steep Taita Hills, between the coast and the highlands, maintain shrines of ancestors' skulls. Their capital, Wundanyi, is a pleasant detour. See p.331

❾ Giriama Witchcraft and hooch aren't unique to the Giriama, but their millions of coconut trees make fine palm wine, while after-dark conversations will have you believing impossible things. See p.425

⑩ Swahili roots Many people on the coast regard themselves as Swahili and speak a rich and complex dialect of the language. The conservative culture of Pate island is particularly fascinating. See p.494

Wildlife

Kenya has more than a hundred species of large native **mammals** and its plains are home to the world's last surviving community of megafauna: the giant animals – including elephant, rhino, lion and giraffe – that dominated the earth approximately one to two million years ago. The so-called "Big Five" (elephant, black rhino, buffalo, lion and leopard) were the hunter's trophies of the early twentieth century, and are still a fixation in the minds of many driver-guides and their clients. But don't ignore the less glamorous animals: there can be just as much satisfaction in spotting a serval or an uncommon antelope, or in noting rarely observed behaviour, as in ticking off one of the more obvious status symbols.

This field guide provides a quick reference to help you identify the larger mammals you're likely to encounter in Kenya – and despite huge losses since the early twentieth century, Kenya still teems with wildlife. While visiting some of the country's forty-odd parks and reserves (see box, pp.74–75) can almost guarantee sightings, if you travel fairly widely, even outside the parks, you're almost certain to see various gazelles and antelopes, zebra and giraffe – and even hippo, buffalo and elephant. Monkeys and baboons can be seen almost anywhere and are a regular menace.

Swahili names are given in brackets. NP: National Park; NR: National Reserve.

BIG CATS

Kenya's **big cats** are some of the most exciting and easily recognizable animals you'll see. Although often portrayed as fearsome hunters, pulling down plains game after a chase, many species do a fair bit of scavenging and all are content to eat smaller fry when conditions dictate or the opportunity arises.

LION (Simba) Panthera leo
Of the large cats, lions are the easiest species to find. Lazy, gregarious and very large – up to 1.8m in length, not counting the tail, and up to 1m high at the shoulder – they rarely make much effort to hide or to move away. They can be seen in nearly all the parks and reserves, and their presence is generally the main consideration in determining whether you're allowed out of your vehicle or not. "Man-eating" lions appear from time to time but seem to be one-off misfits. Normally, lions live in prides of three to forty (usually six to twelve) hunting cooperatively, in the day as well as at night, preferring to kill very young, old or sick animals, and making a kill roughly once in every two attacks. They will happily steal the kills of cheetahs or hyenas. Lions can manage in most habitats, except desert and thick forest, but habitat disturbance can cause them to move into pastoral areas where they often kill goats or cattle and are then killed in turn by herding communities. With fewer than 2000 lions left in Kenya, the problem of keeping *Panthera leo* and *Homo*

sapiens apart is a daily struggle for the Kenya Wildlife Service.

LEOPARD (Chui) Panthera pardus
Possibly the most feared animals in Kenya, and intensely secretive, alert and wary, leopards live – usually solitarily – all across the country except in the most treeless zones. Their unmistakeable call, which sounds something like a big hand saw being pulled back and forth, is unforgettable. Although often diurnal in the parks, they are strictly nocturnal wherever there is human pressure: they sometimes survive on the outskirts of villages, carefully choosing their prey to avoid a routine. They tolerate nearby human habitation and rarely kill people unprovoked. For the most part, leopards live off any small animals that come their way, pouncing from an ambush and dragging the kill up into a tree where it may be consumed over several days – the so-called "leopard's larder". Melanistic leopards are known as black panthers, and seem to be more common in highland areas, such as Mount Kenya and the Aberdare range.

SMALLER CATS

CHEETAH (Duma) Acinonyx jubatus
In the flesh, the cheetah is so different from the leopard, it's hard to see how there could ever be any confusion. Cheetahs are lightly built, finely spotted, with very long legs, small heads and a dark "tear mark" running from eye to jowl. Unlike leopards, which are highly arboreal, cheetahs rarely climb trees – though where accustomed to

vehicles, they climb on them to scan the horizon. They live alone, or sometimes briefly form a pair during mating. Hunting, too, is normally a solitary activity, dependent on eyesight and an incredible burst of speed that can take the animal up to 100kph (70mph) for a few seconds. Cheetahs can be seen in any of Kenya's large parks, and are usually out and about during the day.

1 LEOPARD; 2 CHEETAH; 3 LION; 4 SERVAL; 5 CARACAL >

SERVAL *(Mondo) Felis serval*
The beautiful part-spotted, part-striped serval is found in most of the parks, though it's uncommon and always a special sighting. They normally prefer reed beds or tall grassland near water, and while often nocturnal and solitary, they can sometimes be seen setting off on hunting forays on roadsides or at water margins at dawn or dusk.

CARACAL *(Simba mangu) Caracal caracal*
The aggressive, tuft-eared caracal resembles a lynx, but is more closely related to the serval and the even rarer golden cat. They are seen quite rarely, and while occasionally arboreal, they tend to favour open bush and plains in dry-country zones like Tsavo East NP and Samburu NR. A night drive, however, is the most likely way of seeing one.

SMALLER PREDATORS

GENET *(Kanu) Genetta genetta*
Once encountered, never forgotten, the beautifully marked, sinuous genet thrives in light bush country and even arid areas. It's a fairly common, slender, cat-sized, partly arboreal hunter, with short legs and a very long tail. Reminiscent of an elongated domestic cat, they were in fact once domesticated around the Mediterranean, but cats proved better mouse-hunters. You'll often see genets at game lodges, where they frequently become habituated to humans and can be found draped on a rafter above the bar, or mincing along a deck rail.

AFRICAN CIVET *(Fungo) Civettictis civetta*
A curious, short-legged, terrestrial prowler, about the size of a small dog, the civet is not to be confused with the smaller genet. And while genets are most likely to be seen around lodges, the civet is a solitary nocturnal omnivore that prefers to keep close to woodland and dense vegetation. They're not often seen, but they are predictable creatures that wend their way along the same paths at the same time, night after night, so if there's one in the neighbourhood, you're likely to see it.

HONEY BADGER *(Nyegere) Mellivora capensis*
Also known as the ratel, this widespread, omnivorous, badger-sized animal is notoriously aggressive, even to humans. They sometimes encounter people when raiding beehives or scavenging rubbish dumps – giving rise to one of the possible sources for the myth of the Nandi Bear (see box, p.286). Honey badgers tolerate a very broad range of habitats, are mainly nocturnal and are usually solitary, although they can also be found in pairs. Primarily omnivorous foragers they will tear open bees' nests (to which they are led by a small bird, the honey guide), their thick, loose hides rendering them impervious to the stings.

DWARF MONGOOSE *(Kitafe) Helogale parvula*
An unmistakeable group of animals, made famous by their cutest member, the meerkat (which isn't found in Kenya), mongooses are often seen and always delightful to watch. The main Kenyan species, in order of size, are the dwarf, black-tipped or slender (*Galerella sanguinea*), banded (*Nguchiro; Mungos mungo*), large grey (*Herpestes ichneumon*) and white-tailed (*Kicheche; Ichneumia albicauda*), which is a good-sized, shaggy beast, with surprisingly long legs. Mongooses' snake-fighting reputation is greatly overplayed: in practice they are mostly social foragers, fanning out through the bush like beaters on a shoot, hunting out anything edible – mostly invertebrates, eggs, lizards and frogs.

KENYA'S WILDLIFE WEBSITES

East African Wildlife Society ⓦeawildlife.org. Influential Kenya-based group, centrally involved in the movement to ban the ivory trade. Publishes the excellent *Swara* magazine.
Ecotourism Society of Kenya ⓦecotourismkenya.org. This local organization promotes sustainable tourism by awarding ratings to lodges, tented camps and tour operators.
Friends of Nairobi National Park ⓦfonnap.wordpress.com. Works to keep open the migration route into the park, and raise awareness about the remarkable environment on Nairobi's doorstep.
Green Belt Movement ⓦgreenbeltmovement.org. Grassroots conservation and women's movement founded by the Nobel Peace Prize winner Wangari Maathai, who died in 2011.
Kenya Forests Working Group ⓦkenyaforests.org. Promotes sound forest management and conservation.
Nature Kenya ⓦnaturekenya.org. The website of the East African Natural History Society organizes regular activities and has a good online newsletter.
Wildlife Direct ⓦwildlifedirect.org. Chaired by Richard Leakey, this is where conservation fundraising meets a network of conservationists, including more than fifty bloggers from the field in Kenya.

DOGS AND ALLIED SPECIES

AFRICAN HUNTING DOG (Mbwa mwitu)
Lycaon pictus

The unusual and rather magnificent hunting dog is still extremely rare in Kenya, having been present in reasonable numbers fifty years ago. Its decline was partly due to canine distemper and partly because of human predation and habitat disruption. The good news is that hunting dogs, also known as wild dogs or painted dogs, seem to be on the increase. There are now quite a few packs around the country, and in recent years they have been spotted in the Maasai Mara NR and neighbouring conservancies, in Tsavo West NP and even in Lake Nakuru NP, as well as in the Laikipia range lands where they have held out for decades. They are diurnal, highly nomadic and can range hundreds of kilometres, but if the opportunity exists to see them you'll hear about it.

BLACK-BACKED JACKAL (Bweha) Canis mesomelas

The commonest members of the dog family in Kenya are the black-backed and side-striped jackal. Both species can be seen just about anywhere, usually in pairs, in a broad range of habitats from moist mountain regions to desert, but drier areas are preferred. The black-backed jackal has a distinctive dark "saddle" flecked with white, so it's sometimes known as the silver-backed jackal. Although they usually live in pairs, you can often see family packs of these smartly coated canids playing in and around their dens, and even hunting – a much more common activity than the scavenging after lions with which they're normally associated. The shyer side-striped jackal (*C. adustus*) has smaller ears and a lateral stripe that can be more or less distinctive, while the unmarked golden or common jackal (*C. aureus*) is otherwise very similar, though in Kenya it is mostly restricted to the Maasai Mara and Laikipia.

SPOTTED HYENA (Fisi madoa) Crocuta crocuta

Kenya's biggest carnivore after the lion and leopard is the spotted hyena; it is also, apart from the lion, the meat-eater you will most often see. Although considered a scavenger *par excellence*, the spotted hyena is a formidable hunter, most often found where antelopes and zebras are present. Highly social, usually living in extended family groups, spotted hyenas are exceptionally efficient consumers, with immensely strong teeth and jaws, and they eat virtually every part of their prey, including hide and bones (which explains their distinctive, white droppings). Where habituated to humans, they sometimes steal leather shoes, unwashed pans and trash from tents and villages. Although they can be seen by day, they are most often active at night – when they issue their unnerving, whooping cries. Clans of twenty or so animals are dominated by females, which are larger than the males and compete with each other for rank. Curiously, female hyenas' genitalia are hard to distinguish from males', leading to a popular misconception that they are hermaphroditic. Not surprisingly, in view of all their attributes, the hyena is a key figure in local mythology and folklore.

STRIPED HYENA (Fisi miraba) Hyaena hyaena

Shy, solitary, largely silent and infrequently seen, the striped hyena is a shyer and less common animal than its spotted cousin, although apparently widespread in dry country and occasionally glimpsed very early in the morning trotting along park roads. The stripes can be a good identification guide, but the most obvious identifier is the pointed ears and erect mane of hair or crest along the shoulders.

AARDWOLF (Fisi ndogo) Proteles cristata

This is a much smaller hyena cousin, though it's easily mistaken for a small striped hyena. Widespread but shy and largely nocturnal, it lives all over Kenya, wherever it can find its unusual food supply – harvester termites and other insects, for which it forages solitarily while usually pairing for life.

BAT-EARED FOX (Mbweha masikio) Otocyon megalotis

Bat-eared foxes aren't uncommon, and they're unmistakeable in appearance. Their distribution coincides with that of termites – their favoured diet. Monogamous pairs spend many hours every night foraging, using their sensitive hearing to pinpoint their underground prey. In the cooler months they can also be seen out and about during the day.

ELEPHANTS AND HIPPOS

AFRICAN ELEPHANT *(Ndovu) Loxodonta africana*
Elephants are found throughout Kenya: almost all the big mountain and plains parks have populations. These are the most engaging of animals to watch – their interactions, behaviour patterns and even individual personalities have so many human parallels. Babies are born after a 22-month gestation, with other cows in close attendance. A calf will suckle for up to three years, from the mother's two breasts between her front legs, and grows from helpless infancy, through self-conscious adolescence, to adulthood. The basic family unit is a group of related females, tightly protecting their babies and young, and led by a venerable matriarch. It's the matriarch that is most likely to bluff a charge, and occasionally she may get carried away and actually tusk a vehicle or person. Seen in the flesh, elephants seem even bigger than you would imagine – you'll need little persuasion from those flapping, warning ears to back off if you're too close – but they are at the same time surprisingly graceful, silent animals on their padded, carefully placed feet. In a matter of moments, a large herd can merge into the trees and disappear, their presence betrayed only by the noisy cracking of branches as they strip trees and uproot saplings. Old animals die in their seventies or eighties, when their last set of teeth wears out and they can no longer feed. Grieving elephants pay much attention to the disposal of their dead relatives, often dispersing the bones and spending time near the remains.

HIPPOPOTAMUS *(Kiboko) Hippopotamus amphibius*
Hippopotamuses are highly adaptable and found wherever rivers or lakes are deep enough for them to submerge and have a surrounding of suitable grazing grass – from the humid estuary of the Tana River to the chilly mountain district of Nyahururu, including briny Lake Nakuru in the central Rift Valley and saline Lake Turkana in the semi-desert of the northwest. They spend most of the day in water to protect their thin, hairless skin from dehydration. After dark, they move onto land and spend the whole night grazing, often walking up to 10km in one session. In the Maasai Mara, they wander across the savanna; at Lake Naivasha they plod through farms and gardens; and everywhere they are rightly feared. Hippos are reckoned to be responsible for more human deaths in Africa than any other large animal (mosquitoes being by far the most deadly). Deaths occur mostly on water, when boats accidentally steer into hippo pods, but they can be aggressive on land, too, charging and slashing with their fearsomely long incisors. Hippos can run at 30km/h if necessary and have a small turning circle. Although uncertain on land (hence their aggression when cornered), they are supremely adapted to long periods in water. Their nostrils, eyes and ears are in exactly the right places and their clumsy feet become supple paddles – as can be seen, if you're lucky, from the underwater observatory at Mzima Springs in Tsavo West National Park.

ELEPHANTS AND THE ENVIRONMENT

Local overpopulation of **elephants** is usually the result of old migration routes being cut off, forcing the elephants into reserves – like the Maasai Mara and its neighbouring conservancies – where their massive appetites can appear destructive. Adults may consume up to 170kg of plant material daily, so it's estimated that several thousand tonnes of foliage pass through the Maasai Mara elephant population's collective gut each month. This foliage destruction puts new life into the soil, however, as acacia seeds dunged by elephants are released when dung beetles tackle the football-sized droppings, breaking them into pellets and pulling them into their burrows where the seeds germinate. Elephants also dig up dried-out waterholes with their tusks, providing moisture for other animals. Elephants are **architects of their environment**, setting the inter-species agenda by knocking over trees, creating deadwood habitats for invertebrates and causing hundreds of other impacts, all of which are natural functions in a dynamic ecosystem. The jury is still out on how it works when the wildlife corridors are closed, or the parks fenced in. What is not in doubt is that their **ivory** is increasingly valuable and poaching is on the rise again (see p.353). And when they are closely managed and secured in safe sanctuaries, the elephant populations quickly reach unsustainable levels. The Kenya Wildlife Service is getting proficient at translocating elephants, moving them around to balance the numbers.

1

2

RHINOS

There are two, highly endangered species of rhinoceros in Africa, the hook-lipped or **black rhino**, and the much heavier wide-lipped or **white rhino**, which has two distinct subspecies, southern and northern white rhinos. The shape of their lips is far more significant than any colour difference, as it indicates their respective diets (browsing for the black rhino, grazing for the white) and favoured habitats (thick bush and open grassland respectively). Both species give birth to a single calf, after a gestation period of fifteen to eighteen months, and the baby is not weaned until it is at least a year or sometimes two years old. With a calf only every three to four years, their population growth rate is slow compared with most animals – another factor contributing to their rarity. In fact, for their own protection, the exact number and whereabouts of each species of rhino in all parks and reserves is now a closely guarded secret by all KWS employees.

BLACK RHINOCEROS *(Faru or kifaru)* Diceros bicornis

Black rhinos, which are slightly smaller than white, were a fairly common sight in most of Kenya's parks until the early 1970s. Amboseli had hundreds of magnificent black rhinos, some with graceful horns more than 1m in length. But poaching decimated the population (see p.353), and today there are around 600 black rhinos in Kenya, distributed between Nairobi, Lake Nakuru, Aberdare, Meru and Tsavo West national parks, Maasai Mara NR and, increasingly, the Laikipia conservancies. Black rhinos prefer thick bush, at altitudes up to 3500m. They are solitary and active day and night, taking rests between periods of activity. Notoriously bad-tempered, they have good hearing and sensitive smell, but bad eyesight, making them dangerous at close quarters.

WHITE RHINOCEROS *(Faru or kifaru)*
Ceratotherium simum

Native northern white rhinos ("white" from the Afrikaans *wijd* for the wide mouth) have been extinct for several hundred years in Kenya, but reintroduced southern white rhinos, mostly from South Africa, can be seen in several parks and wildlife sanctuaries. At Ol Pejeta in Laikipia, Kenya also has the last remaining northern white rhinos, brought here from a Czech zoo in 2009, but it's feared the subspecies is doomed as all attempts at breeding have failed. Docile grazers, white rhinos are a savanna species, active day and night like black rhinos. Males tend to be solitary, but females often cluster in small same-sex herds or nursery groups.

ZEBRAS

PLAINS OR BURCHELL'S ZEBRA *(Punda milia)*
Equus burchelli granti

The plains zebra (the Kenya subspecies is called Grant's) has thick stripes and small ears and is found in savanna in most parts of Kenya up to about 4000m. In the far north, they tend to have a very short mane. In Tsavo West and other parts of southern Kenya, they often exhibit the "shadow striping" typical of the species in southern Africa, with fawn stripes alternating between the black ones. Their usual social set-up is a harem of several mares and foals led by a dominant stallion, active day and night, resting intermittently. In Amboseli and Maasai Mara, they gather in migrating herds several thousand strong, along with wildebeest and other grazers.

GREVY'S ZEBRA *(Punda milia)* Equus grevyi

Grevy's zebra is a large, fairly rare equid with very fine stripes and big, saucer-like ears, restricted to arid regions in Tsavo East and, especially Laikipia. These zebras are largely diurnal and live in small territorial herds. Mares with foals and stallions generally keep to separate troops.

PIGS

WARTHOG *(Ngiri or gwasi)* Phacochoerus aethiopicus

The commonest wild pig in Kenya is the warthog, seen all over the country at altitudes up to 2000m. Flighty and nervous, warthogs are notoriously hard to photograph as they're generally on the run through the bush, tails erect, often with their young in single file. They shelter in tunnels (often using old aardvark burrows), and live in family groups, usually of a mother and her litter of two to four piglets. They're diurnal, and principally grazers of grass and herbs, though they also root for tubers. Boars join the group to mate, and are easily distinguished from sows by their big warts, which protect their heads during fights.

BUSH PIG *(Nguruwe mwitu)* Potamochoerus porcus

Two nocturnal pigs, both much rarer than the warthog, are also found in Kenya. The red river hog or bush pig, which resembles a long-haired domestic pig with tasselled hair on its ears and a white-crested back, is found in dense forest, close to agriculture and river margins, and lives in groups of up to twenty. The huge, dark-coloured giant forest hog (*Hylochoerus meinertzhageni*), is a bristly, big-tusked pig that lives in the highlands and is very occasionally seen from tree hotels on Mount Kenya or the Aberdare range.

GIRAFFES

The tallest mammals on earth, **giraffes** are relatively common and unmistakeable and found widely across Kenya in wooded savanna and thorn country. Mild-mannered and non-territorial, they gather in loose, leaderless herds and spend the day browsing on the leaves of trees too high for other species (acacias are favourites), while at night they lie down and ruminate. Bulls test their strength while in bachelor herds by "necking" – using their powerful necks like broadswords. When a female is in heat, which can happen at any time of year, the dominant male mates with her. She gives birth after a gestation of around fourteen months. More than half of all young fall prey to lions or hyenas in their early years.

GIRAFFE *(Twiga) Giraffa camelopardalis*

Kenya has three types of giraffe, differentiated from each other by their pattern and the configuration of their short horns. Most often seen is the Maasai giraffe (*G. c. tippelskirchi*), with two horns and a very broken pattern of dark blotches on a buff or fawn background. This is the giraffe you will see in Maasai Mara, Amboseli and Tsavo West. In northern Kenya, and eastern Kenya roughly northeast of the Tana River, lives the dramatically patterned reticulated giraffe (*G. c. reticulata*), which normally has three or five horns and boldly defined chestnut patches on a very pale background. The reticulated subspecies is seen in the Samburu reserves,

Meru NP and Lewa and Ol Pejeta in Laikipia. The more solidly built Rothschild's giraffe (*G. c. rothschildi*) which has a pattern more like crazy paving (also with well-defined blotches), plain white lower legs, like socks, and usually two horns, is largely restricted in Kenya to Lake Nakuru NP and the Nairobi Giraffe Centre. They all appear able to interbreed, but because they are geographically separated, they very rarely do. There is disagreement among zoologists over whether any of the giraffe's subspecies should be accorded the status of separate species – particularly concerning the reticulated giraffe – but some, like the Rothschild's are extremely rare and in need of protection.

WILDEBEEST AND RELATIVES

The rather ungainly **hartebeest** family includes one of Kenya's rarest antelopes, the hirola or Hunter's hartebeest (*Damaliscus hunteri*) of the lower Tana River. The Coke's hartebeest, however, is found widely in southern Kenya, and topi are practically emblematic of the Maasai Mara, their main habitat. The **wildebeest** is also particularly associated with the Mara.

COKE'S HARTEBEEST *(Kongoni) Alcelaphus Buselaphus cokii*

Hard to confuse with any other antelope except the topi, the Hartebeest has several subspecies, distinguishable by horn shape, two of which live in Kenya – Coke's and Jackson's (*A.b. jacksoni*), which is darker and lives only in western Kenya. Coke's hartebeests live in a wide range of grassy habitats. They're diurnal and the females and calves live in small, wandering herds, while the territorial males are solitary.

TOPI *(Nyamera) Damaliscus lunatus*

An extremely fast runner, (once it accelerates out of bouncy, hartebeest gear), the topi is largely restricted in Kenya to the Maasai Mara, where the subspecies (one of four found across the continent) is *D. l. jimela*. They show a marked preference for moist savanna grasslands, near water, and the females and young form herds with an old male. These male topis are very characteristic of the Mara landscape: often seen standing sentry on abandoned termite hills, they're actually marking their territories against rival males, rather than nobly defending the herd against predators.

BLUE WILDEBEEST OR BRINDLED GNU *(Nyumbu) Connochaetes taurinus*

With its long tail, mane and beard, the blue wildebeest is an unmistakeable, nomadic grazer. An intensely gregarious animal, it lives in a variety of associations within "mega-herds" that can number more than a million animals. During the breeding season, the territorial bulls gather cows into their areas and defend their harems against rivals. Strictly grazers, dependent on pasture and preferring short grass, they are always found near water. It is that dependence that drives their continuous migration, forming mega-herds that shape into columns of animals to follow each other on the scent of new grass, only to dissolve and spread out again when good grazing is reached. With the East African climate changing rapidly, their movements are less and less regular, and hundreds of thousands of wildebeest can be months "early" or "late" in locations along the route that was typical of the mid-twentieth century.

GAZELLES AND ALLIED SPECIES

THOMSON'S GAZELLE (Swala tomi) Gazella thomsoni

The most obvious of the gazelles, the Thomson's gazelle is smaller than the similar Grant's, and distinguished by the black band on its flank. The female has tiny horns. This gregarious, diurnal grazer prefers flat, short-grass savanna near water, and is quite often seen at the roadside in southern Kenya. Thomson's gazelles live in a wide variety of social structures, often massing in the hundreds with other grazers.

GRANT'S GAZELLE (Swala granti) Gazella granti

Larger than the very similar Thomson's gazelle, Grant's is distinguished from it by the white rump patch which extends onto the back. The female's horns are smaller than the male's but not the tiny spikes of female "Thommies". Grant's gazelles thrive on wide grassy plains with good visibility, where they live in small, territorial harems. They can range much further from water than Thomson's, and their geographic range extends further north to encompass the northern parks of Samburu and Meru where Thommies are absent.

GERENUK (Swala twiga) Litocranius walleri

The unmistakeable gerenuk is an unusual browsing gazelle able to nibble from bushes standing on its hind legs (its name means "giraffe-necked" in Somali). Although considered an arid-land specialist, its range encompasses most of Kenya east of the Rift Valley and it's not uncommon. Gerenuks are usually solitary or live in small, territorial harems. Females are hornless.

IMPALA (Swala pala) Aepyceros melampus

The impala, although technically not one of the gazelles, is closely related to them and common in many parts of Kenya. The only antelope with a black tuft above the hooves, the males have long, lyre-shaped horns and the females are hornless. Usually found in open savanna with light woodland cover, impalas are diurnal and make distinctive, high, graceful leaps when fleeing danger. Females live grouped together in large herds that overlap with several male territories. During the breeding season, the males become territorial and separate out breeding harems of up to twenty females, which they vigorously defend from rivals.

GRAZING ANTELOPES

ORYX (Choroa) Oryx gazella callotis

Ranging from open grasslands into waterless wastelands, and tolerant of prolonged drought, this distinctive, rapier-horned antelope is nocturnal as well as diurnal. They live in highly hierarchical mixed herds of up to fifteen, led by a dominant bull. The O. g. callotis subspecies, which lives in Tsavo and Amboseli, is easily distinguished by its luxuriantly tufted ears from the Beisa oryx (O. g. beisa), found in northern Kenya.

SABLE ANTELOPE (Palahala) Hippotragus niger

This very large, handsome antelope lives only in Shimba Hills NP, inland from the south coast. Here it finds its preferred mix of open woodland and tall grassland near water. Sables are hard to confuse with any other antelope:

the females are tan-coloured while the males are glossy black, and both have white bellies and facial markings, stiff manes and huge curved horns that reach 1m or more in length in the males. Active by day and night, sable antelopes live in territorial herds of females and young, dominated in breeding season by the bulls.

ROAN ANTELOPE (Kirongo) Hippotragus equinus

The massive roan antelope, a close relative of the sable but with much shorter horns, is fairly common in much of west and south-central Africa, but restricted in Kenya to Ruma NP south of Kisumu – a sanctuary of tall grassland with plenty of water. Small herds are usually led by a dominant bull, but immature bachelor herds and seasonal pairs are also common.

WATERBUCKS AND REEDBUCKS

COMMON OR BOHOR REEDBUCK (Tohe) Redunca arundinum

Reedbucks and waterbucks are related, and both spend much time in or near water. The medium-sized common reedbuck has a patchy distribution in southern Kenya, living in monogamous pairs or family groups in territories defended by the (horned) male. They subsist on a specialist plant diet that is generally unpalatable to other herbivores.

WATERBUCK (Kuro) Kobus ellipsiprymnus

The rather deer-like waterbuck is relatively common in many

parts of central and southern Kenya, living in open woodland and savanna, near water. There are two subspecies in Kenya: the ringed waterbuck, east of the Rift Valley, which has a white circle on its rump, and the Defassa waterbuck of western Kenya, whose rump is solid white. This is a large antelope, with a tendency to look a bit shaggy and unkempt, and like the reedbuck, its plant diet is unpalatable to other grazers (and can give it a distinctive smell, according to some authorities). Only the males have horns, and they either lead a territorial herd of females and young or maintain a territory that is visited by wandering female herds.

1 THOMSON'S GAZELLE; 2 GRANT'S GAZELLE; 3 IMPALA; 4 ORYX; 5 SABLE ANTELOPE; 6 GERENUK; 7 COMMON REEDBUCK;
8 RINGED WATERBUCK; 9 ROAN ANTELOPE >

DWARF ANTELOPES

KIRK'S DIK-DIK (*Digidigi* or *Dika*) *Madoqua kirkii*
Found all over Kenya, Kirk's dik-dik measures no more than 40cm at the shoulder, and usually pairs for life. You frequently see pairs of this hare-sized antelope, named after its alarm cry, at the roadside in national parks and reserves, and all over Laikipia and northern Kenya. They have quite a distinctive, swollen snout that looks like the beginning of a short trunk. Adults are sometimes accompanied by a single youngster, and occasionally by an older sibling too. If you do a bush walk, you'll come across their territorial boundaries, marked by piles of droppings and black secretions from their facial glands, deposited on grass stems like tiny drops of engine oil.

SUNI (*Suni*) *Neotragus moschatus*
The suni is much less common than the dik-dik, and frequently mistaken for it, though it is even smaller, at just 35cm, and doesn't have the dik-dik's proboscis. Like the dik-dik, they live in monogamous pairs, sometimes with additional non-breeding females forming a small group. They can be encountered almost anywhere there's good, dry forest cover, but their distribution is extremely patchy: forested coastal hills have the largest populations. Sunis tend to be nocturnal and crepuscular, hiding in shade by day, and will habitually freeze when threatened or surprised, before darting into the undergrowth.

SHARPE'S GRYSBOK (*Dondoo* or *Dondoro*) *Raphicerus sharpei*
This is a rarely seen antelope, around 50cm high at the shoulder. It's distinguished from the slenderer steenbok by its light underparts. Only the males have short horns, using them to defend their territories. They pair loosely, not monogamously or for life, and are most likely to be seen in dense thicket adjacent to open grassland where they rest during the day and feed by night.

ORIBI (*Kasia*) *Ourebia ourebia*
This small antelope (the biggest of this group at about 60cm at the shoulder) is patchily distributed in Kenya, mostly in the southwest and the coast north of the Tana, but it's not hard to see where common as it's diurnal and favours open grassland. The oribi is distinguished from the smaller grysbok and steenbok by a black tail and dark skin patch, like a stain, below the eye. Their territorial harems consist of one to four females led by a horned male. Males are noted for their charming foreplay: when the female is in heat, the male pushes his head under her hindquarters and shoves her along on her forelegs like a wheelbarrow.

KLIPSPRINGER (*Mbuzi mawe*) *Oreotragus oreotragus*
With their raised hooves wonderfully adapted for scaling near-vertical rock faces ("rock goat" is the translation of their Swahili name), klipspringers are a distinctive sight in many rockier parts of the country, or wherever there are cliffs and *kopjes*. Being browsers, and not dependent on pasture, they can often be seen far from water in remote, desolate districts, and out and about in the heat of the day. A territorial male (with horns; though occasionally females are also horned) lives with his mate or a small family group, and they often have quite restricted, long-term territories.

STEENBOK (*Dondoo* or *Dondoro*) *Raphicerus campestris*
Despite a height of only 50cm at the shoulder, the surprisingly aggressive steenbok – an inhabitant of dry savanna – defends itself furiously against attackers or, *in extremis*, dashes down any available hole. Male steenboks have horns, but the species is normally solitary, waking and feeding intermittently by day and night, using its huge ears to warn of the first sign of danger.

DUIKERS

The **duikers** (from the Dutch for "diver", referring to their plunging into the bush) are larger than the dwarf antelopes though they appear smaller because of their hunched posture. Uniquely among antelopes and allied species, duikers are omnivorous, feeding not just on leaves, fruit and fungi but also on a range of insects and other invertebrates – and even catching frogs and lizards and snatching birds when the opportunity arises.

COMMON DUIKER (*Nysa*) *Sylvicapra grimmia*
The 60cm-high common duiker is found throughout the country in many habitats, but most species are choosier and prefer plenty of dense cover and thicket. The red duiker and blue duiker are quite widespread, but the tiny Zanzibar duiker is restricted in Kenya to the Arabuko Sokoke Forest near Malindi, the black-fronted duiker to Mount Kenya and Mount Elgon and the yellow-backed duiker to the Mau forest.

BUFFALO AND SPIRAL-HORNED ANTELOPES

Kenya's **big antelopes** are the twisted-horn bushbuck types (*Tragelaphinae*; after the Greek for "billy goat"), though they are all related, surprisingly perhaps, not to goats or the smaller antelopes, but to cattle and **buffaloes**.

AFRICAN OR CAPE BUFFALO (*Nyati* or *mbogo*) *Syncerus caffer*

The buffalo itself is very common and closely related to the domestic cow. Buffalos tolerate a wide range of habitats, up to altitudes of 4000m, but always near water. Their sense of smell is much more acute than other senses. Active day and night, they rest up during the heat of the day. They live in large herds of cows and calves that can number up to three hundred and rarely make much effort to move when vehicles approach. Young bulls often form small bachelor herds, whereas older bulls are usually solitary and can sometimes be dangerous. Although usually ambivalent to the presence of humans, they are often destructive: you don't have to read the papers long before finding an example of buffalos trampling crops or goring a farmer trying to protect his harvest.

COMMON ELAND (*Mpofu* or *mbungu*) *Taurotragus oryx*

Spotted almost as easily as the buffalo, and present in most parks and reserves, is the huge, cow-like eland, with its distinctive dewlap. This highly adaptable mega-antelope – the biggest in Africa – is happy from semi-desert to mountains, but it prefers scrubby plains for its 24-hour lifestyle punctuated intermittently with brief periods of sleep. Non-territorial herds of up to sixty eland is the norm, but temporary gatherings of as many as a thousand aren't unheard of. Despite being so huge, and relatively common, it's still a shy animal, and usually turns and moves away when you stop to say hello. Indeed, elands can be quite skittish, and they're surprisingly good jumpers for a half-tonne beast. Both sexes have straight horns with a slight spiral.

GREATER KUDU (*Tandala mkubwa*) *Tragelaphus strepsiceros*

This is another impressively big antelope (up to 1.5m at the shoulder) with very long, spiral horns in the male. Strikingly handsome and extremely localized, it is shy of humans, tends to be nocturnal and is not often seen in the daytime unless its territory is secure, as on some of the Laikipia conservancies. Your best bet for seeing them is Lake Bogoria NR and semi-arid, hilly or undulating bush country in northern Kenya, sometimes far from water. Male greater kudus are usually solitary; females live in small troops with the young.

LESSER KUDU (*Tandala mdogo*) *Tragelaphus imberbis*

The lesser kudu isn't infrequently seen, where it exists at all, but, like its greater cousin, it's localized and a threatened species. You're most likely to see lesser kudu in Tsavo West NP or Tsavo East NP, where they inhabit dense scrub. Like the greater kudu, lesser kudu females clump together with the young, while the adult males are more solitary. Like the eland, both species are startlingly good jumpers – which somehow ties in neatly with their spring-like horns.

BUSHBUCK (*Kulungu* or *mbawala*) *Tragelaphus scriptus*

This is another notoriously shy antelope – the only usual evidence of a bushbuck in the area is its noisy crashing through the undergrowth and a flash of a chestnut rump as it takes off. With their very variable appearance, even in the same close locality (there are as many as 29 subspecies, and some zoologists consider that the bushbuck is actually at least two different species), they can sometimes be hard to identify: look out for randomly white-spotted or sometimes white-broken-striped flanks. Thick bush and woodland close to water is their principal habitat, and even with this protection they are mostly nocturnal. They tend to be solitary. The male has fairly short, straight, spiralled horns.

SITATUNGA (*Nzohe*) *Tragelaphus spekei*

This large, hirsute, semi-aquatic relative of the bushbuck is found only in one or two remote corners of western Kenya (including Saiwa Swamp NP, where they are easy to see). They are very localized and are not likely to be mistaken for anything else. Usually seen half submerged, it's a challenge to spot their remarkable hooves, up to 18cm long and widely splayed – exactly as if a marsh-dwelling antelope were taking on the characteristics of a lily-trotter. As usual in this genus, only the males have horns.

BONGO (*Bongo* or *ndongoro*) *Tragelaphus eurycerus*

The bongo is a particularly impressive member of this group, now confined to the highlands of Mount Kenya, the Aberdare range and possibly the Cherangani Hills and Mau Escarpment. Your best chance of seeing these stocky, robust, splendidly marked creatures is at Mount Kenya Safari Club, at Nanyuki, which has successfully bred and reintroduced them on the mountain.

PRIMATES

Excluding *Homo sapiens*, there are twelve species of primates in Kenya, most of them diurnal. They range from the pint-sized, slow-motion, lemur-like potto (*Perodicticus potto*), found in Kakamega Forest, to the baboon. Other rare or more localized monkeys include the stocky but distinguished-looking De Brazza's monkey (*Cercopithecus neglectus*), with its white goatee, found almost exclusively in Saiwa Swamp National Park; the Tana River crested mangabey (*Cercocebus galeritus galeritus*), a partly ground-dwelling monkey with a characteristic Mohican-style crest of hair; and the terrestrial Patas monkey (*ngedere; Erythrocebus patas*), a moustachioed plains runner of Laikipia and the dry northwest. Kenya no longer has any great apes (the family to which the gorilla and the chimpanzee belong), although they probably only became extinct in the western forests, of which Kakamega is a relic, in the last 500 years, during the period when the region was being widely settled by humans. There's a large chimpanzee welfare sanctuary in Ol Pejeta Conservancy, but it isn't engaged in breeding.

VERVET MONKEY *(Tumbili) Chlorocebus pygerythrus*

Widespread, common and occasionally a nuisance where used to humans (they will steal food and anything else that looks interesting), the primate you are certain to see almost anywhere in Kenya, given a few trees, is the vervet monkey. This small monkey lives in troops led by a dominant male (easily identified by his sky-blue scrotum), and they have no difficulty adjusting to the presence of humans and their food. The vervet is one of the guenons – typical African monkeys – every species of which has distinctive facial markings and hairstyles.

BLUE OR SYKES' MONKEY *(Nyabu, kima* or *nchima) Cercopithecus mitis*

Almost as common as the vervet in certain areas, notably on the coast, is Sykes' monkey, also known as the blue monkey. Naturally a monkey of the forests, a number of Sykes' troops at Diani Beach have become notoriously accustomed to stealing food from hotel dining tables, and large males will even raid bedrooms. Upcountry populations of Sykes' monkey seem to be more timid.

EASTERN BLACK-AND-WHITE COLOBUS MONKEY OR GUEREZA *(Mbega) Colobus guereza*

You are most likely to see the beautiful, leaf-eating black-and-white colobus monkey in the Kenya highlands, where the Eastern species lives. Strictly diurnal, and almost entirely arboreal (their missing thumb is a distinctive characteristic that aids swinging; "kolobos" means "mutilated" in Greek), they live in small troops and are dependent on thick forest habitat, but also live along water courses and around lake margins in otherwise arid savanna districts. You can see them in the Aberdare and Mount Kenya national parks, in patches of forest among the tea hills northwest of Nairobi, at lakes Naivasha and Nakuru and around Maasai Mara NR. A second, smaller species, the Angolan black-and-white colobus (*C. angolensis*), can also be spotted in the Diani forest on the coast south of Mombasa. Both species are usually seen high in the tree canopy; look out for the pure-white babies. The Tana River red colobus (*Procolobus rufomitratus rufomitratus*) is only found in the remote Tana River National Primate Reserve north of Malindi.

GREATER BUSHBABY OR THICK-TAILED GALAGO *(Komba) Galago crassicaudatus*

In some Kenyan coastal lodges, where there's enough nearby forest, you're quite likely to see this appealing, cat-sized primate – the largest of Kenya's three species of bushbabies – as they sometimes visit dining rooms and verandas. They're strictly nocturnal, roosting in small family groups during the day, and very active hunters and foragers after dark, when their wailing "baby" cries are such a distinctive sound. The tiny Senegal bushbaby (also *komba; G. senegalensis*) is a shy, tree-leaping sap- and insect-eater: it's the big species that want your bread roll or fruit.

YELLOW BABOON *(Nyani) Papio cynocephalus*

On safari you'll have plenty of opportunities to watch baboon troops up close. Large males can be intimidating – disconcertingly so towards women, whom they identify as less physically threatening than men. Troops, averaging forty to fifty individuals, spend their lives, like all monkeys, in clear but mutable social relationships. Rank and precedence, physical strength and kin ties all determine an individual's position in this mini-society led by a dominant male. They favour open country with trees and cliffs, always near water, and their days revolve around foraging and hunting for food (baboons will consume almost anything, from a fig tree's entire crop to a baby antelope found in the grass). There are two species, whose distributions overlap in Kenya: the slenderer yellow baboon in the east and south, and the stockier, heavily maned olive baboon (also *nyani; P. anubis*) in the west and north. Both adapt quickly to humans, are frequently a nuisance and occasionally dangerous.

OTHER MAMMALS

It's unlikely **rodents** will make a strong impression on safari, unless you do a night game drive. In that case you may see the frenzied leaps of a spring hare, dazzled by headlights or a torch. In rural areas off the beaten track you may occasionally see hunters taking home giant rats or cane rats – shy, vegetarian animals, which make good eating.

Kenya has several species of **squirrel**, of which the most widespread are the two species of ground squirrel – striped and unstriped – which are often seen, dashing along the track in front of the vehicle on game drives. The most spectacular squirrel, however, is the giant forest squirrel, with its splendid bush of a tail, and the nocturnal flying squirrel – which glides from tree to tree on membranes between its outstretched limbs. Both are most likely to be seen in Kakamega Forest. Kenya's true flying mammals will usually be a mere flicker over a waterhole at twilight, or sometimes a flash across your headlights. The only **bats** you can normally observe in any meaningful way are fruit bats hanging from their daytime roosting sites. The hammer-headed fruit bat, sometimes seen in Kakamega Forest, has a huge head and a wingspan of more than 1m.

ROCK HYRAX *(Pimbi) Procavia capensis*
Rock hyraxes, which you are certain to see at Hell's Gate NP, on Mount Kenya and in Nairobi NP, look as if they should be rodents. But one of the most memorable bits of safari knowledge imparted by guides is the fact that they share the same prehistoric ancestor as the elephant. Present-day hyraxes are pygmies compared with some of their prehistoric ancestors, which were as big as a bear in some cases. Rock hyraxes live in busy, vocal colonies of twenty or thirty females and young, plus a territorial male. Some areas swarm with the adults and the playful and very independent young. The tree hyrax (*pembere*; *Heterohyrax brucei*) is quite similar, but largely nocturnal: this is the hyrax making the painfully wheezing cry that you sometimes hear at night.

AARDVARK *(Mhanga) Orycteropus afer*
The aardvark is one of Africa's – indeed the world's – strangest mammals, a solitary termite-eater weighing up to 70kg. Its name, Afrikaans for "earth pig", is an apt description, as it holes up during the day in large burrows – excavated with remarkable speed and energy – and emerges at night to visit termite mounds within a radius of up to 5km, to dig for its main diet. It is most likely to be seen when you're out on a night drive in bush country that is well scattered with tall termite spires.

PANGOLIN *(Kakakuona) Manis temminckii*
Pangolins are also very unusual – nocturnal, scale-covered mammals, resembling armadillos and feeding on ants and termites. When frightened, they secrete a noxious liquid from anal glands and roll into a ball with their scales erect (*pangolin* is Malay for "rolling over"). The ground pangolin, the only species found in Kenya (most pangolins are arboreal), lives mainly in savanna and woodland districts.

CRESTED PORCUPINE *(Nungu or nungunungu)* *Hystrix cristata*
This is a really large rodent (up to 90cm in length), rarely seen, but common away from croplands, where it's hunted as a pest, or for its quills. Porcupines are adaptable to a wide range of habitats and often hide in caves during the day, where several may gather, coming out only at night to forage for roots and tubers along their routine pathways.

GOLDEN RUMPED ELEPHANT SHREW *(Sengi) Rhynchocyon chrysopygus*
The insectivorous elephant shrews are worth looking out for, simply because they are so weird. Your best chance of a sighting is of the golden-rumped elephant shrew, at Gedi ruins on the coast, near Watamu, or in the nearby Arabuko Sokoke Forest NP. This fascinating insect-eater is a creature of many parts: the size of a small cat, but built like a giant mouse running on stilts, it has a soft, elongated snout, like a short trunk. "Elephant shrew" captures the look fairly well.

DUGONG *(Nguva) Dugong dugon*
The rarest of all of Kenya's "other mammals" is the dugong, the mermaid-prototype, of which there are believed to be a handful of individuals remaining in Kenyan waters, drifting in the shallows around the Lamu archipelago. They're part of a much depleted population – threatened by deliberate hunting and accidental trawling – that lives all along the Indian Ocean coast, feeding on seagrass (also vulnerable to habitat destruction) and coming up for air every few minutes. Adults usually weigh around half a tonne and reach about 3m in length, and the females give birth, in very shallow water, to metre-long, 30kg calves that suckle for eighteen months.

CURIO STALL

Basics

Getting there

Flying is the only straightforward way of getting to Kenya, unless you're travelling overland from southern Africa. Flights to Kenya are generally most expensive from early July to late October and from mid-December to mid-January. Make reservations as far in advance as possible, especially if you want to travel at these popular times.

Nairobi is the major hub for East Africa and is served by many airlines so there's a competitively priced choice of flights, but the cheaper tickets generally have fixed dates that you won't be able to change without paying an extra fee.

With the exception of the package-holiday **charter airlines** from Britain and Europe, there are no direct flights to **Mombasa** without going to Nairobi first. However, an inclusive package trip can make a lot of sense. Some packages, based around mid-range coast hotels, are relatively inexpensive and, if you choose carefully, you shouldn't feel too constrained. Based on your flight, plus a week of half-board accommodation (dinner, bed and breakfast) they cost from around £700 from the UK. It's worth remembering that you aren't obliged to stay at your hotel all the time: you could use it as a base to make independent trips around the country.

Adding some **safari** travel to a beach package holiday will increase the price by at least £250 per person per day of safari. If you have more time and flexibility, book a safari in Kenya – recommended companies are listed in the relevant sections of the book (see p.79, p.123 & p.404). Alternatively, any of the beach hotels can recommend a safari operator to take you to the closest parks, and reasonable deals are possible.

Flights from the UK and Ireland

London Heathrow is the only British airport with **direct flights to Nairobi**, operated by Kenya Airways (Ⓦ kenya-airways.com) and British Airways (Ⓦ britishairways.com), and taking around nine hours. **Fares** for flights on fixed dates start from around £500 return in low season and rise to above £1000 on key dates in high season. It may well be cheaper, particularly if coming from other UK cities such as Edinburgh or Manchester to take an **indirect flight**, changing planes in mainland Europe (see below) or the Middle East (see p.48).

There are also several **charter operators** with whom you can sometimes get "seat-only" deals to Mombasa out of London (and sometimes one or two UK regional airports) from around £400. Any online or high-street agent can give you a quote.

Flying from Ireland, the choice is to fly to Heathrow or to one of the mainland European cities with direct flights to Kenya (see below). Flights should cost between €850 and €1200, depending on the season.

Flights from the US and Canada

There are no direct flights from the US or Canada to East Africa. The fastest routes to Nairobi are usually two nonstop legs via **London** or another European city such as Amsterdam, Frankfurt or Paris (see below). Other possible but longer connections are available with the Middle Eastern airlines (see p.48), or by going via Johannesburg with South African Airways (see p.48). **Fares** start from around $1400 for a low-season round-trip ticket out of New York, and from $2000 in high season, and from Toronto around Can$1700 in low season and Can$2400 in high season. Shortest journey times via Europe are 17hr from New York and 18hr from Toronto.

Travellers from the **west coast** might want to consider flying via East or Southeast Asia. Kenya Airways has flights between Nairobi and Bangkok, Hanoi, Hong Kong and Guangzhou in China.

Flights via mainland Europe, the Middle East and Africa

Kenya Airways offers direct flights to Nairobi from Amsterdam, Frankfurt and Paris, while European carriers with direct services include Air France (Ⓦ airfrance.com), KLM (Ⓦ klm.com), Lufthansa

---

A BETTER KIND OF TRAVEL

At Rough Guides we are passionately committed to travel. We believe it helps us understand the world we live in and the people we share it with – and of course **tourism** is vital to many developing economies. But the scale of modern tourism has also damaged some places irreparably, and **climate change** is accelerated by most forms of transport, especially flying. All Rough Guides' flights are carbon-offset, and every year we donate money to a variety of environmental charities.

(Ⓦlufthansa.com), Swiss (Ⓦswiss.com) and Turkish Airlines (Ⓦturkishairlines.com).

You can also route to Nairobi with Emirates via Dubai (Ⓦemirates.com), Ethiopian Airlines via Addis Ababa (Ⓦethiopianairlines.com), Etihad Airways via Abu Dhabi (Ⓦetihad.com), Qatar Airways via Doha (Ⓦqatarairways.com) and South African Airways via Johannesburg (Ⓦflysaa.com).

Flights from Australia and New Zealand

There are no direct flights to Kenya from Australia or New Zealand. From **Australia**, South African Airways has some good connections to Nairobi via Johannesburg, while Emirates, Etihad Airways and Qatar Airways also offer decent connections. Another option, with a potential bonus stopover, is from Perth to Mauritius and then direct to Nairobi with Air Mauritius (Ⓦairmauritius.com). From **New Zealand**, Emirates via Dubai is your most obvious bet, but Air New Zealand (Ⓦairnewzealand.co.nz) and Qantas (Ⓦqantas.com) can get you to Kenya in combination with other airlines, such as Kenya Airways or South African Airways from Johannesburg.

Except for the Christmas period, when you will have to pay more, **fares** to Kenya from Australia and New Zealand are generally not seasonal. The lowest-priced return tickets bought from a discount agent or direct from the airline cost around Aus$2000–3500 from Australia or NZ$2400–4000 from New Zealand.

Flights from South Africa

There are several daily **direct flights** to Nairobi from Johannesburg (taking just over 4hr) on South African Airways (Ⓦflysaa .com) and Kenya Airways (Ⓦkenya-airways.com). Round-trip fares start at around R4000.

DISCOUNT FLIGHT AGENTS

Africa Travel UK Ⓦ africatravel.co.uk. Experienced and resourceful.
Airfares Flights Aus Ⓦ airfaresflights.com.au. Fare-comparison site.
AirTreks US Ⓦ airtreks.com. Specialist in round-the-world and multi-sector tickets.
CheapOair US Ⓦ cheapoair.com. Airline consolidator fares and standby-seat broker.
Flight Centre Worldwide Ⓦ flightcentre.com. Flights and safari packages and some of the best Nairobi fare deals.
helloworld Ⓦ helloworld.com.au. Well-priced and user-friendly agent.
North South Travel UK Ⓦ northsouthtravel.co.uk. Excellent personal service and discounted fares, with all profits going to grassroots development charities.
Spector Travel of Boston US Ⓦ spectortravel.com. African

specialist for flights and tours with competitive prices.
STA Travel Worldwide Ⓦ statravel.com. Specialists in multi-sector flights and tours for gap-year travellers and under-26s, though others are catered for.
Trailfinders UK and Ireland Ⓦ trailfinders.com. Long-established, reputable agent, with good-value flights and Kenya safaris.
Travel Bag UK Ⓦ travelbag.co.uk. Discount flight and holiday agent.
Travel Cuts Canada/US Ⓦ travelcuts.com. Popular, long-established student and youth travel organization.
Travelstart South Africa Ⓦ travelstart.co.za. Comprehensive South African site for comparing flight options and prices.
USIT Ireland Ⓦ usit.ie. Irish and Northern Irish student and youth specialists.
World Travel Centre Ireland Ⓦ worldtravel.ie. Flight deals including round-the-world.

KENYA AND AFRICA SPECIALISTS

The international agents and operators listed below will be able to assist you regardless of your home country. Overland tours of East Africa are covered under "Overlanding to/from Kenya" (see p.50); "voluntourism" trips are covered under "Work and volunteering" (see p.95). You can also book an itinerary through companies in Nairobi (see p.123) and elsewhere in Kenya, though if making arrangements through a Kenyan agent, bear in mind that international flights will generally have to be booked separately.

Australia

The Africa Safari Co. Ⓦ africasafarico.com.au. Good, knowledgeable agents for East Africa with personal experience of lodges and tented camps and scheduled and tailor-made safaris.
African Travel Specialists Ⓦ africantravel.com.au. Well-established agent with an excellent reputation and a team of experienced staff, many of whom know Kenya well.
African Wildlife Safaris Ⓦ africanwildlifesafaris.com.au. Upmarket and mid-range safaris, either with set departures or tailor-made, and a good selection of online brochures.
Classic Safari Company Ⓦ classicsafaricompany.com.au. Tailor-made safaris ranging from comfortable to luxurious including mobile camping, riding and walking options.

South Africa

African Budget Safaris Ⓦ africanbudgetsafaris.com. Very knowledgeable and helpful operator with a huge range of overland tours, budget safaris, cheaper accommodation and camping. Frequently advertises discounts and specials.
Go2Africa Ⓦ go2africa.com. A large consultancy team with good service, offering all manner of trips in Kenya and East Africa from mid-range packages to luxury lodges.

UK

Aardvark Safaris Ⓦ aardvarksafaris.co.uk. Committed and enthusiastic tailor-made Africa specialists who spend a lot of time getting to know the high-end camps and lodges they work with.
Adventure Alternative Ⓦ adventurealternative.com. Small,

personal operator, with a strong sense of responsibility and reciprocation, specializing in walking and treks, mountain expeditions, adventure holidays and volunteering trips.

Africa Odyssey Ⓦ africaodyssey.com. Tailor-made tours in East and southern Africa featuring safaris, beach holidays and small lodges off the beaten track.

Birdfinders Ⓦ birdfinders.co.uk. Expertly guided birdwatching tours. Runs an annual 18-day Kenya extravaganza from the UK in Nov/Dec.

Cazenove & Loyd Ⓦ cazloyd.com. Intelligently designed, entirely tailor-made private safaris, relying on clients who know what they're looking for.

Exodus Ⓦ exodus.co.uk. Long-established East African overland and adventure company, with an interesting selection of Kenya escorted tours, including a photographic trip to the Mara and a Mount Kenya climb.

Expert Africa Ⓦ expertafrica.com. Specialists in tailor-made trips, with very strong local knowledge. The Kenya programme is run by Richard Trillo, author of *The Rough Guide to Kenya* since 1987, and the team includes other guidebook writers.

Footloose Adventure Travel Ⓦ footlooseadventure.co.uk. Enthusiastic independent outfit offering a selection of treks and safaris; they'll tailor-make a safari to fit your budget and interests, offer advice and track down flights.

Freeman Safaris Ⓦ freemansafaris.com. Personal, specialist photographic safari operator, using a raft of experience to deliver exceptional trips.

Gane & Marshall Ⓦ ganeandmarshall.com. Africa specialists, with responsible travel credentials and a good Kenya programme, including Mount Kenya and Laikipia.

Hartley's Safaris Ⓦ hartleys-safaris.co.uk. Highly rated safari specialists creating bespoke tours.

Imagine Africa Ⓦ imagineafrica.co.uk. Well-established and reliable outfit with a good reputation for organizing mid- to high-end safaris.

IntoAfrica Ⓦ intoafrica.co.uk. Small, good, eco-minded tour operator, whose trips give a genuine insight into the country while having minimum negative impact on people and environment.

Natural High Safaris Ⓦ naturalhighsafaris.com. Very cool, contemporary consultancy, safari-planner and booking agent, with a focus on experiences rather than mainstream holidays.

On The Go Tours Ⓦ onthegotours.com. Lively and competitively priced range of Kenya tours from no-frills overland camping trips to small group or family safaris.

Original Travel Ⓦ originaltravel.co.uk. Luxury eco-holiday company with a great reputation for delivering off-the-beaten-track arrangements.

Ornitholidays Ⓦ ornitholidays.co.uk. Offers an annual guided birdwatching trip to Kenya – Tsavo and the coast – to coincide with the arrival of many species of migrants.

Rainbow Tours Ⓦ rainbowtours.co.uk. Small operator with long-standing links with Africa, some unusual Kenyan properties and keen and experienced staff.

Safari Consultants Ⓦ safari-consultants.com. Long-established and very personal Africa specialists in tailor-made travel to East and southern Africa.

Steppes Travel Ⓦ steppestravel.co.uk. Innovative company with a

personal approach, specializing in tailor-made trips based in luxury lodges.

Theobald Barber Ⓦ theobaldbarber.com. Experienced, bespoke safari planners, offering a very personalized service.

To Escape To Ⓦ toescapeto.com. Hand-picked property rental, hotels, lodges and camps in Kenya, including mid-priced and family options.

Tourdust Ⓦ tourdust.com. Out-of-the-ordinary and competitively priced trekking and Mount Kenya climbs as well as safaris and good-value beach extensions.

Tribes Travel Ⓦ tribes.co.uk. Highly recommended small company in the vanguard of responsibly operated tourism offering tailor-made arrangements in Kenya using individually reviewed and rated properties.

Wild Frontiers Ⓦ wildfrontierstravel.com. Adventure travel specialist highlighting the travel as much as the destination, with some excellent Kenya tours.

Wildlife Worldwide Ⓦ wildlifeworldwide.com. Tailor-made Kenya safaris, often escorted by well-known guides or conservationists, plus family, adventure camping and walking trips.

US and Canada

The African Adventure Company Ⓦ africa-adventure.com. One of the best agencies in the business with a customized approach, giving first-hand reviews of places to stay and safaris. Has an exceptional knowledge of African wildlife and where and when to see it.

African Horizons Ⓦ africanhorizons.com. Decent range of well-priced mid-range Kenya safaris with flexible departures.

Bicycle Africa Ⓦ ibike.org/bikeafrica. Easy-going small-group cycling tours visiting many parts of Africa, including Kenya.

Born Free Safaris & Tours Ⓦ safaris2africa.com. Long-established operator, with good-value safaris on offer including "Best of Kenya" options.

Good Earth Tours & Safaris Ⓦ goodearthtours.com. An ethically responsible operator that can organize good-value camping or mid-range lodge safaris plus beach extensions.

Journeys International Ⓦ journeysinternational.com. Award-winning ecotourism operator with a handful of Kenya trips, including a mainstream nine-day safari and a Mount Kenya trek.

Ker & Downey Ⓦ kerdowney.com. Renowned and much-commended upmarket travel company, working closely with top Kenya property groups Chell & Peacock and Bush & Beyond.

Micato Safaris Ⓦ micato.com. Kenyan-American family-run tour operator with a variety of bespoke Kenya offerings, mostly utilizing top-end and remote properties.

Mountain Madness Ⓦ mountainmadness.com. Seattle-based adventure travel firm, offering really good-value, well-planned, well-paced Mount Kenya climbs.

Nature Expeditions International Ⓦ naturexp.com. Good-value, flexible educational tours – one just in Kenya, one including Tanzania – with optional lectures on wildlife, natural history and culture. Good for older kids and teens.

Premier Travel & Tours Ⓦ premiertours.com. A good choice of upmarket safaris and escorted tours in East and southern Africa.

Uncharted Outposts Ⓦ unchartedoutposts.com. Highly recommended operator, with many Kenya options, particularly focusing on boutique camps and small lodges.

Overlanding to/from Kenya

With plenty of time and a sense of adventure, **travelling overland** can be a rewarding way of getting to or from Kenya. Central African conflicts have effectively closed routes from West Africa for the time being, and while adventurous **self-drive** overlanders are heading to Kenya from Egypt, taking a boat from Aswan to Wadi Halfa in Sudan, crossing into Ethiopia at Metema and entering Kenya at Moyale or at the northern end of Lake Turkana, this route is not an easy one.

Currently the only advisable route is from **southern Africa**. You can drive by various routes, take the train up through Zambia and Tanzania, go overland by local transport or hook up with an overland operator – any number of which run multi-week tours between Cape Town and Nairobi.

Scrutinizing the operators' websites gives an indication of what to expect from a trip, and given that prices vary widely (anything between $50 and $120 per day, including the local kitty), be sure to research what is included in the price and what is not (many activities cost extra). Also be aware that overlanding is group "participatory" travel (putting your own tent up and down, helping with cooking etc), which can be lots of fun for the adventure, camaraderie and company, or may be your worst nightmare: think carefully whether it will suit you before booking a long tour. While overlanding has traditionally involved camping, thanks to ever-increasing improvement of tourist facilities in Africa, many companies also offer "accommodated" trips – although sometimes this may mean not much more than a bed in a *banda* at a campsite.

Most of our **recommended operators** (see opposite) offer more or less the same classic Nairobi–Cape Town tour, taking eight to ten weeks – the southbound trip starts in Nairobi and does a loop into Uganda and Rwanda to see the mountain gorillas, heads back through Kenya for the parks and then down through Tanzania, Malawi, Zambia, Zimbabwe, Botswana, Namibia and South Africa. The northbound itinerary from Cape Town is exactly the same in reverse. Alternative options that deviate from this route loop through more of Zimbabwe (than just Victoria Falls), travel through Mozambique and into South Africa via Kruger National Park to start and finish in Johannesburg. You don't have to book the entire trip and can do sections to/from Nairobi.

TAKING YOUR OWN VEHICLE INTO KENYA

If you're taking a foreign-registered vehicle into Kenya you'll need to have the following with you at customs:

Vehicle Registration Certificate in the name of the driver (or a certified copy). If it's not in the driver's name, a letter of authorization is required from the registered owner.

Carnet de Passage en Douanes A customs document issued by a driving association in your home country (the RAC in the UK, for example; ⓦ rac.co.uk) that is internationally recognized as entitling the holder to temporarily import a vehicle duty-free.

Foreign Vehicle Permit (also known as a Temporary Import Permit or TIP). Acquired at the border and valid for up to three months (expect to pay $25–40). If you've hired a Tanzanian- or Ugandan-registered vehicle (or you've rented a car in Kenya and are taking it over the border into Tanzania or Uganda) you normally just have to sign a logbook at the border and there's no fee, but ensure that the car rental company gives you the appropriate paperwork.

Third-party insurance is compulsory and the police will ask to see it, both at the border and (if they stop you) in Kenya itself. A short-term policy can be obtained from kiosks at the border posts, or you may already have COMESA (Common Market for Eastern and Southern Africa; ⓦ ycmis.comesa.int) insurance, commonly known as the "Yellow Card", which covers numerous African countries including Kenya. In South Africa this can be purchased from the AA (ⓦ aa.co.za), in other countries from private insurance companies.

Driver's licence This doesn't have to be an international one (unless you are staying for more than three months, after which foreign licences are no longer valid in Kenya) but it does have to have a photo.

Oval sticker It's compulsory to have a sticker showing the origin country of the vehicle (GB, ZA and so on).

Red warning triangle By law in Kenya you must carry one and the police may ask to see it.

For more information contact AA Kenya (see p.52).

OVERLAND COMPANIES

Absolute Africa UK Ⓦ absoluteafrica.com.
Acacia Africa UK and South Africa Ⓦ acacia-africa.com.
African Trails UK Ⓦ africantrails.co.uk.
Dragoman UK Ⓦ dragoman.com.
G Adventures Canada and UK Ⓦ gadventures.com.
Gecko's Adventures Australia Ⓦ geckosadventures.com.
Intrepid Australia Ⓦ intrepidtravel.com.
Oasis Overland UK Ⓦ oasisoverland.co.uk.

Getting around

There's a wide range of travel options in Kenya. If you want to be looked after throughout your trip, you can travel on a shared or exclusive road safari where you sign up to an off-the-shelf or tailor-made itinerary; alternatively you can take an air safari, via scheduled domestic airlines (often in small planes with great visibility), or charter a light plane for your own use. If you want more independence, you can easily rent a vehicle for self-drive or with a driver.

If you're on a budget, you'll find a wide range of **public transport** – though, to be clear, it is all privately operated – from air-conditioned **buses** run by large operators to smaller companies and "saccos" (cooperatives) with a single battered minibus. In towns of any size, crowds of minibuses, operating as shared taxis and referred to as **matatus**, hustle for business constantly. Kenya's **railway** "network" appears to be in terminal decline, but the Nairobi–Mombasa line still runs a couple of services a week.

Flying

Domestic flights in Kenya are thoroughly enjoyable, especially to the national parks, with animals clearly visible below as you approach each airstrip.

The **main operators** are SafariLink (Ⓦ flysafarilink .com), Kenya Airways (Ⓦ kenya-airways.com) and its no-frills subsidiary Jambojet (Ⓦ jambojet.com), Airkenya (Ⓦ airkenya.com), Mombasa Air Safari (Ⓦ mombasaairsafari.com) and 540 Aviation (Ⓦ fly540.com). Destinations served include the main **towns and cities** (Nairobi, Mombasa, Kisumu, Eldoret, Lodwar and Nanyuki), **coastal resorts** (Diani Beach, Malindi, Lamu and Kiwayu) and airfields serving safari clients in the main **parks and reserves** of Amboseli, Maasai Mara, Meru, Tsavo West and Samburu-Shaba, and at Lewa Downs and Loisaba north of Mount Kenya.

Most services are daily and in some cases there are several flights a day, though **frequencies** on certain routes are reduced in low season. Same-day connections can be a problem, too, as flights are routinely cancelled if there are not enough passengers to make them worthwhile, and you will be "bumped" onto the next one. Be aware, too, that flights to the parks and reserves run on circuits, meaning that not all passengers are necessarily going to alight at the same airstrip: the plane might touch down at a few on the route, so flight times and the order of arrival may vary. Nevertheless, flying around Kenya (especially to the parks) saves on long bumpy road trips and each airline endeavours to get you to your destination on time.

Baggage allowance on the smaller planes (those going to safari destinations) is limited to 15kg per person (in soft bags only – rigid suitcases are often not accepted), though this isn't strictly adhered to unless the flight is full. In any event you will be able to make arrangements to store excess baggage while you are on safari.

For some ballpark return **fares** (in high season), reckon on Nairobi–Maasai Mara costing $345, Nairobi–Lamu $375 and Nairobi–Diani Beach (Ukunda) $275. City to city fares with Fly 540, Kenya Airways and Jambojet are much cheaper and are not affected by season, so, for example, the cheapest fare with Fly 540 from Nairobi to Eldoret starts at $82 one-way, while a Jambojet flight from Nairobi to Mombasa costs from only $55 one-way.

Chartering a small plane for trips to safari parks and remote airstrips is worth considering if money is less important to you than time, and is an especially good option for groups or large families. Costs vary depending on the size of the aircraft needed to accommodate the number of passengers, the amount of fuel required and other incidentals such as airport landing fees. Remember also that the plane has to make a round trip, even if you don't. SafariLink and Mombasa Air Safari (see above) will quote for charters; two other excellent charter companies are Tropic Air (Ⓦ tropicairkenya.com), based at Nanyuki airfield, and Yellow Wings (Ⓦ yellowwings.com), based at Wilson Airport in Nairobi.

Car rental and driving

All the parks and reserves are open to private vehicles, and there's a lot to be said for the freedom of choice that **renting a car** gives you. Unless there are more than two of you, though, it won't save you money over one of the cheaper camping safaris.

Before renting, shop around for the best deals and try to negotiate, bearing in mind how long you'll need and the season. July, August and Christmas are busy, so you might want to book ahead. **Rates** vary greatly: some are quoted in Kenyan shillings and others in dollars or euros; some include unlimited mileage while others don't. The minimum age to rent a car is usually 23, sometimes 25.

You can often rent a vehicle with a **driver or driver-guide** supplied by the rental company, which can be more relaxing and a great introduction to the country. This adds around Ksh3000/day to your bill for the driver's salary and daily expenses (plus tip). Obviously fuel is still extra. Be clear precisely what the arrangements are before you set off: it's best to have things in writing.

Check the insurance details and always pay the daily **collision damage waiver (CDW)** premium, sometimes included in the price; even a small bump could be very costly otherwise. **Theft protection waiver (TPW)** should also be taken. Even with these, however, you'll still be liable for an **excess**, usually $500–1000, which you will have to pay if there is any claim. You're also required to leave a hefty deposit, roughly equivalent to the anticipated bill, though normally credit card details will suffice. Assuming you return the vehicle, nothing will be debited from your account. Additionally if in a rental car, you may be asked to produce evidence that the rental car has a **PSV** (passenger service vehicle) licence. You should have a windscreen sticker for this as well as the letters "PSV" written somewhere on the body; if in doubt, check this out with the rental company before you leave.

Being stopped by the **police** is a fairly frequent occurrence; for advice on how to deal with this, see the "Crime and safety" section (see p.85). If you have a **breakdown**, before seeking assistance it is customary to pile bundles of sticks or foliage 50m or so behind and in front of the car. These are the universally recognized "red warning triangles" of Africa – their placing is always scrupulously observed, and you should put them out even if your vehicle is equipped with a real red triangle. Wedging a stone behind at least one wheel to stop the vehicle rolling away is also a good idea.

You might consider joining **AA Kenya** (ⓦ aakenya.co.ke), which offers temporary membership for up to six months for Ksh2000, which includes the usual breakdown and rescue services, where available.

Choosing and running a vehicle

A normal saloon (sedan) car is sufficient if you are driving around Nairobi, up and down the main coastal road or sticking to the major tarred highways between cities. However a high-clearance **four-wheel drive** (4WD) vehicle is recommended for anywhere else. Most car rental companies will not rent out non-4WD vehicles for use in the parks, and rangers will often turn away such cars at the gates, especially in wet weather. Maasai Mara and the mountain parks (Mount Elgon, Mount Kenya and the Aberdare range) are the most safety-minded.

Four-wheel drive **Suzuki jeeps** are the most widely available vehicles, but ensure you get a long wheelbase model with rear seats, room for four people (or five at a pinch) and luggage space at the back. These are more stable than the stumpy short-wheelbase versions. Other good options, also commonly rented out, are the Nissan X-Trail and Mitsubishi Pajero. All three models are dependable, capable of great feats in negotiating rough terrain and can nearly always be fixed by a local repair workshop.

You shouldn't assume that the vehicle is roadworthy before you set off. Have a good look at the engine and tyres, and don't set off without checking the spare wheel (preferably two spare wheels) and making sure that you have a few essential tools, including a tow rope. You should also always carry spare water, and if you are going off the beaten track, also consider spare fuel in a jerrican, a spare fan belt and brake fluid. You are responsible for any **repair** and **maintenance work** that needs doing while you're renting the vehicle, but good car rental companies will reimburse you for spare parts and labour, and expect you to call them if you have a breakdown, in which case they will often send out a mechanic to help.

When you get a **flat tyre**, as you will, get it mended straight away: it costs very little (Ksh100–200) and can be done almost anywhere. Local mechanics are usually very good and can apply ingenuity to the most disastrous situations. But spare parts, tools and proper equipment are rare off the main routes. Always settle on a price before work begins.

At the time of writing, the **price of petrol** (gasoline, always unleaded) ranges from roughly Ksh100–120/litre (£0.65–1/litre), depending on the retailer, the remoteness of the town and Kenya's latest oil imports. There is occasionally a choice of regular or premium, but the latter is the norm. **Diesel** is ten to fifteen percent cheaper. When filling, which is always done by an attendant, check the pump is set to zero. In city petrol stations you can sometimes pay by credit card, but don't count on it as their card reader may be out of action. However in Nairobi, and increasingly at big highway petrol stations, there are ATMs if you need to get cash.

Driving on the roads

You can drive in Kenya with either a valid **driving licence** from your home country, or an international one. A **GPS** SatNav device or smart phone is useful, as road signs tend to be sporadic and there are few detailed, accurate road maps.

Be cautious of abrupt changes in road surface. On busy **tarmac roads**, "tramlines" often develop, parallel with the direction of travel. Caused by heavy trucks ploughing over hot blacktop, these can be deep and treacherous, making steering difficult. Slow down.

Beware of animals, people, rocks, branches, ditches and potholes – any combination of which may appear at any time. It is accepted practice to honk your horn stridently to warn pedestrians and cyclists. **Other vehicles** are probably the biggest menace, especially in busy areas close to towns where matatus are constantly pulling over to drop and pick up passengers. It's common practice to flash oncoming vehicles, especially if they're leaving you little room to pass. Try to **avoid driving at night**, and be extra careful when passing heavy vehicles – the diesel fumes can cut off your visibility without warning.

Officially Kenya **drives on the left**, though in reality vehicles keep to the best part of the road until they have to pass each other.

You should recognize the supplementary meanings of **left and right** signals particularly common among truck drivers. A right signal by the driver ahead of you means "Don't try to pass me", while the left signal which usually follows means "Feel free to pass me now". Do not, however, automatically assume the driver can really see that it is safe for you to pass. In fact, never assume anything about other drivers.

Beware of **speed bumps**, found wherever a busy road has been built through a village, and on the roads in and out of nearly every town. Try to look out for small bollards or painted rocks at the roadside, but usually the first you'll know of speed bumps is when your head hits the roof.

Driving in towns and cities, and especially in Nairobi, you may need to adopt a more robust approach than you would use at home, or risk waiting indefinitely at the first busy junction you come to. There is no concept of yielding or giving way in Kenya: most drivers occupy the road forcefully and only concede when physically blocked by another vehicle or someone in uniform with a weapon. Although it sounds highly confrontational, incidents of "road rage" seem few and far between.

Finding somewhere to **park** is rarely a problem, even in Nairobi or Mombasa. There are council traffic wardens in most large towns from Monday to Saturday, from whom you can buy a 24-hour ticket (the only option) for Ksh50–150. If you don't, your car may be clamped or towed away. Be careful not to park inadvertently on yellow lines, which are often faded to near-invisibility.

Off-road driving

Although there are few parts of Kenya where 4WD vehicles are mandatory, you would be well advised not to go far off tarmac in a two-wheel-drive vehicle. A short cloudburst can transform an otherwise good dirt road into a soft-mud vehicle trap, and even unsurfaced entrance roads and access tracks can become quagmires in the wet. Take local advice if attempting unsurfaced roads in the rainy season.

If you have to go through a large muddy puddle, first kick off your shoes and wade the entire length to check it out (better to get muddy than bogged down). If it's less than 30cm deep, and the base is relatively firm (ie your feet don't sink far), you should be able to drive through. Engage 4WD, get into first gear, and drive slowly straight across, or, if there's a sufficiently firm area to one side, drive across at speed with one wheel in the water and one out. For smaller puddles, gathering up speed on the approach and then charging across in second gear usually works.

It's harder to offer advice about approaching **deep mud**. Drive as fast as you dare, never oversteer when skidding – and pray.

On a mushy surface of "**black cotton soil**", especially during or after rain, you'll need all your wits about you, as even the sturdiest 4WDs have little or no grip on this. It's best to keep your speed down and stay in second gear as much as possible. Try to keep at least one wheel on vegetation-covered ground or in a well-defined rut.

If you do **get stuck**, stop immediately, as spinning the wheels will only make it worse. Try reversing, just once, by revving the engine as far as you can before engaging reverse gear. If it doesn't work, you'll just have to wait for another vehicle to pull you out.

Buses, matatus and taxis

Safety should be your first concern when travelling by public transport: matatus, and to a lesser extent buses, have a bad **safety record**. The most dangerous matatus are those billed as "express" (they mean it). Don't hesitate to ask to get out of the vehicle if you feel unsafe, and to demand a partial refund, which will usually be forthcoming.

Whatever you're travelling on, it's worth considering your general **direction** through the trip and

DISTANCE CHART
Distances are given in kilometres

	Busia	Eldoret	Embu	Garissa	Isebania	Isiolo	Kakamega	Kericho	Kisii	Kisumu	Kitale	Lamu (Mokowe)	Lodwar	Loiyangalani	Malaba
Busia	–	157	537	794	305	534	87	195	223	110	149	1120	445	692	33
Eldoret	157	–	393	650	275	390	97	161	193	117	72	975	365	536	128
Embu	537	393	–	329	460	194	476	344	442	428	463	654	687	566	520
Garissa	794	650	329	–	720	461	710	608	661	699	733	355	966	895	794
Isebania	305	275	460	720	–	526	242	186	87	193	350	1077	649	747	328
Isiolo	534	390	194	461	526	–	437	339	438	423	534	787	711	428	517
Kakamega	87	97	476	710	242	437	–	133	161	49	110	1074	406	640	85
Kericho	195	161	344	608	186	339	133	–	101	82	229	926	530	554	216
Kisii	223	193	442	661	87	438	161	101	–	111	269	984	566	649	246
Kisumu	110	117	428	699	193	423	49	82	111	–	157	1029	455	639	135
Kitale	149	72	463	733	350	534	110	229	269	157	–	1047	299	600	119
Lamu (Mokowe)	1120	975	654	355	1077	787	1074	926	984	1029	1047	–	1313	1223	1100
Lodwar	445	365	687	966	649	711	406	530	566	455	299	1313	–	720	417
Loiyangalani	692	536	566	895	747	428	640	554	649	639	600	1223	720	–	662
Malaba	33	128	520	794	328	517	85	216	246	135	119	1100	417	662	–
Malindi	1032	910	726	345	940	874	992	861	905	945	956	218	1207	1169	1037
Maralal	460	299	338	665	517	198	405	331	426	409	371	970	495	230	428
Marsabit	798	646	406	668	784	256	729	597	696	680	716	1045	797	228	772
Meru	522	385	98	409	524	51	469	337	437	421	457	740	704	413	514
Mombasa	931	794	607	463	874	755	877	745	785	826	863	334	1112	1051	920
Moyale	1125	898	653	969	1035	505	977	845	946	928	965	1297	1054	477	1021
Nairobi	478	313	130	366	343	279	395	264	306	345	380	695	630	569	437
Naivasha	391	224	205	443	325	301	308	177	275	260	305	767	545	484	353
Nakuru	302	157	272	507	296	231	240	108	210	192	227	834	475	453	284
Namanga	619	474	287	523	505	436	650	424	465	510	541	926	794	731	600
Nanyuki	456	311	117	447	449	78	394	263	360	344	382	775	631	431	439
Narok	324	261	259	499	203	365	262	157	164	212	319	823	584	580	347
Nyahururu	362	218	176	505	356	173	299	169	311	250	286	833	536	396	345
Nyeri	464	315	74	405	456	137	403	269	368	353	387	730	637	480	447
Sekenani Gate	338	346	345	584	173	453	279	175	181	231	388	908	680	664	364
Shimoni	1018	874	686	543	899	834	956	824	867	908	945	414	1194	1141	999
Taveta	763	619	431	728	645	580	701	569	611	652	684	575	936	883	742
Voi	784	640	452	622	715	599	722	592	632	672	711	469	959	901	768

Malindi	Maralal	Marsabit	Meru	Mombasa	Moyale	Nairobi	Naivasha	Nakuru	Namanga	Nanyuki	Narok	Nyahururu	Nyeri	Sekenani Gate	Shimoni	Taveta	Voi
1032	460	798	522	931	1125	478	391	302	619	456	324	362	464	338	1018	763	784
910	299	646	385	794	898	313	224	157	474	311	261	218	315	346	874	619	640
726	338	406	98	607	653	130	205	272	287	117	259	176	74	345	686	431	452
345	665	668	409	463	969	366	443	507	523	447	499	505	405	584	543	728	622
940	517	784	524	874	1035	343	325	296	505	449	203	356	456	173	899	645	715
874	198	256	51	755	505	279	301	231	436	78	365	173	137	453	834	580	599
992	405	729	469	877	977	395	308	240	650	394	262	299	403	279	956	701	722
861	331	597	337	745	845	264	177	108	424	263	157	169	269	175	824	569	592
905	426	696	437	785	946	306	275	210	465	360	164	311	368	181	867	611	632
945	409	680	421	826	928	345	260	192	510	344	212	250	353	231	908	652	672
956	371	716	457	863	965	380	305	227	541	382	319	286	387	388	945	684	711
218	970	1045	740	334	1297	695	767	834	926	775	823	833	730	908	414	575	469
1207	495	797	704	1112	1054	630	545	475	794	631	584	536	637	680	1194	936	959
1169	230	228	413	1051	477	569	484	453	731	431	580	396	480	664	1141	883	901
1037	428	772	514	920	1021	437	353	284	600	439	347	345	447	364	999	742	768
–	939	1035	725	118	1292	600	687	756	708	805	742	784	756	827	195	382	249
939	–	345	250	821	577	340	251	212	505	196	345	154	253	429	900	653	663
1035	345	–	309	1010	247	535	620	495	696	335	621	429	394	705	1091	835	858
725	250	309	–	702	557	225	302	372	381	76	357	168	133	442	782	525	548
118	821	1010	702	–	1269	481	568	637	597	692	625	668	640	711	80	265	157
1292	577	247	557	1269	–	783	845	739	939	583	869	679	642	953	1337	1082	1103
600	340	535	225	481	783	–	85	155	161	205	143	185	164	227	560	305	328
687	251	620	302	568	845	85	–	70	252	193	126	98	238	210	651	395	418
756	212	495	372	637	739	155	70	–	322	158	132	64	162	217	720	465	486
708	505	696	381	597	939	161	252	322	–	368	301	348	100	387	672	417	439
805	196	335	76	692	583	205	193	158	368	–	286	94	58	370	763	508	528
742	345	621	357	625	869	143	126	132	301	286	–	191	287	86	234	109	469
784	154	429	168	668	679	185	98	64	348	94	191	–	102	277	747	490	514
756	253	394	133	640	642	164	238	162	100	58	287	102	–	372	712	448	467
827	429	705	442	711	953	227	210	217	387	370	86	277	372	–	788	533	554
195	900	1091	782	80	1337	560	651	720	672	763	234	747	712	788	–	343	235
382	653	835	525	265	1082	305	395	465	417	508	109	490	448	533	343	–	109
249	663	858	548	157	1103	328	418	486	439	528	469	514	467	554	235	109	–

which side of the vehicle will be shadier. This is especially important on dirt roads when the combination of dust, a slow, bumpy ride and fierce sun through closed windows can be unbearable.

Inter-city bus and matatu **fares** are typically around Ksh3–5/km (or if the vehicle is "deluxe" in some way, up to Ksh7/km). Even the longest journey by matatu, the 345km, six-hour journey from Nairobi to Kisumu, should cost no more than Ksh1400 (or Ksh2400 by "deluxe" vehicle). Fares go up and down depending on the price of fuel, and rarely does anyone attempt to charge more than the approved rate. Baggage charges should not normally be levied unless you're transporting a huge load. If you think you're being overcharged, check with other passengers.

Buses

Buses cover almost the whole country. Some, on the main runs between Nairobi and Mombasa, and to a lesser extent the centre and west, are fast, comfortable and keep to schedules; you generally need to **reserve** seats in advance. The easiest procedure is to mention your destination to a few people at the bus park (known as "stage" or "stand" in Kenya) and then check out the torrent of offers, though the large companies have proper ticket offices at or near the bus stations where they list their routes and prices. Once you've acquired a seat on the bus, the wait can be almost a pleasure if you're in no hurry, as you watch the throng outside and field a continuous stream of vendors proffering wares through the window.

Matatus

Along most routes the matatus these days are Nissan or Toyota **minibuses** (in rural areas one or two old-style **pick-up vans**, fitted with wooden benches and a canvas roof, still ply their trade). Matatus are fast and are sometimes dangerous: try to sit at the back, to avoid too graphic a view of blind overtaking. And, at the risk of being repetitious, always ask to get out if you're unhappy with the driving.

Regulations introduced by the Kibaki government in 2003 state that all seats are supposed to be fitted with seat belts (they are often broken); loud music is banned (it is often still played, and is the one saving grace for some passengers); and electronic speed governors are supposed to prevent speeds above 80km/h (they are often broken or deliberately disabled). Passenger numbers are, in theory, strictly limited, but on many routes, especially off the main roads, the old maxim of "room for one more" still applies. *Kitu kidogo*, a "little something" for police officers at roadblocks,

ensures blind eyes are turned towards many infringements. There's more on bribery elsewhere (see p.85), but it's worth pointing out that passengers are never expected to contribute directly.

Matatus can be an enjoyable way of getting about, giving you close contact, literally, with local people, and some hilarious encounters. They are also often the most convenient and sometimes the only means of transport to smaller places off the main roads.

When it comes to making a **choice of matatu**, always choose one that is close to full or you'll have to wait inside until they're ready to go, sometimes for hours. Beware of being used as bait by the driver to encourage passengers to choose his vehicle, and equally of a driver filling his car with young touts pretending to be passengers (spot them by the newspapers and lack of luggage). Competition is intense and people will tell brazen lies to persuade you the vehicle is going "just now". Try not to hand over any money before you've left town. This isn't a question of being ripped off, but too often the first departure is just a soft launch, cruising around town rounding up more passengers – and buying petrol with the fare you've just paid – and then going back to square one.

If your destination isn't on a main matatu route, or if you don't want to wait for a vehicle to fill up (or, indeed, if you just want to travel in style), drivers will happily negotiate a price for the **charter** or rental of the whole car. The sum will normally be equivalent to the amount they would receive from all the passengers in a full vehicle over the same distance.

Taxis and other vehicles

Transport in towns often comes down to **private taxis**. You'll need to discuss the fare in advance: most drivers will want to be earning something like Ksh500/hour (even if stuck in traffic or waiting) plus at least Ksh200/km, and would baulk at driving anywhere for less than Ksh300–400. In some towns, there's also the option of using a **tuk-tuk** (three-wheeled vehicles imported from Asia, on which fares are around half the price of an ordinary taxi). Alternatively, many areas have motorcycle taxis that can carry one or two people without luggage (known as a **piki-piki**), or a bicycle with a padded passenger seat for one (known as a **boda-boda**). Most drivers/cyclists will be straight with you (if surprised to be taking a fare from a foreigner), but if you're in doubt about the correct fare, which is generally around Ksh40/km, asking passers-by will invariably get you a quick sense of the proper price to pay.

MATATU TERMS

The following terms are worth knowing: a **stage or stand** is the matatu yard; a **manamba or turn boy** is the tout who takes the fares and hangs on dramatically; and **dropping** is what you do when you disembark, as in "I'm dropping here".

Trains

Rift Valley Railways runs Kenya's few passenger train services. The overnight **Nairobi–Mombasa** train ran twice a week in each direction at the time of writing, departing Nairobi Mon and Fri at 7pm, and scheduled to arrive in Mombasa around 10am; leaving Mombasa Tues and Sun at 7pm, it is scheduled to arrive in Nairobi around 10am. While this timetable indicates the journey takes around thirteen hours, in reality it usually takes at least up to seventeen hours, and on occasion, the train can pull in anything up to eight hours late. Do not plan any tight connections at either end. The delays are in fact not necessarily caused by the passenger train itself, but by freight trains holding it up on the line. Frustrating as the almost routine delays are, they at least mean you are likely to have a few hours of daylight to watch the passing scene: approaching Nairobi from Mombasa, the animals on the Athi Plains, or approaching Mombasa, the sultry crawl down to the ocean.

Construction of the original line began in Mombasa in 1895 and the railway reached Nairobi in 1899. The China Road & Bridge Corporation (CRBC) is currently building a **new standard-gauge railway** alongside the old narrow-gauge line, which is set for completion in early 2018 (see box, p.322). When rail services are functioning on the new line, passenger trains will travel at a top speed of 120km/h, reducing journey time to an estimated four hours. For that reason those who want to experience the Nairobi–Mombasa sleeper service will need to do it soon.

There used to be a (sporadic) overnight Nairobi–Kisumu service, though this has not been operational since 2012. In the future, however, the new Chinese-built railway is expected to extend from Nairobi to Malaba on the Ugandan border and eventually all the way to Kigali in Rwanda.

The present Nairobi–Mombasa train has three **seat classes**, but only first and second offer any kind of comfort. In first class, you get a private, two-berth compartment; second class has four-berth compartments, which are usually single-sex,

though this may be disregarded if, for example, all four people are travelling as a party; third class has hard seats only and is packed with local passengers because it's half the price of the cheapest bus (even though it takes considerably longer).

The trains are old, the carriages and compartments are far from luxurious, and the toilets are not all European-style, but they begin the journey freshly cleaned, and in a reasonably good state of repair. **Meals and bedding**, available in first and second class only, cost a little extra, and must be paid for when you buy your ticket, though it's normally assumed you will take them: they are included in the fare. The linen is always clean, washing water usually flows from the compartment basins, meals are freshly prepared and service is good. On the Mombasa train, dinner is served in two sittings (7.15pm & 8.45pm). You should go for the first sitting for the best food and service, and the second if you'd rather take your time. Breakfast is served from 6am. Singles and couples will usually have to share their tables with other diners.

You can usually rely on getting **drinks** – bottled water, cold beers and sodas, and sometimes wine, all at fairly standard prices. It's a good idea to **take some snacks** with you – you'll be glad of them if the train rolls in several hours late, which it usually does.

The Rift Valley Railways website (**W** riftvalleyrail .com) includes **schedules** and fares, but is not always entirely accurate. The Man in Seat Sixty-One (**W** seat61.com) is a much more reliable and up-to-date source of information.

Nairobi–Mombasa **fares**, including bedding, dinner and breakfast are as follows: first class Ksh4405, second class Ksh3385, third class (seat only) Ksh680. You need to purchase tickets at the stations, ideally the day before so you can check that the train is running. Tickets can also be **booked** in advance with most travel agents and tour operators in Nairobi and Mombasa: you pay extra as a booking fee, but it's much easier and most can arrange delivery of train tickets to hotels. If you do it this way, expect to pay around $65 for first class and $54 for second class (you can't pre-book third class). Try East Africa Shuttles & Safaris (**W** eastafrica shuttles.com) or Go Kenya Safari Tours & Safaris (**W** kenyatraintravel.com) or ask the tour operator you may already have arrangements with.

Boats and ferries

There's no passenger **shipping** along the Kenya coast apart from small vessels connecting the islands of the Lamu archipelago, and the Likoni car and foot passenger ferry across Kilindini Creek between Mombasa island and the south coast. It's illegal for foreigners to ride on ocean-going **dhows** – and there are few working dhows left – but there are plenty of opportunities to go on short dhow trips from the resorts for fishing, snorkelling or sightseeing.

Hitchhiking

Hitchhiking is how the majority of rural people get around, in the sense that they wait by the roadside for whatever comes, and will pay for a ride in a passing lorry or a private vehicle, the cost being close to what it would be in a matatu. Private vehicles with spare seats are comparatively rare, but Kenyans are happy enough to give lifts, if often bemused by the idea of a tourist without a vehicle.

Highway hitching **techniques** need to be fairly exuberant: beckon the driver to stop with a palm-down action, then quickly establish how much the ride will cost. And be sure to choose a safe spot with room to pull over. Alternatively, use a busy petrol station and ask every driver – the most likely way to get a ride. In terms of **safety**, it's highly unlikely you would run into any unsavoury characters, but do not get in if you think the vehicle is unroadworthy, or the driver unfit to drive.

Hitching rides at the gates of **national parks and reserves** is rarely successful, simply because the passing vehicles will probably be safari vehicles with paying clients on board and they are very unlikely to give someone a free ride. You will have better luck by asking the Kenya Wildlife Services staff at the gates (if it's a KWS park) who may be able to offer you a lift to the park headquarters within the park, which in some cases is close to the KWS accommodation and campsites.

Cycling

If you have enough time and determination, you'll find Kenya's climate and varied terrain make it an interesting – if challenging – country in which to **cycle**. However on main roads be cautious of trucks and matatus, and be very wary about cycling in the cities, especially Nairobi, which is congested with traffic most of the time. It's also not permitted to cycle in the parks and the reserves (for obvious reasons), although some of the smaller game parks that do not have predators allow bikes, including Hell's Gate at Naivasha, Kakamega Forest, Saiwa Swamp and some of the private conservancies such as those on the Laikipia plateau. You also need to consider the **season** – you won't make much progress on dirt roads during the rains – and the **altitude**. Even if you are in good shape at sea level, don't be surprised if you feel lethargic and your legs feel like lead weights for the first couple of days up in the hills.

As well as renting, you can take a bike with you to Kenya, or buy one locally. Most towns have **bicycle shops** selling basic mountain bikes and trusty Indian three-speed roadsters, starting from around Ksh7000. We've mentioned some outlets in Mombasa (see p.404) and Nairobi (see p.123). Whatever you take, and a mountain bike is certainly best, it will need low gears and strongly built wheels, and you should have some essential spare parts and a secure lock.

Buses and matatus with **roof racks** will always carry bicycles for about half the regular fare, even if flagged down at the roadside. Trucks will often give you a lift, too. The Nairobi–Mombasa train also take bikes at a low fixed fare.

Accommodation

There's a huge diversity of accommodation in Kenya, ranging from campsites and local lodging houses for a few hundred shillings a night to luxury lodges and boutique tented camps that can easily cost many hundreds of dollars a night.

All coastal resorts, safari camps and lodges operate **seasonal rates**, approximately divided into high-, mid- and low-season (sometimes called "green season"; see box opposite). Some of the smaller safari camps and lodges close for a couple of months over the March–June period (shutting up shop as soon as Easter has passed), not just due to lack of demand or weather conditions, but to allow for maintenance and refurbishment. Listings throughout the guide show the latest details on months of closure, though these can vary from year to year. All cheap lodgings and standard hotels, however, are non-seasonal and their rates stay the same throughout the year.

Hotels, lodges and tented camps

The term **hotel** covers a very broad spectrum in Kenya (the word *hoteli* means a cheap café-restaurant, not a place to sleep). At the top end are the big tourist and business-class establishments. In the game parks, they're known as lodges. Some establishments are very good value, but others are shabby and overpriced, so check carefully before splurging. Try to reserve the more popular places in advance, especially for the peak season.

At the mid-price level, some hotels are old settlers' haunts that were once slightly grand and no longer quite fit in modern Kenya, while others are newer and cater for the Kenyan middle class. A few are fine – charmingly decrepit or fairly smart and semi-efficient – but a fair few are just boozy and uninteresting.

As a rule, expect to pay anything from Ksh3000–10,000 for a decent double or twin room, with bathroom en suite, known in Kenya as "self-contained" (and abbreviated throughout this book to s/c). Most rooms, even at lower price points, are s/c; if not, this is indicated in our review. Breakfast is usually included, but if you want to have breakfast elsewhere, the price will be deducted. Features such as TV – often with DSTV (satellite) service – floor or ceiling fans and air conditioning will all put the price up, and are sometimes optional, allowing you to make significant savings at cheaper hotels.

Older **safari lodges** may show their age with rather unimaginative design and boring little rooms (those that date back to the 1960s were built when just having a hotel in the bush was considered an achievement). Today, the best of the big lodges have public areas offering spectacular panoramas and game-viewing decks, while the rooms are often comfortable chalets or **bandas**. The most expensive, boutique lodges may have as few as just half a dozen rooms, constructed entirely of local materials, ingeniously open-fronted yet secure, with stunning views, and invigorating open-air showers.

If you want to experience the fun of camping without the hassle, opt for a **tented camp**. These consist of large, custom-made tents erected over hard floors. The walls flap in the breeze and large areas of mosquito screening can be uncovered to allow maximum ventilation (at night, they zip up tight to keep the insects out). All the usual lodge amenities, including electricity (generated by solar panels), are installed, and the furniture is what you'd expect to find in a comfortable hotel, though often with a nod to bush life, such as canvas chairs on the deck and beds made from reclaimed branches of dead wood. At the back, the bathroom

is usually more of a solid-walled structure, with a flush toilet – though the "safari shower" or "bucket shower", using hot water delivered on request by staff to a pulley system outside the bathroom, is a popular anachronism that works very well and saves water. In the centre of the camp, the usual public areas will include a dining room and bar, or in smaller camps a luxurious "mess tent" with sofas and waiters proffering drinks, where you'll eat together with your hosts and the other guests and share the day's experiences in an atmosphere that always has a little *Out of Africa* in it.

Some lodges and camps are surrounded by a discreet, or not so discreet, **electric fence**. This gives you the freedom to wander at will, and is better if you have children in tow, but detracts from the sense of being in the wild. Places that don't have such security may ask you to sign a disclaimer to limit their liability in the event that a large mammalian intruder should abruptly terminate your holiday. In practice, although elephants, buffaloes and other big animals do sometimes wander into camps, serious incidents are exceptionally rare and you have nothing to worry about. After dark, unfenced camps employ escorts – usually tradition-ally dressed, spear-carrying *askaris* (see box, p.61) – to see you safely to and from your tent.

Meals in the safari lodges and camps are generally good, although in the large places the buffets can be a little mediocre. The best lodges have their own organic vegetable gardens and prepare gourmet dinners, fresh bread and excellent pastries in the middle of nowhere.

Almost all of Kenya's upmarket and midrange hotels and beach resorts provide **wi-fi**: it's either free or you pay for a voucher (with a password) at reception. Whether wi-fi is charged or not largely depends on the room rate – the more expensive places usually include it as part of the service. The larger safari lodges and tented camps will also offer wi-fi, though if you need to pay extra be cautious of the cost – it usually uses a remote server and may be expensive, even if just hooking up for an hour or two. Places in remote areas (mountain lodges, small tented camps, out-of-the-way parks and reserves) won't be able to offer wi-fi, and of course neither will establishments at the very cheap end of the scale such as B&Ls.

Boarding and lodgings

In any town you'll find basic guesthouses called **Boarding and lodgings** (for which we've coined the abbreviation "B&L"). These can vary from a mud

---

SEASONS (APPROXIMATE)

Peak Dec 21 to Jan 2.
High July 1 to Oct 31.
Mid Jan 3 to Easter, Nov 1 to Dec 20.
Low/Green/Closed After Easter to June 30.

shack with water from the well to a multistorey building of en-suite rooms, complete with a bar and restaurant, and usually built around a lock-in courtyard/parking area. Most B&L bathrooms include rather alarmingly wired "instant showers", giving a meagre spray of hot water 24 hours a day.

While you can find a room for under Ksh1500 – and sometimes much less – in any town, **prices** are not a good indication of quality. If the bathrooms don't have instant showers, then check the water supply and find out when the boiler will be on. The very cheapest places (as little as Ksh500 or less) will not usually have self-contained rooms, so you should check the state of the shared showers and toilets. You won't cause offence by saying no thanks.

The better B&Ls are clean and comfortable, but they tend to be airless and often double as informal brothels, especially if they have a bar. If the place seems noisy in the afternoon, it will become cacophonous during the night, so you may want to ask for a room away from the source of the din. Moreover, if it relies on its bar for income, security becomes an important deciding factor. Well-run B&Ls, even noisy, sleazy ones, have uniformed security staff and gated access to the room floors. You can leave valuables with the manager in reception, though use your judgement.

Cottages and homestays

Increasingly, it's possible to book **self-catering** apartments, villas or cottages, especially on the coast. Try Langata Link Holiday Homes (🆆 holiday homeskenya.com), Kenya Beach Rentals (🆆 kenya -beachrentals.com) and Kenya Holiday House (🆆 kenyaholidayhouse.com). Uniglobe Let's Go Travel (🆆 uniglobeletsgotravel.com) is a highly recommended agent for accommodation across the spectrum Also, try **Airbnb**, mostly for Nairobi and the coast.

Camping

If you're on a budget and have a flexible itinerary, there are organized **campsites** (campgrounds) in Kenya, but bear in mind that, away from the parks and reserves, they are few and far between and almost non-existent on the coast. There are exceptions, however, such as around the lakes in the Rift Valley, and many hotels in the Central Highlands and Western Kenya allow campers to set up tents on their lawns and will provide bathroom facilities. If you do decide to carry a tent, bring the lightest one you can afford and remember its main purpose is to keep insects out,

---

ACCOMMODATION PRICES

The **accommodation rates** given in this guide are for double- or twin-bed occupancy during the high season (see box, p.59). For peak season (Christmas and New Year) expect to pay another 10–20 percent on top of high season rates.

All cheap lodgings, all Nairobi hotels and most town hotels (unless they're on the coast) are non-seasonal. All coastal resort hotels, safari camps and lodges operate seasonal rates.

The rates have been provided directly by the property and are the non-resident "rack rates" – in other words the regular walk-in rates that you will pay for the night, including taxes (16 percent VAT and 2 percent training levy). If there is more than one class of room, the standard or cheapest option is the one quoted.

For **dorm beds** and **campsites**, the price per person has been given, while for **self-catering** cottages, houses and *bandas*, the price given is for the whole unit.

Children's rates are usually 50 percent of the adult rate when they are sharing with adults, and 75 percent when sharing their own room, and generally apply to kids between 2 and 11 years old; some places have reduced rates for teenagers. However, this does not apply to all venues and there may be different age brackets and costs depending on the establishment.

Agents, online **booking** services and the property's own reservations desk or website may offer cheaper deals for advance bookings. And you can, of course, always ask if they can offer you a discount – for paying by cash; because you're a first-time visitor; because you're a repeat visitor; or for any other plausible reason you care to approach with. Cheap hotels quote their rates in Kenyan shillings, while hotels aimed at the tourist market tend to quote in US dollars or sometimes in euros and occasionally UK pound sterling. You can always settle your bill in Kenyan shillings, but check the exchange rate is fair.

Residents' rates for Kenyan citizens and residents, including expat workers (typically around 30–40 percent discount), are offered at most establishments above the budget bracket. There's no hard-and-fast rule, but most places charging above $80–100 a room have two-tier pricing.

ACCOMMODATION TERMS

a/c air-conditioned
AI all-inclusive
askari or **soja** guard, security officer
banda cottage or chalet
BB bed & breakfast
B&L boarding and lodging, a cheap guesthouse
FB full board (lunch, dinner, bed and breakfast)
fly camp mobile camp
HB half board (dinner, bed and breakfast)
hoteli cheap restaurant or café, *not* a hotel
lodge safari hotel in the bush
long-drop non-flushing toilet – a hole over a deep pit
mabati corrugated-iron roof
package the usual full-board arrangement in high-end safari camps and lodges, with all drinks and activities included
rondavel small, round hut, containing beds but no bathroom
safari shower also known as a bucket shower, a refillable reservoir of hot water above the shower area
s/c "self-contained" room, with en-suite bathroom
star-bed four-poster bed mounted on vehicle wheels, pulled onto a deck at night and guarded by *askaris*
tented camp a camp in the bush, or in a game park, consisting of large, walk-in safari tents with solid bathrooms (see p.59)
tree-hotel animal-viewing lodge on stilts, after the style of *Treetops* (see p.193)

so one made largely of mosquito netting could be ideal.

Kenya's few **privately owned campsites** have toilets and showers with hot water and possibly a restaurant, bar and sometimes a swimming pool. *Askaris* are usually provided to guard tents and vehicles. Some also offer the option of renting a tent, and there may be other accommodation such as dorms and simple twin/double/triples, where bathroom facilities are usually shared with campers. These are often in basic *bandas* but they nearly always have adequate bedding and lighting.

Kenya Wildlife Service (KWS, @ kws.org) manages all the campsites in national parks. Each has one or two very basic "**public campsites**", often located near the gates or the KWS park headquarters further into the park. These generally do not have to be pre-booked – you simply pay for camping on arrival at the gate along with your park entry fees. Current daily per-person rates are $20 ($30 in Amboseli and Lake Nakuru). For that hefty price, you often get little more than a place to pitch your tent and park your vehicle, and showers and toilets that are often rudimentary.

KWS's so-called "**special campsites**", are in reality simply sites which have to be reserved on an exclusive basis for private use, and are often used by

tour operators on camping safaris. Some of them are in particularly attractive locations, but unlike public campsites they have no facilities whatsoever: you need to be entirely self-sufficient to use them. Special campsites attract a flat reservation fee of Ksh7500 (around $75) plus the daily per-person rates ($35, or $50 in Amboseli and Lake Nakuru). To reserve them, contact KWS in Nairobi (@020 6000800), or visit the KWS headquarters at Nairobi National Park Main Gate (see p.144). Camping fees in the major national parks (Aberdare, Amboseli, Nairobi, Lake Nakuru, Tsavo East and Tsavo West) are normally deducted from your pre-paid Safari Card (see p.71).

Opportunities for **wild camping** depend on whether you can find a suitable, safe site. In the more heavily populated and farmed highland districts, you should always ask someone before pitching in an empty spot, and never leave your tent unattended. Far out in the wilds, hard or thorny ground is likely to be the only obstacle. During the dry seasons, you'll rarely have trouble finding dead wood for a fire, so a stove is optional. You can buy camping gas cartridges in a few places in Nairobi (see box, p.129). Camping near roads, in dry river beds or on trails used by animals going to water is highly inadvisable (see p.86). Camping on the beach is illegal unless it's on private property such as in the compound of a beach resort.

Food and drink

For the vast majority of Kenyans, meals are plain and filling. Most people's living standards don't allow for frills, and there are no great national dishes. For culinary culture, it's only on the coast, with its long association with Indian Ocean trade, that a distinctive regional cuisine has developed, with rice and fish, flavoured with coconut, tamarind and exotic spices, the major ingredients. For visitors, and more affluent Kenyans, the cities and tourist areas have no shortage of restaurants, with roast meat, seafood and Italian restaurants the most common options among a range of cuisines that runs the gamut from Argentine to Thai. The "Language" section contains a list of useful food terms (see p.603).

As for **cost**, in the most basic local restaurant, a decent plate of food can be had for less than Ksh300. Fancier meals in touristy places rarely cost more than Ksh2000 a head, though there are a number of establishments where you could easily spend Ksh5000 or more. When checking your bill, remember there's a 16 percent value-added tax (VAT) on food and drink and a 2 percent government training levy in all but the smallest establishments. In most establishments, taxes are included in the prices on the menu, but in some they are extra, basically adding nearly one-fifth to the bill. An "optional" service charge can be added, too, and of course you may want to add a tip (see p.93).

Many restaurants on the coast serve halal food, and elsewhere in the country you'll usually be able to find a Somali-run *hoteli* that has halal meat.

Home-style fare and nyama choma

In any *hoteli* (cheap local café-restaurant) there is always a list of predictable dishes intended to fill customers' stomachs. Potatoes, rice and especially **ugali** (a stiff cornmeal porridge) are the national staples, eaten with chicken, goat, beef or vegetable stew, various kinds of spinach, beans and sometimes fish. Portions are usually gigantic; half-portions (ask for *nusu*) aren't much smaller. But if this is not to your taste, even in small towns, you'll find cafés with a menu of mostly fried food – eggs, sausages, chips, fish, chicken and burgers.

The standard blow-out feast for most Kenyans is a huge pile of **nyama choma** (roast meat, usually goat, beef or mutton). *Nyama choma* is usually eaten at a purpose-built *choma* bar, with beer and music the standard accompaniments, and *ugali* and greens optional. You order by weight (half a kilo is plenty), direct from the butcher's hook or out of the fridge. After being roasted, the meat is brought to your table on a wooden platter, chopped to bite-size with a sharp knife, and served with crunchy salt and *kachumbari* – tomato and onion relish.

Snacks and breakfast

Snacks, which can easily become meals, include samosas, chapattis and miniature kebabs (*mishkaki*). Also look out for *mandaazi* (sweet, puffy, deep-fried dough cakes), and *mkate mayai* ("bread of eggs") in Swahili), a light wheat-flour pancake wrapped around fried eggs and minced meat, usually cooked on a huge griddle. Snacks sold on the street include cassava chips, roasted corncobs, and, in country areas, at the right time of year, if you're lucky, roasted termites (which go well as a bar snack with beer).

Breakfast varies widely. Standard fare in a *hoteli*, or in the dining room of a B&L, consists of sweet tea and a chapatti or a doorstep of white bread thickly spread with margarine. Modest hotels offer a "full breakfast" of cereal, eggs and sausage, bread and jam and a banana, with instant coffee or tea. If you're staying in an upmarket hotel or safari lodge, breakfast is usually a lavish acreage of hot and cold buffets that you can't possibly do justice to.

Restaurant meals

Kenya's seafood, beef and lamb are renowned, and they are the basis of most restaurant meals. **Game meat** used to be something of a Kenyan speciality, most of it farmed on ranches. Giraffe, zebra, impala and warthog all regularly appeared at various restaurants. These days, only captive-farmed ostrich (excellent, like lean beef) and crocodile (disappointingly like gristly fish-tasting chicken) are legal.

Indian restaurants in the larger towns, notably Nairobi and Mombasa, are generally excellent, with *dhal* lunches a good standby and much fancier regional dishes widely available too. When you splurge, apart from eating Indian, it will usually be in **hotel restaurants**, with food often very similar to what you might be served in a restaurant in Europe or North America. The **lodges** usually have buffet lunches at about Ksh1200–2000, which can be great value, with table-loads of salads and cold meat.

VEGETARIAN AND VEGAN FOOD

If you're a **vegetarian** staying in tourist-class hotels you should have no problems, as there's usually a meat-free pasta dish, or various egg-based dishes. In more expensive establishments, vegetarian cooking is taken seriously, with creative options that are more than just stodge increasingly available. If you're on a strict budget you'll gravitate to Indian vegetarian restaurants in the larger towns where you can often eat well and cheaply. Otherwise, it can be tricky, because meat is the conventional focus of any meal not eaten at home, and *hotelis* rarely have much else to accompany the starch; even vegetable stews are normally cooked in meat gravy.

If you're a **vegan**, you'll find there are nearly always good vegetables and lots of fruit at safari lodges and the more expensive hotels. Once again, where you'll struggle is if you're on a strict budget and eating local restaurant food.

Fruit and nuts

Fruit is a major delight. Bananas, avocados, papayas (pawpaws) and pineapples are available in the markets all year, mangoes and citrus fruits more seasonally. Look out for passion fruit (the familiar shrivelled brown variety, and the sweeter and less acidic smooth yellow ones), physalis (cape gooseberries), custard apples and guavas – all highly distinctive and delicious. On the coast, roasted **cashew nuts** are widely available, but not cheap. Never buy any with dark marks on them. **Coconuts**, widely seen at roadside stalls in their freshly cut, green-husked condition, are filling and nutritious.

Drinks

The national beverage is **chai** – tea. Universally drunk at breakfast and as a pick-me-up at any time, the traditional way of making it is a weird variant on the classic British brew: milk, water, lots of sugar and tea leaves are brought to the boil in a kettle and served scalding hot (*chai asli*). It must eventually do diabolical dental damage, but it's quite addictive and very reviving. The main tea-producing region is around Kericho in the west, but the best tea tends to be made on the coast. These days, tea is all too often a tea bag in a cup, with hot water or milk brought to your table in a thermos.

Coffee, despite being another huge Kenyan export, is often just instant coffee granules if ordered in a cheap hotel or restaurant. However local chains of American-style coffee shops have sprung up in Nairobi, Mombasa and Nakuru and it's steadily getting easier to order a latte or cappuccino, often accompanied by a swoosh of air-conditioning and free wi-fi. Prices reflect the modern interiors and the baristas' professional training, and an espresso will cost at least Ksh200 and a frothy coffee up to Ksh400. Nevertheless, the coffee is often excellent, and many chains such as *Java House* and *Dorman's* also sell packets of Kenya-produced coffee beans. Breakfast with a good cafetière of the excellent local roast is also increasingly the norm, especially in upmarket places.

Soft drinks (sodas) are usually very cheap, and crates of Coke, Fanta and Sprite find their way to the wildest corners of the country. The Krest brand (also produced by Coca-Cola) produces a good bitter lemon, tonic and soda, but their ginger ale is a bit watery and insipid; Stoney ginger beer has more of a punch.

Fresh fruit **juices** are available in the towns, especially on the coast (Lamu is fruit-juice heaven). Passion fruit or mango, the cheapest, are excellent, though nowadays are likely to be watered-down concentrate. Some places serve a variety: you'll sometimes find carrot juice and even tiger milk, made from a small tuber (the tiger nut or Spanish *chufa*). Minute Maid is the most popular commercial juice brand (again also owned by Coca-Cola), and comes in small 300ml and large one litre cartons in various flavours. Their drinks are available at supermarkets and many petrol station shops, along with fizzy soft drinks.

Plastic-bottled **spring water** is relatively expensive but widely available in 300ml, 500ml and one-litre bottles. Mains water used to be very drinkable, and in some places still is, but it's safer to stick with bottled (see p.66).

Beer and cider

If you like **lager**, you'll find Kenyan brands generally good. Brewed by East African Breweries, the main lagers are Tusker and White Cap (both 4.2 percent) and Pilsner (4.7 percent), sold in half-litre bottles, with Tusker Malt (5.2 percent) in 300ml bottles. They all cost from a little over Ksh200 in local bars up to about Ksh400 in the most expensive establishments. While Tusker Malt is fuller-flavoured, Tusker, White Cap and Pilsner are all light, slightly acidic, fairly fizzy, well-balanced beers that most people find very drinkable when well chilled. East African Breweries also produce a head-thumping 6.52 percent-alcohol version of **Guinness**. A number of slightly pricier (about ten percent more) imported beers are also available, mostly under the umbrella of South Africa's SABMiller, including Castle Lager, Castle Milk Stout, Castle Lite and US brand Miller Genuine Draft. Also look out for South Africa-produced Savanna Dry, a clear, refreshing and dry-tasting **cider** that is usually thrown into cool boxes along with the beer for sundowners at safari lodges.

A point of drinking **etiquette** worth remembering is that you should never take your bottle away. As bottles carry deposits, this is considered theft, and surprisingly ugly misunderstandings can ensue. Sodas and beer in cans are available in supermarkets, but expect to pay about 10–20 percent more than the bottle price.

Other alcoholic drinks

Most of the usually familiar **wines** sold in Kenya come from South Africa and Chile, with Italy, California, France and Spain also featuring. Locally made wines struggle a little, but Rift Valley Winery makes the increasingly well-known Leleshwa (Ⓦ leleshwa.com).

Kenya Cane (white rum) and **Kenya Gold** (a coffee-flavoured liqueur) deserve a try, but they're nothing special. One popular Kenyan cocktail to sample is the **dawa** ("medicine") – a highly addictive vodka, white rum, honey and lime juice mix, poured over ice and stirred with a sugar stick.

There's a battery of laws against **home brewing** and distilling, perhaps because of the loss of tax revenue on legal booze, but these are central aspects of Kenyan culture and they go on. You can sample pombe (bush beer) of different sorts all over the country. It's as varied in taste, colour and consistency as its ingredients: basically fermented sugar and millet or banana, with herbs and roots for flavouring. The results are frothy and deceptively strong.

On the coast, where coconuts grow most plentifully, merely lopping off the growing shoot produces a naturally fermented, milky-coloured **palm wine** (mnazi or tembo), which is indisputably Kenya's finest contribution to the art of self-intoxication. It's bottled, informally, and usually drunk through a piece of dried grass or straw with a tiny filter tied to the end. There's another variety of palm wine, tapped from the doum palm, called mukoma.

Although there is often a furtive discretion about pombe or mnazi sessions, consumers rarely get busted. Not so with home-distilled spirits: think twice before accepting a mug of **chang'aa**. It's treacherous firewater, and is also frequently contaminated with industrial alcohol, regularly killing drinking parties en masse. Sentences for distilling and possessing chang'aa are harsh, and police or vigilante raids common.

Health

Disease is an ever-present threat to most Kenyans, but health should not be a big issue for visitors. Malaria is endemic and HIV infection rates are high, but so long as you take sensible precautions – remember your malaria pills, clean any cuts or scrapes and avoid food that has been left out after cooking – you should have no problems beyond the chance of minor tummy trouble.

Your doctor or travel clinic is your best first source of advice and probable supplier of jabs and prescriptions. Ensure you consult them at least four weeks prior to your departure from home so that you have enough time for **vaccinations** and/or a course of malaria **prophylactics**. If you're going to Kenya for longer than a short holiday, get a thorough **dental checkup** before leaving home.

Sexually transmitted diseases, including **HIV**, are rife. Using a condom will help to protect you from this and other STDs, including **hepatitis B**, which is quite widespread and can lead to chronic liver disease. One of the biggest hazards is the fierce **UV radiation** of the equatorial sun. Brightness rather than heat is the damaging element, so wear a hat and use high-factor **sunblock**, especially in your first two weeks.

MEDICAL RESOURCES

IAMAT (International Association for Medical Assistance to Travellers) Ⓦ iamat.org. A free-membership non-profit organization, providing travel health info and lists of approved participating doctors and hospitals in Kenya.

International SOS Ⓦ internationalsos.com. Emergency evacuation and assistance to members.

UK

Fit for Travel Ⓦ fitfortravel.nhs.uk. Detailed advice from the NHS for people travelling abroad from the UK.

MASTA (Medical Advisory Service for Travellers Abroad) Ⓦ masta-travel-health.com. The largest network of private travel clinics in the UK.

Nomad Pharmacy Ⓦ nomadtravel.co.uk/pharmacy. Has an online pharmacy and sells travel medical kits and equipment. Several outlets in London, plus Bath, Birmingham, Bristol, Cardiff and Manchester.

Ireland

Tropical Medical Bureau W tmb.ie. More than a dozen travel clinics across Ireland.

US and Canada

Centers for Disease Control and Prevention W cdc.gov/travel. US government official site for travel health.
MEDJET Assist W medjetassist.com. Medical evacuation specialists.
Public Health Agency of Canada W phac-aspc.gc.ca. Traveller's health portal from the Canadian government.

Australia, New Zealand and South Africa

Netcare Travel Clinics W travelclinic.co.za. Travel clinics in the major cities of South Africa, and useful for visitors en route to other African countries.
The Travel Doctor TMVC W traveldoctor.com.au. Travellers' medical and vaccination clinics across Australia and New Zealand and a good source of pre-trip information.

Inoculations

For arrivals by air direct from Europe and North America, Kenya has **no required inoculations**. Entering overland from Uganda or Tanzania, though (or flying via another African country), you may well be required to show an International Vaccination Certificate (IVC) for **yellow fever** on arrival. You may also be required to show an IVC for yellow fever when returning home from a country that requires one (such as Uganda or Tanzania). Effective protection takes some time to develop after vaccination, so plan ahead and start organizing your jabs at least four weeks before departure. A yellow fever certificate only becomes valid ten days after you've had the jab, but is then valid for ten years.

You should ensure that you are up to date with your childhood **tetanus** and **polio** protection: boosters are necessary every ten years and it's as well to check before travelling.

Although not necessary for an ordinary safari-and-beach holiday, if you're going to be exposed to unhygienic conditions – particularly if working locally or travelling extensively – doctors recommend jabs for **typhoid**, **hepatitis A** and **hepatitis B** (or a combined vaccination course).

Malaria

Malaria is endemic in tropical Africa. It's caused by a parasite called *Plasmodium*, carried in the saliva of the female *Anopheles* mosquito. *Anopheles* prefers to **bite** in the evening, and can be distinguished by the eager, head-down position as she settles to bite. *Anopheles* is rarely found above 1500m, which means Nairobi and much of central Kenya are naturally malaria-free, but infected humans are vectors for the disease, meaning that an uninfected *Anopheles* mosquito that bites an infected person can pass malaria on to someone else, so you should assume the whole country is risky. Research has spotlighted a number of areas as having relatively **high levels of malaria transmission**, including the far south coast, around Shimoni, and the Lake Victoria shoreline and the plains inland from it. It can't be stressed enough, however, that you can catch malaria virtually anywhere in Kenya.

Though not infectious, the disease can be very dangerous and sometimes fatal if not treated quickly. The destruction of red blood cells by the *Plasmodium falciparum* parasite can lead to **cerebral malaria** (blocking of the brain capillaries), which can cause a swelling of the brain and induce coma.

Wherever you travel, mosquito bites are almost a certainty and protection against malaria is essential. The best and most obvious method is to reduce your risk of being bitten. Keep your arms, legs and feet covered as much as possible after dusk (long, light-coloured sleeves and trousers are best), and cover exposed skin with a strong repellent. **Deet-based repellents** ("Deet" is the insecticide diethyltoluamide) are best; citronella oil is considered much less effective, and has the disadvantage that elephants are attracted to the smell, and have been known to break into cars and tents to get at it. Sleep under a **mosquito net** (if you're using your own, you might want to impregnate it with Deet) and burn **mosquito coils**, or mosquito-repellent **tablets** on a plug-in electric burner, both readily available in Kenya. Electronic buzzers have been shown not to work.

However much you can avoid being bitten, most medical professionals consider it essential to take **anti-malaria tablets**. The commonly recommended preventatives are the weekly mefloquine (sold as **Lariam**), which has a poor record for side effects, the antibiotic **doxycycline**, taken daily, and atovaquone-with-proguanil, taken daily (sold as **Malarone**), which, while expensive, has few, if any, side effects and can be started just two days before you leave. Your doctor or travel clinic should be able to advise which of these is the best for you, and what the various side effects can be. It's important to maintain a careful routine and cover the period **before and after** your trip with doses.

If you do get a **dose of malaria**, you'll know about it: the fever, shivering and headaches are something like severe flu and come in unpleasant waves, making you pour with sweat for half an hour and then shiver uncontrollably. Typically, the time between being infected and when symptoms start (incubation period) is seven to eighteen days, but it can be up to several weeks. If you suspect anything, even after returning home, seek medical attention immediately. You will be rapidly tested and sold the appropriate treatment. If you are in Kenya and can't get to a doctor, seeing a pharmacist is a good plan B.

If you're visiting Kenya for an extended period, it makes sense to buy further supplies of anti-malarial tablets there. They're all available over the counter and can be much cheaper than at home – a box of one hundred doxycycline, for example, costs less than Ksh1000.

Waterborne diseases

Serious stomach upsets don't afflict a large proportion of travellers. That said, Kenya's once fairly safe **tap water** is increasingly unfit to drink and the supply can be particularly suspect during periods of drought or heavy flooding. Where there is no mains supply, be very cautious of rain- or well water. To purify water intended for drinking, use purifying tablets or, better, iodine (six drops per litre of water, then wait for half an hour), or boil it (if at high altitude, for thirty minutes).

If your stay in Kenya is short, you might as well stick to **bottled water**, which is widely available. For longer stays, think of **re-educating your stomach**; it's virtually impossible to travel around the country without exposing yourself to strange bugs from time to time. Take it easy at first, don't overdo the fruit (and wash it in clean water), don't keep food too long, and be wary of salads. It is also wise to eat food that is freshly cooked and piping hot, even at buffets in safari lodges and beach resorts.

Should you go down with **diarrhoea**, it will probably sort itself out without treatment within 48 hours. In the meantime, and especially with children, for whom it may be more serious, it's essential to replace the fluids and salts lost, so drink lots of water with oral rehydration salts (if you can't get them from pharmacies, use half a teaspoon of salt and eight teaspoons of sugar in a litre of water). It's a good idea to avoid greasy food, heavy spices, caffeine and most fruit and dairy products. Plain rice or *ugali* with boiled vegetables is the best diet. Drugs like Lomotil and Imodium simply plug you up, undermining the body's efforts to rid itself of infection, though they can be useful if you have to travel.

Avoid jumping for antibiotics at the first sign of trouble: they annihilate (what's nicely known as) your "gut flora" and will not work on viruses. But if your diarrhoea continues for more than five days, seek medical help. You should be aware of the fact that diarrhoea reduces the efficacy of malaria and contraceptive pills as they may pass straight through your system without being absorbed.

Bilharzia (medical name schistosomiasis) is transmitted by tiny worm-like flukes that live in freshwater snails and burrow into animal or human skin to multiply in the bloodstream. The snails only favour stagnant water and the chances of picking up the disease are small. The usual recommendation is never to swim in, wash with or even touch lake water that can't be vouched for as schistosome-free. The stagnant and weed-infested parts of Kenyan lakes and rivers often harbour bilharzia, but the danger of crocodile attack means you're unlikely to want any close contact with most inland waters in any case. If you suffer serious fatigue and pass blood, which are the first symptoms of bilharzia, see a doctor: it's quickly curable with the right medication.

Heat and altitude

It's important not to underestimate the power of the **equatorial sun**: a hat and sunglasses are strongly recommended to protect you from the bright light. The sun can quickly burn, or even cause **sunstroke**, so a high-factor sunblock is vital on exposed skin, especially when you first arrive (and it's expensive in Kenya, particularly in hotel shops, so take it with you). Be aware that overheating can cause **heatstroke**, which is potentially fatal. Signs are a very high body temperature, without a feeling of fever but accompanied by headaches and disorientation. Lowering the body temperature (by taking a tepid shower, for example), and resting in a cool place, are the first steps in treatment.

The sun's radiation is stronger at higher altitudes, but the biggest risk if you climb to over 2500m above sea level is **altitude sickness** (see p.171), which may affect climbers on Mount Kenya, and even walkers in the Cherangani Hills.

On the coast, many people get occasional **heat rashes**, especially at first. A warm shower to open the pores, and loose cotton clothes, can help, as can zinc oxide powder. **Dehydration** is another possible problem, so make sure you're drinking enough fluids, especially when you're hot or tired, but don't overdo alcoholic or caffeinated drinks. The main danger sign of dehydration is irregular urination, and dark urine definitely means you're not drinking enough water.

Cuts and bites

The most likely way to hurt yourself on a trip to Kenya is while swimming or snorkelling, as old coral rock can be very sharp. Wear fins or swimming shoes. You should also take more care than usual over minor **cuts and scrapes**. In the tropics, the most trivial scratch can quickly become a throbbing infection if you ignore it. Take a small tube of antiseptic cream (or even better, powder) with you, although these can be also purchased in Kenyan pharmacies.

As for animal bites, **dogs** are usually sad and skulking, and pose little threat, but rabies does exist in Kenya, and can be transmitted by a bite or even a lick, so it's best to avoid playing with pets or strays unless you know the owner and are sure they are safe. Remember too that rabies can also be carried by **monkeys** and baboons, which should never be approached in any case. On the smaller scale, **scorpions and spiders** abound, but are hardly ever seen unless you deliberately turn over rocks or logs. Scorpion stings are painful but rarely dangerous, while spiders – even the big ones – are mostly harmless. **Snakes** are common but, again, the vast majority are harmless. To see one at all, you need to search stealthily. If you walk heavily they obligingly disappear. Larger animals, especially elephants, pose a potential risk to safari-goers, but not one that you need to worry about if you follow the rules (see p.86).

Medical treatment

For serious treatment Kenya has too few well-equipped or well-staffed state hospitals, and travellers with adequate insurance should always head for the **private hospitals** if possible. These can be found in Nairobi, along the coast and in some of the upcountry towns. In most you're expected to pay for all treatment and drugs up front and make a claim from your insurance at a later date – always keep receipts. Among the better private hospitals in Kenya are Nairobi Hospital (Ⓦnairobihospital.org), which is in fact considered the best hospital in East Africa and admits patients with serious medical conditions from all over the region; The Aga Khan University Hospital, Nairobi (Ⓦhospitals.aku.edu); The Aga Khan Hospital, Mombasa (Ⓦagakhanhospitals.org); The Aga Khan Hospital, Kisumu (Ⓦagakhanhospitals.org); Kijabe Hospital on the east side of the Rift Valley near Naivasha (Ⓦkijabehospital.org); Mombasa Hospital (Ⓦmombasahospital.com); Diani Beach Hospital (Ⓦdianibeachhospital.com), which also offers cosmetic surgery for people on holiday at the south coast beach resorts. The best local hospitals are mentioned in relevant parts of the guide.

Kenya's **flying doctors** air ambulance service (☏020 6992299 or 6992000, Ⓦflydoc.org) offers evacuation by air to the nearest suitable hospital, which is very reassuring if you'll be spending time out in the wilds. Tourist membership costs $16 per person per month to cover Kenya and Tanzania, though check whether medical air evacuation (and medical repatriation in general) is already covered under your travel insurance as adequate provision may already have been made; tour operators may also have cover for their clients on organized safaris.

MEDICAL KIT

Items to consider taking on a trip include:
- **Antibiotics** If you are likely to be far from medical help for any length of time, your doctor should be able to prescribe you broad-based antibiotics in case you need to treat a serious bowel crisis or skin infection.
- **Antihistamine cream and tablets** Effective against allergies, itching, skin rashes and insect bites (tablets can also be used to prevent travel sickness).
- **Antimalarial tablets** Essential.
- **Antiseptic cream or powder**
- **Antiseptic wipes** Invaluable for cleaning minor wounds and insect bites.
- **Aspirin or paracetamol**
- **Iodine tincture, with dropper, or water purifying tablets** If you are going off the beaten track and can't get clean or bottled water, these will do the trick.
- **Lip-salve/chap stick**
- **Oral rehydration solutions** Such as Dioralyte.
- **Plasters (Band-Aids)**
- **Tampons** Available in town chemists but expensive, so bring your own supplies.
- **Thermometer** Get a plastic one that sticks on your forehead.
- **Tweezers** Useful for extracting thorns or splinters.
- **Zinc oxide powder** Useful anti-fungal powder for sweaty crevices.

The flying doctors' income goes back into their outreach programme and the African Medical Research Foundation (AMREF) behind it. They have an office at Wilson Airport, from where most of their rescue missions take off.

The media

The press in Kenya is lively and provides reasonable coverage of international news. There are more than a hundred radio stations for music, while satellite TV offers numerous home-grown and international channels, including the BBC, CNN and European sports stations.

Radio and TV

The Kenya Broadcasting Corporation (Ⓦwww.kbc .co.ke) broadcasts **radio** news and current affairs services in English, Swahili and local languages across most of the country. The *Nation* newspaper group runs a news station, Nation FM (96.4FM), while the BBC World Service can be picked up on FM in Nairobi (93.7MHz) and Mombasa (93.9MHz). With so many commercial FM music radio stations, you simply need to find one playing the music you like. For popular newly released music, try Capital FM (98.4FM; Ⓦcapitalfm.co.ke) or Kiss FM (100.3FM: Ⓦkiss100.co.ke). Most radio stations are available on the **internet** – good for pre-departure immersion - and you can tune in at Ⓦradio.or.ke.

Kenyan **television**, much of it imported, carries a mix of English and Swahili programmes. There are three main channels: the stuffy and hesitant state-run KBC, which carries BBC World for much of the day; the upbeat, mainly urban KTN owned by the *Standard* newspaper group, which carries CNN during the night and much of the morning; and the *Nation* newspaper group's channel, NTV. An increasing number of homes, bars and hotels have **satellite TV** on the South African DSTV service (Ⓦdstv.com), which has various movie and sports channels and gives access to Britain's Sky News, BBC and ITV, and numerous other foreign channels.

The press

Kenya is a nation absorbed in its press, though the papers, as everywhere, struggle to hold their own against online media. The leading mainstream **newspaper** is the *Daily Nation* (Ⓦnation.co.ke),

which has reasonable news coverage, including international news and European football results, and a letters page full of insights into Kenyan life. Its main competitor is *The Standard* (Ⓦstandardmedia .co.ke). Both papers are available online. Unfortunately, sharp analysis is in short supply and many editorials and opinion pieces lack bite. For a more critical take on the news, turn to *The Star* (Ⓦthe-star.co.ke), which is much more outspoken but tends to be gossipy. Intelligent weekly *The East African* (Ⓦtheeastafrican.co.ke) covers news from Kenya, Uganda and Tanzania and focuses on economic and political issues in the region.

Of the **foreign press**, one- or two-day-old editions of British, German and US newspapers, and a fair number of foreign magazines, can be found at newsstands and hotel lobby shops in Nairobi and busy areas on the coast in high season.

There are few events **listings** publications and "what's on" portals. The *Daily Nation*, *The Standard* and *The Star* carry (limited) listings, usually on Fridays and Saturdays, but little more than what's showing at the cinemas. Checking Kenya Buzz (Ⓦkenyabuzz .com) is your best bet, though some information about venues is out of date. Other cultural resources include the sprawling Ⓦartmatters.info, the lively blog Ⓦnairobinow.wordpress.com, which has arts events in Nairobi flagged up in good time, and Ⓦkwani.org, Kenya's pre-eminent literary website.

Public holidays and festivals

The main Christian religious holidays and the Muslim festival of Id al-Fitr are observed, alongside secular national holidays. Other Muslim festivals are not public holidays but are observed in Muslim areas. Local seasonal and cyclical events, peculiar to particular ethnic groups, are less well advertised.

On the coast, throughout the northeast, and in Muslim communities everywhere, the lunar **Islamic calendar** is used for religious purposes. The Muslim year has 354 days, so dates recede against the Western calendar by an average of eleven days each year. Only the month of fasting called **Ramadan** and the festival of **Id al-Fitr** – the feast at the end of Ramadan, which begins on the first sighting of the new moon – will have much effect on your travels. In smaller towns in Islamic districts during Ramadan, most stores and *hotelis* are closed

PUBLIC HOLIDAYS AND ISLAMIC FESTIVALS

Note that if a public holiday falls on a Sunday, the following Monday is usually declared a public holiday.

January 1	New Year's Day	**October 20**	Mashujaa Day**
March/April	Good Friday	**December 12**	Jamhuri Day†
March/April	Easter Monday	**December 25**	Christmas Day
May 1	Labour Day	**December 26**	Boxing Day
June 1	Madaraka Day*	**Shawwal 1**	Id al-Fitr (see opposite)

* commemorates the day that Kenya attained internal self-rule in 1963
** also known as Heroes' Day (formerly Kenyatta Day), this honours those who contributed towards the struggle for Kenya's independence or positively contributed to post-independence Kenya
† Republic Day and Independence Day

ISLAMIC FESTIVALS: APPROXIMATE DATES

	2016	2017	2018	2019
Beginning of Ramadan (1st Ramadan)	June 7	May 27	May 16	May 6
Id al-Fitr/Id al-Saghir (1st Shawwal)	July 7	June 26	June 15	June 5
Tabaski/Id al-Adha (10th Dhu'l Hijja)	Sept 13	Sept 2	Aug 22	Aug 12
Muslim New Year's Day (1st Moharem)	Oct 3*	Sept 22**	Sept 12†	Sept 1††
Ashoura (10th Moharem)	Oct 12	Oct 1	Sept 21	Sept 10
Maulidi/Mouloud (12th Rabia I)	Dec 12	Dec 1	Nov 21	Nov 10

*1438 **1439 †1440 ††1441

through the daylight hours, while all businesses will close in time for sunset, to break the daily fast. Public transport and most government offices continue as usual. **Maulidi**, the celebration of the prophet's birthday, is worth catching if you're on the coast at the right time, especially if you'll be in Lamu, where it is celebrated in great style.

There are fewer **music and cultural festivals** than you might expect. Nairobi has a number of regular events (see p.136), usually publicized on Facebook. On the coast, the Mombasa carnival used to take place in November, but has not happened for several years, but the Lamu Cultural Festival (see p.480) is a highly recommended regular fixture. Less than two hours west of Nairobi, Kenya's first annual outdoor music festival, the Rift Valley Festival, has taken root on the shores of Lake Naivasha in late August (see box, p.210) and makes a great tie-in with a Maasai Mara migration safari. If you're visiting in May, do everything possible to catch the extraordinary Lake Turkana Festival – a hugely enjoyable tribal gathering at Loiyangalani (see box, p.533).

Finally the Agricultural Society of Kenya (ASK; ⓦask.co.ke) hosts a series of annual **agricultural** shows in the major towns, featuring livestock and produce competitions, beer and snack tents, as well as some less expected booths, such as family planning and herbalism. These can be lively, revealing events, borrowing a lot from the British farm show tradition, but infused with Kenyan style.

Entertainment and sport

Kenya's espousal of Western values has belittled much traditional culture, and only in remote areas are you likely to come across traditional dancing and drumming that doesn't somehow involve you as a paying audience. If you're patient and a little adventurous, however, you're likely to witness something more authentic sooner or later, especially if you stay somewhere long enough to make friends. On a short visit, popular music and spectator sports are more accessible.

Dance

The hypnotic swaying and displays of effortless leaping found in **Maasai and Samburu dancing** are the best-known forms of Kenyan dance. Similar dance forms occur widely among other non-agricultural peoples. **Mijikenda dance troupes** (notably from the Giriama people) perform up and down the coast at tourist venues, while all-round dance troupes perform a range of "tribal dances" for tourists in hotels all over the country. It's best to ignore any purist misgivings you might have about the authenticity of such performances and enjoy them as distinctive and exuberant entertainments in their own right.

Music

Your ears will pick up a fair amount of current music (see p.580) on the streets or on buses and matatus, but the live spectacle of **popular music** is mostly limited to Nairobi, a few coastal entertainment spots and various upcountry **discos** and "**country clubs**". The indigenous music scene is somewhat overshadowed by soul and hip-hop, reggae (especially in the sacred image of Bob Marley) and a vigorous Congolese contribution, often called **Lingala**, after the language of most of its lyrics.

Theatre and film

Theatrical performances are effectively limited to one or two semi-professional clubs in Nairobi and Mombasa and a handful of upcountry amateur dramatic groups.

Kenya is a frequent location for international **filmmakers**, from *Out of Africa* to Disney's *African Cats*, but there's almost no home-grown industry, and cinema in Kenya revolves almost entirely around imports. The big towns have a few cinemas, including an IMAX in Nairobi, but downloads or DVDs are how most people get their movies, with US and Bollywood box-office hits the staple diet.

Sport

Kenya's **athletes** are among the continent's leaders and the country's long-distance runners are some of the best in the world. It has even been suggested that certain Kalenjin communities may have a genetic make-up which makes them more likely to be strong athletes, but Kalenjins as much as anyone else have played down this idea. What is indisputable is that Kenya has possibly the most successful athletics training school in the world in St Patrick's High School

at Iten, up at an altitude of 2400m in the Rift Valley (see box, p.243). Kenya's ongoing **Olympic success story** is internationally recognized, with a regular clutch of gold and silver in the **track events** – though 2012 didn't match their success in 2008 in Beijing. The most recent achievement was at the 2015 World Athletics Championships, also in Beijing, when Kenya came top of the overall medal table with seven gold, six silver and three bronze medals. This massive triumph, however, was soured a little as two athletes from the Kenyan team were suspended after failing pre-competition drug tests.

Football is wildly popular, with English Premier League teams having millions of devoted fans. You'll see plenty of matatus decorated with the colours of Arsenal, Liverpool or Manchester United, and any small bar with DSTV will show all the big games from Europe and will always be packed. Kenya's national team, the Harambee Stars, have not fared so well, however, and while the country most recently hosted the East and Central African CECAFA Cup in 2009, it hasn't won it since 2002, and neither has it qualified for the Africa Cup of Nations since 2004 (or ever qualified for the FIFA World Cup). Nevertheless, matches played against visiting international teams at Nairobi's Nyayo National Stadium are spirited occasions.

Kenyan **cricket** reached its highest points when the national team beat the West Indies at the World Cup in 1996 and came third overall in 2003. It hasn't progressed much on the international agenda since then, but most matches, played in the Nairobi area, get a good turnout and the game is particularly popular with the Asian communities. Check out Cricket Kenya Ⓦ cricketkenya.co.ke.

Other spectator sports include: **horse-racing** at the racecourse in Nairobi (see p.143), which dates from early colonial times; and **camel-racing**, spotlighted annually at the International Camel Derby in Maralal (see box, p.525).

Car rallies

Once considered "the world's toughest rally", but dropped by the World Rally Championship in 2003, the **KCB Safari Rally** (Ⓦ motorsportkenya.com) blazes a shorter trail across Kenya than it used to, doing a couple of "clover leaf" routes out from Nairobi and back. The rally is usually held on a weekend between Easter and June and uses public roads. Depending on weather conditions, drivers either spin through acres of mud or chase each other blind in enormous clouds of dust.

Another annual motor event, usually held in June, is

the **Rhino Charge** motor race (W rhinocharge.co.ke), which attracts 4WD-drivers from across the globe, though these days it's largely restricted to those who can raise the most funds. Registrations usually close about a year ahead. The challenge is to reach ten control posts in remote locations, whose whereabouts are revealed to the entrants only the night before the event. The funds raised go to Rhino Ark (W rhinoark.org), a charitable trust that works to protect forest ecosystems in Kenya; It has already fenced Aberdare National Park and is now involved in fencing part of the Mau Forest Complex.

Outdoor activities

Kenya has huge untapped potential for outdoor activities, with hiking and climbing particularly good inland and diving and snorkelling the outstanding coastal activities. Walking, running, cycling, horseriding, fishing, windsurfing, kite-surfing, rafting and golf also have strong local followings and are easy for visitors to take part in.

Walking and running

If you have plenty of time, **walking** is highly recommended and gives you unparalleled contact with local people. In isolated parts, it's often preferable to waiting for a lift, while in the Aberdare, Mau and Cherangani ranges, and on mounts Kenya and Elgon, it's the only practical way of moving away from the main tracks. You will sometimes come across animals out in the bush, but buffaloes and elephants (the most likely dangers) usually move off unless they are solitary or with young. Don't ignore the dangers, however, and stay alert. You'll need to carry several litres of water much of the time. You might prefer to go on an organized **walking safari**, at least as a starter. Such trips are offered by a number of companies in Nairobi (see p.123) and by most of the smaller lodges and camps in the private game sanctuaries and conservancies, especially in Laikipia (see p.529). Popular parks where lions are normally absent and you can hike include Hell's Gate and Lake Bogoria. Parks inhabited by lions, but in which you can generally hike, include Aberdare and Mount Kenya.

Kenya produces some of the world's top long-distance runners, and **jogging** and **running** are popular. If you're a **marathon** runner, there are several events to tie your trip in with; these usually offer fun runs and half-marathons too. The Safaricom Marathon (W safaricom.co.ke/safaricommarathon) is the best known, on account of its location, in the prestigious Lewa Wildlife Conservancy north of Mount Kenya, and altitude (an average of more than 1600m), both of which make for a tough and exciting race. Marshals (and helicopters) ensure your safety in the wildlife areas, but you'll be running on dirt tracks through the bush. It usually takes place in June. The Standard Chartered Nairobi Marathon (W nairobimarathon.com) takes place in October, starts and finishes at Nyayo National Stadium, and runs on roads in a circuit around the city.

Climbing

Apart from Mount Kenya (see p.169), there are **climbing** opportunities of all grades in the Aberdare, Cherangani and Mathews ranges, in Hell's Gate National Park and on the Rift Valley volcanoes, including Longonot and Suswa. If you intend to do any serious climbing in the country, you should make contact with the **Mountain Club of Kenya** (W mck.or.ke), which has its clubhouse at the Nairobi Sailing and Sub Aqua Club, behind Langata Shopping Centre, Langata Road, near Wilson Airport (Ksh2500 joining fee, plus Ksh4000 annual membership). A good source of advice and contacts, they usually hold club meetings on the second and last Tuesdays of each month. Safari companies in Nairobi offer everything from simple hikes to technical ascents of Mount Kenya.

Cycling

Cycling is more popular in Kenya than you might expect, given the often steep terrain, and you will even see hardy road riders and mountain bikers –both locals and expats – braving the traffic-clogged streets of Nairobi. But the real joy of cycling in Kenya is out in the bush, on quiet roads in the Rift Valley or Laikipia, or on the coast. Hell's Gate National Park is a popular place to cycle with the wildlife (see p.215). One or two companies sometimes offer tours (see p.123) and you can usually rent bikes at several places on the coast, notably in Diani Beach, Malindi and Watamu; some visitors even bring their own (see p.58).

Caving

Kenya's big attractions for cavers are its unusual **lava tube caves**, created when molten lava flowing downhill solidified on the surface while still flowing beneath. Holes in the surface layer allowed air to enter behind the lava flow, forming the caves. Lava tubes in Kenya include the Suswa caves near Narok and Leviathan cave in the Chyulu Hills, one of the world's biggest lava tube systems, with more than 11km of underground passages. For more information, contact the Cave Exploration Group of East Africa (CEGEA; W cavinginkenya.com) or one of the lodges in the Chyulu area (see p.345).

Riding

There are good opportunities for **horseriding** in the Central Highlands and Laikipia, and active equestrian communities in Nairobi and scattered throughout the country. Bush & Beyond (see p.124), Safaris Unlimited (see p.125) and Safari & Conservation Company (see p.125) offer riding safaris in the Amboseli area, the Chyulu Hills and the Mara conservancies, and Offbeat Safaris (W offbeatsafaris .com) do horseback safaris on the Mara conservancies and on their Deloraine ranch in the Rift Valley (see p.234). The African Horse Safari Association (W africanhorse.com) is a useful resource. **Camel safaris** are popular too (see box, p.529).

Fishing

Some of the highlands' streams are still stocked with **trout**, imported early in the twentieth century by British settlers. A few local fishing associations are still active, including the Kenya Fly Fishers Club (W kenyaflyfishersclub.com). The most logical place for visitors to Kenya to try their hand is in the foothills of Mount Kenya where several lodges offer **fly-fishing**; so too do those on the Laikipia plateau. For **lake fishing**, it's possible to rent rods and boats at lakes Baringo, Naivasha and Turkana (Loiyangalani), and there are luxury fishing lodges on Rusinga and Mfangano islands on Lake Victoria.

Kenya's superb offshore coral reef, with its deep-water drop-offs and predictable northerly currents, is home to many species of large game fish such as tuna, marlin, sailfish and varieties of shark and is very popular for **deep-sea fishing**. The main centres, where fully equipped guided excursions can be arranged, are Shimoni, Kilifi, Watamu and Malindi. The ocean fishing season is usually from August to March.

Diving and snorkelling

Kenya's coastal waters are warm all year round so it's possible to **dive** without a wetsuit and have a rewarding dip under the waves almost anywhere, though the best period is October to April with October, November and March ideal. Most of the dive bases located at Malindi, Watamu, the coast north of Mombasa or Diani Beach will provide training from a beginner's dive to PADI leader level. For underwater photographers, in particular, the immense coral reef is a major draw. The undersea landscape is spectacularly varied, with shallow coral gardens and blue-water drop-offs sinking as deep as 200m, and as there are few rivers to bring down sediment, visibility is generally excellent. There are some useful **guide-books** (see p.598) and, if you plan to do a fair bit of **snorkelling**, it makes sense to bring your own mask and snorkel, though they can always be rented.

Wind- and kitesurfing

Windsurfing has been a feature of the Kenya coast since the 1970s, while Diani Beach (see p.436) and *Che Shale* north of Malindi (see p.470) are increasingly popular among **kitesurfing** enthusiasts. Several schools along the coast offer lessons in both disciplines and rent out equipment to experienced surfers. The coast has excellent conditions from December to February, with the northeast monsoon tending to get up in the afternoon, blowing between 16 and 22 knots (Force 4 to 5 Beaufort), which is ideal for both beginners and experienced riders. While the southeast monsoon, blowing from June through to September, isn't as reliable as the northeasterly, it can offer some exceptional conditions.

Rafting

Both the Tana and Athi rivers have sections that can be **rafted** when they're in spate. Approximate dates are early November to mid-March, and mid-April to the end of August. Savage Wilderness is the main operator (see p.166), and offers single- and multi-day trips.

Golf

Kenya has almost forty **golf clubs**, notably around the old colonial centres of Nairobi, Naivasha, Thika, Nanyuki and Nyeri in the Central Highlands, and Kisumu and Kitale in western Kenya. There are also several courses on the coast, and – the most bizarre – on the scorched moonscape shore of Lake Magadi (see p.153). Green fees vary widely, usually starting at about $30/person per day. Details for all of these can be had from the Kenya Golf Union (W bit.ly/KenyaGolfUnion). For organized upmarket **golfing safaris**, contact Tobs Golf Safaris Ltd (W kenya-golf-safaris.com).

National parks and reserves

About eight per cent of Kenya is formally protected for wildlife and environment conservation, either as national parks (there are 23 on land and another four marine parks) or as national reserves (28, plus six marine ones). The national parks are administered by the Kenya Wildlife Service (KWS) as total sanctuaries where human habitation, apart from tourist lodges, is prohibited. National reserves, run by local councils, tend to be less strict on the question of human encroachment. As well as these formally demarcated areas, the conservation effort is increasingly being supported by private sanctuaries and community wildlife conservancies, where private operators work with the local community to conserve wildlife and the environment while bringing landowners a direct income from tourism.

Most parks and reserves are not fenced in (Lake Nakuru, Aberdare and the north side of Nairobi National Park being exceptions). The wildlife is free to come and go, though animals do tend to stay within the boundaries, especially in the dry season when cattle outside compete for water.

All the parks and reserves are open to **private visits** (though foreign-registered commercial overland vehicles are not allowed in). A few parks have been heavily developed for tourism with graded tracks, signposts and lodges, but none has any kind of transport at the gate for people without their own transport (Nairobi National Park is the one partial exception, with a weekend bus service taking visitors around the park).

In general, without your own transport, you'll have to go on an organized safari. The largest and most frequently visited parks are covered in depth in Chapter 5, with others covered in regional chapters. Our table (see pp.74–75) gives you some idea of what to expect from the major parks.

It's important to bear in mind some simple facts to ensure that you leave the park and the animals as you found them. **Harassment** of animals disturbs feeding, breeding and reproductive cycles, and too many vehicles surrounding wildlife is not only unpleasant for you, but also distresses the animals. If you're camping, collecting **firewood** is strictly prohibited, as is picking any flora. If you

smoke, always use an ashtray. Cigarette butts start numerous bush fires every year.

Entry fees and Safari Cards

National park and reserve **entry fees** are set in US dollars and payable either in dollars (the best approach) or in pounds, euros or Kenya shillings (all often converted at rather poor rates). They are charged per person per 24-hour visit, and as you are charged on arrival, it is helpful to know exactly how long you plan to stay. Your ticket will indicate your time of arrival. One **re-entry** is allowed per 24 hours, meaning you can leave the park to stay overnight outside and return again the next morning.

For most parks and reserves, independent travellers pay – in cash only – at the gate where they enter and receive a paper ticket. However, entry to the eight most popular national parks (see box below) is by a pre-loaded smartcard called a **Safari Card**. You can obtain temporary Safari Cards at various **Points of Issue and Points of Sale (POIPOS**; see box below) with proof of identity. You need to be over 18 (under-18s' fees go on adult cards). Once you've got your Safari Card, you load it with credit, whether in cash or with a credit card (Visa or MasterCard), covering entry fees (per person and per vehicle), as well as any camping fees – the precise sum determined by which park or parks you're visiting and for how long. If you have sufficient credit, your Safari Card is good for entry by any entrance to any Safari Card park. Unused credit is non-refundable, and the card needs to be surrendered on your exit from the park – meaning you have to go to a POIPOS to get a new one if you want to make further visits to Safari Card parks. The whole system seems somewhat complicated, but it's designed to stop large sums of money being held at the gates.

If you're visiting the parks on an organized safari, all this is handled and paid for on your behalf. But if

---

SAFARI CARD POINTS OF ISSUE AND POINTS OF SALE

Aberdare National Park Park HQ, Mweiga
Amboseli National Park Iremito and Kimana gates
Lake Nakuru National Park Main Gate
Malindi Marine National Park Park HQ
Mombasa Marine National Park Park HQ
Nairobi National Park Main Gate
Tsavo East National Park Voi Gate
Tsavo West National Park Mtito Andei Gate

you're travelling independently, it does require some planning and makes last-minute changes of itinerary potentially problematic. Happily, there seems to be enough **flexibility** in the system to allow most gates to process independent visitors who turn up hoping to pay in cash. If your itinerary has gone awry, or you're entering through a minor gate, you can also usually persuade KWS rangers to allow you to travel through the park to a gate where you can rectify your status. Likewise, if you decide to stay another day, you can usually pay the balance owing on departure (see box, p.73).

Note that if you overstay, even by a few minutes, you will very likely have to pay the full 24-hour fee (for a group that could easily be more than $300). If you are genuinely delayed through no fault of your own (such as a vehicle breakdown), it's a good idea to alert the rangers and ask them to radio ahead, as

National Park/ National Reserve	Description	Main attractions	Accommodation
Aberdare NP $65 Safari Card (see p.190)	Forest and montane grassland, access by 4WD only	Hiking; elephant, buffalo, black rhino, giant forest hog, rare bongo antelope	*Treetops* and *The Ark*, KWS cottage, camping
Amboseli NP $80 Safari Card (see p.337)	Small, flat, marshy, dominated by Kilimanjaro	Kilimanjaro; elephant, hyena, buffalo, zebra, hippo, giraffe, cheetah, lion	Lodges, KWS cottages, camping
Arabuko Sokoke NP $25 (see p.454)	Coastal forest, home of pioneering community conservation projects	Walking; Aders' duiker, elephant shrew, birds and butterflies	Camping in the park, hotels in Watamu
Buffalo Springs NR $70 (valid for Samburu and Shaba) (see p.377)	Smallish reserve adjacent to Samburu	Ewaso Nyiro River; lion, elephant, reticulated giraffe, Somali ostrich, gerenuk, crocodile	Lodges
Chyulu Hills NP $25 (see p.345)	Rarely visited volcanic hills near Tsavo West	Hiking, horseriding, cloud forest; black rhino, elephant, buffalo, eland	One lodge and one tented camp outside the park, camping
Hell's Gate NP $30 (see p.214)	Small, scenic park next to Lake Naivasha	Walking, cycling, rock-climbing; zebra, giraffe, buffalo, Thomson's gazelle	KWS campsites
Kakamega Forest NR $25 (see p.307)	Last stand of lowland tropical forest in western Kenya	Walking, birdwatching; great blue turaco, monkeys, chameleons	KWS *bandas*, camping, small lodges nearby
Lake Bogoria NR $50 (see p.234)	Rift Valley soda lake with limited facilities	Hot springs; flamingos, greater kudu	Hotel outside reserve, camping
Lake Nakuru NP $80 Safari Card (see p.224)	Soda lake, accessible by taxi	Lakeshore circuit; flamingos, pelicans, lion, leopard, buffalo, white and black rhino	Lodges, KWS cottage, camping
Maasai Mara NR $80 ($70 if staying in reserve) (see p.356)	Best park for game-watching, and often very busy, surrounded by conservancies with fewer tourists	Wildebeest migration (Aug–Sept); big cats, huge variety of savanna wildlife	Dozens of lodges and tented camps, some budget accommodation and camping outside the gates

the gate you exit through is more likely to waive the excess fee if they have been notified. Don't, however, expect to use this plan to do an extra game drive or stay for lunch: they watch the clock.

Non-residents' park entry fees range from $20 to $80. Kenyan and East African residents' fees range from Ksh350 to Ksh1200. Children's fees apply to anyone over 3 but under 18 and are usually half the price of the adult fee. Throughout the guide, we have *only* quoted adult, non-residents' rates. On top of per person entry fees, there are **vehicle fees**: a car (fewer than six seats) is Ksh350, while a vehicle with six to twelve seats (like a minibus) is Ksh1200. Again your safari operator will be paying this unless you are visiting the parks in your own vehicle.

In the **national reserves** (the main ones are Maasai Mara, Samburu, Buffalo Springs and Shaba), revenue is not controlled by KWS but by rangers

National Park/ National Reserve	Description	Main attractions	Accommodation
Meru NP $75 (see p.382)	Beautiful landscapes, relatively few visitors, increasingly good wildlife	Lion, cheetah, elephant, buffalo, reticulated giraffe, Grevy's zebra, black and white rhino	Lodges and tented camps, KWS *bandas*, camping
Mount Elgon NP $30 (see p.296)	Kenyan slopes of an extinct volcano on the Ugandan border	Hiking; salt lick caves, hot springs, scenery, elephants	KWS cottage and *bandas*, camping
Mount Kenya NP $65 (see p.169)	Kenya's highest mountain, an extinct volcano	Hiking and climbing, high-altitude afro-alpine flora; buffalo, elephant	Hiking huts, hotels around the base
Nairobi NP $50 Safari Card (see p.144)	Close to downtown Nairobi, with a great variety of savanna, streams, gorges and forest	Full variety of plains game, including giraffe, lion, cheetah, black and white rhino (no elephants)	Tented camp, lodge, camping
Saiwa Swamp NP $25 (see p.292)	Smallest park in Kenya, access on foot only	Walking on boardwalks; sitatunga antelope, birdlife	Small treehouse, Sirikwa Safaris guesthouse (11km)
Samburu NR $70 (valid for Buffalo Springs & Shaba) (see p.377)	Peaceful and beautiful park of arid lowlands north of Mount Kenya	Ewaso Nyiro River; leopard, elephant, reticulated giraffe, Grevy's zebra, Somali ostrich, gerenuk, cheetah, Beisa oryx, crocodile	Lodges, tented camps, camping
Shaba NR $70 (valid for Samburu and Buffalo Springs) (see p.381)	Better watered and less visited than Samburu with striking landscapes	Ewaso Nyiro River; elephant, jackal, lion, Grevy's zebra, reticulated giraffe	One lodge, one tented camp
Shimba Hills NR $25 (see p.428)	Forested hills near Diani Beach, with pleasant climate	Views; elephant, sable antelope, leopard, bushbabies	Tree-hotel, KWS *bandas*, camping, accessible from beach resorts
Tsavo East NP $75 Safari Card (see p.351)	Biggest park in Kenya, popular for short safaris from the coast	Mudanda Rock, Lugard's Falls; elephant, hippo, crocodile, lion, zebra, cheetah	Lodges and tented camps, camping
Tsavo West NP $75 Safari Card (see p.346)	Busy and popular core area, surrounded by wilderness	Mzima Springs (underwater hippo-watching), lava flows; elephant, zebra, giraffe, lion, buffalo, lesser kudu	Lodges and tented camps, KWS *bandas*, camping

employed by the local county councils. Fees are comparable to national park fees, and are again strictly for periods of 24 hours. Transactions take place only at the gates or airstrips on arrival.

Seasons

Most of the parks get two **rainy seasons** – brief rains in November or December, more earnest in April and May – but these can vary widely. As a general rule, you'll see more animals during the dry season, when they are concentrated near water and the grasses are low. After the rains break and fill the seasonal watering places, the game tends to disperse deep into the bush. Moreover, if your visit coincides with the rains, you may have to put up with mud and stranded vehicles, making for frustrating game drives. By way of compensation, if your plans include upmarket accommodation, you'll save a fortune at lodges and tented camps in the low season. Most places reduce their tariffs by anything from a third to a half between March and mid-June. And, when the sun shines in the rainy season, the photographic conditions can be perfect.

Getting around the parks

If you're travelling on a **shoestring budget** and don't have access to a vehicle or a tour, then with a lot of luck you *may* be able to get a lift at one of the busier park gates with visitors in a private vehicle, but this is not a common option and you could wait a very long time, even at a relatively popular park. Furthermore, safari operators with paying clients on board simply won't pick you up for free. Also, you still need a plan for where you will stay once you're in the park. The best gates to try are **Voi Gate** of Tsavo East National Park and **Mtito Andei Gate** of Tsavo West National Park. In both cases, if you have to give up, you can easily pick up public transport to get away again by walking back to the highway or into town. Alternatively, head to one of the safari lodges or camps on the outside of the park boundaries and arrange game drives from there. You can also use public transport to reach the **Talek or Sekenani gates** of Maasai Mara National Reserve, again making arrangements to do game drives with local vehicle owners or budget tented camps located just outside the reserve (see p.368).

If you're **self-driving**, or renting a vehicle with a driver, a 4WD vehicle (see p.52) is close to essential in the parks. None of the park roads are paved; most car rental companies will insist you have 4WD to visit them, and rangers on the gates may not allow you to enter in

a 2WD vehicle, especially in wet weather. A night spent stuck in Maasai Mara mud isn't to be recommended; nor is trying to reverse down a boulder-strewn slope in Tsavo West. In any case, a normal saloon will be shaken to bits on the average park road.

Be sensitive to the great damage that can be done to delicate ecosystems by **driving off marked roads**. Even apparently innocent diversions can scar fragile, root-connected grasslands for years, spreading dust, destroying the lowest levels of vegetation and hindering the life cycles and movements of insects and smaller animals, with consequent disruption to the lives of their predators.

The effects of this are especially visible in Amboseli and Maasai Mara, both of which are now ecologically at risk. Use only the obvious dirt roads and tracks (admittedly, it can sometimes be hard to judge whether you're following a permitted route, or simply the tyre marks of others who broke the rule), and if you have a driver, ask him to do the same. Stick to the official maximum **speed limit** posted at the gates, usually 30km/h. **Night driving** between 7pm and 6am is not allowed in Kenyan parks and reserves without permission from the warden.

Park accommodation

If you're travelling independently on a **medium-to-high budget** and staying in lodges or tented camps, it's very wise to make advance reservations as there is often heavy pressure on beds, especially during the high and peak seasons (see p.59). Besides its **campsites** (see p.61) KWS has a limited range of self-catering cottages, houses and *bandas* in most of the parks. See ⓦ kws.org for reservations or take a chance at the gate.

If you're visiting the parks on a **shoestring budget** it may well be worth bringing a **tent** – consider renting or buying one in Nairobi (see p.129). If you don't have one, you will find the budget options fairly limited, and in some parks and reserves a campsite may be the only affordable place to stay, as well as significantly adding to the adventure.

Game drives

If you're on an organized drive-in (road) safari, your driver will conduct morning and afternoon **game drives** – two- to three-hour excursions from wherever you are staying, slowly heading around the park, looking for animals to watch and photograph. If you fly in, you'll use the services of the driver/guides and vehicles at your lodge or camp. Invariably, two game drives per day are included in your safari.

KENYA'S HABITATS

Kenya's **location**, its range of **altitude** and its **climate**, dominated by the Indian Ocean's monsoon winds, have given rise to a diverse range of **ecosystems**. From lowland rainforest to savanna grassland, high-altitude moorland to desert, and coral reef to mangrove swamp, these zones provide equally varied habitats for its extraordinary fauna and flora. With few large **rivers**, Kenya's riverine habitats are restricted, but those that exist – notably the Tana and the Athi-Galana-Sabaki – are extremely attractive to wildlife. The vast, relatively shallow expanse of **Lake Victoria**, fed mainly by rainwater rather than rivers, is low in nutrients, but ideal for papyrus beds and marshes, harbouring birds found nowhere else in Kenya.

LOWLAND FOREST AND WOODLANDS

West of the Rift Valley, the 240 square kilometres of the Kakamega Forest, and a few adjacent outliers, are examples of the "Guineo-Congolan" **equatorial forest**, mainly found only in central Africa and home to many animal and plant species encountered nowhere else in Kenya. Beyond Kakamega, Kenya's once widespread **forests** are now limited largely to the highlands, notably Mount Kenya (see p.169) and the Aberdare range (see p.190), and to a much smaller extent the coast (see box, p.391), where patches of old forest often correspond to the sacred groves or cultural villages of the Mijikenda, known as *kaya* (see box, p.453).

GRASSLANDS

The **wooded savanna** of grassland with scattered trees – East Africa's archetypal landscape – covers large areas of Kenya between about 1000m and 1800m. The main grasslands are in the Lake Victoria basin, which includes the Maasai Mara (see p.356), and east and southeast of Mount Kenya, where the savanna is protected by the national parks of Meru (see p.382) and Amboseli (see p.337) and the better-watered areas of Tsavo East (see p.351) and Tsavo West (see p.346). Dry-season **fires** are quite common – whether natural or deliberately set to encourage new pasture with the first rain – and many of the often broad-leaved and deciduous trees are protected by their cork-like bark. The savanna of the Great Rift Valley is dotted with bird-rich **lakes** – ranging from freshwater Naivasha and Baringo to intensely saline Magadi and Bogoria – which act as a magnet for wintering migrants from Europe and northern Asia.

ARID AREAS

Starting just 30km inland from the Indian Ocean, a vast region known as the **nyika** – "wilderness" – stretches west across the drier areas of Tsavo East and West to the edge of the Central Highlands. Nyika is characterized by an impenetrably thick growth of stunted, thorny trees with scaly bark, such as acacias and euphorbias. Grey for most of the year, they sprout into a brilliant palette of greens during the rainy season. Where the land is lower than around 600m and there's unreliable rainfall and strong winds, the vegetation is sparse and scrubby, with tufts of grass, scattered bushes and only occasional trees, mainly baobab and acacia. In these **semi-arid areas**, where much of the ground is bare and soil is easily removed by the wind, long droughts are common. Kenya's true **desert** habitats are drier still, with very limited plant life and only dwarf trees and bushes. Large areas of northern Kenya consist of bare, stony or volcanic desert with thin, patchy grasses and the odd bush along seasonal watercourses.

If you've booked a lodge or camp yourself, and made your own travel arrangements, you may have to pay extra for game drives (usually around $40–80/person for 2–3hr). If you want exclusive use of the vehicle, expect to pay $150–200 for a drive and up to $350 for a full day. Lodge- or camp-based drives are usually very worthwhile because the drivers know the animals and the area.

The usual pattern is two game drives a day: at dawn and late afternoon, returning just after sunset.

In the middle of the day, the parks are usually left to the animals. While the overhead sunlight makes it a poor time to take photos, the animals are around, if sleepy. If you can put up with the heat while most people are resting back at the lodge, it can be a tranquil and satisfying time.

Rangers can usually be hired for the day: the official KWS rates are Ksh2000 for four hours, or Ksh3500 for up to six hours. If you have room in your vehicle, someone with intimate local knowledge and a trained eye is a good companion.

There are some fairly obvious **rules** to adhere to when watching animals. If you're stopping, switch off your engine and be as quiet as possible, speaking in low murmurs rather than whispering. Obviously, never get out of the vehicle except at the occasional (often rather vaguely designated) parking areas, picnic sites and viewpoints. Never feed wildlife, as it upsets their diet and leads to dependence on humans (habituated baboons and vervet monkeys can become violent if refused handouts). Remember that animals have the right of way, and shouldn't be disturbed, even if they're sitting on the road in front of you. This means keeping a minimum distance of 20m away, having no more than five vehicles viewing an animal at any one time (wait your turn if necessary), and not following your subjects if they start to move away.

To see as much game as possible, stop frequently to scan with binoculars, watch what the herds of antelope and other grazers are doing (a predator will usually be watched intently by them all), and pause to talk to any drivers you pass along the way. Most enthusiastic wildlife-watchers agree the best time of day is just before sunrise, when nocturnal animals are often still out and about, and you might see that weird dictionary leader, the aardvark.

Safaris

At the heart of most visits to Kenya, the safari is the wildlife-watching part of the trip, and usually implies at least an overnight stay. Before anything else, bear in mind that the professionalism and experience of your guide can transform any visit to the parks. Then think about whether you want comfort or a grittier experience, and whether you want the convenience of having it pre-booked as part of a package holiday, or the flexibility of picking and choosing online, or once you're in Kenya. Remember that the parks can be visited independently, allowing you to arrange your own itinerary. If you have the time, this is a good alternative to an organized trip.

Types of safari

Air safaris, using internal flights to get around, will add significantly to the cost and comfort of your trip and give you spectacular views, but a much less intimate contact with Kenya. A week-long air safari will work out in the range of $500–1000 per person per day, assuming four scheduled flights and three different camps or lodges, but will depend on the quality of your accommodation and, to a lesser extent, the size of your party. With air safaris, your actual wildlife viewing – your game drives – will be organized using the vehicles and guides of the lodge or camp you are staying at, which usually means good local knowledge of the park and the particular area, and specially adapted, often largely open, 4WD vehicles.

On a **road safari**, on the other hand, the long drives require minibuses or other closed vehicles with pop-up roof hatches, and your game drives will be conducted in the same vehicle. Though this is a much cheaper option than an air safari, the journeys can be exhausting, and hours of your time are eaten away in a cloud of dust.

Most road safaris take you from one lodge or camp to another, staying two or three nights at each lodge, in two or three parks. Samburu–Nakuru–Maasai Mara would be a typical route. Make sure you have a window seat and ask about the number of passengers and whether the vehicle is shared by several operators or is for your group only. A week's safari by road, staying at lodges or tented camps, will cost in the range of $300–700 per person per day, assuming at least five or six clients.

The alternative to a standard lodge safari is a **camping safari**, again usually travelling by minibus, where the crew (or you, if it's a budget trip) pitch your tents each day. With this kind of trip you have to be prepared for a degree of discomfort along with the self-sufficiency: insects can occasionally be a menace; you may not get a shower every night; the food won't be so lavish; and the beer not so cold. The price should be in the range of $250–350 per person per day, depending on the itinerary and again assuming at least five or six clients.

It's common on camping safaris to spend the hot **middle of the day** at the campsite. Some of these are shady and pleasant, but that's not always the case and, where there are nearby lodges with swimming pools, cold beer and other amenities, it's worth spending a few hours in comfort. Similarly, if you want to go on an early game drive, or spend the whole morning out, don't be afraid to suggest to the tour leader that you skip breakfast, or take sandwiches. Daily routines may be altered to suit the clients easily enough if you ask, though going over-budget on fuel may be an issue.

On better camping safaris, you travel in a more **rugged vehicle** that's higher off the ground – a 4WD Land Rover or Land Cruiser or even an open-sided lorry – giving more flexibility about where you go and how long you stay. The most **expensive camping safaris** come very expensive indeed: you can easily expect to pay $600–1000 per person per day. But you'll be guided by expert guides and usually looked after superbly, with top-quality tents ready for your arrival at your fly-camp every evening, good meals, cold drinks and informed safari chat.

Horseriding, **camel-assisted**, **walking** and **cycling** safaris are also available, and are generally comparable in price with mid-range or expensive conventional safaris. A dawn one-hour **balloon flight** can also be added to any safari to the Maasai Mara – a fantastic experience but not a cheap one, currently costing around $500 per person (see box, p.367).

Booking safaris direct

If you want the flexibility of booking your **own safari**, rather than having a travel agent or operator at home organize the whole trip for you, you will probably be dealing with agents or operators in Nairobi or on the coast, although you could piece the whole trip together yourself direct with camps/lodges and local airlines or car rental companies. It's worth noting that the **minibus safaris** that are included in inexpensive Mombasa-based charter packages venture no further afield than the three national parks easily accessible from the coast: Tsavo East, Tsavo West and Amboseli. Trips north to Samburu or west to the Maasai Mara are usually arranged from Nairobi.

If you have the budget to organize a **tailor-made, exclusive safari**, your only constraints will be the availability of staff and vehicles at the companies you approach. Choosing a **budget safari company**, however, can feel fairly hit-or-miss. Unless you have the luxury of a long stay, your choice will probably be limited by what is available during your visit. If you're booking at the last minute, many companies are willing to offer a discount in order to fill unsold seats.

This is not to recommend the very **cheapest outfits**. You should be somewhat suspicious of any safari to the main parks and reserves that comes in under $250 per day. Some camping operators sell safaris that undercut the competition just to get seats filled, and then have to cut corners to make any kind of profit. The easiest way for them to cut costs is to avoid paying park entry fees, by disguising a one-day, 24-hour park stay, as a **"3-day safari"**: Day 1: leave Nairobi, drive slowly to camp outside park doing "game drive"; Day 2: enter park after breakfast for all-day

RESPONSIBLE TOURISM

Kenya's diverse and fragile environments, its traditional lifestyles and its reliance on tourism make it especially vulnerable to exploitation by insensitive visitors and the local tourist industry. As a first port of call, check out Kenya's main responsible tourism body, **Ecotourism Kenya** (Ⓦ ecotourismkenya.org), which awards bronze, silver and gold eco-ratings to hotels and operators.

game drive; Day 3: enter park again for early game drive, leaving for breakfast before ticket expires, followed by a slow drive back to Nairobi. Nevertheless, if you are aware of how these cheapest safaris work and are happy to pay that price, then this is the most affordable way to go on safari. But before signing up, *always* ask for a full breakdown of what is included in the proposed itinerary, including the number of park tickets and the exact locations and names of the places you will be staying. If you're not satisfied with the itinerary, then you may well have to spend a little more on one with which you are.

KATO

Some **recommended operators** are listed in the Nairobi section (see p.123), but it's difficult to find a company that's absolutely consistent, and this is particularly the case among the budget operators. While unpredictable factors such as weather, illness and visibility of animals all contribute to the degree of success of the trip, and group relations among the passengers can assume great significance in a very short time, it's the more controllable factors like breakdowns, food, equipment and competence of the staff that really determine reputations. If anything goes wrong, reputable companies will do their best to compensate you on the spot.

The Nairobi grapevine and social media are probably your best guide to the latest good deals. Membership of **KATO**, the Kenya Association of Tour Operators (Longonot Rd, off Kilimanjaro Ave, Upper Hill, Nairobi ☏ +254 (0)20 2713386 or 2622961, Ⓦ katokenya.org; see map, p.104) is a good sign, but don't take it as a guarantee. KATO publishes full lists of its members, and can offer advice if you have problems with any of them. The KATO website runs a quotation service, which forwards your needs and interests to their members who then contact you directly by email.

BIRDWATCHING

More than 1100 species of birds have been recorded in Kenya, the second-highest bird count in Africa after the Democratic Republic of Congo. BirdLife International (@ birdlife.org) has recognized sixty Important Bird and Biodiversity Areas (IBAs) in Kenya, in habitats ranging from dense forests and marshy wetlands to arid plains and rich grasslands. Obviously birdwatching can be part of a regular safari to see the larger animals, but some forested parks and reserves – such as **Kakamega** and **Arabuko Sokoko**, as well as the **Rift Valley lakes** – are especially rewarding for even inexperienced birders.

Kenya Birding (@ kenyabirding.me) is a useful resource covering Kenya's birding hotspots. Nairobi-based Nature Kenya (see box, p.116) regularly organizes guided bird walks in the city's forests and rare trips further afield. Other specialists in birding include Birdfinders (see p.49) and Ornitholidays (see p.49), though most tour operators will tailor-make an itinerary for keen clients.

Guides and tips

Leaving aside your choice of itinerary, transport and standard of accommodation, the one aspect of your safari that is right out of your hands once you've booked is the calibre of your **guide**. Since the late 1990s, the Kenya Professional Safari Guides Association (@ safariguides.org) has taken the lead in setting benchmarks for professional guides in Kenya. They hold monthly exams and there are now several hundred accredited KPSGA gold, silver and bronze guides in the country, with a wealth of knowledge about big game and natural history in general.

It's highly rewarding to go out game-watching with **a silver or gold guide**. They can offer memorable insights into animal behaviour and can be astonishingly adept at tracking animals and interpreting their observations: a good guide will know, for example, why two male lions are being chased by a lioness, and what you might expect to find if you discreetly follow the lioness later. **Bronze guides** can be very good, too: they have to wait three years before they can take their silver exam, and many will spend hours every day reading the literature. Many, too, will have worked for years before thinking about getting qualified.

You can check the association's bronze, silver and gold members at the KPSGA website, and it's perfectly fair to ask your company if they have any accredited guides and if so whether they will be guiding your safari. Generally accredited guides will be employed by lodges/camps and tour operators, though many are also freelance and they may be attached to any of the safari operators.

Good guides are far more than animal-spotters: they are often gifted linguists, highly practical in every way and excellent bush companions. Many visitors become close friends of their guides and are drawn back to the same company repeatedly to renew the friendship.

Guides earn reasonable salaries by Kenyan standards, but clients' tips still make up a large proportion of their income, accounting sometimes for more than half their earnings. **Tipping** – of guides, drivers and other staff – can often cause misunderstandings between clients on group safaris and tailor-made trips: some companies even make suggestions in their briefing packs. It's entirely at your discretion, but very roughly each client should budget for around $5–10 per driver-guide per day, and around the same amount per day into the lodge or camp staff tip box, all to be given at the end of the stay or service. You can give a higher amount per client if in a small group, and less in a very large group, or one that includes children. It's best to pay tips in Kenyan shillings that don't have to be converted.

Crafts and shopping

Kenya's most important crafts traditions are metal-working (for jewellery and tools), basketware, beadwork and gourd utensils, all of which go back centuries. The wonderful carvings you'll see all over are usually made specifically for the tourist market.

It's a good idea if possible to buy from **cooperatives and development organizations**. Places such as Kazuri Beads & Pottery Centre (see p.141), Akamba Woodcarvers Village (see p.409), Bombolulu (see p.413) and Malindi Handicraft Co-operative (see p.474) provide their employees with above-average rewards.

What you take home will depend somewhat on how much you can transport. It's easy to get carried away when bargaining: some wooden and soapstone carvings are heavy as well as fragile, and can be hard to cart home. Bigger shops and large cooperatives will ship items for you.

Carvings

From the ubiquitous animals of doubtful appearance to finely chiselled bowls and plates, **wooden carvings** are created in Kenya in their millions, mostly by Kamba carvers (see box, p.315). The most striking carvings are in the dramatic makonde style (after the Makonde people of Mozambique and Tanzania, a group of whom live west of the Taita Hills). Makonde carvings are ostensibly made from endangered ebony, but fortunately most are carved from blackened rosewood or something similar. The other popular carving material is steatite, or **soapstone** – a soft, lustrous stone mined from one area, Tabaka near Kisii (see p.277). Apart from its tendency to snap (which makes soapstone hippos more popular than giraffes), soapstone is one of the most versatile materials, and the industry encompasses a wide variety of plates, bowls, boxes and utensils, as well as decorative items such as chess sets and candlesticks.

Baskets

The Kamba are also big basket-makers (see p.314): **sisal baskets** (*chondo*, or *vyondo* in the plural) come in a huge variety of patterns and can be made from nylon string as well as sisal and, much more rarely, baobab bark twine, with beads woven in. The baskets are all light and functional and, since becoming international fashion accessories, are much more expensive than they were: buying direct from weavers, especially when leather straps and other decorations have still to be added, can be an excellent deal for all.

Beads, tribal items and weapons

Beadwork (*ushanga*, *mkufu*) and tribal **regalia** – weapons such as spears and clubs, shields, drums (*ngoma*), carved stools and headrests, traditional utensils made from gourds (sometimes beaded), cowhorn keepsakes and metal jewellery – are fairly common, but often more expensive when they're

the genuine article rather than made for the tourist industry. The best region if you want to buy metal goods is the north: the Turkana region can yield some fairly spectacular examples of lethal weaponry, crafted indiscriminately for murderous assault or apartment wall. The bracelet-like wrist knives, or *aberait*, used to slash an enemy, are particularly impressive. You can buy **traditional weapons** – clubs, knives, swords, spears and bows and arrows – almost anywhere, and sometimes it can be hard to distinguish between an authentic weapon and an item made for tourists: the old man wandering the streets of Machakos with two bows and a quiver full of beautifully flighted arrows for Ksh20 each is not thinking of your souvenir requirements but of local hunters and security guards.

Toys

Look out for beautifully fashioned, push-along **buses**, **cars** and **lorries** made entirely of wire. These used to have tall rods, fitted with steering wheels, and would be given to lucky boys in rural areas by older brothers and uncles. Today, they're vastly outnumbered by mass-produced (though still hand-made) wire vehicle toys, manufactured as tourist souvenirs. Also widely available are amusing push-along birds, monkeys and cyclists that flap, bob or crank as they're rolled.

Textiles and sandals

Fabrics, although usually imported, bear a certain stamp of authenticity in that they are worn locally and make good-value, practical souvenirs. On the coast, the printed women's wraps – **kanga** – in cotton, and the heavier-weave men's sarongs – **kikoi** – are really good buys, and older ones represent collectable items worth seeking out. *Kangas* are always sold in pairs and are printed with intriguing Swahili proverbs. Local tailors will make them into garments for you at reasonable prices. You can also buy pretty, beaded, leather **sandals**, and the much tougher and more local sandals made from discarded vehicle tyres known as "five-thousand-mile shoes".

Culture and etiquette

Although it's not essential on a short visit, understanding something of the subtle rituals and traditions that underpin everyday life will make a big difference to

---

> **IVORY**
>
> You are very unlikely to be offered any, but you should remember that possession of ivory is strictly illegal in Kenya, and most countries have banned all trade. If it's found by customs you are likely to be imprisoned.

your appreciation of Kenyan culture. And if you're staying for an extended period, you'll need to make some adjustments yourself. There's more detailed information about Kenya's ethnic groups and cultural traditions in boxed sections throughout the guide, as well as a dedicated language section (see p.599).

Greetings

Every contact between people in Kenya starts with a greeting. Even when entering a shop, you shake hands and make polite small talk with the shopkeeper. **Shaking hands** upon meeting and departure is normal between all the men present. Women shake hands with each other, but with men only in more sophisticated contexts. Soul-brother handshakes and other, finger-clicking variations are popular among young men, while a common, very respectful handshake involves clutching your right arm with your left hand as you shake or, in Muslim areas, touching your left hand to your chest when shaking hands.

Traditionally, **greeting exchanges** last a minute or two, and you'll often hear them performed in a formal manner between two men, especially in rural areas. Long greetings help subsequent negotiations. In English or Swahili you can exchange something like "How are you?" "Fine, how's the day?" "Fine, how's business?" "Fine, how's the family?", "Fine, thank God." It's usually considered polite, while someone is speaking to you at length, to grunt in the affirmative, or say thank you at short intervals.

Hissing ("Tsss!") is an ordinary way to attract a stranger's attention, though less common in more sophisticated urban situations. You may get a fair bit of it yourself, and it's quite in order to hiss at the waiter in a restaurant: it won't cause any offence.

"KENYA" OR "KEENYA"?

Although you'll hear "Kenya" most of the time, the second pronunciation is still used, and not exclusively by the old settler set. The colonial pronunciation was closer to the original name of Mount Kenya, "Kirinyaga". This was abbreviated to "Ki-nya", spelt Kenya, which came to be pronounced with a short "e". When Jomo Kenyatta became president after independence, the pure coincidence of his surname was exploited.

If you're **asking questions**, avoid yes/no ones, as answering anything in the negative is often considered impolite. And when making enquiries, try not to phrase your query in the negative ("Isn't the bus leaving?") because the answer will often be "Yes" (it isn't leaving).

Body language, gestures and dress

You are likely to notice a widespread and unselfconscious ease with close **physical contact**, especially on the coast. Male visitors may need to get used to holding hands with strangers as they're shown around the guesthouse, or guided down the street, and, on public transport, to strangers' hands and limbs draped naturally wherever is most comfortable, which can include your legs or shoulders.

It's good to be aware of the **left-hand rule**: traditionally the left hand is reserved for unhygienic acts and the right for eating and touching, or passing things to others. Like many "rules" it's very often broken, at which times you have to avoid thinking about it. Unless you're looking for a confrontation, never **point** with your finger, which is equivalent to an obscene gesture. For similar reasons, **beckoning** is done with the palm down, not up, which if you're not familiar with the action can inadvertently convey a dismissive gesture. Don't be put off by apparent shiftiness in **eye contact**, especially if you're talking to someone much younger than you. It's normal for those deferring to others to avoid a direct gaze.

In Islamic regions on the coast, wearing **shorts and T-shirts** (which are considered fine on the beach) won't get you into trouble, as people are far too polite to admonish strangers, but it's better to dress in loose-fitting long sleeves and skirts or long trousers. Lamu calls more for *kikoi* and *kanga* wraps for both sexes and, because it's so small, more consideration for local feelings. For **women**, even more than men, the way you look and behave gets noticed by everyone, and such things are more important if you don't appear to have a male "escort". Your **head and shoulders** and everything from **waist to ankles** are the sensitive zones, and long, loose hair is seen as extraordinarily provocative, and doubly so if it's blonde. It's best to keep your hair fairly short or tied up (or wear a scarf). **Topless sunbathing** is prohibited.

You'll also need to be suitably attired to enter **mosques** and in practice you should take advice from your guide – you can't enter unaccompanied, and women often won't be able to enter mosques at all.

Beggars

In central Nairobi and Mombasa **beggars** are fairly common. Most are visibly destitute, and many are disabled, or homeless mothers with children. While some have regular pitches, others keep on the move, and all are harassed by the police. Kenyans often give to the same beggar on a regular basis: to the many Kenyans who are Muslim, alms-giving is a religious requirement. This kind of charity is also an important safety net for the destitute in a country with no social security system.

Sexual attitudes

Although there is a certain amount of ethnic and religious variation in attitudes, **sexual mores** in Kenya are generally hedonistic and uncluttered. Expressive sexuality is a very obvious part of the social fabric in most communities, and in Muslim areas Islamic moral strictures tend to be generously interpreted. The age of consent for heterosexual sex is 16.

Female **prostitution** flourishes almost everywhere, with a remarkable number of cheaper hotels doubling as informal brothels. There are no signs of any organized sex trade and such prostitution appears to merge seamlessly into casual promiscuity. If you're a man, you're likely to find flirtatious pestering a constant part of the scene, especially if you visit bars and clubs. With HIV infection rates extremely high, even protected sex is extremely inadvisable. On the coast there's increasing evidence of child prostitution and, apart from the odd poster, little effort by the authorities to control it.

Sex between men is illegal in Kenya, and **homosexuality** is still largely a taboo subject; lesbianism doubly so, although no law specifically outlaws it. Many Kenyans take the attitude that being gay is un-African, although male homosexuality among Kenyans is generally an accepted undercurrent on the coast (*msenge* is the Swahili for a gay man), and nightclubs in Nairobi and on the coast are relatively tolerant. Fortunately, visiting gay couples seem to experience no more problems sharing a room (even when opting for one double bed) than straight travelling companions, and the prevailing mood about gay tourists seems to be "don't ask, don't tell". Nevertheless if you are a gay couple you may have to be discreet. Public displays of affection are out of the question, and while holding hands may not bother anyone, you might be unlucky, so it's best to avoid doing even that.

Gay Kenya Trust (Wgaykenya.com) is a human rights and advocacy organization for gay men, and for the wider LGBT community.

Crime and safety

There's no denying that petty crime is a problem in Kenya, and you have a higher chance of being a victim in touristy areas, where pickings are richer. It's important to bear in mind, though, that most of the large number of tourists who visit the country each year experience no difficulties. Wildlife should not compromise your safety either if you act sensibly (see p.78).

For **official government warnings**, check the travel advisories on the websites of the UK Foreign & Commonwealth Office (Wgov.uk/foreign-travel-advice), the US Department of State (Wstate.gov/travel) or the travel advisory of your own country. But bear in mind that travel advisories have an inherent tendency to be somewhat cautious and nannying, and are only as good as the information fed into them on the ground.

In Kenya, the **Kenya Tourism Federation** is an umbrella organization uniting a number of tourist industry associations. They have a sporadically updated website with security news (Wktf.co.ke).

Avoiding trouble

After **arrival** in Kenya, try to be acutely conscious of your belongings: never leave anything unguarded even for five seconds; never take out cameras or other valuables unless absolutely necessary; and be careful of where you walk, at least until you've dropped off your luggage and settled in somewhere. It's hard not to look like a tourist, but try to **dress like a local**, in a short-sleeved shirt, slacks or skirt and sunglasses, and try not to wear anything brand-new. Wearing **sunglasses** lessens your vulnerability, as your inexperience is harder to read.

In Nairobi and in a few tourist-traffic towns such as Mombasa, Naivasha and Nakuru, **pickpocketing** may occur, and it's a good idea to be alert in busy places like markets and bus stages. Down at the coast, possessions may disappear from the beach, so ensure they are being watched while you swim. When you're out and about, avoid carrying a **bag**, particularly a day-pack over your shoulder, that will instantly identify you as a tourist. And don't wear fancy earrings or any kind of chain or necklace. There's usually less risk in leaving your valuables tucked in your luggage in a locked hotel room, than in taking them with you.

If you're **driving**, it's a good idea never to leave any valuables in a vehicle – if this isn't an option ensure the vehicle is guarded even if it's locked. In towns, there are often official council parking marshals, who you have to pay for an hour or two of parking during the daytime, or at least someone who will volunteer to guard your vehicle for you for a tip (Ksh200 is plenty). At night, ensure you park in a hotel car park, and when there isn't one, ask if they employ an *askari* to guard guests' vehicles outside on the street.

When you have to carry **cash and other valuables**, try to put them in several places. A money belt or pouch tucked into your trousers or skirt is invisible and the most secure, while pouches hanging around your neck are easy targets for grab-and-run robberies and ordinary wallets in the back pocket are an invitation to pickpockets. Similarly, the voluminous "bum bags", worn back to front by many tourists over their clothing, invite a slash-and-grab mugging. You'll be carrying around large quantities of low-value banknotes, so make sure you have a reasonably safe but accessible purse or zip pocket to stuff it all in.

If you do unfortunately get mugged, **don't resist**, as knives and guns are occasionally carried. It will be over in an instant and you're unlikely to be hurt. But the hassles, and worse, that gather when you try to do anything about it make it imperative not to let it happen in the first place. Thieves caught red-handed are usually mobbed, and often lynched, so avoid the usual Kenyan response of shouting "Thief!" ("*Mwizi!*" in Swahili) unless you're ready to intercede instantly once you've retrieved your belongings.

All of this isn't meant to induce paranoia, but if you flaunt the trappings of wealth where there's poverty and a degree of desperation, somebody will try to remove them. If you clearly have nothing on you, and look like you know what you're doing, you're unlikely to feel, or be, threatened.

Cons and scams

On public transport, **doping scams** have occasionally been a problem, with individuals managing to drug tourists and relieve them of their belongings. It's best not to accept gifts of food or drink on public transport, even at the risk of causing offence.

Approaches in the street from "schoolboys" with **sponsorship** forms (education is free but books and uniforms have to be bought) and from "refugees" with long stories are not uncommon and probably best shrugged off, even though some, unfortunately, may be genuine. Also beware of people offering to **change money** on the street, especially in Nairobi, which is usually a trick to get you down an alley where you can be relieved of your cash.

Gangs of scammers who pick on gullible visitors in the Nairobi CBD to work elaborately theatrical cons are another occasional problem. If you find yourself surrounded by a group of "plain clothes policemen" insisting you have been seen talking to a "known terrorist" following a conversation you've had with someone and you need to "discuss the matter" with them, you should agree to nothing and go nowhere.

A particularly unpleasant scam on the **coast** involves a male tourist being approached by children who start a brief conversation, which is then followed up by an adult minder accusing the tourist of soliciting for sex. He then demands a payment or threatens a visit from the police. As with the "terrorist" scams, never agree anything or pay any money and don't be afraid to cause a scene and involve passersby. The groups will quickly melt away.

Police

If you have any official business with the **police**, which is only likely if you have to go to a police station to report a theft, or if you get stopped at police roadblocks when driving (see p.52), then politeness, smiles and handshakes are the order of the day. This will get you a lot further than shouting, stamping your feet or making any kind of demand. Generally the police are very friendly, and in unofficial dealings, especially in remote outposts, will sometimes go out of their way to help you with directions, transport or accommodation.

If you've been **mugged** or had something stolen from a vehicle or hotel room, your first reaction may be to go to the police. Unless you've lost irreplaceable property and need to make an insurance claim, however, this may not be a worthwhile course of action. They rarely do anything about catching petty thieves, and writing a police report of the incident or stamping an **insurance form** will probably cost you a small "fee".

Checkpoints

Being stopped by the police when **driving** is a common occurrence. Checkpoints are generally marked by low strips of spikes across the road, with just enough room to slalom through. Always stop, greet the officer and wait. If you're not waved through, then the police officer may approach and ask to look at your driver's licence and other vehicle paperwork (see box, p.50) – don't be alarmed as this is routine for all Kenyan drivers.

If the police claim that you've committed a **misdemeanour** (for example, exceeding the speed limit, overtaking a truck on a hill, talking on your mobile while at the wheel or having something wrong with your vehicle like a broken headlight), consider first whether you may in fact be guilty of any of these traffic offences (speeding for example is quite easily done in Kenya as the speed limit drops very abruptly even outside the smallest settlement).

If you have done something wrong, then you may be given an **on-the-spot fine**, which the police have every right to ask drivers to pay. The official course of action is to pay the full amount and get a receipt (officers always carry receipt books). However, some of the less scrupulous members of the police force (not all by any means) may instead ask something along the lines of "how much can you pay?" – this is blatant solicitation for a bribe. Unless a receipt is issued, money taken will not be logged and most likely will be slipped into a pocket. If you're prepared to haggle over the sum in this way you may well get away with paying half the official fine, or even less. To do so, though, would be to participate in Kenya's ongoing institutionalized petty **corruption** – you should always ask for an official receipt and thus pay the full amount, and the police (perhaps some of them, a little sulkily) will send you on your way.

If you are sure you have not committed any offence, and the police still ask for "something small" or "money for a soda", politely declining in a friendly manner (so as not to insult their authority) usually does the trick and they'll give up on you.

To help stop corruption in taking fines for traffic offences, there is a new system being rolled out whereby drivers can pay by M-Pesa (see box, p.90), which prevents any cash being exchanged. It has been dubbed *Faini Chap Chap* (corrupted Swahili for "quick fines").

Drug and other offences

Though illegal, **marijuana** (*bhang* or *bangi*) is widely cultivated and smoked, and is remarkably cheap. However, with the authorities making efforts to control it and penalties of up to ten years for possession (or 20 years for trafficking), its use is not advisable. Official busts result in a heavy fine and deportation at the very least, and quite often a prison sentence, with little or no sympathy from your embassy. **Heroin** is becoming a major problem on the coast, and possession of that, or of anything harder than marijuana, will get you in a lot worse trouble if you're caught. The herbal stimulant

miraa or *qat* (see box, p.186) is legal and widely available, especially in Meru, Nairobi, Mombasa and in the north, but local police chiefs sometimes order crackdowns on its transport, claiming it is associated with criminality.

Be warned that failure to observe the following points of behaviour can get you **arrested**. Always stand on occasions when the national anthem is playing. Stand still when the national flag is being raised or lowered in your field of view. Don't take photos of the flag or the president, who is quite often seen on state occasions, especially in Nairobi. And if the presidential motorcade appears, pull off the road to let it pass. Smoking in a public place is prohibited (it's usually okay to smoke outdoors, though not advisable to do so on the street; check before lighting up). It's also a criminal offence to tear or deface a banknote of any denomination, and, officially, to urinate in a public place.

Sexual harassment

Women travellers will be glad to find that machismo, in its fully-fledged Latin varieties, is rare in Kenya and male egos are usually softened by reserves of humour. Whether travelling alone or together, women may come across occasional **persistent hasslers**, but seldom much worse. Drinking in **bars** unaccompanied by men, you can expect a lot of male attention, as you can in many other situations. Universal basic rules apply: if you suspect ulterior motives, turn down all offers and stonily refuse to converse, though you needn't fear expressing your anger if that's how you feel. You will, eventually, be left alone. These tactics are hardly necessary except on the coast, and then particularly in Lamu. Some women mitigate unwelcome attention by adapting their dress (see p.82).

Fortunately you will usually be welcomed with generous hospitality when travelling on your own (many Kenyan women travel alone on public transport) and if you're staying in less reputable hotels, there'll often be female company – employees, family, residents – to look after you.

Terrorism

Unfortunately Kenya has been the scene of various attacks attributed to terrorist elements, which have caused a number of deaths among the civilian population. In recent years, the principal threat to Kenya's internal security has been from **Al-Shabaab**, a militant group of insurgents that has risen out of the civil war that's raged in southern Somalia since

2009 (see box, p.577). Since 2012, Al-Shabaab has carried out grenade and gun attacks in northeastern Kenya and low-income parts of Nairobi and Mombasa. The most high-profile of these were at Nairobi's Westgate Shopping Mall in 2013, when heavily armed gunmen killed 67 (see box, p.108) and at Garissa University College in April 2015, when almost 150 lost their lives.

The terrorist threat in Kenya has led to **travel advisories** by UK, US and other governments cautioning against travel to various regions of Kenya. One of the downsides of this has of course been a significant downturn in tourism, with disastrous consequences for the local economy, jobs and livelihoods. Fortunately it's widely recognized how important tourism is to Kenya and that tourists are rarely the specific targets of terrorism, and as such travel advisories are usually lifted as soon as possible.

The mood in Kenya at the end of 2015, was one of stoicism. Life goes on, you'll be told, and you are still far more likely to be injured in a road traffic accident or catch malaria (both quite remote possibilities) than you are to be caught up in a terrorist attack. You could never rule out the possibility – and there's certainly no strategy for avoiding it – but terrorism is an international threat which is no more likely to affect you during a visit to Kenya than it would were you to stay at home. Needless to say, you'll notice that security at shopping malls and big hotels is high-profile, with airport-style baggage scanners and metal detectors widely in use. And equally you'll notice that people who work in tourism – from hotel owners and tour operators to curio sellers and waiting staff – will be thrilled to have your patronage in what is a difficult time for the industry.

Wildlife dangers

Although **wild animals** are found all over Kenya, not just inside the parks, dangerous predators like **lions** and **hyenas** rarely attack unprovoked, though they are occasionally curious about campfires. More dangerous are **elephants** and **buffaloes**, and you should stay well clear of both, especially of solitary bulls. In the vicinity of lakes and slow-moving rivers you should watch out for **hippos**, which will attack if you're blocking their route back to water, and **crocodiles**, which can be found in most inland waters and frequently attack swimmers and people at the water's edge. Never swim in inland lakes or rivers. More generally, follow park and conservancy rules and, unless signs indicate an area is specifically designated as a nature trail and you're allowed to leave your vehicle, never walk unaccompanied in

areas where large mammals are present.

A persistent and growing problem is the continued, unstoppable damage done by those loutish hooligans, **baboons**. A locked vehicle might be safe but an unwatched tent or an open-fronted lodge room certainly isn't.

Travel essentials

Bargaining

Prices in formal shops are fixed but they aren't in markets or street-side stalls, and generally vendors will attempt to ask tourists for more than an item's real value. **Bargaining** is an important skill to acquire, not just when buying curios and souvenirs but also when negotiating fees for services such as taxi rides and guides, and even for hotel rooms and excursions (though for these last it will usually only work when things are quiet). Remember that if you pay an unreasonable price for goods or services, you'll make it harder for the next person and contribute to local inflation, so always be cautious over your purchases.

You're expected to knock down most negotiable prices by anything from ten percent to a half. **Souvenirs** are sometimes offered, at first, at prices ten times what the vendor is actually prepared to accept. You can avoid the silly asking prices by having a chat and establishing your streetwise credentials. The bluffing on both sides is part of the fun; don't be shy of making a big fuss and turning on the comedy. There are no fast rules, but don't begin if you're in a hurry; don't show interest if you're not thinking of buying; and never offer a price you are not prepared to pay. Equally, as you'll quickly discover if you walk away and aren't called back, if you don't offer enough the vendor simply won't sell it to you.

Costs

Kenya can be expensive for **budget travellers** if you want to rent a car or go on organized safaris, especially in high season. By staying in B&Ls, eating in local places and using public transport, you can get by okay on $30–50 a day. It's always cheaper per person if you can share accommodation – it's not uncommon for hotels in Kenya to have three or four beds in some rooms, and you could ask to stay in a family room even at safari lodges and beach resorts. Getting around by bus and matatu is inexpensive, but you can't use public transport to visit the game parks. Renting a vehicle, and paying for fuel and vehicle entry fees to the parks and reserves, will add at the very least $120 a day to your costs. However, if you're in a group of three or more, it starts to become more reasonable. You could also visit the parks on a cheap camping safari, though check what you're getting for the price – the cheapest companies don't necessarily offer the best value for money (see p.79), and if you're only ever going once it's definitely worth considering spending more. On the coast, there are few cheap hotels away from the expensive all-inclusive beach resorts, but there's the option of negotiating accommodation on a room-only basis or renting a self-catering cottage.

For those on a more **comfortable budget**, an all-inclusive safari with road transport plus accommodation in a lodge or tented camp will cost from around $300 per person per day, and a night in an all-inclusive beach resort from around $120 per person per day; both can rise to well over $1000 per day depending on the level of luxury. Then you need to add the cost of flights, if you prefer to fly between destinations. That said, once you've forked out for those costs, you're likely to find daily expenses refreshingly modest. Drinks in most hotels, tented camps and lodges run from around Ksh200–400 ($2.50–5) for a beer or a glass of house wine, and a main course in a restaurant generally costs around Ksh800–2000 ($8–20). Taxis are reasonably priced, but you need to establish the fare in advance (see p.56).

Customs and duty-free

Duty-free allowances on entering Kenya are one bottle of spirits or wine and one carton of 200 cigarettes (or 50 cigars or 225g of tobacco). If you're stopped at customs, you may be asked if you have any cameras, camcorders or the like. Unless you're a professional with mountains of specialist gear, there should not be any question of paying duty on personal equipment. If you are taking presents for friends in Kenya, however, you are likely to have to pay duty if you declare the items.

Electricity

The mains electricity supply (220–240V) from **Kenya Power and Lighting** is inconsistent and unreliable, and all but the most basic establishments have backup generators and/or solar panels. Some of the more remote safari lodges and tented camps are not on the national grid, and therefore rely solely on generators. They will advise when these are switched on – usually for a few hours in the evening and the early morning. **Wall sockets** are the square, three-pin variety used in Britain. Appliances using other plug fittings will need an adaptor to fit Kenyan sockets (available in major supermarkets), while North American appliances that work only on 110V (most work on 110–240V) will also need a transformer.

Emergencies

For police, fire and ambulance dial ☏999. They often take ages to arrive. Another option in Nairobi if you are on the Safaricom phone network, is to call the Security 911 line (☏911), which sends out an alert for a security vehicle, of which there are more than fifty around the city.

Entry requirements and visas

Most nationals, including British, Irish, US, Canadian, Australian, New Zealand and EU passport-holders, need **visas** to visit Kenya. Nationals from a number of African countries are exempt, including South African passport-holders, who are allowed a visa-free stay of up to thirty days. Children of the relevant nationalities also require visas and pay exactly the same. It's a good idea, however, to check with a Kenyan embassy website to confirm the current situation. Also ensure that your passport will remain valid for at least six months beyond the end of your projected stay, and that it has at least two blank pages for stamps – this is a requirement, not just a recommendation.

Visas can be obtained **in advance** from Kenyan embassies or high commissions, either in person or by post. A **single-entry visa** (valid for ninety days) costs $50 or equivalent. A **transit visa** (allowing you to enter Kenya for a maximum of 72 hours before flying to a neighbouring country) costs $20 or equivalent. If you're not leaving the airport, a transit visa is not required. A **multiple-entry visa** costs $100 and is valid for a year.

In September 2015 a new **eVisa** service was introduced (☏evisa.go.ke) allowing you to upload your passport details and photo, pay for the visa in advance by credit card, and print out an approval form to take with you. The system generally works and in theory should make arrival faster. However, although the plan was to make the eVisa system mandatory, it currently operates alongside the other methods of obtaining a visa, and there is no dedicated queue system at the airport to give those with eVisas any advantage.

It is still usually easier to get your **visa on arrival**. No photos are required and you pay in cash (new notes) only. Download the application form (☏bit .ly/KenyaVisaForm), and have it filled in ready on arrival. Once you have your visa, your passport will be date-stamped with a **visitor's pass** along with a (sometimes barely legible) hand-written endorsement. The standard shorthand for showing the length of stay you have been granted is as follows: "KVP2W/H", meaning "Kenya Visitor's Pass 2-Week Holiday", or however long you have been given.

Surprisingly, a single-entry visa allows **re-entry** to Kenya after a visit to Uganda or Tanzania. For other trips beyond Kenya's borders, unless you have a multiple-entry visa for Kenya (obtainable only at an embassy or on arrival), you will need another visa to get back in.

If you intend to stay beyond the period written in your passport, you should renew the visitor's pass before it expires, assuming your visa is still valid, which should be free. If your visa is also about to expire, you'll need to buy a new one. You can stay in Kenya for a maximum of six months as a tourist, after which time you'll have to leave East Africa. **Visitor's pass and visa renewals** can be done at the immigration offices in Nairobi, Mombasa, Lamu, Malindi and Kisumu; addresses for these are given in the relevant sections in the Guide..

KENYAN EMBASSIES AND CONSULATES

The Kenyan diplomatic missions that readers are likely to find most useful are listed here. There's a full list at ⓦ embassy.goabroad .com/embassies-of/kenya.

Australia 33–35 Ainslie Ave, Canberra ☎ 02 6247 4788, ⓦ kenya .asn.au.

Canada 415 Laurier Ave E, Ottawa, K1N 6R4 ☎ 613 563 1773, ⓦ kenyahighcommission.ca.

Ethiopia Comoros St High 16, Kebelle 01, Addis Ababa ☎ 011 661 0033, ⓦ kenyaembassyaddis.org.

Ireland 11 Elgin Rd, Ballsbridge, Dublin 4 ☎ 01 613 6380, ⓦ kenyaembassyireland.net.

New Zealand Closest representation: Australia.

South Africa 302 Brooks St, Menlo Park, Pretoria 0081 ☎ 012 362 2249, ⓦ kenya.org.za.

South Sudan Hai-Neem, Juba ☎ 0959 099 900.

Sudan Plot 516 Block 1, West Giraif, Street 60, Khartoum ☎ 0155 772 800.

Tanzania Cnr Ali Hassan Mwinyi Rd/Kaunda Drive, Oysterbay, Dar-es-Salaam ☎ 022 266 8285, ⓦ kenyahighcomtz.org.

Uganda Cnr Acacia Ave/Lower Kololo Terrace, Kampala ☎ 041 258 232, ⓔ kenyaahicom@africaonline.co.ug.

UK 45 Portland Place, London W1B 4AS ☎ 020 7636 2371, ⓦ kenyahighcom.org.uk.

US 2247 R St NW, Washington DC 20008 ☎ 202 387 6101, ⓦ kenyaembassy.com; Los Angeles consulate, Park Mile Plaza, 4801 Wilshire Boulevard, CA 90010 ☎ 323 939 2408, ⓦ kenyaconsulatela.com.

Insurance

You'd do well to take out a **travel insurance policy** prior to travelling to cover against theft, loss, illness and injury. It's worth checking, however, that you won't duplicate the coverage of any existing plans you may have. For example, many private medical schemes include cover when abroad.

A typical travel insurance policy usually provides cover for loss of baggage, tickets and cash up to a certain limit, as well as cancellation or curtailment of your journey. Most of them exclude so-called dangerous sports unless an extra premium is paid: in Kenya such sports could mean scuba diving, windsurfing and climbing, though not vehicle safaris. If you take medical coverage, check there's a 24-hour medical emergency number. When securing baggage cover, make sure that the limit per article, which is typically less than $1000, will cover your most valuable possessions, like a camera. If you need to make a claim, you should keep receipts for medicines and medical treatment, and in the event you have anything stolen, you must obtain an official statement from the police.

Internet access

Wi-fi is widely available in urban areas, with free or low-cost access in the airports at Nairobi and Mombasa, some of the modern shopping malls, most hotels and beach resorts, many city coffee

---

ROUGH GUIDES TRAVEL INSURANCE

Rough Guides has teamed up with **WorldNomads.com** to offer great travel insurance deals. Policies are available to residents of more than 150 countries, with cover for a wide range of adventure sports, 24-hour emergency assistance, high levels of medical and evacuation cover and a stream of travel safety information. Roughguides.com-users can take advantage of their policies online 24/7, from anywhere in the world – even if you're already travelling. And since plans often change when you're on the road, you can extend your policy and even claim online. Roughguides.com-users who buy travel insurance with WorldNomads.com can also leave a positive footprint and donate to a community development project. For more information go to ⓦ **roughguides.com/travel-insurance.**

shops and an increasing number of public places (especially in Nairobi, Mombasa, Nakuru and Kisumu). However, don't expect it in rural areas, small, out-of-the-way towns and villages, or at remote tented camps.

While wi-fi in cafés is usually free, at hotels it can either be offered free as part of the service (more often than not in the more expensive places) or is charged for, with access requiring a voucher and password. Charges vary but you shouldn't have to pay more than Ksh100–200 per hour. We have listed in our hotel and restaurant reviews throughout the guide when wi-fi is available, whether free or chargeable.

If you are using a **3G or 4G mobile phone or device**, bear in mind that data charges will be a lot cheaper with a local Kenyan SIM card (see p.91) than using your home service provider's roaming service. If you have a **laptop**, you can buy a Kenyan internet service provider's USB 3G or 4G stick (modem/router) and SIM card (and equally swap the SIM card into your iPad or **tablet**) and use pay-as-you-go data bundles. These can be purchased at any phone shop (Safaricom, Airtel and Orange), all widely found in urban areas, and the set-up cost, currently around $20, is coming down all the time. Ensure everything is fully set up before you leave the shop: fortunately staff at most stores are very professional and helpful.

Despite the decreasing need for them, **internet cafés** can be found in many towns, particularly those with a college or university, and larger conference-style hotels have "business centres" where you can get online. Expect to pay around Ksh1/minute for access.

Laundry

There are virtually no launderettes in Kenya, but all hotels, lodges and tented camps run a **laundry service** for guests. Female underwear is normally excluded except where they have a washing machine (soap powder is provided for guests to do their own). In cheap hotels, you'll easily find people offering the same service (*dobi* in Swahili), but again they often won't accept female, and sometimes male, underwear. If you're camping, you'll find small packets of washing powder widely available, and clothes dry fast in the sun. Beware of **tumbu flies**, however, which lay their eggs on wet clothes where the larvae subsequently hatch and burrow into your skin. As the larva grows, it's painful but harmless, reaching the size of a grain of rice after a few days until it breaks out, leaving a small, round inflamed bump. Not quite *Alien*, but still very unpleasant, and most people don't wait to find out, but burst the swelling and clean it with antiseptic. A good, hot iron should kill the eggs, which is why every item of your clothing will be returned neatly pressed. Don't leave swimming costumes drying outside, but hang them in your shower.

Mail

There are main **post offices** in all the towns and, except in the far north, sub-post offices throughout the rural areas. Run by Posta Kenya, post offices are usually open Mon–Fri 8am–5pm, Sat 9am–noon. Letters and airmailed parcels take about a week to reach Europe and around ten days to North America, Australia and New Zealand. Parcels need to be wrapped in brown paper and string. This needs to be done at the post office as contents are checked to see if export duty must be paid. For all mail costs, there's usefully a cost calculator on Posta Kenya's website (@posta.co.ke). For large or valuable items, always use a courier. FedEx and DHL have branches or agents in all large towns, and Posta Kenya runs its own courier/tracking service from post offices known as EMS (Expedited Mail Service).

The **Poste Restante** service is free, and fairly reliable in Nairobi and Mombasa. Have your family name marked clearly, followed by "Poste Restante, GPO" and the name of the town. You'll need to show your passport at the post office. Packages can be received, too, but many go missing, and expect to haggle over import duty when they're opened in your presence. Ask the sender to mark the package "Contents To Be Re-exported From Kenya".

Maps

There are very few good **road maps** of Kenya. The best available is the Reise Know-How's *Kenia* map (1:950,000; 2012)), printed on rip-proof, waterproof plastic paper, followed by ITMB International Travel Maps' *Kenya* (1:920,000; 2014).

A local company, @touristmapskenya.com, publishes a number of maps including of the **major parks and reserves** highlighting interior roads and junction numbers, plus maps of greater Nairobi and of the Kenyan coast. These are available in bookshops, some large supermarkets like Nakumatt and at park gates.

Money

Kenya's currency, the Kenyan shilling (Ksh), is a colonial legacy based on the old British currency (as in pre-decimal Britain, Kenyans occasionally refer to shillings as "bob"). There are notes of Ksh1000, 500, 200, 100 and 50, and coins of Ksh20, 10, 5, 1 and 50 cents (half a shilling). In Kenya, prices are indicated either by Ksh or by the /= notation after the amount (500/= for example). Some foreign banks stock shillings should you wish to buy some before you leave, but you'll get rates about five percent less than what you might find in Kenya. You can import or export up to Ksh100,000 (you need the exchange receipts if exporting).

Because the Kenya shilling is a weak currency, prices for anything connected to the tourist industry tend to be quoted in **US dollars**. Cash dollars, together with British pounds and euros, are invariably acceptable, and often preferred, as payment. People often have calculators and know the latest exchange rates. If you take US dollar bills to Kenya, be sure they are less than five years old as they won't be exchangeable in many places otherwise.

While most **prices** in this book are given in Kenyan shillings or US dollars, the occasional use of euros or pounds sterling reflects the way hotels and tour operators price their services.

Cards and ATMs

The best way to carry your money is in the form of **plastic**. Credit and debit cards are more secure than cash, can be used to withdraw cash from **ATMs** and increasingly to buy things. Visa and MasterCard are the most common, but Cirrus and Plus cards are also accepted at some ATMs. Also useful are pre-paid currency cards (also known as travel money cards or cash passports) affiliated with Visa and MasterCard, which can also be used to withdraw money at ATMs. As well as at banks, ATMs can also be found at petrol stations and shopping malls. On the street, always find one inside a secure booth or with a guard on duty. ATMs usually offer the best rate of exchange, but home banks charge a fee for withdrawing cash from a foreign ATM and there may be a daily limit.

Visa and MasterCard are widely accepted for tourist services such as upmarket hotels, curio shops and restaurants, flights, safaris and car rental. There's usually a five-percent mark-up on top of the price for the cost of the transaction to the company. Most transactions use chip-and-PIN, but if you're paying by using a manual machine, make sure you've filled in the leading digits with zeros and the voucher specifies the currency before you sign. If it doesn't, it's all too easy for the vendor to fill in a $, € or £ sign in front of the total after you've left.

Exchanging money

You can **exchange** hard currency in cash at banks and foreign exchange ("forex") bureaus all over the country, and also at most large hotels, though for a substantially poorer rate. US dollars, British pounds and euros are always the most easily changed.

THE MOBILE REVOLUTION

The World Bank estimates that about 32 million Kenyans are mobile phone users and of these about 70 percent are mobile money customers. Invented in Kenya and launched in 2007, **M-Pesa** (M for mobile, *pesa* is Swahili for money) is a mobile-phone based branchless and largely cashless bank, which now features all over East Africa and is rapidly spreading worldwide. M-Pesa allows users to make cash deposits and withdrawals into/from their cell phone-based accounts at a network of agents. As well as regular phone shops and airtime vendors, these can be any kind of store, from large supermarkets to small roadside kiosks. These accounts can then be used to transfer money and pay for goods and services such as rent and utility bills using PIN-secured SMS text messages. Newer android apps give transaction history, just as a bank statement would.

The phenomenally popular service has been lauded for transforming Kenya's rural economy – money can be sent and received literally in the middle of nowhere as long as there's cell phone reception – and giving millions of people access to the formal financial system, and for reducing crime in cash exchanges. Although there's little need to sign up if you're travelling with plastic, visitors with Kenyan SIM cards can sign up to M-Pesa with Safaricom, or the equivalent with Airtel (Airtel Money) or Orange (Orange Money), simply by registering with an agent (you'll need your passport). Just about all hotels, airlines and tour operators accept M-Pesa (or equivalent system), as does KWS, giving you the option of loading fees onto a Safari Card or paying for accommodation using the service.

EXCHANGE RATES

At the time of writing, the **rates of exchange** were approximately Ksh157 to £1, Ksh102 to $1 and Ksh111 to €1.

Always check the commission and any charges as they may vary slightly. Many banks and forex bureaus also give over-the-counter cash advances in Kenyan shillings (and in Nairobi or along parts of the coast, in US dollars or pounds) on MasterCard and Visa cards. Travellers' cheques are not worth the trouble.

Banks are usually open Mon–Fri 9am–3pm, Sat 9–11am (some smaller branches are not open every Sat). Forex bureaus usually offer better rates of exchange than banks and are open longer hours (often on Sunday mornings too). Changing money on the street is illegal – ignore any offers as you will most likely be ripped off and run the risk of being arrested if caught. An exception is when entering or leaving Kenya by land from Ethiopia, Uganda or Tanzania, where changing each country's currency to or from Kenyan shillings is deemed acceptable. But be careful with any transaction – always count notes very carefully before swapping, and if at all possible wait to get cash at an ATM.

Opening hours

Shops are generally open Mon–Sat 8am–5pm, with the smaller ones having a break for lunch. In parts of the coast, and especially Muslim areas like Lamu, shops are more likely to close for an afternoon siesta (2–4pm) but they will stay open later in the evening. Muslim-owned shops may also close on Fridays, and correspondingly open on Sundays. Large **supermarkets** have extended hours until at least 7pm every day, and big towns often have at least one 24-hour Nakumatt hypermarket. Small kiosk-type shops (*dukas*) can be open at almost any hour.

Tourism businesses such as travel agents, car rental firms and airline offices are usually open Mon–Fri 8am–6pm, plus Sat 9am–noon. **Banks** are open Mon–Fri 9am–3pm and most open Sat 9–11am, too, while forex bureaus stay open later and some are open on Sunday mornings as well. **Museums** and historical sites are open seven days a week, usually 8.30am–5.30pm. **Post offices** open Mon–Fri 8am–5pm, Sat 9am–noon, though smaller branches will close for an hour over lunch. Most other offices are closed all weekend. Most **petrol stations** stay open late, and there are 24-hour ones on the major highways and in urban areas.

Museums run by National Museums of Kenya (ⓦmuseums.or.ke), such as the National Museum in Nairobi, Fort Jesus in Mombasa and Lamu Museum, are open daily 8.30am–6pm. In **national parks and reserves**, gates are open from sunrise to sunset, and given that Kenya is on the equator, these times stay the same virtually all year round: 6am–7pm.

Phones and mobiles

The need for Kenya's conventional **landline telephone system**, run by Telkom Kenya, is now virtually nil. The vast majority of adult Kenyans (a staggering estimated 90 percent) are mobile phone users, and while businesses still have landlines, they nearly always use an additional cell phone too (you will notice this in the numbers we've given in our listings). Traditional call boxes, where they still exist (even Kenyans have a giggle at the sight of these archaic contraptions), have either been decommissioned or are defunct. If you do need to find a working call box, your best bet will be a post office. Landline **area codes** are all three figures, comprising 0 plus two digits. The subscriber numbers are five, six or seven digits depending on area: Nairobi numbers have seven, while a small northern town may have only five.

Mobile phones

Most of the country has **mobile (cell) phone** coverage. The main exception is the far north, but reception can also be patchy in thinly populated rural areas further south and in the remoter parks and reserves.

Mobile phone services are provided by **Safaricom** (the biggest operator with more than 20 million customers), and its rivals **Airtel** and **Orange**. All mobile phone numbers begin with a four-digit code starting 07, followed by a six-digit number.

Your own mobile will almost certainly work in Kenya on international roaming, but very high charges make using it for calls unattractive for anything but emergencies. There are two easy options: either buy a cheap handset from any mobile phone shop, which will cost around $20, or buy a Kenyan **pay-as-you-go SIM card and starter pack** (around Ksh200) and temporarily replace the SIM card in your mobile. As well as standard mini-SIMs, the cut-down micro-SIMs for iPhones and other smart phones are widely available. Check with your home service provider that your phone is not locked to their network (unlocking, if necessary, can be done anywhere).

Once you have your Kenyan SIM installed (any phone shop, from the airport onwards, will sell you one and put it in your phone), you can buy **airtime** cards literally anywhere, rubbing a scratch number, which you use to key in the top-up. A Ksh1000 card will give you very low-price calls (as low as Ksh4 per minute and Ksh1 per text on the same network) and should last you for a short holiday.

For most short-term visitors to Kenya, it's fairly immaterial whether you choose an Airtel, Orange or Safaricom SIM card. They continually outbid each other for value and flexibility. If, however, you're travelling more widely in **East Africa**, you'll find Airtel's One Network service handy. It allows you to use the same SIM card throughout Kenya, Tanzania, Uganda and several other countries, while topping up in the local currency.

International calls

To **call Kenya from abroad**, dial your country's international access code followed by 254 for Kenya, then the Kenyan area code or mobile phone code (omitting the initial 0), and then the number itself.

Kenya, Uganda and Tanzania have a special telephone code agreement, used just between them, which replaces their international access and country codes with a single three-digit code, ☎005 for Kenya, ☎006 for Uganda and ☎007 for Tanzania. So, if you're calling Kenya from Uganda or Tanzania, you dial ☎005, then the Kenya area code (omitting the initial zero), then the number. Note, however, that on mobiles, no matter where you're dialling from, the codes for Kenya, Tanzania and Uganda are the usual, international +254, +255 and +256.

To **call out of Kenya**, the international access code is 000, followed by the country code followed by the number, omitting any initial 0 (this includes calls to mobiles being used with foreign-registered SIM cards in Kenya).

Photography

Kenya is immensely photogenic, and with any kind of **camera** you'll get beautiful pictures. But if you want good wildlife shots, you'll need one with an optical magnification of at least 10x on a point-and-shoot camera or 400mm-equivalent on a DSLR. Such telephoto capabilities are essential if you want pictures of animals rather than savanna. **Wildlife photography** is largely about timing and patience. Keep your camera always to hand and, in a vehicle, always turn off the engine.

Keep your camera in a dust-proof bag. If it uses a rechargeable **battery**, take a spare – you will always run out of power at the critical moment if you don't. Also take plenty of memory cards with you, or a separate storage device.

Though most people are tolerant of cameras, the superstition that photos capture part of the soul is still prevalent in some areas. When **photographing local people** always be sensitive and ask permission first; not to do so would be rude. If you don't accept that some kind of interaction and exchange are warranted, you won't get many pictures. The Maasai and Samburu, Kenya's most colourful and photographed people, are usually prepared to do a deal (bargain over the price), and in some places you'll even find professional posers making a living at the roadside. Other people may be happy to let you take their picture for free, but will certainly appreciate it if you take their name and address, and send a print when you get home, or email the shot to them.

Note that it's always a bad idea to take pictures of anything that could be construed as strategic, including any military or police building, prisons, airports, harbours, bridges and the president or his entourage. The idea that your photos may show Kenya in a poor light is also common.

Time

Kenya's **time zone** is three hours ahead of Greenwich Mean Time (GMT) all year round (thus two hours ahead of British Summer Time). It's eight hours ahead of North American Eastern Standard Time, and eleven hours ahead of Pacific Standard Time. Take off an hour from these (ie seven hours and ten hours respectively) during summer daylight saving time. Kenya is seven hours behind Sydney and nine hours behind

---

INTERNATIONAL CODES WHEN CALLING FROM KENYA

Australia ☎000+61
Canada ☎000+1
Ireland ☎000+353
Netherlands ☎000+31
New Zealand ☎000+64
South Africa ☎000+27
Tanzania ☎000+255 (☎007 from East African landlines)
Uganda ☎000+256 (☎006 from East African landlines)
UK ☎000+44
US ☎000+1

New Zealand; add an hour to these during summer daylight saving time. South Africa Standard Time is one hour behind Kenya all year round.

Sunrise comes between 6am and 6.40am and **sunset** between 6.10pm and 6.50pm throughout the year. Dawn arrives earliest on the coast and the sun sets latest on Lake Victoria. Because of its equatorial location, there are no short days or long evenings in Kenya.

If you're learning Swahili, remember that "**Swahili time**" runs from dawn to dusk to dawn rather than midnight to noon to midnight: 7am and 7pm are both called *saa moja* (one o'clock) while midnight and midday are *saa sita* (six o'clock). It's not as confusing as it first sounds – just add or subtract six hours to work out Swahili time (or read the opposite side of your watch).

Tipping and gifts

If you're staying in tourist class establishments, **tipping** is expected, though ironically, in the cheapest establishments, where employees are likely to be on very low wages, it is not the custom. In expensive hotels, Ksh100 wouldn't be out of place for seeing you to your room with your bags (and £1, $1 or €1 would also be very acceptable, though the employee has to change the money, which can be difficult; shillings are always better). It isn't necessary to tip waiting staff constantly while staying in a hotel. Fortunately, many hotels have a **gratuities box** in reception, where you can leave a single tip for all the staff – including room staff and backroom staff – when you leave, in which case Ksh500 or Ksh1000 per room per day is about right. In tourist-class restaurants, tips aren't essential, but leaving a tip equivalent to ten percent of the bill for your waiter would be generous. Note that on safaris, tips are considered very much part of the pay and you're expected to shell out at the end of the trip (see p.80).

As for **gifts**, ballpoint pens and pencils are always worth taking and will be appreciated by children. - But never just give them away freely as this just encourages begging – rather donate them in exchange for something, like taking a photograph or having chat and look at the children's school-books. Many visitors take more clothes with them than they intend to return with, leaving T-shirts and other items with hotel staff and others along the way: there's even a website devoted to this concept where your philanthropic instincts can be more precisely honed (ⓦstuffyourrucksack.com). Bear in mind, however, that all this largesse deprives local shops and businesses of your surplus wealth and perpetuates a dependency culture. Assuming you can spare a little, it's always better to make a positive gift of cash to a recognized institution which can go into the local economy while providing local needs at a school, clinic or other organization.

Tourist information

The **Kenya Tourist Board** (KTB; ☎020 2711262, ⓦmagicalkenya.com) has reasonable information on its website. It doesn't run any walk-in offices either in Kenya or abroad, but has franchised its operations to local PR companies, who are often very helpful. In addition to the UK and US offices (see below), there are KTB representative offices in Australia, Canada, China, Dubai, France, Germany, India, Italy, the Netherlands and Scandinavia (addresses at ⓦmagicalkenya.com).

You can always ask practical questions and expect a useful reply – often from the author of this Rough Guide – at the very good online Kenya forums at ⓦsafaritalk.net, ⓦbit.ly/RoughGuidesCommunity, ⓦbit.ly/FodorsKenya, ⓦbit.ly/ThorntreeKenya, ⓦbit.ly/TA-Africaforums or the *Rough Guide to Kenya* blog itself at ⓦbit.ly/ExpertKenya.

Once you're in Kenya, the only official tourist offices are in Eldoret (see p.287), Mombasa (see p.404), Malindi (see p.469) and Lamu (see p.488).

KENYA TOURIST BOARD OFFICES

Australia 35 Grafton St, Bondi Junction, Sydney 2022, ☎02 9028 3577.
Canada c/o VoX International Inc., 2 Bloor St West, Suite 2601, Toronto, Ontario M4W 3E2 ☎416 935 1896, ⓦvoxtm.ca.
UK c/o Hills Balfour, Colechurch House, 1, London Bridge Walk, London SE1 2SX ☎020 7367 0931, ⓦhillsbalfour.com.
US c/o Myriad Marketing, 6033 West Century Boulevard, Suite 900, Los Angeles, CA 90045, ☎310 649 7718, ⓦmyriadmarketing.com.

Travelling with children

Overall, Kenya is an excellent family destination and wherever you go, local people will be welcoming to your children. The **coast** is particularly family-friendly (it was developed as package-holiday destination after all), with good, safe beaches, lots of fun activities and attractions, and the resorts are geared up with facilities like children's swimming pools, kids' clubs, adjoining rooms and babysitting services (usually housekeeping staff), and they serve buffet meals at which even the fussiest of eaters will find something they like.

Safaris

Safaris, on the other hand, may not suit babies and very small children and can be quite a hassle in terms of supervision and organization. It's obviously exciting for them (and you) to see animals, but you may find the overall adventure isn't enough reward with bored, fidgety small children in tow on long, hot and tiring journeys. With a young family, it's probably inadvisable to go on a group safari with other travellers, who may be annoyed by having children in the vehicle. Renting a vehicle with a driver on an exclusive safari is a more feasible option, and gives you the flexibility and privacy you need for toilet stops and other interruptions. Perhaps the easiest parks to visit with small children are Nairobi and Lake Nakuru, where distances are small and you have a good chance of seeing a fair number of animals in just a few hours.

Older children, on the other hand – say above the ages of 10–12 – can be a pleasure to go on safari with: their understanding and enjoyment of the environment and landscapes is more in tune than younger children; they have a great deal more patience; and their enthusiasm for spotting animals can be very infectious. If the children are old enough to enjoy watching wildlife, make sure they have their own binoculars, cameras and checklists. Whatever the ages of your children, it's always a good idea to pick safari lodges that are well set up for family visits. The larger mid-range ones usually have the best child-friendly facilities, and tend to be fenced – the smaller tented camps usually aren't.

Prices and discounts

Children under the age of 11 usually get discounts for **accommodation** (see box, p.60) and good deals can be had, especially if they share a room with parents. However some accommodation has a minimum age limit, and some places, mostly small luxury safari camps and honeymoon retreats on the coast, may not allow children under the age of 16. For other costs, such as entry fees to **museums**, **game parks and reserves**, activities and excursions, children under 16 can expect to pay half the adult price, and kids under 3 are rarely charged anything.

Health and essentials

Health issues (see p.64) figure most prominently in most people's minds, but you can largely discount fears about your children getting a tropical disease in Kenya (remember how many healthy expat children have been brought up there: the biggest health problem for Kenyan children is poverty). It can, however, be very difficult to persuade small children to take **malaria pills**. Be sure to cover children carefully with a Deet-based mosquito repellent early each evening and ensure they sleep under secure nets. Every morning, smother them in a high-factor sunscreen, insist they wear hats and make sure they get plenty of fluids.

In terms of what to bring, disposable **nappies/diapers** and jars of baby food are available from supermarkets (Nakumatt is the best bet), and hotel kitchens usually have a good variety of fresh food and, given some warning, staff will happily prepare it to infants' tastes. If you have a light, easily collaps-ible **buggy**, bring it. Many hotels and lodges have long paths from the central public areas to the rooms or cottages. A **child-carrier** backpack is another very useful accessory. If you're going on safari, you'll need a **car seat** for babies and young children. The right model can also work as an all-purpose carrier, poolside recliner and picnic throne. Unless you're exclusively staying on the coast, bring some **warm clothing** for upcountry mornings and evenings, when temperatures can drop quite low.

Travellers with disabilities

Although by no means easy, Kenya does not pose insurmountable problems for **people with disabil-ities**. While there is little government support for improving access, travel industry staff and passers-by are usually prepared to help whenever necessary. For wheelchair-users and those who find stairs hard to manage, many hotels have ground-floor rooms, a number on the coast have ramped access and larger hotels in Nairobi have elevators. While the vast majority of hotels, lodges and tented camps have at least some rooms that are ramped or with only one or two steps, most only have showers, not bathtubs, and few have any properly adapted facilities.

The majority of safari vehicles, too, are not ideal for people with impaired mobility. **Off-road trips** can be very arduous and you should take a pressure cushion for game drives.

If you're flying from the UK, you can avoid a change of plane by going with BA or Kenya Airways direct from London to Nairobi. All charter flights are direct (if they're not always nonstop, at least you won't need to change), but they only go to Mombasa.

If you're looking for a **tour**, contact the disabled and special needs travel specialists Go Africa Safaris in Diani Beach (Ⓦgo-africa-safaris.com) and the highly recommended Mombasa-based Southern Cross Safaris (Ⓦsoutherncrosssafaris.com; see

> ## THINGS TO TAKE
> - **Binoculars** for each member of your party
> - **Cotton clothes** (loose and few), plus a warm, light, jacket or fleece
> - **GPS** (basic handheld version), or GPS-enabled smart phone, immensely useful in the bush
> - **Multipurpose penknife** (be sure to put it in your checked luggage)
> - **Sheet sleeping bag**, essential in the very cheapest accommodation
> - **Sunglasses, hat and high-factor sun protection**
> - **Torch** (flashlight), ideally a wind-up one
> - **Water shoes** (easy to swim in) to protect your feet

p.404), who are one of the few mainstream companies to offer specialist safaris for people with mobility impairments.

Work and volunteering

It is illegal for a foreigner to work in Kenya without a **work permit**. Extremely difficult to obtain, these are usually only associated with specific skilled professions and must be arranged by the employer before a work contract can be taken up in Kenya. However you are permitted to do **voluntary work**, even while on a short three-month visitor's visa, which can be extended if necessary.

An international **work camp** is no holiday, with usually primitive conditions, and you will have to pay your expenses, though it can be a lot of fun, too, and is undoubtedly worthwhile. Voluntary organizations bring Kenyans and foreigners together in a number of locations across the country – digging irrigation trenches, making roads, building schools or just producing as many mud bricks as possible. Other groups employing volunteers in community projects may focus on HIV awareness, education and women's income generation.

An alternative is to take the more expensive option of a work placement combined with a holiday – commonly known as "**voluntourism**" – on which a few weeks of volunteering might be followed by another week or two on safari or at the beach, or even an extended overland tour. Check out what opportunities are available in Kenya at Ⓦ globalvolunteernetwork.org, Ⓦ gooverseas.com, and Ⓦ volunteerhq.org.

We have also listed some **charities and NGOs** that run programmes in Kenya (see below). The placements, which include basic accommodation, meals and transport in Kenya, start at around $500

for the first two weeks followed by roughly $100 per week thereafter. Voluntourism packages start from about $1750 for two weeks of volunteering followed by a week of holiday. Flights cost extra.

VOLUNTEERING ORGANIZATIONS

Adventure Alternative Ⓦ adventurealternative.com. A good clutch of Kenyan professional electives and gap-year voluntourism opportunities.

Africa & Asia Venture Ⓦ aventure.co.uk. Runs a five-week programme to teach at and refurbish schools near Shimoni on the coast, and longer gap-year projects lasting twelve to sixteen weeks.

Animal Experience International Ⓦ animalexperienceinternational.com. Their Kenyan initiative places volunteers at wildlife conservancies to help conduct wildlife counts, and to assist on water and road improvement projects.

A Broader View Ⓦ abroaderview.org. Teaching and orphanage work, affiliated with a village school outside Mombasa.

Camps International Ⓦ campsinternational.com. Expertly run, community-facing gap-year, school-group, career-break and voluntourism programmes for people of all ages, doing genuinely useful work. Camp Tsavo, on the edge of Tsavo East National Park, is their flagship location, while there are three smaller camps on the south coast. Each offers a number of well-thought-out ecological, conservation and cultural placements.

Kenya Voluntary Community Development Project Ⓦ kvcdp.org. Short-, medium- or long-term placements focusing on health programme, environmental education and community development. Mostly in western Kenya, but arranges voluntourism packages with homestays and resorts on the coast, including Lamu.

Madventurer Ⓦ madventurer.com. Runs two- to four-week projects to help build classrooms or assist teachers at local schools in Rift Valley villages around Nakuru and Naivasha, which can be combined with an overland tour or climbing Kilimanjaro in Tanzania.

Worldwide Experience Ⓦ worldwideexperience.com. Arranges gap-year placements to wildlife conservation organizations. The Kenyan projects are predator research at Koiyaki Guiding School in the Maasai Mara's Naboisho Conservancy, and the rehabilitation of primates at Colobus Cottage at Diani Beach (see p.434).

Nairobi and around

CITY MARKET

1

Nairobi and around

Easily the largest city in East Africa, Nairobi is also the youngest, the most modern, the fastest growing and, at nearly 1700m altitude, the highest. The superlatives could go on forever. "Green City in the Sun", runs one tour-brochure sobriquet, "City of Flowers" another. Less enchanted visitors growl "Nairobbery". The city catches your attention, at least: this is no tropical backwater. Most roads in Kenya, particularly paved ones, lead to Nairobi and, like it or not, you're almost bound to spend some time here. Strolling around the malls in Westlands or negotiating Kenyatta Avenue at rush hour, it's also perhaps easy to forget how quickly you can leave the city and be in the bush.

Apart from being the **safari** capital of the world, Nairobi is an excellent base for Kenyan travel in general. To the coast, it's as little as eight hours by road, an overnight train journey, or an hour if you fly. It takes about the same time to get to the far west and barely two hours to get to the great trough of the **Rift Valley** or the slopes of **Mount Kenya**.

Nairobi County, an area of some 690 square kilometres, ranging from agricultural and ranching land to savanna and mountain forest, used to stretch way beyond the city suburbs, but the city is increasingly filling the whole county. For visitors, most of the interest around Nairobi lies to the **south and southwest**, in the predominantly Maasai land that begins with **Nairobi National Park**, literally on the city's doorstep – a wild attraction where you'd expect to find suburbs, it makes an excellent day-trip – and includes the watershed ridge of the **Ngong Hills** just outside the city in neighbouring Kajiado County. It's a striking landscape, vividly described in Karen Blixen's *Out of Africa* (see p.594). **Southeast**, beyond the shanty suburb of Dandora, are the wide Athi plains, which are traditionally mostly ranching country but nowadays increasingly invaded by the spread of Nairobi's industrial and residential satellites. In the southwest, meanwhile, a much overlooked trip to **Lake Magadi** takes you into a ravishingly beautiful and austere part of the Rift Valley.

Nairobi

NAIROBI is one of Africa's major cities: the UN's fourth "World Centre", East Africa's commercial, media and NGO hub, and a significant capital in its own right, with a population of between three and four million, depending on how big an area you include. As a traveller, your first impressions are likely to depend on how – and where – you arrive. If you've come here overland, some time resting up in comfort can seem an appealing proposition. Newly arrived by air from Europe, though, you may wonder – amid the rash of roadside ads persuading you to upgrade your mobile-phone package or catch the latest TV offering – just how far you've travelled. Nairobi, little more than a century old, has real claims to Western-style sophistication but, as you'll soon find, it lacks a convincing heart. Apart from some lively musical attractions – some of East

DAVID SHELDRICK WILDLIFE TRUST ELEPHANT ORPHANAGE

Highlights

❶ Kibera Take away some added awareness and leave a little extra cash behind on a tour of Kenya's biggest slum district – a sobering but not a depressing experience. **See p.111**

❷ Nairobi National Museum By far the biggest and best museum in the country and a good introduction to Kenyan culture and natural history. **See p.113**

❸ Markets From the bewildering, muddy maze of Gikomba to the tourist-oriented Maasai markets, these are excellent places to sample a slice of Nairobi life, eat street food or pick up souvenirs. **See p.141**

❹ Nairobi National Park On Nairobi's doorstep, the park is home to most of Kenya's big mammals, and the place for classic photos of plains animals against a backdrop of skyscrapers. **See p.144**

❺ David Sheldrick Wildlife Trust Highly regarded elephant and rhino orphanage where you can get on petting terms with tiny pachyderms. **See p.147**

❻ Olorgasailie Prehistoric Site Stark site in the southern Rift Valley, with huge numbers of early hominin stone tools preserved *in situ*. **See p.152**

HIGHLIGHTS ARE MARKED ON THE MAP ON P.100

1

Africa's busiest clubs and best bands – there's little here of magnetic appeal, and most travellers stay long enough only to take stock, make some travel arrangements and maybe visit the **National Museum**, before moving on.

If you're interested in experiencing modern Kenya, though, Nairobi is as compelling a place as any and displays enormous vitality and buzz. The controlling ethos is commerce rather than community, and there's an almost wilful superficiality in the free-for-all of commuters, shoppers, police, hustlers, security guards, hawkers and tourists. It's hard to imagine a city with a more fascinating variety of **people**, mostly immigrants from the rural areas, drawn to the presence of wealth. On the surface the city accepts everyone with tolerance, and, in any downtown street, you can see a complete cross section of Kenyans, every variety of tourist, and migrants and refugees from many African countries.

Nairobi's rapid growth, however, inevitably has a downside. Watch the local TV news, read any paper or talk to a resident and you'll hear jaw-dropping stories of crime and police shootings. Although the city has become safer in recent years, you should certainly be aware of its reputation for **bag-snatching and robbery**, frequently directed at new tourist arrivals (see box, p.108). If you plan to stay in Nairobi for any length of time, you'll soon get the hang of balancing reasonable caution with a fairly relaxed attitude: thousands of visitors do it every year. If you're only here for a few days, you're likely to find it a stimulating city.

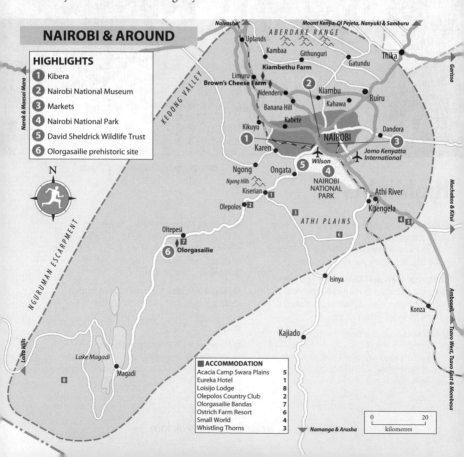

NAIROBI & AROUND

HIGHLIGHTS

1 Kibera
2 Nairobi National Museum
3 Markets
4 Nairobi National Park
5 David Sheldrick Wildlife Trust
6 Olorgasailie prehistoric site

■ ACCOMMODATION

Acacia Camp Swara Plains	5
Eureka Hotel	1
Loisijo Lodge	8
Olepolos Country Club	2
Olorgasailie Bandas	7
Ostrich Farm Resort	6
Small World	4
Whistling Thorns	3

GETTING ORIENTED IN NAIROBI

Nairobi has widespread suburbs but the downtown area of the **Central Business District** – known simply as the CBD or "town" to many Nairobians – is relatively small: a triangle of shops, offices and public buildings, with the train station on the southern flank and the main bus stations to the east. Downtown Nairobi divides into three principal districts bisected by the main thoroughfares of **Kenyatta Avenue** and **Moi Avenue**. The grandest and most formal part of the CBD is the area around **City Square**, in the southwest. This square kilometre is Nairobi's heart: government buildings, banks and offices merge to the north and east with upmarket shopping streets and major hotels. The area's big landmarks are the **Kenyatta International Conference Centre**, with its huge cylindrical tower and artichoke-shaped convention hall, and the blue-glass skyscraper of **Lonrho House**. To the south of this area, towards the train station, stands the **Memorial Park** on the site of the bombed US Embassy.

North of Kenyatta Avenue, there's a shift to smaller scale and lesser finance. The **City Market** is here, surrounded by a denser district of modest shops, restaurants and hotels. The modest-sized **Jeevanjee Gardens** are a welcome patch of greenery, and a little further north is the university district and Nairobi's oldest establishment, the *Norfolk Hotel*, contemporary with the original 1907 rebuilding of the city.

East of Moi Avenue, the character changes more radically. Here, and down towards the reeking trickle of the Nairobi River, is the relatively poor, inner-city district identified with **River Road**, its main thoroughfare. The River Road quarter is where most long-distance **buses and matatus** start and terminate, and where you'll find the capital's cheapest restaurants and hotels, as well as the highest concentration of African-owned businesses. It's also a somewhat notorious area, with a traditional concentration of sharks and pickpockets (see box, p.108). The reputation can be exaggerated, but you can still meet residents of Nairobi who work five minutes' walk away and in all their years in the city have never been to this part of town.

If you're not on a shoestring budget and/or you're not eager to become acquainted with the city centre's gritty soul, then your time in Nairobi is more likely to be spent in one of the **suburbs**: the busy inner suburb of **Westlands** just north of the CBD; the forest-swathed ridges of **Runda** or **Spring Valley** further north; or the well-fed lawns and gardens of **Karen** or **Langata** in the southwest. Many of the city's attractions and most popular hotels, restaurants and bars are also found in these suburbs.

Brief history

Nairobi came into being in May 1899, an **artificial settlement** created by Europeans at Mile 327 of the Uganda Railway, then being systematically forged from Mombasa on the coast to Port Florence – now Kisumu – on Lake Victoria. Although called the "Uganda Railway" there was no connection to Kampala until 1931; before that, Lake Victoria ships provided the link.

Nairobi was initially a supply depot, switching yard and campground for the thousands of Indian labourers employed by the British. The bleak, partly swampy site was simply the spot where operations came to a halt while the engineers figured out their next move – getting the line up the steep slopes that lay ahead. The name came from the local Maasai word for the area, *enkare nyarobi*, "the place of cold water", though the spot itself was originally called *Nakusontelon*, "Beginning of all Beauty".

Surprisingly, the unplanned settlement took root. A few years later it was totally rebuilt after the burning of the original town compound following an outbreak of plague. By 1907, it was so firmly established that the colonists took it as the capital of the newly formed "British East Africa" (BEA). Europeans, encouraged by the authorities, started settling in some numbers, while Africans were forced into employment by tax demands (without representation) or onto specially created **reserves** – the Maasai to the Southern Reserve and the Kikuyu to their own reserve in the highlands.

Nairobi's districts and suburbs

The capital, lacking development from any established community, was somewhat characterless in its early years – and remains so. The **original centre** retains an Asian

1

△ Limuru & Ndenderu △ Banana Hill, Nazareth Hospital, Limuru & Brown's Cheese Farm

N

◁ Kikuyu & Naivasha

RUAKA RD

LIMURU ROAD

GIGIRI

UNITED NATIONS RD

Village Market

1 1 2
3 1

US Embassy

LOWER KABETE ROAD

KITISURU

TIGONI RIDGE RD

Canadian
HC

Karura
Forest

Karura
Forest

MUTHAIGA

Caltex
Plaza

LORESHO

WAIYAKI WAY

WESTLANDS

City
Park

Sarakasi
Dome

2

SEE "WEST NAIROBI" MAP FOR DETAILS

JAMES GICHURU RD

UHURU

Arboretum

Railway
Museum

CBD

Easy
Coach

Railway
Station

2

LUSAKA

Junction Mall

HILL

Nyayo
Stadium

Lenana
Forest
Centre

War
Cemetery

Jamhuri
Park

KIBERA

Wilson
Business
Park

3

3

Racecourse

Forest HQ

Uhuru Gardens
National Monument

SOUTH "C"

POPO RD

7

KAREN

Motherland
Centre

4

Ngong Road
Forest Sanctuary

SOUTHERN BY-PASS

Lengai
House

5

5 7

Wilson
Airport

WHITE GRASS

WINDY RIDGE

5

Rhino
Leisure

Nairobi Safari Walk &
Animal Orphanage

Splash!

Nakumatt Crossroads
Karen Office Park

4

Mamba
Village

10

Main Gate

Hyena Dam

KAREN ROAD

13 8 4

MARULA LANE

9

Karen
Club

Hillcrest
School

11

Bomas of
Kenya

KWS
HQ

Ivory
Burning Site

1A

No. 3
Dam

BUSHYVALE

AA

14

Symbion House

6

LANGATA

Galleria Mall

Langata Gate

7

24A

23C

2

23B

Narogomon
Dam

Olomanyi
Dam

Karen Blixen
Museum

BOGANI ROAD

16 8

13

25D

25C

25B

Impala
Hill

21A

Oloolua
Forest

Oloolua
Forest
Gate

USHIRIKA ROAD

9

Banda
Gate

17

26A

26B

30

29A

River Kisembe

18A

FOREST LINE RD

18

AFEW Giraffe
Centre

19

MUKOMA ROAD

27A

26D

27B

29A

29

28A

28B

Mbagathi
Gate

27C

HYRAX

VALLEY

Maasai
Gate

20

David Sheldrick
Wildlife Trust

River Empakasi

21

Kitengela
Glass

10

MAGADI ROAD

Ongata
Rongai

◁ Ngong Hills & Magadi

GREATER NAIROBI

0   2
kilometres

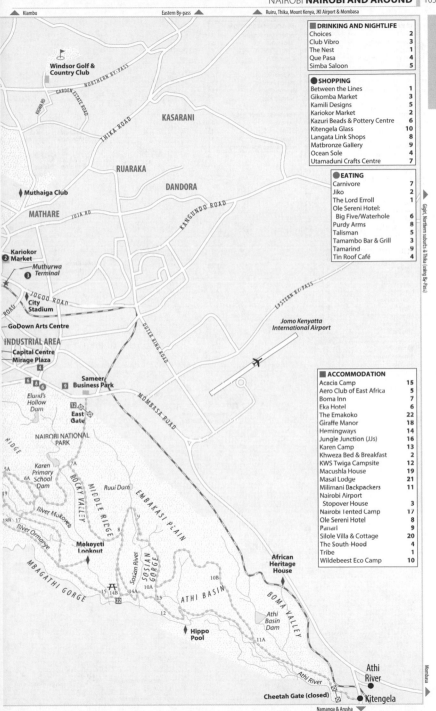

Kiambu Eastern By-pass Ruiru, Thika, Mount Kenya, JKI Airport & Mombasa

■ **DRINKING AND NIGHTLIFE**
Choices	2
Club Vibro	3
The Nest	1
Que Pasa	4
Simba Saloon	5

● **SHOPPING**
Between the Lines	1
Gikomba Market	3
Kamili Designs	5
Kariokor Market	2
Kazuri Beads & Pottery Centre	6
Kitengela Glass	10
Langata Link Shops	8
Matbronze Gallery	9
Ocean Sole	4
Utamaduni Crafts Centre	7

● **EATING**
Carnivore	7
Jiko	2
The Lord Erroll	1
Ole Sereni Hotel:	
Big Five/Waterhole	6
Purdy Arms	8
Talisman	5
Tamambo Bar & Grill	3
Tamarind	9
Tin Roof Café	4

■ **ACCOMMODATION**
Acacia Camp	15
Aero Club of East Africa	5
Boma Inn	7
Eka Hotel	6
The Emakoko	22
Giraffe Manor	18
Hemingways	14
Jungle Junction (JJs)	16
Karen Camp	13
Khweza Bed & Breakfast	2
KWS Twiga Campsite	12
Macushla House	19
Masal Lodge	21
Milimani Backpackers	11
Nairobi Airport	
Stopover House	3
Nairobi Tented Camp	17
Ole Sereni Hotel	8
Panari	9
Silole Villa & Cottage	20
The South Hood	4
Tribe	1
Wildebeest Eco Camp	10

Gigiri, Northern suburbs & Thika (using By-Pass)

Mombasa

Namanga & Arusha

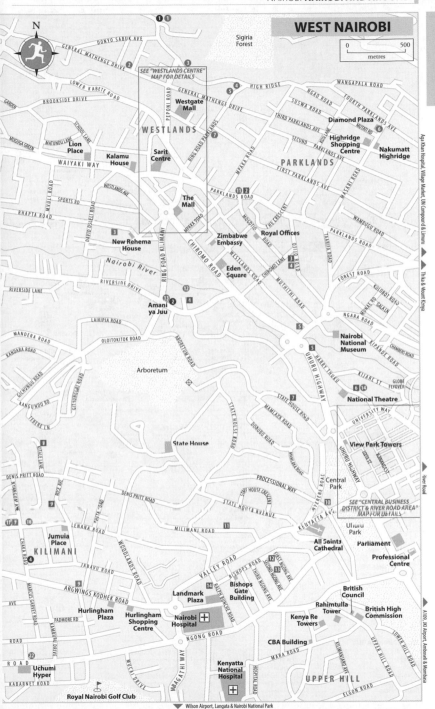

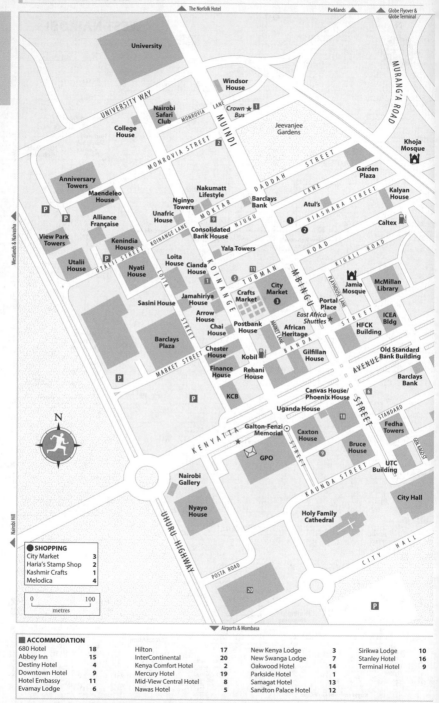

The Norfolk Hotel · Parklands · Globe Flyover & Globe Terminal

University

Windsor House

UNIVERSITY WAY

MURANG'A ROAD

Nairobi Safari Club

MONROVIA LANE

Crown Bus

Jeevanjee Gardens

College House

MONROVIA STREET

MUINDI

DADDAH STREET

Khoja Mosque

Garden Plaza

Anniversary Towers

Maendeleo House

Nakumatt Lifestyle

MOKTAR

Barclays Bank

Atul's

LANE

BIASHARA STREET

Kalyan House

Nginyo Towers

Unafric House

KOINANGE LANE

NJUGU

Caltex

Alliance Française

Consolidated Bank House

Kenindia House

View Park Towers

UTALII STREET

Yala Towers

Loita House

KOINANGE

KIGALI ROAD

Utalii House

Nyati House

Cianda House

TUBMAN

Jamia Mosque

McMillan Library

Jamahiriya House

Crafts Market

City Market

PLAYHOUSE LANE

Portal Place

ICEA Bldg

Sasini House

LOITA STREET

Arrow House

Chai House

Postbank House

East Africa Shuttles

MBINGU

HFCK Building

African Heritage

BANDA

STREET

Barclays Plaza

Chester House

Kobil

Gilfillan House

Old Standard Bank Building

MARKET STREET

Finance House

Rehani House

AVENUE

Barclays Bank

KCB

Canvas House/ Phoenix House

STREET

STANDARD

Fedha Towers

Uganda House

KENYATTA

Galton-Fenzi Memorial

Caxton House

Bruce House

UTC Building

GPO

KAUNDA STREET

City Hall

Nairobi Gallery

Nyayo House

Holy Family Cathedral

UHURU HIGHWAY

CITY HALL

N

POSTA ROAD

Airports & Mombasa

Westlands & Naivasha

Nairobi Hill

● SHOPPING
City Market	3
Haria's Stamp Shop	2
Kashmir Crafts	1
Melodica	4

0 — 100
metres

1

CENTRAL BUSINESS DISTRICT AND RIVER ROAD AREA

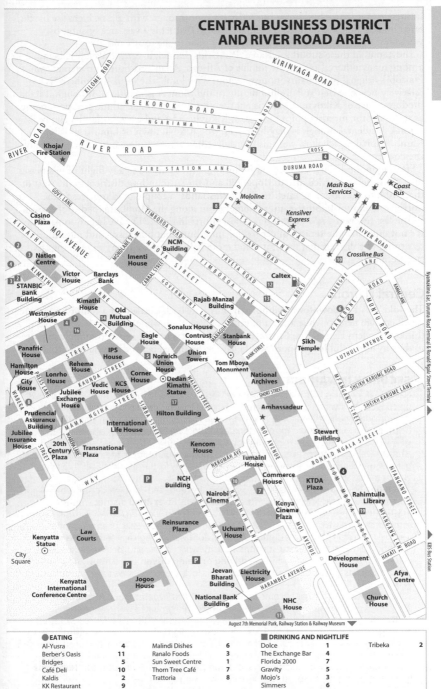

KIRINYAGA ROAD

KILOME ROAD

KEEKOROK ROAD

NGARIAMA LANE

RIVER ROAD

NGARIAMA ROAD

VOI ROAD

Khoja/
Fire Station ★

CROSS LANE

DURUMA ROAD

FIRE STATION LANE

LAGOS ROAD

GOVE LANE

Mash Bus
Services ★

★ Coast
Bus

Casino
Plaza

MOI AVENUE

TIMBOROA ROAD

TOM MBOYA STREET

Moloine ★

LATEMA ROAD

DUBOIS LANE

Kensilver
Express

River Road

KIMATHI STREET

Nation
Centre

Victor
House

Barclays
Bank

Imenti
House

NCM
Building

CABAN STREET

GOVERNMENT LANE

TSAVO LANE

TSAVO ROAD

TAVETA ROAD

★ Crossline Bus

STANBIC
Bank
Building

Kimathi
House

Old
Mutual
Building

Rajab Manzal
Building

Caltex

ACCRA ROAD

GABERONE ROAD

MUNYU ROAD

Westminster
House

STREET

Eagle
House

Sonalux House

MARASHA LANE

Stanbank
House

GABERONE

LUTHULI AVENUE

KANHE LANE

Panafric
House

STREET

IPS
House

Contrust
House

Sikh
Temple

Hamilton
House

Rehema
House

KAUNDA STREET

Norwich
Union
House

Union
Towers

BANK STREET

SHEIKH KARUME ROAD

City
House

Lonrho
House

Corner
House

MFANGANO STREET

Tom Mboya
Monument

MANGO STREET

SHEIKH KARUME LANE

PRESS LANE

WABERA STREET

Jubilee
Exchange
House

Vedic
House

KCS
House

⊙ Dedan
Kimathi
Statue

WUYALI STREET

National
Archives

SHORT STREET

Prudencial
Assurance
Building

MAMA NGINA STREET

SZABI STREET

Hilton Building

Ambassadeur ★

Jubilee
Insurance
House

International
Life House

Stewart
Building

RONALD NGALA STREET

20th
Century
Plaza

Transnational
Plaza

Kencom
House

MARUMAH AVE.

Tumaini
House

MOI AVENUE

MFANGANO LANE

WAY

P

NCH
Building

AGA KHAN WELK

NERHUMA LANE

Commerce
House

Kenya
Cinema
Plaza

KTDA
Plaza

TOM MBOYA STREET

Rahimtulla
Library

MFANGANO STREET

P

Nairobi
Cinema

P

Reinsurance
Plaza

Uchumi
House

Kenyatta
Statue ⊙

Law
Courts

TAIFA ROAD

City
Square

Development
House

HAKATI ROAD

Kenyatta
International
Conference Centre

P

Jogoo
House

P

Jeevan
Bharati
Building

Electricity
House

HARAMBEE AVENUE

National Bank
Building

NHC
House

MOI AVENUE

Afya
Centre

Church
House

August 7th Memorial Park, Railway Station & Railway Museum ▼

Nyamakima Ear, Duruma Road Terminal & Ronald Ngala Street Terminal

EDS Bus Station

● EATING			
Al-Yusra	4	Malindi Dishes	6
Berber's Oasis	11	Ranalo Foods	3
Bridges	5	Sun Sweet Centre	1
Café Deli	10	Thorn Tree Café	7
Kaldis	2	Trattoria	8
KK Restaurant	9		

■ DRINKING AND NIGHTLIFE			
Dolce	1	Tribeka	2
The Exchange Bar	4		
Florida 2000	7		
Gravity	5		
Mojo's	3		
Simmers	6		

1

influence in its older buildings, but today it's shot through with glassy, high-rise blocks. Surrounding the core of the old **Central Business District** is a vast area of suburbs: wealthiest in the west and north, increasingly poor to the south and east.

The names of these **suburbs** – Karen, Parklands, Eastleigh, Spring Valley, Kibera, among many others – reflect the jumble of African, Asian and European elements in Nairobi's original inhabitants, none of whom were local. The term "Nairobian" is a relatively new one that still applies mostly to the younger generation. Although it has a predominance of Kikuyu, the city is not the preserve of a single ethnic group, standing as it does at the meeting point of Maasai, Kikuyu and Kamba territories. Its choice as capital, accidental though it may have been (the Kikuyu town of Limuru and the Kamba capital, Machakos, were also considered), was a fortunate one for the future of the country.

Starting in the 1990s, the Central Business District saw the steady flight of businesses into the suburbs, particularly to **Upper Hill** and the surrounding districts to the west of the CBD; to the booming satellite city of **Westlands**, a couple of kilometres to the northwest; and for kilometre after kilometre out along the **Mombasa road** to the south. In the last few years, however, regeneration efforts in the CBD have begun to pay off. It's not quite like the rebirth of central Johannesburg, but businesses and nightlife are returning to a district that feels safer and more habitable than at any time in the last two decades.

Central Nairobi

The "old" heart of **downtown Nairobi** may only date back a little over a century, but there is still enough here to while away a morning or afternoon while you decide what you think of modern Kenya. The **Central Business District** is not the most cosmopolitan part of the city – that dubious honour would have to be shared between several suburban

---

SECURITY IN NAIROBI

Nairobi isn't nearly as bad as its **"Nairobbery"** reputation would suggest. The city has cleaned up considerably over the past few years: the centre is less threatening, and there are fewer street children, beggars and touts. That said, it pays to take some precautions against crime. It helps to memorize any route you're walking, as lost-looking tourists are easier targets. Keep your hands out of reach, as a handshake can sometimes throw you off guard, and be – rationally – suspicious of everyone until you've caught your breath. It doesn't take long to get a little streetwise. Every rural Kenyan coming to the city for the first time goes through exactly the same process.

At night, be extra vigilant if you're walking in the city centre and don't wander outside the CBD unless you're really clued-up. Be especially wary in the **River Road district**, which in practical terms means anything east of Moi Avenue (and be cautious on Moi Avenue itself). Even some locals avoid walking in the River Road area and taxi drivers are quite often reluctant to venture into certain parts of the district. Obviously, don't walk through any of the **parks** at night.

All the main **bus** and **matatu stations** are somewhat chaotic and ideal for pickpockets and snatch-and-run robberies. If you're **driving or being driven**, avoid displaying phones, cameras, tablets and laptops, and keep your doors locked and windows rolled up, especially at traffic lights.

In recent years Nairobi has become a target for the Somali terrorist group **Al-Shabaab**, as a 2013 attack on Westgate Mall, which killed 67 people, demonstrated with savage clarity; Al-Shabaab grenades also killed or injured dozens of less wealthy Kenyans in a series of attacks on matatus between 2011 and 2013, and the British Foreign Office still advises against travel to Eastleigh, where most of the city's Somali population resides. A profusion of armed guards and metal detectors around malls and other public buildings might not inspire much confidence, but the chances of being caught up in such an attack are still so minute that most Nairobians find that it doesn't pay to spend too much time worrying about it.

malls – but after the dark, anti-democracy period in the 1980s and the collapse of security in the 1990s, twenty-first-century central Nairobi is beginning to feel like a world-class city again. Strolling around here in the daytime is one of the most truly urban experiences you're likely to have in East Africa, as you make your way through streets bustling with harried office workers, students and street vendors. And if you later choose to check out the CBD's nightlife (see p.137), you'll have some idea of where you are.

Kenyatta Avenue

The obvious place to start looking around Central Nairobi is **Kenyatta Avenue.** Originally designed to allow a twelve-oxen team to make a full turn, the broad, multi-laned thoroughfare, planted with flowering trees and shrubs, remains – along with the Kenyatta Conference Centre – the capital's favourite tourist image. The avenue is smartest – and most touristy – on its south side, with would-be moneychangers, itinerant souvenir hawkers and safari touts assailing you from every direction.

The focus of the avenue's eastern end is the *Stanley Hotel's* **Thorn Tree Café**, on the corner of Kimathi Street. The CBD's one proper pavement café, the *Thorn Tree* is an enduring meeting place – despite its prices and a clientele largely made up of *wazungu* and rich business types (see p.131). The thorn tree in question was once Nairobi's main information exchange, with notice boards fixed to its trunk. It was felled in 1997 and replaced with a new sapling and purely ornamental message boards.

Off Kenyatta Avenue, close to Uhuru Highway, is **Koinange Street**, named after the Kikuyu Senior Chief Koinange of the colonial era. The peculiar, caged **Galton-Fenzi Memorial**, where the street meets Kenyatta Avenue, is a monument to the man who founded, of all things, the Nairobi branch of the Automobile Association. In 1926, Galton-Fenzi was also the first motorist to drive from Nairobi to Mombasa.

Nairobi Gallery
Kenyatta Ave and Uhuru Hwy • Daily 8.30am–5.30pm • Ksh1000 • ☎ 020 2216566, ⓦ museums.or.ke

The former **Provincial Commissioner's Office**, the low grey-red building with the dome on the corner of Kenyatta Avenue, in the shadow of Nyayo House, was the register office for births, marriages and deaths during the colonial period. It is now the **Nairobi Gallery**, home to a rotating series of temporary exhibitions, featuring mostly African artists, which can be well worth a visit. Call to ask what's on, or check the National Museums website.

Uhuru and Central parks
Western side of Uhuru Highway • Daily 24hr • Free

Central and **Uhuru** parks – not to be confused with Uhuru Gardens, the independence park on Langata Road (see p.115) – are unfenced and never closed (though it's a distinctly bad idea to visit after dark when they have a reputation for muggings). There are rowing boats for rent in the small murky lake in **Uhuru Park**, which are very popular at weekends and holidays. A poignant **memorial** to the many lives lost in political violence over the past decade can be seen at the roadside verge of Uhuru Park at Kenyatta Avenue, also known as **Freedom Corner**, where the Green Belt Movement (see p.26) have planted "Trees of Peace", each bearing a simple wooden cross with the name of a victim and the words *Saba-Saba*, meaning "Seven-Seven", after the crackdown on pro-democracy demonstrators on July 7, 1990.

City Square
City Square lies on the southern side of City Hall Way, east of Uhuru Highway. Jomo Kenyatta's statue sits benevolently, mace in hand, on the far side of the wide, flagstoned court; his mausoleum, with flickering eternal flames, is on the right as you approach the Parliament building further on. When the flags are out for a conference it all looks very bright and confident.

1

Parliament

Parliament Rd • No tours when Parliament is in session (usually mid-Oct to mid-July Tues, Wed & Thurs 9am–noon & 2.30–4pm)

The legend over the main doors of Kenya's **Parliament** reads: "For a Just Society and the Fair Government of Men." The motto seems finally to be losing its edge of irony, the government having been forced by both national and international pressures to allow greater democracy and accountability in its business. A host of contentious motions is openly debated here, concerning corruption and ethnic violence, and there's even the occasional vote of no confidence in the government.

It used to be possible to sit in the **public gallery**, but these days it's only open to school groups. The guards at the gate can tell you how to get a tour of the building when Parliament is not in session. If you are assigned a guide, make sure you agree about exactly how much you'll pay for the tour.

Kenyatta International Conference Centre

Harambee Ave • Daily 6am–6pm • Ksh350 • ☎ 020 3261000, ⓦ kicc.co.ke

From Parliament, walking down Harambee Avenue along the shady pavement, you come to Nairobi's pride and joy: the thirty-storey, 105m-high **Kenyatta International Conference Centre** or KICC. This, for a long time the tallest building in Kenya, is capped by a revolving restaurant, now closed. It's still worth going to the top, as the view of Nairobi is without equal and a firm reminder of the vastness of Africa. Just 4km to the south, the Mombasa road can be seen trailing through the suburbs and out towards the coast; northwards, hills of coffee and tea roll into the distance towards the Aberdare range. On a clear day you really can see Mount Kenya in one direction and Kilimanjaro in the other. Immediately below you the traffic swarms, and **Jogoo House**, containing government offices, is suddenly seen to be built remarkably like a Roman villa. In 2000 the KICC was overtaken by the nearby 38-storey **Times Tower**, the tallest building in East Africa at 140m, which is occupied by Kenya's tax authority and inaccessible to tourists.

National Archives

Moi Ave, junction with City Hall Way • Mon–Fri 9am–4.30pm, Sat & Sun 9am–4pm • Ksh200 • ☎ 020 2228959

Housed in the striking old Bank of India building on the bend of Moi Avenue across from the *Hilton*, the **National Archives** amount to a museum and art gallery in the heart of the city that few visitors to Nairobi know about. If you want to see the locked archives themselves (mainly books, papers, correspondence and some recordings) you can pay a token fee for a year's access.

The ground floor is a **public gallery** with a range of paintings from Kenya and throughout the African continent; an enormous display of Maasai, Luo, Turkana, Luhya and Ethiopian weaponry; and a wall of tribal photographs. In the centre of the floor there's also a jumbled collection of African ethnographia – musical instruments, masks, weapons and domestic artefacts.

Beyond the first floor and its photograph library, the second floor houses a photographic exhibition of the struggle for **independence** – compelling not just for its content but because this is one of the few public places in the country where Kenyans can be reminded of the period in their history euphemistically called "the Emergency".

Tom Mboya Monument

Facing the National Archives, the **Tom Mboya Monument** commemorates the life of the left-leaning Luo government minister who was assassinated in 1969 close to this spot on Moi Avenue. Mboya's statue, sculpted by Oshoto Ondula, depicts him in Ghanaian robes as presented to him by the first president of Ghana, Kwame Nkrumah, and surrounded by pink flamingos – a curious reference not to his family's lakeside origins but to the plane tickets he bought for students to study abroad after independence.

KIBERA

Kibera is a sprawling mass of shacks, just a few kilometres southwest of Nairobi's city centre. It was long thought to be the largest shanty town in sub-Saharan Africa, home to around one million people; although recent mapping exercises have dramatically reduced the estimated number of residents down to as few as 250,000, the scale of the place can still be difficult for most Westerners to imagine. The slums were a flashpoint during the post-election violence in January 2008, when protestors torched buildings and uprooted the Nairobi–Nakuru railway line that runs right through Kibera, and the area is still the scene of occasional politically motivated riots. There have been no major incidents since, however, and although it's perhaps best not to just wander down there, it's safe to visit if you're accompanied by local residents or NGO workers – a number of local operators even offer morning excursions to the area.

Kibera started at the end of World War I as a village housing Sudanese Nubian soldiers of the demobilized armies of British East Africa. Subsequently, as rural-to-urban migration increased, people moved into the area and began putting up mud-and-wattle structures. Today most residents live in makeshift huts, typically measuring 3m by 3m, with an average of five people per dwelling. Access to electricity, running water and sanitation ranges from zero to very minimal – the occasional makeshift pit latrines are shared between anything from ten to one hundred homes, though foreign donors have constructed some new toilet blocks. The streets are a mass of seemingly endless trenches, alleyways and open gutters clogged with waste and sewage. As well as lacking even the most basic services, Kibera has an HIV infection rate of between fourteen and twenty percent, and the number of orphans rises daily. However, the slum somehow works and is full of small **businesses**, from video cinemas to bakeries. Few residents buy newspapers or own TVs; the community radio station **Pamoja FM** (99.9 FM; ⓦ bit.ly/Pamoja), whose name means "together" in Swahili, provides a vital glue that helps prevent Kibera from ripping apart.

When booking an **escorted visit** to Kibera, make sure before you sign up that you know exactly where your money is going; some businesses are not above running "pro-poor" tourism as part of their activities while pocketing much of the cash supposed to be supporting slum projects. As you visit various premises and community projects, you should find the experience deeply affecting, if not enjoyable, and not without its lighter moments. Good options for a tour include **Kibera Tours** (ⓦ kiberatours.com) or **Explore Kibera Tours** (ⓦ explorekibera.com).

August 7th Memorial Park

Corner Haile Selassie Ave and Moi Ave • **Park** Daily 7am–6pm • Ksh20 • **Memorial centre** Daily 9am–5pm • Ksh150

The **August 7th Memorial Park** occupies the site of the former American embassy, which was bombed by al-Qaeda in 1998 (see p.573). The park is a peaceful refuge from the free-for-all of downtown Nairobi, with grassy lawns and statues built from the rubble. It is also a chilling reminder of the horror perpetrated here. In the centre of the park, near the fountain, a wall commemorates each of the 218 victims of the blast. The memorial centre displays arrefacts from the bombing and a video about the atrocity.

Dedan Kimathi Statue

Opposite the *Hilton Hotel*, on the corner of Kimathi and Mama Ngina streets, stands a statue honouring **Dedan Kimathi**, the Mau Mau freedom fighter who was executed by the British in 1957. The statue – an imposing 2m bronze sculpture atop a 3m base – is hard to miss. Kimathi, sporting the dreadlocks typical of Mau Mau fighters, holds a gun in one hand and his *rungu* (club) in the other. The statue was erected in February 2007 on the fiftieth anniversary of his death.

Jamia Mosque

The **Jamia Mosque** stands near the City Market, north of Kenyatta Avenue. The ornate green-and-white exterior contrasts strikingly with the simple interior, and the central dome appears far larger from beneath than it does from the courtyard outside.

1

MUSEUMS IN KENYA

To keep up with developments in Kenya's museums, contact the **Kenya Museum Society** (0724 255299, kenyamuseumsociety.org), based off Kipande Road, behind the Nairobi National Museum. As well as publishing the excellent annual journal *Kenya Past and Present*, they organize an Affordable Art Show every October, where you can pick up works by local artists at very reasonable prices. You can take out **one-month temporary membership** of KMS for Ksh800, which entitles you to free entry in all NMK museums and sites around the country – a very good deal.

Although most Kenyan towns now have at least one mosque, often financed by Saudi patrons, few are as large or as beautiful as Nairobi's Jamia. It's unlikely that non-Muslims will be allowed in, although polite requests, a genuine interest in Islam and the usual modesty of attire may help.

Jeevanjee Gardens

Corner Muindi Mbingu St and Moktar Daddah St • Daily dawn–dusk • Free

In a reasonably reputable part of the city, **Jeevanjee Gardens** are always worth a visit, especially during a weekday lunchtime when you can picnic on a bench and chat with the office workers not thronging the nearby restaurants. It seems to be an acceptable place to have a **cigarette** in a public place, too. You can also listen to the preachers who have made Jeevanjee their church and the bemused picnickers their congregation. The park contains a curiously small statue, just about recognizable, of **Queen Victoria**, presented to Nairobi by the nineteenth-century business tycoon A.M. Jeevanjee, who founded Kenya's *The Standard* newspaper. And there's a rather good sculpture of the tycoon himself, crafted from heavy, iron wire.

Railway Museum

1km west of the railway station (signposted) • Daily 8am–5pm • Ksh400, including guided tour • 0721 268741, krc.co.ke

Nairobi's privately run **Railway Museum** is a natural draw for rail fans and of more than passing interest for anyone else. The main hall contains a mass of memorabilia, including photos of early stations, of the "Lunatic Express" East African Railway from Mombasa to Lake Victoria being built, pictures of the engineering feats involved in getting the carriages up and down the escarpment, and of strange pieces of hardware, such as the game-viewing seat mounted at the front of the train. Passengers who risked this perch were reminded that "The High Commissioner will not be liable for personal injury (fatal or otherwise)." In the museum annexe, the motorized bicycle inspection trolley is quite a sight, but, as the write-up explains, the experiment in the 1950s "was not really successful", as the wheels kept slipping off the rail.

Outside, exposed to the elements, is the museum's collection of old **locomotives**, most of them built in Britain. You can clamber inside any of the cabs to play with the massive levers and switches. The restriction on forward visibility in some of the engines seems incredible; the driver of the *Karamoja Express* couldn't have had any idea what was in front of him while steaming down a straight line.

Lions figure prominently in the early history of the railway. Look in the shed for first-class coach #12 to learn the story of Superintendent C.H. Ryall. In 1900, two years after the hunt for the "Man-eaters of Tsavo", lion-hunter Ryall had been sent to Kima station to shoot another suspected man-eater. He readied his gun one evening, settled down in the carriage and offered himself as bait. Unfortunately, he nodded off and was dragged from this carriage and devoured while colleagues sat frozen in horror. The coach, together with the repainted loco #301, was used in the filming of *Out of Africa* at Kajiado.

Nairobi National Museum

Museum Hill • Daily 8.30am–5.30pm • Ksh1200, Ksh1500 combined ticket with the snake park (see p.115); free with NMK membership (see box opposite) • ⓦ museums.or.ke • A 30min walk from Kenyatta Ave or a few minutes by bus (#21, #23 or #119)

In 2008, the **Nairobi National Museum** reopened its doors after a three-year, Ksh800 million facelift. The refurbished result is a still partly sparkling, showpiece attraction and a good prelude to any tour around the country. It's easy to reach from the centre of town and provides a solid overview of Kenya's culture, history and wildlife.

Hall of Kenya

The expansive entry hall into the museum, **Hall of Kenya**, is sparsely appointed with some of Kenya's most impressive and unusual artefacts and artworks. In one display case is a Swahili **siwa** from the 1680s. The *siwa*, a ceremonial horn intricately carved from an elephant tusk, was traditionally blown on celebratory occasions as a symbol of unity and was considered to possess magical powers. There is also a **sambu**, a Kalenjin elder's cloak made from the skins of Sykes' monkeys. Beautiful photos of some of Kenya's animals adorn the wall of this hall, and prepare you for the next gallery.

Great Hall of Mammals

Dedicated to Africa's charismatic, endangered **megafauna**, and the plains animals that are still found in some abundance in Kenya, the **Great Hall of Mammals** features some impressive dioramas. In the centre of the room are examples of a giraffe, an elephant, a buffalo, a zebra and an okapi, the strange forest-dwelling relative of the giraffe found only in the jungles of the Democratic Republic of Congo. Along the walls are displays of most of Kenya's mammals, including the big cats, primates and antelopes, with explanations of their habitats, diets and life cycles. Also displayed in this gallery is the skeleton of **Ahmed**, the most famous of the giant-tusked bull elephants of Marsabit, in the north of the country. In the 1970s, when poaching was rampant in northern Kenya, conservationists feared that Ahmed would be targeted because of his enormous tusks. Kenya's first president, Jomo Kenyatta, assigned two rangers to track Ahmed day and night until he died of natural causes at the age of 55. His tusks weighed in at 68kg each. There's a life-size replica of Ahmed in the courtyard between the entrance and the shop.

Just off the Hall of Kenya gallery is a room devoted to **ornithology**, featuring 1600 specimens in glass cases. Kenya's birdlife usually makes a strong impression, even on non-birdwatchers. Look out for the various species of hornbill, turaco and roller, and for the extraordinary standard-wing nightjar, which is frequently seen fluttering low over a swimming pool at dusk, hunting for insects.

Cradle of Human Kind

The unique interest of the Nairobi museum lies in the **human origins** exhibit, **Cradle of Human Kind**, where paleontology displays are housed. Along the walls, skeletons and skull casts of ancient hominins trace primate diversity and the evolution of the human species back millions of years. Of particular importance is the almost complete skeleton of "Turkana Boy", the 1.6-million-year-old remains of an immature male hominin found near Lake Turkana. Hardcore paleontology fans will want to visit the **Hominin Skull Room**, which contains the skulls of some of our ancient ancestors and non-ancestral cousins, such as *Homo erectus*. The understanding of human evolution is itself a rapidly evolving field, with new theories about human origins and ancestry appearing almost yearly, but East Africa is invariably its field-research location.

Cycles of Life

Upstairs, next to the temporary galleries of local art, the **Cycles of Life** exhibit covers Kenya's tribes and cultures, in neatly laid-out displays of artefacts telling the story of each ethnic group from childhood through adulthood to ancestor status. If you're

1

planning on travelling through any of the areas inhabited by pastoral peoples (especially Pokot, Samburu, Maasai or Turkana), then seeing some old and authentic handicrafts beforehand is a good idea.

The room begins with a display of traditional birthing methods and **child-rearing** techniques, including a traditional Pokot child carrier made from monkey skin and children's toys made from discarded scraps of metal. The exhibit moves on to explain initiation and circumcision rituals. On display here is a Maasai warrior outfit, complete with spear and shield. The **adulthood** display contains various clothing and beauty products including beaded necklaces and earplugs used by some of the seminomadic tribes to stretch the earlobes. A display of grave markers and artefacts used to send someone into the afterlife marks the end of the exhibit.

Snake Park

Museum campus • Daily 8.30am–5.30pm • Ksh1200, Ksh1500 combined ticket with the Nairobi National Museum (see p.113) • W museums.or.ke

The **Snake Park**, a reptile exhibit in the grounds of the National Museum, is not nearly as interesting as it should be, with the majority of the serpents housed in dark, glass-fronted tanks and pretty much invisible under their rocks and branches. Only the **pythons**, **tortoises** and an inappropriate American **alligator** have large, well-lit enclosures. Nevertheless, it's worth getting the most out of the visit by taking an informative tour with one of the very willing **guides** hovering around: their services are free (note the "Report corruption" signs everywhere). Perhaps you could ask your guide to explain how the central, open-air enclosure (the one that warns "Trespassers will be Poisoned") manages safely to house highly venomous **boomslangs** – whip-fast tree snakes that the guide gleefully points out, not much more than an arm's length from the crowds of schoolchildren jostling around.

City Park

Limuru Rd • Daily 6.30am–6.30pm • Free • Matatu #11 from Globe Terminal

The biggest and best park in the city centre is **City Park** in the north, a half-hour stroll from the National Museum down Forest Road and Limuru Road. City Park has a wealth of tropical trees and birdlife, including hornbills, several troops of vervet and Sykes' monkeys, a small stream with wooden bridges, gravel paths, shady lawns, and the city's Jewish, Goan and World War I memorial cemeteries. At the weekend, it gets crowded with families. During the week it's delightful, though it's best for women not to visit alone.

Arboretum

Arboretum Rd, off State House Rd • Daily dawn–dusk; guided walks second Sat and last Mon of each month – call to check and arrive at the gate by 9.30am • Free; parking Ksh50; guided walks Ksh100 • ☎ 020 3754904 or ☎ 0733 823045, W nairobiarboretum.org • Matatu #48 from the CBD

Close to the city centre, northwest of Uhuru Park on Arboretum Drive, the **Arboretum** is a lovely place to wander or picnic and, of course, a must if you're botanically inclined. Somewhat overgrown, almost jungly in parts, it contains more than two hundred varieties of tree, and even the odd monkey. There are security notices everywhere so don't take any valuables, but it's guarded and fenced and, since its makeover and the paving of its paths by the Friends of Nairobi Arboretum, it has become essentially another safe area of the city. The Arboretum Café, in the car park just outside the gate, has drinks and snacks.

Uhuru Gardens National Monument

1

Langata Rd, 2km west of Wilson Airport • Daily 8am–6pm • Free entry to pedestrians, parking Ksh200 • Take any matatu to Langata, Karen and Ongata

The point of having a place like **Uhuru Gardens National Monument** – not to be confused with Uhuru Park (see p.109) in the CBD – is presumably to provide a location for national events when required. There isn't any obvious reason to make a special trip here, but if you're killing an hour between flights or appointments – or you've simply had enough of sitting in traffic on Langata Road – then it's certainly somewhere to stretch your legs and inspect some examples of triumphalist post-independence architecture. Most locals come here for a picnic or just to doze.

On the east side of the park is the more striking of the two Uhuru edifices, a towering 24m **obelisk**, opened in December 1986. Its base is decorated with sculptures of a dove of peace perched on the clasped hands of unity, a group of citizens cooperating to put up a flagpole and a barrel-chested worker standing ready to defend the nation with his bare hands.

On the other side of the park, an ambitious **water feature** constructed in 1978 marks a quarter-century of independence in the year that saw the passing of the first president, Jomo Kenyatta. Abstract figures join together to hold up a monstrous, black-tiled diamond, but the lack of running water may be taking something away from the meaning.

Nairobi's forests

A colour map of Nairobi suggests a multitude of cool green spaces around the fringes of the city and, happily, over the last decade the pretty picture has become more of a reality. Two of the most important of Nairobi's forests – the **Ngong Road Forest Sanctuary** in the west and the **Karura Forest** in the north – have been fierce battlegrounds between environmentalists and developers who had hoped to move onto these public lands amid a morass of corruption. As a new road snakes through it, the future of the Ngong Road Forest is still under some doubt, but the safety of Karura and the fine rainforest at **Olooloua**, in the southwest corner of the city, seems assured.

Karura Forest

Main entrance off Limuru Rd, 5.2km from the National Museum; the Sigiria entrance is at the end of Thigiri Lane, off Thigiri Ridge Rd, 4.4km from Westlands roundabout • Daily 6am–6pm • Ksh600, parking Ksh100, guide Ksh300/2hr • ☎ 0724 215423, ⦿ friendsofkarura .org • Matatus to Gachie, Denderu and Limuru serve the main entrance • Ten square kilometres

Where Nairobi's exclusive northern suburbs are divided by forest-flanked ridges and gurgling brown streams, the stretch of indigenous rainforest, gum-tree plantation and marshland that comprises **Karura Forest** has been secured and opened to visitors. Formerly notorious as a refuge for muggers and bush-meat hunters, the forest has had a dramatic image change since the "squatters" who used to live here were talked into moving out and taking jobs as rangers under an initiative headed up by the wife of the former British High Commissioner.

Karura is now a popular area for **jogging**, **dog-walking**, **biking** and **horseriding**. You can buy a map showing the clearly cut trails at the entrance (Ksh500), and although it's a peaceful escape from the city, you won't be alone, as several hundred local residents every day make use of it. The waterfall that is such a feature of Karura publicity is no Niagara, but for a city it's an impressive asset, especially after heavy rain, and you can even swim in the clean pools at the bottom. Some of the grand rainforest trees near the waterfalls have been labelled, so you won't miss the giant sycamore fig, nor the steeple-like Newtonia. Most of the forest's **wildlife** is on the small side, and fairly secretive, but duikers abound and there are three species of monkeys, genets, monitor lizards and more than two hundred species of birds.

1

BIRDWATCHING IN NAIROBI

Birdwatching need not be exclusively a bush pursuit. For any visitor staying in central Nairobi, an impressive sight during the early morning and late evening is groups of **black kites** circling as they move between feeding and roosting sites, and among these are readily identified black-and-white **pied crows**. **Marabou storks**, **sacred ibises** and **silvery-cheeked hornbills** can sometimes be seen flying over the city (dramatically large marabous may also be seen in the thorn trees on Uhuru Highway, near Nyayo Stadium), while flocks of **superb starlings** call noisily from office buildings. The leafier areas of the city are likely to produce even more birds.

The gardens in the grounds of the Nairobi National Museum are an interesting and relatively safe area to start birding. Here, keen birdwatchers may encounter **sunbirds** (variable and Hunter's) and the **cinnamon-chested bee-eater**. Another bird of the gardens is the **African paradise monarch**, a species of flycatcher. In breeding plumage, the rufous males have long tail streamers, which trail behind them like ribbons as they flit from tree to tree.

Nature Kenya organizes bird walks from the National Museum every Wednesday morning at 8.45am for a temporary membership fee of Ksh200. They usually proceed to another part of Nairobi. Longer trips are also offered at least once a month. For more information, contact Nature Kenya at the museum (☎020 3537568 or ☎0771 343138, ⊛naturekenya.org).

Ngong Road Forest Sanctuary

Main entrance on Ngong Rd, 1.5km west of Junction Mall, before you pass Nairobi War Cemetery • Daily 8am–6pm • $10 on foot, $15 with a bicycle, $20 with a horse • ☎ 020 2113358 or ☎ 0729 840715, ⊛ ngongforest.org • Take any matatu to Woodley, Dagoretti or Ngong • Six square kilometres

Formerly off-limits to all but timber thieves, medicinal bark strippers and outnumbered forest guards, the **Ngong Road Forest Sanctuary** is now safe to walk, jog, cycle or ride a horse through, thanks to increased ranger patrols and perimeter fencing. It's a particularly impressive achievement, considering that the **Kibera slum** (see p.111) presses up hard against the forest on its eastern flank – and, indeed, bringing Kibera residents into the forest and engaging people with conserving their natural heritage has been intrinsic to the success of the sanctuary.

This is one of the world's few indigenous forests within a capital city, harbouring more than three hundred species of trees and plants, at least 120 species of birds, and mammals including bushbuck, porcupine, aardvark and, it's said, even hyenas and leopards, unlikely as that seems. One spectacular species you probably will see is the forest's breeding **crowned eagles**, whose unmistakeable bonfire-shaped nests are often visible high in a tree fork.

As you stroll through the glades beneath towering, buttress-rooted forest giants, you'll also spot **red duiker** and tiny **suni** antelope and, floating near the treetops, handsome **swallowtail** butterflies marked with azure and brown that swoop down to visit damp mud patches on the paths. The forest is also the habitat of some of the best **timber** for sculpting tourist souvenirs – in fact, illegal wood collection could well be a threat to its long-term future.

Oloolua Forest and Nature Trail

Entrance at the far southern end of Karen Rd • Mon–Fri 9am–4pm, Sat & Sun 9am–5.30pm • Ksh600 • ☎ 020 3882571, ⊛ primateresearch.org • Citi Hoppa #24 • One square kilometre

Although not quite as extensive as Nairobi's other city forests, **Oloolua Forest** is a very attractive area in a part of the city suburbs that is conveniently close to other attractions including the AFEW Giraffe Centre and the Karen Blixen Museum. The forest serves principally as a primate sanctuary, where the **Institute of Primate Research** looks after a protected zone where they study the habits of olive baboons and vervet and colobus monkeys, as well as breeding and studying other species in captivity as the focus of tropical disease research.

You can drive into the forest reserve, or leave your car at the barrier and walk. You immediately come to a picturesque bridge over the jungle-swathed Mbagathi River.

The forest reserve contains caves (Mau Mau hiding places, naturally), bamboo thickets, a waterfall, papyrus groves and a campsite and picnic area. The marked, 3km **nature trail** takes about ninety minutes to walk, with regular stops to watch monkeys, birds and butterflies. You could drive around slowly in about half an hour.

Bomas of Kenya

Forest Edge Rd (400m north of the junction at Galleria Mall) • Shows Mon–Fri 2.30–4pm, Sat, Sun & holidays 3.30–5.15pm • Ksh600 • ☎ 020 8068400, ☻ bomasofkenya.co.ke • Bus/matatu #15, #125 or #126

Bomas of Kenya was originally an attempt to create a living museum of Kenyan culture, with a display of eleven traditional homesteads (*bomas*) and an emphasis on regional dances. Unfortunately, the place has always had a touristy feel, not helped by the huge indoor **amphitheatre** where dance shows are performed. In fact the vitality of the Bomas is channelled mainly into souvenir-selling and conferences, most famously the constitutional conference of 2003 that led to the so-called Bomas draft constitution calling for decentralized government. The ethnic homesteads re-creating Kenya's vernacular architecture (a guided tour of which is included in the price) are for the most part sadly unkempt. Even so, if you're looking to fill an afternoon, they can be enjoyable enough, particularly on weekends, when they're busier, and when an evening disco sometimes follows the dance show.

Surprisingly, perhaps, the dances are not performed by the appropriate Kenyan tribes; instead, the **Harambee Dancers** do fast costume changes between acts and present the nation's traditional repertoire as professional performers rather than participants. If the acoustics were better and the whole place less of an amphitheatre, the impression would undoubtedly be stronger. As it is, you at least get a very comprehensive taste of Kenyan dance styles, from the mesmeric jumps and sinuous movements of the Maa-speaking peoples, to the wild acrobatics of some of the Mijikenda dances.

AFEW Giraffe Centre

Koitobos Rd, 3km off Langata Road (signposted) • Daily 9am–5.30pm • Ksh1000, children Ksh500 • ☎ 020 8070804 or ☎ 0734 890952, ☻ giraffecenter.org • Citi Hoppa #24

Although it tends to be promoted as a children's outing, the **AFEW Giraffe Centre** has serious aims. Run by the African Fund for Endangered Wildlife, it has successfully boosted the population of the rare **Rothschild's giraffe** from an original nucleus of animals that came from a wild herd near Soy (see p.285). Its other main mission is to educate children about conservation. You'll get some great mug shots from the giraffe-level observation tower, where the creatures push their huge heads through to be fed the pellets you're given to offer them. There are various other animals around, including a number of tame **warthogs**, and a wooded 95-acre **nature sanctuary** across the road – great for birdwatching. If you really like it here, and have deep pockets, consider an overnight stay at the wonderful, country-house-style **Giraffe Manor** (see p.129).

Karen

Always associated with its famous former resident, the author **Karen Blixen** (pen name Isak Dinesen), the suburb of **KAREN** was actually named after her cousin, Karen Melchior, whose father was the chairman of the Karen Coffee Company – the estate that was sold for residential development and named Karen – though most people, including Blixen herself, were not aware of the coincidence.

While the number of African residents is rising steadily, until recently Karen was the quintessential white suburb – a network of five-acre plots spaciously set on eucalyptus-lined avenues amid fields grazed by horses. Still separated from Nairobi by the dense, bird-filled woodland of the Ngong Road Forest (see opposite), Karen is a reminder of

1

how completely the settlers visualized and created little Europes for themselves. In parts, you could almost be in the English shires – or, for that matter, northern California.

If you're driving the most direct route to Karen from the city centre, along Ngong Road, you pass **Jamhuri Park**, the Agricultural Society of Kenya showground (see p.69), the **racecourse** (see p.143) and the **Nairobi War Cemetery**, a peaceful and dignified World War II cemetery set far back from the busy road among shady trees, with pink stonework and carefully tended lawns.

Karen's central **shopping centre**, at the crossroads of the Langata and Ngong roads, officially now called Karen Connection (but usually referred to as Karen *dukas*), includes a growing cluster of safari businesses, banks and other services. The whole area now feels much less like a country crossroads and much more like a town centre, especially with the arrival of the big **Nakumatt Crossroads**.

Karen Blixen Museum

Karen Rd, 3.5km south of Karen crossroads • Daily 8.30am–6pm • Ksh1200, which includes a guided tour, although note that temporary membership of the museum society (see p.112) costs only Ksh800 and allows free entry • ☎ 020 8002139, ⓦ museums.or.ke • Citi Hoppa #24

The **Karen Blixen Museum** is located in the house where much of the action of the author's autobiographical memoir *Out of Africa* (see p.594) took place. The epitome of colonial Africa, the **house** was presented to Kenya by the Danish government as an Uhuru gift at the time of independence, along with the agricultural college built in the grounds – the **gardens**, laid out as in former times, are delightful.

It's a beautiful, well-proportioned home with square, wood-panelled rooms, and the restoration of its original appearance and furnishings has evidently been very thorough. A guided tour is included in the price but can be somewhat rushed, especially at weekends, and there's no guarantee that they'll let you wander around on your own. They certainly don't like you to take photos of the old black and white pictures.

On weekends you may be somewhat suffocated by a surfeit of Mozart (the favourite composer of Karen Blixen's lover, Denys Finch Hatton), and by tour groups complaining about how little Finch Hatton resembles Robert Redford.

ARRIVAL AND DEPARTURE — NAIROBI

BY PLANE

International flights, and domestic Kenya Airways, Jambo Jet and Fly540 services, use Jomo Kenyatta International Airport (NBO; ☎020 6822111, ⓦkaa.go.ke), commonly abbreviated to JKA or JKIA, 15km southeast of the city centre, off the Mombasa Hwy. If you fly into Nairobi on a domestic flight with Airkenya or SafariLink, you'll probably arrive at Wilson Airport (WIL; ☎0724 256837), 5km from the city centre between the CBD and the National Park.

DOMESTIC AIRLINES

Airkenya Wilson Airport ☎020 3916000, ⓦairkenya.com.

Fly540 International House, Mama Ngina St ☎0712 540540 or ☎0722 540540, ⓦfly540.com.

Jambo Jet Sales offices in Yaya Centre and Sarit Centre among others ☎020 3274545 or ☎0711 024545, ⓦjambojet.com.

Kenya Airways Jomo Kenyatta International Airport, with sales offices in Barclay's Plaza, Loita St; Junction Mall, Kilimani; Sarit Centre, Westlands; and Village Market, Gigiri ☎020 3274747.

SafariLink Wilson Airport ☎020 6000777, ⓦflysafarilink.com.

INTERNATIONAL AIRLINES

British Airways, fourth floor, The Citadel, Muthithi Rd, Westlands (☎020 3277400); Brussels Airlines, fifth floor, Bandari Plaza, Woodvale Grove, Westlands (☎020 4443070); Egyptair, Hilton Building, City Hall Way (☎020 2226821); Emirates, 9 West Building, opposite Sarit Centre, Westlands (☎020 7102519); Ethiopian Airlines, Bruce House, Muindi Mbingu St (☎020 2296000); Etihad, third floor, ABC Towers, Wayaki Way (☎020 4259000); Kenya Airways, Superior Arcade, Accra Rd; first floor, Barclays Plaza, Loita St; Yaya Centre; and Village Market (☎020 3274747); KLM, Barclays Plaza, Loita St (☎020 2958210); Qatar Airways, second floor, Barclays Plaza, Loita St (☎020 2800000); South African Airways, mezzanine floor, International House, Mama Ngina St (☎020 2247342); Swiss Airlines, first floor, Regal Plaza, Limuru Rd, Parklands (☎020 3744045).

AIR CHARTER COMPANIES

SafariLink (see above) offers charter flights in a two-seater Cessna 182. Other charter companies, all represented at Wilson Airport, include: Blue Bird Aviation (☎0732 189000, ⓦbluebirdaviation.com); Yellow Wings

(☎0713 467304, ⓦyellowwings.com); and East African Air Charters (☎0735 880011, ⓦeaaircharters.co.ke).

TRAVEL AGENTS

Most travel agents can book you international airline seats, but the following should be able to offer discounted seats: Akarim Agencies, ground floor, Kenyatta International Conference Centre (☎020 2218880, ⓦakarim.net); Bunson Travel, second foor, Park Place, Limuru Rd (☎020 3685990, ⓦbunsontravel.com); Kambo Travel, first floor, Mpaka House, Mpaka Rd, Westlands (☎020 4448505 or ☎0733 595119, ⓦkambotravels.com).

JOMO KENYATTA INTERNATIONAL AIRPORT

Jomo Kenyatta International Airport now sports a brand new terminal, 1A, built after a fire in 2013 destroyed both the arrivals and departure halls. If you're dropping or picking up, there's easy parking, but remember to pay as it leaves before you leave again (Ksh70 short-stay, Ksh250/24hr).

Arrivals JKIA arrivals are normally straightforward; full visa information is given in our Basics chapter (see p.87). There's normally a cursory customs check, where you may be asked what you're bringing into the country, but obvious tourists are usually waved through. If at any stage someone asks you for a bribe or "a little something", refuse politely. If you have a long layover you may want to use the a/c Aspire Lounge at Gate 11 ($30/4hr), which gives you a comfy sofa to curl up on, papers and TV, and unlimited snacks and drinks. For proper pampering there's also a full-blown spa, Sheri Spa, near Gate 15.

Baggage store There's a left-luggage store at terminal 1D.

Money There are Barclays and Equity Bank ATMs outside the arrivals hall, and one or two other bank exchange desks and forex bureaus. Count notes carefully if you're exchanging money.

Mobile phones The airport has mobile phone shops where you can buy a local SIM card.

Food, drink and toilets There's little choice in terms of food and drink: airside, the always busy branch of *Java House* coffee shop near Gate 14 is most people's retreat. There are also cafés near gates 4 and 18, and at the international arrivals hall. The quietest toilets are by Gate 13.

Children There's a children's play room by Gate 11.

Information and assistance There are Kenya Airports Authority customer care counters by gates 6, 11, 15 and 18.

Airport taxis Once you're out of the arrivals hall, a horde of private taxi touts invariably assails new arrivals. Ignore them and walk straight to the waiting cabs lined up outside, or else go to the Kenatco office on the right of the small concourse. If you'd prefer to be met, contact Kenatco directly (ⓦkenatco.com) or a travel agent like Uniglobe Let's Go Travel (see p.124), who can organize a cab. There's a range of generally agreed prices to the city centre, currently around Ksh2000–2500, depending on your bargaining

skills. Trips to Karen and the northern suburbs are more expensive. Taxis don't have meters, so always agree the exact price before getting in (see p.56).

Airport buses There is no public airport shuttle, but some hotels will pick you up if you make prior arrangements. The local Citi Hoppa bus #34 leaves from outside the arrivals hall (roughly every 20min; daily 6am–11pm; Ksh70), entering the city through the eastern suburbs (rather than running straight up Uhuru Hwy) and stopping on Accra Rd or at the nearby *Ambassadeur Hotel*.

WILSON AIRPORT

Wilson Airport is a small facility, right by Langata Rd, and there are always taxis awaiting passengers. Airkenya and SafariLink both have departure lounges with café-restaurants, and there's a branch of I&M bank with an ATM.

REGIONAL DESTINATIONS

Amboseli NP lodges (1–4 daily; roughly 45min; WIL); Diani Beach (2 daily; 1hr 30min; WIL); Eldoret (4 daily; 45min–2hr 30min, depending on route; NBO); Entebbe, Uganda (10 daily; 1hr 20min; NBO); Juba, South Sudan (2 daily; 1hr 45min; NBO); Kilimanjaro (frequent; 45min–1hr 10min, depending on route; WIL, NBO); Kisumu (10 daily; 50min; NBO); Kitale (1 daily; 50min; WIL); Lamu (2 daily; 1hr 10min–2hr, depending on route; WIL, NBO); Lewa Downs (2–3 daily; 1hr; WIL); Loisaba (3 daily; 1hr 45min; WIL); Lokichokio (4 weekly; 1hr 45min; WIL); Maasai Mara NR lodges (7 daily; 1hr; WIL); Malindi (3-plus daily; 1hr–2hr, depending on route; WIL, NBO); Meru NP (2 daily; 50min; WIL); Mombasa (at least 12 daily; 1hr; NBO); Naivasha (1 daily; 15min; WIL); Nanyuki (3 daily; 40min; WIL); Samburu NR (2 daily; 1hr 10min; WIL); Tsavo West NP lodges (1–2 daily; 50min; WIL); Zanzibar (8 daily; 2hr 20min; NBO).

BY BUS

Most bus companies have their booking offices or parking areas in the River Rd district, especially around Accra Rd. The smaller companies operate out of the Country Bus Station (aka "Machakos Airport"), 1.5km east of the city centre just past Wakulima Market, between Pumwani Rd and Landhies Rd (buses #4, #18 or #28 from the *Ambassadeur Hotel* bus stage). There is often a wide range of prices, depending on the vehicle and the services on board, which may include video, snacks and a/c. Always reserve tickets in advance.

DOMESTIC BUS COMPANIES

Coast Bus (aka Coast Air, Coastline, Coast Express, Modern Coast) Corner Accra Rd and Cross Lane ☎0722 206446, ⓦcoastbus.com. One of the best companies. "Oxygen " is their a/c service.

Destinations Multiple daily services between Mombasa (and Malindi) and Nairobi, plus Kisumu, Kakamega, Kitui and points in between.

Crown Bus Lagos House, Monrovia St ☎ 020 2212253 or ☎ 0722 719944, ⊚ crownbus.co.ke.
Destinations Nairobi to Mombasa plus western Kenya.
Easy Coach Haile Selassie Ave ☎ 020 2212711 or ☎ 0738 200301, ⊚ easycoach.co.ke. One of Kenya's biggest bus companies.
Destinations Principally the Rift Valley, Western Kenya and Kampala.
Kensilver Express Dubois Rd ☎ 020 2120935 or ☎ 0722 509918.
Destinations Central Highlands, especially Embu and Meru.
Mash Corner Accra Rd and Duruma Rd ☎ 0723 463685 or ☎ 0733 623260, ⊚ masheastafrica.com. Mash (short for Mashuru) is a major competitor of Easy Coach.
Destinations Mainly along the Mombasa (and Malindi)– Nairobi–Malaba–Kampala axis.

ARUSHA BUS COMPANIES

The following all offer – in theory – daily services from city-centre hotels via Jomo Kenyatta International Airport to Arusha, although in practice, the number of buses actually running depends on demand. If you're boarding at JKIA, you should contact the company well in advance with flight details. Most services leave the CBD at approximately 8am and the airport at 8.30am, arriving in Arusha at 1pm. Prices range from $25–35.
Davanu Shuttle Kingsway Nairobi Centre, Muindi Mbingu St ☎ 020 2630182 or ☎ 0722 787182, ⊚ davanushuttle .com.
East Africa Shuttles House Suite 403, fourth floor, Portal Place, Muindi Mbingu St ☎ 020 2248453 or ☎ 0722 348656, ⊚ eastafricashuttles.com.
Riverside Shuttle Room 1, third floor, Panafric House, Kenyatta Ave ☎ 0722 328595, ⊚ riverside-shuttle.com.

DESTINATIONS

Arusha (8 daily; 6hr); Chogoria (6 daily; 4hr); Dar-es-Salaam (1 daily; 16hr); Eldoret (6–8 daily; 8hr); Embu (frequent; 3hr); Isiolo (4 daily; 6hr); Kakamega (12 daily; 8hr); Kampala (6 daily; 12hr–15hr); Kericho (10–20 daily; 4hr); Kigali (1 daily; 23hr); Kisumu (10–30 daily; 7hr); Kitale (10–15 daily; 7hr); Kitui (4 daily; 3hr); Machakos (frequent; 1hr 30min); Malindi (3 daily; 12hr); Maralal (4 daily; 8hr); Meru (frequent; 5hr); Mombasa (frequent, especially around 7am & 7pm; 8–9hr); Moshi (6 daily; 5hr 30min); Naivasha (frequent; 1hr 30min); Nakuru (10–15 daily; 2hr 30min); Namanga (8 daily; 3hr); Nanyuki (8 daily; 4hr); Narok (6 daily; 5hr); Nyeri (8 daily; 2hr 30min); Thika (frequent; 40min).

BY TRAIN

Riding the Nairobi–Mombasa train, the last remaining long-distance passenger service in Kenya, can be a colourful and interesting experience (see p.57), but in

recent years it has become increasingly unreliable, often subject to delays of up to 24hr. While it's worth taking at least once, be sure not to schedule any onward connections for the following day, and bring some extra food with you just in case.

Arrival The train for Nairobi is supposed to leave Mombasa at 7pm (Tues & Sun), and to arrive at 9.30am the next day. The railway station is virtually in the city centre, with one of Nairobi's biggest matatu stages right in front. Arriving here, you can just walk straight out and follow Moi Ave into town. Watch out for taxi drivers and porters who will more or less kidnap your luggage if you don't prevent them. Otherwise, the main attention you'll attract is from safari touts, who are persistent, but friendly enough, and useful if you need an escort to one of the cheaper River Rd addresses. A small tip agreed between you (say Ksh100) would be appreciated.

Departure The service to Mombasa is scheduled to run twice a week (Mon & Fri), in theory leaving Nairobi at 7pm, arriving in Mombasa at 10am the next morning. If you're planning to take the train from Nairobi, it's important to make a reservation, especially if you want a first-class compartment. While you may get away with leaving this until a couple of hours before departure, it's always advisable to reserve well in advance, especially during busy travel periods like Christmas and New Year. It's best, and cheapest, to buy tickets in person at the station (☎ 0728 787305 or ☎ 0728 787301), but agents (see p.123) can also obtain tickets for you.

BY MATATU

Matatus leave from various terminals as detailed below. There are no matatus to the coast.

DESTINATIONS

Accra Rd Terminal (between River Rd & Duruma Rd) Embu (2hr 30min); Isiolo (5hr).
Accra Rd Terminal (between River Rd & Tsavo Rd) Meru (5hr); Nanyuki (3hr 30min).
Accra Rd Terminal (Dubois Rd area) Busia (9hr); Kakamega (7hr); Kericho (6hr); Kisii (6hr); Kisumu (7hr).
Accra Rd Terminal (River Rd end) Archers Post (1 or 2 daily; 6hr); Nyeri (2hr 30min).
Globe Terminal (by Globe Flyover) Thika (1hr).
Latema Rd Terminal Nyahururu (2 daily; 3hr).
Muthurwa Terminal (by Wakulima Market) Machakos (1hr 30min).
Nyamakima Bar, Duruma Rd Terminal Eldoret (5hr 30min); Gilgil (2hr); Kitale (7hr); Maralal (7hr); Naivasha (1hr 30min); Nakuru (2hr 30min); Narok (4hr).
Railway Station Terminal Magadi (3 daily; 2hr).
Ronald Ngala St Terminal Kajiado (1hr 30min); Namanga (3hr).

1

GETTING AROUND

Getting around Nairobi has been a headache for decades: the lack of transport planning and the absence of any light rail transport means **traffic jams** for four or five hours on weekday mornings and evenings, and serious delays in getting from one suburb to another, except late at night and before dawn. Getting **around the CBD** is so straightforward you won't need much assistance. By day, you'll probably want to walk; by night, you should take a taxi. If you're on any kind of budget, though, it's certainly worth getting to know what passes for the city's public transport system, and look out for the **bus and matatu map** published by *Kenya Buzz* (ⓦ kenyabuzz.com).

BY BUS AND MATATU

The green Citi Hoppa buses which roar around Nairobi all day are cheap (Ksh20–100; pay the conductor) and very unpredictable. Buses are numbered, but bus stops aren't and routes change frequently. Nairobi's matatus – which, like the city's taxis, must bear a yellow stripe – tend to take the same routes as buses and often display the same route numbers. They're generally faster, more dangerous and even more packed, though serious accidents are rare.

TERMINALS

City buses and matatus save you money on getting around, certainly for longer trips out of the city centre, but take some figuring out. They all start and finish their routes at terminals ("stages" or "stands") in the city centre, where they fill up and then head out on their routes – although they are not supposed to drop off or pick up anywhere in the CBD. The terminals are marked on the CBD map (see pp.106–107). From north to south:

Globe Roundabout Journeys to the east and southeast suburbs.

Khoja/Fire Station West and northwest suburbs.

Latema Rd West and northwest suburbs.

Accra Rd Embakasi.

Kencom House Kibera; Ngong; southwest suburbs.

Ambassadeur Hotel Jomo Kenyatta International Airport.

Ronald Ngala St Eastern suburbs.

KBS Bus Station Kiambu and northern suburbs; Dagoretti; southern suburbs.

Railway Station Magadi Rd; Ongata; Kiserian; Kikuyu; Limuru.

Muthurwa Lane Eastern suburbs.

BY TAXI AND MOTORCYCLE TAXI

Taxis By Kenyan standards, Nairobi's private taxis – the registered ones all bear a yellow stripe – are expensive. Cabs, licensed by the Kenya Taxi Cabs Association, crowd around key spots in the city and have generally agreed prices for well-known routes, with the lowest fare for any trip in the city centre around Ksh300. A reliable company is Kenatco, who have a 24hr office at Uchumi House on Aga Khan Walk (ⓣ 020 2506790, ⓦ kenatco.com).

Motorcycle taxis A cheaper option is motorcycle taxis, known as piki-pikis or boda-bodas; they carry only one passenger and charge a fraction of the taxi fare, though for safety reasons they are best used only for short hops.

BY COMMUTER TRAIN

On weekday mornings and evenings, there are several slow and packed commuter rail services between the suburbs of Ruiru, Kahawa, Embakasi, Kikuyu, Stony Athi and the city centre. These aren't much help to most travellers, but a station which opened in 2012 at Syokimau, just south of the international airport, signalled the start of an expansion of services which may one day include a new airport shuttle rail service.

BY CAR

Avoid driving in or through the city if you can. The congestion has to be seen to be believed, and your average speed can be as little as 3km/hr – commuting has become nightmarish, and many city workers spend four hours a day behind the wheel. If you're renting a car, if possible, pick it up at the airport, or have it delivered there, which gives you time to get used to the vehicle and the traffic before joining the city-centre madness. For general driving advice, turn to our Basics chapter (see p.51). The driving itself can be a nerve-racking experience too, though you do get used to it. Watch out for matatus, which lurch into the fray as suddenly as they stop to pick up fares. And beware of roundabouts (traffic circles). These labour under "priority traffic" regulations, which in theory means cars already on the roundabout have priority, but in practice means chaos as nobody is prepared to give way. Try to stay in lane.

Parking Parking in the CBD can be difficult during business hours, though there's usually space at the Loita Street Car Park, next to Barclays Plaza, or at the Kenyatta International Conference Centre (entrance off City Hall Way). If you park on the street, assuming you can find a legal space, you'll need to buy a daily parking ticket (valid 24hr); this ticket is theoretically only payable electronically via mobile money, but in practice the city's uniformed parking wardens seem happy to accept cash. All the private car parks and the 24hr daily parking ticket cost Ksh300/day.

Car repairs Stantech Motors, Shimo la Tewa Rd, off Lusaka Rd, Industrial Area (ⓣ 020 8070403, ⓦ stantechmotors .co.ke), is reliable and recommended.

Leaving Nairobi Driving out of Nairobi, allow plenty of time to get clear of the city traffic. The first bypass, the Northern By-Pass, runs roughly from Gigiri to Jomo Kenyatta International Airport, and the new southern by-pass is nearly complete..

CAR RENTAL

Avis/Budget College House, University Way ☎020 2213330, ⓦavis.com; map p.106.

Central Rent-A-Car 680 Hotel, Muindi Mbingu St☎020 2222888, ⓦcarhirekenya.com; map p.106.

Concorde Car Hire Sarit Centre, Westlands ☎0733 606856, ⓦconcorde.co.ke; map p.132.

Market Car Hire Ground floor, Chester House ☎0722 515053, ⓦmarketcarhire.com; map p.106.

Sunworld Riverside Lane, off Riverside Drive, Westlands ☎020 4445669 or ☎0722 525400, ⓦsunworld-safari.com; map p.105.

BY BIKE

If you plan to cycle in Nairobi, you won't be alone, but you need to keep your wits about you and mirrors are essential. To connect with other urban cyclists, visit ⓦshecyclesnairobi .wordpress.com.

Bikes and Sports Ltd Ground floor, Lavington Green Mall, James Gichuru Rd ☎0700 640775. Repairs and sells both mountain and street bikes, including a selection for children. Mon–Sat 9am–7pm, Sun 9.30am–6pm.

Cycleland Lower ground floor, Sarit Centre, Westlands ☎020 3743550. Offers bike rental (Ksh900/day), with a decent selection of imported bikes, and half-decent mountain bikes for sale starting from around Ksh19,000. Mon–Sat 9am–7pm, Sun 10am–5pm.

INFORMATION

Tourist information Nairobi has no official tourist office, but The Standard and the Daily Nation newspapers are useful sources of current information and special offers, and the free and widely circulated magazines Go Places (ⓦgoplaceskenya .com), Kenya Buzz (ⓦkenyabuzz.com) and Up Magazine (ⓦupnairobi.com) are always worth a look.

Maps If you need a detailed map of the city you probably won't find anything better than the Nairobi A–Z, available from bookshops, although like most maps it's years out of date. Alternatively, the city has now been comprehensively Google-mapped, so if you're prepared to put up with roaming charges or you've got an unlocked phone and a local SIM card (see p.89) your GPS-enabled 3G or 4G mobile phone will be able to guide you around.

SAFARIS

Nairobi is the travel hub of Africa, with a mass of opportunities for **safaris** around Kenya. There are hundreds of safari **operators** and travel agents to provide you with everything you need for your trip; you can also organize your own **self-drive** safari via a number of car rental outlets (see above), who can also provide a driver if needed. One possibility not often considered is **cycling**: Hell's Gate at Naivasha, Kakamega Forest and a number of other small parks allow bikes, and there's a lot of wonderful cycling country besides these areas. At the other end of the budget spectrum, **chartering a plane** offers unequalled opportunities for seeing the country; a few small operators, mostly based at Wilson Airport, will oblige (see p.118). The "Safaris" section in Basics (see p.78) gives general information about safaris and guides.

SAFARI OPERATORS AND TRAVEL AGENTS

The best travel agents are honest and reputable. Many belong to KATO (see p.79), but some who don't are still very good. It's always a good idea to meet staff from the operator you are travelling with before departure. Every other business in Nairobi seems to be a safari outfit, and in the challenging environment of Kenya, spotless reputations are hard to maintain. The businesses we list below, however, rarely come in for criticism. Check whether the advertised safari is actually run by the company in question, as the practice of one company sub-contracting a safari to another is common. Take your time, ask to see their vehicles, ask about the KPSGA qualifications of their guides (see p.80), demand everything in writing including a detailed breakdown of the costs, and don't be pressured into making any decisions until you are ready. Pay particular attention to how many 24hr park/reserve tickets your safari will use. Safari touts who hang around on the street, or at various hotels and lodgings, are keen to take you to operators' offices, but should be avoided – no reputable company uses them. In the lists below, the pricing categories are only a rough guide – per person, all-inclusive except drinks.

UP TO $300/DAY

African Home Safaris Delta Hotel, University Way ☎0722 760661, ⓦafricahomeadventure.com; map p.106. Budget safari operator affiliated to Hostelling International – they also run the Enchoro Wildlife Camp in the Mara (see p.369)

Best Camping Second floor, Amee Arcade, corner Muthithi Rd and Parklands Rd, Westlands ☎0733 603090, ⓦbestcampingkenya.com; map p.132. Long-established operator whose budget camping trips are generally recommended.

Bonfire Adventures Ninth floor, Yala Towers, Koinange St (with branches in Lavington Mall and Ridgeways Mall) ☎020 2067788 or ☎0722 879629, ⓦbonfireadventues.com; map p.106. Kenyan tour company offering pocket-friendly packages and weekend getaways, along with a growing list of international destinations including Tanzania, Uganda and Zanzibar.

Dallago Valley Arcade, Kileleshwa ☎0772 768753, ⓦdallagotours.com; map p.104. One of the few budget companies to have KPSGA-certified guides, Dallago offers

1

good-value camping safaris to Maasai Mara, Lake Nakuru, Samburu and Amboseli.

★**Gametrackers** Seminary Rd, Karen ⓣ 020 2222703, ⓦ gametrackersafaris.com; map p.102. Long-established, popular and consistently good operator with strong northern Kenya credentials.

Ice Rock Mountain Treks and Safaris Fourth floor, NCM Building, Tom Mboya St ⓣ 020 2244608 or ⓣ 0722 301306, ⓦ icerockclimbing.com; map p.107. A small professional setup with knowledgeable guides, mainly dealing with safaris to Mount Kenya, Kilimanjaro, Hell's Gate and other East African destinations. The owner, who used to be a member of the Mount Kenya rescue team, organizes and leads most trips.

★**Savage Wilderness Safaris** Sarit Centre, Westlands ⓣ 020 7121590, ⓦ whitewaterkenya.com; map p.132. Excellent programme of technical climbing and walking trips on Mount Kenya, rafting, and cycling and walking safaris.

Savuka Tours & Safaris Off Kiene Rd, Kileleshwa ⓣ 020 2215256 or ⓣ 0722 415643, ⓦ savuka-travels.com; map p.104. Good-value camping safaris that get favourable recommendations from budget travellers for their good food and driver/guides, though accommodation is basic.

★**Uniglobe Let's Go Travel ABC Place,** Waiyaki Way, Westlands (branch at Karen crossroads) ⓣ 0722 331899, ⓦ letsgosafari.com; map p.104. Consistently impressive, Let's Go are the first and best port of call for independent travellers in Kenya, agents for a large number of homestays and independent lodges throughout the country and operators of well-organized camping safaris.

AROUND $300–500/DAY

Eastern & Southern Safaris Sixth floor, Finance House, Loita St ⓣ 020 2242828 or ⓣ 0716 500001, ⓦ essafari.co.ke; map p.106. Highly regarded safari company that has a reputation for very reliable service.

★**Gamewatchers** Village Market ⓣ 0774 136523, ⓦ porini.com; map p.102. Innovative, ecoconscious operators with a strong list of bronze and silver guides among their staff. As well as running excellent safaris, they also own and manage the outstanding *Porini* eco-camps in the Mara, Amboseli area and Ol Pejeta. Highly recommended.

Nalepo Expeditions Marula Lane, Karen ⓣ 0718 888004, ⓦ africaexpeditions.com; map p.102. Safari operator with a good record and highly professional approach, offering largely tailor-made trips and their own camp in the Mara and other regional destinations, including (unusually) the Loita Hills.

Southern Cross Symbion House, Karen Rd ⓣ 020 8070311, ⓦ southerncrosskenya.com; map p.102. Considering they have a number of silver as well as bronze guides, their lodge and tented camp safaris offer extremely good value for money.

Steenbok Safaris Suite 1G, first floor, Sunrise Plaza, Ruiru (behind Bushgate/Oilibya) ⓣ 020 2432452 or ⓣ 0733 775763, ⓦ steenboksafaris.com. Reputable mid-budget safari outfitter with a decent fleet of vehicles and a car rental operation.

★**Sunworld** Riverside Lane, off Riverside Drive ⓣ 020 4445669 or ⓣ 0722 525400, ⓦ sunworld-safari.com; map p.104. Extremely proficient 4WD specialists with a good fleet of vehicles, bronze and silver driver-guides and a well-organized, walk-in bookings operation.

ABOVE $500/DAY

★**Bush & Beyond** Wilson Business Park, Wilson Airport ⓣ 020 6000457 or ⓣ 020 6005108, ⓦ bush-and-beyond.com; map p.102. Very good bespoke safari organizers (including riding safaris) and reservations agents for a short list of superb camps and lodges. If you know what you want, they know how to deliver.

★**Cheli & Peacock** Lengai House, Wilson Airport ⓣ 0730 127000, ⓦ chelipeacock.com; map p.102. As owners and agents for some of Kenya's very best small lodges and tented camps, C&P have a savvy and personal approach that keeps them at the forefront of safari operation and lodge design: you tend to see it here first. They also have a good number of bronze and silver guides among their staff.

Ker & Downey Safaris Ndalat Rd (south of Langata Link), off Langata South Rd, Karen ⓣ 020 8058032 or ⓣ 0724 252606, ⓦ kerdowneysafaris.com; map p.102. The archetypal old-style safari outfitter (Kenya's oldest, dating from 1946), Ker & Downey are the people to choose if you want a no-expense-spared, tailor-made safari, either fully mobile or using lodges and camps. Many silver and bronze guides work for them.

Micato Safaris Second floor, Almont Park, Church Rd, Westlands ⓣ 020 4445220 or ⓣ 020 4445218, ⓦ micato.com; map p.104. Much lauded Kenyan-American tour operator with off-the-peg and tailor-made trips run by crews who include more bronze and silver safari guides than any other operator in the country – all trips are run by a driver-guide with at least a bronze certificate.

★**Origins Safaris** Fifth floor, Landmark Plaza, Argwings Kodhek Rd ⓣ 020 2042695, ⓦ originsafaris.info; map p.105. Excellent birdwatching trips and a huge range of other safaris, for all interests, with more than twenty bronze and silver guides and one of only four gold guides in the country. Not cheap, but very highly recommended if you have specific interests, with accommodation at well-selected lodges and tented camps.

Safari & Conservation Company Wilson Business Park, Wilson Airport ☎020 2115453, ⊛scckenya.com; map p.102. Safari organizers and agents for a short list of beautiful, owner-managed camps and lodges in some of Kenya's most remote and exciting corners.

Safaris Unlimited ☎0727 535019, ⊛safarisunlimited .com. Horseriding safari specialists, for confident riders

only, covering the Maasai Mara, Loldaiga Hills, Laikipia and other wilderness areas.

Tropical Ice 98 Marula Lane, Karen ☎020 2405573 or ☎0712 282793, ⊛tropical-ice.com; map p.102. High-end adventure safaris combining 4WD vehicles with foot safaris in Tsavo East's elephant country, led by expert safari guides, operating traditional-style, mobile camps.

ACCOMMODATION

It isn't difficult to find **accommodation** in Nairobi, but it can be very expensive. The main question is which area fits your needs. The **Central Business District** is useful for accessing shops and some offices on foot (though many businesses, embassies and other offices are not located here), while if you base yourself further afield, you're likely to need transport or have to rely on the nearest mall. Travellers congregate at a number of different spots around the city and many visitors never set foot in the downtown CBD. If you're arriving in town in the small hours or early in the day, it's worth knowing that most places won't be able to offer you a room before 10am. Bear in mind, too, that **a/c** is not considered essential in Nairobi's climate and you'll only find it at top-end addresses, which also uniformly offer free room safes. All the top-of-the-range places and most backpacker haunts have guarded or enclosed **parking** – only cheap, city-centre lodgings are a problem in this respect. Naturally, leave nothing of value in the vehicle, or attached to it – such as spare wheels, jerricans or roof boxes. **Wi-fi** is increasingly widespread in Nairobi, and all but the cheapest hotels should have it.

MOMBASA ROAD AND JOMO KENYATTA AIRPORT

There are no hotels at JKIA itself and only limited options in the area. The following can be convenient as they are largely clear of city-centre traffic jams, but none is as close to the airport as they would have you believe. If you're driving, remember the Mombasa Hwy is divided along this street, and there are relatively few turning points. As an alternative, consider one of the options in – or just outside – Nairobi National Park (see p.148) – though you will usually have to pay park fees on top – or the excellent *Acacia Camp* near Athi River (see p.151).

Boma Inn Kenya Red Cross Complex, Red Cross Rd, off Popo Rd, off Mombasa Hwy, 13km from JKIA ☎0719 050000, ⊛theboma.co.ke; map p.103. Surprisingly smart sixty-room hotel owned by the Kenya Red Cross. Rooms are on the small side but stylish enough, with DSTV, and there's a gym and sauna. Staying here also gives you access to the pool and restaurant at the five-star *Boma* next door, whose rooms are twice the price. BB $250

Eka Hotel Mombasa Hwy, 12km from JKIA ☎0719 045000 or ☎0732 105000, ⊛ekahotel.com; map p.103. Modern hotel with slick decor and all amenities, aiming to outdo the neighbouring *Ole Sereni* as a relatively convenient airport address at very competitive rates (but with no view of the national park). The best rooms face the pool. Bed only $255

Nairobi Airport Stopover House Oluvimu Rd, South C ☎0722 787182, ⊛nairobiairportstopoverhouse. com; map p.102. Half the name is true – it's definitely a place to stop over. But the bit about the airport is misleading, since it's only 3km from the city centre – not

close enough to be within easy walking distance but still likely to be affected by rush-hour traffic. Nevertheless it's a clean, reliable overnight base at a good price, with kitchen facilities, dorm beds and private rooms that sleep up to four. Dorms $15, BB $38

Ole Sereni Hotel Mombasa Hwy, 12km from JKIA ☎020 3901000 or ☎0731 436405, ⊛ole-sereni.com; map p.103. Glitzy and flamboyant hotel cramming 134 rooms into a limited space directly on the boundary of the Nairobi National Park, with views across the savanna from the restaurant terrace and the more pricey rooms. There's also excellent food and a pool. BB $390

Panari Mombasa Hwy, 11km from JKIA ☎0711 091000, ⊛panarihotels.com; map p.103. Even leaving aside the tired opulence, standard rooms here are absurdly overpriced, though booking ahead can get you major discounts. Lower floors include a small shopping mall, gym, pool and famous ice rink (see p.103), and the upper floors enjoy views out across Nairobi National Park (albeit from a distance). BB $390

The South-Hood House #54, Balozi Estate, off Mombasa Hwy, 12km from JKIA ☎0712 652280, ⊛southhoodvillas.com; map p.103. Small, smart and homey B&B in a residential estate, whose six rooms provide a more affordable alternative to the hotels on the highway. The proprietor is friendly and helpful, and there is a kitchen for those who'd like to self-cater. BB $90

RIVER ROAD AREA

The very cheapest lodgings in Nairobi are around River Rd, the main drag through the city centre's poorest quarter. Despite the constant worry about safety, River Rd is central Nairobi's most stimulating and animated area, and offers a

1

plunge into a world you pass by if you stay in the CBD or out in the suburbs. Choose carefully, as some places have rowdy bars and clubs attached to them, their rooms aren't always terribly clean or secure, and they may not be ideal for solo female travellers.

Abbey Inn Gaberone Rd ☎0727 865625; map p.107. A noisy, boozy place, but the adequate rooms have nets and TVs and are mostly clean and fresh, with tiled bathrooms and electric showers. Unlovely, and with an awful lot of stairs to climb, but there's a handy cybercafé downstairs, as well as a bar and restaurant. BB Ksh1800

Destiny Hotel Duruma Rd ☎0724 954999; map p.107. This four-storey block is conscientiously run, with airy rooms, nets and electric showers. Particularly good value for friendly couples as only single rooms with modestly sized beds are available. There's a TV lounge and cold sodas but no bar or restaurant. Bed only Ksh1000

Evamay Lodge River Rd, at the junction with Duruma Rd ☎0703 949680; map p.107. Very good value for the price, with comfortable rooms that have TVs and mosquito nets. The friendly staff have made some attempt at decoration, and the whole place is clean with good security. BB Ksh2300

★ Khweza Bed & Breakfast South side of Ngara Rd, 200m west of Sarakasi Dome ☎020 2672116 or ☎0717 060045, ⊛khweza.com; map p.103. This may not be as conveniently located as central Nairobi's cheap hotels, but it offers a funkier and probably more comfortable alternative. Rooms are brightly decorated, and there's a pleasant roof terrace with plenty of other travellers to meet. They also organize tours. BB Ksh5500

Mercury Hotel 18 Tom Mboya St ☎0720 553820; map p.107. With walls hung with moth-eaten game trophies, this hotel seems to hark back to the 1970s. Rooms have sporadic hot showers, and there's a pleasant courtyard bar-restaurant (beer Ksh170, soda Ksh70) with a *nyama choma* bar and a bizarre miniature rockery. Bed only Ksh1860

Mid-View Central Hotel Latema Rd ☎0720 484496, ⊛midviewhotels.com; map p.107. Fifty cramped rooms in a hotel that feels a shade more upscale than the other cheapies, with nets, TVs, spotless bathrooms with electric showers, plus a no-prostitution policy. BB Ksh2700

Nawas Hotel Nawas Building, corner Latema Rd and River Rd ☎020 2243148; map p.107. Thirty-six small, neat and very cheap rooms with TVs, nets and electric showers, with a good, friendly restaurant on the first floor. Good value all round. BB Ksh1300

New Kenya Lodge River Rd, at the top of Latema Rd ☎020 2222202 or ☎0733 925208; map p.107. A long-established backpackers haunt, with six small dorms, twelve s/c twin rooms with electric showers and one non-s/c single. Popular communal area, book exchange, two common showers and mosquito nets in the rooms. Budget safaris can be organized here, but check all the details and

"what ifs" before committing. Wi-fi. Dorms Ksh750, rooms bed only Ksh1500

New Swanga Lodge Corner Duruma Rd and Accra Rd ☎0720 215769; map p.107. The green-walled rooms here, though not large, are comfy enough, with nets and electric showers. Convenient for buses and good value, with a decent breakfast, though hardly quiet. BB Ksh1800

Samagat Hotel Park House, Taveta Rd ☎020 2585933; map p.107. In a former apartment block, this has spacious rooms with nets and TVs, the upper ones with views of the CBD's high-rises. Elevators get you to your room and the ninth-floor dining room/TV lounge. BB Ksh2500

Sandton Palace Hotel Taveta Rd ☎020 342104 or ☎0720 629985, ⊛sandtonhotels.co.ke; map p.107. One of the best hotels in the district, although rather overpriced. All 102 rooms, accessed by lift, have TV with DSTV, direct-dial phones, safes, ceiling fans and electric showers in proper cubicles. Basement parking. The similarly appointed and priced sister hotel *Sandton City* is on nearby Duruma Rd. BB $75

Sirikwa Lodge Corner Munyu Rd and Accra Rd ☎0700 020666; map p.107. These rooms above a *miraa* shop have seen better days, and you'll only get hot water in the evenings. Ideally located for enjoying the chaos of the Accra Rd matatu stands, but not quite as comfortable as similar places. Bed only Ksh1500

CENTRAL BUSINESS DISTRICT

The following listings cover the more affluent parts of the city centre, roughly north as far as the museum and west as far as Central and Uhuru parks. Even at the lower end it's always worth discussing the price, and rates on the websites of the international groups can be cheaper by as much as fifty percent if you book online and pay in advance.

680 (Six-Eighty) Corner Kenyatta Ave and Muindi Mbingu St ☎020 315680 or ☎0722 207361, ⊛sentrim-hotels.com; map p.106. Catering mostly to business travellers, the *680* is getting run down but is still very convenient if you want to be right in the CBD, and better value than many other central hotels – assuming you bargain hard for a good rate. Rooms have cable TV but old-style plumbing, and there's safe basement parking. Be sure to ask for a room at the back unless you want to be kept awake by the racket from *Simmers*, opposite. BB $180

Boulevard Harry Thuku Rd, next to the National Museum ☎020 2227567, ⊛sentrim-hotels.com; bus #21, #23 or #119, matatu #104; map p.105. On the fringes of the CBD, and functional rather than extravagant, this well-cared-for hotel dates back to the 1950s and has a distinctly vintage feel to it. There's a good-sized pool (unfortunately getting a little murky), tennis court, TV in all rooms and ample parking. It's always lively with mid-market tour groups. To avoid the noise of Uhuru Hwy, get a room at the back in the middle, overlooking the garden. BB $210

Downtown Hotel Moktar Daddah St ☎ 020 222 4501 or ☎ 0721 417832, ✉ downtownhotel2000@yahoo.com; map p.106. A clean, cheaper and (in some rooms) quieter alternative to its neighbour, the better-known *Terminal*. Rooms are small and the sheets are getting a bit worn, but it remains good value in the Jeevanjee Gardens area. Bed only **Ksh3000**

Hilton Mama Ngina St ☎ 020 2288000, ✇ hilton.com; map p.107. The iconic cylindrical tower is unmistakeable and the lobby impressive, but the impersonal *Hilton* caters more for expense-account travellers than for leisure visitors. Rooms get better the higher you climb, but they all need refurbishing. The "rooftop pool" is nice, but somewhat overshadowed as it's located on the second floor. Facilities include a health club, a spa, four restaurants and a pub. Bed only **$242**

Hotel Embassy Tubman Rd, right behind the City Market ☎ 020 2224087 or ☎ 0716 215928, ✇ hotelembassy-kenya.com; map p.106. Very decent place, with a reliable restaurant serving local dishes and well-maintained, if rather tired, rooms with nets, fans and electric showers. BB **Ksh4500**

InterContinental City Hall Way ☎ 020 3200000, ✇ ichotelsgroup.com; map p.106. More than forty years old and working hard to keep up with its newer competitors, the 376-room *InterContinental* has some surprisingly secluded corners in the grounds and many amenities, including a heated pool, health club, casino, Italian and Indian restaurants, 24hr bar, an ATM in the lobby and good disabled access. BB **$321**

Kenya Comfort Hotel Corner Muindi Mbingu St and Monrovia St ☎ 0737 777777, ✇ kenyacomfort.com; map p.106. Handily located, this large hotel is popular with budget safari operators, and the friendly staff are used to arrivals in the middle of the night. The reasonable rooms come with nets and DSTV, and there's a rooftop terrace, 24hr bar and restaurant, although it's still fairly expensive for what it offers. Bed only **$50**

Norfolk Hotel Harry Thuku Rd ☎ 020 2265000 or ☎ 020 2265555, ✇ fairmont.com/norfolkhotel; map p.105. Nairobi's oldest hotel has had the Canadian Fairmont treatment, which has lightened and freshened it all over, improving standards while diminishing the reason you'd want to stay here – the Edwardian atmosphere. The very comfortable rooms have good beds and flatscreen TVs; facilities include a pool, health club and sauna. Bed only **$284**

Oakwood Hotel Kimathi St ☎ 0735 478924, ✇ madahotels.com; map p.107. An endearing oddity lost amid the skyscrapers, this older two-storey hotel has wood panelling, a wonderful antique lift and good security, and you can't beat the price for this location. There's a relaxing first-floor bar looking across to the touristy *Thorn Tree Café* (see p.131). BB **$100**

Parkside Monrovia St ☎ 020 2214154 or ☎ 0710 420859; map p.106. Facing Jeevanjee Gardens and convenient for buses to Arusha, the *Parkside* is large, secure, and has clean, airy and reasonably pleasant rooms with nets, TVs and electric showers. It can be noisy, however. Bed only **Ksh3500**

Stanley Hotel Corner Kimathi St and Kenyatta Ave ☎ 020 2757000 or ☎ 020 2763000, ✇ sarovahotels.com; map p.107. Complete with its famous *Thorn Tree Café*, this is as central as you can get, and a popular base for tourists and business travellers alike. The rooms are equipped with DSTV, mini-bar and noise-excluding double-glazing, and some are designed for disabled guests. Facilities include a modern gym and sauna and a heated rooftop pool and bar. BB **$505**

Terminal Hotel Moktar Daddah St ☎ 020 2228817 or ☎ 0723 351513, ✇ terminal-hotel.com; map p.106. A long-time backpackers favourite, with large, well-kept rooms (including a few triple rooms for Ksh4500), all with nets and electric showers. Good value, but bring some earplugs to counter the noise from the neighbourhood. Bed only **Ksh3600**

WESTLANDS AND PARKLANDS

Amani Gardens Inn 71 Church Rd, Westlands ☎ 0723 161935, ✇ amanigardensinn.com; map p.104. If you want somewhere clean, safe, comfortable and quiet, this is worth booking far ahead. The nice gardens and decent meals (mains Ksh700) are added incentives, and there's an exchange library and free tea and snacks. As well as standard rooms with shared bathrooms, they also have more expensive s/c rooms. No smoking or alcohol are allowed on the premises. BB **$90**

Dusit2 (D2) 14 Riverside Drive, Westlands ☎ 020 4233000 or ☎ 0787 657000, ✇ d2nairobi.com; map p.105. Impeccably stylish boutique hotel hidden away in a swish new complex off Riverside Drive, filled with modern art and designer furniture. The airy bar serves good cocktails and is one of the most fashionable places in town to be seen. The immaculate rooms are surprisingly good value, and come with all the amenities you'd expect. Bed only **$250**

Jacaranda Hotel Off Waiyaki Way, Westlands ☎ 0711 089000 or ☎ 0733 601613, ✇ jacarandahotels.com; map p.132. Strong selling points include the great location, a couple of minutes' walk to the Sarit Centre mall and other Westlands amenities, plus a good pool in a pleasant garden. Rooms (all with fan and DSTV) are on the small side and most don't have a/c, but the "Garden" rooms are a bit bigger than the rest. BB **$183**

Parklands Shade Hotel Klub House entertainment complex, Ojijo Rd, Parklands ☎ 0717 969500, ✇ klubhouse.co.ke; map p.105. The tiled, no-frills rooms with double beds here are quite decent and serve their purpose of providing a resting place for exhausted *Klub House*

1

partiers (see p.138) – though not all guests are principally interested in sleep, as you may discover. BB **Ksh4000**

★**Sankara** Woodvale Grove, Westlands ☎020 4208000 or ☎0703 028000, ⓦsankara.com; map p.132. The standout accommodation in Westlands, and indeed one of Nairobi's most consistently good hotels, the *Sankara* is efficiently managed and has all the facilities of a five-star establishment, including a glass-bottomed rooftop pool and a spa, while giving off the vibe of a boutique hotel. The 156 rooms are impeccably comfortable, light and well thought-out. Bed only **$290**

Southern Sun Hotel Parklands Rd, next to the Mayfair casino, Parklands ☎020 3740920 or ☎0722 205508, ⓦtsogosun.com; map p.105. Classy, well-maintained, very likeable establishment in a pastiche of Edwardian and Art Nouveau styles (the original building, the *Mayfair*, opened in 1949). The 171 rooms come with a/c, safe and DSTV, while facilities include two pools, spa, gym and plenty of other amenities – all set in several acres of tropical gardens. BB **$324**

UPPER HILL, LAVINGTON, KILIMANI AND KILELESHWA

Many of Nairobi's better-value mid-range and upmarket hotels – often independently owned – are located in a number of relatively affluent suburbs west of the city centre.

Central YMCA State House Rd, 300m from Uhuru Hwy, State House ☎020 2724117 or ☎0729 152816, ⓦkenyaymca.com; map p.105. On the edge of the CBD, the well-equipped *Central YMCA* is popular with female as well as male travellers, offering a choice of dorms and private rooms with nets. There's well-priced if average food (meals Ksh400–600), and secure parking, but the clincher is the range of facilities, including a pool and tennis and squash courts. Long-stay discounts available. BB dorm beds **Ksh1400**, BB **Ksh3200**

★**Fairview** Bishops Rd, Upper Hill ☎020 2881000, ⓦclhg.com; map p.105. A peaceful, rambling country-style place with spacious grounds that are great for birding, plus unusually good security and a wide variety of accommodation across the hundred-odd rooms. The pool and relaxed atmosphere make it popular with families (family rooms have bunk beds for kids), and there's excellent food. Reserve far ahead. BB **Ksh19,600**

Hadassah Hotel Ralph Bunche Rd, near Nairobi Hospital, Upper Hill ☎0733 347700 or ☎0711 444471, ⓦhadassahhotel.com; map p.105. This converted youth hostel still feels a bit cramped and hostel-ish, with rooms on the small and dark side. But it's clean and reasonably priced for its location, and all rooms come with TVs, fridges and canopy mosquito nets. There's a restaurant and bar downstairs. BB **Ksh8000**

Heron Portico Milimani Rd, Upper Hill ☎020 2720740, ⓦtheheronportico.com; map p.105. Close to the city centre but on a leafy, relatively quiet street, this place has had a recent face-lift, giving it a vaguely Middle Eastern flair. Smart, comfortable rooms – with neat bathrooms, DSTV and room safes – rise on five floors around a central atrium. Staff are helpful; there's an adequate restaurant with a large balcony overlooking Milimani Rd, and a nice pool, gym and sauna. BB **Ksh19,550**

★**Ndemi Place** Ndemi Close, off Ndemi Rd, Kilimani ☎0720 226860, ⓦndemiplace.com; map p.104. This attractive, friendly guesthouse is set in a shady garden frequented by troops of Sykes' monkeys, and offers ten homely rooms, all different, as well as a lounge area with a fireplace for chilly Nairobi nights. Some rooms come with bunk beds to accommodate families, and all have mosquito nets. It's very popular and often booked out; reserve well in advance. BB **Ksh8000**

Palacina Kitale Lane, off Dennis Pritt Rd, Kilimani ☎0733 777173 or ☎0720 493747, ⓦpalacina.com; map p.105. This small, upmarket hotel down a quiet lane exudes an air of exclusivity, offering just fourteen spacious, airy rooms that come with jacuzzi tubs, balconies and walk-in closets. There's a pool, bar and good restaurant downstairs, as well as a gym. Long-term guests also have the option of a serviced one- to three-bedroom apartment at "The Residence" (from $2995/month). BB **$498**

Serena Processional Way, between Nyerere Rd and Kenyatta Ave, facing Central Park, Upper Hill ☎020 2822000, ⓦserenahotels.com; map p.105. Dating from the mid-1970s, the 183-room *Serena* is impeccably decked out in Pan-African style, replete with sculptures and wall hangings. Rooms are very comfortable and feature carved furniture, marble bathrooms and African art. Amenities include a health club, pool and shops. A comfortable, safe bet, though don't venture out of the grounds on foot after dark. BB **$501**

Town Lodge 2nd Ngong Ave, Upper Hill ☎020 2881600, ⓦclhg.com; map p.105. A popular and more affordable alternative to its co-owned neighbour, the *Fairview*, whose facilities you can use if you stay here. Rooms can feel a bit sterile, like a small private hospital, but it's very clean, and, in keeping with *Fairview* tradition, security is positively airtight. A pleasant garden and gym complete the amenities. BB **Ksh16,100**

Woodmere Apartments Rose Ave, off Lenana Rd, three blocks from the Yaya Centre, Kilimani ☎020 2712511 or ☎0722 344778, ⓦwoodmerenairobi.com; map p.105. Well-guarded premises with a small pool, sauna, gym and garden. Accommodation ranges from fully furnished, serviced studios with tiny kitchen and loft sleeping area to spacious apartments, with monthly rates available for long-term stays. Daily rates: budget studios **$65**, four-bed apartments **$180**

KAREN AND LANGATA

Most of Nairobi's backpackers and campsites have fled the city centre for the cheaper rents in the suburb of Karen.

CAMPING EQUIPMENT

For camping equipment, try the following outlets: Atul's, Biashara St; map p.106 (☎0722 348258); Rhino Leisure, Rhino House, Karen Rd; map p.102 (☎0722 567257, ⏍rhinoleisure.com); or Xtreme Outdoors, first floor, Yaya Centre, Kilimani; map p.104 (☎0736 411527, ⏍xtremeoutdoors.co.ke).

Acacia Camp Magadi Rd, 1.5km south of Langata Rd, Langata ☎0733 603501, ⏍africatravelco.com; map p.102. Not to be confused with the tented camp at Swara Plains near Athi River (see p.151), this is one of the best-equipped campsites in Nairobi, base of a South African overland company, with small single and double rooms and some dorm beds, all with nets. The site is secure, and the bar is a good place to talk to staff from a number of safari operators. Food is available, and there are laundry facilities and DSTV. Camping $8, dorm beds $10, bed only $36

Aero Club of East Africa Wilson Airport, Nairobi West ☎020 6000482, ⏍aeroclubea.com; map p.102. If you're taking an early flight from Wilson, where better to stay than this old flying club, built in 1929? It's far from fancy – and being close to Langata Rd the traffic noise continues until late at night – but it's safe, decent and reliable and you can get reasonable food from the bar-restaurant and eat on the deck as the planes buzz in and out. There's also a pool. Rates include temporary membership. Bed only Ksh15,100

★**Giraffe Manor** Koitobos Rd, adjacent to the AFEW Giraffe Centre, Langata ☎0733 224446, ⏍thesafaricollection.com; map p.102. Head and shoulders above Nairobi's other places to stay is this wonderfully eccentric Scottish-style manor house built in the 1930s, which sits in the grounds of the Giraffe Centre -- the long-necked creatures have been known to share your breakfast through the windows. Rates include full board, airport transfers and Giraffe Centre entry. Closed mid-April to mid May. Package $1130

Hemingways Mbagathi Ridge, Karen ☎0711 032000, ⏍hemingways-collection.com; map p.102. The trappings of luxury are not wanting at this immaculate new hotel – including spacious rooms, walk-in closets and personal butler services – though the place lacks the historical charm its name might suggest. The restaurant downstairs is highly regarded and some of the rooms, which trail down into the sweeping gardens, enjoy views of the Ngong Hills. Rates are negotiable. BB $750

Jungle Junction (JJ's) Kongoni Rd, Karen ☎0722 752865 or ☎0723 392014, ✉c_handschuh_68@yahoo.com; map p.102. Legendary overlanders' garden hangout and campsite, where you can get your vehicle fixed – or find out who can do it for you. There are facilities for long-term vehicle

storage and a large garden for camping, with clean, communal toilets, showers, kitchen area, washing machine and wi-fi, plus dorm beds and private rooms. Camping from Ksh550, dorm beds Ksh1200, BB Ksh4800

Karen Camp Marula Lane, Karen ☎0723 314053, ⏍karencamp.com; map p.102. A B&B-cum-overlanders' camp with somewhat shabby s/c and non-s/c rooms, permanent tents, dorms and a big lawn for camping, as well as good food and a bar. An OK option if the other backpackers are full. Camping $7, dorm beds $15, BB $40

★**Macushla House** Nguruwe Rd, Langata ☎020 891987 or ☎0733 706178, ⏍macushla.biz; map p.102. Delightfully unpretentious, owner-managed boutique hotel in a forested and secluded part of Langata. Although the grounds are small, the rooms are large and comfortable, and the tightly organized gardens are adorably funky with their quirky ornaments; they attract more than sixty species of birds. Good meals are available in the bar-restaurant (tasty fusion-style dishes from Ksh1000), and there's a pool. BB $230

★**Milimani Backpackers** St Hellen Lane, Karen ☎0718 919020 or ☎0722 347616, ⏍milimani backpackers.com; map p.102. Clean and friendly, with nets, hot showers, s/c and non-s/c rooms and kitchen facilities for self-catering. Good meals are available, and you can meet other travellers in the cosy TV lounge or garden, where you can also pitch a tent. Wi-fi. Camping Ksh1000, dorm beds Ksh1500, bed only Ksh2700

★**Wildebeest Eco Camp** 151 Mokoyeti Rd West, Langata (1.4km west of Galleria Mall, then 1.5km north) ☎020 2103505 or ☎0734 770733, ⏍wildebeestecocamp.com; map p.102. Close to the Ngong Road Forest, this exceptional, family-run house and garden caters across the range, from backpackers to more upmarket guests. Pitch your own tent, take a bed in a dorm tent, stay in a non-s/c room or opt for one of their non-s/c "garden" (Ksh8500) or s/c "deluxe safari" (Ksh11,000) tents. There's a great deck over the pond – superb for birders – and a bar-restaurant, as well as a small pool, a trampoline, table tennis and even a zipline. BB: dorm beds Ksh1250, camping Ksh1000, double Ksh5000

NORTHERN SUBURBS

With the opening of the Northern Bypass, Gigiri can now be reached from JKIA in as little as 45min – or up to around 90min during rush hours.

Tribe Next to Village Market, Gigiri ☎020 7200000, ⏍tribe-hotel.com; map p.102. *Tribe* is popular for its proximity to the UN headquarters and many embassies, but its location isn't ideal for regular trips around the city. The plunging, angular atrium and generous displays of African art are impressive, and the well-selected lounge music and outdoor swimming pool/water feature/sun terrace are fun, but sponsored poolside

1

events can make for very noisy evenings and there are no gardens as such. Standard rooms are super-comfortable, with orthopedic mattresses, flatscreen DSTV and glass-walled bathrooms. Food in the *Jiko* restaurant (see p.136) can be good, but it's not the gastronomic experience you might expect. BB **$275**

EATING

Nairobi has no shortage of eating places. Their diversity is one of the city's best points, and eating out is an evening pastime that never dulls. Admittedly, anything like authentic Kenyan food is generally not highlighted in most restaurants, which concentrate on offering a range of Asian and European cuisines, and spectacular quantities of meat. Included below are one or two of the city's fancier **hotels**, where the food has a good reputation. For further eating **listings**, check out the "Drinking and Nightlife" section (see p.136), which includes a number of venues that double as restaurants. When assessing **prices** (or checking your bill) remember there's a two percent training levy and sixteen percent value-added tax (VAT) on food and drink in all but the smallest establishments. Some include or add a variable service charge as well, which could raise the actual food and drink price by a further eight to ten percent. Most places include these taxes and charges in their menu prices, but some don't. At the more upmarket restaurants in the following listings, it's often a good idea to **reserve a table** or, as an alternative to calling yourself, try the free services of **Eat Out Kenya** (ⓦ eatout.co.ke), a Nairobi-based online startup that makes restaurant bookings for you via your mobile.

MOMBASA ROAD AND AIRPORT AREA

There's a very limited choice of places to eat at the airport itself: the *Nairobi Java House* (see below) by Gate 14 of the international terminal is reliable, has a bar, and is open 24hr. For something a little more upscale, try the *Simba Restaurant* on the top floor of the arrivals building.

Ole Sereni Hotel Mombasa Hwy, 12km from JKIA ☎020 3901000 or ☎0731 436405, ⓦ ole-sereni.com; map p.103. There are two main places to eat here: the *Big Five* restaurant and the *Waterhole* snack bar and terrace – both surprisingly good considering their essentially captive customers. Nibble on sides and starters (Ksh300 and up) or tuck into something mouthwateringly good like the Jack Daniels beef fillet with a *baba ghanoush* and mustard sauce (Ksh1700). Daily: Waterhole 7am–10pm, Big Five 24hr.

RIVER ROAD

The River Rd area has one *hoteli* after another on most streets, generally dishing up standard meals of fried fish, chicken or sausages with chips or *ugali*.

Malindi Dishes Gaberone Rd ☎0722 103410 or ☎0722 555571, ⓦ facebook.com/malindidishes .restaurant; map p.107. Self-service cafeteria with good, cheap Swahili dishes. They've been here for more than

---

QUICK EATS IN NAIROBI: CITY-WIDE CHAINS

Many of Nairobi's best-known eating and drinking venues have multiple venues in the city. This isn't to say that each branch maintains consistent standards, but they're generally fairly predictable. American-style **coffee shop chains**, in particular, have caught on in a big way, with *Java*, *Artcaffé* and a couple of smaller rivals slugging it out for market share.

Artcaffé Village Market, Junction, Oval, Yaya, Karen Crossroads, Lavington Green and Galleria malls; ⓦ artcaffe.co.ke. Artcaffé bakes very good bread and pastries to munch over your emails (free wi-fi) and offers tasty pizzas (around Ksh1100), light meals (around Ksh1200) and excellent coffee (espresso Ksh160), plus drinks. Daily 7.30am–10pm or later.

Creamy Inn Union Towers, corner Moi Ave and Mama Ngina St, plus branches around the city. Serves great ice cream, including a spectacular honey crunch waffle sundae (cones from Ksh100). Hours vary.

Nairobi Java House Transnational Plaza, Mama Ngina St, plus a dozen other branches, including ABC Place on Waiyaki Way, Adams Arcade on Ngong Rd, Capital Centre on Mombasa Rd and at Gate 14, JK International Airport;

ⓦ nairobijavahouse.com. This hugely popular coffee shop has some of the best breakfasts in Nairobi, good-value lunches (Tex-Mex, burgers and salads, all around Ksh600–800), and a great variety of coffees (large cappuccino Ksh270). Daily, with minor branch variations, 7am–9pm.

Steers Muindi Mbingu St opposite Jeevanjee Gardens, plus other branches including Wabera St and Uchumi Hyper on Ngong Rd; ⓦ steers.co.ke. It's something of a miracle that a certain well-known global burger chain doesn't already have three hundred outlets in Kenya, so despite hit-or-miss service and quality, respect to the South African fast-food chain for venturing into Kenya with all their usual beef-based offerings (cheeseburger, chips and soda for Ksh550), plus toasted sandwiches, salads, shakes, juices and great caramel ice cream. Daily 9am–10pm.

thirty years and they know their business: mutton or beef *pilau* costs Ksh200, or there's chicken tikka or fish masala for Ksh300. Daily 6.30am–midnight.

Sun Sweet Centre Ngariama Rd 0737 888880; map p.107. Indian place, large, sparse and slightly lacking in atmosphere, but with excellent vegetarian food including an all-you-can-eat Gujarati *thali* (Ksh500), along with tempting sweets. Mon–Sat 9am–6pm, Sun 7.30am–3pm.

CENTRAL BUSINESS DISTRICT

★**Al-Yusra** Banda St 0712 012012, bit.ly/ Al-Yusra; map p.107. Halal Somali restaurant that gets packed at lunchtime, when worshippers at the nearby mosque come to feast on roast camel (Ksh400), *injera* flatbread and platefuls of fried goat. They also serve Kenyan standards like chicken and *pilau*, with delicious milkshakes (Ksh250) to wash it all down. Daily 6am–9pm.

Berber's Oasis Mezzanine floor, NHC Building, Aga Khan Walk 020 2064809 or 722 853175, berbersoasiskenya.co.ke; map p.107. Worth an outing for its good, filling African dishes – *kisamvu na karanga* (cassava leaves with groundnuts; Ksh700), beef curry and rice (Ksh450) – served in a quirky dining room, plus beer (Ksh150), wine (Ksh250) and cheap cocktails (from around Ksh350). See if they have any *muratina* (home-made honey beer; Ksh120). Daily 6.30am–11pm (last orders 10pm).

Bridges Tubman Rd 0722 424125; map p.106. A certified organic restaurant on a mission to make Kenyans healthier by serving up unusual dishes like amaranth porridge (Ksh110), arrowroot and freshly squeezed vegetable juices (Ksh180). There's muesli for breakfast and curries or delicious chicken "sizzlers" for lunch (Ksh650) – even special dishes for diabetics. Mon–Sat 7am–9pm.

Café Deli Tumaini House, Nkrumah Lane 0721 596801, facebook.com/cafedeli.nairobi; map p.107. Wholesome, reliable, rather old-school bar and restaurant with the feel of a 1950s American diner. As well as all the usual greasy-spoon stuff, they do a good range of African dishes: try the *aliya* (Luo smoked beef; Ksh750) or the fried goat meat. Daily 6.30am–9pm.

Kaldis Kimathi St 020 2000885 or 0725 000784, kaldisafrica.com; map p.107. Urbane coffee shop popular with professionals from the nearby office towers. In the morning pancakes (Ksh300), omelettes and full cooked breakfasts (Ksh500) are on offer, as well as curries, paninis and wraps. The coffee's not bad, either. Sun–Thurs 6.30am–9.30pm, Fri & Sat 6.30am–11pm.

KK Restaurant Standard St 0713 639314; map p.106. A bustling, no-frills local restaurant that serves up a wonderfully flavourful chicken stew (Ksh300), alongside the usual Kenyan staples including *githeri* and fried beef. Despite the size of the place, it can still be hard to find a seat at mealtimes. Mon–Fri 6am–8pm, Sat 6am–4pm.

Lord Delamere Terrace Norfolk Hotel, Harry Thuku Rd 020 2265000 ext. 2056, fairmont.com/norfolk hotel; map p.105. Sooner or later, a people-watching drink and meal at this century-old restaurant is a must – though at times it can feel a bit stuffy and there's not much flavour of 1904 about it. It offers the usual range of pizzas and grills, as well as a handful of more imaginative Kenyan dishes like red snapper with coconut and tamarind (Ksh1600). Daily 6.30–10am, noon–3pm & 6–10pm.

★**Ranalo Foods** First floor, Balfour House, Kimathi St, near the Nation building 020 2249728 or 0721 323238; map p.107. Long-established yet still surprising, this big upstairs self-service dining hall and bar, with a rooftop terrace, specializes in Luo dishes from western Kenya. Fish in coconut (Ksh650), roast beef stew (*athalo*; Ksh550), millet *ugali* and several indigenous vegetables are all recommended. It's invariably packed, and there's always music, often dancing, and occasional live bands. Daily 8am–10pm (later at weekends).

Thorn Tree Café Stanley Hotel, Kimathi St 0719 048182, sarovahotels.com; map p.107. A welcome refuge from street hustlers and a handy meeting place, partly screened from the street by beautiful Kitengela glass (see p.141). The famous notice board is still there (see p.109), though not much used. A pot of coffee costs Ksh400, as does a bottle of beer. The restaurant area inside serves up rather expensive old-school dishes like beef bourgignon (Ksh1560) and some standard Indian dishes. Daily 24hr.

Trattoria Corner Wabera St and Kaunda St 020 2340855, trattoria.co.ke; map p.107. This still gets enthusiastic reviews – and not just from budget travellers having a splurge – and it's great to find a place that's stuck it out in the CBD for more than thirty years and has helped to bring about the area's rejuvenation. The pasta dishes and pizzas (around Ksh1200) are the real thing, and the cakes and ice cream magnificent. Daily 7am–midnight.

WESTLANDS AND PARKLANDS

Behind the Oilibya petrol station on Lower Kabete Rd, there's a useful 24hr food court with branches of *Pizza Inn*, *Creamy Inn*, *My Shop* and *Chicken Inn* – and a terrace on which to consume your calories.

★**360°** ABC Place, Wayaki Way, Westlands 0700 360360, 360degreespizza.com; map p.104. This classy pizzeria serves what is quite possibly the best wood-fired pizza in Nairobi, some with tomato sauce, some without (*pizza bianco*) – try the prosciutto funghi or the bacon and brussels sprouts (both Ksh1200). The pasta dishes (around Ksh900) are also excellent, as are the desserts. Sun–Thurs 11.30am–10pm, Fri & Sat 11.30am–11pm.

About Thyme Corner Peponi Rd and Eldama Ravine Rd, Westlands 0721 850026, about-thyme.com; map p.105. A charming if somewhat pricey restaurant in an atmospheric old house with a beautiful garden, serving

1

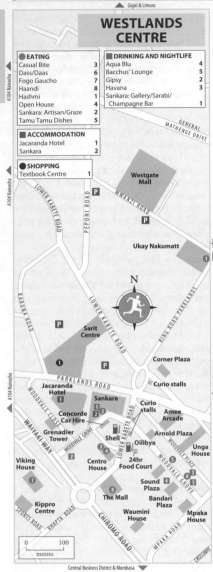

▲ Gigiri & Limuru

WESTLANDS CENTRE

● EATING
Casual Bite	3
Dass/Daas	6
Fogo Gaucho	7
Haandi	8
Hashmi	1
Open House	4
Sankara: Artisan/Graze	2
Tamu Tamu Dishes	5

■ DRINKING AND NIGHTLIFE
Aqua Blu	4
Bacchus' Lounge	5
Gipsy	2
Havana	3
Sankara: Gallery/Sarabi/ Champagne Bar	1

■ ACCOMMODATION
Jacaranda Hotel	1
Sankara	2

● SHOPPING
Textbook Centre	1

Central Business District & Mombasa ▼

English home cooking and a variety of creative fusion dishes like lamb stew with figs (Ksh1600) and tuna steak with wasabi mayonnaise. The soups (around Ksh500) are delicious, and there's a long and tempting dessert menu and a good wine list. Two-course set menus are available for lunch (Ksh1450). Tues–Sat noon–10pm, Sun 10am–3pm.

★**Amaica** Getathuru Gardens, off Peponi Rd, Westlands ☎0724 477663, ⌨amaica.co.ke; map p.105. Just above the Getathuru Stream, near the Sigiria

Forest, this excellent restaurant specializes in Kenyan traditional cuisine, with dishes labelled according to the region in which they originated; if you've ever fancied tasting fried white ants (Ksh500), a western Kenyan delicacy, this is the place to do it. Otherwise try the delicious smoked beef, Luhya bean soup or Luo omena fish in peanut sauce (Ksh850). Daily 9am–11pm.

Amani Garden Café Riverside Drive, Westlands ☎020 4449071, ⌨amaniafrica.org; map p.105. Nice salads (around Ksh600) and lunches – including plenty of vegetarian and one or two vegan options – plus bagels and other snacks, and a children's menu, in a very pleasant shady garden with children's play equipment. Mon–Sat 7.30am–4.30pm.

Asmara General Mathenge Drive, Westlands ☎0721 948020 or ☎0715 179596, ⌨facebook.com/asmaranairobi; map p.105. While the Eritrean food here is top-notch, that isn't the only thing this attractive garden restaurant does well. The soups and salads are very good, made from ingredients grown on Asmara's own farm, and the desserts are worth saving space for. Go for a mixed dish of Eritrean specialities on *injera* flatbread (Ksh1200), or *tsebhi asa* – fish chunks with chilli (Ksh1100). Daily 12.30–3pm & 6.30–10.30pm.

Casual Bite Centro House, Lower Kabete Rd, Westlands ☎0727 468681, ⌨facebook.com/CasualBiteKe; map opposite. As its name suggests, this is a friendly and casual café serving good, reasonably priced food in the heart of Westlands. The salads (Ksh650), sandwiches and house soup make it a good bet for lunch, though there's also more substantial food on offer, including Swahili coconut chicken (Ksh780) and beef sourced from the Ol Peteja ranch in the Central Highlands. Mon–Wed 6.30am–8pm, Thurs–Sat 6.30am–10pm.

Chowpaty Diamond Plaza, Masari Rd, Parklands ☎020 3747575 or ☎0733 714391, ⌨chowpatyrestaurants. com; map p.105. The best location in Nairobi for south Indian, exclusively vegetarian meals, with a huge and inexpensive menu (most dishes Ksh500–600) including a range of good *dosas* (around Ksh500). You can order their food either in the restaurant or in the lively Indian food court out front. Daily 10.30am–11pm.

Dass (also spelt Daas) Woodvale Grove, above Havana, Westlands ☎020 4441632 or ☎0721 208843; map opposite. Up two flights of stairs, this large dining room, with seating around low drum tables, is the real deal in the heart of Westlands: authentic Ethiopian *injera* flatbread covered in dollops of different *wat* (stew; most around Ksh500–600) accompanied at weekends by musicians, poets and other performers. Sun–Thurs 10.30am–11pm, Fri & Sat 24hr.

Fogo Gaucho Viking House, Waiyaki Way, Westlands ☎0729 243202, ⌨fogogaucho.com; map opposite. Recommended and convenient all-you-can-eat meat palace – a Brazilian *churrascaria* – that gives *Carnivore* (see p.134) a run for its money, with lunch at Ksh2000 and dinner at Ksh2150. There's also a mostly vegetarian buffet (Ksh1650) and salad bar. Mon–Sat noon–3pm & 6.30–10.30pm, Sun noon–4pm & 6.30–10pm.

Furusato Corner Ring Rd Parklands and General Mathenge Drive, Parklands ☎0722 488706; map p.105. One of Nairobi's most popular Japanese restaurants – affordable and unpretentious. Choose from the counter and eat either in the restaurant or garden. They do sushi sets from Ksh1250, à la carte sashimi from around Ksh650 for nine pieces and a vegetarian sushi menu for Ksh1300. There's a Korean menu, too, including *kimchi* with pork (Ksh950). Takeaway available. Daily 12.30–3pm & 6.30–11pm.

Golden Spur Southern Sun Hotel, Parklands Rd, Parklands ☎0724 253804, ⓦspurcorp.nl; map p.105. US-style grill house popular with families, complete with huge triptych menus. The decent meals include good ribs (Thurs is all-you-can-eat rib night; Ksh1800), a 500g steak with chips and onion rings (Ksh1250) and a main-course salad buffet (Ksh750). Daily 11am–11pm.

★**Haandi** Mezzanine floor, The Mall, Westlands ☎020 4448294, ⓦhaandirestaurants.com; map opposite. Nairobi's best north Indian restaurant (now with branches in London) specializes in tandoori (clay oven) cooking, with a huge variety of vegetarian and meat dishes from around Ksh1200. Try the *Diwani Haandi* (peas, beans and cauliflower cooked in ginger and garlic; Ksh1150) or *saag* (lamb and spinach; Ksh1200). Daily noon–3pm & 6.30–11pm.

Hashmi Ukay Nakumatt Mall, Ring Rd Parklands ☎020 3748704 or ☎0733 721786, ⓦhashmisbbq.com; map opposite. Casual Indian BBQ joint very popular with local families, serving big, satisfying plates of lamb, beef, mutton and chicken grilled over charcoal. Tandoori dishes like *mushkakis* and *faludas* (Indian milkshakes) are also available, but since it's halal, alcohol is not. *Hashmi* often fills up and doesn't take reservations, but you can always opt for takeaway. Tues–Sun 12.30–2.30pm & 6.30–10pm.

Maxland Wayaki Way, behind the Shell station, Westlands ☎0725 314705; map p.104. One of the best and most authentic *nyama choma* bars in Westlands, *Maxland* fills up on weekends with Kenyans coming for the tasty grilled goat (Ksh750/kg), the whole chickens (Ksh1200) and the live music every Fri and Sat, though it's big enough that you can still find a peaceful spot to enjoy your meat. Sun–Thurs 8am–11pm, Fri & Sat 8am–3am.

Mystique Gardens Ring Rd Parklands ☎0720 984855; map p.105. One of the nicest gardens in town for *koroga*, the East African Indian tradition of communal curry cooking with pre-prepared ingredients. Sit in a *banda* and order the number of chickens you'd like to cook (Ksh1600,

each serving about four people), and the charcoal stove, spices, onions and *rotis* are all provided for you; appetizers can be ordered separately. Wash it all down with ample quantities of beer. Great for groups. Daily 11am–late.

Ocean Basket The Oval, Ring Rd Parklands ☎0770 227538, ⓦoceanbasket.co.ke; map p.105. Nairobi's only branch of this popular South African seafood chain occupies an attractive terrace in the new Oval shopping centre, and serves consistently good combo platters (from Ksh1300), prawns, calamari and daily fish specials. There's sushi as well, but the Japanese restaurants do that better. Daily 11.30am–11.30pm.

★**Open House** Ground floor, Centro House, Westlands ☎0735 621824, ⓦopenhouserestaurant.co.ke; map opposite. Usually packed with local Kenyan Indian families and not at all touristy, this place serves up delicious and well-prepared Indian dishes such as ginger chicken *masala* (Ksh900), Goan fish curry (Ksh890) and light, crispy, buttery *naans*. Daily 11am–3pm & 6–11pm.

Sankara Woodvale Grove, Westlands ☎020 4208000 or ☎0703 028000, ⓦsankara.com; map opposite. There are two main places to eat here: the *Artisan* restaurant and the steakhouse *Graze*. *Artisan* has a very good, pricey wine list and equally pricey food that varies from OK to sublime (burgers, sandwiches and salads around Ksh1400); *Graze*, as you might expect, specializes in steaks served a variety of ways (around Ksh2500), although seared tuna and Watamu lobster make an appearance as well. Artisan daily 6am–10.30pm; Graze daily noon–11pm.

★**Seven Seafood Bar & Grill** ABC Place, Waiyaki Way, Westlands ☎0737 776677, ⓦexperienceseven .com; map p.104. Very appealing, slick and well-presented seafood and salads, and always busy. The fish and crustacea are top-drawer, including Indian Ocean oysters (six for Ksh550), prawns, crab (Ksh1850) and several other daily fish dishes. There's also a range of steaks and salads, including their own delicious interpretation of a *salade niçoise* (Ksh900) and a bigger dinner menu, with very good grills. Mon–Sat noon–11.30pm, Sun 8.30am–11.30pm.

Soi 14 Riverside Drive, next to Dusit2 hotel, Westlands ☎020 4233000 or ☎0787 657000, ⓦsoi.co.ke; map p.105. It may be pricey, but if you're in the mood for top-quality Thai food this is the place to find it. *Soi* serves a delicious green curry (Ksh1400), stir fries, noodle dishes and amazing desserts, including basil ice cream (Ksh650), as well as intriguing cocktails served in teapots for two. Daily noon–2.30pm & 7–10.30pm.

Tamu Tamu Dishes Woodvale Grove, Westlands ☎0728 872944, ⓦbit.ly/TamuTamu; map opposite. Generous portions of cheap and cheerful Swahili-centric food, to be consumed on plastic chairs while watching the nocturnal revellers drift by on Woodvale Grove (fish and chapatti Ksh300, beef and *matoke* Ksh260). Daily 24hr.

1

LAVINGTON, KILIMANI AND KILELESHWA

★**The Arbor** 904 James Gichuru, next to the "Ebru" sign, Lavington ☎0700 506377, ⓦthearbor.wix.com/thearborcafe; map p.104. With its wooden tables and benches scattered around a leafy garden, this has become a deservedly popular place to while away an afternoon. Come for the hearty breakfasts (from Ksh450), gyros or sandwiches, or sample the modest array of Southeast Asian dishes including *laksa* noodles (Ksh750), *pad thai* or coconut with lemongrass. There are plants, crafts and luscious home-made bath products for sale, as well. Tues–Sun 9am–5pm.

Cedars Lenana Rd, Kilimani ☎020 2710399 or ☎0700 045521, ⓦcedarsnairobi.com; map p.105. Excellent Lebanese food, if a little pricey, at Ksh1900 a head for the full *mezze* (serves eight). There's a balcony and terrace, and the dining room – with understated Middle Eastern decor – often has a roaring fire for chilly evenings. Daily 11am–11pm.

★**Habesha** Argwings Kodhek Rd, Kilimani ☎0733 730469; map p.104. Serving some of the best Ethiopian food in town, *Habesha* dishes up large portions of spicy *wat* (stew) of various kinds on huge spongy *injera* flatbreads, shared by the whole table; a mixed dish goes for Ksh850. Dessert is traditionally popcorn, served with coffee, deliciously Ethiopian-style. The best tables are outside in the garden next to the fire pits. Beers Ksh200, Ethiopian wine Ksh1000/bottle. Daily 9am–11pm.

Le Salumeria Hendred Rd, off Gitanga Rd, Kileleshwa ☎0722 530288; map p.104. An intimate little Italian joint hidden away behind Valley Arcade, perfect for knocking back pitchers of house wine (Ksh2100), tucking into home-made pasta (around Ksh900) or enjoying the grilled calamari and prawns (Ksh1400). Look out for specials like *osso buco* or ginger crab. Sun–Fri noon–10.30pm, Sat 6–10.30pm.

Little Sheep Hot Pot Ngong Rd between Adams Arcade and Prestige Plaza, Woodley ☎0736 113333 or ☎0706 304448; map p.104. Great Mongolian hot-pot place, popular with Chinese expats, where you cook your choice of raw veg, fish and meat ingredients in a steaming pot of stock and eat with tasty home-made wheat noodles and soy, ginger, garlic and chilli sauces. Allow Ksh1200/person. Daily 10am–10pm.

Mediterraneo Junction Mall, Ngong Rd, Dagoretti Corner ☎020 3878608 or ☎0734 845077, ⓦwww.mediterraneorestaurant.co.ke; map p.104. Popular and lively Italian with a good wine list, serving everything from pasta to seafood and meat dishes, as well as excellent desserts. Not that cheap, though: with most mains at Ksh1500 and above, you're looking at around Ksh3000/head or more, depending on the wine you choose. Branches at the 9 West Building, Westlands and UN Ave, Gigiri. Daily noon–11pm.

Misono Ground floor, The Greenhouse, Ngong Rd, Kilimani ☎020 3868959 or ☎0722 511229; map p.104. Japanese venue famous for its avocado sauce, with tasty *teppanyaki* hot-plate options (from Ksh2600) as well as sushi and sashimi. It's popular at lunchtime with nearby office workers. Mon–Sat 12.30–3.30pm & 6.30–11.30pm.

Monikos Valley Arcade, Kileleshwa ☎0737 032064, ⓦmonikoskitchen.com; map p.104. A relaxing café and popular brunch spot in a pleasant courtyard, where you can tuck into granola (Ksh650), a full English breakfast (Ksh850) or a good salad. There's more substantial food as well, including the likes of pasta and chicken kiev (Ksh1350), and locals gather here for quiz nights once a month. Daily 7am–10pm.

Osteria del Chianti Lenana Rd, Kilimani ☎0724 277332 or ☎0734 472778, ⓦosteriadelchianti.com; map p.105. Occupying a large compound attached to the *Casablanca* bar (see p.138), Osteria is a lively and straight-up Italian decorated with plenty of bottles and sausages. They do a brisk trade in wood-fired pizzas (Ksh650–1000), either eaten in or delivered. Most other dishes – like chicken or pasta – go for just over Ksh1000. Branches in Village Market, in Karen and in the CBD. Daily noon–11pm.

Pete's Café and Burrito Haven Bishop Magua Centre, George Padmore Lane, off Ngong Rd, Kilimani ☎020 2177453, ⓦpetescoffee.co.ke; map p.104. One of the best independent coffee shops in town, *Pete's* attracts a loyal following of lunching office workers and creative types who come for the pleasant terrace, good coffee (Ksh200 for a cappuccino), sandwiches and signature *burritos* (around Ksh600). Mon–Sat 7am–7pm.

The Thai Place Acacia Courts, Ngong Rd, Kilimani ☎0723 733713, ⓦthethai.place; map p.104. A quirky little restaurant in a private house, run by an expat with a taste for Thai food. The menu is small but the dishes – including chicken satay and curries – are satisfying and surprisingly good value, with most mains going for around Ksh600. The cocktails (Ksh500) are recommended, and strong. Reservations advisable. Daily noon–10pm.

Tokyo Kolloh Rd, off James Gichuru Drive, Lavington ☎0722 485556, ⓦfacebook.com/tokyonbi; map p.104. Nairobi's newest Japanese restaurant is set in a wooden house, where you can eat a fairly small but tasty selection of traditional dishes including good sushi platters (from Ksh1990), *teppanyaki* sets (from Ksh2200), bento boxes and a creative list of *maki* rolls, including a "bonsai roll" made of salmon skin. Daily 11am–3pm & 5.30–11pm.

KAREN AND LANGATA

Carnivore Langata Rd, Langata ☎0733 611608 or ☎0722 204647, ⓦtamarind.co.ke; map p.102. Nairobi's

1

most famous restaurant no longer serves game meat (Kenya banned it in 2004), and seats more than four hundred, so it's not a refined experience, but go in a party frame of mind and you'll probably enjoy it. The all-you-can-eat menu (lunch Mon–Sat Ksh3400; Sun lunch & dinner Ksh3600; under-12s half-price; under-5s free) includes farmed samples of chewy camel and fishy/chickeny crocodile, but the very good ostrich, beef and lamb, carved off the roasting sword, are usually excellent, and what you should fast for. There's an all-you-can-eat fish and vegetarian menu, too (lunch Ksh2850; dinner Ksh2950). Go early to choose a good table, and don't be tempted by early evening distractions of potatoes and sausages. Daily noon–3pm & 6–9.30pm.

★**Purdy Arms** 61 Marula Lane, Karen ☎0712 007001, ⓦpurdyarms.com; map p.102. A friendly local pub whose expansive gardens host an organic farmers' market every Sat (9am–3pm), and whose food is consistently good. The fish and chips (Ksh950), burgers, pizzas and soups are best enjoyed from the sunny veranda, or from a picnic table out on the lawn; inside, locals carry on drinking well into the evening. Daily 6am–late.

★**Talisman** 320 Ngong Rd, Karen ☎0705 999997, ⓦthetalismanrestaurant.com; map p.102. One of Nairobi's best restaurants, with pleasant gardens children can run around in, artworks on show, a really nice terrace and funky colonial-oriental decor. The menu features a diverse variety of international dishes – their celebrated feta-and-coriander samosa starter (Ksh750) is almost a Kenyan foodie cliché, and turns up all over the country. Reserve ahead and allow about Ksh3500/person. Tues–Sun 9am–midnight.

Tamarind Blixen Coffee Garden, Karen Rd, Karen ☎0719 346349, ⓦtamarind.co.ke; map p.102. Nairobi's best seafood restaurant, with a kitchen run by Julius Mugo, head chef here for more than twenty years, and waiting staff overseen by Alex Mtundo, who has been here ten years longer than that. The bill will depend on whether your tastes are simple or you tuck into the oysters and lobster, but don't expect much change from Ksh3000/person, without drinks. Wines (from Ksh2750/bottle) include a good selection from South Africa. Reservations essential. Daily 6.30–11pm.

Tin Roof Café Thogoto Mutarakwa Rd, Karen ☎0706 348215, ⓦsouk-kenya.com; map p.102. Sandwiches, crêpes, cakes and good breakfasts served in a quaint old house in a eucalyptus grove, where you can eat on the covered porch or tucked into a cosy window seat. Most mains (Ksh950) come garnished with a variety of scrumptious home-made salads, and the cappuccinos (Ksh200) are pleasingly frothy. Daily 8am–5.30pm.

NORTHERN SUBURBS

Jiko Tribe hotel, next to Village Market, Gigiri ☎020 7200000, ⓦtribe-hotel.com; map p.102. *Jiko* is the *Tribe* hotel's main restaurant, serving an array of European dishes that range from golden onion confit (Ksh800) to pasta, burgers and rib-eye steaks (Ksh1700), plus a few Kenyan sides like coconut rice and *sukuma wiki*. Considering the setting it's not overpriced, but the food can be hit or miss. Daily 24hr.

The Lord Erroll Ruaka Rd, Runda Estate, behind Village Market, Gigiri ☎0721 920820 or ☎0733 579903, ⓦlord-erroll.com; map p.102. Colonial-style house with an old-fashioned, mahogany-panelled bar (the *Highlander*), two dining rooms and a terrace. Food and service are excellent, and there are good imported wines to accompany the French-with-a-touch-of-Swiss menu, which includes such specialities as Vienna schnitzel (Ksh1650) and deep-fried camembert (Ksh700). Daily noon–2.30pm (Sun 3pm) & 6–9.30pm.

Tamambo Bar & Grill Top floor, Village Market, Gigiri ☎020 7124005 or ☎0722 385089, ⓦtamarind.co.ke; map p.102. Modern African brasserie serving very good African and European food. Try the lamb *tagine* (Ksh1300) or the Kachos – Kenyan nachos made with cassava. There's an appealing terrace as well as the main restaurant, and the bar serves excellent frozen *dawas*. Live music some weekends. Daily 11am–11pm.

DRINKING AND NIGHTLIFE

Promoting bands in Nairobi is as precarious a business as anywhere and, given the volatile nature of the music business, **venues** and bands change at a moment's notice. Check out ⓦnairobinow.wordpress.com, ⓦupnairobi.com and ⓦfacebook.com (most clubs and bands have a Facebook account even if they have no website) and look at the *Nation* newspaper on Fri and Sat for one-off gigs. As for drinking, one or two of the more interesting **bars** in the city's fancier hotels are included in the listings below.

Hours and entrance fees Most clubs are open nightly and often on weekend afternoons – and in some cases never close at all. Starting times vary considerably for live music: on weekdays, 8pm wouldn't be too early to turn up, while at weekends even the warm-up act may not begin before 10pm, and some shows may not get rolling until midnight. Earthy, local clubs have free entry or very cheap entrance fees, while in the glitzier places, men still sometimes pay more than women; around Ksh200–400 as against Ksh100–200.

Security In recent years, downtown Nairobi's after-dark reputation as a dead zone, where nobody moved except by taxi, has been transformed by more street lighting and simple numbers: the clubbier streets are often streaming

1

GAY NAIROBI

Homosexuality may be illegal in Kenya (see p.83), but that doesn't stop gay men and lesbians coming out – and going out – and Nairobi is increasingly tolerant of lesbian, gay, bisexual and transgendered people. Still, gays and lesbians should be cautious, as the popular (and political) mood changes quickly and it can be difficult to predict how Kenyans will react to overt displays of affection. At the time of writing a handful of bars and clubs were extending a cautious welcome, or at least turning a blind eye: *Gipsy* (see p.138), the *Exchange Bar* at *The Stanley* (see below) and *Mercury Lounge* (see p.138).

with people, especially at weekends, so there's no reason to feel threatened. Take the usual precautions you would in any city, by not carrying anything with you that you don't need or would hate to lose. Other than that, make the most of a rejuvenated night-time Nairobi. Do be warned though that, male or female, if you're not accompanied by a partner of the opposite sex, you soon will be.

MOMBASA ROAD

★**Choices** Baricho Rd, Industrial Area ☎ 0722 521986, ⓦ bit.ly/ChoicesNairobi; map p.102. The place to be on a Thurs night, when a rotating cast of up-and-coming Kenyan bands takes the stage at this hopping local pub In the Industrial Area. DJs take over during the rest of the week, spinning club hits, oldies and whatever else they fancy. There's good *nyama choma* to keep the punters happy, and plenty of beer (Ksh250). Entry free. Daily noon–3am; live music Thurs 8–11pm.

Club Vibro Mai Mahiu Rd, Nairobi West (off Langata Rd between Nyayo Stadium and Wilson Airport) ☎ 0705 101030; map p.102. Popular and friendly Congolese club with live music on weekends and every Wed; some big names have played here over the years, and the dancing can get pretty wild, fuelled by cheap local beer (Ksh180). Congolese DJs play on nights when there's no band. Cover Ksh100 Fri and Sat. Sun–Thurs 10am–3am, Fri & Sat 24hr.

CENTRAL BUSINESS DISTRICT

Dolce Cianda House, Koinange St ☎ 0774 675396, ⓦ bit.ly/DolceNairobi; map p.106. Slick, smooth *Lingala* and soul dinner-dance place for a glitzy crowd, with a deafening sound system. Fun if you're in the right mood, but quite pricey. Beer Ksh300; cover Ksh400 Fri and Sat. Tues–Sun 5.30pm–late.

The Exchange Bar First floor of the Stanley Hotel, corner Kimathi St and Kenyatta Ave ☎ 0719 048186, ⓦ sarovahotels.com; map p.107. This historic bar certainly looks the part, with its leather armchairs, polished wood railing and palm-leaf fans. It may feel like a nineteenth-century gentlemen's club, but this was once the site of Nairobi's first stock exchange; it's still a good spot to sip decent whiskey (from Ksh525) or indulge in afternoon cocktails (around Ksh600). Daily 9am–11pm.

Florida 2000 First floor, Commerce House, Moi Ave ☎ 020 2229036 or ☎ 0726 110968, ⓦ floridaclubskenya .com; map p.107. Also known as *F2*, this dark cavern of a club attracts desperate-looking businessmen and offers rather unambiguous entertainment, pumped up with what they call "most exotic floor shows". For some local women, this means grabbing drunken *wazungu* and persuading them to part with their money. Be relaxed, but beware. Beer Ksh200, cover Ksh300. Mon–Sat noon–6am.

Gravity Kimathi St ☎ 0720 608914, ⓦ facebook.com/ GravityLoungeke; map p.107. Established club attracting a mature, professional crowd with its slick decor – think white leather and a reflective staircase – and boasting a more spacious people-watching balcony than most of the Kimathi St bars. Thurs is African night and on Sun they play soul, but otherwise expect a mix of African house and techno. Basic local food is available, and beers go for Ksh220. Daily 7.30am–3.30am.

Mojo's Banda St ☎ 0732 755153, ⓦ bit.ly/ MojosNairobi; map p.107. Possibly even more popular than *Tribeka* next door, *Mojo's* packs out on weekends with lively patrons downing cocktails (Ksh400) and shouting happily over the pounding music, or squeezed onto the balcony. Theme nights include rock (Tues), African night (Wed) and old school (Thurs), and during the day tired office workers even turn up for lunch. Daily 8am–4am.

Simmers Corner Muindi Mbingu St and Kenyatta Ave; map p.106. Large and laidback, the CBD's only *nyama choma*-style joint, where you can get a plate of chicken and chips for Ksh480, is very popular with office workers deferring the misery of commuting home. Music, dancing and frequent live bands. Daily 7am–late.

Tribeka Corner Banda St and Kimathi St ☎ 0708 322222, ⓦ tribeka.co.ke; map p.107. Very busy double-storey bar-restaurant, flashing with sports screens, banging with music and heaving with sweaty, and mostly young, bodies – and with a balcony overlooking this lively corner (the name stands for Triangle Below Kimathi). Theme nights include karaoke (Mon), live music (Wed) and reggae (Thurs), and local beers go for Ksh230. Daily 24hr.

WESTLANDS AND PARKLANDS

Aqua Blu First floor Krishna Centre, Woodvale Grove, Westlands ☎ 0729 888833 or ☎ 0789 888833,

1

w aquablu.co.ke; map p.132. Somewhere between a lounge and a club, this water-themed nightspot features fountains, a glass-topped bar and plenty of blue lighting, pulling in a glitzy crowd with guest DJs every weekend. Prices are reasonable considering the setting – beers go for Ksh250, and cocktails for around Ksh500. Tues–Thurs 3pm–2am, Fri–Sun 3pm–late.

Bacchus' Lounge Woodvale Grove, Westlands 📞0721 493859; map p.132. Popular bar and club that's relaxed and welcoming. Music includes rock (Tues), hip-hop (Wed), techno (Thurs) and dance music (Fri and Sat). Beers and wine both Ksh250. Mon & Sun 4.30pm–midnight, Tues–Sat 4.30pm–5am.

Gipsy Woodvale Grove, Westlands 📞0733 730529, w gipsybar.com; map p.132. As well being a friendly terrace bar, rendezvous and hangout, popular with *wahindi* and *wazungu*, *Gipsy* is a good place to eat late, with a vaguely Spanish-styled menu, including steaks (Ksh1300), seafood (Ksh1200) and burgers and veggie meals (Ksh1000). Mon–Sat 10am–3pm & 5pm–late, Sun 3pm–late.

Havana Opposite Bandari Plaza, Woodvale Grove, Westlands 📞0723 265941, w havana.co.ke; map p.132. Dark and smoky Latin restaurant and bar, with a chic young crowd attracted by good Mexican-inspired food (mains around Ksh900) and cheap cocktail pitchers (mojitos Ksh2000/litre). Daily noon–3am.

★**Juniper Social** Muthangari Drive, off Wayaki Way, Westlands 📞0707 612585, w facebook.com/ thejuniperkitchen; map p.104. Run by an Australian with knack for upcycled decor, this wildly popular restaurant and bar occupies an elegant old Westlands house and garden strewn with pallet furniture and carefully sourced antiques. It gets especially lively on weekends, when expats and well-heeled Nairobi youth flock to sip cocktails out of jars (Ksh700), listen to poetry and dance on the back porch. The light lunches, including a variety of creative salads, are delicious. Tues–Thurs & Sun 11am–midnight, Fri & Sat 11am–3am.

Klub House (K1) Junction Chiromo Rd and Ojijo Rd, Parklands 📞0717 969500, w klubhouse.co.ke; map p.105. Huge, gated, quintessentially Kenyan drive-in entertainment complex (part of the highly successful Kahama empire). Inside you'll find the double-storey wooden *Klub House* itself ("Paradise" downstairs, and "Heaven" upstairs with six pool tables and beers for Ksh275); the *Karwash* snack bar with valeting services on one end and snacks on the other; the *Pitcher & Butch* live music venue, pub and *nyama choma* grill (*mbuzi* arm Ksh1650/kg), which sometimes has working wi-fi; and a hotel, the *Parklands Shade* (see p.127), for when you just have to crash. Daily 24hr.

Mercury Lounge ABC Place, Waiyaki Way, Westlands 📞020 4451875 or 📞0722 309947, w mercurylounge .co.ke; map p.104. Cool designer watering hole with a

curved wooden bar and dark green and purple leather furniture, with DJs spinning Afro-pop, hip-hop and rock. Cocktails cost from Ksh500, and there's tapas-style food alongside heavier dishes such as pepper steak (Ksh1250). Mon–Sat 4pm–late.

Sankara Woodvale Grove, Westlands 📞020 4208000 or 📞0703 028000, w sankara.com; map p.132. There are three bars in this hotel (see p.128): the *Gallery* wine bar and patisserie on the first floor (with probably the best wine selection in Nairobi); the slick, rooftop *Sarabi* with its glass-bottomed swimming pool; and the seventh-floor *Champagne Bar*. All daily 2pm–1am.

Tree House Westlands Rd, by Museum Hill Overpass 📞0786 776600, w treehousenairobi.wordpress.com; map p.105. On weekend nights up to two thousand people pack into this landmark venue built around a giant mahogany tree, lured by live music, reasonable prices (beer Ksh250, wine Ksh300, burgers Ksh700) and guaranteed crowds. Tues–Sat 11am–4am.

Vineyard Rhapta Rd, Westlands 📞0772 332270, w facebook.com/theVineyardWineBar; map p.105. Relaxed garden pub by day, where you can enjoy a beer (Ksh250) or a *shisha* (Ksh1000) on a wine-barrel table under the trees; at night the young Westlands throngs take over, downing shots and swarming onto one of several dancefloors inside. There's food too – pizzas and such – but the real action starts after dinner. Daily 11am–6am.

LAVINGTON AND KILIMANI

★**Brew Bistro** Piedmont Plaza, Ngong Rd, Kilimani 📞020 4183382 or 📞0771 152350, w thebigfivebreweries.com; map p.104. Microbrewery terrace bar and restaurant. Go for the interesting beer (Ksh400 for half a litre of the bar's own brew), the buzz and the scene of Nairobians paying to be seen – and keep your fingers crossed that the food, when it comes, will be as good as it sometimes is: waiting staff are frequently swamped. Tues–Thurs 4pm–midnight, Fri & Sat 4pm–3am, Sun 11am–midnight.

Caribea Komo Lane, off Wood Ave, Kilimani 📞020 2108579 or 📞0703 993123, w caribea.co.ke; map p.104. Casual *koroga* restaurant and bar with a nice garden for hanging out and a collection of *bandas* out back, often filled with locals munching on chicken and drinking bottles of hard liquor, though beers (Ksh250) are available too. Daily 10am–late.

Casablanca Lenana Rd, Kilimani 📞0724 277332 or 📞0734 472778, w facebook.com/casablanca.nairobi; map p.105. Moroccan-themed bar attached to *Osteria* restaurant, with an oasis-style garden that has grown a bit seedy in recent years. There are the requisite palms, cushions, *shishas* and smoky dancefloor, but ladies of the night are much in evidence. Beers Ksh300, cocktails Ksh700. Mon–Sat 5pm–late.

Kengeles Lavington Green shopping centre, James Gichuru Drive, Lavington ☎020 2587343; map p.104. Popular sports bar serving pub food like burgers, steaks and toasted sandwiches, as well as buffalo wings (Ksh680), all washed down with beer (Ksh250) to a loud, nonstop music accompaniment, including the occasional live band. Daily 8am–late.

Level 8 Roof of the Best Western, corner Rose Ave and Arwings Kodhek Rd, Kilimani ☎0722 292700 or ☎0732 292700, ⊛bestwestern.co.ke; map p.105. Drinks here are pricey (beer Ksh450), but the selling point is that both the bar – decked out in white leather and plush velvet wallpaper – and the more relaxed rooftop restaurant above it, offer stunning views over western Nairobi. Go for happy hour (5.30–7.30pm) and catch the sunset. Daily 5pm–2am.

KAREN AND LANGATA

Que Pasa Karen Shopping Centre, Ngong Rd, Karen ☎0711 222222, ⊛quepasa.co.ke; map p.102. Restaurant and pub with vaulted ceilings and a bewildering mix of culinary offerings, ranging from pizza to Thai food to

lobster. But the real action gets going late here, as Karen residents stream in after dinner to down cocktail pitchers (Ksh2000) and imported beers like Leffe and Windhoek. Mon–Thurs 9am–midnight, Fri & Sat 9am–5am, Sun 9am–1am.

Simba Saloon Carnivore restaurant, Langata Rd, Langata ☎0733 611608 or ☎0722 204647, ⊛tamarind.co.ke; map p.102. A successful melding of bands and DJs in a pleasant outdoor environment with a very spacious dancefloor, and reasonably priced drinks (beer Ksh250). There's frequent live music, both Kenyan and international, and big names like Baaba Maal and Youssou N'dour have played here. The adjacent *Carnivore Gardens* concert venue holds up to fifteen thousand people. Daily noon–midnight, later on concert days.

NORTHERN SUBURBS

The Nest Tribe hotel, next to Village Market, Gigiri ☎020 7200000, ⊛tribe-hotel.com; map p.102. *The Nest* is the *Tribe* hotel's very comfy, open-air rooftop cocktail (Ksh600) and *shisha* (Ksh1000) bar. They also do light meals for around Ksh1000. Daily 4pm–midnight.

ARTS AND CULTURE

After years of stagnation, the Nairobi **arts scene** seems to be finally finding a rhythm of its own, independent of the tourist market, which had previously driven much of it. Although still modest by international standards, it is well worth discovering. Besides checking out the theatres and arts centres listed below, your first base should be the excellent arts-scene blog ⊛ nairobinow.wordpress.com, which posts news of up-and-coming performers, shows and events. Also worth having a look at are the theatre pages in the Thurs edition of *The Standard* and the *Nation* on Fri and Sat. A selection of **cinemas** is listed in the Directory (see p.143).

★**African Heritage House** Mombasa Rd ☎0721 518389, ⊛africanheritagebook.com; map p.103. This appointment-only treasure-trove of beautiful items collected by an American Africaphile and Kenya resident includes superb musical instruments such as thumb pianos and lyres – well worth a special visit. Meals are available if booked in advance. Tours cost $40 for up to four people, including tea, or $35/person with lunch or dinner. It's also possible to stay the night (BB $265).

Alliance Française Corner Loita and Monrovia streets, Central Business District ☎0727 600622, ⊛afkenya .or.ke; map p.106. There's a constant stream of activity here – events, shows, films and forums.

★**Banana Hill Art Studio & Gallery** Raini Rd, Banana Hill ☎0733 882660 or ☎0711 756911, ⊛bananahillartgallery.com; map p.100. Very worthwhile contemporary Kenyan painting and sculpture based around a community of artists.

★**GoDown Arts Centre** Dunga Rd, Industrial Area ☎0732 117000, ⊛thegodownartscentre.com; map p.102. A not-for-profit organization including an art gallery, dance studio and performance space presenting everything from classical music by local musicians to visiting overseas artists.

Goethe-Institut Maendeleo House, corner Loita St and Monrovia St, Central Business District ☎020 2224640, ⊛goethe.de/kenya; map p.106. The German overseas cultural mission hosts monthly movies, concerts and events.

Italian Institute of Culture Fifth floor, Grenadier Tower, 1 Woodvale Close, Westlands ☎020 4451266, ⊛www.iicnairobi.esteri.it; map p.132. Beautiful event and exhibition space that does as much to promote African culture as support Kenya's lively and long-settled Italian community.

Kenya National Theatre Opposite the Norfolk Hotel, Harry Thuku Rd, Central Business District ☎020 2672843 or ☎0726 008677, ⊛bit.ly/ KenyaNationalTheatre; map p.105.Built in 1952, the theatre was refurbished in the early 2000s with government and private funding. It has now been restored in all its Art Deco glory, hosting productions with a special emphasis on African theatre, and Kenyan drama in particular.

★**Kuona Trust** Likoni Close, off Likoni Lane, off Dennis Pritt Rd, Kilimani ☎0721 262326 or ☎0733 742752, ⊛kuonatrust.org; map p.104. Active for many years, this visual arts centre brings together Kenyan and international artists and performers for residencies, workshops and events.

1

Live at the Elephant 3 Kanjata Rd, off James Gichuru Drive (North), Lavington ☎0721 946710, ⓦfacebook.com/LiveAtTheElephant; map p.104. This leafy Lavington garden hosts regular concerts by mostly Kenyan musicians, as well as occasional alfresco film screenings. Events tend to be pricey, but are very popular with expats and well-heeled young Kenyans.

Michael Joseph Centre Safaricom HQ2, Waiyaki Way, Spring Valley ☎0722 005890, ⓦsafaricom .co.ke/michaeljosephcentre; map p.104. Gallery and performance space, funded by the mobile phone company, that increasingly hogs the limelight in Nairobi's arts universe, with an eclectic variety of shows from classical European music to Kenyan hip-hop and theatre.

Phoenix Players Professional Centre, Parliament Rd, Central Business District ☎020 2225506, ⓦwww. phoenixtheatre.co.ke; map p.105. This small theatre has assumed the mantle of Nairobi's leading playhouse. Its energetic repertory company, the Phoenix Players, formed in 1948, stages contemporary works by Kenyan and foreign playwrights and classics adapted for Kenya – always worth catching and sometimes outstanding.

★**Sarakasi Dome** Ngara Rd, opposite the post office, Ngara ☎020 2694026 or ☎0722 814133, ⓦsarakasi .org; map p.102. Built in 1952 as a circus (*sarakasi*) venue, then the Shan Cinema for many years, this is now a Dutch-owned venue and renovated performance space for the very active Sarakasi Trust and their vibrant Sarakasi Players, promoting contemporary African art, music and dance.

SHOPPING

Commerce is Nairobi's *raison d'être*. The city is the best place in East Africa to buy **handicrafts**, with the widest, if not the cheapest, selection, and there are also some lavish **produce markets**, enjoyable even if you only want to browse. The upper part of Moi Ave is Nairobi's busiest ordinary shopping street, with some colonnaded shopfronts still remaining. A certain amount of **bargaining** is expected at all Nairobi's markets and many independent shops.

SHOPPING MALLS AND SUPERMARKETS

Nakumatt There are branches of Nakumatt, Kenya's number-one supermarket and hypermarket chain, all over the city. There's no bargaining, of course, but you can buy everything from beans to solar panels, and the erstwhile Nakuru Mattresses Co. does deliver on variety and – usually – price. Some branches are open 24hr, including Nakumatt Ukay in Westlands, Nakumatt Ngong Rd at Prestige Plaza and Nakumatt Lifestyle on the corner of Monrovia and Moktar Daddah streets near Jeevanjee Gardens in the CBD.

Shopping malls Nairobi now has the dubious distinction of having more shopping malls – over twenty, and counting – than any other African city outside South Africa. Despite the trauma of the 2013 Al-Shabaab attack on Westgate (which reopened in summer 2015), Kenyans still flock to the malls, possibly due to the fact that Nairobi life has become inextricably centred around them; generally providing a hassle-free environment for getting on with ordinary shopping and business, for practical matters they're difficult to avoid. You'll find most of the malls stuffed into the western and northern suburbs, where they cater to the expat and wealthy Kenyan markets. All include banks, travel agents, specialist food suppliers and an assortment of cafés and restaurants. The biggest and most popular – Westgate in Westlands, Village Market in Gigiri, Junction and Yaya Centre on Ngong Rd in Kilimani, Galleria in Langata – are major landmarks. Shops in the malls generally don't open until 9am or even 10am and then remain open until 7pm or 8pm. The malls themselves are usually open by 7am for breakfast and coffee outlets.

CRAFTS AND FABRICS

For the exhausting business of buying crafts and curios, it's advisable to be quite focused and decide what sort of items you're interested in buying before stepping into a shop or looking at a stall: if you merely browse you'll often be hassled mercilessly by the majority of shopkeepers and stallholders (see p.86). There are dozens of curio shops and you might get a good deal at almost any of them, though you should never accept their first price, and always bargain hard. Upmarket places are almost all located the city's suburban malls. In the CBD they're clustered on Standard, Kaunda and Mama Ngina streets. At some of the fancier places you can browse for ages undisturbed, but at cheaper outlets dilly-dallying is not encouraged and the pressure may be on to part with your money. As well as the following shops, City Market has a number of crafts stalls, but the sales pressure can be intense. For fabrics, Biashara St ("Commerce Street") is the traditional home in Nairobi of cloth merchants, and many of them are still there.

Haria's Stamp Shop 38 Biashara St ☎0731 868246, ⓦhariastamp.com; map p.106. This old place has an excellent and very reasonably priced range of fabrics, including *kikois* and *kangas*. Mon–Sat 9am–5pm.

Kamili Designs Langata Rd, Karen, near Karen Hospital ☎020 2430495 or ☎0701 928656, ⓦkamilidesigns.com; map p.102. This textile workshop sells locally designed, hand-printed fabrics in typically bold and colourful patterns, available both by the metre and as cushions, bedspreads and the like. Mon–Fri 9am–5pm.

Kashmir Crafts Biashara St ☎0735 007013; map p.106. If you are in no hurry and after something unique, but not necessarily Kenyan, this is worth a visit, with a great selection of carvings, masks and jewellery from across the continent at very reasonable prices. Daily 9am–5.30pm.

Langata Link Shops Langata Link, Langata South Rd, Karen ☎0738 651042 or ☎0724 539342, ⓦfacebook .com/langatalinkshop; map p.102. A collection of ten or so shops selling high-quality crafts like leatherwork, clothing, jewellery and bath products, including some items, such as beautiful home-made pottery, that are hard to find elsewhere. Mon–Fri 8am–5pm, Sat & Sun 9.30am–5pm.

Matbronze Gallery 2 Kifaru Lane, Langata ☎0733 969165, ⓦbit.ly/MatbronzeGallery; map p.102. Gallery and shop selling beautifully wrought bronzework by artist Denis Mathews, some of it small enough to take home as gifts. There's also a pleasant garden café where you can admire some of the larger pieces. Mon–Fri 8am–5pm, Sat 8am–5.30pm, Sun 9.30am–5.30pm.

COMMUNITY CRAFT CENTRES

Nairobi has a number of craft shops with charitable status, or associated with development or self help projects. Although sometimes a little expensive (and they don't go in for bargaining), they often have unusual and well-made stock, some of which finds its way into charity catalogues overseas. A few are a little way out of town, but well worth making special journeys to visit, and they can be good tonics if you're suffering from curio shop fatigue.

Amani ya Juu Riverside Drive ☎020 4449071, ⓦamaniafrica.org; map p.105. This project employs women who have been marginalized by poverty and war. It's great for gifts, including colourful handmade clothes and bags. Mon–Fri 9am–4pm, Sat 10am–4pm.

★**Kazuri Beads & Pottery Centre** Mbagathi Ridge, Karen ☎020 2328905 or ☎0720 953298, ⓦkazuri .com; map p.102. Kazuri, which means "small and beautiful", employs nearly a hundred formerly destitute women who make an extraordinary variety of handmade, mostly ceramic, jewellery and beads. You can watch the whole process from shaping and colouring to firing, and there's also a pottery showroom. It's expensive, but the stuff is lovely. Workshops: Mon–Fri 8am–4.30pm, Sat 8am–1pm; shop: Mon–Sat 8.30am–6pm, Sun 9am–5pm.

★**Kitengela Glass** Off the Magadi road, south of Nairobi National Park ☎0734 287887, ⓦkitengela .com; map p.102. Inspiring community of glass-blowers and craftspeople in a photogenic creative village. Visitors are welcome and you can observe, browse and buy, unhassled, lots of beautiful work, and plenty of quirky rejects, although you'll need your own transport to get here. Daily 8am–5pm.

Mikono Craft Shop Gitanga Rd, Lavington ☎020 3874152, ⓦjrsea.org; map p.104. The outlet of the Jesuit Refugee Service, with well-made work (including especially beautiful patchwork textiles) from refugees, and

superb Mozambican carvings. Mon–Fri 8.30am–1pm & 2–5pm, Sat 9am–3pm.

★**Ocean Sole** Marula Lane, Karen ☎0707 339952, ⓦocean-sole.com; map p.102. This innovative company recycles the old flip-flops that wash up on beaches, working with slum-dwellers to sculpt them into colourful rubber giraffes, warthogs, Christmas ornaments, doorstops and a host of other playful objects. Their shop is a great place to find unique gifts, particularly for children. Mon–Sat 9am–5pm.

Spinner's Web Getathuru Gardens, off Peponi Rd, Westlands ☎020 2072629 or ☎0731 168996, ⓦspinnerswebkenya.com; map p.105. A large shop selling a lot of good stuff – crafts, textiles, woollen goods and jewellery, much of it made by self-help groups and individuals, including Meru's Makena Textile Workshop. Mon–Fri 9.30am–6.30pm, Sat & Sun 9.30am–5.30pm.

Utamaduni Crafts Centre Bogani East Rd, Langata ☎0722 205028, ⓦutamadunicraftshop.com; map p.102. Eighteen individual craft shops in one large house, opened by Richard Leakey in 1991 (a portion of the profits goes to the Kenya Wildlife Service). It has everything you might want, much of it made on site or from street kid projects. Quality and prices are high, and the attached *Verandah* restaurant is excellent. Daily 9am–6pm.

Woodley Weavers Chaka Rd, Kilimani ☎0733 612028, ⓦwoodleyweavers.com; map p.105. Known to many as the "rug gallery", this place has a variety of rugs made by local women, often single mothers from the Kibera slum, using local wool, cotton and plant dyes; all rugs cost Ksh350/square ft. Mon–Fri 9am–6pm, Sat 10am–4pm.

MARKETS

City Market Muindi Mbingu St; map p.106. Though it doesn't offer the city's lowest prices, for a colourful and high-quality range of fruit and vegetables (plus separate meat and fish sections) this is the obvious option in the CBD, though many erstwhile greengrocer's stalls have switched to overpriced crafts. Beware of bag-snatching while browsing. Mon–Fri 7.30am–6.30pm, Sat 7.30am–3pm, Sun 8.30am–noon.

Gikomba Market Off Landhies Rd, past the Country Bus Station; take any bus or matatu for Jogoo Rd and get off at Gikomba; map p.103. The largest general market in Nairobi, this is a spot that few tourists ever see, a labyrinth of muddy alleyways, courtyards and open sewers. It's also a place to experience an exhilarating slice of Nairobi life, and just about anything can be found on sale, from school uniforms to industrial-size ovens. Gikomba is gutted by fires from time to time, most recently in June 2015, but the traders are always swift to rebuild. Come with someone who knows the place; it's very easy to get lost and Gikomba can be unsafe. Daily dawn–dusk.

Kariokor Market Ring Rd, Ngara; bus/matatu #4, #6, #14, #15, #30, #31, #32, #40, #42 or #46/46B; map p.103.

1

MAASAI MARKETS

If you're after **Maasai crafts** (whether traditional beaded jewellery or items made up for the tourist industry), or carvings and crafts in general, the city's various Maasai markets are recommended, though they are no longer the cheap, hot tip they once were. Initiated downtown opposite the post office in the mid-1990s, the original group of Maasai and other women from rural areas (as well as a number of men) were moved several times by city council *askaris* and now convene to display their wares at various places throughout the week. You'll sometimes find prices well below those in the tourist markets, with good deals on the simpler designs of beaded jewellery, baskets and gourds. But more usually you'll have to bargain hard to get what seems like an acceptable price. All the markets are open roughly from 8am to 3pm.

Tues Kijabe St, behind the *Norfolk Hotel*.
Wed Capital Centre, Mombasa Rd.
Thurs Junction Mall, Ngong Rd.

Fri Rooftop car park at Village Market, Gigiri.
Sat Law Courts car park, off City Hall Way.
Sun Yaya Centre, Kilimani.

Named after the wartime "Carrier Corps", Kariokor is closer to an oriental bazaar than most markets in Kenya, with permanent booths for the traders. Inside, there's as much manufacturing and finishing going on as selling – you'll find sisal weavers, leather workers, makers of tyre-rubber sandals ("5000-mile shoes" – about Ksh300 a pair and surprisingly comfortable), carpenters, toy-makers (look out for locally made wire-and-fabric contraptions – cars, bicycles, flapping birds – which are sometimes beautiful works of art), tailors and traditional healers with various remedies and charms. Kariokor is certainly the best place in Nairobi to buy baskets (*vyondo*), made with sisal, coloured with natural or artificial dyes, with garish plastic, or with cord manufactured from the bark of the baobab tree. The cord baskets can be truly exquisite, with tiny beads included in the tight weave.

CLOTHES AND MATUMBA

You'll find clothes shops all over the city, but more interesting for visitors is the *matumba* phenomenon, the secondhand clothes stalls that are found in markets and spilling over roadsides across the city. These are entirely supplied through a murky chain of international connections whose first link is the donation of unwanted clothes to "charity" clothes collection companies in Europe and the US. *Matumba* is big business and a serious challenge to local clothing manufacturers: the vast majority of Kenyans buy most or all of their clothes at these stalls. One of the easiest *matumba* markets to navigate is Toi Market, behind Adam's Arcade on Ngong Rd, although prices here tend to be a bit higher than elsewhere.

BOOKSHOPS

Just a few years ago there was barely a handful of decent bookshops in Nairobi. Now they're everywhere, with most malls having at least one. The shelves tend to be packed with school and college books, but the best of them have excellent ranges of local and imported fiction, gift books, travel guides and maps.

Between the Lines Village Market, Gigiri ☎0708 098188; map p.102. A good place to come for fiction, cookbooks, African literature and even a few graphic novels. Mon–Sat 9.30am–7pm, Sun 10am–5pm.

Bookstop Second floor, Yaya Centre, Arwings Kodhek Rd, Kilimani ☎0722 520160, ⍟bookstopltd.co.ke; map p.104. An excellent selection of fiction and nonfiction, including a good number of maps, run by staff who know their wares. Mon–Sat 10am–6.45pm, Sun 10.30am–6pm.

Textbook Centre Sarit Centre, Westlands ☎0734 940940 or ☎0720 539539, ⍟textbookcentre.com; map p.132. Aimed mostly at schoolchildren, but with a modest selection of novels, guidebooks and biographies as well. Mon–Sat 9am–6.45pm, Sun 10am–6pm.

MUSIC

Although many of the most iconic record stores have closed, Nairobi is still a great place for music fans, especially if you have a taste for Kenya's stunning variety of ethnic musical strands – not to mention the plethora of recordings from elsewhere in East and Central Africa, especially Congo. In addition to Melodica, look out for tiny hole-in-the-wall music shops near markets selling CDs or, increasingly, individual MP3s.

Melodica Tom Mboya St ☎0721 580721, ⍟melodica .co.ke; map p.107. This dusty, pleasingly old-school music shop is a good place to get your hands on some rare LPs of African artists, as well as CDs of music from across the continent. Mon–Sat 9am–5.30pm.

SPORTS AND ACTIVITIES

Climbing Blue Sky Climbing, sixth floor, Diamond Plaza, Parklands (☎0736 236745, ⍟blueskykenya.org) has a set of indoor climbing walls; the club also organizes climbing, hiking and kayaking trips around Kenya. Equipment rental available.

Diving Nairobi Sailing and Sub-Aqua Club, off Langata Rd, opposite Wilson Airport (⍟diveclubkenya.com). BSAC training and trips to coastal and lake diving sites.

Football (soccer) Nyayo Stadium, at the junction of

Uhuru Hwy and Langata Rd (☎020 201 3704), is the national stadium as well as being the headquarters of the Football Kenya Federation and home ground of Nairobi's top premier league team, AFC Leopards. The season runs from Feb–Nov, and seats start at Ksh200.

Golf Karen Golf & Country Club, Karen Rd (☎020 3882801, ⓦkarencountryclub.org); Muthaiga Golf Club, Muthaiga Rd (☎020 2368440, ⓦmuthaigagolfclub.com); Royal Nairobi Golf Club, Mucai Drive, off Ngong Rd (☎0718 810810, ⓦroyalnairobigc.com); Windsor Golf & Country Club, Kigwa Rd (☎020 8647000, ⓦwindsorgolfresort.com).

Horse racing The Kenya Jockey Club's racecourse is on Ngong Rd (☎0722 414598, ⓦjockeyclubofkenya.com); take bus #24 or matatu #111. Races are held every Sun, with general viewing free or grandstand entry for Ksh200.

Horseriding Malo Stables, Mudodo Lane, Karen (☎0722 203063, ⓦmalostables.com); New Muthaiga Stables, Thigiri Rd off Thigiri Ridge Rd, Gigiri (☎0721 421728 or ☎0788 291896).

Jogging The jogging trails through the golf course at the Windsor Golf & Country Club are useful, and you can also jog in many parks and suburban streets, often in the company of others; contact the Nairobi Hash House Harriers (☎0723 203427, ⓦnhhh.co.ke) for information about running with them.

Karting GP-Karting, in Langata next to *Carnivore* (see p.135), has a 500m circuit, with rides from Ksh130 (Tues–Sun 9am–6pm; ☎020 6008444 or ☎0733 666333, ⓦgpkarting.co.ke).

Skating Panari Sky Centre, Mombasa Rd (daily 11am–10pm; Ksh800/hr, including skates).

Swimming Many hotel pools are open to the public for a fee. Alternatively, try Splash! water park next to *Carnivore* in Langata (Wed–Fri 10am–5pm, Sat & Sun 10am–6pm; adults Ksh400, children aged 2½-plus Ksh350; ☎020 2405799, ⓦsplash.co.ke; see p.135).

DIRECTORY

American Express Hemingways House, Karen Office Park, Langata Rd (☎020 2295000, ⓦexpresstravel.co.ke).

Banks and foreign exchange There are branches of Barclays, Equity Bank, Kenya Commercial Bank (KCB) and Standard Chartered everywhere, most with ATMs. All banks are closed on Sun, except those at the airport, but most ATMs operate daily 24hr. The Central Bank of Kenya publishes a list of licensed independent forex dealers at ⓦcentralbank.go.ke/index.php/forex-bureaus.

Cinemas The major malls all have modern multiplex movie theatres showing recent mainstream releases. Seats cost around Ksh400–650. Daily programmes can be found online or in the *Nation* and *Standard* newspapers. Venues include: Century Cinemax, Junction Mall, Ngong Rd (☎0700 326726, ⓦcenturycinemaxe.com); Fox Cineplex Sarit, Sarit Centre, Westlands (☎020 3753026, ⓦfoxtheatres.co.ke); IMAX, 20th Century Plaza, Mama Ngina St (☎0737558802 or ☎0737 558785, ⓦimax.or.ke); Star Flix Prestige, Prestige Plaza, Ngong Rd (☎0708 251275).

Dentists Peter Griffiths & Associates, Haven Court, off Wayaki Way, Westlands (☎020 4443391 or ☎0722 736439, ⓦthedentalpractice.co.ke); Skye Dental, fourth floor, Junction Mall, Ngong Rd (☎0734 816470, ⓦskydental.co.ke).

Doctors and hospitals Aga Khan Hospital, Third Parklands Ave (☎020 3662000); Nairobi Hospital, Argwings Kodhek Rd (☎020 2846000).

Embassies, high commissions and consulates Australia, ICIPE House, Riverside Drive, off Chiromo Rd (☎020 4277100); Burundi, first floor, Co-op Trust House, Lower Hill Rd off Bunyala Rd (☎020 2719200); Canada, Limuru Rd, Gigiri (☎020 3663000); DR Congo, twelfth floor, Electricity House, Harambee Ave (☎020 2229772); Egypt, 24 Othaya Rd (south), off Gitanga Rd, Kileleshwa B (☎020 3870298); Eritrea, second floor, New Rehema House, Rhapta Rd (☎020 4443164); Ethiopia, State House Ave, Nairobi Hill (☎020 2732052; visas only issued for entry by air); France, fifteenth floor, Barclays Plaza, Loita St (☎020 2778000, ⓦambafrance-ke.org; can issue visas for some francophone countries in West Africa); Germany, Ludwig Krapf House, 113 Riverside Drive (☎020 4262100, ⓦnairobi.diplo.de); Ireland, Eden Square, Chiromo Rd (☎0729 000353); Italy, ninth floor, International Life House, Mama Ngina St (☎020 2247750, ⓦambnairobi.esteri.it); Madagascar, AACC Building, Westlands (☎020 4452410); Malawi, Sports Rd, off Waiyaki Way, Westlands (☎020 4440569); Mozambique, third floor, Bruce House, Standard St (☎020 2221979); Netherlands, Riverside Lane, off Riverside Drive (☎020 4288000, ⓦkenia.nlembassy.org); New Zealand, Hon. Consul, Nairobi Business Park, Ngong Rd (☎020 8045100); Rwanda, Limuru Rd, Gigiri (☎020 7121321, ⓦkenya.embassy.gov.rw); Seychelles, Professional House, Kuwinda Rd, Karen (☎020 2016322); Somalia, Likoni Lane off Dennis Pritt Rd, Kilimani (☎020 2736618, ⓦsomaliaembassynairobi.com); South Africa, third floor, Roshanmaer Place, Lenana Rd (☎020 2827100); Spain, third floor, CBA Building, corner Mara and Ragati roads, Upper Hill (☎020 2720222); South Sudan, sixth floor, Bishops Gate Building, 5th Ngong Ave (☎020 2711384); Sudan, Kabarnet Rd, off Ngong Rd (☎020 3875133); Tanzania, ninth floor, Reinsurance Plaza, Taifa Rd (☎020 2311948); Uganda, Riverside Paddocks, off Riverside Drive (☎020 4445420), visa section: Uganda House, Kenyatta Ave; UK, Upper Hill Rd, off Haile Selassie Ave (☎020 2873000, ⓦukinkenya.fco.gov.uk); US, United Nations Ave, Gigiri (☎020 3636000, ⓦnairobi.usembassy.gov); Zambia,

1

Nyerere Rd, by Central Park (☎020 2724796); Zimbabwe, 2 Westlands Close, Westlands Rd (☎020 3744052).

Internet access There are internet cafés all over the city and plenty of wi-fi hot spots too, including in most hotels and many restaurants. In the CBD, try the many places round the junction of Loita St and Monrovia St. Most coffee-shop chains (see p.130) offer free wi-fi.

Libraries McMillan Memorial Library, Banda St (Mon–Fri 9am–5pm, Sat 9.30am–1pm); British Institute in Eastern Africa, Laikipia Rd, off Arboretum Drive, Kileleshwa (☎020 8155186, ⊛biea.ac.uk; visits by arrangement).

Optician Optica, Jubilee Insurance Building, Kaunda St, with other branches around town (☎020 2220516, ⊛opticakenya.com).

Pharmacies Mimosa Pharmacy, ground floor, Junction Mall, with other branches around town (☎020 3873763); Shah Chemists, Sarit Centre, Westlands (☎0720 994464).

Post office The GPO is on Kenyatta Ave, offering poste restante and the usual services (Mon–Fri 7.30am–6pm, Sat 9am–1pm).

Vaccinations Cholera, yellow fever, typhoid and hepatitis jabs can be obtained from the Inoculation Centre, City Hall, City Hall Way (Mon–Fri 8.30am–12.30pm & 2–4pm; ☎0722 769654).

Visitor's passes/visas Visitor's pass extensions can be obtained at Nyayo House, Posta Rd, behind the GPO (Mon–Fri 8.30am–12.30pm & 2–4pm; ☎020 2222022).

Nairobi National Park

Daily 6am–6pm • $50 with Safari Card (see p.73) • Park and Kenya Wildlife Service Headquarters ☎020 2423423 or ☎0726 610508, ⊛kws.org

Notwithstanding the hype, it really is remarkable that the plains and woodland making up **Nairobi National Park** should exist almost uncorrupted within earshot of Nairobi's downtown traffic, complete with more than eighty species of large mammals, including all the giant savanna species with the exception of the elephant – it boasts the greatest density of **megafauna** of any city park in the world. There is, in fact, no comparable park anywhere. In contrast to the pitted streets of the city, gridlocked with traffic, here is a haven of tranquil wilderness where humans have only temporary landing rights.

The park is a good place to spend time during a flight layover, or before an afternoon or evening flight, and you have a high chance of seeing certain species, especially black rhino, which might well elude you in the bigger Kenyan parks. Although it is fenced along its northern perimeter, the park is open to the south, in theory allowing migrating herds, and the predators that follow them, to come and go more or less freely. For all the low-flying planes and minibuses, you have a greater chance of witnessing a kill here than in any other park in Kenya.

Around the park

The first couple of hours after dawn are always best for **game-watching**. Try asking the rangers on arrival and you'll get the latest news: "Number 12 for a cheetah; lions at number 20…", the numbers referring to the road junctions, marked on every map of the park. The highest point in the western part of the park, **Impala Hill**, is a good spot to pause and scan the park with binoculars. It's also a picnic site, with toilets.

The Mbagathi or Athi River, forming the park's **southern boundary**, is its only permanent river and fringed with the yellow acacias that early explorers and settlers dubbed "fever trees" because they seemed to grow in the areas where malaria was most common. Flowing into the Mbagathi, several of the park's seasonal streams are dammed to regulate the water supply; in the dry season, these **dams** – all located on the northern side of the park where the streams come down off the Embakasi plain to the north – draw the densest concentrations of animals. **Hippos** can usually be viewed at a pretty pool at the confluence of the Mbagathi and Athi rivers (junction 12), beyond the "Leopard Cliffs", which has the added attraction of a **nature trail** and **picnic site** where you can leave your vehicle and disappear into the thickets for closer communion

FROM TOP KENYATTA AVENUE, NAIROBI (P.109); YELLOW-BILLED STORKS, LAKE MAGADI (P.153) >

1

with nature (there's usually an armed ranger on guard). As you're wandering, watch out for **crocodiles** in the river – to an untrained eye they can look very much like submerged logs – and **monkeys** in the bushes.

Cheetah Gate, in the far southeast of the park, is permanently closed, but it's worth driving down here to visit the lovely **Mokoyeti picnic site** at junction 14B, near the Leopard Cliffs where the Mokoyeti stream flows into the Mbagathi, just below Mbagathi gorge. This route gives you a chance to drive through the open savanna country favoured by **zebra** and **antelope**. Impossibly tall **giraffe** browse from the underside of flat-topped acacia trees; bevies of graceful, high-heeled **impalas** vault across the track ahead of your vehicle; stocky **eland** munch the sward; **ostriches** appear to float above the landscape like giant feather dusters; and fearsome phalanxes of **buffalo** turn and face you as you drive by.

Ivory Burning Site

If you're looking for a spot to **picnic**, head a couple of kilometres in from the main gate to the first fork. There's a shady site on the left, beside the **Ivory Burning Site**, the location of the 1989 public burning of twelve tonnes of ivory by President Moi to mark the start of a major, very successful offensive on ivory poaching and smuggling led by the then-director of the Kenya Wildlife Service, Dr Richard Leakey.

Big cats

If you arrive early, start if possible at the western end of the park, where most of the woodland is concentrated. If you're very lucky, this is where, just after dawn, you're most likely to see a **leopard**, perhaps back from a nocturnal foray into Langata, hunting for guard dogs. Such forays are becoming a bit of a problem: 2012 saw two lionesses on the loose in this affluent part of suburban Nairobi, one of which, with four cubs, was eventually shot by Kenya Wildlife Service rangers (the cubs were saved).

Lions, usually found in more open country, are generally best located by checking with the rangers at the gate: their excursions into suburban areas are blamed by some authorities on the high proportion of male lions in the park, causing vulnerable females with cubs to leave and pick on domestic animals and livestock. Such a scenario led to the killing, also in 2012, of two lionesses and four cubs in Kitengela, a densely populated area outside the southeast corner of the park, by Maasai youths who were incensed that their livestock had been attacked. With only around two thousand lions in the whole country, the killings caused a public outcry and also drew criticism for KWS for failing to respond quickly enough with a darting team.

There are usually a few **cheetahs** in the park, though seasonal long grass can make

---

THE NAIROBI MIGRATION

Until the end of the twentieth century, Nairobi National Park witnessed the second-largest **herbivore migration** after that of the Mara and Serengeti, with thousands of wildebeest and zebra streaming in from the south in July and August for the good grazing. Before 1946, when the park was created, only the physical barrier of Nairobi itself diverted what was a general northward migration on towards the Aberdare range and the foothills of Mount Kenya. The erection of fences along the park's northern perimeter closed that migration route, while the steady encroachment of housing, industry, farms and livestock grazing along the southern boundary is also tightening the **wildlife corridor** there. The wildebeest you see nowadays are mostly sedentary individuals that stay in the park all year, and the migration has been reduced, in most years, to a trickle. Conservationists are, however, determined to keep the southern corridor open, claiming that to fence the park (partly a response to fears about lion and rhino poaching) would effectively suffocate its ecosystem, which depends on free-ranging wildlife to be sustainable. The **Friends of Nairobi National Park** (☎0723 690686, ⊛fonnap.wordpress .com) have the full story on this and much more about the park.

seeing them very difficult and they are inclined to move in and out between the park and the big rangelands south of the built-up area around Athi River.

Rhinos

It's much easier than spotting spotted cats to see some of the park's **black rhinos**. Nairobi National Park has one of the largest populations anywhere in Kenya, attesting in part to the perseverance of the David Sheldrick Wildlife Trust (see below). You'll also see nice groups of the much more docile and approachable **white rhinos** (again, there are at least fifty), easily distinguished from the other species not by colour but by their grazing habits and wide (*weid* in Afrikaans) mouths; quite different from the hook-lipped features of the black rhino that likes to lurk in dense bush and uses its almost prehensile upper lip to browse trees and shrubs.

Birdlife

The park's **birdlife** is staggering: four hundred-plus species have been seen here, including migrant rarities from European latitudes as well as the rich local avifauna flitting and chattering all around – babblers, weavers, flycatchers and widow birds. Even if you're fresh off the plane and ornithologically illiterate, the first glimpses of ostrich, secretary bird, crowned crane and the outlandishly hideous marabou stork never fail to impress.

Animal Orphanage

Inside the Main Gate • Daily 8am–6pm • $25 • ☎ 020 2587411, ⊛ kws.org

Mainly intended for children, the **Animal Orphanage** is moderately interesting if you're fed up with seeing wildlife only from a distance. Here, a motley and shifting collection of waifs and strays, protected from nature, has for some years been allowed to regain strength before being released. That, anyway, was the idea, though many of the inmates seem to be established residents and it appears doubtful whether "this orphanage is not a zoo", as the sign claims. At least it's a zoo with a difference, with as many wild monkeys outside the cages as in them, and good opportunities for meeting and petting the tamer inmates.

Nairobi Safari Walk

Inside the Main Gate • Daily 9am–5.30pm • $25 • ☎ 020 2587437 or ☎ 020 2587435, ⊛ kws.org

More inspiring than the Animal Orphanage is the **Nairobi Safari Walk**. Showcasing Kenya's great ecological diversity, the walk simulates the country's wetlands, savanna and forest in a captivating, seminatural environment. This is the closest you can come to seeing captive animals behaving as they would in their natural habitats. The boardwalks to the open-air pens, observation points and platforms are clearly signposted and full of useful information about the animals.

David Sheldrick Wildlife Trust

Access via the park's Banda Gate, signposted "Sheldrick", a 5min drive (park fees are waived if you're only driving through to visit the DSWT orphanage) • Daily 11am–noon and, by private arrangement, from 4pm onwards for "foster parents" sponsoring a minimum of $50; office open Mon–Fri 9am–5pm • Ksh500 • ☎ 020 2301396, ⊛ sheldrickwildlifetrust.org

The **David Sheldrick Wildlife Trust** elephant and rhino orphanage, inside the western end of the park, offers a chance to see staff caring for **baby elephants**, and sometimes baby **rhino**, which have been orphaned by poachers, or have been lost or abandoned for natural reasons. The trust is run by Daphne Sheldrick in memory of her husband, the founding warden of Tsavo National Park, and, during the hour-long open house, the elephant keepers bring their juvenile charges up to an informal rope barrier where you can easily touch them and take photos.

After many years of trial and error, Sheldrick and her staff have become the world's experts on hand-rearing baby African elephants, sometimes from birth, using a special

1

milk formula for the youngest infants and assigning keepers to individual 24-hour guardianship of their charges, a responsibility that includes sleeping in their stables. Without the love of a surrogate family and plenty of stimulation, orphaned baby elephants fail to thrive: they can succumb to fatal infections when teething, and, even if they survive, can grow up disturbed and unhappy and badly prepared for reintroduction to the wild.

Rehabilitation is one of the Sheldrick Trust's major preoccupations. For rhinos, which mature at twice the speed of elephants, this involves a year or more of walks with their keeper, introducing the orphan's scent, via habitual dung middens and "urinal" bushes, to the wild population. Many of Nairobi National Park's rhinos grew up in the Sheldrick nursery; the last surviving member of Amboseli's famous long-horned rhino herd was rescued by the Trust in 1987 and is now a successful breeding female, having been released in Tsavo East. In the case of elephants, which mature at about the same rate as humans, the process of reintroduction is more attuned to the individual: outgoing animals are encouraged while young to meet wild friends and potential adoptive mothers, again through walks with their keepers, most often in Tsavo National Park. More traumatized elephants take longer to find their feet. Matriarchs who were Sheldrick orphans themselves, such as Eleanor at Tsavo East, have been responsible for adopting many returnees.

ARRIVAL AND INFORMATION   NAIROBI NATIONAL PARK

The park is accessible via the **Main Gate**, Langata Rd; **Langata Gate**, Magadi Rd; **East Gate**, Mombasa Rd (enabling you to avoid retracing your route from the park's western end if you're going to the airport or the CBD); **Banda Gate**, Magadi Rd (David Sheldrick Wildlife Trust only); and **Maasai Gate**, Ongata–Kitengela Rd. The Mbagathi Gate, Magadi Rd, and Cheetah Gate, Mombasa Rd, are closed to the public.

By matatu and hitchhiking Early birds can get an early #125 bus or #126 matatu from Nairobi to the main gate; after 7am you can use any bus or matatu going down Langata Rd. Once at the main gate, either hitch a lift (which may take some time), or, on the weekend, take the KWS park shuttle (Sat & Sun only; leaves from Development House, Tom Mboya St, at noon; $50).

By car You can self-drive in a rental car: 4WD is preferable, but not essential in dry weather, while a sat nav or a smartphone with GPS is useful for navigation.
Tours Any tour operator will fix you up with a half-day tour – try East Africa Shuttles (☏ 020 2248453, ⊚ eastafricashuttles.com), which charges $110 for 4hr, including park fee (see p.120).

ACCOMMODATION

Park **fees** are payable if you're staying at most of the following, but a huge benefit to overnighting in the park if you're using one of the airports is the dramatic reduction in driving time. East Gate is a reliable 15min drive from JKIA at any time of day, while Main Gate is just 5km from Wilson airport, or about an hour's drive in a worst-case scenario.

★**The Emakoko** Mbagathi Gorge, Nairobi National Park, accessed exclusively through the park ☏ 0774 309752, ⊚ emakoko.com (reservations ☏ 020 6000457, ⊚ bush-and-beyond.com); map p.103. Very attractive owner-managed designer lodge on the south side of the national park, on the banks of the Mbagathi River near the confluence of the Emakoko and Mokoyeti streams, with very large, light, cottage rooms, plus pool. Rates include very convenient airport transfers, game drives and drinks. Park fees payable. BB $\underline{\$760}$
KWS Twiga Campsite East Gate, Nairobi National Park (reservations – not normally necessary – with KWS ☏ 0726 610508, ✉ reservations@kws.go.ke); map p.103. Pleasant and secure campsite with good showers and toilets, cooking area and helpful rangers.

You will probably need a vehicle to camp here, as walking the 200m from the gate is not allowed. Park fees payable. Camping $\underline{\$20}$
Masai Lodge Just outside Nairobi National Park, between the Kiserian and Mbagathi gorges, less than 2km west of Maasai Gate, or accessible from Ongata Rongai ☏ 0736 160888 or ☏ 0774 160888, ⊚ maasailodge.com; map p.102. Minutes from the park, in a pre-eminent position in the steep, rocky valley of the Mbagathi, looking north across the gorge, this long-established lodge is looking a bit ragged these days and could use a bit of refurbishment. Still, it's cheaper than some of the other options in the area, with reasonable rooms (some with great views), a pool, well-stocked bar and a kitchen that needs plenty of advance notice (order

meals the day before). BB Ksh10,000

★**Nairobi Tented Camp** In the densely wooded western part of Nairobi National Park ☎0774 136523 or ☎0733 884298, ⓦnairobitentedcamp.com; map p.102. Traditional-style tented camp (the only one in the park) with top-notch meals in the lovely mess tent and excellent animal-spotters and guides available for 4WD game drives (extra). It's also very convenient for the DSWT elephant orphanage, just 5km away (see p.147). Rates include soft drinks. Park fees payable. BB $260

★**Silole Villa & Cottage** Above Kingfisher Gorge, Silole Sanctuary, outside Nairobi National Park, west of Maasai Gate ☎0721 646588, ⓦsilolesanctuary .com; map p.102. Set in a private, four-hundred-acre wildlife sanctuary that extends to the riverside boundary of the park. Choose between the three-bedroom villa (sleeping five), either self-catering or with private chef, plus all meals and soft drinks; and the purely self-catering, thatched cottage, with two s/c double rooms, plus loft space for adventurous kids to bed down. Whole cottage Ksh10,000, whole villa self-catering Ksh15,000, whole villa FB Ksh30,000

Ngong Hills

About 2km from Ngong police station • Daily dawn–dusk • Ksh500 (plus negotiable security escort fee) • Matatu or bus #111 or #126

The town of **NGONG**, the jumping-off point for the **Ngong Hills**, is 8km beyond Karen shopping centre; turn right after the police station in Ngong. If you have the chance, stop on the way at **Bulbul**, 4km from Karen, and take a look at the pretty mosque of this largely Muslim village. As often happened in Kenya, Islam spread here through the settlement of discharged troops from other British-ruled territories, in this case from Nubia in Sudan. Ngong itself is basically just a small junction town with limited shops and services and the rough D523 road trailing out to the west towards the Maasai Mara.

The Ngong Hills are revered by the Maasai, who have several traditional explanations of how they were formed. The best-known says that a giant, stumbling north with his head in the clouds, tripped on Kilimanjaro. Thundering to the ground, his hand squeezed the earth into the Ngongs' familiar, knuckled outline. An even more momentous story explains the Ngongs as the bits of dirt left under God's fingernails after he'd finished creating the earth.

The walk along the sharp spine of the Ngong Hills was once a popular weekend hike and picnic outing, easily feasible in a day, although, unfortunately, the hills got a reputation for muggings in the 1980s, curtailing independent expeditions, and KWS rangers usually now provide an **escort** (negotiable, from Ksh3000/ranger for the day). The views, of Nairobi on one side and the Rift Valley on the other, are magnificent, and despite the wind farm at the northern end of the hills, the forested slopes are still inhabited by buffalo and various species of antelope. With a car – and it has to be 4WD if it's been raining – you can get to the summit, **Point Lamwia** (2459m), which offers a 360-degree view. If you want to walk, and are reasonably fit, allow a minimum of three hours to get to the top and back to your car. Alternatively, you could organize transport to meet you west of Kiserian, on the C58 Magadi road, and spend four to five hours traversing the length of the peaks, a walk of about 15km.

On the ridges below the summit, on privately owned land, almost due east of the highest point, is the **Finch Memorial**, Karen Blixen's tribute to the man who took her flying.

North of Nairobi

North of the city the land is distinctive, with narrow valleys twisting up into the Kinangop plateau, some still filled with jungle and, it's said, leopards. In spite of that, the steep slopes here are high-value real estate, still being developed as exclusive suburbs, planted with shady gardens and festooned with security signs. To the **northwest** lies largely Kikuyu farmland, densely cultivated with corn, bananas, tea and the cash crop insecticide plant, pyrethrum.

1

Brown's Cheese Farm

Tigoni, 21km northwest of Village Market (map p.100) • Thurs–Sat 12.30–4pm (advance booking essential) • Ksh3600/person for a minimum of six people, including cheese tasting and a three-course lunch • ☎ 0728 999654, ⓦ brownscheese.com • Coming from Nairobi, turn left off the road to Tigoni just beyond the Kentmere Club; the farm is about 100m down this road

Brown's Cheese Farm, an artisanal family cheese-maker, has cracked the art of producing something exceptional while making its production the basis for a fascinating visit. You can buy a huge variety of their cheeses here, too. Cheese, which you quickly learn is all about keeping the harvest season's calories for the lean season, is created here using biodynamic principles. The explanation of the process rolls around as you stroll through the admirably cottage-sized factory from the warm steel milk pans to the deliciously mysterious storage rooms. Tours finish in the family dining room overlooking the biodynamic kitchen garden, where everything grows by the principles set out by Rudolf Steiner (no artificial additives, planting with the moon and no tilling or weeding, everything being dug back in). Guests sample a slate of delicious **cheese morsels** with home-made crackers and a glass or two of wine, followed by an excellent three-course **lunch**: you really should skip breakfast if you're visiting Brown's.

Kiambethu Tea Farm

Tigoni, 22km northwest of Village Market (map p.100) • Lunch and afternoon tea (advance booking essential) Ksh3000/person (minimum four people) • ☎ 0729 290894 or ☎ 0733 769976, ⓦ kiambethufarm.co.ke • Coming from Nairobi, turn right off the road to Tigoni at the Kenchic processing plant, then drive past Limuru Girls' school; the farm is on the left

A visit to the working **Kiambethu Tea Farm** gives you the opportunity to sample the charmingly time-warped settler lifestyle (albeit a third-generation, naturalized one) over a very good lunch. The farmhouse is set in a glorious highland garden, with sweeping lawns and a colourful riot of flowers and tropical birds. To work up an appetite you take a stroll with the owners up the lane, past bushes full of chameleons to the edge of one of the tea fields, where a swathe of neatly plucked shrubs plunges into the valley. A little further, there's a relict patch of highland rainforest – standing proud in a sea of tea bushes – where you'll be escorted on a short forest walk, during which you've a good chance of seeing some of Kiambethu's resident colobus monkeys.

Southeast of Nairobi

Until a couple of decades ago, **Athi River**, 25km southeast of Nairobi, consisted of a train station and the Kenya Meat Commission processing plant. Then the real-estate marketeers got to work and suddenly the dusty plains around the river became a desirable commuter neighbourhood. But the meat factory was still there, and so the developers invented the new suburb of **Kitengela**, a few kilometres further south, beyond the smell of the factory, where Maasai herders roamed and the wildebeest and gazelle herds – and the odd cheetah – moved in and out of the Nairobi National Park.

Today, driving into Kitengela up the A104 from the Tanzanian border, the new town is a harbinger of Nairobi: what was Maasai pasture lands in the 1990s has become a wide main street lined with canteens, petrol stations and soaring apartment blocks, as well as unplanned shanties. Just as well, then, that a few kilometres outside this burgeoning residential zone, the **Lukenya Plains** are still home to cheetah and most other plains species, and they have some protection in the shape of **Swara Plains Sanctuary** – a former game ranch (see opposite).

★**Acacia Camp Swara Plains** 11km southeast of the Kitengela junction (turning for the A104 Namanga and Arusha), turn right at Small World (see below) and follow signs ☎0723 557914 or ☎0717 062855, ⓦswaraplains.com; map p.100. The former Hopcraft Ranch, which once supplied game meat to *Carnivore* (see p.134), is now a wildlife conservancy roamed by wildebeest, giraffe and zebra, and offers the perfect solution if you want to avoid Nairobi on your first or last night. Spacious s/c *bandas*, with decent bathrooms (get a renovated one), nets, electricity and plug sockets, encircle a pretty garden, with a pleasant bar-restaurant to one side. Casual meals are available (Ksh1500–2000) – the food is surprisingly good, though

you should call a day in advance to book. Overnight camping and *banda* rates include the conservancy fee of Ksh600/person. Camping Ksh1600, BB Ksh 8500

Small World 11km beyond the Kitengela junction (turning for Namanga and Arusha), signposted on the south side of the highway at the entrance to Swara Plains ranch (see above) ☎0734 818340, ⓦklubhouse.co.ke; map p.100. A perfectly OK place to spend the night, either as a prelude to driving straight to Tsavo or Mombasa the next morning or because you left it too late to reach Nairobi. The small s/c cottages have double beds and there's also wi-fi, a garden restaurant and bar, plus live music some weekends. Bed only Ksh4000

The southern Rift Valley

The journey south from Nairobi down into the hot, sparsely inhabited southern districts of the **Rift Valley** takes you first to the prehistoric site at **Olorgasailie**, then on to the dramatic salt lake of **Magadi**, and finally to the **Nguruman Escarpment** and the remote nature conservancy at **Shompole**. The scenery opens out dramatically as you skirt the southern flank of the Ngong Hills and descend steeply down the escarpment; if you're travelling by public transport, try to get a front seat, as giraffe and other animals are often seen.

Kiserian and around

KISERIAN, 15km southwest of Nairobi National Park's main gate, is your last chance to buy decent provisions, as there's not much available further south. Once a tiny Maasai trading post tucked below the Ngong Hills, Kiserian is now the final gasp of Nairobi's sprawling suburbs, barely separated from **Ongata** – the burgeoning dormitory suburb south of Karen. The drive south from here, over the southern spine of the Ngongs, is truly spectacular.

ACCOMMODATION AND EATING   KISERIAN AND AROUND

There are several basic **B&Ls** in the centre of Kiserian, or you can head east to *Whistling Thorns* or the Ostrich Farm Resort or press on to Olepolos. There's a pleasant picnic site at *Olepolos Country Club* some 12km southwest of Kiserian.

Eureka Hotel Town centre, Kiserian ☎0720 819165; map p.100. A lively restaurant and bar set in a garden, serving local dishes for around Ksh300, with occasional live music and decent (if small) s/c rooms around a courtyard in back. Alternately, you can pitch a tent in a field nearby. Camping for two Ksh1000, BB Ksh1700

Olepolos Country Club Magadi road, Olepolos, 13km southwest of Kiserian ☎0714 032122, ⓦbit.ly/OlepolosCountryClub; map p.100. Pleasant rural picnic and camping site, *nyama choma* garden (goat meat Ksh800/kg) and bar (sometimes with live music and Maasai dancers) on a hillside with fantastic views out over the southern Rift Valley. There are also adequate rooms, which enjoy great views as well. Camping Ksh500, BB Ksh4000

Ostrich Farm Resort Maasai Ostrich Farm (go 21km southeast of Kiserian junction on the Isinya road then turn left and take the farm road a further 10km; also accessible from Athi River) ☎0733 140141, ⓦmaasaiostrich.com; map p.100. A curious combination of ostrich farm and Kenyan-country-club-style resort, incorporating pleasant, shady gardens with very overpriced s/c tented chalets with electric showers, and a glittering swimming pool, usually accompanied by country music warbling from speakers through the trees. As well as touring the farm and eating the excellent but pricey low-cholesterol meat, you can also ride the birds (Ksh500 during the week, Ksh300 on the weekend), though the warning that "Maasai Ostrich Resort is not liable for any incident that may occur

1

during riding" is probably enough to deter most would-be ostrich jockeys. Camping Ksh1000, BB Ksh10,450

★**Whistling Thorns** 12km southeast of Kiserian junction on the Isinya road ☎0722 721933, ⓦwhistlingthorns.com; map p.100. Very pretty country guesthouse, campsite, gardens and restaurant that could practically be in Wales or Oregon if it wasn't for the Maasai jewellery for sale and the prospect of running into wandering elephants in the neighbourhood (a herd walked

up here from Amboseli in 2012). The rooms, which range from cottages to safari tents, are basic but comfortable, and the whole setup is so relaxing that they're worth every penny; the food, if somewhat hit or miss, is hard to dislike when eaten on the terrace overlooking the garden and delightful swimming pool. There's lots of variety on the menu, including fish, coconut chicken and veggie options (Ksh800–1500), good desserts and a reasonably priced bar. Camping Ksh800, room only Ksh5000

Olorgasailie Prehistoric Site

Signposted 3km south of Oltepesi, then 1.6km from the main road • Daily dawn–dusk • Ksh500 • ⓦ museums.or.ke

Between 400,000 and 500,000 years ago, the wide, shallow lake east of what is now **Olorgasailie Prehistoric Site** was inhabited by a species of hominin, probably *Homo erectus* of the Acheulian culture (after St Acheul in France, where it was first discovered). The site is endowed with numerous pathways, boardwalks and informative signs, and is a peaceful place to stay, though most people just stop here for an hour or two. The guided tour around the excavations (included in the entrance charge; tip welcomed) is not to be missed. The museum and accommodation are just above the excavations, on a ridge overlooking the former lake.

The **early people** who lived at Olorgasailie made a range of identifiable stone tools: cleavers for skinning animals; round balls for crushing bones, perhaps for hurling or possibly tied to vines to be used, like gauchos, as *bolas*; and heavy hand axes, for which the culture is best known, but for which, as Richard Leakey writes, "embarrassingly, no one can think of a good use." The guides tell you they were used for chopping meat and digging. This seems reasonable, but some are very large, while hundreds of others (particularly at the so-called "factory site") seem far too small, the theory being that they were made by youngsters, practising their toolmaking.

Mary and Louis Leakey's team did most of the unearthing here in the 1940s. Thousands of the **stone tools** they found have been left undisturbed, *in situ*, under protective roofs. Perhaps the most impressive find, however, is the fossilized leg bone of an extinct **giant elephant**, dwarfing a similar bone from a modern elephant placed next to it. It was long hoped that human remains would also be uncovered at Olorgasailie, but despite extensive digging none has been found – providing more scope for speculation.

Today, sitting with a pair of binoculars and looking out over what used to be the lake can yield some rewarding **animal-watching**, especially in the brief dusk. Go for a walk out past the excavations towards the gorge and you may see baboons, duiker, giraffe, eland and even gerenuk if you're lucky – Olorgasailie is the westernmost extent of their range in southern Kenya.

ARRIVAL AND DEPARTURE · · · · · · · · · · · · OLORGASAILIE PREHISTORIC SITE

By matatu If you don't have your own transport, find out when the next matatu along the road between Lake Magadi and Nairobi will be passing by, as they are few and far between.

By car If you're driving, bear in mind that the road from Kiserian to Oltepesi, which marks the end of the steep descent to the Rift Valley floor, is badly potholed. Thereafter it's reasonably smooth for most of the way to Magadi.

ACCOMMODATION

Olorgasailie Bandas Olorgasailie Prehistoric Site ⓦmuseums.or.ke; map p.100. Simple *bandas* – four new and presentable with twin beds, bedding, nets and kerosene lamps; four old and decrepit with beds and bedding only. Separate tepid shower and long-drop toilet

blocks are also available, plus a couple of sit-down loos for site visitors. Maasai women sell firewood for Ksh200–300/bundle, but that is the only commodity available on site apart from occasional sodas. Camping Ksh600, old *bandas* Ksh1800, new *bandas* Ksh2000

SHOPPING

Contacts with Maasai are good at Olorgasailie and there's jewellery for sale under a sponsored shelter. You can cultivate further friendships – and collect some scant provisions – at the cluster of desolate *dukas* at **Oltepesi**, 3km back along the Nairobi road, where they also have warm beer and soft drinks.

Lake Magadi and around

Lying in a Rift Valley depression 1000m below Nairobi, **Lake Magadi** (ⓦlakemagadi .com) is a vast shallow pool of soda (sodium carbonate), a sludge of alkaline water and crystal trona deposits, and one of the hottest places in the country. Magadi is also the second-largest source of soda in the world, after the Salton Sea in the US. At Magadi, the Magadi Soda Company – formerly an ICI business, now owned by the Indian company Tata – operates the very model of a **company town**, on a barren spit of land jutting out across the multicoloured soda. The company's investment here is guaranteed – hot springs gush out of the earth's crust to provide an inexhaustible supply of briney water for evaporation. Everything you see, apart from the homes of a few Maasai on the shore, is owned and run by the corporation. You pass a company police barrier where you sign in and enter over a causeway, past surreal pink salt ponds, often crowded with flamingos. Now on company territory, visitors are advised by a sign that "it is dangerous to walk across the lake surface", just in case you were contemplating a stroll across the soda. Note that some of the company police are touchy about you taking photos of the factory installations. Despite this, the atmosphere here, somewhat surprisingly because of the nature of the work and harshness of the environment, is relaxed and welcoming. By comparison with the rest of Kenya, the company pays its seven hundred staff high wages, starting at around Ksh40,000 per month; people tend to get drunk a lot, and staff accommodation and many services are free.

Many visitors come to Magadi specifically for its **birdlife**. There's a wealth of avifauna here, including, usually, large numbers of flamingos at the southern end of the lake. At this end, there are also freshwater swamps, which attract many species.

Around the lake

The lake lies behind the police station, which stands on the highest point of the peninsula. If you look the other way (to the west), the road to the left leads to the "management" end of town, where a dozen or so senior staff live in shady villas and where there's a strange, barren golf course; to the right, the town slopes gently down to a crusty shore where most of the Kenyan employees live in gaunt blocks of apartments. There's also a church, a mosque, schools and a swimming pool, poolside bar and *nyama choma* kiosk.

For most of the year, on the eastern side where you first arrive, you can watch the **sweepers** in rubber boots shovelling the by-product, sodium chloride, or common salt, into ridges on the technicolour "fields" (after heavy rain, the dilute solution removes the need for manual labour in the lake and all the work is done by dredging machines). Common salt crystallizes on top of the sodium carbonate, and is then loaded onto tractor-drawn trailers and taken away to be purified for human and animal consumption.

Magadi **soda**, used principally for glass-making, is Kenya's most valuable mineral resource. The dried soda is exported, first by rail to Mombasa via Kajiado and Konza, thence, much of it, to Japan. Despite the relatively high wages, however, you wonder how anyone can be persuaded to work in this lurid inferno: the first rains here are usually so-called phantom rain, the ground so hot that the raindrops evaporate before hitting the surface. It's important to wear sunglasses and a hat while out in the sun, and bring plenty of drinking water.

1

Magadi hot springs
Ksh1000, plus Ksh1000 to camp, plus Ksh1000 for a guide

With your own vehicle you can drive south from Magadi town, around the lake to the **hot springs** in the southwest corner. You'll be stopped at the checkpoint outside Magadi Sports Club on the way out of town and asked to pay the admission fee, plus camping or guide fees (a guide is optional, but recommended if you don't already know the way).

It's a further, straightforward 14–15km to the hot springs, reached by driving south along the eastern shore of the lake. The precise route you take will depend on how much water is flowing into the lake from the higher ground to the south. Depending on the time of year, you'll be able to cut across sandy, desert-like areas, following other vehicle tracks, but don't venture onto unknown surfaces without a good guide.

At the **hot springs**, you'll be able to park near the water's edge and camp nearby if you are fully equipped. Local Maasai will appear to sell jewellery. The springs bubble up into the shallow waters of the lake itself and create deep pockets of perfectly mixed bathing water. Do take great care to find the right spot, however, and don't attempt to bathe without getting clear confirmation that it is safe to do so.

The **birdlife** here is fascinating, and if you're a photographer you will delight in the contrast of pink flamingos, shimmering water and the austere, background landscape.

Shompole Conservancy

From the Magadi hot springs, you can drive west to the Ewaso Nyiro River at the foot of the Ol Choroi plateau, also known as the **Nguruman Escarpment**. Forget about trying to take a 4WD up the rough track beyond the river, over the escarpment and on to the Mara. People have done that in the past, but the whole area is privately owned Maasai land and, for the moment at least, not accessible.

This whole area focuses around the 142-square-kilometre **Shompole Conservancy**, an ecotourism venture involving the Maasai Shompole Group Ranch. Access to the highly appealing *Shompole Lodge* is usually by chartered plane to their private **airstrip**, but the lodge closed in 2011 after a dispute with the community, and it's not clear when it will reopen.

If you have a guide it's straightforward enough to drive right **around the lake** up the west shore, joining the Magadi–Nguruman road after 18km. You then drive east on the good gravel road back to Lake Magadi, crossing the northwest arm of the lake on a causeway and driving right through the industrial part of town – a fascinating clash of railway tracks and furnaces, rusting pipework and traditionally dressed Maasai.

ARRIVAL AND DEPARTURE

LAKE MAGADI

By matatu There are matatus between Magadi town and Nairobi (2 daily; 3hr) and Olorgasailie (2 daily; 1hr). The first matatu to Nairobi leaves at 5am. There are no regular vehicles south of Magadi. Everyone waits for lifts either in a passing vehicle, or on the back of a motorbike. If you don't have your own transport, you should wait in town and see what turns up.

By car Apart from along the main Magadi–Nguruman road (which isn't much used and is in good condition), driving south of the lake it's best to go with a guide: even with GPS, the tracks change so often that you shouldn't rely on satellite imagery or previous tracks – routes around the lakeshore and across areas that have dried out are very unpredictable.

INFORMATION AND TOURS

Services There's a Co-operative Bank with ATM on Duka Hill Rd, in the building behind the Total station. Note that there's very patchy mobile coverage in this part of Kenya.

Tours Magadi Adventures (☎ 0717 999228), the Magadi company's tourism wing, organizes custom tours of the area that can include a game drive, a visit to the hot springs and a return trip from Nairobi, part of which involves a special single-carriage train organized by the company. Two-day tours cost around Ksh12,000/person.

ACCOMMODATION AND EATING

MAGADI TOWN

There is really only one hotel in Magadi, run, as is everything else, by the company. If you're fully self-sufficient, you could possibly camp almost anywhere south of the town (pay your camping fee of Ksh1000/ person at the Magadi Sports Club), but it's baking hot during the day and a favourite haunt for baboons, so hardly ideal territory; a better option is to pitch your tent at the hot springs, or near the *MSC*'s safari tents (see below). For provisions and limited fresh food, Magadi has barely any shops, but there is a daily market. On the western shore of the lake, local Maasai will sell you *pombe* (bush brew), fermented from a base of roots, herbs and honey. It's a lot cheaper than beer, and stronger, too.

Magadi Sports Club (MSC) Southern end of Magadi town, reservations through the company ☎0717 999228 or ☎0735 604796, ⍟lakemagadi.com. The only option in town for proper rooms, which are comfortable enough with nets and a/c. There's also a bar-restaurant and a nice swimming pool in the garden; if you're not staying here you'll be charged a Ksh500 temporary membership fee to eat or swim. The *MSC* also runs a slightly regimented camp of a/c safari tents (s/c) a further 1km out of town, where you'll find fewer amenities but a better view. Room reservations essential. Safari tents **Ksh3000**, BB **Ksh6000**

New Flamingo Club Southern side of Magadi town, signposted east of the road ☎020 6999280. Local watering hole popular with old Maasai men nursing bottles of cheap booze, with food (around Ksh300) available if ordered well in advance and a pleasant enough terrace. Daily 8.30am–1am.

Swimming Pool Club Magadi town centre. A lower-key option than the *MSC* for rest and recuperation, with decent *hoteli* food (Ksh150–300) and ample cold sodas and beers (Ksh150) to consume on the terrace, not to mention the large, somewhat murky pool – it's Ksh100 to swim, if you can find someone to unlock the gate. Daily 6am–midnight.

SHOMPOLE CONSERVANCY

Loisiijo Lodge Shompole Conservancy ☎020 3533338 or ☎0722 515377, ⍟loisiijolodgeshompole.org; map p.100. While *Shompole Lodge* remains closed, this is the only accommodation inside Shompole Conservancy. The former *Shompole Bandas* have been revamped as a beautiful self-catering or catered lodge tucked under fig trees on the banks of the Ewaso Nyiro, sleeping a total of fifteen people. If you're self-catering, you get the services of a cook and other staff included, but unless you book the whole lodge ($485/night) you can only confirm a stay within 48 hours of arrival. Self-catering **$100**, FB (minimum two-night stay) **$290**

The Central Highlands

TRIBAL DANCERS, KATARINA

The Central Highlands

Travelling through the Central Highlands, Kenya's political and economic heartland, offers some great rewards. Mount Kenya, Africa's second-highest peak, gave the colonial nation its name and presents plenty of scope for hiking. Walks lower down and in the Aberdare range are easier but still dramatic, with better chances of seeing wildlife. Travel itself is never dull here, and the range of scenery is a spectacular draw in its own right: primary-coloured jungle and *shambas*, pale, windswept moors and dense conifer plantations, all with a mountain backdrop. People everywhere are friendly and quick to strike up a conversation, the towns are animated and the markets colourfully chaotic. Most roads are in good shape, and bus and matatu journeys are invariably packed with interest and amusement.

After the main game-viewing areas and the coast, the circuit provided by the **Mount Kenya ring road** is one of the most travelled in Kenya, and there are always a few tourist vehicles to be seen. Apart from the high forests, moors and peaks, little of this remains wild country, with *shambas* steadily encroaching upon the ridges. The Kikuyu, Meru and Embu peoples have created an extraordinary spectacle of cultivation on the steep slopes, gashed by the road to reveal brilliant red earth.

As you travel, the mountain is a constant, looming presence, even if you can't often see much of it. With a base 80km across, Mount Kenya is one of the largest free-standing volcanic cones in the world. The twin peaks are normally obscured by clouds, but early in the morning and just before sunset the shroud can vanish suddenly, leaving them magically exposed for a few minutes. To the east and south, the mountain drops steeply away to the broad expanse of Ukambani (Kamba-land) and the Tana River basin. Westwards, and to the north, it slopes away more gently to the rolling uplands of Laikipia.

The **Aberdare range**, which peaks at 4001m, is less well known than Mount Kenya. The lower, eastern slopes have long been farmed by the Kikuyu (and more recently by European tea and coffee planters), and the dense mountain forests covering the middle reaches are the habitat of leopard, buffalo, some six thousand elephants and a few small herds of critically endangered bongo antelope. Above about 3500m, lions and other open-country animals roam the cloudy moorlands. Melanistic forms, especially of leopard, but also of serval cat and even bushbuck, are also present.

The park stretches 60km along the length of the peaks, with the Salient on the lower slopes reaching out east. Like Mount Kenya National Park, it attracts the worst of the weather: rainfall up here is high, often closing the park to vehicles in the wet season, although in the Salient the "tree-hotel" **game lodges** – *The Ark* and *Treetops* – stay open all year. The towns of **Naivasha** and **Nyeri** are the usual bases. **Nyahururu**, the other important town in the region, has **Thomson's Falls** as a postcard attraction, and is also the setting-off point for a wild cross-country journey to Lake Bogoria, 1500m below in the Rift Valley (see p.234). Also from Nyahururu begins the main route to Maralal and Loiyangalani on the eastern shore of Lake Turkana (see p.516).

MOUNT KENYA

Highlights

❶ **Sagana River rafting** Test the class III, IV and V whitewater rapids and bungee jump above Kenya's longest river. **See p.166**

❷ **Trout Tree** Enjoy delicious fresh fish and a treehouse setting among fig trees at this quirky restaurant. **See p.169**

❸ **Climbing Mount Kenya** Africa's second-highest mountain is a highly recommended trekking area, with various routes and diverse flora and fauna. **See p.170**

❹ **Nanyuki** Good hotels and restaurants, a beautiful climate and one of the most agreeable small towns in Kenya. **See p.180**

❺ **Animal orphanage** Find a century-old tortoise, rare, breeding bongos, and Liberian pygmy hippos at the Mount Kenya Wildlife Conservancy. **See p.180**

❻ **Aberdare range** Sensational views and a particularly good chance of seeing elephants and buffaloes in a compelling highland environment. **See p.190**

❼ **Horseriding** Take a guided equestrian tour of Mount Kenya's lush green foothills – Sandai offers guided tours and there are a number of other options in and around the area. **See p.197**

HIGHLIGHTS ARE MARKED ON THE MAP ON P.160

2

KENYA'S HIGHLAND FORESTS AND MOORS

Kenya's main **highland forests** are on mounts Kenya, Elgon and Marsabit, on the Aberdare range and on the Mau Escarpment. The characteristic natural landscape in the highlands is patches of evergreen trees separated by vast meadows of grasses – often wire grass and Kikuyu grass. The true highland forest, typically found only above 1500m, contains different species of trees from lowland forest, and does not normally grow as tall or dense. Typical species include camphor, *Juniperus procera* (the East African "cedar") and *Podocarpus*. The better-developed forests are found on the wetter, western slopes of the highlands. Above the forest line, at altitudes of 2500m and higher, are stands of giant bamboo, while along the lower, drier edges of the highlands, the stands of trees tend to be interspersed with fields of tall grass, where commonly you also find various species of olive.

Brief history

The Central Highlands are utterly central to Kenyan history. The majority of British and European settlers carved their farms from the countryside around Mount Kenya. Later, and as a direct consequence, this was the region that saw the development of organized anti-colonial resistance culminating in Mau Mau.

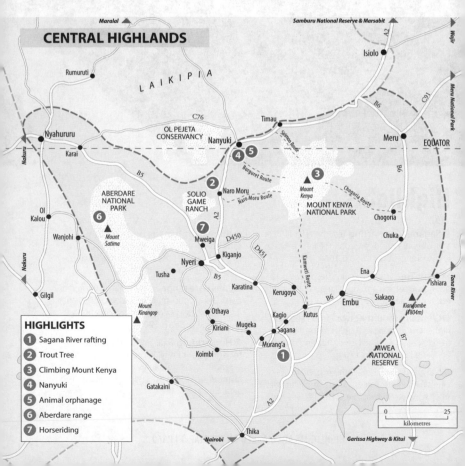

CENTRAL HIGHLANDS

Maralal

Samburu National Reserve & Marsabit

Wajir

A2

Isiolo

Rumuruti

L A I K I P I A

Meru National Park

C91

B6

C76

Timau

OL PEJETA CONSERVANCY

Nyahururu

Nanyuki

Meru

EQUATOR

Karai

Sirimon Route

B6

B5

Burguret Route

Mount Kenya

2 Naro Moru

3

Chogoria Route

ABERDARE NATIONAL PARK

SOLIO GAME RANCH

Naro Moru Route

MOUNT KENYA NATIONAL PARK

Chogoria

Ol Kalou

6

A2

7

Chuka

Wanjohi

Mount Satima

Mweiga

D450

Kamweti Route

Kiganjo

D451

Nyeri

Ena

Ishiara

Tusha

B5

Tana River

Gilgil

Karatina

Kerugoya

B6

Mount Kinangop

Othaya

Kagio

Siakago

Kiangombe (1804m)

Embu

Kutus

Kiriani

Mugeka

Sagana

B7

Koimbi

Murang'a

1

MWEA NATIONAL RESERVE

Gatakaini

A2

HIGHLIGHTS

1 Sagana River rafting
2 Trout Tree
3 Climbing Mount Kenya
4 Nanyuki
5 Animal orphanage
6 Aberdare range
7 Horseriding

0   25
kilometres

Nairobi

Thika

Garissa Highway & Kitui

Until independence, the fertile highland soils ("A more charming region is not to be found in all Africa," thought Joseph Thomson, exploring in the 1880s) were reserved largely for Europeans and considered, in Governor Eliot's breathtaking phrase, "White Man's Country". The **Kikuyu peoples**, skilled farmers and herders, had held the land for several centuries before the Europeans arrived. They were at first mystified to find themselves "squatters" on land whose ownership, in the sense of exclusive right, had never been an issue in traditional society. They were certainly not alone in losing land, but, by supplying most of the "Mau Mau" fighters for the Land and Freedom Army (see p.564), they were placed squarely in the political

2

THE KIKUYU

The ancestors of the **Kikuyu** migrated to the Central Highlands between the sixteenth and eighteenth centuries, from northeast of Mount Kenya. Stories describe how they found various hunter-gatherer peoples already in the region (the **Gumba** on the plains and the **Athi** in the forests), and a great deal of intermarriage, trade and adoption took place. The newcomers cleared the forests and planted crops, giving the hunters gifts of livestock, honey or wives in return for using the land.

Likewise, there was trade and intermarriage between the Kikuyu and the **Maasai**, both peoples placing high value on cattle ownership, with the Maasai depending entirely on livestock. During bad droughts, Maasai would raid Kikuyu herds, with retaliation at a later date being almost inevitable. But such **intertribal warfare** often had long-term benefits, as ancient debts were forever being renegotiated and paid off by both sides, thus sustaining the relationship. Married Kikuyu women enjoyed a special immunity that enabled them to organize trading expeditions deep into Maasai-land, often with the help of a *hinga*, a middleman, to oil the wheels.

Like the Maasai, the Kikuyu advanced in status as they grew older, through named age-sets and rituals still important today. For Kikuyu boys, **circumcision** marks the important transition into adulthood (female circumcision, or clitoridectomy, is illegal and rarely performed today). In the past, boys would grow their hair and dye it with ochre in the style of Maasai warriors (in fact, the Maasai got their ochre from the Kikuyu, so it may really have been the other way around). They also wore glass beads around their necks, metal rings on their legs and arms, and stretched their ear lobes with earplugs. Women wore a similar collection of ornaments, and between initiation and marriage, a headband of beads and discs, still worn today by most Maasai women.

Traditionally, the Kikuyu had no centralized **authority**. The elders of a district would meet as a council and disputes or important decisions would be dealt with in public, with a party to follow. After their deaths, elders – now known as ancestors – continued to be respected and consulted. Christianity has altered beliefs in the last few decades, though many churchgoers still believe strongly in an **ancestor world** where the dead have powers over their living descendants. The Kikuyu traditionally believed that the most likely abode of God (Ngai), or at least his frequent resting place, was Mount Kenya, which they called **Kirinyaga** (Place of Brightness). Accordingly, they used to build their houses with the door always looking out towards the mountain, hence the title of Jomo Kenyatta's book, *Facing Mount Kenya*.

Today, the Kikuyu are at the forefront of Kenyan **development** and, despite entrenched nepotism, are accorded grudging respect as successful business people, skilled media operators and formidable politicians. There is considerable political rivalry between the Kiambu Kikuyu of the tea- and coffee-growing district north of Nairobi and the Nyeri Kikuyu, based in the fertile area of Othaya who rely on a more mixed economy.

The **GEMA** (Gikuyu, Embu and Meru Association), created in 1971 to further Kikuyu interests, at first concerned itself primarily with countering Daniel Arap Moi's ascent to the presidency, and although it was banned in 1980, it is believed to continue to operate clandestinely throughout Kenya.

The emergence in Kikuyuland in the early 2000s of the secret and violent **Mungiki** cult, somewhat modelled after the colonial era's Mau Mau independence movement but based primarily around extortion and gangster operations rather than emancipation, brought terror to slum districts in parts of Central Kenya. In a twist of jaw-dropping chutzpah, its leader escaped justice, declaring himself a born-again Christian. He is now wooed by mainstream politicians, while Mungiki has become a deeply corrupting force within the political process.

limelight. In return, they received a large proportion of what used to be known as the "Fruits of Independence". Today, most of the land is in African hands again, and it supports the country's largest rural population. There's intensive farming on almost all the lower slopes and much of the higher ground as well, beneath the national parks of Mount Kenya and the Aberdare.

Thika

THIKA, a bustling Nairobi satellite just off the main road to Mount Kenya, is not redeemed by the profusion of flame trees you might expect from its famous literary connection, Elspeth Huxley's *The Flame Trees of Thika*, recording her family's move there in 1913. It's a surprisingly laidback, friendly sort of place, with a bit of light manufacturing, but best known for its pineapples. The fruit was introduced in 1905 and thousands of acres flourish here, mostly owned by Del Monte and easily confused with the sisal also grown in the area.

The town centre is compact and straightforward, although there are no major attractions. If you're passing through, it's worth visiting the **Blue Post hotel**, where the grounds include a small **zoo** (Ksh100), the best viewpoints for the **Chania and Thika Falls**, a clutch of well-stocked, competitively priced **curio shops** and a small children's playground and boating pond.

ARRIVAL AND DEPARTURE

By car The completion of an eight-lane superhighway connecting Nairobi and Thika has eased congestion along this route – the 50km drive should take around 1hr. The road narrows to one lane after Thika but remains in good condition until past Nyeri.

By bus and matatu Frequent buses and matatus ply the busy Nairobi–Thika route (1hr). Matatu stands line the highway at all major junctions. Most buses and matatus carry on to Murang'a (1hr), Embu (1hr 30min), Nyeri (1hr 30 min) and Naro Moru (2hr).

INFORMATION

Services ATMs include those at Barclays and Standard Chartered, and other services include the Netstop Cyber Café (Mon–Sat 7am–8pm; Sun 11am–7pm) on Uhuru St, a Tuskys supermarket (Mon–Sat 7.30am–9pm, Sun 8.30am–8pm) also on Uhuru St, The Chemists pharmacy (Mon–Sat 8am–6pm, Sun 9am–4pm; ☎0701 882396), and a market east of the town centre, past the street stalls at the stadium roundabout.

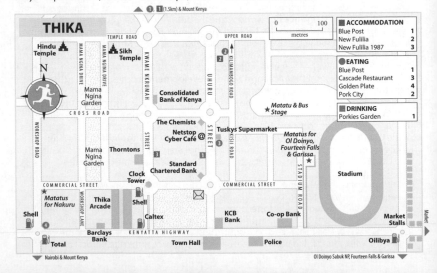

ACCOMMODATION

Blue Post Just to the east of the Nairobi–Murang'a road, 1.3km north of the turning to downtown Thika ☎0725 999538 or ☎0721 578245, ✉bph.info @heritagehotels.co.ke. Dating from 1908, older than Thika itself, this has modest, tourist-class rooms, with good nets and small TVs, though they're overpriced. Coming from Nairobi, take the slip road signposted "Thika Coffee Mills 3km" and traverse the A2 on the flyover to reach the hotel. The relatively primitive bathrooms do have instant showers but no tubs, and don't expect hot water in your basin. Room only `Ksh5100`

New Fulilia Uhuru St ☎0720 003863. Reasonably clean lodgings right in the centre of town, though the fifty-odd rooms are small and dark, and only one has two beds. There's a frenetic bar downstairs, plus *nyama choma* and a decent *hoteli*. Room only `Ksh900`

New Fulilia 87 Kwame Nkrumah St ☎0711 331892. A more basic alternative to its sister establishment, this noisy courtyard-style B&L has plenty of small, windowless singles on offer with electric showers and nets, but only a couple of rooms with two beds. There's also a busy, ground-floor *hoteli* and second-floor bar. Room only `Ksh800`

EATING

Blue Post Just to the east of the Nairobi–Murang'a road, 1.3km north of the turning to downtown Thika ☎0725 999538 or ☎0721 578245. Popular local venue, especially at weekends, with its tables on the lawns and sweeping views of the Chania and Thika Falls. The restaurant offers good lunchtime buffets (Ksh1500) and various dinner dishes like goat chops (Ksh700) and vegetable lasagne (Ksh400). Daily 6.30am–11pm.

Cascade Restaurant Uhuru St ☎0720 663719. This clean and friendly two-storey local joint is a safe bet for fast food (fish and chips Ksh170, chicken and chips Ksh240) and has a pleasant, bustling atmosphere. Mon–Sat 6.30am–8pm.

★**Golden Plate** Kenyatta Highway, across from Total ☎0722 268620. Busy, clean, friendly and well-run *hoteli* on a crowded street corner with plenty on the menu and a pleasingly old-fashioned feel, complete with wood panelling, big windows and ceiling fans. *Kienyeji* chicken stew goes for Ksh240. Daily 6.30am–7.30pm.

Pork City Kisii Rd ☎0722 366047 or ☎0711 487775. Basic but friendly butchery with an attached restaurant specializing in pork (Ksh500/kilo), although they'll also serve you beef, chicken and even rabbit (Ksh600/kilo). Daily 8am–9.30pm.

DRINKING

Porkies Garden Uhuru St ☎0713 188762. Food is on offer (*bhajias* Ksh120, whole tilapia Ksh400), but this is more bar than restaurant. There's a covered courtyard offering live English football on four TV screens, a pool table and balcony good for people-watching over a beer (or three). Daily 24hr.

Fourteen Falls

Daily 9am–5pm • $4, vehicles $5 • Head for the village of Kilima Mbogo, 18km east of Thika, along the Garissa road; some matatus stop at Kilima Mbogo, while others go on to the village of Donyo, 4km off to the south, down a dirt track that passes 900m from the entrance to Fourteen Falls

The trip to **Fourteen Falls** on the Athi River, close to Ol Donyo Sabuk National Park, is popular with locals. Donyo, on the south side of the river, is a busy centre, with dozens of *dukas* and *hotelis*.

Fourteen Falls is a broad cascade, plunging 30m over a precipice with many lips, hence the name. The falls are modestly spectacular after rain, when they flood into a single, thundering red cataract. You may end up with breathtaking photos, but will have to experience the stench of what is sadly becoming an increasingly polluted ecosystem due to upstream development. The boat-crossing to the viewpoint to watch locals jump off the falls is well worth the modest entrance fee.

Ol Donyo Sabuk National Park

$30 • ⊕ kws.org • Matatus run to Kilima Mbogo village, 18km east of Thika along the Garissa road; the park gate is 2km further on – follow the signpost by the teacher training college

Seen from a distance, **Ol Donyo Sabuk**, "Big Mountain" in Maa, also known as Kilima Mbogo ("Buffalo Mountain" in Kikuyu), is not especially inspiring, and at 2146m it's not high in Kenyan terms. The attractions of the national park become apparent when you approach the gate, as the flat, dry scrubland gives way to red soil, cool air and fine views. The national park encloses the entirety of the mountain, and protects diverse birdlife and indigenous forest, though the mammals – buffaloes, Sykes' and colobus monkeys and porcupines – make themselves scarce in the thick vegetation.

Walking the 9km track from the gate to the summit requires being accompanied by an armed ranger (Ksh1500). Beyond signboard #8, at the 7km mark, on the left, you come to the grave of Sir William Northrup MacMillan, the fattest of famous settlers, whose intended burial place on the summit had to be abandoned when his modified tractor-hearse's clutch burned out. He rests here with his wife, maid and dog. Between the MacMillans' graves and just below the summit, the track winds steeply up through dense forest. The occasional clearings offer good views, including a huge oxbow in the Athi River and, when the air is clear enough (usually Dec & Jan), Mount Kenya and Kilimanjaro. The vegetation at the summit is more open, with shrubs and grassland, spoilt by a humming grove of communications towers.

ACCOMMODATION
OL DONYO SABUK NATIONAL PARK

Sabuk Guest House 1km south of the gate ☎020 2062503, ✆ reservations@kws.go.ke. Very large and nicely situated old home, formerly the MacMillans' ranger residence. It's a charming place with satellite TV and full kitchen for up to ten. Whole house **$300**

Turacco campsite By the gate ☎ 020 2062503 or main KWS reservations ☎ 0726 610508, ✆ reservations@kws .go.ke. This campsite offers shady lawns, free firewood, good showers and toilets and a nice picnic spot. **$20**

Murang'a

Established as the administrative outpost of **Fort Hall** in 1900, **MURANG'A** has since come to be thought of as the "Kikuyu Homeland" because of its proximity to Mukuruwe wa Nyagathanga, a sort of Kikuyu Garden of Eden. At the beginning of the twentieth century, Fort Hall consisted of "two grass huts within a stone wall and a ditch". Although a British military base, it was never a settlers' town; Fort Hall district was outside the zone earmarked for white settlement and most of it comprised the "Kikuyu reserve". Colonel Richard Meinertzhagen, an officer in the King's African Rifles, posted here in 1902, found time, when not shooting animals (or people), to write, "If white settlement really takes hold in this country it is bound to do so at the expense of the Kikuyu who own the best land, and I foresee much trouble." That said, Meinertzhagen helped put down some of this trouble, launching "punitive expeditions" from Fort Hall with his African troops (see box, p.286).

The present-day town, perched above the busy Mount Kenya road, is a small commercial centre, bustling energetically, and outwardly a happy enough place, despite its notoriety as an area of Mungiki gang violence (see box, p.161). But this won't impact in any way on your visit, and there's no reason not to call in. There's even a bit of sightseeing in the **CPK Cathedral**, formerly the Church of St James and All Martyrs. The cathedral features an unusual mural sequence which depicts the life story of an African Christ in an African landscape. The murals were painted by the Tanzanian artist Rekiya Elimoo Njau in 1955 – the year the church was founded by the Archbishop of Canterbury – as a memorial to the thousands of Kikuyu victims of Mau Mau attacks.

Mukuruwe wa Nyagathanga

In Kikuyu mythology, it was at nearby Mukuruwe wa Nyagathanga that God made husbands for the nine daughters of Gikuyu and Mumbi, spiritual ancestors of all the

Kikuyu people. The husbands, who became the ancestors of the nine Kikuyu clans, were found by Gikuyu under a large fig tree. Although the original *mukuruwe* (fig tree) disappeared long ago, you can take a matatu to nearby **Mugeka** and walk from there to **Gakuyu** village if you'd like to see the site.

ARRIVAL AND DEPARTURE
MURANG'A

There are three main onward travel options from Murang'a: clockwise around Mount Kenya via Karatina; anticlockwise around the mountain via Embu (see p.187); or up to Nyeri and the Aberdare range (see p.190). The main route from Murang'a to Nyeri goes north via the town of Sagana, where it joins the A2 highway. But if you're not in a hurry, you should take either of the two minor roads leading out of Murang'a to the west. Both are in good condition, and much more pleasant to travel on than the main highway; they join at Kiriani. Frequent buses and matatus run from Murang'a to Thika (1hr), Nairobi (2hr), Embu (1hr) and Nyeri (1hr) from the bus station off Gichinga Lane.

INFORMATION

Services Barclays and KCB both have ATMs and there's internet access at the Post Office, off Kenyatta Highway.

There's a Mathai supermarket at the western end of Market St.

ACCOMMODATION

Murang'a has several recommended lodgings providing bed and breakfast at knock-down prices; however, there is nowhere upmarket.

★**Golden Palm Breeze Hotel** On the highway in Kenol town, about 10km from Thika ☎0712 619342. The most modern building en route to Murang'a from Thika, with manicured gardens and small but immaculate rooms with DSTV and wi-fi. Room only **Ksh2000**

Murang'a Courtyard Kangema Rd ☎0721 166878. Nine small but pleasant and clean rooms, each with a small double bed and a mosquito net, over a popular bar-restaurant which, fortunately, quietens down after about 11pm. Very affordable, but you get what you pay for. BB **Ksh1000**

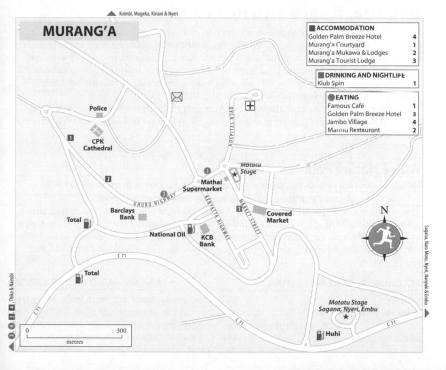

MURANG'A

Koimbi, Mugeka, Kiriani & Nyeri

■ ACCOMMODATION	
Golden Palm Breeze Hotel	4
Murang'a Courtyard	1
Murang'a Mukawa & Lodges	2
Murang'a Tourist Lodge	3

■ DRINKING AND NIGHTLIFE	
Klub Spin	1

● EATING	
Famous Café	1
Golden Palm Breeze Hotel	3
Jambo Village	4
Mamu Restaurant	2

Police
CPK Cathedral
Matatu Stage
Mathai Supermarket
Barclays Bank
Total
National Oil
KCB Bank
Covered Market
Total
Huhi

HOSPITAL ROAD
UHURU HIGHWAY
KENYATTA HIGHWAY
MARKET STREET

Matatu Stage
Sagana, Nyeri, Embu

N

0   300
metres

C71

Thika & Nairobi

Sagana, Naro Moru, Nyeri, Nanyuki & Embu

Murang'a Mukawa & Lodges Uhuru Highway ☎ 0723 701409. A cut above the other lodgings, with a nice terrace bar with views across the hills. The clean rooms come with nets and small balconies, though there are a lot of stairs to climb to reach them. BB **Ksh1600**
Murang'a Tourist Lodge 2km down the Thika road

☎ 0726 495060. Somewhat run-down hotel right on the main road, which nonetheless manages to be clean and agreeable. Rooms are dark but come with nets and electric showers, and there's a handy *nyama choma* bar downstairs. BB **Ksh1500**

EATING

Famous Café Uhuru Highway ☎ 0719 542741. A good joint for a tea and snacks with samosas (Ksh45) and *mandaazi* served on cheerful checked tablecloths, though it's a little cramped and surrounded by a cacophony of traffic. Daily 6am–8pm.
Golden Palm Breeze Hotel Off the Thika–Muranga'a highway ☎ 0712 619342. This is a great stop on the way to Murang'a. It's a popular weekend spot for locals, with a full *nyama choma* restaurant, a nice garden and four separate bars featuring live music on weekends. Hearty meals – including goat *choma*, a half-chicken or a whole

tilapia – go for around Ksh700. Daily 6am–late.
Jambo Village 300m south of Muranga Tourist Lodge ☎ 0718 153331. Lively *nyama choma* (Ksh600/kg) spot on the outskirts of town that's packed on weekends, with a family-friendly atmosphere, music and decent chicken and chips (Ksh1200 for a whole chicken). Daily 8am–11pm.
Marmu Restaurant Uhuru Highway ☎ 0721 141513. A busy spot offering a good range of snacks and local dishes, with a nice terrace out front for watching the street life. Mains around Ksh200. Daily 7am–7pm.

DRINKING

Klub Spin Market St ☎ 0720 849056. Boozy and friendly, this is the closest you'll get to a nightclub in Murang'a. Beers go for Ksh180, and pork is available if you're in the

mood for something more substantial (Ksh440/kg). Mon–Fri 5pm–3am, Sat & Sun 2pm–3am.

Sagana, Kagio and Karatina

SAGANA has some accommodation and a good activities camp nearby (see below), but little else to recommend it. Seven kilometres northeast of here, the market (Tues & Fri) at the village of **KAGIO** is recommended for animated scenes and wonderful fruit and vegetables. South of here, the land levels out into a series of intricately irrigated **rice paddies**, part of the Mwea rice scheme, originally a resettlement area for landless farmers supported by Japanese NGOs.

Heading north along the main highway, you pass through the feverish commercial centre of **KARATINA**. Its market (Sat and Tues–Thurs) is one of East Africa's biggest cattle and produce sales.

Wajee Nature Park

Take the main A2 road from Karatina to Nyeri, turning west 3km northwest of Karatina at Tumu Tumu onto the Gakonya road; then go south about 17km via Mukurweini and Mihuti · Ksh300 · ☎ 0720 615471, ⓦ wajeenaturepark.co.ke · 25 acres

The sanctuary of **Wajee Nature Park** is a magnet for ornithologists, who can spot more than a hundred bird species here, including the rare endemic Hinde's babbler, as well as owls, hornbills, monkeys and porcupines. While the camping facilities and cottages are very basic, the surrounding nature trails and apiary are of particular interest and well worth a visit.

ACCOMMODATION AND EATING   SAGANA, KAGIO AND KARATINA

SAGANA
★**Savage Wilderness Camp** On the east bank of the Sagana river, 7km south of Sagana on the Nairobi road signposted to the west ☎ 0737 835963, ⓦ savage wilderness.org; map p.160. This adventure activities

base, run by Savage Wilderness Safaris (see p.124), specializes in whitewater rafting and also has a 60m bungee jump over the river, nature walks, zipline and an artificial rock-climbing wall. The shaded, grassy campsite is entirely powered by a home-made hydroelectric system.

There's plenty of space to pitch your own tent; other options include renting a small tent (with bedding and mattress) or a large one (with bedding and two camp beds), or getting a double cottage. An extra Ksh2250 gets you breakfast, lunch, dinner and two beers/sodas. Per person: camping **Ksh1000**, small tent **Ksh1350**, large tent **Ksh1500**; whole cottage **Ksh4650**

KARATINA

Express Restaurant On the main road 100m south of Uchumi supermarket ☎0725 099817. Cosy local joint with the standard Coca-Cola-branded tables serving up snacks (*mandaazi* and chai Ksh70) as well as a small range of sandwiches and burgers (Ksh150–200). Daily 6.45am–10pm.

Ibis Opposite Uchumi supermarket, off the main road ☎0774 312566, ✉Kihuria@ibishotel.co.ke. The hotel

offers the bare necessities, with small but adequate rooms equipped with TVs, nets and electric showers. There's also a restaurant and bar on the ground floor. Room only **Ksh1000**

Hotel Starbucks Next door to Ibis, off the main road ☎0721 466577, ⒲hotelstarbucks.com. Small, clean rooms, good security and satellite TV. You can eat fast food at *Chicken Inn* downstairs (6am–midnight), à la carte and buffet at *Stings* restaurant upstairs (6am–last customer) and drink at *Casper's Bar*, whose nice veranda looks onto the main street. Room only **Ksh2000**

WAJEE NATURE PARK

Wajee Nature Park Campsite ☎0720 615471, ⒲wajeenaturepark.co.ke; map p.170. The campsite here also offers rather run-down garden accommodation with four triple rooms, hot water and a kitchen with gas and firewood. Camping **Ksh300**, triple room **Ksh1500**

Southern Mount Kenya

The *Castle Forest Lodge* can arrange a hiking trip for $165 a day all-inclusive, regardless of the size of the party, via *Mackinder's Camp* and Point Lenana, terminating either in Naro Moru (4–6 days) or Chogoria (6–9 days)

Relatively few tourists approach Mount Kenya from the park's southern boundary, which offers some excellent accommodation options and great basecamp hiking. If you're keen to try an unusual approach to the summit, consider the **Kamweti route** which begins at the road-head, a steep 8km north of *Castle Forest Lodge* (see below). This southern part of the mountain shelters the last remaining wild **bongos** on Mount Kenya, as researchers' night-surveillance cameras proved in 2008.

Thego Fishing Camp

Camping Ksh300, day-trips Ksh100 • ☎0716 465831

Along the Chaka route, 7km from the highway, you pass *Thego Fishing Camp*, a pretty spot by the Thego stream with camping allowed, but without electricity. If you don't already have a fishing licence, you can get one here for Ksh200, giving you three months' worth of fishing, and allowing you up to six fish per day (if you're lucky).

ACCOMMODATION

★**Castle Forest Lodge** Southern slopes of Mount Kenya, 40km from Sagana via Kagio ☎0721 422908 or ☎0722 314918, ⒲castleforestlodge.com; map p.170. A private home built for British royalty before World War I, this nestles in a fragrantly piny forest clearing at 2100m. Remotely sited and personally managed by its Dutch leaseholder, it is far from the main road and overlooks a waterhole regularly visited by elephants. Even if you're simply passing by, there are few nicer ways to spend an afternoon than sitting on the veranda with tea and home-made cakes. The old house has several modest, comfortable rooms with camphor-wood floors. In the grounds there are three bungalows, each sleeping four; an arc of stylish, individually decorated double and twin cottages with fireplaces; a self-catering "bush hut" 9km from the main house; and the option

SOUTHERN MOUNT KENYA

of DIY camping. The *Lodge* uses an impressive hydro system from the nearby waterfall for electricity, good-value meals are available, and there's a well-stocked bar. In between sleeping and eating, you can walk in the woods, sit by the waterfalls of the Karute stream (a short walk from the house through beautiful thick forest), fish the stream for trout or take a horse out for a ride. Make sure you take a guide if venturing deep into the forest – in 2010 two visitors were killed by a charging elephant 5km from the main lodge. To get here from Sagana, take the C73 towards Embu. After 18km, you reach Kutus; continue east on the C73 for 400m, then turn left on the tarmac D458 signposted "Castle Forest Lodge 22km." After 2km, turn left onto an excellent road which eventually becomes a forest track in reasonable condition. Camping **$8**, bush hut **$100**, BB **$116**, FB **$160**

2

2

★**Serena Mountain Lodge** Mount Kenya National Reserve, on the southwest slopes of Mount Kenya ☎020 2842000 or ☎0771 109637, ⓦserenahotels.com; map p.170. The best of Kenya's three highland tree-hotels, set at an altitude of 2200m. Reminiscent of an old-style ski lodge in its cosy, dark wood design, it has public balconies facing the forest-encircled, floodlit waterhole and excellent food. The lodge is inside the Mount Kenya National Reserve and you pass through KWS's Kihari gate, where you'll need to pay the standard entry fee (see p.169). Visit the underground bunker for close-up waterhole views. It's a 40min drive from the A2: from Karatina, drive 3km northwest and take the right (east) turning at Tumu Tumu, then follow directions for 31km; from Kiganjo, head north 4km, take the right (east) turning at the market centre of Chaka and drive 27km to the lodge. Both routes are paved and in good shape and join at Sagana State Lodge, a well-guarded presidential retreat with excellent game viewing 14km short of *Serena Mountain Lodge*. FB ̄$304

Naro Moru

Heading north up the A2 towards Naro Moru from Kiganjo, you emerge from the folded landscape of Kikuyu cultivation onto a high, windswept plain. Here, you're crossing one of Kenya's great animal migration routes, severed by human population pressure. Until 1948, when the two mountain parks were created, every few years used to see a mass migration of **elephants** from one side to the other. When the parks were opened, it was decided to keep the elephants away from the crowded farmlands in between, so an 8km-long ditch was dug across their route.

The road climbs gently and steadily to nondescript **NARO MORU**, which stands on the watershed between the Tana and the Ewaso Nyiro river basins. Built around its now disused train station, Naro Moru is the most straightforward base for climbing Mount Kenya, either independently or on an organized trek.

ARRIVAL AND DEPARTURE   NARO MORU

By bus and matatu Frequent matatus to and from Nanyuki (30min) and Nyeri (45min) pass through Naro Moru. Transport also connects Naro Moru with Nairobi (3hr).

By car The A2 highway connects Naro Moru with Nanyuki and Nairobi and is in good shape.

INFORMATION

Guided treks *Naro Moru River Lodge* and *Bantu Mountain Lodge* (see below) run guided treks. Another recommended outfit in Naro Moru is Mount Kenya Guides and Porters Safari Club (☎020 3524393, ⓦmtkenyaguides.com), whose office is 6km along the Naro Moru trail, about 3km before the youth hostel.

Services The town has a post office and KCB bank with ATM, but no Barclays.

ACCOMMODATION

The area around Naro Moru and the route north to Nanyuki offers a good variety of **accommodation**. If you're camping, the rather exposed campsite at *Naro Moru River Lodge* is the obvious destination. There's not a lot in the **food** department in Naro Moru; the centre's offerings are strictly in the beans and chapatti line. Besides the *Trout Tree Restaurant*, your best bet for something classier is the lodges – try the *Naro Moru River Lodge*.

Bantu Mountain Lodge 8km north of Naro Moru ☎0718 136539 or ☎0720 745338, ⓦmountainrock kenya.com; map p.170. A mid-range trekking base rated for its grounds full of indigenous trees and its organized treks using its own mountain bunkhouses – there's also horseriding (Ksh1000/hr) and escorted walks on offer. The lodge's standard rooms are vastly overpriced for non-residents (residents pay half), and you might want to upgrade to "superior" ($110) for the quaintly preferable furnishings and fireplace. You can also camp in the grounds, which are fitted out with a dodgy "sky walk", a pond for boating and even an ancient-looking set of carnival swings. All rooms have TVs and prices are highly negotiable. BB ̄$100, camping ̄$10

Blueline Hotel 3km up the road to Mt Kenya National Park's Naro Moru gate ☎0722 887395, ⓔbluelinehotel naromoru@yahoo.com; map p.170. One of the best budget hotels in town, offering basic but cosy rooms complete with small porches and colourful quilts, alongside a small courtyard with safari animals painted on the walls. Rooms are priced per person, so it's good value for single travellers. The small restaurant in the front is popular with locals, but the place is generally quiet unless the bar really gets going. Room only per person Ksh1500

★**Colobus Cottages** 1km south of Bantu Mountain Lodge, then 2km west of the A2 ☎0722 840195 or ☎0753 951720, ⓦcolobuscottages.com; map p.170. Three delightful solar-powered cottages on the banks of the Burguret stream, built and managed by the man who built the *Trout Tree* restaurant. The cottages come with natty decor and fireplaces, perched above a stream for trout fishing overlooking colobus-laden trees. There's a treetop bar and restaurant (breakfast and lunch Ksh800, dinner Ksh1500), though the cottages also come with kitchens and BBQs for self-caterers. Per person Ksh3500

Mount Kenya Hostel 9km up the well-signposted track to Mount Kenya National Park's Naro Moru gate ☎0722 598974, ⓦhihostels.com; map p.170. This excellent family-run hostel has comfortable if basic dorms and camping, with hot showers and a well-equipped kitchen. A good place to hire guides and porters, or to team up with others for climbing the mountain. The friendly owner can also arrange conservation-related volunteer opportunities in the local community, and rents out a handful of attractive four-person cottages scattered among the *shambas* nearby. Dorm Ksh1000, cottage Ksh2000, camping Ksh400

Mount Kenya Royal Cottages 1km south of Nanyuki airport, just off the A2 ☎0728 816392, ⓦthokozela .co.za; map p.170. Highway-side stopover with spacious, nicely furnished cottage-style rooms with cosy duvets, TV and hot water. Family-friendly restaurant with bar and gardens, serving traditional Kenyan dishes. BB Ksh6000

★**Naro Moru River Lodge** Signposted 1.5km northwest of the town centre ☎0724 082754 or ☎0737 102955, ⓦnaromoruriverlodge.com; map p.170. The town's upmarket base, this is also the area's main climbing rendezvous, with a pricey but decently stocked kit-rental shop. It has a welcoming atmosphere, pretty gardens along the Naro Moru stream and superb birdwatching, as well as a sauna, squash, tennis, a pool and mountain bike rental (Ksh500/hr). Although some rooms need refurbishment, most have fireplaces and balconies and are reasonable value for money, as are the ten self-service cottages (most sleep 6 or 7 at around $40 per person); there's also room to camp. The *Lenana Bar* and *Kinnyaga* restaurant are busy hangouts on the weekend, with hearty breakfasts and lunches, and good dinners (lunch and dinner both $23). Camping $15, BB $107

★**Trout Tree** About 9km north of Naro Moru, just past Bantu Mountain Lodge ☎0726 281704, ⓦtrout-tree .com; map p.170. Built on wooden platforms among giant fig trees, overlooking trout ponds, this unique restaurant serves very good fish (Ksh950 for a whole trout) in a variety of styles. You can also stay here in the adorable three-bedroom "creaky cottage", a rustic wooden cabin with a fireplace and good kitchen facilities, which sleeps up to six. Daily 10am–4pm. Cottage Ksh12,500

Mount Kenya National Park

$65 • ⓦ kws.org • 715 square kilometres

An extinct volcano some 3.5 million years old, **Mount Kenya** is Africa's second-highest mountain, with two jagged peaks. Formed from the remains of a gigantic volcanic plug – it rose more than 7000m above sea level until a million years ago – most of its erupted lava and ash have been eroded by glacial action to create a distinctive, craggy silhouette. The peaks are permanently iced with snow and glaciers, the latter in retreat due to climate change. On the upper slopes, altitude and the equatorial location combine to nurture forms of **vegetation**, seemingly designed by some 1950s science-fiction writer, that exist only here and at one of two other lofty points in East Africa. When you first see them, it's hard to believe the "water-holding cabbage", "ostrich plume plant" or "giant groundsel."

Europeans first heard about the mountain when the German missionary **Johann Ludwig Krapf** saw it in 1849. His stories of snow on the equator were not taken seriously, but in 1883 the young Scottish traveller Joseph Thomson confirmed its existence to the outside world. The Kikuyu, Maasai and other peoples living in the region had venerated the mountain for centuries, and park rangers still occasionally report finding elderly Kikuyu high up on the moorlands, drawn by the presence of God – Ngai – whose dwelling place this is. It is not known, however, whether anyone had scaled the peaks before Sir Halford Mackinder reached the higher of the two, **Batian**, in 1899. Another thirty years passed before **Nelion**, a tougher summit, was conquered. Both were named by Mackinder's expedition after nineteenth-century Maasai *laibon*, or ritual leaders.

The **KWS-managed national park** encloses all parts of the mountain above 3200m plus stretches down the Naro Moru and Sirimon streams. Inside this area fees have to be paid, and strict rules control your activities. Outside this zone, surrounding the

2

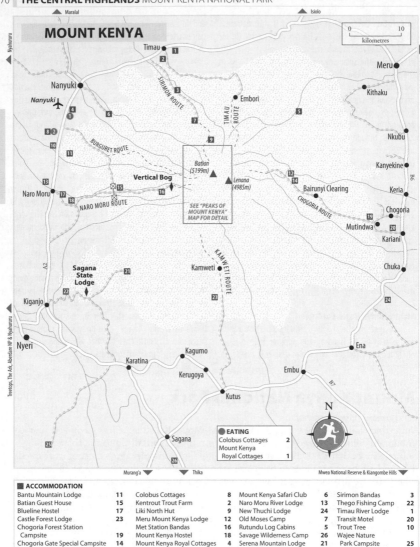

ACCOMMODATION

Bantu Mountain Lodge	11	Colobus Cottages	8	Mount Kenya Safari Club	6	Sirimon Bandas	3
Batian Guest House	15	Kentrout Trout Farm	2	Naro Moru River Lodge	13	Thego Fishing Camp	22
Blueline Hostel	17	Liki North Hut	9	New Thuchi Lodge	24	Timau River Lodge	1
Castle Forest Lodge	23	Meru Mount Kenya Lodge	12	Old Moses Camp	7	Transit Motel	20
Chogoria Forest Station		Met Station Bandas	16	Rutundu Log Cabins	5	Trout Tree	10
Campsite	19	Mount Kenya Hostel	18	Savage Wilderness Camp	26	Wajee Nature	
Chogoria Gate Special Campsite	14	Mount Kenya Royal Cottages		Serena Mountain Lodge	21	Park Campsite	25

national park, lies the Mount Kenya National Reserve, in which your movements are normally only limited by your inclinations and equipment – though on some access roads, such as the one for *Serena Mountain Lodge* (see p.168), fees are payable even in the reserve. Various specialist **guidebooks and maps** are available to help you explore on your own (see p.598).

Climbing Mount Kenya

There are **four main routes** up Mount Kenya. From the west, the **Naro Moru trail** provides the shortest and steepest way to the top. The **Burguret** and **Sirimon trails** from the northwest are less well trodden; Sirimon has a reputation for lots of wildlife, while

Burguret passes through a long stretch of dense forest. The fourth trail, **Chogoria**, is a beautiful, much longer ascent up the eastern flank of the mountain, on which you have to carry tents. In practice, Naro Moru, Sirimon and Chogoria account for nearly all hikes; if you want to use any other route, you have to inform the warden in advance (this can be done by radio by the rangers at any park gate).

The technical peaks of **Batian** (5199m) and **Nelion** (5189m) are accessible only to experienced, fully-equipped mountaineers, and the easiest route is Grade IV, making them a lot more testing, for example, than most of the routes up the Matterhorn. If you want to climb these peaks, you should join the Mountain Club of Kenya (see p.71), who will put you in touch with the right people, and can give reductions on accommodation charges.

Anyone who is reasonably fit can scale the third-highest peak, **Point Lenana** (4985m). The climb has acquired a reputation for being fairly easy, and lots of people set off quite unprepared for high-altitude living – a quarter of attempts fail for this reason. Above about 4000m the mountain is often foggy or windy and freezing cold, wickedly so after dark. The air is thin, and it rains or snows, at least briefly, almost every day, though most precipitation comes at night.

Mount Kenya's **weather** is notoriously unpredictable. There are days when it's fairly clear even during the rainy seasons, but driving up the muddy roads to the park gates may be nearly impossible. If it's really bad, you probably won't be allowed in anyway. The most **reliable months** are February and August, although January and most of July can be fine, too.

What to bring

Above all, it's essential to have a really **warm sleeping bag**, ideally with an additional liner and/or a Gore-Tex bivouac bag, capable of keeping you warm below freezing point. One **thick sweater**, or better still, several thinner ones, and either a **windproof jacket** or a down- or fibre-filled one are also essential, as is a **change of footwear**, as you're bound to have wet feet by the end of each day. **Gloves** and a **balaclava** or **woolly hat** are also handy. A light cagoule or anorak is good to have, as is a set or two of thermal underwear for the shivering nights. A **torch**, ideally a wind-up one, is always handy, especially if you're camping. An **emergency foil blanket** is advisable, weighs next to nothing and packs down very small. Another prerequisite is a **stove**, as you'll be miserable without regular hot drinks. Firewood is not available and cannot be collected once you enter the park (no burning is allowed). For **food**, dehydrated soup and chocolate are perhaps the most useful. The *Naro Moru River Lodge* (see p.169) has a **rental** shop where you can get just about anything, though at prices that may make you wish you'd simply bought it in Nairobi (see box, p.129).

Altitude and health

The various ascents themselves are mostly just steep hikes, if rough underfoot in parts. It's the **altitude** rather than the climb that may stop you reaching the top. Much more relevant than the training programmes that some people embark on is giving yourself enough time to acclimatize, so that your body has a chance to produce extra oxygen-carrying red blood cells.

Above 3000–4000m, you will be well outside your normal comfort zone and are likely to notice the effects of altitude. You may want to take Diamox (acetazolamide) to speed up your acclimatization and keep painkillers handy for headaches, which are fairly normal at first, especially at night. Keeping your **fluid intake** as high as possible will also help – three to five litres a day is recommended. Most water sources on the mountain are reckoned to be safe (one or two exceptions are noted). It's highly recommended to avoid alcohol while climbing.

The effects of altitude can be largely avoided if you **take your time** over the trek, as minor symptoms gradually disappear. Going up the Naro Moru route, you shouldn't attempt to climb from the base of the mountain (that is, from Naro Moru town at 2000m) to Point Lenana (just under 5000m) in less than 72 hours. Four or five days is much better, especially if you've just arrived in Kenya and are used to living at sea level. Assuming you allow a day to get down again, giving yourself just under a week for the whole trip is a good idea. If you can, climb for an hour or two higher than the altitude you are going to sleep, or spend two nights at the same altitude.

The symptoms of **altitude sickness**, also known as acute mountain sickness, vary between individuals, and appear unrelated to how fit you are – indeed, fit young men often suffer the most acute symptoms. If you climb too fast, extreme breathlessness, nausea, disorientation and even slurred speech are all possible. If someone in your group shows signs of being seriously tired and weak, you should descend a few hundred metres. If the symptoms develop into unsteadiness on the feet and drowsiness, **descend rapidly** until the symptoms improve. The effects of altitude, especially on bodies tuned only to sea level, are remarkable, and they can quickly become very dangerous and even fatal if high-altitude pulmonary or cerebral oedema (water in the lungs or brain cavity) develop.

ARRIVAL AND DEPARTURE   MOUNT KENYA NATIONAL PARK

Getting to the Mount Kenya area is an easy trip from Nairobi up a busy highway. If you're not driving, you could buy a bus ticket from Nairobi direct to any of the towns in this section, or make Thika (see p.162) or Murang'a (see p.164) a first destination before heading around the mountain. Naro Moru (see p.168), a popular base for climbing the mountain, lies on its west side, while Nanyuki (see p.180), 25km further north, offers a good alternative hiking base and is the closest commercial airstrip to the park. On the eastern slopes, Chogoria (see p.176), between Meru and Embu, offers arguably the finest route up the mountain. Or you could head up to the southern slopes, where *Castle Forest Lodge* (see p.167) is an excellent, low-key staging post.

INFORMATION, ENTRY AND COSTS

KWS operates a sign-in/sign-out system and you register your details and plans at your gate of entry. This is where you pay fees for your anticipated stay ($65 per 24hr, $255 for 4-day package, $315 for 5, $380 for 6; no refunds). You can change your plans once on the mountain, or extend your stay and pay the balance on departure, but you must leave by one of the three main gates – Naro Moru, Sirimon or Chogoria – and formally sign out. It's a bad idea to use any alternative exit: KWS will look for you and eventually organize an air search if you don't show up. Stories circulate of people being pursued to Nairobi and beyond for non-payment of huge rescue service bills.

Costs Climbing Mount Kenya is a fairly expensive business, though still significantly cheaper than Kilimanjaro. Doing the trek independently from Naro Moru, the cheapest possible four-day trip (three up, one down) for two people, including park fees, overnight accommodation, transport to the road-head and a basic self-catering food budget of $10/day, but excluding any equipment rental, would cost around $380/person. Organized trips start from around $50/person per day, not including park fees, and many guides will include cooked meals in their packages; be sure to check in advance whether or not this is the case. Note that the

multi-day fees (see above) for national park entry include camping fees.

Guides and porters It's now obligatory to hire a certified guide to climb Mt Kenya. Porters are optional, but climbing with the help of members of the local community can be a way of giving back and of showing respect. Expect to pay around $10–20/day per porter. Every guide needs to have an official KWS guiding permit. Ask to see it, and don't be fobbed off with local guiding association cards. It's best to agree terms in writing in advance and to pay half or two-thirds of the wages up front and the balance on safe delivery back to base. You can hire guides and porters in Naro Moru at

KEEPING MOUNT KENYA CLEAN

The Kikuyu and other tribes venerated Mount Kenya as the dwelling place of God. It was believed that if you went up to the peaks you would find him, and medicine men and diviners routinely trekked up the mountain to seek miraculous cures or spiritual inspiration. Nowadays, it's mainly tourists, some 15,000 each year, who tread in their steps. Few of them, it seems, particularly respect, never mind venerate, the old mountain deity, and many tonnes of rubbish are left behind every year. Take all your trash back down with you.

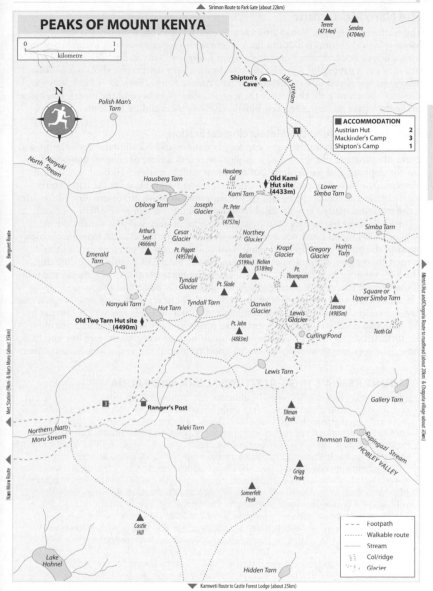

PEAKS OF MOUNT KENYA

Naro Moru River Lodge, Bantu Mountain Lodge, Mount Kenya Hostel or the Mount Kenya Guides and Porters Safari Club (see p.168), in Nanyuki at the *Peak View Hotel* (see p.182) and in Chogoria at the *Transit Motel* (see p.179).

ACCOMMODATION

With a tent, you can camp anywhere in the park – the only practical advantages of the campsites at the *Met Station Bandas*, *Mackinder's* and various other designated campsites on the mountain are water pipes and long-drop toilets. Accommodation on the mountain includes some basic lodges with limited facilities and a number of rudimentary mountain huts which provide little more than shelter and bare bunks with thin mattresses. Accommodation inside the park is given in the relevant route accounts.

The Naro Moru route

The earth road between **Naro Moru** town (see p.168) and the road-head at the Meteorological Station is a 26km haul. There are no regular matatus; private transport with a driver, booked with *Naro Moru River Lodge*, will set you back $90. If you walk, you may get a paying lift some of the way, but the very light traffic thins out as you head east, and if you don't get transport past *Mount Kenya Hostel* after 9km, you should allow five hours to walk the rest of the way. Another 9km beyond the hostel, you come to the **park gate** and usually a few buffalo chewing their cud on the lawn.

From the park gate to the Meteorological Station

From the park gate, you leave the conifer plantations and occasional *shambas* behind as the road twists and climbs through shaggy forest into a zone of colossal **bamboo**. Look out for elephant and particularly **buffalo** if you walk this stretch, though you'll more often see just their droppings and footprints. If you find buffalo on the path, you're advised to lob stones at them, and they're supposed to move out of the way. Much safer is the tried and trusted retreat-steadily-without-taking-your-eyes-off-them approach.

The final ascent to the Met Station is a 3km series of steep hairpins usually driveable only in a 4WD (and often not at all when wet). You start to get some magnificent views out over the plains from up here, while right under your nose you may find a three-horned **chameleon**, stalking cautiously through the foliage like a miniature dinosaur. The high forest is their favourite habitat. **Lions** and **black panthers** – the melanistic form of the leopard found at high altitudes – can occasionally be seen in this area.

With an early start, it's physically perfectly possible to reach *Mackinder's Camp* in one day, but unless you're already well acclimatized, you'll probably feel very below par by the time you get there. It's far better to take it easy and get used to the Met Station's 3050m altitude, or, if you have a tent, climb an hour or so up to the tree line and camp there. The mountain's weather is another good reason to stop at the Met Station. After

---

MOUNT KENYA'S HIGH-ALTITUDE FLORA AND FAUNA

The mountain's vegetation is zoned by **altitude**. Above about 2000m, *shambas* and coniferous plantations cease and the original, dense cloud forest takes over, with the best areas on the mountain's southern and eastern, rain-facing slopes. At 2400m, forest gives way to giant bamboo, with clumps up to 20m high. The bamboo, a member of the grass family, appears impenetrable, but dark-walled passages are kept open by elephants and buffalo. Again, it's the south that has the best bamboo areas; on the dry, northern slopes, there's very little of it.

Above the bamboo at about 2800m you come into more open country of scattered, twisted *Hagena* and St John's wort trees (*Hypericum*), then the tree line (3000m) and the start of peculiar, Afro-Alpine moorlands – look out for the striking scarlet-tufted sunbird. Above about 3300m, you reach the land of the giants; giant heather, giant groundsel, giant lobelia. Identities are confusing: the cabbages on stumps and the larger candelabra-like "trees" are the same species, giant groundsel or tree senecio, an intermediate stage of which has a sheaf of yellow flowers. They are slow growers and, for such weedy-looking vegetables, they may be extraordinarily old, up to 200 years. The tall, fluffy, less abundant plants are a species of giant lobelia discovered by the explorer Teleki and found only on Mount Kenya. The name plaque below one of these (there's a nature trail along the ridge above the Naro Moru stream) calls it an "ostrich plume plant" (*Lobelia telekii*), and it's the only plant that could fairly be described as cuddly. The furriness, which gives it such an animal quality, acts as insulation for the delicate flowers.

Any nights you spend up in the mountain huts will normally be shared with large numbers of persistent **rodents**, which you won't see until it's too late. Remember to isolate your food from them by suspending it from the roof. The familiar diurnal scavengers that you'll see are **rock hyraxes**, which are especially tame at *Mackinder's Camp*; the welfare service provided to them by tourists preserves elderly specimens long past their natural lifespan. Hyraxes are not rodents; the anatomy of their feet indicates they share a distant ancestry with elephants. You're likely to come across other animals at quite high altitudes, too, notably **duiker antelope** on the moorlands.

midday, it often gets foul, and the infamous **vertical bog** (not far beyond the Met Station) is no fun at all in heavy drizzle and 20m visibility.

The Teleki Valley

An early start from the Met Station should see you to *Mackinder's Camp* (see below) by lunchtime, before the clouds start to thicken up. In fair weather the vertical bog en route is not as daunting as it sounds: you keep to the left of the red-and-white marker posts where it isn't as wet. In wet conditions, however, it can be ghastly, as the rosette plants hold just enough icy water to reach certain parts in a bracing manner whenever you slip. As you reach the bog, you enter another vegetation zone, that of **giant heather**. Beyond and above the bog, the path follows a ridge high above the **Teleki Valley** with the peaks straight ahead, rising brilliantly over a landscape that seems to have nothing in common with the hazy plains below.

For *Mackinder's*, you follow the contours across the valley side and jump, or cross by stepping stones, over the snowmelt Northern Naro Moru stream. The peaks of **Batian** and **Nelion** tower magnificently over the valley, with a third pinnacle, **Point John**, even closer. There's usually a fresh icing of snow every morning, but early sunlight melts most of it by midday.

Point Lenana

If you want to climb straight to **Point Lenana**, you're likely to be able to join at least one group leaving from around 2am the following morning. Leaving this early, with a three- to five-hour hike ahead of you, allows you to get to the summit by dawn for a fabulous view, in the right conditions, from northern Kenya on one side to Kilimanjaro on the other.

On the final ascent to Point Lenana, a 500m **via ferrata** steel cable and ladder system, bolted into the rock, was installed by KWS and Rift Valley Adventures in 2012. This "iron road" – the highest via ferrata in the world – allows safer and steadier climbing, and more route options, on the final stretch – assuming you have a harness and carabiners. Still, it's not advisable to rush into doing this final ascent. For most people, day three is better spent getting acclimatized in the Teleki Valley, and not making the climb to Point Lenana until the morning of the fourth day. Note that spending your third night on the mountain at *Austrian Hut*, just below Point Lenana, is not a good idea if you're not used to the altitude.

The **descent** doesn't take long. After summiting, you can get all the way down to Naro Moru in one day, assuming you have transport arranged at the Met Station or manage to find a lift there. If you're not ready to go straight back down, you might want to do the circular **hike around the peaks** (see p.179).

ACCOMMODATION   **THE NARO MORU ROUTE**

As well as the huts listed below there are others in various states of repair, owned by the MCK and reserved for members.

Austrian Hut At 4785m ⓦkws.go.ke; map p.173. *Austrian* is usually staffed by KWS rangers. Reserve in advance or pay at the gate. Bed only per person Ksh2000
Batian Guest House At 2400m near the park gate ⓣ020 3568763, ⓦkws.go.ke; map p.170. A KWS-run, self-service guesthouse, once the home of the former park warden. Needs to be booked well in advance. Six beds in four bedrooms. Whole house $180
Liki North Hut At 3990m ⓦkws.go.ke; map p.170. This hut has been so poorly maintained – at the time of writing it didn't even have a roof – that the only real option here is to camp in the nearby field, which you can do at no extra cost.

Mackinder's Camp At 4200m. Book via ⓣ0724 082754, ⓦnaromoruriverlodge.com; map p.173. Alpine stone hut with bunk beds that's owned by *Naro Moru River Lodge*. Set at 4200m, virtually at the head of Teleki Valley, it's certainly no hotel, but does provide some warmth and the company of other climbers, Kikuyu guides and porters. It can be booked in advance, or on arrival if they have space. Bed only per person $30
Met Station Bandas At 3050m. Book via ⓣ0724 082754, ⓦnaromoruriverlodge.com; map p.170. Basic self-catering bunk beds. Like *Mackinder's*, it's owned by *Naro Moru River Lodge* and can be booked in advance, or on arrival if there's space. Bed only per person $22

The Chogoria route

The **Chogoria trail** is scenically superior to the others, but it's also the longest route. You should allow a *minimum* of five days from Chogoria village up to Point Lenana and down the west side to Naro Moru, or six days if you're returning to Chogoria. Note that the Chogoria route is a camping-only trek: you have to show you have tents for your party when passing through the park gate.

Chogoria village

The muddy, Land Rover-choked village of **CHOGORIA** off the B6 highway is your first target. Public transport sometimes drops passengers on the highway (a 1km walk into Chogoria village) and sometimes drives into the small centre.

Up to the park entrance

The road from Karaa/Kiriani meets the one from Chogoria 5km west of the highway at a rural junction hamlet called **Mutindwa**. From here, it's about 26km to the park gate. En route, some 2km from Mutindwa at Chogoria Forest Station, there's a decent campsite (see p.178).

If you're driving, 4WD is vital on this steep track, but even with it, getting up to the park gate in wet weather can't be guaranteed. If you haven't got your own vehicle, you can charter transport at the *Transit Motel* or elsewhere in Chogoria. Expect to pay around Ksh2000 for a ride on the back of a motorbike or around Ksh8000 to charter a Land Rover for your group. It's a good idea not to pay in full until you get up to the gate. You may prefer to walk up in any case, as it helps you acclimatize. There's exciting, dense rainforest along much of the road, and you're likely to see colobus monkeys, hyenas, buffaloes and lots of elephant dung. The next available campsite is only a clearing in the forest, at a place called **Bairunyi Clearing**, 15km further up the track, with no water. The national park's **Chogoria Gate** is 9km further up the increasingly steep and rough track, flanked by giant, creaking bamboo forest.

Meru Mount Kenya Lodge and the road-head

Just before the gate for the camping-only Chogoria Route, there is good *banda* accommodation at *Meru Mount Kenya Lodge* (see p.178); you can also camp by the gate or follow the main track up from here to a special campsite (see p.178).

Both the main track and a side branch, via the site of the old *Urumandi* hut, eventually meet up at the **road-head**, 7km further on. The side branch is the more interesting walk, but tougher on vehicles. The road-head, with a small parking area, is on the north side of the Nithi stream and there's another very pleasant **campsite** here, with good stream water.

There are good walks round about, useful for acclimatizing to the 3000m-plus altitude. Short scrambles from the road-head take you to the four sets of waterfalls at **Nithi Falls**, while longer walks (3–6hr round trip) take you north to **Mugi Hill**, **Lake Ellis** and the flat-topped peak known as the **Giant's Billiard Table** or Mount Kilingo.

Minto's to Point Lenana

From the road-head (a 3hr trek from *Meru Mount Kenya Lodge*), all wheels are abandoned as you slog on foot up towards *Minto's Hut*, a six-hour stint away in the high moorlands. The route tracks along the axis of an ascending ridge, then flattens onto the rim of the spectacular **Gorges Valley**, carved deep by glaciation. There are unobstructed and encouraging views up to the peaks as you hug the contours of the valley wall.

Minto's Hut, at 4300m is, like *Mackinder's* on the west side of the mountain, a three- to five-hour hike from Point Lenana. Situated by the four small **Hall Tarns**, it's perched above the larger **Lake Michaelson** at the head of the valley below – a very beautiful place, inspiringly set off by giant groundsel, lobelia plants and weird volcanic formations

OPPOSITE THOMSON'S FALLS (P.198) >

inhabited by rock hyraxes. The hut is only for porters. Beware of the tarn water, which is not pure; boiling it at this altitude (water boils at 85–90°C) will kill fewer bugs than usual, so if you need to drink it you should use purifying tablets or iodine.

On the morning of day three you have two options. The first is to head up to the ridge west of *Minto's* and follow it, through pretty scenery, to **Simba Tarn**, below Simba Col. From there, head due south around the peaks and past little **Square Tarn** before turning right to follow the contours for a tough kilometre to the so-called **Curling Pond** (matches have been held on the ice here) and *Austrian Hut*. If you're thinking of a short cut straight up to Square or Upper Simba Tarn, note that it's very steep. Alternatively, from *Minto's* make for the base of the ridge extending east from Point Lenana, then tackle the cruel scree slope to the south for a ninety-minute scramble up to a saddle, followed by a straight drop to the head of the **Hobley Valley** with its two tarns. From here, it's just an hour across to the base of Lenana Ridge, behind which, again, is *Austrian Hut*.

Mercifully, whichever route you choose, this day's hike is a short one and at this altitude (over 4000m) you'll be glad to spend the rest of the day at one of the huts, recuperating for the final ascent. Considering the altitude, a safer and probably more comfortable option would be to spend a second night acclimatizing at the base of Simba Tarn, followed by a pre-dawn assault on Point Lenana on day four. As on the Naro Moru approach, the via ferrata on the approach to Lenana is a big help (see p.175).

After the climb to Lenana, you have a ninety-minute **descent** from *Austrian Hut*, tracking back and forth over miserable scree, to the Teleki Tarn at the head of the Naro Moru stream. *Mackinder's*, and the scent of civilization, is just an hour away down the valley. But if you can resist that lure, and it is still early in the day, and if you have enough food and water, you can continue around the west side of the peaks to **Hut Tarn**, then up and down over the ridges to the site of the former *Kami Hut*, at the head of the Sirimon route on the north side. If you feel acclimatized, there's no problem making it from *Minto's* to Point Lenana and on down to the Met Station in one day.

ARRIVAL AND DEPARTURE
THE CHOGORIA ROUTE

By bus Buses connect Chogoria with Embu (several daily; 1hr 30min); Meru (several daily; 1hr); Nairobi (several daily; 4hr).

INFORMATION AND TOURS

Guides There are several porter/guide associations in Chogoria, most of whose members are extremely pushy. The most reliable is the Mount Kenya Chogoria Guides Association (☎ 0733 676970 or ☎ 0722 950479), based at the *Transit Motel*. Expect to negotiate a wage of around $13/day per porter.

Services Chogoria has a KCB bank with ATM, but no Barclays.

ACCOMMODATION

You'll have to pay daily park fees to stay anywhere within the boundaries of the park, which includes all the lodgings below except for the *Transit Motel*. If the phone numbers provided below don't work – reception on the mountain can be poor – the Mount Kenya Chogoria Guides Association (see above) can make bookings for you. Note that *Minto's Hut* is not open to tourists – once you've passed the gate to the park, the only accommodation on the ascent is in your own tent. On your descent, the *Austrian Hut* and *Mackinder's Camp* offer beds (see p.175).

Chogoria Forest Station Campsite 2km from Mutindwa ☎ 0721 744454; map p.170. Decent site on the edge of the park, dominated by a fine, huge-leaved *Anthocleista zambesiaca* tree. Firewood is available. Camping Ksh300
Chogoria Gate Special Campsite Up the main track from Chogoria Gate, reserve via ☎ 0726 610508, ⊛ kws.go.ke; map p.170. This is a beautiful place to camp, near *Meru Mount Kenya Lodge*. Camping charges included in park entry fee.
★**Meru Mount Kenya Lodge** At 3015m, just before Chogoria Gate ☎ 0729 390686; map p.170. The very good and beautifully located *bandas* of *Meru Mount Kenya Lodge* are just before the gate. Firewood is available for the fireplaces in each *banda*, and there's a basic shop that usually has beer. The lodge is often visited by buffaloes, and you may see elephants at the nearby waterholes. Whole *banda* per person Ksh1500, camping Ksh500

Transit Motel 1.5km off the main road south of Chogoria at Karaa Market ☎0721 973133 or ☎0725 609151, ⓦfacebook.com/transitmotelchogoria; map p.170. By far the best of several lodgings near Chogoria Village, with spacious rooms, each with its own balcony, and a rooftop bar with views of Mount Kenya and the surrounding tea fields. There's also a garage where you can leave your vehicle while you climb the mountain, a cheerful restaurant and an expanse of grass for pitching a tent. To get here, alight from your bus or matatu at Kiriani stage, 3km south of the Chogoria turnoff. Camping **Ksh300**, BB **Ksh2400**

The Sirimon route

2

The **Sirimon route** leads up from the A2 highway from a point some 14km east of Nanyuki. The route climbs over the northern moorlands, giving superb views of the main peaks as well as the twin lesser peaks of Terere (4714m) and Sendeyo (4704m), which have small glaciers of their own.

There are certain advantages in using this trail: it's the driest ascent, the scenery is more open, and it's renowned for wildlife. *Bantu Mountain Lodge* (see p.168) offers all-inclusive **guided tours** up to Point Lenana using this route, as do other Naro Moru and Nanyuki operators. Note that if you're looking to team up with others, you're much less likely to find company here than on the Chogoria or Naro Moru routes as, apart from the huddle of *dukas* on the highway 9km below the park gate, there isn't any real base to start from.

ACCCOMMODATION	THE SIRIMON ROUTE

Accommodation consists of the *Sirimon Bandas* at the gate, *Old Moses Camp* at the road-head (3400m up and accessible only by 4WD) and *Shipton's Camp* bunkhouses at 4200m.

Old Moses Camp At 3400m ⓦmountainrockkenya .com; map p.170. Alpine huts, formerly known as *Judmeier's Camp*, with basic bunk beds. Both huts have a kitchen and dining area with a clean and well-maintained bathroom. Owned by *Bantu Mountain Lodge*. Bed only **Ksh2000**
Shipton's Camp At 4230m ⓦmountainrockkenya .com; map p.173. Just below the main peak and used often for the night before the final summit hike, this mountain hut offers basic bunk beds. Owned by *Bantu Mountain Lodge*. Bed only **Ksh2500**
Sirimon Bandas At 2650m, just outside the gate ☎020 3568763, ⓦkws.go.ke; map p.170. KWS-run operation with two four-bed *bandas* together with a campsite. Whole *banda* **$80**

Treks around the peaks

Though most people head straight up to Point Lenana, trekking round the peaks is an even more exhilarating experience, with the bonus of exploring some of the tarns and glacial valleys on the north side. It is reckoned to be easier to do this anticlockwise in two or three days. If you want to do it in one day, however, set off clockwise from *Mackinder's* via the site of the former *Two Tarn Hut* next to **Hut Tarn**, set in a glorious and eerily silent col beneath the glaciers and scree. The walk from here round to Point Lenana is very much a switchback affair but, as long as the mists stay away, the scenery is fairy-tale. If you're fairly fit and acclimatized, it should take eight to ten hours. Both the *Two Tarn Hut* and *Kami Hut*, on the north side of the peaks, have been demolished, but you can still camp at both sites.

Other routes: Burguret and Kamweti

The trails described above represent only the most obvious and well-trodden of the mountain's possibilities. With time and the right gear, you could **hike** the moorland and peaks area for as long as you liked. Note, however, that you must be fully self-sufficient, you must inform the rangers at the park gate where you buy your tickets of the route you intend to take, and you must exit and sign out via one of three approved gates, paying any fees owed.

Burguret

Bantu Mountain Lodge's preferred route used to follow the **Burguret River** up from the lodge through thick bamboo forest and moorland, but this is now mostly overgrown and hard to follow without a guide. The lower trail passes a clutch of caves described as a "Mau Mau conference centre" (the lodge offers half-day hikes or mountain-bike trips on this trail).

Kamweti

The southern flanks of the mountain seem to have largely escaped the notice of hikers, but there are several forest stations in the vicinity of Embu and plenty of scope for exploration. Most of the southern slopes were a designated "Kikuyu reserve" during the colonial period, so few European climbers created routes up here, but the **Kamweti route** from *Castle Forest Lodge* is becoming more popular (see p.167).

Nanyuki

North of Naro Moru, the A2 runs across the yellow-and-grey downs, scattered with stands of tall blue gums, roamed by cattle and overflown by brilliant roller birds, before dropping to **NANYUKI**, the gateway to Laikipia and parts of northern Kenya. You might be forgiven for expecting something momentous to take place at the **equator**, just south of town. There's a sprouting of curio shops and signs ("This sign is on the Equator") and even an "Equator Professor" who claims to demonstrate the Coriolis effect of the earth's rotation using a bucket of water and a matchstick (aided by sleight of hand). In the northern hemisphere a large body of still water in a perfectly formed vessel would gurgle through a plug hole anticlockwise, whereas in the southern hemisphere it would flow clockwise – though in practice the direction of flow is controlled by the operator because the Coriolis effect is too tiny to have an impact, especially anywhere near the equator itself where the effect is zero. The demonstration is free; the "certificate" comes for a fee.

Nanyuki has the dual distinction of being Kenya's air-force town and playing host to the British Army's training and operations centre. And although in recent decades it has taken in thousands of refugees, escaping from rural poverty and ethnic violence, it remains very much a country town in atmosphere, and an oddly charming one; a wide, tree-lined main street and the mild climate lent by its 2000m altitude bestow an unfamiliar, cool spaciousness that seems to reinforce its colonial character. Yet the town is becoming popular with foreign and Kenyan investors, and **real-estate prices** have doubled in recent years. The town's modern Nakumatt supermarket and assorted new coffee shops and restaurants are a sign of things to come.

Brief history

The first party of **settlers** arrived in the district in 1907 to find "several old Maasai *manyattas*, a great deal of game and nothing else". Nanyuki is still something of a settlers' town and European locals are always around. The animals, sadly, are not. Although you may see a few grazers on the plains, the vast herds of **zebra** that once roamed the banks of the Ngare Nanyuki (Maasai for "Red River") were decimated by hunters seeking hides, by others seeking meat (particularly during World War II, when eighty thousand Italian prisoners of war were fed a pound of meat each day), but most of all by ranchers protecting their pastures.

Mount Kenya Wildlife Conservancy

At Mount Kenya Safari Club, 8km southeast of the town centre • Ksh1500 • ⓦ animalorphinagekenya.org

As the zebra herds dwindled, so lions became a greater threat to livestock and the predators retreated, under fire, to the mountain forests and moors. These days, the

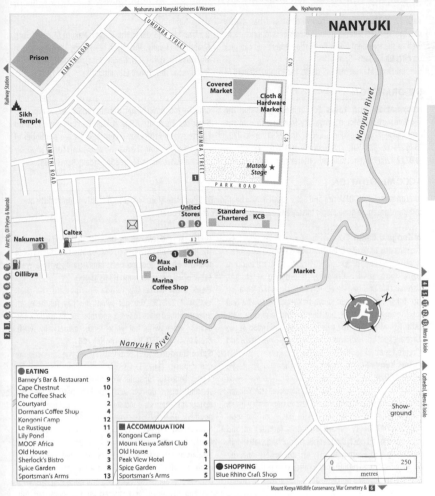

NANYUKI

2

● EATING
Barney's Bar & Restaurant	9
Cape Chestnut	10
The Coffee Shack	1
Courtyard	2
Dormans Coffee Shop	4
Kongoni Camp	12
Le Rustique	11
Lily Pond	6
MOOF Africa	7
Old House	5
Sherlock's Bistro	3
Spice Garden	8
Sportsman's Arms	13

■ ACCOMMODATION
Kongoni Camp	4
Mount Kenya Safari Club	6
Old House	3
Peak View Hotel	1
Spice Garden	2
Sportsman's Arms	5

● SHOPPING
| Blue Rhino Craft Shop | 1 |

Mount Kenya Wildlife Conservancy, War Cemetery & ▼

non-profit **Mount Kenya Wildlife Conservancy** is doing good work with waifs and strays and has an active **bongo breeding programme** which is now working on reintroductions. The conservancy, resembling something out of *Dr. Doolittle*, hosts llamas, pygmy hippos, cheetahs, adorable patas monkeys and even the late William Holden's 100-year-old tortoise.

Nanyuki Spinners and Weavers workshop

Located about 1km down the Nyahururu road, on the left • ☎ 020 6232062, ⓦ nanyukispinnersandweavers.org
This women's group employs more than 130 local women and sells their rugs and blankets, woven on hand looms, at decent prices (Ksh500–10,000). It's a recommended trip, and they appreciate visitors.

ARRIVAL AND DEPARTURE   NANYUKI

By plane Nanyuki's airfield is 9km south of the town centre on the way to Naro Moru and has several scheduled flights a day to and from Nairobi. It's also the home of local charter company Tropic Air (☎ 020 2033032 or

2

☎0722 207300, ⓦtropicairkenya.com) and has a very pleasant bar-restaurant serving Kenya's best cappuccino, as well as the excellent North Road shop where you can pick up gifts (daily 8am–5pm).

Destinations Maasai Mara (2 daily; 1hr 15min); Nairobi (2 daily; 40min).

By bus Meru (3 daily; 1hr 30min); Nakuru (1 daily; 5hr); Nyahururu (1 daily; 3hr); Nyeri (2–3 daily; 1hr 30min).

By matatu Isiolo (1hr); Nakuru (5hr); Nairobi (3hr 30min); Nyahururu (3hr); Timau (30min).

INFORMATION

Information and tours For guides/porters for the Sirimon route up Mount Kenya, try Montana Treks in the *Peak View Hotel* building (☎06220 32731 or ☎0722 231697) or Rift Valley Adventures (☎0707 734776 or ☎0712 426999, ⓦriftvalleyadventures.com), who can also organize mountain biking, climbing and abseiling trips.

Services There are ATMs at KCB, Barclays and Standard Chartered, all in the town centre. There are a number of internet cafés along the road near *Dormans Coffee Shop*; try the one above *Marina Coffee Shop* (daily 8am–8pm).

ACCOMMODATION

You can camp at MOOF Africa and Spice Garden. Also bear in mind that Naro Moru (see p.168) is only a 20min drive away, and there are some good places to stay and eat between the two town centres.

★**Kongoni Camp** 1km north of the town centre on the way out to Meru, then 200m off the highway south ☎0702 868888 or ☎062 2031225, ⓦkongonicamp .com; map p.181. Campsite, fine-dining restaurant, pizzeria, café and bar, deservedly popular as a celebration spot for returning Mount Kenya trekkers. The *bandas* and hotel rooms aren't huge, but they're clean and cosy, with instant showers, and the overall setting and mood of the place are spot on. Highlights include stone-oven pizzas and a "tented spa". Wi-fi. BB Ksh12,500

Mount Kenya Safari Club 8km southeast of the town centre ☎020 2265555, ⓦfairmont.com/mount-kenya -safari; map p.170. Founded by Hollywood star William Holden, this lavish resort hotel offers extraordinary levels of comfort, but seems to relate little to its local environment. Plenty of activities and facilities in and around the hotel, including tennis, riding, bird walks, golf, swimming and visiting the stylish art gallery and the not-to-be-missed wildlife conservancy (see p.180). Good-value online advance purchase deals available. Wi-fi. Room only $533

Old House Haile Selassie Rd, 1km south of the town centre ☎0722 697868 or ☎020 3526007. A clutch of

cool, clean, modern cottages, overlooking the gardens and the little Nanyuki River, each divided into two comfortable rooms with TVs (but no nets, fans or a/c), with a well-established bar-restaurant. BB Ksh5000

Peak View Hotel Lumumba St, opposite the park ☎020 2175218. You get what you pay for here, an unembellished place to sleep, and most rooms are dark and airless, albeit with hot water and, theoretically, wi-fi. Breakfast is Ksh150. Room only Ksh700

Spice Garden South of town just off the highway, by Old House ☎0771 233838, ⓦspicegardennanyuki .com. Series of upscale s/c tented cottages behind a spacious open garden with modern bar, lounge and restaurant. There's a good selection of Indian meals and a good bar. BB Ksh7000, camping Ksh1500

Sportsman's Arms North side of town ☎062 32348 or ☎0734 944077, ⓦsportsmansarmshotels.com. An old establishment, with various parts renovated, improved or neglected. The old cottages ooze atmosphere but main-block rooms are better equipped and quite spacious, with TVs and balconies. Decent-sized outdoor pool, hot tub, sauna and fitness centre (Ksh500 for non-guests). Wi-fi. BB Ksh7600

EATING

★**Barney's Bar & Restaurant** Nanyuki airfield, 9km south of the town centre ☎0723 310064, ⓦlerustique.co.ke/aboutbarneys.php. The people here have created an effortlessly cool ambience on a veranda overlooking lawns next to the runway. Drop in for great coffee or a big English breakfast, or call ahead for a list of the day's specials. It's a little pricey (salads, pizzas and sandwiches all go for around Ksh700), but everything is fresh, tasty and really well prepared and they have the nicest loos in Nanyuki – pity it's not open later. Wi-fi. Daily 7am–7pm.

Cape Chestnut South of the town centre ☎0705 250650, ⓦwww.capechestnut.com. A popular local

rendezvous in a homely wooden house tucked away in the wood, offering English-style home cooking, with daily vegetarian soup specials and a rotating menu of main dishes for around Ksh800–900. To get here, turn left 300m before the road to *Mount Kenya Safari Club* and continue for 700m. Mon–Thurs & Sat 8.30am–5pm, Fri 8.30am–midnight, every other Sun 10am–4pm.

The Coffee Shack In the town centre ☎0702 689163. A funky and colourful little café decorated with local art and serving up good breakfasts (full breakfast Ksh950), burgers and sandwiches (Ksh750) made with fresh home-made bread. Loaves of the bread are for sale as well, alongside a variety of fresh cakes and pastries. Mon–Sat 6.30am–6pm.

Courtyard By the corner of Lumumba St and Kenyatta Ave ☎0701 563719. An intimate little café tucked away in a courtyard on an otherwise-busy corner, scattered with potted rosebushes and serving wood-fire pizzas (Ksh400), calzones, salads and sandwiches. Daily 7am–9pm.

Dormans Coffee Shop By Barclays on Main St ☎0702 787890, ⓦdorman.co.ke. Nanyuki's branch of the national café chain serves up tasty smoothies, cakes, burgers and sandwiches (around Ksh650), with plenty of house coffee to wash it down (Ksh150). Wi-fi. Mon–Sat 7am–7pm, Sun 8am–7pm.

★**Kongoni Camp** 1km north of town on the south side of the Meru road ☎0702 868888 or ☎062 2031225, ⓦkongonicamp.com. This popular bar-restaurant has the feel of a hunting lodge, where you can eat in the welcoming high-ceilinged timber and *mabati* bar/fine dining room, or at tables in the garden. Pizza from Ksh450, fillet mignon Ksh1350. Wi-fi. Daily 7am–10pm, later for the bar.

★**Le Rustique** North side of town, 500m beyond Sportsman's Arms ☎0721 609601, ⓦlerustique .co.ke. One of Nanyuki's most charming and sophisticated restaurants, serving wonderful fresh crêpes (from Ksh650) alongside mouth-watering dishes like slow-cooked lamb (Ksh950), snapper with a sauce of blue cheese and leek, and a temping list of French-inspired desserts. There's a good wine list as well, or you can choose a bottle from the wine shop just next door. Wi-fi. Daily 8am–10.30pm.

★**Lily Pond** Ol Pejeta Rd ☎0727 918243 or ☎0724 675453, ⓦlilypondartscentre.com. This restaurant and bar is a wonderful retreat, perched above a pond full of purple flowering lilies. The open seating areas are spread throughout a series of walkways and there's a colourful main bar, the whole reminiscent of a Frida Kahlo dream set in an eighteenth-century fairy tale. Try their quiche (Ksh700) and burgers (Ksh600). Open late on weekends

with a well-stocked bar. Wi-fi. Mon–Thurs 10am–6pm, Fri–Sun 10am–midnight.

MOOF Africa On the Naro Moru road 3.5km from Nanyuki ☎0733 664103, ⓦmoofafrica.com. Mount Kenya Organic Farming's slow-food restaurant serves fresh tilapia, free-range chicken, fresh juices and home-grown organic produce (mains around Ksh600). It's also a great educational visit, with much to teach about permaculture in tropical countries. Fishing and workshops can be organized on the organic farm, which supplies many local restaurants including Dormans and Barney's. You can also camp here for Ksh1000. Wi-fi. Daily 8am–8pm, or later if it's busy.

Old House Off Haile Selassie Rd, 1km south of the town centre ☎0722 697868 or ☎020 3526007. Pub and restaurant which does good food, with curries from Ksh450, *nyama choma* at Ksh500/half-kilo and snacks in the Ksh100–450 range. A great spot for a pint with the locals. Daily 6am–11pm.

Sherlock's Bistro Located in the Nakumatt complex on Main St ☎0786 667409. Spacious sports bar and lounge with tables downstairs spilling out into the parking area, and an extensive and good value menu including enormous pizzas (Ksh450) and Mexican food. Wi-fi. Daily 6.30am–midnight.

Spice Garden South of town just off the highway, by Old House ☎0771 233838, ⓦspicegardennanyuki .com. Restaurant and bar serving mostly Indian food, with a few Chinese dishes thrown in for good measure; most dishes – including butter chicken, palak paneer and kung pau chicken – go for Ksh690. Daily 7.30am–11pm.

Sportsman's Arms North side of town ☎062 32348 or ☎0734 944077, ⓦsportsmansarmshotels.com. Time appears to have stood still for seventy years in the downstairs pub at this old hotel, while their deck restaurant conforms more to twenty-first-century norms. There are à la carte meals for around Ksh700, and lunch and dinner buffets for Ksh1000. Wi-fi. Restaurant daily 6.30am–10.30pm; bar daily 10am–11.30pm, later on weekends.

SHOPPING

Blue Rhino Craft Shop Main St, next to Dormans Coffee Shop ☎020 2324836. Superior bric-a-brac, crafts

and souvenirs, including some lovely leatherwork and home-made bath products. Mon–Sat 9am–5pm.

Timau

Leaving Nanyuki eastwards, the ring road skirts closer to the mountain than at any other point in its circumference. The extremely fertile land here is for the most part covered by rolling wheatfields and commercial estates; many people work on the acreages of poly-covered flower and vegetable fields.

After 19km you come to the high-altitude village of **TIMAU**, unremarkable but for two outstanding stopover possibilities with accommodation.

ARRIVAL AND DEPARTURE

TIMAU

By public transport Frequent buses and matatus connect Timau with Nanyuki (30min), Meru (1hr 30min) and Isiolo (1hr 30min). Both accommodation options would require a taxi or a long walk from the main road.
By plane The nearest airport is located just south of Nanyuki.

ACCOMMODATION AND EATING

★ **Kentrout Trout Farm** 3km to the south of Timau up a rough, signposted track (4WD in rainy weather) ☎ 072 357672 or ☎ 072 0804751, ✉ kentroutltd@gmail .com; map p.170. A delightful retreat, the gardens, river and indigenous forest teeming with birdlife and colobus monkeys. The restaurant (daily 8am–9pm) offers delicious alfresco lunches (trout with soup and salad Ksh1000), the ingredients for which are grown or bred on the farm. There are three somewhat shabby but characterful rooms in a rambling old ranch house, plus two stone cottages for rent, all with their own fireplaces. Room only **Ksh3000**

★ **Timau River Lodge** 2km east from Timau and 1km off to the south ☎ 0721 331098 or ☎ 0716 703111, ⊛ timauriverlodge.webs.com; map p.170. The dream of a charming Afghan couple, this lodge (a diverse collection of rustic log, mud and underground houses) was built to run on ecological principles. There's a communal cooking area with ancient Scottish cast-iron ovens, and children will adore the loft bedrooms in the largest *bandas*. You can camp anywhere you like (tents and bedding are an extra Ksh1500 per person). Trout fishing is on offer, and there are secluded waterfalls and river pools for bathing in, plus a huge expanse of forest to explore. Per person rates: camping **Ksh750**, FB **Ksh5250**, HB **Ksh4000**, BB **Ksh3250**, self-catering **Ksh2500**

East to Meru

After Timau, the scenery acquires a real grandeur as you pass along the southern fringes of the Lewa Wildlife Conservancy (see p.508). The 70km from Timau to Meru couldn't illustrate better the amazing variety of climate and landscape in Kenya. The road climbs steeply to almost 3000m, passing alternative routes to the peaks and giving unparalleled views of them in the early morning. A spectacle you might not have guessed at, however, is the panorama that spreads out to the north as the road drops once again. On a really clear day, after rain has settled the dust, this is devastatingly beautiful. Even on an average day, you can see as far as the dramatic mesa of **Ol Olokwe**, nearly 100km north in the desert. Isiolo (see p.541) lies out there, too, first stop on the way to the northern wilderness. East of the Isiolo and Lewa turnoff, the road to Meru suddenly plunges through verdant jungle, with glimpses through the trees of the Nyambeni Hills and volcanic pimples dotting the plain. Road signs tell you to slow down and beware of elephants crossing (a warning blithely ignored by most motorists).

ACCOMMODATION

EAST TO MERU

Rutundu Log Cabins On northeast side of Mount Kenya; no telephone, but reservations ☎ 0727 232445 or ☎ 0731 325797, ⊛ rutundu.com; map p.170. On the moorland shore of little Lake Rutundu at 3000m, beneath the dramatically flat-topped Rutundu hill, this rustic retreat is the perfect place for getting away from it all – and even better if you want to have large trout for dinner every night. The comforts are elementary, yet it's exclusive at the same time – and given huge cachet as the place where Prince William proposed to Kate Middleton. Self-catering, in two cabins sleeping up to four in total (extra beds $75 each); park fees payable on top of the nightly rate. From Timau go about 20km east until you reach the North Imenti petrol station, and 300m beyond that, the 1.5hr, 4WD-only track – or you can charter a helicopter from Lewa or Nanyuki. Exclusive use **$570**

Meru

The moist, jungle atmosphere around **MERU**, with wood smoke curling up against a background of dark forest, is reminiscent of parts of West Africa, and a change of mood after the dryish grasslands on the northwest side of the mountain. **Meru oak** is the commercial prize of this forested eastern side of the mountain, though judging by the number of active sawmills at the upper end of the town, supplies won't last much longer. The forest still comes almost to the town's edge, however, with tall forest giants still looming high, and paths lead off to cleared *shambas* where, for a year or two, just about anything will grow.

Meru town stretches for several kilometres down the mountain slopes, with great views from the upper (**Makutano**) half of town over the densely settled lower areas. The municipal **market** is large, and it's the obvious place to sample the excellent agricultural produce of the district: they grow the best **custard apples** in Kenya here, and you won't find cheaper, bigger or better bunches of *miraa* anywhere (see box, p.186). Meru is also a good base for forays into the nearby **Meru National Park**, 67km east of town.

Meru Museum

Daily 8.30am–5.30pm • Ksh500 • Ⓦ museums.or.ke

The tiny but fascinating **Meru Museum** is a treat. It occupies the oldest stone building in town, a former District Commissioner's office, where you're likely to be the only visitor, except at weekends when they also do special film shows for local children. The emphasis is on the traditional culture of the Meru people: small ethnographic exhibits, pick-up-and-feel blocks of fossilized wood, stone tools from a prehistoric site at Lewa Downs and some woeful stuffed animals. There's a particularly good **herbal pharmacopoeia** – a collection of traditional medicinal plants growing in the garden, where you can see what a *miraa* bush looks like – and the museum's **Meru homestead** is well presented.

If you're interested in the Meru tribe, ask at the museum about the **Njuri-Ncheke traditional courthouse**, approximately 9km north of Meru on the road to Maua. The Njuri-Ncheke is a semi-secret society of elders sworn to preserve and uphold traditional cultural structures and religion.

ARRIVAL AND INFORMATION
MERU

By bus and matatu Meru is a hub for transport south, west and east. Numerous bus and matatu companies have their offices between the mosque and *miraa* trading area, and most major destinations are served from the main stage, with the exception of Embu, vehicles for which leave from the western end of Moi Ave.

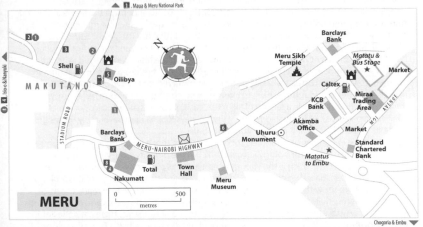

MERU

■ ACCOMMODATION				● EATING		■ DRINKING
Alba Hotel	8	Nevada Palace Hotel	3	Alba Hotel	4	**AND NIGHTLIFE**
Blue Towers	5	Rocky Hill Inn	4	Rocky Hill Inn	3	Simba Wells	1
Meru Safari Hotel	6	Three Steers	2	Three Steers	1	
Meru Slopes	7	White Star	1	Zulu Roasters Cabanas	2	

2

Bus destinations Embu (several daily; 2hr 30min); Maua (3 daily; 1hr 30min); Mombasa (daily; 12hr); Nairobi (several daily; 6hr); Nanyuki (3 daily; 2hr); Thika (several daily; 5hr).

Matatu destinations Isiolo (1hr 30min); Maua (several daily; 1hr 30min); Nairobi (6hr); Nanyuki (2hr).

Services All three main banks have ATMs here, and nearly all the hotels in town have wi-fi.

ACCOMMODATION

In keeping with its market-town functions, Meru has no shortage of accommodation, with a couple of new, classier options having recently been added to the usual clutch of B&Ls.

Alba Hotel Up the hill behind Nakumatt ☎ 0722 795173, ⓦ albahotels.co.ke. Meru's only high-end hotel still feels relatively small and intimate, offering 51 elegantly decorated rooms with all the amenities and views over the Nyambeni Hills. There's a pool (Ksh500 for non-guests) and gym, as well as a decent restaurant and bar (see opposite). Wi-fi. BB Ksh10,200

Blue Towers At the junction of Meru-Maua Rd in Makutano ☎ 0701 160961, ⓔ bluetowershotel@yahoo .com. Decorated with paintings and posters, this offers excellent value, with TVs, nets and safes in every room, as well as a safe place to leave your car. Deluxe rooms, with enormous bathrooms, cost only a few hundred shillings more. Wi-fi. Room only Ksh2100

Meru Safari Hotel Tom Mboya St ☎ 0725 259852, ⓔ merusafari@yahoo.com. Large hotel, with a rather institutional feel and smallish rooms with instant showers, but clean and comfortable enough, with a nice terrace bar-restaurant that serves very decent food. BB Ksh2000

Meru Slopes Just up the hill next to Nakumatt ☎ 0711

620219, ⓔ mslope@yahoo.com. A slick, business-like hotel catering to Meru's many conference-goers, with good security and a bar/restaurant serving Kenyan food. Rooms come with elegant canopy nets over the beds and free tea and coffee, as well as DSTV. Wi-fi. BB Ksh6500

Nevada Palace Hotel By Makutano's shopping centre, along the Meru–Nanyuki road ☎ 0723 444611, ⓦ nevadapalacehotel.co.ke. A large and very pink tower of a hotel with small but surprisingly cosy and attractive rooms set around a cavernous central courtyard. There's a bar and restaurant as well, and DSTV is on offer. Wi-fi. BB Ksh2500

Rocky Hill Inn 8km northwest of Meru on the Nanyuki road ☎ 0724 534761. An ornate creation with chalets almost hidden among the landscaping and overgrown gardens, this has an unreliable water supply, but its non-s/c rooms are fairly spacious and, for the moment, exceedingly cheap (plans are under way to add en-suite bathrooms, at which point prices will inevitably rise). Endearingly weird and worth a visit. BB Ksh500

MIRAA

Throughout Kenya, and especially in the Central Highlands and on the coast, you'll often see people selling and chewing what looks like a bunch of twigs wrapped in a banana leaf. This is **miraa**, more commonly known abroad by its Somali name **qat**, a natural stimulant that is particularly popular among Somalis, Somali Kenyans and Yemenis. The shrub (*Catha edulis*) grows in the hills around Meru (the world centre for its production), and the red-green young bark from the shrub's new shoots is washed, stripped with the teeth and chewed, with the bitter result being something of an acquired taste (it's sometimes taken with bubble gum to sweeten it). *Miraa* contains an alkaloid called cathinone, a distant relative of amphetamine, with similar **effects**, though you have to chew it for some time before you'll feel them. When they do kick in, they include a feeling of alertness, ease of conversation and loss of appetite. Long-term daily use can lead to addiction. It's not always looked upon favourably, with signs prohibiting the chewing of it in many hotels and bars.

Miraa comes in bundles of a hundred sticks called "kilos" (not a reference to their weight) and various **qualities**, from long, twiggy *kangeta*, which is the ordinary, bog-standard version, to short, fat *gisa kolombo*, which is the strongest. As it loses its potency within 48 hours of picking, it's wrapped in banana leaves and transported at speed. Street stalls selling it often display the banana leaves to show that they have it, and the best place to buy *miraa* in many towns is where the express matatus arrive from Meru. The use of *miraa* by bus, truck and matatu drivers goes a long way towards explaining why they have so many accidents. There are no **legal restrictions** on the use of *miraa* in Kenya, although imams have issued a *fatwa* (legal judgement) condemning it as an intoxicant, like alcohol, which means that it is forbidden to true believers. In fact, in most countries (including the UK), *miraa* is a controlled narcotic, the possession of which is a criminal offence.

Three Steers Along Nanyuki road, 200m from the Makutano junction ☎0728 588005, ⓦnairobipacific hotels.com. This large motel-type complex was in the process of adding a newer, fancier wing at the time of writing, but the older rooms are quite functional if somewhat pricey, with nets, TVs and instant showers. Safe parking, and wi-fi. BB Ksh6000

★**White Star** Moi Stadium Rd, 800m east of the Makutano junction ☎0701 160962, ❷bluetowershotel @yahoo.com. Sister hotel of the *Blue Towers* and similarly decorated with animal murals, this cosy little lodge offers excellent value (though the restaurant doesn't serve alcohol). Standard rooms are large and airy, with dark wood furnishings, TVs, safes and nets ("Hippo" is the best), while deluxe rooms have four-poster beds with a separate shower and tub. There's safe parking, and wi-fi. Room only Ksh1700

2

EATING

Meru doesn't have any outstanding places to **eat**, but most places are reasonably cheap. Most of the hotels also have good restaurants that serve a selection of African dishes. If you're **self-catering**, there's a huge new Nakumatt at the upper, Makutano, end of town. Makutano district is also the centre for **nightlife**.

Alba Hotel Up the hill behind Nakumatt ☎0722 795173, ⓦalbahotels.co.ke. The most up-market dining experience in Meru around the hotel pool, though the menu isn't quite as sophisticated as the setting. There are curries and pastas on offer, as well as lamb chops, T-bone steak (Ksh1300) and even lobster (Ksh2500), alongside a good selection of liquors you can enjoy in the restaurant itself or the attached bar. Wi-fi. Daily 6.30am–11pm.

Rocky Hill Inn 8km northwest of Meru on the Nanyuki road ☎0724 534761. At the weekend, you might want to venture here for *nyama choma* on the terraces tucked into this charmingly overgrown garden restaurant. They even do a bring-your-own deal: you supply the animal, they do the rest. Goat *choma* Ksh600/kg, whole chicken Ksh1500 and whole

duck, when available, Ksh3000. Daily 6.30am–midnight.

Three Steers Along Nanyuki road, 200m from the Makutano junction ☎0728 588005, ⓦnairobipacific hotels.com. The chef at this hotel is Indian and the good-value Indian-inspired dishes include plenty of vegetarian options (mains around Ksh500), but there's also a *nyama choma* bar outside and a large, round disco hall with live music on weekends. Daily 6.30am–11pm.

Zulu Roasters Cabanas At an outdoor courtyard opposite the mosque ☎0734 428392. You can't go far wrong with the *nyama choma* at this friendly local hangout, where you can stuff yourself with chicken and chips, ugali and plenty of roast goat (Ksh650/kg); try the "special *githeri*" with black beans and peas. Daily 7am–10pm.

DRINKING AND NIGHTLIFE

Simba Wells 50m from the Makutano Junction, along the Meru–Embu Highway ☎ 0723 515084, ⓦsimbawells .com. Always jam-packed during the weekends, this multi-level bar and nightclub, whose decor gives it a vaguely Pirates of the Caribbean flavour, is the most famous nightspot in Meru. They have expensive beer (Ksh200), great *nyama choma* (Ksh800/kg) and a large terrace, plus a dancefloor downstairs. Daily 8am–4am.

Embu and around

The fast road from Meru to Embu swoops around the eastern slopes of Mount Kenya, as a vibrant collage of picturesque landscapes unfolds before you. Five kilometres south of Meru, you cross the **equator**, and it's indicative of the lack of tourism round here that there's not a single curio stand, let alone a "Professor Coriolis" (see p.180). Hundreds of streams, the run-off from luxuriant rainfall blown in by the southeast monsoon, cut deeply into the volcanic soil of this eastern flank of the mountain. As a result, this side has a much broader covering of jungle, which extends, *shambas* permitting, down to the level of the road and beyond. Driving along, you plunge from one green and tan gorge to the next – early in the morning (the safest time to travel) you can sit back and admire the scenery. Sit on the right side of the vehicle for glimpses of snow-capped peaks, normally visible at this time of day. Most public transport between Meru and Embu stops at **Chogoria**, a base for the eastern Mount Kenya ascent (see p.176), although if you're staying overnight you might consider continuing to the livelier market town of **CHUKA**.

There's very little to get excited about at **EMBU**, and it's not obvious why it was chosen as the capital of Embu County. Without the apparatus of a county headquarters, the town wouldn't amount to much, although its proximity to Mount Kenya has resulted in a fair range of accommodation, mostly in the form of small motels.

ARRIVAL AND DEPARTURE

EMBU AND AROUND

Most public transport between Meru and Embu stops at Chogoria (50min from Embu) and Chuka (35min from Embu). Heading south, transport from Embu along the Kangonde route goes to Thika, with only a few matatus bound for Kitui (2hr). The trip to Nairobi via Sagana is covered by dozens of buses and matatus. If you want to climb **Mount Kenya** from Embu, the closest route is via the idyllic *Castle Forest Lodge* (see p.167).

By bus from Embu Meru (several daily; 2hr); Nairobi (several daily; 2hr 30min); Sagana (several daily; 1hr); Thika (several daily; 1hr 30min).

By matatu from Embu Isiolo (3hr 30min); Meru (2hr 30min); Nairobi (2hr 30min); Sagana (1hr); Siakago (1hr).

ACCOMMODATION

CHUKA

Godka Hotel About 500m north of Chuka on the Meru road ☎0740 085222. Reasonable, airy rooms with good-sized bathrooms, TVs and nets. There's a basic restaurant and a *nyama choma* bar in the garden that's a popular place for locals to drop by for a drink. Wi-fi. Room only **Ksh2000**

New Thuchi Lodge South of Chuka ☎0726 656841, ✉karueinvestco@yahoo.com; map p.170. Relatively upmarket local haunt with beautifully tended tropical gardens, a large pool, well-kept rooms with nets and TVs and very spacious two-bedroom cottages. There's a restaurant as well, but order well in advance. To get here, turn off the main B6 road 8km south of Chuka at Kathegeri, and take the easterly direction on the E652 signposted "Kigumo 7km". The lodge is 3km down this decent earth road. Room only **Ksh1500**

EMBU

★**Izaak Walton Inn** At the top end of town, on the way out northwards, towards Meru ☎0712 781810, ⓦizaakwaltoninn.co.ke. By far the best place in Embu is a colonial-era former farmhouse, now an assemblage of green-*mabati*-roofed and newer buildings, with pleasant gardens, welcoming staff and an enthusiastic local clientele. Rooms are clean and comfortable, with nets and TVs, and mix colonial features with more modern fixtures and fittings. There's quite a range to choose from, so check several rooms before deciding. It's also a good place for a drink or meal. Wi-fi. BB **Ksh4300**

Kryptonite Hotel Opposite Embu Municipal Council Offices ☎0728 398455, ✉thekryptonitehotel@gmail .com. Spacious and rooms with modern bathroom fittings and attractive decor, including frosted glass doors leading onto small balconies. There's laundry service and ample, secure basement parking, as well as a sunny restaurant on the first floor. Wi-fi. BB **Ksh3000**

EATING AND DRINKING

As well as the options listed below, Embu also has a number of decent *hotelis* doing reliable food.

Izaak Walton Inn At the top end of town, on the way out northwards, towards Meru ☎0712 781810, ⓦizaakwaltoninn.co.ke. It isn't cheap, but this is the most sumptuous food selection in town, with tables spread across the lawn or the veranda of this old farmhouse. There are some good vegetarian options, sandwiches (Ksh500 for a club sandwich) and a meaty "Izaak Walton platter" for Ksh1200. Inside you'll find a cosy wood-panelled bar with a nice big fireplace. Wi-fi. Restaurant daily 7am–11pm;

bar daily 8am–last customer.

Pearl Springs Hotel One street back from the main road, near the Kryptonite Hotel ☎0722 547978. Popular first-floor restaurant with a sunny wrap-around terrace, serving good-value Kenyan dishes like big plates of chicken and chips (Ksh300), as well as steak and lamb chops, though not everything is always available. Wi-fi. Daily 6.30am–11pm.

The Kiangombe Hills

The relatively modest altitudes of the **Kiangombe Hills** (Kiangombe peak is 1804m), east of Embu, aren't enough to lure climbers, but the unspoilt district, upstaged by Mount Kenya and ignored by tourists and travellers, is worth a visit if you have an interest in mysterious folklore. The hills are the home of the **Mbere**, who are related to the Kikuyu, Embu and Meru, and have a reputation in Kenya as possessors of magical powers. Some villages have elderly sages called **Arogi**, credited with terrifying abilities, though others – the **Ago** – have more beneficent gifts like the ability to foretell the future or find missing goats. The identity of these "witches" is at best a hazy and mysterious one which people aren't in any hurry to talk about and is further confused by the supposed existence in the hills of a race of **"little red men"** whose diminutive size (estimated at 1.2m) and fleeting appearances in the bush have led more imaginative scientists to suppose that they might be *australopithecines*, or ape-men, hanging on into the twenty-first century. They and the Ago-Arogi may be just part of the "old people" mytho-history of central Kenya, which is at least partially based on the real, ancient and probably Cushitic-speaking peoples of two thousand or more years ago. Such, anyway, are the stories that might draw you from the main highway.

Siakago

SIAKAGO, 25km east of Embu, is the main centre of the Kiangombe Hills. Siakago isn't a ki-Mbere word and its derivation is uncertain. It may well have derived from "Chicago", after a group of American anthropologists based themselves here in the 1930s and started the ape-men stories. It's a pleasant and relaxed one-street town, all deep-red earth, green vegetation and colourfully painted shop fronts. As well as basic services, there's a noisy little market (main days Tues & Fri), which mostly sells livestock at extortionate prices, and several mission churches set amid the huts and *shambas* on the outskirts.

Exploring the hills

The Kiangombes rise behind Siakago and look deceptively easy to **climb**. In fact, it's a stiff hike to the top, better as a two-day trip with an overnight camp in the hills. You start with a 10km hike to **KUNE**, northeast of Siakago, followed by a 2km walk to a **forest station**, where you'll find the start of the main approach to the summit area. You should pick up a **guide** at the forest station (expect to pay around Ksh1500), which may have to be coordinated in Siakago or Kune the day before. From the forest station, ignore the disused vehicle track winding into the hills; it soon becomes difficult to follow. Instead, use the **footpath** leading straight up from behind the huts, which takes you in about four hours to the peaks area. Much of your way is likely to be impeded by thick vegetation and you'll find following the overgrown trail can be tiresome, so ensure someone in your party has a *panga* to trail-blaze it with. As you climb, human population quickly thins out; this is "red-people" territory and traditionally feared by the Mbere.

ARRIVAL AND INFORMATION   THE KIANGOMBE HILLS

By matatu Siakago can be reached from Embu by matatu (around 30min).

By car From the north, take the B7 road from Embu, turning off at Musonoke, to Siakago. You can also reach

Siakago from Kitui (see p.317) in about 2hr.

Services Siakago has a scattering of *hotelis* (usually combined with butchers), a petrol station and two B&Ls.

Mwea National Reserve

$25 • ☎ 020 2052727, ⊕ kws.org • 42 square kilometres

The **Mwea National Reserve**, 35km south of Siakago, is well worth the effort if you're looking for solitude and want to avoid the touristy atmosphere of some other parks and reserves. It's a beautiful area with a wealth of ornithological interest and wildlife including giraffes, buffaloes, antelopes and elephants, though the big beasts can be hard to see. With your own tent you can camp either by the main gate or on the sloping site near the shore of the reservoir, though swimming is highly inadvisable – the crocs have a mean reputation.

By car The easiest way to get to the reserve is via the tarmac B7 Embu–Kangonde road. Some 15km south of Embu, the signposted *murram* road off the B7 to the reserve is passable all year round. Further along the B7, on the south side of the hydroelectric Kamburu dam, another signposted road heads in via Masinga Dam from just before the village of Kaewa: the first 11km are tarmac, the remaining 12km *murram*, liable to be impassable in wet weather. One kilometre to the left, at the end of the tarmac, is the hilltop *Masinga Dam Resort*.

ACCOMMODATION

Masinga Dam Resort 1km from Masinga Dam ☎ 0728 054584, ⓦ masingadamresort.co.ke. The resort is located on a hilltop, overlooking the reservoir. It has a pool and a choice of rooms – both prefab s/c tents and rather impersonal suites with better views, with meals available in the restaurant. Room only: tents $̲1̲6̲, rooms $̲4̲5̲

Aberdare National Park

$65 with Safari Card (see p.73) • ☎ 020 2046271 or ☎ 0707 325852, ⓦ kws.org • 767 square kilometres

Aberdare National Park splits into two different environments: the **high moorland and peaks** which form its bulk, and the lower **Salient** to the east where the vegetation is dense rainforest and there is considerably more wildlife.

In order to protect the park's **wildlife,** in particular its black rhinos (one of the largest populations in Kenya), but mainly to arrest the conflict between wildlife and humans, which most visibly manifested itself in the trashing of crops and homes fringing the park by "rogue" or "rampaging" elephants, the KWS has built a 388km electric fence to encircle the national park and the forests of the Aberdare Conservation Area, with the support of **Rhino Ark** (ⓦ rhinoark.org) and the annual Rhino Charge **motor race** (see p.70).

The high park

The high moorlands have some exceptional **walking** and include **three peaks**, Lesatima (the highest at 4001m) in the north, Il Kinangop (3906m) in the south, and Kipipiri (3349m), an isolated cone outside the park above the Wanjohi Valley in the west. They can be climbed relatively easily, given good weather conditions. It takes about three hours to climb Lesatima and two hours back down again. *Sandai* (see p.197) organizes climbs, or ask the Mountain Club of Kenya in Nairobi for details (see p.71). *El Paraiso* (see p.193) can also arrange guiding. Hiking in the park is allowed only with the approval of the warden, so apply in good time. You may be required to take a guide (whom you'll have to pay).

Unless you're planning several days of walking, fishing or camping, the most straightforward visit to the moorlands is to spend a day driving through from one side to the other between the **main gates**, Matubio and Ruhuruini. There are two other eastern gates further from Nyeri (Wandere and Kiandongoro) and two at the remote north end of the park (Shamata, accessible from Nyahururu, and Rhino Gate, from the B5 Nyeri–Nyahururu road), but there's no reliable route through the park between north and south, and the small circuit of tracks in the north is very rough. Driving via the park from Naivasha to Nyeri (or vice versa) is easy enough in good weather with 4WD. If conditions are less than ideal, however, and you get stuck, you could be in for a long day, or a miserable night. You need to check **road conditions** with the rangers at the park gates. Surfaces are mostly red *murram*, though there are also a few, very steep, rocky sections. It's usually permissible to wander a short distance from your car, though the lion situation changes from time to time.

Naivasha to Matubio Gate

From Naivasha, follow the signs for the national park via the Uplands road as if going to Nairobi, as far as the junction for Kinangop on the east side of town. From here,

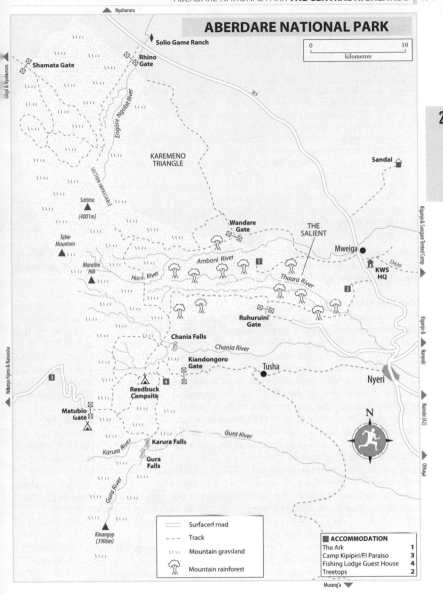

you climb about 14km, on reasonably intact tarmac, past the National Youth Service camp to Karima, where you turn left onto a good dirt road. After another 5km or so, you reach Kipipiri junction, where you keep right.

At **Ndunyu Njeru** centre, you pass the last chance of fuel and the final stop of matatus up from Naivasha. Back on the route to the gate, the road finally runs out of reasons to continue except to the national park itself, becoming a narrow, quite acceptable, tarmac switchback, and climbing through the vegetation zones, with increasing evidence of elephants (dung everywhere), to pitch out finally through the

2

HISTORY OF THE ABERDARE RANGE

The Kikuyu called these mountains Nyandarua ("drying hide", for their silhouette) long before Joseph Thomson, in 1884, named them after Lord Aberdare, president of the Royal Geographical Society. In their bamboo thickets and tangled forests, Kikuyu **Mau Mau guerrillas** hid out for years during the 1950s, living off the jungle and surviving thanks to techniques learnt under British officers during the Burma campaign in World War II, in which many of them had fought. Despite the manhunts through the forests and the bombing of hideouts, little damage was done to the natural habitat, and Aberdare National Park remains one of Kenya's most pristine forest reserves.

On the western side, the range drops away steeply to the Rift Valley. It was here, in the high Wanjohi Valley, that a concentration of settlers in the 1920s and 1930s created the myth of the glamorous, decadent **Happy Valley** out of their obsessive, and unsettled, lives. There's not much to see (or hear) these days. The old wheat and pyrethrum farms were subdivided after independence and the valley's new settlers are more concerned with making their market gardens pay. The memories live on only among veteran *wazungu*. The Kinangop plateau was settled by Europeans, too, but in 1950 the high forest and moorland here was declared **Aberdare National Park**.

highest extent of the forest at Matubio Gate, on the threshold of the moorland. Along the last 7km there are some excellent views back down to Lake Naivasha. Allow two to three hours to get this far.

Matubio Gate to Ruhuruini Gate

Allowing four hours from Matubio Gate to Ruhuruini Gate gives time enough, in good weather, for visits to Chania Falls and Karura Giant Falls. Proper access to the top of the **Karura Falls** (there's no way down to the bottom) was built only in 1992, by the British Army's Royal Engineers. They created two superb, dizzy, timber viewpoints, one on each side, from which you can look across through dripping, Afro-Alpine vegetation to the babbling, 4m-wide Karura stream as it plunges over the abyss, dropping nearly 300m in three stages. To the south, the distant veil of the **Gura Falls**, a kilometre or two across the yawning canyon, seems to make for a surfeit of dramatic beauty.

The much lower, sheer drop of the **Chania Falls** has rickety access walks and platforms (be careful), and you can gaze from the top, or the bottom, and even contemplate a swim in the pool. It was near here, in 1984, that an American tourist was badly mauled by a lion, an incident that so unnerved the park's authorities that for many years there were tough rules on unaccompanied walking. In 2000, this was followed by a cull of more than a hundred lions, many of which had been relocated from Solio Ranch. The cull was intended to rebuild the safe reputation of the park and give various herbivores, such as the giant forest hog and bongo, a chance to increase their endangered populations. In the case of the giant forest hogs, that has been rather *too* successful, but the bongos are still recovering only slowly.

The 15km east to **Ruhuruini Gate** descends in a breathtaking helter-skelter through the cloud forest, with stunning views across jungle-cloaked valleys. The road down to Nyeri from the gate is in good condition and you soon reach tarmac.

The Salient and the Tree-hotels

Kenya's most famous hotel, **Treetops**, was hosting Princess Elizabeth in February 1952 when she became **Queen Elizabeth II** on the death of her father George VI. The original tree house she stayed in was burned down in 1955 by Mau Mau freedom fighters; the present, much larger, construction is an ugly box, built on stilts, with a few trees growing through it. The main Nyeri road passes by just 3km away, and *shambas* and villages are easily visible: this is no jungle hideaway. Both tree-hotels, *Treetops* and *The Ark* (see opposite), are located in the controlled area called **the Salient**, a lower-altitude extension of the Aberdare National Park. Depending on the season, mist and low temperatures can affect both lodges: take warm clothes.

The problem at *Treetops* is clear when you survey the scene from the open-air "top deck": it is a victim of its own success. The laying of **salt** by the waterhole guarantees the nightly arrival of heavyweight camera fodder, but has brought about the destruction of all the nearby forest by elephants. The current scene – tree-planting areas enclosed by electric fences and acres of mud – is neither popular with visitors nor good for wildlife. That shy forest antelope, the bongo, hasn't put in an appearance since 1988. Despite the lack of cover, black rhino are seen often and leopard two or three times a month. But efforts to encourage hardwood forest regeneration behind the electric wires seem doomed to fail – they've been trying for more than thirty years.

ARRIVAL AND GETTING AROUND

Naivasha (see p.190 & p.210) and Nyeri (see below) are the usual bases.

By car Driving in the park is beautiful, with waterfalls and sensational views more than compensating for comparatively scarce wildlife. On the west side of the park, Matubio Gate is a 50km drive from Naivasha. On the east, distances from Nyeri are: Ark Gate 28km, Treetops Gate 29km, Ruhuruini Gate 20km, Kiandongoro Gate 30km and Wandare Gate 47km.

By plane The nearest airstrip is located at Mweiga along

ABERDARE NATIONAL PARK

the Nyeri–Nyahuru road next to Sasini Estate Farm.

By matatu Ndunyu Njeru is the final stop of matatus up from Naivasha, and from the last few kilometres to the park gate you will need to hire private transport. It's relatively easy to get around the lower parts of the range, with regular bus and matatu services between the villages. To head over the mountains and through the park, however, you need your own 4WD vehicle unless you're prepared to wait for a lift for days (you could try the *Outspan Hotel* in Nyeri). Few organized tours venture up here.

ACCOMMODATION

THE HIGH PARK

There are fairly few accommodation options in the high park; at the time of writing the two Tusk Camp Bandas and the Sapper Hut were closed for renovation, and it's unclear when they will reopen.

Camp Kipipiri/El Paraiso About 9km north of Ndunyu Njeru centre ☎0722 715853, ⓦoutdoorafrica.org. A pleasantly rustic, multi-monikered adventure centre, offering camping, meals, guided walks and safaris. Bronze guide. Camping Ksh1000, with tent hire Ksh3000

Fishing Lodge Guest House Some 2km inside the Kiandongoro Gate, located on open moors above the Magura River; reserve through KWS ☎020 6000800 or ☎0726 610533, ⓦkws.org. Two stone-built, *mabati*-roofed cottages, each with three bedrooms and sleeping a total of seven people, with a central, open-fire cooking and eating area. There's also a basic campsite nearby where you can pitch a tent. You need to take food and firewood; wood-fired boiler tanks outside produce hot water. Camping $30, whole house $210

THE TREE-HOTELS

The Ark The Salient ☎0733 779904 or ☎0733 779913, ⓦmarasa.net. The normally good game-viewing here is helped by the wide variety of viewing points. Accommodation is a little more spacious than at *Treetops*, and since recent renovations the lodge has become exceedingly cosy; the rooms are quite small, but all have a healthy dose of charm and luxury. Dinner is usually excellent, and you eat breakfast up here before returning to the affiliated *Aberdare Country Club* in Nyeri. Children under 7 not accepted. BB $305

Treetops The Salient ☎061 2032425 or ☎0722 207762, ⓦaberdaresafarihotels.co.ke. This tall, thin lodge, only 6m from front to back, has something of the creaking atmosphere of a wooden ship, and the corridors and standard rooms are very cramped. The entire place has undergone noticeable renovations (all rooms are now s/c), which have brought the hotel up to par with its royal reputation, but it still brings to mind a *Travelodge* made of wood. Dinner remains notoriously variable – excellent and copious one night, like a school dinner the next. Children under 5 not accepted; unsuitable for wheelchair-users. BB $352

Nyeri

The self-styled capital of Kikuyu-land – a title the Kikuyu of Kiambu might dispute – **NYERI** is the administrative headquarters of Nyeri County and a lively, chaotic and friendly highland town, whose name derives from the Maa word *nyiro*, meaning "reddish brown", after its earth. An attractive trading centre, it nestles in the green hills where the broad vale between Mount Kenya and the Aberdare range drops towards Nairobi. Tumultuous markets, scores of *dukas* and even a few street entertainers lend it an air of irrepressible commercialism.

Another former British military camp, Nyeri emerged as a market town for European coffee growers in the hills and for settlers on the ranching and wheat farms further north. Nyeri was also the last home of Robert **Lord Baden-Powell**, founder of the worldwide scouting movement, whose cryptically named Paxtu cottage, now a small museum (open on request; $8), stands in the grounds of the *Outspan Hotel* and whose grave and memorial are to be found on the north side of town in the cemetery.

ARRIVAL AND DEPARTURE — NYERI

By bus and matatu The bus stage and main matatu stages are on Kimathi Way.

Bus destinations Nairobi (2–3 daily; 2hr 30min); Sagana (2–3 daily; 1hr).

Matatu destinations Eldoret (5hr); Kisumu (7hr); Nairobi (2hr 30min); Nakuru (3hr).

By car A signposted route leads west from Nyeri, past the *Outspan* (see opposite), up into the Aberdare range and to the park's Kiandongoro Gate in the high moorland. In the

other direction, the road splits out of town, forking south to Murang'a via Othaya, Kiriani and Koimbi (a good road all the way), or continuing east to the A2 highway and the quickest return route to Nairobi via Sagana. A fourth route takes you northwest out of town, splitting in two after 2km. Take the right fork for the A2 highway for Naro Moru and Nanyuki, via Kiganjo. Fork left to take the B5, which sweeps past the road for Aberdare Park's Ruhuruini Gate, the track for *Treetops*, the turning to the right (east, on the

NYERI

■ ACCOMMODATION	
Aberdare Country Club	1
Batian Grand	9
Central	4
Green Hills	8
Maru B Court	5
Outspan	6
Sandai	2
Solio Lodge	3
The White Rhino	7

● EATING	
Greenoak	1
Outspan Hotel	2
The White Rhino	3

■ DRINKING	
New Mukaro Club	2
Outdoor juice bars	1

D439) for the *Aberdare Country Club*, Mweiga (8km from Nyeri), and, finally, the track up to *The Ark*. About 1km south of Mweiga, on the east side of the road, is the national park's KWS headquarters, the only point of sale for Smartcards in the highlands.

INFORMATION

Services Nyeri has branches of all the banks, including Barclays, KCB and Standard Chartered, all with ATMs. Internet access is widely available, especially along Market St.

Guides Alpine Swift Expeditions, Raipha House, Nanyuki bus stage ☎0722 805657, ✉alpineswiftexpeditions @yahoo.com. Run by John Ndetwa, this outfit is very highly recommended for Mount Kenya climbs.

ACCOMMODATION

Batian Grand Market St ☎0722 265863, ⊛batian hotel.com. Ageing but acceptable block of small rooms around a central courtyard, with big beds, nets and TVs in every room. There's a *nyama choma* bar in the courtyard which, combined with the road noise, means the upper floor rooms are much quieter. Conscientiously run but overpriced. BB **Ksh3400**

Central Kanisa Rd ☎0716 626222 or ☎0712 286333, ✉anne.kagwe@gmail.com. Secure rooms, all with instant showers, some with balconies and TVs. The newer rooms are good value and breakfast is included. It's the best place in Nyeri for *kienyeji*, and there's occasional live music at weekends. Wi-fi. BB **Ksh1600**

Green Hills Bishop Gatimu Rd, 1km south of town ☎061 2030604 or ☎0716 431988, ⊛greenhills.co.ke. A decently run, busy hotel with around a hundred comfortable rooms, equipped with canopy nets, bathtubs and DSTV. This is mostly a conference base, with a big gym and aerobics suite, a pool and extensive gardens and lawns. Wi-fi. BB **Ksh8100**

Maru B Court Off Kimathi Way ☎0720 850303. Reasonable for the price, with good security and busy bar-restaurant below. The small rooms and come with electric showers and tiny TVs, but no toilet seats. BB **Ksh1800**

Outspan Off the Kiandongoro Gate road (2km west of the clock tower on Kanisa Rd) ☎061 2032424 or ☎0722 207762; reservations through ⊛aberdaresafari hotels.com. Built in 1927 and set in splendid grounds, the stately *Outspan* (the base for visits to *Treetops*) is comfortable enough, but has the irritating flaws of its era which won't endear it to visitors expecting international standards; there are, for example, no fans, nets, a/c or room safes. The showers can be iffy, and some rooms are on the small side. The new (Chania) wing rooms are larger, with better showers and fireplaces, while the rooms in the old building have the most character (especially those downstairs, with balconies) and lovely garden views. Activities include a chilly pool, guided bird walks, the neighbouring nine-hole golf course and various excursions. Wi-fi. FB **$290**

The White Rhino Kenyatta Rd ☎0736 046784, ⊛whiterhinohotel.com. One of the largest and most reliable hotels in Nyeri. The nightclub within the same compound is busy (and gets especially noisy on weekends) but the rooms are nicely finished with satellite TV and bathtubs. There's also a pleasant terrace restaurant and attached fast-food joint (see below). Wi-fi. BB **Ksh7000**

EATING

Nyeri has a number of interesting restaurants as well as a cheese factory (from which lots of produce is available locally).

Greenoak Kimathi Way. Very good value, serving up top-quality fried meat (mutton at Ksh480/kg), plus stews, curries and snacks like *bhajias* (Ksh130). If the weather's okay, the first-floor terrace-bar, overlooking the commotion below, is fun too, and serves alcohol. Daily 6am–11pm.

Outspan Hotel Off the Kiandongoro Gate road (2km west of the clock tower on Kanisa Rd) ☎061 2032424 or ☎0722 207762. This atmospheric pile welcomes day-visitors for its excellent buffet lunches (Ksh2100), or for tea on the lawn and a swim in the pool (Ksh400). The hotel's

Tavern Bar is pleasant enough for a beer in the evening in civilized surroundings. Wi-fi. Restaurant daily 7–9.30am, 12.30–2.30pm & 7.30–9.30pm; tavern daily 3–11pm.

The White Rhino Kenyatta Rd ☎0736 046784 ⊛whiterhinohotel.com. Nyeri's most put-together fast-food joint, selling burgers and pizza (around Ksh500) – they're nothing special, but it's the cleanest hoteli in the centre. The hotel's restaurant offers meaty mains for Ksh400–900, and the bar/nightclub within the same complex is very popular with the locals. Wi-fi. Fast food daily 24hr; restaurant daily 6.30am–11pm.

DRINKING

As well as a number of bars, Nyeri has a clutch of **juice bars** near the Standard Chartered bank, which do very nice, tall glasses of avocado, beetroot and regular fruit juices for around Ksh50.

New Mukaro Club Opposite the Mathai supermarket. A pleasant open-air boozer occupying a terrace strewn with dusty potted palms, offering a limited menu of food (mostly pork, at Ksh520/kg) but plenty of local beer (Ksh140). Daily 9am–11pm.

Around Nyeri

The extraordinary density of **cultivation** in the tightly spaced *shambas* around Nyeri (crops include maize, cassava, sugar cane, millet, squash and citrus fruits, as well as tea, coffee and macadamia nuts) is partly a hangover from white settlerdom, when a rapidly growing population was deprived of huge tracts of land and forced to cultivate intensively. Partly, too, it's the result of land consolidation – the "rationalization" of fragmented land holdings into unitary *shambas* that took place in the 1950s, turning people who had held traditional verbal rights into deed-holding property owners. It's also the simple consequence of an excellent climate and soil, plus a birth rate reckoned to be one of the highest in the world.

There's no doubt that the changes which have taken place in Nyeri District have been some of the most profound and rapid anywhere in the country. Even the villages of Kikuyu-land are nearly all innovations of the last sixty years, the irreversible effects of the Emergency. Until then, the Kikuyu had mostly lived in scattered homesteads among their crops and herds. British security forces, unable to contain open revolt in the countryside, began the systematic internment of the whole Kikuyu population into fenced and guarded villages, forcing the guerrillas into the high forests, and the villages of today have mostly grown from such places.

North of Nyeri, the B5 passes several routes into Aberdare National Park, including the tracks for the tree-hotels. Eight kilometres from Nyeri you'll find the hilltop centre of **Mweiga**; several ranches offer good spots to relax and watch wildlife in the vicinity.

Sangare Conservancy

Conservancy fee $55 • ☎ 0733 642320, ⊕ sangareconservancy.com • From Nyeri, head north towards Mweiga, turn east onto the D439 and drive 5km past the *Aberdare Country Club*; from the Kiganjo side, take the *murram* D439 road, which branches off the A2 3.5km north of Kiganjo and 20km south of Naro Moru

The main draw of **Sangare Conservancy**, north of Nyeri, is its **birdlife**, with migratory pelicans, glimpses of crowned eagles and black-headed herons squawking loudly in the trees. There are usually some elephant and buffalo in the vicinity, as well as zebra, gazelle, hyena, Sykes' and colobus monkeys and the occasional leopard, while darkness brings a fantastic chorus of frogs and toads.

Solio Game Ranch

$80 • ☎ 0725 804273 • Well signposted 30km north of Nyeri off the main road to Nyahururu; you can also visit the ranch by joining a trip from Sandai or the *Aberdare Country Club* • 70 square kilometres

Solio Game Ranch lies a few kilometres north of Mweiga, off to the right. Privately run, the Solio more or less single-handedly saved the Kenyan black rhino from extinction, breeding them here for subsequent translocation into the national parks and other Kenyan reserves. The project has so far proved its worth: the population of black rhinos has tripled while the numbers of white rhinos have done even better.

ACCOMMODATION   AROUND NYERI

Aberdare Country Club 11km out on the Nyahururu road near Mweiga, then signposted 3km along the D439 murram road ☎ 0733 779904 or ☎ 0733 779913, ⊕ marasa.net. Parts of this former farmhouse date from 1930, and much of it, such as the dining room in the old house, is still attractive. The 47 rooms are in 22 cottages, built in the 1960s and still furnished comfortably, if not stylishly, while the old "Nursery Wing" has spacious family rooms with older fittings. The whole property, which has just completed significant renovations, sits on the 50-square-kilometre ACC game sanctuary, with warthogs, bushbuck, suni and even the odd leopard, together with 170 species of bird. Activities include a heated pool, tennis and game walks. It's under the same ownership as *The Ark* (see p.193), and tours often take in both. FB $305

★**Sandai** 11km northeast of Mweiga ☎0733 734619, ⓦafricanfootprints.de. This German-family-run farmhouse is a charming and relaxing rural homestay, with comfortable and very attractive rooms. Activities include horseriding (from $25), day hikes to the Aberdares, overnight excursions, painting and yoga. The five one- to four-bedroom self-catering cottages are also beautifully furnished, with fireplaces and kitchens. To get here from Mweiga, head north for 4.2km from the town centre – note the white tyre in the earth on the east side of the road, marked "Sandai 7km" (beneath a

sign announcing "St Joseph Mahiga Secondary School"). Follow this for 5.3km, turn left and after a further 600m right onto a road marked by a white tyre planted in the earth, marked "Sandai 7km". Camping Ksh500, whole cottage Ksh7000, FB $190

Solio Lodge Solio Game Ranch, 30km north of Nyeri ☎0725 804273, ⓦthesafaricollection.com. Opened in 2010, this exclusive farm and safari getaway on one of Kenya's oldest conservancies has just six large and luxurious cottages, complete with high thatched roofs and modern glass-walled bathrooms. Highly recommended, assuming price is not an issue. Conservation fee $80. Closed first half of Nov. FB $1760

Nyahururu (Thomson's Falls)

Like Nanyuki, **NYAHURURU** is almost on the equator, and it shares much of Nanyuki's character. It's high up (at 2360m, Kenya's highest town), cool and set on open savanna lands with patches of indigenous forest and plenty of coniferous plantation. Since the splendid B5 road to Nyeri was completed, Nyahururu has been less cut off, but it's still something of a frontier town for routes north to Lake Turkana and the desert. A tarmac road goes out as far as Rumuruti and then the fun begins (see p.524).

Joseph Thomson gave the town its original name when he named the nearby waterfall after his father in 1883. Many still call it "T. Falls", and not just the old settlers you might expect. Thomson's Falls was one of the last settler towns to be established. The first sign of urbanization was a hut built by the Narok Angling Club in the early 1920s to allow its members to fish for the newly introduced trout in the Ewaso Narok, Pesi and Equator rivers. In 1929, when the branch rail line arrived, the town began to take shape. The line has closed now, but the hotel built in 1931, *Thomson's Falls Lodge*, is still going strong, and Nyahururu remains an important market town, and is not really a tourist centre. The **market** is well worth a browse, especially on Saturdays. It sprawls out over most of the district west of the stadium, an indication of the town's rapid growth over the last couple of decades.

NYAHURURU

0 — 200 metres

ACCOMMODATION
Bettan Hotel & Lodge	5
Equator Lodge	4
Laikipia Comfort Hotel	3
Nyaki	2
Safari Lodge	6
Thomson's Falls Lodge	1

EATING
Emms Café	3
Frima Café	2
Star Point	4
Waterfalls Resort	1

2

The falls

On the northeast outskirts of town, **Thomson's Falls** are pretty rather than spectacular, though they can be dramatic when the Ewaso Narok is in flood after heavy rain. The falls are a popular stopoff for tourists travelling between the Samburu and Maasai Mara game reserves, and the hotel lawns above the falls get crowded with picnickers from town at weekends. Uniformed council officials have taken to extracting an "entrance fee" of Ksh200 from unwary tourists: only pay if they can give you an official ticket or receipt. Otherwise tell them you have business at the hotel, whose grounds overlook the falls. The path leading down to the bottom of the 75m falls is somewhat dangerous, especially when wet, and you should ensure there have been no recent incidents of robbery. Don't attempt to climb up again by any other route, because the cliffs are extremely unstable.

Excursions around Nyahururu

With a couple of hours to spare, you can walk down into the forested valley, following the **Ewaso Narok River** northeast of town. If you want to try this, cross the road bridge first, then look for a way downstream. The spray-laden trees are shaken periodically by troops of colobus monkeys, and chameleons are always around. The area is also fruitful for ornithologists. A much shorter stroll also takes you over the bridge and then past the electricity substation, beyond which the first trail you come to leads to the top of a hill with a communications tower and a skeletal lookout post. Excellent views from here stretch south towards Ol Kalou and the marshy trough of Lake Ol Bolossat.

A longer excursion takes you in quest of the highest-located **hippos** in Kenya. A kilometre from the turning off to *Thomson's Falls Lodge* on the Nyeri road, you come to a small cluster of *dukas* on the right. Walk down towards the houses closest to town and, about 300m from the road, you emerge by a swampy area fed by Lake Ol Bolossat. The area immediately by the access path is thick with reeds, but walk round the lake to the clump of trees and you can shin up one of these and select a natural observation platform. Sit and watch and you may see as many as half a dozen or so hippos. If you don't find them here, then they're likely to be in Lake Ol Bolossat itself, which has its north shore some 15km south of Nyahururu on the road to Aberdare National Park's Shamata gate.

ARRIVAL AND DEPARTURE
NYAHURURU

By matatu Matatus run down the impeccably surfaced B5 road to Nyeri (1hr 30min) through forested valleys and over immense plains of swaying grass. Other destinations include Maralal (3hr), Nairobi (4hr), Naivasha (2hr) and Nakuru (1hr).

By bus Nakuru (4 daily; 1hr); Nyeri (6 daily; 1hr 30min).

By car The mostly unsurfaced C76 road to Ol Pejeta

Conservancy and Nanyuki begins at Karai, 15km east of Nyahururu; the B5 road eastwards to Nyeri sweeps through the Aberdare foothills, and westwards it descends the escarpment to Nakuru, via the Subukia valley, following the route to Lake Bogoria (see p.231); lastly, the reasonably quiet C77 road to Gilgil and the Rift Valley heads south out of town, crossing the equator.

INFORMATION

Services The town has branches of KCB and Barclays, both with ATMs. Internet access is at Clicks Cybercafé (Mon–Sat

8am–6pm) in the Mima Centre, among quite a few other places.

ACCOMMODATION

Bettan Hotel & Lodge Kenyatta Ave ☎0722 305013 or ☎0702 608609. Basic, dark rooms around a busy central courtyard, with TVs and nets but no toilet seats. There's a popular 24hr restaurant on the first floor, whose balcony is always full of people drinking *chai* above the bustling commerce below. Good service. Room only **Ksh1000**

Equator Lodge Sharpe Rd ☎0710 205809. A handful of basic, small rooms, with TVs, electric showers and nets, only two of which come with two beds. It also has a very good-value restaurant and bar out front, with a sunny terrace on which to eat good breakfasts and meat dishes (Ksh100–200). There's safe parking in the courtyard. Room only **Ksh700**

Laikipia Comfort Hotel Opposite the Cooperative Bank on the way to Nyahururu Catholic Church ☎0724 894414, ✉laikipiacomfort@gmail.com. One of the newer hotels in Nyahururu, this is very clean, with bright tiled rooms around a four-storey central courtyard and good customer reception. BB Ksh2100

Nyaki North side of town, across from Nyahururu Steak House ☎065 2022313. The reasonable, well-lit rooms are on the top floor of this friendly place, with nets, TVs and instant showers, but they don't include breakfast (add Ksh500 per person). There's a restaurant on the first floor and a bar on the second. Room only Ksh1800

Safari Lodge Near the bus stage ☎065 2022334 or ☎0722 305735. Relatively spacious, clean and cosy rooms, some with balcony and all with TV, instant shower and nets. There's an alcohol ban here, and safe parking. Probably the best of the cheapies. Room only Ksh1100

★**Thomson's Falls Lodge** ☎0716 108833, ⊛thomsonsfallslodge.co.ke. Abidingly pleasant, friendly old hotel that dates back to the 1930s, with a highlands-farmhouse atmosphere and log fires in the rooms, which include nets, lots of polished floors and old-style bathtub-showers. The pleasant gardens overlook the falls themselves, beyond an observation platform roamed by camels, horses and groups of schoolchildren. The camping price includes hot showers and ample firewood. Wi-fi. Camping Ksh1000, BB $100

EATING

Emms Café Below Cyrus Lodging, opposite the market ☎0722 241148. Next to the main bus station along the busy Nairobi highway, this is a very clean local eatery with excellent service. Pilau with beef Ksh240. Mon–Sat 6.45am–6.30pm.

Frima Café Located right in town next to St Martin's Catholic Church on the road to Nyeri ☎0716 120414. A simple local joint that has developed a reputation for good, fresh food. The perfect place to enjoy your morning *mandaazi* with chai, or the usual range of Kenyan dishes like *githeri* (Ksh80), chicken or whole tilapia (Ksh250). Mon–Sat 6.30am–9pm.

Star Point On the road south towards Gilgil, 5km from the town centre by the Suera service station ☎0720 756350. This is a slightly upmarket restaurant and *nyama choma* joint, where you can stuff yourself on lamb *choma* (Ksh550/kg), whole tilapia (Ksh400) or *muteta* (meat broth with vegetables). There's a nice panoramic view of the Aberdares, and rose scents from the flower gardens next to the tents. Live music on weekends. Daily 6am–7.30pm.

Waterfalls Resort Near Thomson's Falls ☎0708 243065. Friendly and popular *nyama choma* spot serving up delicious roast meat with a fully stocked bar; 1kg of grilled meat Ksh600. There's ample space for outdoor dining and large groups, with seating in *bandas* and tables scattered around the garden. Daily 7am–midnight.

The Rift Valley

HELL'S GATE NATIONAL PARK

The Rift Valley

Kenya's Rift Valley is only part of a continental fault system that runs 6000km across the Middle East and Africa from Jordan to Mozambique. Perhaps Kenya's most important topographical feature, it is certainly one of the country's great distinguishing marks, acting as a human and natural divide. With its spectacular scenery of lakes and savanna, it has come to be seen as a monumental valley of teeming game and Maasai herders, a trough of grasslands older than humanity. Although the iconic image is not – or at least is no longer – entirely borne out by reality, the valley certainly is magnificent, a literal rift across the country, with all the stunning panoramas and gaunt escarpment backdrops you could wish for, and the plains animals are still abundant in places. Nevertheless, much of the game has been dispersed by human population pressure onto the higher plateaus to the southwest, and today most of the Maasai live further south.

3

At least the Rift Valley's **historical influence** cannot be diluted. People have trekked down it, generation after generation, over perhaps the last two or three thousand years, from the wetlands of southern Sudan and the Ethiopian highlands. Some of the more recent immigrants were the ancestors of the **Maasai** (see p.362), who dominated much of the valley and its surroundings for several centuries before the Europeans arrived. Until the beginning of the twentieth century the Maasai lived on both sides of the valley, and the northern **Ilaikipiak** group were a constant threat to trading caravans coming up from the coast. With European settlement, the Maasai were forced from their former grazing grounds in the valley's turbulent bottleneck and confined to the "Southern Reserve" (now Amboseli National Park) for much of the colonial era. Although many have now returned to the valley, and many towns retain their ancient Maa names, the Maasai are at their most conservative and traditional in southern Kenya.

The parts of the Rift Valley covered in this chapter offer several exceptional lakes, lots of scenic, twisting roads, and some of central Kenya's wildest areas. Highlights of the **central Rift Valley** include the scenic freshwater **Lake Naivasha**; the dramatic cliffs of **Hell's Gate** and nearby craggy crater rim of **Mount Longonot**; the shallow, alkaline **Lake Elmenteita**; and the busy **Lake Nakuru National Park**, with its lovely fever-tree-lined lake shore and almost guaranteed rhino sightings. In addition, there are several interesting **prehistoric sites** in this area with a refreshing rawness about them.

Heading into the **northern Rift Valley** away from Nakuru, the land drops away gently, and, as the road descends, so temperatures rise, the terrain dries up and human population becomes sparser. Although this region isn't far from Nakuru or Nairobi, and is not necessarily a difficult journey, it has a bright, harsh beauty: freshwater **Lake Baringo** and saline **Lake Bogoria** – currently the most likely place in Kenya to see

BLACK RHINO, LAKE NAKURU NATIONAL PARK

Highlights

❶ Lake Naivasha and Hell's Gate National Park A hauntingly atmospheric freshwater lake near the sheer red cliffs of Hell's Gate, where the plains have good wildlife, and whose ravine makes for spectacular hiking. **See p.205**

❷ Lake Nakuru National Park Lake Nakuru's picturesque combination of woods, grasslands and lakeshore offers some of Kenya's easiest game-driving with a good chance of seeing rhinos and leopards. **See p.224**

❸ Hyrax Hill If you don't visit any other Stone-Age site in Kenya, try to take an hour out for a wander around the eerily evocative Hyrax Hill, just outside Nakuru. **See p.230**

❹ Lake Bogoria The often overlooked Lake Bogoria – with steaming hot springs, greater kudu antelope and remote campsites – makes a wonderful retreat, and in recent years has been the location for the Rift Valley's vast flocks of flamingos. **See p.234**

❺ Lake Baringo A beautiful freshwater oasis in the dry northern Rift Valley, with plenty of hippos, crocs, almost five hundred bird species and a clutch of excellent places to stay. **See p.237**

❻ The Kerio Valley The road between the Tugen Hills and the Elgeyo Escarpment drops more than 1000m into the Kerio Valley. With spectacular views it is one of the Rift's most scenic drives. **See p.244**

HIGHLIGHTS ARE MARKED ON THE MAP ON P.204

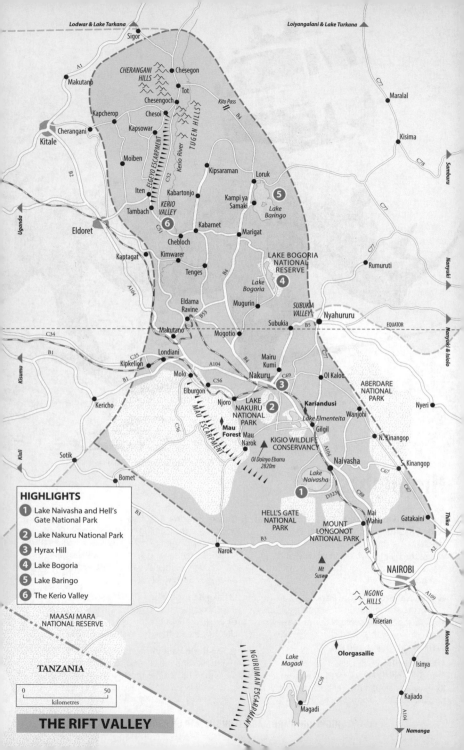

HIGHLIGHTS

1. Lake Naivasha and Hell's Gate National Park
2. Lake Nakuru National Park
3. Hyrax Hill
4. Lake Bogoria
5. Lake Baringo
6. The Kerio Valley

THE RIFT VALLEY

Lodwar & Lake Turkana
Loiyangalani & Lake Turkana

CHERANGANI HILLS

Sigor
Chesegon
Makutano
Tot
Chesengoch
Kito Pass
Kapcherop
Chesoi
Kapsowar
Cherangani
Kitale
Moiben
Iten
Kabartonjo
Tambach
KERIO VALLEY
Kipsaraman
Loruk
Kampi ya Samaki
Lake Baringo
Eldoret
Kabarnet
Marigat
Chebloch
Kimwarer
LAKE BOGORIA NATIONAL RESERVE
Kaptagat
Tenges
Lake Bogoria
Rumuruti
Eldama Ravine
Mugurin
SUBUKIA VALLEY
Makutano
Mogotio
Subukia
Nyahururu
EQUATOR
Kipkelion
Londiani
Mairu Kumi
Molo
Nakuru
Ol Kalou
ABERDARE NATIONAL PARK
Elburgon
Njoro
LAKE NAKURU NATIONAL PARK
Kariandusi
Wanjohi
Nyeri
Kericho
MAU ESCARPMENT
Mau Forest
Mau Narok
Lake Elmenteita
Gilgil
N. Kinangop
Sotik
KIGIO WILDLIFE CONSERVANCY
Ol Doinyo Eburru 2820m
Naivasha
S. Kinangop
Bomet
Lake Naivasha
Mai Mahiu
Gatakaini
Narok
HELL'S GATE NATIONAL PARK
MOUNT LONGONOT NATIONAL PARK
Mt Suswa
NAIROBI
MAASAI MARA NATIONAL RESERVE
NGONG HILLS
Kiserian
Olorgasailie
Isinya
TANZANIA
Lake Magadi
Kajiado
Magadi
Namanga

Uganda
Kisumu
TANZANIA

Maralal
Kisima
Samburu
Nanyuki & Isiolo
Thika
Monbasa

0   50
kilometres

flamingos in their thousands – are alluring targets and distinctively different, both from each other and from the lakes further south. This northern region also includes the spectacular **Kerio Valley**, which deserves a special recommendation as an unusual route north if you're heading for the west side of Lake Turkana.

Apart from **Naivasha**, **Nakuru** and the string of towns up the Mau Escarpment (**Njoro**, **Elburgon** and **Molo**), the area covered in this chapter contains few places larger than a village. Though there is usually somewhere to lay your head, this is a region where, if you're on a budget, a **tent** will be worth its extra weight, and good walking shoes are a definite advantage.

GETTING AROUND   THE RIFT VALLEY

Roads and transport are generally fine on the valley floor around Naivasha and Nakuru, but northwards, once you leave the main Nakuru–Baringo–Kabarnet axis, you can expect long waits, next-to-no buses and infrequent matatus.

By car Driving between Nairobi and Naivasha, both the Uplands Road (A104) and the Escarpment or Lower Road (B3) are in good shape, though if you're climbing the steep and winding B3 back towards Nairobi on a busy day, it can be slow going in the fumes and traffic. North of Nakuru,

there are three possible routes up to Lake Turkana (see p.516), two of them joining with the Kitale–Lodwar road west of the lake, and the third curving up to Maralal for the east side. You will need a 4WD, spare fuel and water and some flexibility in your schedule.

By bus or matatu Most public transport between Nairobi, Naivasha and Nakuru uses the Uplands Road. North of Nakuru there's reasonable public transport as far as Marigat, though it thins out beyond Lake Bogoria and dries up almost completely north of Lake Baringo.

Nairobi to Naivasha

Many travellers' first proper view of the Rift Valley is from the souvenir-draped **B3 Escarpment Road**, originally built by Italian prisoners-of-war during World War II. This flirts with the precipice before dropping steeply down to the Rift through candelabra euphorbia and spikey agave. The little **chapel** at the bottom, also Italian-built, and often used as a picnic site, seems fitting in this Mediterranean scene. From here the B3 continues north to Mai Mahiu, where it turns westwards to Narok, while the C88 continues to Naivasha.

The alternative route, the more northerly **A104 Uplands Road**, crosses a broad, bleak plateau, where roadside traders sell rhubarb, plums, carrots and potatoes, and where, in the wet season, you can find yourself driving over a thick carpet of hailstones between gloomy conifer plantations. All this contrasts dramatically with the dusty plains of the Rift Valley. When you start descending, get out your binoculars and you can pick out herds of gazelle, Maasai with their cattle and, bizarrely, a satellite-tracking station.

On the escarpment section of both roads, souvenir stands sell crafts and small sheepskins (the latter often excellent value, though they're not always very well cured, so don't last long).

Lake Naivasha

Naivasha, like so many Kenyan place names, is a corruption of a local Maasai name, this time meaning heaving or rough water, *E-na-iposha*, a pronunciation still used by Maa-speakers in the area. The grassy lakeshore was traditional Maasai grazing land for two centuries or more, prior to the lake's "discovery" by Joseph Thomson in 1884. Before the nineteenth century was out, however, Thomson's "glimmering many-isled expanse" had seen the arrival, with the railway, of the first European settlers. Soon after, the *laibon* Ole Gilisho, whom the British had appointed chief of the Naivasha Maasai, was persuaded to sign an agreement ceding his people's grazing rights all around the lake – and the country houses and ranches went up. Today the Maasai are back, though very much as outsiders, either disputing grazing rights with the many European landowners still left here, working their herds around the boundary fences or labouring on the vast horticultural farms around the lake.

The **lake** is slightly forbidding – grey and placid one minute and suddenly green and choppy with whitecaps the next – but is hugely picturesque, with its purple mountain backdrop and floating islands of papyrus and water hyacinth. It is fresh water – Lake Baringo is the only other example in the Rift – and the water level has always been prone to mysterious fluctuations. At the beginning of the twentieth century, Naivasha completely dried up and the former lakebed was even farmed, until heavy rains a few years later caused it to return, swallowing up the newly established estates. Then again in 1945, the lake almost disappeared again from drought, but since the 1950s water levels have maintained a depth of at least half a metre, rising to 6m at times.

The fast lakeside road has brought tens of thousands of migrant workers to the **farming estates**, where they grow vegetables and flowers, mostly in giant polythene greenhouses, for export by air to European supermarkets (see box, p.209). Since the late 1980s, great stretches of acacia scrub have been cleared for the expansion of the farms, and ugly lines of squalid field-hand housing have sprouted in the dust at **KARAGITA**, now the largest lakeshore settlement. But despite the development, and the ever-growing encroachment of farms and jobseekers, Lake Naivasha is still a place of considerable natural beauty. The lakeshore retains some patches of fairly unspoilt savanna and woodland, and boasts plenty of local wildlife. Even today, you can still see the odd giraffe as it lopes down to Crescent Island, or families of waterbuck or zebra munching on the lawns of the lakeside properties, and the area's climate, with a light breeze always drifting through the acacias, along with the many hiking possibilities around the lake, makes it hard to beat as a first stop out of Nairobi.

On the northeastern side of the lake, **NAIVASHA TOWN** has little to offer as a place to stay, and unless you arrive late in the day, you may as well head straight down to the lake. If you plan to spend any time in the area, however, you may want to go into town to get fuel and cash and stock up on essentials first.

Crescent Island Game Sanctuary

2km down a dirt road off Moi South Lake Rd, 6km from the A104 junction • Daily 8am–6pm • Guides available (free; tips appreciated) – ask the ticket-seller • $30, cars Ksh300 • ☎ 0733 579935 or ☎ 050 2021030, ⊕ crescentisland.co • The island is connected to the shore by a narrow causeway on the private land of *Sanctuary Farm* (see p.312); alternatively, take a boat trip (Ksh3000) from any of the resorts or campsites along the lakeshore and arrange to be picked up later in the day • Two square kilometres

A very popular short trip is a visit to **Crescent Island Game Sanctuary**. The "crescent" is the outer rim of a volcanic crater, which forms a deep bay, the deepest part of the lake. At first you may think there's nothing much on the island (which has actually been a

---

WILDLIFE OF LAKE NAIVASHA

One of the lake's most interesting features is its **wildlife**, especially its protected **hippo** population. Despite their bulk, hippos are remarkably sensitive creatures, with good night vision – always follow the advice at the lodges and campsites about where to venture after dark. You can also see **giraffes**, floating blithely through the trees, taking barbed wire and gates in their stride, and zebra, waterbuck, wildebeest and even the occasional eland are often spotted grazing in the farms and expansive grounds of the lodges and campsites that line Moi South Lake Road. Naivasha has extraordinary **birdlife** of all kinds, too, from grotesque, garbage-scavenging marabou storks to pet-shop lovebirds, doves cooing in the woods, weavers and warblers twittering in the acacia trees and splendid fish eagles, whose mournful cries fill the air like seagulls. On the water, the papyrus swamps are alive with kingfishers, herons and jacanas, while Lake Oloiden, once a bay of the main lake and now a separate saline lake, frequently attracts wayward flamingos.

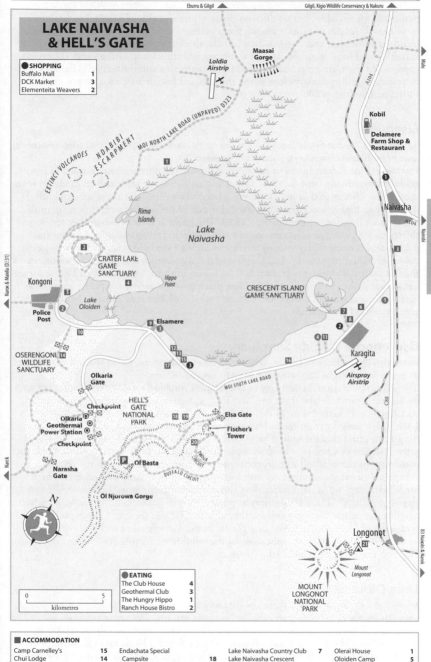

LAKE NAIVASHA & HELL'S GATE

● SHOPPING

Buffalo Mall	1
DCK Market	3
Elementeita Weavers	2

Eburru & Gilgil ▲

Gilgil, Kigio Wildlife Conservancy & Nakuru ▲

Maasai Gorge

Loldia Airstrip

MOI NORTH LAKE ROAD (UNPAVED) D323

NDABIBI ESCARPMENT

EXTINCT VOLCANOES

Rima Islands

Lake Naivasha

CRATER LAKE GAME SANCTUARY

Kongoni

Lake Oloiden

Police Post

Hippo Point

CRESCENT ISLAND GAME SANCTUARY

Elsamere

OSERENGONI WILDLIFE SANCTUARY

Olkaria Gate

HELL'S GATE NATIONAL PARK

Checkpoint

Olkaria Geothermal Power Station

Checkpoint

Narasha Gate

Ol Basta

Ol Njorowa Gorge

BUFFALO CIRCUIT

Elsa Gate

Fischer's Tower

Kobil

Delamere Farm Shop & Restaurant

Naivasha

A104

Karagita

Airspray Airstrip

Malu ▶

A104 / Nairobi

3

C88

B3 Nairobi & Narok ▶

Longonot

Mount Longonot

MOUNT LONGONOT NATIONAL PARK

MOI SOUTH LAKE ROAD

Narok & Maida (D:31) ◀

Narok ◀

N

0   5
kilometres

● EATING

The Club House	4
Geothermal Club	3
The Hungry Hippo	1
Ranch House Bistro	2

■ ACCOMMODATION

Camp Carnelley's	15	Endachata Special		Lake Naivasha Country Club	7	Olerai House	1
Chui Lodge	14	Campsite	18	Lake Naivasha Crescent		Oloiden Camp	5
Crater Lake Tented		Fish Eagle Inn	12	Camp	6	Oloongonot	
Camp	2	Fisherman's Camp	13/17	Lake Naivasha Sopa Resort	16	Campsite	21
Elsamere	9	Hippo Point	4	Naiburta Public Campsite	19	Panorama Park	3
Enashipai Resort & Spa	8	Kiangazi House	10	Ol Dubai Public Campsite	20	Sanctuary Farm	11

peninsula for decades), but you'll soon come across a wealth of wildlife, including hundreds of species of birds – among them pelicans and fish eagles – as many as four hundred wildebeest and two hundred impala, more than one hundred zebra, a variable-sized herd of giraffe, as well as hippos, waterbuck and Grant's and Thomson's gazelles. As there are no predators, walking is permitted and the terrain is flat and open so you can get surprisingly close to the animals – although watch for hippos along the shoreline (see box, p.206).

Elsamere

Moi South Lake Rd, 22km from the A104 junction • Daily 9am–6pm • Ksh850 • Lunch served 1–2.30pm; Ksh1560, including entry fee • Tea served 3–5pm; included in the entry fee • ☎ 050 2021055, Ⓦ elsamere.com

Elsamere is the former home of Joy Adamson who, together with her husband George, achieved worldwide fame for their pioneering conservation work and relationship with the lioness Elsa, as told in Joy's bestselling book *Born Free*, which was subsequently made into a highly successful film. Joy did much of her writing at Elsamere up until her murder by a former employee in 1980. The house is now a field-studies centre and the focus for Lake Naivasha's environmental research. It offers accommodation (see p.211) and is open to day visitors who can watch an aged video about the Adamsons, visit the small museum of Adamson memorabilia and enjoy a civilized afternoon tea on the lawns. Book ahead if you want to have lunch. Although the house and museum are somewhat shrine-like, the garden is a fine place to while away a couple of hours with a pair of binoculars, and a troop of black and white colobus monkeys can be seen in the acacias around the grounds.

Oserengoni Wildlife Sanctuary

Moi South Lake Rd, 30km from the A104 junction • ☎ 050 2020792, Ⓦ oserengoniwildlife.com • Visits are restricted to guests staying at Oserengoni's *Kiangazi House* (see p.212), or *Chui Lodge* (see p.211). • Forty square kilometres

The worthwhile conservation area of **Oserengoni Wildlife Sanctuary** covers 30,000 acres on a former ranch inland from the lakeshore, as well as a 3000-acre wildlife corridor that links Hell's Gate National Park (see p.214) with the lake, crossing the Moi South Lake Road. Judging from the polythene horticulture so prevalent in the area, you might not guess that the same Dutch family behind the biggest flower farm in Kenya – the Zwagers of Oserian – have set aside this area of land as a sanctuary. Although the proximity of the lake and its burgeoning population can't be ignored, the reserve comprises an extensive wild area with a good array of big mammals and excellent birdlife (birders won't need reminding about the rare grey-crested helmet shrike that can be seen here). There are significant populations of giraffe, buffalo, eland, hartebeest, gazelles and zebra, and the guides will be able to find you some of Oserengoni's species translocated from northern Kenya – greater kudu, Grevy's zebra and Beisa oryx. Even if you're not staying, you may spot some of the wildlife wandering across Moi South Lake Road en route to or from the lake (there are signs).

Lake Oloiden

At Kongoni, off Moi South Lake Rd, roughly 30km from the A104 junction

Lake Oloiden was formerly part of Lake Naivasha but it is now separated from its southwest shore by a stretch of elevated land. The distance between the two lakes is about 200m, although the fluctuations in Naivasha's water levels mean that this figure is always changing (for example during unprecedented flooding in 2012–14 the two lakes actually joined up). Normally covering an area of about five square kilometres, the lake is home to several families of hippos and is a breeding ground for the common and white-necked cormorant. Unlike Naivasha, it is a saline lake (*oloiden* means "salty" in the

NAIVASHA'S FLOWER POWER

The high equatorial sun that ensures straight stems, together with the availability of fresh water, means that flower-growing is a multimillion-dollar business around Lake Naivasha. Kenya is the largest supplier of **flowers** to supermarkets across the European Union (responsible for around 35 percent) – mostly roses, carnations, chrysanthemums and lilies – and the industry is a major foreign currency earner for the country, employing hundreds of thousands of people. However floriculture uses up large quantities of water, and the blame for significant **reductions in water levels** of the lake has been largely blamed on the flower firms since they arrived in Naivasha in the late 1980s. Additionally, given that the number of people living near the lake has risen at least fivefold since the late 1970s (mostly workers on the farms), there has been a growing **pollution** problem too, and sewage waste (as well as the toxic runoffs from pesticides) has in the past put the future of the lake's delicate ecosystem into question.

However, awareness of the lake's conservation issues has grown, and many of the dozen or so horticulture companies are now addressing their responsibilities. Established in 2007, the **Lake Naivasha Water Resource Users Association** (LANAWRUA; ⓦ lanawrua.org) now monitors Naivasha's lake levels and promotes water-wise practices and good management, aiming to ensure that water resources are reasonably shared between the ecosystem, wildlife, livestock and commercial flower-growing. Most flower-growing companies have adopted computerized drip-irrigation to optimize their water efficiency, and now use geothermal steam to purge diseases in their greenhouses instead of artificial pesticides.

While wages are still low, the majority of larger farms now adhere to the exacting social and ecological standards demanded by European supermarket companies and their consumers. Currently five of the Naivasha companies are certified by Fairtrade (ⓦ fairtrade.org.uk), with more expected to follow suit. And production processes are becoming more sophisticated. Once the blooms are cut, they are also packaged here, and in some cases even the barcode indicating which particular branch of a supermarket the flowers are destined for is logged by workers in Kenya, before they are transported to the airport (usually Eldoret) to be freighted.

Maa language) and has an underground inlet containing volcanic ash – the cause of its salinity – which produces a blue-green algae. When water levels are low it therefore attracts a few wayward flamingos from the other Rift Valley lakes. To visit the lakeshore, stop in at *Oloiden Camp* (see p.211) or have lunch at the *Ranch House Bistro* (see p.213).

Crater Lake Game Sanctuary

Off Moi North Lake Rd, 38km from the A104 junction, and 8km north of Kongoni and 5km beyond Oserengoni · $25 · ☎ 050 2020613, ⓦ craterlake.co.ke

The **Crater Lake Game Sanctuary** is a straightforward target for a short trip, perhaps with a picnic or lunch at the *Crater Lake Tented Camp* (see p.211), but preferably with your own vehicle as few matatus go beyond the village of Kongoni along the unpaved Moi North Lake Road. A small **game sanctuary** has been set up all round the teardrop-shaped crater lake, with various tracks you can follow, though the one to the crater rim is only for hikers or 4WD vehicles. The birdlife is exceptional and there's a host of wildlife in the vicinity, including black and white colobus monkeys, giraffe, zebra and bushbuck.

The jade lake is quite breathtaking: the Maasai consider its deep alkaline waters good for sick cattle, and it's also favoured as a sacred place. From the main viewpoint on the west rim it's a ten-minute scramble up to the highest point. There are not many places where you can get down to the crater floor – the easiest trails are on the southwest side near the lovely *Tented Camp* and campsite. The property was formerly part of the Ndabibi Estate that belonged to Lady Diana Delamere and it contains the hilltop grave where she was buried in 1987 alongside her third and fourth husbands, Gilbert Colville and Thomas Delamere; all were key figures in the hedonistic "Happy Valley" set of British settler aristocrats in the 1940s.

THE RIFT VALLEY MUSIC FESTIVAL

Taking its cue from Malawi's increasingly popular Lake of Stars festival, the annual **Rift Valley Music Festival** is Kenya's first international music festival, and has taken place every late August since 2010, at Fisherman's Camp on the shores of Lake Naivasha (ⓦ riftvalleyfestival.co.ke). Energetic and dance-oriented on the Saturday, it turns more low-key and family-friendly on Sunday when the mood is blankets, picnics and beer. The highly recommended festival features mostly Kenyan artists and a few international acts playing from a single, central stage to an audience of a few thousand. There's also a craft market, open-air cinema and children's play area with face-painting, bouncy castle and the like. You can stay anywhere around the lake and walk, cycle or get a matatu every day, or book ahead if you want to stay on-site. Advance day tickets (excluding camping fee) cost Ksh2000 and weekend tickets Ksh4000)

ARRIVAL AND DEPARTURE   LAKE NAIVASHA

A road runs all the way around the lake, branching off from the main A104 Naivasha–Nakuru highway 3km north of Naivasha town. Distances in kilometres given in the reviews below refer to the distance from the lake road junction with the A104. The southern part of the lake road – the paved, 30km-long **Moi South Lake Road** – is where you'll find most of the lake's accommodation and other facilities. Beyond Kongoni village, you hit the dust and potholes of **Moi North Lake Road**, which loops for 35km (a 1–2hr drive) around the northern side of the lake before rejoining the A104 highway 9km north of Naivasha town.

By air A daily SafariLink service flies from Nairobi's Wilson Airport to Loldia airstrip on the west side of the lake (continuing to Maasai Mara and then directly back to Nairobi). It's also possible to charter small planes to the short Airspray airstrip on the lake's southeast shore.

By matatu Most matatus crowd in a mass up Kenyatta Avenue in Naivasha town.
Destinations Eldoret (4hr); Kisumu (6hr); Nairobi (1hr 30min); Nakuru (1hr 15min).

Buffalo Mall, Gilgil & Nakuru

NAIVASHA TOWN

Total

Jamia Mosque
Total

MBARIA KANIU ROAD

Bus & Matatu Stand

POSTA LANE

Railway Station   KCB
Barclays
STATION LANE

CHOTARA ROAD

KARIUKI

MOI AVENUE

BIASHARA ROAD

Municipal Market

Shell
Lakeshore Matatu Stand
Sera Centre
Naivasha District Hospital

KENYATTA AVENUE

MAMA NGINA ROAD

Oilibya

Naivas Supermarket

Wholesale Market

● **EATING**
Cool Breeze Café   6
Jolly Café   5
La Belle Inn   3
Mother's Kitchen   4
Njambi's   2
Sweet Banana   1

■ **ACCOMMODATION**
Ken-Vash Hotel   4
La Belle Inn   5
Lakeside Tourist Lodge 1
Viewers Park Hotel   2
Wambuku   3

● **SHOPPING**
Rift Valley Leather   1

0   250
metres

Panorama Park

GETTING AROUND

By matatu or hitchhiking Regular matatus shuttle between the lake and Naivasha town, and you can also hitchhike down to the lake fairly easily. However no public transport goes along Moi North Lake Road beyond the end of the tar at Kongoni village so to reach *Olerai House* or the Crater Lake Game Sanctuary, for example, your only option is to take one of the piki-pikis that hang around the village.

By bike A good way of exploring the lakeshore and Hell's Gate National Park, bicycles can be rented from several of the more independent traveller-oriented camps and a number of roadside operators including at the Elsa Gate of Hell's Gate (around Ksh500/day).

By boat All the lakeshore establishments offer motorized boat rides for bird- and hippo viewing and to transfer you over to Crescent Island, usually for Ksh3000–5000/hr with room for up to seven passengers. Check the life vests before you embark and make sure the crew have radios or reliable cell phones to contact shore in the event a swell rises on the lake – boating mishaps are common here.

INFORMATION

Banks There's a full showing of banks with ATMs (including Barclays and KCB) on Moi Ave in Naivasha town. Closer to the lake itself, there's a KCB ATM at Karagita (3.5km from the junction), and KCB and Barclays ATMs at DCK Market (just before *Carnelly's*).

ACCOMMODATION

There's a wide variety of excellent accommodation **around the lake** along Moi South Lake Road – everything from frugal *bandas* and camping to stately hotels and homestays. Most are open to day visitors to enjoy the lakeshore, lunch and perhaps a boat trip, and many Nairobi people do just that, especially at the weekends. There's not much to choose between the lodgings in **Naivasha town** itself and they are surprisingly pricey for what you get. The few listed below are at least adequate, but there's little reason to stay in town when the lake is so tantalizingly close.

AROUND THE LAKE

BUDGET

★ **Camp Carnelly's** Moi South Lake Rd, 17.9km from the junction ☎ 050 5050004 or ☎ 0722 260749, ⓦ campcarnelleys.com; map p.207. Funky backpacker den with s/c *bandas* sleeping up to six (Ksh8000–14,000), basic non-s/c twin rooms, dorm bunks and camping. The welcoming and convivial ambience, with a relaxing lounge area decked out in cushions, makes it a firm favourite among the independent and overland crowd. The *Lazy Bones* bar-restaurant does things like smoothies, wood-fired pizzas and nachos, plus an excellent Naivasha crayfish curry. Camping **Ksh600**, dorm bed **Ksh1000**, room only **Ksh3000**

Fish Eagle Inn Moi South Lake Rd, 18.2km from the junction ☎ 020 2067025, ⓦ fisheagleinn.co.ke; map p.207. Middle-of-the-road resort establishment with a variety of accommodation options, including dull but well-equipped "standard rooms" (with nets and hot water), dorms and camping, although most campers head for the nicer campsites at nearby *Fisherman's* or *Carnelly's*. There's a small pool (Ksh500 for campers and day visitors) and the restaurant/bar serves reasonably priced but unmemorable grills and fish from the lake. Wi-fi. Camping **Ksh700**, dorm bed **Ksh1000**, BB **Ksh9800**

Fisherman's Camp Moi South Lake Rd, 18.2km from the junction ☎ 020 2139922 or ☎ 0726 870590, ⓦ fishermans camp.com; map p.207. This long-established budget hideaway has one of the best lakeside locations, right by the water's edge and set in a magnificent grove of giant fever trees full of monkeys. Besides camping (tents, mattresses and bedding can be rented), there's a choice of simple three- and four-person s/c *bandas* (Ksh2000 per person, minimum of Ksh6000 at weekends) with fridge and small stone patios, and the six-person *Kasuku Cottage* (Ksh2500 per person, minimum of Ksh10,000 at weekends) has two bedrooms, a fully equipped kitchen and spacious veranda. Avoid the "top" camp; it's on the cliffs on the other side of the road and its several rudimentary *bandas* are infrequently used and a little forlorn. The good thatched bar/restaurant serves breakfast, fish and chips, pizza, burgers and Kenyan stews/curries and there's a lounge area upstairs. Wi-fi. Camping **Ksh700**, room only **Ksh5000**

Oloiden Camp Moi North Lake Rd, 1km beyond Kongoni and then 800m to the lakeshore, 27km from the junction ☎ 0702 993131, ⓦ oloidencamp.com; map p.207. A peaceful campsite right on the shore of Lake Oloiden with picnic tables and fire grills, this also has pre-erected dome tents and mattresses for hire (about Ksh2500 for two people all up with the camping fee), hot showers and clean flushing toilets. There's also a basic bar serving simple grilled chicken and fish and the like. Camping **Ksh700**

MID-RANGE TO EXPENSIVE

Chui Lodge Oserengoni Wildlife Sanctuary, Moi South Lake Rd, 30km from the junction ☎ 0722 200596 or ☎ 0707 645630, ⓦ chuisafaricollection.com; map p.207. One of the only two accommodation options in Oserengoni, this intimate, very upscale little lodge offers just eight two-person cottages made from local materials and decorated with hand-crafted furniture. There's a heated pool overlooking a waterhole, and the beautiful dining room, lounge and bar area features African art and antiques. Game drives are included in the price. Wi-fi. FB **$850**

Crater Lake Tented Camp Crater Lake Game Sanctuary, off Moi North Lake Rd, 38km from the junction and 8km north of Kongoni ☎ 050 2020613, ⓦ craterlake.co.ke; map p.207. Tucked away on the shore of the green crater lake (see p.209), this is in an idyllically peaceful spot. The fifteen twin and double tented rooms and family *bandas* have a rustic charm with handmade beds and little wooden verandas over the lake, and there's a pool and a floating restaurant. The birding is superb, with birdbaths everywhere, so your subjects effectively come to you – and don't miss the silent electric boat trip. You can also camp, and equipment (tents with bedding and cooking gear) is available for hire. Wi-fi. Camping **Ksh1000**, FB **$229**

Elsamere Moi South Lake Rd, 20.7km from the junction ☎ 050 2021055, ⓦ elsamere.com; map p.207. The former home of Joy Adamson (see p.384) offers comfortable, English holiday home-style rooms in spacious cottages, each with a veranda facing the lake, and dinner is hosted in the house's dining room. Very friendly and relaxing and activities include bike hire and boat trips. Reservations advisable. Wi-fi. FB **$198**

Enashipai Resort & Spa Moi South Lake Rd, 3.6km from the junction ☎ 051 2130000, ⓦ enashipai.com; map p.207. A luxury complex with a slightly Mediterranean feel and pretty, well-maintained grounds. Its forty-plus rooms are opulently furnished, with big beds and a nod to African style, while the four- and five-bedroom cottages are each large enough to house several families. Facilities

3

include a large heated pool, gym and sauna, along with all the restaurants and bars you might need. FB **$480**

Hippo Point Moi South Lake Rd, 23km from the junction ⓣ0733 993713, ⓦhippopointkenya.com; map p.207. One of the most unusual and elegant places to stay on the lakeshore, *Hippo Point* is centred around Dodo's Tower, a 35m-high folly built in 1993 by the owners of this colonial estate (Dodo and Michael Cunningham-Reid). The tower's four doubles and one single are decorated with antiques and handmade local furniture, and have lovely views from the top balconies. There are eight more rooms in the manor house built in 1932. Pool, excellent food and, as the property is not fenced, it shares the wildlife from Oserengoni Wildlife Sanctuary as it ventures down to the lakeshore at Hippo Point. Wi-fi. FB **$1300**

3

★**Kiangazi House** Oserengoni Wildlife Sanctuary, Moi South Lake Rd, 30km from the junction ⓣ0722 200596 or ⓣ0707 645630, ⓦchuisafaricollection.com; map p.207. The other accommodation at Oserengoni, and equally as stylish and personable as *Chui Lodge*, *Kiangazi* is a quintessential colonial-style country house, with seven rooms (either in the main house or garden cottages), a broad veranda overlooking the southwest corner of the lake, a pool and a nearby waterhole. As at *Chui*, the meals are superb and are accompanied by excellent wines, and game drives are included. FB **$850**

Lake Naivasha Country Club Moi South Lake Rd, 3.8km from the junction ⓣ0703 048000 or ⓣ0703 048200, ⓦsunafricahotels.com; map p.207. This grand old lady with sweeping lawns and a colonial-style lounge/terrace was built in 1937 and served as a staging post for Imperial Airways' flying boat service from Durban to London until 1950. It's a little too old-fashioned (especially its bathrooms) for some visitors (think more 1980s than 1930s), but it's got good facilities and there's always wildlife (so much so you have to have an escort after dark) on the lovely 55-acre site. Its most expensive rooms (from FB$500) are at the newer *Kiboko Luxury Camp*, with eight plush tents built on elevated walkways along the lakeshore and its own dining room. Pool gym, spa, camel and boat rides. Wi-fi. Ecotourism Kenya Bronze Award. FB **$320**

Lake Naivasha Crescent Camp Moi South Lake Rd, 1.9km from the junction (plus 1km down to the site) ⓣ020 2321135, ⓦcrescentcamp.com; map p.207. Expansive stretch of grass under yellow acacias, with twenty enormous and very comfortable safari tents on stilts with huge built-in bathrooms and wooden floors and verandas. A special touch is the "turn-down" service and hot water bottles on a cool evening. Good and generous buffet food and attentive staff. Wi-fi. FB **$360**

★**Lake Naivasha Sopa Resort** Moi South Lake Rd, 8.6km from the junction ⓣ020 3750235 or ⓣ0704 300301, ⓦsopalodges.com; map p.207. With ostentatious public areas sprawling from an impressive euphorbia grove, this is one of the better large mid-range options and has 84 rooms in double-storey cottages arranged in a crescent, each with terraces/balconies, DSTV and bathtubs. Good for families as the rooms connect. Facilities include two swimming pools, tennis courts, stables for horse-riding and a buffet restaurant (lunch Ksh1750). Wi-fi. Ecotourism Kenya Bronze Award. FB **$275**

★**Olerai House** 19km along Moi North Lake Rd from the A104 turn-off 9km north of Naivasha ⓣ0731 596437, ⓦelephantwatchportfolio.com; map p.207. Located on the north shore of the lake in a small, private wildlife sanctuary with plenty of plains game, this is the former home of Iain and Oria Douglas-Hamilton, who have been instrumental in elephant conservation for decades (they still live on the estate and also operate *Elephant Watch Camp* in Samburu National Reserve; see p.379). There are six rooms and a self-catering cottage, all full of cool touches and idiosyncratic design ideas, in bungalows surrounding the main, flower-covered house. The cooking is superb, and uses ingredients from the organic garden. Wi-fi. FB **$700**

★**Sanctuary Farm** At the head of Crescent Island, 1km down a dirt road off Moi South Lake Rd, 6km from the junction ⓣ0722 761940, ⓦsanctuaryfarmkenya.com; map p.207. With its 400 acres of wooded grounds roamed by zebra, giraffe and wildebeest, it's no wonder this place has become a favourite among expats and NGO workers. The ten rooms are in a converted old polo stable, all nicely decorated with a sense of privacy that's hard to find elsewhere and there's a communal lounge with a fireplace. Rates are with or without meals so you can bring the price down by cooking in the self-catering kitchen (Ksh2000 per day). There's also a shady campsite with hot showers and you can hire decent-sized tents with bedding (minimum total cost for a pitch Ksh7000). Day visitors are welcome at *The Club House* (see opposite). Wi-fi. Camping **Ksh2000**, room only **$255**

NAIVASHA TOWN

Ken-Vash Hotel Posta Lane ⓣ0716 198481; map p.210. Lacking in atmosphere, but reasonably comfortable and very clean, with decent nets, DSTV in all sixty-odd rooms, and – strangely – carpeted throughout. It's a bit old-fashioned, but the service is good and there's safe parking. BB **Ksh3200**

★**La Belle Inn** Moi Ave ⓣ020 3510404, ⓔinfo@labelleinn.com; map p.210. Popular and atmospheric old staging post on the main street through town, built in 1922, with a variety of good-value, homely, English-BB-style rooms with nets and TV, set around a garden courtyard. Rooms are mostly spacious and well furnished and the whole place is well looked after, though the bathrooms are tatty, with old plumbing and hot water only in the mornings and evenings. Safe parking. Wi-fi. BB **Ksh5000**

Lakeside Tourist Lodge Moi Ave ☎ 050 2020856 or ☎ 0722 524565, ⓦ lakesidetouristlodge.com; map p.210. Ignore the name – it's nowhere near the lakeshore – but this large, pleasant place on the north side of the town centre has good, clean, bright s/c rooms with nets and DSTV (some on the first floor have balconies) and efficient service. Go for a window room, as inside rooms are small and dark – and negotiate on the price, which is steep. The restaurant is another place to try Naivasha fish and crayfish. BB **$55**

Panorama Park Off Koinange Rd on the south side of town ☎ 050 2030128 or ☎ 0712 091777, ⓦ lakenaivasha panoramapark.co.ke; map p.210. Set on a cliff edge, this local holiday and wedding/conference resort has old-fashioned but neat little rooms with nets, DSTV and instant showers, each occupying half a rondavel. The grounds are attractively landscaped with plenty of flowers, there's a

(vaguely) Africa-shaped pool, and the glass-walled restaurant boasts gorgeous views across the lake. Note that it's Christian-run so no alcohol is served. Rates are somewhat confusing and highly negotiable. BB **$140**

Viewers Park Hotel Moi Ave ☎ 0708 211070 or ☎ 0738 376437 ⓦ viewersparkhotel.co.ke; map p.210. A fairly new purple-painted four-storey hotel just north of the main drag, although the furnishings inside are cheap and a bit haphazard. The decent tiled rooms have nets, electric showers, DSTV (some also have balconies) and there's a small ground-floor cafeteria-type restaurant. Safe parking can be arranged with an *askari*. Wi-fi. BB **Ksh2500**

Wambuku Moi Ave, next to the post office ☎ 050 2030287; map p.210. Big and impersonal with a facade of large mirrored doors opening onto balconies, the *Wambuku* has stuffy, rather cramped s/c rooms with nets, TV and old-style showers (hot water evenings only). Still, it's central and not bad value for Naivasha. BB **Ksh1200**

EATING

You can drop in for meals and drinks at all the camps and lodges **around the lake** expect to pay around Ksh1750–2250 for a buffet lunch at Lake *Naivasha Country Club*, *Enashipai Resort & Spa* or *Crater Lake Tented Camp*. These also charge casual visitors an additional fee of around Ksh300–500 for a swim in the pool. Good and cheaper casual meals can be found at the pleasant thatched restaurants at *Camp Carnelly's* and *Fisherman's Camp* and you can also stop at *Elsamere* for lunch or afternoon tea. In **Naivasha town** there's a clutch of cheap, local places to eat on Moi Avenue north of the Total petrol station.

AROUND THE LAKE

The Club House Sanctuary Farm, at the head of Crescent Island, 1km down a dirt road off Moi South Lake Rd, 6km from the junction ☎ 0722 761940, ⓦ sanctuaryfarmkenya.com; map p.207. Set in a characterful old wooden polo club on stilts overlooking a meadow filled with wild game at *Sanctuary Farm* (see opposite), this offers finely presented gourmet dishes using lots of locally sourced food and homegrown veggies. Lunch (Ksh 2500), afternoon tea (Ksh750) and dinner (Ksh3000), and you must book ahead, as there are set menus for all meals. Wi-fi. Daily 8am–10pm.

Geothermal Club KenGen complex, 19.6km from the junction; map p.207. A picturesque place to grab a drink or a bite to eat, with great views and a short list of (mostly Kenyan) daily specials, scrawled on a blackboard out front. The swimming pool itself, fed by the geothermal spring, is pretty murky. Mains from Ksh400. Daily 7am–11pm.

The Hungry Hippo 1.2km from the junction ☎ 0707 967124, ⓦ bit.ly/TheHungryHippo; map p.207. No lake views and on the inland side of the road, but nonetheless popular in the evenings with Naivasha's expat crowd for its beer garden, British pub-style atmosphere and reasonably priced meals like fish and chips, burgers, pizzas and the odd

special like Thai curry (from Ksh750). Wi-fi. Daily 11am–11.30pm.

★**Ranch House Bistro** At Kongoni, off Moi South Lake Rd, 26.9km from the junction ☎ 0700 488475, ⓦ bit.ly/RanchHouseBistro; map p.207. Housed in converted farm buildings, this is a simply lovely spot set amid green lawns on Lake Oloiden's shoreline and you may well see a waterbuck or giraffe wander by. The short but carefully thought-out à la carte menu offers the likes of crumbed brie, sticky pork ribs, peppered steak, burgers with blue cheese or roasted vegetable gnocchi; otherwise opt for a thin-crust pizza. Mains Ksh750–1100 (on Sun there's a set menu or curry buffet; Ksh1200). Also has excellent coffee, a good choice of wine, plus a farm shop (Mon–Sat 8.30am–6.30pm, Sun 8.30am–1pm). Contact in advance for lunch and a game drive on the property (Ksh4000). Wi-fi. Tues–Thurs & Sun 10am–6pm, Fri & Sat 10am–10pm.

NAIVASHA TOWN

Cool Breeze Café Kenyatta Ave; map p.210. Sun-filled little wooden box of a café, vaguely reminiscent of an American diner and surrounded by foliage. There's basic Kenyan food on offer for around Ksh250, as well as baked goodies like samosas and *mandaazi*. A good spot for coffee

3

or breakfast. There are a few off-street parking spaces at the back. Daily 6.30am–9.30pm.

Jolly Café Naivasha Silver View Hotel, Kenyatta Ave ☎0716 660022; map p.210. At the front of the *Silver View* hotel, this lively *hoteli* has lots of reliable staples (main dishes around Ksh200–300) and *chai* for Ksh30. The rooms themselves are only very basic B&Ls; there are better places to sleep. Mon–Sat 6.30am– 10pm, Sun 7am–10pm.

★**La Belle Inn** Moi Ave ☎020 3510404; map p.210. A long veranda stretches along the whole front of the building here, giving a good vantage point to watch the comings and goings in town. It serves great fried breakfasts (Ksh750), grilled steaks, chicken and fish – including barbecued tilapia, spiced crayfish, Naivasha bisque and the like, all for around Ksh600 – and there's usually a vegetarian choice as well. They also have a good pastry chef and fresh bread, pies, cakes and croissants in the shop. The *Happy Valley Bar*

(6.30–11pm) gets quite lively and a band plays on Sat night. Daily 8am–10pm.

★**Mother's Kitchen** Kariuki Chotara Rd, opposite Naivas Supermarket ☎0721 220100, ⓦmothers kitchencafe.biz; map p.210. A Naivasha institution, this big, cheery canteen is always heaving with locals. Various rice and stews and chicken and chips are available, served with tasty side salads and vegetables from Ksh400 per heaped plateful. Come hungry. Daily 5am–10pm.

Njambi's Moi Ave; map p.210. Wonderful little street-side juice bar with terrace tables and fruit strung about, offering freshly squeezed juices for only Ksh40 per glass and fruit salads to take away. Also sells cold sodas, tea and coffee. Mon–Sat 6.30am–7.30pm.

Sweet Banana Moi Ave, north of Total petrol station; map p.210. The best in a string of cheap *hotelis* along this stretch of road, with great *nyama choma* from Ksh100, along with the usual local dishes. Daily 6am–10.30pm.

SHOPPING

For food shopping in **Naivasha town**, there are plenty of small supermarkets dotted around – try Naivas (Mon–Sat 8.15am–6pm, Sun 8.15am–3pm) on Kariuki Chotara Rd. You can pick up good picnic food like bread, pastries and pies at *La Belle Inn* (see above), and get fruit at the *dukas* across the road. There's always a cluster of curio hawkers around *La Belle Inn* offering various works, some quite good, while **around the lake**, the best hotel gift shop for general souvenirs is at *Lake Naivasha Sopa Resort*.

Buffalo Mall 3km north of town at the A104 junction ☎0716 328384, ⓦbuffalomallnaivasha.com; map p.207. Opened in 2015, this offers mostly fashion and phone shops. A food court is also promised, but at the time of writing the best reason to stop is for coffee at *Java House* (daily 6.30am–9pm) and the enormous and flashy Tusky's Supermarket (daily 8am–8pm). Mon–Sat 9am–8pm, Sun 10am–8pm.

DCK Market (aka Sulmac dukas) 17.6km from the junction, just before Carnelly's; map p.207. Near the main entrance to the Sulmac flower plantation (one of the biggest in the area) this small market has some useful *dukas* for fruit and veggies and is also good for second-hand clothes. Daily 7am–6pm.

Elmenteita Weavers 4.3km from the junction, and then 800m along the signposted track ☎0733 603652, ⓦelmenteitaweavers.com; map p.207. A very friendly weaving shop, with looms behind the showroom, selling carpets and rugs, *kangas* and *kikois*. Also an outlet for Fired Earth (pottery) and Cedar Creations (wooden home crafts), and the excellent little farm shop sells home-made pickles and chutneys, fresh eggs and butter, meat including turkey and duck, crayfish from the lake and some wine. Daily 9am–5.30pm.

Rift Valley Leather La Belle Inn, Moi Ave ⓦriftvalleyleather.co.ke; map p.210. This outlet shop of the Karen-based company in Nairobi sells an excellent range of high-quality leather goods, including safari-style bags and holdalls, wallets and belts. Daily 8.30am–6pm.

Hell's Gate National Park

$30 • Daily 6am–6pm • ☎050 50407, ⓦkws.org

Named after the narrow break in its tall basaltic cliffs, **Hell's Gate** was the outlet for the prehistoric freshwater lake that stretched from here to Nakuru and which, it's believed, would have supported early human communities on its shores. Today it's a spectacular and exciting park, the red cliffs and undulating expanse of grassland providing one of the few remaining places in Kenya where you can walk among herds of **plains game** without having to go a long way off the beaten track. Buffalo, zebra, eland, hartebeest, Thomson's gazelle and baboons are all usually seen, as (more rarely) are servals – one of the most elegant of cats – and, high on the cliffs, small numbers of klipspringer ("cliffjumper") antelope. Visitors to Hell's Gate cannot fail to notice the large numbers of hyrax that scamper about the rocks, resembling large, plump, brown guinea pigs. The birdlife is also good: on the valley floor secretary birds and ostriches are easiest to identify, and look out for vultures, Verreaux's eagles and augur buzzards on the higher cliffs, which also provide a nesting site for thousands of Nyanza and mottled swifts.

The park is also home to **Olkaria Geothermal Power Station**, the first productive geothermal installation in Africa. The underground temperature of the super-heated, pressurized water reaches 304°C, making it one of the hottest sources in the world. Although the whole complex is working at full tilt, the impact on the local environment appears to be small, and it certainly doesn't spoil the landscape.

Exploring the park

The best time **to arrive** in the park is dawn, when most animals are about, and you should try to avoid the midday hours, as the heat away from the lake can be intense. You'll need to carry plenty of water and some food. There is a KWS kiosk at **Elsa Gate** where you can buy water and maps. The most popular route through the park is to enter at Elsa Gate and drive, walk or cycle right through, along the main tarmacked road along the valley beneath the cliffs. You can either return the same way or exit from the **Olkaria Gate**, a distance of about 14km. (Alternatively, you can enter at Olkaria and exit from Elsa; see below). Immediately on passing Elsa Gate, you'll see the rock known as **Fischer's Tower**, named after the German explorer who arrived at Lake Naivasha via Hell's Gate. The rock is a volcanic plug, the hard lava remaining from an ancient volcano after the cone itself has been eroded.

Branching off the main route there are two alternative loops around the park, signposted as the Twiga Circuit and the Buffalo Circuit. The **Twiga Circuit** heads left and uphill from just inside Elsa Gate to the base of Fischer's Tower, where there's a picnic site – a good place to see rock hyrax scuttling among the rocks. The grassy hillocks around here are a favourite not only with giraffe (*twiga*) but with eland too. Branching off Twiga is the **Buffalo Circuit**, which ploughs through thick bush. Don't go anywhere near the buffalo, as they can be unpredictable and dangerous. Both tracks are insanely dusty in the dry season, but when the dust clears, the views out over Hell's Gate and across to the Aberdare range are magnificent.

Further south along the main road is a car park and nearby viewpoint, a good place to picnic and take shelter from the sun. From here you can look up at the park's second volcanic plug, known as **Ol Basta** or the Central Tower; a short trail leads around its north side. Close to the car park, another path leads down into the deep, tangled **Ol Njorowa Gorge**, or Lower Gorge, beneath Ol Basta; it's steep, so proceed with care, especially in the wet season when the rocks can become slippery, and flash floods can be very dangerous. This dramatic sandstone ravine is a beautiful place for an hour or two's hike; the stream that meanders along its base is fed by hot-water springs and the sheer, narrow water-eroded walls are streaked with red and golden hues.

ARRIVAL AND DEPARTURE	HELL'S GATE NATIONAL PARK

The main entrance road to Hell's Gate is off Moi South Lake Road, 16km from the junction with the Nairobi road/A104 (3km north of Naivasha town itself); **Elsa Gate** is 1.5km along this track. It's possible to get a **lift** at weekends, as a fair number of vehicles visit, though there are far fewer during the week. If you're **driving**, be aware of the need for high clearance on the Twiga and Buffalo circuits. **Cyclists** are better off entering by the **Olkaria Gate**, which makes for an easier downhill ride to Elsa Gate; the road to Olkaria Gate is 28km from the junction (5km south of Moi South Lake Road). The third entrance to the park is the more remote and little-used **Narasha Gate**, in the southwest corner.

ACCOMMODATION

There are three KWS campsites in the park. Reservations can be made through KWS in Nairobi ☎ 020 6000800 or through the warden (☎ 050 50407, ⓦ kws.go.ke). Pay at the park gates. Given that there is no other accommodation within the park, campers virtually have it to themselves after the gates close at 6pm, though it's far cheaper to camp on the lakeshore and visit for the day.

Endachata Special Campsite Across the gorge on the northern cliffs; map p.207. A "special campsite" that must be reserved in advance (for a fee of Ksh7500). There are no facilities to speak of, but the site is exclusive and boasts great views of waterholes frequented by giraffe and zebra. $35

Naiburta Public Campsite Across the gorge on the northern cliffs; map p.207. Close to Endachata and with similar views of the waterholes, this public campsite is

fitted out with cooking sheds, picnic benches, drinking water and latrines, though you have to bring your own firewood. $20

Ol Dubai Public Campsite On the clifftop south of Fischer's Tower; map p.207. This shady and superbly sited public campsite is probably the nicest place to camp, and the best place for large groups. Facilities include cooking sheds, drinking water and latrines, but bring firewood. $20

3

Mount Longonot National Park

$30 · Daily 6am–6pm · ☎ 050 50255, ⓦ kws.org

The prominent cone of the dormant volcano **Mount Longonot** (2777m) looms high above Lake Naivasha, flanked by thorny savanna slopes and visible for many kilometres around. It's a relatively easy ascent, worth climbing for the fabulous views in every direction as you circle the rim.

Up the mountain

To start your ascent of the mountain, head for **Longonot village** on the old Nairobi road. About 500m south of the village, just beyond the railway bridge, a 4km dirt road leads to the national park gate at the base of the mountain. You can leave your car safely here (remember to take ample water with you).

There's only one straightforward route up to the crater rim, a 3km trail that takes about an hour. At the top you can collapse (the last section is rather steep) and look back over the Rift Valley on one side and the enormous, silent crater on the other. Joseph Thomson, the first *mzungu* up here in 1884, was overcome:

The scene was of such an astounding character that I was completely fascinated, and felt under an almost irresistible impulse madly to plunge into the fearful chasm. So overpowering was this feeling that I had to withdraw myself from the side of the pit.

Avoiding the same urge, it's now possible to scramble down **into the crater**, where exciting encounters with buffalo aren't uncommon: a 1937 guidebook observes that "any attempt to descend into the crater is accompanied by hazard". You should preferably be accompanied by a guide if you want to go down to the crater floor.

Walking the crater rim

Most climbers walk around the **crater rim**. The anticlockwise route is easier because the climb to the summit on the western side is quicker and steep sections easier to negotiate. It doesn't look far, but allow two to three hours to circumnavigate the 2km-diameter bowl. Longonot's name comes from the Maasai *oloonong'ot*, "mountain of many spurs" or "steep ridges", and you soon find out why. The cone is composed of very soft volcanic deposits that have eroded into deep gulches and narrow ridges: much of the path is over crumbly volcanic tufa worn into a channel so deep and narrow that it's difficult to put one foot in front of the other.

Until recently, Longonot's crater was famous for its steam jets; the volcano is classed as "senile", rather than extinct. Although the pockmark-like vents from which steam issues are still visible in several places around the rim and on the crater walls, emissions of steam have decreased since the Olkaria geothermal power station went on line, though the hot-air currents are said still to be sufficient to deflect light aircraft.

ARRIVAL AND DEPARTURE   **MOUNT LONGONOT NATIONAL PARK**

Matatus between Nairobi and Naivasha using the lower road (the B3 as far as Mai Mahiu where it turns off towards Narok, and then the C88 to Naivasha) go through the village of Longonot. From Naivasha town it's 21km south to Longonot – take any matatu bound for Mai Mahiu. The park gate is 4km to the southwest of the village and clearly signposted.

ACCOMMODATION

The nearest formal accommodation is in Naivasha, from where the park is an easy day-trip.

Oloongonot Campsite At the park gate ☎ 050 50255; map p.207. There's a spot to pitch your tent as you enter the park, where you'll find a cooking shed, latrines and drinking water, as well as a few *dukas* selling drinks and basic food. There are no official campsites on the mountain itself, and if you want to sleep there you'll have to get formal permission in advance from the rangers. **$20**

Lake Elmenteita and around

After the A104 leaves Naivasha town, it passes alongside the marshy northern reaches of Lake Naivasha, again clustered with flower greenhouses, to the west, before passing through flat sheep-farming country. After **Gilgil**, 32km beyond Naivasha, you'll start to catch glimpses of **Lake Elmenteita** on the left. Often overlooked by people rushing from Lake Naivasha to Lake Nakuru, the area around the lake offers some off-the-beaten-track attractions, including the **Kariandusi** prehistoric site and wildlife viewing from the lodges in and around the **Soysambu Conservancy**.

Kigio Wildlife Conservancy

On the A104; the turnoff is signposted 15km north of Naivasha and 500m before the Gilgil toll station • $25 • ☎ 0702 975923 • Fourteen square kilometres

Just 1km off the road between Naivasha and Gilgil lies the **Kigio Wildlife Conservancy**, a former cattle ranch. Established in 1997, Kigio has a good conservation record, with the herd of **Rothschild's giraffe** relocated here in 2002 now breeding sustainably and providing stock for other reserves. The conservancy is entirely fenced except along its riverbank side and rarely contains any large predators, which means that you can walk or cycle here safely. The large mammal count is very healthy and includes hippo, buffalo, impala, Thomson's gazelle, eland, waterbuck, zebra and warthog, and more than 250 species of birds, including ostriches. The reserve is a great place to visit even just for a few hours, but you can also stay at one of the lodges here (see p.219) as an alternative to basing yourself at Naivasha. As well as wildlife-viewing (by car, on foot or with mountain bikes) and riverside birding, Kigio offers hikes up the densely wooded Kasuki gorge, with river swims and rock-jumping just 1.5km downstream from the *Malewa Wildlife Lodge*.

Gilgil

GILGIL, just south of Lake Elmenteita, is as dull a town as you could find anywhere, with fragile-looking *dukas* and dusty streets scavenged by goats. On the outskirts lie the serried, pastel-coloured ranks of housing for the local Gilgil Telecoms Industries

3

workers. Still, you're bound to pass this way en route to Nakuru, and Gilgil can be a good spot to stock up on provisions and take a quick peek at the old war cemetery. Other than that, there is little need to veer off the A104 to the town proper.

Gilgil Commonwealth War Cemetery

On entering Gilgil from the Naivasha direction, take the turning right on to the C77/Nyahururu road for 2km, then turn left on the dirt track after crossing the rail line; the cemetery is another 400m • Mon–Fri 6am–6pm; outside of these hours the gate is locked

Of more than forty cemeteries in Kenya tended by the Commonwealth War Graves Commission, this is one of the most meticulously kept and a good place to stop for a picnic and some moments of contemplation. There are 227 graves here from the East African campaign of World War II. Whether by accident (which doesn't seem likely) or design, the African graves are all at the bottom of the slope, and record no personal details apart from name, age and rank. The graves of British soldiers are higher up, the stones inscribed with family messages. As well as graves from World War II, there are also about thirty from "the Emergency" – poignant reminders of lives lost between 1959 and 1962 after the British government's futile attempt to prevent the inevitable.

Lake Elmenteita

Beyond Gilgil, the fast A104 sweeps the eastern wall of the Rift Valley and pushes up high above **Lake Elmenteita**. The name of this shallow soda lake derives from the Maasai *Ol muteita* ("place of dust"), reflecting its tendency to shrivel to a huge white salt pond. Elmenteita's setting is spectacular and primeval, framed by the broken caldera walls of several extinct volcanoes, which resemble a reclining human figure. The Maasai know these peaks as Elngiragata Olmorani ("Sleeping Warrior") – a name that is ironically fitting, since the lake and its lands were expropriated from the Maasai at the start of the colonial period by Lord Delamere (the caldera is now also known as "Delamere's Nose"). You can get a good view from the big "parking lane" viewpoint – if you survive the occasionally desperate assaults by curio sellers.

The lake itself is a good site for flamingos, especially since Lake Nakuru has been out of favour, and sees an estimated four hundred bird species in all (eighty of which are waterfowl). Pelicans can always be found here, and Elmenteita is the only breeding ground in East Africa for the great white pelican, which nests on some rocky islands in the lake. Like Lake Nakuru, Elmenteita has no outflow, and its accumulated alkaline salts make it uninhabitable for all but one species of fish, the indomitable *Tilapia grahami*. Nearly all the land around the lake is now part of the private, fenced **Soysambu Conservancy**, which occupies the original farm of colonist and aristocrat Lord Delamere, and is accessible from the camps and lodges around the lakeshore.

Kariandusi

Signposted off the A104, 11.7 km north of Gilgil and 1.5km east of the highway • Daily 8.30am–5.30pm • Ksh500 • ⊕ bit.ly/Kariandusi

A number of prehistoric sites are scattered around the lake's shores. The Acheulian site of **Kariandusi** is characterized, like Olorgasailie (see p.152), by heavy hand-axes and cleavers. The site consists of just two small excavated areas cleared by Louis Leakey in 1928–31 and 1947, each displaying a scattered assortment of stone tools, many of them made of the black glassy volcanic rock, obsidian.

The small **museum** explains the formation of the Rift Valley and has comparative skull specimens of various distant human ancestors. Neither Kariandusi nor Olorgasailie demonstrates any signs of permanent habitation, and it's been suggested that they were simply places where the kill was habitually butchered and consumed, the tools being made on the spot and left for the next occasion. Nothing much is known about the toolmakers themselves, apart from the fact that they obviously had a formidable grip. The most likely candidate is a primitive form of *Homo erectus*, an early hominin whose remains have been found at Olduvai Gorge in Tanzania alongside Acheulian artefacts.

Soysambu Conservancy

Daily 6.30am–6.30pm (24hr for lodge guests) • Adult $47, children (3–12) $24 • Pre-booked guides to go in your own vehicle Ksh1200/4hr • ☎ 0711 235039, ⓦ soysambuconservancy.org • From Naivasha, turn left off the A104 15.4km after Gilgil, (3.4km after the *Sunbird Lodge* sign) and after 200m turn right to the main gate; from Nakuru, turn left off the A104 after 24km and follow the road around under the road bridge to the gate • Nineteen square kilometres

Lord Delamere moved down from Nakuru to Elmenteita in 1906, where he continued his experiments with sheep and cattle ranching (see p.221). He named his farm "Soysambu", Maasai for "striated rock". Today's **Soysambu Conservancy** was proclaimed in 2007 on land around the lake still owned by the Delamere family, including about three-quarters of the shoreline. Although the family still farm – with beef and dairy farming, hay-baling and agri-forestry among their agricultural operations – the conservancy has also been restocked with wild animals and is now home to more than 15,000 head of plains game including zebra, eland, waterbuck and buffalo, as well as a breeding population of Rothschild's giraffe; other naturally resident mammals include black-backed jackal, bat-eared fox, warthog and baboons. Although the original ranch was fenced, some fences have been taken down to allow game corridors – both between Soysambu and Lake Nakuru National Park and south towards Lake Naivasha.

It's possible to follow the dirt roads around the conservancy in your own vehicle (with or without a guide), but most visits start at one of the lodges and camps inside or just outside the boundaries. As well as game drives (at night too, as it's not a national park) the conservancy is good terrain for walks and horse-riding (there are stables).

ARRIVAL AND DEPARTURE

LAKE ELMENTEITA AND AROUND

By matatu The best way to get to and from Gilgil by public transport is to catch one of the numerous matatus that ply the A104 between Naivasha and Nakuru. To veer off the A104, you'll need private transport.

INFORMATION

Services Gilgil town has a few small supermarkets, a KCB with ATM, several petrol stations, but not much else. The Kobil petrol station and Delamere Farm Shop and Restaurant on the A104 (9km after Naivasha and 21km before Gilgil) is a better stop for drivers and saves veering off the main road and going into Gilgil at all. There is also the option of getting everything you need at Naivasha's Buffalo Mall (see p.214).

ACCOMMODATION

The places to stay on or near **Lake Elementeita** are either within the boundaries of the Soysambu Conservancy or just outside but offer excursions into the conservancy. Remember that conservation fees apply (see above) whether you are staying overnight or visiting for the day.

KIGIO WILDLIFE CONSERVANCY

Kigio Wildlife Camp In the conservancy ☎ 0702 975923, ⓦ porini.com. This has eleven very comfortable tents, plus a family cottage, surrounded by fever trees and perched above the Malewa River. The dining area and bar is in a glade facing a cliff face that is alive with colonies of bee-eaters and other birds. Nature walks, fishing and bike rental are all included in the rates. Wi-fi. Ecotourism Kenya Bronze Award. FB $380

Malewa Wildlife Lodge In the conservancy ☎ 0702 975923, ⓦ porini.com. Riverside bush eco-lodge with delightfully eccentric accommodation in four cottages and five river suites all made from reclaimed timber with mud walls and thatched roofs. The main lounge has an open fireplace and dining terrace, and the same activities as at *Kigio Wildlife Camp* are on offer. Wi-fi. Ecotourism Kenya Bronze Award. FB $380

Malu 14km north of Naivasha; after Kobil turn right and then drive 11km ☎ 050 2030181 or ☎ 0720 899530, ⓦ malu-kenya.com. South of (and note not in) Kigio Wildlife Conservancy, this country retreat is located in an indigenous cedar and olive forest with breathtaking views of Lake Naivasha and Mount Longonot. Accommodation is in cottages, family chalets and a unique "treehouse", plus there's good farm food. Activities include donkey-cart rides, mountain biking and horse-riding. Wi-fi. FB $375

GILGIL

Hotel Freci 200m from the A104 on the C77 Nyahururu road ☎ 0725 726266, ⓦ facebook.com/HFRECI. An outwardly unremarkable motel, but inside, the pastel-coloured rooms are comfortable (and come in a variety of bed configurations), with electric showers and nets. There's a busy bar-restaurant, with main meals around Ksh500 and a wide choice of snacks. BB **Ksh2500**

Hotel Horns On the A104 behind Shell petrol station ☏ 0706 975922, ⓦ hotelhorns.com. A little cheaper than the *Freci* but noisier as it's on the main road, though you can ask for a quieter room at the back which overlooks the walled garden and good-sized swimming pool (an unexpected plus). Rooms are clean and comfortable, with reliable hot showers, though furnishings are old and worn. Decent local food and secure parking. Matatus drop off outside. BB **Ksh2800**

LAKE ELMENTEITA

Jacaranda Lake Elmenteita Lodge Signposted on left 6km after Gigil, then 1 km down a good dirt road ☏ 050 50836, ⓦ jacarandahotels.com. Housed in a red-brick building that was Kekopey Ranch (originally built by early settler Lord Galbraith Cole in 1916), this is one of the oldest lodges on the lake and certainly the most historic. The 33 rooms (with DSTV) are in brick cottages at the back, though the decor is a bit old-fashioned. There are nice views from the terrace of the *Lord Cole Restaurant*. Wi-fi. HB **$210**

Lake Elmenteita Serena Camp Signposted on left 13.5km after Gigil, then 800m down a good dirt road ☏ 0732 123333, ⓦ serenahotels.com. This plush Serena offering opened in 2011 on the north shore of the lake and now offers the most luxurious accommodation in the region with 24 tented suites, all with lake views and colonial-style furnishings, and a central dining, lounge and bar area with an attractive semi-circular pool. Activities include day and night game drives and nature/bird walks. It lies within the Soysambu Conservancy; conservation fees are included in the rates. Wi-fi. Ecotourism Kenya Gold Award. FB **$569**

Punda Milias Camp Signposted on left 27km after Gigil (15km before Nakuru), then 3km down a bumpy dirt track ☏ 0733 245915, ⓦ nakurucamp.co.ke. North of Elementeita and not on the lakeshore, this affordable and secluded backpacker's option is nevertheless still on the northern boundary (outside) of the Soysambu Conservancy. Accommodation spans four s/c tents, plus eight *bandas*, ten "dorm" beds in a huge mess-style tent, a

campsite with dome tents (Ksh3000 for two) – or bring your own tent – that all share bathrooms with hot showers. The rustic bar serves good food and has a nightly bonfire and there's a small pool. Activities include game drives into the conservancy and safaris to Lake Nakuru National Park. Camping **Ksh600**, dorm beds **Ksh900**, room only *banda* **Ksh3500** s/c tents **Ksh8500**

The Sleeping Warrior Signposted on left 4km after Gigil then follow signs down a dirt road for 6km ☏ 0727 067418 or ☏ 0735 408698, ⓦ sleepingwarriorkenya .com. Overlooking the southeastern edge of the lake and Soysambu Conservancy, this lodge is divided into a camp with eight comfortable (though slightly old-fashioned) s/c safari tents at the bottom of a steep hill, and a smarter lodge with ten well-spaced spacious stone cottages at the top. There's a pool at the lodge, and plenty of wildlife (buffalo are regulars visitors to the tented camp), and game drives and guided walks are on offer. Note that the access road is rough rock and high clearance is essential. Wi-fi. FB: Camp **$250**, Lodge **$330**

Soysambu Campsites 3.4km after the Sunbird Lodge sign, turn left off the A104 and after 200m turn right to the main gate ☏ 0711 235039, ⓦ soysambu conservancy.org. There are two campsites within and run by the conservancy itself (therefore conservation fees apply). Nestled among acacia trees, *Simon's Campsite* overlooks Lake Elmenteita and faces south with a view of the Sleeping Warrior crater and Mount Eburu. It is named for Simon Combes, the renowned wildlife artist, who hosted artist safaris on this site. A little north of the lake, *Monkey Bridge Campsite* is in a pleasant wooded location next to the Meroroni River. Both have pit latrines, taps (but not for drinking water) and firewood. Camping **$24**

★Sunbird Lodge Signposted on left about 12km after Gigil, then 800m down a dirt road ☏ 0715 555777, ⓦ sunbirdkenya.com. Outside but adjacent to the Soysambu Conservancy, this has fourteen rooms in cute, spectacularly sited cottages on grounds that ramble down the hillside towards the lake. All come with wide balconies boasting the best views hereabouts, while the common areas are comfortably cosy, with soft couches and firepits, and there's a pool. You can drop in for (a pre-arranged) lunch ($25). Wi-fi. FB **$390**

Nakuru

Kenya's fourth-largest city (though it projects a noticeably busier and more energetic image than Kisumu, the third), **NAKURU** is a noisy, dusty and hustly place and a major transport hub for the Rift Valley. It's also the closest jumping-off point for visits to the justly celebrated **Lake Nakuru National Park** and the vast **Menengai crater** (whose *shamba*- and conifer-cloaked southern flank you'll have passed if approaching Nakuru along the A104 highway from Naivasha), as well as the departure point for trips to **lakes Bogoria** and **Baringo**, and the **northern Rift Valley**.

Lake Baringo & Lake Bogoria (B4) — Rift Valley Provincial General Hospital, Lake Baringo & Lake Bogoria

NAKURU CENTRE

DRINKING AND NIGHTLIFE

Club Dimples	1
Enigma Lounge	3
Summit Resort	5
Taidy's	2
Whistles Guava	4

ACCOMMODATION

Avenue Suites Hotel	3
Bontana Hotel	7
Carnation	8
Eagle Palace Hotel	9
Kivu Resort	10
Merica	5
Midland	1
Mid-Rift Hotel	2
Shik Parkview	4
Waterbuck	6

EATING

El-Bethel Cana Meeting Place	10
Gilani's	8
Java House	7
Kitchen Planet	9
Midland	1
Ming Yue	6
Moca Loca Coffee & Lounge	5
Nakuru Coffee House	3
Oyster Shell	2
Sisima Coffee	4

10 (800m), 5 & Nakuru National Park (3km)

Modern Nakuru is still largely a workaday farmers' town, with unadorned old seed shops and veterinary paraphernalia much in evidence on the main street, like a little Nairobi without the flashy veneer, its streets frequently undergoing ear-shattering repairs. The town can appear intimidating at first, and most visitors on their way to the national park stay in one of the lodges there. Still, Nakuru has some positive aspects: the **market** is animated and a pleasure to look around (though it, too, has its fair share of hassle), and there's a glimmer of charm remaining in the colonnaded old streets and jacaranda-lined avenues at the edge of town.

Brief history

Nakuru came into existence on the thrust of the Uganda railway and owed its early growth, at least in part, to Hugh Cholmondeley, 3rd **Baron Delamere** (1870–1931). A wealthy landowner from Cheshire in the north of England, Lord Delamere was the territory's first "white settler", arriving in 1897 having walked over 1000km south from Berbera on Somalian coast. Delamere went on to dedicate his fortune to pioneering farming methods in the Rift Valley, advised and assisted by the Maasai (with whom he had a great rapport), and in 1903 he acquired four hundred square kilometres of land on the lower slopes of the Mau Escarpment. This was followed in 1906 by another two-hundred-square-kilometre block on the other side of the lake which he called Soysambu (see p.219). Eager to share the empty vistas with compatriots – though preferably with other Cheshire or Lancashire men

– he promoted in England the mile-square plots being offered free by the Foreign Office. Eventually, some two hundred new settler families arrived and Nakuru – a name that as usual could mean various things, including "Place of the Waterbuck" (Swahili) and "Swirling Dust" or "Little Soda Lake" (Maasai) – became their country capital. It lies on the unprepossessing steppe between the lake and the flanks of Menengai crater. This desolate shelf has a nickname: "the place where the cows won't eat grass", the pasture's iron deficiency explaining Delamere's decision to move his herds down to Soysambu.

ARRIVAL AND DEPARTURE   NAKURU

Nakuru's **matatu and bus stages** are packed together at the east end of the town centre, with cheap lodgings all around, although better places to stay can be found within easy walking distance. The national park gate and campsite (5km) is a bit of a slog without transport – take a taxi, tuk-tuk or piki-piki.

By bus The town's bus companies all run regular and frequent services to Nairobi, as well as Eldoret, Kisumu, Kitale and other points west. Alternatively, you can take the quieter road west (see p.231) through the highland towns of Njoro, Elburgon and Molo. Buses between Nairobi and Kampala in Uganda (11hr) stop In Nakuru, one of the few scheduled stops. Easy Coach (office at Kobil petrol station Kenyatta Ave; ☏ 0738 200312, ⓦ easycoach.co.ke) has a daily service; check times as new legislation in both Kenya and Uganda is currently prohibiting cross-border buses from traveling at night.

Destinations Eldoret (6–10 daily; 2hr 30min); Kakamega (2 daily; 4hr); Kisumu (6–8 daily; 5hr); Kitale (2 daily; 5hr); Nairobi (10 daily; 2hr 30min).

By matatu Heading southwards, you can get to Narok (for the Maasai Mara) by matatu up the fantastic Mau Escarpment (allow a day to get there). In the other direction, matatus make the spectacular climb up to Nyahururu through the Subukia Valley. A string of matatus runs daily to Marigat at Lake Baringo, as well as to Kabarnet in the hills to the west.

Destinations Eldoret (2hr 30min); Kabarnet (2hr); Kericho (2hr); Kisumu (4hr); Kitale (3–4 daily; 5hr); Marigat (1hr 30min); Nairobi (2hr 30min); Narok (3 daily; 5hr); Naivasha (1hr 15min); Nyahururu (1hr 30min).

By car Most of the Rift Valley's major roads go through Nakuru and are in good condition: the B5 heads to Nyahururu through the Subukia Valley; the B4 to lakes Bogoria and Baringo; and the A104 cuts through Nakuru as GK Kamau Highway along its northern fringe.

ACCOMMODATION

You're spoilt for choice for **hotels**, though few places stand out, and the throbbing of discos from Wednesday to Sunday can also be a nuisance. Nakuru's hotels see few tourists as such (most go straight to the national park) so you should always try to negotiate to get the residents rate. For **campers**, the only option is to go to the national park (see p.228) though you'll have to pay entry fees.

Avenue Suites Hotel Kenyatta Ave ☏ 051 2210607. Good-value, friendly place with fifty spacious rooms, all with electronic room keys, nets, TV, reasonable bathrooms, and most with distinctive semi-circular balconies (you'll spot the place quite easily) and views down over Nakuru's main street, although this also makes it noisy. The Ming Yue Chinese restaurant (see opposite) occupies the building's entire second floor. Wi-fi. BB Ksh2700

Bontana Hotel Tom Mboya Rd ☏ 051 2210134, ⓦ bontanahotel-nakuru.com. Located in a quieter, residential part of town, this hotel is restful but rather dull, and its furnishings are slightly the worse for wear. The rooms are a good size, though, and all have balconies (those on the upper floor enjoy nice views), and the good-sized pool is another redeeming feature on a hot Nakuru day. Secure parking. Wi-fi. BB $110

Carnation 1st floor of a building on Mosque Rd ☏ 051 2215360. An old, rundown establishment in an especially

busy part of town (the street below is clustered with overflowing shops) but rooms have nets and tiled bathrooms with reliable hot water, CCTV cameras monitor the hallways and a basic breakfast of bread and eggs is included. Beware of the hustly tour and taxi touts here. BB Ksh1600

★ Eagle Palace Hotel Oginga Odinga Ave ☏ 0770 766674, ⓦ eaglepalacehotel.com. A newly built glass tower in a quietish part of town so everything is modern and fresh. Get one of the rooms above the fourth floor for views of Lake Nakuru National Park. The decent restaurant is Muslim-owned (no alcohol or bacon for breakfast). Wi-fi. BB $80

Kivu Resort Off Flamingo Rd, 1.5km before the main park gate ☏ 0726 026894, ⓦ kivuresort.co.ke. Conference venue-style hotel with good-value, nicely decorated, chalet-style rooms set in a garden with a 25m swimming pool and kid's playground (very popular with locals on weekends), plus a reasonable restaurant and bar. Wi-fi. BB Ksh5500

Merica Cnr Court Rd/Kenyatta Ave ☎051 2216013, ⓦmerica.co.ke. Busy modern town hotel, built on the central-courtyard model, with nearly one hundred large, bright rooms with nets, a good restaurant, large pool with poolside pizza restaurant and live music in the bar at weekends. Base rates are expensive but highly negotiable. Wi-fi. BB $185

Midland GK Kamau Highway ☎051 2212125, ⓦmidlandhotel.co.ke. Some like the old-style ambience and service of this colonial hotel (some parts date back to 1906 when it was the *Nakuru Railway Hotel*, although most of it comprises 1950/60s blocks), while others don't like the poky rooms. Nevertheless they are well kept and offer DSTV, and a member of staff pops a morning newspaper under the door. Good restaurant (see below), secure parking and car-washing. Wi-fi. BB Ksh9000

Mid-Rift Hotel Gusii Rd ☎020 2439270. One of the better cheap joints in this quarter of town, with light and spacious rooms with nets and TV plus filling breakfasts, but like the *Avenue Suites* and the *Shik Parkview* it can be incredibly noisy thanks to all the piki-pikis and tuk-tuks along its stretch of the main street. BB Ksh1800

Shik Parkview Kenyatta Ave ☎020 2614381. Straightforward B&L, with reasonably airy s/c and non-s/c rooms, some on the small side and with squat toilets, but very clean. There's also a very busy restaurant and great views of downtown Nakuru from the roof terrace, and security is good. Room only Ksh800

Waterbuck West Rd ☎051 2215672, ⓦwaterbuck .co.ke. Just behind the Westside Mall, the *Waterbuck* can be noisy (get a room overlooking the courtyard and not the road), but the rooms have nets, a/c, DSTV, decent bathrooms and balconies. There's a pool and friendly bar area, often full of Kenyan families at weekends. Secure parking. Wi-fi. BB $95

EATING

Finding good **food** is fairly easy in Nakuru, and getting a **coffee** is no problem at all. As a guide, the older, more down-at-heel establishments are bunched towards the east end of town near the train station, while the west end, especially along Kenyatta Avenue, tends to be more upmarket.

El-Bethel Cana Meeting Place Moi Rd. This cheery eatery is a good standby for rice, stews and cold sodas (mains around Ksh350). There's also a pleasant outside seating area, and lots of decorative plants. Daily 6.30am–6.30pm.

Gilani's Club Rd ☎051 2211745, ⓦgilanis.co.ke. In this long-established Indian-owned supermarket, the 1950s-style cafeteria has a rather unusual view down on to the supermarket shelves from its mezzanine-floor location. Serves cheap pastries and cakes, juices, tasty Indian snacks and lunchtime curries (from Ksh350). Mon–Sat 8.15am–7pm, Sun 10am–6.30pm.

Java House Westside Mall, Kenyatta Ave ☎0702 811525, ⓦnairobijavahouse.com. The reliably good *Java*, Kenya's top coffee chain, has a branch next to Nakumatt in this new swishy mall. The pastries and muffins, English breakfasts and lunches like chicken or steak and chips are decent value for the quality, but there are cheaper places to get a coffee. Wi-fi. Daily 7am–10pm.

Kitchen Planet Watalii Rd ☎0726 096575. This pavement café boasts a pleasantly leafy outdoor terrace and serves salads, curries and pizzas alongside the expected fried meat. Wildly popular with locals. Mains around Ksh500. Daily 7am–9pm.

Midland GK Kamau Highway ☎051 2212125, ⓦmidlandhotel.co.ke. *Flamingo Grill* is the main hotel restaurant with reasonable continental and oriental dishes (the grilled tilapia fish is good), some South African wines and good service; budget on about Ksh1400 for a two-course meal. The

outside thatched *Terrace* bar offers tasty barbecued chicken. Wi-fi. Daily 7am–10pm (Terrace bar till midnight).

Ming Yue Avenue Suites Hotel, Kenyatta Ave ☎051 2215151. Second-floor restaurant with a leafy balcony and good, authentic Chinese food including sizzling pork or beef, sweet and sour chicken, and several varieties of noodles and fried rice. Amazingly fast service and good value if you share a few dishes (from Ksh500). Daily 11am–10pm.

★**Moca Loca Coffee & Lounge** Kenyatta Ave ☎0708 084839, ⓦbit.ly/MocaLocaCoffee. Up two flights of stairs this stylish a/c place (red chandeliers and black leather couches) comes with views down Kenyatta Ave. Excellent, generous breakfasts and main meals (from Ksh700) include salads, pizzas, toasted sandwiches, burgers and tasty versions of Kenyan dishes like beef stew with kale and *ugali*. Wi-fi, and the electric sockets come in handy for charging. Daily 8am–10pm.

Nakuru Coffee House Moi Rd ☎0702 644533. This old-style diner-café offers real coffee, and is a good choice for tasty pastries, as well as mains like roast chicken and chips and passable pizzas (around Ksh550). Daily 6.30am–7.30pm.

★**Oyster Shell** Hill Climb Rd, Milimani, 2km east of town (roughly behind the Naivas Supermarket on the A104) ☎0714 129997. Set in a house in the Milimani suburb, away from the town chaos, this place has excellent meat, fish and vegetarian European and authentic Indian food from Ksh900 (try the T-bone, pork chops, butter

3

chicken or paneer dishes). They take a little long to prepare but there's a pleasant leafy garden and (late) bar to enjoy while you wait. Take a taxi as it's not easy to find. Daily 10.30am–midnight.

★**Sisima Coffee** Kenyatta Ave ☎0789 712978, ⊛sisimacoffee.co.ke. If you haven't yet infused enough caffeine in Nakuru, this is another excellent choice, and also offers a menu of tasty soups, salads, sandwiches, juices, freshly made crêpes with ice cream, divine chocolate cake and a good range of drinks, including South African wine by the carafe. It's upstairs and has comfy lounge chairs. Wi-fi. Daily 8am–10pm.

DRINKING AND NIGHTLIFE

Club Dimples Kenyatta Ave, opposite Westside Mall ☎0722 332888, ⊛bit.ly/ClubDimples. Hung with kitsch mirrors and disco balls, this popular club with pool tables has been around for decades and pumps out a mix of rock, rumba and reggae. Entry Ksh200. Wed–Sun 7pm–late.

Enigma Lounge Kenyatta Ave, opposite Barclays Bank ☎0722 434450, ⊛enigmalounge.yolasite.com. Modern bar and club above the shops, playing a mix of African and Western dance tunes. On weekend afternoons it's quite a lively place to watch European football. Mon–Thurs 5–11pm, Fri & Sat 2pm–3am, Sun 2pm–midnight.

Summit Resort Flamingo Rd, near the national park main gate ☎0710 547164, ⊛bit.ly/SummitResort. The open-air dancefloor at this large, friendly complex gets packed at weekends with patrons of all ages getting down to Western and Kenyan pop and golden oldies. There are also several different dining areas (grills plus excellent *mutton choma* for Ksh250 for a half-kilo) and a swimming pool (Ksh200). Mon–Thurs 8am–11pm, Fri–Sun 8am–3am.

Taidy's Cnr Oginga Odinga Ave/Gusii Rd ☎051 2211409, ⊛bit.ly/TaidysNakuru. This tatty but lively open-air terrace bar overlooking a busy corner is a Nakuru institution. The beer's always cold and there's a (mostly fried) menu of meat and grilled chicken, served with chips or chapatti from Ksh400. Daily 8am–3am.

Whistles Guava Cnr Moi/Government roads ⊛bit.ly/WhistlesGuava. Polished (though oddly named) bar/club with every alcoholic drink imaginable behind the bar, a dancefloor, lounge areas and regular events including hotly contested karaoke competitions with prize money. Wed–Sat 6pm–3am.

DIRECTORY

Banks Scattered all over Nakuru, most of them with ATMs.
Hospital If you need medical attention, avoid Nakuru's public Rift Valley Provincial General Hospital if at all possible and instead head to the private Avenue Healthcare Nakuru Clinic, in the Polo Centre on Kenyatta Ave (Mon–Fri 8am–8pm, Sat & Sun 9am–3pm; ☎0722 226446), which has doctors and a pharmacy.
Markets The main produce market, near the train station, has the full range of fruit and vegetables, but watch out for pickpockets and petty thieves. Nakuru's curio market is in front of Standard Chartered Bank on Kenyatta Ave; it has a good choice, and prices are reasonable.
Pharmacies There are lots of pharmacies at the eastern end of Kenyatta Ave, as well as in Westside Mall.

Shopping malls and supermarkets The new Westside Mall, on the corner of Kenyatta Ave and West Rd (☎020 2664071, ⊛westsidemall.co.ke) has a vast branch of Nakumatt (Mon–Sat 8am–10pm, Sun 9am–9pm), which sells everything you may need, plus thirty smaller shops and cafés, a branch of DHL and a multistorey car park which makes it easy to pull in if driving past on the A104. Elsewhere in town, reasonable supermarkets include Tuskys on Kenyatta Ave (daily 7.30am–9pm) and Gilani's on Club Rd (Mon–Sat 8.15am–7pm, Sun 10am–6.30pm), while the big branch of Naivas (Mon–Sat 8am–8pm, Sun 9am–6pm) on the A104 at the B5/Nyahururu turnoff is also easily accessible from the A104.

Lake Nakuru National Park

Daily 6am–7pm • $80 Safari Card (see p.73) • ☎051 8012070, ⊛kws.org • 188 square kilometres

Just 5km outside Nakuru, **Lake Nakuru National Park** is one of the most popular in the country and a must-see for wildlife enthusiasts, offering one of the best chances in Kenya of spotting black and white rhinos. With more than 300,000 visitors each year, this is one of Kenya Wildlife Service's two "premier parks" (the other being Amboseli). Though not large, it's a beautiful park, the terra firma mostly under light acacia forest and well provided with tracks to a variety of hides and lookouts; the contrast between these animated woodlands and the soda lake with its primeval birds give it a very distinctive appeal. And while there is very good accommodation within the park boundaries, it's also one of the easiest parks to visit for the day, with or without a vehicle. The easy-to-follow topography and signposted tracks mean you really can't get lost and it's a pleasure to drive around, which takes about three hours.

However, the park has undergone some quite remarkable changes in recent years due to the significant **flooding** that has affected all the Rift Valley lakes. Heavy seasonal rain swelled Nakuru by, it's estimated, at least one-third in 2012, 2013 and 2014 (the 2015 long rainy season was a relatively light one in comparison). As a result, not only has the lake's surface area and shape changed considerably, but the park's infrastructure has been altered too (and probably permanently): KWS lost two campsites; the Main Gate had to be moved to higher ground (you'll see the old gate buildings being lapped by the waves); and the marshy floodplain region at the southern end of the lake is now under deep water.

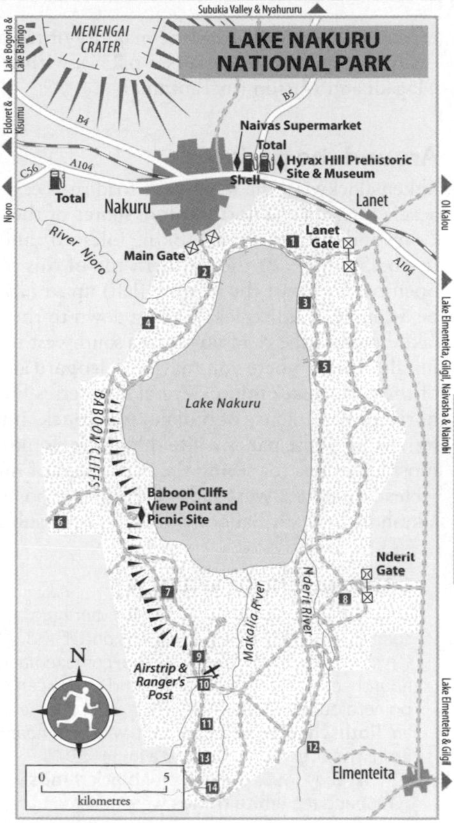

KWS has undertaken a major redesign of the park's road layout and facilities as, unlike the other lakes like Ba-ringo and Naivasha, water levels are not expected to go down at Lake Nakuru anytime soon. There are several reasons for this. First, again unlike the other lakes, Nakuru has no outlet. Additionally, as well as the unprecedented heavy rains over the last few years, some underground springs have recently been discovered on the lake bed, suggesting that the lake is also fed from beneath the ground. Finally, it's thought that recent initiatives to stop human encroachment on the Mau Forest Complex on the western edge of the Rift Valley (see box, p.233), from which Nakuru receives much of its rainfall, have caused significantly more water to find its way down the escarpment to the lake.

LAKE NAKURU NATIONAL PARK

■ ACCOMMODATION

SC: special campsite, no facilities		Naishi Guest House	9
Chui SC	13	Naisha SC	10
Flamingo Hill Camp	4	Pelican Public Campsite	2
Kampi ya Nyati SC	3	Reedbuck SC	7
Lake Nakuru Lodge	8	Rhino SC	11
Lake Nakuru Sopa Lodge	6	Sarova Lion Hill Game Lodge	5
Makalia Public Campsite	14	Wildlife Clubs of	
Mbweha Safari Camp	12	Kenya Guest House	1

So what does all this mean for the fauna in Lake Nakuru National Park? Not a great deal in fact: while the animals have lost much of their grazing land, they are also thriving from the constant source of fresh water and flourishing habitat. Lake Nakuru however no longer supports its formerly vast population of **flamingos** – several decades ago, up to two million lesser flamingos (maybe a third of the world's population) could be seen here massing in the warm alkaline water to feed on the abundant blue-green algae cultivated by their own droppings. The rising water levels have caused a big drop in salinity, and the flamingos have simply flocked elsewhere. This has happened many times in the past (notably in the 1970s and again in the 1990s when the lake water was especially high) and today the majority of the gloriously pink, massed flocks are more easily seen at Lake Bogoria (see p.234), with scattered communities also at Elmenteita, Magadi and Natron (in Tanzania).

Around the park

Taken clockwise, the main park road runs east of the Main Gate via the lightly wooded acacia forest of the **northeastern shores** of the lake, past the *Sarova Lion Hill Game Lodge* and into an exotic-looking forest of candelabra **euphorbia** – great cactus-like trees up to 15m high. At the southern end of this zone you come into a stretch of more open country, past the turning (left) up to *Lake Nakuru Lodge*. From here there used to be a couple of side tracks leading down to the (now vanished) mudflats and the lakeshore but the road now turns southwest into the southern park's dense acacia jungle. This is where you may see a **leopard** and – if they overcome their shyness – one of the park's **black rhino**. Several kilometres further, the road opens again onto wider horizons with plenty of buffalo, waterbuck, impala and eland all around. You're likely to see one of the park's **white rhino** here, looking for good grazing, and this is also the most likely area for seeing the park's herd of introduced **Rothschild's giraffe**.

Heading up the **west shore** is no longer possible as the road that ran along the lakeshore beneath Baboon Cliffs has been submerged. Instead, a new road has been cut

---

LAKE NAKURU'S WILDLIFE

Fortunately, in view of the flamingos' vanishing act (see p.225), there's a lot more to the lake's spectacle than the pink flocks it was once famous for. There's a good number of **mammals** which are very easily seen and often come remarkably close to vehicles. **Hippos** have flourished in the less briny water, and by day can be seen snorting and splashing at various points around the lake. Nakuru has also become a popular venue for introduced species: there are **Rothschild's giraffe** from the wild herd near Kitale, and **lions** and secretive **leopards** from wherever they're causing a nuisance.

In the early 1990s, a number of **black rhinos** were relocated from Solio Game Ranch (see p.196), and ten **white rhinos** were donated by South Africa in 1994. These have bred exceptionally well, but despite the electric fencing around the entire perimeter of the park, Nakuru has not avoided the scourge of recent rhino poaching and it sadly lost five in 2014. Each rhino is now heavily guarded by armed KWS rangers and, as in other KWS parks, population numbers are no longer made available to the public. Nevertheless, as a visitor to the park, you have a very good chance of spotting one, and both KWS rangers and lodge staff will point you in the right direction.

Nakuru is in fact Swahili for "place of the waterbuck", and the park is indeed **waterbuck** heaven. With only a handful of lions and small numbers of leopards to check their population, the large, shaggy beasts number several thousand, and the herds (either bachelor groups or a buck and his harem) are large and exceptionally tame. **Impala**, too, are very numerous, though their instinct of fear means you rarely witness the graceful flight of a herd vaulting through the bush.

The two other most often seen mammals are **buffalo** – which you'll repeatedly mistake for rhinos until you get a look through binoculars – and **warthog**, scuttling nervously in singles and family parties everywhere you look. Elephants are absent, but you're likely to see **zebra**, **dik-dik**, **ostrich** and **jackal** and, in the southern part of the park, **eland** and **Thomson's and Grant's gazelle**. More rarely you can encounter **reedbuck** down by the shore and **bushbuck** dashing briskly through the herbage. Along the eastern road, near *Lake Nakuru Lodge*, are several over-tame **baboon troops** to be wary of. The park is also renowned for its very large **pythons** – the patches of dense woodland in the southwest, between the lakeshore and the steep cliffs, are a favourite habitat.

Finally, though the reduced salinity may have put paid to flamingo numbers, the higher water levels have attracted other species of **birds** to Lake Nakuru in large numbers, including pelicans, fish eagles, herons, egrets, hammerkops and grebes.

that leaves the shore and ploughs north, through thick forest with many tall trees and dense undergrowth, up to **Baboon Cliffs View Point and Picnic Site**, which is well worth a stop for a full view of the now swollen lake; you may be accompanied by rock hyrax and large troops of vervet monkeys (keep car doors and windows shut). From here the road goes past the turnoff to the new *Lake Nakuru Sopa Lodge* and then it's a gentle descent back to Main Gate.

ARRIVAL AND DEPARTURE   LAKE NAKURU NATIONAL PARK

The park has three gates: Main Gate, Lanet and Nderit. The relocated **Main Gate**, the park's headquarters and the Point of Issue and Point of Sale (POIPOS) for Safari Cards, is on the southern edge of Nakuru town, about 4km from the centre. Entering through **Lanet Gate**, on the northeast side of the park, gives the most direct access from Naivasha or Nairobi and allows you to avoid the congestion of Nakuru town. The 1.5km dirt road to Lanet Gate branches off the A104; if coming from Naivasha it's about 3km before entering town proper – if you cross the railway bridge, you've overshot. **Nderit Gate**, in the southeast corner, is useful only if you're driving cross-country from the Soysambu Conservancy and Lake Naivasha or over the Mau Escarpment from Narok. Note that if you enter through either Lanet or Nderit gates, you will be issued with a gate pass and then will have to go to the Main Gate at some point during your visit in order to pay fees onto a Safari Card.

GETTING AROUND

By car This is one of the easiest parks to drive around; animals are easily spotted and the main gravel roads are in good condition. KWS ranger/guides are available at the Main Gate to go with you in your own vehicle for Ksh2000/4hr (easily enough time to see the whole park).

By taxi You can also see the park by taxi; some of the taxi drivers around Nakuru town know the park very well. Ask at the hotels for a recommended driver. With some hard bargaining you can count on around Ksh2500 for a 3–4hr

trip, with park fees on top (including Ksh1600 in fees for the car and driver).

By KWS game drives Another alternative is to hire a KWS six-seater safari vehicle from the Main Gate with a driver/guide. These cost a flat rate of Ksh5000/4hr (excluding park fees) so are cheaper if you can summon a group together. Open and much higher than taxis, aiding better viewing, these also have the advantage of an accompanying knowledgeable guide.

ACCOMMODATION

Any of the lodges in the park will pick up visitors who arrive at the Main Gate by public transport (see above) for a small fee, or for free if they are out on game drives with their guests. Park lodges either include game drives in their rates or offer them as extra for about $35 per person for 3hr.

Flamingo Hill Camp Signposted to the right, 2.5km southwest of the Main Gate ☏ 020 2062424 or 0712 138444, ⊛ www.flamingohillcamp.com. This neat mid-range tented camp is just on the edge of the fenced boundary (you can sometimes hear the distant traffic at night) but has a proper safari camp atmosphere: you can see animals at a waterhole from the pool area. The 29 thatched tents are spacious and spread around the gardens, and there's reasonable buffet food. Low-season rates drop to $105 per person and there are also triple and family rooms. Wi-fi. FB **$305**

Lake Nakuru Lodge Southeast corner of the park ☏ 0720 404480, ⊛ lakenakurulodge.com. On a wooded rise in shady gardens, based around an old Delamere Estate house, *Lake Nakuru Lodge*'s main selling point is a good, large pool (non-guests $8) and uninterrupted views across the savanna with a distant glimpse of a corner of the lake. On the downside, most of the rather discordantly decorated *banda*-style rooms are fairly small and dark, though the family rooms are large, with big bathrooms. Wi-fi. FB **$400**

Lake Nakuru Sopa Lodge 14km from the Main Gate ☏ 020 3750235, ⊛ sopalodges.com. The newest lodge in the park was opened in 2015 on the western side of the park and has fantastic views from its ridgetop position. Rooms are in spacious semi-detached thatched cottages with balconies and floor-to-ceiling windows, and there's an especially lovely pool facing the lake, though the gardens have yet to mature. **$380**

★**Mbweha Safari Camp** Just outside the park, a 15min drive from Nderit Gate ☏ 0721 373994 or 0702 692648, ⊛ atua-enkop.com. Ten private cottages tucked among euphorbias, all made from local materials and with private verandas and views of the Eburru and Mau ranges. There's also a sunken lounge and bar area looking out onto the pool and a small waterhole, and a fantastic restaurant. As well as game drives into the park, this is also well located for exploring the Soysambu Conservancy (see p.219), and they offer bike rides, bush dinners and sundowners. Wi-fi. FB **$370**

Naishi Guest House Southwest part of the park; bookings through KWS ☏ 020 6000800, ⊛ kws.go.ke.

A popular and peaceful twin-gabled country house surrounded by savanna, with a fully equipped kitchen and four bedrooms to suit a self-catering group of up to eight (two triples in the main house, and two singles in a separate annexe). Firewood and kerosene lamps are provided and the generator is fired up from 7pm to 10pm. There's a good front terrace, and spotlights shine on a small waterhole at night. Expect to see zebra, impala and the occasional lion. Whole house **$250**

Sarova Lion Hill Game Lodge On the park's eastern slopes, high above the lake ☎ 020 2767000 or 0709 111000, ⊛ sarovahotels.com. One of Sarova's less exciting lodges, with typically high standards but undistinguished (albeit comfortable) rooms in grey block cottages ranged along the hillside among the trees. All come with a large double plus a single bed and good nets, but few other embellishments. Meals are excellent and slightly cheaper than at *Lake Nakuru Lodge*. There's a good-sized pool and massages are available. FB **$281**

Wildlife Clubs of Kenya Guest House 3.5km east of the Main Gate ☎ 020 2671742, ⊛ wildlifeclubsofkenya.org. Set in a renovated old farmhouse, this guesthouse is aimed at Kenyan students but is open to anybody when there's no group staying, and represents the only truly budget option in the park. Facilities are simple and the six rooms have single beds (it sleeps eighteen in total), and there's a fully equipped kitchen and dining room. **Ksh1250** per person

CAMPSITES

Camping rates are high, thanks to Lake Nakuru's standing as one of KWS's top-league parks. Special campsites must be reserved in advance through KWS (⊛ kws.org) in Nairobi on ☎ 020 6000800, or the Lake Nakuru Main Gate (☎ 051 2217151), though it's a good idea to reserve a spot

at the public sites as well. Fees are paid at the gates on arrival. As well as ranger-guided game drives (see p.227), you can also arrange tent and other equipment rental from the Main Gate, the only KWS park where you can do this: a two-person dome tent with a small fold-up table and two chairs costs Ksh1000; bedding for two Ksh350; kitchen stuff (frying pan, cutlery, crockery etc) Ksh650; and a gas stove Ksh1500.

Makalia Public Campsite At the southern tip of the park. The somewhat elusive *Makalia* is in a wonderful location straddling the stream of the same name, close to a waterfall (hence its other name of *Waterfalls*), though it has the same poor facilities as *Pelican* (see below). Very few organized tours come down this way, but should you feel isolated you may be reassured to know there's a ranger station fairly close by. **$30**

Pelican Public Campsite At the old Main Gate. Formerly called *Backpackers'*, this is the park's main public campsite. It sits on a grassy patch under fine old yellow acacias but the meagre facilities – cold showers, unpleasant squat toilets and communal tap – are a let-down. Beware the audacious vervet monkeys and baboons here. **$30**

Special campsites Since the floods, KWS has cleared spaces for several new special sites: *Kampi ya Nyati* (Buffalo Camp), next to the lake in the northeastern part of the park; *Reedbuck*, beneath the southern end of Baboon Cliffs; *Naisha* near the airstrip; and *Rhino* and *Chui*, which are 1km apart in the southern part of the park beyond the airstrip. These have no facilities but are in areas where there's plenty of animal action, and given that they are booked for exclusive use, you'll have whichever one you choose all to yourself. Be sure to bring all your own food, water and firewood. **$50**

Menengai crater

The crater rim is 8km from the centre of Nakuru

Containing an enormous caldera, **Menengai crater** is 12km across and nearly 500m deep in places, a spectacular sea of bush-covered lava whose black waves are frozen solid. The crater was the site of a battle around 1854 in which the Ilpurko Maasai defeated the Ilaikipiak Maasai, whom they considered upstarts disrespectful to Batian, the *laibon* (paramount chief) of the time, after whom the highest peak of Mount Kenya was named. At intervals throughout the nineteenth century these **Maasai civil wars** flared up over the issue of true Maasai identity. In this case, it wasn't simply a matter of honour but also of grazing rights in the Rift Valley, especially around Lake Naivasha and on the scarp slopes. The Ilpurko were herders, while the Ilaikipiak from the north grew crops as well. Both had been preparing for battle for some time and it is said that hundreds of Ilaikipiak *morani* were hurled over the crater rim to their deaths. The place retains a sinister reputation – even the normally fearless Maasai traditionally consider it to be the dwelling place of devils and evil spirits – and local people prefer not to go near the edge.

A century later, at the highest point of this windy crest, the Rotary Club erected a signpost. Apart from informing you that Nairobi is 140km away and Rome 2997km in the opposite direction, it also points out that the crater wall is 2272m above sea level and its area covers some 90 square kilometres – the whole dramatic extent of which you can see before you descend into the crater itself. You'll also get fantastic views over Lake Nakuru if you walk down the dirt road along the south side of the gum-tree plantation.

ARRIVAL AND DEPARTURE   MENENGAI CRATER

By taxi There's no public transport to the crater but there's always the option of getting a taxi and asking the driver to wait (allow roughly Ksh50/hr).

By car Head up Menengai Drive and take the fourth left turn (Crater Climb) through the suburbs above town towards the telecommunications tower 4.5km up the hill. Turn right at the tower, following the track for 20min to a

fire lookout tower on the bare cliff, from where the crater spreads out beneath you.

On foot Allow 3hr to reach the crater rim from Nakuru on foot, and at least another hour to hike down to and up from the crater floor. Try to go up in a group, as muggings are a possibility.

Hyrax Hill

3.5km from Nakuru centre, off the north side of the Nairobi road • Daily 8.30am–5.30pm • Ksh500 • ☎ 051 2217175, ⓦ museums.or.ke • Matatus for Lanet and Gilgil will drop you at the turnoff, from where it's a 600m walk to the small museum where you pay the entrance fee • It's usually possible to camp here either free or for a small fee (staff facilities only)

An easy target outside Nakuru, **Hyrax Hill** has been a human settlement site for at least three thousand years, with finds dating from the Neolithic period immediately before the modern era. Named for the hyraxes that once scampered over this ancient tongue of lava, the prehistoric settlement site was discovered by Louis Leakey in 1926, and subsequently excavated by Mary Leakey ten years later and by others between 1965 and 1987.

The Northeast Village

The path leading out to the right of the museum winds its way around the north side of the hill to an excavated pit dwelling or "sunken enclosure", with baulks left in place to show the depth of material that was removed during the digging. There are thirteen similar depressions in this "**Northeast Village**", but it's uncertain exactly how they were used. They have yielded a tremendous quantity of pottery shards, tools made from flakes of obsidian and animal-bone fragments. The absence of postholes normally needed to support a roof suggests they may have been shelters for livestock, but just as plausibly, a roof might have been added whenever needed, leaving no trace, and animals and people may have shared the shelters.

It's believed the inhabitants would have been semi-nomadic Sirikwa- or Nandi-speaking (Kalenjin) herders. Today, the Kalenjin mostly live further west, and, in the case of Hyrax Hill, may have been forced to flee by an expanding Maasai population from the north.

THE GAME OF BAU

For a less dramatic, but more accessible, impression of life at Hyrax Hill, the **game of bau**, cut into the rock close to the museum, is a delightfully fresh record. *Bau* is the Bantu name for a game of skill and – depending on the rules used – amazing complexity that has been played all over Africa for a very long time. Two people play, moving pieces (cowries, seeds or pebbles) from one hole to another to win. There are a number of these "boards" around the hill; the one near the museum is a particularly good example.

The fort

Following the path towards the top of the hill, you come to an exposed "**fort**" facing out towards Nakuru, which consists of a circle of hefty boulders enclosing a flattened area. It may have been an Iron Age lookout post, but there's no way of being certain, or of knowing how old it might be, since no artefacts have been found. From here, you can scramble over the volcanic boulders to the summit, where you get a good view of the southern part of the site and the lake. Now several kilometres away, Lake Nakuru once extended, probably as fresh water, right to the base of the hill and across much of the Rift Valley, turning Hyrax Hill into a peninsula or even an island.

Burial sites

A hundred metres down the hillside, in a fenced-in shelter, the massive stone slab which sealed a **Neolithic burial mound** has been removed to display part of a skull and some limb bones. The remains of a further nineteen Neolithic skeletons were discovered north of this, beneath a more recent Iron Age occupation area marked by the two stone circles (which were hut foundations). Nineteen Iron Age skeletons were also discovered, overlying the Neolithic graves, mostly of young men, possibly slain warriors, apparently buried unceremoniously or in a hurry, their skulls and limbs in tangled heaps. The coincidence of nineteen skeletons at each level may be just that – coincidence. Or perhaps the Iron Age survivors who buried their young men knew about the ancient Neolithic graves beneath.

The Subukia Valley

North of Nakuru, the tarred, good B5 to Nyahururu (see p.197) through the **Subukia Valley** is a particularly scenic route, an ascent of the Rift that, for sheer grandeur, comes close to the Naivasha escarpment. If you're driving, note that the turnoff, which is 2.5km east of Nakuru along the A104 towards Nairobi, is not clearly signposted – turn left at the Shell petrol station by *Kunste Hotel*. From here it's 59km to Nyahururu, the road passing after 37km through the village of **SUBUKIA**, just 4km north of the equator, which has a scattering of *hotelis* and *dukas*, and a filling station.

The Subukia Valley itself was the Maasai's "Beautiful Place" (Ol Momoi Sidai) and its lush pastures were their insurance against the failure of the grass up on the Laikipia plateau. But they were evicted in 1911 to the "Maasai Reserve" and the way was clear for **settler families**. It's easy to see why the Europeans chose this high valley, despite its isolation, with its soft, arcadian beauty far removed from the windy plateaus above or the austere furnace of the Rift Valley floor below.

It's entirely possible to visit Nyahururu and Thomson's Falls on a day-trip from Nakuru – a good option if you don't plan to venture further into the Central Highlands. Several buses and matatus run daily between Nakuru and Nyahururu (see p.197).

West of Nakuru

West of Nakuru, the **A104** is a busy, often dangerous highway along which trucks, buses and matatus thunder at top speed over a surface which varies, unpredictably, from perfect to perfectly awful. It's hair-raising if you're driving yourself or with a driver, and even more wearing on the nerves if you're travelling by public transport.

Heading into Western Kenya, the **C56** offers a scenic and much quieter alternative to the main highway, climbing gradually up to the towns of **Njoro**, **Elburgon** and **Molo**, in ascending order of altitude and size, before continuing through the **Mau Forest**

3

THE KALENJIN PEOPLES

The **Kalenjin** form the majority of the population in the central part of the Rift Valley. Their name, actually a recent adoption by a number of peoples speaking dialects of Nandi, means "I tell you". The principal Kalenjin are the **Nandi**, **Terik**, **Tugen**, **Elgeyo**, **Elkony**, **Sabaot**, **Marakwet** and **Kipsigis**, and, more contentiously, the Pokot. They were some of the earliest inhabitants of Kenya and probably absorbed the early Bushmen or Pygmy peoples who had already been here for 200,000–300,000 years.

Primarily **farmers**, the Kalenjin have often adapted their economies to local circumstances. The first Kalenjin were probably herdsmen, and the pastoral **Pokot** group still spurn all kinds of cultivation, despising peoples who rely on anything but livestock – they call the **Marakwet**, living against the western Rift escarpment, *Cheblong* ("The Poor"), for their lack of cattle. The **Okiek** provide another interesting clue to the past. Hunter-gatherers, they live in scattered groups in the forests of the high slopes flanking the Rift and traditionally regard wild fruits and vegetables as barely palatable, though maize and gardening have been introduced and they now keep some domestic animals too. The Okiek and other groups in Kenya who live mostly by hunting have often been called **Ndorobo** or Wandorobo, deriving from the Maasai term "Il Torobbo", again meaning "poor people without cattle" – though today this is considered a highly derogatory term.

Many Kalenjin played key roles in the founding of the Kenya African Democratic Union (KADU – now disbanded), but the most famous of Kalenjin in recent years was Kenya's second president, Daniel Arap Moi, a **Tugen** from Baringo District. As he was from a small ethnic group, his presidency at first avoided the accusations of tribalism levelled so bitterly against Kenyatta. But Moi's firm grip on the reins of power was increasingly exercised through the Kalenjin-dominated civil service, rather than the more ethnically mixed cabinet. In 1992, when democratic elections first took place, there were tribal clashes, often coordinated from behind the scenes, with the "ethnic cleansing" of non-Kalenjin (usually Kikuyu incomers) from the Rift Valley by groups of surprisingly well-organized young men. Similar incidents were repeated at election time in 1997 and 2002, while in 2007 post-election tensions resulted in retaliatory violence by Kikuyu groups against supporters of Raila Odinga, which included the Kalenjin, especially around Nakuru and Naivasha.

(see box opposite) towards Kericho. This is a gentle land of small towns, colonial manors and conifers, and although most travellers see nothing more of it than the road, the area offers a couple of rural accommodation options and is worth a detour.

Njoro

The turn-off to **NJORO** and the Mau Escarpment lies 5km west of Nakuru, and is usually marked by a police roadblock. From here, it's 13km to Njoro, the hometown of **Egerton University** (the main campus is 5km out of town on the road to Narok), which has several other campuses scattered through the highlands. The jacaranda-fringed main road runs straight past the "centre" of town – a great acreage of mud (or, at best, dust), backed by a humble row of *dukas* and *hotelis*. Beyond the Narok junction, there's another and more soulful Njoro of wooden-colonnaded, tin-roofed, one-storey *dukas*. Here you'll also find a KCB bank and the Njoro Farmers Petrol Station, a Shell garage. On the other side of town, past timber yards, is flat cereal country, with herds of dairy cattle and racehorses between the lines of gum trees and copses of acacia.

Kenana Knitters

5km from Njoro along the C56 • Mon–Fri 8.30am–5pm, and at other times by prior arrangement • ☎ 0715 262303, ⓦ bit.ly/KenanaKnitters

Just outside Njoro on Kembu Farm, and just a short walk from *Kembu Campsite and Cottages* (see p.234), you'll find the buzzing workshop of **Kenana Knitters**, a non-profit women's cooperative which makes toys and other knitted items primarily for export, although you can see how they put them together (and buy some of the finished products). The handmade blankets, clothing and stuffed animals are all made from organic cotton, home-grown wool and plant dyes, and many of them are really quite beautiful.

Elburgon

Seventeen kilometres along the C56 west of Njoro, the town of **ELBURGON** is a good deal bigger than Njoro, and higher up. You're into seriously muddy, conifer country here, and the buildings, characteristically chalet-style, are built of dark, weathered planks. Elburgon used to be a thriving timber town on the fringes of the Mau Forest, but because of large-scale deforestation, the government has implemented a ban on logging and the settlement is not as prosperous as it once was (although of course the forest is faring much better).

Molo

West of Elburgon, the road winds and dips through patches of the Mau Forest for 13km to **MOLO**, with glimpses of railway viaducts across the valleys (the Nairobi–Kisumu line that is currently not operational), until it emerges, still higher up, among the cereals and pyrethrum fields. Molo (famous for its lamb) straggles for several kilometres down into a broad valley across the rail tracks and up the other side onto Mau Summit Road, where you'll find a post office, banks and several petrol stations.

MAU FOREST COMPLEX

Spreading across the Mau Escarpment, a fault scarp running along the western edge of the Rift Valley and down to the lakes on the valley floor, and covering an area (disjointed in places) of about 4200 square kilometres is the **Mau Forest Complex**, Kenya's largest closed-canopy indigenous montane forest ecosystem. As large as the forests of Mount Kenya and the Aberdares combined, the Mau Forest Complex receives some of the country's highest rainfall, and is the Rift Valley's most important water catchment area, feeding twelve rivers that flow into five major lakes: Baringo, Nakuru, Turkana, Victoria and Natron (in Tanzania).

Widespread encroachment by unplanned settlements, cash-crop farming and illegal logging has, however, destroyed an estimated quarter of the complex since the late 1990s and for many years Mau has been synonymous with Kenya's illegal charcoal trade. The pace and severity of **degradation and destruction** has generated increasing concern and publicity, and since 2008 various stakeholders have been involved in the forest's restoration and protection. The government has been fairly forcible, banning logging and (controversially) evicting communities (Raila Odinga was especially proactive during his term as prime minister) and today the Kenya Forest Service (KFS) and the African Wildlife Foundation (AWF) are both managing tree-planting projects and have initiated moves to get a southeastern section of the complex re-gazetted as a protected area. Already there is evidence that an increasing quantity of water is making its way down to Lake Nakuru, for which this area serves as the headwater catchment zone.

The most significant development began in 2013 (and is still ongoing) when Rhino Ark (@rhinoark.org), a charitable trust attempting to tackle the challenges facing Kenya's forest ecosystem, in collaboration with the KWS, began constructing the Mau Eburru **electric fence** on the slopes of the highest peak in the Mau Forest Complex, **Ol Doinyo Eburru** (2820m), which lies to the west of lakes Naivasha and Elmenteita. When finished it will enclose and protect the **Eburru Forest Reserve**, one of 22 blocks in the complex. Rhino Ark completed its hugely ambitious project of fencing the Aberdare National Park in 2009 (see p.190). The purpose of the proposed 50km-long Mau Eburru electric fence is the same – to stop encroachment of human activity into the forest.

3

CROSSING THE EQUATOR

On the way up from Nakuru to lakes Bogoria and Baringo on the B4, you'll pass through the village of **Mogotio**, which lies on the equator. On the left (heading north) look out for the **Equator Monument**, a giant metal spinning globe erected in 2009. For a tip, the friendly tour guide here will spin the globe and tell you everything you'll ever need to know about the equator – from which countries it passes through to an explanation of the "Coriolis effect", an acceleration imparted by the Earth's rotation which causes draining water to (supposedly) flow counterclockwise north of the equator and clockwise to the south. As well as Mogotio, there are equator-crossing roads and signs near (from west to east) Meru (see p.187), Nanyuki (see p.180), Nyahururu, Eldama Ravine and Kisumu, but none as elaborate (or informative) as the Mogotio spinning globe.

On towards Lake Baringo

If you're continuing from Molo towards **Lake Baringo** in your own vehicle, you can avoid doubling back to Nakuru by heading north to the A104 from Molo and turning northwest towards Eldoret. After 5km, when you reach Makutano, take the surfaced B53 to the right, which goes through some wonderful mountain scenery via **Eldama Ravine**, where you can turn right and join the B4 to the lake.

ACCOMMODATION AND EATING   **WEST OF NAKURU**

Deloraine House 34km from Nakuru off the A104; turn right 1km past Salgaa, then right again, and follow signs to the house ☎0704 909355, ⓦ offbeatsafaris.com. Exquisitely chilled and stately colonial pile built in 1920 on a vast estate beneath the Mount Londiani forest, just a few kilometres northwest of – but a million miles from – the straggling truck-stop of Salgaa (Rongai). The long shady terrace looks east across luxuriant borders and lawns and there's a large swimming pool, lovingly maintained stables with eighty horses and a gentle Happy Valley atmosphere. The rooms are baronial and the meals delicious, copious and garden-fresh. It particularly appeals to riders, who often stay here as part of a safari with Offbeat (see p.72). Full-board packages including riding. Wi-fi. **$840**

★**Kembu Campsite and Cottages** 5km from Njoro along the C56 to Elburgon, 18km from the A104/C56 junction west of Nakuru, and then 1.2km from the main road (well signposted) ☎0722 725003, ⓦ kembucottages.com. Set on an 800-acre, family-run working farm with great views and wonderful hospitality, with accommodation in a variety of spacious, relaxing cottages, some dating back to the 1920s and 1930s,

including a delightful "Tree House" and an old wooden train carriage, "Cobb's Carriage". A good spot to hang out for a few days, it's also popular with overland groups, and has fresh farm produce for sale, excellent food and a convivial bar-restaurant ensuring regular company. *Kembu*, incidentally, is Kikuyu for chameleon, and you can find little Van Hoehnell's chameleons all around the site. Prices range from Ksh5900 for Cobb's (non-s/c) up to Ksh16,500 for a fully s/c cottage sleeping four, or you can camp (tents and bedding are available to rent). Wi-fi. Fantastic value, and great for families. Camping **Ksh550**, room only **Ksh9000**

Ziwa Bush Lodge 16km from Nakuru on the way to Njoro and 6.3km from the A104/C56 junction, and then 3km from the main road (well signposted) ☎07076 98822, ⓦ ziwalodge.com. A peaceful farm retreat, this lodge is owned by an Australian couple who also run a children's home on the same property. Accommodation is in eight double/twins and one family unit made from local stone with canvas walls and thatched roofs; each has a veranda overlooking a magnificent wheat field with a distant view of Nakuru town. Good wholesome farm food (hopefully lamb chops will be on the menu), great hospitality and there's a pool. Wi-fi. FB **$200**

Lake Bogoria National Reserve

Daily 7am–7pm • $50 plus Ksh300 per vehicle • ☎0732 370114 or ☎0700 404462

One of the least-visited lakes in the Rift Valley, despite being a globally recognized Ramsar wetlands site since 2002, **Lake Bogoria** is a body of saline and alkaline water entrenched beneath towering hills, 60km north of Nakuru. With the fluctuating water levels of Lake Nakuru, more reliable Lake Bogoria has become the favoured feeding ground of tens (at times hundreds) of thousands of **lesser flamingos**, and the lakeshore is one of the few places where **greater kudu** antelope can easily be seen. But the lake is worth visiting as much for its physical spectacle as for the wildlife: a largely barren, baking wilderness of scrub and rocks, from which a series of furious **hot springs** erupts on the western shore, and the bleak walls of the Siracho range rise from the east.

The lake

Hidden in its deep bowl, Lake Bogoria – when approached from the village of **Mugurin** to the south – is only visible when you're almost on top of it. The final stretch of the track leading down to the southern Emsos Gate is steep and rocky as well as being savagely beautiful, the landscape transformed into a strident dazzle of red and blue and splashes of green. The lake itself, a glistening pool of soapy blue and white, usually has a mirage of pink flamingos tinting its shores.

While the reserve's **paved road** between the northern Loboi Gate and the Loburu hot springs is in good condition, the **east shore road** has been quite impassable for years, owing to a huge rock fall coupled with higher water levels, so there is no circuit round the lake. If you're driving northwest from Emsos Gate, there's a river bed to negotiate before you reach the tarmac, for which 4WD is essential. It may be best to take a ranger who knows the road: ask at the gate.

The Loburu hot springs

However you enter the reserve, you're bound to want to see the **hot springs**, a series of boiling water spouts on the shore. Although they hardly touch Yellowstone or Rotorua standards, "hot springs" is a tame appellation for this very impressive, terrifying and photogenic phenomenon. Depending on the lake level, one or more of the springs may break the surface of the lake (while the others show their presence by the agitated green water above them, some steam and a strong smell), or they may all be visible from the shore.

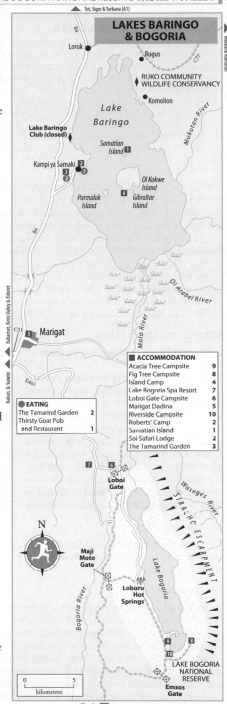

LAKES BARINGO & BOGORIA

Tot, Sigor & Turkana (A1)

Loruk

Rugus

RUKO COMMUNITY WILDLIFE CONSERVANCY

Komolion

Lake Baringo

Lake Baringo Club (closed)

Samatian Island 1

Kampi ya Samaki

Parmalok Island

Ol Kokwe Island

Gibraltar Island

Mukutan River

Ol Arabel River

Molo River

Marigat

C51

E461

Kabarnet, Kerio Valley & Eldoret

Nakuru, & Nairobi

■ **ACCOMMODATION**

Acacia Tree Campsite	9
Fig Tree Campsite	8
Island Camp	4
Lake Bogoria Spa Resort	7
Loboi Gate Campsite	6
Marigat Dadina	5
Riverside Campsite	10
Roberts' Camp	2
Samatian Island	1
Soi Safari Lodge	2
The Tamarind Garden	3

● **EATING**

The Tamarind Garden	2
Thirsty Goat Pub and Restaurant	1

Loboi Gate

Waseges River

SIRACHO ESCARPMENT

N

Maji Moto Gate

Bogoria River

Loburu Hot Springs

Lake Bogoria

LAKE BOGORIA NATIONAL RESERVE

Emsos Gate

0   5 kilometres

Moqotio

Maralal & Rumuruti

3

3

> ## LAKE BOGORIA'S WILDLIFE
>
> Although there's plenty of wildlife in and around Lake Bogoria, it tends to make itself scarce, with the exception of the flamingos at the hot springs. Most animals – including buffalo, hyena, klipspringer, impala, dik-dik, zebra, warthog and Grant's gazelle – prefer the remote and inaccessible eastern shore, though you may see **greater kudu** just about anywhere. The **flamingos**, for some curious reason – possibly chemical – tend to flock in their greatest numbers to the shallows on the western shore, where the hot springs flow into the lake (they appear immune to the heat). The Bogoria **fish eagles** have made a gruesome adjustment to their fierce, fishless environment: they prey on flamingos. Overall, birdwatching here is tremendous, with other birds to look out for among the 373 recorded species including avocets, transitory pelicans and migratory steppe eagles.

With normal water levels, the springs burst up from huge natural cauldrons of super-heated water not far below the ground and drain into steaming rivulets that cut through the crusty earth, continuously collapsing and reforming their courses down to the lake. Even at midday, when the sun glares like a furnace, clouds of steam drift across this infernal scene. Near the lakeshore, the macabre bleached skeletons of flamingos lie strewn in the sand and, in the background, the dull thundering of the springs fills the air. It's like some water garden in Hell.

Picnickers sometimes think it's fun to boil eggs and heat tins of food in the pools, but the consequences of a fall can be messy and even fatal: over the years a number of people have slipped and died as a result. An *askari* has been posted to watch out for visitors, but if you scald yourself, help might still be a long time coming.

ARRIVAL AND DEPARTURE   LAKE BOGORIA NATIONAL RESERVE

FROM NAKURU VIA MOGOTIO TO EMSOS GATE

The B4 road north from Nakuru runs 20km to the west of Lake Bogoria and carries little traffic – tortoises in the road present the greatest hazard to motorists. The reserve is signposted to the right, 36km from Nakuru at Mogotio (fill up on petrol here), from where a good *murram* road, easily motorable in the dry season, cuts across to the lake. Some 23km from this junction, shortly after Mugurin, you fork left for the western Maji Moto Gate (an incredibly rough 17km further, bringing you to the hot springs and tarmac lakeshore road), or right/straight ahead for the southern Emsos Gate (an equally rough 13km), which brings you to the wooded part of the reserve, from where a further rough track leads to the springs. Depending on the season, you may need 4WD beyond Mugurin, and there's no public transport.

FROM NAKURU TO LOBOI GATE

The far easier, quicker and usual option is to continue northwards up the B4 to the signposted junction a few kilometres before Marigat (see opposite). From here, a fast tarmac road, the E461, takes you straight to the Loboi Gate 20km further on. There are plenty of matatus between Nakuru and Marigat, but only infrequent matatus between Marigat and Loboi village.

GETTING AROUND

Though most visitors **drive** along the (potholed) tarmac road between Loboi Gate and the Loburu hot springs, you're also allowed as far as the springs **on foot** or **by bicycle**; you might be able to rent bikes from locals at Loboi Gate (about Ksh700/day).

ACCOMMODATION

The rigour of Lake Bogoria's landscape is relieved by three shady **campsites** at the southern end of the lake, though they're difficult to get to unless you have 4WD and are sometimes closed after flooding; check the situation in advance by phoning the gate (📞 0723 370114 or 📞 0700 404462). If they're shut, the gate staff will point you to other places to camp on higher ground, though there will be no facilities. There's also a fourth campsite, rather easier to access, at Lobio Gate. Camping fees are paid at the gates. Take insect repellent and a good tent with an inner mesh lining – be aware that this area can be very hot (even at night) and there are aggressive mosquitoes and lake midges. There's just one other accommodation option near Loboi Gate, though it's not cheap; the best option for budget travellers is to visit Lake Bogoria as a day-trip en route (after a very early start) from Nakuru to Baringo, although a lot of matatu-hopping is involved.

LODGES AND RESORTS

Lake Bogoria Spa Resort 3km before Loboi Gate ☎ 0710 445627, ⓦ lakebogoria-hotel.com; map p.235. It has an unattractive exterior, and is essentially no more than an ordinary town hotel stranded in the bush, but this resort's 55 rooms and cottages have been refurbished to a comfortable level and have a/c (a bit of a godsend in Bogoria's hot valley), nets and TV. Rates are high; negotiate for the resident's rates. There are also twenty pre-erected tents of varying standard (some are old); campers use the pool bathrooms. The resort's best feature is its naturally replenished thermal spring pool, always a steady 37°C; day visitors can stop for a swim (Ksh500) and a buffet lunch (Ksh1800). Wi-fi. Tents BB $45 per person, rooms HB $282

CAMPING

Acacia Tree Campsite 1.5km past Riverside Campsite, a 30min walk from Emsos Gate; map p.235. A pretty spot on the lakeshore, shaded by acacias and frequented by kudu. Water and latrines are provided here, which makes the site better equipped than most. $15

★Fig Tree Campsite 3.5km from Emsos Gate; map p.235. An absolute delight, though the magnificent glade of giant fig trees that shades the site is a favourite haunt of baboons that gorge themselves day and night. Buffalo also graze near here and are not to be trifled with. Bring your own food – a few basics are usually available just outside Emsos Gate – though water isn't a problem, since a permanent brook, clear and sweet, runs right through the site and provides a natural spa. $15

Loboi Gate Campsite Loboi Gate; map p.235 You can camp at Loboi Gate, next to the Environmental Education Centre, just outside the reserve. It's not the most picturesque place, but there are latrines and usually water, and the handful of small shops at the gate can provide you with basics like eggs, biscuits and drinks; bring any other food and supplies yourself. $15

Riverside Campsite 2km from Emsos Gate; map p.235. The most basic of the three campsites, on the banks of a river that serves as the camp's only water source. Weaver birds breed nearby, and you can hear them in the trees at night. $15

Lake Baringo

An internationally recognized Ramsar wetlands site since 2002, **Lake Baringo** is a peaceful and beautiful oasis in the dry-thorn country, rich in **birdlife** and with a captivating character entirely its own. Depending on lake levels, the waters are either heavily silted with the topsoil of the region and appear a rusty red or streaky yellow or (if the lake is full of fresh water that has run down from the catchment areas in the hills) it runs through a whole range of colours from coral to purple to a brilliant aquamarine, according to the sun's position and the state of the sky. On the lakeshore are villages inhabited by the **Il Chamus** (Njemps) people, who live by an unusual mixture of fishing and livestock-herding, breaking the taboo on the eating of fish, which is the norm among pastoralists. Speaking a dialect of Maa – the Maasai language – these fishermen paddle out in half-submerged dinghies made from the spongy and buoyant saplings of the fibrous *ambatch* tree that grows in profusion around the lake.

Like Lake Nakuru and the other Rift Valley lakes, Baringo has experienced unprecedented flooding since 2012, which reached a peak in mid-2014 when the surface area of the lake was believed to be over 300 square kilometres, well over double its pre-2012 dry season level. Schools, farms, even whole villages were submerged by the rising water, and many thousands of people displaced and forced to higher ground. The 2015 rainy season proved to be drier in comparison and at the time of writing waters had receded about 10m from their 2014 record high.

Marigat

Some 100km from Nakuru, the small district town of **MARIGAT** ought to be the hub of the Baringo–Bogoria tourist circuit, but it's a bland, dust-blown little place. The town's major landmark is an impressive bright green and white **mosque** funded by a wealthy Saudi, with two tiers of large windows and a capacity that obviously exceeds the area's Muslim population.

Kampi ya Samaki

The lakeside village of **KAMPI YA SAMAKI** ("Fish Camp"), 17km beyond Marigat and 2km from the main B4 road, is the de facto capital of Lake Baringo. There are very few facilities in the scruffy little settlement itself: a small post office, but no bank and little in the way of shops. There's not a whole lot to do here, either, apart from a small **reptile park** (daily 8am–6pm; Ksh200), signposted at the entrance to the village, where you can see some local snakes, lizards and tortoises at close range.

Around the lake

Lake Baringo is fresh water (Naivasha being the only other non-saline Rift Valley lake), so its fish support a wide variety of **birds** and there are also sizeable populations of crocodiles and hippos. Though you rarely see much more than ears and snout by day, **hippos** come ashore after dark to graze; on a moonlit night their presence can be unnervingly obvious, though even in pitch darkness they're too noisy to be ignored. Although it used to be commonly understood that Baringo **crocodiles** were too small to pose a danger to swimmers, what constitutes a dangerous size in a Nile crocodile is perhaps a reckless debate. Swimming is certainly highly inadvisable.

Although you can walk (be careful) along the shore at various points, the best way to enjoy Lake Baringo is by motorboat (see opposite). The motorized canoes used are ideal for shallow water cruising, allowing you to access reed beds and river mouths and to get close to the hippos, crocodiles and birds.

Ruko Community Wildlife Conservancy

Ksh500 per person • Conservancy Office in Kampi ya Samaki ☎ 071 773034, ⓦ rukokenya.org • 75 square kilometres

Established in 2008 on the northeastern shore of Lake Baringo, the **Ruko Community Wildlife Conservancy** is managed by Pokot and Il Chamus (Njemps) people. Its name derives from the first two letters of the two local villages – Rugus, where KWS maintains a ranger post, and Komolion – that donated the land for the conservancy's creation. Resident animals include warthog, ostrich, zebra and

---

BIRDWATCHING AT LAKE BARINGO

Baringo's 470 species of **birds** are one of its biggest draws, and even if you don't know a superb starling from an ordinary one, the enthusiasm of others tends to be infectious. Former Baringo ornithologist Terry Stevenson holds the world record "bird-watch" for 24 hours – 342 species. Baringo's bird population rises and falls with the seasons (the dry season is the leanest time for birders), but the lakeshore resounds with birdsong (and frogs) at most times of year. It's surprisingly easy to get within close range of the birds – some species, such as the starlings and the white-bellied go-away bird, are positively brazen and may even perch on your breakfast table. There are some interesting marshy areas south of the (now closed) *Lake Baringo Club* where you should see some unusual species such as the white phase of the paradise flycatcher, grey-headed bush shrike, violet wood hoopoe and various kingfishers. Hippos commonly graze here, too, even in daylight hours. Wherever you're staying, an early-morning birding boat trip along the lake's reedy shore is likely to be on offer, possibly in combination with a visit to the **Goliath Heronry** and one or two **hippo** and **croc** haunts. Afternoons can profitably be used for a trip out near the main road under some striking red cliffs, an utterly different habitat where, apart from hyraxes and baboons, you can see several species of hornbill, sometimes the massive nest of a hammerkop (wonderful-looking birds in flight, resembling miniature pterodactyls with their strange crests) and, with luck, the rare Verreaux's eagle. The most dedicated birders should definitely take the opportunity to spot Baringo's nocturnal birds on a night bird walk from *Roberts' Camp* (see p.240). Your highly trained guide may find you a nightjar, Heuglin's courser, white-fronted scops owl or the curiously named spotted thick-knee.

waterbuck, and a number of grazing game have been translocated here by KWS, including impala and eight **Rothschild's giraffes** which were brought up from the Soysambu Conservancy near Lake Naivasha in 2011. Quite uniquely they were transported across the lake four at a time by barge, the first instance of giraffes being carried across water in Kenya. The photographs were so extraordinary that they became an internet sensation.

Originally occupying a peninsula that jutted out into the lake, the conservancy's land area has shrunk and is now an island. Motorboat excursions include a bush walk on this so-called **Giraffe Island**, accompanied by the resident Pokot and Njemps scouts, who will also help you feed the giraffes.

ARRIVAL AND DEPARTURE   LAKE BARINGO

Approaching **from the south**, the lake can be reached by matatu via the town of Marigat. Travelling **north of Marigat** is a hit-or-miss affair without your own transport: there's no public transport either to Maralal or to Tot from here, but you could try to hitch. If you're driving north of Baringo, note that there is **fuel** at Marigat, but none after that until Maralal or Archer's Post (going northeast), and (going northwest) not until you hit the A1.

From the south: by matatu via Marigat Regular matatus from Nakuru go up to Marigat, where you'll have to change to another to reach Kampi ya Samaki. Travelling back from Kampi ya Samaki, there are one or two matatus direct to Nakuru at around 6am; otherwise change at Marigat.

Destinations from Marigat Kabarnet (45min); Kampi ya Samaki (30min); Loboi (30min); Nakuru (1hr 30min).

From the northeast: by road to or from Maralal The highly recommended but rough road from Marigat to Maralal (one day) or the rougher continuation to Samburu National Reserve (best done over two days) are only viable with your own vehicle – there's no public transport on these routes. The Maralal route starts by swinging north off the B4 at Loruk, about 15km north of the Lake Baringo turnoff, leaving tarmac and tourism behind, and taking you up into the rugged country of the Lerochi plateau, dotted with Tugen and Pokot settlements. When the air is clear, there are stunning

views back over Baringo. After two to three hours, you join the Rumuruti–Maralal *murram* road (C77), then go north as far as Kisima, where you choose between a short journey onwards on the C77 to Maralal or some inspiring but wheel-shattering driving along the C78/79 east to Archer's Post and Samburu (see p.377).

From the northwest: by road to or from the A1 From Loruk the B4 road heads northwest and up the steep and difficult Kito Pass to Tot (122km from Marigat), where there's a route south along the Elgeyo Escarpment to Iten (see p.243). The B4 itself continues along the northern spurs of the Cherangani Hills via Sigor to its junction with the A1 – 56km west of Tot and about 20km north of Ortum. Don't be fooled by the road classification: though *murram*, this part of the B4 varies in quality and is steep in parts, and a 4WD vehicle is required. There are only sporadic matatus between Tot and Sigor, after which transport improves; there are also matatus to/from Makutano near Kapenguria on the A1 (see p.294).

INFORMATION

Services Marigat town has a KCB bank with ATM on the main street. Fuel stations include a smart new Shell at the B4 junction to town, and an equally new Petro at the Kabarnet turnoff on the B4 1.5km further south.

TOURS AND ACTIVITIES

Motorboat trips Excursions by motorboat can be arranged directly with the boatmen at the jetty at Kampi ya Samaki or at the lodges, but the best option is either *Roberts' Camp* (see p.240) or Lake Baringo Boats and Excursions, a community-run tour company opposite *Roberts' Camp* (☏ 0721 548657). Both offer the same prices and often use the same excellent guides. Expect to pay around Ksh3000/hr for a boat carrying up to seven people, but (given that Baringo can get rough) make sure that life jackets are provided and that no more than seven passengers are carried. Most boatmen know their birds and are old hands at luring fish eagles by tossing

them fresh fish – take your camera for spectacular close-ups as the eagles swoop down for the bait. Trips can also take in the Ruko Community Wildlife Conservancy for an extra Ksh500 per person conservancy fee on top of the boat charge.

Walks *Roberts' Camp* and Lake Baringo Boats and Excursions also offer bird walks, either along the lakeshore or up in the cliffs above Kampi ya Samaki (Ksh500 per person for 2hr). Keen birders will want to combine a walk with a motorboat trip as the two habitats attract different species. There's also an additional night bird walk (see box, p.240) for Ksh600/hr.

3

ACCOMMODATION

The lakeside accommodation was much affected by Baringo's newly shaped perimeter but the places that have remained open are adapting and refurbishing.

★**Island Camp** On the southern tip of Ol Kokwe Island ☎0728 478638 or 0724 874661, ⊛islandcamp .co.ke; map p.235. Opened in 1972 and considered to be one of Kenya's first "tented camps", *Island Camp* is today not as luxurious as some but has real atmosphere and rustic charm and a simply outstanding location – dense with birdlife and with expansive views directly over the lake, which lulls you to sleep with its lapping just metres away. There are sixteen tents varying from modest twins to massive doubles with their own plunge pool, excellent food and hospitality and there's a good-sized (if chilly) pool. *Island* offers the same excursions as the shore-based places (see p.239) as well as guided island walks, a sundowner trip ($36 with drinks) to Gibraltar Island – a red sandstone uninhabited rock off Ol Kokwe – and kayaks for hire ($10/hr). Rates include boat transfer from the jetty at Kampi ya Samaki, which has a secure car park. Wi-fi. FB $400

Marigat Dadina Near the roundabout in Marigat ☎0735 359351; map p.235. There's little point in staying In Marigat unless you're too late for a matatu connection to Kampi ya Samaki. This has fairly well-kept rooms around a dusty courtyard, though the singles and doubles (both s/c and non s/c) are rather small and cell-like. There are plenty of *hotelis* on the same street for basic food. Room only Ksh800

★**Roberts' Camp** 1km south of Kampi ya Samaki ☎0717 176656 or 0733 207775, ⊛robertscamp .com; map p.235. A lovely campsite in a large, acacia-shaded garden dipping into the lake, with lots of space, good facilities and great birding. Accommodation includes dome tents (which can be rented with bedding), two twin *bandas* and a pair of walk-in safari tents with electricity (sharing bathrooms with campers; warm water only), plus one s/c self-catering cottage (Ksh11,000 for six people). At the heart of the camp is the *Thirsty Goat* pub (see opposite). Matatus from Marigat will drop off on the corner right outside. Wi-fi. Camping Ksh700,

dome tents Ksh2000, BB Ksh8000

★**Samatian Island** ☎0722 207772 or 0722 706895, ⊛samatianisland.com; map p.235. Set on a minuscule private island, this is a wonderfully peaceful and relaxing self-catering lodge, where birds hop and flit everywhere and there are fantastic, ever-changing lake views in every direction. The two double/twin and two family *bandas* are very spacious and fully open-plan, with no windows or walls to block out the idyllic natural environment. Guests can bring their own food and drink and self-cater – there's a kitchen and dining area – or the staff will cook, and there's also the option of organizing the boatman to take you across to nearby *Island Camp* (see above) for (pre-arranged) lunch or dinner. The minimum rate per night is Ksh14,000 for 1–4 people plus Ksh4000 per extra person up to the capacity of eight, and you must book for a two-night stay. Rates include boat transfer from the jetty at Kampi ya Samaki; parking can be arranged. Ksh14,000

Soi Safari Lodge Kampi ya Samaki ☎0704 704 411621, ⊛soisafarilodge-lkbaringo.com; map p.235. A big, rather plain construction, although the new thatched roofs make it look a bit more safari-like, offering rooms with a/c, nets and TV (hot water mornings and evenings only). It's adequate, reasonably priced and (since the floods) now unexpectedly has lakeshore access, but is predominantly aimed at the local conference market. The large pool (non-residents Ksh300) is surrounded by about an acre of crazy paving. Wi-fi. HB $205

The Tamarind Garden On the left of the road 1km before Kampi ya Samaki ☎0702 2649446, ✉tamarindgarden@hotmail.com; map p.235. A peaceful spot in a gated garden with a dozen small but spotless concrete rooms with nets and fans; as the building is under thatch, they are refreshingly cool in the Baringo heat. You can also camp on the grass, surrounded by flowering trees. Camping Ksh1000, BB Ksh5000

EATING

Highly recommended is the excursion across to *Island Camp* by boat for a buffet lunch, afternoon tea and swim at the lovely pool (Ksh2500) – a wonderful way to splurge a little if you're on a budget – but you must let the camp know you're coming over in advance (the trip can be organized at *Roberts' Camp*). *Soi Safari Lodge* also offers filling but mediocre buffets for breakfast (Ksh1200), lunch (Ksh1800), dinner (Ksh2000), but again try and give them notice.

The Tamarind Garden On the left of the road 1km before Kampi ya Samaki ☎07022 649446; map p.235. With lovely gardens and large open thatched restaurant/ bar, this is a relaxing spot for a drink or meal. Good

breakfasts, and the coffee is the genuine article. The main meals, like spaghetti bolognese, pork chops, steak or tilapia fish from the lake, are tasty and good value (from Ksh500). Daily 7am–9.30pm.

Thirsty Goat Pub and Restaurant Roberts' Camp, 1km south of Kampi ya Samaki ☎ 0717 176656, ⓦ robertscamp.com; map p.235. Occupying a pleasant patio with hippos grazing nearby, this is the best focus for food and drink in the area and there's always a buzz here. Full English breakfasts and main meals like tilapia fish and chips, pizza, beef and beer stew and a vegetarian option go for around Ksh600–800. Wi-fi. Daily 7am–9pm, bar later.

The Kerio Valley

The rollercoaster route up the western wall of the Rift Valley makes a good alternative to the busy A104 to Eldoret. West from Lake Baringo, it climbs up into the **Tugen Hills**, drops down into the **Kerio Valley** and then rises again to the Elgeyo Escarpment (see p.245) that marks the rim of the Cherangani Hills (see p.246). On the way, the spectacular escarpments offer semi-tropical vegetation on their lower slopes and higher forested crests, while the Kerio River gorge itself cuts through dry-thorn bush on the hot valley floor. It's the high altitude around **Iten** that attracts Kenyan (and international) long-distance runners, but it must be the incredible views that inspire them to rise early to conquer the hills.

Kabarnet

Lying 52km west of Marigat on the good, tarred C51, **KABARNET** has a superb setting on the **Kamasia massif** – the slab also known as the Tugen Hills, which remained upstanding on the brink of the Kerio Valley when the rest of the area sank – and the route up the escarpment offers breathtaking views back over the Rift Valley floor. Frequent matatus make the climb from Marigat, the road soaring and plunging through at times almost alpine scenery. Kabarnet has good transport connections to surrounding towns, and makes for a good jumping-off point for excursions into the Kerio Valley.

Despite its dramatic location, the town of Kabarnet itself is fairly featureless and dull. From a small nucleus of administration buildings and *dukas* on the hillside in colonial times, it has expanded in every direction since becoming capital of Baringo District, undoubtedly related to its status as former president Daniel Arap Moi's home town (he was born in Sacho, 30km away). There's little to detain you, though you will find fuel stations, a post office, banks with ATMs, a well-stocked market and a few supermarkets.

Kabarnet Museum
100m south of the C51, turnoff opposite the Kobil petrol station • Daily 9am–6pm • Ksh500 • ☎ 053 21221, ⓦ museums.or.ke

The only point of interest in town, the small **Kabarnet Museum** features exhibits on human evolution, headdresses from around the country and artefacts and homesteads of the Tugen, Pokot and Il Chamus peoples who inhabit the region.

Kabarnet to Iten

From Kabarnet, it's about 90km on the C51 to Eldoret (see p.284) across the hot and fascinating **Kerio Valley**. The excitement of this route builds only after you leave Kabarnet town and plunge into the valley, a drop of 1000m in not much more than the same distance. There are magnificent views as the road rolls through **Chebloch**, crossing the muddy-brown Kerio River at Chebloch Gorge, after which the road turns sharply up the **Tambach escarpment** on the western side of the Kerio Valley. A turn right just before the hamlet of **Biretwo** is the start of the lonely trans-valley route north to Tot (see p.246). Also before Biretwo, look out for the **Torok Falls**, looming high above and to your left at the top of the Tambach escarpment. They're worth a visit if you like waterfalls; count on a good half-day if you're hiking up. The

THE KERIO VALLEY
AND CHERANGANI HILLS

ascent of the escarpment is equally spectacular by road, after which there are a couple of worthy reasons to stop at **Iten** – Kenya's famous running centre– to admire the valley from the western escarpment, and perhaps pull on a sweater, given the increase in altitude.

An alternative trans-valley route begins at the turnoff east of Kabarnet, running south to **Tenges** on a surfaced road that twists spectacularly along the spine of the Tugen Hills, with lovely views across the valley. You'll find some public transport to Tenges from Kabarnet, but very little when you turn right, west, for **Kimwarer** down in the valley. Kimwarer is more easily reached via a better road that meets the C51 just west of Chebloch. Kimwarer itself is a company town for the fluorspar mine at the head of the Kerio River (fluorspar – calcium fluoride – is used in the manufacture of steel, aluminium and cement). With nothing but bush, Kalenjin herders and the occasional party of honey-hunters round about, Kimwarer's tidy managerial villas and staff quarters come as a surprise.

Iten and around

3

After a few more hairpins and a spectacular viewpoint (with obligatory curio and drinks stall), the C51 road finally levels out at **ITEN**, a busy little market town on the rim of the Tambach escarpment at an altitude of 2400m. Its name derives from one Joseph Thomson, who in 1883 christened it "Hill Ten" when he was marking the number of hills he had conquered in his exploration of the Rift Valley. Today Iten is the main centre on the west side of the Kerio Valley with a cool climate and some beautiful walks in the area. There is fuel, a KCB bank with ATM and a small market (known for its leather goods). The town is known primarily as a training ground for **runners**: the famous St Patrick's High School (see box below) can be seen just after the main shops on the road north to Kapsowar.

A stop at the *Kerio View Hotel* just beyond Iten (see p.244), even for just a coffee or meal, is one of the highlights of a drive through the Kerio Valley – from its location on the very lip of the Tambach escarpment, the staggeringly vast view takes in the entire valley below. Beyond Iten it's another relatively flat 35km to Eldoret through dairy-farming country (you'll notice the black and white heads of Friesian cows over the fences). Alternatively the intrepid can head north along the Elgeyo escarpment (see p.245).

RUNNING IN ITEN

The remarkable **St Patrick's High School** in Iten must be the world's top school for runners, having produced middle-distance stars such as Peter Rono, Wilson Kipketer, Ibrahim Hussein and – more recently – David Rudisha, while its associated athletics camps have produced female runners such as Lydia Cheromei, Susan Chepkemei and Lornah Kiplagat. The phenomenon dates back to the 1970s, when an Irishman, **Colm O'Connell**, recognized the students' potential and set out to turn them into world-class athletes, developing a training programme which Iten's runners still follow to this day. The remarkable prowess of these runners, in particular those from the Kalenjin group, is something that sports scientists have yet to explain fully, but has a lot to do with running at altitude, as well as physiological factors and a diet high in complex carbohydrates. But the town's reputation has spread, and these days elite athletes come from all over the world to do their high-altitude training in Iten, several hundred passing through each year to run up and down the Kerio Valley and absorb the atmosphere of champions. If you're interested in pursuing some serious athletics, either contact the **High Altitude Training Centre** (see p.244) direct, or get in touch with UK-based **The Kenya Experience** (Ⓦtraininkenya.com), which organizes all-inclusive training "holidays" at the centre with coaching, personal training and physiotherapy (from £1300 for two weeks, excluding flights).

North down the Kerio Valley

For most of the year the Kerio valley floor, wooded and not much cultivated, resonates with dry heat and the rattle of cicadas and crickets. Climatic conditions are best in the few months of vivid greenery after the long rains, in theory from April to June – and fiercest in February and March, just before they break. On the valley floor, **Lake Kamnarok National Reserve** once protected the lake of the same name and its large population of Nile crocodiles, but a severe drought in 2007–2008 caused the lake to dry up and it has never recovered; the crocodiles are long gone and at best the former lake becomes a marshy area after heavy rains. However there are still some small antelope in the area and the birdlife is good.

There's a dearth of public transport through the valley off the main Kabarnet–Iten C51 road, but drivers may enjoy the solitude of following the C52 road north from **Biretwo to Tot** on the west side of the reserve. It has a broken *murram* surface as far as Chesongoch, after which it's very rough, and note that the villages along the way have no facilities for travellers, and only limited supplies. If you have a sturdy 4WD, however – and perhaps camping equipment – it's worth attempting this 90km route as it follows one of Kenya's most beautiful valleys. Once in Tot, you join the B4 road, which heads east to Marigat or northwest to the A1 (see p.246). There's also an alternative route between Iten and Tot that runs along the top of the Elgeyo Escarpment via Chesoi and Chesongoch (see opposite).

ARRIVAL AND DEPARTURE   THE KERIO VALLEY

KABARNET

By matatu The bustling stage is in front of *Hotel Sinkoro*, with frequent connections to a number of towns in the area.

Destinations Eldoret (1hr 45min); Iten (1hr); Marigat (45min), with onward connections (see p.239); Nakuru (2hr 30min); Tenges (1hr).

KABARNET TO ITEN

Plenty of matatus ply the C51 between Kabarnet and Eldoret via Iten. Occasional matatus run between Iten and Kapsowar but only sporadic transport (overloaded 4WDs) beyond there to Chesoi and Tot on the B4. Between Tot and Sigor there are only 1–2 matatus a day (if you're lucky) but at Sigor you can catch a matatu on to Makutano, near Kapenguria on the A1 (see p.295).

ACCOMMODATION

KABARNET

Kabarnet has a dearth of accommodation so try not to plan an overnight here. The old colonial *Kabarnet Hotel*, 1km above the town off the Nakuru road, is still there and the bar is open, but other than that it's virtually derelict. Some building work appears to have been started, though, so by all means look in.

Sinkoro Hotel Kipsunya Rd, by the matatu stage ☎ 053 22243. A rambling basic B&L above a row of shops with large, light and clean rooms with hot showers, though those facing onto the matatu stage are noisy. There's also a bar and a passable restaurant serving local food. BB <u>Ksh1000</u>

ITEN AND AROUND

High Altitude Training Centre (HATC) Off the C51, just before the red arch marking the entrance to Iten from the Eldoret direction ☎ 0772 700701, ⊛ hatc-iten .com; map p.242. If you're an athlete rather than a tourist, you'll already know about Lornah Kiplagat's training camp, but if you'd simply like to stay in Iten and do some running and training, or just relax, it's open to all-comers. There's

accommodation in single/double/triple rooms with hot showers, a dining room serving three healthy buffet meals per day and a comfortable lounge with DSTV, plus a 25m pool, gym, sauna, 400m running track and a physiotherapy clinic. Additionally, for ordinary mortals, the *Iten Club* is a separate drop-in restaurant that offers pizza, burgers, Kenyan food and beer. Rates vary enormously depending on how long you stay and how many people in a group but start from Ksh3500 per person per night. Wi-fi. FB <u>$75</u>

★ **Kerio View Hotel** Just before HATC on the C51 (towards Eldoret) turn left and follow Kerio View Rd for 800m ☎ 020 2039559 or 0722 781916, ⊛ kerioview .com; map p.242. The best place to experience the beauty of the Kerio Valley, in an unbeatable location on top of the Tambach escarpment (2630m) with sweeping views to the valley floor 1000m below. Accommodation is in simply furnished s/c cottages and *bandas* sleeping up to four, and the very cool, glass-fronted bar-restaurant is a great place for a meal even if you're not staying (mains Ksh400–900; daily Kenyan lunch/dinner buffet Ksh1000, continental lunch/dinner buffet Ksh1650). Activities include hiking (the very fit can attempt the descent to the valley floor),

and it's Kenya's top paragliding spot (though there are no paragliding options for the casual visitor). Wi-fi. BB $95
Lelin Overland Campsite 6km out of Iten on the C51 towards Kabarnet, just south of Kessup ☎0722 900848; map p.242. A friendly overlanders' place with a grassy campsite plus very basic beds in five thatched *bandas*, all sharing flush loos and wood-fired hot showers. There's a bar but food is rarely available: it's advisable to bring your own and ask for it to be cooked. The views are magnificent but do consider whether you really want to camp at this altitude – it can get very cold at night. Camping Ksh700, room only Ksh2200
TooGuestHouse On the main road a few metres west of the municipality building ☎0728 723954 or 0733 373886, ⓦtooguesthouse.com; map p.242. This friendly setup has simple but neat brick rooms with tiled bathrooms

and reliable hot water arranged around a grassy courtyard. Decent bar/restaurant where you may meet Kenyan athletes since it's an affordable base for some high-altitude training. Wi-fi. BB Ksh3400

KIMWARER
Sego Safari Lodge 2km west of the Kerio River bridge over Chebloch Gorge turn left (south) and continue for about 8km (32km from Kabarnet via the C51) ☎0722 407470 or 0788 715259, ⓦsegosafarilodge.co.ke; map p.242. Owned by the *Eldoret Wagon Hotel* (see p.287), this simple lodge is a little off the beaten track and a little down at heel, but clean and welcoming, with s/c cottages, a small pool and restaurant offering a limited menu. You can camp here too. Camping Ksh700, BB Ksh3500

The Elgeyo Escarpment

The long, lush shelf of the **Elgeyo Escarpment** looms some 1500m over the floor of the Kerio Valley, providing some of the most spectacular panoramic views of the Rift Valley you'll find anywhere. Access to the northern stretches of the escarpment is difficult, and few tourists make it this way, so intrepid souls are likely to have mountain towns like Kapsowar and Chesoi all to themselves.

Iten to Chesoi

Roughly 50km north of Iten, your first logical destination along the escarpment is picturesque **KAPSOWAR**, which has a couple of B&Ls, a market, a post office, a branch of KCB and a petrol station (though neither cash nor fuel can be totally guaranteed from either of these). It is also where public transport ends; frequent matatus do the run from Eldoret to Kapsowar, but after that the going gets too tough for the rickety minibuses to handle. However there is the odd battered old-style pick-up van ferrying people and goods to and from the next major settlement along the escarpment, **CHESOI**, 20km from Kapsowar by road, though only 8km as the crow flies. Quite

---

THE MARAKWET IRRIGATION SYSTEM

The rocky, almost perpendicular slopes along the Elgeyo Escarpment around Chesoi are the best places from which to view the surviving sections of the Marakwet's ancient **irrigation system.** The Marakwet – part of the broadly related Kalenjin group of peoples – may have arrived on these slopes as long ago as a thousand years, and their irrigation system has been dated to be at least 500 years old. The system once stretched north–south for over 40km, diverting water from the gushing streams coming down from the Cherangani Hills. The water was channelled into a branching system of furrows and aqueducts made from hollowed-out logs supported by earth mortar and foliage. Complex, unwritten laws ensured that each Marakwet sub-clan was fairly provided for by the system, which irrigated intensive, luxuriant gardens at their tiny *shambas* and provided water for their livestock.

Still operational, the irrigation channels routinely get damaged by heavy rains, when rocks and dirt become trapped and create blockages, and ongoing repair work is needed to keep the streams flowing in the right direction. Many are now reinforced by cement and pipes have been laid along the original furrows. Some still run under the main escarpment road, and any local around Chesoi will show you the channels clinging to the hillside above the village.

unexpectedly, the road between the two settlements is tarred, presumably simply to maintain communication between them.

The land up here warps and buckles like a rumpled patchwork quilt and is dotted with **Marakwet homesteads**, the huts unusual in being built of stone (there's a limitless supply up here), giving them an ancient-looking permanence rarely seen in Kenyan rural architecture. The Cherangani Hills (see below) stretch away to the west, and a thousand metres below, spreading like a grey-green carpet into the haze, are the scrubby, bush-covered plains of Pokot and south Turkana. Dozens of tiny wisps of smoke from charcoal burners combine to smudge out the distant peaks of Mount Kenya to the southeast.

Chesoi to Tot

From Chesoi, the scenic escarpment road descends the 25 breathtaking kilometres down to **Tot** via Chesongoch. Once in Tot (no facilities) you're on the B4 road which heads south down the steep Kito Pass to Marigat (122km) and Lake Baringo (see.p.237) and north via Lomut and Sigor to the A1 (56km) at its junction about 20km north of Ortum and just south of the Marich Pass (see p.295). Going south, the tarmac only starts at Loruk, about 15km before the Lake Baringo turnoff. Make sure you have enough petrol for any of these routes as there are no fuel pumps along the way.

The Cherangani Hills

Forming an undulating upland plateau to the west of the top of the Elgeyo Escarpment and to the east of the A1 road between Kapenguria and the Marich Pass, the **Cherangani Hills** are wild, thickly forested and hardly explored. Cherangani's forests are important water-catchment areas and sit astride the watershed between the Lake Victoria and Lake Turkana basins. Higher up, they merge into mountain moorland and giant Afro-alpine vegetation: superb hiking country where you're very unlikely to meet any other walkers. Parts of the hills are also accessible by car, most notably along the scenic **Cherangani Highway circuit**.

Hiking the Cheranganis

The hills are on a forested escarpment which is surrounded on three sides by sheer cliff faces, but they are criss-crossed by walking paths and the ease of finding your way around and the undemanding terrain make this excellent country for relaxing hill walking. The paths cross open farmland, pass through sheltered valleys and wind their way up to forested peaks. If your hiking plans are more ambitious, try to get hold of the relevant Survey of Kenya 1:50,000m-scale maps and set off, suitably equipped, over the high central districts of the massif. There are several peaks up here: the highest elevation of the Cheranganis is the Kameleogon peak on Mount Chemnirot (3580m), the fourth highest mountain in Kenya after Mount Kenya, Mount Elgon and Mount Satima in the Aberdares. The best base for exploring this area is *Barnley's Guesthouse* (see p.291), with the *Marich Pass Field Studies Centre* (see p.295) offering a less expensive alternative. You can hire local guides at either.

The Cherangani Highway circuit

The scenic D327 road from Makutano through **Kapsait** and **Kaibichbich** is known as the "**Cherangani Highway**", and the northern stretch forms part of a driving circuit. The road suffers landslides, and you should check on its current condition before setting out – *Barnley's Guesthouse* (see p.295) should be able to advise. Note too that the route crosses the 3000m contour, with accompanying decreased oxygen supplies, and that car engine performance may be adversely affected by the altitude – it is essential to carry extra supplies of fuel as consumption is heavy.

Starting at the junction on the A1 near Kapenguria, you can drive down through Kaibichbich to a junction north of Kapsait, where you take a left, passing through Kapsangar towards the peak of Kalelaigelat. Another left turn takes you northwest through **Sina** and back to meet the A1 at **Chipkorniswa**. The hills between Sina and the villages of **Parua** and **Tamkal** to its north can also be hiked, with footpaths connecting the three villages, although you'll need a guide to follow them. All three villages are connected to the A1 by *murram* roads. If you are going to Tamkal, it's worth trying to coincide with market day, which is Tuesday.

3

Western Kenya

KITUM CAVE, MOUNT ELGON NATIONAL PARK

Western Kenya

Like the tiers of a great amphitheatre, western Kenya slopes away from Nairobi, the major game parks and the coast, down to the stage of Lake Victoria. Cut off by the high Rift wall of the Mau and Elgeyo escarpments, this region of dense agriculture, rolling green valleys and pockets of thick jungle is one of the parts of the country least known to travellers. Although more accessible than the far north, or even some of the major parks, it has been neglected by the safari operators – and as a tourist, that may well work to your advantage. You can travel for days through lush landscapes from one busy market town to the next and rarely, if ever, meet other tourists.

It's not easy to see why western Kenya has been so ignored, and there's a great deal more of interest than the tourist literature's sparse coverage would suggest. While the west undeniably lacks teeming herds of game stalked by lions and narcissistic warriors in full regalia, what it offers is a series of delightfully low-key, easily visited attractions. For a start there are **national parks**: at **Kakamega Forest**, a magnificent tract of equatorial rainforest bursting with species found nowhere else in Kenya; at **Saiwa Swamp**, where access on foot allows you to get quite close to the rare sitatunga antelope; at **Ruma**, where a lush valley harbours reticulated giraffe, roan antelope and black rhinos; and at **Mount Elgon**, an extinct volcano to rival Mount Kenya in everything but crowds.

Lake Victoria is the obvious place to make for in the west, sprinkled with out-of-the-way islands, populated by exceptionally friendly people, and with the region's major town, **Kisumu**, on its shores. The **Western Highlands** rise all around Lake Victoria in a great bowl, dotted with a string of busy towns. While **Eldoret** and **Kakamega** are essentially route-hubs with little for visitors to do, **Kisii** has a couple of good excursions, the tea capital **Kericho** is certainly worth an overnight stay, and **Kitale** has some interesting museums. Away from the towns, much of the west, even in areas of intensive farming, is ravishingly beautiful: densely animated jungle near Kakamega and Kitale, regimented landscapes of tea bushes around Kericho and many areas of swamp and grassland alive with birds.

Ethnically, the region is dominated by the **Luo** on the lakeshore, but there are Bantu-speaking **Luhya** in the sugar lands, north of Kisumu, and **Gusii** in the formidably fertile Kisii Hills. Other important groups speak one or another of the Kalenjin languages, principally the **Nandi**, around Eldoret, and the **Kipsigis** in the district around Kericho. And of course there are thousands of migrants from other parts of Kenya.

GIRL WITH NILE PERCH, RUSINGA ISLAND

Highlights

❶ Kisumu Museum Action-packed taxidermy and cultural illumination at one of Kenya's best regional museums. **See p.256**

❷ Ruma National Park Verdant national park, home to rare roan antelope, Rothschild giraffes and black rhinos. **See p.267**

❸ Thimlich Ohinga Like a scaled-down Great Zimbabwe, this is the most impressive site of stone wall enclosures in western Kenya. **See p.267**

❹ Islands in the lake Prehistoric and historical sites vie with Nile perch-fishing trips and pure relaxation at Rusinga and Mfangano islands in Lake Victoria. **See p.268**

❺ Tea country Kericho, the most important centre for tea production in the whole of Africa,

is surrounded by an endless rolling sea of brilliant green plantations. **See p.280**

❻ Saiwa Swamp National Park Home to the unusual sitatunga antelope, rare monkeys and a huge variety of birds, Saiwa Swamp can only be explored on foot. **See p.292**

❼ Mount Elgon One of Africa's biggest extinct volcanoes, Elgon's slopes include the mysterious Elkony caves, whose walls are gouged by elephants for minerals. **See p.296**

❽ Kakamega Forest This unique patch of lowland rainforest off the tourist trail preserves wildlife that has more in common with central Africa than Kenya. **See p.306**

HIGHLIGHTS ARE MARKED ON THE MAP ON P.252

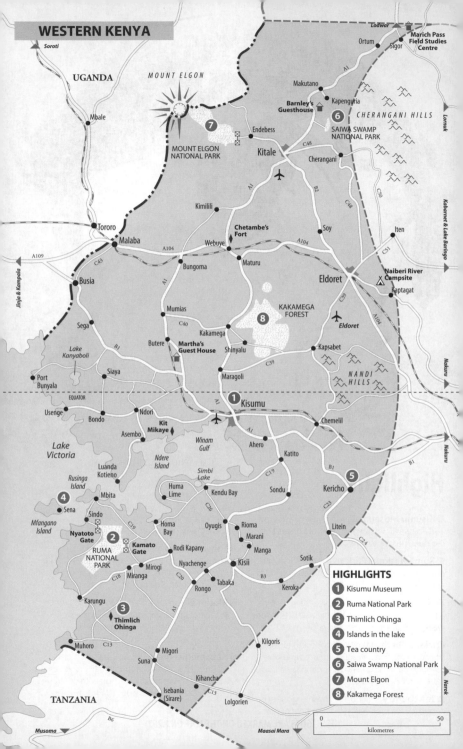

GETTING AROUND

Travel is generally easy. The region has a high population and plenty of roads (many of which are in excellent condition), so you'll rarely have long to wait for transport, and although the west has only a handful of luxury or international-class hotels, there is no lack of good, modest **lodgings**. If you like to plan ahead, one obvious circuit begins in Kisumu and runs through **Kisii**, **Kericho**, **Eldoret**, **Kitale** and **Kakamega**. You could also head southwest from Kisumu to **Rusinga Island**, then further south along a spectacular, hilly stretch of the Lake Victoria coast, through **Ruma National Park** and back up to Kisii, or even east to the Maasai Mara.

TRAVEL AROUND LAKE VICTORIA

Lake Victoria is the obvious place to make for in the west, but frustratingly few main roads get really close to its shores – the best drive is the scenic route from Mbita to Sindo. Most travellers arrive in Kisumu, which used to have ferries linking it with several Kenyan ports, as well as ports in Tanzania and Uganda. Unfortunately, all services – apart from a ferry across the mouth of the Winam Gulf between Luanda Kotieno and Mbita – are suspended, because low water levels, and stretches clogged by water hyacinth, make navigation unsafe. Currently, the only transport from Kisumu to other lakeshore towns is by road. If you want to get out on the lake, the best place to head for is Mbita, which has regular ferries to Mfangano Island, one of the least-visited corners of Kenya, with the added attraction of some wonderful prehistoric rock art.

WALKING IN THE WESTERN HIGHLANDS

There are some good walking areas in the Western Highlands: at Saiwa Swamp National Park and Kakamega Forest National Park, for example, both areas where visiting on foot is essential to appreciate the forest environment. For well-equipped hikers, Mount Elgon is also a major temptation, sharing much of Mount Kenya's flora and fauna, but with very few visitors. There's more wonderful walking country in the high Cherangani Hills, though you need to build in some extra time for accessing them.

4

Kisumu

In the sultry atmosphere of **KISUMU**, a distinctive smell from the lake – fish, mud and rotting vegetation – drifts in on a vague breeze from central Africa. More laidback than any other big town in Kenya, Kisumu was founded as a rail town and lake port, becoming the country's third-largest town as its fortunes rose with the growth of trade in colonial East Africa and the newly independent nations. It suffered badly following the East African Community's break-up, however, and throughout the 1980s and early 1990s the port was mostly dormant. Kisumu's position might lead you to expect a bustling waterfront and a lake-facing atmosphere, although in fact the town has now turned its back on the water, focusing instead on the commercial centre and land links to the rest of Kenya. Although some commercial shipping has resumed, and the port sporadically buzzes with loading or unloading (and people looking for a lift to Uganda or Tanzania), low water levels and water hyacinth have held back progress.

Even if the time-warped atmosphere of a place that's been treading water for three decades may not be much comfort to its inhabitants, Kisumu is one of the few upcountry towns with real character. It's a tranquil, easy-going place, where even the *manambas* at the bus station are unusually calm. Any anticipation of claustrophobia is quickly soothed by the spacious, shady layout. If you've just come from Nakuru, the

LAKE VICTORIA HEALTH HAZARDS

Although going out on the lake is fun, it is, unfortunately, a disease-ridden body of water, and even though there aren't always clouds of mosquitoes, the **malaria** risk is quite high. Snails carrying **bilharzia** also flourish in the reeds around the fringes of the lake, and although the Luo wash and swim in it and sail their vividly painted, dhow-like mahogany canoes on it, the danger of bilharzia is all too real. It's very rare to get the disease after brief contact with infected water, but you should avoid getting wet, as far as possible, if you're fishing or boating, and don't even think about swimming.

KISUMU

■ ACCOMMODATION

Acacia Premier	12
The Duke of Breeze	8
Impala Eco Lodge	16
Imperial	10
Kiboko Bay Resort	15
Kisumu	11
Lake Side Guest House	7
Lake View	9
New East View	6
New Victoria	2
Palmers	4
Perch	1
St Anna Guesthouse	17
St Johns Manor	13
Sooper Guesthouse	5
Sunset	14
YWCA	3

● EATING

Al-Noor Cafeteria	5
Barista	12
The Duke of Breeze	7
Green Garden	4
Haandi	10
Kenshop Cyberstation	8
The Laughing Buddha	11
Oriental	9
Senorita	6
Simba Club	1
Suprim Sweet	3
Tilapia Beach	2
The Yacht Club	13

● SHOPPING

HOPE	1
Pendeza Weaving	2
Sarit Bookshop	4
Tourist Market	3

■ DRINKING AND NIGHTLIFE

The Duke of Breeze	5
Havannaz	1
Octopus Bottoms Up	2
Railways Institute	6
Ramogi Bar	4
Signature	3

contrast is striking. It's a good idea to find somewhere to stay soon after arriving, before starting any energetic wanderings, as it gets tremendously hot here.

Brief history

The **train line** from Mombasa reached the lake by 1901, reassuring the British public who were having serious doubts that the "Lunatic Line", as it was dubbed, would ever reach completion. But the first train only chugged into the station at **Port Florence**, as Kisumu was originally known, in 1903 when the Mau Escarpment viaducts were completed. By then, European transport had already arrived at the lake in the form of a steamship brought up from Mombasa piece by portered piece, having steamed out from Scotland in 1895. Many of the ship's parts were seized en route from the coast and recycled into Nandi ornamentation and weaponry, and it was five years before a complete vessel could be launched on its maiden voyage across the lake to Port Bell in Uganda.

By all accounts Kisumu was a pretty disagreeable place in the early years. Apart from the endemic sleeping sickness, bilharzia and malaria, the climate was sweltering and municipal hygiene primitive. But it quickly grew into an important administrative and military base and, with the consolidation of the colonies in the 1930s and 1940s, became a leading East African entrepôt and transport hub, attracting Asian investment on top of the businesses that had been set up at the rail terminus when the Indian labourers were laid off. Kisumu's rise seemed unstoppable until 1977, when the sudden **collapse of the East African Community**, more or less overnight, robbed the town of its *raison d'être*. The partial reformation of the community in 1996 brightened prospects, and by 1999 the port was relatively busy, thanks largely to UN World Food Programme transit goods destined for war-torn Rwanda and Congo.

Since then, however, Kisumu has again seen a downturn in its fortunes due to the decline of the local **sugar** industry, sugar cane being the surrounding region's main cash crop. Dumping of subsidized sugar by the EU led to a worldwide crash in prices, and this in turn forced the closure of sugar refineries at nearby Muhoroni and Miwani, which were the mainstays of the local economy. More recently, parts of Kisumu were badly hit during the post-election **clashes** in 2007–08, though recovery since then has been rapid.

4

THE LUO

The **Luo** are the second-largest ethnic group and one of the most cohesive "tribes" in Kenya. Their distinctive language, Dholuo, closely resembles the Nuer and Dinka languages of southern Sudan, from where their ancestors migrated south at the end of the fifteenth century. They found the shore and hinterland of Lake Victoria only sparsely populated by hunter-gatherers and scattered with occasional clearings where Bantu-speaking farmers had settled over the previous few centuries. Otherwise, the region was wild: untouched grassland and tropical forest, dense with heavy concentrations of wildlife.

The Luo were swift invaders, driving their herds before them from water point to water point, always on the move, restless and acquisitive. They raided other groups' cattle incessantly and, within a few decades, had forced the Bantu-speakers away from the lakeshore. Despite the conflict, **intermarriage** (essentially the buying of wives) was common and the pastoral nomads were greatly influenced by their Bantu-speaking in-laws and neighbours, ancestors of the present-day Luhya and Gusii.

The Luo today are best known as fishermen, a lifestyle that had sustained them while migrating along the rivers, but they also cultivate widely and still keep livestock. Culturally, they have remained surprisingly independent, and are one of the few Kenyan peoples who don't perform circumcision. Traditionally, children had six teeth knocked out from the lower jaw to mark their initiation into adulthood, but the operation is hardly ever carried out these days. **Christianity** has made spectacular inroads among the Luo, with an estimated ninety percent being believers, but it does not seem to have destroyed their traditional culture quite as thoroughly as it has elsewhere. Despite the ubiquity of Gospel singing, **traditional music**, especially the playing of the *nyatiti* lyre, is still very much alive and well worth listening out for.

Kisumu Market

By the bus station • Daily dawn to dusk

Kisumu's **market** is the biggest and best in western Kenya. It's an absorbing place to wander, crammed with fruit and vegetables (including some oddities like breadfruit) and all the usual household paraphernalia – pots and plates, reed brushes, wickerwork and wooden spoons. The market is such a success that it has mushroomed out into the adjacent municipal park, much to the consternation of the local authorities.

Jamia Mosque

Otieno Oyoo St

The calls to prayer from Kisumu's green-and-white **Jamia Mosque** sound odd in such a heavily Christian region, but Islam is well established here and is an important regional influence dating from well back into the nineteenth century. This orthodox Shafi'ite mosque was built in 1919, though the women's section on the right was only finished in 1984. The beautiful long mats inside are from Saudi Arabia.

The Port

Ksh100 • Paul Waswa (☎ 0720 406954; Ksh200 per person for a tour) is a helpful guide and can tell you all about water hyacinth and shipping movements

If you're interested in **visiting the port**, it's easy enough to go down there, buy a "port visitor" ticket at the port gates and wander along the dock. There is, in truth, practically nothing to see, although if a ship is in port the scene can be quite animated. Your visit may be improved, however, by having a local guide to stroll with you, especially if you want to take photos.

Kisumu Museum

Busia Rd • Daily 8.30am–6pm • Ksh500 (see p.112) • ☎ 057 2020332, ⦿ museums.or.ke

Foremost among the town's sights is the engaging and ambitious **Kisumu Museum**. Set in a large garden with carefully labelled trees, the main gallery happily mingles zoological exhibits with ethnographic displays. Apart from the rows of trophy-style game heads around the walls, the **stuffed animals** and preserved insects and crustaceans are displayed with considerable flair and imagination. Particularly good use has been made of old exhibits from Nairobi's National Museum. A free-swinging vulture, for example, spins like a model aircraft overhead while, centre stage, a lion is caught in full, savage pounce, leaping onto the back of a hysterical wildebeest in the most action-packed piece of taxidermy you're ever likely to see.

The **ethnographic** exhibits are illuminating, too. The Maasai aren't the only people who take blood from their cattle for food: Kalenjin peoples like the Nandi and the Kipsigis once did the same, and even the Luo lived mostly on cow's blood mixed with milk before they arrived at Lake Victoria and began to cultivate and fish. In separate halls from the main gallery are a small, but worthwhile **aquarium**, illustrating the problem of fish depletion in the lake (see what your tilapia looked like before it became a curry), and a **snake house** with a fairly comprehensive collection of Kenyan species. Outside, the tortoise pen and croc pond seem rather pointless extras. The crocodiles, getting extremely large, are fed on Monday evenings at around 5.30pm.

Impala Sanctuary

3km southwest of town • Daily 6am–6pm • $25 • ☎ 020 3530417, ⦿ kws.org

For a fine walk out of town, follow any road heading southwest and you'll pass the entrance to the small **Impala Sanctuary**. Here, more than twenty tame impala (said to be the remnants of wild herds from the early railway days) run free, with vervet monkeys and plenty of birdlife in the dense woodland. A single main footpath (no cars allowed) runs through the kilometre-long sanctuary from end to end, taking you between the lakeshore and a few cramped pens and cages that contain a pair of bored **leopards**, an **ostrich** and a **hyena** that looks as if it might well escape from its insecure confinement. More of a city park than a nature reserve, the sanctuary is worth a visit for the chance to stretch your legs in the shade and stroll near the lakeshore. And, cages aside, it's a pleasant place for an hour or too and a good escape from the heat. Train buffs will be pleased to find a bit of old **rail line** along the lakeshore at the far end.

Hippo Point

800m south of the Impala Sanctuary past the yacht club • Boat trips cost around Ksh2500/hr for a boat seating up to six people

Riotously hued sunsets can be seen from the rock-strewn shore at **Hippo Point**. There's a strong, warm breeze at dusk, and it's a curious sensation to experience this giant body of water without the characteristic smell of the ocean in the air. Hippos are still seen here, and the small crowd of friendly local boatmen will offer to take you out to view them. They use "long shaft" outboard motors for manoeuvrability in the shallows and, as well as hippos, can often show you spotted-necked otters in the area. As a contribution to local environmental restoration, they've planted a patch of what they call "freshwater mangrove", or ambatch, as in Lake Baringo.

Dunga

2km south of Hippo Point, on the headland

Beyond the Impala Sanctuary, most people make for the Luo fishing village of **Dunga**, a picturesque settlement and home to the Dunga Environmental and Eco-Tourism Team (DECTTA), the main focal points of the pleasant little beach. DECTTA have taken a new approach to the problem of earning a sustainable living based on more than just increasingly uncertain fishing, branching out into tourism and educational activities as well. They share a small office, just up the road from the beach, with the **Dunga Wetland Pedagogical Centre** (daily 8am–5pm; ☏0726 701042, ✉wetlandcentre @ecofinderkenya.org), whose friendly staff are happy to provide information on local

4

LAKE VICTORIA'S DISCOVERY AND EXPLORATION

The westward view from Kisumu gives you little sense of the vastness of **Victoria Nyanza** (**Lake Victoria**). From the shores of the narrow Winam Gulf it's difficult to grasp the fact that there's another 300km of water between the horizon and the opposite shore in Uganda, and an even greater distance south to Mwanza, the main Tanzanian port. Victoria, the second-largest freshwater lake in the world after Lake Superior, covers a total area of nearly 70,000 square kilometres – almost the size of Scotland or Nebraska – of which only a fraction is in Kenya.

It was barely five centuries ago that the **Luo** first settled beside the vast equatorial lake they called **Ukerewe**, and the lake remained uncharted and virtually unknown outside Africa until well into the second half of the nineteenth century. Then, in the midst of the race to pinpoint the **source of the Nile**, the lake suddenly became a focus of attention. When English adventurer **John Hanning Speke** first saw Ukerewe in 1858, he was convinced that the long search was over, and promptly renamed the lake after his Queen. In 1862 he became the first person to follow the Nile downstream from Lake Victoria to Cairo, and triumphantly cabled the Royal Geographical Society in London with the words "The Nile is settled." Sceptics, however, doubted the issue was settled, countering that Lake Tanganyika was the true source, and it took a daring circumnavigation of Lake Victoria in 1875, led by the American journalist **Henry Morton Stanley**, to prove Speke right. Sadly, Speke did not live to enjoy the vindication – he was killed in a shooting accident in 1874.

ecology and assist you with any lake activities you might want to pursue, from night fishing to birdwatching. There's also a gift shop.

ARRIVAL AND DEPARTURE KISUMU

Kisumu is the west's transport hub, well connected to the rest of the country by **bus** and **matatu** and excellently positioned for exploring the region – all the towns covered in this chapter are within a half-day's journey.

By plane Kisumu airport (☎057 2531186 or ☎057 2524399) is 4km out of town off the Busia road. There are always a few cabs around until the last flight of the day arrives; the current standard fare into town (15min) is Ksh1000. There are currently daily flights to Nairobi (1hr) with Fly540 (☎0707 540560), Jambo Jet (☎0711 024545) and Kenya Airways (☎0734 102665).

By bus and matatu The bus and matatu stage is on Gumbi Rd, at the intersection of Kenyatta Ave and Otieno Oyoo St, with services to more or less everywhere in western Kenya and further afield to Nakuru, Nairobi and Mombasa. Modern Coast Bus, behind the matatu stage (☎0716 817400), runs overnight buses to Mombasa (three

nightly; 14hr), via Nairobi, arriving at Mombasa in the morning. EasyCoach, United Mall, Gumbi Rd (☎0728 200307), runs buses to Nairobi (6 daily; around 7hr).

Matatu destinations Busia (2hr 30min); Homa Bay (2hr 30min); Kakamega (1hr 30min), some continuing to Kitale (4hr); Kendu Bay (1hr 30min); Kericho (2hr); Kisii (2hr 30min); Luanda Kotieno (2hr 30min);) Mbita (3hr 30min); Nairobi (6hr); Nakuru (3hr 30min).

Bus destinations Kitale (2 daily; 4hr); Mombasa (6 daily; 14hr); Nairobi (roughly hourly; 6hr); Nakuru (roughly hourly; 5hr) via Kericho (2hr).

By car If driving in Kisumu, you're likely to encounter parking wardens – it costs Ksh100/24hr to park anywhere.

ACCOMMODATION

There's a wide choice of places to stay, with a good number of modest, mid-range **hotels**, though prices tend to be higher than usual. Temperature, humidity and mosquitoes will conspire to give you an uncomfortable night if you don't have a net or a fan (preferably both), so it's worth paying a little more for them. It's worth noting too that most hotels in Kisumu have a 9.30am checkout time.

INEXPENSIVE

The Duke of Breeze Off Kenyatta Ave ☎0717 105444, ⓦthedukeofbreeze.com. A very popular budget option with enormous, clean rooms in a concrete tower block, though it suffers a bit from traffic noise. Rooms come with fans, nets and instant showers, and a handful have been spruced up with colourful curtains and funky fabrics. But it's the rooftop bar (see p.260) that makes it such a hit. Wi-fi. BB Ksh3300

★**Lake Side Guest House** Kendu Lane ☎0725 468797. This cosy little guesthouse offers some of the best value in town, offering nicely appointed rooms with ceiling fans, lock-up cupboards and good showers. A pleasant terrace out front overlooks the street and the lake, as do some of the rooms. Room only Ksh1400

Lake View Alego St ☎0721 778287 or ☎0716 058080. Despite the name there are no exceptional views here, though with its corner position, the *Lake View* does offer some breeze and also has a very congenial bar. Rooms come with nets and hot water but no fans. Wi-fi. BB Ksh1500

New East View Omolo Agar Rd ☎0722 556721, ⓔneweastview@yahoo.com. A quieter alternative to the nearby *Palmers*, with 29 well-kept, scrupulously clean rooms with bathtubs. Showers are old-style, but there is safe parking, as well as a tiny café. Wi-fi. BB Ksh2500

★**New Victoria** Gor Mahia Rd ☎057 2021067 or ☎0727 225577. Perennially popular with travellers, this

well-maintained and efficiently run hotel is bright and cheerful inside and out. Most rooms have balconies, and rooms 206–209 have good lake views; there are also a few non-s/c singles (Ksh1100) for those on a tight budget. The very good breakfasts alone are worth the visit. Wi-fi. BB Ksh2700

Palmers Omolo Agar Rd ☎0722 999691. Handy for the bus and matatu stand, and with safe parking, this friendly place is nicely furnished, offering rooms with TVs, fans and big windows (though some of the singles are quite small). There's also a breezy café at the side. Wi-fi. BB Ksh3500

Perch Corner of Mark Asembo Rd and Obote Rd ☎0722 974607, ⓔhotelperch@gmail.com. A cavernous block in the industrial area behind the port, this is reasonably comfortable, and the rooms (some with lake views) have nets, TV and instant showers, but no fans, and the inward-facing rooms are very dark. There's a busy bar-restaurant, safe, basement parking and rates that are slightly pricey, but just about acceptable. BB Ksh4500

St Anna Guesthouse Signposted on the left, 450m south between Tom Mboya Rd and Ring Rd, next to Care Kenya, Milimani Estate ☎057 2024792 or ☎0734 600119, ⓦstannaguesthouse.com. Tricky to find but worth the effort, offering 59 well-kept, value-for-money rooms with solar-heated showers and TV. Although managed by Franciscan sisters, it's open to all and has no guest requirements beyond refraining from alcohol. The top-value restaurant serves filling staples. Safe parking. Wi-fi. BB Ksh3400

★**Sooper Guesthouse** Oginga Odinga Rd ☎0725 281733 or ☎0723 292781, ✉kayamchatur@yahoo .com. Living up to its name, *Sooper* offers some of the best cheap lodgings in Kisumu, with light, clean rooms with instant showers, nets, fans and TV – the best rooms are the two at the front sharing a balcony overlooking the street. Cold drinks, snacks and breakfast are available, and there's a kind of roof terrace good for a cold drink on a warm night. Room only Ksh1300

YWCA Off Ang'awa Ave ☎0703 963973, ✉ywcakisumu @ywcakenya.org. Friendly, cheap but rather bland, with a canteen, one double room and five-bed dorms, as well as a broad expanse of dusty earth (plus a bit of wiry grass) on which to pitch a tent, but the campsite is on a busy corner near the market so there's a fair bit of traffic noise. It's popular with conferences and school groups, so book ahead. Dorm beds Ksh450, BB Ksh1700, pitches Ksh250

MID-RANGE AND EXPENSIVE

Acacia Premier Jomo Kenyatta Ave ☎057 2055000 or ☎0726 774304, ⊛acaciapremier.com. This brand-new top-end hotel is the most luxurious in town, boasting cool modern design and facilities that include a spa, a gym and a pool terrace with views of the lake. The attractive, airy rooms come with wood floors and networked TVs through which you can watch pay-per-view movies and (theoretically, at least) settle your bill. Wi-fi. BB Ksh16,500

Impala Ecolodge Inside the Impala Sanctuary ☎057 2533040, ⊛impalaecolodge.com. A high-end retreat offering its guests the kind of exclusive safari atmosphere normally found in game parks, and with prices to match. The cottages, all with private wooden decks and lake views, are attractively furnished using local materials, and there's an elegant bar-restaurant on site. Wi-fi. BB $310

Imperial Jomo Kenyatta Ave ☎057 2020002 or ☎0721 240515, ⊛imperialhotelkisumu.com. Once the top hotel in town, the *Imperial* has been seriously out-classed

by the newer *Acacia Premier*, and is looking a bit old-fashioned these days. But it's also cheaper, and the seventy rooms are comfortable, with big, hanging mosquito nets, DSTV, a/c and proper showers. The modest-sized courtyard pool (non-residents Ksh400) is a good place for a dip, though it's closed during mealtimes. Wi-fi. BB Ksh10,920

★**Kiboko Bay Resort** 1.5km south of the Impala Sanctuary, between Hippo Point and Dunga ☎0733 532709 or ☎0724 387738, ⊛kibokobay.com. A very pleasant tented camp with a beautiful location on the lakeshore, offering nine luxurious safari tents equipped with mains electricity, generator backup, nets, fridges, well-equipped bathrooms with solid walls and floor fans, plus a pool (non-residents Ksh500) and terrace by the lake. A popular alternative to staying in town, and a great spot for lunch at weekends. Wi-fi. BB Ksh12,000

Kisumu Jomo Kenyatta Ave ☎057 2024157 or ☎0733 500036, ⊛kisumuhotel.net. Average-sized rooms with TV, a/c and old-style baths and showers – those on the ground floor are a bit dark. There are three bars and a moderately priced restaurant, and the small pool (11am–6pm, non-residents Ksh250) is nicely situated on a shaded terrace. Wi-fi. BB Ksh6500

St Johns Manor Off Got Huma Rd ☎057 2023245 or ☎0734 141666, ⊛lesavannacountrylodge.com. Attractive, tile-floored rooms in a quiet, residential street, with nets, a/c, DSTV and good views (from the upper floors). Staff are friendly, and facilities include a restaurant, lounge (though no bar) and a large pool (non-residents Ksh350). Wi-fi. BB Ksh6000

Sunset Aput Lane, 2.5km south of the town centre ☎0733 411001, ⊛sunsethotel.co.ke. Above and behind the Impala Sanctuary, this five storey complex dating from the 1960s is fraying around the edges but offers great lake views and beautiful sunsets from rooms on floors 2–4, most of which have small balconies as well as TV, floor fans and a/c. The business centre has decent internet, and there's also a pool (11am–6pm; non-residents Ksh250). Wi-fi. BB Ksh5600

EATING

Kisumu has lots of good **places to eat**, but it's worth starting early as many places close shortly after dusk. For **budget food**, the best deal in town is the fresh fried tilapia dished up in a series of *hotelis* down by the lakeside at the far northern end of Oginga Odinga Rd, served with either *ugali* or *chapattis* and a lump of shredded *sukuma wiki*. There are a number of good **supermarkets** including the 24hr Nakumatt Nyanza at Mega Plaza, as well as several decent **bakeries** – Victoria (Mon–Sat 7am–6.30pm, Sun 7am–2pm), by the *New Victoria Hotel* on Gor Mahia Rd, has probably the best selection of cakes and pastries in western Kenya.

Al-Noor Cafeteria Swan Centre, Oginga Odinga Rd ☎0722 802894. Popular halal café with streetside seating and an eclectic array of offerings, ranging from Indian dishes (Ksh600–850) to sandwiches, pizzas and *nyama choma*; or you can just opt for a plate of chips from the "chipsy den". There's real coffee here as well, with espresso

drinks from Ksh200. Daily except Tues 10am–midnight. **Barista** Ground floor of the Acacia Premier, Jomo Kenyatta Ave ☎057 2055000 or ☎0726 774304, ⊛acaciapremier.com. The most stylish place in town to sip an iced cappuccino (Ksh270) or a blueberry smoothie, with sleek modern furnishings and good wi-fi. There's also an excellent selection of teas and pastries, as well as panini – try the one made with spice-rubbed roast beef (Ksh600). Daily 6.30am–11pm.

★ **The Duke of Breeze** Top floor, Duke of Breeze hotel, off Kenyatta Ave ☎ 0717 105444, ⊛ thedukeofbreeze .com. A breezy rooftop escape from the city, strewn with lounge pillows and wafting music that gets steadily livelier as the night wears on. The eclectic menu ranges from Mongolian stir-fry (Ksh600) to fajitas, or you can get three courses for Ksh1500. Stunning views, and a great spot for sundowners or a *shisha* (see below). Daily 4–9pm.

Green Garden Odera St ☎ 0727 738000 or ☎ 0731 809108. Very popular NGO and traveller haunt on an unpromising side street, serving a long menu of dishes in the pretty palm-filled courtyard dining area – pizzas, vegetarian dishes and grills for Ksh450–550 – accompanied by a wonderful range of African music. Daily 8am–10pm.

Haandi Ground floor, Mega Plaza, Oginga Odinga St ☎ 0733 224788, ⊛ haandirestaurants.com/kenya.php. Part of a chain of upmarket Indian restaurants, serving dishes like chicken korma, malai kofta and a range of Punjabi specialities. The food is good, but expect to spend at least Ksh1100 per person, without drinks. Daily 11am–3pm & 6–11pm.

Kenshop Cyberstation Oginga Odinga Rd ☎ 057 2502999. An excellent place for breakfast or tea, with real espresso coffee (from Ksh200) and fresh juices, plus pies, sandwiches, pizzas, snacks and even a very tasty fish burger (Ksh300). It's also right next to Kenshop Supermarket's excellent bakery, which has nice fresh loaves. Mon–Sat 8am–6pm, Sun 9am–3pm.

★ **The Laughing Buddha** fourth floor, Tuf Foam Mall, Jomo Kenyatta Ave ☎ 0728 270013. Sophisticated vegetarian café on a rooftop terrace with gorgeous views over the lake, serving a delicious mix of Eastern and Western dishes (think falafel, pasta and sizzling fudge brownies). The desserts and milkshakes (Ksh350) are divine, and you can wash it all down with wine or herbal teas. Mains Ksh350–500. Tues–Sun 10.30am–11pm.

Oriental Upstairs, al-Imran Plaza, Oginga Odinga Rd ☎ 057 2025462 or ☎ 0722 289185. All the usual Chinese favourites, like beef with broccoli and chilli garlic prawns, plus some Thai starters; good but a bit pricey, with most dishes Ksh600–1000. Daily 11am–11pm.

Señorita Oginga Odinga Rd ☎ 0733 744588. A friendly local joint with a long and varied menu of Indian and African dishes (mains around Ksh500), good for steaks and stews. But there's not much atmosphere and nothing Spanish or Latino on offer, despite the name. Mon–Sat 9am–6pm.

★ **Simba Club** Jomo Kenyatta Ave ☎ 0733 532709. The Sikh Union's restaurant is open to non-members, with an excellent menu of tandoori dishes and curries. Specialities include Amritsari fish (in a tandoori-style marinade, but fried rather than baked; Ksh500) and paneer à la Simba (cooked with corn, mushrooms and green peppers; Ksh550). Friday evening is the best time to go, when there's a good-value buffet (Ksh750) and the place is full of families relaxing into the weekend. Daily 11am–3pm & 7pm–midnight.

Suprim Sweet Paul Mbuya Rd ☎ 0722 822135. A casual little vegetarian café serving a small menu of spicy Indian thalis (from Ksh300), Indian snacks and a selection of syrupy sweets that you can order by the kilo. Mon–Sat 7.30am–6pm, Sun 8am–1pm.

Tilapia Beach Down a dirt road at the northern end of Oginga Odinga Rd. The pick of the fish-fry *hotelis* and a shade more upscale than the rest, where you can gorge yourself on fresh tilapia, *ugali* and chips (from Ksh1000) in peaceful lakeside *bandas*. Daily 8.30am–11pm.

The Yacht Club Next to the Impala Sanctuary ☎ 057 2021450. Gorgeous location with tables overlooking the lake, where you can dine on Indian food or pizza (from Ksh400) while watching fishing boats drift by. Visits require temporary membership (Ksh500, or Ksh100 Fri & Wed evenings). Daily 9am–midnight.

DRINKING AND NIGHTLIFE

Kisumu has good nightlife, with the chance to catch **live bands**, and sometimes even big-name stars. More run-of-the-mill **discos** are plentiful, too. The regional music speciality is *ohangala*, based on Luo folk music, which is just as danceable as the alternatives of Congolese Lingala, or *benga*, which is also largely a Luo creation (see p.580).

The Duke of Breeze Top floor, Duke of Breeze hotel, off Kenyatta Ave ☎ 0717 105444, ⊛ thedukeofbreeze .com. A restaurant by day, this breezy rooftop turns into a relaxed bar in the evening, and on the weekends DJs spin a mix of East African and international hits on a make-shift dancefloor. You can smoke a shisha here (Ksh500), and cocktail specials include the "Obama" (tequila, Cointreau, rum and ginger ale) and the "Black Mamba" (vodka, lemon and Coke). Sun–Thurs 4–11pm, Fri & Sat 4pm–1am.

Havannaz Down a dirt road just off Omino Crescent.

Little more than a large shed filled with plastic tables and chairs, this is one of the best places to come for live music, with Congolese bands and various local artists playing nightly into the wee hours. Beer is Ksh170, and there's *nyama choma* if you're feeling peckish. Daily 8.30am–2am or later (music from 6.30pm).

Octopus Bottoms Up Ogada St. A pick-up joint of the first order, so not for the faint-hearted, but relaxed enough if you just want to mingle over a beer or two (Ksh180). The restaurant is often empty, but there are pool tables, the disco is always lively, and the roof terrace is a popular, breezy rendezvous, albeit with dire service. Open 24hr.

Railways Institute New Station Rd. Rough, rowdy and wildly popular local joint by the train station, with a house band playing rumba and *benga* to punters dancing or lounging in plastic chairs; beer from Ksh170. Daily 9am–1am (music from 5pm).

Ramogi Bar Kendu Lane. A satisfyingly seedy and friendly little hole in the wall, with comfy armchairs and table football, plus plenty of local characters eager to share a cheap beer or five (Ksh140). Daily 10am–11pm.

Signature fourth floor of a building on Makasembo Rd. Kisumu's poshest club and the most popular place to dance, featuring a sleek bar, white leather sofas, a modern sound system and plenty of disco lights. Gets very crowded at weekends. Ksh200 cover on Fri & Sat. Mon–Fri 4.30pm–5am, Sat & Sun 1.30pm–5am.

SHOPPING

HOPE Airport ☎0710 663990. The UN-award-winning Hyacinth Ornament Production Enterprise (HOPE) trains disabled women to create handicrafts out of Lake Victoria's endless supply of water hyacinth, whose fibres are used to fashion bags, jewellery and clothing, which you can purchase at this small stall outside the arrivals hall. Daily 8am–5pm.

Pendeza Weaving About 3km along the Nairobi road (go past the chief's camp and look for a small white sign on the right) ☎0734 587253, ⊚pendezaweaving .com. Another worthwhile visit for hand-woven cotton crafts such as tablecloths, bedcovers, dresses and Christmas ornaments. Daily 8am–5pm.

Sarit Bookshop Oginga Odinga Rd, corner of New Station Rd ☎057 2021222. A selection of novels in English and Swahili, including some African literature, and a handful of Kenya guidebooks and birding guides. Mon–Fri 8.30am–5.30pm, Sat 8.30am–1.30pm.

Tourist Market Busia Rd, by Kisumu Museum. The best place to find craft sellers. Things to buy here include heavy, three-legged Luo stools (the best are intricately inlaid with beads, and dark brown from repeated oiling), plus bangles, carvings and rows of soapstone knick-knacks.

DIRECTORY

4

Banks and exchange The town is full of banks with ATMs – and there's also a KCB ATM at the airport. For changing money try Victoria Forex, on Central Square near Barclays (Mon–Fri 8.30am–4.30pm, Sat 8.30am–12.30pm), or PEL Forex in al-Imran Plaza, Oginga Odinga Rd (Mon–Fri 8.30am–4.30pm, Sat 9am–12.30pm).

Birdwatching Lake Victoria Sunset Birders is the local birding group (☎0734 994938 or ☎057 2024162, ⊚lvsb.50megs.com). You can join up for Ksh500 and participate in their internationally recognized monitoring work or simply go on one of their regular bird walks – the area along the golf club shore and the 120 acres of Dunga swamp are very productive.

Car rental and travel agents Rav4s and similar small 4WDs are available from around Ksh5500/day. Try Piepercaps, Awori House, Alego St ☎0722 344148, ⊚piepercaps.org; Kisumu Travels, Central Square ☎0722 206020, ⊚kisumutravels.com; or Zaira Tours, Ogada St ☎0734 788879, ⊚zairatoursafrica.com. Integritour (☎0700 517969 or ☎0720 647864, ⊚integritour.com) is a very well-regarded operator and agent, based on the ground floor of the *Duke of Breeze Hotel*; it claims to be the first responsible tourism operator in western Kenya and offers a number of tours, including safaris to the Maasai Mara.

Golf Nyanza Golf Club (☎0704 133131, ⊚nyanzaclub .com) is on the lakeshore, the first left down the airport road, about 4km from the town centre. A round of eighteen holes costs Ksh1500.

Hospitals The main treatment centre is Nyanza Provincial General Hospital northeast of the centre on Jomo Kenyatta Ave ☎057 2020801. The best private hospital is the Aga Khan Hospital on Otieno Oyoo St ☎057 2020005.

Immigration The Immigration Department, first floor, Reinsurance Plaza, behind Alpha House on Oginga Odinga Rd (☎057 2024935), is generally helpful, usually stamping visitors' pass extensions on the spot.

Internet access There are numerous places around town, and several in the Mega Plaza on Oginga Odinga Rd. Kenshop Cyberstation (see opposite) is good, or try Moscom on the mezzanine floor of Mega Plaza.

Kisumu Show The annual Agricultural Society of Kenya show is held in the first week of August, 6km north of town on the Miwani road (off to the east of the Kakamega road).

Library Off Gumbi Rd, behind the bus and matatu station ☎020 2158368 (Mon–Fri 8am–6.30pm, Sat 8.30am–5pm).

Mobiles Safaricom Service Centre, mezzanine floor, Mega Plaza, Oginga Odinga Rd ☎0722 002546 (Mon–Fri 8am–6pm, Sat 8am–3pm).

Pharmacies Several are open late and on Sundays. Try Winam, Mega Plaza, Oginga Odinga Rd ☎057 2023167 (daily 7am–10pm), and A-Z Pharmacy, Ang'awa Ave, 100m from the clock tower ☎0722 988725 (Mon–Sat 8am–6pm, Sun 8am–noon).

Police Omolo Agar Rd ☎057 2024719.

Swimming Forget the lake – bilharzia, hippos and crocs are all unfriendly – and instead swim at the *Sunset*, *St Johns Manor*, the *Kisumu*, *Acacia Premier* or the *Imperial*. The small fee is sometimes waived if you have a meal.

Siaya and the road to Uganda

Heading **northwest out of Kisumu**, down a broad avenue of flame trees, you pass first the Sunni Muslim, Ismailia and Hindu cemeteries then Nyanza Golf Club, and emerge into the rolling plains of **Siaya County**, home to herbalists and a reasonable base for exploration. The **C27** to Bondo and Usenge is a very pretty road, in good shape and well worth the trip, and there's a constant stream of matatus and buses to the town of **Busia**, on the Ugandan boarder.

The easy route to **Mbita** (see p.270) ends with a short ride aboard the small car ferry (8am, 11am, 3pm & 6pm; 45min) from **Luanda Kotieno**, reached by turning south off the C27 at **Ndori**.

Kit Mikaye

1km south of the C27 highway (signposted off the highway 14km west of Kisian junction)

Kit Mikaye is a locally famous landmark and minor pilgrimage site. Meaning Place (*kit*) of the First Wife (*mikaye*), it's the largest balancing act in a landscape of giant boulders. This scenic, rocky spot is where the first wife of the Luo is supposed to have rested on the tribe's journey south from Sudan, and local women often visit for cures and meditation. Back on the C27, there's another huge boulder-pile directly by the north side of the road.

Kisumu tour operators, including Integritour (see p.261), organize trips to Kit Mikaye and can provide a thorough explanation of its cultural significance.

Siaya

The district capital, **SIAYA**, locally known as Tat Yien ("Roof of Herbs"), has a large community of traditional **herbalists** and is a well-known healing (and bewitching) town. There isn't much to see or do in Siaya itself, but as one of the largest towns in the area it's not a bad base for expeditions in the region, including nearby Usenge.

INFORMATION, ACCOMMODATION AND EATING   SIAYA

There's a KCB bank with **ATM**, as well as the useful Siaya Self Service **supermarket** and plenty of **cybercafés** – try the centrally located Jamat Cyber Café, 100m from the market (daily 8am–6pm; Ksh1/min).

Mwisho Mwisho Tourist Hotel Equity Bank building, 1km from the centre on the road to Kisumu ☎0717 553359 or ☎0736 000363, ✉info@mwishohotel.com. If you're staying overnight you'll probably end up at this noisy place, which offers unexciting but good-value rooms with nets, and the occasional live band. They also serve food, but meal service is rather slow. BB Ksh1750

Usenge

At the end of the C27 road from Kisumu, **USENGE** (or Usengi) is a good target if you're planning an exploration of the district, and a town of pre-colonial historical significance in its own right. The nearby hill, **Got Ramogi**, is by tradition the site where the first Luo arrived at the lake from further north. It's not a hard climb to the top for a satisfying view over Yala Swamp, Lake Sare and the land that the Luo fought for and eventually won from the Bantu-speakers at the end of the fifteenth century. Usenge itself is a pretty town, but there are no banks, few services and not much in the way of accommodation.

Busia

The **road to Busia** is in good shape these days, and is lined with colourful scenes of everyday rural life, including women, often in brilliantly pleated floral-print dresses,

GEM OF AN IDEA

In the early **colonial period**, the Luo benefited from some inspired, if dictatorial, leadership. They had inherited the institution of the *ruoth* (king or chief) from the original immigrants from Sudan. The *ruoth* of Gem, a location just east of Siaya, was Odera Akang'o, an ambitious and perceptive young man with an almost puritanical attitude to his duties. He had a private police force to inspect farms and report any idleness to him, and he regularly had his subjects beaten or fined for "unprogressive" behaviour. He introduced new crops and, under British protection, made himself quite a sizeable fortune. He was widely feared.

In 1915, the colonial government sent him, with two other chiefs, to Kampala. He returned full of admiration for the European education and health standards there, and ashamed of Gem and Luoland in general. Fired with enthusiasm, he applied his style of schooling and hygiene, bullying his subjects into sending their children to classes and keeping their shirts clean, while the British turned a blind eye. The results were rapid educational advances in Gem, which is still considered a progressive district today. Odera, unfortunately for him, was employed by the British to use his methods on the Teso people in Uganda, where they singularly failed. He was accused of corruption and sent into internal exile, where he died.

carrying huge head-loads of bananas, sugar cane and baskets. **BUSIA**, on the Uganda border, is surprisingly bearable for a border town. It boasts more services and less hassle than Malaba, the frontier post on the rail line further north, and is a much more pleasant place to cross.

4

ARRIVAL AND INFORMATION
BUSIA

Moneychangers on both sides of the border will change Ugandan and Kenyan shillings, or give either for dollars, euros or pounds, but check the rates in advance. There are also Barclays and KCB banks with ATMs.

By bus Several daily from Busia to Nairobi (8hr) via Kisumu (2hr). Most companies run one morning and one evening service.

By matatu There are frequent matatus to Kisumu (2hr 30min), Malaba (1hr), some going on to Bungoma (3hr), and morning departures to Kitale (4hr 30min) and Nairobi (8hr 30min). On the Ugandan side, frequent matatus run to Jinja (2hr) and Kampala (4–5hr).

ACCOMMODATION

Blue York Bulanda Rd, south of the main drag ☎ 0721 696078. Clean, tidy rooms around a small but well-manicured courtyard. The restaurant is a pleasant place for a meal or a drink, with a bit of outdoor seating. Wi-fi. BB **Ksh2500**

Breeze Hotel Just south of the main road ☎ 0707 461665, ⊚ thebreezehotel.com. One of the Busia's newest hotels and very popular with NGO workers. The rooms are modern and comfortably furnished, but the real selling point

is the big pool surrounded by tacky concrete animals and bizarre faux-rock formations, where you can feast on *nyama choma* and relax with a drink. Wi-fi. BB **Ksh3500**

Farm View Hospital Rd, 1km south of the main drag ☎ 0725 341248, ⊚ farmviewhotel.com. The farm on view may be just a field of maize, but this quiet complex has a nice countryside feel to it nonetheless. The good rooms come with nets and TV, and there's a kids' play area in the shady garden. Wi-fi. BB **Ksh3500**

South Nyanza

The territory south of Kisumu is interesting to explore and easy enough to get around, if you're willing to go by matatu. Highlights include the agreeable little town of **Kendu Bay**, the main town of **Homa Bay**, the unjustly overlooked **Ruma National Park**, the intriguing ruins of **Thimlich Ohinga**, the islands of **Rusinga and Mfangano** and, down near the Tanzanian border, the one-street town of **Migori**. The **lakeshore** west of Migori is remote and, in parts, beautiful, with **Karungu Bay** and the scenic route via **Sindo** to **Mbita** a rewarding side trip.

Kendu Bay

The best route from Kisumu to **KENDU BAY** is straight along the lakeshore from Katito, south of Ahero. There's a wealth of interest in the surrounding Luo countryside, most of it until recently a rural backwater, with scenes of fishing boats and compounds of square, thatched mud-brick houses (a fairly recent change; traditionally they were round). Although Kendu Bay has a good deal of intrinsic charm, there's little to offer the casual visitor in the town itself. The old part, 500m off the Kisumu–Homa Bay main road, has one notable building in the gorgeous **Tawakal mosque**. You can look around it, though there's not much to see, and climb on the roof. The smaller **Jamia mosque** is less ornate, but older, built in 1902.

Simbi Lake

About 4km west of the centre of Kendu Bay (a 45min walk or take a boda-boda): follow Homa Bay road past the turning to Oyugis and Kisii; 2km beyond, over the river bridge before you reach Kanyadhiang, turn right down the dirt road and continue another 15min along the river's left bank before climbing to the lake's rim

Kendu Bay's local fame comes from the curious **Simbi Lake**. The lake and the nearby Ondago Swamp have been adopted as June and July feeding grounds by a couple of thousand **lesser flamingos**, refugees from Lake Nakuru. Although some locals and officials would like to exploit the attraction, it remains a tranquil beauty spot with a footpath around the rim, the only commerce being the odd local selling sugar cane. Even without the flamingos, this is unquestionably a weird body of water: around 70 acres of bright green, alkaline water, sunk 20–30m below the surrounding land and less than 2km from Lake Victoria itself. It has no apparent source and its origins are somewhat mysterious: it looks like a huge meteorite crater.

It's only a couple of kilometres around the perimeter path – an easy half-hour walk. The little lake's shores are almost devoid of vegetation. It's of volcanic origin and is apparently extraordinarily deep. According to one local belief, visitors should throw money in to avoid bad luck. Whatever the natural explanation, it seems plausible that the area was inhabited when the lake was formed, and that a natural disaster accounts for the legends.

An interesting new twist on the fame of Simbi is the claim by locals from the hamlet of **KANYADHIANG** (just south of the bridge on the C19 road) that their village is the true birthplace of Barack Obama Senior, father of the US president, rather than Kogelo on the other side of the Winam Gulf, and hence the rightful location of any western Kenya Obama museum – though when this book went to press Barack Obama had less than a year left in office, and there was still no sign that such a museum would ever be built.

ARRIVAL AND INFORMATION

By matatu You'll have no difficulty getting a matatu to or from Oyugis or Homa Bay. The obvious alternative route is the lakeshore road from Kendu Bay to Katito, where it meets the A1 between Kisii and Kisumu.

THE LEGEND OF SIMBI LAKE

According to legend, the **origins of Simbi Lake** are to be found in the story of an elderly woman, travelling alone, who was refused hospitality one rainy night at the village that once occupied the site of the lake. A big beer party was going on and she was ignored. Only one woman would allow her to warm herself, and the old woman insisted she and her family leave the village with her. The young woman tried in vain to persuade her husband to come with them, fearing the old lady's revenge for her ill-treatment. So the two women left alone. Later that night there was a tremendous cloudburst and the rain came down so hard that the village was swamped to become Simbi Lake. Further variations on the story (there are many) improve on the theme of drunkenness and debauchery to give a Sodom and Gomorrah ring to the tale. Other lakes in Kenya have similar tales of origin.

By boat The ferry dock (a pier partly made of concrete-filled barges) is about 1km from the old town, but there were no boat services at the time of writing due to low water levels in the lake.

Services There's a Total petrol station on the main road by the junction with the road to Oyugis, and a post office about 100m west of the junction, but no banks or ATMs.

ACCOMMODATION, EATING AND DRINKING

Club Big Five At the petrol station ☎ 0728 852977. Decorated with pink paint and Disneyesque concrete trees and animals, this restaurant serves excellent fish (Ksh300) and its nightclub has music (occasionally live) every night, though it's only really busy on Saturday. Daily 11am–10pm (club open later).

Hotel Maryland Just south of the petrol station ☎ 0720 892622. Comfortable and reasonably priced rooms, with tiled floors and nets, set behind an ostentatious-looking restaurant. At the moment the showers are cold, but there are plans to upgrade them to the instant variety. Room only ~~Ksh800~~

Milimani Bar & Lodging In the old town, before the mosque ☎ 0733 989062. B&L with eight basic, dark, non-s/c rooms with bucket showers and solar-powered electric lights. Not terribly comfortable, but dirt cheap (singles are only Ksh400) and bearable for one night. Room only ~~Ksh600~~

Homa Bay

At first glance a scruffy and unremarkable place, the small port town of **Homa Bay**, the region's main centre, is one of the friendliest towns in Kenya, and also a good base for visits to Ruma National Park, Rusinga Island and Simbi Lake. The town, admittedly, has nothing much of interest, just a few potholed streets and the unusual straw-hat-shaped **St Paul's Catholic Cathedral**, atop a low hill behind town, with its central altar-in-the-round and great views from the back of the pews. However, if you're into **traditional Luo music**, Homa Bay is the place to track down tapes of *nyatiti* (lyre), *orutu* (single-stringed bow fiddle) and *onand* (accordion) music, as well as the ubiquitous gospel pop.

Homa Bay used to have a busy port, but in 1997 this, and much of the shoreline, became hemmed in by more than 1km of **water hyacinth**. The weed infestation happened quickly, trapping some boats. Ferries were suspended, and people sold off their vessels. The hyacinth was eventually cleared mechanically, and fishermen keep the remainder at bay by hand, but the port is a shadow of its former self.

Got Asego

The hike up **Got Asego**, the impressive conical hill on the east side of town, is recommended. The hill is the highest of dozens of volcanic plugs (cores of old volcanoes) in the area; from its table-sized summit, you'll have a 360-degree panorama of the lakeshore and surrounding plains. It is remarkable how little of the land is not used. Luo thatched huts are interspersed with tin-roofed

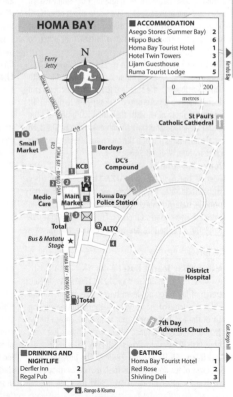

HOMA BAY

N

■ ACCOMMODATION
Asego Stores (Summer Bay)	2
Hippo Buck	6
Homa Bay Tourist Hotel	1
Hotel Twin Towers	3
Lijam Guesthouse	4
Ruma Tourist Lodge	5

0   200
metres

St Paul's
Catholic Cathedral

Ferry
Jetty

Small
Market

Barclays

KCB

DC's
Compound

Medio
Care

Main
Market

Homa Bay
Police Station

Total

ALTQ

Bus & Matatu
Stage

HOMA BAY – RONGO ROAD

District
Hospital

Total

7th Day
Adventist Church

■ DRINKING AND NIGHTLIFE
Derfler Inn	2
Regal Pub	1

● EATING
Homa Bay Tourist Hotel	1
Red Rose	2
Shivling Deli	3

▼ **6** , Rongo & Kisumu

Kendu Bay

Got Asego hill

homesteads, a patchwork of small plots and agave hedges. Take binoculars and you can see more: clumps of papyrus drifting across the lake, and traffic along the road where it snakes east to Kendu Bay.

It takes about an hour to reach the top from the centre of town (actual ascent 30–45min), an easy climb but best tackled late in the afternoon (early morning ascents, though cooler, can be treacherous thanks to dew on the rocks). Head up the Rongo road, turn left 500m south of the Total petrol station and turn right up the *murram* road after Homa Bay School. The hill itself is best approached up the northwest ridge, where there's a well-defined footpath.

ARRIVAL AND DEPARTURE   HOMA BAY

Most of the town is strung out along the main street, the C20, which starts at the jetty and runs uphill. The little town centre fills a small grid of dusty streets between this main road and the higher, residential area to the east.

By bus Numerous bus companies run services to Nairobi (10hr); there are also three daily buses to Kisii (1hr 30min) and Kericho (3hr), as well as two that go as far as Mombasa (18hr).
By matatu Matatus leave Homa Bay from the stage on the main road, serving Kendu Bay (30min), Kisii (1hr

30min), Kisumu (2hr), Mbita (45min) and Migori (2hr). If you can't find a direct vehicle to Kisii, then take a Migori matatu and get off at Rongo on the A1 highway, where you can soon find a Kisii-bound vehicle coming up from the south.

ACCOMMODATION

★**Asego Stores (Summer Bay)** Next to the mosque, opposite the KCB bank ☎0733 268718. Nice, bright lodgings, basic but clean, with ground-floor single rooms, one triple and a giant double in a quirky turret of sorts, all set around a courtyard-style dining area. There are squat loos, and the showers come in a bucket (hot water on request). Room only **Ksh800**
Hippo Buck Rongo Rd, 2km south of the town centre ☎0723 262000, ⊛hippobuck.com. Competing with *Homa Bay* (below), the standard rooms are functional and clean, though a bit overpriced; the superior rooms ($100) are considerably nicer, with their own balconies, and the dining area, food and staff all improve the stay. The deep canal that gushes through the courtyard after heavy rain is a nice feature. Wi-fi. BB **$40**
Homa Bay Tourist Hotel Near the old port, just west of the main road ☎0727 112615, ⊛homabay touristhotel.com. Twenty-three renovated rooms in this formerly state-run hotel (with TVs, nets, floor fans and instant showers), and six roomy safari tents facing the lake (Ksh8500). The grounds are very attractive, and there's a

good restaurant. Wi-fi. BB **Ksh6800**
Hotel Twin Towers Just east of the main market ☎0775 612195 or ☎0722 688212, ⊜twintowers .homabay@yahoo.com. A cool, impersonal mid-range hotel offering comfortable, good-value accommodation in smallish rooms with TVs, fans and balconies. The covered parking garage could be a selling point if you're driving, though in the evening it doubles as a bar. Wi-fi. BB **Ksh2300**
Lijam Guest House Off the main paved road skirting the eastern side of town ☎0720 932829. A simple and quiet three-storey guesthouse straddling a dirt lane, with decent tiled rooms on one side and a friendly bar/restaurant on the other. The rooms come with nets and electric showers, and there's safe parking in the courtyard. Room only **Ksh1200**
Ruma Tourist Lodge South end of town backing onto the Total station ☎0701 238422, ⊜evansochieng85 @yahoo.com. Small, but clean and pleasant rooms set apart from a very congenial outdoor bar-restaurant, with safe parking. The enormous, rustically furnished "special rooms" are worth the extra Ksh400. Wi-fi. Room only **Ksh1000**

EATING

★**Homa Bay Tourist Hotel** Down near the old port, just west of the main road ☎0727 112615. A gorgeous stretch of lawn sloping down to the lake, sprinkled with tables in patches of shade, with a flamboyant tree growing out of the bar. The perfect spot for a drink cooled by the offshore breeze, or a lunch of European dishes like lamb chops (Ksh500) or sandwiches (Ksh450). Daily 24hr.
Red Rose KCB Rd ☎0722 788558. The best spot for a breakfast of tea and delicious fresh *mandaazi*, though it's not bad for other meals as well, and it's open late for

dinner. Chicken, fish, beef and curry go for Ksh180–300, and the generous front porch is great for people-watching. Mon–Fri 8am–11pm.
Shivling Deli Next to Shivling Supermarket, behind the Total station. This spare little café really isn't much more than a supermarket deli counter spruced up with plastic chairs, but it's one of the most popular spots in town for local staples like pilau, *githeri*, beef stew and roast chicken; a plate of chicken and chips goes for Ksh350. Mon–Sat 8am–7.30pm, Sun 8am–5pm.

DRINKING AND NIGHTLIFE

Homa Bay is not especially hot on **nightlife**, but it does have a few bars worth checking out in the evening.

Derfler Inn On the main road. A disco playing *benga* and other local sounds well into the wee hours, with a psychedelic interior of green and orange walls and faux leather sofas; the terrace out front is good for a sundowner (beer Ksh160) and a chat with the locals. Daily 5pm–6am.

Regal Pub KCB Rd. An intimate first-floor bar with a wrap-around balcony and black walls covered in graffiti. The music varies depending on the clientele, though there isn't much space to dance. Beers Ksh150. Daily 5pm–4am.

DIRECTORY

Banks There are Barclays and KCB ATMs, both east of the main road.
Internet ALTQ is small, but it can get you online (Mon–Sat 8am–5pm).

Pharmacy Medio Care (☎ 0723 247626; daily 7.30am–9pm).
Shopping The shopping chains haven't yet reached Homa Bay, but Shivling Supermarket (Mon–Sat 8am–7.30pm, Sun 8am–5pm) has most of what you might need.

Ruma National Park

25km southwest of Homa Bay • $25 • Contact the park warden in the DC's compound in Homa Bay (Mon–Fri 8am–4pm) on ☎ 0724 511333, 🌐 kws.org • 200 square kilometres

The Lambwe valley's tsetse-fly-ridden bush, protected as **Ruma National Park**, is one of the few places in Kenya where you can see **Jackson's hartebeest** and two extremes of the antelope family: the miniature **oribi** and the enormous, horse-like **roan**, which is found only here. Roans are extremely rare, and the best place to see them is among the park's western grasslands, which are often hit by community fires that spread into the park from the west – they like the fresh grazing on burnt ground. Ruma also has about seventy beautiful **Rothschild's giraffes** which aren't too hard to see above the tall grass. You'll have more difficulty spotting **leopards**, the park's only large predators, and you'll be very lucky to spot one of Ruma's prize denizens, the **black rhinos** translocated from Mugie ranch in Laikipia in 2012 (see p.514).

4

ARRIVAL AND DEPARTURE
RUMA NATIONAL PARK

Ruma isn't really practical without your own vehicle as it is tricky to reach by public transport – the busiest matatu route, Homa Bay to Mbita, skirts it by 11km – but if you're driving it's worth the effort, as you're virtually guaranteed to have the park to yourself. There are two main gates, **Kamato**, in the east, with the park HQ and the *Oribi Guest House* (signposted, 25km from Homa Bay), and the more remote **Nyatoto** in the northwest, on the road between Mbita and Karungu (24km from Mbita; the road crosses the park). If you're coming along the A1 from Migori or Kisii, look for a signposted *murram* road leading straight to Kamato gate.

ACCOMMODATION

Fig Tree Campsite 200m from Kamato gate and park HQ ☎ 020 6000800, ✉ reservations@kws.go.ke. Public campsite on a flat stretch of grass, shaded by a few acacia trees and frequented by buffalo and bushbuck. Bring all your own equipment, food and water, although toilets, showers and firewood are provided. $20
Nyati Campsite Around 200m from Kamato gate, near the Fig Tree Campsite ☎ 020 6000800, ✉ reservations @kws.go.ke. Similar to *Fig Tree*, except that this is a

"special campsite" – reserve in advance and pay the booking fee, and you'll have it all to yourself for up to a week. Bring all your own supplies, as there are no facilities whatsoever. Booking fee per group Ksh7500
Oribi Guest House Just outside the gate ☎ 020 6000800, ✉ reservations@kws.go.ke. Self-catering cottage on the Kanyamwa Escarpment, with three double rooms sharing a bathroom, solar power and a fully equipped kitchen. Whole cottage, room only $100

Thimlich Ohinga

Daily • No set hours or entry price, but tips welcome

An archeological site of potentially huge significance, **Thimlich Ohinga** is considered one of the greatest stone enclosures in East Africa, and for sheer visual impact you won't find a more impressive or atmospheric ancient site anywhere in Kenya away from the coast.

The precise meaning of "thimlich ohinga" in archaic Luo is open to interpretation, but it is generally held to mean "scary, walled enclosures", though some say the "scary" is a reference to the wild bush country from which the occupants of the site were protected. It's estimated the compounds were built around the fifteenth century by a people whose history has been forgotten, but were almost certainly Bantu-speaking predecessors of the Luo. It probably came to be occupied by Luos displaced in inter-clan fighting in the early eighteenth century, within a few decades of their arrival here. Elsewhere in the district, successive generations of various communities have used stone enclosures and, in some places, modern Luo families have their homesteads inside the remnants of such walls.

Covering an area of 52 acres, the site is the most striking example of a style of architecture whose remnants are scattered across South Nyanza. Similar to the dry-stone enclosures of southern Africa (of which Great Zimbabwe is the classic example), the biggest structure is a **compound** about 150m in diameter, inside which are five smaller enclosures, probably used as cattle pens, and at least six house pits, the sites of former dwellings. The walls, which range in height from 1m to 4.2m, are built from a combination of natural boulders and dressed stone, the latter used particularly in the construction of the low doorways through the walls. A combination of gradual excavation and continued restoration work means it's a little hard to get a clear grasp of the whole layout of the site (and there's no map or guidebook), but there are at least four large walled enclosures, each with smaller enclosures inside them.

ARRIVAL AND DEPARTURE   THIMLICH OHINGA

You really need your **own transport** to get to Thimlich Ohinga. If you're very determined and intrepid you could try reaching the site by a combination of matatus and hitchhiking (or walking), but there's nowhere to stay and barely anywhere to eat, so you'll need a tent and supplies in case you can't get there and back in a day.

From Migori The easiest approach to Thimlich Ohinga is from Migori. Follow the Tanzania road for 4km to reach Soma and the junction for Muhoro Bay, where there's a National Cereals and Produce Board depot. Take the turnoff on the right (west) onto *murram* here and continue for a couple of kilometres from the depot to reach another junction. Turn right here and drive straight on via Suna and Macalder, across a big bridge over the Migori River and then (exactly 4.8km further on) over a smaller bridge across the Gucha. A further 800m west is a place called Ayego (or Ombo). Turn right (north) onto a basic farm/bush track, in fair condition and a bit stony in dry weather but liable to be tricky in the wet. Continue north for 12.3km, following the ridge to the west of the Gucha River valley, as far as another junction at another small location, Masara. Turn right here onto a broad stretch of *murram*, following a fence, and 200m further you'll find the entrance to the site (a total of 55km from the Cereals Board

Depot). You can also reach Thimlich Ohinga, using the last part of these directions, by driving east from Karungu (the junction at Ayego is 21.2km east of Karungu). If you don't have your own vehicle, it's possible to get most of the way to the site using the occasional matatus that ply between Migori and Karungu, getting out at Ayego. But you might have to walk that last 12km.

From Kisii or Homa Bay via Miranga From Kisii (105km) or Homa Bay (60km), head for Rodi Kopany on the C20 between Homa Bay and Rongo, where you take the C18 southwest, through Mirogi and Ndhiwa to Miranga. You should be able to make it this far by matatu from the Homa Bay/Rongo road. Just beyond Miranga's shops, a signpost shows the direction of Thimlich Ohinga down a rough *murram* track, driveable in an ordinary car when dry, but requiring 4WD in the wet. The site is about 30km south of here, and there is no public transport.

Rusinga Island and Mbita

Much easier to reach and explore than Ruma National Park or Thimlich Ohinga is **Rusinga Island**. The narrow channel between **Mbita** and the island was bridged by a **causeway** in 1984, so driving around Rusinga is quite feasible.

Mbita and the causeway

The shabby town of **MBITA**, straddling either side of the causeway, is very unprepossessing indeed, but things improve once you get onto the island. The building of the causeway – partly over two dumper trucks that fell into the lake during the operation and couldn't be recovered – has had some unwanted side effects. Vervet monkeys now move onto the island to raid crops, and fish have become scarce on the Kisumu side of Rusinga because the causeway blocks the current, turning the water there into a stagnant pond. A bridge to replace the causeway (under construction at the time of writing) should hopefully reverse some of the damage to the ecosystem and the livelihoods that depend on it.

Rusinga Island

Small and austerely beautiful, **Rusinga Island** has high crags dominating its desolate, goat-grazed centre, and a single dirt road running around the circumference. Life here is difficult, with drought commonplace and high winds a frequent torment. The occasional heavy rain either washes away the soil or sinks into the porous rock, emerging lower down where it creates swamps. Ecologically, the island is in very dire straits: almost all its trees have been cut down for cooking fuel or to be converted into lucrative charcoal. These conditions make harvests highly unpredictable and most people fish to make ends meet (although the causeway has forced them to make longer fishing trips), either selling the catch on to refrigerated lorries or bartering directly for produce with traders from Kisii. Yet the islanders, in common with their mainland cousins, remain an unfailingly friendly and cheerful bunch, more than happy to make contact with wayward travellers.

If you're interested in making a contribution to the welfare and development of the Rusinga community, you might like to look in at the permaculture project and education centre at **Badilisha Ecovillage** near the lakeshore at Kaswanga, on the north side of the island, 9km from Mbita, that brings together green-minded volunteers from around the world to work with AIDS orphans, in local schools doing support work or working the land on the permaculture project, founded on the principles of sustainability and respect for the environment. You can stay here for a night or a couple of months (see p.272), and the stays make for an excellent way of getting to know local issues in a remote and challenging rural setting.

The island is rich in **fossils**, and was the site of Mary Leakey's discovery of a skull of *Proconsul africanus* (a primitive anthropoid ape), which can be seen in the National

LAKE VICTORIA'S ECOLOGY AND ECONOMY

Lake Victoria fills a shallow depression (no deeper than 80m) between the Western and Eastern Rift valleys, yet it is not part of the Rift system. Until the 1960s, it was home to around five hundred different species of brilliantly coloured tropical fish, known as haplochromines or **cichlids**, all of them endemic – unique to the lake. Scientists, puzzling over how such a dazzling variety of species came to evolve in this largely uniform environment in the space of no more than a million years, have suggested that, at some stage in its history, the lake must have dried into a series of small lakes in which the fish evolved separately. Lake Victoria's cichlids are popular aquarium fish, and one of the commonest larger species, the tilapia, is a regional speciality, grilled or fried and served whole.

In the early 1960s a voracious carnivore, the **Nile perch**, was introduced to the lake, and proceeded to eat its way through the cichlid population, driving some species close to extinction, though many have held on in parts of the lake which were too shallow for perch or in smaller lakes around the main one. For local people, the introduction of the perch, which can reach a weight of 250kg, has been a bit of a Trojan horse: while they're consumed locally and sold for export (good news for the lakeshore economy), traditional fishing and processing have been hit hard by the arrival of modern vessels and factories joining in the feast and taking their profits elsewhere.

The lake has other problems, however. **Algae** have proliferated due to industrial and sewage pollution, depriving the lake of oxygen. More than three million litres of human waste drain into the lake every day, and the Swedish development agency, SIDA, estimates that Kenya, with the smallest share of the lake's shoreline, is its main polluter. As well as suffering a dramatic fall in oxygen levels, the lake is becoming so murky that the remaining cichlids are unable to identify mates, so that hybridization is occurring. Meanwhile, the building of the causeway between Mbita and Rusinga Island has turned the Winam Gulf into even more of a pond, with only one outlet, inhibiting currents and making its water even less healthy.

Another threat comes from the **water hyacinth**, originally native to Brazil. This floating weed grows quickly around the lakeshore and spreads like a carpet across the surface, blocking out the light, choking the lake to death and snaring up vessels. Since the mid-1990s, Homa Bay, Kendu Bay and Kisumu have all at times been strangled by kilometre-wide cordons of the weed, inhibiting passage to all but the smallest canoes, with disastrous results for the local economy. Solutions have included the promotion of products (furniture, paper, even building materials) made from harvested hyacinth. In 2001, mechanical clearance enabled passenger ferries to resume, only for falling water levels to cause their suspension once more. There's been a resurgence of the invasive weed since 2006, and the nutrient run-off following occasional heavy rains spreads the deadly canopy even further.

Museum (see p.113). It was also the family home of **Tom Mboya** (see below), the civil rights champion, trade unionist and charismatic young Luo politician who was assassinated in Nairobi in 1969, a turning point for the worse in Kenya's post-independence history, sparking off a crisis that led to more than forty deaths in widespread rioting and demonstrations.

Tom Mboya's mausoleum

Daily 8am–5pm • ☎ 0711 469435 • Take a boda-boda (Ksh100 one way) or walk (allow 4hr). From the Mbita causeway, aim for the crags in the centre of the island, skirt them to the right and then walk down to rejoin the road on the other side of the Tom Mboya Memorial Health Centre; the mausoleum's conical silver roof is visible just off the road. By car: turn right 11.7km from the causeway (signposted "Kolunga Beach"), then right again after 150m; the mausoleum is 600m further on

Built in the shape of a bullet to recall the manner of his death, **Tom Mboya's mausoleum** is on family land at Kamasengre on the north side of the island, about 11km by dirt road from Mbita, or roughly 6km directly across the island. It contains various mementos and gifts Mboya received during his life, including a cup won in a dancing competition and the briefcase he was carrying when he was murdered. The inscription on the grave reads:

THOMAS JOSEPH MBOYA
August 15th 1930 – July 5th 1969
Go and fight like this man
Who fought for mankind's cause
Who died because he fought
Whose battles are still unwon!

You don't have to know anything about the man to be impressed. In any other surroundings his memorial might seem relatively modest, but on this barren, windswept shore, it stands out like a beacon. Members of Mboya's family live nearby and are happy to see foreign visitors. They maintain the mausoleum themselves so always appreciate donations, though these are not obligatory. If you're interested, take a look at the rather good folder of press cuttings about Mboya.

Hippo Bay
Fifty metres past the Tom Mboya Secondary School, on the north side of the island, the path to the right takes you through *shambas* of millet and maize to a seasonally grassy lakeside called **Hippo Bay**. Here you can watch nesting fish eagles as well as, usually, hippos. If you're lucky, you may see the pretty and little-known spotted-necked otters that live around Lake Victoria and nowhere else in Kenya.

4

ARRIVAL AND DEPARTURE   RUSINGA ISLAND AND MBITA

The town of Mbita is as far as you can go by public road transport. There are, however, some wooden "engine boats" connecting Mbita daily (until around 5pm) with Takawiri Island, as well as a car ferry to Luanda Kotieno and another to Mfangano Island.

By matatu A steady stream of matatus plies the Homa Bay–Mbita route throughout the day, but they're often packed; the road, at least, has been recently resurfaced and is smooth the whole way. There are some good lakeshore views (and access if you're driving and want a break) for a couple of kilometres south of Luanda (29km from Homa Bay's Mbita junction). From Kisumu, it can be quicker to get a matatu to Luanda Kotieno (see p.262), from where there are ferries over to Mbita (at 8am, 11am, 3pm & 6pm; 45min; matatus leave Kisumu 3–4hr earlier to connect). Matatus complete the journey to Kisumu via Asembo and Ndori – usually a faster way of reaching Kisumu than going via Homa Bay.

By ferry Leaving Mbita, you can take the car ferry across the Winam Gulf for the short 10km ride to Luanda Kotieno. The ferry goes four times a day (currently 7am, 10am, 2pm & 5pm), returning 2hr later (passengers Ksh150, cars Ksh800). There's also a car ferry service to Sena on Mfangano Island (2 daily; 1hr 30min).

ACCOMMODATION

One of the great perks of staying overnight in this area is to catch the impressive spectacle at dusk when fishermen on the lake put out hundreds of hurricane lamps to attract tiny *omena* fish (making "more light than Nairobi" as one waiter put it). The wonderful *Lake Victoria Safari Village*, 2km from Mbita, was under renovation at the time of writing; ask at *Elk Lodge* (see opposite) to see whether it has reopened.

RUSINGA ISLAND
Badilisha Ecovillage About 2km north of Rusinga Island Lodge ☎0738 015009, ⓦbadilisha.net. Local homestays are organized for Badilisha volunteers or travellers just passing through, which include bed and board. You can also turn up at Badilisha and camp, and at the time of writing they were in the process of constructing some simple double rooms. Meals and shared showers and toilets are provided. FB: camping $\overline{\$3}$, doubles or homestays per person $\overline{\$8}$

Rusinga Island Lodge On the north side of the island, 10.5km from the causeway coming via the north side, 9.5km via the south side. ☎0716 055924 or ☎0734 402932, ⓦrusinga.com. A luxurious rustic retreat, most of whose clients fly in from the Maasai Mara to the lodge's airstrip. Part fishing lodge, part spa retreat, part watersports club, part birders' paradise (369 species have been recorded), this is a sumptuous and relaxing escape with comfortable, safari-style cottages and large bathrooms. Much of the produce for the sixteen guests is grown on site. There's also the chance to do a fossil walk to the site where Mary Leakey discovered *Proconsul africanus*. FB package for two including all activities (but not flights) $700

★ **Wayando Beach Eco Lodge** On the north side of the island, 4km from the causeway ☎ 0723 773571 or ☎ 0708 593513, ✆ wayandobeachclub.com. A gorgeous collection of individually decorated s/c *bandas*, all brightly painted and inlaid with coloured glass, dotted around a garden planted with fruit trees and strung with hammocks. You can camp here too, either in your tent or theirs, with excellent facilities that include composting toilets, open-air showers and a congenial little restaurant, much of whose produce is organically grown on site. A path leads directly down to the lakeshore. Room only camping, own tent Ksh950 per person; BB: camping with tent rental Ksh1500 per person, *banda* Ksh8260

MBITA

Elk Lodge Across the square from the matatu stand ☎ 0720 716665. A friendly little guesthouse offering clean s/c doubles and non-s/c singles, set around a patio garden with flowers and pawpaw trees. There's no hot water, but they may be able to provide some in a bucket, and the *hoteli* at the front is the best in town. Room only Ksh700

Patroba Ogweno Lodge Behind the Elk Lodge ☎ 0733 731638. Tiny but good-value rooms set around a concrete courtyard, with cold-water showers and safe parking. It's not quite as cosy as the *Elk* or *Viking*, but the well-appointed downstairs rooms are nice and cool. Room only Ksh500

Viking Rest House 20m from Elk Lodge and run by the same lady ☎ 0720 716665, ✆ safarikenya.net/viking .htm. The non-s/c rooms here are smaller than the ones at the *Elk*, but they're well maintained, the mosquito nets are good and the whole place has been freshly painted in cheerful blue and white. The bar at the front gets lively, but never too loud. Room only Ksh600

Mfangano Island

Ksh500/day for a guide

Said to have been inhabited for centuries, enigmatic **Mfangano Island** is out of range of the smallest fishing boats, and, aside from a handful of motorbikes, largely without vehicles. This may be about to change, though, since a twice-daily ferry service from Mbita and the newly completed ring road around the island have gone a long way toward opening up Mfangano to the outside world. The island is populated by a curious mixture of immigrants from all over Kenya, administered by a chief and three sub-chiefs with help from a trio of policemen. Monitor lizards swarm on the sandy shores and **hippos** are much in evidence out in the water.

Larger and more populous than Rusinga, with a similarly rugged landscape but better vegetation cover, Mfangano's greatest economic resource is still the lake itself. As on Rusinga, the local **fishing techniques** are unusual: the islanders fish with floating kerosene lamps hauled shorewards, or towards a boat, to draw in the schools to be netted. Despite the new road, many local residents still rely on a network of temporary **footpaths** that are constantly changing course; you can use these paths to walk through the interior of Mfangano, though it's always easier if you have a guide.

Sena

The chief's camp and capital of Mfangano, Sena has a couple of small *dukas* and *hotelis* and a post office. About 1km north of the centre lies the **Abasuba Community Peace Museum** (hours vary, but if you call in advance they'll open up for you; Ksh500; ☎ 0723 898406), which displays cultural artefacts such as traditional cooking pots and farming implements. The helpful staff can also organize guided excursions to the island's main sights, and can even arrange transport from Mbita. For further information, contact museum director Jack Obonyo on the number above.

Rock paintings

The main sites (at Kwitone and Mawanga) are close to Ukula on the north coast • Ksh500 guiding fee to be taken to them from Sena, and Ksh200 entry fee at each site

The island's **rock paintings** are certainly worth the trip alone. Thought to be at least a thousand and possibly four thousand years old, they are believed to have been painted by the island's original hunter-gatherer inhabitants who were displaced in around the sixteenth century by Luo incomers, who were themselves displaced a couple of centuries ago by a Bantu people called the Abasuba.

The Abasuba Community Peace Museum, which publishes an excellent pamphlet explaining the local rock art, can arrange trips to two sites, **Kwitone** and **Mawanga**, featuring prehistoric rock paintings comprising reddish spirals and whorls, some with rays up to 50cm across, that at first sight could come from any Von Däniken paperback. The paintings were probably used for rainmaking ceremonies, and all kinds of rituals and taboos are still supposed to apply to people visiting them – a period of sexual abstinence, for example, and not telling anybody that you are coming to the site before you actually do so.

ARRIVAL AND DEPARTURE   MFANGANO ISLAND

By boat The cheapest way of reaching Mfangano is on the ferry that shuttles back and forth twice a day between Sena and the western shore of Mbita (Ksh200). The ferries leave Mfangano at 7.30am and 2pm, and leave Mbita at 11am and 5pm; the trip takes 1hr 30min, so a day-trip would be too rushed to be really practical. Hiring a boat for the day gives you more flexibility, but will set you back about Ksh4000.

ACCOMMODATION

Abasuba Community Peace Museum 1km north of Sena ☎0723 898406. The museum allows camping on its grounds (and can provide tents and mattresses), or you can stay in a traditional Abasuba hut. Breakfast is an extra Ksh250, and other meals can be prepared on request. Camping `Ksh500`, room only `Ksh1000`

Gethsamane Guesthouse On the lakeshore just beyond the museum ☎0724 005910. A simple wooden barn of a building crammed with bunk beds, each with a mosquito net, and cold-water showers. It's rustic, but the lakeshore location is lovely. Food can be cooked to order. Bunk bed per person `Ksh800`

Mfangano Island Beach Club 3km from Sena on the eastern side of the island ☎0725 379288. A collection of simple thatched-roof concrete s/c *bandas* right at the water's edge, unadorned except for mosquito nets, with attached bathrooms equipped with electric showers and a restaurant that serves basic Kenyan food. The rooms may be unlovely, but the location is splendid, and it's a good place to pitch a tent. BB: camping `Ksh800`, *banda* `Ksh3500`

Mfangano Island Camp ☎0733 268888, ⊛governors camp.com. Accommodation at the top end of the spectrum is provided by this exclusive camp (sleeping 12) comprising a huddle of clay-and-thatch buildings laid out in the shape of a Luo homestead, but fitted out in deluxe style and overlooking a private bay. Most of the camp's visitors fly in from the Maasai Mara on a day-trip (fishing and birding in the morning, lunching and lounging in the afternoon), but some stay on to enjoy the beautiful setting, gourmet food and attentive service. Closed April & May. FB packages (including a boat with driver at your disposal; flights extra) `$1030`

Mbita to Sindo and Karungu

Continuing south beyond Mbita to Sindo and Karungu is slow going by matatu. The road can be very difficult during the rains and, at the best of times, there's only a limited demand, so one daily departure is the norm. Karungu is better linked with Migori: the stretch between Sindo and Karungu, while remote and beautiful in parts, is best done in your own 4WD.

Some of the most scenic landscapes in western Kenya are to be found around the **Gembe Hills**, south of Mbita. As you approach **SINDO** from the north, the little lakeside town, with the impressive towering backdrop of the **Gwasi Hills**, soaring nearly 1000m above the level of the lake, makes for some memorable views which seem to have more in common with the Greek islands than with equatorial Africa.

The road then turns inland, between the Gembe and Gwasi hills, and runs down to **KWOYO** and the northwestern Nyatoto Gate entrance to Ruma National Park (see p.267). The narrow public road, mostly of treacherous black cotton soil, follows the eastern border of the park, just inside the fence line. If you can take your eyes off the road you're likely to get some excellent free game-viewing, and can expect to see Rothschild's giraffe and various antelope out on the grassy plain to the east. After you leave the park zone, the road improves to a wider, stonier surface, and you should be able to keep up a decent speed to Karungu.

Seventy kilometres from Mbita, **KARUNGU** is a small town on the lakeshore, greatly occupied with *omena* catching and drying, with one or two basic lodgings and *hotelis*. All the streets in the town seem to have been surfaced, but the road out to the east, to Suna and Migori, is *murram*.

Migori

Spread out along the A1 highway for 4km, the "border town" of **MIGORI** is the last major settlement before Tanzania – although the actual border crossing is a further 23km down the road at Isebania. It's more of a western highlands town than you might imagine, with conifer-covered hills rising up to the east. Market days are interesting for the variety of peoples and for traditional activities untainted by tourism. Although Migori is just 80km from the Maasai Mara, the state of the road (see p.364) doesn't make it an ideal jumping-off point for visits to the park. But it can still make for a pleasant stopover en route to Tanzania.

East of Migori to the Maasai Mara

Much of the **C13** road east to the Maasai Mara (see p.364) is in a pretty dreadful state, and, if you're driving, it should only be attempted in a 4WD. Some matatus do parts of this route, and one or two services go right through to Narok and back, which, if you're on a budget, is one way of visiting the Maasai Mara without paying for the privilege. You won't enter the reserve itself, but you will see some wildlife en route, especially in the great conservancy areas north of the reserve, though it's a long and uncomfortable journey.

The Maasai Mara junction is at **Suna**, 4km south of Migori down the A1, where the *murram* road to Karungu also meets the highway. From here, it's 22km to the **Kihancha** turning (keep on straight: the small town is to the right) and you cross the Migori River 2km later. Halfway between Kihancha and Lolgorien, the road improves to fair-to-good *murram*, with the odd rough patch. You reach **Lolgorien**, 46km from Suna, and another 20km sees you at the top of the escarpment above the Oloololo Gate, with the plains of the Mara spread out to the east. Allow at least two hours to get here.

ARRIVAL AND INFORMATION   MIGORI

By bus and matatu Buses and matatus run to Nairobi (8hr) via Kisii (2hr), Kericho (3hr 30min) and Nakuru (5hr 30min) leaving early morning or evening, and there are also morning buses to Eldoret (8hr), and frequent matatus to Homa Bay (3hr 30min), Kisumu (4hr 30min) and Kisii (2hr). Heading down to Tanzania, there are direct buses to Mwanza mornings and

---

ROLE-PLAY AMONG THE KURIA

Kihancha is the capital of the **Kuria** people, who live in scattered rural communities. The Kuria have an interesting, quasi-matriarchal system found in various parts of Africa which essentially allows women of means to "marry" younger women in order to be provided with children. In practice, an older woman who can't have children may invite a younger woman into her home. The young "bride", in turn, chooses a male partner, often in secret, to father her children, who are brought up by the two women without the involvement of the father or the older woman's husband (if she has one – she may also be a widow, or simply unmarried). In any case, the older woman lives like a male elder – attending to light business affairs but essentially waited upon hand and foot from dawn to dusk. It's a system with much to recommend it, especially when it takes care of unmarried mothers (who are barred from marrying men), who come into the family as "wives" – surrogate mothers – and whose children are automatically adopted. Ironically, despite these apparently female-controlled arrangements, it's male children that women-families want, and men who inherit land.

4

evenings, but otherwise you'll have to take a matatu to the border post at Isebania (also called Sirare, and served by direct matatus from Kisumu), or at Kianja, cross on foot and take an onward vehicle from the other side.

Services The town has a Barclays with an ATM, as well as one or two small supermarkets.

ACCOMMODATION AND EATING

There are one or two decent, modest **hotels** in Migori, but water supplies are sporadic, and even cold water may not be available on tap. If you're looking for something cheaper than the *Girango*, try one of the B&Ls around the matatu stand and north of the bridge.

Girango At the south end of town ☎ 0721 273878. Friendly and peaceful, with quiet rooms equipped with couches and TV. Basic local food (mains around Ksh300) is served in the pleasant garden, and there's safe parking. Room only Ksh1500

Heritage Hotel Near the matatu stage. Once famous for the quality of its food, this restaurant has seen better days, but it's still a good option for chicken, fish and meat dishes (all around Ksh350). Daily except Sat 6am–10pm.

Kisii and around

Headquarters of the **Gusii** people, and district town of a region vying with Nyeri in having the fastest-growing population in the country, **KISII** is a prosperous, hard-working trading centre in the hills. Notoriously muddy and rubbish-strewn,

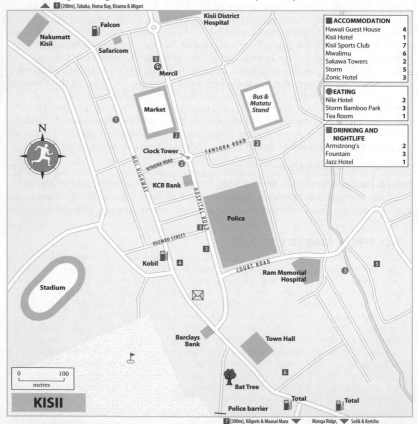

ACCOMMODATION
Hawaii Guest House	4
Kisii Hotel	1
Kisii Sports Club	7
Mwalimu	6
Sakawa Towers	2
Storm	5
Zonic Hotel	3

EATING
Nile Hotel	2
Storm Bamboo Park	3
Tea Room	1

DRINKING AND NIGHTLIFE
Armstrong's	2
Fountain	3
Jazz Hotel	1

KISII

with a minor reputation for hassle which really only reflects the friendliness of the locals, the town is undergoing something of a makeover, with its sloping streets gradually being resurfaced with paving blocks. Kisii is most famous for its fine **soapstone**, though there's little to be seen in the town itself. The best locality for watching the carvers and making on-the-spot purchases is **Tabaka**, some way south. One thing you may notice if you stay overnight in Kisii is the occasional **earth tremor** – the town lies on a fault line and minor earthquakes are not uncommon. Wildlife enthusiasts will want to check out the tree full of **giant bats** in the government compound between Moi Highway and the Sports Club at the southern end of town.

Tabaka

TABAKA is one of the most important centres in the world for **soapstone** (steatite) production. Most of the carvings are bought up by buyers from curio shops in Nairobi and elsewhere, but shops selling the carvings now line the road through the little town, and are happy to sell directly to visitors.

Beyond Tabaka centre are four **quarries**, with two main ones, the first on the left, and the other further down on the right. There must, however, be vast reserves of stone under the ground all over the district. The stone emerges in a variety of colours and densities: white is easiest to work, shades of orange and pink harder, and rosy-red the hardest and heaviest. A number of families have become full-time carvers, but for most people it's simply a spare-time occupation after agriculture, a way of making a few shillings. You'll even see children walking home from school carving little animals from chips of stone. The professional carvers often specialize in a variety of designs from chess sets and traditional animals, to vases, cups and human figures. The stone is dampened to bring up the colour and make it easier to work, and then waxed to retain the lustre.

ARRIVAL AND DEPARTURE   TABAKA

By car The turnoff for Tabaka is at Nyachenge, 18km west of Kisii on the A1 Migori road. A sign to the left, if coming from Kisii, points to the St Amillus Tabaka Mission Hospital and Kisii Soapstone Carvers Co-operative Society. From here it's 5km into the village (6km to the Co-operative Society) on a rough dirt road that's treacherous in wet weather, though an ordinary car can make it when it's dry. Coming by matatu from Kisii, it's best to get one that goes direct to Tabaka, even if that means waiting. The alternative is hanging around just as long at the halfway point, or a long walk from Nyachenge. The last matatus from Tabaka back to Kisii leave around 5pm.

Manga Ridge

The lavishly fertile district around Kisii gets rain all year, in remarkable contrast to the semi-arid lowlands of the lakeshore just a few kilometres away. A walk to the dramatic escarpment cliff of **Manga Ridge** is a good way of getting into the countryside. It's a two- to three-hour walk north of the town, wonderful either in the early morning, or, if you can arrange a lift back, the late afternoon.

Leaving Kisii on the Kericho road, turn left into Manga Road at the bottom of the hill, 500m after Barclays, and follow the road as it sweeps you towards and then alongside the ridge. After about 5km you can cut down one of the tracks across the lush valley to your left and continue straight up the escarpment (several hundred metres high). Beware of snakes lurking among the rocks and grass on the upward scramble. Alternatively, you can continue along the road for a further 5km to come up behind the ridge. From here it's a ten-minute hike up to the edge, where a path follows the cliff for a kilometre or two. Magnificent views out over Kisii and down to Lake Victoria are your reward. It's possible to get a matatu to the village of **Manga** from Kisii town (in front of *St Jude's Guest House*), but make it clear you want to get off at the ridge.

GUSII HISTORY AND CULTURE

The Bantu-speaking **Gusii** (after whom Kisii is named) were only awakened to the brutal realities of British conquest in 1905, when they rebelled, pitching themselves with spears against a machine gun. It was "not so much a battle as a massacre", one of the participants recalled, leaving "several hundred dead and wounded spearsmen heaped up outside the square of bayonets". In 1908, after the District Commissioner was speared in a personal attack, the same thing happened again, only this time the Gusii were trying to escape, not attack. Crops were burned and whole villages razed to the ground. **Winston Churchill**, at the time the Under-Secretary of State for the Colonies, telegraphed from the Colonial Office: "Surely it cannot be necessary to go on killing these defenceless people on such an enormous scale."

The Gusii were totally demoralized. In a few brief years, the fabric of their communities had been torn apart, hut taxes imposed, and cattle confiscated to be returned only in exchange for labour. And then came World War I. Kisii was the site of the first Anglo-German engagements in East Africa, and thousands of men were press-ganged into the hated **Carrier Corps**.

It seems extraordinary that the exceptionally friendly people of Kisii are the grandchildren of the conscripts. The powerful, millennial religious movements that burst among them during the colonial period under the name Mumboism may partly account for the very strong ties of community they've maintained against all odds. Prophets and medicine men have always been important here, and even in today's superficially Christianized society, the Gusii have solidly kept their cultural identity. The practice of **trepanning**, for example, which involves tapping a small hole in the skull to relieve headache or mental illness, seems to be as old as the Gusii themselves. "Brain operations" are still performed, clandestinely, but apparently quite successfully.

Witchcraft and **sorcery** also continue to play important roles in the life of the town and its district, and often make headlines. The growing influence of Christianity has led to spates of **lynchings** of suspected witches. Residents are often reticent to come forward as witnesses, which can lead to an interesting collision of worldviews in the media. On one occasion the local police chief was quoted as saying "We hope we can get them [the witches] and if possible charge them in court. This way we shall save their lives."

Kisii to Sotik and Kericho

The town of **SOTIK** is nothing more than a couple of petrol stations. But **KEROKA**, halfway between Kisii and Sotik, has become a sizeable town and has a huge **Sunday market** drawing people from many kilometres around.

Museum of History, Art and Science of the Kipsigis People

Kapkatet, 12km east of Sotik and 150m off the north side of the road • Mon–Fri 9am–5.30pm, Sat & Sun 9am–6.30pm • Ksh500 • ☎ 0714 718276, ✉ tumpaul45@yahoo.com

Travelling along the road to Sotik, it's worth stopping at **KAPKATET** to take a look around the little **Museum of History, Art and Science of the Kipsigis People** (see p.278). The museum comprises a diverse little collection of traditional garments, tools, weapons, containers and musical instruments, all well lit and well captioned, with pronunciation guides, putting many of the country's official national-museum collections to shame. Look out for the young girls' circumcision cloaks and for the *chepchingilit* – bells that would have been worn by sheep or goats (and by girls, after their operations and only removed after marriage). Finally, there's a fascinating and pretty successful attempt to recreate a cross-section of a traditional Kipsigis home, with wooden sliding door ("with a peephole for anticipating attacks").

ARRIVAL AND DEPARTURE   KISII AND AROUND

Kisii is something of a route hub, with both regional and national bus and matatu services passing through. If you're heading to **Tanzania**, you can take bus and matatu services throughout the day to the border crossing, variously known as Isebania or Nyabikaye on the Kenyan side, and Serira, Sirare or Siria on the Tanzanian.

By matatu Plenty of matatus run throughout the day, most departing from the main stage in front of the market. These include three or four useful early-morning departures roughly for Narok via the B3, passing the junctions for the C12 and C13 Maasai Mara access roads. Other destinations include Eldoret (3hr 30min); Homa Bay (1hr 30min); Kericho (1hr 30min); Kisumu (2hr 30min); Migori (2hr); Nairobi (5hr 30min); and Rongo (45min).

By bus There are numerous bus services to and from Kisii, with most buses pulling into and departing from the matatu stage. Services include Homa Bay (4 daily; 1hr 30min); Migori (6 daily; 1hr 30min); Mombasa (4 daily; 13hr); and Nairobi (roughly hourly; 5hr).

By car If you're driving and are planning to take the route to the Maasai Mara via Kilgoris and Lolgorien, note that the road to the Mara is difficult beyond Kilgoris, even with 4WD, and the section down the Oloololo Escarpment can be impossible after rain. Heading for the north or east of the reserve, the fastest route is via Sotik and Bomet.

ACCOMMODATION

You'll find plenty of places to **stay**, although some are pretty awful, and most are noisy, especially on Wednesdays and weekends when bars and discos are at their loudest, and women travelling alone will want to avoid cheaper places. Water supplies are notoriously erratic and you should be prepared for power fluctuations during heavy rain, so have some candles handy.

Hawaii Guest House Moi Highway ☎0718 777582. Cheap, secure and clean place that has improved enormously after a recent facelift. The s/c doubles and s/c or non-s/c singles are all comfortably furnished, though some are dark and rather cramped; a good deal overall. Room only **Ksh1000**

Kisii Hotel Moi Highway, 200m north of Nakumatt on the road to Kisumu ☎0734 002044. Ramshackle but quiet, with an agreeable, creaking colonial atmosphere and helpful staff, the *Kisii* belies outward appearances with its twelve spacious, clean rooms with nets, TV and instant showers. There's guarded parking and a huge and beautiful bird-filled garden, perfect for relaxing with a cold beer, though the food in the restaurant isn't great. BB **Ksh1500**

Kisii Sports Club Heading south, turn right 300m past the Total station, then right again ✉kisiisportsclub @gmail.com. The club is open to all, with seven good-sized, clean and well-furnished rooms with nets, TV and instant showers. There's a golf course, squash court and pool on site, though it costs extra to use them, and the peaceful grounds have lots of space for kids to run around on the lawns. BB **Ksh2500**

Mwalimu Moi Highway ☎0717 687880, ✉ceo @ourupower.com. This large, labyrinthine concrete block at the southern end of town was once a teachers' hostel and is still owned by the teachers' union. The rooms are comfortable enough, with nets and electric showers, and downstairs there's a restaurant and bar with sports on TV. Wi-fi. BB **Ksh2250**

Sakawa Towers Hospital Rd ☎0737 347374. This six-storey block, with great town views from the roof and upper floors, offers good value, although there are a lot of stairs to climb. All the rooms have balconies, but some are small and cramped, so be choosy. Wi-fi. Room only **Ksh1000**

Storm Court Rd ☎0727 630021, ✉hotel-storm.com. The quietest hotel in Kisii offers a choice of adequate rooms with nets, TV and instant showers, plus some more expensive suites, and an outside bar and *nyama choma* joint. Good value and well managed. Wi-fi. Room only **Ksh1125**

Zonic Hotel Hospital Rd ☎0710 782421. The most upscale option in town, this is still a fairly dour place, though the rooms are at least reasonably priced and there's an elevator to take you to them. All rooms come with balconies and some with tubs, and downstairs you can eat either in the pleasant streetside café or around the pool. Wi-fi. BB **Ksh2500**

EATING

Despite the noxious drain smells, the overflowing **market** is the first base for hungry travellers. Kisii is also blessed with a big **supermarket**, Nakumatt Kisii (daily 8.30am–8.30pm).

Nile Hotel Hospital Rd. A very popular first-floor terrace restaurant, offering huge portions of Kenyan staples, plus a few more unusual items like sandwiches (around Ksh200) and salads. The wrap-around balcony is a great place for hanging out and people-watching. Daily 6.30am–9.30pm.

Storm Bamboo Park Court Rd ☎0727 630021, ✉hotel-storm.com. A garden bar and restaurant that provides a welcome oasis from the chaos of downtown Kisii, where you can tuck into Indian and African dishes at tables under the trees; locals come here to drink well into the night. *Nyama choma* costs Ksh600/kg. Daily 7.30am–midnight.

Tea Room Moi Highway ☎0722 112111. True to its name, this packed little eatery does a gorgeous cup of milky, sweet *chai*, along with snacks and all the usual local dishes (mains Ksh180–300). Open 24hr.

DRINKING AND NIGHTLIFE

Armstrong's Ground floor, St Jude's Guest House. A long bar with a congenial atmosphere, plus several screens of sports (usually English football) and good music; beer Ksh140. Daily 10am–10pm.
Fountain Ogembo St. Cavernous, multi-level bar playing African tunes and showing sports on wide-screen TVs. They

also serve grilled meats, chicken and fish for around Ksh300. Daily 9am–midnight.
Jazz Hotel Hospital Rd ☎0727 710828, ⊛bit.ly /jazzsports. Perennially popular and relaxed venue, with big windows overlooking the busy street and an eclectic mix of sounds; beer Ksh150. Daily 6am–midnight.

DIRECTORY

Banks There's a KCB on Hospital Rd, and a Barclays on Moi Highway; both have ATMs.
Hospitals The main hospital is Kisii District in the northern part of town, at the end of Hospital Rd (☎058 30564); the

private option is Ram Memorial Hospital on Court Rd (☎058 30236).
Internet access Mercil, in the basement of the Keiko Building on Hospital Rd (daily 8am–6pm; 50 cents/min).

Kericho and the tea country

Kericho, named after the early English tea planter John Kerich, is Kenya's **tea capital**, a fact that – with much hype from the tourism machine embellished by the presence of the *Tea Hotel* – is not likely to escape you. Its equable climate and famously reliable, year-round afternoon rain showers make it the most important tea-growing area in Africa. While many of the European estates have been divided and reallocated to small farmers since independence, the area is still dominated by giant tea plantations.

Kericho

Compact **KERICHO** town seems as neat as the serried rows of bushes that surround it. The central square has shady trees and flowering shrubs – a bandstand would make it complete – and even the matatu park has lawns around it. It's a gentle, hassle-free place

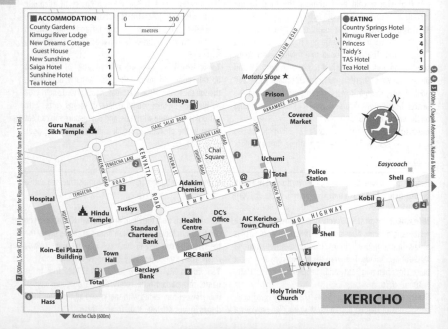

■ACCOMMODATION
County Gardens 5
Kimugu River Lodge 3
New Dreams Cottage Guest House 7
New Sunshine 2
Saiga Hotel 1
Sunshine Hotel 6
Tea Hotel 4

●EATING
Country Springs Hotel 2
Kimugu River Lodge 3
Princess 4
Taidy's 6
TAS Hotel 1
Tea Hotel 5

KERICHO

to wander, the people mild-mannered, and is in many ways an oddity. Clipped, clean and functional, there's little of the shambolic appearance of most upcountry towns. With so many people earning some sort of salary on the tea plantations or in connection with them, and so few acres under food or market crops, the patterns of small-town life are changed here. Most workers live out on the estates, their families often left behind in their home villages. Kericho is above all an administrative and shopping centre, and a relay point for the needs of the estates. The produce market is small, trading is limited and most places seem to close early. The town suffered badly during the 2007–08 election violence, with dozens killed and around 20,000 displaced. Things are calm now, but some say the historical resentment behind the violence remains, and that there is still tension between Kipsigis – the original inhabitants – and Kikuyus over land ownership.

There's a substantial Asian population in the town: note the vast Sikh **Gurdwara**, the Guru Nanak Temple, whose superb gardens are worth a stroll. Many of the streets have a vaguely Oriental feel, with single-storey *dukas* fronted by colonnaded walkways where the plantation "memsahibs" of fifty years ago presumably did their shopping. This curious, composite picture is completed by the grey stone **Holy Trinity Church**, with its small assembly of deceased planters in a miniature cemetery. Straight out of the English shires, it tries so hard to be Norman that it's a pity to point out that it was only built in 1952. Unfortunately (at least from an aesthetic point of view) it is now overshadowed by the modernist **AIC Kericho Town Church**, with its welcoming perimeter of razor wire.

ARRIVAL AND DEPARTURE
KERICHO

Kericho has hassle-free travel options in every direction: southwest to **Kisii** and **Migori**, east over the Mau Escarpment to **Nakuru via Molo** (see p.233), or northwest to **Kisumu** and **Kapsabet**. Heading south to the **Maasai Mara**, the first part of the route, to Bomet, follows a good road through splendid farming country and then links with the highway to Narok (see p.355). For travel eastwards, Nairobi and Nakuru buses and matatus generally originate in Kisumu and Kisii and pass through Kericho throughout the day and night. Kericho is fairly compact, fortunately, since there are few taxis and if you don't have your own vehicle **getting around** town is only possible by walking or flagging down a passing boda-boda.

By matatu Matatus arrive at the main stage, on the north side of the centre opposite the market. Leaving Kericho, there are services to Eldoret (3hr); Kisii (1hr 30min); Kisumu (1hr 30min); Molo (1hr 30min); and Nairobi (4hr) via Nakuru (2hr).

By bus Buses in both directions pass through town on the Moi Highway; you can pick them up around the Total station, where several bus companies also have offices. The EasyCoach office is at Oilibya (☎0726 354306; 24hr). Destinations include Busia (2 daily; 4hr); Kisumu (roughly hourly from 11am–6pm; 1hr 30min); and Nairobi (7 daily; 5–6hr) via Nakuru (2hr).

ACCOMMODATION

★ **County Gardens** Signposted down a dirt road behind the AIC Church ☎0715 850661, ✉thecounty gardens@gmail.com. A wonderfully homely little cottage with a cosy communal sitting room and a handful of bright rooms with flowered bedspreads. It feels just like a private house, down to the hot-water bottle in your bed, with meals cooked on request and an expansive garden. BB **Ksh2500**

Kimugu River Lodge Off Moi Highway, opposite the Shell station, 700m northeast of the centre ☎0720 861079, ✉kimuguriverlodge@yahoo.com. Take the signposted turning and follow the track for 600m to reach this rather downmarket-looking but peaceful place, with a great location above the Kimugu River. The rooms in brick- and wood-panelled alpine-style chalets come with lots of hot water and are simple but comfortable, while those in the new block, which are twice the price, have fireplaces. There's also a

decent bar and excellent Indian restaurant. BB **Ksh2500**

New Dreams Cottage Guest House Moi Highway, 700m west of the Total station on the south side of the road ☎0716 290880, ✉newdreamscottage@gmail.com. British-style B&B with attentive management, offering ten rooms with big nets, carpets, instant showers and DSTV. A safe choice, and all very cosy, but strictly no alcohol served or allowed to be consumed on the premises. Wi-fi. BB **Ksh3000**

New Sunshine Tengecha Rd ☎0724 146601, ✉sun shinehotelltd@gmail.com. The budget branch of the bigger *Sunshine Hotel* (see p.282), this is a well-run place that's easily the best in the town centre, with small, neat, extremely clean rooms with TV, nets and instant showers (although some face inward and are quite dark). There's a busy *hoteli* downstairs serving good buffet breakfasts, and safe courtyard parking. Wi-fi. BB **Ksh2700**

4

Saiga Hotel John Kerich Rd ☎051 8011711. A surprisingly large establishment hidden away behind the shops, with a selection of very cheap s/c and non-s/c rooms, hot water and parking in the yard. Rooms have nets and electric sockets but no fans, and most have inward-facing windows (the best are a handful of brighter one at the end). But it's decent value given the low price. Room only Ksh600

Sunshine Hotel Moi Highway ☎052 2021285 or ☎0721 700358, ⓦsunshinehotel.co.ke. A good mid-range business-traveller hotel, efficient and bright, whose rooms boast modern bathrooms with electric showers; some have tubs. There are nice views from the upper floors of sheep-grazed fields and the tea bushes beyond. Some rooms come with balconies, and a few of the deluxe rooms even have heaters for chilly Kericho nights. Wi-fi. BB $83

Tea Hotel Moi Highway ☎0714 510824, ⓔinfo @teahotel.co.ke. Built in 1952 by the Brooke Bond tea company, and at one time the best place in town, the *Tea Hotel* has been in slow decline ever since, though with its wooden floors and elegant French windows it still retains a faded charm. Standard rooms are large and comfortable enough, with instant showers and nets but no fans or a/c, and would be quite overpriced if you weren't also getting the beautiful gardens and large swimming pool (non-residents Ksh200). Choose your room carefully as the main house can be noisy. You can also camp using room showers or the pool-changing facilities. Wi-fi. Camping Ksh500, BB $95

EATING

If you're buying food, you'll find Kericho's **market** is best at weekends, when there's a greater variety of fruit, vegetables, snacks and spices at good prices. The town's best **supermarkets** are Tusky's (daily 8.30am–8.45pm) and Uchumi (daily 7.30am–8.45pm). Kericho has its fair share of cheap and fairly ungastronomic *hotelis*, heavy on the chips and *ugali*.

Country Springs Hotel Kenyatta Rd ☎0721 848497. A friendly little diner crammed with tables that gets quite busy at mealtimes, probably because it's one of the best options in town for cheap staples; pilau goes for Ksh150. Daily 6am–9pm.

★**Kimugu River Lodge** Off Moi Highway, opposite the Shell station, 700m northeast of the centre. The best food in town (and not expensive), with an extensive menu of mainly Indian food (most dishes around Ksh500) including chicken *methi*, *malai kofta* and a wonderful crayfish *masala* (Ksh700); food is cooked to order, so it can take some time. You can dine overlooking the Kimugu River, where colobus monkeys sometimes come to frolic in the trees. Daily noon–midnight.

Princess Off Moi Highway, opposite the Shell station, 700m northeast of the centre. A popular local drinking spot with a nice garden in which to unwind with a beer (Ksh170), as well as a few lounge-like rooms with sofas for those looking for more privacy. Sun–Thurs 11am–10pm, Fri & Sat 11am–2am.

Taidy's Moi Highway, just past the Hass petrol station ☎0712 385555. Branch of the excellent Nakuru restaurant, with the same thick menu of pizzas, burgers, grilled meat and Indian food (pizzas and grills Ksh500, other dishes around Ksh300). The attached sports bar turns into a fairly classy club on weekends. Restaurant daily 6am–late, bar daily 3pm–late.

TAS Hotel Moi Rd ☎0728 782005. The busiest and best-value of the Moi Rd *hotelis*, always lively and packed with workers at lunchtime. Tuck into a full breakfast for just Ksh180, or fish stew with *ugali* for Ksh250. Daily 6.30am–9pm.

Tea Hotel Moi Highway ☎0714 510824. For an upmarket hotel, the menu here isn't particularly expensive, filled with old-school options like steaks, pork chops and roast chicken (around Ksh600); for lunch, you can opt instead for a three-course set menu for Ksh700. Otherwise the gardens are a nice spot for tea for two; if you'd rather have good strong, boiled-in-the-pot African tea, ask for *chai majani*. Daily 7–9.30am, 12.30–2.30pm & 7.30–10pm; drinks available 7am–10pm.

DIRECTORY

Banks The three main banks are on Moi Highway at the Kisumu end of town; all have ATMs.

Hospital Kericho boasts good medical facilities including the superior Central Hospital, 1km past the *Tea Hotel* on the Unilever tea estate.

Internet access There are several cybercafés on Moi Rd, including Online Kinyozi (daily 8am–8pm).

Pharmacy Adkaim Chemists (☎0721 759977; Mon–Sat 7.30am–7.30pm, Sun 8.30am–7pm); there are no late-opening or night pharmacists.

Around Kericho

This is **tea country**: Kenya is the world's third-largest producer after India and Sri Lanka, and the biggest exporter to Britain. As you gaze across the dark green hills, you might pause to consider that the land, now covered in vast regimented swathes of tea bushes, was, until not much more than a century ago, virgin rainforest, only a tiny part

TEA

Tea (*Camellia sinensis*) is a psychoactive shrub originally native to China. Its effects are said to have been discovered by the legendary third millennium BC Chinese emperor Shen Nung, who was apparently taking a cup of hot water in the shade of a shrub when one of the buds fell into it, making him an invigorating drink. For centuries the Chinese had a monopoly on tea, but with its rise in popularity at home, the British were keen for an independent source of supply, and eventually managed to smuggle some cuttings to India. In Kenya, tea was first grown in 1903, though it was nearly twenty years before commercial production got under way. Kenyan teas are known for their strength and full flavour, and are a major component of most commercial blends sold in the UK and Ireland. Kenya's other main customers are Egypt, Pakistan and Afghanistan.

Tea **production**, though not complicated, is very labour-intensive. Picking continues throughout the year, and you'll see the pickers moving through the bushes in their brilliant yellow-and-green ((KETEPA/Kenya Tea Packers) plastic aprons, nipping off the top two leaves and bud of each bush (nothing more is taken) and tossing them into baskets. Working fast, a picker can collect up to 70kg in a day, though half that is a more typical figure; the piece-rate is set at around eight shillings per kilo picked. After withering, mashing, a couple of hours' fermentation and a final drying in hot air, the tea leaves are ready for packing and export. The whole process can take as little as 24 hours.

Tea can be harvested three years after planting, and in the first year of production it must be picked every eight days, then every fourteen days in the second year and every seventeen in the fourth, after which the bush must be pruned to keep it at the right height for picking, which can begin again after three months. Weeding is not necessary as the foliage is sufficiently dense to prevent other plants from growing under it.

The stimulating **effects** of tea are due to the presence of caffeine, and a cup of strong tea can contain as much caffeine as a cup of medium-strength coffee. The effect feels different because it is moderated by other alkaloids such as thebaine, which is a relaxant. Because the human body requires fluid to process caffeine and thebaine, tea depletes the body of water, even though it appears to quench your thirst. Like beer, therefore, strong tea should not be taken as a fluid against dehydration.

4

of which, the Kakamega Forest, survives. The estates were first set up after World War I with tea bushes imported from India and China.

The tea estates

The factories generally operate daily except Mon (the day after the pickers' day off), though they might be open every day during the rainy season; visits to tea factories are best booked several days in advance • Tours last 2hr (Ksh200 per person, plus the price of transport if required); alternatively, you can just take a tour of the tea fields combined with a nature walk (Ksh200 per person)

It is possible to **visit the tea estates** on a guided tour (enquire in the lobby of the *Tea Hotel*). The *Tea Hotel*'s guide can also be hired for **birding** excursions in the neighbourhood at Chagaik Arboretum, and to **Lelartet Cliff**, which is also home to a large number of red colobus and black-and-white colobus monkeys.

Kimugu Valley

Down in the **Kimugu Valley**, behind the *Tea Hotel* and *Kimugu River Lodge*, you can get some idea of what the land was like before the settlers arrived. Although vast swathes have recently been cleared for cultivation, most of the valley is still a deep, tangled channel of sprawling trees and undergrowth, with shafts of sunlight picking out clouds of butterflies. The cold brown waters of the Kimugu flow down from Chagaik Dam and allegedly harbour **trout**.

Chagaik Arboretum

Drive or get a lift in the Nairobi direction, past the KETEPA buildings, then take the right turn to Chagaik Dam, 6.5km from the *Kimugu River Lodge* (marked with a small white signpost saying "Kericho Forest Station"), then the first left, after which it's a 5min walk to the arboretum • Daily 7.30am–5.30pm • Free

A curious sight amid the closely cropped tea bushes, the graceful **Chagaik Arboretum** consists of acres of beautiful trees from across the tropics and subtropics, tumbling steeply down through well-tended lawns to a lily-covered lake. Inside the arboretum, a plaque reads "Founded by Tom Grumbley, Tea Planter 1946–75". Don't miss the magnificent stands of bamboo on the banks. Entry to this haven of landscaped tranquillity is unrestricted and you can picnic or rest up as long as you like, though there are gardeners around who won't let you camp. It gets quite popular at weekends and holidays when families come out here to enjoy the space and air. Across the lake, thick **jungle** drops to the water's edge. Mysterious splashes and rustles, prolific bird and insect life, and at least one troop of colobus monkeys are a surprising testament to the tenacity of wildlife in an environment hemmed in on all sides by the alien ranks of the tea bushes.

Eldoret and around

The direct journey from Kericho to Eldoret through the **Nandi Hills** is one of the most varied and spectacular in the west, through countryside that is often far wilder than you'd expect, including bleak mountainous scrublands and jungle-packed ravines. Midway, you cross the Kano Plains and you may have to change transport at **Chemelil**, a major crossroads in the Nyando valley, down in the flat sugar lands. Beyond, the road zigzags northwards into high tea country again, the homeland of the **Nandi**, the fiercest early opponents of the British, and the haunt of a crypto-zoological mystery known as the **Nandi bear** (see box, p.286). The only town of any size before Eldoret is **Kapsabet**, which has a couple of banks, a market and a handful of reasonable lodgings, but nothing to warrant a stopover unless, again, you need to change matatus. If you're

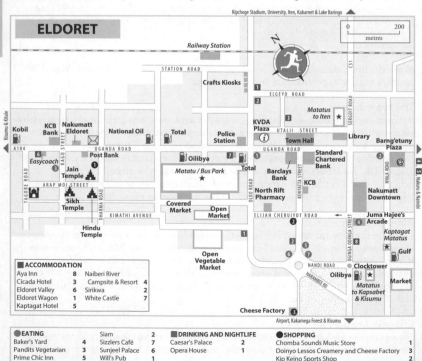

ELDORET

Kipchoge Stadium, University, Iten, Kabarnet & Lake Baringo

Railway Station

STATION ROAD

Crafts Kiosks

ELGEYO ROAD

Matatus to Iten

KVDA Plaza

UTALII STREET

Town Hall

Library

Barng'etuny Plaza

Kobil

KCB Bank

Nakumatt Eldoret

National Oil

Total

Police Station

Standard Chartered Bank

Easycoach

UGANDA ROAD

Post Bank

UGANDA ROAD

Oilibya

Total

Barclays Bank

Nakumatt Downtown

Jain Temple

Matatu / Bus Park

North Rift Pharmacy

KCB

ARAP MOI STREET

Sikh Temple

KIMATHI AVENUE

Covered Market

Open Market

ELIJAH CHERUIYOT ROAD

Juma Hajee's Arcade

Hindu Temple

Kaptagat Matatus

Gulf

Open Vegetable Market

NANDI ROAD

Clocktower

Oilibya

Matatus to Kapsabet & Kisumu

Market

Cheese Factory

Airport, Kakamega Forest & Kisumu

ACCOMMODATION

Aya Inn	8	Naiberi River	
Cicada Hotel	3	Campsite & Resort	4
Eldoret Valley	6	Sirikwa	2
Eldoret Wagon	1	White Castle	7
Kaptagat Hotel	5		

EATING

Baker's Yard		Siam	2
Pandits Vegetarian	3	Sizzlers Café	7
Prime Chic Inn	5	Sunjeel Palace	6
		Will's Pub	1

| | 4 | | |

DRINKING AND NIGHTLIFE

Caesar's Palace	2
Opera House	1

SHOPPING

Chomba Sounds Music Store	1
Doinyo Lessos Creamery and Cheese Factory	3
Kip Keino Sports Shop	2

0   200
metres

driving, you might pause at the **Kingwal Swamp**, north of Kapsabet (the road passes right through it), where more than sixty **sitatunga** antelope (see p.292) hang on in an unprotected wetland area.

Although more bustling than Kericho, and somewhat healthier and pleasanter than Nakuru, **ELDORET** really has hardly anything to differentiate it from dozens of other highland centres, though as Kenya's fifth-largest town, it's a good deal bigger. The **Uasin Gishu Plateau** all around is reliably fertile cereal, vegetable and stock-raising country; wattle plantations provide the tannin for the town's leather industry; the Raymond, Rivatex, Raiply and Ken-Knit **textile factories** provide employment; and **Moi University** has proved a shot in the arm for local schools. Eldoret's prosperity is shown clearly enough by the windows of Eldoret Jewellers on the main road.

Though there are no sights as such to keep you here for very long, you may well find Eldoret a useful stopover, and it's refreshingly unthreatening and friendly despite its size. The town's affluence is reflected in a wide variety of places to stay, eat and drink, and enough nightlife to see you through an evening or two.

Brief history

Eldoret was initially a backwoods post office on Farm 64, later chosen in 1912 as an administrative centre because the farm's soil was poor and the deeds were never taken up by the owner. The name started as Eldare (a river), was then Nandi-ized to Eldaret, and finally misprinted in the *Official Gazette* as Eldoret.

Before the town existed, the area was settled by **Afrikaners**. They gave it much of the dour worthiness that seems to have characterized its first half-century and which is perceptible even today – though most of the Boers trekked on after Kenya's independence. In the era of **President Moi**, whose roots were in nearby Kabarnet, Eldoret was a special focus for investment and development: this is when its university was founded and its "international" airport opened. Although most modern inhabitants are Kalenjin-language-speakers from the Elgeyo and Nandi tribes, there are also Somali-speakers, the remnants of the European settler community and a long-established and respected Asian community (Juma Hajee's supermarket, now a shopping arcade, is the oldest business in the town).

In addition, there are enough immigrants from the rest of Kenya for Eldoret to have been a brutal flashpoint in the **post-election violence** of 2007–08. This culminated in the massacre of more than forty Kikuyu people, including many children, in an arson attack on the Assemblies of God church in the suburb of Kiambaa, where they had taken refuge. Outwardly, Eldoret has already recovered from the trauma of the clashes: most Kikuyu fled the area, as did members of many other non-Rift Valley and non-western Kenya tribes, some of whom seem resigned to staying in internally displaced person (IDP) camps in the district for years. But the anger released did nothing to resolve the tensions that remain.

Beyond Eldoret

Beyond the small centre of **Kaptagat** and **Kaptagat Forest**, which has a few trails and is a nice place for walks, runs the unpaved route down to the fluorspar mine at **KIMWARER**. Believe it or not, this used to be the main way across the Kerio Valley, and although it no longer sees much traffic, you can usually hitch a ride with a lorry travelling to or from the mine – an incredible hairpin descent that seems to go on forever. Route details for the Kerio Valley continue in the Rift Valley chapter (see p.241).

In the other direction (northwest) out of Eldoret, the only real town is **SOY**, 9km past the B2/A104 junction, formerly a tiny community but now a sizeable centre. Beyond Soy, the road continues through **MATUNDA**, formerly the train station of Springfield Halt (18km past Soy and 25km short of Kitale), and the small trading centre of **MOI'S BRIDGE**, 21km short of Kitale.

THE NANDI AND THE NANDI BEAR

At the end of the nineteenth century, the **Nandi** (dialects of whose language are spoken by all the Kalenjin peoples) were probably in the strongest position in their history. Their warriors had drummed up a reputation for such ferocity and daring that much of western Kenya lived in fear of them. Even the Maasai, at a low point in their own fortunes, suffered repeated losses of livestock to Nandi spearsmen, whose prestige accumulated with every herd of cattle driven back to their stockades. The Nandi even crossed the Rift Valley to raid Subukia and the Laikipia plateau. They were intensely protective of their own territory, relentlessly xenophobic and fearful of any adulteration of their way of life. Foreigners of any kind were welcome only with express permission.

With the killing of a British traveller, Peter West, who tried to cross their country in 1895, the Nandi opened a decade of guerrilla warfare against the British. Above all, they repeatedly frustrated attempts to lay the rail line and keep communications open with Uganda. They dismantled the "iron snake", transformed the copper telegraph wires into jewellery and took whatever livestock and provisions they could find. Despite increased security, the establishment of forts, and some efforts to reach agreements with Nandi elders, the raiding went on, often costing the lives of African soldiers and policemen under the British. In retaliation, a series of **punitive expeditions** shot more than a thousand Nandi warriors (about one young man in ten), captured tens of thousands of head of livestock, and torched scores of villages. The war was ended by the killing of Koitalel Arap Samoiei, the *Orkoiyot* or spiritual head of the Nandi who, having agreed to a temporary truce, was then murdered at a meeting with a delegation led by the British officer Richard Meinertzhagen, who shot him in cold blood (see p.594). As expected, resistance collapsed. His people had believed Koitalel to be unassailable and the Nandi were subsequently hounded into a reserve and their lands opened to settlers.

Traditionally keepers of livestock, the Nandi have turned to agriculture with little enthusiasm and focus instead on their district's milk production, the highest in Kenya. *Shambas*, however, are widespread enough to make your chances of seeing a **Nandi bear**, the source of scores of yeti-type rumours, remote. Variously said to resemble a bear, a big wild dog or a very large ape, the Nandi bear is believed to have been exterminated in most areas. But in the less accessible regions, on the way up to Kapsabet, many locals believe it still exists – they call it *chemoset*. Exactly what it is is another matter, but it doesn't seem to inspire quite the terror you might expect; the occasional savagely mutilated sheep and cattle reported in the press are probably attributable to leopards. A giant anthropoid ape, perhaps a gorilla, seems the most likely candidate for the original *chemoset*, and the proximity of the Kakamega Forest may account for the stories. This is a surviving tract of the rainforest that once stretched in a continuous belt across equatorial Africa and is still home to many western and central African species of wildlife (though not giant apes). The *chemoset* possibly survived up until the early twentieth century in isolated valleys. Whatever the truth, if you camp out in the Nandi Hills, you won't need reminding to zip your fly-sheet.

ARRIVAL AND DEPARTURE   ELDORET AND AROUND

Eldoret sprawls widely and inelegantly in all directions, stretching some 10km along the highway. The whole place can be a real bottleneck, and it can easily take 30min to get through town from one end to the other. If you want to **park** here you'll need a ticket, sold by the parking wardens all over town (Ksh100; valid 24hr). Heading directly **to Uganda** by bus or matatu, there's little to delay your progress to Malaba on the border, via Webuye and Bungoma. For the **Kakamega Forest**, take a bus or matatu going to Kisumu via Kapsabet, and get off at the D267 turning about 20km west of Kapsabet (signposted "Kisieni 12km"), from where you might be able to hitch a lift; otherwise it's a walk of about 3hr to the *Forest Guest House*.

By plane Eldoret airport (☎053 2063377) is 16km south of town on the Kapsabet road and has five daily flights with Fly540 to Nairobi, and two with Jambo Jet (1hr).

By matatu The main matatu stage is at the east end of Arap Moi St. Matatus from the main stage run to Kakamega, Kisumu, Kitale and Kaptagat. Matatus for Iten and Kabarnet (with connections to Lake Baringo and Lake Bogoria) leave from the stage on the corner of Oginga Odinga and Utalii streets using the spectacular Tambach Escarpment route.

Destinations Cherangani (1hr 30min); Kabarnet (2hr) via Iten (45min); Kakamega (2hr); Kaptagat (1hr); Kitale (2hr); Malaba (4hr).

By bus The EasyCoach office is next to the Eldoret Valley on Uganda Rd (☎0738 200308), from where buses run four times a day to Nairobi (8hr) via Nakuru (3hr).

Destinations Kitale (6 daily; 1hr 30min); Malaba (2 daily; 3hr); Nairobi (6–8 daily; 8hr) via Nakuru (3hr).

INFORMATION

Tourist office On the second floor of KVDA Plaza ☎ 053 2032086. Mostly an administrative office without much in the way of handouts, but staff are very helpful and happy to provide information on local attractions. Mon–Fri 8am–5pm.

Banks Barclays, Standard Chartered and KCB all have

ATMs. There's also Safari Forex in KVDA Plaza (Mon–Fri 8.30am–4.30pm, Sat 9am–1pm), but they don't take small bills.

Internet There are numerous internet cafés in Barng'etuny Plaza including Sphere Internet Cafe (Mon–Sat 9am–6pm).

ACCOMMODATION

ELDORET

Eldoret has no shortage of accommodation, though cheap places tend to be grubby or clearly intended for "short-term guests". Campers should consider heading out to the lovely *Naiberi River Campsite & Resort* (see below).

Aya Inn Oginga Odinga St ☎ 0708 046117. A friendly place with clean purple-walled rooms, nets and instant showers, though couples have to get cosy as the beds are only barely wide enough for two. There's good security and safe parking, and the two rowdy but good-natured bars aren't bad options for a drink. Wi-fi. BB Ksh1200

Cicada Hotel Just off Utali Rd ☎ 053 2061081 or ☎ 0733 907640, ⊛ cicada.co.ke. This is a somewhat impersonal mid-range hotel in a tiled tower block, but the smallish rooms are still comfortable, and come with TVs and nets. A good buffet breakfast is included, and there's safe parking in the basement. Wi-fi. BB Ksh4500

Eldoret Valley Uganda Rd ☎ 0722 816108. Small but scrupulously clean rooms in an orderly B&L established by its friendly owners more than thirty years ago. The little café out front, which also serves as reception, has decent Kenyan fare and is a good place for tea. BB Ksh900

★**Eldoret Wagon** Elgeyo Rd ☎ 053 2062270, ⊛ eldoretwagonhotel.co.ke. Helpful, friendly and charmingly old-fashioned but professionally managed, the *Wagon* has 102 light, airy rooms, with nets, TV and instant showers, and a *nyama choma* bar. The Eldoret Jambo Casino is by the front gate and the whole place gets quite lively at weekends. Unusually, they take most credit cards. Very good value. Wi-fi. BB Ksh3800

Sirikwa Elgeyo Rd ☎ 0728 680000, ⊛ sirikwahotel .com. The town's "premier" hotel, this monolithic and faintly pompous pile is fairly bright and clean, although rooms are tired and overpriced. Discounting the pool, which is in good shape (non-residents Ksh200), the more low-key and much cheaper *Eldoret Wagon*, opposite is a better bet any day. Wi-fi. Room only $100

White Castle Uganda Rd ☎ 053 2061362, ⊛ eldoret

whitecastlemotel.com. Although first impressions are very unpromising – a bland modern building on the noisy main road through town – the rooms turn out to be better than average, spacious and comfy, but with old-fashioned showers. There's a lift, and even a sauna and health club. BB Ksh2150

BEYOND ELDORET

Kaptagat Hotel 1km off the main road 5km east of Naiberi River Campsite ☎ 0722 778654. More sedate than the *Naiberi River Campsite*, this colonial anachronism survives from the days when British aristocrats roamed the neighbourhood. The hotel is set in extensive and beautiful grounds, and there's excellent birdwatching from the terraces of the cottages, which come with wooden floors, open fires and the dodgy bathroom plumbing you'd expect from such an old establishment. There's also a bar and TV lounge, and meals can be rustled up. BB Ksh4000

★**Naiberi River Campsite & Resort** 16km east of Eldoret, 400m off the Kaptagat Rd ☎ 0722 686512, ⊛ naiberi.com. A popular stop for independent overlanders and tour trucks heading for Uganda, with a scenic location above the small Naiberi River and comfortable, cabin-style rooms, plus dorms (with good, shared showers and toilets) and camping. The centrepiece is a sprawling and enjoyable pub-restaurant built into the hillside, incorporating streams and waterfalls, a central fireplace and the remains of what are said to be Sirikwa cave dwellings or animal pens (see p.230). The chef cooks up excellent, sizzling hot-plate dishes and other meals. It's a delightfully relaxing place to hang out for a day or two, the hilly grounds leading down to the river, and a sparkling (if chilly) swimming pool making it hard to leave. Driving here, turn east towards Kaptagat 3km southeast of Eldoret town centre on the Nairobi road then drive 15.3km and *Naiberi* is on your left. Call ahead for a lift from town. Room only: camping Ksh700, dorm bed Ksh2500; BB: double Ksh9400

EATING

Eldoret has plenty of good places to grab a bite, with a clutch of established snack bars, several options for dinner and one or two evening haunts. For your own supplies, head for the markets west of Oloo Rd, or a branch of the Nakumatt **supermarket**: choose between the big 24hr Nakumatt Downtown in Oginga Odinga St, or Nakumatt Eldoret on Uganda Rd (daily 8.30am–8.30pm).

Baker's Yard Juma Hajee's Arcade, Elijah Cheruiyot Rd ☎0733 782150. Excellent hole-in-the-wall bakery tucked into an old brick arcade, tempting you in with the aroma of warm bread. There are also biscuits, pies, cakes and pastries for sale (Ksh40–120), and good filter coffee. Mon–Sat 9am–7pm.

★**Pandits Vegetarian** Kago St ☎0729 039099. Charming snacks and sweetmeats shop, and an excellent place for vegetarian Indian meals including thalis and some good lunch specials. Mains around Ksh380, or a whole thali for Ksh450. Mon–Sat 8am–6pm, Sun 8am–5pm.

Prime Chic Inn Kenyatta St ☎0723 589632. Fast-food place often teeming with Eldoret youth, with high standards and keen prices, offering chicken, burgers, fry-ups and chips every which way. They'll deliver as well. Half a chicken goes for Ksh440. Open 24hr.

Siam Nyala Rd, corner of Uganda Rd ☎053 2060402. The Chinese dishes, with the accent on chilli, aren't bad, and include specials like shredded honey chicken (Ksh600) and Gong Bau prawns. What makes it really good value are the great-value lunchtime specials: Ksh550 for a main dish, a spring roll and a drink. Mon–Fri 11am–3pm & 6–10.30pm, Sat & Sun 11am–10.30pm.

Sizzlers Café Kenyatta St ☎053 2031259. Popular American-style diner with quirky retro decor, offering speedy, high-quality burgers (Ksh230), curries, excellent samosas, ice cream and other desserts. Mon–Sat 9am–6pm.

★**Sunjeel Palace** Kenyatta St ☎0720 554747. Operating very much in British-style Indian-restaurant mode, this is where Eldoret's Asian community often comes for a good meal out, usually ordering ahead (allow at least 30min) from a selection of fine curries (veg and non-veg), plus good *naan*. Mains Ksh450–600. Daily 11.30am–11pm.

Will's Pub Uganda Rd ☎0703 730666. Mostly patronized by local businessmen, this murky cave of a pub is all wood panelling and dark corner tables. It's a good place for a beer, but also for solid Kenyan food and snacks, including tasty meat samosas. Full breakfasts Ksh350, half-chicken Ksh500. Mon–Sat 7am–11pm, Sun 9am–10pm.

DRINKING AND NIGHTLIFE

The following places charge a small entry fee at weekends but are free during the week.

Caesar's Palace Kenyatta St. A revamped disco, loud and enjoyable, with pool tables and cheap beer (Ksh160). It's generally packed at weekends when they play soul, ragga and hip-hop, with live English and European football on screen. Mon–Fri 3pm–3am, Sat & Sun 2pm–3am.

Opera House Oloo Rd ☎0717 549072. Very firmly established nightspot (pronounced "O-pair-a", not "Oprah"), with pink and white walls and plenty of mirrors, whose DJs play mostly Afri-pop and dancehall music. Daily 4pm–5am.

SHOPPING

Chomba Sounds Music Store Dharma Rd ☎0722 747675. A hole-in-the-wall place that's more of a kiosk than a shop, but which is nonetheless the best place in town to find sounds from the region – including traditional Luo, Kalenjin, Kikuyu and Maasai music, as well as contemporary Kenyan pop. It comes in the form of CDs or MP3s, which they'll load onto a flash drive if you bring one. Mon–Sat 8.30am–6.45pm.

★**Doinyo Lessos Creamery and Cheese Factory** At the end of the track south of Kenyatta St. This little place has been making top-quality European-style cheese, yogurt and ice cream since 1964, and although they don't have a shop per se, you can buy their products directly from the factory window (Ksh974 for 250g of gruyere, Ksh32 for a cup of fresh yogurt). Daily 8am–6pm.

Kip Keino Sports Shop Kenyatta St ☎0723 878086. Set up by athlete and Christian philanthropist Kepchugi Keino. Keino's double gold at the 1964 Olympics blazed a trail that has since been followed by other Kenyan runners, mainly from around Eldoret. It's a small place, but still good for sports equipment and clothing. Mon–Fri 8am–5pm, Sat 8am–1pm.

Kitale

KITALE is smaller than Eldoret, and not much more exciting, but has more going for it from a traveller's point of view, primarily as the base for visits to **Mount Elgon**, Kenya's second giant volcanic cone, and the superb, very underrated hiking country in the area. It's also an obvious springboard for the **Cherangani Hills**, and a straightforward departure point for trips to the west side of **Lake Turkana**. There's a **national park** nearby – the little-known but easily accessible **Saiwa Swamp**, which can only be explored on foot. In addition, the town also has two **museums** and a couple of other sites to visit.

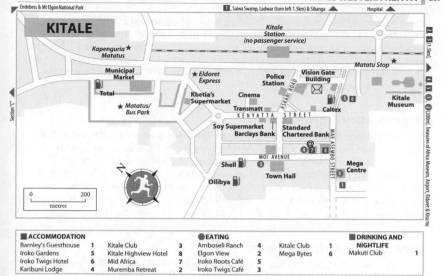

■ ACCOMMODATION			● EATING					■ DRINKING AND
Barnley's Guesthouse	1	Kitale Club	3	Amboseli Ranch	4	Kitale Club	1	**NIGHTLIFE**
Iroko Gardens	5	Kitale Highview Hotel	8	Elgon View	2	Mega Bytes	6	Makuti Club	1
Iroko Twigs Hotel	6	Mid Africa	7	Iroko Roots Café	5				
Karibuni Lodge	4	Muremba Retreat	2	Iroko Twigs Café	3				

The town's present population is a mix of tribes, including Nandi, Pokot, Marakwet, Sabaot and Sengwer, as well as a few Luhya, Kisii and Kikuyu and an influential Asian community. Like most towns in the Rift Valley and western Kenya, it was seriously affected by the post-election clashes of 2007–08, but managed to make a swift recovery.

Brief history

Originally Quitale, a relay station on the old slave route between Uganda and Bagamoyo in Tanzania, the modern town was founded in 1920 as the capital of Trans-Nzoia District. When the first white settlers arrived after World War I, this vale of rich grasslands between Mount Elgon and the Cherangani Hills was supposedly almost uninhabited. But just a few years earlier it had been a Maasai grazing area, and a group of people who consider themselves Maasai still live on the eastern slopes of Elgon. With the arrival of the rail line in 1925, the town and the region around it began to flourish, with a fantastic array of fruit, cereals, vegetables and livestock, and all the attendant settler paraphernalia of agricultural and flower shows, church fetes and gymkhanas. This heady era lasted barely forty years, but the region's **agriculture** is still famous; almost anything, including such exotic fruit as apples and pears, can be grown here. The Kitale Show is held each year in late October or early November.

Kitale Museum

Southeast of the town centre on the road to Eldoret • Daily 8.30am–5.30pm • Ksh500 • ☎ 054 30996, ⓦ museums.or.ke

Originally the "Stoneham Museum", a collection opened to the public by a lieutenant-colonel on his Cherangani farm in 1927, the **Kitale Museum** was transferred here in 1972. For the most part, Stoneham's curious collections are just that: collected curiosities in striking contrast to the recent, more educationally motivated, Kenyan additions.

The main hall contains interesting **ethnographic displays** on Pokot, Elkony (Elgon), Luhya, Maasai, Turkana and Luo, with artefacts such as Kamba carvings (including skin-covered animals and smooth polished abstracts); a Pokot goat bell made from a tortoise shell; and intricate Turkana belts and beadwork. In the small room to the right of the entrance in the main building is an old piano and accordion and a collection of traditional **musical instruments**, which really are becoming museum pieces as younger generations embrace more cosmopolitan musical genres (though you can buy CDs of traditional Luhya music in town). Outside, the re-creations of Nandi and Luhya **homesteads** make an interesting point of comparison with the realities of present-day villages.

Agroforestry Project

Next to the Kitale Museum (though the entrance is 300m further east) • Mon–Fri 8am–5pm • Free • ☎ 054 31498 or ☎ 054 30283

The Swedish Co-operative Centre's **Agroforestry Project** was set up to educate cultivators in Trans-Nzoia and West Pokot about the basics of tree planting. This accomplished, it now deals with soil erosion and overgrazing, and offers practical advice to farmers on the selection of species best suited to local conditions. There's a small gallery and demonstration *shamba*, showcasing sound techniques for increasing crop yield.

Treasures of Africa Museum

1.7km from the town centre, northeast of the main road to Eldoret, 200m past the Kitale Club • Mon–Sat 9.30am–5pm • Ksh500 • ☎ 054 30867 or ☎ 0722 547765

The quirkiest of Kitale's sites is the **Treasures of Africa Museum**. Run by John Wilson, a retired former colonial administrator from Uganda, the museum displays cultural artefacts, mainly from the Karamojong pastoralists of northern Uganda. The exhibits are arranged in robustly un-scientific fashion to illustrate the proprietor's case, based on supposed linguistic parallels between Karamojong and other languages, such as Gaelic, that a single worldwide farming culture existed tens of thousands of years before what is normally believed to be the case. The curator-proprietor is usually on hand to explain his theory in person, but if you want to be sure of a guided tour – and the visit is fascinating – it's best to call in advance of your visit.

Kitale Nature Conservancy

About 5km north of Kitale en route to Saiwa Swamp and Kapenguria • Daily 8am–6pm • Ksh800 • ☎ 0720 309108

The **Kitale Nature Conservancy** is a small zoo ostensibly geared toward conservation, but the real focus is on its bizarre collection of natural freaks and oddities – five-legged cows and the like – that would normally be slaughtered at birth. It's all a bit grotesque and some locals claims that the animals aren't cared for as well as they should be, but if you can stomach it the place is still morbidly fascinating.

ARRIVAL AND DEPARTURE   KITALE

By plane The airport is 6km southwest of town, off the A1 road to Webuye. There's currently one daily flight to Nairobi with Fly540 (1hr 15min).

By matatu Matatus spill out from the stage near the municipal market onto the adjoining main road, and there's a smaller gathering of Nissans bound for Eldoret, Kakamega and Kisumu opposite the Kitale Museum on the corner of the Lodwar road. For Mount Elgon, the closest destination is Endebess, reached quickly enough by regular matatus, from where you'll have to hire a motorbike or taxi. Southwards, Kisumu is no more than 3hr away down the busy and bumpy A1.

Destinations Cherangani (30min); Eldoret (1hr 45min);

Endebess (30min); Kipsaina (30min); Kisumu (4hr); Makutano for Kapenguria (1hr); Nairobi (6–7hr) via Nakuru (4hr).

By bus Most buses leave from the bus park in the west of town, or the streets around it. Eldoret Express run regular buses to Nairobi (8hr) via Eldoret (1hr 30min) and Nakuru (4hr), leaving when full – roughly every hour – from the main bus park. There are also services to Lodwar (6 daily; 12hr) and Mombasa (1 daily; 18hr). The road to Lodwar for Lake Turkana (see p.517) is in such an appalling condition beyond Marich that it might as well not be paved at all. There are several buses a day (but no matatus), most in the afternoon. Remember to take water, and also to stock up on provisions, as you'll only find more basic stuff on sale further north (fresh fruit and vegetables are expensive and poor quality in Lodwar).

By car If you're driving yourself, be sure you've got plenty of food and water in case of a breakdown, and note that there is nowhere to get fuel between Ortum and Lodwar.

INFORMATION

Services The local branches of Barclays and Standard Chartered banks, both on Kenyatta St, have ATMs. For internet access, try the cyber café in the *Mid Africa Hotel* (daily 8am–7pm).

ACCOMMODATION

In town, there are quite a few cheap lodgings, the very cheapest of which are at the grubby north end of town, past the market. For mid-range hotels, you're spoilt for choice, but there's nothing top-end. You can camp at *Karibuni Lodge*. *Barnley's Guesthouse* (p.294) near Saiwa Swamp is also an excellent option for those who don't mind being based a bit further afield.

Iroko Gardens 3km out of town on the road to Eldoret ☎0722 696563, ✉irokohotels@gmail.com. A quiet guesthouse set in a nice garden; not a bad option if you don't mind being a bit out of town. The standard rooms are on the small side, but at the time of writing a new block of fancier rooms was under construction, each with its own kitchen. There's also a restaurant and bar on site. BB **Ksh2000**

★**Iroko Twigs Hotel** Mak Asembo St, behind Iroko Twigs Café ☎0726 370293, ✉kmuyundo@yahoo.com. Conveniently located right in the centre of town (but with safe parking), these are the most luxurious and sophisticated rooms in Kitale, decked out with wood floors, gleaming new bathrooms, DSTV and enormous double beds. The only downside is that inward-facing windows make them a bit dark. Most credit cards accepted. Wi-fi. BB **Ksh3500**

★**Karibuni Lodge** Milimani district, 2km from the town centre (heading for Eldoret, turn left at Total) ☎0706 043618, ⟁karibunikitale.com. A very nice place catering to NGOs and backpackers, with camping, dorm beds and both s/c and non-s/c rooms with nets and hot water set in pleasingly rustic cabins scattered throughout the garden. The owner does a good line in locally sourced home cooking, including vegetarian options. Guests also have use of the kitchen. Wi-fi. Camping **Ksh350**, dorm bed **Ksh500**, BB **Ksh3000**

Kitale Club 1.5km out on the road towards Eldoret ☎0726 610241, ✉reservation@kitaleclub.co.ke. On the site of the former slave headquarters, offering old cottages with cement floors, a new block with larger rooms and wooden floors, and new cottages with wooden floors, TVs and fireplaces. The price includes temporary membership and access to club facilities including the golf course (Ksh1000) and pool (Ksh200). The club rules are slightly stuffy – they include a ban on mobile phones in the clubhouse – but if that doesn't bother you this can be a pleasant place to stay. BB **Ksh5300**

Kitale Highview Hotel Moi Ave ☎723 652006, ✉kitalehighview@795.com. Friendly high-rise hotel with good, breezy and relatively clean rooms with nets, and a decent balcony restaurant. The luxury rooms, which cost slightly more than the ordinary ones, are much bigger and come with a sitting area. Safe parking. BB **Ksh1800**

Mid Africa Moi Ave ☎0727 277077, ⟁midafricahotel .com. A relatively slick multistorey hotel popular with business travellers, though these days it's starting to look a bit tired. Still, there's a reasonable restaurant and rooftop *nyama choma* bar, and the rooms (some with balconies) have DSTV. Wi-fi. BB **Ksh3000**

Muremba Retreat Wamalwa St, Milimani district, 2km out of town ☎0722 716070, ⟁kenya-kitale-accomodation-muremba.com. A cosy house in a big garden with seven rooms, all quite comfortable, though the best are the two rooms in the wooden cottage with a sauna. Staff are attentive, and the breakfast is very good; other meals are available as well if ordered in advance. Wi-fi. BB **Ksh5000**

EATING

Kitale has several quite good **places to eat**, including the local *Iroko* franchise, and after dark a number of places provide for drink and lively conversation. The best places to stock up on provisions are the big new Nakumatt Kitale on Mak Asembo St (Mon–Sat 8.30am–9.30pm, Sun 10am–9pm) and Khetia's near the bus park (daily 8am–7.30pm).

Amboseli Ranch Roof of the Mid Africa hotel, Moi Ave ☎0727 277077. Cheerful rooftop *nyama choma* bar with views of Mt Elgon (on a clear day) plus football matches on TV; a nice spot for a sundowner over a plate of roasted meat (Ksh800/kg). Mon–Fri 3pm–midnight, Sat & Sun 2pm–midnight.

Elgon View Eldoret road, 1km southeast of the centre ☎0722 553144. The most upscale restaurant in town, with views of the mountain from the garden at the back and a menu of Chinese-inspired dishes (Ksh350–1000) alongside tasty Indian offerings (around Ksh500), including plenty of vegetarian options. Daily 11.30am–10pm.

4

★ **Iroko Roots Café** Moi Ave. A perennial favourite for cheap but tasty Kenyan food, always packed with a mix of locals and tourists dining on delicious stews, curries and pilau (Ksh80–250); sometimes sandwiches and soups are available as well, but the focus is on well-cooked Kenyan food. Daily 6am–8pm.

Iroko Twigs Café Mak Asembo St ☎0726 370293. Sister establishment to *Iroko Roots*, always busy and equally nice, but with more Western food on the menu – think soups, salads and sandwiches, as well as lamb chops and pizzas (though not wood-fire); most dishes around Ksh350. Daily 6.30am–9.30pm.

Kitale Club 1.5km out on the Eldoret road ☎0726 610241. Serves a mix of Indian and European dishes, all heavy on the meat, in a rather old-fashioned dining

room; dishes are around Ksh450, but there's a Ksh500 minimum spend to eat here, the money loaded onto a temporary membership card. Less hassle are the two bars, including an atmospheric wood-panelled sports bar and a lounge with expansive views onto the golf course. Daily 6.30am–10pm.

Mega Bytes Mega Centre on Mak Asembo St, next to Nakumatt ☎0714 069599. Putting aside the atmosphere that comes with eating in a mall, there is decent Indian food here, with a fair number of vegetarian dishes on offer – including aloo goby (Ksh500) and crunchy aubergine – as well as seafood (mostly prawns and fish) and fresh-squeezed juices (Ksh150). Daily 9am–9pm.

DRINKING AND NIGHTLIFE

Makuti Club Entrance down a dirt road off Kenyatta St ☎0722 218786. The most popular club in town, with DJs spinning a mix of East African and Western rock

music. Step off the dancefloor for a game of pool or a greasy plateful of *nyama choma*; beer is Ksh180. Daily 24hr.

4 Saiwa Swamp National Park

$25 • ☎0732 480586, ⓦ kws.org • 1.9 square kilometres

Created specifically for the protection of the **sitatunga**, a rare and vulnerable semi-aquatic antelope, **Saiwa Swamp National Park** is the smallest in the country and is rarely visited, despite its accessibility, which is a pity. The requirement that you walk (rather than drive) around the jungle and swamp, plus the chance of seeing the antelope as well as various monkeys and birds, makes it an exciting and interesting day out. If you're staying at *Barnley's* (see p.294), think about hiring a guide there for the trip, which is worthwhile and not at all expensive.

Wildlife-watching

You're almost bound to see one of the park's **sitatunga**, an unusual species of antelope which lives most of its life partly submerged in water and weed. Similar in size and general appearance to the bushbuck, the sitatunga is reddish-brown with a slightly shaggy coat and very large ears, while the males have spiral horns. The sitatunga's most unusual features (usually hidden in water) are their strangely splayed and elongated hooves, evolved, it's believed, to help prevent them from sinking as they pick their way gingerly through their native swamps. It's hard to see how much help these feet really are in keeping the antelope from sinking into the swamp, as the hooves are only moderately elongated: the theory makes sense, but evolution has a little more work to do here. Due to poaching, numbers in the park are down from more than seventy in the 1980s to fewer than twenty at the last count.

Sitatunga can be found in scattered locations throughout western and central Africa, but in Kenya they are restricted to Saiwa Swamp, the Kingwal Swamp south of Eldoret (see p.285), and a few spots around Lake Victoria. Only at Saiwa Swamp, however, have they grown really used to humans. They can be watched from **observation platforms**, which have been built in the trees at the side of the swamp – two on the east side, two on the west. These somewhat precarious, Tarzan-esque structures enable you to spy down on the life in the reeds, while one of them – *Treetop House* – has been

converted into a snug overnight stay (see below). The best times for sitatunga-spotting are early morning and, to a lesser extent, late afternoon.

The drier parts of the park also shelter **bushbuck**, easily distinguished from the sitatunga by their terrified, crashing escape through the undergrowth as you approach. As well as the antelopes, Saiwa Swamp is a magnet for ornithologists, with a number of unusual **bird species**, including several turacos, many kingfishers and the splendid black-and-white casqued hornbill. Most conspicuous of all are the **crowned cranes** – elegance personified when not airborne, but whose lurching flight is almost as risible as their ghastly honking call.

A delightful, easily followed, **early-morning walk** takes you across the rickety duckboards over the swamp and along a jungle path on the eastern shore. Here you're almost bound to see the park's four species of **monkey**: colobus, vervet, blue and the distinctively white-bearded de Brazza's monkey.

ARRIVAL AND DEPARTURE   SAIWA SWAMP NATIONAL PARK

By matatu The park is 11km from *Barnley's Guesthouse* (see below), and easily reached by matatu from there or from Kitale. The park lies to the east of the main Kitale–Lodwar road, near the village of Kipsaina, 17.5km from Kitale. Matatus from Kitale will drop you at Kipsaina (10 daily; 30min), from where it's Ksh50 each way by boda-boda, or a signposted 4.8km walk to the park gates.

By car If you're driving straight to the park from Kitale, you can also turn right 11.5km north of Kitale (signposted "Sibanga") for Saiwa Swamp's main gate (7km).

ACCOMMODATION

★**Barnley's Guesthouse** (also known as Sirikwa Safaris) Signposted off to the right 23.1km north of Kitale on the A1 ☎0723 917953 or ☎0737 133170, ✉ sirikwasafaris.com; map p.252. One of the finest homestays in the country, and the best place to stay around Kitale if you have your own transport or you're heading north anyway. Based around an old farmhouse and superb gardens situated on a tree-covered hill, *Barnley's* offers camping in three furnished tents with electricity or rooms in the fine old house, with full-on highlands atmosphere and shared facilities – or you can pitch your own tent in the gardens. Excellent meals (Ksh500–1500) are cooked to order and eaten with the charmingly informative hosts. Given notice, the Barnleys will organize just about anything, and can also provide excellent guides (Ksh800/ day for a field guide, Ksh2400/day for the ornithologist) – perfect companions for the Saiwa Swamp, or for a trip to the Cherangani Hills for anything from a day to a week. Camping **Ksh500**; BB: furnished tents **Ksh3600**, rooms **Ksh7200**

Park campsite Just inside the main gate ☎020 6000800, ✉ reservations@kws.go.ke. You can pitch a tent on this stretch of lawn, which has basic facilities including cooking *bandas*, firepits, toilets and hot showers. It's also a good spot for a picnic. **$20**

Treetop House Just inside the main gate ☎020 6000800, ✉ reservations@kws.go.ke. A one-bedroom stilted house sleeping two, with great views from the front deck; perfect for dawn birdwatching and animal-spotting. Water tends to go off after 6pm. **$50**

Kapenguria

KAPENGURIA, off the highway north of Saiwa Swamp, is surprisingly small given its status as the capital of West Pokot District and is notable only for its role of minor notoriety in colonial history. You can find out more about this at the Kapenguria Museum, which is interesting enough to warrant a day-trip.

Kapenguria Museum

Kapenguria town centre • Daily 8.30am–5.30pm • Ksh500 • ⊕ museums.or.ke

This excellent museum occupies the prison where Jomo Kenyatta and his colleagues were detained during their parody of a trial. Their individually named cells have been restored, and contain copies of contemporary press reports, photos, depositions and the charges laid against each of the "Kapenguria Six" (some almost laughably nebulous). All six defendants were found guilty of belonging to Mau Mau and sentenced to seven years in jail with hard labour. More visually interesting are the **ethnographic displays** of local cultures, including well-described photographs of traditional circumcision dances and initiation groups, musical instruments and a telling series on the changes wrought by modern life. Look out for the chisel for removing teeth, and the small horn "for sucking after making incisions on both sides of the head if one has a headache". In the museum grounds are some traditional Pokot family compounds, which the museum caretaker will explain to you.

ARRIVAL AND DEPARTURE   KAPENGURIA

By matatu Matatus from Kitale will drop you on the main A1 road at Makutano, 5km from Kapenguria, which is the main town in the western Cherangani Hills and has more services than Kapenguria itself (the turning for Kapenguria is a couple of kilometres further north). If you're heading

towards the Kerio Valley (p.241) on the other side of the Cheranganis you'll find plenty of matatus between Makutano and Lomut, especially on market day in Sigor (Thurs) or Lomut (Sat), with fewer onwards to Tot, unless you coincide with the weekly market at Chesegon (Wed).

INFORMATION AND ACTIVITIES

Banks There's a Barclays, plus a KCB ATM opposite the Total station.
County Craft Makutano, on the Kitale road ☎0716 192177. Run by a local artist named Alfred, this little curio shop also hosts art classes (Ksh1000–3000/day) in which you can learn to make your own batiks, carvings, candles

and fabric paintings. Classes can last as long as you want, ranging from one-day workshops to intensive three-month courses; prices vary according to the number of days involved and the cost of the materials. But whether you're looking for a taste of African art or trying to master a craft, this is a good place to start. Mon–Fri 7am–5.30pm.

ACCOMMODATION AND EATING

There's nowhere to stay in Kapenguria itself, but nearby Makutono has a handful of tolerable options, and is only 5km away.

Hotel Kalya On the road to Lodwar, just past Oilibya on the right ☎0721 944992. Tiny but immaculate hoteli serving a range of good-value *ugali* and chapatti dishes for around Ksh100, as well as tall glasses of freshly pressed mango and avocado juice (Ksh40). Daily 5.30am–9pm.
Sebit Resort Club West of the main road and north of the Total station ☎0725 567984. Located behind a lively and colourfully painted bar and *nyama choma* joint, these

rooms are unexceptional, but at least they're clean and well kept, with nets and TV. BB **Ksh1000**
Tegla Hotel Behind an unmarked orange gate next to the Total station ☎0724 762911. Owned by Olympic marathon runner Tegla Loroupe, this B&L offers very simple rooms that are getting pretty tatty and run-down. Their one redeeming quality is the price, and the fact that there's a tiny area to park at the front. Single rooms only **Ksh500**

Ortum and the Marich Pass

North of Makutano, the A1 enters the truly spectacular countryside of West Pokot proper, winding up the western ridge of Lelan forest, then plunging steeply to the Marun (or Moruny) River. After some 45km you reach **ORTUM**, beautifully positioned beneath the heights of the Cheranganis close to the **Marich Pass**, a jumping-off point for a hike into the hills. If you're heading north by car, Ortum has the last petrol before Lodwar, though it's better to fill up at Makutano to be on the safe side. **Mount Sekerr** (or Mount Mtelo, 3354m) is the peak that looms to the northwest – it's a three-day hike to the top and back down. Nearer Marich, 3206m **Mount Koh** to the southeast is a one-day hike if you've got 4WD to get halfway up; two full days otherwise.

ACCOMMODATION   ORTUM AND MARICH PASS

There are several cheap B&Ls in the village and no shortage of *hotelis*.

★ **Marich Pass Field Studies Centre** On the banks of the Marun River, signposted 1km down a track south of the Lodwar road, 1km north of the trading centre of Marich (which is at the junction of the A1 road to

Lodwar and B4 road to Sigor, Tot and the Kerio Valley) ☎0722 139151 or ☎0718 767874, ⊕www.gg.rhul .ac.uk/marichpass; map p.252. An excellent base, with a lovely shaded campsite, some good cottages with mosquito nets, including two cottages adapted for wheelchair use, and dorm beds. Firewood, stoves and lamps are available for a small charge. The food is basic but wholesome, and Ethiopian food is available with two days notice (order all dishes well in advance; Ksh300–650); drinking water comes pure from the well. Even if you're not staying, it's well worth dropping in for a picnic (admission Ksh200), as the centre is surrounded by dense bush, quivering with bird and animal life, and guides will help you on excursions around the hills, to Pokot homesteads and to the local markets (tours Ksh750–1100). Camping **Ksh550**, BB dorm bed **Ksh600**, BB **Ksh1700**

★**Mount Mtelo View Campsite** 120km north of Kitale, a 4hr hike or 1hr drive from Marich Pass Field Studies Centre ☎0737 941400, ⦿bit.ly/mtelo -campsite. For anyone in search of solitude and tranquillity, this campsite and handful of brightly painted non-s/c *bandas*, all overlooking the broad expanses of the Rift Valley, certainly fit the bill. The garden is slung with hammocks, and you can spend your time relaxing or hiking with guides from the community. Meals are cooked on site. To get there you'll have to drive (4WD only) or hike, or call in advance and the owner will arrange a pickup. Camping **Ksh400**, *bandas* **Ksh800**

Mount Elgon National Park

$30 • ⦿kws.org

Straddling the Kenya–Uganda border, **Mount Elgon** is hidden in clouds most of the time, its precise outline hard to discern. The name comes from the Maasai **Ol Doinyo Ilgoon**, meaning "Breast Mountain", and, like Mount Kenya, it's an extinct volcano, around whose jagged and much-eroded crater rim the flat-topped peaks crop up like stumpy fingers of an upturned hand. The two mountains are comparable in bulk, but Elgon is lower. It's below the snowline and less precipitous, which is encouraging if the thought of tackling the "loneliest park in Kenya" was putting you off.

The highest of the peaks, **Wagagai** (4321m; there's also nearby Little Wagagai, at 4298m), is across the caldera in Uganda, but the most evocatively shaped peaks (Sudek, 4176m; Lower Elgon, 4301m; Koitoboss, 4187m; and Endebess Bluff, 2563m) belong to Kenya. Part of the east side of the mountain is enclosed within the confines of **Mount Elgon National Park**. Outside this zone is a forest reserve, with some restrictions on movement due to the presence of poachers and cattle rustlers. The park itself, however, is open for business.

Exploring the park

The easiest way to visit Elgon is by driving in at the main Chorlim Gate, staying just inside the park and visiting the nearby **caves and forest**. There are several relatively easy circular drives and short hikes in this lower part of the park. On the **moorland** and towards the **peaks**, the smoothing effects of erosion make **hiking** relatively easy, and there's some bracing walking country. **Driving** within the park, it's possible to get to within 4km of Koitoboss peak with a 4WD vehicle, but it needs to be an extremely sturdy, high-clearance vehicle, and you'll need steely nerves as it's a steep, rocky and extremely muddy ride up to the road-head where the summit trail starts. Indeed, the route is often completely impassable (Jan–Feb is the best time), and even the area near Chorlim Gate can be extremely treacherous, with slippery tyre-ruts and ample opportunities to bog down or even roll your vehicle.

The mountain also has good **rock-climbing** – the best routes are on the cliffs of Lower Elgon, Sudek and the nearby pinnacles – but you must be properly equipped. You'll also need to clear your plans with the KWS rangers. Up inside the caldera (technically in Uganda), the **warm springs** by the Suam River provide a tempting bath.

Wildlife

The **vegetation** on Mount Elgon is similar to Mount Kenya's, and equally impressive, with bamboo and podocarpus forests (the latter more accessible than Mount Kenya's)

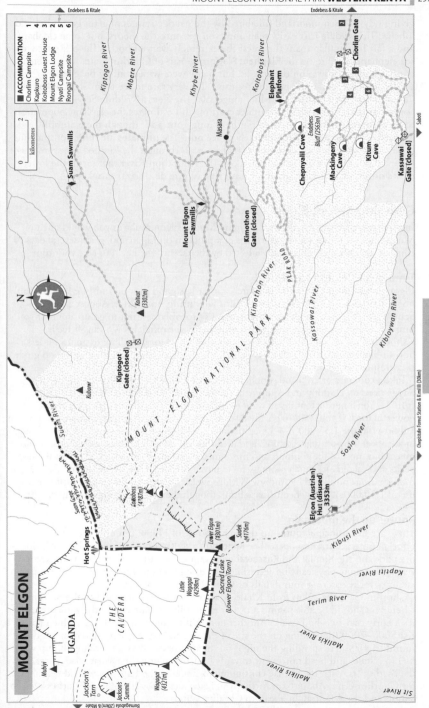

MOUNT ELGON

giving way to open moorland inhabited by the strange statues of giant groundsel and lobelia. The **wildlife** isn't easily seen until you get onto the moors, but some elephant and a fair few buffalo roam the forest (be extremely wary of both). The best place to see elephants used to be the **Elephant Platform** north of Chorlim Gate, where herds congregated to browse on the acacias, but many were wiped out by poachers in the 1980s, and the remainder became reclusive. It's very rare to see them at the **Elkony Caves**, where they regularly used to gouge salt. The Kenya Wildlife Service is confident that poaching is now under control, and estimates the elephant population to be around two hundred. The lions have long gone and, though there are still **leopards** and **servals**, you're not likely to see one. The **primates** are more conspicuous: blue monkeys and black-and-white colobus crash through the forested areas, troops of olive baboons patrol the scrub, and along the Kimothon River that forms the lower park's northern boundary, there's a scattering of rare de Brazza's monkeys.

Climbing Mount Elgon

In most respects, you should treat a trip up Mount Elgon much as you would one to Mount Kenya. However, **altitude** is less of a problem on Elgon and, given several days to climb it, few people will be badly affected by the ascent. The key is to take your time.

Timing, guides and equipment

Elgon is best from December to March, rather less good in June and July, and probably not worth visiting when the heaviest rains fall during April, May, August and September. This is a lonely mountain and it's probably best not to go up alone. If you hire a **guide** to accompany you at Chorlim Gate, the official KWS ranger fee is Ksh3000/day (or Ksh1500/half-day). You might find locals willing to go up for less, but, unlike Mount Kenya, there is no guiding industry here, and finding a good guide is correspondingly harder.

Take a **compass** or GPS and supplies for at least two to three days of self-sufficiency. Suggestions on clothing and equipment can be found in the Mount Kenya section (p.171). You'll need a **tent** if you want to explore beyond the lower park area, and a powerful **torch** if you want to go any distance into the caves. If you are planning more than a short visit, the 1:35,000 KWS map (usually available at Chorlim Gate, but better bought in advance) is better than nothing, and useful for the roads and trails, though it sketchily misses out most of the contours and mixes metric and imperial spot heights. For the high peaks and caldera, it's much more useful to have the topographically accurate *Mount Elgon Map & Guide* published by Andrew Wielochowski (the map of the caldera itself is at a useful 1:50,000; ⓦewpnet.com/maps.htm), though the practical details are dated.

Routes up the mountain

There are five **principal routes** up the Kenyan side of Elgon, but only the route via **Chorlim Gate** is currently open. The **Kimothon** and **Kiptogot** routes on the north side of the park and the **Kimilili** and **Kassawai** routes up the south side have been closed for years. They may physically be accessible, but using them to enter the park (there are no facilities for registering your details or paying) is not permitted.

Chorlim Gate lies 22km from Kitale. Matatus run from Kitale to **Endebess**, from where you should be able to find a taxi or motorbike to take you to the gate; otherwise it's a fairly easy two-hour walk. Another option is to hire a taxi in Kitale, which costs Ksh5000–7000 (depending on the size of the vehicle) either for a full day or for the round trip if you're spending the night on the mountain. If you're driving, fill up with fuel in Kitale, and head northwest towards Endebess along the tarmac road. After 9km the road splits, with the tarmac continuing to Endebess and a *murram* road bearing left for Chorlim Gate. About 6km further you reach a crossroads (right to Endebess, left to **Saboti** and the A1, straight ahead to Chorlim Gate).

MAYHEM ON MOUNT ELGON

Despite the tranquillity inside the national park, communities around the southern slopes of Mount Elgon have been embroiled in land disputes with the government since colonial times, and wracked by violent episodes over the past two decades. The most recent began in 2005 with the formation of the **Sabaot Land Defence Force**. Formed to resist a forced resettlement programme, the SLDF rapidly degenerated into a brutal **insurgency** that terrorized unsupportive Sabaot villagers and Okiek tribespeople alike, with murder, mutilations and rape, and is estimated to have displaced 66,000 people and killed more than six hundred. Early in 2008, as the world watched the post-election clashes in Eldoret, Kisumu and Naivasha, the Kenyan military went on a **rampage** in the southern Elgon foothills, arresting every Sabaot man over the age of 15, torturing and raping villagers suspected of involvement with the SLDF and, according to the local MP, Fred Kapondi, killing more than 150 people. As reported by Human Rights Watch, the Red Cross and the UN Special Rapporteur on Extrajudicial, Summary or Arbitrary Executions, Philip Alston, it seemed that the Kenyan armed forces believed they could get away with murder, and, if anyone noticed, the even worse atrocities committed by the SLDF would cover for them. In May 2008, the army cornered and shot the SLDF's military commander, 25-year-old Wycliffe Komon Matakwei, and arrested or killed most senior members of the militia, though questions remain about their funding and political control. For now, the insurgency seems to be over, but the issues of landlessness, official abuses and legal whitewash persist, as do rumours that the SLDF itself remains secretly in operation.

Once inside the park, install yourself near the gate at one of the campsites or *bandas*, or at the self-catering *Koitoboss Guest House*. These are the obvious bases for visiting the **Elkony Caves** (see below). For **Koitoboss Peak** (4187m), follow the driveable track or "Peak Road" into the moorlands to the road-head on the southern border of the park at 3500m, allowing three to four hours to cover the 30km. You leave your vehicle here, and it's a three-hour hike up the upper Kimothon valley to the pass at the southern base of Koitoboss peak, where there are flat (but cold and windy) places where you can camp. You can then make the one-hour scramble to the top, or take a two- to three-hour diversion to the Suam warm springs in the caldera.

Elkony Caves

Perhaps Elgon's most captivating attraction is the honeycomb of **caves** on the lower slopes. Some of these were long inhabited by one of the loosely related Kalenjin groups, the **Elkony** (whose name, in corrupted form, was given to the mountain), and used both as living quarters and as livestock pens at night. There is evidence that the caves had a ritual function as well – **Chepnyalil Cave** contains a structure that might have served as an altar or shrine, and its walls are painted with a red-and-white frieze of cattle. The caves are also linked with Luhya circumcision ceremonies, in which boys spent their month-long initiation period covered from head to toe in the white diatomite powder found in the area, before returning home as men. The Elkony were officially evicted from the caves by the colonial government, who insisted that they live in the open "where they could be counted for tax", but several caves were still occupied by extended families within living memory.

The largest and most spectacular cave is **Makingeny Cave**, close to the road and marked by a cascade falling over the entrance. It makes a good hike teamed up with its neighbour, **Kitum Cave**, a twenty-minute hike to the south. Early explorers believed that some of the caves were artificial, one report referring to "thousands of chisel and axe marks on the walls". In fact, generations of elephants were responsible: the well-signposted Kitum Cave was the mineral fix of local elephants, and on rare occasions they still walk into the cave at night to gouge the salt-flavoured rock from the walls with their tusks. If you're exceptionally lucky, a night vigil at Kitum Cave may be repaid by a visit from the elephants; but if not, the thousands of bats and the sounds of the forest are good compensation.

ARRIVAL AND DEPARTURE   MOUNT ELGON NATIONAL PARK

Access to the national park is easy, with two or three **matatus** most days from Kitale. If you **drive** in, you can park and hike on your own, but if you don't have your own vehicle you will need to sign a waiver form at the gate.

Crossing into Uganda If you want to cross the mountain into Uganda, make arrangements in advance with the senior warden (☎020 3539903, ✉menp@swiftkenya .com), who will coordinate with the Ugandan park authorities on the west side of the mountain; you'll be asked to pay park fees on the Ugandan side as well, and it's best to have a Ugandan visa before you cross. You'll need to hire a Kenyan ranger to accompany you as far as the warm springs on the border, where you are handed over to the care of a Ugandan ranger (or vice versa if coming the other way). If you don't already have a visa you will also have to visit Suam to complete border formalities before going through the park. The Suam border post is easily reached by road, and a lot more easy-going than those further south at Malaba and Busia. Suam is accessible by regular matatus from Kitale and Endebess. On the Ugandan side, there are matatus to Kapchorwa and thence to Mbale, where you'll find onward transport to the rest of Uganda.

ACCOMMODATION

Inside the park itself and on the slopes of the mountain, **camping** is the obvious option. The **bandas** and **guesthouse** are more comfortable and are often available on the day, but it's best to book in advance with KWS (☎020 6000800, ✉reservations@kws.go.ke).

Kapkuro 1km from the gate, in a clearing in the woods. Four good s/c *bandas*, each with a bedroom with one double and one single bed, a basic kitchen and a bathroom with hot water delivered in a bucket when required – but no electricity. BB $40
Koitoboss Guest House Just up from Chorlim Gate. If you want something more comfortable than Kapkuro, and with electricity, there's the old warden's house, which has been converted into a self-catering guesthouse set in a garden full of impala, bushbuck and waterbuck. It comes with six double beds, a well-equipped kitchen with a big fridge, two bathrooms and the generator electricity from 7pm to 10pm. A very nice spot, though a little pricey for fairly basic comforts. Whole house $180
Mount Elgon Lodge 1.5km outside the park on the track between Chorlim Gate from Kitale ☎0724 390380 or ☎0722 875768. Although it's an interesting old pile, you can't get away from the fact that the main house is desperately run-down and the ten cottage rooms in the garden only slightly less so. Camping in the grounds is an accepted, and very acceptable, alternative to taking a room (it includes use of bathroom and showers), and the food is actually pretty good. Be sure to order lunch or dinner in advance (Ksh550) and get them to show you round the old house. FB: camping Ksh600, double Ksh5400
Public campsites Near Chorlim Gate. There are three public campsites near Chorlim Gate – *Chorlim*, *Rongai* and *Nyati*. Of the three, Chorlim has the best facilities. But if you're going to be hiking deep into the park, camping in the wild is your only option. $20

Malaba and the road to Uganda

Although it's the least interesting part of western Kenya to look at – mostly undulating **grasslands** and Kenya's largest **sugar-cane** fields – the route through Malaba is a good

---

ELIJA MASINDE'S CULT OF THE ANCESTORS

In the 1940s and 1950s, there was a resurgence of **Bukusu resistance** and nationalism in the *Dini ya Msambwa* (Cult of the Ancestors) movement, spearheaded by the charismatic prophet-rebel, **Elija Masinde**. The heart of the movement was in the Elgon foothills between Kimilili and the Ugandan border. It called for the eviction of all *wazungu* and the transfer of their property to Africans. As the *Dini* spread, there were violent confrontations with colonial forces, and a number of deaths. Masinde was sent into internal exile but, since he was by then a folk hero, his followers kept the sparks of resistance alive throughout the more organized uprising of Mau Mau in the Central Highlands, until independence was finally obtained. The movement collapsed in the early years of *uhuru*, when Masinde was allowed home to Kimilili and his continued denouncements of all authority and claims to divine inspiration began to lose their coherence. Until his death in the 1990s he could still be seen on the streets of Kimilili, a rather terrifying figure shouting at the wind.

alternative to that via Busia (see p.262) for travellers passing between Kenya and Uganda, and when passenger rail services resume it will undoubtedly become the main border crossing point, as indeed it once was.

If you're making your way to the south from this district down towards Kakamega and Kisumu, the busy A1 will take you through some fine stands of tropical forest, heralding the **Kakamega Forest** to the southeast.

Chetambe's Fort

Perched above the drab town of **Webuye**, at the junction of the A1 and the A104, are the lonely remains of **Chetambe's Fort**. This was the site, in 1895, of a last-ditch stand by the Bukusu group of the Luhya tribe against the motley line-up of a British punitive expedition, which had enrolled Ugandan, Sudanese, Maasai and even other Luhya troops. A predictable massacre, in this case by Hotchkiss gun, took place, with negligible losses on the attackers' side and equally few survivors among the defenders. How the British managed to storm the scarp in the first place, however, is a mystery: presumably the Bukusu were all inside their walled fort at the top. Resistance among the Bukusu continued right up until independence (see box opposite).

The "fort" itself is quite unimpressive, and in fact not easy to make out: all that remains these days is a circular field covering several acres, surrounded by a shallow ditch. The spot where the British placed their deadly gun, opposite the fort's main entrance, is just west of the water tower and is now marked by a small concrete memorial, dated May 11, 1988 (the day the emplacement was declared a monument). The people who live nearby are glad to show visitors the site, and can tell you stories from their grandparents of finding bones in the compound area, of women coming here to weep in the evenings and of animal sacrifices to the dead warriors.

ARRIVAL AND DEPARTURE **CHETAMBE'S FORT**

The fort sits on top of the steep scarp that rears up beyond Webuye, 8km from the main A104 road.

By car From the *Webuye Falls Resort*, the local *hoteli* north of the A104, keep straight on along the *murram* road, passing the KBC transmitter towers. Bear left at a couple of small junctions, keeping to the top of the ridge. 5.1km from the resort you reach a T-junction. Here you turn sharp left and, after 400m, you reach the end of the track and the site of the fort.

By foot Alternatively, you can hike straight up the steep escarpment on foot. The trail head begins 1.5km north of the A1 Kitale road's junction with the A104, where there's a *murram* turning to the right (east) near a grove of trees and some buildings. Scramble directly up the scrubby hillside for 400m to reach the top of the ridge. The fort is 200m in front of you.

To the border: Bungoma and Malaba

The only town of any size between Webuye and the Ugandan border is **BUNGOMA**, a surprisingly animated commercial town, with its Sharriffs Centre **shopping plaza** and bustling, arcaded main street. There's a Barclays **ATM** (the first you'll find if you're coming from Uganda), but no special reason to stop.

If you're heading **south from Bungoma** on the C33, the road is good all the way to Mumias. **West of Bungoma**, the tarmac is smooth and the scenery unexciting until you reach the border crossing at **MALABA**. This is less used by passenger road traffic than Busia, but it's where most freight, as well as the (presently freight-only) rail line, crosses the border with Uganda. Endless lines of lorries choke the roads on both sides; for some, it can take days to get across. Fortunately, pedestrians can cross without difficulty. Official formalities are relatively simple, and moneychangers are on hand on both sides of the border. Try to find out the current rates in advance, watch out for scams and count the currency you're buying carefully before handing yours over.

ARRIVAL AND ACCOMMODATION   MALABA

Whether you're arriving in Kenya or departing for Uganda, you'll find the point where your **bus** drops you on one side of the border to where the bus picks you up on the other side is a long walk and it can be confusing, especially at night: it's a good idea to have a companion for the crossing, especially if you can't find a boda-boda or piki-piki to speed you across. There are several grimy budget **guesthouses** on the Kenyan side, although nothing as comfortable as what you'll find in the other border town, Busia (see p.262), and few people hang around.

By bus and matatu There are several bus companies doing the run to Nairobi via Eldoret. Matatus on the Kenyan side serve Bungoma, Kisumu and Eldoret; on the Ugandan side, they run to Tororo, Jinja and Kampala.

Jaki Guest Hotel On the south side of the main drag about 500m from the border post ☎ 055 54004.

Probably your best bet in Malaba, quiet and set back from the street, with cheap and simple doubles and singles (singles cost just Ksh500, and some have beds big enough for two). There are also pricier and fancier doubles in the main block. Room only **Ksh1000**

Mumias

MUMIAS was originally *Mumia's*, capital of the Luhya-speaking mini-state of **Wanga**, and well established by the middle of the nineteenth century at the head of an important caravan route to the coast. **King Mumia**, who came to power in 1880, was Wanga's last king and the present-day town stands on the site of his capital. His ten-thousand-strong army, half of them dispossessed Maasai from the Uasin Gishu plateau, was largely responsible for smashing Bukusu resistance at Chetambe's Fort fifteen years later (see p.301).

Even at the beginning of Mumia's reign, Europeans were beginning to arrive in the wake of Arab and Swahili slave-traders, who in turn had been settling in since the 1850s with the full accord of the Wanga royal family. By 1894 there was a permanent British sub-commissioner or collector of taxes posted here. King Mumia had always welcomed strangers, and he allowed the slavers to continue their work on other Luhya groups (notably the Bukusu), but he was unprepared for the swift usurpation of his authority by the British, whom he'd assumed were also there to trade. He was appointed "Paramount Chief" of a gradually diminishing state and then, as an old man, was retired without his real knowledge. He died in 1949, aged 100, and with him expired, almost without notice, Kenya's first and only indigenous upcountry state.

Modern Mumias is now a charming and lively little market town. The central **mosque** (by the junction of the Bungoma and Kakamega roads) was built in King Mumia's honour and its Koran school is just one of about 25 around the town. Mumias has long been a centre of Islam, famous for its coastal ways. Today, however, women in *buibuis* (the long, black coverall of the coast) are rarely seen, and Islam is losing ground to Catholicism, exemplified by the town's impressive Catholic church 2km down the Kakamega road.

ARRIVAL AND INFORMATION   MUMIAS

By matatu Matatus run from Mumias to Kisumu (2hr), Kakamega (40min), Bungoma (30min) and most other places in the district. Leaving Mumias there's a good road to Kisumu via Butere.

By bus Buses run to Kisumu (daily; 2hr), Kakamega

(4 daily; 40min) and Nairobi (2 daily; 8hr), and there are two daily services direct to Mombasa (16hr).

Services Mumias has KCB and Barclays banks with ATMs, and a handful of petrol stations.

ACCOMMODATION AND EATING

There are a couple of places to stay and eat, and numerous places to get a drink in the evening – although you might want to give *Club Hookers* a miss.

Crossroads Café Across the street from the matatu stage ☎0702 138699. Breakfasts, snacks, *nyama choma*, chicken and fish (mains Ksh300) served in a room that looks like it's been decorated for Mardi Gras, complete with crenellated pink walls, silk flowers and a non-functional fountain. Mon–Sat 5am–10pm.

Jembe Guest House Behind the matatu stage ☎0714 430863. The quieter of the two options in central Mumias, this characterless concrete tower houses very basic rooms that are certainly run-down, with only cold-water showers on offer, but are also dirt-cheap and convenient for transport. Room only Ksh600

★ **Martha's Guest House** Mundeku, 25km south of Mumias ☎0771 645330, ⊛marthasguesthousekenya .com; map p.252. Built by railway employee James Shiraku Inuyundo in 1935 and officially opened as a guesthouse by Princess Margaret in 1956, this is the quirkiest place to stay between Lake Victoria and Mount Elgon, with charming grounds, attentive service, good food and accommodation in a variety of non-s/c rooms in the main house and creatively themed chalets in the

large gardens (including a Princess Margaret Suite and an Obama Suite) – pricey, but full of character. A fascinating little museum (Ksh50 entry) crams more into one tiny hut than some of the national museums manage in a large building. To reach *Martha's*, heading south from Mumias past Butere, ask to be dropped at Khumailo. A signboard on the left indicates "Martha's Guesthouse 5km away." About 4km down this dirt road you'll see another sign pointing down a small track; it's 400m down the track, behind an anonymous green gate. Just 200m further along the dirt road, the grove of large trees on the left is Omulundu, a sacred grove of the Luhya elders, never to be cut. BB Ksh1500

St Mary's Guest House Behind St Mary's Hospital on the Kakamega road just outside town ☎0726 712382. Friendly guesthouse in the quiet hospital grounds, mainly used by visiting doctors but happy to welcome travellers as well. It's surprisingly cool and relaxing for such an institutional place, with the French windows of the spacious rooms opening out onto a garden. Most rooms are s/c, but a few are not. FB Ksh3600

Kakamega

KAKAMEGA is the headquarters of the **Luhya**, a loosely defined group of peoples whose only clear common denominator is a **Bantu language**, spoken in more than a score of vernaculars, which distinguishes them from the Luo to the south and the Kalenjin to the east. Numerically, the Luhya (also spelt Abaluhya or Luyia) are Kenya's second-largest ethnic group, and most are settled farmers.

Kakamega itself was founded as a buying station on the ox trail known as **Sclater's Road**, which reached here from the coast in 1896. Historically, its only fame came in the 1930s, when gold was discovered nearby and more than a thousand prospectors came to the region; however, very few fortunes were made. In the early 1990s Kakamega became the first town in Kenya to use the bicycle taxis known as boda-bodas, now almost a nationwide institution. Today it's a lively place, but with little to detain casual visitors. If you're passing through in August in an even-numbered year, however, it's worth being aware that some of the Luhya communities in the district are swept up in exuberant boys' **circumcision parties** – though the actual chop is usually done in hospital and the initiates themselves tend not to be the ones doing the partying. A more sedate event, the **Agricultural Society of Kenya annual show**, takes place at the town's showground every November.

ARRIVAL AND DEPARTURE   KAKAMEGA

The obvious routes out of the area lie along the **A1**, heading either north to Kitale or south to Kisumu – the latter is a real roller-coaster drive, particularly the final 8km descent over the Nyando Escarpment. An alternative onward route heads straight through the Kakamega forest via Shinyalu and out to Kapsabet, where you join an excellent tarmac highway, the **C39**, to Eldoret and rejoin the **A104**. There's also a paved road west to Mumias, with regular public transport.

By matatu Most matatus leave from the main stand on Sudi Rd, although those for Mumias have their own stand on Mumias Rd.

Destinations Kericho (3hr); Kisumu (1hr); Kitale (2hr 30min); Mumias (40min); Webuye (1hr).

By bus Coast Buses (☎0722 206453) runs direct daily services to Mombasa at 5.30pm (14hr), while the comfortable Easy Coach (☎056 30837 or ☎0738 200313) departs for Nairobi at 8.30am and 8pm (8hr). There are also a number of buses to Kisumu (8–10 daily; 1hr).

ACCOMMODATION

If you arrive here late in the day (or after around 2.30pm in a 2WD vehicle, when the rain often starts to fall), you may want to stay in town rather than arrive in the forest after dark.

Hotel Frelian Mumias Rd ☎0723 461111, ⊚bit.ly /frelian. The secure parking, clean and comfortable rooms (some with good views, all with electric showers) and *nyama choma* in the evenings make this a reasonable choice, though the noisy bar downstairs is something of a drawback. Room only Ksh1400

Golf Hotel Khasakhala Rd ☎0728 833974 or ☎0731 338705, ⊚golfhotelkakamega.com. Well-insulated rooms (nets and TVs, bathtubs and old-style showers, but no fans or a/c) in a comfortable, tourist-standard hotel from the late 1970s, its pretensions comically clipped by

the vultures hopping over the lawns. There's a large pool and gift shop, but rates for non-Kenya residents are too high. BB $126

Kakamega Guest House Along the road to Webuye, next to the Total station ☎0710 548 416 or ☎0710 548388, ⊚kakamegaguesthouse.co.ke. A big concrete tower of a hotel aimed primarily at business travellers, with spacious rooms equipped with nets, TVs and balconies – the bright corner rooms are the best. The downstairs restaurant serves beef stew, curries and the like. BB Ksh3000

EATING

In addition to the hotel dining rooms, there are some good, cheap **restaurants** in Kakamega. As for **drinking** places with character, you're spoilt for choice. For supermarkets, Tusky's on Kisumu Rd (daily 8am–9pm), and Yako Supermarket on Kenyatta Ave (daily 7.45am–8.30pm), should do the job.

★**Alberin@Lawino** Cannon Awori St ☎0701 818050. An innovative eatery specializing in western Kenyan cuisine

KAKAMEGA

("Our mission: to contribute to a healthy and safety nourishment, through indigenous African cuisines"), *Lawino* serves local dishes such as *alya* (smoked beef; Ksh250) and *isindu* (quail; Ksh200), all of it very reasonably priced. Daily 24hr.

Golf Hotel Khasakhala Rd ☎0728 833974. A reasonably priced option, considering its poolside location in the town's most upscale hotel, offering decent à la carte European food, including burgers and meal-sized salads (around Ks400), plus lunchtime buffets (Ksh1100). Daily 6.30am–9.30pm.

Wayside Palace Hotel Kenyatta Ave, next to the clock tower ☎0721 281697. A warm and friendly café (though it isn't much to look at), with great breakfasts and good local fare like tilapia (Ksh350). Mon–Sat 6am–7.30pm, Sun 9am–6pm.

DRINKING AND NIGHTLIFE

Hotel Frelian Mumias Rd ☎0723 461111, ⊚bit.ly/frelian. Below the guesthouse of the same name, this is one of the town's liveliest drinking holes, with some outdoor seating and music that pounds until around 1am. The attached restaurant serves the usual range of chicken and beef dishes, plus roasted mutton (Ksh180/quarter kilo). Daily 6–midnight, bar until 1am.

Sagittarius Mumias Rd ⊚bit.ly/sag-lounge. A cavernous bar and nightclub hung with numerous TV screens, which opens up its dancefloor every night for a mix of reggae, rumba, R'n'B and Lingala music. Daily 8am–2am.

DIRECTORY

Banks There are Barclays and Standard Chartered banks in town, both with ATMs on Kenyatta Ave.

Books Vaghela bookshop (☎0721 223799; Mon–Sat 8am– 6pm, Sun 8.30am–12.30pm), on Mumias Rd, has a small selection of Kenyan and other African fiction, though it mostly sells schoolbooks.

Internet Kakamega Cyber Café (daily 8am–8pm), by the

SomKen station on Sudi Rd, has fast connections.

Market The municipal market, next to the bus station, is very lively, particularly on Wed & Sat, when the stalls are swelled by produce from outlying rural areas. Among the local produce on offer you'll find natural remedies and medicines made from forest plants.

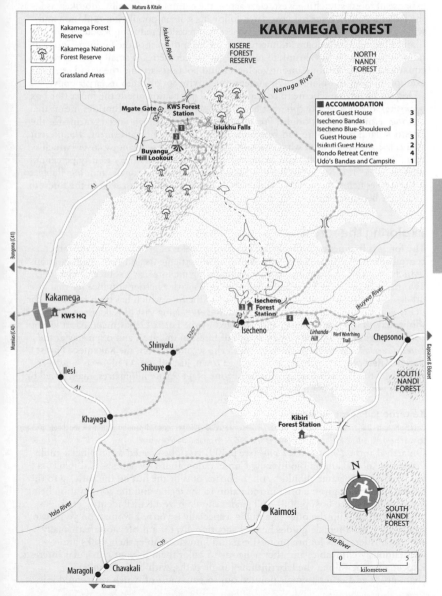

KAKAMEGA FOREST

Kakamega Forest Reserve

Kakamega National Forest Reserve

Grassland Areas

KISERE FOREST RESERVE

NORTH NANDI FOREST

Maturu & Kitale

Isiukhu River

Nanugo River

Mgate Gate

KWS Forest Station

Isiukhu Falls

Buyangu Hill Lookout

ACCOMMODATION

Forest Guest House	3
Isecheno Bandas	3
Isecheno Blue-Shouldered Guest House	3
Isukuti Guest House	2
Rondo Retreat Centre	4
Udo's Bandas and Campsite	1

Kakamega

KWS HQ

Shinyalu

Shibuye

Ilesi

Khayega

Isecheno Forest Station

Isecheno

Lirhanda Hill

Rirri Watching Trail

Chepsonoi

Ikuywo River

SOUTH NANDI FOREST

Kibiri Forest Station

Yala River

Kaimosi

SOUTH NANDI FOREST

Maragoli Chavakali

Kisumu

Bungoma (C41)

Mumias (C40)

Kapsabet & Eldoret

D267

A1

C39

Yala River

0   5
kilometres

N

Kakamega Forest

230 square kilometres

The nearby **Kakamega Forest** is one of western Kenya's star attractions, and if you have any interest at all in the natural world, it's worth going far out of your way to see. Fortunately, it's fairly easy to get to Kakamega Forest from Kisumu or, if you've been in the Mount Elgon region, from Webuye along a scenically forested stretch of the A1.

Some 400 years ago, Kakamega Forest would have been at the eastern end of a broad expanse of forest stretching west, clear across the continent, virtually unbroken as far as the Atlantic. Three hundred years later, following human population explosion and widescale cultivation, the forests everywhere had receded, reducing Kakamega to an island of some 2400 square kilometres, cut off from the rest of the Guineo-Congolan rainforest. Today, it has shrunk to just 230 square kilometres, a small patch of relict equatorial jungle, famous among zoologists and botanists around the world as an example of how an isolated environment can survive cut off from its larger body.

Despite a laudable scheme to educate the local population about the forest (see box opposite), the lack of any coherent backing or action from the authorities means that its long-term future isn't bright. Pressure from local people, who need grazing for their livestock, land to cultivate and firewood, amounts to a significant threat. The present area is less than a tenth of what it was in 1900, and its closed canopy cover (which indicates the forest's health and maturity) has dropped from ninety to fifty percent of the total area. This has led to the degradation of the natural habitat, and, inevitably, to some species being threatened, while others, like the leopard, last seen in the forest in 1992, are becoming extinct.

Exploring the forest

The forest is fragmented, interspersed with open fields of grassland, and the larger, central area has cultivated stream margins, small settlements and even tea plantations (which give the locals an alternative to plundering the forest as a source of income). Two main areas can be visited, though one comes with a heftier entrance fee than the other, and their names are confusingly similar. The first, which has been accessible for many years, is the central **Kakamega Forest Reserve**, lying east of Kakamega town, somewhat off the beaten track, and managed by the Forest Department. Most visitors come to part of one of the densest stands of forest in this area, and often stay at the *Forest Guest House* in the glade at its edge. The second section, the **Kakamega Forest National Reserve**, is northeast of Kakamega town, just off the A1 highway, and very easy to get to. This is a strictly controlled zone of 44 square kilometres, maintained by KWS more or less like a national park.

Kakamega Forest Reserve

Daily 8am–6pm • Daily "recreation" charge of Ksh600 • Guides cost Ksh500–1000 per person, depending on the walk you choose, plus any tip you care to add (Ksh300 for 3hr is about right) • ☎ 0731 790955, ⓦ kakamegarainforest.com

On arrival at the *Forest Guest House* (see p.309) you'll be greeted by an official guide (a member of Kakamega Biodiversity Conservation Tour Operatorsv– KaBiCoTOa for short), whose name should be on the board outside the hut on the path up to the house. You will be given a brief introduction to the region and the conservation being done by KEEP (see box, p.308) – all guides should have a KEEP identity card.

It's best to take up the offer of a **guide**, especially if you're a woman on your own (there are several female guides here). Exceptionally, for a profession that usually attracts hustlers, this lot are professional and knowledgeable; their walks are tremendously enjoyable, and they're happy to tailor them to your particular interests. Expect a wander along the labyrinthine jungle paths, with birds, monkeys, chameleons and other animals pointed out to you, most of which you would miss if

THE WILDLIFE OF KAKAMEGA FOREST

The Kakamega Forest is a haven of shadowy gloom for more than three hundred species of birds, 45 percent of all the butterfly species ever recorded in Kenya and seven species of primates, as well as snakes, various other reptiles and untold varieties of insects. Many of these creatures are found nowhere else in East Africa because similar habitats no longer exist. The fear now is that even this tiny surviving track of rainforest is in grave danger of being eliminated.

BIRDS

Among the commoner **birds** are the noisy and gregarious black-and-white-casqued hornbill and the very striking, deep violet Ross's turaco. You may also see familiar-looking African grey parrots and, circling above the canopy on the lookout for unwary monkeys, the huge crowned hawk eagle. Kakamega's avian stars, however, are the **great blue turacos**, glossy, turkey-sized birds like dowagers in evening gowns. They're easily located by their raucous calls: a favourite spot at dusk is the grove of very tall trees down by the pump house. They arrive each evening to crash and lurch among the branches as they select roosting sites.

MAMMALS

The forest draws mammal-watchers as well, particularly for its **monkeys**. Troops are often seen at dusk, foraging through the trees directly opposite the *Forest Guest House* veranda. Apart from the ubiquitous colobus, you can see Sykes' monkeys and the much slimmer black-cheeked white-nosed monkey (most easily recognized by its red tail). They're often seen milling around with the hornbills. You may also see pairs of giant forest squirrels capering in the treetops – the deep booming call you sometimes hear in the morning is theirs.

At **night**, armed with a powerful torch, you might catch a glimpse of bushbabies, palm civets, genets or even a potto, a slow-moving, lemur-like animal whose name aptly conveys its appearance and demeanour. The forest is also home to several species of fruit bat, of which the hammer-headed fruit bat (*Hypsignathus monstrosus*) is the largest in Africa, with a wingspan of a metre and an enormous head. Other nocturnal Kakamega specialities are the otter shrew, which lives in some of the forest streams, the tree pangolin (a kind of arboreal scaly anteater) and the flying squirrel.

REPTILES

The forest's reptiles are legendary, but few people actually see any **snakes**, and you're much more likely to come across **chameleons**. Reptiles spend a good deal of time motionless, especially when frightened, and to see snakes in the dense foliage you have to be experienced. Visible or not, however, snakes are abundant and you certainly shouldn't walk in the forest in bare feet or sandals: the sluggish gaboon viper, growing to a metre or more in length, and fatter than your arm, is a dangerous denizen of the forest floor, though not an animal that seeks confrontation. To avoid a serpentine encounter, simply walk heavily: snakes are highly sensitive to vibration and will flee at your seismic approach.

---

you went on your own. A pair of **binoculars** is more or less indispensable if you're out to watch birds.

If you have time for more than one daylight walk, you could ask a guide to show you the way to **Lirhanda Hill**, via a trail that's rich in medicinal plants. You will be shown the leaves, berries and saps that forest dwellers chew, swallow or anoint themselves with to treat various ailments. Lirhanda Hill itself is a lookout point, offering fine views over the whole expanse of forest, with the sombre bulk of Mount Elgon glowering in the distance. Cutting into the hillside near the top is a gold-mining shaft, long disused and now home to a large colony of bats. With a powerful torch and a steely nerve you can grope your way along the tunnel to meet them at close quarters.

Kakamega Forest National Reserve

Entrance to the reserve is via a signposted *murram* road some 16km northeast of Kakamega town along the A1, at a junction with a cluster of shops and *hotelis* set back from the road • $25 • ☏ 056 30603, ⓦ kws.org

Driving south down the A1 road to Kakamega from its junction with the A104 at Maturu, you enter the thick tree cover of the Kakamega forest region after about

14km. Although parts are cleared and there's no lack of people about, it's a very different environment from just about anywhere else in Kenya.

Kakamega Forest National Reserve is the part of Kakamega Forest managed by the Kenya Wildlife Service. If you've got your own vehicle, it's easier to get around this part of Kakamega forest than the Kakamega Forest Reserve central zone. The deepest and most interesting part of the forest is, in fact, a fair walk from the KWS-run *Udo's Bandas and Campsite* (see opposite), though a number of driveable and walkable tracks begin just beyond *Udo's*. You have free run of the national reserve on foot. The main trail is well signposted and there are numerous branches and "exit" trails that allow for a relatively quick return when you've had enough of the deep forest.

The most significant difference between the National Reserve here and the Forest Reserve further south is the age of the growth. Many of the **trees** are colossal. In addition, the climate is generally drier and there's a greater diversity of habitat, including ancient forest, young forest and areas of scrub. It's an impressive area and, as in the southern forest, there's a huge variety of bird and plant life, and many monkeys.

An easy excursion from the forest station is to the **Isiukhu Falls**, a rather feeble waterfall 1.5km away along a rocky path. Alternatively, you could head for **Buyangu Hill viewpoint**, a precipice with a spectacular vista east across the forest to the Nandi Escarpment. To reach the viewpoint tower, don't stop when you get up to the coniferous trees. Walk through them another 100m or so and you'll see it, up a steep rise (an easy scramble).

A longer walk leads to the **Kisere Forest Reserve**, 5km from Mgate Gate: a separate, outlying part of the main reserve, four kilometres square and home to de Brazza's monkeys and other species, as well as some superb examples of the prized Elgon olive timber tree. Ask the rangers for directions.

ARRIVAL AND DEPARTURE   KAKAMEGA FOREST

BY CAR

Whichever of the two approaches described below you take, track surfaces get treacherously slippery in wet weather. Given the predictable afternoon rains, this limits you to arriving between 10am and 2pm, when the road is at its driest. Even so, 4WD is advisable.

From Kakamega via Khayega From Kakamega, the easiest approach road is from Khayega, 7km south of Kakamega on the A1. The junction is marked by signposts for the Arap Moi Girls' School and the Office of the President. From here, an earth road leads 6km to Shinyalu. Keep right at Shinyalu and continue for another 5.3km to Isecheno, turning left just after the barrier and a signposted arrow. From the barrier, it's less than 1km up the trail to the *Forest Guest House*.

From Eldoret via Kapsabet Approaching from Eldoret via Kapsabet, the road into the forest starts at Chepsonoi, on the C39 where you take the right turning (west), signposted "Kisieni 12km D267".

BY PUBLIC TRANSPORT

From Kakamega From Kakamega, the cheapest way of reaching the forest on public transport is to catch a matatu to Shinyalu (there are occasional matatus from Khayega to Shinyalu too, or you could take a boda-boda from there). Alternatively, a private taxi from Kakamega to Shinyalu (or the *Forest Guest House* if you're lucky) will cost Ksh1500–2000. It's a lovely hour-long walk to Isecheno from Shinyalu, while Shinyalu itself often has a cattle auction and a major market on Saturdays, when it's worth pausing an hour to soak up the atmosphere of cowboys in the jungle.

"KEEP OUR FOREST"

The Kakamega Environmental Education Programme, or **KEEP** (Ⓦ keep-kakamega.or.ke), was set up by the guides at *Forest Guest House* to combine visits to the forest for local schoolchildren with their school lessons. They hope that by convincing the children of the importance of the forest, the message will spread into the community. A tree nursery has been started to demonstrate basic tree-planting techniques, alongside information on waste recycling and efficient use of firewood. In addition, a butterfly farm has been set up, with the aim of breeding local butterflies to frame and sell as souvenirs, generating income for the local community from the forest itself. Other sustainable projects in the pipeline include bee keeping and snake farming (for antivenin). They're always looking for volunteers – contact them through the website above.

From Eldoret Any bus or matatu heading from Eldoret towards Kisumu via Kapsabet, Chavakali and Maragoli will pass the turning for Isecheno at Chepsonoi. From here, if you don't get a lift, it takes about 3hr to walk through the magnificent forest to the Central District HQ at Iescheno.

INFORMATION

For all matters relating to Kakamega Forest visit the **Kenya Wildlife Service** office in Kakamega ($\bullet$ 056 30603; Mon–Fri 8am–5pm): go past the *Golf Hotel*, right at the roundabout, follow the road past the DC's office (which it's behind) to the next junction, turn left and it's on the left after 50m.

ACCOMMODATION

If you stay in one of the Isecheno places (the *Forest Guest House* or *Isecheno Bandas*) the closest reliable **supplies** are at the *dukas* about 3km away on the road to Shinyalu, meaning that it's best to bring your own food. For candles and simple staples – bananas, *chai*, mineral water, biscuits, sodas and sometimes beer – there's a small *duka* (open daily) on the way to the pump house. They also cook inexpensive meals to order, given a few hours' notice.

Forest Guest House Central District HQ $\bullet$020 2315979 or $\bullet$0721 711293. If you're not too fussy about comforts this wooden chalet is a delight – a kind of budget *Treetops* without the crowds. There are four twin rooms up on the first floor, with a long veranda facing the wall of forest. There's basic bedding, but you might bring a blanket or sleeping bag, as it can get decidedly chilly early in the morning. There's no electricity, but each room has a functioning bathroom and toilet. BB $\underline{Ksh1000}$

Isecheno Bandas Next to the Forest Guest House $\bullet$0726 951764, $\textcircled{w}$kakamegarainforest.com. KEEP's own *bandas* are located right next to the *Forest Guest House*, but instead of going to the park, the money is used locally for KEEP's ongoing community conservation projects. There are five cute, non-s/c *bandas*, with beds, blankets, sheets and pillows, and a separate shower (hot water on request) and toilet block. As at the *Forest Guest House*, you can either bring food and firewood to self-cater, or make arrangements locally to have meals provided. BB $\underline{Ksh1800}$

Isecheno Blue-Shouldered Guest House 500m south of the Central District HQ $\bullet$0722 886833, $\textcircled{e}$blueshouldered@yahoo.com. Quirky little homestay named after the blue-shouldered robin-chat, one of Kakamega's unusual birds. Sleeping five people in three rooms, the house has a veranda from where you can watch monkeys in the trees opposite. There are also ten bunk beds in a spacious dorm, all with nets and separated from the main house in a well-appointed *banda*. Meals are made to order (or bring food and cook your own in the spotless kitchen), and forest walks available (the owner is a Kakamega guide). Dorm beds $\underline{Ksh900}$, BB $\underline{Ksh1800}$

Isukuti Guest House 1.2km from the main gate, Just before Udo's as you come into the reserve $\bullet$020 6000800, $\textcircled{e}$reservations@kws.go.ke. This guesthouse has four beds in two rooms, a bathroom and kitchen, and is a good deal more spacious and comfortable than *Udo's*, but lacks atmosphere. Book In advance with KWS. BB $\underline{\$60}$

Rondo Retreat Centre 2.5km east of the Isecheno junction $\bullet$0735 894474, $\textcircled{w}$rondoretreat.com. Kakamega Forest's most upmarket option, situated in a fine old sawmiller's house built in 1948. This "Christian sanctuary for nature lovers" – owned by a group called the Trinity Fellowship – has wonderful, bright bedrooms in cottages set among cool lawns. It's fresh and elegant, with just enough clutter and lack of uniformity to make it feel homely. There's great birdwatching, butterfly-spotting and flower-enjoying too, but they don't serve alcohol (though you can bring your own). HB $\underline{Ksh20,000}$

★**Udo's Bandas and Campsite** 300m from the northern reserve boundary and under 2km from Mgate Gate $\bullet$020 6000800, $\textcircled{e}$reservations@kws.go.ke. Named after the ornithologist Udo Savalli, these six simple thatched non-s/c rondavels (five twins and one quad), with bedding, nets and padlocks on the doors, come with a few pieces of cane furniture, but no other comforts, plus basic cold showers and long-drop toilets nearby. It's basic, but the forest environment touches it with a little magic. Book in advance with KWS. Camping $\underline{\$20}$, BB $\underline{\$60}$

4

The national parks and Mombasa highway

LIONS IN THE MAASAI MARA

5

The national parks and Mombasa highway

This chapter covers the well-travelled route from Nairobi to Mombasa and a number of detours off it, along with the country's most visited game parks: Maasai Mara, Amboseli, Meru, Chyulu Hills, Tsavo East and West, and a trio of reserves in the north – Samburu, Buffalo Springs and Shaba. The Mombasa highway (the A109) is Kenya's most important thoroughfare and overall is in good condition, although with a constant stream of heavy trucks it can be a hair-raising drive. With scenic interest marginal for much of the journey, the temptation is to head straight for the coast, stopping only at the Amboseli or Tsavo national parks. But there are some rewarding diversions off the highway, which are not greatly explored: east into Kamba country and the pleasant towns of Machakos and Kitui, or west towards the base of Kilimanjaro and the Taita Hills.

Together with the coast, the **game parks** in this chapter are the most visited parts of Kenya, and the country's archetypal image. This is not to take anything away from their appeal, for visiting any of them is an exceptional experience. In the 24,000 square kilometres covered by the nine parks, animals hold sway. Their seasonal cycles and movements, most spectacularly in the Maasai Mara's **wildebeest migration**, are the dominant plots in the natural drama going on all around. Seeing the wildlife isn't difficult, but it does require some patience and an element of luck that makes it exciting and addictive.

It's likely that you will either already be booked on a safari, or you'll book one once in Kenya, either from the coast or from Nairobi. Popular alternatives are to **rent a vehicle**, with or without a driver, or, if you're alone or there are just two of you, and especially if you're on a limited budget, to take a **no-frills camping safari**. There are details on the ins and outs of booking safaris in "Basics" (see p.78), and plenty of operators in Nairobi (see p.123) and Mombasa (see p.404).

Ukambani

One very good way to start a trip heading towards the coast, if you're in no particular hurry, is to take an excursion right into the heart of **Ukambani**, the land of the Kamba people.

HOT AIR BALLOON OVER WILDEBEEST, MAASAI MARA

Highlights

❶ Umani Springs This stunning yet affordable designer lodge nestles deep inside the Kibwezi forest, just a short drive from the Mombasa highway. **See p.324**

❷ The Taita Hills The densely cultivated and untouristy Taita Hills rise steeply from the dry plains. Visit the skull caves, where the heads of Taita ancestors are interred. **See p.331**

❸ Amboseli National Park Seeing *that* view of Kilimanjaro towering above the elephants in the marshes and grazing plains game is the highlight of this easy-to-visit park. **See p.337**

❹ Mzima Springs A remarkable oasis, bubbling with crystal-clear water and inhabited by hippos, crocodiles and a variety of other species, some of which can be seen from the underwater viewing chamber. **See p.347**

❺ The migration At any time of the year, the Maasai Mara yields an extraordinary wildlife spectacle, but a visit during the annual wildebeest migration can be truly awe-inspiring. **See p.363**

❻ Mara Naboisho Conservancy A shining example of conservation, community involvement and superb safari experiences. **See p.373**

❼ Meru National Park Despite being home to the Big Five, Meru remains little visited, making game drives here an almost personal adventure. **See p.382**

HIGHLIGHTS ARE MARKED ON THE MAP ON P.314

5

Machakos

The biggest town in Ukambani, with a population of roughly 150,000, the bustling, good-natured trading centre of **MACHAKOS**, is, after Nairobi, the main urban focus for the Kamba people. Imperial British East African Company's first upcountry post, Machakos was established in 1889, and is therefore ten years older than Nairobi, 65km to the northwest; the capital was moved to Nairobi in 1899 as Machakos was bypassed by the Uganda Railway, then under construction.

Distinctly friendly, Machakos has a backdrop of green hills and a tree-shaded, relaxed atmosphere to its old buildings that is quickly endearing. The weaving of **sisal baskets** (*vyondo*) is a visible industry and a major occupation for many women, either full-time, or behind the vegetable stands in the market. Machakos effervesces and it's a great place to visit for the day or to overnight from Nairobi, especially on the major market days of

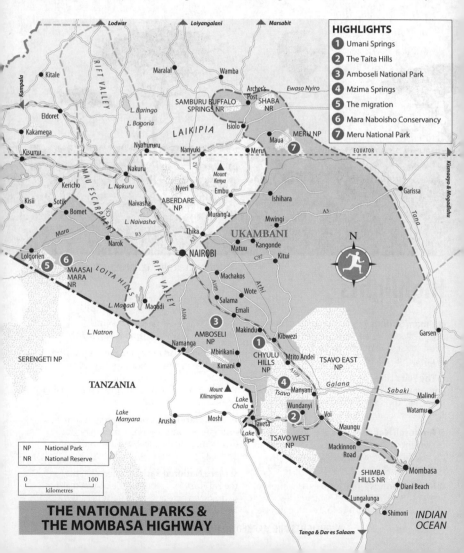

HIGHLIGHTS

1. Umani Springs
2. The Taita Hills
3. Amboseli National Park
4. Mzima Springs
5. The migration
6. Mara Naboisho Conservancy
7. Meru National Park

| NP | National Park |
| NR | National Reserve |

0 ——— 100
kilometres

THE NATIONAL PARKS & THE MOMBASA HIGHWAY

Monday and Friday. Look out for (though you can scarcely miss) the truly splendid and quite venerable **mosque** and the fine, upstanding **Catholic cathedral**, Our Lady of Lourdes. Despite its significance, you can walk round the compact centre of Machakos in twenty minutes.

Machakos People's Park

1.5km west of town off the approach road from the Mombasa highway • Thurs 2–9pm, Fri 10am–10pm, Sat & Sun 10am–11pm (closed Mon–Wed) • Free

Only really worth mentioning as it's signposted everywhere, the huge **Machakos People's Park** was opened in 2014 as a public recreation area. It features grassy lawns,

---

THE KAMBA

The largely dry stretch of central Kenya from Nairobi to Tsavo and north as far as Embu has been the homeland of the **Kamba people** for at least five centuries. Also called the Akamba or Wakamba, they moved here from the regions to the south in a series of vague migrations, in search, according to legend, of the life-saving **baobab** tree, whose fruit can stave off the worst famines, and whose trunks hold large quantities of water.

With a diverse economy in better years, including mixed farming and herding as well as hunting and gathering, the Kamba slowly coalesced into a distinct tribe with one (Bantu) language. As they settled in the hilly parts, the population increased. But drier areas at lower altitudes couldn't sustain the expansion, so **trade** for food with the Kikuyu peoples in the more fertile highlands region became a solution to the vagaries of their generally implacable environment.

In return for farm produce, the Kamba **bartered** their own manufactured goods: medicinal charms, extra-strong beer, honey, iron tools, arrowheads and a lethal and much-sought-after hunting poison. In the eighteenth and nineteenth centuries, as the Swahili on the coast strengthened their ties inland, **ivory** became the most important commodity in the trade network. With it, the Kamba obtained goods from overseas to exchange for food stocks with the highland tribes.

Long the **intermediaries** between coast and upcountry, the Kamba acted as guides to Swahili and Arab caravans, and led their own expeditions. Settling in small numbers in many parts of what is now Kenya, they were naturally enlisted by the early European arrivals in East Africa. Their broad cultural base and lack of provincialism made them confident travellers and employees, and willing porters and soldiers. Serving alongside British troops during **World War I** gave them insights into the ways of the Europeans who now ruled them. Together with the Luo and Kikuyu, they suffered tens of thousands of casualties in the white men's wars. Even today, the Kenyan army has a disproportionately high Kamba contingent, while many others work in the police and as private security guards.

In the early years of **colonialism**, the Kamba were involved in occasional bloody incidents, but these were usually more the result of misunderstandings than any concerted rebellion. Although there was a major ruckus after an ignorant official at Machakos cut down a sacred *ithembo* tree to use as a flagpole, on the whole their trade networks and diplomatic skills helped to ease their relations with the British. As early as 1911, however, a Kamba movement rejecting European ways had emerged. Led by a widow named **Siotune wa Kathake**, it channelled opposition to colonialism into frenetic dancing, during which teenage girls became "possessed" by an anti-European spirit and preached radical messages of non-compliance with the government. Later, in the 1930s, the Ukamba Members Association (one of whose leaders was **Muindi Mbingu**) was formed in order to pre-empt efforts to settle Europeans in Ukambani and reduce Kamba cattle herds by compulsory purchase. Five thousand Kamba marched in peaceful protest to Kariokor market in Nairobi – a show of collective political will that succeeded in getting their cattle returned – and the settlers never came to Ukambani in any numbers.

Wamunyu, midway between Machakos and Kitui, was the birthplace of the modern Kamba **woodcarving industry**. Kamba men who served in World War I were introduced to the techniques of wood sculpture by the Makonde ebony carvers of the Tanganyikan coast. Today, the vast majority of woodcarvings in Kenya are still produced by Kamba artists, often in workshops far from Ukambani.

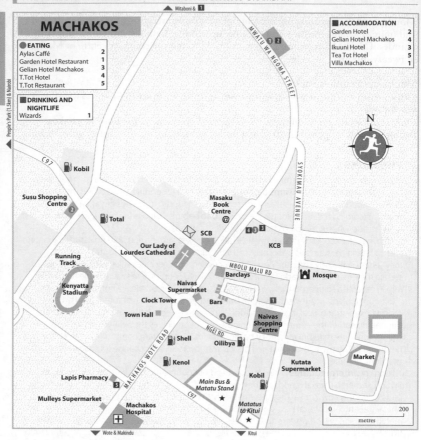

paved walkways, fountains, an ornamental lake and some fairground rides for small children and is a popular venue for picnics at the weekend.

ARRIVAL AND DEPARTURE MACHAKOS

By bus and matatu There's a steady stream of buses to Nairobi (2hr), Mombasa (8hr) and Voi (6hr), leaving from the main stage in the centre of town. The bus stand for Kitui (1hr 30min), which has connections for Thika, Embu and Mwingi, spreads around the corner of the Kitui road (C97).
By car It's a 1hr 30min drive (depending on the traffic) from Nairobi to the Machakos turnoff on the Mombasa highway (A109) and then a further 15km (20min) into town.

ACCOMMODATION

Garden Hotel Mwatu Wa Ngoma St, 1km north of .the town centre ☎0722 585637, ⍟gardenhotel .co.ke. In the quieter part of Machakos, with views of the Iveti Hills, this large hotel has carpeted rooms with nets and TV, but it's old-fashioned, with dated fixtures and fittings, so feels overpriced for what you get. BB **Ksh5500**
★**Gelian Hotel Machakos** Mwatu Wa Ngoma St ☎0710 551611, ⍟gelianhotel.com. In a brand-new eight-storey tower block, this well-designed and comfortable hotel has good views across town. The

hundred-plus neat and modern rooms have made-for-hotel furnishings, DSTV, safes and a/c, and there's a swimming pool, gym and restaurants. All up, the best in town and with excellent service. Wi-fi. BB **$150**
Ikuuni Hotel Between Mwatu Wa Ngoma St and Syokimau Ave, near KCB ☎0711 465344. Busy watering hole and restaurant sitting right in the shadow of the *Gelian Hotel*, with five s/c (double bed) and five non-s/c (mix of twin and double) rooms – all well kept, if nothing out of the ordinary, with nets, TVs and hot

water (most of the time). Basic *hoteli* meals are available. S/c BB Ksh2800

Tea Tot Hotel Machakos Wote Rd, opposite Machakos Hospital ☎044 20577 or ☎0718 009684, ⓦteatot.co.ke. To enhance the confusion of there being two restaurants in town called *Tea Tot*, there's also a hotel of the same name. The spotless and neatly kept, if plain, rooms have nets, DSTV and electric showers and there's a restaurant serving basic meals on a balcony. BB Ksh5200

Villa Machakos Off Kangundo Rd, 1.5 km north of Machakos centre ☎0707 038048 or ☎0718 770066, ⓦvillamachakos.co.ke. Near Machakos Golf Club, this is another new setup so everything is (for now) fresh and neat. The nine nicely decorated rooms have DSTV and tea and coffee facilities, plus there's a small restaurant with garden tables serving breakfast, sandwiches and hot meals such as curries or steaks. Wi-fi. BB $80

EATING

★**Aylas Caffé** Susu Shopping Centre, opposite Kobil ☎0703 249189. Slick new café with an even slicker coffee machine offering cappuccinos and lattes made from Java coffee beans, plus food including a full English breakfast (Ksh500), sandwiches and salads (Ksh250) and more elaborate main meals like T-bone steak or whole tilapia (Ksh700). There are sunny courtyard tables and you can park outside. Wi-fi. Daily 8am–10pm.

Garden Hotel Restaurant Mwatu Wa Ngoma St, 1km north of the town centre ☎0722 585637, ⓦgardenhotel.co.ke. Good-value snacks and main meals, including salads (Ksh200), sandwiches (Ksh150–250) and buffets (Ksh900). The outside garden bar is very pleasant but the inside restaurant is rather gloomy. Daily 10am–11pm.

★**Gelian Hotel Machakos** Mwatu Wa Ngoma St

☎0710 551611, ⓦgelianhotel.com. Currently the best in town but with prices to match, this smart new hotel has a bakery in the lobby for snacks, sandwiches and pastries, and a bar next to the pool, while the main restaurant offers European-style dishes (from Ksh800) and weekend buffets (Ksh1200). Wi-fi. Daily 7am–10pm.

★**T.Tot Hotel** Ngei Rd ☎0735 135558. This canteen-style place is deservedly busy with a steady turnover of satisfied customers tucking into pilau (Ksh200), chapattis and soup (Ksh110), kebabs (Ksh80), fruit salad (Ksh60) and the like, served by efficient staff. Daily 6am–9.30pm.

T.Tot Restaurant Ngei Rd. The newer neighbour, slightly undercutting the more established *T.Tot Hotel*, with *sukuma nyama* (Ksh100), chapattis and soup (Ksh110), fruit salad (Ksh50) and other dishes. Daily 6am–9.30pm.

DRINKING AND NIGHTLIFE

For a cold beer, there are a number of bars lining the little square north of Ngei Road (turn up the side street alongside the Naivas Shopping Centre), where there are plastic chairs and tables to sit out. Most are so-called sports bars.

Wizards Off Syokimau Ave, behind Naivas Shopping Centre ⓦbit.ly/WizardsMachakos. On the first floor above a row of small shops, this is a popular local pub for

watching football, while the club/disco section gets very lively on Fri & Sat nights (entry Ksh200–300). Daily 7am–late.

DIRECTORY

Banks Barclays, Standard Chartered and KCB all have ATMs.

Markets and supermarkets Apart from the town's many produce markets, there are several well-stocked supermarkets, including the twin Naivas supermarkets on

Ngei Road in the town centre.

Pharmacy Lapis Pharmacy (Mon–Sat 8am–8pm, Sun 11am–6pm), next to *Tea Tot Hotel* reception, is a good chemist.

Kitui

The small town of **KITUI** is a busy trading centre, its streets lined with arcaded shops, although it has no sights. Like Machakos, 100km to the west on the C97, it has sizeable populations of coastal Swahili and Somali people, descendants of the traders and travellers who criss-crossed Ukambani in the nineteenth century. The town's mango trees were planted then, and are a reminder of the trading tradition.

Kitui was the home village of **Kivoi**, the most celebrated Kamba trader, who commanded a large following that included slaves. It was Kivoi who met the German missionary **Ludwig Krapf** in Mombasa, and who guided him to Kitui in 1849, from where he became the first European to set eyes on Mount Kenya.

ARRIVAL AND DEPARTURE

By bus and matatu The bus and matatu stage is right in the middle of town, 450m from the junction with the B7.

Destinations Kibwezi (4hr); Machakos (1hr 30min); Mombasa (5 nightly; 8hr); Nairobi (several daily via Thika; 4hr); Thika (2hr), where you can connect to Embu.

By car The B7 road heads north to Kangonde (57km from Kitui), where it joins the A3. Tarred and in good condition, the A3 leads northeast to Mwingi and Garissa and west to Matuu and Thika. Using the B7, A3 and A2 route via Thika, you can reach Nairobi in under 3hr. Travelling south, the Kitui–Kibwezi section of the B7 is a slog of 3hr-plus – some 20–30km at each end is reasonably graded but the rest is mostly rough gravel and in poor condition. If you'd rather drive on tarmac, it's better to use the longer route (4hr) via Machakos and the Mombasa highway.

ACCOMMODATION

Kitui-Mwingi Parkside Motel 800m northwest of Kitui centre ☎044 4423026 or ☎0701 023026, ⓦ kituiparkvilla.com. Formerly *Parkside Villa* (and still being rebuilt at the time of writing), this large hotel is currently the best in town, though it mainly hosts seminars, conferences and weddings, so can be busy and noisy. Set in blocks and cottages in a large garden compound, the 100-plus decent rooms have nets, DSTV and electric showers. The Kamba Cultural Centre crafts shops (see opposite) are at the front. There are plans to build a pool. Wi-fi. BB **Ksh3200**

Rosen Guest House Mbusyani Rd ☎0711 772843. Small and neat B&L with a few rooms, of which #5 (very small) and #6 (slightly more room), with a shared balcony overlooking the street, are easily the best, although there is only one barely double bed in each. Nets, TVs, electric showers; the parking in front is guarded by an *askari*. BB **Ksh1100**

Talents Guest House Northwest of Kitui centre ☎0711 963222. Clean if somewhat cramped rooms, with electric showers, nets and TVs. Also safe courtyard parking and, as it's on a cul-de-sac, a pleasant, paved area to sit outside at the front of the hotel. BB **Ksh2200**

EATING

Flavours/Flavas Kitui centre. Co-owned with *Talents Guest House*, with a first-floor terrace that is Kitui's best people-watching address. Meals are appetizing and well presented by switched-on staff (chicken mixed grill Ksh350, beef stew with *githeri* Ksh300). Mon–Sat 7am–9pm (closed Sun).

Kitui-Mwingi Parkside Motel 800m northwest of Kitui centre ☎044 4423026 or ☎0701 023026, ⓦ kituiparkvilla.com. If you're driving, this is the best option to pull into (even if not staying) as it has a secure gated car park. Food encompasses good breakfasts and local dishes, and decent non-Kenyan food like meatballs and spaghetti (Ksh700) or steak and chips (Ksh700). The bar (behind a metal grill) gets lively and a band plays on the little stage on Fri and Sat nights. Daily 6am–11pm (later on Fri & Sat).

Parkside Hotel Mbusyani Rd. Busy and popular, with a terrace as well as indoor tables and offering nourishing staples such as *githeri* and *matoke* (Ksh150), chicken pilau (Ksh300) and fruit salad (Ksh100). Daily 6am–9.30pm.

Riverside Bar & Hotel Kalundu Market, 1km from central Kitui. A big *nyama choma* joint owned by

Kitui-Mwingi Parkside Motel that's dead during the day, but lively every evening, when they play music. Take your pick of goat (Ksh400/kg) or chicken (Ksh700 whole) with *sukuma* (Ksh50), washed down with cheap beer or South African box wine. Daily 24hr.

SHOPPING

Kitui Kamba Cultural Centre Front grounds of the Parkside Villa Hotel. Row of crafts shops, each selling a particular output of the local crafts industry, including baskets, woodcarvings and jewellery. Prices are fixed

but fair (medium *vyondo* sisal baskets Ksh800), and each item is identified with its creator so the money goes back to the right people. Mon–Sat 8am–5.30pm, Sun 2–6pm.

DIRECTORY

Banks KCB and Barclays have ATMs.
Markets and supermarkets The biggest and best-stocked supermarket in town is Naivas on Mbusyani Road

in the town centre (Mon–Sat 6.45am–8.30pm, Sun 7.45am–8.15pm). Happy Family and Kitui supermarkets are long-standing standbys.

The Thika–Garissa Road

The A3 is an important artery to the east and is in good condition for most of the way (323km) between Thika (see p.162) and Garissa (see p.540), though expect lots of police roadblocks. It may look like an alternative route to the coast to the obvious, traffic choked Mombasa highway on the map, but it would be very ill-advised to head this way under current circumstances (see box, p.541). In the event that things improve for casual travellers, we've included here a couple of stop-offs with facilities for drivers.

A thriving trading centre 62km beyond Thika, **MATUU** is busiest at the top of the hill, near the easternmost of the town's two communications masts, where you'll find most shops and businesses, though its one good hotel (and petrol stations and bus passenger cafés) are all on the A3.

Another 67km on, **MWINGI** has a surprisingly attractive location in an area of rocky hillocks and woodland. Coming from the Thika direction, you first see the town more than 10km before you arrive, spread out across the boulder-dotted hills. Mwingi offers plenty of small places to eat and a decent hotel.

ARRIVAL AND INFORMATION THE THIKA–GARISSA ROAD

By bus and matatu There's no shortage of vehicles passing along the highway, though as usual pickings thin out in the afternoon. They take around 4hr from Mwingi to Nairobi (or the reverse) via Thika, and 3hr from Matuu. Vehicles run frequently between Kitui and Matuu (less than 1hr).

By car It's an easy drive of around an hour from Thika to Matuu, and a further hour's drive will see you in Mwingi. From there, allow 3hr to reach Garissa.

Services Matuu's KCB and Equity banks have ATMs; Mwingi has a KCB ATM. Both have a couple of small supermarkets.

ACCOMMODATION AND EATING

MATUU

Ndallas Hotel On the A3 out towards Thika ☎0713 662662, ⓦbit.ly/NdallasHotelMatuu. The biggest establishment in Matuu with rooms of varying quality (avoid paying even more for a deluxe room: they have carpets, which are hard to keep clean), though they all have nets, DSTV and hot water (in theory, 6pm–6am). Also has pleasant terraces, a bar and restaurant and safe parking. BB **Ksh3100**

MWINGI

Legacy Hotel Mwingi Off the A3 in the middle of town, just south of the KCB ☎0701 075402, ⓦlegacyhotelmwingi.com. The best option along the stretch by far, and well priced, this hotel offers neat rooms with modern furnishings, nets, DSTV, tiled bathrooms, and a bar-restaurant. The leafy gardens have a *nyama choma* spot in a pagoda-style structure and a welcome and well-kept pool. Secure parking; wi-fi. BB **Ksh2500**

5

Nairobi to Namanga

The A104, which used to be the main route to Amboseli National Park – now mainly accessed via Emali (see p.322) – links Nairobi with Arusha in Tanzania. Going south, the largely dull Kapiti plains are broken only by the **Maasai Ostrich Farm** (see p.151), signposted 7km off to the west, 15km south of Athi River. Further south still and about 80km from Nairobi, in the gentle hills where Maasai country really begins, is the district capital of **KAJIADO**. Set among sisal spikes and acacias, it's a friendly market town, where Maasai in all their gear mix with other Kenyans, and there's a fascinating daily **market**, where everyday Maasai commodities such as vegetables, spices, millet, sandals and blankets are traded. The scenic interest picks up south of Kajiado, as the road snakes into the hills, giving views of the conical Mount Meru in Tanzania (4565m), and, if the sky is clear, your first glimpses of Kilimanjaro.

Namanga

The hot frontier town of **NAMANGA** sits on the Kenya–Tanzania border, nestled in a wooded valley between steep hills, 160km south of Nairobi and 130km north of Arusha. It's a big **Maasai** trading centre, and Maasai women hawk armloads of beaded jewellery and other crafts around the dusty car park and at the petrol stations at the border. They can be a little aggressive, but with a bit of good-natured haggling you can get a decent price and put a little money into the local economy.

Namanga lies mostly in Kenya, and crossing the (24hr) border can be hectic (it's often busy) but the process is fairly easy.

ARRIVAL AND INFORMATION NAMANGA

By bus and matatu There are frequent services to Nairobi (4hr) and Arusha (3hr), plus the Nairobi–Arusha–Nairobi "shuttle" buses (see p.120) passing through, which often have the odd empty seat.

Services There's a KCB with ATM about 500m before the border. Ignore the illegal black-market moneychangers at the border: wait until you get to a bank in Arusha to get Tanzanian shillings as there's little opportunity to spend any money before you get there.

ACCOMMODATION

Namanga River Hotel On the right as you arrive in town ☎0733 440089 or 0722 440089. A colonial-era oddity, composed of wooden cabins set amid pretty gardens, this was once the halfway house on the old safari trail between Nairobi and Arusha. The place has a likeable atmosphere, and rooms have nets and decent bathrooms, but uncertain hot water. The restaurant is reasonable (lunch Ksh750) and meals are served in the garden. You can also camp in the grounds, using the shower provided and toilet block. Camping <u>Ksh700</u>, BB <u>Ksh4300</u>

The Mombasa highway

The **Mombasa highway** (A109) is the main road linking Nairobi and Mombasa, and for the majority of its distance (482km) runs adjacent to the Nairobi–Mombasa rail line, a branch of the historic Uganda Railway (see box, p.322). It's regarded as the busiest (and most dangerous) road in the country thanks to the constant stream of trucks carrying goods along it from the port of Mombasa to be distributed in Nairobi and beyond.

The largest town on the highway is the sisal-processing centre of **Voi**, about two-thirds of the way to Mombasa. Before and after Voi are a string of smaller highway service towns, not much more than a scruffy line of petrol stations, *dukas* and roadside vendors, though they provide an opportunity for a break from the hectic drive. There are, however, several wildlife-related places where you might think about stopping over for a day or two, including the **Kibwezi Forest** and **Ngutuni Game Sanctuary** – as well as

Tsavo East (see p.351) and **Tsavo West** (see p.346) national parks.

As you travel south down the highway, you may, in exceptionally clear conditions, see Kilimanjaro, either on the stretch between the small settlements of Sultan Hamud and Kiboko, or to the west of the Tsavo River. Your best chances are in the early morning or late afternoon.

GETTING AROUND THE MOMBASA HIGHWAY

By bus and matatu Try to avoid using matatus for travelling on the highway, as their constant stopping for passengers makes them more dangerous than usual. There's little need to use them anyway as going by bus you can always ask to be dropped at the towns along the highway if you want to make a stopover or take a detour. Most buses break their journeys at Voi and Mtito Andei, and most companies will give you a part-refund on the full fare if you alight early.

By car Don't expect to drive fast on the highway – the hundreds of trucks plying this route sometimes slow progress down to little more than 40kmph at times. Be very wary about overtaking and only do so when you are sure there is a long clear view. The journey from Nairobi to Voi can take up to 5hr, while Mombasa is roughly a 7hr drive, not counting congestion at either end. There are big filling stations at all the towns along the highway, although the gaps that sometimes catch drivers out are the 65km stretch between the junction for Machakos and Sultan Hamud, and the 97km between Mtito Andei and Voi.

Athi River to Emali

Heading southeast from central Nairobi, the road runs along the east side of Nairobi National Park, passing the turnoff to the airport on the left, and then goes through the industrial zone on the south side of the city until it reaches the town (although really a suburb now) of **Athi River**. Here is a tangled junction where the A104 branches off for **Namanga** (on the Tanzanian border) and **Arusha**. The highway continues southwest, skirting the Kapiti Plains on your right into semi-arid open country.

After Athi River it's just over 40km to the junction with the C97 towards Machakos see p.314). Beyond is the dreary drive to the truckers' stopover of

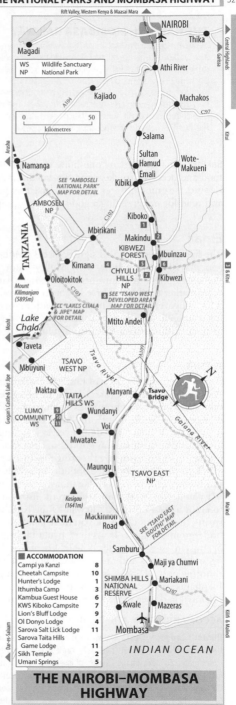

THE NAIROBI–MOMBASA HIGHWAY

5

THE NAIROBI–MOMBASA RAILWAY

Views along from the Mombasa highway are far from scenic at present, as the Chinese are building a new standard-gauge railway alongside the old narrow-gauge line. This massive $13.8 billion rail project, which began in December 2014, will eventually replace the existing line and is part of a package of deals signed between Kenya and China in 2013. Construction is well underway on Kenya's biggest engineering project since independence, and when it's completed (scheduled to be 2018), the new line is expected to cut travel time from Nairobi to Mombasa to four hours for passengers, and eight hours for freight trains. When all the temporary road- and rail-side equipment has been removed, the landscape should hopefully return to its bush-like state.

Salama, the first of many one-horse towns on the way to Mombasa, providing lodging, food and beers for truckers and lost-looking Maasai. The next settlement, **Sultan Hamud**, isn't much bigger, but does have fuel pumps (though no formal filling station) and roadside *dukas* selling a good variety of prepared fruit and other snacks.

Emali

The first centre of any real significance is **EMALI**, which lies on the boundary of Kamba and Maasai territory. It has a big Mulleys Supermarket (with parking outside), which is the last stop for provisions before Amboseli National Park and the biggest formal supermarket until Voi. Three kilometres east of Emali, just after the new Chinese railway flyover, a sharp turn to the south marks the start of the fine new C102 highway, for Amboseli, the western flanks of the Chyulu Hills, Oloitokitok (on the northern slopes of Kilimanjaro) and the Chyulu Gate of Tsavo West National Park.

Kiboko

At the petrol-station oasis of **KIBOKO**, 160km from Nairobi, there's accommodation on offer in the shape of *Hunter's Lodge*, named after Scottish-born **John Alexander Hunter** (aka J.A. Hunter) – a notorious "white hunter" between the early 1900s and the late 1950s. After World War II, the Makueni area southeast of Machakos (including present-day Kiboko) was designated as a Kamba resettlement area, and the Kenya Game Department sent in Hunter to clear it of unwelcoming rhinos – which he did (living up to his name) by shooting 996 black rhinos. In later years, before his death in 1963, he became concerned about the possible extinction of the wildlife he had so assiduously hunted, and spoke in favour of conservation.

If you need a break from driving, the lush gardens at *Hunter's Lodge* are a good place to enjoy a meal or drink. They sit by the Kiboko River, fed by the nearby Kiboko spring (hotel staff can walk you there in a few minutes), which are fed in turn by an underground channel from the Chyulu Hills and believed to be linked to the Mzima Springs in Tsavo West (see p.347). Just above the source (surrounded by ancient giant fig and fever trees and more modern pump stations) are the remains of Hunter's shooting post where he sat with his rifle waiting for elephants to come to drink. Elephants still occasionally make their way to the same spot from the Chyulu Hills National Park (see p.345), although usually at night and they are rarely seen.

ACCOMMODATION AND EATING   **KIBOKO**

Hunter's Lodge Mombasa highway ☏ 0727 209209, Nairobi reservations ☏ 020 6005072, ⊛ madahotels .com; map p.321. Set among 25 acres of lovely grounds full of birdlife (over a hundred species) and vervet monkeys, the *Lodge* was completely revamped in 2015. It now boasts 62 neat, tiled rooms with excellent hot showers and balcony or terrace. The highlight here is the massive pool, which uses the crystal-clear water from the Kiboko spring (non-guests can swim for Ksh500). It also serves reasonable meals, such chicken or tilapia (Ksh750), peppered steak or pork chops (Ksh850) and toasted sandwiches (Ksh450) to the passing trade. Wi-fi. BB **$160**

NATIONAL PARKS AND KWS SAFARI CARDS

Independent travellers who plan to visit **Amboseli**, **Tsavo West** or **Tsavo East national parks** can pick up temporary **Safari Cards** (see p.73) at the main gates to each park. The Points of Issue and Points of Sale (POIPOS) are the Iremito and Kimana gates of Amboseli, the Voi Gate of Tsavo East, and the Mtito Andei Gate of Tsavo West. Cards need to be surrendered at the gate on exit.

If you want to enter by any of the parks' other (minor) gates, you'll either need to have called at a POIPOS and had the appropriate funds loaded on to a card in advance, or you can get a "gate ticket" and pay when you exit through one of the main gates. If you plan to enter *and* exit through non-POIPOS gates, you will still have to go to a POIPOS at some point during your visit to pick up and load payment on to a Safari Card as gate staff *cannot* accept cash. Additionally, if you decide to stay another day longer than the period already paid for, you can pay the balance owing on departure. None of this applies to **non-Safari Card parks**, such as Chyulu Hills National Park, where you pay in cash on arrival.

Makindu and around

Twenty minutes southeast of Kiboko, you pass the Sikh temple at **MAKINDU**, sometimes strung with what look like Christmas lights, and prettily unmistakeable. The Sikh community here dates back to 1899 and the construction of the rail line. The temple was formally opened in 1926 and, in 1998, the Sikh community opened the hospital behind.

South of Makindu, the road to Mtito Andei has grand, sweeping views south over the Chyulu Hills and glimpses of lava flows and strange rock outcrops just to the north, although the east view is marred by the heavy construction sites of the Chinese rail line. The Kibwezi district is well known for its **basketware** which you'll be offered by countless sellers along the road.

ACCOMMODATION   MAKINDU AND AROUND

Sikh Temple Mombasa highway, corner of Wote Rd ⓦ sikhtemplemakindu.com (no tel); map p.321. With sixty clean and comfortable s/c rooms, most with three beds, the temple is rarely full and welcomes tired souls escaping the highway any time up to 9pm. Meals are available too (daily 7am–9pm). There are no formal charges, so you should leave whatever you feel is appropriate: any excess supports the community hospital. HB **Donation**

Kibwezi and around

KIBWEZI is a Kamba trading town off the highway at the junction for the rough B7 road to Kitui. There are a few shops, including a small **supermarket** and a **market** where you can occasionally buy spiky green **soursops**. One of those fruits you either love or loathe, the soursop is related to the custard apple, but larger and tarter. Also at Kibwezi is the turnoff to the Chyulu Hills National Park (see p.345); the Kithasyo Gate is signposted off the west side of the highway 1.5km south of town; the gate is 9km from here.

Continuing south along the A109 from Kibwezi, the altitude drops below 900m above sea level and, at this lower altitude, you start to see large **baobabs** along the highway. Some are said to be more than a thousand years old. In the past, they were credited with all manner of spiritual powers and associations (see box, p.449), and oral history has it that the Kamba were drawn to this area by the sponge-like centres of their trunks, which are a vital source of liquid during droughts. In the low sunlight of early morning or late afternoon, the baobab landscape, with Kamba women working tiny plots of maize between the huge trunks, is one of the highway's most beautiful sights.

INFORMATION   KIBWEZI AND AROUND

Services There's a KCB bank with an ATM in town. A small branch of Kitui Happy Family supermarket stocks the essentials, and a basic produce market has fruit and veg.

ACCOMMODATION

If you're lucky, you'll be booked at the extraordinary self-catering lodge, *Umani Springs*, in the Kibwezi Forest (see below). Campers can make for the KWS *Kiboko Campsite* at the Chyulu Hills National Park gate (see p.345).

Kambua Guest House Kibwezi town; 2.3km from the highway cross the rail tracks, then follow the road north around the back of the town for 1.5km; signposted) ☎ 0720 260250, ⓦ bit.ly/KambuaGuestHouse. Bright rooms in fairly new thatched rondavels with tiled bathrooms, nets, TV and a/c, plus a shady terrace and pleasant gardens. They also do meals. HB **Ksh3500**

The Kibwezi Forest

Daily dawn–dusk • Ksh1000 • 58 square kilometres

Contiguous with the Chyulu Hills National Park (see p.345), the **Kibwezi Forest** is one of the largest groundwater woodlands in Kenya. This tropical forest ecosystem could not be supported by Kibwezi's low rainfall, but is largely dependent on the springs seeping up from the base of the Chyulu Hills through the area's porous bedrock and volcanic soil. The forest is managed by the David Sheldrick Wildlife Trust on behalf of the Kenya Forest Service. Despite being just a few kilometres from the highway, it's a gloriously unspoilt area, and the only sounds you'll hear in the dense woodland are the calls of forest birds and the crashing around of the odd large mammal by day and an impressive cacophony of frog and insect noise at night.

Forest wildlife includes a good number of **elephants and buffaloes**. In 2014 the David Sheldrick Wildlife Trust began using the Kibwezi Forest as an orphan relocation site for elephants with disabilities from leg injuries, the *Umani Springs* stockade providing a gentler environment for them to habituate themselves back to the wild than the broader plains of the main re-release site in Tsavo East (see p.354). Also around *Umani Springs* you can often see **crocodiles**, and the area has become famous for some exceptionally large rock **pythons**. Even if you don't see any of these, the forest **birdlife** and extraordinary insect life (more then 230 species of **butterfly** have been recorded) make it a compelling area to explore.

ARRIVAL AND DEPARTURE   KIBWEZI FOREST

By bus or matatu You'll need to be dropped off at the Kibwezi junction, or ideally at the forest road entrance, 4km northwest of the Kibwezi junction. From here you'll have to walk or perhaps get a lift with the rangers.
By car The easiest entrance to Kibwezi Forest is signposted off the south side of the highway, 4km northwest of the Kibwezi junction. From here it's 700m to the forest rangers' gate, where you sign in, then a further 8.6km of rough track to *Umani Springs* lodge, which is sited close to the boundary of the Chyulu Hills National Park. With a high-clearance 4WD you can drive over the hills through the park to *Ol Donyo Lodge* and the C102 road to Amboseli, but you'll need to advise *Umani Springs* in advance so they can arrange for a guide to show you the way.

ACCOMMODATION

★ **Umani Springs** Kibwezi Forest, 9.3km from the Mombasa road ☎ 0733 891996, reservations through ⓦ sheldrickwildlifetrust.org; map p.321. Once a modest tented camp, *Umani Springs* has been entirely rebuilt as a chic, self-catering designer lodge, and is one of the most graceful and delightful in Kenya. Set deep in the forest, shaded by huge fig and acacia trees, it combines real bush living with very high levels of comfort, including solar power with generator backup, a very competent team of staff and an excellent cook (who can prepare anything for which you bring ingredients). Ten beds in three spacious houses are enhanced by extensive decking, dry-stone lava block walls for the outdoor showers, broad lawns, a large spring-fed swimming pool and comfy tree-swings. You need to bring drinking water and food, but it's possible to stock up adequately in Kibwezi. Self-catering, whole lodge **$600**

Mtito Andei

Busy and noisy all day and night thanks to the trucks, **MTITO ANDEI**, or "Vulture Forest", is a big sprawl of service stations and snackeries, roughly at the midway mark between Nairobi (233km) and Mombasa (250km). Many of the buses shuttling between the two break here for up to an hour. The settlement rises out of the dry country by the northern boundaries of both Tsavo West and Tsavo East national parks, with the "twin" Mtito Andei Gate lying on both sides of the highway. The KWS information centre is on the Tsavo West side (see p.348).

INFORMATION

Banks There are at least three KCB ATMs in town, the most convenient of which is on the main road opposite the Total petrol station.

ACCOMMODATION AND EATING

Only very simple **B&Ls** are on offer among the petrol stations frequented by weary truck drivers and "twilight ladies". About 1km north of town is a clutch of signposted **hotelis** (no rooms), which are rest stops for the buses with cafés and toilets. The best of these is the *Titanic Hotel* (daily 6am–10pm) with a cafeteria selling samosas, chapattis, chicken and chips and the like (from Ksh300) plus cold sodas, tea and coffee. The Shell and Total petrol stations have shops for drinks and snacks.

The Tsavo River

From Mtito Andei to Voi, the road runs through national park country. When you cross the **Tsavo River**, 49km south of Mtito Andei, you're in the spot where two **man-eating lions** played havoc with the building of the rail line in 1898, while engineers grappled with the river crossing. The lions seem to have been preternaturally lucky, since they eluded Colonel Patterson's various weapons for nearly a year and killed 28 Indian labourers in that time. The Field Museum in Chicago has the two stuffed man-eaters on display.

You're unlikely to see lions at the roadside these days, but between the Tsavo River and Manyani you may well come across **elephants**, always a brick-red colour, thanks to the soil. The Tsavo bridge marks the northern side of a 10km-wide animal migration corridor linking Tsavo East and Tsavo West, and thus also effectively connecting the northern Kenya ecosystem with that of southern Kenya. Note that **Tsavo**, although marked as a town or village on some maps, is neither; it's just a bridge, a virtually disused, slightly eerie train station, plus a lengthy viaduct across the valley for the new rail line. The Tsavo Gate of Tsavo West National Park is on the north side of the old bridge (see p.349).

ACCOMMODATION AND EATING   THE TSAVO RIVER

Loyk Tsavo Camp (see p.355), in Tsavo East National Park, is accessed opposite the Tsavo Gate of Tsavo West National Park.

Man Eaters Lodge Off the highway, 1km to the northeast on the south bank of the Tsavo River, accessed by crossing the rail tracks by the old station ☎ 020 7125741 or ☎ 0722 201240, ⌨ maneaterslodge .com; map p.352. Consisting of thirty tents along a bend in the Tsavo River in a private concession just inside the park (no park fees payable), this has tent-style rooms with good nets and verandas, decent bathrooms with electric showers and generator electricity. You can also stop for lunch (Ksh1500) and a swim in the excellent pool. Wi-fi. HB **$165**

Manyani

Some 13km south of the Tsavo bridge, and 2km south of Tsavo East National Park's Manyani Gate (see p.354), the nondescript highway centre of **Manyani** marks the southern side of the animal migration corridor. This has a number of *dukas* and basic *hotelis* refuelling weary travellers. **Manyani prison**, on the west side of the road, was an infamous Mau Mau detention centre (see p.566), the British deciding to

5

establish a holding camp in the middle of wild-animal country to deter inmates from escaping. Also in Manyani is the **Kenya Wildlife Service Field Training School**. Established in the early 1990s, it trains the KWS armed uniformed wing in paramilitary skills for anti-poaching duties.

Mbulia Conservancy

Access from the Mombasa highway, Tsavo West or by air to Kilaguni airstrip • 120 square kilometres

Bordering Tsavo West National Park, the private, exclusive-use **Mbulia Conservancy** is an important dispersal area for Tsavo's elephants and buffaloes. A tourism initiative established in 2012 as a joint project between Mbulia Group Ranch and New African Territories (the owners of the one camp here), it formally protects what was previously a bottle-neck area on the edge of Tsavo, employing game scouts to protect the wildlife and contributing conservancy and bed-night fees to the local community for social projects.

ACCOMMODATION	MBULIA CONSERVANCY

Kipalo Hills 13km south of Manyani or 22.4km north of Voi, then another 10km to the lodge ☎ 0722 701601, ⊚ africanterritories.co.ke; map p.352. This exclusive camp sits perched on a rocky *kopje* and offers sweeping views of the Tsavo West plains to the north, south down to the Taita Hills and in clear weather to distant Kilimanjaro. The eight tents, which all feature locally made wooden furniture and broad decks, can each accommodate up to two adults and two children, and are set well apart from one another – all in all, a very peaceful experience. There's a pool, mess tent for dining and drinks, and activities include guided walks and day and night game drives, as well as fly-camping in the conservancy and day-trips into Tsavo West. Conservancy fee ($58 per person) not included in rates. FB **$900**

Voi

With a population of around 50,000, **VOI** is the biggest town between Nairobi (329km) and Mombasa (155km). It's a short way from the highway to the east, connected by two access roads, one from the Nairobi side to the west, and one from the Mombasa side 5km to the southeast. You drive through Voi to reach the Voi Gate of Tsavo East National Park, 5km to the northeast of the town centre.

Unless you're going into the park, there's no compelling reason to stay or even stop in Voi town itself, though it's a welcome break from the hectic traffic on the main road and the **Commonwealth War Cemetery**, with its graves from the Anglo-German campaigns of World War I, is interesting. If you do stay, however, you'll find it's a pleasant enough place, especially on the south side of town, where most of the street grid has been neatly block-paved and there is a lively market around the bus park.

ARRIVAL AND DEPARTURE	VOI

By bus and matatu The bus and matatu stand is in the middle of town, around which are several bus kiosks. Coast and Taheed run services to both Mombasa and Nairobi. Buses between Mombasa (2–3hr from Voi) and Nairobi (5–6hr from Voi) come in all day – the heaviest concentration arriving and departing in the middle of the day. Some Mombasa-bound buses continue on to Malindi (6hr). Buses from Mombasa to Taveta (2hr) also stop at Voi. Matatus go to Mombasa (2hr) and Taveta (2hr), as well as Wundanyi in the Taita Hills (last departure around 5pm; 1hr 30min).

By car Voi is around 5hr from Nairobi or 2hr from Mombasa. If you'd rather keep on the road than come into town, but still need a break or a bite to eat, the 24hr Petro Plus filling station on the east side of the highway, just south of the Nairobi junction, has a café-restaurant, *Poa* (also 24hr), and a shop (daily 7.30am–9pm).

By train The train to Mombasa (5hr; first class Ksh1370, second class Ksh600) departs – in theory – at 4am on Mon and Fri, while the Nairobi-bound train (10hr; Ksh3035 and Ksh2330) passes through town – again, in theory – at 11.20pm on Tues and Sun. The station (☎ 043 2030098) is 10min walk from the town centre.

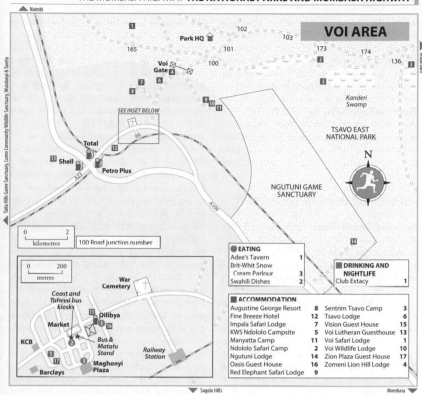

VOI AREA

● EATING
Adee's Tavern	1
Brit-Whit Snow	
Cream Parlour	3
Swahili Dishes	2

■ DRINKING AND NIGHTLIFE
Club Extacy	1

■ ACCOMMODATION
Augustine George Resort	8	Sentrim Tsavo Camp	3
Fine Breeze Hotel	12	Tsavo Lodge	6
Impala Safari Lodge	7	Vision Guest House	15
KWS Ndololo Campsite	5	Voi Lutheran Guesthouse	13
Manyatta Camp	11	Voi Safari Lodge	1
Ndololo Safari Camp	2	Voi Wildlife Lodge	10
Ngutuni Lodge	14	Zion Plaza Guest House	17
Oasis Guest House	16	Zomeni Lion Hill Lodge	4
Red Elephant Safari Lodge	9		

INFORMATION

Services Voi has plenty of filling stations, a couple of supermarkets (though none of the big chains) and several banks with ATMs; the easiest to pull in at is Barclays as it has its own car park, while KCB is on the opposite side of the road.

ACCOMMODATION

While there are a few places to stay and eat in Voi, most visitors go to one of the several safari camps or lodges – mostly budget to mid-market places popular on short safaris from the coastal resorts – near the Voi Gate that lie just outside the perimeter fence of the park. If you don't have your own transport, the best way to reach them is to hop in a piki-piki (or tuk-tuk if you have luggage) from the bus stand. You can organize game drives into Tsavo East from any of these. Voi Gate also provides access to several camps and lodges within the park, including *Ashnil Aruba Lodge*, *Sentrim Tsavo Camp* and *Voi Safari Lodge* (see p.355).

VOI TOWN

Fine Breeze Hotel On the main road about 200m after Barclays bank going towards the Nairobi junction ☎ 0714 447638. A reasonable place in a five-storey block: rooms have clean, tiled modern bathrooms, electric showers, nets and balconies. Avoid those facing the main road, though, as the hotel shares a compound with a bar that can be noisy (or fun depending on your mood). Secure parking. Room only **Ksh1850**

Oasis Guest House Voi centre ☎ 024 514257. A very basic place with cheap, clean, s/c rooms that oddly shares an alleyway with a car wash where you can park safely. You can get a chapatti-and-*chai* local breakfast in the tiny attached café. Room only **Ksh1000**

Vision Guest House Voi centre ☎ 0722 660113. Similar to the *Oasis*, with very basic but cheap s/c rooms with nets, plug sockets and electric showers. Ask for an upstairs room at the back for less street noise. You can eat breakfast at *Adee's Tavern* across the road (see p.328). Room only **Ksh900**

Voi Lutheran Guesthouse Signposted 1km before the junction to Voi if coming from the north

5

☎020 2668607, ⊛voiguesthouse.com. Newly built and run by the Voi Lutheran Mission, with all profits used to fund work with local orphaned children, this guesthouse sleeps forty in s/c doubles and non-s/c family rooms with bunk beds, with reliable solar hot water and neat Maasai souvenir decor. Meals and game drives into the park can be arranged. BB Ksh2700

Zion Plaza Guest House Voi centre ☎0726 039439. Clean, secure and breezy rooms with fans, nets and DSTV in a tall salmon-pink block – look up from Barclays bank and you'll see it on the next side street east. Street parking with an *askari* guard can be arranged. Room only Ksh1500

BETWEEN VOI TOWN AND TSAVO EAST

VOI GATE

Augustine George Resort 1km from Voi town junction ☎0723 455370 or ☎0721 919925, %Eaugustinegeorgeresort2@gmail.com, ⊛bit.ly/ AugustineGeorgeVoi. Pleasant, Christian-run place in a complex of thatched cottages. Rooms have fans, electric showers and TVs – most have double beds only. Good-value meals from Ksh450, coffee bar but no alcohol. BB Ksh4000

Impala Safari Lodge 1km from junction ☎0750 153694, ⊛impalasafarilodge.com. Budget safari camp on a cramped plot, with six closely spaced, tile-floored tents, two cottages sleeping up to six and a pool. Breakfast included, buffet lunch/dinner Ksh900. Wi-fi. BB Ksh10,000

Manyatta Camp 4.5km from Voi town junction ☎0722 201240 or 0722 206998, ⊛manyattacamp .com. Sharing the same large plot as the co-owned *Voi Wildlife Lodge* (see below), this is the more expensive, tented-camp side of the operation, with a view over a seasonal stream and a nominally more "bush" atmosphere, undermined by pumping music around the pool and restaurant and the paved floors and private plunge pools for each of the tents. Wi-fi. FB $212

Red Elephant Safari Lodge 4.3km from Voi town junction ☎0727 112175, ⊛red-elephant-lodge.com. The main "safari rooms" in thatched huts are very basic, but the four "bush houses", facing the park fence and a waterhole, are bigger and much nicer ($23 extra). The reasonably pleasant, shady grounds are spoilt by a backyard-style, above-ground pool, but the thatched restaurant/bar has comfortable lounge areas and a campfire is lit at dinner. Wi-fi. FB $85

Tsavo Lodge 3km from Voi town junction ☎0720 423136 , ⊛tsavolodgesandcamps.com. Though this is a little down at heel with raggedy tents and peeling paintwork, the eight rooms and six tents set within a walled compound are nevertheless very good value. You can also camp, using the electric showers in the main toilet block. The thatched bar serves basic meals from Ksh600 or you can walk to one of the other lodges to eat. Camping Ksh1000, BB Ksh2500

Voi Wildlife Lodge 4.5km from Voi town junction ☎020 2048954 or 0733 201240, ⊛voiwildlifelodge .com. Industrial-sized lodge of 178 rooms, featuring acres of concrete, that faces the park fence much as a beach resort faces onto the ocean. There is a vast buffet restaurant (awful food) and it even has its own church, mosque and temple. Even though it's way overpriced for non-residents, it gets the thumbs up for its decent rooms with verandas/balconies, nets and ceiling fans; two pools; and the fact that you're guaranteed to see literally dozens of elephants at the floodlit waterhole just over the fence from the bar area and elevated walkway. Wi-fi. FB $195

★**Zomeni Lion Hill Lodge** 4km from Voi town junction ☎020 8030828 or ☎0735 877431, ⊛lionhilllodge.com. The best option in this area, perched on Mlima ya Simba ("Lion Hill") with wonderful views across the park. The modern lodge has eight thatched rooms and four tents (verandas, nets, fans, tiled bathrooms) and serves good food in the vast open thatched dining room at the top of the hill. Wi-fi. FB $160

EATING

On the way in/out of the park, you can stop at either *Zomeni Lion Hill Lodge* or *Voi Wildlife Lodge* for a buffet lunch (around Ksh1600).

★**Adee's Tavern** At Oilibya, Voi centre. Spotless and friendly upstairs café/restaurant that is part of the petrol station. Everything here is super-cheap – breakfast items like chapatti, eggs and beans go for Ksh80 each, chicken, beef or veggie stews from Ksh200 and there are a couple of noodle (tasty if not authentic) Chinese dishes from Ksh350. Daily 7am–8pm.

Brit-Whit Snow Cream Parlour Post office street, next to Maghonyi Plaza, Voi centre ☎0787 209661, ⊛bit.ly/Brit-Whit. Unfathomably named ice-cream

parlour and café in modern premises with plastic tables, a/c and a few handy parking spots on brick paving outside. Ice cream by the scoop or tub, plus fried chicken or burgers and chips and fresh juices. Daily 11am–9pm.

Swahili Dishes Post office street. Does excellent, coastal-style rice and beans (Ksh100), goat *biriani* (Ksh200), *bhajias* (Ksh20) and the like, and they usually have fresh juices on the go (Ksh70). Daily 7am–6pm.

Club Extacy Across from Barclays Bank. The open-air terrace at the front is popular with local boozers and football fans for the TVs, cold-ish beer and fried food. The dancefloor inside wakes up more at weekends with occasional live music and karoke (entry Ksh150). **Open 24hr.**

Ngutuni Game Sanctuary

Signposed 5km south of Voi on the east side of the highway • Exclusive to overnight guests or lunch visitors • Daytime game drives included in rates, tip expected; night drives $20 per person • Any Mombasa-bound bus or matatu will drop you at the gate • 45 square kilometres

Beyond Voi, the **Ngutuni Game Sanctuary** is tucked into the space between the boundary of Tsavo East National Park and the highway. Though a former ranch, it feels as though it's deep in the bush and has plenty of game including **elephant**, **lion** and large numbers of **buffalo**. A good network of driveable trails criss-crosses the thorn bush, and if you have your own vehicle, you can usually take a ranger for a game drive: alternatively go on one of the lodge's morning and afternoon game drives. As it's outside the park, night drives are also available to see the shyer nocturnal animals. While the sanctuary doesn't match Tsavo East or West for spectacle or a sense of wilderness, it makes for a good stopover between Nairobi and Mombasa, or an affordable base for exploring the area.

Ngutuni Lodge ☎ 043 2030747, ⓦ rexresorts.com; map p.327. Constructed from large timber poles, with thatched roofs and elevated decking, the lodge is a good safari overnighter that is popular with mid-market tour groups. Rooms are a decent size and very comfortable (they could possibly do with a/c at this altitude, but the fans work well enough), with balconies facing the waterhole, which is floodlit at night. The lodge prides itself on good cooking, and staff are friendly and helpful. Wi-fi. FB **$202**

Maungu

After Voi, the road veers across the relentless **Maungu Plains**, also known as the **Taru Desert**, a plateau of "wait-a-bit" thorn and occasional baobabs which forms another, though less significant, migratory corridor for wildlife passing between Tsavo East and the southern plains of Tsavo West. Scenically dreary for much of the year, the plains come alive with colour after heavy rains, and during May and June can be carpeted in flowers. The small town of **MAUNGU** itself, 30km southeast of Voi, is again a sprawl of ramshackle buildings and roadside *dukas* serving the passing trucks.

⋆ Rock Side Camp 10km from Maungu down a rough signposted track on the west side of the highway ☎ 020 2041443, ⓦ rocksidecamp.com; map p.352. Popular with German visitors and hosted by the owners who live on site, this hotel lies in the shadow of an imposing *kopje* (Mount Kasigau) which you can climb – it takes about an hour. There are wooden *bandas* and larger bungalows, a semi-open lounge/bar, good food and a pool. Great views of the Taita Hills and there's a surprising level of visiting wildlife. FB **$177**

Mackinnon Road

Some 11km south of Tsavo East National Park's Buchuma Gate, the first place you might stop for refreshments is the long sprawl of **MACKINNON ROAD**, distinguished by its huge and beautiful **mosque** and the neighbouring burial place of Sayyed Baghali Shah Pir Padree – a holy man who worked on the railway – right alongside the rail track. By tradition, vehicles are supposed to hoot their horns in salutation as they pass the shrine. The town's odd name derives from an original ox-cart route that preceded the Uganda Railway – the Mackinnon–Sclater road from Mombasa to Busia that was built around 1890 by the British East Africa Company.

5

Samburu, Mariakani and Mazeras

East of the small settlement of **SAMBURU** (no connection with the national reserve in northern Kenya of the same name), the land is peopled mostly by members of the large **Mijikenda** ethnic group, their distinctive, droopy, thatched cottages often replaced nowadays by more formal square ones, and increasingly also whitewashed and tin-roofed in the coastal manner. The **Duruma** Mijikenda of this district herd cattle, make charcoal and grow some sisal – there's little else they can do in such a dry region.

The tiny centre of **Maji ya Chumvi** ("salt water") and the growing Mombasa satellite and truckers' town of **MARIAKANI** ("place of the *mariaka*", the Kamba arrows used in nineteenth-century wars against the Maasai), with its huge steel-rolling mill, bring you closer to the coastal domain.

The coast mood really takes over at **MAZERAS**, a largely Duruma town (see p.423). From this point onwards, the landscape has a quite different cast, with its mango trees, bananas and cassava, and – encouraging for weary travellers – the sublime sight of thousands of **coconut palms**. The route from Mazeras to the north heads along a ridge through the Mijikenda back country (see p.423). The main road plunges on, down the scarp to the Indian Ocean and Mombasa.

ARRIVAL AND DEPARTURE

SAMBURU, MARIAKANI AND MAZERAS

BY CAR

If you're driving to or from the coast but looking to avoid the traffic of Mombasa and its crowded suburbs, there are alternative routes for 4WD vehicles.

To Kilifi and the north coast A short cut, along the C107, leads out of the centre of Mariakani, heading more or less due east for 19km through the rolling Mijikenda back country to Kaloleni (see p.425), and then for a further 35km northeast through pretty forest and farmland to rejoin the coastal highway a few kilometres south of Kilifi creek. You can also take the turning north from Mazeras to Kaloleni, via Rabai and Ribe (see p.425). Allow 2hr from Mariakani or Mazeras to Kilifi, more after heavy rain.

To Kwale and the south coast For Kinango, Kwale and/or Diani Beach, turn off the highway at Samburu or Mariakani to take the back country route over the Shimba

Hills (see p.428). Allow 1hr 30min to Kinango, another hour to Kwale and 30min more to Diani Beach.

BY BUS AND MATATU

Coming by public transport from the Nairobi direction to the coast (or the reverse), you can skip Mombasa by asking to be dropped at Samburu, Mariakani or Mazeras.

To Kilifi and the north coast If your destination on the coast is Kilifi or further north, then you'll need to get a matatu to Kaloleni from either Mariakani or Mazeras, both of which see vehicles leaving all morning. Onward connections to Kilifi get fewer later in the day.

To Kwale and the south coast To do the Kinango "short cut" to the coast, avoiding Mombasa city, you're likely to have to spend a night in a cheap B&L in Samburu or Mariakani before getting one of the few daily matatus that leave very early for Kinango and Kwale (see p.429).

The Voi–Taveta road and southern Tsavo West

The A23 road from **Voi to Taveta** follows the old rail line, a 110km branch off the Nairobi–Mombasa railway constructed in 1914 as a vital supply line for British forces fighting the *Schutztruppe* in German East Africa (now Tanzania). At the time of writing this once painfully rocky road was being tarred; scheduled to be completed by mid-2016, this will make access from the Mombasa highway to the Tanzanian border at Taveta much quicker and easier. The middle section of the A23 forms a 37km-long corridor through the southern arm of Tsavo West National Park, where drivers are quite likely to spot elephants and plains game from the road. Although technically you enter the park at Maktau and leave it again at Mbuyuni, you don't pay any fees to drive along this stretch.

The only settlement of note on the A23 is **MWATATE**, which lies 26km from Voi on the southern side of the Taita Hills. From 1900 to 1912 this was the headquarters of the whole district before administration was moved to Voi, and now is a ramshackle place with a population of no more than three thousand, serving the sisal estates near town. It is from Mwatate that you can veer off up into the Taita Hills (see below). Beyond Mwatate, the two attractions off the A23 before the Tsavo West boundary at Maktau Gate are the Taita Hills Wildlife Sanctuary (see p.332) and Lumo Community Wildlife Sanctuary (see p.333), both signposted to the south of the road.

Access to Tsavo West

The **Maktau Gate** to Tsavo West is 32km beyond Mwatate, a "twin" gate on either side of the road. From the south gate the park track leads 43km through the rarely visited southern section of Tsavo West to Jipe Gate (see p.336), while from the north gate the track heads up to the Tsavo River, connecting via the one bridge to the network of roads in the "Developed Area" of the park.

Alternatively you can also head north into the Developed Area through Ziwani Gate (see p.349). The road off the A23 to the gate arrows north 72km west of Mwatate (and 14km east of Taveta), mostly following the park boundary, with wildlife much in evidence. After 20km, you'll find Ziwani Gate on the right and *Voyager Ziwani Camp* (see p.351) on the left. Note that this route can be closed when heavy rains damage the Tsavo river bridge in the park.

The Taita Hills

Though largely unvisited, the **Taita Hills** region, accessed via the A23, has a fascinating and distinct culture. Despite the name, the hills don't have any real connection with the Taita Hills Wildlife Sanctuary, which lies on the rolling plains to the south of the A23 road.

From the junction at Mwatate, the C104 twists for 14km into precipitous and beautiful hills, striped with cliffs, waterfalls, intense cultivation and patches of thick forest, and rising to the (sometimes chilly) height of 2200m. The climate of the area is strongly affected by its proximity to the ocean, roughly about 100km away as the crow flies, and is so agreeable that during the 1950s the colonial administration briefly moved the district headquarters to **Wundanyi** from Voi to escape the harsh plains. Today there's a high population density, reasonable prosperity and a strong sense of community up here. Most of the welcoming **Taita people** speak the Taita language, a member of the coastal Bantu family related to Swahili and Mijikenda.

Wundanyi

Regular matatus up from Voi pitch through the fertile chasms on the switchback road to the attractive little district capital of **WUNDANYI**. There's not much to the place – bar a research station recently established by the University of Helsinki, it's really just a main street and a side street – but conifer trees on the slopes, and a babbling brook running past Wundanyi's football field, reinforce the feeling of departure from the thorn bush and scrub on the plains below. Further enhancing that feeling, the locally notorious Shomoto Hill, from which Taita criminals were hurled to their deaths under traditional law, rises up to the west.

The cave of skulls

1.5km outside town on the road to Werugha and Mbale, hidden in a banana grove just below the road

The sense of suspended reality in Wundanyi is accentuated by **Mwanda** – the **cave of skulls**, one of many ancestor shrines in the hills (there's one for each clan). In this niche rest 32 skulls, exhumed from their graves: Taita burial practice dictated that

5

when a person died, they were interred for a year after which their bodies would be exhumed and the skull severed from the rest of the body and taken to a sacred cave, to be buried "properly" among the ancestors. Rather than looking for the cave yourself and possibly making a cultural *faux pas*, ask one of the hotels to provide a guide.

Traditionally, the shrine was an advice centre where life's perplexities were resolved by consultation with the dead, and where sacrifices were made in times of drought. The advance of Christianity at the beginning of the twentieth century eroded some of the reverence that the Taita once had for these shrines (and traditional dances and rituals have almost disappeared), but they are left undisturbed nonetheless.

ARRIVAL AND INFORMATION   WUNDANYI

Entering town, turn right at the T-junction just before the bridge, and, after passing the Shell petrol station, the KCB (ATM) and the post office, take the first left around the back of the large football field. This leads to the centre of town around the *Lavender Garden Hotel*. If you don't turn left, continuing up the hill brings you to the market and matatu stand.

By matatu There are direct connections with Voi (1–2hr) and Mombasa (3–4hr), most of them leaving Wundanyi in the early morning. For Taveta (allow at least 2hr), you'll have to change vehicles down on the A23 at Mwatate

(around 30min–1hr).
By car It's a straightforward drive up to Wundanyi from the Voi–Taveta road. Allow 1hr to reach the town from Voi.

ACCOMMODATION AND EATING

There's a limited number of places to **stay** and **eat**. You'll find street food on Wundanyi's big market days, Tues and Fri.

Hebron Guest House On the road to Werugha/ Mbale just out of town (at the bridge, turn right and cross the stream and take the right fork after 600m; it's 100m from the fork) ☎0723 058078. The accommodation provided for Finnish scientists/students at the Taita Research Station (which explains the sauna) is very nice, clean and well run, and has a peaceful location, but can't be relied upon as it may well be full if a group is visiting. There are dorm beds as well as single and double rooms, plus hearty meals of meat, rice, veg and fruit (Ksh700). Dorm bed **Ksh1000**, room only **Ksh2000**

Lavender Garden Hotel Overlooking the football field ☎0715 876473 or ☎0700 478556, ⓦbit.ly/ LavenderGardenWundanyi. Under the same ownership as *Lake Jipe Safari Camp* (see p.337), this bright, mid-range hotel has good rooms with nets, DSTV and nice bathrooms with electric showers. Try to get a room at the

front for sunset views from the balcony across the valley to the local landmarks of Wesu Rock and Shomoto Hill. The restaurant is the best place to eat in town for continental food. BB **$56**

★**Taita Rocks Hotel** Just a few metres before the bridge on entering the town, close to the Deputy Governor's office and police station ☎0722 955214 or ☎0716 221950, ⓦbit.ly/TaitaRocks. This fairly new venture is the best place to settle into if you're interested in finding out more about the Taita people: the owner is knowledgeable, and can organize walks to see the skull caves and Shomoto Hill. It has sweeping views down into the valley and well-kept rooms with DSTV in chalets dotted around the hilly well-manicured garden. Under a generous thatched roof, the lovely restaurant-bar serves food including grilled chicken, fish (and unusually) rabbit. You can also camp (negotiable rates). HB **Ksh 3500**

Taita Hills Wildlife Sanctuary

Entry is off the south side of the A23, signposted 15.5km west of the junction for Wundanyi in Mwatate • $35 • Night game drives 7pm & 9pm (2hr; $30) • 113 square kilometres

One place attracting major tourist traffic in this district, particularly visitors on fleeting air safaris from the coast, is **Taita Hills Wildlife Sanctuary**, which isn't in the Taita Hills at all, but in the hillocky lowlands west of Mwatate. Set up in 1973 by the *Hilton* hotel chain, the sanctuary is now owned and managed by Sarova Hotels, who successfully balance wildlife and human needs in an environment that, while not being fully natural, seems to work well for both.

For most of the year, the sanctuary is full of wildlife. There are more than fifty species of **large mammals** and three hundred species of birds here, and the sanctuary's small size means the rangers always have a good idea of where the key animals can be seen. It's not uncommon to spot two dozen species in a morning game drive, among them lions, cheetahs, large herds of elephant and buffalo, and all the other southern plains grazers. During the drier times of the year, when the animals are not dispersed, the water sources beneath *Salt Lick Lodge*, on the southern side of the sanctuary, provide waterhole game-viewing, including a very good ground-level hide, far better than you could hope to experience at *Treetops* or *The Ark* (see p.193).

ACCOMMODATION
TAITA HILLS WILDLIFE SANCTUARY

★**Sarova Salt Lick Lodge** Inside the sanctuary, 7km beyond the Game Lodge ☎ 020 2757000 or ☎ 0728 608765, ⓦ sarovahotels.com; map p.321. Built on stilts over a chain of waterholes, this looks from a distance like a clump of mushrooms sprouting from the bush. The semicircular rooms occupy turret-like, conical-roofed houses, linked by aerial walkways, their walls built of cemented and painted sandbags, all in keeping with the sanctuary's World War I battle history theme. Architecture aside, remarkable animal-viewing is the hallmark of *Salt Lick*. As you sip your beer over the heads of elephants drinking from the waterhole below, you're literally within touching distance of dozens of trunks, while the underground tunnel to a hide brings you eye level with their feet. Few lodges in Kenya offer this kind of access.

Pachyphile heaven. Wi-fi. FB $251
Sarova Taita Hills Game Lodge 500m from the road, just before the sanctuary gate ☎ 020 2757000 or ☎ 0728 608765, ⓦ sarovahotels.com; map p.321. Built in the shape of a German fort, Sarova's other property at Taita Hills has comfortable rooms with balconies, nets and fans. Ordinary but copious meals are complemented by a very good pool, and poolside animal-watching over the fence into the sanctuary. It's good value for money, and although *Salt Lick* has the edge in terms of a game experience, the daily drives from the lodge do pull in there to enjoy the waterholes. Non-guests can stop here for the buffet lunch (Ksh2000), and look in at the small World War I museum, without paying the sanctuary fee. Wi-fi. FB $204

Lumo Community Wildlife Sanctuary

Entry is off the south side of the A23, signposted 23.5km west of the junction for Wundanyi in Mwatate • $35 • ⓦ lumoconservancy.com • 460 square kilometres

Comprising Lualenyi Ranch, Miramba Communal Grazing Area and Ossa Group Ranch (hence LU-M-O), **Lumo Community Wildlife Sanctuary** is one of Kenya's most successful community conservation initiatives. And with simply outstanding panoramic views from its *Lion's Bluff Lodge*, it is a real draw for coast-based safaris.

More than four times the size of Taita Hills Wildlife Sanctuary, Lumo shares its boundary, and visitors are able to do game drives in both areas. There are usually plenty of **elephants** to be seen, together with most of the other species of plains game common in the southern Kenyan parks. **Predators** tend to be elusive, but sightings of lion, cheetah and leopard are well noted and passed on – so you're unlucky to miss them if they're in the area. Night drives can sometimes include some real rarities, such as **aardwolf** and **serval**, of which Lumo has recorded melanistic – all black – individuals.

As well as mammals, Lumo is a bit of a paradise for ornithologists, with an estimated 400-plus species of **birds**, include rare endemics like the Taita apalis, Taita thrush and southern banded snake eagle. There's a resident ornithologist at *Lion's Bluff Lodge* who is just as happy going out with novice birders as he is with experienced enthusiasts.

ACCOMMODATION
LUMO COMMUNITY WILDLIFE SANCTUARY

Cheetah Campsite About 8km from the A23 ☎ 020 268580 or ☎ 0729 265018, ⓦ lumoconservancy.com;

map p.321. Well-maintained campsite with showers, toilets, drinking water and firewood included in the rate,

5

and the option of sleeping in a four-bed shelter under mosquito nets. Tents, bedding and kitchen equipment are available to rent, and campers can use the lodge restaurant and bar and join the optional activities. You need to hire the services of the rangers while you are in camp (Ksh2000/24hr). Camping $10, shelter $30 per person

★**Lion's Bluff Lodge** About 8km from the A23 (steep in parts; 4WD required) ☎0717 555498 or ☎0722 782627, ⊛lionsblufflodge.com; map p.321.

This community-owned lodge, spectacularly sited at the end of a dramatic ridge, has stunning sunsets and sunrises and good views of Kilimanjaro in clear weather. The comfortable thatched tented *bandas* have jutting balconies on platforms suspended from one side of the steep slope, and are linked by timber bridges. There's also a bar, dining room, viewing terrace and community handicrafts shop, and activities include bush walks, game drives and cultural visits to local villages. Wi-fi. FB $240

Taveta

Twenty-three kilometres beyond Tsavo West's Mbuyuni Gate, the town of **TAVETA** lies, like Lake Jipe (see p.336), within the curious kink of Kenya that juts into Tanzania. This kink was created in 1881 when Queen Victoria "gave" Mount Kilimanjaro to her German grandson, the Crown Prince of Prussia (later to become Kaiser Wilhelm II), necessitating an adjustment to the border so that Kilimanjaro fell in German East Africa.

Some 109km from Voi, and right on the (24hr) Tanzanian border, Taveta has the petrol stations, basic B&Ls and roadside *dukas* typical of a busy frontier town. For a few moments' reflection, visit the **World War I cemetery** at the entrance to town, next to the post office, which holds 127 graves of both British and German casualties. The only paved street in town (the end of the A23) crosses the old rail line and heads straight for the border post, but the town's real main street runs north from the paved road immediately west of the rail tracks crossing.

ARRIVAL AND DEPARTURE   TAVETA

By bus and matatu There are plenty of buses and matatus connecting Voi and Taveta (2hr), several daily vehicles to/from Mombasa (5hr) and one or two early morning departures to/from Oloitokitok (3hr) 79km to the north, near the eastern end of Amboseli National Park.

By car If you're driving to Oloitokitok (turn north off the A23 4km east of Taveta), note that the *murram* road can be very rough going, and can be impassable in the rains, even with a 4WD. Voi to Taveta should by the time you read this be smooth tar all the way (if it's not then there'll be roadworks) and shouldn't take more than 1hr 30min. Bear in mind though, that the middle stretch goes through Tsavo West so keep your speed down and look out for game.

Onwards to Tanzania The Kenya/Tanzania crossing is

one of the new "one-stop" border posts, meaning that customs and immigration procedures for both countries are in the same building, and is in Holili, on the Tanzanian side. From Holili, frequent matatus go to Moshi (37km; 40min) and Arusha (118km; 2hr). On the way, the road passes through Himo, 10km beyond Holili, which is the junction for the main B1 road going south to Dar es Salaam. Moneychangers on both sides of the border exchange Kenyan shillings for Tanzanian shillings (and vice versa), but, as ever, beware of scams and make sure you know the rate. The better option is to use the ATMs at banks in Taveta (the road leading up to the border has both a Barclays and a KCB with ATMs) if you need Kenyan shillings, and if possible wait until you get to Moshi to get Tanzanian shillings.

ACCOMMODATION

Lake Challa Hotel 400m past the market ☎043 5352240 or ☎0735 849170. This hotel has excellent-value rooms – the best in Taveta – around a bright internal courtyard, with nets, TV, fans and electric showers. The restaurant serves good food, including decent omelettes for breakfast, and next door (and under the same management) is a large, relaxed garden bar offering cold beer, snacks and DSTV. Parking. BB **Ksh2000**

Triple J Paradise On the main street just before the old border buildings on the western side of town ☎0725 095220. Much inferior alternative to the *Challa* with tiled rooms (nets, fans) on four floors, some of which have balconies with Kilimanjaro views, and a simple ground-floor restaurant serving *nyama choma*, local *matoke* stew and the like. BB **Ksh1200**

Lake Chala

A four-square-kilometre crater lake north of Taveta, **Lake Chala** has one shore in Kenya and the other in Tanzania. Very deep, remarkably clear and blue, it is a bewitchingly beautiful landscape, completely unsuspected from the plains below. Chala is still paddled over by a few friendly fishermen in their dugouts and is spiritually significant, with **lake monster** stories part of local folklore. From the 100-metre-high crater rim, it's a steep descent to the lake and good walking shoes are advised. You might spot monitor lizards, baboons and vervet monkeys, and if lucky, a dik-dik or bushbuck. The bird list numbers more than 250 species, including peregrine falcons, which nest in Chala's cliff-faces.

The lake, which is filled and drained by underground streams fed by the waters running off Kilimanjaro, is bilharzia-free. It was also once believed to be free of crocodiles. However, a crocodile killed a young British traveller swimming here in 2002, and you are very strongly advised not to enter the water. While locals swear the crocodile responsible was killed a few years later, there's no reason to think the reptiles won't colonize the lake again. They are resourceful survivors, and have been known to crawl overland for long distances.

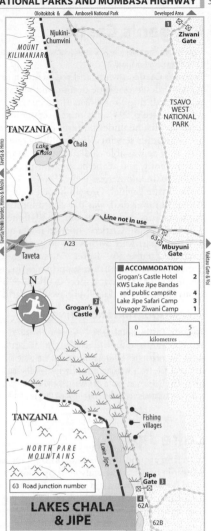

ARRIVAL AND DEPARTURE   LAKE CHALA

By bus or matatu Local vehicles are most frequent on market days: Wed and Sat in Taveta; Tues and Fri in Njukini-Chumvini north of Lake Chala; and Tues and Sat in Oloitokitok, far to the north, near the eastern end of Amboseli National Park.

By car Lake Chala is just west of the rough road between Taveta and Oloitokitok. Exactly 7.4km north of the junction outside Taveta (the junction is 3.6km east of the rail crossing), you'll find a stone cairn in a triangle of stones by the road, the start of the 1.3km motor track that scrapes over bare rock up the side of the crater to the rim (high-clearance 4WD essential). From the top, it's another 800m along the south rim to the ruins of the *Lake Chala Safari Lodge*.

ACCOMMODATION

The Kenyan side of Lake Chala has no accommodation. You can **camp wild** for free in the slightly eerie ruins of *Lake Challa Safari Lodge* (people come here from Nairobi), although there are no facilities and you'll need to bring drinking water. The village of Chala, 4km north of the cairn on the road at the base of the hill, has the closest simple supplies. To find out whether the old lodge, which closed after the crocodile incident, is being restored, contact the *Lake Challa Hotel* in Taveta (see opposite), which has the same owner.

5

Grogan's Castle

Head east from Taveta along the A23, turning right 6.6km from Taveta rail crossing; the 800m track leading up to *Grogan's Castle* starts 6.8km down this *murram* road

Grogan's Castle, a white and red mansion on an isolated hill rising from the plain, certainly deserves a little detour on the way to Lake Jipe. This extraordinary residence was built during World War II by Ewart Grogan, one of the most influential early colonists (see p.594). His mixed reputation was founded on a walk from the Cape to Cairo, which he undertook in 1898, on a notorious public flogging that he carried out on three of his servants (nearly killing one of them), and on his wealth: his status was such that he was able to dictate terms to the governor of Kenya before he even arrived in the colony, and at the peak of his prosperity his holdings extended to more than 2500 square kilometres.

The "castle", which Grogan hoped would become a government agricultural training school (it never did), was run down for decades, during which time it provided roosts for birds, bats and insects, but in 2010 the current owner, the high-profile former Taveta MP, Basil Criticos, opened it as a quirky hotel. It's an enigmatic building, part hacienda, part folly, with huge arched windows. The enormous circular main lounge gives spectacular 360-degree views out towards Kilimanjaro to the north, the Pare Mountains to the southwest and Lake Jipe to the south. It's a completely unique place, where you can share the sheer exuberance of Grogan's vision – and even sleep in his room (Room 1) and use his claw-foot bath.

ACCOMMODATION AND EATING   GROGAN'S CASTLE

Grogan's Castle Hotel ☎0735 671006 or ☎0717 330228, ⊕ groganscastlehotel.com; map p.335. Don't expect luxury but this old creaky house is a fun place to stay, and the team working here is very friendly and hospitable. The six vast rooms all have nets and piping hot water in the showers or baths, and although they're a little sparsely furnished, some have four beds, making them a little better priced for a family/group. The comfortable lounge, with its wraparound views, has books on Ewart Grogan, there's a little plunge pool, and the food is unexpectedly good, served *en groupe* at Grogan's colossal dining table. HB **$210**

Lake Jipe

Covering around thirty square kilometres, **Lake Jipe**, like Lake Chala, straddles the Tanzania border, and is also fed by Kilimanjaro's snowmelt, which passes via Lake Chala's underground outlet, as well as by streams flowing off the Pare Mountains across the border in Tanzania. Unlike Chala, Lake Jipe's shores are flat and thickly carpeted in reed beds and the surrounding swamps can extend for a kilometre or more from the lakeshore: when exploring the bush around the lake, you should keep a sharp eye out for **hippos**.

Several villages along the northern shore make a living from fishing, while the southeastern shore lies inside the almost unvisited southern section of Tsavo West National Park. The **Jipe Gate**, where you can enter the park, is directly on the shore 43km south of Taveta, and the friendly rangers here (they have little to do) can offer a boat (Ksh1500/hr) for a spot of crocodile- and hippo-spotting. Despite the sometimes vicious mosquitoes, this is a peaceful and rewarding spot, and a paradise for birders.

ARRIVAL AND DEPARTURE   LAKE JIPE

By taxi If you don't have your own vehicle, get a taxi in Taveta for the day, which will cost around Ksh500/hr.

By car Head east from Taveta along the Voi road (A23), turning right 6.6km from Taveta rail crossing. The road down to the northern tip of Lake Jipe (27km) runs straight over the flat land between the A23 and the lake. It's an area prone to flood, and the cambered *murram* road can be very slippery when wet.

ACCOMMODATION

KWS Lake Jipe Bandas and public campsite Just inside Jipe Gate ☏0720 968527, ⊛kws.org; map p.335. Lovely, peaceful spot on the lakeshore with just three simple twin *bandas*, which have bedding and nets, toilets, hot showers, small kitchens equipped with gas cookers and solar power. Firewood is provided by the warden; bring food and drinking water. Boat trips on the lake can be organized. Camping $\overline{\$30}$, whole *banda* $\overline{\$50}$

Lake Jipe Safari Camp Just outside Jipe Gate ☏0717 356016, ⊛lakejipesafaricamp.com; map p.335. Located

500m from the lakeshore along the fence of Tsavo West, this new and friendly setup has the same owners as the *Lavender Garden Hotel* in Wundanyi (see p.332). The comfortable tents and *bandas* (same price) have a flush toilet, warm shower, nets and little veranda, though you can't see the lake (the view of the Pare Mountains makes up for it). The restaurant-bar serves decent food given the remote location, a campfire is lit in the evenings, and very refreshingly there's a swimming pool. You can also negotiate to camp. FB $\overline{\$120}$

Amboseli National Park

$80 with Safari Card (see p.73) • ☏ 020 8029705, ⊛ kws.org • 392 square kilometres

Amboseli, the Maasai's "Place of Dust", is a small and very popular park, and often full of visitors. Scenically, however, it is redeemed by the stunning spectacle of **Kilimanjaro** towering over it and – in those clichéd but irresistible photos taken with telephoto lenses – appearing almost to fill the sky. In the right light, the snowy massif, washed coral and orange, is devastatingly beautiful. Sunrise and sunset are the most likely times to see the mountain, especially during the rainy season when the air is much clearer, but for the most part it remains tantalizingly shrouded in a thick shawl of cloud.

On the animal side, Amboseli is **elephant** country *par excellence*. You will see large herds, and some individuals with big tusks. Predators, apart from hyenas and jackals, are relatively scarce, lions are almost absent, thanks to the revenge wrought by the Maasai upon the expulsion of them and their herds from the park (see p.340), but good numbers of herbivores are present. In the dry season, most of the animals crowd into the impenetrable marshy areas, and patches of hardy acacia woodland where food plants are available. But during and shortly after the rains the picture is different, with the animals more dispersed and the landscape greener.

In the dry season, Amboseli can seem a parched, unattractive place, with Kilimanjaro disappointingly hazed into oblivion. Heading straight for the park's centre at Ol Tukai, with its lodges, workers, filling station, fences and barriers, doesn't improve first impressions. During the rains, however, it all looks far more impressive, with the shallow and seasonal **Lake Amboseli** partially filled, and a number of other seasonal lakes and ponds – the temporary home of small flocks of flamingos, pelicans and other migratory species – scattered across the landscape.

Ol Tukai

Ol Tukai is a central oasis of trees and vegetation, a kind of "human reserve", fenced off from the rest of the park. KWS's elementary support services are located here, alongside *Ol Tukai Lodge* (see p.342) and the now-closed and derelict *Amboseli Lodge*. Game drives pass through the complex as it links several of the park's central routes, and *Ol Tukai Lodge* itself is an ideal place to take a break for coffee or a (pre-arranged) lunch with spectacular views across the animal-studded plains to the east.

Game drives

Small enough to explore easily in two or three game drives over a couple of days, Amboseli is mostly open country with good visibility. There's always a concentration of animals around the swamps and along the driveable tracks which follow their

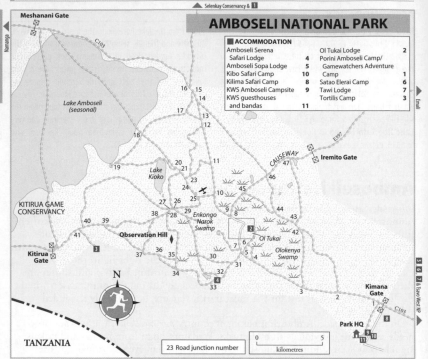

fringes. These marshes are permanent enough to keep **hippos** in Amboseli all year, and the park is also home to hundreds of **elephant** and **buffalo** and a raucous profusion of **birdlife**. **Lake Kioko**, between Lake Amboseli and Ol Tukai – most easily seen along the track between junctions #21 and #26 – is a particularly worthwhile oasis, and similarly **Olokenya swamp**, with its seasonal lakes north and east of Ol Tukai, is always worth slow exploration. **Birdlife** is abundant, particularly around the swamps and seasonal lakes. About 420 species have been recorded in the park.

Lions are fairly rare though they're not particularly shy and are often seen around **Observation Hill**, in the southern part of the park a few kilometres after the airstrip, and Lake Kioko. **Cheetahs** are spotted frequently in the woods south of Olokenya swamp towards Kimana Gate, and there are often dozens of **giraffes** among the acacias. Look out, too, for the beautifully formed, rapier-horned **fringe-eared oryx** antelope, and for the **gerenuks**, stretching their long necks up to forage in the trees.

The open plains are scoured by **zebra** and haphazard, solitary **wildebeest**. The two species are often seen together – a good deal from the zebras' point of view because in a surprise attack the predator usually ends up with the less fleet-footed wildebeest. There are tail-flicking **gazelles** out here, too, of both species: the open country provides good protection against cheetah ambushes.

To get *that* photograph of Kilimanjaro plus elephants, you need to start early – the mountain is usually covered by a mass of clouds by 10am, even if the sky is blue and clear. The best spots are at Ol Tukai and Olokenya, where elephants feed in the swampy areas. Observation Hill is another good place to stop, with the swamps of **Enkongo Narok** a brilliant emerald sash to the east, and Kilimanjaro a pervasive sky-filler to the south. You can get out and walk around up here and there are toilets.

5

VISITING THE MAIN PARKS

The first realization of where you are in Kenya's **big parks** – among uncaptured, and for the most part unfenced, wild animals – can be truly arresting. It may take you a day or two to adjust, as your normal, human-centric view of the world is re-balanced towards an environment in which big creatures hunt, die, mate, feed and enjoy themselves all around you in a wilderness landscape not much changed in centuries. Which parks you choose to visit can seem at first like a pin-in-the-map decision: any of them can provide a store of amazing sight and sound impressions (see pp.74–75).

Amboseli, **Tsavo West** and **Tsavo East**, all in southern Kenya, are three of the most accessible parks, with ever-busy game lodges, well-worn trails, large numbers of tourists and big herds of animals. Amboseli, with its picture-postcard backdrop of Mount Kilimanjaro and guaranteed elephants, is an instant draw, but the flat landscape and lack of tree cover means you may be sharing the stunning vistas with dozens of very noticeable safari vehicles. Tsavo East, in contrast, is so huge you can usually escape company completely, although its sheer size makes the same easy for the animals, too. Tsavo West is also huge, but better watered, allowing higher concentrations of wildlife in a varied landscape that includes hills, woodland springs and lava flows. On the other hand, the bush and woodland landscape can make animal-viewing harder. The little-visited **Chyulu Hills National Park**, to the north and effectively an extension of Tsavo West, has smaller populations of animals because of its altitude, but those lucky enough to stay in one of the two luxury lodges on its perimeter will find exploring here on foot or horseback rewarding.

Maasai Mara has the most fabled reputation of Kenya's parks, with horizons of wildlife on every side in a rich, rolling landscape of grasslands and wooded streams. Although it is somewhat isolated in the southwest, it is well worth the effort and cost of getting there, especially if you can arrange your visit during the yearly **wildebeest migration**. This takes place over an eight- to ten-week period, roughly between early July and early November, and is usually at its most spectacular at the end of August.

North of Mount Kenya, on the fringes of Kenya's desert region, the adjoining national reserves of **Samburu** and **Buffalo Springs**, and, just to the east, **Shaba National Reserve** share the bounty of the Ewaso Nyiro River system. These reserves have a number of animal varieties not found in the southern parks, including northern races and species of giraffe, zebra, various antelope and ostrich. Each of the reserves is small, even compared with Amboseli, which lends an impression of great concentrations of animals and birds, especially in the dry season when water sources are magnets for the wildlife.

Over to the east of Mount Kenya, the Kenya Wildlife Service's rescue and relaunch of **Meru National Park**, which in the 1990s had fallen into the hands of bandits and poachers, has been an impressive piece of work. Verdant Meru is one of the country's most beautiful parks, and still relatively unvisited, despite having, among its few places to stay, some of the very best options in the country – at both the luxury and budget ends of the spectrum – and nowadays some of the best wildlife-viewing.

GETTING AROUND THE PARKS

Read through the advice about safaris, and particularly **guides** (see p.80), before signing up for a safari. If you're **driving**, the numbered junctions ("#17", "#158" and so on) and clearly defined *murram* roads and tracks make most parts of the parks relatively easy to get around, so long as you have a map (though the painted numbers on some cairns are illegible and many maps are out of date). Never drive off-road, which is not only illegal and can draw fines, but is hugely damaging and causes soil erosion. Don't ignore the **distances** involved, especially in the large parks: at 40km/h, the speed limit in all the parks and reserves, it can take a long time to make a few centimetres of progress on the map, and of course you'll want to stop frequently to watch the wildlife. If you set off somewhere, be sure you have time to get back to base by nightfall, as all the parks **close their gates** at 7pm, and you are not allowed to drive around after that time. If you are changing camp, inform the management at your destination about your movements. Except at the designated nature trails and picnic sites, or where there's an obvious parking area, you should stay in your vehicle all the time, even if you break down – rangers will eventually find you.

5

AMBOSELI'S HISTORY

What is now Amboseli was part of the **Southern Maasai Reserve** at the turn of the last century. Then tourism arrived in the 1940s and the Amboseli Reserve was created as a wildlife sanctuary. Unlike Nairobi and Tsavo national parks, created at the same time and sparsely inhabited, Amboseli's swamps were used by the Maasai to water their herds and they saw no reason not to continue sharing the area with the wildlife and – if necessary – with the tourists. In 1961, the Maasai District Council at Kajiado was given control of the area. But the combined destructive capacities of cattle and tourists began to tell in the 1960s and a rising water table in the following decade brought poisonous alkali to the surface and decimated huge tracts of acacia woodland.

Kenyatta declared the 400-square-kilometre zone around the swamps (the present-day Amboseli) a **national park** in 1970 – a status that formally excluded the Maasai and their cattle, although in practical terms the park staff could do nothing to keep them out. Infuriated, the Maasai all but exterminated the park's magnificent long-horned black rhinos over the next few years, seizing on Amboseli's tourist emblem with a vengeance (the surviving rhinos were translocated). They also obliterated a good part of the lion population, which has still not recovered. Not until a piped water supply was set up for the cattle did the Maasai finally give up the land. For years, compromise appeared to be the order of the day, and, in the dry season, you'll see numerous herds of cattle and their herders encroaching well into the park unhindered, as they always did. Tensions rose in 2012, however, after a Maasai boy was killed by a buffalo and a number of animals, including elephants, were speared in retribution.

The **erosion** of Amboseli's grasslands by circling minibuses did a great deal of damage in the 1980s, turning it into a vehicle-clogged dustbowl that appealed little to animals or tourists. A concerted programme of environmental conservation, road-building and ditch-making was initiated, and this, combined with the toughest approach of any park to off-road driving (including fines and expulsions), has improved the situation enormously.

Selenkay Conservancy

West off the C102 between the Mombasa highway and Amboseli's Iremito Gate • Access exclusive to Gamewatchers Safaris clients on two- or three-night fly or drive packages from Nairobi • 60 square kilometres

North of the park proper and only accessible by air or with a driver-guide who knows the way, the **Selenkay Conservancy** is one of Kenya's pioneering community conservation success stories. Here, Gamewatchers Safaris, one of the country's most environmentally sound safari operators, co-manages *Porini Amboseli Camp* and *Gamewatchers Adventure Camp* (see p.342) with the local Maasai community. With a maximum of eighteen visitors at each, there are no time-serving, long-distance staff here: you're looked after by local warriors, generating direct income for their families.

Although the Selenkay (also spelled Selengei) area is bushy, with few stretches of open savanna, and wildlife is much less habituated to vehicles than in the park, the **game-viewing** can still be good, with predators frequently seen, as well as elephants, several species of antelope, and often the more infrequently observed mammals – there's a porcupine den close to the camp, for example. And the beauty of being here is the chance to go on game walks with your Maasai hosts, as often as you like. Down in a sandy area near the seasonal **Merueshi River**, they do sundowners and bush dinners, while their tree platform, near a waterhole, is a regular bush breakfast and sundowner spot.

ARRIVAL AND DEPARTURE · AMBOSELI NATIONAL PARK

BY CAR

Most drive-in visitors to Amboseli approach via the beautifully smooth, fast and quiet Emali road, which takes you from the Mombasa highway to the eastern end of the park. Don't take the slower route from Nairobi that uses the A104 to Namanga. If

you're coming from Arusha to Amboseli, however, you drive north towards Nairobi and turn right after the border at Namanga.

From Emali The C102 swoops south through Maasai grazing concessions and mixed farmland towards Oloitokitok. Keep a look out, if the sky is clear, for the unmistakeable shape of Kilimanjaro on the horizon, often directly ahead. It's 59km from Emali to the junction for Iremito Gate and a further 21km on the gravel E397 to the gate itself: this is the fastest route to the centre of the park at Ol Tukai. Alternatively, it's 90km from Emali to the eastern, Kimana Gate, junction, and then 22km more on the gravel C103 road to Kimana Gate: this gives you the quickest access to the camps outside the park.

From Namanga The horribly corrugated C103 road from Namanga to Meshanani Gate is comfortable only at more than 60km/h, and very wearing once you're inside the park, where the well-enforced speed limit is 40km/h. From the gate it's roughly another 20km to Ol Tukai.

Between Amboseli and Tsavo West Many independent travellers connect Amboseli with Tsavo West on a wildlife-viewing itinerary – the process is similar in both directions. From Amboseli, the C103 road leaves the park's east side at Kimana Gate and meets the C102 highway 22km east of the gate, and 5km south of the trading centre of Kimana. The junction for the continuation of the C103 east of the highway is well signposted just over 3km further south. As you head east, it quickly

becomes a reasonably smooth *murram* road. Tsavo West's Chyulu Gate is 66km from the junction.

BY BUS AND MATATU

There is no public transport to the gates (and little chance of getting a lift into the park from them), so budget travellers usually sign up for a cheap safari instead (see p.123). However buses and matatus from Nairobi or Mombasa will get you as far as Kimana or Oloitokitok on the east side, from where you'll have to arrange a pickup or, at a pinch, hop on a piki-piki to the lodges near Kimana Gate, where you can organize a game drive. On the west side of the park, buses and matatus from Nairobi will only get you as far as Namanga.

BY PLANE

There are daily Airkenya and SafariLink flights between Nairobi's Wilson Airport and the park's only airstrip (2–3 daily; around 1hr; around $165 one-way, $285 round trip). Mombasa Air Safari also has a daily flight to Amboseli from Mombasa via Diani Beach (daily; around 1hr 30min; around $370 one-way, $490 round trip), which then continues on from Amboseli to the Mara.

ACCOMMODATION

There are two **lodges**, a luxury **tented camp**, and basic **KWS accommodation** within the boundaries of the park, while the rest of the camps and lodges are just outside the park near Kimana Gate in the southeast. These have good access from the C102 from Emali and are in game-rich areas with Kilimanjaro views, but bear in mind that the park's $80 daily fee allows only one exit and re-entry per 24hr, which may restrict the number of game drives you can do inside the park itself.

INSIDE THE PARK

Amboseli Serena Safari Lodge Southern park area, near the Enkongo Narok swamp ☎020 2842000 or ☎0734 699838, ⓦserenahotels.com. *Serena's* adobe-style architecture is neatly arranged in a jungle of tropical plants and creepers, though unfortunately (and unfathomably) it does not have Kilimanjaro views. However standards are high in the modestly sized rooms, adorned with animal murals, and there's 24hr electricity, as

well as a large and inviting pool, and good wildlife-viewing from the terraces. A bronze guide and an Ecotourism Kenya Silver Award. Wi-fi. FB **$392**

KWS Amboseli Campsite 2km south of Kimana Gate within the park ☎020 8029705, ⓦkws.org. Shady sites with a view of Kili, but like the KWS guesthouses and *bandas*, it's right on the fence line of the KWS staff village. Good facilities include Western-style toilets, hot showers and taps (but not for drinking water), a kitchen hut with

KILIMANJARO'S GLACIERS

The most glorious views of **Kilimanjaro** are often on clear mornings during the rainy season. At these moments, when the dust in the air has been washed away and the clouds separate, the whole mountain seems to glow in the sky. Heavy rain often falls on the upper slopes in the form of snow, leaving a thick white topping and creating the impression that all is well with the atmosphere. It is of course an illusion: the glaciers are melting. The solid 10,000-year-old ice that rests on the peaks and once smothered the mountain with an icecap more than 20km across, has been steadily disappearing since Kilimanjaro was first seen by outsiders, and glaciers now cover only about one-tenth of the area they did when German geographer Hans Meyer made the first ascent of the peak in 1889. From the late nineteenth century until the 1980s, the melting effect was slow, reducing the ice cover by about one third over the course of the century; but another third has vanished in the last thirty years, and glaciologists now variously estimate that the mountain is likely to be ice-free at some point between 2030 and 2060.

5

caretaker, firewood and electric lights. Pay for camping at the gate. $30

KWS guesthouses and bandas By the park HQ, just inside the park, 2km south of Kimana Gate ☎045 62225 or KWS reservations in Nairobi ☎020 600800, ⓦkws.org. KWS manages two self-catering houses where you reserve the whole house – *Kilimanjaro Guest House* (six beds) and *Kibo Guest House* (four beds) – and five twin-bedded *bandas* (Nyati, Simba #1 and #2 and Chui #1 and #2). Bedding, warm water, firewood and security are provided (plus gas for cooking and generator electricity in the houses, and kerosene lighting in the *bandas*), but you need to bring everything else. *Kibo House* $240, *Kilimanjaro House* $200, *banda* $90

Ol Tukai Lodge Ol Tukai area ☎045 622275 or 0726 249697, ⓦoltukailodge.com. Set among tall trees and lawns, *Ol Tukai Lodge* has stylish, rustic architecture, beautiful communal areas and accommodation in well-furnished wooden cottages. Half the rooms look out beyond the low-key electric fence towards the Amboseli plains (rooms #1–48, "Elephant View"), and the rest look out towards Kilimanjaro (#49–80, "Mountain View"). There's a stunning pool from which you can see plenty of game, and Maasai dances most evenings. Wi-fi. Ecotourism Kenya Bronze Award. FB $450

Tortilis Camp In Kitirua Game Conservancy, just outside the southern park boundary, but accessible only via the park ☎0730 127000, ⓦtortilis.com. Set around a low hill, and named after the *Acacia tortilis* trees of the area, with stunning views of Kilimanjaro, this camp, surrounded by a sensitively low electric fence, is one of Cheli & Peacock's oldest. While not quite offering the same boutique feel as most of the others – it's a little larger and less informal – the seventeen tent-*banda* combinations are stylish enough and there's a separate house suitable for a family. Perks include good meals on the terrace (they grow their own veg), a lovely pool, superb birdlife and waterhole game-viewing, plus game drives and walks (a gold and four bronze guides). Wi-fi. Ecotourism Kenya Gold Award. FB $712

OUTSIDE KIMANA GATE

Amboseli Sopa Lodge 5km east of Kimana Gate ☎045 622334, Nairobi reservations ☎020 3750235, ⓦsopalodges.com. A mid-range option popular for safaris from the coast, with spacious and comfortably furnished rooms in thatched cottages in a very pleasant garden setting, with good views of Kilimanjaro and a pool. *Hemingway's Bar*, perched on top of massive boulders at the highest point of the property, is a good place for sundowners. Wi-fi. Ecotourism Kenya Bronze Award. FB $270

★**Kibo Safari Camp** 2km south of Kimana Gate

☎020 2672834 or ☎0721 380539, ⓦkibosafaricamp .com. Easily the best-value mid-range option, and with friendly staff to boot. The large tents are arranged in six rows fanning out into the gardens from the main thatched, stone-built central area, and all face the mountain. There's a pool and massages available, plus an extensive choice of buffet food and Maasai entertainment in the evenings. For those getting here under their own steam, game drive vehicles can be arranged for $100 for up to six people. Wi-fi. FB $240

Kilima Safari Camp 500m east of Kimana Gate ☎020 6005072 or 0722 741161, ⓦmadahotels.com. Owned by the operators of *Fig Tree Camp* in the Mara, this very different beast – a huge investment incorporating a lofty public area with a viewing tower topping the acres of thatch, a splendid pool and flamboyant "tent" and chalet designs – was opened in 2009. There are negatives, though: too much furniture, uncomfortable beds, not enough shade on site and it does seem hauntingly empty when there are not many guests around. Ecotourism Kenya Silver Award. FB $580

Satao Elerai Camp 10km southeast of Kimana Gate ☎020 2434600 or 0729 403566, ⓦsataoelerai.com. Like its sister camp in Tsavo East, *Satao Elerai* is a very comfortable, stylish, well-run, safari camp that isn't mass market, but with fourteen tents isn't quite small enough to be boutique. Great views of Kilimanjaro – when the mountain isn't being coy – are complemented by competent (bronze) guiding in the private, game-rich Elerai conservation area as well as game drives into the park. Wi-fi. Ecotourism Kenya Silver Award. FB $460

★**Tawi Lodge** 4km northeast of Kimana Gate ☎020 2300943 or ☎0722 745552, ⓦwww.tawilodge.com. On the 24-square-kilometre Kilitome Conservancy (a collaboration between the Dutch owners, local Maasai and the African Wildlife Foundation), which acts as a corridor between the park and the Chyulu Hills, this is the area's most luxurious and intimate offering. The spacious, Kilimanjaro-facing cottages each have a fireplace and freestanding bath plus a broad deck. Also available are excellent gourmet food, a spa, a heated pool overlooking a waterhole, sundowner trips and camel rides on the conservancy. Wi-fi. Ecotourism Kenya Gold Award. FB $604

SELENKAY CONSERVANCY

★**Porini Amboseli Camp/Gamewatchers Adventure Camp** 37km south of Emali, then 34km on bush tracks to the west (very difficult route to follow without a guide) ☎0774 136523, ⓦporinisafaricamps.com. These two camps in the Selenkay Conservancy (see p.340) are co-owned by Gamewatchers Safaris and the Maasai and offer an intimate and highly enjoyable experience. *Porini Amboseli*

5

Camp has just nine comfortable and spacious walk-in tents, each with solar lighting, full bathrooms and outdoor furniture under shadecloth. *Gamewatchers Adventure Camp* is the budget alternative, with small dome tents with mattresses – guests either bring their own sleeping bag and towel or hire them – and bathrooms in cubicles behind the tents with flush toilet, washbasin and "bladder" shower. The same activities are offered from both camps – game drives on the conservancy and in Amboseli, bush walks, sundowners and village visits. Package for two, including transport and conservancy fee: 2 nights *Porini Amboseli Camp* **$2880**, 3 nights *Gamewatchers Adventure Camp* **$1940**

Oloitokitok

With Kilimanjaro towering in front of you, the C102 highway slices across the plains, curves through the pretty, spring-fed oasis of Kimana and then climbs up to the Maasai country town of **OLOITOKITOK** at an altitude of 1700m. You'll pass through Oloitokitok (also known as Loitokikok) if heading direct to Taveta from Nairobi or planning to cross the border to Tanzania via the foothills of Kilimanjaro. It's also a potential place from which to start a climb up the mountain.

Although it's ignored by 99 percent of tourist traffic, this one-street hill town is in a stunning location, closer to Kilimanjaro than anywhere else in Kenya – Kibo Peak is just 25km from Oloitokitok as the crow flies. It's a relaxed place to settle into if you're interested in finding out more about the Maasai, as this is their easternmost major centre. Markets happen on Tuesdays and Saturdays. There's a customs post on the north side of town (you'll be waved through unless you're going to **Tanzania**), but the actual border is 8km further south at Illasit, on the road to Taveta.

ARRIVAL AND DEPARTURE   OLOITOKITOK

By bus and matatu There are plenty of connections with Emali (2hr), as well as less frequent services to Taveta (3hr). For transport direct to Nairobi (4–5hr), be prepared for an early start.

By car Oloitokitok is 104km from Emali (around a 1hr 30min drive), 79km from Taveta (2hr 30min) and some 230km from Nairobi (around 4hr).

INFORMATION

Services KCB, on the C102 as it goes through town, has an ATM. The most reliable petrol station for fuel is Oillibya up the hill from the C102 in the market area. You can get snacks and drinks from *dukas* around here.

ACCOMMODATION AND EATING

★ **Kibo Slopes Cottages** 700m down a track branching off the main road to the east, immediately south of the customs post (on the left side of the road if you're coming from the Emali direction) ☎ 0729 308767, ⓦ kibocottages.com. Superior to everywhere else in town, with clean and tidy s/c rooms in brick cottages set in rows in flowery gardens. There's a bright bar and restaurant – you may see Kili from the patio –and you can stop for lunch if passing by (main courses such as pan-fried tilapia or vegetable pasta Ksh650–850, toasted cheese sandwich Ksh160). It's a

well-established base for climbing Kilimanjaro (ⓦ kiboslopessafaris.com; given that the ascent starts over the border, allow for a Tanzanian visa and make sure you have a yellow fever certificate). They can also organize local drivers for transfers to the lodges at Amboseli's Kimana Gate. Wi-fi. BB **$70**

Safaris Guest House 100m from the Oilibya petrol station ☎ 0728 244514. Christian-run lodgings with small s/c rooms with nets, sockets and electric showers. It's very simple but the house is tidy, clean and well run. **Ksh1000**

From Oloitokitok to Taveta

The tarmac continues invitingly south out of Oloitokitok to the Tanzanian border crossing and market town of **Illasit**, where it veers off to the south towards Moshi in Tanzania. The road that continues in a southeasterly direction to Taveta starts well, with graded grey gravel skirting the flanks of Kilimanjaro, at least as far as the dispersed centre of **Njukini-Chumvini**. From here to **Lake Chala**, however, it's in a poor state and often impassable after heavy rain, even with 4WD. From Chala to **Taveta** (see p.334) it's much better.

Much of the scenery along this route is beautiful, the landscape changing from scrubby cattle pasture to plots of sisal and maize – marking the end of Maasai territory – and patches of acacia woodland, cut by streams and dotted with swamp. There are only a few settlements, acting as market centres for Maasai and Taveta farmers, but **Rombo** is notable for its very fine mosque with its soaring minaret.

Chyulu Hills National Park

$25 (see p.73) • ⓣ 0711 574766, ⓦ kws.org • 741 square kilometres

The **Chyulu Hills National Park**, which follows the spine of the geologically recent Chyulu Hills lava ridge – only formed around 500 years ago – and shares a border with Tsavo West to the south, is one of Kenya's least visited and least developed national parks. Aside from the wildlife and the glorious scenery (the hills took the role of the less impressive Ngong Hills for the filming of *Out of Africa*), the main attraction is **Leviathan Cave**, the world's second-longest lava tube. You can explore Leviathan from *Umani Springs* lodge in Kibwezi Forest (see p.324). **Wildlife** in the Chyulus is fairly sparse because of the altitude (1500–2160m), but the plains between the highway and the hills are often speckled with game, including giraffe, buffalo, eland, zebra and wildebeest. In the glades of the forested hills themselves you may spot elephant and giant forest hog. The crest of the Chyulus is wreathed in mossy cloud forest, constantly watered by the clouds that make the landscapes here so ravishingly beautiful. On a clear day, the haloed peak of Kilimanjaro rises to the west.

ARRIVAL AND GETTING AROUND — CHYULU HILLS NATIONAL PARK

By car A high-clearance 4WD is required to get into the park. Inside the park, you'll preferably have a guide: there are few rough tracks and the terrain is steep and hard going. The easiest access is via Kithasyo Gate, signposted off the west side of the Mombasa highway, 1.5 km south of Kibwezi, and then another 9km (gate around a 5hr drive from Nairobi). Alternatively, you can drive into the hills from *Ol Donyo Lodge* or *Campi ya Kanzi* (see below).

By plane SafariLink flies from Nairobi Wilson via Tsavo West to *Ol Donyo Lodge* airstrip daily in the morning (1hr–1hr 30min; around $215 one-way and $340 round trip), with a second, afternoon flight in high season.

ACCOMMODATION

There is no accommodation within the park boundaries except for the **campsite** at Kithasyo Gate. The two upmarket options in the foothills of the Chyulus are both on Maasai group ranches adjoining the park and are normally accessed by plane.

★Campi ya Kanzi Southern end of the Chyulu Hills, 12km north of the C103 Amboseli–Tsavo West road ⓣ 045 622516, ⓦ maasai.com; map p.321. Passionately conceived, award-winning Maasai–Italian eco-collaboration on the 1130-square-kilometre Kuku Group Ranch, which was constructed without tree-felling and is entirely powered from renewable sources, sourcing water with a huge rain-water catchment area and using organic produce from their own garden, dairy cows and hens. Accommodation is in thatched cottages with balconies and rollup canvas walls, and Kanzi House, a villa for families and groups. Each has furniture made from reclaimed wood, plus luxuries like Italian bed linen. There's also a pool, and activities include walks with the Maasai, horse riding and (for extra) scenic flights over the Chyulus. Two bronze guides. Ecotourism Kenya Gold Award. Conservancy fee $100. Package **$1900**

KWS Kiboko Campsite At the park HQ 200m into the park from Kithasyo Gate, 9km west of Kibwezi ⓣ 0711 574766, ⓦ kws.org; map p.321. Not much more than a clearing in the bush, with cold showers and long-drop toilets, but a pleasant spot and convenient for self-drive campers going down the Mombasa highway. You need to be self-sufficient, but KWS rangers live behind the campsite and will be able to organize firewood. Camping **$20**

★Ol Donyo Lodge On the western flank of the Chyulus, 29km east of Mbirikani on the C102, reservations through Great Plains in South Africa ⓣ +27 (0)87 3546591, ⓦ greatplainsconservation.com; map p.321. On the 1110-square-kilometre Mbirikani Group Ranch, this astonishingly chic bush lodge

5

has extremely stylish and spacious suites, all with roof terraces where you can sleep under the stars if you choose, outdoor showers, private views and eight with their own plunge pools. Guests eat separately or together, sometimes with the owners, legendary safari pilot Richard Bonham and family. Included are guided walks, mountain biking, horse riding and day and night game drives. Conservancy fees are included in rates. Wi-fi. Package. **$2430**

Tsavo West National Park

$75 with Safari Card (see p.73) • ☎ 020 2384417 or ☎ 0720 968527, ⊛ kws.org • 7065 square kilometres

The combined area of **Tsavo West and Tsavo East national parks** makes this by far the biggest wildlife reserve in Kenya, and one of the largest in the world, sprawling across 20,812 square kilometres of dry bush country. It's the same area as Wales, and two-and-a-half times bigger than Yellowstone National Park in the US.

Of the two Tsavos, **Tsavo West**, encircled by roads and encroaching human populations, is the most visited and the most developed. Yet within its vast 7000 square kilometre extent, the popular part that receives nearly all visitors is a "mere" 1000 square kilometres, known as the **Developed Area**, located between the Tsavo River and the Mombasa highway. Here, a combination of magnificent landscapes and good access and facilities (*Kilaguni Serena Safari Lodge* and *Severin Safari Camp* both welcome casual visitors, and *Kilaguni* has fuel supplies) attracts visitors in large numbers, while the well-watered, volcanic soils support wooded grasslands and a great quantity and diversity of animal life – though it's not always easily seen.

The Developed Area

Across the hilly **Developed Area**, there's an unending succession of fantastic views across the plains, dotted with volcanic cones and streaked with forest at the water margins. When the animals are abundant, every turn in the track seems to bring you face to face with zebra, giraffe, huge herds of buffalo, casual prides of lions – descendants of the "man-eaters of Tsavo" (see p.325) – or methodical, strolling elephants, almost orange from the dust. An unusual species to look for is the beautiful and shy **lesser kudu** antelope – always, it seems, running away.

One large mammal you're less likely to see is the black rhino. In the 1960s, Tsavo had as many as nine thousand **black rhinos** – the biggest population in Africa. By 1981, they had been poached to barely one hundred individuals across Tsavo West and East. Though the situation later improved, like everywhere else in Africa rhino poaching is unfortunately rife once again today.

The little circuit that takes you around the foot of **Rhodesian Hill** is recommended, and **Poacher's Lookout**, near *Severin*, is a very promising place for a quiet scan with binoculars. There's a thatched shelter on this prominent hilltop, where you can sit in the breeze. Note that the summit is 4.5km from junction #32, not 2km as marked.

Ngulia Rhino Sanctuary

At the eastern end of the Developed Area • Daily 4–6pm (get there early as it's at least a 1hr 30min drive back to the Developed Area) • Free

Covering around ninety square kilometres and surrounded by an electric fence, **Ngulia Rhino Sanctuary** was established in 1986. Access is currently possible only for two hours in the afternoon. You may see one of the sanctuary's **black** and **white rhinos**, though the thick bush makes them hard to spot. Sadly Ngulia has not been without incidents: in 2013, and again in 2014, poachers penetrated the sanctuary and several rhinos were lost. As a result, KWS has since moved some of the animals out of the sanctuary and dispersed them more widely in the park – a strategy simply to disguise their whereabouts. As with the other parks, KWS does not publish any information about how many rhinos are resident.

5

Mzima Springs

500m south of junction #11, 48km from Mtito Andei and close to both *Kilaguni Serena Safari Lodge* and *Severin Safari Camp*

The biggest attraction in Tsavo West is **Mzima Springs**. This stream of crystal-clear water is a delightful, and popular, spot, so you're advised to arrive very early to avoid a possible tour-bus atmosphere. With luck, some of the night's animal visitors may still be around, while the luxuriant growth around the water reverberates noisily with birds and monkeys.

You can walk around freely, as elephants and predators rarely visit, and there are **KWS rangers** posted by the car park to look after you, but make sure you're not close to the water's edge, where large crocodiles lurk. Equally be sure that you're not between a hippo and the water, especially early or late in the day, or during wet weather. They seem settled in their routine, content to snort and flounder en masse, but are notoriously irritable animals.

There are two large pools, connected by a rush of rapids and shaded by stands of spectacular trees. These include date and raffia palms, water berries and figs, whose submerged roots absorb nutrients from the springs and whose fruit is a source of food for monkeys (vervet and Sykes') and birds. At the side of the top pool, a circular underwater **viewing chamber** has been built at the end of a short pier. With luck (and it doesn't happen on every visit), you'll see the unforgettably comic tip-toeing of an underwater hippo, or the sinuous, streamlined stealth of a crocodile in motion, as well as the blue swirl of large fish.

Mzima Springs' water is filtered to aquarium transparency by the lava of the **Chyulu range**, just to the north of here: the porous rock absorbs the water like a sponge and gravity squeezes it out into the springs. A direct pipeline from Mzima to Mombasa, completed in 1966, is the source of most of the city's **drinking water**. Engineers devised a way of taking water from beneath the lava, but above the spring, preserving the area's integrity. There are one or two signs of the pipeline, but most are unobtrusive.

You don't have to be a botanist to enjoy Mzima's two **tree trails**, with examples of various trees labelled with their common uses and their English, local and botanical names. It's easy to spend a couple of hours in the area: try to sit for a while completely alone on the bank and you'll begin to piece together the ecological miracle of the place, as the mammals, birds and other creatures forget about your presence. .

Game-viewing at the lodges

Kilaguni Serena Safari Lodge (see p.350) off junction 8, about 30km from Mtito Andei Gate • **Severin Safari Camp** (see p.350) off junction #36, 8km from Mzima Springs

You may not be staying in the relative luxury of **Kilaguni Serena Safari Lodge** or **Severin Safari Camp**, but a visit to either can be highly rewarding, for the pleasure of sitting on the terrace with a cold beer, or having lunch (allow $25), while you watch the enthralling natural circus going on a few metres away. At acacia-shaded *Severin*, guests and wildlife are on exactly the same level, making the experience very intimate, while the **waterholes** at *Kilaguni*, spread beneath the panorama of the Chyulu Hills, are a well-known magnet for animal visitors.

At *Kilaguni*, dazzling **birds** hop everywhere, **agama lizards** skim along the walls (the miniature orange and blue dragons are the males in mating colours), **hyraxes** scamper between the tables, and **dwarf mongooses** are regular visitors. Out by the waterholes, scuffling **baboon troops**, several species of **antelope** and **gazelle**, **buffalo**, **zebra**, **giraffe** and **elephant** all provide a constant spectacle, with the possibility of the occasional kill adding tension. At dusk, **bats** swoop, while **genets**, **jackals** and **hyenas** lurk near the floodlights, drawn by the smell of dinner – though, thankfully, the lodge has stopped the practice of baiting them with meat scraps.

5

The camp at *Severin*, meanwhile, seems to be absorbed by its environment, and there's nothing to stop the animals treating the whole place as their own. Signs warn visitors not to stray off the paths, but you'll need little reminding, as families of **warthogs** trot past the terrace, **impala** and **giraffe** nibble audibly, and **lion kills** take place close to reception. Unlike *Kilaguni*, which is fenced, guests at *Severin* have to be escorted to and from their tents after dark.

Birding at Ngulia Safari Lodge

8km west of Tsavo Gate, 6.5km south of junction #18 (see p.350)

Ngulia Safari Lodge is a stopover on the annual southern migration of hundreds of thousands of European **birds**, but the reasons for its attraction for the birds – apart from its isolated lights – aren't really known. Kenyan and overseas ornithologists and amateur birders gather at the end of November for a fortnight to identify and ring the birds that are trapped in mist nets to build up a picture of their migration routes. The count has been between 10,000 and 20,000 per year since the activity began in 1969. If you'd like to participate, contact the lodge or your national birdwatching organization for information.

Lava flows and caves

Shetani lava flow starts about 10km east of junction #29 and continues east for more than 1km – the caves are 5.5km up the high-clearance-only track that climbs the flank of the volcano, north of junction #26B; after 5km, start looking out on the right side of the track for an oil drum, and a fig tree that covers the entrance

The lava that purifies Mzima's water can be seen in black outcrops all around the Developed Area of Tsavo. The main park road from Amboseli to Chyulu Gate runs right across the spectacular **Shetani lava flow**. The eruption that spewed it out two hundred years ago was evidently a cataclysmic event for local people, and is still the focus of stories about fire and evil spirits (*shetani* means "devil" in Swahili). People are said to have been buried under the hot lava, and legend has it that their plaintive cries can be heard on certain nights.

At several places you're allowed out of your vehicle to explore the lava, which is brittle, honeycombed and unstable. After only two centuries, very few plants have yet taken hold. The **caves** are certainly worth investigation, and they sometimes contain the bones of various unlucky animals that have stumbled in and been unable out again. You'll need a powerful torch, however, to get very far.

Chaimu Crater

Nature trail 6km southeast of junction #9

At the foot of the extinct **Chaimu volcano**, you can leave your vehicle and climb up to the crater rim – a steep scramble through the scree that delivers magnificent views across the park. Although it doesn't look high, it can be surprisingly hard work and you shouldn't attempt it in the heat of the day. There are no rangers here, so you need to be acutely aware of your surroundings and watch out for large mammals.

ARRIVAL AND DEPARTURE   **TSAVO WEST NATIONAL PARK**

Nearly all visitors to Tsavo West come by private vehicle or on a road or air safari.

By bus and matatu There are no bus or matatu services into Tsavo West National Park itself. The small service town of Mtito Andei (see p.325), midway between Mombasa and Nairobi and walking distance from Mtito Andei Gate, is easily reached by public transport. If you've booked accommodation at one of the lodges in the Developed Area, they will pick you up from

the gate for a fee. It's not a good idea to be dropped at Tsavo Gate, the southern gate on the Mombasa highway located where the highway crosses the Tsavo River, as there is no settlement there, and you could wait a very long time before getting a lift into the park.

By car Allow 4–5hr to reach Mtito Andei from either Nairobi or Mombasa. Fill up before entering the park and

APPROXIMATE DRIVING TIMES IN TSAVO WEST

From Mtito Andei Gate: 1hr to *Kilaguni*; 1hr 30min to *Severin*; 2hr to *Finch Hatton's*.

From Tsavo Gate: 40min to *Ngulia*; 2hr 30min to *Kilaguni* and *Severin*; 3hr to *Finch Hatton's*.

From Chyulu Gate: 1hr to *Kilaguni*; 1hr 30min to *Severin*; 2hr 30min to *Ngulia*; 2hr to *Finch Hatton's*.

From Ziwani Gate: 2hr 30min to *Kilaguni*; 2hr to *Severin*; 2hr 30min to *Finch Hatton's*; 3hr to *Ngulia*.

From Maktau Gate: 2hr to *Kilaguni*; 1hr 30min to *Severin*; 2hr to *Finch Hatton's*; 3hr to *Ngulia*.

take drinking water. *Kilaguni* lodge has a small filling station (daily 7am–4pm & 6–7pm; prices about ten percent above the pump price in Mtito Andei). The information centre at Mtito Andei gate has interesting background about Tsavo West, as well as a small shop selling cold drinks: other gates have few, if any, facilities. Coming from the coast direction, the quickest access is Tsavo Gate, in the southeast of the Developed Area; allow 2–3hr to get there from Mombasa. Another option is Maktau Gate (see p.331) on the newly tarred Voi–Taveta road (A23), which is the most straightforward route to the Developed Area if coming from Tanzania. Access via Chyulu Gate (see p.341) and Ziwani

Gate (see p.331) is possible, but bear in mind the warning about the small Tsavo river bridge in the park, which is apt to be closed after heavy rains. Once you're in the park, you'll soon come to appreciate your dependency on the marker cairns at the numbered junctions.

By plane There are at least daily flights from Nairobi Wilson on SafariLink and Airkenya to *Kilaguni* and/or *Finch Hatton's* airstrip, depending on demand (around 1hr; around $215 one way, $345 round trip). You can fly daily to the same airstrips from Mombasa and Diani Beach with Mombasa Air Safari (around 1hr 30min; around $370 one way, $490 round trip).

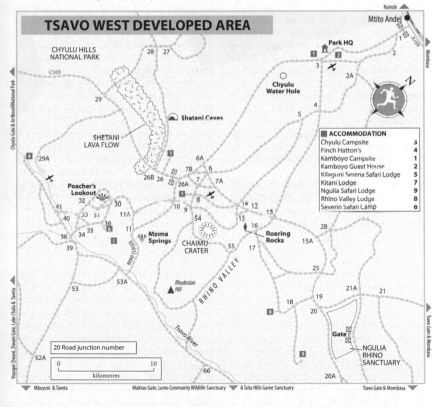

TSAVO WEST DEVELOPED AREA

CHYULU HILLS NATIONAL PARK

Park HQ

Chyulu Water Hole

Shetani Caves

SHETANI LAVA FLOW

Poacher's Lookout

Mzima Springs

CHAIMU CRATER

Roaring Rocks

Rhodesian Hill

RHINO VALLEY

Tsavo River

■ ACCOMMODATION
Chyulu Campsite	3
Finch Hatton's	4
Kamboyo Campsite	1
Kamboyo Guest House	2
Kilaguni Serena Safari Lodge	5
Kitani Lodge	7
Ngulia Safari Lodge	9
Rhino Valley Lodge	8
Severin Safari Camp	6

Gate

NGULIA RHINO SANCTUARY

20 Road junction number

0 — 10
kilometres

Nairobi

Mtito Andei

Mombasa

5

ACCOMMODATION

A lack of modestly priced accommodation is less of an obstacle in Tsavo West than in most of the other main parks. There are three public KWS **campsites** within the park – the two reviewed below plus another on the lakeshore at Lake Jipe (see p.337). In addition, there are several KWS-designated "special campsites" along the north bank of the Tsavo River – though remember these have no facilities of any kind and have to be organized in advance through KWS (see p.61). If you're not equipped to camp but can bring food supplies, you can take advantage of the mid-priced self-catering options in the shape of the *bandas* at *Rhino Valley Lodge* and *Kitani Lodge*, and the house rental at *Kamboyo Guest House*, near the park headquarters. All accommodation reviewed here is marked on the "Tsavo West Developed Area" map (see p.349), with the exception of *Voyager Ziwani*.

CAMPSITES

Chyulu Campsite Just outside Chyulu Gate, north of junction #26. Basic European-style toilets, running water for the showers and shacks for pitching your tent under (assuming it's a smallish dome tent). $20

Kamboyo Campsite Just north of junction #3, near the park HQ not far from Mtito Andei Gate. Nice enough, with plenty of easy pitches under shady trees, and a promising-looking shower and squat toilet block. Unfortunately the water here is not to be relied upon, though, so you need to bring your own. $20

TENTED CAMPS AND LODGES

Finch Hatton's 9km south of junction #29, 65km from Mtito Andei Gate ⓣ 0720 444419, ⓦ finchhattons.com. *Finch Hatton's*, named after the aristocrat who introduced royalty to the bush, has recently reopened after a two-year redevelopment, and is now once again living up to its long-established reputation. Managed with great flair and expertise, the camp offers lavish tented suites (choose #16, at the far end by the viewing platform). As Mozart (Denys Finch Hatton's favourite composer) tinkles above the evening frog chorus, you're served multi-course dinners of exceptionally good food. Best of all is the site's truly remarkable natural environment, which is similar to Mzima Springs. There's a good pool, and extra treats include spa treatments and bush breakfasts. Their own airstrip is 3km away. Wi-fi. FB $862

Kamboyo Guest House 2km northeast of junction #3, by the park HQ ⓣ 0726 610508, ⓦ kws.org. Well located, above a small waterhole, with views to the south from the large upstairs balcony and ground-floor veranda, this spacious, clean and decently furnished house can sleep up to eight. There's a lounge with a log fire, and facilities include a fully equipped kitchen with gas cooker and generator (7–10pm). Whole house $240

Kilaguni Serena Safari Lodge Off junction #8, about 30km from Mtito Andei Gate ⓣ 020 2842000 or ⓣ 0734 699865, ⓦ serenahotels.com. Dating from 1962, the oldest park lodge in Kenya is a perennial favourite with many repeat visitors, as much as anything for its prime site and terrific wildlife ambience, with a spectacular panoramic overlook of two floodlit waterholes. There's a busy atmosphere and it's very often full, but standards are high for the price. The well-laid-out rooms are either in a double-storey block or a string of thatched cottages, most facing the wildlife action, with views towards the Chyulu Hills and Kili from the balconies or verandas. Modest pool, gift shop, children's activities and evening Maasai entertainment. Wi-fi. Ecotourism Kenya Silver Award. FB $342

★**Kitani Lodge** 1.5km from Severin Safari Camp, off junction #36, 8km from Mzima Springs ⓣ 041 2111000 or ⓣ 041 2004153, ⓦ severin-hotels.com. Also known as *Kitani Bandas*, and competently managed by *Severin*, this delightful self-catering camp comprises eight comfortable s/c *bandas*, each sleeping up to three, with nets, good kitchens with gas cookers and electric sockets, and a firepit (firewood provided). *Bandas* #3 and #4 have the best views of Kili, but all share the intimate connection with the Tsavo environment. Guests can go to the main camp to eat or use the pool, spa and wi-fi (you'll need to drive or call them to arrange transport). Whole *banda* $123

Ngulia Safari Lodge 48km west of Tsavo Gate, 6.5km south of junction #18 ⓣ 0733 333400, ⓦ safari-hotels.com. Somewhat isolated in the more hilly eastern side of the park, where the immediate area has less wildlife appeal than the other lodges, this 1970s apartment-block-style lodge offers small and dated rooms, with nets and floor fans but no other frills. There are redeeming factors though: it's well maintained, with a small pool; the two small waterholes by the terrace attract buffalo and a host of birds; and there are tremendous views over the plains far below. Casual visitors are welcome. Wi-fi. FB $270

Rhino Valley Lodge 3.5km west of junction #18 ⓣ 0725 517832, reservations ⓣ 0721 328567, ⓦ tsavolodgesandcamps.com. Nestled on the steep north slopes of Ngulia Hill, *Rhino Valley Lodge* offers sweeping vistas from the terrace bar-restaurant and has a waterhole opposite *bandas* #4, #5 and #6. But like *Ngulia Safari Lodge*, you don't get the concentrations of wildlife you find around *Kilaguni* or *Severin*. There are six *bandas* and a family room with fully equipped kitchens, six more basic *bandas* with no kitchen, plus ten stone-and-thatch rooms with balconies. Electricity, powering sockets and fridges, is supplied 6–11am and 5–8.30pm. Self-catering *bandas* $110, FB *bandas* $180, FB rooms $240

★**Severin Safari Camp** Off junction #36, 8km from Mzima Springs ⓣ 020 2684247 or ⓣ 0733 645444,

Ⓦ severinsafaricamp.com. Enthusiastic, hands-on German management is responsible for the distinctive flavour of this very cool, thoughtfully conceived camp of tents and luxury *bandas*, sprawled on a flat, bushy plain, teeming with wildlife. Casual visitors are welcome for meals that are well out of the ordinary (Ksh2000; try the cook-your-own hot stone grill with dipping sauces), the superb pool and the rejuvenating spa, all witnessed by a ceaseless parade of giraffes, antelopes, warthogs and birdlife attracted by the camp's five waterholes. Bush walks and night drives are on offer. Tent #16 and *banda* #3 have the best views. Wi-fi. Ecotourism Kenya Silver Award. FB **$326**

Voyager Ziwani Just outside Ziwani Gate, about 40km south of the Developed Area, most easily reached from the Taveta–Voi road (see p.335) ☎020 2688982, Nairobi reservations ☎020 4446651, Ⓦ heritage-eastafrica.com; map p.335. In a glorious location in a private sanctuary on the Sante River, dammed to create a hippo and crocodile pool, *Ziwani* has 25 good-quality and well-spaced-out tents under thatched roofs. Although a good hour's drive south of the park's main attractions (from which it is sometimes cut off when floods wash away the crossing points over the Tsavo River), the local bonuses such as early-morning walks and night game drives more than compensate. It's also one of the best lodges for children: Heritage Hotels' excellent Adventurers' Club has a programme here. Wi-fi. Ecotourism Kenya Bronze Award. FB **$364**

Tsavo East National Park

$75 with Safari Card (see p.73) • Ⓦ kws.org • 13,747 square kilometres

Northeast of the highway, the rail line, and the apparent natural divide that separates Kenya's northern and southern environments, lies **Tsavo East National Park**. Although it is the larger part of the combined Tsavo parks, the sector north of the **Galana River** has few tracks and is much less visited. South of the river, the great triangle of flat wilderness, with **Aruba Dam** in the middle, is popular with safari operators, since it offers a pretty sure chance of seeing plenty of animals, in a very open environment, just half a day's drive from most coastal resorts.

Apart from some tumbled **crags and scarps** near Voi, and the rocky cleft of the Galana River (fed by the Tsavo and the Athi), Tsavo East is an uninterrupted **plain of bush**, dotted with the crazed shapes of baobab trees. It's a forbiddingly enormous reserve and at times over the last three decades has seemed an odd folly, especially since its northern area was closed to the public for many years due to the long war against elephant and rhino **poachers** (see box, p.353)

Although there's a steady stream of minibus safaris coming up from the coast, and the emptiness of the park is no longer as overwhelming as it was, Tsavo East's vastness still means that for much of the time you will still have the pleasure of exploring the wilderness completely alone. It's easy to get away off the two or three beaten tracks, and you may find something special – a **serval** perhaps, or a **lesser kudu**. After decades of poaching, **rhinos** are very rare in Tsavo East, but you may be lucky enough to spot one grazing quietly somewhere, especially north of the Galana. By contrast, you are absolutely certain to see a lot of Tsavo East's delightfully colourful **elephants**, be they huge, dusty-red adults, or little chocolate babies fresh out of a mud bath.

Game drives along the Galana

The **Galana River** itself, with its fringing cordon of branching **doum palms**, creates a captivating backdrop, the sandy river bed often dotted with wildlife in the dry season. West of junction #110, above the confluence of the Tsavo and Athi rivers and the start of the Galana, is **Observation Hill**, while downstream, east of junction #160, are the gently spectacular **Lugard's Falls**, where you're allowed to park and clamber around the bizarrely eroded rocks. Even in relatively dry conditions, the falls, progressing from foaming rapids to narrow cascades gouged deep into the rock, are quite impressive.

A kilometre east of the falls, another short diversion takes you to **Crocodile Point**, something of a letdown as the crocs are hard to see unless you get up close, which you're no longer allowed to do. **Hippos** are easier to spot from the vantage point.

5

Game drives south of the Galana

Most **game drives** from the camps near the Galana River use the main dirt road along the south bank of the river as an introduction, and then strike south along the roads following tributary *luggas*, up into the higher bush country between the Galana and Voi rivers. Heading south from the Galana, any of the park roads from junctions #150, #111, #110, #161, #163, #108 or #174 can yield good results. **Buffalo Wallows Lugga** (junction #110, then #159) is often rewarding, with the chance of seeing a leopard, and plenty of birdlife. Lions, and occasionally cheetahs, can be seen along these watercourses.

Some 20km further southwest, just north of junction #158, **Mudanda Rock** is particularly recommended. Resembling a scaled-down version of Australia's Uluru, it towers above a natural dam which, during the dry season, draws elephants in their hundreds.

Game-viewing near Voi

Starting out from the relatively busy Voi area (see p.326 and map, p.327), the wooden margins of the seasonal **Voi River** often hide a profusion of wildlife, and this area is one of the most promising in the park. Try the KWS **Ndololo Campsite** at junction #103, the pretty **Aruba Dam** at junction #105 (roughly 30km east of Voi Gate) and the **Kanderi Swamp loop** at #174. The river's marshy fringe is an excellent spot for birdwatching, and is a favourite with elephant and buffalo, and lions are sometimes spotted too. The *Ashnil Aruba Lodge* (see p.354) is close to the dam on the river's north bank. After rains in swampy areas, keep your windows up when driving through the tall grass and undergrowth, not only for security against the bigger animals, but as a defence against the tsetse flies that may mistake your vehicle for a large animal.

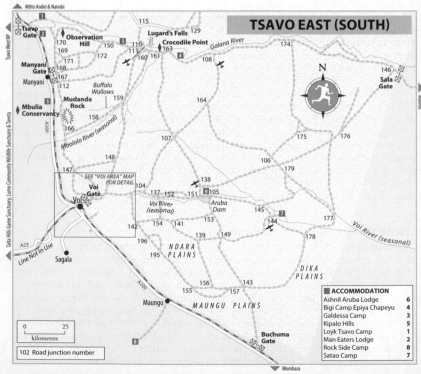

TSAVO EAST (SOUTH)

■ **ACCOMMODATION**

Ashnil Aruba Lodge	6
Bigi Camp Epiya Chapeyu	4
Galdessa Camp	3
Kipalo Hills	5
Loyk Tsavo Camp	1
Man Eaters Lodge	2
Rock Side Camp	8
Satao Camp	7

102 Road junction number

5

TSAVO'S POACHING WARS

In Tsavo, as throughout the country, the question of how to manage the **elephants** is still paramount. While several other countries permit trophy hunting, it has been illegal in Kenya since the 1970s and the policy here is to hunt the poachers and allow the elephants to reach their own natural balance within the defined park territory. Zoologists are divided about whether there is an optimal elephant population for a park like Tsavo, especially as natural weather patterns and now climate change are so significant. The destruction by elephants of Tsavo East's fragile woodlands and ongoing human–elephant conflict in the farmlands around the perimeter (the park boundary is fenced around Voi) are perennial concerns.

Such questions have been submerged for many years by the overbearing problem of ivory **poaching**, which at one time looked like it would wipe out the elephants completely. In 1967, the combined Tsavo parks' elephant population was more than 30,000. It dropped to 5300 in 1988, and today stands at between 11,000 and 12,000. Elephants are long-lived and intelligent animals with complex kinship patterns, and the social structure of the herds in many districts was badly distorted in the 1980s, with many older animals killed and too many inexperienced younger elephants unable to fend for themselves or to act as role models for infants. The poachers had changed too; they were no longer marginalized Kamba farmers killing an occasional elephant with an old gun or poisoned arrows – rather this was a new breed of well-connected gangster, equipped with automatic weapons, wiping out whole family groups in a single attack.

Kenya's response, its first **ivory burning**, organized for President Moi by the new Kenya Wildlife Service director **Richard Leakey** in 1989 (see p.146), caused so much worldwide publicity that it triggered an international ivory trade ban that remains in force today among countries that are members of CITES – the Convention on International Trade in Endangered Species. The ban stopped much of the ivory trade in its tracks, and had an immediate effect on the numbers of new elephant corpses being logged in Tsavo East. Equally dramatic was the unprecedented aggression with which the KWS started performing their duties under their bluntly pragmatic boss, with poachers liable to be shot on sight and Leakey adamant that there was no alternative.

Leakey went too far for some and left the KWS after an unexplained, near-fatal plane crash (see box, p.571). But the **ivory pyre** was a winning idea: in 2011, President Kibaki lit 6.5 tonnes of ivory and in March 2015, a mound of more than 15 tonnes of tusks was set ablaze by President Kenyatta to mark World Wildlife Day. At a time when other countries are stockpiling seized ivory, and Kenya's reputation for corruption and mismanagement could hardly be worse, these burnings were intended to symbolize to the world that the country is committed to putting its ivory beyond commercial use.

Kenyans in the **conservation community** are sceptical: the lobby group Wildlife Direct (𝕎 wildlifedirect.org) reported that over a recent five-year period only seven percent of convictions for ivory and rhino horn offences resulted in jail terms, despite a maximum ten-year sentence. The treatment of arch smuggler **Feisal Mohammed Ali**, regarded as Kenya's "ivory kingpin", is telling too: having finally been arrested in Tanzania and extradited to Kenya, he was bailed by a Mombasa court in August 2015.

Despite the lack of will at home, the future for Kenya's elephants may be a little rosier because of a change of mind in a powerful partner: in March 2015, amid international outrage at the consequences of its citizens' huge appetite for ivory, **China** imposed a ban on ivory imports and the price of raw ivory fell from more then $2000/kg to $1100/kg.

Tsavo East's **black rhinos** are much further down the path to annihilation. The Tsavo region was once a bastion of the black rhino in Africa, with estimates in the 1960s of between 6000 and 9000 in this region alone. And those numbers were already down, thanks to the savage groundwork in rhino extermination that started after World War II, when the colonial government sent in one **J.A. Hunter** to clear the Kamba resettlement area between Nairobi and Tsavo of unwelcome animals (see p.322). The rest were all but eliminated during Tsavo "killing fields" period in 1970s and 1980s.

The concept of **saving the rhino** has become a national cause in Kenya and ranches and sanctuaries around the country play a leading role in breeding future generations. But as long as there is a market for the horn for pseudo-medicinal use, as there is still in China and increasingly in **Vietnam** – and with its price at up to $60,000/kg – rhinos will remain under extreme threat.

5

Don't assume the flat expanses between **Buchuma Gate** and the Voi River will be devoid of interest. Try alternative routes to the main arteries – for example the remote loop across the **Dika plains** from junction #143 to *Satao Camp*, where elephants are often abundant and cheetahs not uncommon.

Visiting Tsavo East's northern sector

The park's **northern sector** is most easily accessed from Mtito Andei Gate East, but in the dry season it's also possible to reach the northern sector over the Galana River bed at junction #160, the only crossing point. Beware of mistaking mud for the smooth rock bed: unwitting drivers sometimes get stuck. On the western side of the northern sector lies a huge, ancient lava flow, in the shape of the **Yatta plateau**, stretching from Mtito Andei towards the Galana River, above the east bank of the Athi River.

ARRIVAL AND DEPARTURE   TSAVO EAST NATIONAL PARK

There is no public transport into the park itself, but it's perfectly feasible to be dropped by a **bus or matatu** at one of the gates on the Mombasa highway (A109), or in Voi. Getting a lift into the park is, as always, difficult, but you can organize a pickup from one of the lodges.

BY CAR
If you're going independently, and assuming your trip along the Mombasa highway goes relatively smoothly, the journey from Nairobi might take 4hr (to Mtito Andei Gate) to 5hr (Voi Gate), and the trip from Mombasa 2hr (Buchuma Gate) to 4hr (Mtito Andei Gate). Distances inside Tsavo East are huge – think of it as a small country – and there is little infrastructure, so help can be a long time coming. Only just out of Voi (see p.326), Voi Gate is the park HQ, where you get Safari Cards (see p.73), and the town itself has all the facilities you may need. Most of other gates have limited or zero facilities, although busy Buchuma Gate has a decent-sized curio shop.
From gates on the Mombasa road From north to south: Mtito Andei Gate East gives access to the northern

sector; Tsavo Gate is used for *Loyk Tsavo Camp* (30min); Manyani Gate for *Galdessa* (30min) and *Bigi Camp Epiya Chapeyu* (1hr); Voi Gate (see map p.327) for *Voi Safari Lodge* (15min), *Sentrim Tsavo* and *Ndololo* (both 30min), *Ashnil Aruba* (1hr) and *Satao* (1hr 30min); and Buchuma Gate for *Ashnil Aruba* or *Satao* if driving up from Mombasa (both 1hr 30min).
From Sala Gate On the east side of the park, Sala Gate is 105km due west of Malindi. The first 40km stretch over coral rock road surface is quite jarring, but the remaining 65km over red *murram* and gravel is mostly fairly smooth, though heavy rain can cause delays. Allow 3hr to reach the gate, and be prepared to make a fixed 7am start from the police barrier outside Malindi. Once at Sala Gate, it's a good 1hr 30min to *Epiya Chapeyu*, *Ashnil Aruba* or *Satao*.

ACCOMMODATION

Tsavo East's **accommodation** options are more numerous and varied than you might expect. Our listings include most of those inside the park itself, but outside the park you'll find cheaper options, as well as one or two good lodges and tented camps, around Voi and off the Mombasa highway (see p.326 & p.327). As at Tsavo West, there are several KWS-designated **special campsites** dotted around the park ($35), though remember these have no facilities of any kind and have to be organized in advance through KWS (see p.61).

ITHUMBA AREA
Ithumba Camp In the northern sector 98km from the Kibwezi turnoff on the Mombasa highway (A109), Nairobi reservations through the David Sheldrick Wildlife Trust ☎ 020 2301396, ⊕ sheldrickwildlifetrust. org; map p.321. As well as KWS, much of the hard work in re-establishing elephants in Tsavo East (see box, p.353) has been done by the David Sheldrick Wildlife Trust based in Nairobi (see opposite). If you "adopt" an orphan (minimum $50 per year) you can make arrangements to visit this release facility in the far north of the park. There's also a camp here, with four twin tents with partially open stone

bathrooms and a communal thatched *boma* with lovely views from the upper deck over the mess area. You need to bring food yourself – the kitchen has gas for cooking and lighting, although resident staff will cook if requested. Sponsors can visit the juvenile elephants in the stockades where they are prepared for their eventual release into the park proper, and bush walks accompanied by the KWS rangers stationed here can be arranged. Self-catering **$200**

SOUTH OF THE GALANA
Ashnil Aruba Lodge Off junction #105, 30km from Voi Gate, 40km from Bachuma Gate and 66km from Sala

Gate ☎ 020 3566970 or ☎ 0717 612499, ⓦ ashnilhotels .com; map p.352. Although located in a prime location by Aruba Dam, this fenced lodge's poor design has most of the 52 brick-built, motel-style chalets facing the dry savanna. Nevertheless, the deck and lounge do overlook the busy dam, and there's good food and service and a lovely pool. It's also well priced. Wi-fi. FB **$280**

Bigi Camp Epiya Chapeyu South bank of the Galana River, 12km west of junction #108, 10.5km east of junction #110 (Lugard's Falls) ☎ 0733 743210, ⓦ epiya-chapeyu-camp.com; map p.352. Also known as *Bigi Camp*, this unstuffy, Italian-run camp (*Epiya Chapeyu* means "The man with the hat" in Waliangulu, in reference to the nearby rock on the Yatta plateau) in a lovely location close to the banks of the Galana River, has eighteen closely spaced tents with nets and verandas (the better ones in the front row face the river). Not fancy, but extremely good value, and casual visitors are welcome for lunch (Ksh1800). FB **$220**

★ Galdessa Camp 4km north of junction #111 on the south bank of the Galana ☎ 0734 283810 or ☎ 040 3202217, ⓦ galdessa.com; map p.352. This spectacular, Italian-owned boutique camp is stunningly conceived and located above the river. With a wonderful ambience, lavish and comfortably furnished *banda*-tents, good, hearty, Italian cooking and great attention to detail, it's by far Tsavo East's best camp. It's situated in one of the few areas of Tsavo East where you have a chance of spotting black rhino, and elephants are nearly always seen crossing the river here. The accommodation is divided into *Main Galdessa*, which has eleven tents, and *Private Galdessa*, with three; the latter can be booked exclusively for a family or group of up to six. Wi-fi. FB **$620**

KWS Ndololo Campsite Near the Kanderi swamp off junction #103, right next to Ndololo Safari Camp and 7km from Voi Gate ☎ 043 2030049, ⓦ kws.org; map p.327. Popular and well-shaded public site with clean loos and showers, a communal kitchen/food preparation area, and helpful *askaris* who will sell you firewood. Pay at the gate. **$20**

Loyk Tsavo Camp West bank of the Athi River, 9km from Tsavo Gate ☎ 0713 077755 or ☎ 0771 725812, ⓦ loykhotels.co.ke; map p.352. With its eco-friendly architecture (some of the double beds are made from reclaimed wood), decent tents and little beach next to the river with hammocks strung out in the trees, there's a relaxed, rustic feel here. It's not a wildlife-rich area, but you'll see hippos, crocs and elephants. FB **$380**

Ndololo Safari Camp Near the Kanderi swamp off junction #103, 7km from Voi Gate ☎ 043 30050, ⓦ tsavolodgesandcamps.com; map p.327. Lying on the forested banks of Voi River, this mid-range place has twenty well-spaced tents under *makuti* roofs, with tiled and solid-paved floors, small terraces, nets and decent plumbed-in bathrooms. Popular with overnight visitors from the coast, it's nothing fancy, but relatively good value. Wi-fi. FB **$200**

★ Satao Camp Off junction #144, around 45km from Voi or Buchuma Gate and 60km from Sala Gate ☎ 043 2030204 or 020 2039571, ⓦ sataocamp.com; map p.352. A long-established mid-range Tsavo camp deservedly popular with safari-goers from the coast, *Satao* has a fine, low-key ambience and good service and food. Spread out beneath big trees, its thatch-covered tents are simply decorated but have large stone bathrooms and verandas. The atmosphere will suit you if you want to relax in the bush and enjoy the wildlife — elephants, occasional lions and lots of plains game are attracted to the waterhole. Ecotourism Kenya Bronze Award. Wi-fi. FB **$388**

Sentrim Tsavo Camp Off junction #136, 11km from Voi Gate ☎ 0720 211961, ⓦ sentrimhotels.net; map p.327. The tents at this fenced camp have solid floors and walls, cheap furniture and hotel-style bathrooms, and there are also three cottages (for guests who want to lock themselves in from the wildlife). The buffet meals are mediocre, but the pool is a redeeming feature, as is the good game viewing from the raised platform above the waterhole, which is spot-lit at night. Go for tents #3 or #4, which have views of the waterhole. Wi-fi. FB **$230**

Voi Safari Lodge 4.5km from Voi Gate ☎ 0733 333400, ⓦ safari-hotels.com; map p.327. Not to be confused with the brashly oversized *Voi Wildlife Lodge* outside the park (see p.328), this 53-room lodge is quite busy enough, and similar in many respects to its sister establishment, *Ngulia Safari Lodge* in Tsavo West (see p.350). Despite the shortcomings of its dated style (it first opened in 1967), it's is a perennial favourite for its good pool, two floors of smallish rooms banking onto a tree-covered hill, near-guaranteed game-viewing from the terrace and the magnificent panorama plunging to the horizon. Wi-fi. FB **$260**

Narok

NAROK is the funnel through which the majority of road transport enters the Maasai Mara. It's a bumpy, hustly mess, but is the last guarantee of fuel, a cold drink or almost anything for more than 80km before you enter the reserve. If you arrive here after 5pm, you may well end up having to stay the night, as you won't have time to get into the reserve itself by nightfall (the gates close at 7pm).

5

Despite its touts and garish tourist bazaars full of carvings and beads, the town is lively and interesting, always full of Maasai on shopping expeditions or doing business at the market.

ARRIVAL AND DEPARTURE   NAROK

By bus and matatu The main bus and matatu stage is 300m north of the town's main junction (with the B3 from Nairobi and the C57 south towards Mau Narok). There are frequent vehicles to and from Nairobi (3hr) and several vehicles a day along the C12 to Sekenani and Talek (villages by the Maasai Mara reserve gates of the same names; allow 2hr, and much longer after rain) and along the C13 to Mara Rianta (for Musiara Gate; allow

3hr, and again much longer after rain) and on to Lolgorien (4hr-plus) and Migori (5hr-plus), beyond the western side of the reserve.

By car On a good day Narok is 2hr from Nairobi, once you've cleared the city traffic. There are several filling stations here with good repair facilities. Fill up, and check your tyres and oil: there are no full-service filling stations south of Narok.

ACCOMMODATION

Kims Breeze Hotel North side of the road about 2km after the centre towards the Mara ☎0700 351444, ⓦkimsbreezehotel.webs.com. A cheery complex of low concrete blocks set in gardens (plus car park). The rooms are fairly bare but have nets, tiled bathrooms and reliable hot water. Filling local meals and the likes of chicken and chips (Ksh400) are served. BB **Ksh1500**

Maralink Hotel At the Total petrol station, north side of the road about 1km towards the Mara ☎0729 466708 or ☎0771 301070, ⓦcentrino.co.ke/mara. Belying its breeze-block exterior appearance, this fairly new place has neat, fresh rooms with modern

made-for-hotel furnishings, nets and DSTV. The dining room offers a generous buffet breakfast, and there's a nice garden bar at the back. Plans are afoot to build a pool. Wi-fi. BB **$76**

Seasons Hotel Narok South side of the road as you enter Narok (left, coming from Nairobi) ☎0718 323213, ⓦseasonshotelskenya.com. A surprisingly smart hotel, although it's a little pricey for non-residents, with well-maintained, smallish rooms with DSTV and electric showers in reasonable bathrooms, plus the chance of a dip in a sometimes sparkling pool. Hearty, varied buffet meals (Ksh900). Wi-fi. BB **$115**

EATING

River Breeze Place At the Kenol petrol station on the main road ☎0724 452943, ⓦbit.ly/RiverBreezeNarok. A stopover for refreshments and fuel for safari vehicles, this glorified petrol station shop has a garden with tables and a children's playground, and offers sodas, tea and coffee, and snacks such as toasted sandwiches, samosas and chips. Daily 6am–10pm.

Stage View At the bus and matatu stage. A spotlessly clean transport café on two floors overlooking all the vehicles (as the name suggests). The full breakfast includes sausage, samosa, chapatti, eggs and a huge milky coffee for only Ksh250. Main courses from Ksh350. It's a good place to sit with luggage while waiting for a matatu to arrive, which you'll probably be able to see from the window. Daily 6am–7pm.

DIRECTORY

Banks Banks in Narok that have ATMs include KCB, situated on the north side of the main road (right, coming in from Nairobi), 300m west of Kobil; and Barclays, which is found on the south side of the main road, just past the post office.

Markets and supermarkets Narok's main market is on the north side of the town centre, to the right as you go through town towards the Mara. The best supermarket in town is Naivas (daily 7am–6pm), north of the junction and opposite the bus and matatu stage.

Maasai Mara National Reserve

Inside reserve $70, outside reserve $80 (see p.74); vehicle fees: fewer than 6 seats Ksh 400; 6–12 seats Ksh1000 • No single official website, but see ⓦmaratriangle.org and ⓦmaasaimara.com • 1510 square kilometres

For a long list of reasons, **Maasai Mara** is the best game reserve in Kenya. Set at nearly 2000m above sea level, the reserve is a great wedge of undulating **grassland** in the remote, sparsely inhabited southwest of the country, right up against the Tanzanian border and, indeed, an extension of the even bigger **Serengeti National Park** in Tanzania. This is a land of short grass and croton bushes (Mara means "spotted", after

> **HOW TO VISIT THE MAASAI MARA**
>
> The vast majority of visitors arrive in the Maasai Mara on pre-booked air or road **safari packages**, which can work out cheaper than making independent arrangements. If you're travelling on a budget, you'll have to accept that the reserve is not a cheap option and even organized **budget-camping safaris** (see p.123) can seem expensive. While it is just about possible to access the area by public transport (see p.364), and then camp or stay in budget establishments, the experience is likely to leave you wishing you'd saved a little more before coming here. There's also a third option if you can afford it; there's nothing to stop you **renting a vehicle**, ideally with an experienced driver-guide (see p.80), and visiting the region entirely independently, while staying at camps or lodges you've booked directly.

the yellow crotons dotted on the plains), where the wind plays with the thick, green mantle after the rains and, nine months later, whips up dust devils from the baked surface. Maasai Mara's climate is relatively predictable, with ample rain, and the new grass supports an annual **wildebeest migration** of half a million animals from the dry plains of Tanzania.

At any time of year, the Mara has abundant wildlife. Whether you're watching the migration, a pride of lions hunting, a herd of elephants grazing in the marsh or hyenas squabbling with vultures over the carcass of a buffalo, you are conscious all the time of being in a realm apart. To travel through the reserve in August or September, while the wildebeest are in possession, feels like being caught up in the momentum of a historic event. There are few places on earth where animals hold such dazzling sway.

With its plentiful vegetation and wildlife, the reserve's **ecosystem** might at first appear resilient to the effect of huge numbers of tourists. However, the Mara is the most visited wildlife area in Kenya, and the balance between increasing tourist numbers and wildlife can't be maintained indefinitely. Off-road driving kills the protective cover of vegetation and can create dust bowls that spread like sores through the effects of natural wind and water erosion and become muddy quagmires in the rains.

Human population increase is also a threat: the **animal numbers** in the Mara are still huge by comparison with most other parts of Africa, but the enormous herds of every species – not just wildebeest – that were here after independence are gone, as Kenya's population has quadrupled. With the land subdivided and sold off, the old ecosystem, in which the Maasai and their herds mingled with the wildlife, is beyond being challenged: local people no longer tolerate lions and hyenas near their homes, or buffalo where their children are walking to school, or elephants raiding their corn. The answer, in an imperfect world, is **wildlife conservancies** for the wildlife and ranching and settlement areas for people.

The reserve and the conservancies

In terms of structuring your visit, think of the national reserve in three parts. In the west you have the **Mara Triangle**, between the Mara River and the Oloololo Escarpment. This lush, green area is only accessible from Oloololo Gate in the north, or by crossing the Mara New (Purungat) Bridge in the far south. It's administered by the Mara Conservancy on behalf of Narok County Council (@maratriangle.org). The rest of the national reserve, the **Narok side**, is administered directly by Narok County Council (@narok.go.ke) and consists of the **Musiara sector** in the north and the **Sekenani sector** in the centre and east. The Musiara sector, bounded by the Mara and Talek rivers, is the location of *Governors' Camp* and *Mara Intrepids* and has some of the most photogenic wildebeest river crossings. The Sekenani sector, the largest portion of the reserve, is bordered by the Talek, Mara and Sand rivers, and has *Keekorok Lodge* – the oldest lodge in the reserve – in its centre.

5

THE HISTORY OF THE MAASAI MARA

When the reserve was created, today's familiar scene of plentiful wildlife looked very different. Traditionally, the **Maasai** lived in some harmony with the wildlife, hunting only lion, as a ritual exercise, and, in times of famine, the beasts they called "wild cattle" – the eland and buffalo. When the first European **hunting safaris** made the Mara world-famous in the early years of the last century, the white hunters were ransacking a region recently deserted by the Maasai. Smallpox had ravaged the Maasai communities and rinderpest had torn through their cattle herds.

By 1961, the white hunters had brought the Mara's lion population down to nine, and the Maasai Mara was created as a game sanctuary to be administered by the Maasai District Council at Narok. In 2001, management of the **Mara Triangle** was handed over to the **Mara Conservancy**, a non-profit management company which has demonstrated full transparency with gate receipts, had major success against poachers and improved road maintenance. Meanwhile, the management of the **Narok side** has been shambolic: the draft of a much mooted management plan for the whole reserve has been "under review" for years.

Outside the reserve proper to the north, most of the Maasai **group ranches** east of the Mara River have been converted from pasturelands to wildlife conservancies, and all of them now have their own entry fees, usually levied by the camps and lodges where guests are staying and added to the bill. Safari operators and local community leaders have transformed much of the largest group ranch, Koiyaki, into the **Mara North**, **Olare Motorogi** and **Mara Naboisho** conservancies, and as the community-led (rather than tour operator-led) model for managing wildlife and tourism proves increasingly successful, the trend looks set to continue.

Outside the reserve, roughly a dozen **conservancies**, **group ranches** and **private game ranches**, usually run in partnership with the local Maasai communities, offer wildlife-viewing that is often the equal of what you'll see in the reserve proper – increasingly reflected in their management practices, conservation work and prices. Some of them, including the Mara North and Mara Naboisho conservancies, only permit game drives for visitors staying at their camps and lodges, the aim being to limit visitor numbers and exclude drive-in minibus tours.

Game drives

The Maasai Mara is the one part of Kenya where the **concentrations of game** that existed in the nineteenth century can still be seen, even if it's true numbers have hugely diminished overall. The panorama sometimes resembles one of those wild-animal wall charts, where groups of unlikely-looking animal companions are forced into the artist's frame. You can see a dozen different species in one gaze: gazelle, zebra, giraffe, buffalo, topi, kongoni (Coke's hartebeest), wildebeest, eland, elephant, hyena, jackal, ostrich and a pride of lions waiting for a chance. The most interesting areas, scenically and zoologically, tend to be westwards, signalled by the long ridge of the Oloololo Escarpment. If you only have a day or two, and you're inside the reserve, you could do worse than spend most of your time here, near the **Mara River**.

It sometimes seems, however, that wherever there are animals there are **people** – in minibuses, in Land Cruisers, in rented Suzukis, often parked in ravenous, zoom-lens-touting packs around understandably irritable lions, leopards and cheetahs (the official limit is five vehicles around an animal at any one time). This popularity is highly seasonal, and can be overbearing around Christmas and during the migration, but it need not spoil your visit. If you aren't driving yourself, encourage your driver to explore new areas (obviously not off-road) and perhaps stress you'd rather experience the reserve in its totality than tick off animal species.

5

Lions and other predators

Big brunette **lions** are the best-known denizens of the Maasai Mara. There are now between six hundred and eight hundred in the greater Mara ecosystem, but their numbers are believed to have dropped significantly in the past thirty years, thanks to hunting and the reduction in the number of wildebeest and other game they depend on for survival. They are relatively easy to find, however, and there are usually several prides firmly in possession of their territories in the Musiara and Sekenani sectors, as well as in the Triangle. Instinctively, the lion use the Mara's river and stream meanders and many confluences as "lobster pots" to corner their prey in ambushes, and it is sometimes possible to watch them hunt, as they take very little notice of vehicles. The **Mara Lion Project** and **Mara Cheetah Project** (ⓦkenyawildlifetrust.org) work across the ecosystem, following in the footsteps of the ground-breaking **Mara Predator Project**, whose "Living With Lions" database (ⓦlivingwithlions.org) made use of visitors' photos and observations.

While lions seem to be lounging under every other bush, finding a **cheetah** is harder, although they can sometimes be seen on the *murram* mounds alongside the Talek–Sekenani road). These are usually solitary cats – slender, unobtrusive, somewhat shy and vulnerable to harassment by wildlife-watchers. Cases of Mara cheetahs using vehicles as look-out hills – first noted only in the 1990s – have become common, as they lose their fear and adapt to close human scrutiny. Their natural hunting times are dawn and dusk, but some cheetahs prefer to hunt during the middle of the day, when the humans are shaded in the lodges. This is not a good time of day for the cheetah, which expends terrific energy in each chase and may have to give up if it goes on for more then thirty or forty seconds. When they move, cheetahs exhibit marvellous speed and agility and, if you're lucky enough to witness a kill, it's likely to take place in a cloud of dust a kilometre from where the chase began.

Leopards, are seen increasingly often in the daytime, and there are plenty of them. Leopard Gorge, in the Mara North Conservancy, is an obvious place to look. Their deep, grating roar at night – a grunt, repeated – is a sound which, once heard, you carry around with you.

By the early 1990s, **wild dogs** were thought to have been extinct in the greater Serengeti-Mara ecosystem, but in 2013 a couple of packs were spotted in Olare Motorogi and Mara North conservancies. Sightings remain rare though.

VISITING MAASAI VILLAGES

One diversion you're likely to be offered, especially if travelling on an organized safari, is a visit to a **Maasai** *enkang*, usually incorrectly called a *manyatta* (an *enkang* is an ordinary homestead, a *manyatta* a ceremonial bush camp). Forget about the authenticity of tribal life: this is the real world. Children and old people are sick, young men have moved to the towns, and everyone wants your money. Unprepared and uncomfortable, most visitors find the experience depressing or a bit of a rip-off, or both. You'll pay around $30 per person if organized by your lodge, camp or safari driver, or around Ksh1000 per person if you arrange it yourself, for the right to have a look around, peer inside some dwellings, and be on the receiving end of a determined sales pitch to get you to buy souvenirs. Because of the supposed sales opportunity, safari drivers have for decades paid a tiny fee to the headman of their chosen village and kept the bulk of the cash for themselves. A number of initiatives are now changing this, however, and the best operators and camps have worked hard to make the experience less mercantile and more worthwhile for both parties. Visitors can play their part, too, by not just standing and staring, or snapping away on a camera, but by actually sitting down and talking to the Maasai (there will always be people who speak a little English), which may well transform the interaction into a shared experience full of interest and laughter.

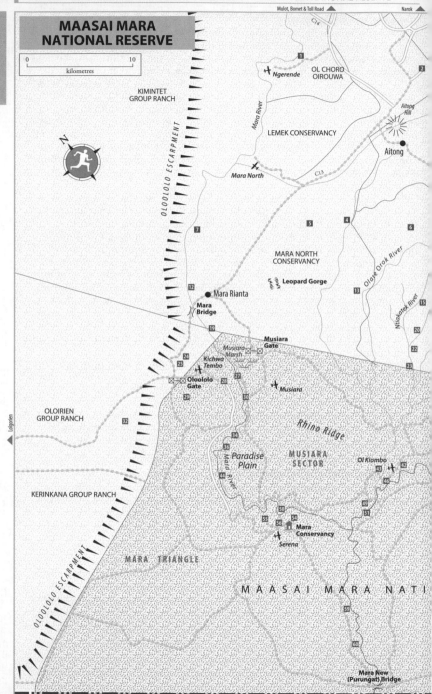

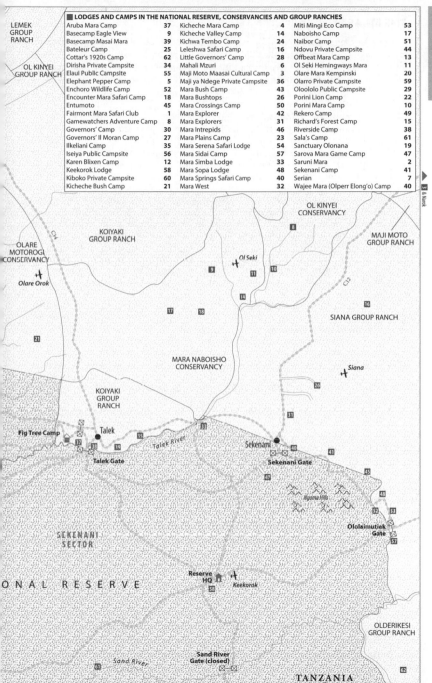

■ **LODGES AND CAMPS IN THE NATIONAL RESERVE, CONSERVANCIES AND GROUP RANCHES**

Aruba Mara Camp	37	Kicheche Mara Camp	4	Miti Mingi Eco Camp	53
Basecamp Eagle View	9	Kicheche Valley Camp	14	Naboisho Camp	17
Basecamp Masai Mara	39	Kichwa Tembo Camp	24	Naibor Camp	51
Bateleur Camp	25	Leleshwa Safari Camp	16	Ndovu Private Campsite	44
Cottar's 1920s Camp	62	Little Governors' Camp	28	Offbeat Mara Camp	13
Dirisha Private Campsite	34	Mahali Mzuri	6	Ol Seki Hemingways Mara	11
Elaui Public Campsite	55	Maji Moto Maasai Cultural Camp	3	Olare Mara Kempinski	20
Elephant Pepper Camp	5	Maji ya Ndege Private Campsite	36	Olarro Private Campsite	59
Enchoro Wildlife Camp	52	Mara Bush Camp	43	Oloololo Public Campsite	29
Encounter Mara Safari Camp	18	Mara Crossings Camp	50	Porini Lion Camp	22
Entumoto	45	Mara Explorer	42	Porini Mara Camp	10
Fairmont Mara Safari Club	1	Mara Explorers	31	Rekero Camp	49
Gamewatchers Adventure Camp	8	Mara Intrepids	46	Richard's Forest Camp	15
Governors' Camp	30	Mara Plains Camp	23	Riverside Camp	38
Governors' Il Moran Camp	27	Mara Serena Safari Lodge	54	Sala's Camp	61
Ilkeliani Camp	35	Mara Sidai Camp	57	Sanctuary Olonana	19
Iseiya Public Campsite	56	Mara Simba Lodge	33	Saruni Mara	2
Karen Blixen Camp	12	Mara Sopa Lodge	48	Sekenani Camp	41
Keekorok Lodge	58	Mara Springs Safari Camp	40	Serian	7
Kiboko Private Campsite	60	Mara West	32	Wajee Mara (Olperr Elong'o) Camp	40
Kicheche Bush Camp	21				

LEMEK GROUP RANCH

OL KINYEI GROUP RANCH

→ A1 & Narok

OL KINYEI CONSERVANCY

8

KOIYAKI GROUP RANCH

OLARE MOTOROGI CONSERVANCY

Olare Orok

Ol Seki

9   11   10

14

MAJI MOTO GROUP RANCH

C12

16

SIANA GROUP RANCH

17   18

21

MARA NABOISHO CONSERVANCY

Siana

26

KOIYAKI GROUP RANCH

31

33

Fig Tree Camp   Talek

37 15   Talek River

38 39

Talek Gate

Sekenani

40

41

Sekenani Gate

45

47

48

Ngoma Hills

52   51

Ololaimutiek Gate

57

SEKENANI SECTOR

...NAL RESERVE

Reserve HQ

58   Keekorok

OLDERIKESI GROUP RANCH

Sand River

Sand River Gate (closed)

61   62

TANZANIA

5

THE MAASAI

After deep reflection on my people and culture, I have painfully come to accept that the Maasai must change to protect themselves, if not their culture. They must adapt to the realities of the modern world for the sake of their own survival. It is better to meet an enemy out in the open and to be prepared for him than for him to come upon you at home unawares.

Tepilit Ole Saitoti, writing in *Maasai* (Elm Tree Books/Abrams)

Of all Kenya's peoples, the **Maasai** have received the most attention. Often strikingly tall and slender, dressed in brilliant red cloth, with beads, metal jewellery and – for young men – long, ochred hairstyles, they have a reputation for ferocity fed by their somewhat arch superiority complex. Traditionally, they lived off milk and blood (extracted, by a close shot with a stumpy arrow, from the jugular veins of their live cattle), and they loved their herds more than anything else, rarely slaughtering a beast. They maintained rotating armies of spartan warriors – the **morani** – who killed lions as a test of manhood. And they opposed all interference and invasion with swift, implacable violence. The Maasai scorn of foreigners was absolute: they called the Europeans, who came swaddled in clothing, *iloridaa enjekat* or "those who confine their farts". They also derided African peoples who cultivated by digging the earth – the Maasai even left their dead unburied – while those who kept cattle were given grudging respect so long as they conceded that all the world's cattle were a gift from God to the Maasai, whose incessant cattle-raiding was thus righteous reclamation of stolen property. **Cattle** are still at the heart of Maasai society. There are dozens of names for different colours and patterns, and each animal among their three million is individually cherished.

Some of this noble savagery was undoubtedly exaggerated by Swahili and Arab slave and ivory traders, anxious to protect their routes from the Europeans. At the same time, something close to a **cult of the Maasai** has been around ever since Thomson walked *Through Masai Land* (see p.595) in 1883. In the early years of the colony, Governor Delamere's obsession with the people and all things Maasai spawned a new term, "Maasai-itis", and with it a motley crop of romantic notions about their ancestors, alluding to ancient Egypt and Rome, and even to the lost tribes of Israel.

The Maasai have been assailed on all sides: by uplands farmers expanding from the north; by eviction from the tourist/conservation areas within the Maasai Mara boundaries; and by a climate of opposition to their traditional lifestyle from all around. Sporadically urged to

Rhinos, hippos and elephant

The Mara has the country's only indigenous **black rhino** population – meaning that it has not been affected by translocations to and from the region – though numbers are small and every calf born is a victory. Finding them is often difficult, but rangers and lodge staff are certain to know their whereabouts and point you in the right direction.

Maasai Mara's other heavyweights are about in abundance. The Mara River surges with **hippo**, while big families of **elephant** traipse along the forested river and stream margins and spread out across the plains when there's plenty of vegetation to browse.

Grazers

Among all these outstanding characters, the herds of humble grazers can quickly fade into the background. It's easy to become blasé when one of the much-hyped "big five" (elephant, rhino, buffalo, lion, leopard) isn't eyeballing you at arm's length – but those are the hunter's trophies and not necessarily the photographer's. **Warthog** families like rows of dismantled Russian dolls, **zebra** and **gazelle**, odd-looking **hartebeest** and slick, purple-flanked **topi** are all scattered with abandon across the scene. The topi are particularly characteristic of the Maasai Mara, being almost confined in Kenya largely to this reserve: there are always one or two in every herd standing sentry on a grass tussock or an old termite mound. Topi and **giraffe** – whose dream-like, slow-motion grow crops, go to school, build permanent houses and generally settle down and stop being a nuisance, the Maasai face an additional dilemma in squaring these edicts with the fickle demands of the **tourist industry** for traditional authenticity. Maasai dancing is *the* entertainment, while necklaces, gourds, spears, shields, *rungus* (clubs), busts (carved by Kamba carvers) and even life-sized wooden *morani*, to be shipped home in a packing case, are the stock-in-trade of the souvenir shops. For the Maasai themselves, the rewards are fairly scant. Few make much of a living selling souvenirs, but enterprising *morani* can do well by just posing for photos, and even better if they hawk themselves in Nairobi or down on the coast.

Many men persevere with the status of **warriorhood**, though modern Kenya makes few concessions to it. The *morani*, arrested for hunting lions and prevented from building *manyattas* for the *eunoto* transition in which they pass into elderhood, have kept most of the superficial marks of the warrior without being able to live the life fully. The ensemble of a cloth tied over one shoulder, together with spear, sword, club and braided hair, is still widely seen, and after circumcision, in their early days as warriors, young men can still be encountered out in the bush, hunting for birds to add to their elaborate, taxidermic headdresses. But there is considerable local frustration and, when the pasture is poor, the *morani* have little compunction about driving their herds into the reserve to compete with the wildlife.

Maasai culture is still coming to terms with the idea of individual land ownership, but all the land outside the reserve is now subdivided into thousands of separate title deeds held by families. The new wildlife **community conservancies**, run in partnership with safari industry partners (such as Ol Kinyei and Mara North), provide a steady source of income, and cattle herds, while still being a big deal for status and inheritance, are beginning to stabilize.

The **lifestyle** is changing: education, MPs and elections, new laws and new projects, jobs and cash, all impinge on Maasai communities – with mixed results. The traditional Maasai staple diet of curdled milk and cow's blood has largely been replaced by *ugali*. Many Maasai have taken work in the tourist lodges and tented camps while others end up as security guards in Nairobi. For the majority, who continue to live semi-nomadic lives among a welter of constraints, the future would seem to hold little promise. But that stubborn cultural pride – the kind of hauteur that keeps a cattle-owner thoroughly impoverished in cash terms, while he counts his 220 beasts – may yet insulate the Maasai against the social upheavals that seem certain to rock the lives of many Kenyans in the future. For further information, see ⓦ maasai-association.org.

canter is one of the reserve's most beautiful and underrated sights – are often good pointers for predators in the vicinity: look closely at what they're watching.

The wildebeest migration

It is the annual **wildebeest migration**, often billed as one of the seven natural wonders of the world, that has planted Maasai Mara so firmly in the popular imagination. The numbers are far down from their peaks of over a million wildebeest in the 1960s and 1970s, but still an average of nearly half a million animals swell the Mara's sedentary population ever year.

With a lemming-like instinct, the herds gather in their hundreds of thousands in May and June on the withering plains of the Serengeti to begin the long journey northwards, following the scent of moisture and green grass in the Mara. They arrive in July and August, streaming over the Sand River and into the Sekenani side of the reserve, gradually munching their way westwards towards the escarpment in a milling mass, and turning south again, back to the Serengeti, in October and November. Never the most graceful of animals, wildebeest seem to play up to their appearance with unpredictable behaviour; bucking like wild horses, springing like jack-in-the-boxes or suddenly sprinting off through the herd for no apparent reason.

5

The **Mara River** is their biggest obstacle. Heavy rains falling up on the Mau Range where the river rises can produce a brown flood that claims thousands of animals as they try to cross. Like huge sheep (they are, in fact, most closely related to goats), the brainless masses swarm desperately to the banks and plunge in. Many are fatally injured on rocks and fallen branches; others are skewered by flailing legs and horns. With every surge, more bodies bob to the surface and float downstream. Heaps of bloated carcasses line the banks; injured and dying animals struggle in the mud, while vultures and marabou storks squat in glazed, post-prandial stupor.

The migration's full, cacophonous impact is awesomely melodramatic – both on the plains and at the deadly river crossings. This superabundance of meat accounts for the Mara's big lion population. Through it all, **spotted hyenas** scamper and loiter like psychopathic sheepdogs: a quarter of a million wildebeest **calves** are born in January and February before the migration, of which two out of three perish in the Mara without returning to the Serengeti.

ARRIVAL AND DEPARTURE   MAASAI MARA NATIONAL RESERVE

BY PLANE

Access from Nairobi is most straightforward by the scheduled daily air services on SafariLink (Ⓦ flysafarilink .com) and Airkenya (Ⓦ airkenya.com). Unless otherwise noted, flights land at one or more of the nine airstrips in the reserve and adjoining conservancies, depending on passenger requirements, so flight times and the order of arrival vary. Every lodge and camp has a preferred airstrip and will transfer guests accordingly. The other option is to use Governors Aviation (Ⓦ governorscamp. com/governors-aviation), which flies daily between Nairobi's Wilson Airport and the Musiara airstrip.

From Nairobi SafariLink and Airkenya flights cost $200 one-way, $345 round trip, including taxes (less in low season) and leave from Wilson Airport. Governors Aviation fares are $220 one-way, $385 round trip (again less in low season). Flying time is 45min–1hr 30min.

From Naivasha In the high season, SafariLink routes one Mara-bound Nairobi flight a day via Naivasha (Naivasha–Mara around 40min; $145).

From Laikipia and Samburu In the high season, SafariLink and Airkenya fly to the Mara from Nanyuki/Lewa Downs/Loisaba/Samburu/Shaba (1–2hr; around $385; southbound only).

From the coast Mombasa Air Safari (Ⓦ mombasaairsafari .com) flies to the Mara airstrips daily in the high season from Mombasa via Diani Beach (around 3hr; $350 one-way, $460 return; same price from both airports), via Tsavo West and Amboseli, and from Malindi (2hr 15min; also $350 one-way, $460 return).

From Migori SafariLink flies daily in the high season between the Mara and Migori on the Tanzanian border (30min; $238 each way), avoiding hours of bumpy road travel for passengers visiting the Serengeti and the Mara on the same safari.

BY CAR

Although hard-surfaced roads have made advances into the region, the final approaches to the reserve – and all the routes inside it and in the adjoining conservancies – still have a gravel or dirt/mud surface. If you drive, give yourself plenty of time, use a high-clearance 4WD vehicle, and check that you know the precise location and final directions for your lodge or camp. If you're coming that way, make sure you top up with fuel in Narok, though in the reserve area it is usually available at Talek village (where there is also a KCB ATM) and sometimes at *Fig Tree*, *Keekorok*, *Sarova*, *Serena* and *Simba* lodges. If you intend to do a lot of game-driving, it's a good idea to carry a jerrycan of spare fuel.

FROM SOUTHWEST KENYA AND TANZANIA

Entry is not permitted directly from Tanzania's Serengeti National Park at the Sand River Gate into the Maasai Mara, and there are no other gates or routes between the two.
Via Lolgorien Most people coming from Tanzania cross the border at Sirari-Isebania and head north 20km to Suna-Migori, before turning east on the unsurfaced C13 road (see p.275 and map, p.252) towards the Mara. Once you reach Lolgorien, 46km from Suna, the road is mostly good *murram* all the way through to the Mara, with turnings to the long-closed *Olkurruk Mara Lodge* after 65km and *Mara West* camp after 66km. After 70km you reach the junction for the road down to Oloololo Gate. Keep going northeast and you cross the Mara River, climb up to the straggling settlement of Mara Rianta and then reach the turning down to the Musiara Gate.

FROM NAIROBI

From Nairobi, take the lower road (B3) towards Naivasha, down the escarpment, turning left at the unpleasantly burgeoning truck stop of Mai Mahiu (see map, p.204; allow 1–2hr to cover this 50km from Nairobi, depending on

5

traffic and where you start from). The B3 continues from Mai Mahiu to Narok (92km), is in excellent condition (surfaced) and shouldn't take more than an hour.

Via Narok to the Sekenani, Talek and Ololaimutiek gates Once through Narok, if you branch left onto the C12 highway 3.2km after the bridge in Narok town, the road makes its way south towards Sekenani Gate and the eastern section of the reserve. From the C12 junction, the first 23km are excellent tarmac, but at the end of that comes Kenya's most notorious road – the 58km to Sekenani Gate, on a mix of corrugated *murram* (which isn't too bad at a decent speed) and scraped older tarmac (where you're driving on rocky road foundations). In anything but a top-of-the-range 4WD, it's a miserably uncomfortable 1hr 30min–2hr trial. You reach Talek Gate from Sekenani Gate by following the Talek River on a reasonable road for 18km. For Ololaimutiek Gate, turn left at the little junction settlement of Ngoswani (35km from the C12 junction, before you reach Sekenani Gate), then drive 16km southeast, before swinging right, to the south and southwest, reaching Ololaimutiek after approximately another 30km.

Via Narok to the Musiara and Oloololo gates For access to the western end of the reserve from Nairobi, you start by taking the decent B3 highway from Narok to Sotik. West of the C12 junction (3.2km west of the bridge at the bottom of the hill in Narok town), there are two main turnings south off the B3. The first is just past Ololulunga, 28km west of the C12 junction, signposted to *Fairmont Mara Safari Club*. This route goes via the small centres of Ngorengore and Lemek and becomes the rutted and often muddy C13. The second turning off the B3 is exactly 50km from the C12 junction, just south of Mulot. Here, a private toll road (Ksh500) takes you south, a few kilometres away from the east bank of the Mara River towards *Fairmont Mara Safari Club* and others outside the reserve, and ultimately joins the road from Kaboson (see below) and then the C13 at Aitong Hill. Unless you're advised differently as you approach the region, or when planning your trip, use the toll road if you can, in preference to the tortuous public road. About 2km further west along the C13 from Aitong Hill, the road to Talek Gate (34.5km) forks south, via Aitong village, while the C13 continues for 25km straight across the plains to the Mara bridge. The turning for Musiara Gate is 3.7km before the bridge; the turning for Oloololo Gate is 5.8km after it.

FROM KISUMU, KERICHO OR KISII

Approaching the Maasai Mara from Kisumu, Kericho or Kisii (see p.279), all routes converge on the overgrown village of Bomet, with its three streets running around the back of the Kobil petrol station, a small market, a few meagre *hotelis* and *dukas*, a KCB (with ATM), a post office and some very basic lodgings. If you get stuck in Bomet, stay at the decent, newly built *Brevan Hotel* (☎0721 366821, ⊛brevanhotel.com; BB Ksh4000) on the hill above town, which has passable rooms, electric showers, a restaurant and a car park.

Via Bomet and Mulot on the B3 Southeast of Bomet, the surfaced B3 heads for Narok, crossing the headwaters of the Mara River. The easiest route into the reserve is via the toll road from the Mulot junction, a right (south) turning, 25km southeast of Bomet.

Via Bomet and Mulot on the C14 A shorter but rougher alternative is the unpaved C14 for Sigor and Kaboson. The first important turning for this route is right, exactly 4km after crossing the river on the south side of Bomet. After a further 19km, take the right fork to Kaboson, and 8km later, just outside Kaboson where the road turns west towards Kilgoris, turn left and drive another 10km on the C14 to cross the Mara River. You then join the C13 after a further 13km, by the prominent Aitong Hill.

BY BUS AND MATATU

There are a few **matatus** and **buses** making daily runs from Narok through the group ranches along the C13 via Mara Rianta to Lolgorien, and occasionally as far as Migori. Matatus also run several times daily to Sekenani and Talek gates (about 2hr, although they can take up to 4hr depending on road conditions); ensure you get to the matatu stage in Narok before noon. You're likely to see a good deal of plains game along the way – so long as you can see out of the window – so you could, at a pinch, get a flavour of the Mara district ecosystem without paying any reserve or conservancy fees.

BY TAXI

An option for independent travellers is to take a taxi from Narok to one of the budget camps around Talek and Sekenani, though ensure the vehicle is sturdy enough and preferably has high clearance for the rough *murram* road – the budget camps will likely be able to recommend a taxi driver. A one-way trip will cost approximately Ksh5000 to Talek/Sekenani, depending on your negotiating skills.

GETTING AROUND

Organized drives As well as the usual 2–3hr game drives ($70–100/person) available at most lodges and the larger tented camps, you can often find $30–50/person game drives (depending on vehicle and group size) at the budget camps near the eastern gates. If there's only one or two of you, ask at the camp if you can join another group.

Vehicle rental You may find someone with a serviceable van, pickup or 4WD vehicle by asking around the villages at Talek, Sekenani or Ololaimutiek gates or in the neighbouring budget campsites. You might also be able to pick up a vehicle in Narok, though bear in mind the extra costs: you'll need to allow for the extra

5

BALLOON FLIGHTS

At around $450–500 per person (half price for children under 12; no under-4s) for the one-hour flight followed by breakfast with sparkling wine (it's never champagne, whatever the label says), **balloon safaris** are the ultimate safari treat – even watching the inflation and lift-off from the ground is spectacular. It's a highly enjoyable and very memorable experience, especially as you float above the trees along the Mara River, but photographic opportunities can be limited by low light, and the fact that you mostly fly quite high – so don't bank on every shot being a winner.

The flights take place in the usually calm conditions immediately after dawn, but if the wind is up, they don't fly at all and you get a refund. If you're not staying at a lodge or camp with a launch site, the operators will come and pick you up (usually between 4 and 5.30am). After breakfast you do a game drive on your way back to your lodge, normally returning 9.30am–10.30am.

You can arrange a balloon flight when booking your safari, or leave it until the last minute, either booking directly through an operator or at one of the lodges or camps, when **two-for-one deals** are sometimes available – an advantage of leaving it till later. However it is *essential* to pre-book during the wildebeest migration.

BALLOON OPERATORS

Adventures Aloft Balloon Safaris ⓦbit.ly/ AdventuresAloft. Launch sites at *Fig Tree Camp* (west of Talek Gate) and in the Siana Conservancy.
Balloon Safaris ⓦballoonsafaris.co.ke. Launch sites just south of Talek Gate and Siana, Naboisho and Olare Motorogi conservancies.
Governors' Balloon Safaris ⓦgovernorscamp .com. Launch site behind *Little Governors' Camp*.

Hot Air Safaris ⓦmaraballooning.com. Launch site just north of Talek Gate.
Skyship Co. ⓦskyshipcompany.com. Launch site just outside Oloololo Gate.
Transworld Safaris ⓦwww.transworldsafaris .com/ballooning. Launch sites at *Sarova Mara, Mara Serena* and *Fairmont Mara Safari Club*.

2–4hr (approximately $50 each way from Narok), and possibly a rate for the driver's overnight stay. Expect to pay around $100/day for, say, a Suzuki 4WD (which fits three plus a driver) up to around $175/day for a Land Cruiser (which will fit up to nine plus driver) – though remember that, if there are enough of you, taking a larger vehicle can work out cheaper per person, assuming costs are shared equally.

Roads and driving Graded roads, with improved surfaces and theoretically unbreachable banks and ditches alongside them to deter off-road driving, have been laid in various parts of the reserve, especially in the east. There is also a reasonable all-weather road from Talek Gate to Sekenani Gate, inside the reserve. During the rains, however, and for some weeks after, the western parts of the reserve can be treacherous. In many parts of the reserve and conservancies, it can be hard to know what is a road and what is a set of wheel tracks leading nowhere. Apart from wanting to avoid off-road driving, it is easy to get lost. If you don't have a guide with you, it's a very

good idea to have a GPS or a smart phone – the mobile network is good in many areas.

River crossings, bridges and fords The Mara Triangle and Narok sides of the reserve are effectively separated by the Mara River. Only two bridges span the Mara River: the Mara Bridge on the C13 road just outside the reserve in the north, and the Mara New Bridge (or Purungat Bridge) on the southern boundary, by the Tanzanian border. These bridges are the only points where you can cross the Mara, not counting the foot-passenger dinghy at *Little Governors'*. On the Narok side of the reserve, crossings over the Talek are also limited. There are bridges by *Mara Simba*, west of Sekenani Gate, and at Talek Gate, and three fords – one near *Rekero*, one by Ol Kiombo airstrip and one at *Mara Intrepids*. After rains, the fords are often impassable for anything from a few hours to several days. In that event you have to drive around to the north to "Double Crossing", near the confluence of the Olare Orok and Ntiakatek rivers, where two narrow fords are usually passable.

RESERVE AND CONSERVANCY FEES

As with the other parks and reserves, the advantages of visiting the Mara with a safari operator, rather than independently, is that they take charge of your national reserve and conservancy **fees**, adding the cost to your bill or including the charges in your accommodation rate. Most visitors staying in the reserve don't venture north into the conservancies and group ranches, while visitors staying in conservancy-based camps usually make just one, full-day trip into the reserve proper, especially during the migration, when some camps cover this cost themselves, usually including one reserve ticket per three-day stay. All tickets are valid 24hr from entry and the time of departure is

5

closely monitored to ensure you pay again if you overstay. Remember, even if you're a shoestring camper, you are expected to pay reserve or conservancy fees, depending on which bit of grass (or dust) your tent is pitched on. That said, there are a few properties where guests are not expected to pay fees unless they enter the reserve – right outside Talek Gate, for example.

Reserve tickets Daily fees to visit the reserve are $80/person for 24hr if staying outside the reserve and $70 if staying inside the reserve. Payments for the Narok side are transferable to the Mara Triangle sector and vice versa. Mara Triangle entry points (Oloololo Gate, Mara New Bridge and Serena airstrip) take Visa credit and debit cards as well as cash. For entry to the Narok side of the reserve (the gates at Musiara, Talek, Sekenani and Ololaimutiek, plus Musiara, Kichwa Tembo, Ol Kiombo and Keekorok airstrips), it is easiest to pay in cash. In theory there is a system in place for payment to made online with a Visa card through,

bizarrely enough, KAPS (Kenya Airports Parking Services; ⓦ kapstickets.com), though in reality this is only a useful tool for safari operators – it's best for independent travellers to pay on arrival.

Conservancy tickets These usually cost the same as, or a little more than, reserve tickets, and are not usually valid for the reserve itself (although some conservancies include a certain duration inside the reserve for each visitor). The four most active conservancies (Mara North, Olare Motorogi, Ol Kinyei and Naboisho) are exclusive to the guests in their lodges and camps, and include the fees in their daily rates.

ACCOMMODATION

When deciding **where to stay** in the Mara region, don't be unduly swayed by whether a lodge or camp is inside the **reserve proper**: the **conservancies** and **group ranches** outside the reserve have excellent wildlife-viewing and their own special features, and are often much less crowded than the busiest parts of the reserve. If you're visiting for the migration, at some point you're going to want to head towards the Mara River to try to witness one of the famous wildebeest crossing points. For this, accommodation on the western side of the reserve might be a good idea, and it tends to be at a premium at that time. There's a lot to be said, however, for camps that are far from others, such as *Offbeat Mara*, *Mara Porini*, *Naboisho* or *Sala's*, that give you those moments early in the morning when it's just you, the animals and the sun coming up over the plain.

Accommodation types The Mara region's hundred-plus lodges and camps, scattered across the national reserve and the adjoining conservancies, vary greatly in style, atmosphere and price: one person's sumptuous luxury will be another's garish opulence, while a place that seems delightfully informal and in keeping with the environment to one visitor may feel a bit plain and unpolished to another. It is worth taking the time to choose carefully and compare a few that you think might appeal.

What is included Regardless of how long you stay, all the lodges and camps, with the exception of the budget places outside the reserve, operate on at least full board (FB) basis, and their rates include all meals. They normally expect guests to arrive for lunch and leave after breakfast. Some provide a "package", which includes all meals and drinks, two or more game drives per day and other activities where available. The majority of guests on "package" will fly in, while most of those on full board will be on drive-in safaris, with a driver/guide accompanying them for the whole trip: except where noted, all the mainstream lodges and camps have vehicles and driver-guides on site. Most of the camps and lodges on the conservancies include conservancy fees in their rates, whereas most places in the reserve itself exclude reserve fees.

Rates and booking Reservations are essential, especially

at popular times (Christmas/New Year and the July–Oct migration season). The mid-range to luxury lodges and tented camps vary greatly in price, and offer vastly different levels of service. There's nothing intrinsically cheaper about sleeping under canvas: the cheaper places are pack-'em-in lodges, while the most expensive establishments are boutique tented camps, often with award-winning guides among the staff.

CAMPSITES

Campers at public or private campsites (which are unfenced) have to have two rangers per campsite on overnight security duty, at a cost of Ksh2000 each. It is not permitted for campers to stray more than 25m from the campsite, and within camp be wary of baboons, which are prone to grab anything that looks inviting, whether edible or not, and dash off with it to examine it later.

PUBLIC CAMPSITES

There are three public campsites managed by the Mara Conservancy, charging $30 per adult and $20 per child per night (available on a first-come first-serve basis – no booking possible; payment in cash). Most have only the most basic facilities: though firewood can usually be bought, bring everything else with you, including water.

You can expect some good-natured pestering by rangers and others, who will try to extract money by guiding you on game drives in your vehicle. Note that the Oloolo and Musiara gates have no nearby settlements (the village of Mara Rianta is a few kilometres to the north), while outside the Talek, Sekenani and Ololaimutiek gates, are ramshackle "villages" of *mabati* houses, where there are a few shops and bars.

Elaui/Iseiya Public Campsites Near the Triangle's Iseiya headquarters by Mara Serena Safari Lodge. Despite being close to human activity, the *Iseiya* and *Elaui* public campsites' only facilities are long-drop toilets. **$30**

Oloololo Public Campsite At Oloololo Gate. Welcoming campsite with (cold) showers, (long-drop) toilets and wonderful views of the escarpment. You can drive to nearby Mara Rianta village for basic supplies, and firewood can be purchased at Oloololo Gate. **$30**

PRIVATE CAMPSITES

The Mara Triangle has five private campsites – *Dirisha*, *Kiboko*, *Maji ya Ndege*, *Ndovu* and *Olarro* – in excellent locations along the Mara River, but they have no facilities whatsoever: you'll need to be completely self-sufficient. Each is for exclusive use, and there's a Ksh10,000/week booking fee in addition to the $40 (children $20) daily fee, though note that tour operators are given priority at *Kiboko* and *Ndovu* between June and October. Bookings and enquiries can be made at ⓦ bit.ly/TriangleCamping. You can also book a private campsite in the greater Mara region through Campsite Bookings (☎0733 602048 or 0733 239226, ⓦ campbookings.com), who manage seven campsites on the Talek, Olare Orok and Ntiakatek rivers, just outside the reserve. Like the private campsites in the reserve there's a weekly booking fee (in this case Ksh36,000) plus a Ksh2000 (children Ksh1000) per day camping fee. Again you need to bring everything you need with you.

BUDGET TENTED CAMPS AND BANDA SITES

The following places are outside the Talek, Sekenani and Ololaimutiek gates and offer simple tents or basic *bandas* with beds and bedding, and usually the possibility of pitching your own tent, too. Most have electricity provided by generators, which are on from early morning until about 10pm in the evening. All camps light bonfires in the evening, which can be shared with the Maasai *askaris*. If the site is physically outside the national reserve boundary, you should only need to pay fees to enter the reserve on game drives.

OLOLAIMUTIEK GATE

Enchoro Wildlife Camp Ololaimutiek Gate ☎0710 322787, ⓦ enchorowildlifecamp.com. A cut above the cheapies near this gate, located in a shady site, with decent-sized, s/c ridge tents under shelters, and a bar-restaurant offering filling set meals. Dorm beds FB **$60**, FB **$130**

Mara Sidai Camp Ololaimutiek Gate ☎0722 584290, ⓦ marasidaicamp.com. Another good budget option, on a wooded site, with neat little ridge tents under shelters, spanning twins, doubles, triples and five-bed family tents, each with (tiny) bathrooms attached, and a small bar-restaurant. FB **$160**

Miti Mingi Eco Camp Ololaimutiek Gate ☎0735 867454 or ☎0722 335734, ⓦ mitimingiecocamp.com. A busy and well-looked-after place: the 25 small s/c tents have thatched roofs, flagstone floors and concrete bathrooms, and there's an on-site bar-restaurant, though set meals are a little plain. FB **$90**

SEKENANI GATE

Mara Explorers 3.5km before Sekenani Gate and 300m from the road ☎0706 856216, ⓦ maraexplorers .com. Good backpacker's option, which can be accessed by matatu (get off before the gate) or by taxi (the camp will give you a contact for a Narok taxi driver). The large camping area has cooking huts, long-drop loos and warm bush showers, and tents and mattresses can be hired ($12); dorm beds and double/twin s/c walk-in tents are also available. There's a thatched lounge area with meals

---

CASUAL MEALS AND DRINKS

With all camps and lodges taking care of their clients' **food and drinks**, and the majority of visitors on organized safaris, pre-booked independent trips or doing DIY camping safaris, there are no independent **restaurants** in the Mara. As an independent visitor, or simply a safari client who wants to spend a few hours *not* game-watching, then if you head to one of the larger lodges or camps, you will normally be welcomed for breakfast, drinks, lunch or afternoon tea (dinner isn't an option inside the reserve, where night-driving is not allowed, though in theory it would be in the conservancies). It might be best to call a day ahead to check they can cater for you: smaller, hosted camps will usually decline because they won't have adequate supplies and wouldn't want you to intrude on their guests, while the big lodges (*Fig Tree*, *Keekorok*, *Mara Simba*, *Mara Sopa*, *Sarova* and *Serena*) will very likely be able to provide for you without advance notice.

5

available (add $30 per person for FB). Camping $8, dorm bed $20, s/c tent $80

Mara Springs Safari Camp 3km from Sekenani Gate, above the Sekenani River ☎0722 511752, ⒲mountainrockkenya.com/marasprings. Large site, with a number of options including basic ridge tents, permanent tents with built-in WC and shower, plus using your own tent. The ablutions blocks are basic, but clean. Bar-restaurant in a large mess tent (meals to order $15). Camping $10, FB: budget tent $100, s/c tent $160

Wajee Mara (Olperr Elong'o) Camp 1km north of Sekenani Gate, then 2km east ☎0713 938938, ⒲wajeemaracamp.com. A shady site with decent toilets and showers, good security and a restaurant-bar. Camp, hire a ridge tent or sleep in one of the larger, double s/c tents on concrete plinths. There's also one s/c cabin where their description of the "liberal use of plywood" is not wrong. Camping $20, FB: tent $90, cabin $120

TALEK GATE

★**Aruba Mara Camp** East bank of the Talek, 100m from Talek Gate ☎0723 997524, ⒲aruba-safaris.com. Well-run German-Kenyan operation, offering terrific value for money (if you're happy being in the busy Talek area) with super-big, comfortably furnished tents with brick bathrooms, and a shady campsite with good ablutions; pre-erected tents can also be hired. The bar-restaurant serves good, varied buffet meals (breakfast $7, dinner $15). Camping $7, pre-erected tents $28, FB including two game drives $260

Riverside Camp Talek Gate ☎0726 030846, ⒲riversidecampmara.com. Close to where the Narok matatus stop, this place has neat *bandas* with tiled bathrooms, some with good river views, plus a campsite with decent ablutions. You can use the camp kitchen or eat at the dining room and bar (breakfast Ksh1000, dinner Ksh1500). Camping $10, *banda* $80

LODGES AND CAMPS IN THE NATIONAL RESERVE

The accommodation inside the reserve includes affordable mainstream lodges such as *Mara Simba* and one of the most expensive camps in the region, *Mara Explorer*. Inevitably, key routes, river crossings and animal-viewing spots can become crowded in the reserve, especially over Christmas and during the migration. Reserve fees of $80 per person per 24hr are not included in the rates given.

THE MARA CONSERVANCY (MARA TRIANGLE)

★**Little Governors' Camp** West bank of the Mara, in the Mara Triangle just upstream from Governor's Il Moran (Musiara airstrip) ☎020 2734000, ⒲governorscamp.com. Accessed from the Musiara sector by a rope-pulled boat

across the Mara, and hidden in the trees, with wonderful birdwatching, this has seventeen tents, all facing an oxbow marsh of the Mara. There's no fence and plenty of animal action, with elephants, buffaloes and hippos keeping the *askaris* very busy. Wi-fi. Ecotourism Kenya Silver Award. FB $1400

Mara Serena Safari Lodge On a hilltop in the Mara Triangle, above the Mara River (Serena airstrip) ☎0732 123333, ⒲serenahotels.com. Located on a saddle overlooking the Mara River, close to the migration crossings, this lodge is intriguingly designed, based on a re-creation of two Maasai *enkangs*, with smallish but appealingly cellular, cave-like rooms with nets. Most have good views. Pool, spa and gym. Wi-fi. Ecotourism Kenya Silver Award. FB $638

MUSIARA SECTOR

Governors' Camp East bank of the Mara, near Musiara Gate (Musiara airstrip) ☎020 2734000, ⒲governorscamp.com. Close to the fantastic game-viewing of the Musiara marsh, this large, busy, highly regarded operation (the main camp of the group) has 37 tents: 28 face the river and nine face the plains, of which six are family-sized. Meals and drinks are taken in the lavish mess tents. One silver and many bronze guides. Wi-fi. Ecotourism Kenya Silver Award. FB $1240

Governors' Il Moran Camp East bank of the Mara, just upstream from the main Governors' (Musiara airstrip) ☎020 2734000, ⒲governorscamp.com. The ten huge, steel-framed tents, mounted on heavy concrete plinths, all face the river (though unfortunately the camp footpath runs in front of tents #1–5) and are more spacious and better furnished than the main camp. Bathrooms include Victorian-style claw-foot baths, and dining is either in the mess tent or alfresco on the river bank. Wi-fi. Ecotourism Kenya Silver Award. FB $1590

Mara Bush Camp Close to Ol Kiombo airstrip, on the banks of the Olare Orok River ☎020 4445669, ⒲marabushcamp.com. Run by the excellent Sunworld Safaris (see p.124) and operating mostly for the wildebeest migration, this is a twelve-tent seasonal camp. Tents have four-poster beds, nets and decks, and offer good value for money. Also comfortable lounge and dining mess tents. Ecotourism Kenya Silver Award. Closed April–June & mid-Nov–mid-Dec. FB $570

Mara Crossings Camp East bank of the Mara (Musiara airstrip) ☎020 2062424 or ☎0729 329488, ⒲maracrossingscamp.com. Hidden in a thicket right on the river bank, close to one of the wildebeest crossings (as the name suggests), this is so secluded many new drivers have trouble finding it. The eight tents, decorated with Kenyan textiles, have verandas with river views, and there's a mess tent with comfy leather sofas; in good weather the communal dining table is set up alfresco in varying

CELEBRITY BIG CAT

Originally, it was **The Marsh Lions**, by Brian Jackman and Jonathan Scott, first published in 1982, that captured the public imagination with its tales of the characters in the Kichwa Tembo, Miti Mbili and Marsh prides living in the Musiara and Mara North areas. Given names like Notch, Scar and Shadow, the anthropomorphism provided a hook for readers into the lives of big cats that a traditional natural history account might have struggled to achieve. The makers of Disney's 1994 film **The Lion King**, who visited Kenya on safari during their research phase, seem to have had the same idea, keeping their movie grounded – as far as the cartoon world allows – in the lives of real animals, and making *The Lion King* into the top-earning title in box office history for both stage productions and films.

Presenting real lion behaviour, while treating the cats as the subjects of a reality TV show – and later as celebrities – was the concept behind the BBC's **Big Cat Diary**, which started airing, more or less live, during the migration season of 1996. Feeding, and then indulging, a huge audience appetite, *Big Cat Diary* – later *Big Cat Live* – followed the fortunes of the Mara's lions, leopards and cheetahs and ran until 2008, becoming one of the BBC's most popular shows. Safari met soap opera in another feline film phenomenon in 2011, Disney's **African Cats**, a much-hyped cinema release that blended remarkable documentary footage with a part-fictional storyline – the equivalent of *The Hills* or *The Only Way is Essex*, but with real manes.

The intense fascination with the minutiae of the lives of a few individual lions has clear conservation benefits for the future survival of big cats in Kenya, especially in the most touristed areas. Because of their international fame, the Mara's big cats are recognized as important (and adorable) characters worthy of protection, not persecution. The risk is, however, that it may divert attention away from the wider conservation story of Africa's lions, leopards and cheetahs that will never have their own television show.

---

locations around camp. FB **$710**

Mara Explorer North bank of the Talek River, just upstream from sister camp Mara Intrepids (Ol Kiombo airstrip) ☏020 4446651, ⊚heritage-eastafrica.com. Upmarket sister of *Mara Intrepids*, this boutique camp is very peaceful, with seven double and three twin open-plan tents, all with decks facing the river, and open air bathtubs. As it's unfenced, guests use radios to summon the *askaris* after dark. Free transfers available to *Intrepids'* pool. Wi-fi. Ecotourism Kenya Silver Award. Package **$1344**

Mara Intrepids North bank of the Talek, just downstream from sister camp Mara Explorer (Ol Kiombo airstrip) ☏020 4446651, ⊚heritage-eastafrica.com. This shady camp of thirty tents (all with four-poster beds and nets) on a bluff overlooking the river is a perennial family favourite – the *huge* family tents have a double, a twin and a large living area (room for up to six). Popular Adventurers' Club for children and teens, watchtower (very good for migration photos) and pool. FB rates include game drives but not drinks. One bronze guide. Wi-fi. Ecotourism Kenya Silver Award. FB **$1132**

★**Rekero Camp** North bank of the Talek (Ol Kiombo airstrip) ☏020 2324904, ⊚rekero.asiliaafrica.com. In a prime location for the migration, this excellent camp has nine large tents, one for a family, spread along the banks of the Talek in the middle of the reserve and very close to its confluence with the Mara. You can enjoy convivial evenings with fellow guests, guides and hosts in the stylish canvas communal areas, one of which is built on a deck jutting out over the river. One silver and four bronze guides. Ecotourism Kenya Silver Award. Closed April & May. Package **$1740**

SEKENANI SECTOR

Keekorok Lodge In the heart of the reserve's Sekenani sector (Keekorok airstrip) ☏020 2345463, ⊚sunafricahotels.com. This 101-room lodge is the oldest in the reserve, dating from 1963. Although the smallish rooms and furnishings are showing their age, the Keekorok ecosystem adjusted long ago to the lodge's presence, and there's good game-viewing in the vicinity. The hippo bar and elephant deck, out on the boardwalk in the papyrus swamp, are a bonus. Good pool, and the best curio shop in the Mara. Wi-fi. FB **$448**

Mara Simba Lodge South bank of the Talek River, 6km northwest of Sekenani Gate (Keekorok airstrip) ☏020 4444401, ⊚simbalodges.com. A typical mid-range large lodge, this has 84 identical hotel-style rooms in blocks of four, with fans, all overlooking the river, and seventeen cabin-style "tents". Public areas are on decks ranged out over the Talek. Often one of the busiest lodges in the Mara, with an international mix of guests, and in low season it's the cheapest big lodge in the reserve itself by some margin. Pool. Wi-fi. FB **$390**

Naibor Camp 1km downstream from Rekero, on the

5

Talek, close to its confluence with the Mara (Ol Kiombo airstrip) ☎ 020 2679594 or 0729 406582, ⊕ naibor.com. Sumptuously comfortable camp (with boutique offspring *Little Naibor* and *Naibor Wilderness*) on a densely wooded bend in the river, *Naibor* is immaculately located for migration-watchers as well as birders and luxury-seekers. Lots of shade, figwood furniture and light canvas. Massage and beauty treatments available on your private deck. Wi-fi. Ecotourism Kenya Bronze Award. Package $1130

Sala's Camp Far south of the Sekenani sector, at the confluence of the Sand and Keekorok rivers (Keekorok airstrip) ☎ 0725 675830 or ☎ 0731 914732, ⊕ thesafaricollection.com. Location is the real draw of *Sala's*. Far to the south of the reserve, hugging the edge of the Serengeti, it's the first camp to see the migration arrive and the last to see it leave. With just seven very comfortable tents, and no other camps in the area, it's exceptionally peaceful, and there's always a good communal group-dinner-campfire atmosphere, accentuated by the camp being unfenced. Closed May & Nov. Package $1276

Sarova Mara Game Camp Off the main C12 entrance road, 2km inside Sekenani Gate (Keekorok airstrip) ☎ 050 222386 or ☎ 0773 610405, ⊕ sarovahotels.com. The most accessible of the reserve's camps and lodges is well managed and always busy and welcoming, with plenty of nice touches, such as vegetarian options at every meal. The seventy tents are comfortable, the large pool and verdant gardens are fun – it's one of the best family options – though it's not the cheapest mid-range place around. Wi-fi. Ecotourism Kenya Silver Award. FB $499

LODGES AND CAMPS IN THE CONSERVANCIES AND GROUP RANCHES

Camps and lodges in the conservancies and group ranches outside the reserve are able to offer guided walks and night drives. Not all do so, and night drives are being discouraged in some areas, though using red/orange lights is much less stressful for the animals than bright spotlights. Walking, however, although strictly a daytime activity, is highly recommended if you get the chance. You will need to sign a disclaimer, and will usually be accompanied by an armed guard.

KIMINTET GROUP RANCH AND OLOOLOLO GAME RANCH

Carved out of the Kimintet Group Ranch, on the west bank of the Mara, the ten-square-kilometre private Oloololo Game Ranch adjoins the main reserve, with access to the Mara Triangle, via the Oloololo Gate, just minutes away. Ranch fees (but not national reserve fees) are included in overnight stays.

Bateleur Camp On the western edge of the ranch beneath the Oloololo Escarpment (Kichwa Tembo

airstrip) ☎ +27 (0)11 8094300, ⊕ andbeyond.com. Discreetly fenced, situated on the fringe of a belt of African greenheart forest, with superb birdlife, this is more exclusive than its co-owned neighbour, *Kichwa Tembo*, but eye-wateringly expensive. The eighteen very comfortable cabin-style "tents" have vintage/explorer-style decor, huge bathrooms and an armchair-furnished deck overlooking the plains, and are tucked into two wings among the trees on either side of a small lap pool. Ecotourism Kenya Silver Award. Package $2470

★ **Kichwa Tembo Camp** Adjoining Bateleur (Kichwa Tembo airstrip) ☎ +27 (0)11 8094300, ⊕ andbeyond .com. Emerging from the trees at the foot of the Oloololo Escarpment, this long-established favourite has excellent food and is justifiably famous for employing female driver-guides. The forty tents have been recently refurbished in contemporary style; the larger, luxury tents have the best views, though cost $190 extra and are much further away from the guests' area and pool. Great for children, with a lovely decked pool and large lawns facing the plains. Wi-fi. Ecotourism Kenya Bronze Award. Package $900

Sanctuary Olonana West bank of the Mara (Kichwa Tembo airstrip) ☎ 020 2487374, ⊕ sanctuaryretreats .com. At the foot of the Oloololo Escarpment, this lavishly appointed eco-camp (solar power, waste management and indigenous tree planting, for example) has comfortable public areas and fourteen huge tented rooms with spectacular views over the river. Another good option for children. Pool and spa. Wi-fi. Ecotourism Kenya Gold Award. Package $1700

MAJI MOTO GROUP RANCH

Northeast of the national reserve, stretching towards the Loita Hills, this 600-square-kilometre group ranch (no fees, free access) is the closest in the Mara ecosystem to Narok, making access to it much quicker and easier than to the national reserve: you're just a 3hr drive from Nairobi on a good day. There has been little tourism or conservation development in this region, which includes the hill peaks of Lolua (2249m) and Olekijapi (2232m). Wildlife numbers are lower, too, though day-trips into the reserve proper can be arranged.

★ **Maji Moto Maasai Cultural Camp** ☎ 07721 778424 or 0717 699676, ⊕ majimotomaasaicamp.com. This Slovene-Maasai-owned small camp has an inspiring hillside location. Accommodation is in Maasai huts or modest-sized dome tents, both furnished with comfy mattresses and bedding; you can also pitch your own tent for a rate that includes meals and activities. Staffed by charming Maasai from the Maji Moto community, its attraction, as much as wildlife, is Maasai culture – understanding it and participating in it, with fun warrior training/play-fighting for willing participants, making it ideal for adventurous families. Limited solar power, no generator, kerosene lamps, simple meals, evening supply of hot water for bucket showers from the hot springs delivered by donkey. Bush walks, mountain-bike rides and bathing in the springs included; game drives into the reserve extra. FB Camping $40, tents $160, huts $200

MARA NABOISHO CONSERVANCY

The 211-square-kilometre Mara Naboisho Conservancy (W maranaboisho.com) was formed, like Olare Motorogi and Ol Kinyei, out of former group ranches by persuading the five hundred-odd Maasai landowners to move out of their two hundred square kilometres, while hosting small numbers of high-paying safari-goers, employing Maasai staff and paying a monthly fee to every Maasai family based on bed-nights. You can see the success of Naboisho (which means "coming together" in Maa) in the huge populations of animals roaming the glorious landscapes here – elephants and giraffes everywhere and as many as seventy lions. Entry is exclusive to Naboisho camp and lodge guests, and conservancy fees are included in rates.

★**Basecamp Eagle View** Above a tributary of the Talek (Ol Seki airstrip) ☎ 0733 333909, W basecampexplorer.com. With laudable ecological features such as compost loos and solar power, this has eight large tents and two family units arranged around a bluff with views on all sides, and there's a large dining area and a superb sundowner terrace. The camp overlooks a waterhole that often attracts predators and elephants. They also set up a fly wilderness camp a short distance across the valley with dome tents, solar showers, bush meals and Maasai guides for walking safaris. Wi-fi. Ecotourism Kenya Silver Award. Package $880

★**Encounter Mara Safari Camp** Banks of the Olmorijo River (Ol Seki airstrip) ☎ 020 2324904, W encountermara.asiliaafrica.com. This award-winning, engagingly hosted camp has ten vast, luxuriously furnished tents in a contemporary style and lies in a prime game area with sweeping views of Naboisho's plains. Expert local Maasai guides lead bush walks which can also take in their nearby village, Enooronkon. Group dining is a chance to relive days (and nights) of full-on game drives. One silver guide. Ecotourism Kenya Silver Award. Package $1390

Kicheche Valley Camp Above the Moliband Stream (Ol Seki airstrip) ☎ 020 2493569, W kicheche.com. Tucked into a wooded corner of the conservancy, this is the most architecturally innovative of the Kicheche camps, with just six luxuriously appointed platform tents dotted across the hillside; all sides of each tent open out, allowing you to sleep under just a mosquito net. Also a spacious lounge tent above a spring that draws animals, and the food is particularly good here. Treats include massages on your deck. Wi-fi. Ecotourism Kenya Silver Award. Closed April–May. Package $1580

★**Naboisho Camp** Central area of the conservancy (Ol Seki airstrip) ☎ 020 2324904, W naboisho.asiliaafrica .com. The sister camp to *Rekero*, inside the reserve, this is the most luxurious of the Naboisho conservancy's handful of tented camps, with eight large canvas suites (one for families), magnificent rainfall-shower outdoor bathrooms and hosted dining in the huge mess tent. Game walks are a standout feature (the manager is a top South African guide) and the game close to camp can be heart-stoppingly impressive, with lion kills and other encounters being frequent events. Ecotourism Kenya Silver Award. Package $1990

Ol Seki Hemingways Mara In the hills on the eastern side of the conservancy (Ol Seki airstrip) ☎ 020 2295011, W hemingways-mara.com. Stylish camp with vintage decor touches. The twelve canvas, almost round tents have open walls on three sides, and are set well apart from each other on a wonderful rocky promontory overlooking the Isupukiai stream. There's also a deck perched right on boulders offering sweeping views of the plains below. Wi-fi. One bronze guide. Ecotourism Kenya Silver Award. Package $1409

MARA NORTH CONSERVANCY

The 320-square-kilometre Mara North Conservancy (MNC; W maranorth.com), northwest of the reserve, is classic savanna bush country, the land broken into ridges by bush-choked *luggas*, with high densities of game. The conservancy (part of the Koiyaki Group Ranch) is the home range of several much-studied lion prides, including the Acacia pride and the Gorge pride, named after the iconic Leopard Gorge, 5km northeast of Musiara Gate. Access by road is fairly straightforward as the C13 runs through the

---

MAASAI/MASAI – WHAT'S IN A NAME?

The spelling of the name "Maasai" can provoke passion among various authorities, with claims that there are different spellings for the people (Maasai) and the reserve (Masai Mara). In fact the spelling of the people and the reserve with one "a" preceded the first attempt to write down the Maa language, which uses standard international orthography for a long "a" (W bit.ly/MaaDictionary). The written form of the Maa language is still not much used, but the double-a spelling of the word Maasai is increasingly considered the standard form, even though the name was originally spelt most commonly with one "a".

5

conservancy en route to Oloololo Gate. Away from the main road, however, there is a strict cap on visitor and vehicle numbers and game drives are exclusively for MNC camp and lodge guests. Conservancy fees are included in the rates given below.

Elephant Pepper Camp Off the C13 (Mara North airstrip) ☏ 0730 127000, ⊛ elephantpeppercamp .com. In a dense grove of elephant pepper trees, with eight lovely tents pitched in two wings each side of the stylish central area, this is owned by boutique safari operator Cheli & Peacock, on a private lease of four square kilometres. The camp uses a non-permanent construction (no cement) for minimal impact and is entirely solar-powered; they have one silver and two bronze guides. Wi-fi. Ecotourism Kenya Gold Award. Closed April 1–June 15. Package $\overline{1172}$

★**Karen Blixen Camp** East bank of the Mara (Mara North airstrip) ☏ 0773 063863 or ☏ 0711 579001, ⊛ karenblixencamp.com. This Danish-owned unfenced camp has 22 tents along the river or on raised platforms. It's eco-friendly, with grey-water recycling and gas water-heaters for each tent, and the gardens are planted with only indigenous trees and shrubs. The public areas are furnished in a 1920s Karen Blixen-era style, and there's a lovely pool shaded by acacia and wild olive trees. Wi-fi. One silver and four bronze guides. Ecotourism Kenya Silver Award. Package $\overline{1242}$

★**Kicheche Mara Camp** "Acacia Valley", on the west bank of the Olare Orok (Mara North airstrip) ☏ 020 2493569, ⊛ kicheche.com. Lying in a wildlife-rich valley above a stream, Kicheche Mara has long been one of the Mara ecosystem's standout camps. There are eight comfortable and roomy tents, two of which can be family tents, with hot-water bucket showers to order. Like all the Kicheche camps, it's a perennial favourite with photographers, assisted by Kicheche's excellent management and guides, three of whom have silver accreditations and one bronze. Dinner is taken communally in the mess tent. Wi-fi. Ecotourism Kenya Gold Award. Closed April–May. Package $\overline{1400}$

★**Offbeat Mara Camp** On the Olare Orok stream (Mara North airstrip) ☏ 0704 909355 or 0704 909356, ⊛ offbeatsafaris.com. A hidden jewel in the Mara, this exceptional, boutique tented camp is unusually informal, unpretentious and enjoyable. The six reasonably sized tents are very private and surrounded by untramelled bush – no clipped lawns or electric fences here, nor any other vehicles around, just fantastic wildlife right in front of you. Charming hosts, outstanding staff, three bronze guides and excellent, generous meals and wine. Wi-fi. Package $\overline{1270}$

★**Saruni Mara** Far to the north, past Aitong (Ngerende airstrip) ☏ 020 2180497 or ☏ 0735 950903, ⊛ sarunimara.com. One of the most stylish lodges in the

Mara, with just six, roomy, breezy thatched cottages and a family villa overlooking a bird- and game-filled valley far to the north of the Mara plains, which you can see through a cleft in the hills. With very good food, awesome showers and the "Masai Wellbeing Space" (free massage with each booking), this is a highly recommended base, especially if you're as happy doing local game walks as game drives. One silver and four bronze guides. Wi-fi. Ecotourism Kenya Silver Award. Package $\overline{1798}$

Serian Spanning the Mara, 6km north of the C13 road (Mara North airstrip) ☏ 020 2663397, or ☏ 0718 139359, ⊛ serian.com. One of the region's most attractive and individual camps, with seven tents on the east bank and four more (called *Ngare Serian*) across the river via a splendid suspension bridge. The super-comfortable tents are dubbed "marquees" and bathrooms are daringly "adjoining" rather than en-suite. A private driver-guide for each tent is part of the package, as are stays in a nearby tree house and fly camp if required. Wi-fi. Four bronze guides. Package $\overline{1490}$

OLARE MOTOROGI CONSERVANCY

The 142-square-kilometre Olare Motorogi Conservancy (OMC; ⊛ mmconservancy.com) is unusual for its highly focused Mara conservation work and the success of its community integration. It sets the benchmarks for sustainable Mara tourism – there is a maximum of 94 beds in its six camps which equates to a ratio of one game-viewing vehicle for every 8.5 square kilometres. Funds are channelled from visitors to the Maasai landowners, who also have access to the conservancy's grasslands during times of drought. Tusk Trust and the International Fund for Animal Welfare are both donors, and the wildlife-viewing is exceptional. All the predators are present, and with about forty lions in two formidable and regularly seen prides, it has some of the best lion-watching in the Mara ecosystem.

★**Kicheche Bush Camp** In the southeast of the conservancy (Olare Orok airstrip) ☏ 020 2493569, ⊛ kicheche.com. This extremely popular camp offers six luxurious tents, with huge bedrooms, built-in safari showers and large, very private verandas – all furnished in a fresh, minimalist way. Luxury aside, it's the attentive management, superb food and top-class guiding that makes a stay here so special. Avid photographers appreciate the little touches like beanbags in the open-sided vehicles, and the much prized ability of the driver-guides to always offer you just the right angle. Ecotourism Kenya Silver Award. Wi-fi. Closed April & May. Package $\overline{1290}$

★**Mahali Mzuri** In the north of the conservancy (Olare Orok airstrip); reservations ☏ +44 (0)20 8600 0430, ⊛ virginlimitededition.com/en/mahali-mzuri. Opened in 2013 by Virgin boss Richard Branson, and perched on the side of a lush valley, the twelve super-luxurious tents here have vast steel and canvas igloo-like roofs and are so far apart it's a good five-minute walk from the furthest one to the main structure. The food, served at a shared dining table, is superb – romantic bush dinners can also be arranged – and other features include a 12m infinity pool and a separate spa down on the valley floor. Obviously a hefty price-tag matches the sumptuousness of it, but this is up there among Kenya's most luxurious safari experiences. Wi-fi. Package **$2140**

Mara Plains Camp Ntiakatek River (Olare Orok airstrip); reservations ☎ +27 (0)792 845945, @ greatplainsconservation.com. Tucked into woodland, surrounded by open savanna, this has seven elegant hexagonal tents on decks (two facing the plains, five the river), with early-explorer-style decor and Swahili-style touches such as large carved Lamu doors. Again a super-expensive and top-end option but the high price tag is justified by the superb views from the front of the camp that go clear across the migration grazing grounds. Run by film and photography pros who share their expert knowledge. Wi-fi. Ecotourism Kenya Gold Award. Package **$2730**

Olare Mara Kempinski Banks of the Ntlakatek River (Olare Orok airstrip) ☎ 0703 049000, @ kempinski .com. Ambitious and fancy fenced tented camp, with lodge-like central areas and a good-size pool. Hardwood floors, decks with guard rails above the river bank and tiled bathrooms all make the twelve huge, well-spaced tents feel more like hotel rooms, but the staff are particularly nice and it will suit you if you want less of a "bush" experience. Pool. Silver guide. Wi-fi. Package **$1390**

★ **Porini Lion Camp** By the Ntiakatek River (Olare Orok airstrip) ☎ 0774 136523, @ porini.com. Fine eco-camp managed in collaboration with the local Maasai community, in a brilliant game-viewing area particularly renowned for big cats. It's far from other camps, but close enough to the reserve to visit. The ten very spacious and airy tents are run as responsibly as possible, with full recycling, and the staff, all from the local community, are paid significantly higher wages than the norm. Guests eat together. Ecotourism Kenya Gold Award. Closed mid-April to end May. Package **$1320**

Richard's Forest Camp By the Ntiakatek River (Olare Orok airstrip) ☎ 0733 700014, @ richardscamp.com, Nairobi reservations ☎ 0735 579999, @ scckenya.com. Owned and hosted by Richard Roberts, a pilot and guide, and his energetic fun-loving team, this is a very enjoyable bush camp tucked away in a pretty tract of forest. The eight individually decorated tents have solar lighting and hot water by the big bucketful, and you can relax in the cosy sitting room with log fire. A good option for a group or a couple of families. Closed May & Nov. Package **$990**

OL CHORO OIROUWA CONSERVANCY

Bounded by the Mara River, the 69-square-kilometre Ol Choro Oirouwa is a largely pristine area. It's away from the

routes of most visitors, and while it's also off the wildebeest migration route, the relative absence of other tourist vehicles makes game drives very rewarding.

Fairmont Mara Safari Club East bank of the Mara, off the C14 (Ngerende airstrip) ☎ 020 2265555, @ fairmont .com. Modish, rather formal tented camp, with fifty riverside tents, in shady grounds linked by concrete paths. It's a peaceful base, with a beautiful public deck area and heated pool, and very large, tile-floored, rather-too-closely-spaced tents, with four-poster, netted beds and city-hotel amenities. Rates include two game drives, but no drinks. One bronze guide. Wi-fi. Package **$639**

OLDERIKESI GROUP RANCH

The remote Olderikesi group ranch has only one, spectacular, camp. The district is teeming with wildlife (including some huge lions), especially since the camp negotiated an agreement with the Maasai stakeholders in the area to create a "no cattle" zone around the camp in exchange for the community charges levied from visitors.

★ **Cottar's 1920s Camp** On Olderikesi GR, close to the Tanzanian border (Keekorok airstrip) ☎ 0733 773377, @ cottars.com. The finely tuned colonial atmosphere (antiques, oriental carpets, porcelain and crystal), organic kitchen gardens and ten huge, sumptuous tents are just the icing on the cake, for this is one of the best wildlife camps in Kenya, in a game-rich area, with a low human population density. The five-bedroom house is contemporary in style, and very private, so appeals to families. Also a 25m pool, and three gold guides plus one bronze. Wi-fi. Ecotourism Kenya Gold Award. Package **$1980**

OL KINYEI CONSERVANCY

Established in 2005, the 67-square-kilometre Ol Kinyei was the Mara's first community-owned conservancy. Formed in partnership with Gamewatchers Safaris, it demonstrated that landowners could make a living from tourism, and the model has since been replicated all over the greater Mara region. Happily bypassed by the lines of vehicles driving between Narok and Sekenani Gate, this is an area rich in game in which guided walks and a good degree of cultural immersion are the norm. The nearest airstrip is Ol Seki in the Naboisho Conservancy.

Gamewatchers Adventure Camp About 5km from Porini Mara Camp (Ol Seki airstrip) ☎ 0774 136523, @ porini.com. Budget version of *Porini Mara*, with accommodation in small dome tents. The rest of the experience, with local guides and all activities including game drives, game walks and a Maasai village visit, is the same as the more expensive base. Rates include conservancy fee but not drinks. Three-night minimum stay. Package **$600**

★ **Porini Mara Camp** 5km west of the C12 road (Ol Seki airstrip) ☎ 0774 136523, @ porini.com. Like other *Porini* camps, in the Amboseli area and further west in the

5

Mara – such as *Porini Lion* (see p.375) – this eco-camp is run in partnership with the local community. Unfenced, it has just six very nice tents and a communal mess. Game walks are a popular feature and guests eat together, creating an intimate atmosphere that's a million miles from the Mara's mainstream lodges. Ecotourism Kenya Gold Award. Closed mid-April to May. Package **$1240**

OLOIRIEN GROUP RANCH

Most of the land of this huge group ranch lies west of the Oloololo Escarpment, far from the main areas of the reserve, and as a consequence the district is relatively little visited. To the south of the one, spectacularly sited, lodge lies the abandoned *Olkurruk Mara Lodge*, built to house Sidney Pollack and his actors Robert Redford and Meryl Streep during the filming of *Out of Africa* in 1985.
Mara West 5km (a 20–30min drive) from Oloololo Gate (Kichwa Tembo airstrip; transfers $30) ☎0733 420601 or ☎0708 459400, ⊛marawest.com. Perched on the crest of the Oloololo Escarpment, with stunning sunrise views over the Mara Triangle, this camp is unusual as it tries to cater for all budgets – and does so quite successfully. Accommodation ranges from economy round, mushroom-like walk-in tents (*bandas*) under thatched roofs with shared bathrooms, to standard safari tents with brick bathrooms and eight very comfortable en-suite chalets with roll-up canvas walls, hardwood floors and French doors. Maasai staff and guides are outstandingly friendly. Rates include meals but exclude transfers from the airstrip and activities – though these are very fairly priced (from $55 for a game drive and $25 for a game walk). Alternatively you can opt for an all-inclusive rate. FB: *banda* **$180**, safari tent **$580**, chalet **$820**

SIANA GROUP RANCH AND CONSERVANCY

The vast Siana Group Ranch stretches from Sekenani Gate to Ololaimutiek Gate and contains a great range of habitats, from shelving plains to forested hills, including the peak of Trevor (1904m) on the north side. The wider ranch area includes a number of budget camps and banda sites, especially near Sekenani Gate. The core Siana Conservancy, established in 2010, is a minibus-free area to which access is only permitted for guests of the lodges in its perimeters (including *Entumoto*, *Leleshwa Safari Camp* and *Mara Bushtop*). More safari lodges are expected to join in, and the area extended, as the conservancy matures.
Entumoto Between Sekenani and Ololaimutiek gates (Keekorok airstrip) ☎0713 400903 or ☎0713 400903, ⊛entumoto.com. A Swedish-Maasai collaboration in a tranquil, forested valley in the Ngama Hills, right on the border of the national reserve. The enormous platform tents, with acres of decking, ostentatious furnishings and built-in fireplaces, are

ranged up the hill – in some cases a good 5min walk from the mess tent and lounge; the four largest have separate lounges and can accommodate four adults and four children. Exceptionally good food, partly from an organic veg garden. Pool; wi-fi. Package **$1080**
★**Leleshwa Safari Camp** On a tributary of the Talek (Siana airstrip) ☎0715 931471, ⊛leleshwacamp.com. Accessed from its parking area by a footbridge across the deep cleft of the densely wooded Ropile River, *Leleshwa* is enjoyably hosted, has tons of bush atmosphere, great food, top guiding and thousands of acres to explore. The seven tents are large, without being self-consciously massive, and well furnished, with tiled bathrooms. There's lots of game in camp – escorts are essential after dark. They also operate a seasonal mobile camp during the migration and a Maasai-led hiking safari and mobile camp in the Loita Hills. Closed May 1–15. Wi-fi. Package **$1320**
Mara Bushtops Northeast of Sekenani Gate (Siana airstrip) ☎020 2137862 or ☎0733 490209, ⊛bushtopscamps.com. Highly regarded camp with twelve tents – based around the old home of Mara hunting and safari legend Glen Cottar – on a fine north-facing hillside, with a tremendous vista from the pool deck and the best wine cellar in the Mara. The area around the camp has outstanding game, including regularly playing host to denning wild dogs. One bronze guide, personal room butlers and a spa. Wi-fi. Ecotourism Kenya Silver Award. Package **$1980**
Mara Sopa Lodge Outside Ololaimutiek Gate (Siana airstrip) ☎020 2516160 or ☎020 2416485, ⊛sopa lodges.com. Equalling *Keekorok* (see p.371) in size, this has a hundred spacious rooms in cottages and impressive public areas, and there's a good pool overlooking the wooded valley. But it's more of a resort than a game lodge, there's little wildlife to see from here, even with binoculars, and it's a fair drive to the central parts of the reserve. Nonetheless its facilities will suit families, and it's well priced. Wi-fi. FB **$344**
★**Sekenani Camp** On the reserve boundary 6km southeast of Sekenani Gate (Keekorok airstrip) ☎020 891169 or ☎0722 147810, ⊛sekenani-camp.com. Unusual and affordable camp on a ridge in the forest. It's built at the source of the Sekenani River, which gathers at a rock pool at the camp's eastern end and flows through the site in front of the accommodation – there are fifteen tents in all, constructed on raised platforms and accessed through tunnels cut through the trees. The area sees elephants, buffaloes and lots of birdlife. Well worth considering if you've been to the Mara before and want somewhere a little different. Well-led walking safaris; pool and wi-fi. FB **$462**

TALEK AREA OF KOIYAKI GROUP RANCH

The mostly mainstream camps and lodges along the north bank of the Talek are often thought of as being inside the reserve. In fact they are all in the southernmost part of

Koiyaki Group Ranch, which means that bush walks are possible – though the human pressures are such that there's not a lot of bush left in the area. Access into the reserve itself is easy via Talek Gate and the Talek bridge, with the plains of the Sekenani sector and the confluence of the Talek and Mara rivers equally close.

★**Basecamp Masai Mara** North bank of the Talek, close to Talek Gate (Ol Kiombo airstrip) ☎ 0733 333909, ⓦ basecampexplorer.com. One of the Mara's most eco-friendly places to stay, this runs on solar energy, uses composting toilets and recycles all waste. The twelve comfy tents with verandas, Kilgoris-grass-thatched roofs and

open-air showers, seem to grow out of the environment. Good food and welcoming Maasai staff and guides from the nearby Talek village. Wi-fi. FB $\underline{\$680}$

Ilkeliani Camp North bank of the Talek (Ol Kiombo airstrip) ☎ 0733 258120 or ☎ 0704 084444, ⓦ ilkeliani.com. Spacious and eco-friendly establishment, sensibly priced and popular with mid-range tour groups. The fifty-acre compound holds seventeen nicely decorated, well-spaced tents looking out onto the Mara plains. Mess tent for communal dining and a viewing platform over the river for sundowners. One bronze guide. FB $\underline{\$364}$

Samburu–Buffalo Springs national reserves

$70, car Ksh1000 (see p.75) • ⓦ samburucouncil.com/reserves.htm • 165 square kilometres

Up in the north of the country, in the hot, arid lowlands beneath Mount Kenya, **Samburu National Reserve** was set up around the richest stretch of the Ewaso Nyiro (or Uaso Ngiro) River in the early 1960s. Although the river usually stops flowing for a month or two around January, the combination of near-permanent water and forest shade on the banks draws plentiful wildlife in the dry season and maintains many of the less migratory species all year round.

While the wildlife spectacle doesn't always match that of the southern parks, the peace and scenic beauty of Samburu is unquestionable and, in the kind of mood swing which only an equatorial region can produce, the contrast with the fertile farming country of the Highlands just a few dozen kilometres to the south couldn't be more striking. In the background, the sharp hill of **Koitogor** rises in the middle of Samburu Reserve, making a useful reference point. And on the horizon, 30km to the north, looms the gaunt red block of **Ol Olokwe** mountain. **Buffalo Springs National Reserve**, the continuation of Samburu on the south side of the river, and Shaba National Reserve (see p.381), further downstream to the east, are often treated as if they were just part of "Samburu". They remain distinct reserves with their own entrance fees, but will allow common game drives across them, which means you will only have to pay $70 once per 24-hour period. That said, the Samburu–Buffalo Springs bridge crossing near the Samburu headquarters has been washed away more than once in recent years by flooding, though it's presently operational. If the bridge is out of action, to get into the reserve from the opposite side, you have to go back to the highway and cross the bridge there, via Archer's Post – a 45km diversion.

Adjoining Samburu are two community conservancies supported by the Northern Rangelands Trust. To the north is the 95-square-kilometre **Kalama Community Wildlife Conservancy** ($116, including access to Samburu-Buffalo Springs; ⓦ nrt-kenya.org/kalama), of which a core 31 square kilometres is a crucial wildlife migration corridor, with just one, very high-end, boutique lodge, *Saruni Samburu* (see p.380). To the northwest of the reserves lies the **West Gate Community Conservancy** ($58; ⓦ nrt-kenya .org/west-gate), which covers an even larger district of semi-arid grazing land, but has a very small core conservancy area of less than 10 square kilometres around the exclusive *Sasaab* lodge (see p.380).

Exploring Samburu–Buffalo Springs

Except during and immediately after the rains, scrubby bush country takes up most of the reserve district, but there are some large acacia thickets, especially in the eastern

5

part of **Buffalo Springs**. The **springs** themselves are a welcome target: two pools of clear if weedy water, the smaller of which has been sanitized with concrete for the benefit of swimmers and, most of the time, the exclusion of crocodiles (be sure to check before jumping in). The larger one is the water supply for the town of Archer's Post. While looking out for crocs, you should also beware of lions, which sometimes rest under the bushes by the neighbouring natural waterhole.

The dry-country ecosystems are prone to large variations in animal populations as they move in search of water and grazing, which means that Samburu's **wildlife** can occasionally be disappointing. Some visitors, however, have tremendous luck and Samburu–Buffalo Springs can provide consistently excellent animal-watching. The best areas are often along the south side of the river in Buffalo Springs Reserve, opposite *Samburu Game Lodge*. Poaching wiped out the rhinos from here years ago, but **lions** are often seen.

Meanwhile, the locally burgeoning **elephant herds** have ruined some sections of the riverine forest. Various rare or more localized races and species compensate, though, and are often seen here in large numbers. Among these, the **reticulated giraffe** with its beautiful jigsaw marking, **Grevy's zebra** (the large, finely striped species that has a bushy mane and outsized ears), the **Somali ostrich**, which has blue rather than pink legs, and the **gerenuk**, the antelope that stands on its hind legs to reach foliage, are all common and conspicuous. Samburu's **birdlife** is diverse and prolific and includes the ferocious **martial eagle**, pygmy falcon, Egyptian goose and several species of hornbill.

ARRIVAL AND DEPARTURE SAMBURU–BUFFALO SPRINGS NATIONAL RESERVES

If you're circling Mount Kenya, Samburu Reserve is close at hand, a couple of hours north of Nanyuki. The entrance to Samburu, **Archer's Post Gate**, is 3.5km west of the main road in Archer's Post itself and is clearly signposted. Most visitors explore Buffalo Springs on game drives from the lodges in Samburu, though the **Buffalo Springs Gate** is just 3.5km south of Archer's Post on the A2. The turnoff from the A2 to **Ngare Mara Gate** is 21km south of Archer's Post (and 25km north of Isiolo), from which it's 2.6km to the gate itself.

By bus and matatu Public transport runs down onto the hazy plain as far as Isiolo (see p.541) from where there are also regular services to Archer's Post (35km). There is no public transport into the reserves, but you might be lucky with a lift from a KWS employee, assuming you are going to camp near the reserve HQ. If you've made plans to stay at one of the lodges, they should be able to pick you up from Archer's Post.

By car The fast new road to Merille (see p.544) means there is no longer any requirement for an escort for the short continuation to Archer's Post. It's a good idea to fill up with fuel before leaving Isiolo, but Archer's Post now has filling stations too.

By plane Airkenya and SafariLink both fly from Nairobi to Samburu and Shaba (at least daily; 1–2hr depending on routing; about $230 each way, $395 round trip). In addition, depending on season and demand, Airkenya flies one-way from Meru to Samburu (daily; 30min; $183) and both airlines fly one-way from Samburu to Maasai Mara (daily; 1hr 30min–2hr; about $385).

ACCOMMODATION

There's an increasing range of **lodges** and **tented camps** in Samburu–Buffalo Springs, though in recent years they've often seemed too many for the number of visitors. In the 2010 and 2011 floods, the Ewaso Nyiro burst its banks and swamped all the riverbank lodges and camps in Samburu and Buffalo Springs. Several were rebuilt, though one – *Serena Samburu* – has remained closed ever since.

CAMPSITES

Reserve Headquarters campsites Although Samburu officially has several public campsites along the banks of the Ewaso Nyiro, between the bridge and park headquarters, most are essentially just cleared spaces shaded by trees. The two closest to the reserve HQ, located on little sandy beaches, are the best bet as they have long-drop toilets and

cold showers. The baboons at the campsites are beyond being an amusement and you need to leave your tent under guard, which can be organized at the reserve HQ (around Ksh500/day). The fact that baboons sometimes fall victim to crocs at the water's edge (keep an eye out and on no account swim) seems less distressing after you've been in the area for a day or two. Both campsites are a 5min walk from

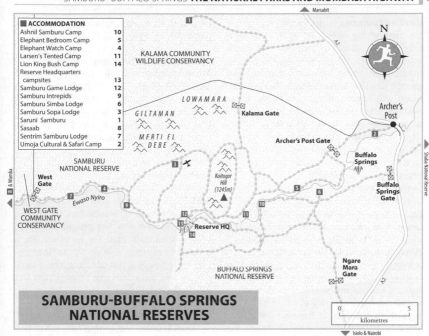

Marsabit

N

■ ACCOMMODATION
Ashnil Samburu Camp	10
Elephant Bedroom Camp	5
Elephant Watch Camp	4
Larsen's Tented Camp	11
Lion King Bush Camp	14
Reserve Headquarters campsites	13
Samburu Game Lodge	12
Samburu Intrepids	9
Samburu Simba Lodge	6
Samburu Sopa Lodge	3
Saruni Samburu	1
Sasaab	8
Sentrim Samburu Lodge	7
Umoja Cultural & Safari Camp	2

KALAMA COMMUNITY
WILDLIFE CONSERVANCY

LOWAMARA

GILTAMAN   Kalama Gate

MERTI EL
DEBE

SAMBURU
NATIONAL RESERVE

West
Gate

Ewaso Nyiro

WEST GATE
COMMUNITY
CONSERVANCY

& Wamba

Koitogor
Hill
(1245m)

Reserve HQ

BUFFALO SPRINGS
NATIONAL RESERVE

Archer's
Post

Archer's Post Gate

Buffalo
Springs

Buffalo
Springs
Gate

Shaba National Reserve

Ngare
Mara
Gate

**SAMBURU-BUFFALO SPRINGS
NATIONAL RESERVES**

0   5
kilometres

Isiolo & Nairobi

Samburu Game Lodge (ask your guard to accompany you), where you can book yourself onto a morning or evening game drive ($70) and use the restaurant and pool. Camping fees are paid at the gate. **$30**

LODGES AND TENTED CAMPS
OUTSIDE SAMBURU RESERVE
Umoja Cultural & Safari Camp 1.2km from the centre of Archer's Post (off the road to the reserve's Archer's Post Gate) ☎0721 659717, ⓦumojawomen. or.ke. A delightfully different setup, founded by the charismatic women's rights campaigner Rebecca Lolosoli as an offshoot of her village for abused women, this has simple, simply furnished s/c *bandas* with nets, plumbed-in bathrooms and mains power, plus a campsite, kitchen, shady bar-restaurant above the river (meals Ksh500–1000) and an eight-seater vehicle with driver to rent for game drives ($200/day). Given that Buffalo Springs is across the river, it is not unusual to see wildlife such as elephants in the distance. Passing visitors are also welcome to drop in to visit the Samburu *manyatta* where most of the women live and sell their handicrafts. Camping **$10** twin *banda* **$38**

SAMBURU NATIONAL RESERVE
Elephant Bedroom Camp 7km from Archer's Post Gate ☎0702 692648 or ☎020 4450036, ⓦatua-enkop .com. This beautifully furnished and very appealing luxury camp has twelve light, airy tents with their own plunge pools spread out along the river and shaded by doum palms. Meals are taken either in the vast mess tent on stilts or at dining tables set out on the sandy beach. Very attentive staff, excellent food and great guides for walks and drives. Elephants really do come right up to the bedrooms. Wi-fi. Package **$810**

★**Elephant Watch Camp** 23km from Archer's Post Gate ☎0731 596437 or ☎0713 037886, ⓦelephantwatchportfolio.com. Elephant specialist Saba Douglas-Hamilton's camp sits on the sandy river bank and has six superb and variously shaped tents with massive nets and rambling, open-air bathrooms; each is individually fitted out with decor and furnishings largely made from trees felled by elephants. As well as the usual game activities, guests can visit the Douglas-Hamiltons' Save the Elephants research centre, and can organize day and overnight hikes to the top of Ol Olokwe mountain. Wi-fi. Closed April & Nov. Package **$1260**

Larsen's Tented Camp 11km from Archer's Post Gate ☎064 31374 or 0720 626367, ⓦwildernesslodges .co.ke. A comfortable mid-range tented camp with twenty spacious tents on a fenced plot, all facing the river, each with wooden floors and verandas and stone bathrooms. There's a nice open-air massage suite, looking across to Koitogor rather than the river, and a pool. Excellent service and good guiding, although the decor could do with a bit of attention. Wi-fi. FB **$596**

5

Lion King Bush Camp 16.5km from Archer's Post Gate, just west of the reserve HQ ☎0711 227626 or 0710 350782, ⊛lionkingsafari.com. This friendly, unpretentious rustic camp is owner-managed by Nahim, an adventurous Samburu enthusiast. Accommodation is in ground-level walk-in tents under shade cloth (not tented rooms), with outside washbasins and bladder showers, plus there's a thatched lounge, bar and dining area next to the river. Game drives are available in the camp vehicle (3hr; $30 per person). With half-board rates of $95 per person, this is Samburu's most affordable option, and if you get to Archer's Post by public transport, you can arrange to be picked up from there. FB $220

Samburu Game Lodge 16.7km from Archer's Post Gate, near the reserve HQ ☎064 30781 or ☎0720 626366, ⊛wildernesslodges.co.ke. The oldest lodge in Samburu (1962), this is very well sited on a heavily wooded broad bend of the river. The rooms, in blocks and thatched chalets, come with excellent views and no fence (the bank provides an adequate boundary along most of the river frontage). It's still popular, but very tired, and in need of an overhaul. Nice pool with shaded surrounds. Ecotourism Kenya Bronze Award. Wi-fi. FB $360

★**Samburu Intrepids** 20.7km from Archer's Post Gate ☎0713 136482, ⊛heritage-eastafrica.com. Built on stilt platforms (for when the river floods), in a dense riverside thicket, the 28 pleasant, modestly sized, river-facing tents here have good bathrooms and wooden floors. The double-sized family tents, excellent Adventurers' Club for children and teens and good pool make it a great family option. Fine, expansive, public deck areas reach over the river bank and are shot through with indigenous trees. Two bronze guides. Wi-fi. Ecotourism Kenya Silver Award. FB $486

Samburu Sopa Lodge Away from the river, on the road to Kalama Conservancy, 20.7km from Archer's Post Gate ☎0721 258278, ⊛sopalodges.com. Popular and affordable lodge, with sixty simple, comfortable rooms in two crescents of fifteen semi-detached cottages curling around the waterhole, which draws wildlife regularly. It's pleasant and welcoming enough, with efficient and friendly staff and a sparkling blue pool. The main drawback is its location, on the thorny hillside, 5km from the river. Wi-fi. Ecotourism Kenya Bronze Award. FB $270

Sentrim Samburu Lodge 27.7km from Archer's Post Gate ☎0735 231533, ⊛sentrimhotels.net. Almost destroyed in the 2010 floods, this has been relocated on slightly higher ground above the river, with accommodation in 21 simple cabins. In the far west of the reserve, it's not yet attached to the grid so a generator is fired up during peak times. The lodge also doesn't offer organized game drives – only walks ($35 per person) – but you can arrange for the guides to go with you in your own vehicle. Nonetheless it's moderately priced (from $75 per person in low season), friendly and there's a little pool and thatched restaurant-bar. FB $240

BUFFALO SPRINGS NATIONAL RESERVE

Ashnil Samburu Camp 12km from Ngare Mara Gate ☎020 3566970 or ☎0717 612499, ⊛ashnilhotels.com. On the Ewaso Nyiro across from Samburu, this fenced camp's thirty tents have hot, single-layer canvas roofs, though there are fans and shaded verandas. Also a small pleasant pool surrounded by grass and a central thatched dining/lounge/bar area, where the buffet food is adequate but a little mediocre. FB $334

Samburu Simba Lodge 5.3km from Ngare Mara Gate and 7km from Buffalo Springs Gate ☎020 4444401 or ☎0722 603303, ⊛simbalodges.com. On a bluff, set back from a flood meander of the Ewaso Nyiro, this sprawling lodge has seventy modern, high-ceilinged rooms spread between seven huge villas. The result looks like a Californian residential development, an impression enhanced by the gym and two pools, though it may appeal to those who prefer hotel-style accommodation with buffet meals. Wi-fi. FB $360

KALAMA COMMUNITY WILDLIFE CONSERVANCY

★**Saruni Samburu** 8km north of Archer's Post, then through the Kalama Conservancy gate on the highway and 11km to the west, or accessed from Samburu National Reserve via the Kalama Gate ☎0735 950903 or ☎020 2180497, ⊛sarunisamburu.com. This sensuous rock-and-steel vision of an architect and designer, clinging to a high, rocky cliff, is unlike anywhere else in the Samburu district. It's completely beguiling: sit and gaze at Mount Kenya far to the south, swim in the pool, and recharge your spiritual batteries. It's expensive but rates drop considerably in quiet periods, and note that two of the five tented villas can accommodate up to four people. Wi-fi. Ecotourism Kenya Silver Award. Package $1560

WEST GATE COMMUNITY CONSERVANCY

★**Sasaab** North bank of the river, 15km west of Samburu reserve's West Gate ☎020 5020888 or ☎0731 914732, ⊛thesafaricollection.com. Situated atop a high hill overlooking the Ewaso Nyiro, this lodge has breathtaking, uninterrupted views across the Northern Frontier District. With heavy Moroccan influences in its design, each of the nine lavish rooms has more than 100 square metres of space, and a private plunge pool. The lodge has a spa, and activities on the conservancy include camel rides, engaging village visits, walks and game drives, plus full-day drives into Samburu. It has its own airstrip for charter flights and SafariLink will touch down here on request. Wi-fi. Ecotourism Kenya Gold Award. Package $1740

Shaba National Reserve

5

$70, car Ksh1000 (see p.75) • ⓦ samburucouncil.com/reserves.htm • 239 square kilometres

On the other side of the Isiolo–Archer's Post A2 road from Samburu–Buffalo
Springs lies the **Shaba National Reserve**, where Joy Adamson experimented with the
release of hand-reared leopards. Highly recommended, Shaba is much less visited
and less developed than Samburu or Buffalo Springs and therefore feels more
peaceful and solitary. If you're driving, you're likely to enter the reserve at
Natorbe Gate (6km from the A2 highway junction a couple of kilometres south of
Archer's Post) on a road that rolls up and down through a **lava field**. The landscapes
of Shaba are a lot more varied than you might expect, with the dramatic bulk of
Bodich mountain rising behind the river to the north, and steep hills, culminating
in **Shaba** peak, pressing in on the south.

For animals, **Shaba** is quite the equal of its two neighbours, with lots
of elephant, jackal, lion and plains game, including beautifully marked
Grevy's zebra, reticulated giraffe and the gerenuk. Exploring in Shaba is very
different from Samburu, where game drives tend to focus on the river; in
Shaba there are scattered natural springs around which the wildlife concentrates
– ideal places to park up, switch off the engine and spend some time watching and
waiting. Unlike Samburu and Buffalo Springs, where tracks are generally flat and
well graded, those in Shaba are topped with gritty volcanic sand and a 4WD is
usually required.

ARRIVAL AND DEPARTURE

SHABA NATIONAL RESERVE

By car, bus or matatu For driving to Shaba or trying to
reach the reserve by public transport, the same details
apply as for Samburu/Buffalo Springs (see p.377). The
turnoff to the main entrance to the reserve, Natorbe Gate,
is 2.7km south of Archer's Post and 800m north of Buffalo
Springs Gate. You can usually get fuel at *Sarova Shaba
Game Lodge*.

By plane You'll arrive on one of SafariLink's
twice-daily flights from Nairobi Wilson (around $230
one-way, $395 round trip) at *Sarova Shaba*'s airstrip, just
inside the reserve. Flight times vary, depending on the
routing, averaging 1hr–1hr 30min.

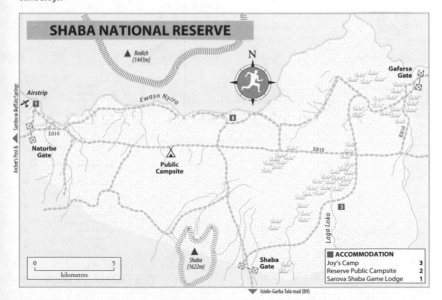

SHABA NATIONAL RESERVE

Bodich
(1443m)

N

Gafarsa
Gate

Airstrip

Samburu = Buffalo Springs

Ewaso Nyiro

E810

Archer's Post &

Natorbe
Gate

E810

Public
Campsite

Laga Loko

Shaba
(1622m)

Shaba
Gate

0   5
kilometres

■ **ACCOMMODATION**
Joy's Camp   3
Reserve Public Campsite   2
Sarova Shaba Game Lodge   1

Isiolo–Garba Tula road (B9)

5

ACCOMMODATION

★Joy's Camp 26km east of Natorbe Gate ☎0725 957321, ⓦjoyscamp.com. Whatever you might feel about the late Mrs Adamson (see p.384), who made her home here for a while, never has a camp been so aptly named. The ten palatial, Bedouin-style tents, gleaming with soft fabric and glass details, and perfectly spaced along a 1km stretch of buffalo-grazed marsh, seem to breathe relaxation. The birdlife is fantastic and the swimming pool, meals and generally chic ambience are sublime. Families can be accommodated by putting extra beds in the tents, but really it's the perfect honeymoon camp. Wi-fi. Ecotourism Kenya Gold Award. Package **$706**

Reserve Public Campsite 9km from Natorbe Gate, on the banks of the Ewaso Nyiro. There are two simple campsites in Shaba, neither with any facilities – this is the better-sited of the pair. Pay for camping at the gate. **$30**

Sarova Shaba Game Lodge 2km northeast of Natorbe Gate, on the banks of the Ewaso Nyiro ☎0728 603590, ⓦsarovahotels.com. Very attractively landscaped, with a superb swimming pool and streams running through public areas, this comfortable mid-range option has 85 rooms arranged in two-storey chalets with balconies/verandas overlooking the river. Popular with tour groups. Wi-fi. Ecotourism Kenya Silver Award. FB **$256**

Meru National Park

$75, car Ksh350, with Safari Card (see p.75) • ☎061 2303094 or ☎0786 348875, ⓦkws.org • 870 square kilometres

Something of a conservation miracle, **Meru National Park** was dragged back from a state of near decimation from poaching in the early years of the 2000s. Visitors have returned, but not as yet in force, and of the main parks covered in this chapter, it is the least visited and most unspoilt and pristine. Safaris in Meru are still an exclusive experience, and you're unlikely to see many other vehicles while out on game drives.

Abundantly traversed by streams flowing into the Tana River on its southern boundary, and luxuriantly rained upon, the rolling jungle of tall grass, riverine forest and swamp is lent a hypnotic, other-worldly quality by wonderful stands of prehistoric-looking doum palms. True, the **animals** aren't always as much in

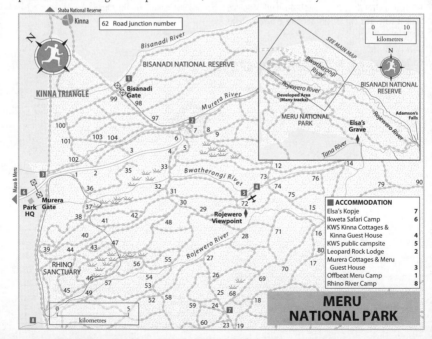

evidence here as they can be in some other Kenyan parks, though in recent years the wildlife numbers have been much improved. There are increasingly frequent sightings of all the Big Five – the huge herds of buffalo and elephant are seen regularly; the park has a healthy lion population (no doubt some descendants of Elsa); large numbers of leopards captured in the stock-raising lands of Laikipia have been released here in recent years; and the handful of rhinos (both black and white), translocated here from other protected areas in Kenya in 2002, have grown steadily in numbers since. After visiting some of the less bushy parks, where the animals can be spotted from far away, Meru's intimate, unusual landscape is quickly entrancing.

Kora National Park, and the three national reserves south and east of Meru – **Bisanadi**, **Mwingi** and **Rahole** – are all in the Land-Rover-expedition category, a total of 4500 square kilometres of scrub and semi-desert, and dense forest where they fringe the Tana River. Because of the history of poor security in the area (though there have been no recent incidents), you do need to check out the situation very carefully with KWS in Meru National Park if you're considering entering the Kora area.

Exploring the park

Meru's many tracks are all good gravel and most **junctions** have signposts and numbered cairns. A popular hook for a fairly long drive is the loop down to the grave of Elsa the lioness, on the banks of the Tana. And there are plenty of other enticing areas to investigate without going too far. Driving in through Murera Gate, for example, turn immediately sharp left up to the "**Kinna Triangle**", cross the Murera stream at junction #102 and pass a stupendous fig tree on your left. You then enter a beautiful area of thick vegetation, tall trees and high grass.

The Rojewero River

The **Rojewero River**, the largest of the park's twelve main streams, is an interesting watercourse: densely overgrown banks flash with birds and monkeys and dark waters ripple with hippos, crocs and freshwater turtles. Large and very visible herds of **elephant, buffalo** and **reticulated giraffe** are common, as are, in the more open areas, **gerenuk, Grevy's zebra** and **ostrich**. Predators were once scarce, though numbers seem to be on the up, and **lion** (which prey mainly on Meru's big herds of buffalo) and **cheetah** are increasingly seen, when they are not hidden in the long grass – the smaller grazers must have a nerve-wracking time of it here.

Rhino Sanctuary

On the right when you enter the park at Murera Gate • Free with national park ticket • 4WD only • 84 square kilometres

Meru's successful **rhino sanctuary** has been enlarged and is now protected by a fence. The couple of dozen white rhinos are doing well, though the few black rhinos suffer somewhat from tsetse flies. Finding the rhino in such a large area requires sharp eyes and a certain amount of luck, but these days they are monitored around the clock by KWS armed rangers, and the gate staff should be able to point you in the right direction.

| **ARRIVAL AND DEPARTURE** | **MERU NATIONAL PARK** |

Getting to Meru is straightforward by air, or if you're driving. Public transport requires a bit more effort.

By plane Most visitors fly with Airkenya from Nairobi Wilson (daily; 1hr–1hr 30min; $255 each way). You can also fly with Airkenya *from* the park on to Samburu (daily 30min; $183), but not the other way round.

By car If you're driving from Nairobi, use the 225km route via

Embu around the east side of Mount Kenya to Meru town (see opposite), allowing 4hr, then the straightforward route from Meru town via the C91 and Maua to the park's Murera Gate (a further 72km, all tarmac; allow another 1hr to the park). Gradually, the highlands scene gives way to the lank grass,

5

THE ADAMSONS

Meru is the area where the passionate animal lovers and recluses **George and Joy Adamson** (he a hunter turned game warden, she a gifted watercolourist and writer) released their most famous lioness **Elsa** back into the wild in the late 1950s – a story that became the bestselling book and film, *Born Free*. After the couple separated, the misanthropic Joy conducted a series of long-term experiments with orphaned cheetahs and leopards in Shaba National Reserve – years of dedicated, lonely work cut short by her murder in 1980. George, meanwhile, moved to **Kora National Park**, adjoining Meru, where he lived in the bush and continued to work with orphaned lions. He was also murdered, in 1989, by poachers.

termite cathedrals and scattered trees and streams that characterize the park's savanna. Fill your tank and jerrycan at Maua (which has Barclays and KCB ATMs and a branch of Uchumi Supermarket). There is usually fuel available about 5km outside the park on the Maua road as well.

By bus and matatu From Meru town there are frequent buses and matatus to Maua, 1hr into the Nyambeni Hills on a tarmac road, through steep tea terraces and plantations of *miraa*. From Maua, however, few matatus run the whole 30km stretch to the park gate, and although there's excellent budget accommodation in the park, you may find it hard to get there.

ACCOMMODATION

Most drive-in visitors head straight to one of the campsites or lodges in the park. If it's late in the day, however, you might want to stay the night in the busy little *miraa*-trading centre of Maua.

MAUA

Ikweta Country Inn Signposted just after KCB, then about 500m to the right of the main road ☎0700 113118, ⊛ikwetacountryinn.com. The sister operation to *Ikweta Safari Camp* (see opposite), this is an excellent lunch stop (Ksh500–900 for main meals) or place to stay if you don't manage to make it all the way to the park. The rooms are modern and bright and set in pretty gardens along the small Mboone River. Smaller budget twins and triples are in an annexe (from Ksh1300 per person). Wi-fi. BB **Ksh3900**

Maua Basin Hotel Signposted 300m off to the left as you arrive in town ☎0725 723659 or ☎0720 175415, ⊛mauabasinhotel.com. Doesn't look much from the outside but this is a reasonable option. Rooms are in two wings, "Museum" and "Basin" – all have nets, though the latter have more light. The hotel's *Hotsprings* restaurant has a long menu (Ksh300–500 for most dishes), and there's secure parking; for a tip you can get your car washed. Wi-fi. BB **Ksh3300**

IN THE PARK

CAMPSITES AND KWS ACCOMMODATION

★**KWS Kinna Cottages & Kinna Guest House** Near the airstrip, 18km from the gate ☎061 2303094 or ☎0786 348875, ⊛kws.org. A shady site by the Bwatherongi River: the five one- or two-bedroom cottages have very large rooms, nets and bathrooms but no cooking facilities, while the *Kinna Guest House*, with two en-suite bedrooms and beds in the huge lounge, is big enough to sleep ten (and has a kitchen). The most appealing feature is the excellent swimming pool in the

middle of the site, complete with recliners. Cottage $80, whole guesthouse $250

KWS public campsite Near the airstrip. KWS's public campsite is located on a stretch of open ground running down to Bwatherongi River, close to the *Kinna Cottages & Kinna Guest House* – campers can use the swimming pool. There are toilet and shower blocks, and firewood is plentiful. $20

KWS special campsites Dotted around the park, reservations in Nairobi ☎020 600800, ⊛kws.org. None of the special campsites has any facilities except supplies of firewood. Reserve ahead (booking fee Ksh7500). $35

Murera Cottages & Meru Guest House By Murera Gate ☎061 2303094 or ☎0786 348875, ⊛kws.org. Four cottages with three beds (one double, one single in each), and a shared barbecue area. Larger groups can be accommodated in the nearby *Meru Guest House*, which sleeps five and has a kitchen. Cottage $80, whole guesthouse $150

LODGES AND TENTED CAMPS

★**Elsa's Kopje** On Mughwango hill, reservations through Elewana Collection in Nairobi ☎0730 127000, ⊛elewanacollection.com. One of Kenya's best lodges, the charm of *Elsa's* is partly down to its stunning rocky hilltop location, with a 360-degree panorama that simply drives away cares. But the details are all spot-on, too – excellent hosts, an infinity pool cleaved from the rock; birds, comical hyraxes and lizards everywhere; outrageously good food and wine; and completely delightful cottages, each open-fronted to let in the sky, with its own private deck among the shrubs and crags.

5

There's also an exclusive two-bedroom house with its own pool. Four bronze guides for bush walks and day and night game drives. Wi-fi. Ecotourism Kenya Gold Award. FB **$870**

Ikweta Safari Camp Outside the park just before Murera Gate on the left ☎0705 200050, ⓦ ikweta safaricamp.com. This comfortable, exceptionally friendly camp offers affordable access to Meru National Park while maintaining an intimate feel. Its ten en-suite tents have nice safari-style decor and little wooden decks, each facing east towards the park for great sunrise views over the bush. The camp runs off mains electricity, has a pool and can arrange game drives into the park. If you're using public transport, you may be able to arrange a lift between here and *Ikweta Country Inn* in Maua. Wi-fi. FB **Ksh15,300**

Leopard Rock Lodge Inside the park, 10km from Murera Gate ☎0733 920082 or ☎0736 333100, ⓦ leopardmico.com. The comfortable cottages at this Italian-owned lodge have grand four-poster beds swathed in nets and overlook the Murera River, while the thatched central dining/lounge *boma* has its own waterhole. The charming pool is surrounded by palms and grassy lawns, and the six-course dinners feature good Italian cuisine. Almost in the luxury bracket (and priced as such) but some of the decor is a little dated. One bronze guide. FB **$880**

Offbeat Meru Camp 1.3km east of junction #99 at the edge of the park in the Bisanadi National Reserve ☎0704 909355 or ☎0704 909356, ⓦ offbeatsafaris .com. This traditional yet stylish and comfortable tented camp above the Bisanadi River is excellently run and a great base from which to explore the park. With only seven tents (with flush toilets and bucket showers) the team's approach to safaris is flexible, and the communal dinners with other guests are sociable affairs. Pool. Closed April, May and Nov. FB **$850**

★ **Rhino River Camp** Outside the park, though accessed via the Rhino Sanctuary, 14km from Murera Gate ☎0732 809287 or ☎0733 621179, ⓦ rhinorivercamp .com. Nestling in the shade of dense forest, with eight spacious, stylishly minimalist private cottages. The decking and private gazebo outside each lends the camp a restful and appealingly Zen aesthetic. The lovely pool area is tucked into a canopied patch of forest by a stream. Package **$940**

The coast

LAMU WATERFRONT

The coast

The coast is a world apart from "upcountry" Kenya and in many ways it feels like a different country. For a start, Mombasa, Kenya's second city, is a much easier place to enjoy than Nairobi. With its sun-scorched, colonnaded streets, this is the quintessential tropical port – steamy and unbelievably dilapidated – and it's fun to shop here, stroll the old city's alleys or visit Fort Jesus. To the north and south of Mombasa there are superb beaches and a number of tourist resort areas, but nothing, as yet, highly developed in the Florida or Canary Islands sense. You can certainly enjoy yourself having a lazy time at a beach resort, but there's a lot more to the coast than recliners, swimming pools and buffet meals.

Most obviously, the beaches are the launch pad for one of the most beautiful **coral reefs** in the world. With rented equipment, you can do some spectacular dives, but even with a simple snorkel and mask, which are easily obtained, you can discover what really is another world. The two most spectacular areas are enclosed in **marine national parks**, around Watamu and Malindi, and at the island of Wasini.

The string of **islands** that runs up the coast – Wasini, Funzi, Chale, Lamu, Manda, Pate and Kiwaiyu – are all very much worth visiting. Apart from their beach and ocean attractions, most of them have some archeological interest, which is also a constant theme on the mainland: the whole coast is littered with the **ruins** of forts, mosques, tombs and even one or two whole towns. Some of these – including **Fort Jesus**, the old town of **Lamu** and the ruined city of **Gedi** – are already on the tourist circuit, but there are dozens that have hardly been cleared and make for compelling excursions if you're feeling adventurous.

Islam has long been a major influence on the coast, and the traditional, annual fast is widely observed during the month of **Ramadan**, when no food or drinks are consumed

WATAMU

Highlights

❶ Fort Jesus Seven centuries of coastal history are on show in Mombasa's fascinating castle-museum. **See p.397**

❷ Tiwi Beach The reef is close to the shore here, and there are some excellent, low-key cottage developments. **See p.429**

❸ Kaya Kinondo Explore, with a knowledgeable community guide, the first sacred forest to be opened to visitors. **See box, p.434**

❹ Wasini A tiny, undeveloped island community, with wonderful diving and snorkelling. **See p.447**

❺ Arabuko Sokoke Forest Reserve East Africa's largest tract of indigenous coastal forest offers excellent guided walks and the chance to see monkeys, birds and butterflies. **See p.454**

❻ Gedi Try to visit this lost city first thing in the morning or as the sun goes down, when the ruins are at their most atmospheric. **See p.456**

❼ Watamu The stunning bays, islets and casuarina-shaded beaches are matched by glorious coral gardens and good diving opportunities. **See p.459**

❽ Lamu A compelling, history-soaked city-state and UNESCO World Heritage Site, with no roads or vehicles. **See p.477**

HIGHLIGHTS ARE MARKED ON THE MAP ON P.390

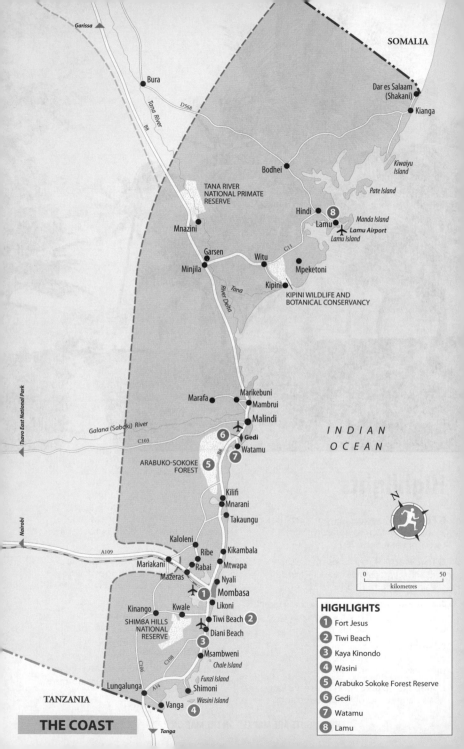

SOMALIA

Garissa

Bura

Tana River

D568

B8

Dar es Salaam
(Shakani)

Kianga

Kiwaiyu
Island

Bodhei

Pate Island

TANA RIVER
NATIONAL PRIMATE
RESERVE

Hindi

Mnazini

Lamu **8**

Manda Island

Lamu Airport
Lamu Island

Garsen

Witu

C11

Minjila

Mpeketoni

River Tana

Kipini

KIPINI WILDLIFE AND
BOTANICAL CONSERVANCY

River Delta

Marafa

Marikebuni

Mambrui

Malindi

INDIAN

Tsavo East National Park

Galana (Saboki) River

C103

B8

6 **Gedi**

7 Watamu

OCEAN

ARABUKO-SOKOKE
FOREST

5

Kilifi

Mnarani

Takaungu

Kaloleni

Nairobi

A109

Ribe

Kikambala

Mariakani

Rabai

Mtwapa

Mazeras

Nyali

1 **Mombasa**

Kinango

Kwale

Likoni

SHIMBA HILLS
NATIONAL
RESERVE

Tiwi Beach **2**

Diani Beach

3

Msambweni

Chale Island

C106

C108

Lungalunga

A14

Funzi Island

Shimoni

Vanga

Wasini Island

4

TANZANIA

Tanga

THE COAST

N

0   50
kilometres

during daylight hours. Visiting the coast at this time might leave a slightly strange impression of a region where everyone is on night shift, but in practical terms it usually makes little difference. The end of Ramadan is marked by major **festivities**, as are several other Muslim holidays throughout the year (see p.69).

Resort areas

Although **travel advisories** in recent years (see p.83) have led to a serious decline in tourism, plenty of visitors do treat the coast as their main destination in Kenya, combining it with a short safari inland. There are four main **resort areas**. First and foremost is the suburban district north of Mombasa island, often known as **North Coast**, around thirty minutes to an hour from Mombasa's Moi International Airport; 100km further north comes **Watamu**, about two hours from the airport; and lastly **Malindi**, another twenty minutes beyond Watamu. South of Mombasa, the main focus of the **south coast** is Diani Beach, some 40km from the airport (about a ninety-minute drive on a good day – the ferry linking Mombasa to the south coast can delay you). Apart from the odd small development, the rest of the coast is largely untouched by tourism.

In many areas along the coast the sea is very shallow at low tide, and in some places it's impossible to **swim** except at high tide; it's useful to consult **tide tables** (see ⓦcoastweek.com/tides.htm). The protected lagoon inside the reef is free of currents and safe for swimming when the tide is high enough. Beyond the reef, however, conditions can be radically different. If you're planning to head out – to dive or go deep-sea fishing, for example – always check that your boat has a useable life jacket for each passenger.

ENVIRONMENT AND WILDLIFE ON THE COAST

The hundreds of kilometres of sandy **beach** that fringe Kenya's low-lying coastal strip are backed by **dunes** and coconut palms, traversed by scores of streams and rivers. Flowing off the plateaus through tumbling jungle, these waterways meander across a narrow, fertile plain to the sea. In sheltered creeks, forests of **mangrove** trees cover vast areas and create a distinctive ecological zone of tidal mud flats.

Most of Kenya's **lowland forests** are on the coast and along the banks of the lower Tana River. The rainforests, all threatened by human incursion, include Witu Forest near Lamu, the Mida-Gedi Forest near Watamu, the Sabaki River Forest near Malindi, several forest fragments in the Shimba Hills, and the Ramisi River Forest on the southern coast. Several of the *kaya* sacred areas (see p.453), such as Kaya Diani and Kaya Kinondo, are similar, although they're too small to have a rainforest microclimate. The most important area of natural forest is the **Arabuko Sokoke Forest Reserve** (see p.454), south of Malindi. Arabuko Sokoke is unique in that it comprises a largely unbroken block of 420 square kilometres of coastal forest, consisting of Brachystegia woodland (containing a huge variety of birdlife), dense Cynometra forest and zones of mixed lowland rainforest that are very rich in plants, mammals and insects.

Wildlife on the coast is in keeping with the region's lush, intimate feel. The big game of upcountry Kenya is more or less absent (Shimba Hills National Reserve southwest of Mombasa is an exception), but smaller creatures are abundant. **Monkeys** are especially common, with troops of baboons by the road, vervet and Sykes' monkeys frequenting hotel gardens and spectacular Angolan colobus monkeys inhabiting the forests behind Diani Beach. **Birdlife** is prolific – if you have even a mild interest you should bring binoculars. On the **reptile** front, snakes, those brilliant disguise artists, are rarely seen (except in a number of snake parks), but lizards skitter everywhere, including upside down on the ceiling at night, and bug-eyed chameleons waver across the road, sometimes making it to the other side. So do **giant millipedes**, up to 30cm long: these harmless scavengers have been nicknamed "Mombasa Express", after the famously slow train. **Insects** are here in full force (although thankfully efforts to eradicate mosquitoes are paying off), and the glorious **butterflies** of the Diani and Arabuko Sokoke forests are attractive participants in the coast's gaudy show.

6

SEASONS ON THE COAST

The coastal region of Kenya, with its monsoon climate, is the area most affected by the **seasons**. The **best months** overall for weather and water visibility are usually October, November and March, though it can be very hot in March in the build-up to the somewhat unpredictable "long rains" between April and June. The **long rains** count as low season – while the beaches tend to be damp and the weather overcast (and some hotels close completely) at this time, you can make big savings on prebooked holidays or, if you're travelling independently, reduce your accommodation costs by fifty percent or more. The **water clarity** is still reasonably good for diving, at least at the start of the rains. During **peak season**, which coincides with the Christmas, New Year and Easter holidays, accommodation prices often double, or even triple.

The **sea temperature** is warm to very warm all year round, averaging 25–30°C, but underwater visibility varies greatly, from as little as 5m between June and September to as much as 30m in December. As for the Indian Ocean's **monsoon winds**, they always blow onshore: the dry, moderate *kaskazi* wind blows onto the beaches from the northeast from November to April; then the moister and stronger *kusi* blows in from the southeast from May to October. The changeover period is often very gusty. In this season large quantities of **seaweed** often sweep up onto the beach. In July, August and September there is generally quite a strong breeze, with choppy seas. From December to February, on the other hand, it's hot and dry, and much calmer.

A word of warning to anyone on a shoestring budget: tempting as it can be, **sleeping out** on the beaches is nearly always unwise because of the danger of robbery. Although there are one or two very remote areas where you might get away with it, you'll usually have to find a room or pitch your tent at one of the few campsites.

ARRIVAL AND DEPARTURE   THE COAST

By plane Many visitors arrive at Moi International Airport (see p.402) in Mombasa. Flying to Diani Beach, Mombasa, Malindi, Lamu or Kiwaiyu from Nairobi will save you at least a day's travel. Note that only the flights to Mombasa and Diani Beach, with occasional views of Kilimanjaro, are interesting in themselves. On the other hand, flying up to Lamu from Malindi offers stunning views over jungle and reef (see p.469).
By train When it was a reliable twice-daily service, the overnight train journey (see p.57) between Nairobi and Mombasa used to be a Kenyan travel highlight. While its infrequency (twice a week) and notorious unreliability

make it difficult to recommend unreservedly (elephants on the line and more mundane problems mean it's often up to 24 hours late), it's a trip worth doing at least once.
By bus The constant stream of buses from Nairobi to Mombasa provides the cheapest transport, and you can stop anywhere en route if you want to explore. It's best to travel on a day bus rather than take a night bus, to reduce the chance of an accident on the very busy highway.
By car Except for a stretch south of Voi, the Nairobi–Mombasa highway is in good condition (see p.320). Again, you're strongly advised to avoid driving after dark.

Mombasa

Sleazy, hot and physically tropical in a way that could hardly be more different from the capital, **MOMBASA** is the slightly indolent hub of the coast, with a sense of community and depth of history that Nairobi lacks. The city centre – neatly isolated by the sea from its suburbs – is faded, flaking and occasionally charming, like a small town that was once great.

While it's a chaotic city, the atmosphere, even in the commercial centre of what is one of Africa's busiest ports, is relaxed and congenial. Rush hours, urgency and paranoia seem to be Nairobi's problems (as everyone here will tell you), not Mombasa's. And the gaping, marginal slums of many African cities hardly exist here. **Miritini** and **Chomvu**, and especially **Likoni** and **Changamwe**, are burgeoning mainland suburbs that the municipality has more or less abandoned, but the brutalizing conditions of Nairobi's Kibera are absent.

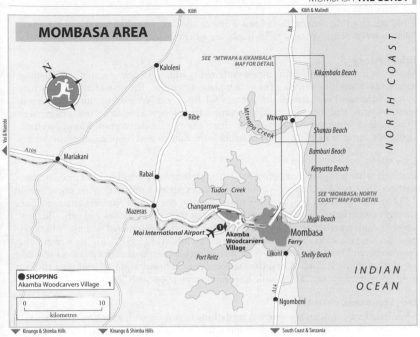

MOMBASA AREA

Ethnically, Mombasa is perhaps even more diverse than Nairobi. The Asian and Arab influence is particularly pervasive, with fifty mosques and dozens of Hindu and Sikh temples lending a strongly oriental flavour. Still, the largest contingent speaks Swahili as a first language and it is the **Swahili civilization** that accounts for Mombasa's distinctive character. You'll see women wearing head-to-foot *buibuis* or brilliant *kanga* outfits, and men decked out in *kanzu* gowns and hip-slung *kikoi* wraps.

Arriving in Mombasa by plane or train in the morning, there's ample time, if you don't find the heat too much, to head straight out to the **beaches** – the nearest is Nyali Beach on the north coast mainland (see p.410). But you might want to spend a day or two in Mombasa itself, acclimatizing to the coast, catching the cadences of the coast's "pure Swahili", or *Kiswahili safi*, and looking around Kenya's most historic city.

Mombasa doesn't have a huge number of sights, but most visitors will want to check out its main one, the museum-monument **Fort Jesus**, in the shadow of which lies the **Old Town**, an atmospheric hive of narrow lanes, mosques and carved Swahili doorways. In the modern town centre, the **tusk arch** that features on so many postcards is not wildly exciting, though fans of 1930s architecture might appreciate one or two of the

---

SECURITY IN MOMBASA

Street crime, though it hardly approaches Nairobi's level, is still a problem in Mombasa, and you should be wary of displaying any valuables or accepting invitations to walk down dark alleys (which should be avoided at all times anyway). The Likoni ferry and the chaotic area around the junction of Jomo Kenyatta Avenue and Mwembe Tayari Road are two hotspots for **pickpocketing** and bag snatching. It's also not unknown for pickpockets to stalk tourists along Moi Avenue and around Fort Jesus. While as a general rule, Mombasa is a far less neurotic city than Nairobi – even after dark, when you'll see Mombasans taking a stroll, old men conversing on the benches in Digo Road and many shops staying open late – it's still important to stay alert and avoid taking risks.

buildings from that era on **Digo Road**. Further afield, the **baobab forest** and **Mbaraki Pillar**, a seventeenth-century pillar tomb, are worth a visit.

Brief history

Mombasa is one of East Africa's **oldest settlements** and, so long as you aren't anticipating spectacular historical sites, it's a fascinating place to wander. The island has had a town on it, located somewhere between the present Old Town and Nyali Bridge, for at least seven hundred years, and there are enough documentary snippets from earlier times to guess that some kind of settlement has existed here for at least two thousand years. Mombasa's own optimistic claim to be 2500 years old comes from Roman and Egyptian adventure stories.

Early tales

Precisely what was going on before the Portuguese arrived is still hard to discern. **Ibn Battuta**, the roving fourteenth-century Moroccan, spent a relatively quiet night here in 1332 and declared the people of the town "devout, chaste and virtuous, their mosques strongly constructed of wood, the greater part of their diet bananas and fish". But another Arab traveller of a hundred years later found a less ordered society. "Monkeys have become the rulers of Mombasa since about 800 AH [1397 AD]," he wrote. "They even come and take the food from the dishes, attack men in their own homes and take away what they can find. When the monkeys enter a house and find a woman they hold congress with her. The people have much to put up with."

Early Portuguese visitors

Mombasa had considerably worse depredations to put up with after **Vasco da Gama**'s expedition, full of mercenary zeal, dropped anchor on Easter Saturday 1498. After courtesy gifts had been exchanged, relations suddenly soured and the fleet was prevented from entering the port. A few days later, richer by just one sheep and "large quantities of oranges, lemons and sugar cane", da Gama went off to try his crude diplomacy at Malindi, and found his first and lasting ally on the coast.

Mombasa was visited again in 1505 by a fourteen-strong Portuguese fleet. This time, the king of Mombasa had enlisted 1500 archers from the mainland and people stored arsenals of stone missiles on the rooftops in preparation for the expected **invasion** through the town's narrow alleys. The attack, pitching firearms against spears and

---

MOMBASA: THE SHAPE OF THE CITY

Mombasa is an island, linked to the mainland by two causeways to the west, by a bridge to the north, and by a ferry to the south. You need to be prepared for poor first impressions: coming in by road over the **Makupa Causeway** from the airport or Nairobi, the erstwhile showcase **Kenyatta Avenue** is a shabby scene of crumbling facades and out-of-date hoardings, smothering the street from its start, via the triumphalist Independence Roundabout, to its final disintegration in the diesel-laden environment of the Mwembe Tayari bus parks.

At the city's heart, however, is the much more appealing **Old Town** – a lattice of lanes, mosques and cramped houses sloping gently down to the once-busy dhow harbour. **Fort Jesus**, an impressive reminder of Mombasa's complicated, bloody past, still overlooks the Old Town from where it once guarded the harbour entrance. From the Old Town, clustered all around you, and mostly within easy walking distance, lies the whole expanse of downtown, **modern Mombasa**, with its wide streets and relative lack of high-rise buildings.

For **orientation** purposes, think of Digo Road, with the main market and GPO, as the city's spine: head up it to the north and you cross Nyali Bridge to the main Mombasa beach resorts; go down it to the south, as Nyerere Avenue, and you come to the Likoni ferry to the south coast mainland. East of Digo Road is the Old Town and one or two sedate streets of government offices. West of Digo Road you have, from north to south: Jomo Kenyatta Avenue, leading to the airport and the Nairobi highway; Haile Selassie Road, leading to the train station; and Moi Avenue, Mombasa's main tourist strip, with its famous tusk arch, known simply as "the Tusks".

poisoned arrows, was brutal and overwhelming, and the king's palace (of which no trace remains) was seized. The king and most of the survivors slipped out of town into the palm groves that then covered most of Mombasa island, but 1513 Mombasans had been killed – as against five Portuguese.

The king attempted to save Mombasa by offering to become a vassal of Portugal, but the request was turned down, the Portuguese being unwilling to lose the chance to loot the town. The victors picked over the bodies in the courtyards and broke down the strongroom doors until the ships at anchor were almost overladen. Then, as a parting shot, they fired the town. The narrow streets and cattle stalls between the thatched houses produced a conflagration that razed Mombasa to the ground.

Portuguese occupation

In 1528, the Portuguese returned once again to wreck and plunder the new city that had been built on the ashes of the old. In the 1580s, it happened twice more. On the last occasion, in 1589, there was a frenzied **massacre** at the hands of the Portuguese on one side and – coincidentally – a marauding tribe of cannibal nomads from the interior called the Zimba on the other. The Zimba's unholy alliance with the Europeans came to a treacherous end at Malindi shortly afterwards, when the Portuguese, together with the townsfolk and three thousand Segeju archers, wiped them out.

Remarkably, only two years after this last catastrophe, Mombasa launched a major land expedition of its own against its old enemy, Malindi. The party was ambushed on the way by Malindi's Segeju allies, who themselves stormed and took Mombasa, later handing over the town to the Portuguese at Malindi. The Malindi corps transferred to Mombasa, the Malindi sheikh was grandly installed as sultan of the whole region, and the Portuguese set to work on **Fort Jesus**, dedicated in 1593.

Once completed, the fort became the focus of everything that mattered in Mombasa, changing hands a total of nine times between the early seventeenth century and 1875. The first takeover happened in 1631, in a **popular revolt** that resulted in the killing of every last Portuguese. But the Sultan, lacking support from any of the other towns under Portuguese domination, eventually had to desert the fort, and the Portuguese, waiting in Zanzibar, reoccupied it. They held it for the rest of the seventeenth century while consolidating their control of the Indian Ocean trade.

Omani rule

Meanwhile, the **Omani Arabs** were becoming increasingly powerful. As Dutch, English and French ships started to appear on the horizon, time was running out for the Portuguese trading monopoly. Efforts to bring settlers to their East African possessions failed, and they retreated more and more behind the massive walls of Fort Jesus. Between 1696 and 1698 Fort Jesus itself was besieged into submission by the Omanis who, with support from Pate and Lamu, had already taken the rest of the town. After 33 months almost all the defenders – the Portuguese corps and some 1500 Swahili loyalists – had died of starvation or plague.

Rapid disenchantment with the new Arab rulers spilled over in 1728 into a mutiny among the fort's African soldiers. The Portuguese were invited back – for a year. Then the fort was again besieged, and this time the Portuguese gave up quickly. They were allowed their freedom, and a number were said to have married and stayed in the town. But Portuguese power on the coast was shattered forever.

The new Omani rulers were the **Mazrui** family, who soon declared themselves independent of Oman, outlawing slave-trading in Mombasa and directly challenging the **Busaidi** family who had just seized power in the Arabian homeland.

British takeover

Intrigue in the Lamu archipelago led to the Battle of Shela (see p.480) and Lamu's unwittingly disastrous invitation to the **Sultan of Oman**, Seyyid Said, to occupy its own

6

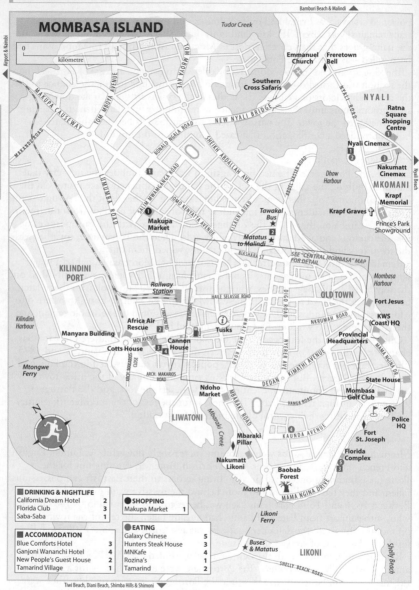

MOMBASA ISLAND

DRINKING & NIGHTLIFE
California Dream Hotel	2
Florida Club	3
Saba-Saba	1

SHOPPING
Makupa Market	1

ACCOMMODATION
Blue Comforts Hotel	3
Ganjoni Wananchi Hotel	4
New People's Guest House	2
Tamarind Village	1

EATING
Galaxy Chinese	5
Hunters Steak House	3
MNKafe	4
Rozina's	1
Tamarind	2

fort. From here, and by now with **British** backing, the Busaidis went on to attack Mazrui Mombasa repeatedly in the 1820s.

There was a hiccup in 1824 when a British officer, **Captain Owen**, fired with enthusiasm for defeating the slave trade, extended British protection to Mombasa on his own account, despite official British support for the slave-trading Busaidis. Owen's "Protectorate" was a diplomatic embarrassment and – not surprisingly – did not last long. The Busaidi government was only installed when the Swahili "twelve tribes" of Mombasa fell into a dispute over the Mazrui succession and called in

Seyyid Said, the Busaidi leader. In 1840, he moved his capital from Oman to Zanzibar and, with Mombasa firmly garrisoned, most of the coast was soon in his domain. Surviving members of the Mazrui family went to Takaungu near Kilifi and Gazi, south of Mombasa.

British influence was sharpened after their guns quelled the mutiny in 1875 of al-Akida, "an ambitious, unbalanced and not over-clever" commandant of Fort Jesus. Once British hegemony was established, they leased the **coastal strip** from the Sultan of Zanzibar and Fort Jesus became Mombasa's prison, which it remained until 1958. It was opened as a museum in 1962.

6

Independence on the coast

Mombasa has played a key role in Kenya's first fifty years of **independence**, as Kenya's second city and East and central Africa's most important port. Before independence, the coast had been leased by the British from the Sultan of Zanzibar, but the possibility of a federal union with the former Kenya Colony was soon buried by Jomo Kenyatta and the upcountry political elite of the 1960s. Since 1999, the **Mombasa Republican Council**, a group that claims "Pwani si Kenya" ("The coast is not Kenya"), has campaigned for independence for the coast and against the marginalization of coastal interests by Nairobi. Their movement, however, has been tainted by its linkage with Islamic extremism, which also has found some appeal in poorer areas, and in recent years Somalia's terrorist group Al-Shabaab has succeeded in making some common cause with the coast's disaffected youth. In August 2012, the assassination of a Muslim cleric in Mombasa led to riots as local youths fought street battles with police brought down from Nairobi (see p.577); the extrajudicial killings of several other religious leaders since then have only served to heighten tensions between authorities and the local community.

Fort Jesus

Off Nkrumah Rd • Daily 8am–6pm • Ksh1200 • ☎ 041 2220058 or ☎ 041 2225934, ⊕ museums.or.ke

For all its turbulent past, **Fort Jesus**, a classic European fortress of its age, is today a quiet museum-monument. Surprisingly spacious and tree-shaded inside its giant walls, it retains a lot of its original character, despite having been much repaired over the centuries. The curious angular construction was the design of an Italian architect and ensured that assailants trying to scale the walls would always be under crossfire from one of the bastions.

The best time to visit is probably first thing in the morning. Look out for the restored **Omani House**, in the far right corner as you enter the fort, and climb up to the flat roof for a wonderful view over Mombasa. Interesting in their own way, too, are the uncomfortable-looking, wall-mounted **latrines**, overhanging the ditch just south of the Omani House, which would presumably have been closed in with mats. It is immediately obvious that Fort Jesus was not so much a building as a small, fortified town in its own right. The ruins of a church, storerooms and possibly even shops are up at this end and, to judge by some accounts, the main courtyard was a warren of little dwellings. Captain Owen described it in 1824 as "a mass of indiscriminate ruins, huts and hovels, many of them built wherever space could be found but generally formed from parts of the ruins, matted over for roofs".

Most of the archeological interest is at the seaward end of the fort, where you'll find the **Hall of the Mazrui** with its beautiful stone benches and eighteenth-century inscription. A nearby room has been dedicated entirely to the display of a huge plaster panel of **wall paintings**, made with carbon and ochre by bored Portuguese sentries. Their subjects are fascinating: ships, figures in armour (including the captain of the fort wielding his baton), fish and what seems to be a chameleon. Oddly enough, there's nothing obscene.

6

Airport & Nairobi

Nyali Bridge & North Coast

MUYAKA ROAD

BIBI WA SHAFI ROAD

FAZA ROAD

BIASHARA STREET

JOE KADENGE STREET

JOMO KENYATTA AVENUE

Mash Bus

Modern Coast Bus

Total

Tahmeed

Simba Bus

BARINGO ROAD

FAZA ROAD

Sikh Temple Complex ④

Kaloleni Buses & Matatus

Kobil

②

MACKAWI ROAD

GEORGE MORUKA STREET

ABDEL NASSER ROAD

BUNGOMA STREET

①

BIASHARA STREET

War Monument

③

⑥

JOMO KENYATTA AVENUE

MWEMBE TAYARI ROAD

BAJUNI ROAD

DURUMA ROAD

④

KWA SHIBU ROAD

RAHA LEO STREET ③

③

Public Health Dept

HOSPITAL STREET

MSANIFU KOMBO STREET

KONZI RD

TURKANA STREET

⑩

⑪

⑫

TANGANA ROAD

Swaminarayan Temple

HAILE SELASSIE ROAD

AGA KHAN ROAD

⑥

SHIMONI STREET

⑯

Oilibya

KWA SHIBU ROAD

Total

⑤

Omar Husein Cycloduka

KCB

Fatemi House ⑰

Kenya National Library

MSANIFU KOMBO STREET

TAITA ST.

GUSII STREET

TURKANA STREET

Tuskys Bandari

MAUNGANO ROAD

MAUNGANO ROAD

⑱

⑲

MACHAKOS ROAD

LIONS CLUB MOMBASA PWANI ROAD

WHITE FARMER'S RD

MERU ROAD

MERU ROAD

CHEMBE ROAD

Farways Safaricentre

Railway Station

Mombasa Uni Plaza

Reinsurance Plaza

Jubilee Insurance Building

Equity Bank

BUNJU ROAD

Uhuru Gardens

Glory Car Hire

Tusks ⓘ

Regal Chambers

Freed Building

Barclays Bank

Gapco

Ketty Tours

@

Diamond Arcade Pharmacy

Diamond Trust House

MOI AVENUE

②

⑧

Commercial Bank of Africa

③

Google Cyber

NGONYO ROAD

CUSTOM HOUSE ROAD

Kilindini Docks

MOI AVENUE

㉑ ⑳

Kobil

KAMUNDE LANE

MOHDAR MOHAMED HABIB ROAD

Wimpy Building

Sairose Pharmacy

WAKATWA ROAD

④

MNAZI MMOJA ROAD

MII MYA ROAD

GIBSON NGOME RD

SAUTI YA KENYA ROAD

Hare Krisna Temple ④

Mombasa Sports Club

CHIEF ALI BIN NAAMAN ROAD

⑩

Playing Fields

MAKARIOS ROAD

DEDAN KIMATHI AVENUE

Little Theatre Club

Commonwealth War Cemetery

● EATING	
Blue Room	12
Café Stavrose	19
Corner Café	3
Fayaz Bakery	6/13
Gelato Divino	14
Huseini Bakery	11
Island Dishes	8
Jahazi Coffee House	5
Kassim Café	2
New Chetna	6
New Overseas Chinese Korean	21
New Recoda Café	9
Old Town Zanzibar Restaurant	7
Pwani Dishes	10
Seif-Halwa	1
Shehnai	17
Singh	4
Splendid View	18
Tarboush Café	15
Temptations	20

Likoni Ferry & South Coast

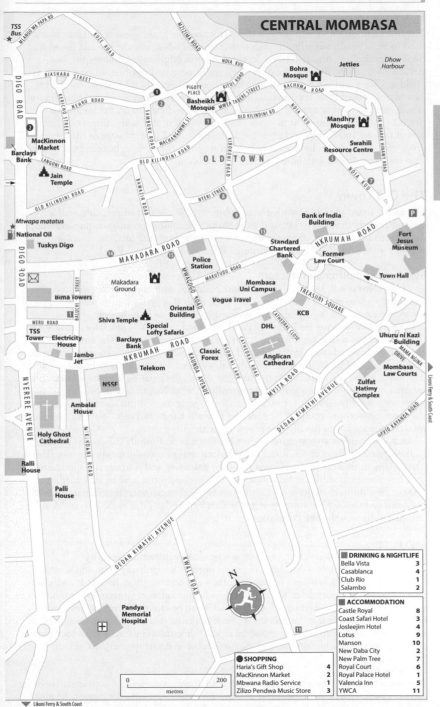

CENTRAL MOMBASA

TSS Bus ★

MLANGO WA PAPA RD

KUZE ROAD

MZIZIMA ROAD

NDIA KUU

BIASHARA STREET

KITUI ROAD

BACHUMA ROAD

Bohra Mosque

Jetties

Dhow Harbour

DIGO ROAD

KERICHO STREET

NEHRU ROAD

SAMBURU ROAD

PIGOTT PLACE ❶ ❷

Basheikh Mosque

MWEA TABERE STREET

WACHANGAMWE ST.

OLD KILINDINI RD

NDIA KUU

Mandhry Mosque

MacKinnon Market ❷

Barclays Bank

LANGONI ROAD

Jain Temple ♣

WACHANGAMWE ST.

❶

OLD TOWN

Swahili Resource Centre ❺

SIR MBARAK HINAWY ROAD

NDIA KUU ❼

OLD KILINDINI ROAD

BAWAZIR ROAD

KIBOKONI ROAD

NYERI STREET ❽

❾

Bank of India Building ❶❸

NKRUMAH ROAD

P

Fort Jesus Museum

Mtwapa matatus

DIGO ROAD

National Oil ★

Tuskys Digo ❶❹

MAKADARA ROAD ❶❺

Police Station

KWAGOGO ROAD

MAKUTUDU ROAD

Standard Chartered Bank ❶❸

Former Law Court

Town Hall

BALUCHI STREET

Bima Towers

Makadara Ground

Shiva Temple ♣

Oriental Building

Mombasa Uni Campus

Vogue Travel

TREASURY SQUARE

KCB

MERU ROAD

TSS Tower

Electricity House

Jambo Jet

Barclays Bank

Special Lofty Safaris

NKRUMAH ROAD ❼

Telekom

KAUNDA AVENUE

Classic Forex

NGOMENI LANE

CATHEDRAL ROAD

DHL

CATHEDRAL CLOSE

Anglican Cathedral

MVITA ROAD

Uhuru ni Kazi Building

MAMA NGINA DRIVE

Mombasa Law Courts

Zulfat Hatimy Complex

NSSF

NYERERE AVENUE

Ambalal House

N KISDANI ROAD

❾

DEDAN KIMATHI AVENUE

DAVID KAYANGA ROAD

Holy Ghost Cathedral

Ralli House

Palli House

Pandya Memorial Hospital

DEDAN KIMATHI AVENUE

KWALE ROAD

N

❶❶

Likoni Ferry & South Coast

6

0 — 200 metres

▼ Likoni Ferry & South Coast

■ DRINKING & NIGHTLIFE
Bella Vista	3
Casablanca	4
Club Rio	1
Salambo	2

■ ACCOMMODATION
Castle Royal	8
Coast Safari Hotel	3
Josleejim Hotel	4
Lotus	9
Manson	10
New Daba City	2
New Palm Tree	7
Royal Court	6
Royal Palace Hotel	1
Valencia Inn	5
YWCA	11

● SHOPPING
Haria's Gift Shop	4
MacKinnon Market	2
Mbwana Radio Service	1
Zilizo Pendwa Music Store	3

6

Fort Jesus Museum

The **museum**, on the eastern side of the fort where the main soldiers' barracks block used to be, is small, but still manages to convey a good idea of the age and breadth of Swahili civilization, and also has a decent display of Mijikenda ethnography (see p.424). Most of the displays are of pottery, indigenous or imported, some from as far afield as China and some of it more than a thousand years old. Look out for the big carved door taken from the Mazrui house in Gazi (p.442) and also the extraordinary whale vertebra used as a stool. The museum has a good exhibit on the long-term project to recover as much as possible from the wreck of the *Santo Antonio de Tanna*, which sank in 1697 while trying to break the prolonged Omani siege of the fort. Some seven thousand objects have already been brought to the surface, but the bulk of the ship itself remains nine fathoms deep in the harbour.

The Old Town

From Fort Jesus, the **Old Town** is an easy objective. While first impressions – of a quarter entirely devoted to gift and **curio shops** – are none too encouraging, the shops don't extend far into the district. Further west, away from the fort, the stores are smaller, with a couple of genuine antique shops along Kibokoni Road.

Mosques and other architecture

The Old Town is not, in fact, that old. Most buildings date from the nineteenth century, and though there may be foundations and even walls that go back many centuries, you'll get a clearer guide to the age of the town from its twenty or so **mosques**.

The **Mandhry Mosque** on Bachawy Road, founded in 1570, is officially the oldest in the city, and has a striking minaret, but it's rarely open to visitors. The **Basheikh Mosque** on Mwea Tabere Street, painted green and white, is also acknowledged to be very old – dating from "about 1300", they'll tell you, though this may be exaggerated. Just south of the old town along the seafront stands the gigantic **Burhani Masjid** – the mosque of the Bohra community, renowned traders of Indian origin. Entering the mosques is usually all right for men if you're properly dressed (no shorts) and take your shoes off. Sometimes you may be expected to wash hands and feet. Women, however modestly dressed, will usually be politely refused.

Much of the other **architecture** in the Old Town is profoundly influenced by the Indian-style Zanzibari tastes of the Busaidi occupiers of the nineteenth century. This is particularly noticeable in the elegant fretwork **balconies** and shutters still maintained on a few houses, notably on **Ndia Kuu**. For older relics, you'll have to look further – there are a number of quite ancient tombs along the seafront, especially towards the northern end of the Old Town, some of which have pillars; this is the part of Mombasa considered to pre-date the Portuguese.

Jain temple

Entrance on Langoni Rd • Daily 10am–12.30pm • Free; remove shoes and anything made of leather before entering

The sublime **Jain temple** – intricate icing sugar outside, scrupulously clean and scented within and decorated in dozens of pastel shades – was built in 1963. Jainism is an Indian religion, pre-dating but related to Buddhism, and commonest in Gujarat (original home of the majority of Kenyan Asians), which holds all life to be sacred. The temple interior is ornamentally magnificent: the painted figurines of deities in their niches are each provided with a drain so they can be easily showered down, while around the ceiling, stylized pictures portray scenes from a human life, including a familiar snake temptation in a garden.

Dhow harbour

The **dhow harbour**, along the shores of the Old Town, is somewhat overrated. There are usually one or two boats in port but you can no longer expect to see dozens, let alone

DHOWS AND DHOW CRUISES

Dhows are found in a variety of forms along the East African coast. The word is a generic Arabic term referring to the lateen-rigged vessels used in the Indian Ocean – a term which itself comes from the triangular, fore-and-aft "Latin" rigged sails of Roman vessels, in which the sail was suspended from a long yard mounted on the mast. Far from being based on ancient tradition, however, the highly manoeuvrable, dhow style of sailing rig in the Indian Ocean may have derived, secondhand, from Vasco da Gama's caravels that appeared in Mombasa at the end of the fifteenth century and had virtually the same setup. You can see similar vessels – feluccas – on the Nile.

Today, the large Kenyan trading dhows, known in Swahili as **jahazi**, are used less and less for transport and are more often bought up by tourist businesses. The *mashua* is a plank boat like a small *jahazi*, while the smaller *ngalawa* – double-outrigger dugout canoes with a small sail rigged high on the short mast – are the little boats that ferry passengers and whose captains normally potter about in the lagoon along the beaches, offering trips out to the reef. These cruises are an excellent way to get an insight into Mombasa's seafaring traditions – and see the city from some unusual angles.

La Marina Mtwapa, north shore of the creek, east of the bridge ☏020 2434726 or ☏0723 223737, ⓦ facebook.com/la.mombasa. This Mtwapa restaurant (see p.423) offers a number of regular dhow excursions, including sunset dinner cruises on Mtwapa Creek, which include dinner and live entertainment ($95), and twice-monthly "champaign cruises" to a small sand island in the Indian Ocean.

Tamarind Tamarind Jetty, Mkomani ☏041 4474600 or ☏0725 959552, ⓦ tamarind.co.ke. The excellent *Tamarind* restaurant (see p.396) has outfitted two old *jahazis*, the *Nawalilkher* and the *Babulkher*, for Swahili seafood dinners under sail ($93), with live music accompaniment.

hundreds, of dhows, even at the end of the northeast monsoon in April, traditionally the peak time for arrivals: seasonal variations are less important now that the big *jahazis* have engines. Nor are you likely to have the opportunity to go aboard one of these exotic vessels, though a number of big dhows have been converted as **dinner-cruise vessels** (see above). Still, the area is an enjoyable place for a stroll, especially at weekends, when families dress up to go for a walk and children leap around in the sea below Fort Jesus.

Walks around Mombasa

Taking a walk, or a stroll, with plenty of cold-drink stops, is a time-honoured Mombasan diversion. You will probably want to see that immortal double pair of **elephant tusks** arching over Moi Avenue. To get to them, you have to run the gauntlet of curio booths that come and go and sometimes almost conceal the cool hideaway of **Uhuru Gardens**, with its Africa-shaped fountain. And when you reach the Tusks, you may regret your determination to view them close up – they're revealed to be grubby aluminium.

Mama Ngina Drive

If you have the time and inclination for an **oceanside walk**, the 2km route around the breezy, seaward side of the island along **Mama Ngina Drive** makes a fine late afternoon stroll, especially on weekends and public holidays, when it seems to become the meeting place for half of Mombasa's Indian population – you'll even find food stalls and street entertainers. There are lots of places to sit and watch the waves pounding the coral cliffs through the break in the reef. On the clifftop, protruding from the far side of Mombasa Golf Club's **golf course**, are the stumpy, insignificant remains of **Fort St Joseph**, built in 1826 to defend Mazrui Mombasa against the attacks of the Busaidi Omanis. At the southern end of Mama Ngina Drive is an extensive stand of enormous **baobab trees**, frequently associated with ancient settlements on the coast. You can get back to the city centre on a matatu from the busy stage east of the Likoni ferry dock.

Mbaraki Pillar

To the west of the Likoni ferry roundabout, the **Mbaraki Pillar** is a huge pillar tomb that's supposedly the burial place of a seventeenth-century mainland sheikh, the chief of one of the "twelve tribes" (see p.396). The pillar's 8m height is impressive enough, but it is dwarfed these days by nearby warehouses. To get to it from the ferry area, turn left immediately before Ndoho Market, then follow the road round to the left about 200m, before branching right down a broad, dirt road between warehouses for a further 200m, behind the Nakumatt Likoni supermarket. The pillar is on the right, near the cliffside, with a small mosque alongside.

6

ARRIVAL AND DEPARTURE   MOMBASA

If you've never been to Africa before, flying into Mombasa throws you into the place more quickly than arriving in Nairobi's cosmopolitan embrace. You may even experience some level of **culture shock** from the poverty, the heat, the noise and the general upfront nature of everything. Mombasa remains a much easier place to navigate, though, however you are doing so, including by driving in your own vehicle or renting a car on arrival (see p.404).

BY PLANE

Moi International Airport is situated in the Port Reitz district of the mainland, some 10km from the city centre. Visas are available on arrival (see p.87). The airport has several ATMs, and bank booths for exchanging money are just outside the customs area.

AIRLINES

Fly540 Ground floor, Mombasa Trade Centre ☎ 041 2319078 or ☎ 0710 540540, ⓦ fly540.com.

Jambo Jet Electricity House, Nkrumah Rd ☎ 0711 024545, ⓦ jambojet.com.

Kenya Airways City Mall, Nyali ☎ 041 2125251 or ☎ 0734 105251, ⓦ kenya-airways.com.

Mombasa Air Safari Moi International Airport ☎ 0701 400400 or ☎ 0734 500500, ⓦ mombasaairsafari.com.

AIRPORT TRANSPORT

Buses and matatus There is no bus service from the airport into town. The nearest matatu service is 1km away – to get there, walk to the first row of small shops at the road junction for Magongo, where you can pick up a matatu to the GPO.

Taxis Several taxi companies which service the airport, including Kenatco (☎ 0720 108222) and Karibu Taxi Service (☎ 0722 318485), have fixed rates – these are posted up near where their representatives wait, or they'll show you on request. As in Nairobi, prices hover somewhere between Ksh100/km and Ksh150/km, and the price to the centre of Mombasa starts from Ksh1000–1200, depending on the street you want. Fares are also fixed for the beach resorts, depending on your hotel: Nyali Ksh1700; Bamburi Ksh2000; Mtwapa Ksh3000.

Car rental You can also arrange to have a prebooked car rental vehicle meet you. Avis/Budget has a desk at the airport, and most rental companies will oblige, though you'll usually need to visit their office in town to complete the paperwork and pay the deposit.

Parking There's never any problem with airport parking in the car park just outside the terminal building (Ksh60 for the first hour, Ksh30 for every hour after that).

DEPARTURE

If you're heading to Moi International Airport from the south coast, be prepared for delays at the Likoni ferry which can easily add an hour to your journey time. Domestic departure tax is always included in the price of tickets, as is the international departure tax of $40 in the case of most airlines – though some charter companies (including Thomson/First Choice) exclude it, forcing the passenger to pay directly on departure.

Destinations Diani Beach/Ukunda (daily; 15min); Maasai Mara (daily; 2–3hr), via Amboseli and Tsavo West (1–2hr); Malindi (daily; 30min); Nairobi (18–20 daily; 1hr).

BY BUS

BUS COMPANIES

Bus company booking offices are spread along Abdel Nasser Rd (for the north coast as far as Lamu) and Jomo Kenyatta Ave and Mwembe Tayari Rd (for Nairobi, the south coast and Tanzania). You can buy through-tickets to central and western Kenya on Modern Coast and Mash, but all services go via Nairobi, usually requiring a change of buses. Competition on all routes is fierce, and some operators are more reputable than others. The safest is reckoned to be Modern Coast, which also has a good reputation for comfort, while there's little to choose between the bus companies running up and down the coast. For reasons of safety and comfort, the overnight journey to Nairobi isn't recommended.

Mash Mwembe Tayari Rd ☎ 0717 088588, ⓦ mash.ssanics.com.

Destinations Nairobi (every morning and evening; Ksh1200–2300).

Modern Coast Mwembe Tayari Rd ☎ 041 3433166, ⓦ coastbus.com.

Destinations Kilifi (daily, early morning; Ksh400); Malindi (daily, early morning; Ksh400); Nairobi (every morning and evening; Ksh1200–2000).

Simba Coach Jomo Kenyatta Ave, opposite Kobil ☎ 0707 471410.

Destinations Lamu (1 daily; Ksh1000).

Tahmeed Jomo Kenyatta Ave ☎ 0729 356561.

Destinations Dar es Salaam (4 daily; Ksh1500); Lamu (every morning; Ksh1000); Nairobi (5 daily; Ksh1400).

Tawakal (Pwani Tawakal) Abdel Nasser Rd ☎ 0722 550111, ⊛ pwanitawakal.co.ke.

Destinations Lamu (every morning; Ksh1200), via Malindi (Ksh300).

TSS Abdel Nasser Rd ☎ 0704 137202.

Destinations Lamu (every morning; Ksh1000), via Malindi (Ksh350).

DESTINATIONS

Busia (2 daily; 16hr); Dar es Salaam (6 daily; 12–14hr), via Tanga (6hr); Kisumu (9 daily; 14hr); Lamu via Kilifi and Malindi (6 daily; 8hr); Malaba (1 daily; 16hr); Malindi via Kilifi (approximately hourly; 2hr); Nairobi (frequent, but especially around 7am and 7pm; 8–10hr).

BY TRAIN

Though the service now runs only twice a week and is often subject to long delays, the night train (see p.57) between Nairobi and Mombasa can be an interesting experience, as long as you're not in a hurry. Mombasa station sits at the west end of Haile Selassie Rd, 1km from the city's main north–south thoroughfare, Digo Rd. Swarms of taxis await the train's arrival – Ksh300–400 is the going rate between the station and any city-centre hotel.

Arrival The train leaves Nairobi at 7pm (Mon & Fri) arriving, in theory, in Mombasa at 10am the next morning. **Departure** The train for Nairobi leaves Mombasa at 7pm (Tues & Sun), and arrives, in theory, at 9.30am the next day. However, don't count on making any further transport connections until at least the next afternoon. You can also disembark at around midnight in Voi, for Tsavo East National Park. It's best to buy tickets in person from the station when the train arrives. The station is open only on Tues and Sun (☎ 0728 787294), roughly from 8am until the train departs.

BY MATATU

Matatus to the north coast beaches (Kenyatta, Bamburi and Shanzu), and on to Mtwapa, leave from opposite the Tusky's

Digo supermarket at the end of Haile Selassie Rd and along the nearby area of Digo Rd as far as the GPO. Matatus going through to Malindi (in principle these don't drop or pick up until north of Mtwapa) congregate at the south end of Abdel Nasser Rd, near the junction with Mackawi Rd, by the mosque. Matatus for Kaloleni and Voi leave from the Kobil station at the junction of Mwembe Tayari Rd and Jomo Kenyatta Ave. If you're heading south of Mombasa, you'll need to get a matatu to the Likoni ferry (see p.403), and pick up onward transport on the other side.

Destinations Bamburi (20–30min); Kaloleni (1hr 30min); Malindi (2hr); Mazeras (1hr); Mtwapa (45min).

BY CAR

Driving into Mombasa Leave plenty of time to get into and out of Mombasa on the Nairobi road – traffic jams and hours of delays are becoming frequent between the island and Mazeras. Delays can also be bad over the Nyali bridge on the Malindi road, and while waiting for the Likoni ferry when coming from the south coast.

Parking It is usually easy to find a parking space, though you shouldn't leave anything valuable in your vehicle or leave it unguarded on the street overnight. Uniformed parking wardens patrol the streets, and will sell you a Ksh100 ticket which you display under your windscreen, entitling you to park as many times as you like over the course of the following 24hr. Beware of faded yellow "no parking" road markings on some kerbs: there are some corrupt wheel-clamping teams on the prowl, ready to take advantage of unwary visitors.

TO AND FROM LIKONI

By ferry and matatu The 24hr Likoni ferry connects the south coast to Mombasa island (10min; 4am–1am every 15min; 1am–4am hourly; pedestrians and cyclists free, cars Ksh150). T-shirted guards look out for pickpockets, but it's still wise to keep valuables tucked away and your car windows up. Rush hours can create long tailbacks of traffic waiting to cross in both directions, so leave plenty of time if you have a flight to catch. While main bus services use the ferry, if you're travelling by matatu, you change vehicles and cross on foot. The other ferry across Kilindini Creek, the Mtongwe ferry (daily 5–10am & 3–9pm), is a free commuter service, but only for foot passengers.

Matatu destinations from Likoni Diani Beach (45min); Kwale (40min); Lungalunga (2hr); Msambweni (1hr); Shimoni (1hr 30min); Ukunda (30min).

GETTING AROUND

With no municipal bus services, city transport comes down to **taxis** and more informal transport. Getting around the city centre **on foot** is easy enough, and sometimes faster than using transport, especially at rush hour.

By taxi Kenatco (☎ 0720 108222, ⊛ kenatco.com), based at the Mombasa Trade Centre, Nkrumah Rd, runs a reliable

24hr taxi service with fixed prices. Most taxi fares on the island range from Ksh200 for a short hop to a top fare of about Ksh400, depending on distance (cabs are all unmetered, so always agree the fare before setting off).

By matatu Matatus run from the GPO to Nyali Bridge, Tudor Docks and the Likoni ferry (Ksh20–40 per hop).

By tuk-tuk or piki-piki Tuk-tuks charge Ksh100–250 per ride for the whole vehicle (seating up to three plus luggage), while piki-pikis (motorbike taxis) usually cost

Ksh100–200 on the island.

By bike Mombasa has bike tours (see p.000) but no bike rental. However, Omar Husein Cycloduka, Haile Selassie Rd near Maungano Rd (Mon–Sat 8.30am–1pm & 2–6pm; ☎ 0770 112345), has a good selection for sale. Heavyweight roadsters with racks start from Ksh6000, while mountain bikes range between Ksh8000 and Ksh12,000.

INFORMATION AND TOURS

Tourist office Operated by the Kenya Coast Tourist Association, the tourist information office is on Moi Ave, next to the Tusks (Mon–Fri 8am–5pm, Sat 9am–1pm; ☎ 041 2225428, ⊛ thekenyacoast.org; see p.398). Although offering little in material terms, the staff are helpful, and can advise you on transport and accommodation.

Bike the Coast Go-Kart Track, Bamburi; map, p.411. This small, Swiss-owned operator (☎ 0722 873738, ⊛ bike thecoast.com) specializes in half-day bicycle tours – an unusual and highly recommended option, although the tours that go inland require a bit of leg work.

SAFARIS

Mombasa is important as a **safari hub**; the majority of safaris starting from the coast visit Tsavo East or Tsavo West. With a number of daily flights further afield, however, even the Maasai Mara is accessible for a short safari, though less than two nights isn't recommended. Expect to pay at least $400/person for a two-day, one-night safari to Tsavo East, depending on the lodge or camp included and the size of your group. Air safaris to the Maasai Mara start at around $1000 for one night, including the flight. Safaris should always include all transport and transfers, meals, park fees for the full duration of your stay, and a two- to three-hour game drive every morning and evening while in the park – be sure to do your research when you book (see p.79).

Kenya Wildlife Service Mama Ngina Drive (daily 6am–6pm; ☎ 041 4311745). Point of issue and point of sale for National Park Smartcards.

SAFARI OPERATORS AND TRAVEL AGENTS

African Quest Safaris Mezzanine floor, Palli House, Nyerere Ave ☎ 041 2227052 or ☎ 0722 703852, ⊛ africanquest.co.ke; map p.399. Large operator offering competitively priced lodge safaris.

★**Farways Safaricentre** Msanifu Kombo St ☎ 0733 773434 or 0734 855261, ✉ mr.jiva@gmail.com; map p.398. Good value and very personal service from a small, long-established agent with an excellent network of operator contacts, including car rental, Zanzibar trips, accommodation bookings and safaris.

Glorious Safaris Nilnkatha Building, next to Bella Plaza, Nyali ☎ 041 476518 or ☎ 0733 239412, ⊛ glorioussafaris.com; map p.411. Busy operator with strong British ties, offering competitively priced local excursions and safaris to Tsavo East and West.

Ketty Tours Ketty Plaza, Moi Ave ☎ 041 2315178 or ☎ 041 2312204, ⊛ www.kettytours.co.ke; map p.398. Solid operator with good experience and a large rental fleet.

★**Lofty Tours** Lofty House, Kwa Shibu Rd ☎ 041 2220241 or ☎ 0722 412186, ⊛ lofty-tours.de; map p.399. Conscientious German-Kenyan operator running its own safaris. The main draw is experience and the Land Cruisers, a more personal way of travelling than minibus.

Pollman's Tours and Safaris Pollman's House, Malindi Rd, Bamburi, north of Mombasa ☎ 041 2014980 or

☎ 0722 202070, ⊛ pollmans.com; map p.411. One of the biggest operators (you'll see their vehicles everywhere), with reliable, mainstream safaris.

★**Southern Cross Safaris** Southern Cross Centre, off Nyali Bridge (northbound, mainland side, immediate first exit on the left) ☎ 020 2434600, ⊛ southerncrosssafaris.com; map p.396. Highly respected operators and agents, with four bronze and ten silver guides and their own camps (called *Satao* camps).

Vogue Tours & Travel Nkrumah Rd, opposite DHL ☎ 041 2223613, ✉ info@voguetravelkenya.com; map p.399. Professional travel agents worth visiting for cheap flights to Europe and Asia.

INDEPENDENT SAFARIS: CAR RENTAL

Renting a car for an independent safari, prices tend to be a little cheaper in Mombasa than in Nairobi, especially if you deal with a local company. Most of the safari operators also rent vehicles with or without a driver. Expect to pay from around Ksh3000–4000/day (Ksh15,000–21,000 for a saloon car).

Avis/Budget Mombasa Mombasa Car Hire, Ratna Square, Nyali ☎ 041 4220465; Moi International Airport ☎ 0736 750006, ⊛ avis.com; map p.411. This big international rental company is reliable, if somewhat pricey compared to the local competition.

Distance Tours & Car Hire Cnr Mt Kenya/Links roads, Nyali ☎ 0717 074056 or ☎ 0724 956579, ⊛ distance tours.com; map p.411. Centrally located fleet-owner with a good reputation.

Glory Car Hire Moi Ave, next to the tourist office ☏ 041 2313561, ⊕ glorykenya.com; map p.398. Well-known company with good prices – saloons from around Ksh3500/day.

Unik Car Hire & Safaris Meru Rd ☏ 041 2226310, ⊕ uniksafaris.com; map p.398. Well-established Kenyan business with a range of cars and safairs on offer.

ACCOMMODATION

None of Mombasa's main resort hotels is located on the island, and barely any of the city's hotels are of international standard. Note that **water supplies** in Mombasa are unreliable, and many cheap places feature the telltale buckets and plastic basins that indicate that water sometimes has to be carried up. Even when the pipes are working, hot water is rare in budget hotels, but in this climate you're unlikely to miss it. Some places aiming for higher standards have the instant electric showers that are widespread in the highlands. If you're travelling on a budget and don't mind staying on the north mainland, you might find the two **backpackers hostels** in Nyali the best options (see p.412). And if you want top-class comforts and service, then look at the *Tamarind*, also in Nyali, but a short journey from the city (see p.412).

BUDGET LODGINGS

Coast Safari Hotel Raha Leo St ☏ 0717 357558; map p.398. This professionally run hotel is a cut above basic, with 41 fairly small, clean, well-maintained rooms with fans, TV and nets, and a decent restaurant on the ground floor. Very convenient for long-distance buses. BB **Ksh1500**

Josleejim Hotel Duruma Rd ☏ 020 2038814 or ☏ 0735 318850, ⊕ josleejimhotel.kbo.co.ke; map p.398. Sizeable, friendly place with reasonable facilities, including safe parking. The comfortable rooms, with nets, fans, clean sheets and even small balconies, make it good value. Room only **Ksh1300**

New Daba City Mwembe Tayari Rd, next to Coast Bus ☏ 0722 472982; map p.398. Clean and respectable cheapie right next to most of the bus companies, with nets but no hot water. Good value if you're counting the pennies. **Ksh1200**

New People's Guest House Abdel Nasser Rd, by the main bus and matatu offices ☏ 0722 471032; map p.396. Big, noisy, long-established, very male-dominated block, with good security and a busy *hoteli* on the ground floor. No frills, but the rooms are tolerable and it's handy if you're taking a morning bus to Lamu. **Ksh800**

YWCA Corner Kaunda Ave and Kiambu Ave ☏ 0727 806979, ⊕ ywcakenya.org; map p.399. Pleasant ambience with good security and a cafeteria (6am–8pm), open to men (downstairs) as well as women (upstairs), and couples can share rooms. Best value for long stays, but book ahead. No curfew, no guests in rooms. Additional one-off charges for all guests: Ksh200 admission fee or Ksh300 annual subscription. BB **Ksh1780**

HOTELS

Blue Comforts Hotel Archbishop Makarios Rd ☏ 0734 537363, ⓔ info@kettytours.co.ke, ⊕ bluecomforts .com; map p.396. Very blue, good-value standby owned by Ketty Tours (see opposite), with a breakfast terrace off the street at the front. All rooms have nets, TVs and fans, though you can upgrade to one with a/c for an extra Ksh1000. BB **Ksh2000**

Castle Royal Moi Ave ☏ 041 2220373 or ☏ 0720 843072, ⊕ sentrim-hotels.com; map p.398. Mombasa's most venerable hotel, formerly the *Palace*, dating from 1909. Period on the outside, modern on the inside, with 68 a/c rooms with fan, DSTV and corridors open at both ends to allow a through breeze. All it lacks is a pool. Wi-fi. BB **$135**

Ganjoni Wananchi Hotel Archbishop Makarios Rd ☏ 0717 357790; map p.396. Popular, upcountry-style hotel aimed primarily at business travellers, with a busy bar and restaurant and competitively priced rooms with TV and fans (or a/c for a Ksh1200 supplement). BB **Ksh2500**

★**Lotus** Corner Mvita Rd and Cathedral Rd ☏ 041 2313207 or ☏ 0722 612517; map p.396. Located on a quiet corner not far from Fort Jesus, with a vaguely oriental feel, and overflowing with greenery. It's not surprising that the plain but very neat, clean rooms with a/c and TV are often full. Wi-fi. BB **Ksh6500**

Manson Mohdar Mohamed Habib Rd ☏ 041 2222419 or ☏ 0722 610615, ⊕ mansonhotel.com; map p.399. Large, clean rooms of variable size in a seven-storey block, some with balconies, some with fans, others with a/c (Ksh300–600 extra). TV lounge and bar-restaurant on the ground floor. Secure, and good value. BB **Ksh2700**

★**New Palm Tree** Nkrumah Rd ☏ 020 8025682 or ☏ 0715 442017, ⊕ newpalmtreehotel.com; map p.398. Once quite a grand place, this still has hags of charm, despite the modernization that includes a cybercafé in the foyer (daily 9am–7pm; Ksh1/min). Alcohol is prohibited. Rooms are spacious and clean, with fans, a/c and nets. There's also a sunny first-floor courtyard. A good deal, and worth reserving. Wi-fi. BB **Ksh3100**

Royal Court Haile Selassie Rd ☏ 041 2230932 or ☏ 0722 412867, ⊕ royalcourtmombasa.co.ke; map p.398. Modern business-class hotel close to the station, with good-sized rooms with spotless bathrooms, facing out over town. Rooftop bar-restaurant, plunge pool and gym. Wi-fi. BB **Ksh9800**

★**Royal Palace Hotel** Old Kilindini Rd ☏ 0717 620602 or ☏ 0736 663011, ⊕ royalpalacehotelmombasa.com; map p.399. The best and one of the only places to stay in the atmospheric heart of the Old Town, this friendly and well-managed hotel is decorated with wildlife art, and its rooms (with fans and nets) come painted in stripes, hearts or leopard print. A highlight is the rooftop terrace, where breakfast is served. BB **Ksh2600**

Valencia Inn Haile Selassie Rd ☎041 2312399, ⌨ sanvalenciakenya.com; map p.398. A relatively smart conversion in a convenient, central location, with a/c and DSTV. The rooms with balcony at the front are worth the Ksh500 supplement. Wi-fi. BB **Ksh5000**

EATING

Mombasa is well supplied with good, **cheap restaurants**. Especially if you're newly arrived from upcountry, they are one of the city's chief delights, with a discernible cuisine involving coconut, fish, chicken, rice and beans, and incorporating Asian flavours. Most places are open daily, but when there's a closure day it's usually Monday. You can also enjoy tasty **snacks** and drinks to go in various parts of the city. During the day, for example, you can get green coconuts (drink the coconut water, then scoop out and eat the jelly-like flesh), sugar-cane juice freshly pressed from the cane and cuplets of *kahawa thungu* (thick bitter coffee, usually flavoured with ginger or cardamom). After dark, by the bus **stalls** up Abdel Nasser Rd and along Jomo Kenyatta Ave and Mwembe Tayari Rd, as well as on other busy corners, you'll find what are effectively full meals for around Ksh100–200, including *nyama choma* (roast meats), chapattis, spicy little chicken kebabs and freshly fried potato and cassava chips and crisps.

SNACK AND JUICE BARS

Fayaz Bakery Jomo Kenyatta Ave ☎0786 252502; map p.398. "Baking since 1911" reads the sign of this old-school bakery, which offers a good range of cakes and biscuits, with fruit muffins (Ksh65) as well as local specialities such as passion cake. There's another branch on Makadara Rd. Mon–Sat 9am–8.30pm, Sun 10am–6pm.

Huseini Bakery Turkana St; map p.398. Nice selection of cakes and snacks, including their house speciality cookies – *nan khatai*, a light biscuit with nuts (from Ksh80/bag). Mon–Sat 9am–12.30pm & 2.30–7.30pm.

Kassim Café Nehru Rd, just off Pigot Place, Old Town ☎0723 512780; map p.399. A hole-in-the-wall café serving the usual *bhajias*, chapatti and *manzazi*, along with good home-made milkshakes, fresh juices and *pan* (see box opposite) at Ksh25 each – it's a favourite meeting spot for older men, and a good place to sample a *pan* counter and get a flavour of the neighbourhood. Daily 6am–6pm.

MNKafe Off Kaunda Ave ☎0711 665233 , ⌨ mnkafe .com; map p.396. Chic little café specializing in luscious desserts and proper espresso drinks, including iced coffee. There are at least a dozen cupcake flavours behind the counter (Ksh120–150), and a long list of Belgian waffles on offer (from Ksh260), with toppings like diced green apples and peanut butter fudge. The breakfasts are good, too. Tues–Thurs 10am–10pm, Fri & Sat 10am–11pm, Sun 1–10pm.

Seif-Halwa Mackawi Rd ☎0727 997808; map p.398. Fresh, gooey, intensely sweet and scented *halwa* is made here daily in the traditional way in a huge pan. Buy a little for a snack or a lot for presents (from Ksh500/kg). Hours vary with speed of business, but officially Mon–Sat 8.30am–noon & 2.30–6pm, Sun 8.30am–noon.

Temptations Moi Ave ☎0722 346500; map p.398. Delicious home-made ice cream served in a sleek, modern split-level coffee house, a good place to escape the heat and hassle of Moi Ave. Most scoops are Ksh100; "premium" scoops Ksh150. Daily 2–11pm.

SWAHILI CUISINE

★**Island Dishes** Kibokoni St; map p.399. Wonderful Swahili dishes, including fish with coconut (from Ksh300), *mkate mayai* ("Swahili pizza"; Ksh150) and several vegetarian options, plus juices from date to passionfruit (Ksh60). There are mango and chilli sauces on the table if you like it hot, or tamarind if you prefer it sweet and sour. Daily 8am–11pm.

★**Jahazi Coffee House** Ndia Kuu ☎0738 277975, ⌨ facebook.com/jahazicoffeehouse; map p.399. Beautifully decorated Canadian-Kenyan venture in an eighteenth-century Old Town house, serving snacks and delicious spiced coffee with cardamom (Ksh100) in a cool environment of cushions and carpets. Swahili lunch or dinner (Ksh1000–1700) available if ordered in advance. Daily except Sat 7am–2pm; later if dinner is ordered.

New Recoda Café Kibokoni St ☎0720 436709; map p.399. Something of an Old Town institution (though moved from its original location), this small, cheap and very traditional café serves dishes like biryani (Ksh350), *mishkaki* and coconut prawns (Ksh400); the selection depends on what's been cooked that day, and there may or may not be an actual menu. Try the fresh juices, including ginger, mango and beetroot (Ksh50). Daily 6am–11pm.

Splendid View Maungano Rd ☎0721 450403, ⌨ bit .ly/SplendidViewMombasa; map p.398. Forget about the view of the *Splendid Hotel* (it's not a splendid view) and concentrate on the excellent house specialities – chicken biryani (Ksh350), garlic chicken and *pili pili* prawns (Ksh650) – perhaps leaving room for a *faluda* for dessert. Mon–Fri 11am–2pm & 5–10.30pm, Sat 11am–2.30pm & 5.30–11pm, Sun 5–10.30pm.

★**Tarboush Café** Makadara Rd ☎0724 664443; map p.399. Perennially busy grill and coast-style diner, its pavement terrace always crowded with a broad spectrum of locals and visitors. The beef *shawarma* pitta (Ksh240), chicken tikka (Ksh280) and beef *mishkaki* (Ksh250) are popular, and they do a good range of *naan* bread (Ksh80–110) and gorgeous juices. You can order takeaway as well. Daily 7am–11pm.

FAST FOOD AND HOTELIS

Blue Room Haile Selassie Rd ☎0721 786868, ⊛blueroomonline.com; map p.398. Large, self-service food hall that's been attracting a devoted clientele for decades with its fans and clean, tiled surfaces, with a menu dominated by burgers and pizzas (both from Ksh550), a good range of chicken and beef dishes and quite a few vegetarian choices, plus home-made ice cream (Ksh130/scoop). Their free wi-fi is a bonus, and there's also a cybercafé on the premises. Daily 7am–10.30pm.

Corner Café Corner Jomo Kenyatta Ave and George Morura St; map p.398. Popular and lively place, with tables on the pavement as well as inside the tiny premises, offering a small range of incredibly cheap and filling dishes and snacks, including *pilau* (Ksh150) and *ugali* with beef stew (Ksh130). Daily 7am–8pm.

Gelato Divino Makadara Rd ☎0722 415401; map p.399. A streetside barbecue joint painted pink and white like a birthday cake, which nonetheless manages to attract throngs of men in the evenings. The speciality here, aside from grills, is Yemeni food like *mandi* (Ksh450) and goat soup (Ksh300), though as the name suggests they serve ice cream as well, alongside milkshakes and "authentic" Italian coffee. Daily 8am–midnight.

★**Pwani Dishes** Turkana St ☎0729 841415; map p.398. Cheap and cheerful diner offering lots of stews and basic Kenyan dishes, with large servings and low prices. Try the coconut fish curry (Ksh170) or masala chips (Ksh190). Daily 7am–10pm, closed Fri noon–1.15pm.

INDIAN COOKING

Café Stavrose Maungano Rd ☎0722 410909; map p.398. A small place that's been serving Indian snacks, tikka dishes and kebabs for years, on Formica tables under whirring ceiling fans. *Bhajius* Ksh100 a plate, lunches around Ksh300. Mon–Fri 9am–7.30pm, Sat 9am–3pm.

★**New Chetna** Haile Selassie Rd ☎0770 010380; map p.398. A long-time favourite for Indian sweets on the left, and tasty South Indian vegetarian dishes at low prices on the right. On offer are well-made *bhajias* and other snacks and dishes (around Ksh120–200/plate) and a superb all-you-can-eat buffet-style *thali* (Ksh400); the food can be very hot, so approach with caution. Daily 8am–8pm.

Shehnai Fatemi House, Maungano Rd ☎0722 411711 or ☎0722 871111, ⊛facebook.com/Shehnai Restaurant; map p.398. Mughlai specialities with a good reputation, in a spacious and light interior with somewhat regal furniture. You're spoilt for choice: try *achar gosht* (mutton cooked in spices and flavoured with pickles; Ksh680), or *malai tikka* (oven-baked chicken marinated in cream and black pepper; Ksh680). Prices exclude VAT and service charges, so count on adding an extra 25 percent to your bill. Tues–Sun noon–2pm & 7–10.30pm.

Singh Mwembe Tayari Rd ☎0723 735881, ⊛bit.ly/SinghRestaurantMombasa; map p.398. A bit of a walk from the centre of town, but very close to all the long-distance buses, and with an a/c room to cool off. Well worth a visit for their extremely tasty, freshly prepared Punjabi curries, both meat and veg. Most mains under Ksh700. Tues–Sun noon–2.30pm & 7–10.30pm.

INTERNATIONAL CUISINE

Galaxy Chinese Florida Complex, Mama Ngina Drive ☎0726 894002; map p.398. Above the *Florida* club, this restaurant enjoys a wonderful position on the waterfront. The Cantonese and Hainanese seafood is rather inconsistent and relatively pricey, with pan-fried whole fish Ksh1000–1200/dish, but the location makes up for it. Daily 11am–2.30pm & 6–11pm.

New Overseas Chinese Korean Moi Ave, 200m west of the Tusks ☎0724 101544; map p.398. Good-value Cantonese and Korean cooking, focusing on seafood, with more expensive specialities including steamed crab, tuna *sashimi* and *kimchi* (spicy pickled cabbage) soup, all at around Ksh600–800. Daily 11am–3pm & 5–11pm.

PAN SHOPS

Highly characteristic of Mombasa are the Indian **pan shops**, often doubling as tobacconists and corner shops. Worth trying at least once, *pan* is a natural digestive and stimulant that encourages salivation. Its main ingredient is chopped areca palm nut, flavoured with your choice of sweet spices and other ingredients, syrup and white lime, selected from a display of dishes. The whole ensemble is wrapped in a peppery-tasting, dark-green leaf from the betel vine, known as *pan* in Urdu and Hindi. Including ground tobacco is another option, but best avoided by novices. Pop the triangular parcel in your mouth and munch – it tastes as exotic and unlikely as it sounds – spitting out the copious juice as you go. It is worth noting, however, that *pan*, with or without tobacco, has various adverse effects on **health**, including gum damage and tooth decay, and is known to be carcinogenic. Two of the best *pan* counters in town are at the *New Chetna* restaurant (see above) and *Kassim Café* (see opposite).

Old Town Zanzibar Restaurant Ndia Kuu ☎0727 723364; map p.399. Positioned to catch tourist spillover from Fort Jesus, this little Old Town restaurant offers a menu based around seafood – coconut fish (Ksh700), chilli garlic crab (Ksh900) and the like – along with curries and snacks. Pricey, but not a bad option for lunch. Daily 8am–9pm.

DRINKING AND NIGHTLIFE

Mombasa doesn't have **bars** on every street corner, but there are one or two watering holes scattered around the city: the *Lotus Hotel* on Cathedral Rd (see p.405) is one of the nicest places in town for a civilized beer. There are several **nightclubs** on the island, too, though the busiest nightlife is in the resort area north of Mombasa, especially in Mtwapa (see p.422) and around Kenyatta Beach (see p.416). Most of the city clubs are free, but on popular nights (Wed, Fri & Sat) you'll occasionally encounter entry charges of Ksh100–300. Long before the clubs get busy, a stroll around the generally safe Old Town will uncover one or two **coffee-sellers** serving black *kahawa* from traditional high-spouted jugs.

CLUBS AND LIVE MUSIC

Unless you want to be repeatedly accosted by prostitutes (or, if you're a woman, by men who are convinced that they are the missing person in your life), it's best to visit most of the following clubs with at least a companion, if not in a group.

Bella Vista Next to Shell, on the corner of Moi Ave and Aga Khan Rd; map p.398. Busy, local sports bar and restaurant (grills, pasta, salads; mains from Ksh450), *Bella Vista* attracted notoriety in 2012 when it was the subject of a grenade attack, but continues to be one of the most popular venues in the city centre. Loud rock and no single shots (doubles Ksh200) can make for a rowdy atmosphere, especially on Fri and Sat nights, but Sun daytimes are mellow, with people having brunch and listening to soul and R&B. Entry Ksh300 on disco nights. Daily 24hr.

California Dream Hotel Corner Moi Ave and Liwatoni Rd ☎0721 485258; map p.396. Formerly the alluringly named *Jam Rescue Hotel*, this has live Congolese rumba music on Sat nights from 8pm. Beer Ksh180, sodas Ksh50, wine Ksh200. Daily 24hr.

Casablanca Mnazi Moja Rd, just off Moi Ave ☎0722 867774; map p.398. This draws a big mixed crowd to a lively terrace, and prostitutes gather here in force, especially upstairs. They can be a pain, or a laugh, depending on your mood. Relatively expensive drinks and food; beer Ksh220. Daily 24hr.

Club Rio Baluchi St; map p.399. A symphony of pink cane furniture, this is one of central Mombasa's only DJ clubs. Fri and Sat nights are packed, and drinks tend to become more expensive as the night wears on (beers normally Ksh200), but other nights can be deserted. Live music, when there is some, is in the second-floor *Calypso Bar*, though the main bar hosts karaoke nights every Thurs. Generally hassle-free, and gay-friendly. Daily 24hr.

Florida Club Mama Ngina Drive, overlooking the ocean, 2km from the city centre ☎041 2313127, ⓦfloridaclubskenya.com; map p.396. This attempts to create a slick impression, with floor shows and glitter, but is similar in most respects to its Nairobi namesake (free until 7pm, then men Ksh300, women Ksh200 or free on Wed). The terrace above the ocean is a nice feature, as is keg beer, and there's a pleasant little casino. DJs start around 7pm, with shows at 10pm and midnight. Daily 24hr.

Saba-Saba Corner Jomo Kenyatta Ave and Ronald Ngala Rd; map p.396. The bar at the front isn't very inspiring, but head out to the open terrace at the back, where the action is. There's often live music, even in the day, and always a sweaty, local atmosphere. Beer Ksh170. The entrance is unmarked; look out for the plants on the first-floor terrace. Daily 24hr.

Salambo Moi Ave; map p.398. By day a dozy bar with limited snacks, this comes to life at night as the city centre's only really local disco. On most nights there's a mix of Congolese sounds, soul and reggae, with midnight shows, acrobats, dancing and beauty contests. Beer Ksh170. Daily 24hr.

ARTS AND CULTURE

Cultural and artistic life in Mombasa is a bit limited. The **Alliance Française** (Freed Building, corner of Moi Ave and Kwa Shibu Rd; ☎041 2225048, ⓦafkenya.or.ke) occasionally sponsors events, but you can't guarantee anything.

Cinemas The closest and best cinema on the coast is the Nyali Cinemax at Nyali Plaza, with four screens (map p.411). **Libraries** Kenya National Library, Msanifu Kombo St (Mon–Fri 8am–6.30pm, Sat 8.30am–5pm; ☎020 2158397); Fort Jesus Museum (archeology; Mon–Fri 8am–12.30pm & 2–4.30pm). **Swahili Resource Centre** on Sir Mbarak Hinawy Rd (hours vary, but usually Mon–Fri 8.30am–4.30pm, Sat 9am–1pm; free) offers one of the few avenues to exploring Swahili culture for casual interested visitors. **Theatre** The Little Theatre Club, Mnazi Moja Rd (☎041 2229258, ⓦbit.ly/LTCMombasa), hosts productions by coastal drama groups, as well as music performances. Seats around Ksh200–300.

SHOPPING

Mombasa is a good city for shopping, with a generally wide choice, and fewer hassles as you window-shop than in Nairobi. Once you know where to go for **crafts**, the business of buying **souvenirs** improves markedly. The usual rules apply when **bargaining** – don't start the ball rolling if you're not in the mood, and never offer a price you're not prepared to pay. If you want quite a few items, it's worth looking out for a well-stocked stall and then, as you reach one near-agreement after another with the stallholder, add a new item to your collection. This way you should be able to buy well-finished *vyondo* (sisal baskets) in the range of Ksh600–1000, small soapstone items for Ksh150–500 and simple bracelets and necklaces for around Ksh100 or less. It's much harder to estimate what you should pay for carvings, as the price depends as much on the workmanship as on the size of the piece. Take a look in Haria's (see below) for an idea.

SOUVENIRS

The main tourist street is the stretch of Moi Ave between the Tusks and Digo Rd, and the pavement is periodically lined with souvenir stalls (their abundance fluctuates seasonally and with the fortunes of the tourist industry). Sisal baskets, soapstone, beadwork and fake ebony carvings make up most of what's on offer. Those at the Digo Rd end of Moi Ave tend to be the most aggressive at touting their wares, and getting past without stopping is not easy, while if you do halt, making cool decisions can be difficult. The line of stalls on Chembe Rd seems to be in something of a backwater, and they're more fun to deal with.

FABRICS AND HOUSEHOLD GOODS

Mombasa is a good place to buy the coast's famous fabrics. For the latest *kanga* wrap designs check out the shops in Biashara St (especially the section between George Morura St and Digo Rd), where new designs are sold before they become available anywhere else in Kenya. It's worth checking prices in several shops before buying, and perhaps going in company so you can bargain for several lots at once (they are always sold in pairs and you should be looking to get a pair for around Ksh1000). Woven *kikoi* wraps go for around Ksh500 each. West of Mackawi Rd, Biashara St shifts from textiles to a less gaudy section of household goods – winnowing trays, coconut graters, palm bags, mats, spoons, furniture and the like. More mundane, perhaps, but just as interesting to browse.

CRAFTS AND CARVINGS

Akamba Woodcarvers Village Near the airport; coming from the airport, it's on the left about 300m before you reach Magongo Rd, the main road leading into the city ☎020 2654362 or ☎041 3432241, ⊛akambahandicraftcoop.com; map p.393. If you want to buy carvings, consider making a special trip to this enormous "woodcarvers' village". While it may appear that the art of woodcarving has been reduced here to not much

more than a human conveyor belt, the village is in fact a cooperative, with willing members who are only too pleased to see visitors. Daily 8am–6pm.

★**Haria's Gift Shop** Next to the Hare Krishna Temple, Mohdar Mohamed Habib Rd ☎041 2220198 or ☎0722 640780; map p.398. This is the best place in Mombasa for crafts, and, unusually, they accept most major credit cards. Haria's consistently offers good deals and you may even be able to get things here more cheaply than on the street. Mon–Sat 9am–6pm.

MARKETS

MacKinnon Market Digo Rd; map p.399. The city centre's main market has a splendid abundance of tropical fruit, including such exotics as jackfruit, soursops, custard apples and baobab seeds. Behind the market, there are several good sweet shops and a row of stores devoted to spices, coffee and tea. Daily 7am–6pm.

Makupa Market Corner Majengo Rd and Salim Mwamganga Rd; map p.396. In the heart of the island's low-income housing district, this colourful, multipurpose market has a busy, almost rural atmosphere and is well worth a visit. Daily 7am–6pm.

MUSIC

Mombasa is as good a place as any to stock up on a few CDs or MP3s. Prices are low: expect to pay between Ksh100 and Ksh1000 for a CD, depending on how legitimate the copy is, or around Ksh10/song for MP3s.

Mbwana Radio Service Just off Pigott Place in the Old Town ☎0721 520058; map p.399. The best place for traditional Mijikenda music and Mombasa *taarab*, as well as traditional songs from the Wa-Bajuni people of Lamu district. Mon–Sat 7am–6.15pm.

Zilizo Pendwa Music Store Up an alley just off Raha Leo St ☎0722 728552; map p.398. Try this hole-in-the-wall shop for Kikuyu and other regional Kenyan sounds, as well as the ubiquitous gospel pop. Mon–Sat 7am–6.30pm.

DIRECTORY

Banks There are one or more branches of each of the three main banks in the city centre, all with ATMs. Classic Forex

on Nkrumah Rd (Mon–Fri 8.30am–5pm, Sat 8.30am–2pm) offers reasonable exchange rates.

6

Consulates Tanzania, twelfth floor, TSS Tower, Nkrumah Rd (Mon–Fri 8am–3pm; ☎041 2228595, ✉tancon@ africaonline.co.ke).

Golf Mombasa Golf Club (☎0718 845611, ⓦ mombasagolfclub.com) offers nine holes and costs Ksh1500. Alternatively, try Nyali Golf and Country Club (see p.411).

Hospitals Pandya Memorial Hospital, Dedan Kimathi Ave (☎041 2313577 or ☎0722 206424), is hygienic and efficient, and has an ambulance service, as does St John's Ambulance Service (☎0733 930000, ⓦstjohnkenya.org). Africa Air Rescue (AAR) Health Centre, Pereira Building, Machakos St, off Moi Ave (☎041 2229045), is open daily 24hr. Mombasa Hospital (ⓦmombasahospital.com) is the biggest private hospital on the coast.

Immigration You can get visitor's pass extensions at the immigration office in the Zulfat Hatimy Complex, next to the Mombasa Law Courts on Dedan Kimathi Ave (☎041 2311745 or ☎041 2222676).

Internet access Try Google Cyber on Moi Ave near the Tusks (Mon–Sat 7am–7pm; around 1Ksh/min) among many others.

Mobile phones Safaricom's main customer centre on Moi Ave (Mon–Fri 8am–5.30pm, Sat 8.30am–2pm) is efficient and very helpful.

Pharmacies The staff at Diamond Arcade Pharmacy, Diamond Trust House, Moi Ave (Mon–Fri 8:30am–5.45pm, Sat 9am–1pm; ☎0771 802607), are helpful. Sairoce Pharmacy, also on Moi Ave, is open late (Mon–Sat 7am–10pm, Sun 9am–10pm; ☎0733 320201).

Supermarkets Nakumatt Likoni, Mbaraki Rd, near the Likoni ferry (daily 24hr), and Nakumatt Cinemax, Nyali (daily 24hr); Tuskys Bandari, Haile Selassie Rd and Tuskys Digo, Digo Rd (both Mon–Sat 8am–midnight, Sun 7.30am–9.30pm).

Vaccinations For yellow fever, you first have to go to the Town Hall, Treasury Square, and pay (Ksh600), and then to the Public Health Department in Msanifu Kombo St, opposite the end of Hospital Rd (Mon–Fri 8am–4.30pm, closed lunchtime).

North of Mombasa

While the **north coast** is busier, brasher, and much less pastoral than the **south coast**, the resorts are closer to the airport and Mombasa city and there are more targets for day-trips. It's just not as appealing if you simply want to stretch out on the beach. The resorts start with Nyali, just ten minutes' drive from the city centre.

Nyali and around

Along with some of the north coast's main hotels, **NYALI**, the comfortable resort suburb of Mombasa on the north side of Tudor Creek, has a few minor points of interest. This was the site of **Johann Ludwig Krapf**'s first missionary toehold on the east coast (see p.425) – four years before Livingstone arrived in Africa, in May 1844, Krapf landed at Nyali with his wife and baby daughter to start work as the first missionary in what is now Kenya. His wife died of malaria on July 13, their baby the next day. The pathetic **graves** can be found in Mkomani on the seaward side of Cement Road, 700m south of the *Tamarind* restaurant (see p.413). Opposite the graves, on a small knoll, is the stone **Krapf Memorial** in a quiet, tended garden.

Freretown Bell

The **Freretown Bell**, at the Nyali Road junction, is a replica of the one erected by the Society of Freed Slaves in the 1880s to warn the people of Freretown (named after Sir Bartle Frere, who founded the freed slave community here) of any impending attack by Arab slavers. The original bell hung silently under its small stone arch until the 1920s when it was removed for safekeeping to the nearby Emmanuel Church (Freretown's parish church, erected in 1889), where it is still in use.

Nyali Beach and around

Nyali Beach is often crowded at weekends and holidays but, although fairly narrow, the sand is white and the palms offer some good shade. You can swim here until the tide is more than halfway out, but high tide can almost cover the beach, especially at the northern end – which does mean, however, that body-boarding is sometimes possible when the waves come in over the reef. The reef itself is a fair way out, and most people take a boat rather than try to swim. There are several points of access, but the easiest is by the entrance to *Nyali International Beach Hotel*.

Shiva Cave

One curiosity at the southern end of Nyali Beach is the so-called **Shiva Cave**, containing several *lingams* (phallic representations of the Hindu god Shiva) in the form of stalagmites, and a rock formation resembling the elephant-headed Hindu god Ganesh. The site was discovered by an Indian doctor, who treated a local farmer who had been attacked by a swarm of bees in the cave, after the farmer had found his cow rubbing her udders on the stalagmite – a set of circumstances rich with Hindu symbolism. The area, which includes a pleasant ledge overlooking the ocean, is maintained as a temple by the local Hindu Union, but visitors are welcome – remove your shoes first.

Mamba Village, Botanical Garden and Aquarium

Links Rd • Daily 8am–6pm • Ksh800 • ☎ 0729 403670

Behind Nyali Beach and the hotels, you can't miss **Mamba Village**. Despite the name, the focus here isn't on venomous snakes; this is the biggest crocodile (*mamba*) farm in Kenya. Several pools in a former quarry are home to thousands of crocodiles at all stages of growth, alongside a collection of snakes – cobras, pythons and mambas, among others. The overall effect – croco-burgers in the snack bar, five o'clock Pavlovian bell-ring feedings and unlimited saurian souvenirs – is tacky, and the crocodile trail sits unhappily with the skin-farming half of the "village", which is not on show. Also part of the empire is the adjacent **Botanical Garden and Aquarium**, while **horseriding** is offered by the same organization further down Links Road (beach rides Ksh1000).

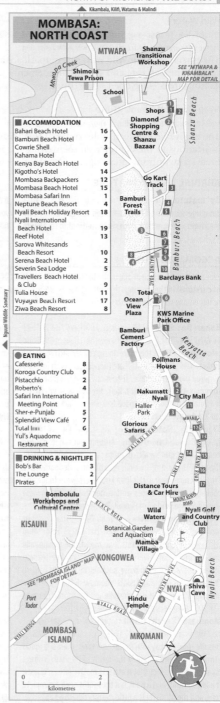

MOMBASA: NORTH COAST

Kikambala, Kilifi, Watamu & Malindi

MTWAPA

Shanzu Transitional Workshop

SEE "MTWAPA & KIKAMBALA" MAP FOR DETAIL

Mtwapa Creek

Shimo la Tewa Prison

School

Shanzu Beach

Shops

Diamond Shopping Centre & Shanzu Bazaar

6

■ **ACCOMMODATION**
Bahari Beach Hotel	16
Bamburi Beach Hotel	7
Cowrie Shell	3
Kahama Hotel	6
Kenya Bay Beach Hotel	6
Kigotho's Hotel	14
Mombasa Backpackers	12
Mombasa Beach Hotel	15
Mombasa Safari Inn	1
Neptune Beach Resort	4
Nyali Beach Holiday Resort	18
Nyali International Beach Hotel	19
Reef Hotel	13
Sarova Whitesands Beach Resort	10
Serena Beach Hotel	2
Severin Sea Lodge	5
Travellers Beach Hotel & Club	9
Tulia House	11
Voyager Beach Resort	17
Ziwa Beach Resort	8

Go Kart Track

Bamburi Forest Trails

Bamburi Beach

MALINDI ROAD

Barclays Bank

Total Ocean View Plaza

KWS Marine Park Office

Bamburi Cement Factory

Kenyatta Beach

Pollmans House

● **EATING**
Cafesserie	8
Koroga Country Club	9
Pistacchio	2
Roberto's	4
Safari Inn International Meeting Point	1
Sher-e-Punjab	5
Splendid View Café	7
Total Inn	6
Yul's Aquadome Restaurant	3

Nakumatt Nyali

City Mall

Haller Park

Glorious Safaris

MWAMBA DRIVE

MOUNT KENYA ROAD

LINKS ROAD

■ **DRINKING & NIGHTLIFE**
Bob's Bar	3
The Lounge	2
Pirates	1

Bombolulu Workshops and Cultural Centre

KISAUNI

Distance Tours & Car Hire

Wild Waters

Nyali Golf and Country Club

BEACH ROAD

Botanical Garden and Aquarium

Mamba Village

MOUNT KENYA ROAD

KONGOWEA

SEE "MOMBASA ISLAND" MAP FOR DETAIL

Port Tudor

NYALI ROAD

LINKS ROAD

MOYNE DRIVE

NYALI

Hindu Temple

Shiva Cave

Nyali Beach

NYALI BRIDGE

MOMBASA ISLAND

MKOMANI

Nguuni Wildlife Sanctuary

0   2
kilometres

Wild Waters

Links Rd • Tues–Fri 10am–6pm, Sat & Sun 10am–6pm; April, Aug & Dec daily 10am–10pm • Ksh1200, Ksh250 for non-sliders; children pay the same as adults • ☎ 0726 337000, ⓦ wildwaterskenya.com

The fifteen slides at **Wild Waters** waterpark are a big hit with children and energetic adults. The bar, café and various amusements – including bumper cars, dry slides and gaming areas – are open until 10pm.

Nyali Golf and Country Club

Across the road from Mamba Village • ☎ 0726 414477, ⓦ nyaligolf.com

The enjoyable eighteen-hole course at **Nyali Golf and Country Club** is – despite stuffy indications to the contrary on the website – open to visitors. In addition to the golf, there's a swimming pool, squash, tennis and a bar-restaurant.

ARRIVAL AND DEPARTURE	NYALI AND AROUND

By matatu A constant stream of matatus ferries passengers back and forth between the city centre and the Freretown junction, with some continuing south into Nyali.

By tuk-tuk or taxi For when you don't fancy cramming yourself inside a matatu or want door-to-door service, tuk-tuks and boda-bodas are always available, as are conventional cabs.

ACCOMMODATION

Whether you're staying in one of the big Nyali hotels or not, all of them will arrange dhow trips and scuba and snorkelling **excursions**. In the evenings they put on bands, acrobat shows and other **entertainments**. Practically every hotel and hostel on this stretch of the coast has wi-fi.

Bahari Beach Hotel Mount Kenya Rd ☎ 0722 206933 or ☎ 0733 477022, ⓦ baharibeach.net. Built in 1971 and refurbished in 1997, this place doesn't have much character and can feel stuffy. But staff are friendly, and with just one hundred rooms it's smaller than many of its neighbours. In common with most Nyali hotels, the rooms – which are reasonably spacious and have balconies – lack sea views. HB **Ksh14,880**

Kigotho's Hotel Links Rd ☎ 0704 414425, ⓦ kigothoapartments.com. Although it's not on the beach, this is quite a nice place to stay, and good value for the area. The bright, spacious apartment-style rooms have fans (but no nets or a/c), plus a kitchenette with fridge and cooking facilities. There's an inexpensive bar and *nyama choma* on site, and a small pool. Room only **Ksh5000**

Mombasa Backpackers Mwamba Drive – no sign, but look for "69" on the black gate ☎ 0701 561233. Large setup with well-thought-out dorms (two mixed, one female-only and one male-only) with a bar-dining room, free tea and coffee, and a nice swimming pool set in a shady garden. Private non-s/c single and double rooms with fan and nets are also available in a house on the grounds. Room only: camping **Ksh500**, dorm beds **Ksh1000**, doubles **Ksh2500**

Mombasa Beach Hotel Mount Kenya Rd ☎ 041 4471861 or ☎ 0722 203143, ⓦ safari-hotels.com. Despite the clumsy 1970s architecture, there's a good atmosphere here – largely the result of its shady, clifftop location and the fact that it attracts mostly African guests. It has good staff and a pool, but the rooms need a complete refit, and the place feels a little overpriced. HB **$125**

Nyali Beach Holiday Resort Bungalows Rd ☎ 041 4472325 or ☎ 0725 849111, ⓦ nbhr.co. Mediterranean-style development right by the beach, with two pools. Most of the 24 large, clean rooms, with a/c, nets and TVs, face both the pool and the beach, as do the self-catering apartments or "cottages". Restaurant, pool bar and safe parking. BB **Ksh12,000**

Nyali International Beach Hotel Bungalows Rd ☎ 020 2648100 or ☎ 0727 228344, ⓦ nyali-international.com. Pleasant and bustling, this is one of the coast's oldest hotels, dating from 1946, with two good pools, five restaurants and extensive gardens. The standard Garden View rooms are OK, but only the marginally more expensive rooms have sea views; a good deal all round. BB **Ksh8000**

Reef Hotel Mount Kenya Rd ☎ 041 4471771, ⓦ reefhotelkenya.com. Once one of Nyali's best, this large and still-friendly 1972 resort is holding up (though the lawn is looking a little ragged), and even its peak-season prices are not excessive. Off-season, if you're not too fussy, it's even better value. There's a good mix of guests and fairly basic food. BB **$120**

★**Tamarind Village** Cement Rd, Mkomani ☎ 041 4474600 or ☎ 0725 959552, ⓦ tamarind.co.ke. Spacious, secure and extremely comfortable, one- to three-bedroom serviced apartments, all with wonderful views across Tudor Creek to Mombasa island, the Old Town and the lights on Nyali Bridge. The *Tamarind* and *Harbour* restaurants are on hand, plus two swimming pools. Room only **Ksh16,000**

★**Tulia House** Just off Links Rd ☎ 0711 955999, ⓦ tuliahouse.com. A very sociable backpackers in a two-storey house, with a pool and a leafy garden, offering dorm beds, a handful of private s/c doubles and a shed filled with sleeping hammocks. Meals are available, and the friendly manager organizes regular games and group excursions – beer pong, movie nights, bowling and snorkelling, among others. Room only: hammock Ksh800, dorm Ksh1200, doubles Ksh4000

Voyager Beach Resort Mount Kenya Rd ☎0720 201155, ⓦheritage-eastafrica.com. With its impressive,

ship-themed communal areas and generally high standards, this is easily the best hotel in Nyali and very good value. It's also very big (236 rooms), with a fun-loving, largely German and Kenyan clientele enjoying three restaurants, four bars, nightly shows and 24hr drinks. It's not quiet, and the relentless nautical theme can be wearing. Facilities include tennis, a PADI diving school (ⓦbuccaneerdiving.com) and all the watersports you'd expect. Al $218

6

EATING

Although growing in number, independent **restaurants**, **bars** and **clubs** are still a bit thin on the ground in Nyali: people tend to check out the hotels, go into Mombasa or explore further north (see p.418).

Hunters Steak House Cement Rd, Mkomani ☎041 474759. When you've had enough coconut fish curry, this is the place for an old-school meat fest, with the tenderest, and possibly most expensive, steaks on the coast (Ksh1600–2500). There's an a/c indoor area, plus garden tables. Wed–Mon 11.30am–2.30pm & 6.30–midnight.

Koroga Country Club Mvita Rd ☎0716 608080. The *koroga* principle is about bringing your friends and family to a place where all the necessary ingredients and cooking utensils are on hand – and then paying to cook the meal yourself. It seems a very male pastime (why can't you do that at home?), but it's popular in Kenya. Here, a watered-down version of *koroga* is also on offer – you order; they cook; you eat (it doubles as a restaurant, in other words). Well-prepared curries start from Ksh500; expect a bill of Ksh1000–2000 a head with drinks, rice and *naan*. If you

want to do real *koroga*, call ahead – prawns Ksh2550/kg, whole chicken Ksh1200 – and find a good spot in the lovely garden. Prices exclude VAT. Daily 11am–11pm.

Rozina's Ratna Square ☎041 4470219 or ☎0724 984373. *Rozina's* covers a range of tastes with nods to India, the UK and US as well as Swahili roots – think pizzas, burgers, seafood and grills. Eat well for under Ksh1500. Daily 11am–10.30pm.

★**Tamarind** Cement Rd, Mkomani ☎041 4474600 or ☎0725 959552, ⓦtamarind.co.ke. With a sublime location above Tudor Creek that offers great views across to Mombasa Old Town, this is unequivocally the best restaurant in the Mombasa area and one of the few places specializing in seafood and doing it really well. Tempting dishes and a pricey wine list mean you're unlikely to come away from dinner with change from Ksh5000 a head. Daily noon–2.30pm & 6–10pm.

From Nyali Bridge: Malindi Road

Beyond the Freretown Bell and the junction for Nyali – always jostling with people trying to get transport to their shifts at the hotels – the main coast road, **Malindi Road**, ploughs through an area of burgeoning suburban growth. This is the Kenya coast that doesn't appear in the brochures, ignored by the resort developers because it's too far from the sea: the primitive living conditions and milling activity here can come as a shock if you're fresh off the plane. There are two very worthwhile destinations in this area, however – **Bombolulu** and **Haller Park** – both recommended whether you're travelling independently or exploring from your beach hotel.

Bombolulu Workshops and Cultural Centre

Just off Malindi Rd, 3km north of Nyali Bridge • **Workshop** Mon–Fri 8am–12.45pm & 2–4.30pm • Free • **Showroom** Mon–Sat 8am–6pm • Free • **Cultural centre** Mon–Sat 8am–4pm • Ksh750 • ☎020 2399716 or ☎0723 560933, ⓦapdkbombolulu.org

Bombolulu is a crafts training school and manufacturing centre, employing more than 150 disabled people, mostly polio victims, in its five handicraft workshops. The **jewellery workshop** is the programme's biggest money-spinner, with hundreds of original designs in metal and local materials, including old coins and seeds, exported to the US and Europe, where you'll come across them in charity gift catalogues. The **showroom** is an excellent place to buy crafts, with somewhat lower prices than you'll find in the souvenir shops. Tragically, a devastating fire in March 2015 destroyed several buildings and all the crafts stock. Although there were no injuries, Bombolulu's recovery will be hard. Visits and purchases are now more important than ever.

6

SWAHILI COASTAL CULTURE

For perhaps two thousand years, **foreign ideas** have been shaping the society, language, literature and architecture of the coast. Immigrants and traders from **Arabia**, **Persia** and **India** have been a subtle and gradual influence here. They would arrive each year in March or April on the northeast monsoon, stay for a few months, and return in September on the southerly monsoon.

Some, either by choice or mishap, would be left behind. Through intermarriage from the earliest times, a distinct ancient civilization called **Swahili** emerged. Swahili, a name thought to derive from the same Arabic root as *sahel*, meaning edge or coast, is also a Bantu language. Known to its speakers as **Kiswahili** (and correctly written kiSwahili), it is one of the most grammatically mainstream of the huge family of Bantu languages, and very typical of the family. Like all old languages used by trading peoples, Swahili contains strong clues about who its speakers mixed with – it's full of Arabic-derived words and peppered with others of Indian, Portuguese and English origin.

The Swahili are not a "tribe" in any definable sense – they are the result of a mixed heritage: families who can trace their roots to foreign shores in the distant past tend to claim superior social status. And, while Swahili culture is essentially **Muslim**, people's interpretation of their religion varies according to circumstance.

THE TOWNS

Like the Swahili language, it used to be thought that the **towns** of the coast began as Arab or even Persian trading forts. It is now known that Mombasa, Malindi, Lamu and a host of lesser-known settlements are essentially ancient African towns that have always tolerated immigration from overseas. With the odd exception, however, efforts to compromise their independence were met with violent resistance. When the Portguese arrived at the end of the fifteenth century, cultural memories of the Moorish occupation of their own country were still

Haller Park

Malindi Rd, 5km north of Bombolulu • Daily 8am–5pm (last entry 4.30pm); feeding time 11am & 3pm for giraffes, 4pm for hippos, 4.30pm for crocodiles • Ksh1400 • ☎ 0722 410064 or ☎ 0733 410064, ⓦ owenandmzee.com

Haller Park (also called **Baobab Adventure and Bamburi Nature Park**) is the outcome of an unusual attempt to rehabilitate a quarry. The Bamburi Cement Factory, whose giant kilns are visible from far and wide, and whose familiar brown sacks are seen all over Kenya, has been scouring the land here for limestone since 1954. In 1971, it began a concentrated programme of tree-planting in an effort to rescue the disfigured landscape, putting a small-is-beautiful principle into conservation practice, making a modest but terrifically successful contribution in a land of huge wildlife parks. Later, as the project gained momentum, fish breeding was established, and large numbers of mammals and birds introduced, including several **hippos**. One of the hippos, **Owen**, is an orphan of the 2004 Indian Ocean tsunami, washed out to sea from his Galana (Sabaki) River home, and later famously befriended here by **Mzee**, an elderly giant tortoise.

The footpaths twist through dense groves of casuarina, a tree known for its ability to withstand a harsh environment, across ground which is mostly below sea level, permanently moist with salty water percolating through the coral limestone rock. The fish-farming side of the operation experiments with different types of **tilapia**, a freshwater fish highly tolerant of brackish conditions, many tons of which now reach shops and restaurants every year, including the park's own restaurant.

Bamburi Forest Trails

Entrance on Malindi Rd, 4km north of Haller Park, opposite the turning for Bamburi Beach Hotel • Daily 8am–6pm (last entry 5pm) • Ksh600; bike rental Ksh300/hr

On a similar theme to Haller Park, and also managed by Bamburi Cement, are the newer **Bamburi Forest Trails**. Intended mainly for joggers and cyclists, there are four looping tracks; bicycles can be rented for use on the trails. There's also a Butterfly Pavilion.

fresh. Accommodation to Islam was not on their agenda and, despite a long acquaintance with the coast, they never established an enduring colonial presence. They fared better in Goa on the Indian coast, further along the same monsoon trading route.

THE SLAVE INHERITANCE

Historically, **slavery** on the coast was quite different from the kind of slavery associated with the Atlantic slave trade. Although refugee and convict slaves were not uncommon, pawn-slavery was a more structured version of the institution. For example, the **Mijikenda** peoples (see p.424), who lived in the coastal hinterland, maintained close links with the coastal towns, trading their produce and providing armed forces when the towns were under threat, and receiving, in exchange, goods from overseas, especially cotton cloth and tools. As traders, the Swahili periodically accumulated surpluses of grain on the coast at times of severe drought inland. In exchange for famine relief, Mijikenda children or marginalized adults would then be taken to the towns by their relatives and fostered with Swahili families with whom they had links – to become pawns, or in effect domestic or farm slaves. Later, they married into their adoptive families, or paid off the debt and returned inland. But sometimes circumstances altered and, for various reasons, a small number of these indentured labourers were sold overseas, though the trade was always fairly insignificant.

When, in the late eighteenth century, the **slave trade** itself became a major aspect of commerce, and the available foreign goods (firearms, liquor and cloth) became irresistible, then any trace of trust in the old arrangements vanished. The weak and defenceless were captured and sold to slavers from the coast, often to end up on Dutch or French plantations in the Indian Ocean, or in Arabian households. And, with the domination of the Sultan of Oman on the coast in the early nineteenth century, and the large-scale migration of Arab families to East Africa, slaves from the far interior were increasingly set to work on their colonial coastal farms and plantations. When the British formally freed the slaves in 1907, they became a new social class in Swahili society.

Nguuni Sanctuary

5km inland from Haller Park • Prebooked visits only, through Haller Park's main office • Ksh500 • ☎ 0721 357876, ⓦ thebaobabtrust.com

Nguuni Wildlife Sanctuary is the third of Bamburi Cement's sites, well known for its herds of farmed **eland** and **oryx antelope** and its ostrich farm. The sanctuary also has more than twenty ponds and lakes, making it a diverse and attractive ecosystem and good for bird-spotting.

ARRIVAL AND DEPARTURE   FROM NYALI BRIDGE: MALINDI ROAD

By matatu Matatus from Mombasa GPO or Abdel Nasser Rd come along this way, usually travelling as far as Mtwapa town on the other side of Mtwapa Creek.

EATING

Cafesserie Ground floor, City Mall, Malindi Rd ☎ 020 2023769, ⓦ cafesserie.com. Urbane café with high ceilings and a vaguely French flavour, managing to create a sophisticated ambience despite sitting in a mall parking lot. They make good, expensive pastries, and breakfasts such as muesli (Ksh450) and eggs Benedict (Ksh700), plus continental offerings along the lines of sandwiches, salads and pizzas. Daily 7.15am–midnight.

Splendid View Café Malindi Rd ☎ 0721 514565. Sister establishment to the *Splendid View* in downtown Mombasa (see p.406), this café may sport an ostentatious facade, but inside it serves a similar array of cheap and cheerful snacks, curries and tandoori dishes (chicken biryani Ksh450), to eat in or take away. Tues–Sun noon–2pm & 7–10pm.

DRINKING AND NIGHTLIFE

Bob's Bar Birgis Complex, near City Mall ☎ 0787 914448. Also known as *Murphy's Irish Pub*, this is a convivial place for a drink (beer Ksh240), with a mix of tourists and locals, flatscreens for sports and good live music, usually on Sun, as well as karaoke every Mon. Daily 24hr.

The Lounge Ground floor, City Mall, Malindi Rd. This popular, slick, modern lounge bar has plenty of terrace seating and music that gets steadily louder as the night wears on. There's no dancefloor per se, but DJs still come in from Nairobi to play on weekends, when the place gets packed. Beer Ksh250, cocktails from Ksh680. Mon–Thurs & Sun 5.30pm–2am, Fri & Sat 5.30pm–5am.

North coast beaches

Kenyatta and Bamburi beaches, together with **Shanzu** just to the north, are the heart of the north coast. If you're just coming for a day-trip, there should, in most cases, be little difficulty in visiting a hotel and using its facilities. The exceptions are the all-inclusive places, which naturally charge admission (usually around Ksh4000 for the day or evening, including lunch, pool access and all drinks). The beaches themselves are entirely public; it's access to them that has been progressively restricted by the hotel developers. Either way, *Sarova Whitesands* (see below) and *Serena Beach* (see p.419) are the nicest hotels along this stretch.

6

Kenyatta and Bamburi beaches

Kenyatta Beach is almost the only beach in the country where you'll see droves of ordinary Kenyans by the seaside. There's a great family atmosphere here – and consequently little or no hassle. The water goes a long way out at low tide, exposing plenty of coral pools and vast stretches of sand for undisturbed walks. There are **sailing boats** for rent and trips offered (check they have life jackets), and at the fringes under the low coconut trees **peddlers** sell ice creams and sodas, snacks and drinking coconuts, while others rent out inflated car inner tubes. For something different, try the Swiss-run **go-kart track** and **bulldozing arena** (yes, bulldozing) at the northern end of Bamburi, just off the main road (Tues–Sun 4–10pm; karting/10min Ksh1500 (adults), Ksh500 (children); bulldozing/30min Ksh1700 (adults), Ksh1500 (children); ☏0721 485247, ⍟mombasa-gokart.com).

Nearly thirty beach hotels throng the 6km shoreline that makes up **Bamburi Beach**. The coconut-shaded sands tend to be buzzing with visitors and beach boys, but at least the sea is swimmable until the tide is more than halfway out and there are decent **snorkelling** spots towards the northern end, past *Severin Sea Lodge* – although a deep channel separates the reef from the shoreline all the way from Nyali to Shanzu.

ARRIVAL AND DEPARTURE   KENYATTA AND BAMBURI BEACHES

By matatu Matatus from Mombasa GPO or Abdel Nasser Rd come along this way, usually going as far as Mtwapa town on the other side of Mtwapa Creek before returning to the city.

ACCOMMODATION

Bamburi Beach Hotel Bamburi Beach ☏041 5485611 or ☏0722 203600, ⍟bamburibeachkenya.com. Unexceptional mid-sized resort hotel with a nice freeform pool, but slow service. On the plus side, most rooms have sea views. Facilities include a PADI diving school, glass-bottomed boats, snorkelling, squash courts and a gym. Most guests are on AI. HB Ksh9500

Cowrie Shell Bamburi Beach ☏0733 888779 or ☏0729 061000, ⍟cowrieshell.co.ke. A block of well-furnished, very high-standard self-catering apartments at the northern end of the beach, ranging from studios to spacious three-bedroom affairs, all with balconies and kitchens. There's a pool in the central courtyard, and a bar/restaurant near the beach for those who don't feel like cooking. Only the three-bedroom apartments have sea views. Room only Ksh7000

★**Kahama Hotel** Malindi Rd, Bamburi Beach ☏0729 949171 or ☏0725 961788, ⍟kahamahotel.co.ke. The former *Octopus Hotel*, just back from the beach, is pretty good all round for the price, with 32 decent, spacious rooms with nets and TVs and a nice pool. The *Pitcher and Butch* sports pub is here, with regular music nights and live bands. The rates prove a very good deal, though they're bumped up about 300 percent at Christmas. BB Ksh5950

Kenya Bay Beach Hotel Malindi Rd, Bamburi Beach ☏041 5487600 or ☏0725 991500, ⍟kenyabay.com. One of the old generation, better maintained than many others, but starting to look a bit worn around the edges. Although it feels smaller than most Bamburi hotels, it still has 106 rooms (a/c, nets, TV, safe), very good staff and a good mix of nationalities. There's a watersports centre, and for the price you can't really complain. BB Ksh7040

Neptune Beach Resort Off Malindi Rd, Bamburi Beach North ☏041 5485701, ⍟neptunehotels.com. Refreshingly lacking in pretension, this hotel is simply furnished and well maintained, a fun package destination with excellent food, good staff, lots of activities and watersports, and a cheerful atmosphere. BB $162

★**Sarova Whitesands Beach Resort** Malindi Rd, Bamburi Beach ☏020 2128000 or ☏0719 022000,

6

ⓦsarovahotels.com. One of the biggest hotels in Kenya, with the longest seafront on the north coast and not a *makuti* roof in sight. The grounds include extensive, interconnecting pools and busy restaurants, and the rooms all have nets, a/c, DSTV and large safes. On offer are all the activities you'd expect. HB $246

Severin Sea Lodge Off Malindi Rd, Bamburi Beach ☏041 2111805, ⓦseverinsealodge.com. Large, well-run resort hotel, with excellent sports and watersports and incredibly motivated staff. Rooms have the lot – a/c, TV, nets, safes and balconies. The *Imani Dhow* restaurant is a converted, beached Zanzibari *jahazi*. Great value for fifty weeks of the year: prices more than double over Christmas/New Year. Eco-Tourism Kenya Bronze Award. HB $102

Travellers Beach Hotel & Club Malindi Rd, Bamburi Beach ☏041 5485121, ⓦtravellersbeach.com. Big,

package-tour setup that crams a lot of rooms into the half-board *Beach* on one side and the all-inclusive *Club* on the other. You can swim into the lobby then slide out again, but you can't go on the beach at high tide, when it's submerged: four pools and lots of activities compensate. Dull gardens, and somewhat tenement-like room blocks, though the rooms are spacious and well appointed. They have a very good Indian restaurant, the *Sher-e-Punjab* (see below). HB $274

Ziwa Beach Resort Malindi Rd, Bamburi Beach ☏0721 777969 or ☏0733 474482, ⓦbamburiresort.com. Budget beach hotel just above the sands, with a cheap bar, a deck and murky green pool. The airy rooms are decked out in rustic style, with reed walls, wooden decks, a/c and nets, and you can self-cater in the basic kitchens provided. The handful of sea-view rooms are the same price as the rest, but non-resident rates are still too high. Room only $100

EATING

In addition to the **hotel restaurants** there are plenty of other eating and drinking places, most of which line the unpretty **Mombasa–Malindi road**. The majority offer free transport from nearby hotels.

Roberto's Bamburi Beach, behind the Indiana Hotel ☏0773 433777, ⓦrobertosmombasa.com. Refreshingly unpretentious and reasonably priced Italian restaurant just above the shoreline, and one of the only places in town where you can find good wood-fired pizzas (from Ksh600) and home-made pasta (from Ksh850). The ice cream is made fresh every morning, as well. Mon–Fri 9am–1pm & 2–6pm, Sat 9am–2pm.

Sher-e-Punjab Travellers Beach Hotel & Club, Malindi Rd, Bamburi Beach ☏041 5485121, ⓦtravellersbeach .com. Unusual among the hotel restaurants for having a reputation for style and quality. Vegetarian (*paneer* tikka, vegetable kebabs), chicken (*jalfrezi*, korma) and Mughlai (*rogan josh*, Mughlai biryanis) dishes, and a very good-value Sun lunchtime buffet (Ksh1750) including vegetarian options. Count on Ksh1200–1500 a head if ordering à la

carte. Daily 12.30–2.30pm & 7.30–10.30pm.

Total Inn Behind the Total garage, Ocean View Shopping Plaza, Malindi Rd, Bamburi Beach. If you wondered where hotel staff can afford to eat, the answer is in places like this: basic African dishes like *matumbo* and *sukuma*, plastic chairs, and not a lobster in sight. Most items are less than Ksh100. Daily 6.30am–6pm.

Yul's Aquadome Restaurant Next to Bamburi Beach Hotel, Malindi Rd, Bamburi Beach ☏0715 01211, Waquadrom-yuls.com. Very reliable spot, based at Yul's watersports centre, with one of the longest (and most consistently available) menus on the coast, and now more than twenty years old. Great pizzas (from Ksh790) and steaks, excellent boneless chicken tikka and naan bread (Ksh1190), and very good ice cream. Gets busy at weekends. Daily 9am–11pm.

DRINKING AND NIGHTLIFE

Pirates Kenyatta Beach ☏0787 890490. For many people, the main attraction on Kenyatta Beach is this combination of restaurant and breezy bar. The restaurant serves good, if not

cheap, Kenyan dishes and seafood (mains Ksh400–700), and the beach bar is the venue for popular nightly discos, with a mixed crowd and a variety of music. Daily 9.30am–2am.

DIRECTORY

Banks There are Barclays and KCB ATMs in City Mall, and another Barclays in the Bamburi shops just north of the *Sarova Whitesands Beach Resort*.

Post office There's a small post office branch in the

Bamburi shops.

Supermarkets The best-stocked supermarket in the area is the large Nakumatt in City Mall, although there's another in Mkomani.

Shanzu Beach

At the northern end of the stretch of coast between Mombasa island and Mtwapa Creek, **Shanzu Beach** is dominated by exclusive (if not particularly upmarket) holiday clubs. It does have a couple of other attractions, however, and it's possible to swim even at fairly low tide, with very good **snorkelling** for much of the year.

6

RESPONSIBLE SNORKELLING, DIVING AND FISHING

Coral reefs are the world's most fragile ecosystems. A reef is a living entity: every cluster of coral consists of thousands of individual organisms called polyps, constantly growing outwards as the older ones die and calcify and become covered in new growth. Solid though it seems, coral is extremely sensitive to sea temperature increases, and of course very vulnerable to physical damage by tourists or fishermen. When snorkelling, diving or fishing, it's worth bearing the following points in mind:

When mooring a boat, ensure you use established buoys, or drop anchor well away from the coral.

Dive and swim carefully, and never touch the coral. Even gentle abrasions can kill some polyps and coral suffocates if covered with silt or sand thrown up by a careless swipe of fins. If you wear fins, use them only in open water and use your hands to swim when near coral.

Don't feed the fish, as it may cause stress and encourages dependency. It also destabilizes the food chain and can cause some species to become aggressive (just like monkeys).

Don't collect souvenirs. Collecting shells, dead coral and starfish disrupts the ecosystem and is illegal in most countries, including Kenya – as is all trade in sea-turtle products. Getting caught when you arrive home can land you in serious trouble. Buying marine souvenirs, rather than collecting them yourself, is no better, although they are widely for sale. Although the law is not enforced, selling shells is illegal.

Big-game fishing (the season runs July–April) reduces the population of natural predators, increasing the populations of their prey, in turn increasing pressure on organisms further down the food chain. Among the sportfishing fraternity, falling catch rates have spurred talk of introducing quotas. Happily, most boat charterers now operate a tag-and-release policy.

Shanzu Transitional Workshop for Disabled Young Women

1.3km east of Malindi Rd • Mon–Sat 9am–6pm • ☎ 0733 994007

The **Shanzu Transitional Workshop for Disabled Young Women** is run by the Mombasa Girl Guides. Here, a group of women get on-the-job training in practical crafts skills, turning out a small selection of well-made clothes (including great Bermuda shorts), jewellery and leatherwork, all of which is for sale.

ARRIVAL AND INFORMATION   SHANZU BEACH

By matatu Matatus for Shanzu from Mombasa GPO or Abdel Nasser Rd usually go as far as Mtwapa town on the other side of Mtwapa Creek before returning to the city. Some pause at the junction of the Malindi Rd and Shanzu Rd, others turn down towards the coast proper and drop and pick up at Shanzu shops.

Services Next to *Sonia Apartments*, in Shanzu, you'll find lots of shops, including a cybercafé at Kay Adventure Tours (Mon–Sat 8.30am–6.30pm).

ACCOMMODATION

Mombasa Safari Inn Shanzu Tourist Rd ☎ 0733 430996 or ☎ 0733 925736. One of the few cheapies in Shanzu, in the little "town centre" itself – friendly, and with adequate rooms that come with nets, fans and cold showers. It has a popular outdoor bar and restaurant. Room only **Ksh1500**

★ **Serena Beach Hotel** Shanzu Beach ☎ 041 5485721 or ☎ 0732 125000, ⍟ serenahotels.com. Beautifully put together with a melange of Moorish and Swahili design, this is the standout proposition on this stretch of coast, and indeed anywhere between Mombasa and Mtwapa. As in all *Serena* hotels, the standard rooms (all with a/c, DSTV and safes) are on the small side and drinks are pricey. Activities, most of them free to guests, include floodlit tennis and a/c squash courts, snorkelling, kayaking and sailing. Kids are well looked after. PADI diving school. Eco-Tourism Kenya Bronze Award. HB **$385**

SEA TURTLES ON SHANZU BEACH

Several parts of Shanzu Beach, notably at *Serena Beach Hotel*, are popular egg-laying sites for **sea turtles**. There are educational talks about these endangered marine reptiles at the hotel (Tues 7pm), where the ban on motorized watersports is enforced (much of this sea area is a marine national park).

EATING

Shanzu is pretty tacky when it comes to eating places and watering holes, with most places catering purely for a captive market of **package tourists**. Don't expect to find any ordinary Kenyan establishments.

Pistacchio Shanzu Tourist Rd ☎0722 713611 or ☎0721 221017. This is the place to come for live music with your meal, with entertainment of some sort every evening except Tues. Most of the specialities are Italian, mainly pizza (from Ksh650) and pasta, though there are grills as well, including crocodile (Ksh945). Painfully touristy (even the menu is in German), but fun if you're in the right mood. Daily 8.30am–11pm.

Safari Inn International Meeting Point Shanzu Tourist Rd ☎0722 671475, ⓦfacebook.com/Safari InnMombasa. A cheery *makuti*-roofed bar and restaurant with a mellow atmosphere. It's not a bad place to eat, with menu offerings that span the globe – from German and Swiss to Thai and Chinese ("so people don't get bored"). Most mains under Ksh1000. Daily 8am–2.30am.

Mtwapa and around

Mtwapa Creek marks the edge of Greater Mombasa, where tropical suburbia, with its villas, supermarkets, clubs, restaurants – and poverty – is more or less left behind. North of here, the road heads with fewer distractions up to Kilifi, Watamu and Malindi.

The town of **MTWAPA** itself is in many ways the most distinctive of the road towns leading north out of Mombasa – and it's certainly the fastest growing. The most obvious reasons to pause here are **boats** and **big fish** – the beautiful **creek** is a focus for yacht owners and game-fishermen – but there are also some good spots for eating, drinking and rambunctious nightlife. Plus, if you have a few hours to spare, don't overlook the fascinating **ruins of Jumba la Mtwana** and **Mtwapa Heritage Site** just north of the creek mouth.

Jumba la Mtwana

The sign for the 3km access road is 2km north of Mtwapa Creek bridge • Daily 8am–6pm • Ksh500 • ⓦ museums.or.ke • If you're travelling by public transport along the coast highway and are dropped off at the junction, you have a good chance of getting a lift down the access road

Well worth stopping for, and worth an excursion in their own right, are the **ruins** of **Jumba la Mtwana**. The remains of a wealthy fourteenth- or fifteenth-century **Swahili settlement**, this national monument – one of three between Mombasa and Malindi – covers a small area, in an enchanting setting among baobabs and lawns, just above the beach; there's a small, single-room **museum** of photos and artefacts from the site, and a beautiful restaurant, *Monsoons* (see p.422).

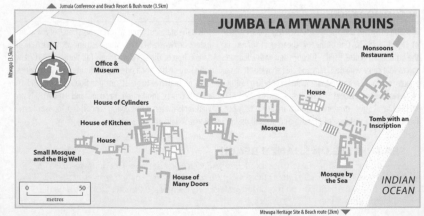

Jumuia Conference and Beach Resort & Bush route (3.5km)

JUMBA LA MTWANA RUINS

Mtwapa (3.5km)

N

Office & Museum

House of Cylinders

House of Kitchen

House

Small Mosque and the Big Well

House of Many Doors

Mosque

House

Mosque by the Sea

Monsoons Restaurant

Tomb with an Inscription

INDIAN OCEAN

0   50
metres

Mtwapa Heritage Site & Beach route (2km)

The phrase *jumba la mtwana* means "house of the slave", but the site has been deserted for some five hundred years and probably had a different name in the past. This seems a strange place for a town, right on an open shore with no harbour, and it's possible the inhabitants were pushed here by raiding parties from inland groups, and relied on Mtwapa Creek as a safe anchorage for the overseas traders who would have visited yearly. Jumba is fortunate in having good water, but why it was deserted, and by whom, remains a mystery.

The site

6

Compared with Gedi, further north (see p.457), Jumba's **layout** is simple. Though it lacks the eerie splendour of that much larger town, it must once have been a sizeable settlement; there were three mosques within the site and a fourth just outside. Most of the population would have lived in mud-and-thatch houses, which have long since disintegrated. In Swahili culture, building in stone (in fact, coral "rag" of different densities) has traditionally been used for mosques, and was the preserve of certain privileged people, principally the long-settled inhabitants of a town. Newcomers would almost always build in less durable materials appropriate to their shorter-term stake in the community.

The **people of Jumba** seem to have been very religious and hygienic – virtues that are closely associated in Islam. Cisterns and water jars, or at least the remains of them, are found everywhere among the ruined houses, and in most cases there are coral blocks nearby which would have been used to squat on while washing. The latrines are all stone-lined with long-drops. Of course, it is possible that the poorer people of Jumba lived in squalor in their mud huts, yet even the **House of Many Doors**, which seems to have been a fifteenth-century lodging house, provided guests with private washing and toilet facilities.

Mosque by the Sea

The best of Jumba's mosques is the **Mosque by the Sea**, which is right behind the beach itself, and shows evidence of a separate room for women, something that is only just becoming acceptable again in modern mosques. The cistern where worshippers washed is still intact, with coral foot-scrapers set nearby and a jumble of tombs behind the north wall, facing Mecca. One of these has a Koranic inscription carved in coral on a panel facing the sea and must have been the grave of an important individual: "Every soul shall taste death. You will simply be paid your wages in full on the Day of Resurrection. He who is removed from the fire and made to enter heaven, it is he who has won the victory. The earthly life is only delusion."

Jumba Beach

Jumba Beach is a good place to while away an afternoon – in fact, late afternoon, when the atmosphere hangs among the ruins like cobwebs, is probably the best time to come. Strange but attractive **screw pines** grow in the sand, aerial-rooted like mangroves. It's a good spot for a swim and a picnic: there are toilets and showers by the ticket office.

Mtwapa Heritage Site

To the north of Mtwapa Creek mouth • ⓦ tinyurl.com/kjb2up • Easily reached on foot from Mtwapa town – take the track to the right by the huge baobab tree on the way down to the beach

The virtually unexcavated ruins at **Mtwapa Heritage Site** sit in twelve acres of thick forest behind Mtwapa's tiny beach. Old Mtwapa dates from the twelfth century and scattered here are the remains of more than sixty houses, a mosque and a tomb. Although it's a gazetted monument (in other words, protected by law), there's no physical protection of the site, and its security looks uncertain. Enjoy the strange jungle ruins while you can: if you come down here soon after dawn, you'll also see plenty of monkeys, hornbills, monitor lizards and even dik-diks.

ACCOMMODATION | MTWAPA AND AROUND

★ **Sweet Lodge** East of the main road, just north of the market ☎ 0723 014675 or ☎ 0720 382016. Clean, properly managed and reasonably comfortable, this is the best B&L in Mtwapa, with quiet, scrupulously clean s/c and non-s/c rooms with fans and nets around a landscaped courtyard. There are larger rooms in a second block across the street, but they tend to be dark. Cold showers only. BB **Ksh1000**

EATING

★ **La Marina** On the north shore of Mtwapa Creek, east of the bridge ☎ 020 2434726 or ☎ 0723 223737, ⊛ lamarinarestaurant-mombasa.com. Mtwapa's top restaurant, serving conventional meals on the creek shore – a very atmospheric spot for dinner (expect to spend at least Ksh2000/head). They also offer dhow cruises, with a barbecue lunch or dinner and music and other entertainments. To get here, turn right at the signboard 550m north of the bridge, and head along the dirt track for 1.5km. Daily 10am–10pm.

★ **Monsoons** Jumba la Mtwana ruins ☎ 041 2012666 or ☎ 734 663370, ⊛ letseat.at/Monsoons. Serving seafood by the seashore near the House of the Slave, this new establishment makes for a great excuse for a trip to the ruins. Good, Italian-styled mains from under Ksh1000,

including linguine with crab and chilli (Ksh1000), various lobster dishes (around Ksh2500) or fillet steak (Ksh1200). Tues–Sun 11am–6pm.

The Moorings On the north side of Mtwapa Creek, west of the bridge ☎ 0736 547923 or ☎ 0723 032536, ⊛ themoorings.co.ke. This floating restaurant, in a fine, breezy location, is a good place for talk and tales – and to hook up with others, either in person or via the noticeboard. They have reasonably priced drinks and snacks, and a largely seafood menu that vies with *La Marina* (see above) for quality – though it's less consistent. They also organize sundowner dhow cruises for $25/person. Main courses Ksh750–3000. To get here, turn left 300m north of the bridge. Tues–Sun 10am–11pm.

DRINKING AND NIGHTLIFE

Bahnhof 300m north of Mtwapa Creek bridge on the west side of the road. Formerly German-owned sports bar, with big screens, pool tables, DJs and plenty of cold beer. It's usually heaving to the point of overflowing on a Sat night, but always a good place to catch the local vibe. Beer Ksh150. Daily 24hr.

Casuarina Nomads 300m north of Mtwapa Creek bridge on the east side of the road ☎ 0713 918920. Although often full of prostitutes, the pleasant, *makuti*-roofed *Casuarina* is a perennial favourite among locals and more adventurous tourists and expats, with a good

atmosphere, discos, occasionally traditional dancers at weekends, and good, chargrilled meat and seafood (from Ksh500) at all hours. Ksh100 entry charge from 10pm Wed–Sun. Daily 24hr.

Lambada North side of Mtwapa, north of Casuarina ☎ 0733 777557. Industrial-strength mega-club – one of the coast's biggest – with pool, sunken dancefloor and plastic-covered sofas, as well as theme nights and live music at weekends. It's a mild-mannered restaurant by day, serving *nyama choma* (beef Ksh1200/kg) and other local dishes. Daily 24hr.

SWAHILI PROVERBS AND SAYINGS

The Swahili are renowned for the imagery, rhythm and complexity of their **proverbs**. *Kangas* always have some kind of adage printed on one side and these are often traditionally Swahili. For more *kanga* aphorisms, see ⊛ glcom.com/hassan/kanga.html.

Haraka, haraka: haina baraka Haste, haste: there's no blessing in it (very commonly heard).
Nyumba njema si mlango A good house isn't (judged by) its door.
Mahaba ni haba, akili ni mali Love counts for little, intelligence is wealth.
Faida yako ni hasara yangu Your gain is my loss.
Haba na haba kujaza kibaba Little by little fills the jug.
Kuku anakula sawa na mdomo wake A chicken eats according to her beak.
Mungu alihlolandika, haliwezi kufutika What God has written cannot be erased.
Heri shuka isiyo kitushi, kama shali njema ya mauwa Better an honest loincloth than a fancy cloak (of shame).
Mke ni nguo, mgomba kupalilia A wife means clothes (like) a banana plant means weeding.

Kikambala

If you're staying in Mombasa or one of the north coast resorts, the low-key resort area around **KIKAMBALA**, a few kilometres north of Mtwapa, is about as far as you'd want to come for a day-trip. Parts of the coastal strip here are still thickly forested and the beach itself is a glorious white expanse, though it's 2–3km from the highway. With the countryside here being very flat, the sea goes out for nearly 1km, and the lagoon isn't deep enough to swim in except at high tide. The Israeli-owned *Paradise Hotel* at Kikambala was the location of an al-Qaeda **suicide bombing** in 2002 in which sixteen people died, including two Israeli children and five members of a Giriama dance troupe. The tragic episode achieved notoriety when the hotel was rebuilt, but the dancers' families received scant compensation.

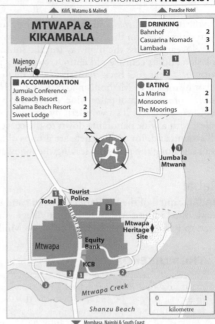

MTWAPA & KIKAMBALA

■ DRINKING
Bahnhof 2
Casuarina Nomads 3
Lambada 1

Majengo Market

■ ACCOMMODATION
Jumuia Conference
& Beach Resort 1
Salama Beach Resort 2
Sweet Lodge 3

● EATING
La Marina 2
Monsoons 1
The Moorings 3

Jumba la Mtwana

Tourist Police
Total
Mtwapa Heritage Site
Equity Bank
Mtwapa
KCB
Mtwapa Creek
Shanzu Beach

0   1
kilometre

ARRIVAL AND DEPARTURE   KIKAMBALA

By matatu Mtwapa-based matatus from Mombasa GPO or Abdel Nasser Rd usually go only as far as Mtwapa town before returning to the city. From Mtwapa, you'll need to find another matatu going down towards the Kikambala hotels. Vehicles normally approach the beach properties from the northern access road, 7.4km north of Mtwapa Bridge (signposted for the *Sun'n'Sand Hotel*).

Coming from the south, you can also cut down to the beach from the turning in Majengo, 5.3km north of Mtwapa Bridge, a sandy road that heads straight to the *Jumuia Conference & Beach Resort*. Such vehicles can be fairly infrequent, so the alternative would be to get to one of those junctions and then hop on a piki-piki or boda-boda.

ACCOMMODATION

The Kikambala **hotels** are virtually the last on the coast north of Mombasa until you reach Kilifi. There are few independent restaurants or bars at Kikambala, and most people stick to their hotels.

Jumuia Conference & Beach Resort Beachfront road, Kikambala (5.3km north of Mtwapa Bridge, then 3km along murram) ☎0738 713444, ⓦwww.resortjumuia .com. Formerly known as *Kanamai*, this sprawling, pretty place under the coconuts, run by the National Christian Council of Kenya, has been comprehensively updated in recent years. The rooms, while not cutting-edge-elegant, are spacious and well furnished, with good fans and nets.

Large pool. BB Ksh7000
Salama Beach Resort Beachfront road, Kikambala (just south of Jumuia) ☎0735 453253, ⓦsalama-beach-resort.com. Cool, attractive, German-owned bungalow-style hotel, right by the beach, with an infinity pool. Rooms have terraces and a/c (small supplement), and their *Maridadi* restaurant has a good reputation. Minimum stay three nights. BB €118

Inland from Mombasa

MAZERAS is just 20km up the hill from Mombasa. If you're coming from Nairobi, this small town marks the end of the long vistas of scrub; it's perched right on the edge of the steep scarp, amid bananas and coconuts. If you're travelling by road, it isn't a bad idea to break your journey here and savour the new atmosphere. The *hotelis* serve good, flavourful, coastal *chai* and there is a slightly unkempt **botanical garden** (daily 6am–6pm; free) on the Mombasa side of town, which makes a good break for the travel-weary. Across the highway (on the southwest side) and up the hill a little way is a **mission** and its century-old church, signs of an evangelical presence in the hills behind Mombasa that goes back, remarkably, more than 150 years.

For historians of Methodism and the Church Missionary Society or, perhaps more likely, connoisseurs of palm wine, the **road to Kaloleni**, 22km north of Mazeras, is a required sidetrack. It's a wonderfully scenic drive in its own right, looping through lush vales, with a wide panorama down to the coast to the east. Masses of **coconut trees** sway all around and, invariably, there are groups of flamboyantly dressed Mijikenda women walking along the roadside: leaving the highway you're instantly back in rural Kenya.

Rabai

RABAI, capital of the **Wa-Rabai Mijikenda** and site of the earliest Christian mission to be established in East Africa, is the first village you come to, 4.5km from Mazeras, on the road to Kaloleni. It's also one of only two Mijikenda villages still occupying its original

---

THE MIJIKENDA

The principal people of the coastal hinterland region are the **Mijikenda** ("Nine Tribes"), a loose grouping whose Bantu languages are to a large extent mutually intelligible, and closely related to Swahili. They are believed to have arrived in their present homelands in the sixteenth or seventeenth century from a quasi-historical state called Shungwaya, which had undergone a period of intense civil chaos. This centre was probably located somewhere in the Lamu hinterland or in the southwest corner of present-day Somalia. According to oral tradition, the people who left it were the Giriama, the Digo, the Rabai, the Ribe, the Duruma, the Chonyi, the Jibana, the Kauma and the Kambe (not to be confused with the Kamba of the highlands around Machakos).

All these tribes now live in the coastal hinterland, the **Giriama** and the **Digo** being the largest and best known. Like so many other Kenyan peoples, the Mijikenda had age-set systems that helped cut across the divisive groupings of clan and subclan to bind communities together. And these involved some fierce traditions: the installation of a new ruling elders' age-set, for example, required the killing and castration of a stranger. This, like most of the milder practices of tribal tradition, was abandoned in the early twentieth century.

The Mijikenda have always had a diverse **economy**. They were cultivators, long-distance traders, makers of palm wine (a Digo speciality now diffused all over Mijikenda-land), hunters, fishermen and herders – the Duruma especially and, at one time, the Giriama, were almost as fond of cows as the Maasai. They still maintain local market cycles. These are four-day weeks in the case of the Giriama: days one and two for labour, day three for preparation, and day four, called *Chipalata*, for the market.

Despite acquiring all the trappings of modern life along with most Kenyan peoples, the Mijikenda have been unusually successful at maintaining their cultural identity. They warred with the British in 1914 over the imposition of taxes and the demand for porters for World War I. And they have preserved a vigorous conservative tradition of adherence to their old beliefs in spirits and the power of their ancestors. While this is very apparent from the resurgence of interest in preserving their traditional sacred groves, or *kayas* (see p.453), and getting graveposts (*vigango*) returned from foreign collections, it's also notable in the relative ease with which you can pick up CDs of **traditional music**, especially in Mombasa: wonderful rhythms and some very delicate *chivoti* flute melodies.

If you're a little off the beaten track, are really interested and have time to spare, even casual enquiries will elicit invitations to **weddings** or **funerals**, where the old traditions – and music – are still very much the centrepieces, despite a veneer of Christianity or Islam. Many Mijikenda have found conversion to **Islam** helpful in their dealings with coastal traders and businessmen. The conversion seems to be the latest development in the growth of Swahili society, and that change is probably the biggest threat to Mijikenda cultural integrity.

kaya (see p.453). A German pastor, the Reverend **Johann Ludwig Krapf**, came here in 1846 after losing his family at Nyali (see p.410), and left his mark on the community when, 41 years later, the imposing **St Paul's church** was erected. The centre of the village, marked by a cluster of schoolrooms and sports fields, lies 500m off the main road on the right as you come into Rabai from Mazeras. For the church and museum, fork left after 200m.

Rabai National Monument

Opposite the entrance to St Paul's • Daily 8am–6pm • Ksh500 • ⓦ museums.or.ke

6

The first church to have been built in Rabai (1846–48), and the first church in Kenya, now houses the modest **Rabai National Monument**. Not the most exciting place in Kenya, it contains a few well-presented photographs but little else. The entrance fee, however, includes a guided tour and explanation, with visits to a full-scale replica of the *kaya* (tourists are not allowed to wander through the real one), and the village's nearby viewpoint over the countryside. Adjacent to the museum is the house where Krapf used to live, and the nearby cottage of Johann Rebmann, Krapf's proselytizing partner, is used as a school room. Between them, the two missionaries managed to explore a great deal of what is now Kenya without the demonstrations of firepower so many of their successors thought necessary. Krapf worked out the grammar of the Swahili language and contributed a partial translation of the Bible (not published in full until 1890).

Ribe

RIBE (the main village of the Wa-Ribe Mijikenda) is more substantial than Rabai, but harder to get to. Some 7km northeast of Rabai, a road snakes up to the right from the deep valley floor: Ribe village – a few small shops and a basic bar-restaurant – is 1.5km along here.

Ribe cemetery

Fifteen minutes' walk from Ribe centre, through the *shambas* and dense undergrowth, is a tiny **cemetery**, regularly cleared of weeds and creepers, near the site of Ribe's Methodist mission, itself crumbled to its foundations and now completely overgrown. It isn't hard to find, and worth visiting if only to take a look at the pathetic graves of those few **missionaries** who struggled all the way here before succumbing in what must have been nearly impossible conditions. They were often very young: the Reverend Butterworth, whose carpentry skills ensured him a welcome on arrival, died aged 23, just two months after coming ashore; they used his new tools to make the coffin. It isn't surprising that the cemetery faces out to sea: towards Mombasa, supplies, the mail and new settlers.

Kaloleni

The paved road from Mazeras comes to its end at **KALOLENI**. On the way, you pass through dense coconut groves where many of the trees have been initialled to avoid ownership disputes. The tapping of **palm wine** (*mnazi*), banned by the government, is still widely practised here, with the **Giriama** section of the Mijikenda leading the field. They call palm wine "the mother of the coconut", since tapping the trees for juice hinders formation of the nuts.

Tapping is done by cutting off the flower stem, binding it tightly and allowing the sap that would have produced new coconuts to collect in a container – usually a baobab pod – tied to the end. Here it ferments rapidly and has to be regularly collected. Variations in the local demand for *mnazi*, which is most often drunk at community gatherings like weddings and funerals, and in the coastal market for *copra* (the dried coconut flesh used in soap and oil manufacture), tend to influence the owners of trees in their decision whether to tap or to grow *copra*. You will see trees incised with step-notches (enabling the tapper to reach the top), that end several metres below the crown, indicating that a tree has been left for several years to develop coconuts.

Although, strictly speaking illegal, **palm wine** is locally available up and down the coast. In Kaloleni, it usually comes in plastic mineral water bottles, and costs about Ksh100 for a litre. You drink it (discreetly) through a reed straw with a coconut-fibre filter.

ARRIVAL AND DEPARTURE INLAND FROM MOMBASA

By bus and matatu There are frequent buses and matatus from Mombasa to Kaloleni via Rabai (from the Jomo Kenyatta/Mwembe Tayari junction), which makes it an easy day-trip from the coast. If you arrive in Kaloleni before mid-afternoon, you'll be able to catch a matatu further north to Kilifi, and from there back to Mombasa or onwards to Malindi. Leaving Kaloleni, there are frequent buses and matatus back to Mombasa via Rabai and Mazeras, or to Mariakani, for Nairobi, and less

frequent matatus north to Kilifi, 40km away (catch these at the bottom of the hill by the Kilifi junction).
By car and bike Fuel isn't always readily available in Kaloleni, so drivers need to fill up in Mombasa or Mariakani. The road from Kaloleni to Kilifi is particularly memorable for its scenes of local life in the coconut groves and forests – it's a great route to drive (see p.330) or cycle along, though sometimes difficult after heavy rain.

The south coast

South of Mombasa, a continuous strip of beach runs between Likoni and Msambweni, backed by palms and broken once or twice by small rivers. Along the 100km stretch of coast south from Mombasa to the Tanzanian border there's just one highly developed resort area, **Diani Beach**. South of Diani, the coast is little known and, in most tour operators' minds at least, nobody stops again until they reach **Shimoni**. This is great news if you have the time to go searching out untrodden beaches. With your own vehicle, or on an organized trip, you can also visit the **Shimba Hills National Reserve** and the neighbouring **Mwaluganje Elephant Sanctuary**, either overnight or on an easy day-trip excursion.

Along with the rest of the coast, the hotels in this area have been hard hit in recent years by the precipitous drop in foreign tourism; most are still open for business, though **prices** tend to be lower than usual.

Likoni and Ngombeni

The fact that you have to take the **Likoni ferry** (see p.403) to get to the south coast emphasizes its separation from Mombasa, and the queues and usual delays have tended to deter hotel developers a little. **LIKONI** itself is a busy suburb of Mombasa, straggling down the southbound road for nearly 5km. A coast road, served by infrequent matatus, runs around the creek mouth to the east to **Shelly Beach**, facing the ocean. Named for its shells and once a popular local resort area, the beach is narrow and the sea here only feasible for swimming at high tide. With the closure of the big *Shelly Beach Hotel*, all the local alternatives have also closed.

A little further south, as you leave the outskirts of Likoni, a turning to the east down to the ocean at the straggling village of **Ngombeni** is the first of several sidetracks off the highway that enable people with their own vehicles to find private coves and beaches, many of them backed by patches of coastal forest. You need a 4WD vehicle and an adventurous spirit – and possibly GPS. It's surprising how uninhabited the immediate coastline is, and how many unspoilt beaches are waiting to be discovered.

ACCOMMODATION LIKONI AND NGOMBENI

There is no resort development between Mombasa and Tiwi Beach, but **private homes** are popping up in one or two spots.

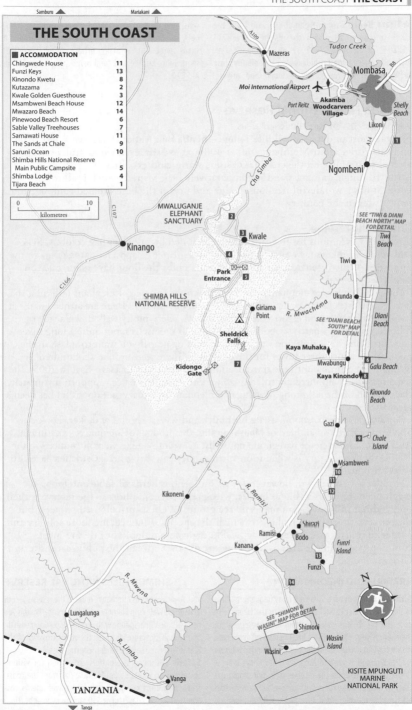

THE SOUTH COAST

■ ACCOMMODATION

Chingwede House	11
Funzi Keys	13
Kinondo Kwetu	8
Kutazama	2
Kwale Golden Guesthouse	3
Msambweni Beach House	12
Mwazaro Beach	14
Pinewood Beach Resort	6
Sable Valley Treehouses	7
Samawati House	11
The Sands at Chale	9
Saruni Ocean	10
Shimba Hills National Reserve Main Public Campsite	5
Shimba Lodge	4
Tijara Beach	1

6

★**Tijara Beach** East of Ngomeni (5.5km from the Likoni ferry ramp, then 3km towards the sea) ☎0734 755754 or ☎0722 701701, ⓦtijarabeach.com. Idyllically located coastal hideaway, conveniently close to Mombasa but completely secluded and private, consisting of four, well-spaced, luxury cottages (fans, nets, sea breezes but no a/c), set in gardens around a shady pool. The virtually private beach, excellent snorkelling, birdlife and coral caves are a bonus. Wi-fi. Al **$870**

Shimba Hills National Reserve

Daily 6am–6pm • $25 • ⓦ kws.org • 310 square kilometres

Kenya's most underrated wildlife refuge, **Shimba Hills National Reserve** is less than an hour's drive from Mombasa and, at 400m above sea level, wonderfully refreshing after the humidity on the coast (take some warm clothes). The hilly park of scattered jungle and grassland is comparatively little visited, which is all to the good. It has a wonderful treehouse lodge and one of the best-situated camping and *banda* sites in the country.

Around the reserve

The reserve is famous for its thick **forest**, inhabited by **primates** like colobus, Sykes' and vervet monkeys, as well as bushbabies and greater galagos; **leopards** range in the same area. Other predators are rare in Shimba Hills: the lions have gone, but you might see a **serval**.

You are likely to see **elephants**, especially from the vantage of Elephant Hill or at the nearby **Sheldrick Falls**, particularly if you go early in the day. There are armed guards at Elephant Hill who will escort you to the falls. It's a very pretty walk down a steep hillside, and then a partly wooded trail to the falls themselves, but quite a long hike back up again. Take drinking water, and swimming gear if you want to splash in the pool. Allow about three hours for the excursion. There were around six hundred elephants in Shimba until the translocation of half of them to Tsavo East in 2005. The remaining three hundred are still arguably more than Shimba can support: fortunately, the creation of the adjoining Mwaluganje Elephant Sanctuary (see opposite) has been a great success.

Buffalo are fairly common, as are **bushbuck** and several species of **duiker**. Look out also for the park's small herd of **Maasai giraffe**, the product of a tentative experiment. Although Shimba never had giraffe naturally, a few individuals were introduced in the 1990s, though the jury is still out on whether they can thrive here. **Ostriches** have also been introduced.

Shimba is best known, however, for its indigenous herds of **sable antelope**, magnificent animals as big as horses, with great, sweeping horns. The reserve is their only habitat in Kenya. You may well see groups of chestnut-coloured females, but the territorial, jet-black males, for which the species is named, are more solitary and harder to find. If you have a guide he'll know where to look, but they're most commonly seen in the area overlooking the ocean, between the public campsite and Giriama Point.

ARRIVAL AND INFORMATION SHIMBA HILLS NATIONAL RESERVE

Arrival and departure There are fairly frequent matatus to the small district capital of Kwale from the Likoni ferry dock, but no obvious way of getting to the reserve from there unless you're lucky with a lift. The reserve's main gate is 3km beyond Kwale, along the elephant-dunged *murram* road to Kigango. If you're driving, it's best to have a high-clearance 4WD to enter the reserve itself. You should get away with an ordinary car in dry weather, but some reserve roads may be too rough for it: the rangers at the gate will tell you. An adventurous alternative route to the reserve (or out of it) links Kwale with Shimoni via Kidongo Gate. For this you need GPS or a smartphone with Google Maps/Google Earth, and a high-clearance 4WD for the rocky crossing of the Ramisi River and several other tricky stretches.

Safaris The most straightforward option for visiting Shimba is on a safari from Mombasa or from the coast. Trips from most coastal hotels and travel agents cost about $150 for a day-trip or $300 for an overnight trip.

ACCOMMODATION

Sable Valley Treehouses On the southeastern slopes below the reserve ☎0733 435341 or ☎0706 754216, ⊚ sableretreat.com. Highly attractive and offering very private, elevated rooms (just two among the trees), with your own staff, in a superb location. Package $500

Shimba Hills National Reserve Main Public Campsite 3km from the main gate; reservations through KWS in Nairobi ☎0726 610508, ⊜ reservations@kws.go.ke, ⊚ kws.org. The main public campsite is located at one of the best vantage points in the reserve. a thickly forested bluff

hundreds of metres above the coconut-crowded coastal plain. It's worth spending the night up here just for the sunrise. Room only: camping $20, twin *banda* $80

★ **Shimba Lodge** ☎0711 367345, ⊚ shimbalodge.net. Like *Treetops* (see p.193), *Shimba* is a "tree-hotel", though much better than the original. The standard rooms with shared ablutions are basic, but when there are bushbabies on the branch outside and a fish eagle in the trees, you don't spare too much thought for luxuries. The best feature is the tree-level walkway and platform. FB $190

Kwale

KWALE, the capital of the district of the same name, is quite a pleasant, bustling little hill town, with lots of shade and reasonable facilities, including ATMs and fuel.

ARRIVAL AND DEPARTURE KWALE

By matatu There are matatus all day to Likoni (Ksh80) and Kombani (the junction for Tiwi and Ukunda; Ksh50). Occasionally matatus go to Kinango and from there to

Mariakani and Samburu on the Mombasa–Nairobi highway.
By car If you're driving, allow a good hour between Kinango and Kwale, especially after rain.

ACCOMMODATION

★ **Kutazama** On the Goloni ridge 6km north of Kwale ☎0723 4023433 or ☎0733 708309, ⊚ kutazama.com. This owner-managed boutique lodge is a stunning place to stay, blending with the landscape and full of tribal artefacts. It has just two, very luxurious and secluded, guest villas, each with a deck and spa pool, and the services of your own chef and butler. Breathtaking views, walks in the area and a split-level infinity pool overlooking a great

loop of the Cha Shimba River make this a perfect honeymoon hideaway. Package €700

Kwale Golden Guesthouse Town centre, on the north side of the tarmac ☎0722 326758, ⊚ kwalegolden guesthouse.com. The best option in Kwale town, offering very clean rooms with nets, ceiling fans and electric showers (smaller rooms are a little cheaper). Breakfast is a motel-style buffet. BB Ksh1500

Mwaluganje Elephant Sanctuary

Northwest of Shimba Hills National Reserve; the main gate is beyond the Shimba Hills park entrance, 14km west of Kwale, then 2km along a signposted track to the right • Daily 7am 6pm • $15 • ☎0722 995837, ⊕ elephantmwaluganje.co.ke • You can get here on an organized tour with several Mombasa-based operators, including Lofty Tours (see p.404), or with your own transport, which enables you to drive around the sanctuary

Mwaluganje Elephant Sanctuary, situated on the slopes of the privately owned Goloni Escarpment, is a remarkable success story of community ecotourism, created in 1995 to defuse conflict between the local Duruma farmers and the district's elephants, which had made a habit of trashing crops and killing farmers. After consultation between the local people, KWS and the Eden Wildlife Trust, 240 square kilometres were set aside for the sanctuary, separated along a third of its boundary from farmland with electric fencing, but with a corridor left open to Shimba Hills to keep the elephants' migration route open. The low-lying areas around the Manolo River are dominated by baobab, while thick Brachystegia forest covers the escarpment's flanks, and harbours one of the densest concentrations of elephants in Africa. You're guaranteed to see elephants, and, in time, it's hoped that threatened species can be relocated here from other parts of Kenya. Other mammals are thin on the ground, but there's prolific birdlife.

Tiwi Beach

The first real magnet on the coast south of Mombasa is **Tiwi Beach**, which lies a couple of kilometres east of the main road. Popular among budget travellers having a bit of a

6

splurge, Tiwi rates as genuine tropical paradise material and also attracts lots of Kenya resident families down from Nairobi. The reef lies just offshore, and there are good **snorkelling** opportunities at high tide, especially at the northern end. With the exception of the large *Amani Tiwi Beach Resort* at its southern end, Tiwi is still cottage territory, with a handful of plots vying for business. The main drawbacks (though you might think they're advantages) are the relative isolation of the beach from Mombasa and Diani, and the lack of restaurants and bars outside the cottages and guesthouses. The clear pluses are fewer tourists and fewer beach boys. In the dry season, you can walk to the south end of Tiwi Beach and wade across the Mwachema River to Diani Beach and the strange **Kongo Mosque**, right next to the *Indian Ocean Beach Resort*.

ARRIVAL AND DEPARTURE   TIWI BEACH

By car If you're driving, there are two access roads down to Tiwi Beach from the main south coast highway. The northern road (signposted for *Sand Island* and *Hill Park*) is a narrow sandy track some 17km from the Likoni ferry; the second, about 1.5km further south, has a bigger clump of signboards and is much wider.

By public transport If you've been dropped at either of the access roads (see above) to Tiwi Beach by matatu,

you're strongly advised not to walk, especially if you have luggage with you: the roads through the cashew woods have seen a number of robberies over the years. Waiting for a ride won't be a huge problem, certainly on the southern access road, where you should get a taxi (Ksh500) and can easily pick up a piki-piki (Ksh100–200). Alternatively, most of the beach properties will happily pick you up for free from the main road if you contact them in advance.

ACCOMMODATION

Tourism **seasons** here tend to reflect the school holidays of the regular, Kenyan resident clients of most of the properties: at Christmas and Easter, advance booking is still a good idea. There isn't much in the real **budget** range, but the extra expense is well worth it if you choose carefully. It's tricky to stay in a **self-catering** cottage without your own vehicle, though some people manage on fruit and fish from vendors and the occasional lift to the shops. Self-catering cottages usually offer the services of a cook/housekeeper for Ksh1000/day.

Amani Tiwi Beach Resort Tiwi Beach ☎ 020 2152088 or ☎ 0724 257105, ⓦ amanitiwibeachresort.com. The beach's only large tourist hotel, with more than two hundred comfortable rooms and a 167m pool, one of the longest in Kenya, which snakes through the garden. Facilities include five restaurants, four bars, a gym and a tennis court, as well as a dive centre and windsurfing on the beach. Wi-fi. HB **$115**
★ **Coral Cove Cottages** Tiwi Beach ☎ 0722 732797, ⓦ coralcove.tiwibeach.com. Spacious two-bedroom self-catering cottages with good bathrooms and an attractive, palm-shaded beach, all decorated with care and bathed in

a laidback mood provided by low-key but helpful management. Dogs and cats, rescue parrots and a troop of vervet monkeys are all part of the atmosphere. The sea here is shallow, good for children, and favoured by egg-laying turtles. Cottage self-catering **Ksh8600**
Hillpark Hotel Tiwi Beach ☎ 040 3300012 or ☎ 0722 328365, ⓦ hillparktiwibeach.com. The former *Maweni Beach*, *Capricho* and *Moonlight Bay* properties, amalgamated under a single management, include self-catering cottages and hotel rooms, a restaurant and a good pool and pool bar. *Maweni* has a variety of cottages with stunning sea views in

---

THE DIGO

Most of the people who live along Kenya's southern coastal strip are **Digo**, and their neat rectangular houses, made of dried mud and coral on a framework of wood, are a distinctive part of the lush roadside scene. Digo women tend to dress very colourfully in multiple kangas. Although they belong to the Mijikenda group of peoples, the Digo are unusual in traditionally having **matrilineal inheritance**: in other words they traced descent through the female line, so that a man would, on his death, pass his property on to his sister's sons rather than his own. It is an unusual system with interesting implications for the state of the family and the position of women. However, the joint assault of Islamic and European values over the last century has shifted the emphasis back towards the male line, and in many ways, women in modern Digo society have less freedom and autonomy than they had a hundred years ago. The site of one of the Digo's ancestral villages, a sacred forest at Kaya Kinondo, near Diani Beach, can be visited with a Digo guide (see p.434).

beautiful gardens roamed by dik-diks; *Capricho* is slightly pricier, with well-designed vault-roofed cottages and plenty of cool space; and *Moonlight Bay* has four cottages and a restaurant. Wi-fi. BB **$100**, cottage self-catering **$110**

★**Olerai Beach House** Tiwi Beach ☎0707 705073 or ☎0722 512476, ⊛holidayhomeskenya.com. Delightful, very spacious family beach house with excellent staff, superb swimming pool and rock water slide, gardens, a coral cave area for shady table-tennis sessions and a virtually deserted beach front. Sleeps eight to twelve, either on self-catering basis, or all-inclusive with exceptionally good meals. Whole house self-catering **Ksh30,000**, AI per person **Ksh12,000**

★**Sand Island Beach Cottages** Tiwi Beach ☎0722 395005, ⊛sandislandbeach.com. These nine cosy, whitewashed self-catering cottages are all sea-facing and come in different sizes, sleeping two to six people each. The long-established, shady site is very attractive, with the sand island exposed at low tide just metres across the lagoon, and safe swimming possible at all states of the tide. The ruins of old slave quarters stand in the grounds. Wi-fi. Cottage self-catering **Ksh9700**

Twiga Lodge Tiwi Beach ☎040 3205126 or ☎0721 577614, ✉twigakenya@gmail.com. Lively, secure and good value, this hostel and campsite trades on a reputation

Diani Beach

Diani Beach ought to fulfil most dreams about the archetypal palm-fringed paradise. The sand is soft and brilliantly white; the sea is turquoise and usually crystal-clear; the reef is a safe thirty-minute swim or a ten-minute boat ride away; and, arching overhead, the coconut palms create pools of cool shade and keep up a perpetual slow sway as the breeze rustles through their fronds. While competition for space always threatens to mar Diani's paradisal qualities, the recent downturn in tourism has knocked out some of the hotels, while the droves of hustlers, or "beach boys" (see p.432), dwindled to a few relatively easily brushed-off diehards. **Security** has been tightened up, with *askaris* posted all the way along the beach outside every property, and tight security at hotel entrances.

Running 300m behind the beach and separated from it by bush, the **Diani Beach road** feels – in the high season – like Kenya's number-one strip. Fortunately, forest and scrubby bush separate the road from the shore, although more of the **Diani Forest** disappears every year as one new plot after another is cleared.

established in the 1970s, and is perennially popular with budget travellers and overlanders with their own vehicles. The budget rooms are simple but good value (some have verandas), and the superior rooms, which cost twice as much, are big, bright and airy. You can also camp. The bar-restaurant does decent meals (8am–9pm), and the bar stays open as late as the last customer. Room only: camping **Ksh400**, double **Ksh3000**

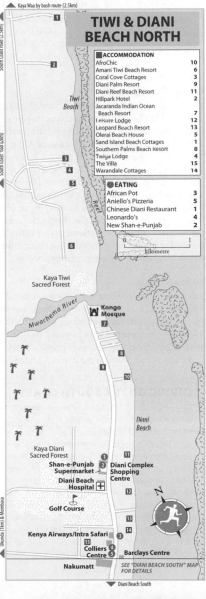

▲ Kaya Waa by bush route (2.5km)

South Coast road (2.5km)
South Coast road (2km)
Ukunda (3km) & Mombasa

TIWI & DIANI BEACH NORTH

Tiwi Beach

■ ACCOMMODATION	
AfroChic	10
Amani Tiwi Beach Resort	6
Coral Cove Cottages	3
Diani Palm Resort	9
Diani Reef Beach Resort	11
Hillpark Hotel	2
Jacaranda Indian Ocean Beach Resort	7
Leisure Lodge	12
Leopard Beach Resort	13
Olerai Beach House	5
Sand Island Beach Cottages	1
Southern Palms Beach Resort	8
Twiga Lodge	4
The Villa	15
Warandale Cottages	14

● EATING	
African Pot	3
Aniello's Pizzeria	5
Chinese Diani Restaurant	1
Leonardo's	4
New Shan-e-Punjab	2

Reef

0 ———— 1
kilometre

Kaya Tiwi Sacred Forest

Mwachema River

Kongo Mosque

Diani Beach

Kaya Diani Sacred Forest

Shan-e-Punjab Supermarket
Diani Beach Hospital ✚
Diani Complex Shopping Centre

Golf Course

Kenya Airways/Intra Safari

Colliers Centre
Barclays Centre

Nakumatt

N

SEE "DIANI BEACH SOUTH" MAP FOR DETAILS

▼ Diani Beach South

6

6

BEACH BOYS AND SAFETY

Spending some peaceful time on the beach can sometimes seem virtually impossible because of the **hustlers** plying their wares, their camel rides, their boat trips or just themselves. Fortunately, the problem has abated in recent years, but a few beach-boy pesterers, in theory all licensed in some way, still hang on. People have different ways of dealing with them. Ignoring their greetings is considered rude, and may well not deter them. One solution is to strike up a friendship of sorts with one beach boy, to buy at least something, or to go on a boat trip. Once you have a friend, and have done some business, you should find you can then use the beach with fewer hassles from the others. It's not so easy for single women, but the principle for most situations still applies – don't fight it. There is no need, incidentally, to feel physically threatened on the beach. Every hotel has its *askaris* (security guards) posted along the boundary between the hotel plot and the beach, and they usually stay alert to the slightest sign of trouble – which is rare indeed.

Along Diani Beach

Enjoying yourself on Diani isn't difficult and there are plenty of activities on offer (see p.435). As on other beaches in Kenya, all of Diani Beach is open to the public, and there are **access paths**, some signposted, between many of the hotels: if you can't find one, you can always access the beach by visiting one of the hotels. If you're doing something that depends on having enough beach (football or volleyball) or sufficient sea depth (wind- or kitesurfing, or snorkelling in the lagoon), it's worth checking the **tides** (see p.391), as the lagoon often drops to ankle depth at low tide, while at high tide all but a thin strip of the beach is generally under water.

If you're on Diani Beach in early June, look out for the local community fundraiser, **Diani Rules** (Ⓦdianirules.com), which you're liable to get roped into. From goat races to dhow races, Frisbee tournaments to volleyball, it's all grist to the mill and part of a three-day party that generally swirls around *Forty Thieves* beach bar and one or other of the hotels, usually raising money for Kwale District Eye Centre.

Kongo Mosque

At the far north end of the beach, at the mouth of the Mwachema River; it's most easily reached through the grounds of the Jacaranda Indian Ocean Beach Resort • No set opening hours • A small donation for the upkeep of the mosque is expected

For a short cultural excursion, visit the **Kongo Mosque**. Surrounded by venerable baobabs, the mosque sits beyond the *Jacaranda Indian Ocean Beach Resort*'s boundary fence and the inevitable *askari*. Also known as **Diani Persian Mosque**, the building is enigmatic and disconcerting, the barrel-vaulted mosque with its five

DIVING ON THE SOUTH COAST

Many hotels on the south coast have **dive centres**, where you can do everything from a basic beginner lesson plus two assisted dives (around €165) to a full course giving you an internationally recognized PADI qualification (€500 for the Open Water Diver). Before choosing a centre, take time to compare their equipment, and ask them about their environmental policy, safety procedures and general experience. They should at the very least have up-to-date PADI accreditation, and ideally be affiliated to Scuba Schools International (SSI). One of the oldest and best-established outfits, with an excellent reputation and good equipment, is **Diving the Crab** (Ⓣ0723 108108, Ⓦdivingthecrab.com), which has several dive bases on Diani Beach. **Diani Marine**, which runs the *Diani Marine Village*, also has an excellent reputation.

If you already have scuba certification, two-dive boat trips cost around €110, including equipment. If you're a complete novice, you can often take a free dip in the pool wearing diving equipment, to test your affinity. If you're qualified, but haven't dived for a while, you should take a pool check at one of the hotels' PADI schools, which is usually free of charge, before going out to sea.

heavy wooden doors brooding like a huge tomb under the trees, although recent unattractive extensions have somewhat altered its character. Named after the former forest of the area, the mosque is thought to be the one remaining building – maybe the only stone one – of a **Wa-Shirazi** settlement here (see p.444) that grew up in the fourteenth or fifteenth century around the first safe anchorage south of Mombasa. If you want to have a close look, take photos, or even have a chance of going inside if you're suitably dressed, you should first introduce yourself to one of the elders who are usually sitting nearby.

Diani Forest

For a walk, or a jog, head south along the Diani Beach road, which has more shade than the northern stretch. Towards the end of the tarmac surface are some wonderful patches of jungle, comprising the dwindling **Jadini** or more correctly **Diani Forest** ("Jadini", disappointingly, turns out to be an embellished acronym made from the initials of members of a white settler family who once owned most of the land around here). There's the almost obligatory snake park, but if you'd like to search for some **animals** in the wild rather than support this venture, then take one of several tracks leading off inland that will take you straight into magnificent areas of hardwood forest, alive with birds and butterflies, and rocking with vervet and colobus monkeys. The most impressive stands of forest are the isolated *kayas*, or **sacred groves**, of which there are at least three along the Diani Beach road: **Kaya Diani**, on the north side of the Leisure Lodge golf course (easy to drive or walk to the edge of the forest, and several trees have plaques proclaiming the grove's status); **Kaya Ukunda**, west of the entrance to *Diani Sea Lodge*; and **Kaya Kinondo**, south of *Pinewood Beach Resort*. Kinondo is the first *kaya* to be officially opened to visitors (see p.434).

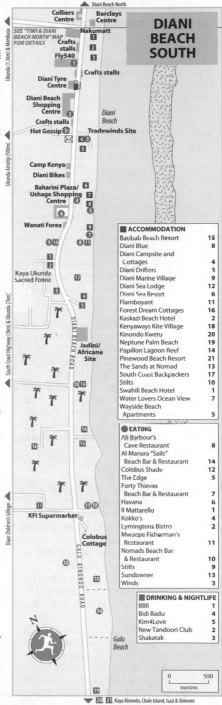

ACCOMMODATION

Baobab Beach Resort	15
Diani Blue	8
Diani Campsite and Cottages	4
Diani Drifters	3
Diani Marine Village	9
Diani Sea Lodge	12
Diani Sea Resort	6
Flamboyant	11
Forest Dream Cottages	16
Kaskazi Beach Hotel	2
Kenyaways Kite Village	18
Kinondo Kwetu	20
Neptune Palm Beach	19
Papillon Lagoon Reef	14
Pinewood Beach Resort	21
The Sands at Nomad	13
South Coast Backpackers	17
Stilts	10
Swahili Beach Hotel	1
Water Lovers Ocean View	7
Wayside Beach Apartments	5

EATING

Ali Barbour's Cave Restaurant	8
Al Manara "Sails" Beach Bar & Restaurant	14
Colobus Shade	12
The Edge	5
Forty Thieves Beach Bar & Restaurant	7
Havana	6
Il Mattarello	1
Kokko's	4
Lymingtons Bistro	2
Mwaepe Fisherman's Restaurant	11
Nomads Beach Bar & Restaurant	10
Stilts	9
Sundowner	13
Winds	3

DRINKING & NIGHTLIFE

BBII	1
Bidi Badu	4
Kim4Love	5
New Tandoori Club	2
Shakatak	3

6

VISITING KAYA KINONDO

Kenya's first *kaya* or **Mijikenda sacred forest** (see box, p.453) to open to visitors is the Digo tribe's **Kaya Kinondo** (daily 8am–5pm; Ksh1000; ☎0722 446916 or ☎0720 050147, ⓦkaya-kinondo-kenya.com), behind Kinondo Beach, at the southern end of Diani Beach. Kaya Kinondo was first inhabited by the Digo in 1560 and abandoned as a village site in 1880.

There's an interpretation centre by the entrance that is well worth spending fifteen minutes looking around before you set off on your forest walk. To enter the forest itself, you visit with a Digo guide from the centre (no independent wanderings allowed), wrapped in a *kaniki* (indigo-dyed calico sarong) that you will be loaned. Photography is encouraged (except at the grave sites near the centre), but you are expected to show deep respect for the impressive forest environment – which means no running around and no kissing and cuddling. Behave as if you were in a church or mosque and you won't go far wrong. As soon as you leave the sunlight and enter the cathedral-like gloom of the understorey, a hush tends to fall on proceedings, as you concentrate on stepping over the buttress roots of forest giants and avoiding contact with trailing creepers or ant-covered surfaces.

There's a more light-hearted side to the experience, in any case, as tree-hugging (transmit all your cares and fears to the tree) and stories of "herbal Viagra", aphrodisiac essences and cures for back pain in pregnant women are all part of the two-hour nature walk as you're accompanied, if you're lucky, by someone of seemingly limitless knowledge. The animals you'll see, apart from monkeys, are mostly smaller denizens of the undergrowth, but no less worth spying for that – fiery red squirrels, slow-flying shade-loving butterflies and giant millipedes and, possibly, an elephant shrew snuffling through the leaf litter with its probing proboscis.

Colobus Cottage

6.8km south of Nakumatt • Mon–Sat 8am–1pm & 2–4.30pm • Guided tours Ksh750 • ☎0711 479453, ⓦcolobusconservation.org

Diani's **Angolan colobus monkeys**, whose population is estimated at around 1500, have come in for special attention since the early 1990s, as concern has mounted over land encroachment and deaths from speeding cars. The resultant campaign, spearheaded by Colobus Conservation, has put up warning signs, speed bumps and ingenious wire, rope and wood "colobobridges" at known danger spots over the road, which the monkeys quickly learnt to use. You can pick up more information at **Colobus Cottage**, where they also run a rescue centre for injured animals, and learn about Colobus Conservation's active campaigns to halt illegal tree-felling by local hotel owners; their one-hour guided tours of the centre also include a walk through the coastal forest. They also welcome **volunteers** here.

ARRIVAL AND DEPARTURE   DIANI BEACH

By public transport If you're coming to Diani by public transport from Mombasa, first take the Likoni ferry (see p.403) and then catch a matatu for Diani Beach. If there are no direct matatus, get one to Ukunda (see p.441), and then take a connection down to the beach road.

By taxi From Mombasa, taxis cost around Ksh4000 to Ksh5000, depending on your final destination.

By plane Ukunda (Diani Beach) airstrip is right in the thick of things, less than a 10min drive from most hotels along the beach (just west of the beach road, 1.5km

south of the junction). Taxis are always waiting (estimate a minimum fare of Ksh700 and allow a total fare of Ksh150/km for more than 3km), but most hotels will include a free transfer if you've booked a room. There are daily flights to Nairobi with SafariLink (ⓦflysafarilink .com), Jambo Jet (ⓦjambojet.com) and Airkenya (ⓦairkenya.com), and to Maasai Mara and Amboseli with Mombasa Air Safari (ⓦmombasaairsafari.com); MAS also offers connections to Mombasa for its services to Malindi.

GETTING AROUND

Car rental Try Glory Car Hire, Diani Beach Shopping Centre (☎0734 437536 or ☎0723 293333, ⓦglorykenya.com); Kenpal Travel, next to the post office (☎0728 765000, ⓦkenpal.net); or Neslo Tours and Safaris in Ushago Food Court (☎0722 454854 or ☎0717 054265,

ⓦneslosafaris.com), which offers vehicles from Ksh2500/day. **Taxis** Most hotels have taxis in their forecourts, and there's a stand opposite Barclays Bank. Also, try Diani Beach Shopping Centre, where the chairman of the taxi drivers' association is based.

SAFARI OPERATORS AND AGENTS

There are various **safari agents** and operators in the shopping centres along the strip. The following are all worth checking out, although you should always be clear whether you are talking to the operator of the safari in question or simply an agent who is selling it.

Bush2Beach ☎040 3202575 or ☎0722 411566, ⓦbeach2bushkenya.com. Highly regarded for its photographic safaris – they're expensive, though, starting from $4490/person.

DM Tours & Safaris Diani Beach Shopping Centre ☎0722 470382, ⓦdmtours.net. A very wide range of well-organized safaris with landcruisers less than four years old, and a maximum of four passengers.

Intra Safaris ☎0738 719966 or ☎0700 278922, ⓦintrasafaris.com. A well-established safari operator and airline agent.

JT Safaris (aka "The Orange Hut") 8.7km south of Nakumatt opposite Neptune Palm Beach Hotel ☎020 2191922 or ☎0731 110522, ⓦjulius-safaris.com. This outfit has a very good reputation, and can arrange safaris to parks all over Kenya.

ACTIVITIES

Bicycle rental When you tire of the beach and the sea, or of lying under the palm trees, you could rent a bicycle and go off exploring, from about Ksh700/half-day. Bicycle rental outlets come and go: ask at your hotel. Diani Bikes, next to Fun Sport Club on Beach Road, rents out its blue bicycles at negotiable rates (Ksh1500/day is the usual figure quoted; ☎0713 959668, ⓦdianibikes.com).

Boat/canoe trips A trip to the reef on one of the outrigger canoes is highly recommended. The crews know all the good spots for snorkelling, and it should cost you Ksh1000 for up to three hours of pottering about with a captain and one crew. One of the best areas is directly opposite *Baobab Beach Resort*, about 300m out towards the reef, where there is a cluster of coral heads. You can arrange a trip through any hotel reception, or directly on the beach. There are a number of dhow-trip operators, too (see box below).

Diving See box, p.432.

Golf There's an 18-hole course at *Leisure Lodge* (see p.437).

Microlight flights You can take a 20–30min flight (one person plus the pilot), scudding low over the reef and coastal jungle. Coastal Microlights will collect you from your hotel – a 20min trip is around Ksh5000 inclusive.

Skydiving Skydive Diani (☎040 3204320, ⓦskydivediani.com), a relatively new outfit, offers tandem jumps over the beach from 300m, as well as four- to five-day courses that allow you to jump solo; tandem jumps cost $350.

Snorkelling Most hotels offer snorkelling gear (free to all-inclusive guests, or rentable for about Ksh1000). You can float out across the lagoon towards the reef but need

---

DHOW, SNORKELLING, DOLPHIN AND WHALE SHARK TRIPS

Several **excursion operators** are based at Diani Beach and the surrounding area. They pick you up from your hotel either for free or for a nominal extra charge. For the most part, the dhows are not under sail but are powered by on-board or outboard motors. All can be booked direct, or though your hotel. Always ensure there's a usable life jacket for each passenger.

★**Charlie Claws** Diani Beach Shopping Centre ☎0722 205156 or ☎0722 205155, ⓦwasini.com. Day-long dhow, snorkelling and dolphin-searching trips at Kisite Mpunguti Marine National Park, with a seafood lunch at the outfit's own restaurant at the northwest end of Wasini island, which also has a large, landscaped swimming pool. $135 including park fees, drinks, lunch, community visits and all equipment, with pickup from north or south coast, or direct from Shimoni. Scuba-diving, if you're qualified or want to try, costs an additional $30 for one dive, or $50 for two. Closed May 1–June 15.

East African Whale Shark Trust ☎0720 555222, ⓦgiantsharks.org. EAWST organize in-water, whale shark encounters, especially during the peak whale shark season (Feb–March). Prices vary depending on group size and duration, but expect around $150/person.

Paradise Divers Wasini island ☎0718 778372, ⓦparadisediver.net. Well-managed, Hungarian-owned dive and boat operation with a basic tented camp and restaurant on the northeast corner of Wasini. They offer five-day, ten-dive packages from €280.

★**Pilli-Pipa Dhow Safaris** Colliers Centre ☎0722 205120 or ☎0724 442555, ⓦpillipipa.com. Small-group dhow day-trips to Kisite Marine Park for outstanding snorkelling (field guides, masks, snorkels and fins provided), with a late lunch of crab, good wine and Swahili food at a private house on the north side of Wasini island. Departures most days at 8.45am from Shimoni jetty; $135, including marine park fees, all equipment and transfers. Closed May.

6

to be a reasonably confident swimmer: there are no strong currents nor any real danger, but the reef is 600–1000m away and swimming back on the ebb tide can be tiring. A number of companies offer snorkelling trips (see box, p.435).

Wind- and kitesurfing The sheltered lagoon behind the reef is ideal for windsurfing (Ksh2500/hr or often free to all-inclusive guests) and kitesurfing (one-day courses from Ksh11,500). There are kite schools at the *Kenyaways* and *Sands at Nomad* hotels.

ACCOMMODATION

Although there are some good **hotels** north of the Ukunda junction, the much longer beachfront to the south retains some flicker of the pre-hotel era, and this is where most of the remaining forest is. To the north, the scene is brasher and more spoilt. Some all-inclusives are open to casual visitors: you'll pay from Ksh2000 to Ksh4000 for a daytime wristband, including lunch and normal activities. Nearly every hotel in Diani offers free wi-fi. **Budget accommodation** along the beach is sparse, although there are three or four places to **camp**. If you're with your family or in a group, **renting a cottage** is invariably better value than taking hotel rooms, and gives you the chance to cook local food – or have it cooked for you. Most places are regularly visited by fruit and fish vendors and someone to cook and look after the house or apartment for you is usually available for an additional Ksh1000 or so/day. The distances in the following listings are from the Ukunda junction on the Diani Beach road, next to Nakumatt.

CAMPING AND BUDGET ROOMS

Diani Campsite and Cottages 1.4km south ☎0722 683900, ⓦdianicampsite.com; map p.433. Once something of an institution when it was *Dan Trench's* (Trench was the elderly character who opened up Diani Beach in the 1960s), this site fell on hard times, but its new incarnation is a popular standby, with one- to four-bedroom self-catering cottages, most with kitchens and nets, plus double rooms, a pool and the busy *Winds* bar-restaurant (see p.440), as well as a kitesurfing school on site. Campers can use cooking facilities. Room only: camping with own tent Ksh500, camping with rented tent Ksh1000, double Ksh3000, cottage Ksh4500

★**South Coast Backpackers** 6.4km south, then 500m inland ☎0700 713666 or ☎0715 614038, ⓦdianibackpackers.com; map p.433. This full-on party place occupies a surprisingly luxurious villa, with tropical gardens, a fine pool and plenty of fellow travellers to share the bar and restaurant. Accommodation only: camping

with own tent Ksh500, camping with rented tent Ksh700, dorm Ksh1050, double Ksh2600

★**Stilts** 3km south, opposite Ali Barbour's Cave restaurant ☎0722 523278, ⓦstiltsdiani.com; map p.433. Just over the road from the beach, but right in the bush, with five rustic non-s/c *bandas* on stilts, three s/c cottages with nets and fans, well-shaded pitches for camping, plenty of wildlife and a good bar-restaurant. There's solar lighting in rooms and no electric sockets except in cottages – charge your batteries at the bar, where there's also a personal safe for each guest. Room only: camping Ksh500, double Ksh2800, cottage Ksh3600

Wayside Beach Apartments 1.4km south ☎0716 341812, ⓦwaysidebeachapartments.com; map p.433. Fairly spacious Mediterranean-style one- to three-bedroom self-catering apartments, basically furnished, in a building around a good pool and bar-restaurant, but not right on the beach. €50

DIANI WILDLIFE

If you're a **birdwatcher**, Diani's hotel gardens offer spectacular entertainment, though the status of the Diani forest's threatened species is uncertain. Look out for southern banded snake-eagle, spotted ground-thrush, plain-backed sunbird and Fischer's turaco, all of which have been seen here, though the spotted ground-thrush not since the 1980s.

You're unlikely to come across **snakes**. Whether harmless green tree snakes, egg-eating snakes or pythons (the commonest species), or more rarely venomous mambas, those that get anywhere near the hotels tend to be bludgeoned to death by enthusiastic *askaris* who also use their sling shots to keep the local monkeys on the run.

The Diani Beach forest used to be the haunt of **leopards**, but they haven't been seen in this part of the coast for decades now. Venture into the woods at night, however, preferably with a guide, and you will see eyes in the dark – usually those of **bushbabies**.

The most iconic of Diani's wildlife are its rare Angolan colobus monkeys (see p.42). Of the other monkeys, **baboons** are most common, and can be quite aggressive. Their adopted diet of hotel leftovers means they've multiplied greatly, and are not afraid of humans, so keep your distance. Overly tame **Sykes' monkeys** are also becoming a nuisance: don't leave things on your hotel balcony, and close your windows if there's food in the room.

HOTELS AND COTTAGES NORTH OF THE UKUNDA JUNCTION

AfroChic 2.3km north ☎0733 645564, ⊛elewana collection.com; map p.431. A large, Mediterranean-style house packed with Lamu-style furnishings, with just ten cool and spacious rooms with balconies, each differently styled. While it's undoubtedly more chic than Afro, this is a comfortable, personable place to stay, with top attention to detail and first-class food – as you'd expect at this price. It suits many honeymooners making a first trip to Kenya. Room safes, tea and coffee, DSTV and DVDs. FB $726

Diani Palm Resort 2.4km north ☎0729 472883 or ☎0721 459433, ⊛dianipalm-hotel.com; map p.431. Although it's on the landward side of the road, the beach is just 400m away, and this part-Swiss-managed hotel offers all the essentials, with less fuss and at far less expense than most of its neighbours. The 35 rooms are fresh and clean (if a little basic), with nets, TV and fridge, with a handful of one- to two-bedroom apartments for self-caterers. There's a reasonably priced bar-restaurant on site, and a pool. Room only Ksh3000

Diani Reef Beach Resort 1.5km north ☎0724 503322 or ☎0734 786300, ⊛dianireef.com; map p.431. Built in the 1970s and revamped in 2005, this is one of the largest hotels on the coast, on a steep stretch of beach, with three restaurants, five bars and 143 rooms, all cool and comfortable, but with little to distinguish them bar the size of their balconies. The two pools may not be the largest on the coast, but facilities are good, and include the *Evanes* casino, *Sins* nightclub and *Maya* spa. HB $280

Jacaranda Indian Ocean Beach Resort 3.4km north ☎0709 979000, ⊛jacarandahotels.com; map p.431. The northernmost property on Diani Beach, on a huge plot opened in 1992 with – at the time – state-of-the-art, Lamu-style rooms, which have recently been modernized in a way that makes them feel a little bit less special. But it's still a lovely place, and the rambling gardens are popular for weddings. The one hundred rooms have fridges, safes and tea-making kits; those upstairs have balconies looking out across the baobab-studded gardens. On the down side, the pool is too shallow and rather exposed. HB $260

Leisure Lodge 1km north ☎041 2011131 or ☎040 3203624, ⊛leisurelodgeresort.com; map p.431. One of the earlier Diani hotels (1971) but slickly revamped, and in a striking location on low cliffs hollowed by bat-filled caves, above a fine, tree-shaded beach. Five pools soak up the guests from 253 rooms and there's a casino and an 18-hole golf course. Standard rooms lack sea views, but come with a/c, nets and DSTV. PADI diving school, windsurfing school and tennis. HB $280

Leopard Beach Resort 700m north ☎0733 202721 or ☎0724 255280, ⊛leopardbeachresort.com; map p.431. Once stylish, this big resort hotel, set in lush gardens

with ponds and waterfalls, is still regularly updated. There's always a good atmosphere and generally decent food. Superior rooms and cottages have sea views, but overall the 158 rooms (plus new villas with private pools) vary a lot in standard. Steps lead down to the beach. Two relatively modest pools, a PADI diving school and a nice spa complete the picture. HB €220

Southern Palms Beach Resort 2.7km north ☎0733 333366, ⊛southernpalmskenya.com; map p.431. Bright, welcoming package hotel, with a spring in its step. The average-sized rooms, with screened windows (no nets), TV, fridge and safe, are perhaps a bit blandly cosmopolitan (and fourth-floor rooms are a bit of a climb), but the overall, fun approach, with two enormous, 80m freeform pools, four restaurants, five bars and a kids' club, make it ideal for families. Windsurfing, floodlit tennis courts, squash, gym. HB €200

The Villa 500m north ☎0774 307907 or ☎0700 025869, ⊛thevillakenya.com; map p.431. It isn't directly on the beach, but this boutique hotel aims for cool, modern seaside luxury, with suites (some with private plunge pools) decorated in beige and white, and much of the Swahili-style furniture made in their own workshop. There's also a bigger pool on the patio and a spa on-site. BB $150

Warandale Cottages 600m north ☎0724 923585, ⊛warandale.com; map p.431. These six self-catering cottages are extremely pleasant, fresh and spacious. Three are sea-facing, others (cheaper) are set back among the trees, with the advantage of more likely bushbaby and monkey sightings. A daily cook/cleaner is included with each cottage. Ksh8000

HOTELS SOUTH OF THE UKUNDA JUNCTION

Baobab Beach Resort 5.9km south ☎020 2057093 or ☎0733 333303, ⊛baobab-beach-resort.com; map p.433. The 1970s *Robinson Club Baobab* is now an elegant and well-kept all-inclusive, part of the big TUI group, located at the southern end of Diani Beach on a coral rock promontory. With 239 rooms, including the 2008 *Maridadi* wing (much bigger rooms) and the separate *Kole Kole Resort* (south of the promontory), it's a busy place, on a sizeable plot – though sadly they have cleared much of the indigenous forest. It has a reputation for good food and is popular with Brits. Clients have access to all three parts of the resort, including a total of five pools. Diving the Crab PADI diving school is located on site. Eco-Tourism Kenya Bronze Award. AI $276

★**Diani Blue** 2km south ☎0723 644945, ⊛dianiblue .co.ke; map p.433. Cool, light, airy, boutique guesthouse, right by the beach, with just six rooms with nets, fans and a/c, and water heated by solar panels. All have pool and sea views. They capture rainwater, separate and recycle all waste, and donate a percentage of income to community

6

projects. Pool and excellent seafood meals at the waterfront restaurant, *The Edge* (see opposite). BB **$250**

Diani Drifters 400m south ☎0713 028226, ⓦdianidrifters.com; map p.433. Rustic whitewashed cottages fabulously located on a cliff above the beach, with fully equipped kitchens, a chef on hand to cook if you don't want to and seafood available from passing fishermen. Cottages range from studios to three-bedroom affairs, all simply decorated and with private porches. Good value. Room only **Ksh3500**

★**Diani Marine Village** 3km south, next to Forty Thieves ☎0707 629061 or ☎0707 629060, ⓦdianimarine.com; map p.433. A great-value dive base, and whether you're diving or not, the spacious rooms, with fans and nets (no a/c), the fine pool and pool snack bar, and the great breakfasts in the Kilimanjaro *banda* all make it well worth considering. They also have a number of self-catering villas. BB **€78**

Diani Sea Lodge 3.3km south ☎040 3203438 or ☎0711 387028, ⓦdianisea.com; map p.433. Large, German-owned, slightly downmarket, Mediterranean-style version of the *Diani Sea Resort*, owned by the same people. The rooms are a letdown: most are small, in bungalows set back in the gardens, though they were getting a facelift at the time of writing. Pool and children's pool, gym, tennis court, crazy golf, windsurfing and PADI diving school. Mainly German clientele. AI **Ksh13,800**

Diani Sea Resort 1.9km south ☎040 3203438 or ☎0711 387028, ⓦdianisea.com; map p.433. Built in 1991 and much more cheerful than its sister hotel (see above), with good service, nice staff and plenty of things to do. As with the *Lodge*, most guests are German, many on long stays. Great pool, gym, tennis and squash courts, crazy golf, windsurfing and PADI diving school. AI **Ksh15,500**

Flamboyant 2.8km south ☎0733 411110 or ☎0720 843585, ⓦflamboyant.co; map p.433. Large family house adapted as a stylish and comfortable hotel, sleeping twenty guests in a variety of a/c rooms with fans and nets. Free laundry, as well as a good pool in a small, pleasant garden, and watersports such as kayaking and kitesurfing on offer. BB **Ksh17,000**

Forest Dream Cottages 5.5km south (and then 800m into the forest) ☎0721 554359, ⓦforestdream.com; map p.433. Funky, boutique "eco-resort" of simple yet stylish *makuti*-roofed cottage rooms around communal lounge areas, set among the trees, plus rooms in a rather incongruous Moroccan-themed villa. Some of the rooms are rather dark, but the whole place is enthusiastically run and very committed to the protection of the Diani forest and its wildlife. Great for families. Solar water heating, nice pool, free bikes, tennis and volleyball. BB **€102**

Kaskazi Beach Hotel 300m south ☎040 3203725 or ☎0715 400370, ⓦkaskazibeachhotel.co.ke; map p.433. A sprawling place that's well run and competitively priced, successfully balancing package-tour prices with a friendly atmosphere. While the 190 rooms are ready for a refurb, the public areas are still stylish enough, decorated with Arabic motifs and white-tiled floors. There's also the sad little ruined seventeenth-century "Diani mosque" in the garden, which is basically just an old wall. HB **$170**

Kenyaways Kite Village 7.5km south, on Galu Beach ☎0728 886821 or 0726 126204, ⓦthekenyaway.com; map p.433. A selection of nicely done, light, well-furnished rooms – including some larger and more deluxe options – in and around this former family home; good value all around. The big thing here is kitesurfing (the h20 Extreme kite school is based here). There's also a pool. Minimum two nights. BB **$100**

★**Kinondo Kwetu** 12km south, on Kinondo beach ☎0710 898030, ⓦkinondo-kwetu.com; map p.433. Far south of Diani Beach proper, the very private *Kinondo Kwetu* ("Our Home at Kinondo") mixes Scandinavian cool and Kenyan warmth in a beguiling combination, with lots of African art, sumptuous fabrics and dark wood, catering for a maximum of 38 guests. The breeze-cooled rooms, none of which locks (or needs to), have stylish, bright interiors; there's excellent cuisine, charming Swedish hosts, and almost nobody on the beach (though note the beach is narrow, the reef far out and the lagoon shallow at low tide). Sauna, yoga and non-motorized watersports, plus a PADI diving school and riding stables. Closed May & June. AI **$560**

Neptune Palm Beach 8.7km south, on Galu Beach ☎020 3549971 or ☎0716 016000, ⓦneptunehotels.com; map p.433. Decent but overpriced rooms in tightly packed rows of two-storey cottages (few with sea views), set back from the beach in a long stretch of tidy garden that has been extended seawards to the point where there is no beach left at high tide; sunbeds are laid out on the grass. Reasonable facilities include an enormous pool surrounding the bar, and a spa. AI **$250**

Papillon Lagoon Reef 5.5km south ☎020 2331338 or ☎0725 204777, ⓦrexresorts.com; map p.433. Middle-market, mid-sized, all-inclusive hotel, with 150 rooms and a good reputation for value-for-money stays, but inconsistent service and food. Rooms, eighteen of which have sea views, are spacious and comfortable, with a/c and fans, useful safes (Ksh150 extra) and balconies. Free diving demos available in the pleasant pool. AI **$176**

★**Pinewood Beach Resort** 10.8km south, on Galu Beach ☎0734 699723 or ☎0723 957080, ⓦpinewood-beach.com; map p.433. Well-managed, Mediterranean-style resort hotel on a quiet stretch of beach south of the main Diani strip, all set in pretty gardens. Take an ordinary room and eat in the restaurant, or a suite and get the services of your own chef thrown in; there's also one three-bedroom family suite. The 58 rooms are in cottages with two doubles upstairs and one suite downstairs, with great a/c, nets and safes. There's a good gym and watersports down on the beach, as well as a congenial beach bar. HB $258

★ **The Sands at Nomad** 4.8km south ☎ 0725 373888, ⓦ thesandsatnomad.com; map p.433. Appealing hotel with 37 cool, well-designed rooms, suites and cottages (though standards and prices vary greatly: the sea-facing rooms and luxurious beach cottages are much more expensive) tucked among baobabs close to the shore, with very personal service. There's a good beach bar and restaurant, the HQ of the Diving the Crab PADI diving school, a 5m-deep pool (good for dive training) and a kitesurfing school. Closed May & June. BB $264

Swahili Beach Hotel 100m south ☎ 020 2661708 or ☎ 0707 730753, ⓦ swahilibeach.com; map p.433. This spectacular resort development sports vaguely Mediterranean exteriors and Swahili chic interiors in two-storey clusters around the landscaped grounds. The soaring lobby brings to mind an enormous mosque, while the cascading swimming pool – starting near reception and descending in eight tiers to the beach, embellished by fake rocks and imported palm trees – is pure Sun City. The rooms themselves are spacious and very comfortable, though the reliance on white moulded plaster decor also makes them a bit austere. Huge spa and gym. HB $335

★ **Water Lovers** 2.2km south ☎ 0735 790535 or ☎ 0727 008840, ⓦ waterlovers.it; map p.433. Both friendly and trying to be ecofriendly, this boutique beach lodge lies in a coconut grove more or less on the seashore, the centrepiece being a small infinity pool above the sands. There are six cottage-style suites, a villa and a four-bedroom penthouse, all largely powered by solar panels. Service is excellent, with superb attention to detail, including an iPhone dock in each room and complimentary iPads preloaded with movies. The good Mediterranean-slanted restaurant goes in for local produce and home cooking; order in the morning if possible. BB €262

EATING

The following listings, with distances given from the Ukunda junction, include some of the best, and best-value, places to eat. Finding food for **self-catering** is straightforward enough, with stalls along the beach road, fish and fruit vendors doing the rounds of most likely sites and several supermarkets, including a Nakumatt (see p.441).

NORTH OF THE UKUNDA JUNCTION

African Pot 300m north ☎ 072 644707; map p.431. A pleasant bar serving cold beer and well-prepared Kenyan food (kebabs Ksh200, avocado salad Ksh200, beef masala Ksh525, green banana in coconut sauce Ksh180), plus a pool table. Daily 7.30am–midnight.

Aniello's Pizzeria Just south of Colliers Centre ☎ 0717 590523; map p.431. A reliable standby for pasta (around Ksh700), meat and fish, but most people come for the good wood-fired oven pizzas (from Ksh600) served in a casual setting. Daily 10am–10pm.

Chinese Diani Restaurant Diani Complex Shopping Centre, 1.5km north ☎ 0720 418563; map p.431. Good Chinese restaurant, but fairly pricey (beef with oyster sauce Ksh720, special fried rice Ksh340). Free pickup from hotels. Daily 11.30am 10.30pm.

Leonardo's Colliers Centre ☎ 0720 501707, ⓦ leonardos-restaurant-diani.com; map p.431. This fancy Italian joint is all wood and wicker with a giant thatched roof, serving pasta and pizza (Ksh700–900), other mains (around Ksh1200), home-made ice creams (Ksh200/scoop), plus good coffee. Charcoal-grilled meat and fish are prepared next to the pizza oven. Supervised children's play area. Daily 10.30am–11.30pm, last food orders 10.15pm.

New Shan-e-Punjab Diani Complex Shopping Centre, 1.4km north ☎ 0733 728279; map p.431. This Punjabi restaurant and snack bar features an open-air garden, serving vegetarian and non-vegetarian dishes like *gosht Punjabi roganjosh* (Ksh700). Very good value, with most dishes around Ksh500–800. Free transfers from anywhere in Diani. Daily 12.30–9pm.

SOUTH OF THE UKUNDA JUNCTION

★ **Ali Barbour's Cave Restaurant** 2.8km south ☎ 0714 456130, ⓦ alibarbours.co; map p.433. Bizarrely built inside a 150,000-year-old coral cave – you enter the restaurant at ground level and descend a staircase. The lavish French and seafood menu includes lobster (Ksh3950), chilli crab and Madagascar steak (Ksh1650), all well presented. The dress code is smart casual – no shorts. Daily 6.30–10pm.

Al Manara "Sails" Beach Bar & Restaurant 7.8km south ☎ 0716 863884, ⓦ almanararesort.com; map p.433. This classy beachside restaurant is one of the best regarded in Diani, with a menu that changes weekly and features pastas, meat dishes and seafood standbys like fresh oysters (Ksh500 a dozen). Starters around Ksh700, most mains Ksh1500. Reservations recommended. Daily except Tues 12.30–3pm & 6.30–11pm.

Colobus Shade and **Mwaepe Fisherman's Restaurant** 6.4km south ☎ 0725 860274; map p.433. Right by Diani's main fish-landing jetty, these two identical seafood-only beach restaurants, which share a shack under a baobab tree, both offer the catch of the day, with rice, potatoes, salad and chapatti (Ksh800) – and knockout service. Beer Ksh200 and even wine by the bottle from Ksh1000. Daily 10am–8pm.

The Edge 2km south, at Diani Blue ☎ 0723 644945, ⓦ dianiblue.co.ke; map p.433. Fine dining around the pool or just above the beach, weather permitting, in an intimate little restaurant serving a three-course set dinner menu (Ksh2500) or à la carte seafood, including ginger crab (Ksh1300). Lunch choices are more in the line of soups and salads (Ksh900), though there are also heavier options like pasta and fish. Daily 10am–8.45pm.

★ **Forty Thieves Beach Bar & Restaurant** 2.8km south ☎0712 294873, ⓦdiani.co/beachbar; map p.433. This famous local watering hole – bare feet, sand underfoot and loud chatter – is a good place for a daytime drink and perfect in the evening when the beachfront is floodlit. Live band, roasts and curry buffet on Sun. Dishes range from fish and chips (Ksh800) to big salads (Ksh850), pizzas (Ksh700) and grills. Beers Ksh300, wine Ksh200. English football and other sport on TV; quiz nights; pool tables. Daily 8am–late.

Havana Baharini Plaza, 2.1km south ☎0706 601421, ⓦhavana.co.ke; map p.433. A branch of the popular Nairobi bar/restaurant (and with Nairobi prices), this Cuban-themed place serves hearty breakfasts (full English for Ksh720), seafood, sandwiches and even a touch of Tex-Mex like *huevos rancheros* (Ksh820). It's also a lively place for a drink. Daily 8am–1am.

Il Mattarello 600m south ☎0727 311638; map p.433. A friendly and casual little Italian joint with a short menu (the highlight is the home-made ravioli from Ksh900, which you can also order uncooked to take away), though you can choose nearly anything from their pasta and pizza cookbooks and they'll try to make it for you. Pizzas from Ksh700. Daily 9am–10pm.

★ **Kokkos** Across from Baharini Plaza, 2km south ☎0721 565567, ⓦfacebook.com/KokkosCafeBistro; map p.433. A chic and breezy café filled with the buzz of grinding coffee beans, and probably the best spot in Diani for brunch, offering tasty French toast (Ksh300) and egg-and-bacon sandwiches. It's worth stopping in later for one of the gourmet burgers

(around Ksh800), a salad or just a good cup of coffee and a pastry. Tues–Sat 9am–11pm, Sun 10am–10pm.

Lymingtons Bistro Diani Beach Shopping Centre, 1.2km south ☎0732 900700; map p.433. Popular for grills, burgers (Ksh500) and an odd assortment of international dishes like Thai beef and schnitzel, as well as a wide variety of meal-sized salads for Ksh800 or less. They have a bar, too. Mon–Sat 10am–10pm.

★ **Nomads Beach Bar & Restaurant** The Sands at Nomad, 4.8km south ☎0735 373888, ⓦthesandsat nomad.com; map p.433. Popular beach bar with snacks, pizzas (from Ksh700), seafood and its famous Sunday lunch curry buffet (Ksh1500), a real family affair with regular live jazz or a one-man band. Part of the restaurant is devoted to excellent Japanese food – allow around Ksh2000/person. Daily: restaurant 7.30am–10.30pm; beach bar 6.30am–11pm.

Stilts 3km south, opposite Ali Barbour's Cave Restaurant ☎0722 523278, ⓦstiltsdiani.com; map p.433. The pleasant tree-level bar-restaurant at this popular backpackers (see p.436) offers main dishes at Ksh450–700 (curries, steaks, fish), snacks and sandwiches and a daily local cuisine "money saver", such as beans and chapattis, for Ksh250. Daily 8am–11pm.

Sundowner 7km south ☎0725 498281; map p.433. A cheap and unpretentious restaurant and bar, serving good African dishes, curries (Ksh400), seafood ("Maasai Fish" – breaded and fried fish fillet Ksh400) and a few random Austrian dishes like *frikadellen* (Ksh450). Beers Ksh160. Daily 8am–9pm.

Winds Diani Campsite and Cottages, 1.4km south ☎0722 683900, ⓦdianicampsite.com; map p.433. Popular diner and TV bar at *Diani Campsite and Cottages* (see p.436) offering fry-ups and sandwiches for around Ksh350, as well as grills (Ksh600) and seafood. Daily 6am–11pm.

DRINKING AND NIGHTLIFE

Apart from predictable **hotel discos**, there are several independent **nightclubs** along the road, each with its own idiosyncrasies, all with at least a trace of sleaze. Couples will usually be ignored, but single men can expect lots of business-like propositions, and women without male partners will be constantly chatted up. None of the discos starts to warm up before 11pm. Entry prices range from free to Ksh100 depending on the season, the night and the entertainment. The distances given below are from the Ukunda junction.

MUSIC AND DANCING IN DIANI

The big entertainment usually touted in these parts, **Giriama dancing**, is perhaps not something to go out of your way for, but is fun if you happen upon it. A couple of professional troupes work the hotels, performing acrobatically to the accompaniment of superb drumming. You're also likely to happen across **Maasai dancers**, invariably the real thing, although they aren't native to the coast. The guttural polyphonic singing is fascinating, though the performances usually end with a "Maasai market" where they sell overpriced (and not necessarily very Maasai) trinkets. More seldom seen are the **Taarab bands** (see p.583), who sometimes play in hotel dining rooms on special occasions or public holidays. All these entertainments are seasonal; you will find much less going on when it's quiet.

GETTING AROUND DIANI BEACH AT NIGHT

To get around Diani Beach at night without your own vehicle, you'll have to rely mostly on **taxis**. Any restaurant or hotel will call one for you: they never take more than a few minutes, but always agree the price firmly before getting in. Ksh500 is about the lowest fare, with Ksh150/km being about right for journeys of more than a few kilometres. While everyone will warn you about walking on the beach at night, under a full moon it's a pleasure that's hard to resist. With no valuables, especially in a group, you're very unlikely to have any problems.

6

BBII 3.4km south (then 300m inland); map p.433. The place to come when you're tired of being a tourist, this is a nice local pub with outdoor tables and a bar behind a cage in the approved fashion. Beer Ksh160, sodas Ksh50. Daily 5pm–2am.

Bidi Badu 3.3km south, on the beach ☎ 0700 833818, ⓦ bidibadu.com; map p.433. This congenial beach shack, filled with rickety wicker furniture and a vaguely Rasta vibe, is a popular hangout for locals intent on a few drinks and a good time (beer Ksh200). You can eat here too, mainly cheap seafood grills featuring octopus (Ksh500) or coconut prawns. Daily 10am–4am.

★ **Kim4Love** 3.5km south, on the beach ☎ 0722 889844, ⓦ kim4love.net; map p.433. Set amid the eerie ruins of the *Two Fishes* hotel, demolished by fire in 1999, this beach bar-restaurant comes alive on weekend afternoons when Kim – the "ambassador of love" – plays with his band to a relaxed crowd of "richest and poorest without boundaries". Great-value food (dishes Ksh250–490). Daily 8am–midnight or later at weekends.

New Tandoori Club 3.5km south, opposite Diani Sea Lodge; map p.433. Popular all-day TV bar and hangout, with an attached disco, the *Baharini*. Although they no longer serve food, the pool tables and regular parties make it a popular local rendezvous. Beer Ksh200. Daily 24hr.

Shakatak 3.5km south, opposite Diani Sea Lodge ⓦ shakatak-kenya.com; map p.433. Although it's got a decent wooden dancefloor, pool tables and a/c, this is a bit of a dive, but it does play the best music mix on the strip – there's sometimes a Ksh100 cover charge on weekends. You can eat here reasonably cheaply if you want – it's mostly Kenyan food. Beers Ksh200, wine Ksh250. Daily 7pm–4am.

DIRECTORY

Banks and exchange Barclays by the Ukunda junction has a 24hr ATM; KCB has an ATM at Nakumatt; and there's a Wanati Forex in Shree Plaza (Mon–Fri 9am–5pm & Sat 9am–1pm).

Internet access Available at several places. The best is Hot Gossip just south of the Diani Beach Shopping Centre (Mon–Sat 8.30am–5.30pm). Others include Forty Thieves Cyber, at the beach bar of the same name (see opposite), 2.8km south of the Ukunda junction (daily 9am–9pm).

Medical services The small, modern Diani Beach Hospital (☎ 0722 569261, ⓦ dianibeachhospital.com), next to Diani Complex Shopping Centre, is recommended. One of the best hospitals on the coast, they have an Outpatients department and a 24hr pharmacy. In an emergency call ☎ 0700 999999.

Mobile phone service For Safaricom dongle or SIM card issues, visit the Safaricom service centre at Nakumatt, first floor (Mon–Sat 9am–7pm, Sun 10am–4pm).

Pharmacy The prosaically named The Chemist is next to Nakumatt (Mon–Sat 8am–9pm, Sun 8am–8pm).

Post office By the airport entrance road, 1.4km south of Nakumatt.

Supermarkets The Nakumatt, on the junction of the main Diani road and the road to Ukunda, should have most of what you need (Mon–Sat 9am–9pm, Sun 10am–8pm). KFI Supermarket, at the junction for *South Coast Backpackers*, is one of several alternatives (Mon–Sat 9am–1.30pm & 2.30–6pm), as is Shan-e-Punjab Supermarket, next to the *New Shan-e-Punjab* restaurant (Mon–Sat 9am–6pm).

Ukunda

Until a few years ago just a village on the highway, **UKUNDA** is now a scruffily burgeoning town and the main service centre for the Diani Beach resort hotels, strung out along the Likoni–Lungalunga road, with a post office, a number of banks with ATMs, several petrol stations, various places with internet access, and hundreds of *dukas*, kiosks and *hotelis*. Only marginally touched by tourism, except insofar as many of its residents work in the hotels, Ukunda has a life of its own. If your holiday isn't otherwise adventurous, it's worth a visit to see something of Kenya a little more authentic than the strip.

6

South to Shimoni

South of *Neptune Palm Beach Hotel* (see p.438), the Diani Beach road returns to gravel, although it continues, in a driveable condition, past one or two secluded properties around Kinondo, and past Kaya Kinondo itself. There's little transport down here, so you're likely to be driving or walking. You get to a hard right-hand bend, then 100m later a sharp left turning for Chale Point. **Chale Island** is 4km further south, and 300m offshore. The island, once an uninhabited beauty spot, was acquired in the early 1990s by a property developer, with the help of two local MPs, despite being public land and a gazetted Mijikenda *kaya*. The resulting resort, the largely Italian-patronized *Sands at Chale*, owned by *The Sands at Nomad* in Diani, angered local people and wiped out acres of natural vegetation. But the owners claim the development has been sensitive, that only a third of the island has been built upon and that the other part is a nature reserve; there are plans to eventually open it up to day visitors. If, instead of driving down to Chale Point you keep straight ahead, you emerge, after exactly 3km of slightly rough-and-ready coral rag road, onto the main highway down to Tanzania, at a point 13km south of Ukunda.

Gazi

Down the main coastal highway south of Ukunda, **GAZI** is next, a sleepy little village just off the road. It was once headquarters of the Mazrui leader **Sheikh Mbaruk ("Baruku") bin Rashid**, who acquired a reputation for torturing prisoners after half-suffocating them in the fumes of burning chillis. The story was perhaps intended to discredit him, as he was the principal figure behind the **Mazrui Rebellion** of 1895, an uprising against British authority that saw Mbaruk flying a German flag at his house and supplying his men with arms donated by the Germans. The British had to send for troops from India and fighting continued for nine months before an Omani puppet regime was re-established and the rebels crushed. Mbaruk died in exile in German Tanganyika. His mansion is now a primary school, which you can look around out of school hours. More than 150 years old, it was obviously a very grand place – the heavy ceiling timbers show that it once had an upper storey – but is now sadly neglected.

There are two turnings to Gazi, which lies between the road and the shore. The first is 3.1km from the Chale island/Diani South turning. The village itself lies back from a deep, mangrove-filled bay and has no beach to speak of. **Gazi Beach**, about 2km south of the village, is more promising. Local women in Gazi manage the **Gazi Women's Mangrove Boardwalk** (daily 9am–4pm), a 250m trail through the mangroves, which is worth visiting, especially for birdwatchers; all donations support the community.

Msambweni

Six kilometres south of Gazi is **MSAMBWENI**, a sizeable village with a famous leprosarium. The road to the beach goes through the village, following the coast for several kilometres before turning back to the highway. The **beach** is lovely – low cliffs and less uniformity than Diani – and there are no beach hassles down here, but the tide goes out for kilometres, with lots of rock pools, so it's not ideal for snorkelling or for most watersports.

Funzi Island

Funzi Island is separated from the mainland by a narrow channel that you can walk across at low tide. Unlike exclusive Chale, you can easily camp on the island if you're equipped for a fair amount of self-sufficiency, and Diani operators (see p.435) run bird- and crocodile-watching day-trips here. The village of **Funzi** is at the southern end, about 6km from the mainland, and there are **beaches** and sections of reef scattered close to the forested shore on both sides of the island.

Shirazi

The tiny and very old settlement of **SHIRAZI**, also known as Kifunzi (which means "little Funzi"), sits on the shore about 2km east of Ramisi. Any of the tracks through the sugar fields on the left of the road will take you to the hamlet – a scattering of houses in the jungle and a small harbour among mangroves.

Like many villages on the coast, Shirazi is a backwater in every sense. The people cut a small quantity of *boriti* (mangrove poles), though much less than they used to; they fish; and they also grow produce in their garden plots, which are continually being raided by monkeys. But the setting is memorably exotic and worth the 2km detour from the main road. They may not have cold sodas at Shirazi, but they do have coconuts and tranquillity.

Just a couple of hundred metres south of Shirazi rests the enigmatic hulk of a **Friday mosque**, its *mihrab* still standing. Though by the beginning of the twentieth century it had already been abandoned, the mosque stood empty for some years – elders in Shirazi, who describe how earlier inhabitants were routed by the Maasai and fled to the Comoros Islands, remember when the mosque was still intact.

Ramisi

Beyond Shirazi the coastal highway passes through verdant regions of parkland, with borassus, doum and coconut palms (borassus palms are the ones with a bulge in the trunk, like pythons that have swallowed a goat) interspersed with swampy dells. Further south, the landscape becomes one of rolling fields of sugar cane, culminating in **RAMISI**, which was the coast's main sugar-producing area until the closure of its factory in the 1970s.

ACCOMMODATION   **SOUTH TO SHIMONI**

There's limited accommodation along this section of Kenya's coast, but what is here is exceptionally good. You ideally need your own transport, though you could manage with taxis. Several of the places are **self-catering** houses, with staff.

CHALE ISLAND

The Sands at Chale ☎ 0725 373888, ⊚ thesand satchaleisland.com. Owned by *The Sands at Nomad* in Diani, this resort caused some controversy when it appeared in the 1990s (see p.442). There's a package feel to it which you wouldn't expect in the location, but they do offer eco-tours of the surrounding mangrove forest. HB $218

MSAMBWENI

Chingwede House Chelsoon, Msambweni Beach ☎ 0733 633332, ⊜ nicole.church49@gmail.com, ⊚ bit.ly/ChingwedeHouse. Fine self-catering house sleeping eight, with a *makuti* roof and a big pool out front, sharing the same plot as *Samawati* (see below). Whole house, self-catering £230

★ **Msambweni Beach House** Msambweni Beach, 6km from the highway ☎ 020 3577093 or ☎ 0723 697346, ⊚ msambweni-beach-house.com. A fabulous boutique hotel, the pride of its Belgian owner-designer, rising from the edge of the highest cliffs on the Kenyan coast above a remote beach complete with caves and a private dining area. Closed May. AI $774

Samawati House Chelsoon, Msambweni Beach ☎ 0722 818128, ⊚ samawati.co.ke. Beautiful Arabesque-style house sleeping up to eight, with a large pool, sharing a big plot with *Chingwede House* (see above) on the palm-studded shore southeast of the village. Whole house, self-catering $360

Saruni Ocean Msambweni Beach, 4km from the highway ☎ 0735 950903 or ☎ 020 2180 497, ⊚ saruniocean.com. One of the coast's most beautiful and luxurious new additions, this offers six sea-facing villas, split into very spacious, private

---

THE WA-SHIRAZI

The people of Shirazi call themselves **Wa-Shirazi** and are the descendants of a once-important group of the Swahili-speaking people. During the fifteenth and sixteenth centuries, they ruled the coast from Tiwi to Tanga from their eight settlements on the shore, one of which is believed to have been this village. Around 1620, these towns were captured by the Wa-Vumba, another Swahili group. The Wa-Shirazi, now scattered in pockets along the coast, speak a distinctive dialect of Swahili. Historians used to think that they originally emigrated from Shiraz, in Persia, but it now seems likely that very few of them have any Persian ancestry and that the name was adopted for political reasons.

a/c suites. Vast infinity pool, spa, yoga and pilates, inventive and personalized cuisine – and a very quiet beach. **$900**

FUNZI ISLAND

Funzi Keys West coast of Funzi island ☎ 0733 900 446, ⓦ thefunzikeys.com. Attentively managed creek-shore resort accessible only by boat or charter flight, surrounded by sand spits and mangroves, and consisting of enormous, open-plan, stone and thatched cottages. Tons of Robinson Crusoe charm is the main appeal, though most activities, even non-motorized, cost extra. No ocean beach on site. Closed March 15–June 30. AI **$440**

Shimoni

In the 1980s, the US had its eye on **Wasini** – the rocky sliver of an island just offshore from the village of **SHIMONI** – as a potential naval base. Fortunately the idea was shelved, and Shimoni, 14km down a picturesque sand and mud road from the highway, remains relatively untouched and fascinating. Most visitors only pass through when coming here for dhow trips to Wasini and the Kisite-Mpunguti Marine National Park, but it's worth an hour or two of your time – especially if you're a keen fisher, as this is one of the world's most renowned **game-fishing** areas. The Pemba Channel (the Tanzanian island of Pemba lies 50km offshore) is considered one of the world's very best stretches of sea for hunting big fish: **marlin** weighing a quarter of a tonne (550lb) and **tiger sharks** close on half a tonne race through these waters, marlin at recorded speeds of more than 100km/hr.

If you're driving down to Shimoni yourself it's worth calling at *Mwazaro Beach* hotel (see p.446), which welcomes casual visitors for meals or drinks. *Mwazaro*, which means "prayer place", is on a beautiful, lonely beach, opposite the delta of the Ramisi River, with forests of **mangroves** all around (eight of the nine species native to Africa can be found here and the owners of Mwazaro have replanted some ten square kilometres), excellent **snorkelling** at the nearby reef and creek- and sea-trips available.

If you can, try to be in Shimoni first thing: an auction takes place at the **fish auction house** by the jetty every morning. Depending on the night's catch, it can be an interesting event, as the seas in the Pemba Channel are rich in fish, though major captures like marlin and shark are rarely on the slab.

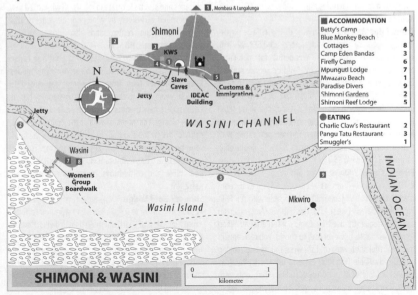

SHIMONI & WASINI

6

The slave caves

Just east of the jetty • Daily guided tours 8.30am–6pm • Ksh400

The "**slave caves**" after which Shimoni was named (*shimo* means "cave" in Swahili) have achieved fame locally, if not much further afield, through the melodramatic warblings of Kenyan-born singer Roger Whittaker's song *Shimoni*, which was recorded in the caves. Based on the evidence of iron rings in the rocks, it's believed that they were used to store slaves prior to shipment to Zanzibar. Historians from the National Museums of Kenya are looking for further evidence, and with 5km of silted-up caverns to excavate they may have some way to go. These are caves into which you descend from ground level. Once you're down, shafts of sunlight pierce through holes in the forest floor to illuminate the stalactites and dangling lianas quite beautifully.

The ruined two-storey building opposite the caves ticket office was formerly the headquarters of the **Imperial British East African Company**, dating from 1885.

ARRIVAL AND DEPARTURE — SHIMONI

By matatu There are direct matatus from Likoni to Shimoni, but they can be infrequent, and tend to run mostly early in the morning. Vehicles for Lungalunga will drop you at the junction where you shouldn't have much trouble getting a lift.

By cargo dhows There is a possibility of getting a slow cargo dhow from Shimoni to Pemba (6–7hr; Ksh4000) and sometimes straight to Zanzibar (24hr; Ksh7000); if you've lined up a passage, you should report to the customs and immigration offices in Shimoni.

ACCOMMODATION

Betty's Camp 500m west of the village centre ⓣ0722 434709, ⓦbettys-camp.com. Aiming at the budget game-fishing market, this place has its own boats and jetty, and offers a choice of small, non-s/c safari tents, with floor fans, or modest rooms with ceiling fans in a quaint rondavel with a breezy, top-floor lounge area. There's a pleasant little pool (a surprising Ksh750 for non-guests), but the whole place is still a bit overpriced for the facilities and standards. BB: tent $89, double $105

Camp Eden Bandas 300m west of the village centre, at the National Park headquarters ⓣ0723 929766, ⓔreservations@kws.go.ke. Wonderful for naturalists and managed by the local Kenya Wildlife Service rangers, *Camp Eden* is a group of seven airy and clean, if fairly rudimentary *bandas* in the forest; five of them s/c, two non-s/c (the latter have basins outside, but share squat loos and showers). There's mains electricity, but it's best to bring your own drinking water. You can also camp, with rented tents available for an extra Ksh500. Room only: camping $20, *banda* $50

Firefly Camp 700m east of Shimoni village centre ⓣ0722 244694 or ⓣ0724 442555, ⓦshimonibackpackers.com. Managed by the people who run Pilli-Pipa Dhow Safaris (see p.435), this gap year/voluntourism camp is frequently used by Camps International. When space is available, however (call to check), you can camp in this beautiful spot, with cold showers, toilets and cooking facilities available (Ksh1000 extra to use the kitchen), as well as a handful of more comfortable safari tents with beds. There's even a nice pool, with a bar alongside. Room only: camping Ksh500 plus Ksh1000 per tent; AI safari tent €45

★**Mwazaro Beach** 1km off the Shimoni road, 7.5km from the highway ⓣ0701 935007, ⓦmwazaro-beach.com. "Where God makes holidays" is how the German owners describe this eco-resort at a Digo *kaya*, where approval was sought and granted for the low-key, sustainable development of thirteen non-s/c *makuti* cottages and seven s/c coral rag rooms, all with fitted nets, and powered exclusively by wind and solar energy. It's a major kitesurfing centre, and also serves excellent Zanzibari set meals. HB $80

Shimoni Gardens 1.5km west of the village centre ⓣ0722 630658, ⓔc.kanini@yahoo.com. This modest little resort set back from the shore was closed for several years and had fallen into disrepair, but its enthusiastic new owners are in the process of sprucing up the s/c stone cottages, as well as the non-s/c reed and cane rooms on the top floor of a stilted house; it should soon be a pleasant and low-key place to stay. There's a separate beach bar-restaurant closer to the shore, with a pool table and cold drinks (open 24hr). Room only Ksh2500

Shimoni Reef Lodge 300m east of the village centre ⓣ0727 486961 or ⓣ0716 182934, ⓦshimonireeflodge.com. Aimed less at sportfishermen than at divers. Pleasant accommodation in ten whitewashed split-level cottages with separate bedroom and lounge areas, floor fans and nets, or in a two-bedroom self-catering cottage. The food is rather average, but it's served on a lovely terrace overlooking the sea. Salt-water pool. HB $150

EATING

Smuggler's Just west of the slave caves ☎0723 219723. An upcountry-style bar-restaurant where you can usually get chicken, beef or goat, either stewed or roasted, sold by weight (beef Ksh600/kg, goat Ksh700/kg), accompanied by rice, *ugali* or chapattis. They also sell juices and do good breakfasts. Daily 9am–11pm.

Wasini Island and offshore

Only 5km long and 1km across, **Wasini Island** has about a thousand inhabitants, and is totally adrift from the mainstream of coastal life. There are no cars, nor any need for them; you can walk all the way around the island in a couple of hours on the narrow footpaths through the bush. With something of Lamu's cast about it, Wasini is completely undeveloped, and people tend to be conservative in dress – something you should be sensitive to while visiting (don't wander around in a swimming costume).

Wasini village

The village of **WASINI**, an old Wa-Vumba settlement, is built in and around its own ruins. It's a fascinating place to wander and there's even a small pillar tomb that still has its complement of inset Chinese porcelain. The **beach** in front of the village (and in fact the shores all round the island) – littered with shells, pottery shards, pieces of glass and scrap metal – are a beachcomber's paradise that you could explore for hours. Be wary of pocketing sea shells or any artefacts, though (see p.419).

The coral gardens and the boardwalk

Daily dawn–dusk • Ksh200

Behind Wasini village is a bizarre area of long-dead **coral gardens**, raised out of the water by changing sea levels, but still flooded by twice-monthly spring tides. The **boardwalk** through the gardens was built by a local women's group to help conserve the mangroves and corals, with funds going towards education and healthcare in the village. Walking among these eerie grottos, with birds and butterflies in the air, gives you the surreal impression that you're snorkelling on dry land. The ground is covered by a short swathe of sea grass – the tasty *mboga kokoni* (sea vegetable) – and patrolled by fleets of small crabs with enormous right claws. Beyond the coral gardens, the boardwalk continues into the four types of mangroves growing here, providing an excellent chance to visit an environment that's usually inaccessible.

Mkwiro

MKWIRO, at the eastern end of Wasini, is still largely a fishing village. The inhabitants have traditionally had little contact with Wasini village, but the arrival of a diving business means they are now also engaging with the tourist economy.

Kisite-Mpunguti Marine National Park

Park fee $25 • ⓦ kws.org

Wasini has ideal conditions for **snorkelling**, with limpid water all around, and the waters offshore are the most likely area on Kenya's coast for seeing dolphins. Several operators (see p.435) run full-day trips in large dhows to the reefs around Kisite island, part of **Kisite-Mpunguti Marine National Park**, which is actually made up of Kisite National Park, which covers 11 square kilometres, and Mpunguti National Reserve, which has less protection and covers 28 square kilometres. The area is renowned for having some of the best snorkelling in Kenya. Similar trips, on a more ad hoc basis, can be arranged with boat captains at the dock in Shimoni: depending on the number in your party, demand on the day and the kind of vessel provided, the price for a three-hour trip could range from Ksh10,000 for a small boat to Ksh17,000 for a dhow, excluding park fees. You'll get the most out of the trip by getting down here as early as

6

possible, adding lunch to the deal, and making a whole day of it. Always check that there are enough life jackets, and that they're usable.

The boats normally go out of the Wasini channel to the east, then turn south to pass the islets of **Mpunguti ya Chini** and **Mpunguti ya Juu** ("little" and "great" Mpunguti) on the port side. Some 5km further southwest, **Kisite Islet**, a coral-encircled rock about 100m long, is the usual destination and anchoring point. The best parts of the Kisite anchoring area are towards the outer edge of the main coral garden. There are fish and sea creatures in abundance here, including angel fish, moray eels, octopuses, rock cod or grouper and some spectacularly large sea cucumbers up to 60cm long. At certain times of the year, however, the water is less clear, and repeated anchorings have destroyed much of the coral in at least one small area. Ask the crew if you'd like to try to find a better area: the **Mako Koke Reef**, the other main part of Kisite marine park, is about 4km further west. The KWS headquarters near the jetty, where you buy **park tickets**, has a good display of information about local marine wildlife.

ARRIVAL AND DEPARTURE · WASINI ISLAND

Snorkelling cruises Operators take prebooked lunchers across the channel in their boats (see box, p.435).

By motorboat You can rent a private motor boat from the jetty to take you across to Wasini Island (Ksh500–1000 depending on your bargaining skills).

By taxi boat The local boat "matatus" are really the same kind of vessel as the private motor boats (Ksh200–300), though you may have to wait for more passengers to arrive before they'll leave; you can find them at the jetty.

ACCOMMODATION

★**Blue Monkey Beach Cottages** Wasini village ☎0715 756952 or ☎0722 532230, ⓦwasini.net. Although technically in Wasini village, these two gloriously rustic cottages still feel hidden away, built entirely of coral rag and shells, perched above the tides and prettily decorated with driftwood and flowering bougainvillea. As on the rest of Wasini there's no electricity or running water, but solar lights and bucket showers keep you from feeling deprived. Meals cost extra, but the simple food is excellent, prepared with local ingredients; if you're lucky you can feast on a succulent giant mangrove crab. Owners can arrange a boat transfer from Shimoni (Ksh250). Room only Ksh2900

Mpunguti Lodge Wasini village ☎0700 010026.

Commonly known as *Masood's*, this is a simple, rustic affair with ten basic rooms and only occasional electricity, though flush toilets and showers have been installed and rainwater tanks provide water for most of the year. A fire tore through the lodge a few years back and the facilities, including the bar and restaurant, have yet to recover. Rooms are overpriced, but the views are certainly lovely. Room only Ksh3000

Paradise Divers Northeast corner of Wasini ☎0718 778372, ⓦparadisediver.net. Tents under *bandas*, some more solid s/c rooms and a restaurant, with long-stay packages and casual stays by the day available. Extra charges for ad hoc diving, snorkelling or boat trips. FB €120

EATING

There are only two real **restaurants** on Wasini, though both are owned by tour operators and can only be visited as part of an organized excursion.

Charlie Claw's Restaurant Wasini ⓦwasini.com. This open-air restaurant, with a lovely pool, is the location at the western tip of the island, where *Charlie Claw's* dhow excursions set down for a lavish seafood lunch. Lunch only, booked with excursion (see p.435).

Pangu Tatu Restaurant Wasini ⓦpillipipa.com. Pilli Pipa's seafood lunch base, set in a shady grove of hole-riddled old reef on the north shore of Wasini, with a menu that includes crab, sea grass, polenta and good wine. Lunch only, booked with excursion (see p.435).

Vanga

Kenya's southernmost settlement, **VANGA**, around 100km south of Likoni, is the largest coastal town to have been left alone by the tourist industry. There are odd matatus from Likoni and Ukunda, but no lodgings and no formal *hotelis*, so take supplies. You should be able to find someone in the village who'll organize accommodation for you in a private home.

ONWARDS TO TANZANIA

If you want to get to **Dar es Salaam** on the same day, you'll need to be at the border post at **Lungalunga**, 18km from **Vanga**, by 9am. After completing formalities on the Kenyan side, take a matatu or taxi or walk the 6km to Horohoro on the Tanzanian side. By *dala dala* (matatu) the journey to Tanga takes two to three hours from Horohoro, where you may have to change vehicles for a further five-hour journey to Dar. There are moneychangers at both border posts, but ascertain the current rate before starting negotiations, and always check the notes carefully before handing yours over. If you're buying Tanzanian shillings with Kenyan, you usually get the best rate on the Tanzanian side, and in fact you'll get them at a better rate here than you will in Tanga or Dar.

6

The big old house on the seafront is a nineteenth-century **British customs house**, in the care of the National Museums of Kenya. Many of the other houses in the village were constructed during **World War I** by General Paul von Lettow-Vorbeck, to billet troops he had recruited in German East Africa to fight the British. It is said that the cache of gold from which he paid them is buried under a baobab tree, but that it is cursed: several people are said to have defied the curse and not survived.

Assuming you haven't come in search of buried treasure, there are still things to do in Vanga: **dugout canoes** can be rented very cheaply for wobbly punting trips through the mangroves.

ARRIVAL AND DEPARTURE   VANGA

By car To get here you travel down one of the country's most beautiful roads, the quiet highway that swoops across green plains and baobab-dotted hillsides from the Shimoni junction to the border town of Lungalunga. Here, you'll need to stop to explain your movements to officials. Midway between the customs check and the immigration barrier you turn left to start the 17km *murram* road to Vanga. The track skims the Tanzanian border past *shambas* and tunnels through tall forest. Vanga itself is in the mangroves, approached along a causeway that regularly floods on the spring tide, despite the sea wall.

From Kilifi to Malindi

The landscape is a diverse collage along the 100km swathe of coast between Mtwapa Creek and **Malindi**. First, between Kikambala and Kilifi lies a major **sisal-growing** area, focused around the small town of **Vipingo**, which has just one or two *dukas* and *hotelis*, but not much else. As far as the eye can see, arrow-straight rows of fleshy-leafed, cactus-like sisal plants stretch in every direction, the remaining **baobab trees** standing out bizarrely. A few kilometres inland sits the Vipingo Ridge golf resort (wvipingoridge.com) and the new Vipingo airstrip, served by daily Safarilink flights (wflysafarilink.com).

Towards **Kilifi**, the road bucks through a hilly area and the baobabs grow more profusely amid the scrub. **Kilifi Creek** and **Takaungu Creek** are both stunning, the clash

BAOBAB STORIES

The **baobab**'s strange appearance has a number of explanations in Kenyan mythology. The most common relates how the first baobab planted by God was an ordinary-looking tree, but it refused to stay in one place and wandered round the countryside. As a punishment, God planted it back again – upside down – and immobilized it.

Baobabs may live for more than two thousand years, putting them among the longest-lived organisms that have ever existed. During a severe drought, their large green pods can be cracked open and the nuts made into a kind of flour. The resulting "hungry bread" is part of the common culture of the region. Even in normal times, they have their uses: the tangy white pith of the fruit is boiled with sugar to make a popular bright red sweet that you will see on sale at street stalls.

6

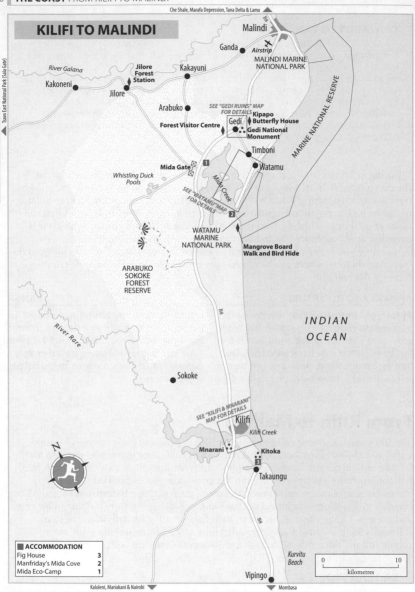

of blue water and green cliffs almost unnatural. As you approach the turning for **Watamu**, thick, jungly forest (the **Arabuko Sokoke Forest Reserve**) and mangrove swamp characterize the district around **Mida Creek**. Further north, there's a more populated zone of *shambas* and thicket as you approach **Malindi**.

There is lots of scope for **beach hunting** along this part of the coast. Malindi and, to some extent, Watamu have been developed, but Kilifi functions largely as a Giriama market centre and district capital, while Takaungu seems virtually unknown, a throwback to pre-colonial days. There's also superb snorkelling at the **marine national**

parks at Watamu and Malindi – local divers reckon Watamu has the better coral, and Malindi better fish, but it's partly a matter of luck and your experience on the day. Lastly, the ruined town of **Gedi**, deep in the forest near Watamu, is one of the most impressive archeological sites in East Africa.

Takaungu

Ten kilometres south of Kilifi, there's a turn-off to the east to **TAKAUNGU**. It's an enchanting place – a quiet, composed village of whitewashed Swahili houses on a high bluff above **Takaungu Creek**, with a perfect, ocean-facing **beach** 1km east of the village. There are three mosques and one or two small shops and *hotelis*, but no official lodgings.

6

Takaungu Creek

Takaungu Creek is startlingly beautiful – sometimes, depending on the light, it's almost the colour of Blue Curacao – and absolutely transparent; the small swimming beach on the stream is covered at high tide, but you can still dive from the rocks. Upstream, the creek disappears between flanks of dense jungle. The small, free, council-operated **passenger ferry** provides a slow service across the narrow creek to the Kilifi side; from there, it's a 5km (90min) walk through the sisal fields to Kilifi bridge.

ARRIVAL AND DEPARTURE   TAKAUNGU

By matatu Although there are a couple of matatus most days from Mombasa direct to Takaungu, if you get dropped off at the turning by a Kilifi-bound vehicle, the chances of a lift down to Takaungu are relatively slim.

Luckily it's not too far (5km) to walk.
By plane SafariLink (⊚flysafarilink.com) has daily flights from Nairobi Wilson to Vipingo airstrip, via Diani airport.

ACCOMMODATION AND EATING

If you want to **stay** in the village and you speak a little Swahili, people will put you up for a very reasonable price. Supplies are variable: women around the village will prepare food if you ask, and especially if you supply the ingredients. There's no produce market, but there's a small **fish market** by the creek – be there when the catch arrives to get the best of it.

Fig House North side of the creek ☎0722 415447, ⊚fighousekenya.com. A beautiful self-catering hideaway (sleeps 8 11) with staff, pool and private tunnel to the creek
shore – it's accessible by road from the Kilifi side. Whole house, self-catering **£400**

Kilifi and around

Kenya's coastline was submerged in the recent geological past, resulting in the creation of the islands and drowned river valleys – the creeks – of today. **KILIFI**, a small but animated town, is on such a creek. When the Portuguese knew it, Kilifi's centre was on the south side of the creek and called **Mnarani** (still the name of the village on that side). Together with Kitoka on the north side of Takaungu Creek, and a settlement on the site of the present town of Kilifi, these three constituted the mini-state of Kilifi.

In recent decades, as the **Giriama** tribe of the Mijikenda (see p.424) has expanded, Kilifi has become one of their most important towns. Giriama women used to be quickly noticed by everyone for their unusual dress, incorporating a padded backside, although this is now only seen in rural areas. Older women still occasionally go topless but younger women cover up, at least in town. The Mijikenda peoples, and the Giriama especially, are known as great sorcerers and practitioners of witchcraft, and Kilifi still frequently sees enough serious witchcraft accusations to be reported in the local press.

The town is draped along the north side of the creek to the east of the bridge. If you're driving you'll probably pass it by. Even most bus and matatu travellers only see it

6

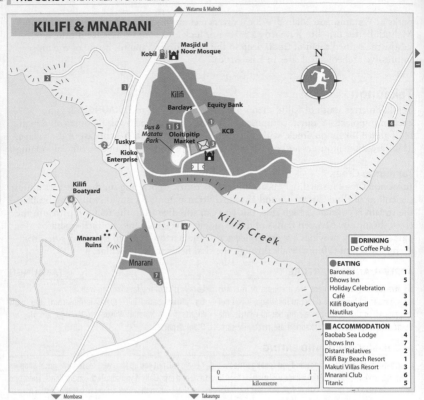

from the inside of the vehicle while more fares are being picked up. But staying the night is a perfectly good plan and certainly better than arriving late in Malindi. There's little of **sightseeing interest** in Kilifi itself, other than the two main **mosques** – one a stumpy shed in the town centre, the other a newer and attractively minareted blue, green and white temple, the Masjid ul Noor, at the north junction. More interesting are the **Mnarani ruins** across the creek.

Mnarani ruins

Under the trees high above the water near the old ferry landing and then up a rather steep flight of steps • Daily 7am–6pm • Ksh500

The small site of the **Mnarani ruins** is archeologically famous mainly for the large number of inscriptions found on its masonry, all in a difficult form of monumental Arabic. They can be seen in several places, in particular in the well-preserved *mihrab* of the main mosque. Just behind this is a very tall octagonal white pillar tomb, which dominates the remains. In front of the mosque, a precipitous well plummets right down to creek level. A little way removed from the main mosque (signposted in front of the office), a smaller mosque is hidden away among the baobabs. As a whole, the site is pretty, though if you're not a specialist its most memorable aspect is its superlative position.

The Kilifi beaches

The **beaches** around Kilifi are mostly accessible only through private property, and the best are up on the open coast to the northeast of the town. Along this 10km tarred road, however, there are several fairly recent developments.

THE MIJIKENDA KAYAS

Each Mijikenda tribe (see box, p.424) has a traditional **kaya** central settlement, a fortified village in the forest ranging from 12 acres to three square kilometres in extent, usually built on raised ground some distance from the coast, but sometimes right by the shore. Some Mijikenda peoples built only one *kaya* while others built secondary *kayas* or even whole clusters. The *kayas* are considered to be the dwelling places of ancestral spirits, although they are now sacred glades rather than fortified villages.

In theory, each *kaya* contains a *fingo* – a charm said to derive from the Mijikenda's ancestral home of Shungwaya. Most *fingo* have been lost or stolen for private collections of "primitive art" or loft-converters' ideas of interesting *objets d'art* – like the **grave posts** called *kigango* (*vigango* in the plural) that also used to be a feature of every *kaya*.

Today, many *kayas* are neglected, but still remembered and visited by tribal elders. Along with the belief in their sacred qualities comes a local conservation tradition: undisturbed and uncultivated, they represent a unique biological storehouse on the East African coast. A WWF-backed botanical research programme, the Coastal Forest Conservation Unit, run by the National Museums of Kenya, is slowly mapping out the *kaya* ecosystems. In 2008 the *kayas* were collectively inscribed as a **UNESCO World Heritage Site** (ⓦ whc.unesco .org/en/list/1231). More than twenty have so far been given legal status and paper protection, and elders are being encouraged to reassert their authority over them before property developers move in. There may be more than fifty altogether, though some could be so small that they will disappear under the bulldozer before anyone remembers them. The first *kaya* to open to visitors is **Kaya Kinondo** on Diani Beach (see box, p.434).

ARRIVAL AND DEPARTURE

By bus and matatu There's no shortage of transport to Mombasa and Malindi. Northbound, most buses to Lamu and Garissa pass through around 8am.

KILIFI AND AROUND

By plane SafariLink (ⓦ flysafarilink.com) has daily flights from Nairobi Wilson to Vipingo airstrip, via Diani airport.

ACCOMMODATION

KILIFI TOWN

Dhows Inn Mnarani, at the south side of the bridge ☎ 020 8088833 or 0722 375214. Big, clean, good-value rooms in the pleasant garden, each with two large beds, fan, nets and electric sockets, plus little porches or balconies. The main downside (or advantage, depending on your mood) is that the bar out front can pretty lively on weekends, so the place isn't terribly quiet. BB __Ksh2000__

★ **Distant Relatives** Around 2km west of Makuti Villas Resort, above Kilifi Creek ☎ 0770 885164, ⓦ kilifibackpackers.com. Hands down the best backpackers on the coast, this chilled-out retreat is good enough reason in itself to visit Kilifi. It offers s/c cottages with beautiful open-air bathrooms, s/c rooms, non-s/c safari tents and a fantastic *makuti*-roofed dorm with a tree growing in the middle, all scattered throughout a stand of coastal forest overrun by dogs, ducks, chickens and pet rabbits. There's a good pool and welcoming common areas, and although it's not right on the beach, it's a 5min walk to a perfect swimming spot through forest frequented by monkeys. The hostel is run as an eco-lodge, using composting toilets and growing its own permaculture produce. Wi-fi. Room only: camping __Ksh500__, dorm __Ksh1000__, safari tents __Ksh1500__, doubles __Ksh4000__, cottages __Ksh5000__

Makuti Villas Resort North side of the bridge, west of the highway ☎ 041 7522371 or ☎ 0734 873704, ⓦ makutivillas.com. Budget tourist-class establishment, with 36 sizeable rooms with nets, TV, ceiling fans and good bathrooms, a pleasant pool and a warm welcome. Their pizzas are usually very good, too. Wi-fi. BB __$67__

Mnarani Club South side of the creek, entrance near the bridge ☎ 041 7522318, ⓦ mnarani.co.za. Comfortable package resort, overlooking Kilifi Creek from expansive gardens, with an international mix of clients, decent food and good service and entertainment. There are two categories of rooms; it's worth paying a bit extra for the more spacious and breezy "Creek" rooms, with stable doors, windows on two sides, a/c and fridge. The views over the creek from the hotel's infinity pool are glorious, and there's a private beach. Wi-fi. BB __$150__

Titanic Town centre, reception at the back of the hotel at street level ☎ 0726 363437, ⓦ hoteltitanic-kenya .com. This big central lodging house with the unpromising name offers a seemingly unlimited variety of rooms. Go for the top floor if you want any kind of view (rooms are all the same price), though they tend to be small up there. All have fans, TVs and good nets, and the better rooms are very spacious. Non-residents' rates are way overpriced, but highly negotiable. BB __€45__

6

KILIFI BEACH

Baobab Sea Lodge 3.2km along the coast road from the highway ☎0731 964016, ⊛madahotels.com. Attractively sited amid densely planted gardens and baobabs, in a pleasant position on a bluff above the shore just north of the creek mouth. Tennis courts and a good pool with lots of shade, but no sea-swimming at low tide. The rooms, while simple, are spacious and attractively furnished, with a/c, good nets, fans, fridges and safes, but only a few have sea views. Wi-fi. FB **$202**

★**Kilifi Bay Beach Resort** 6.5km along the coast road from the highway ☎0725 888560, ⊛madahotels.com. The best of Kilifi's hotels, with a stunning location right down on the beach (the best rooms have stupendous sea views; all have balconies), mature tropical gardens with coconut palms, a freeform pool for when the tide is out, great four-poster beds, spacious *makuti*-roofed communal areas, good service and decent breakfasts. Diving and watersports can be arranged. Wi-fi. FB **$221**

EATING

Baroness By the KCB bank ☎0722 900971. One of the town centre's more upmarket venues, a popular bar-restaurant where local dishes are joined by pepper steak with chips (Ksh400) and chicken curry (Ksh200) served at tables in a cool courtyard. Daily 7am–11pm.

Dhows Inn Mnarani, at the south side of the bridge ☎020 8088833 or ☎0722 375214. Good meals, including stews, chicken and fried fish at around the Ksh400 mark. In the evening it's often quite lively, as are the neighbouring bars. Beer Ksh150. Daily 7am–11pm.

Holiday Celebration Café On the ground-floor terrace of the Watergate Hotel ☎0722 739482. Busy diner serving up spaghetti and meat sauce (Ksh250), kebabs (Ksh60) and Spanish omelettes (Ksh120) to a hungry local clientele. Daily 6.30am–10pm.

★**Kilifi Boatyard** Kilifi Creek shore, south side, accessible via a dirt road from the old main road, 1km inland, then 2km down a steep gravel road to the waterfront ☎0722 442334, ⊛kilifiboats.com. With fine views of the creek and the dramatic bridge, this informal bar-restaurant is popular with Kilifi's seaside-settler and sailing community, making it *the* place for making contacts if you have any plans for Indian Ocean crewing, or want to make contacts for sea-fishing excursions. They turn out fresh and simple seafood dishes, including fish and chips (Ksh750), great crab samosas and full English breakfasts (Ksh650), and there's a noticeboard for exchanging news and trading kit. Daily 7.30am–6.30pm.

Nautilus North shore of Kilifi Creek, just west of town ☎0713 762748 or ☎0724 341034, ⊛facebook.com/nautilusrestaurantkilifi. Attractive, Swiss-run floating restaurant with lovely sunset views over the creek, and a focus on French- and Swahili-influenced seafood: oysters (Ksh900/24), crab and prawn flambé (Ksh1500) and prawns in spicy coconut milk (Ksh1300). There are a few meat dishes as well, including a tempting steak topped with brie and cranberries. Tues–Sun 11am–3pm & 6–11pm.

DRINKING

De Coffee Pub Town centre, behind Titanic hotel ☎0726 363437, ⊛hoteltitanic-kenya.com. Beloved of locals and travellers alike, this bar/club is hopping on weekends, when beers are more expensive (Ksh200). But there are discos every night, and the spacious split-level outdoor seating area, pool table and live sports on TV make it a popular place to congregate. There's food, too – mostly grills and the like, for around Ksh500. Daily 6am–11pm, much later on weekends.

DIRECTORY

Banks Barclays, Equity and KCB all have ATMs.

Internet access There are several internet cafés; the one beneath the *Titanic* hotel is the best bet (Mon–Sat 8am–5pm).

Post office Near the market.

Shops Kilifi's Oloitipitip Market is always bursting with fresh fruit and vegetables; the Tuskys on the road to Malindi (daily 9am–8.30pm) is the best place to stock up on everything else. Kioko Enterprise, next to Tuskys (Mon–Sat 8am–8pm, Sun 8am–1pm), has a good range of wines and spirits, plus cold drinks.

Arabuko Sokoke Forest Reserve

Whether driving or walking, head first for the Forest Visitor Centre, 1.5km south of the Watamu junction on the Malindi–Mombasa road • Daily 6am–6pm • $15 • ☎0729 295382 or ☎0723 314416, ⊛kenyaforestservice.org

The cashew trees lining both sides of the road north of Kilifi soon give way to tracts of jungle where monkeys scatter across the road and hornbills plunge into the cover of the trees. This is the **Arabuko Sokoke Forest Reserve**, the largest patch of indigenous coastal

ARABUKO SOKOKE FOREST WILDLIFE

Beside **elephants** (usually evidenced by their dung), **Sykes' monkeys** and **yellow baboons**, the forest also shelters two rare species of mammal. The 35cm-high **Aders' duiker** is a shy miniature antelope that usually lives in pairs, and the extraordinary **golden-rumped elephant shrew** (see p.44), which has been adopted as the symbol of the forest, is a bizarre insectivore, about the size of a small cat, that resembles a giant mouse with an elongated nose, running on stilts. In one of those mystifyingly evolved animal relationships, it consorts with a small bird, the **red-capped robin chat**, which warns it of danger and in turn picks up insects disturbed by the shrew's snufflings. Your best chance of seeing a shrew is to look for its fluttering companion among the tangle of branches: the shrew will be close by. Elephant shrews can usually be seen (but not for long – they're very speedy) on the walk along the Nature Trail close to the Visitor Centre, or along the sandy tracks further inside the forest. You may also spot one darting across forest trails ahead of you. The exceedingly rare **Sokoke bush-tailed mongoose** is unlikely to put in an appearance – there have been no sightings since the mid-1980s.

The forest is also home to six globally threatened **bird species**, including the small **Sokoke scops owl**, which is found only in the red-soiled Cynometra section of the forest, and the **Sokoke pipit** – both very hard to spot, although guides can help locate them. The other endangered birds are the **Amani sunbird**, **Clarke's weaver**, the **East Coast akalat** and the **spotted ground thrush**, a migrant from South Africa. As well as its wealth of mammals and birds, the forest is, in Africa, second only to the Okavango Delta in Botswana for the diversity of its **frog** population, a fact very much in evidence after heavy rain.

forest in East Africa. At one time it would have covered most of the coastal hinterland behind the shoreline settlements, part of an ancient forest belt stretching from Mozambique to Somalia. There are some 420 square kilometres to explore here, though you'll need a vehicle, or a few days for some walking. A tiny part of the area (six square kilometres in the far north) was declared a national park in 1991.

The bans on cutting timber and clearing bush for agriculture aren't popular with **local residents**, many of whom see the forest as a useless waste of land. To combat this ill feeling, the Kenya Wildlife Service, National Museums of Kenya and a forest support group, the Friends of Arabuko Sokoke (⊕watamu.net/foasf.html), have pioneered a number of projects to make **conservation** worthwhile for the community, including butterfly farming (see p.459), a bee-keeping scheme in which villagers are given low-cost beehives to produce honey from forest flowers (it's sold at the Forest Visitor Centre), and the harvesting of medicinal plants under licence.

Exploring the forest

There are several ways to **explore the forest**, either on foot or by car. A nature trail leads from the Visitor Centre around the first part of the forest, and after rain, this area is spectacularly adorned with the nests of the aptly named foam nest tree frogs. It takes most of a morning, but it's an easy walk and makes an excellent introduction to the forest and its medicinal uses. Take water and insect repellent. Another easy walk is to the Tree House, a viewing platform high up a tree by a former sand quarry, from which you get superb vistas over the forest.

There are also several driving routes, ideally with 4WD, which are also suitable for bikes. The main route starts at the Mida entrance, 2km south of the Visitor Centre on the main Mombasa–Malindi road, and goes up to the viewpoint through Brachystegia forest – look out for the rare Amani sunbird on the way. From the viewpoint, which looks east over the forest to Mida Creek and the Indian Ocean, a walking track continues a further 2km to a second viewpoint that looks west onto Cynometra forest and a large, exposed escarpment. There are other paths along the western edge of **Whistling Duck Pools**, at the junction between the Brachystegia and Cynometra forest on the main driving track between the Mida entrance and the viewpoints. These ponds are a favourite haunt for white-faced whistling ducks, little grebe and open-billed storks, as well as the odd elephant.

6

Guides Walking in the forest is best in the morning or late afternoon, and although this isn't the Amazon, a degree of preparation is a good idea if you plan on venturing far down any of the tracks leading off the main road. The Forest Visitor Centre, 1.5km south of the Watamu junction on the Malindi–Mombasa road, has official guides available to escort you (Ksh1500 for a one- to three-hour

walk for up to four people; Ksh1800 for a birdwatchers' walk). You can also book them for fantastic night walks, which would be impossible on your own.

Maps The Visitor Centre maps are adequate for the main trails but a GPS unit would be helpful if you're venturing off the main trails (though the signal can be weak under the trees).

ACCOMMODATION

Aside from the **official campsite** you can also camp at a number of attractive spots within the reserve, including the Tree House, a large platform in the branches with enough space for a two-person dome tent, though there are no facilities so you'll have to be totally self-sufficient. All cost $15/person.

Campsite Beside the Forest Visitor Centre, 1.5km south of the Watamu junction on the Malindi–Mombasa road ☎0729 295382 or ☎0723 314416.

Not much more than a patch of sandy earth, but it does come with toilets, running water and cold showers. Camping $15

Mida Creek

Southeast of the Arabuko Sokoke forest, **Mida Creek**, which extends inland from the coast to the main road, is an interesting and unusually accessible area of tidal mud, grassland and mangrove forest, and is popular with naturalists.

Mida Creek Mangrove Board Walk and Bird Hide

3km south of the Arabuko Sokoke Forest Visitor Centre, and signposted about 500m off the main road • Daily dawn to dusk • Ksh300, plus Ksh300/hr for a guide (up to four visitors)

The main target in Mida Creek is **Mida Creek Mangrove Board Walk and Bird Hide**. You park at the little information hut, then pay your fees and are escorted out through the mangroves to commune with the tidal ecosystem for as long as you like. If you're a keen birder, you might want to check the tides before your visit (see p.391). The best time to see waders, such as crab plovers, is as the tide comes in.

ACCOMMODATION

Manfriday's Mida Cove Mida Creek south shore, most easily reached by boat from Temple Point on the Watamu side – they will meet you there or at Malindi Airport (see p.469) ☎0721 734171 or ☎0721 388401, ✪manfridays.com. If you want Robinson Crusoe-esque remoteness, without sacrificing your comforts, these four individually serviced villas around a pool above the beach at the mouth of Mida Creek will fit the bill. HB $188

★**Mida Eco-Camp** Next to the board walk ☎0729 213042, ✪midaecocamp.com. This Giriama community project with private UK input is a charming and welcoming

gem of a place. The handful of quirky rooms in various formats (nets, shared toilets and showers, solar power, but no plug sockets in the rooms) is complemented by a blissfully relaxing, open-air tree-platform lounge area where everyone congregates for a cold beer while watching the sunset. The community's Giriama dance troupe often performs in the evening. Meals are highly recommended (Ksh550–800) and the staff, who all benefit directly from every guest, will go out of their way to look after you. They particularly welcome children. Camping with own tent Ksh300, camping with rented tent Ksh600, BB Ksh1800

Gedi ruins

4.3km north of Watamu • **Ruins** Daily 8.30am–6pm • Ksh500 • **Observation platform** Daily 7am–6pm • Ksh100 • ☎0723 359652, ✪museums.or.ke • Any Mombasa- or Malindi-bound bus or matatu can drop you off at the Kobil station at Gedi junction, where the Malindi–Mombasa road meets the turn-off for Watamu; the junction is a 10min walk from the site, which is clearly signposted

The dense forest in the area may help to explain the enigma of **GEDI**. This large, thirteenth- to seventeenth-century Swahili town was apparently unknown to the Portuguese, despite the fact that they had a strong presence only 15km away in Malindi

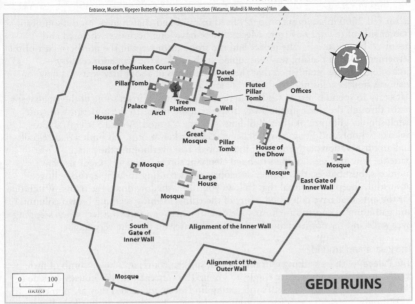

Entrance, Museum, Kipepeo Butterfly House & Gedi Kobil junction (Watamu, Malindi & Mombasa)1km

House of the Sunken Court

Pillar Tomb

Dated Tomb

Fluted Pillar Tomb

Offices

Palace

Tree Platform

Arch

Well

House

Great Mosque

Pillar Tomb

House of the Dhow

Mosque

Mosque

Mosque

East Gate of Inner Wall

Large House

Mosque

South Gate of Inner Wall

Alignment of the Inner Wall

Alignment of the Outer Wall

Mosque

0   100
metres

GEDI RUINS

6

for nearly a hundred years, during a time when Gedi is judged to have been at the peak of its prosperity. Baffingly, Gedi, sometimes spelled Gede, is not mentioned in any old Portuguese, Arabic or Swahili writings and it has to be assumed that as it was set back from the sea and deep in the forest its scale and significance were never noticed.

The **ruins** are confusing, eerie and hauntingly beautiful, especially in the late afternoon. Even if you're not that interested in historical sites, don't miss this one. Forest has invaded the town over the three centuries since it was deserted, and baobabs and magnificent buttress-rooted trees tower over the dimly lit walls and arches.

Gedi has a sinister reputation and local people have always been uneasy about it. Since 1948, when it was opened to the public, it has collected its share of ghost stories and tales of inexplicable happenings. Some of this cultural baggage may derive from the supposed occupation of the ruins in the eighteenth century by the **Oromo** (probably ancestors of the Orma, who live along the Tana River). At the time, the violent and unsettled lifestyle of the Oromo was a major threat to the coastal communities. Even today, Gedi tingles spines easily, particularly if you are on your own. James Kirkman, the archeologist who first worked at the site, remembers: "when I first started to work at Gedi I had the feeling that something or somebody was looking out from behind the walls, neither hostile nor friendly but waiting for what he knew was going to happen."

The more time you spend at Gedi, the further you seem from an answer to its anomalies. The display of pottery shards from all over the world in the small **museum** shows that the town must have been actively trading with overseas merchants, yet it is 5km from the sea and 2km from Mida Creek; and the coastline has probably moved inland over the centuries, so it might previously have been even further away. At the time, with the supposed Oromo threat hanging over the district, sailing into Mida Creek would have been like entering a lobster pot. The reasons for Gedi's location remain thoroughly obscure and its absence from historical records grows more inexplicable the more you think about it.

The site

The **town** is typical of medieval Swahili settlements. It was walled, and originally covered just under a quarter of a square kilometre – some 45 acres. The majority of its estimated 2500 inhabitants probably lived in mud-and-thatch huts, on the southern, poorer side of town, away from Mecca. These have long been overwhelmed and dissolved by the jungle. The palace and the stone town were in the northern part of the settlement. When the site was reoccupied at the end of the sixteenth century – archeologists have established that there was a hiatus of about fifty years – a new inner wall was built, enclosing just this prestigious zone.

It's easy to spend hours at Gedi, and rewarding to walk down some of the well-swept paths through the thick jungle away from the main ruins. In the undergrowth, you catch spooky glimpses of other buildings still unexcavated. ASSETS, the Arabuko Sokoke Schools and Ecotourism Scheme (⚇assets-kenya.org), has built a nature trail and an **observation platform**, high in a baobab tree overlooking the palace. With patience you may see a **golden-rumped elephant shrew** (see p.44). Gedi also has monkeys, bushbabies, tiny duiker antelope and, according to local legend, a huge, mournful, sheep-like animal that follows you like a shadow down the paths. Watch out for the **ants** that have colonized many of the ruins, forming seething brown columns and gathering in enormous clumps. Be careful where you put your feet when stepping over walls and try not to stand on the walls themselves: they are very fragile.

The Palace and around

The **Palace**, with its striking entrance porch, sunken courts and honeycomb of little rooms, is the most impressive single building. The concentration of **houses** outside its east wall is where most of Gedi's interesting finds were made and they are named accordingly: house of the scissors, house of the ivory box, house of the dhow (with a picture of a dhow on the wall). If you have been to Lamu, the tight layout of buildings and streets will be familiar, although in Gedi all the houses had just one storey. As usual, sanitary arrangements are much in evidence: Gedi's toilets are all of identical design, and superior to the long-drops you still find in Kenya today. While many of the houses have been modified over the centuries, these bathrooms seem original. Look out for the **house of the sunken court**, one of the most elaborate dwellings, with its self-conscious emulation of the palace's courtyards.

The Great Mosque

Gedi's **Great Mosque**, one of seven on the site, was its Friday mosque, the mosque of the whole town. Compared with other ruined mosques on the coast, this one is very large and had a *minbar*, or pulpit, of three stone steps, rather than the usual wooden construction. Perhaps an inkling of the kind of people who worshipped here – they were both men and women – and their form of Islam, comes from the carving of a broad-bladed **spearhead** above the arch of the mosque's northeast doorway. Whoever they were, they were clearly not the "colonial Arabs" long believed by European classical scholars to have been the people of Gedi: it's hard to believe that Arabs would have made use of the spear symbol of East African pastoralists.

Tombs

Near the mosque is a good example of a **pillar tomb**. These are found all along the coast and are associated with men of importance – chiefs, sheikhs and senior community elders. The fact that this kind of grave is utterly alien to the rest of the Islamic world is further indication that coastal Islam was distinctly African for a long time. Such tombs aren't constructed any more, although there's one from the nineteenth century in Malindi. It looks as if the more recent waves of Arab immigration to the coast have tended to discourage what must have seemed to them an eccentric, even barbaric, style. The **dated tomb** close to the ticket office gives an idea of Gedi's age. Its epitaph reads 802 AH – or 1400 AD. Also by the office, the **museum** exhibits various finds from the site, including imported artefacts such as Chinese Ming vases and even Spanish scissors.

Kipepeo Butterfly House and Farmers' Training Centre
By the entrance to Gedi ruins • Daily 8am–5pm • Ksh200 • ☏ 0719 671161, ⓦ kipepeo.org

Kipepeo Butterfly House and Farmers' Training Centre (*kipepeo* means "butterfly" in Swahili) helps local residents benefit from the proximity of the forest by exploiting the overseas market for exotic butterflies as preserved specimens and subjects in walk-through butterfly houses. Local people net the adult butterflies in the forest, and the eggs laid by the females are harvested. When hatched, the caterpillars are maintained on their food plants until they pupate, at which point the pupae (chrysalises) are brought to Kipepeo to be shipped to foreign customers, and the breeders are paid. Visitors can see the insects at various stages of their life cycle, and the centre also provides information on the Arabuko Sokoke Forest (see p.455), and sells local handicrafts and honey. Morning is the best time to come, when the butterflies are most active and you have a chance of seeing them emerging, and their wings expanding.

Watamu and around

WATAMU can at first sight seem a bit superficial, consisting simply of a small agglomeration of hotels, a strip of beachfront private homes, a compact village shaded by coconut trees, and the beach. There are good reasons to come here, however, including the superb **marine park**, some interesting **wildlife** initiatives, youthful nightlife (sporadically) and the beautiful **beach** itself. Watamu is comfortable with tourists, and despite tourism's high profile, there's a discernibly easier-going atmosphere here than at Diani, Malindi or along Mombasa's north coast. As most of the beach is within the marine park, KWS regulations tend to be more strictly enforced to keep hawkers away.

This is an exceptional shoreline, with three stunning bays – **Watamu Bay**, the **Blue Lagoon** and **Turtle Bay** – separated by raised coral cliffs and dotted with tiny, sculpted coral islets. Watamu is good for **diving** – and a good place to get qualified, with several diving schools. Out in the **Watamu Marine National Park**, when the visibility is good, the submerged crags of living coral gardens and their swirls of brilliant fish are still magically vivid, although like elsewhere they are suffering from contact damage and the steady rise in sea temperature.

Watamu village
Watamu village is a weird mixture of unhurried fishing community and Europhile souvenir centre. The traditional rubs elbows with the pseudo-hip; Samburu and Maasai *morani* in full ochred splendour stand around waiting for photographers to approach them; and the worshippers wandering in and out of the large **Jamia Mosque** seem quite unfazed by it all.

Bio-Ken Snake Farm
1.3km north of Watamu post office • Daily 10am noon & 2–5pm • Ksh750 • ☏ 0707 577748, ⓦ bio-ken.com

North of the village, **Bio-Ken Snake Farm** is a superb little reptile park with a large collection of snakes, some lizards, plus a few tortoises and terrapins. It's an interesting visit – they have some very impressive creatures here – and staff are very well informed (and one is a silver-level safari guide). They also run specialized **snake safaris** all over Kenya, when you can encounter some of the country's more impressive species in their natural habitats.

Watamu Marine National Park
Daily 6am–6pm • $20 • ⓦ 020 2335459, ⓦ kws.org

The **Watamu Marine National Park** stretches along the coast from the Blue Lagoon to Mida Creek. On the one hand, this **total exclusion zone** for fishermen has not been greeted with rapture by all local people. On the other, tourists come in large numbers and Watamu hasn't gone far wrong in identifying their needs. This is a highly rated

6

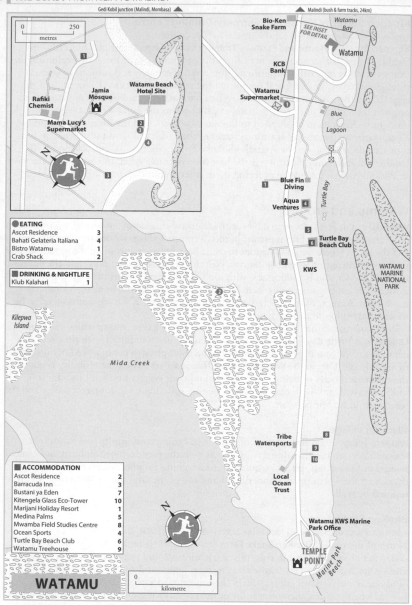

Gedi Kobil junction (Malindi, Mombasa) ▲   ▲ Malindi (bush & farm tracks, 24km)

Bio-Ken Snake Farm

SEE INSET FOR DETAIL

Watamu Bay

Watamu

KCB Bank

Watamu Supermarket

Blue Lagoon

Rafiki Chemist

Jamia Mosque

Watamu Beach Hotel Site

Mama Lucy's Supermarket

Blue Fin Diving

Aqua Ventures

Turtle Bay

Turtle Bay Beach Club

KWS

WATAMU MARINE NATIONAL PARK

Kilepwa Island

Mida Creek

Tribe Watersports

Local Ocean Trust

Watamu KWS Marine Park Office

TEMPLE POINT

Marine Park Beach

● EATING

Ascot Residence	3
Bahati Gelateria Italiana	4
Bistro Watamu	1
Crab Shack	2

■ DRINKING & NIGHTLIFE

Klub Kalahari	1

■ ACCOMMODATION

Ascot Residence	2
Barracuda Inn	3
Bustani ya Eden	7
Kitengela Glass Eco-Tower	10
Marijani Holiday Resort	1
Medina Palms	5
Mwamba Field Studies Centre	8
Ocean Sports	4
Turtle Bay Beach Club	6
Watamu Treehouse	9

WATAMU

0   1
kilometre

0   250
metres

snorkelling and **diving** territory, where the reef is reasonably close to shore, still mostly in good condition and the water crystal clear in the right season. Harmless **whale sharks** also occasionally visit the area, as do dolphins – a highlight for any diver. Boat trips can be arranged in quest of these, and it's become accepted practice to pay only a nominal charge for the trip if you're unsuccessful. Check the terms carefully before signing up with any of the dive operators (see box opposite).

6

WATAMU DIVING AND WATERSPORTS

From October to March, when the water is clearest, the diving possibilities are extensive, with as many as sixteen diving sites off Watamu, compared with Malindi's five. **Turtle Reef**, a few hundred metres offshore, offers big shoals of surgeon and parrot fish around high coral heads. Further out, a popular site is **Moray Reef**, where at least one very large moray eel has become used to visiting divers. Further north, a good spot for beginners is the shallow **Drummers Reef** site, where you can see blue-spotted rays, napoleon wrasse and scorpion fish, and, fairly often on the landward side, **turtles**. There are three dive centres at Watamu; the best plan is probably to visit all of them and make your own assessment of their competence and suitability.

If you're a qualified diver, each dive will cost around $50–60 including equipment, or somewhat less with your own equipment. There are reductions if you book a series of dives, and small supplements for night- and wreck-dives. If you haven't dived for a while, you should be asked to do a check-out dive (usually free) or a one-day refresher. If you're a beginner, you can do either a one-day, one-dive course (around $120), or opt for a PADI course of four dives over five days – leading to Open Water certification – for around $500. Remember that **marine park fees** are extra ($20/day, payable at the KWS Marine Park office at the end of the beach road, or to your operator).

DIVE OPERATORS

Aqua Ventures Based at Ocean Sports, on the beach ⓣ042 2332420, ⓦdiveinkenya.com. Long-established leading operator, with PADI Open Water certification for $590. BSAC Premier Centre (the only one in Kenya), used by the British army for dive training. Underwater digital camera for rent at Ksh1500/dive. They run kayaking trips as well.

Blue Fin Diving Next to Blue Bay Village ⓣ0722 261242, ⓦbluefindiving.com. Based in Watamu Nov–April and Malindi July–Nov, but offering diving year-round (from intro dives to PADI Open Water certification – €360) from many of Watamu's hotels.

Tribe Watersports Across from Mwamba Field Studies Centre ⓣ0718 553355, ⓦtribe-watersports.com. Relatively new outfit whose speciality is kitesurfing, with highly experienced instructors, although they also offer windsurfing, paddleboarding, kayaking and bodyboarding. Three-day beginner kitesurfing course $330; kitesurfing equipment rental from $35/hr.

Turtle Bay Beach Club On the beach ⓣ0733 295487, ⓦturtledive.com. Single dives for qualified divers with own equipment: €38; PADI Open Water certificate: €475.

The coral gardens

If you've never taken a swim before in a shoal of coral fish, the spectacle can be breathtaking: every conceivable combination of colour and shape – and a few inconceivable ones – is represented. The ostentatious dazzle of some of them, especially the absurd parrot fish, can be simply hilarious. The most common destination is the "**coral gardens**", a kilometre or two offshore, where the boat drifts, suspended in five or six metres of scintillatingly clear water. Here, over a group of giant coral heads, where fish naturally congregate, you enter the unusual park. If you dive to the sea floor, you'll get an intense experience of sharing the undersea world with the fish and the coral. Watch out for the small, harmless octopuses that stay motionless until disturbed and then jet themselves across the sea bed – they're brilliant masters of disguise, altering their form and colour to match their surroundings. For people who prefer not to go in the water, the glass-bottomed boats provide an alternative view – but it's often a slightly murky and narrow one.

ARRIVAL AND INFORMATION — WATAMU MARINE NATIONAL PARK

Watamu KWS Marine Park Office The park headquarters and ticket office – you buy your own park tickets if you're using a private boat – is down at the south end of the Watamu road at Temple Point.

Diving See box, above.

Snorkelling trips Ocean Sports (see p.463) runs glass-bottomed boat snorkelling trips, costing $38/person (including park fees) for a 2hr trip in a glass-bottomed boat combining the coral gardens with, at high tide, a trip along Mida Creek. Masks, snorkels and fins are provided, but remember to take plenty of sun cream.

Private boats If you're not on a prebooked trip, you can haggle with the boatmen along the beach or outside the park headquarters. They start at around Ksh1000 for two hours, not including park fees ($20).

Watamu beach

Watamu beach is beautiful, with its coral outcrop islands within swimming distance of the hotel gardens. Although they mostly started as **fishing** and **diving** centres (see p.461), many of the hotels are getting involved with **community and environmental projects** that channel tourist excursion money into the local economy.

Local Ocean Trust

Beach Rd, about 5km south of Watamu village • Mon 2–4pm, Tues–Fri 9.30am–noon & 2–4pm, Sat 9.30am–noon • Ksh300 • ☎0717 578723 or • ☎0713 759627, ⊚watamuturtles.com

Among environmental initiatives, one in which many hotels participate, and which individual tourists can contribute to, is the Watamu **turtle watch scheme** run by **Local Ocean Trust**. This project protects the eggs of threatened marine turtles from poaching by paying local people to guard nests. The same group also pays fishermen to hand in turtles that have got ensnared in fishing nets for treatment of their injuries and release back into the sea – anything from eight hundred to a thousand turtles every year. The **Turtle Rehab Centre** has some shady quarantine pools where you can usually "meet" recovering turtles.

August brings lots of sea grass to Watamu, and turtles mate and lay in the same month. The **eggs**, which are buried en masse on the beach in pits dug by the females with their flippers, and then covered in sand, take sixty to 75 days to incubate, so October and November are commonly the months when nests usually hatch. Watamu's turtles are mostly the green and hawksbill species. Despite extensive research and observation, it is still not known where the babies go after hatching. What is clear is that only one in a thousand survives to maturity.

Visitors can sponsor a turtle for release or a nest for guarding (you can see the nest sites if you walk down the Watamu peninsula towards Temple Point). The Local Ocean Trust is informed when nests that are being guarded start to hatch, so, if you contact them, you may be able to go and see the baby turtles scuttling down the sand like tiny clockwork toys. Mwamba Field Studies Centre (see opposite) is a good place to be based if you don't want to miss anything.

ARRIVAL AND DEPARTURE | WATAMU AND AROUND

By bus and matatu Getting to Watamu is easy, with frequent matatus making the run from Malindi. Buses and matatus ploughing up and down the coast highway will drop you at the Gedi junction, leaving you to walk, hitch a lift, wait for a local matatu, or take a tuk-tuk or cab for the last, dead-straight, 6km.

FISHING IN WATAMU

The **game-fishing season** runs from July to April (there is no legal season as such, but few boats go out in the rough seas in May and June), with the main season for **billfish** – those with spikes on their snouts, including sailfish and black, striped and blue marlin – roughly November to mid-March. Other species commonly hooked include wahoo, kingfish, dorado, bonito, giant trevally and various sharks, including some big tiger sharks and bull sharks. If you're fishing between July and October, before the wind swings round, it's good to be aware that conditions can be rough – it's not for the faint-hearted. While some fish are caught for eating and invariably killed and sold by the crew (yellow fin tuna particularly), all captains have a policy of tag-and-release for sharks and billfish. The fish are tagged for migration research, and a small bounty paid for delivery of tags from recaptured fish. In addition to the official trip providers listed below, a number of Watamu-based **independent boat owners** offer a day's fishing from around $500, usually for a group of four or five, with lunch and drinks included.

TRIP PROVIDERS

Alleycat ☎0722 734788, ⊚alleycatfishing.com. Full days from around $700–900 depending on the season.
Tarka ☎0722 282573, ✉tarka@swiftmalindi.com. Ten-hour day-trips from $500.

Tribe Watersports Beach Rd, across from Mwamba Field Studies Centre ☎0718 553355, ⊚tribe-watersports.com. Full days of deep-sea fishing from $640, depending on the season.

GETTING AROUND

By bike Bicycle rental is offered by a number of outlets, especially in high season when it gets quite competitive (Ksh500–1000/day, depending on season and number of days). Bikes are a great way of getting to know Watamu, with the Gedi ruins and anywhere on the beach road easily reachable in 30min or so.

ACCOMMODATION

There are several accommodation options in the village itself – everything from humble B&Ls to a pleasant holiday hotel. If you have a tent, you can **camp** at *Ocean Sports* or *Mwamba Field Studies Centre*. Watamu's **beach hotels and lodgings** are a mixed bag. Several focus on watersports, with diving and game fishing the main activities. The famous *Hemingway's*, next to *Ocean Sports*, was closed for major redevelopment at the time of writing. The big fishing competition in the first or second week of March can make accommodation scarce, but May and June usually see excellent low-season rates. Matatus usually only go as far south as Turtle Bay, where piki-pikis or tuk-tuks can be rented to take you further south. As in most beach resort towns, you'll find wi-fi virtually everywhere.

VILLAGE ACCOMMODATION

Ascot Residence Village centre ☏042 2232326 or ☏0721 267761, ⓦascotresidencehotel.com. Good-value double rooms and two-room studios (sleeping four), all with nets and fans but no a/c, and a large pool; the apartments come with nice patios and kitchens for self-caterers. The pleasant, breezy public areas get fairly lively in high season and there's a small casino/gaming room. Most guests are Italian. BB **€50**

Marijani Holiday Resort North of the village ☏0735 258263, ⓦmarijani-holiday-resort.com. Friendly, very informal German-run place, with nine comfortable and good-value rooms (four-poster beds, nets, fans, spotless bathrooms) in two stylish houses. All rooms have fridges, some have kitchens. BB **Ksh4000**

BEACH HOTELS AND OTHER ACCOMMODATION

Barracuda Inn On the beach ☏0707 578688 or ☏0701 028754, ⓦbarracuda-inn.com. Unusual hotel with impressive *makuti*-vaulted reception, well worth considering for its location on the shore of the Blue Lagoon, and its great views. Ground-floor rooms are more spacious – all have a/c – and there's a pool. Largely Italian guests. BB **Ksh8500**

Bustani ya Eden West of the road, not on the beach ☏0710 813313. Plain, tidy, comfortable, chalet-style rooms, with fans and nets, set in a garden bursting with bougainvillea. It's attached to a locally renowned bar-restaurant, with reasonably priced seafood and African dishes. BB **Ksh2500**

Kitengela Glass Eco-Tower Just above the beach ☏020 6750602 or ☏0736 761533, ⓦkitengelaglass .co.ke. As much a work of art as viable accommodation, this concrete tower, built around a slender doum palm tree, has had nearly every centimetre of its surface covered in bits of recycled glass, bottles, driftwood and paintings by the creative people behind Nairobi's Kitengela Glass (see p.141). Each floor serves as an open-plan double bedroom (non-s/c), with no door or windows, and beds that hang from the ceiling or, in the case of the "sky bed", project out over the forest canopy. Not for those looking for privacy, but nonetheless a completely unique place to sleep. Kitchen facilities in a separate building. Room only **Ksh13,000**

Medina Palms On the beach ☏0713 181658, ⓦmedinapalms.com. Brand-new Moroccan-styled resort that's attractive though somewhat ostentatious (as are its prices), with fifty self-catering apartments lining a geometric series of pools leading down to the shore. The airy apartments, with their white walls and whitewashed furniture, come with kitchens and between one and five bedrooms; most face the pool and gardens, not the sea. There's also a restaurant, a gym and plenty of watersports on offer. Room only **$355**

★Mwamba Field Studies Centre Just above the beach ☏020 335865, ⓦarocha.org. This friendly guesthouse is run by the Christian conservation group A Rocha, though it is open to all and is only evangelical about the environment. They have 22 beds in various clean, simple rooms with nets and hot-water showers, as well as camping pitches. Snorkelling gear, bird walks and turtle watching are all available and it's close to the nearly deserted beach. Meals are available, eaten communally. Room only: camping **Ksh500**, doubles **Ksh3000**

Ocean Sports On the beach ☏034 195227 or ☏0724 389732, ⓦoceansports.net. Slightly macho place, whose reputation ("Open Shorts") has sailed before it for years. During holiday times it swarms with young Anglo-Kenyans doing their own thing, but the staff are great, as is the food, and it's right above the beach, with a great deck. All 29 rooms have nets, fans, a/c and safes and pleasantly rustic bathrooms, but foam mattresses on the beds are disappointing. There's an adjoining campsite plus tennis, squash, a pool and a PADI diving school (see p.461). Camping **Ksh800**, BB **$150**

★Turtle Bay Beach Club On the beach ☏0721 830604, ⓦturtlebay.co.ke. Expertly run, all-inclusive holiday club, full of happy holidaymakers, mainly British and Kenyan. Lots to do, lots to eat, and plenty of cheap booze. The gardens are cramped, but facilities include three pools, tennis, PADI diving and windsurfing schools (see p.461), free bicycles and some watersports. Staff and management actively participate in local community and environmental initiatives – they have a gold rating from Ecotourism Kenya. Al $212

★ **Watamu Treehouse** Just above the beach ☎0702 810055 or ☎0733 628490, ⍵treehouse.co.ke. Unquestionably the most beautiful place to say in Watamu, this spectacular structure has been hailed as one of the world's best treehouses. It has just seven open-plan rooms (with nets and fans) in two whitewashed towers with fantastic views out over the forest towards the sea, all whimsically decorated in twinkling coloured glass. Rooms are designed to provide maximum privacy with as few actual doors as possible, with waist-high walls that give the impression you aren't indoors at all. The *Treehouse* serves as a yoga retreat (though you don't have to be a yogi to stay here), with daily yoga classes, and the owner also arranges kayaking trips. There's a small pool in the garden. BB $170

EATING

Ascot Residence Village centre ☎042 2232326, ⍵ascotresidencehotel.com. With its small private gazebos set in the garden, this restaurant caters mainly to Italian couples looking for a romantic dinner. The wood-fired oven produces very authentic pizzas, and the wine list is moderately priced. Pizzas from Ksh550, seafood dishes from Ksh900. Tues–Sun 11.30am–2pm & 6–10pm.

★ **Bahati Gelateria Italiana** Village centre ☎0724 079856. Outstandingly good home-made *gelati* and pastries in this very popular and polished Italian-run ice-cream parlour (Ksh120/scoop) and snack-café that has grown from tiny beginnings to fill a whole block. Perfect for a dawn breakfast of hot croissants and cappuccino. Wed–Sun 7am–6pm.

Bistro Watamu By the supermarket. A popular stop-off for local *wazungu*, this serves very nice, freshly ground coffee (Ksh100), cakes (Ksh150), toasted sandwiches (Ksh220), and shakes and juices (around Ksh200). Daily 8am–5pm.

★ **Crab Shack** West of Turtle Bay, in the mangrove swamp ☎0725 315562. Accessed via a picturesque boardwalk though the mangroves, this community-run restaurant serves amazing crab samosas (two for Ksh200), whole crabs (Ksh800) and a number of other seafood dishes, including oysters, on stilted wooden platforms overlooking Mida Creek. To get here follow the dirt road heading west from Turtle Bay, which eventually turns into little more than a footpath. There's a Ksh300 fee for the boardwalk, though it's waived if you're having a meal. Daily 8am–10pm.

DRINKING AND NIGHTLIFE

Klub Kalahari Signposted off the beach road ☎0714 893989, ⍵facebook.com/klubkalahari. Watamu's best local nightspot, this lively bar is a great place to meet local people, with DJs in season and occasional live music. There are also two restaurants, *Sky Gardens* and *Roof Top*, both serving *nyama choma* (Ksh390/half kg) and seafood. Club daily 7pm–late, Sky Gardens daily 11am–11pm, Roof Top daily 6pm–midnight.

DIRECTORY

Banks There's a KCB bank, with an ATM, in Watamu village.
Pharmacy Rafiki Chemist in the village, near Mama Lucy's supermarket (daily 6am–9pm).
Post office Coming into Watamu itself, you pass the post office before reaching the beach road T-junction.
Supermarkets Watamu Supermarket (daily 8am–7pm) and Mama Lucy's supermarket (daily 6.10am–8pm) are both well stocked, but there's no big-name supermarket in town.

Malindi and around

When Vasco da Gama's fleet arrived at **MALINDI** in 1498, it met an unexpectedly warm welcome. The king of Malindi had presumably heard of Mombasa's attempts to sabotage the fleet a few days earlier and, no friend of Mombasa himself, he was swift to ally himself with the powerful and dangerous Portuguese. Until they finally subdued Mombasa nearly one hundred years later, Malindi was the Portuguese centre of operations on the East African coast. Once Fort Jesus was built, Malindi's ruling family was invited to transfer their power base there, which they did, and for many years Malindi was virtually a ghost town as its aristocrats lived it up in Mombasa under Portuguese protection.

Malindi's reputation for **hospitality** to strangers has stuck, and so has the suggestion of sell-out. It has an amazingly salacious reputation, and although recent travel advisories have hit Malindi hard, a quick glance in some of the bars suggests that the **sex safari** is still in full swing, mostly dominated by Italians. With many hotels and tourist activities quoting prices in **euros**, Malindi is slipping towards cultural anonymity: it can't seem to make up its mind whether it wants to be a Mombasa or a Lamu – and while its old centre clings on to some Swahili character, it lacks Lamu's self-contained tranquillity. Although it makes a good base for visits to Gedi and the Arabuko Sokoke Forest, and for a trip to Lamu, it remains unashamedly geared towards beach tourism. Consequently, whether you enjoy Malindi or not depends a little on how highly you rate the unsophisticated parts of Kenya, and whether you appreciate a fully fledged resort town for its facilities or loathe it for its tackiness. It also

6

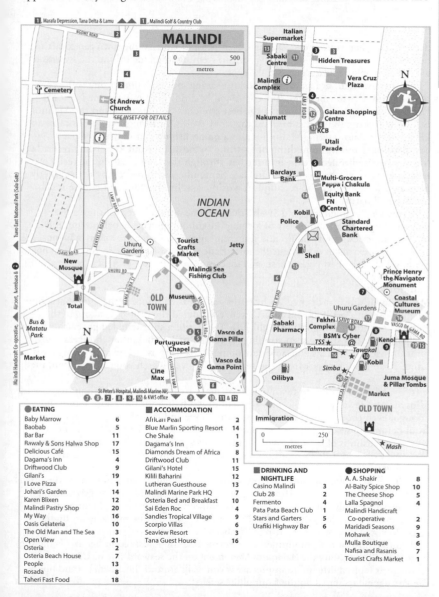

● EATING	
Baby Marrow	6
Baobab	5
Bar Bar	11
Rawaly & Sons Halwa Shop	17
Delicious Café	15
Dagama's Inn	4
Driftwood Club	9
Gilani's	19
I Love Pizza	1
Johari's Garden	14
Karen Blixen	12
Malindi Pastry Shop	20
My Way	16
Oasis Gelateria	10
The Old Man and The Sea	3
Open View	21
Osteria	2
Osteria Beach House	7
People	13
Rosada	8
Taheri Fast Food	18

■ ACCOMMODATION	
African Pearl	2
Blue Marlin Sporting Resort	14
Che Shale	1
Dagama's Inn	5
Diamonds Dream of Africa	8
Driftwood Club	11
Gilani's Hotel	15
Kilili Baharini	12
Lutheran Guesthouse	13
Malindi Marine Park HQ	7
Osteria Bed and Breakfast	10
Sai Eden Roc	4
Sandies Tropical Village	9
Scorpio Villas	6
Seaview Resort	3
Tana Guest House	16

■ DRINKING AND NIGHTLIFE	
Casino Malindi	3
Club 28	2
Fermento	4
Pata Pata Beach Club	1
Stars and Garters	5
Urafiki Highway Bar	6

● SHOPPING	
A. A. Shakir	8
Al-Baity Spice Shop	10
The Cheese Shop	5
Lalla Spagnol	4
Malindi Handicraft Co-operative	2
Maridadi Seasons	9
Mohawk	3
Mulla Boutique	6
Nafisa and Rasanis	7
Tourist Crafts Market	1

SEA AND WATER CONDITIONS IN MALINDI

Malindi's shoreline can get very windy around September, and during June, July and November the beach becomes covered in **seaweed** – though the seaweed is clean and perfectly harmless, and in fact prevents erosion of the beach (clearing it is prohibited within the limits of the marine park), many hotels clear their beachfronts daily. It's also worth knowing that the headland of **Vasco da Gama Point** marks a locally important division. To the north, the sea water is often reddish-brown and cloudy – full of the soil erosion brought down by the Galana (Sabaki) River, especially after rain – and, to the south, the Marine Park encloses a zone of often aquarium-clear water.

---

depends on when you're here. During December and January, the town can sometimes be a bit nightmarish, with everything African seeming to recede behind the swarms of window-shopping tourists and Suzuki jeeps.

Fortunately, Malindi has some important saving graces. Number one is the **coral reef** south of the town centre. The combined Malindi/Watamu Marine National Park and Reserve encloses some of the best stretches on the coast, and the Malindi fish have become so used to humans that they swarm in front of your mask like a kaleidoscopic snowstorm. Malindi is also a **game-fishing** centre with regular competitions, and it's something of a surfing, windsurfing and kitesurfing resort, too. Good-sized rollers steam into the bay through the long break in the reef, opposite the town, between June and late September, whipped up by the southerly monsoon (*kusi*) wind. The surfing isn't world class, but it's fun, and good enough for boogie boards.

Meanwhile, an interesting old **Swahili quarter**, one or two historical sites, a busy market, shops, *hotelis* and plenty of lodgings just about manage to balance out the tourist boutiques, beauty salons and real-estate agencies. As for the **Italian influence**, the new resident expats have brought the town riches that nowhere else in Kenya can boast – and some of the best pizzas, pasta and ice cream in the whole of Africa.

Malindi town

Malindi town was first opened up by settlers as a seaside resort in the 1930s, at a time when ocean air, "sea level and sanity" were considered the proper antidote to the grind of making a living in the highlands. The last of a sun-wrinkled generation from a bygone area can still be seen strolling on **Lamu Road**, which, though increasingly built up with little malls and new developments, is happily still shaded by big trees. Lamu Road is set far back from the **seafront**, however, which you can't see from the town centre.

Today, taking a walk into town is still the main pastime, and not without its idiosyncratic rewards. The old part of Malindi is a half-hour diversion: interesting enough, even though there's nothing specific to see and few of the buildings date from before the second half of the nineteenth century. But the juxtaposition of the workaday business of the old town with the *mzungu*-mania only a couple of minutes' walk away on Lamu Road produces a schizophrenic atmosphere that perfectly epitomizes this place.

Malindi's **archeological sites** are fairly scant. The two **pillar tombs** in front of the Juma (Friday) Mosque on the waterfront are fine upstanding examples of the genre, though the shorter one only dates back to the nineteenth century. This being Malindi, their appearance is sometimes described as "circumcised", though Islamic scholars on the coast do not of course accept the phallic label.

Malindi's most notable monuments are Portuguese, the most recent bequest being the ugly 1959 **Prince Henry the Navigator Monument** on the seaward side of Uhuru Gardens. It looks a little more impressive if you walk around the other side and notice the Portuguese red cross on the front of the sail.

> **MALINDI'S BEACHES**
>
> The beach near the town centre, several hundred metres east of Lamu Road, is windswept and less appealing than you might imagine. For more of a seaside atmosphere, the seafront **Vasco da Gama Road** further south is pleasant, especially in the late afternoon. For the real McCoy, beach-wise, you need to go further south of the town centre to the aptly named **Silversands Beach**, complete with its reef-fringed lagoon, palm trees and inevitable beach boys.

Town museum

6

Vasco da Gama Rd • Daily 8am–6pm • Ksh500, including same-day entry to the Portuguese Chapel and Vasco da Gama Pillar (see below) • ⓦ museums.or.ke

A nineteenth-century trader's shop on the waterfront – the **House of Columns** – was opened as the **town museum** in 2004. With a preserved coelacanth fish downstairs, and some photographs of archeological sites on the coast upstairs – plus a good series of wall posters explaining Vasco da Gama and the Portuguese period on the coast – there is not quite enough to justify the entry fee on its own. The occasional temporary exhibition is a bonus, and the fee does include entry to Malindi's two Portuguese sites. There's also a small collection of old Malindi photos, alongside various traditional objects used by the local Mijikenda and Taita people, tucked away in an annexe down the road.

Portuguese monuments

Both daily 8am–6pm • Ksh500, including same-day entry to town museum (see above)

The **Vasco da Gama Pillar**, far out on a coral outcrop on Vasco da Gama Point, and dating from 1499, makes a good target for a stroll. Once threatened by coastal erosion, the outcrop has been reinforced and the pillar itself – a typical Portuguese *padrao*, or standard, of its era that would have carried the Portuguese coat of arms – is regularly whitewashed. The **Portuguese Chapel** on Vasco da Gama Road is a tiny cube of a church now covered with *makuti*, whose foundations were laid in the sixteenth century on the site of a Portuguese burial ground. There are a number of old burial sites in the grounds as well as more recent graves with inscriptions.

Malindi Marine National Park

Daily 6am–6pm • $20 • ⓦ kws.org • Boat trips: you should find a little room for discussion but won't be able to knock down prices much below the current going rate of Ksh2000 (excluding park fees) for 2hr, especially at peak seasons (in fact your outing may be somewhat curtailed if you bargain too ruthlessly); glass-bottomed boats Ksh3000–5000 for 2hr • Six square kilometres

Trips out to the **marine park** can be arranged with the boat-trip salesmen who make their rounds of the beaches and hotels most mornings. Alternatively, make your own way down to the park office and very pretty beach at **Casuarina Point**, 5km from town, where you can choose your boat and captain. Be sure to check out the condition of masks and snorkels, and insist on a set for each member of the party.

The national park takes in the loveliest areas of coral garden, between 1km and 4km offshore, and the trip is worth every shilling you finally agree on. The **snorkelling** itself is sublime. Look out for the unusual weedy scorpionfish, an array of beautiful sea horses and the bizarre-looking Spanish dancer – a huge and colourful sea slug. Unless you have a mortal fear of snorkelling, don't bother with the **glass-bottomed boats**, which generally have small, not very clear windows.

Marafa Depression

Ksh1000 community fee • To get to Marafa, take the road out of Malindi heading north, turn left on the other side of the Galana (Sabaki) bridge and from there go via Marikebuni and Magarini (about 80km round trip); alternatively, a handful of matatus run to Marafa village every day, or you could rent a cab and negotiate the price – between Ksh5000 and Ksh10,000; to get to the gorge itself, fork right at the end of Marafa village, and the canyon is about 500m along on the left, hidden until you're right at its edge

Northwest of Malindi, the **Marafa Depression** is the remains of a large sandstone ridge, now reduced by wind, rain and floodwater to a series of gorges, where steep gullies and narrow arêtes alternately eat into or jut from the main ridge wall. The colours of the exposed sandstone range from off-white through pale pink and orange to deep crimson, all capped by the rich tawny topsoil. It's particularly dramatic at sunset.

"**Hell's Kitchen**" is the common nickname for this impressive landscape, though the locals call it Nyari – "the place broken by itself" – and tell numerous moralizing stories about its dark origins. The main one sets the word of a monotheistic, all-powerful deity against traditional wisdom, and tells how the people of a village that once stood here were warned by God about a forthcoming miraculous event. They were commanded to move out, and all did so, except one old woman, who refused to believe such nonsense. The village and the old lady disappeared a short while later, leaving Nyari.

At the lip of the gorge, it's easy to descend the steep path to the bottom, where you can count on spending an hour or two exploring the natural architecture of what looks like an early *Star Trek* set.

ACTIVITIES AROUND MALINDI

Snorkelling, **diving** and board-based watersports – **surfing**, **windsurfing** and **kitesurfing** –are Malindi's touristic *raison d'être*. Unfortunately, diving is somewhat marred by the Galana (Sabaki) River's outpouring of thousands of tonnes of prime red topsoil from the upcountry plateaus. The cloudy water prevents any coral growing north of Vasco da Gama Point and the sea in this north part of Malindi is muddy-brown from November to January. The good diving and snorkelling season, in the coastal area starting from Vasco da Gama Point southwards, lasts only from July to October. During the April to June long rains, it's low season and not great for clarity, while between November and March, silt makes the water too murky, and the larger hotels usually organize daily excursions for their guests to dive or snorkel in Watamu.

DIVE CENTRES AND DIVING SCHOOLS

There are two main dive centres in Malindi, and you should probably visit them both before deciding which one to use. Remember marine park fees are extra ($20/day). The Watamu account (see p.461) has more general advice and information.

Blue Fin Diving Sandies Tropical Village, 3km south of Malindi, on Casuarina Rd ☎ 0722 261242, ⓦ bluefindiving.com. Based in Malindi July–Nov, in Watamu Nov–April, with year-round diving (from intro dives to PADI Open Water certification – €360) from many of Malindi's hotels.

Upinde Mariposa Restaurant, south along the beach from Scorpio Villas ☎ 0723 962123 or ☎ 0735 418570, ⓦ upindediving.com. One-day introduction courses and five-day PADI Open Water qualification courses – €330.

KITESURFING

Malindi is one of the world's kitesurfing hot spots. Learning at *Che Shale* (see p.470), the beach lodge that is partly responsible for the development of the sport, costs €340 for a three-day (9hr) residential course, on top of your accommodation. The best seasons are January to April and July to mid-October.

SNORKELLING

Seasonal variations aside (see above), with your own gear you can snorkel in the lagoon, or snorkel out to the inside edge of the reef anywhere north of the marine park. At the park boundary at Casuarina Point the reef hugs the shore, and it runs north to its conclusion off Vasco da Gama Point, where it's more than 900m from the beach. If you find conditions not as good as you'd hoped, it's easy to check out nearby Watamu (see p.459). Some local divers believe Watamu's coral is superior, but Malindi has a greater diversity of fish.

SURFING

Malindi Bay is the main surfing beach (June to the end of September, when the swell is on), and surfboards are available from some of the tourist hotels in town. The beach here is a good 5–10min walk from the road. There are several public access points, and some hotels will allow use of their beach access for a small fee, which means you can use their pool and leave your things on their guarded premises.

ARRIVAL AND DEPARTURE

BY PLANE

Malindi Airport is barely 3km south of the town centre; you can walk into Malindi in half an hour. Matatus heading to the main stage (halfway between the airport and the town centre) will pick you up on the main road just outside the airport; otherwise, taxis charge around Ksh1200 to most beach hotels, or Ksh500 into town. If you need to park at the airport, you can do so safely (Ksh60/hr).

AIRLINES AND DEPARTURES

Aeronav Air Service Malindi Airport (☎ 020 6007892 or ☎ 0722 754580, ⓦ aeronavaircharter.com). Charter services and a daily scheduled flight to Maasai Mara in the high season (90min).

Airkenya Malindi Airport (☎ 042 2120411 or ☎ 0713 981490, ⓦ airkenya.com). Daily flights to Nairobi Wilson (45min).

Fly540 North Coast Travel Services, opposite the FN Centre, Lamu Rd (☎ 042 2130312, ⓦ fly540.com). Daily to Nairobi JKIA (1hr) and Lamu (30min).

Kenya Airways Blue Marlin Shopping Arcade, Lamu Rd (☎ 0723 786314, ⓦ kenya-airways.com). Flies daily to/from Nairobi JKIA (1hr).

Mombasa Air Safari Southern Sky Safaris, Malindi Complex (☎ 042 2130547, ⓦ mombasaairsafari.com). Flights on most days to/from Mombasa (35min) and Maasai Mara (90min).

MALINDI AND AROUND

BY BUS AND MATATU

If you're arriving from Mombasa, you'll end up at the main bus station and matatu area, about a 10min walk south of town along the Mombasa road; a taxi to the centre shouldn't cost more than Ksh400, or Ksh1000 to the furthest beach hotels (half that for a tuk-tuk). Leaving Malindi, there are frequent services to Gedi, Watamu, Kilifi and Mombasa, and infrequent local matatus and buses for points inland from the main bus station and matatu park. In addition, some matatus for Watamu leave from the town centre by the old market in Mama Ngina Rd. Coming from Lamu or Garissa, you'll be dropped by the bus companies' booking offices in the town centre between the market and the high street. Bus services to Lamu start off from Mombasa, and pass by their Malindi booking offices in the centre of town by the old market at around 9am or 11pm each day, reaching the Mokowe jetty for the short crossing to Lamu approximately 5–6 hours later; tickets cost Ksh800–1000. Tawakal is the current market leader, tends to be the most reliable and runs two to three services daily.

Bus companies Companies travelling to Lamu include Simba Coach (☎ 0774 471112), Tahmeed (☎ 0711 756970), Tawakal (☎ 0705 090122) and TSS (☎ 0722 921334).

GETTING AROUND

Car rental There are no full-service car rental firms in Malindi. Try Glory Car Hire, Tours and Safaris at Multi-Grocer Shopping Centre (☎ 0722 829937 or ☎ 0734 007777, ⓦ glorykenya.com), which offers self-drive saloons from around Ksh3000/day. Otherwise, private taxi and 4WD owners will meet your requirements: ask your hotel front desk. Prices for saloons with driver start from Ksh5000/day around town.

Taxis With no formal taxi companies in town, your best bet is to find taxis congregated outside big hotels or supermarkets; your hotel can also call one for you. Tuk tuks are cheaper, boda-bodas cheaper still.

INFORMATION

Tourist office On Lamu Rd, at the very back of the Malindi Complex building, on the first floor (Mon–Fri 8am–12.30pm & 2–4.30pm; ☎ 042 2120747 or ☎ 042 2120689). Staff don't have much in the way of information, but are the people to contact if you have a serious complaint about a hotel, safari operator or restaurant.

ACCOMMODATION

There's plenty of accommodation on offer, though over Christmas room availability can be tight. The cheap town lodgings also fill up during Maulidi and at the end of Ramadan. Tourist establishments usually vary their prices seasonally by up to fifty percent, and many close during May and part or all of June. You can **camp** in the KWS compound near the Marine Park office.

BUDGET ROOMS AND CAMPING

Dagama's Inn Vasco da Gama Rd, on the seafront ☎ 0701 864446. A variety of rather run-down rooms, most s/c, with nets and peeling paint. Best are the two front rooms overlooking the beach, with a balcony, which aren't bad considering the price. Room only **Ksh1000**

Gilani's Hotel Vasco da Gama Rd, on the seafront ☎ 0722 646872. Above the restaurant there are twelve rooms, some of which have four-poster beds with nets and fans, balconies and sea views, making this good budget value. No hot water. BB **Ksh1900**

Lutheran Guesthouse Lamu Rd, town centre ☎ 0723 766278, ⓔ lutheranmalindi@gmail.com. Set in a large garden, with double, triple and quad rooms (clean and mosquito-netted with fans and TVs), plus two self-catering bungalows, each for four people. There's a

6

no-alcohol policy. Room only doubles Ksh1200, bungalows Ksh2500

Malindi Marine Park HQ 5km south of the town centre ☎0790 484973, ✉reservations@kws.go.ke. The Marine Park HQ's campsite is a bit far from town, but worth considering if you want to do a lot of snorkelling in the marine park. There are toilets and showers, but no restaurant, so you'll need to be self-sufficient to stay here – much easier if you have a vehicle. Camping §20

Tana Guest House Uhuru Rd. While basic, the *Tana* is well kept and very cheap, with nets and fans, and is handy for buses to Lamu. Rooms in the main block (s/c and non-s/c) can be hot, but there are slightly dearer, "special self-contained" rooms around a quiet courtyard at the back. Good, busy ground-floor *hoteli* with plenty of choice. Room only Ksh600

HOTELS IN THE TOWN CENTRE AND NORTH

North of town, all the upmarket hotels have pools, but the beach is some 500m east of Lamu Rd and relatively little used. Watersports are very limited at most of these hotels: with no reef offshore, there's no snorkelling, and the current makes windsurfing only feasible if you're experienced. One exception is the excellent *Che Shale*, a 30min drive from Malindi, north of Mambrui. All of the below have wi-fi.

African Pearl Lamu Rd ☎0725 131956, ⓦbit.ly/AfricanPearlMalindi. Twenty spacious rooms in a characterful – if verging on tired – older house decorated with garish paintings, plus four self-catering cottages with kitchens. The best rooms – which are good value – are comfortable and have large verandas (most are a/c too). Good pool and a bar-restaurant (with *nyama choma*) at the front near the road. BB Ksh3500, cottage Ksh5000

Blue Marlin Sporting Resort Lamu Rd ☎0733 363875, ⓦbluemarlinmalindi.com. Chaotically managed but reasonably comfortable and stylish, and very affordable, complex of 31 furnished apartments in the heart of town, with a gym and a pool on site. If you want to be right in the thick of things, this is a good bet. Ksh7000

★**Che Shale** 24km north of Malindi, and 6km off the main road (transfer Ksh2500 from town) ☎0722 230931, ⓦcheshale.com. Literally on the beach – and what a beach – this is one of Kenya's best mid-budget beach bases, opened in 1978, but now reinvented as a kitesurfing centre. With just five s/c, palm-mat and wood *bandas*, sand underfoot and cool owner-manager hosts, staff and fellow guests, this is the archetypal beach hideaway. The separate *Kajama bandas*, 200m north, are the non-s/c, budget option. Closed May & June. BB Kajama €90, Che Shale €160

Sai Eden Roc Lamu Rd ☎0734 598620 or ☎0723832371, ⓦsaiedenrochotel.co.ke. Large old

package-tour place now catering to conference-goers, with huge and largely untended gardens stretching several hundred metres down to the dunes and beach. Friendly management and mostly German and Kenyan guests. A/c, or smaller rooms with fans. BB Ksh8000

Seaview Resort Lamu Rd ☎042 2130427 or ☎0735 432371, ⓦmalindiseaviewresort.com. Low-key development in a pleasant, wooded setting. The big rooms, with a/c, fans and TV, are quite nicely done, and there's a modest pool and a path down to the beach. Self-catering cottages are also available (sleeping up to four). Good value. BB Ksh6500, self-catering cottage Ksh6000

HOTELS SOUTH OF TOWN

Protected by reefs, the area south of town is where the greatest development has taken place in the last few years, with one resort hotel after another reaching almost down to Casuarina Point. Most are Italian-owned or -managed, and Italian visitors comprise the majority of guests. Taxis shouldn't cost more than Ksh1000 from town to Casuarina Point, or Ksh400 to the *Driftwood*, and less by tuk-tuk. Distances are from Uhuru Gardens in town. All of the below have wi-fi.

★**Driftwood Club** 2.7km south, on Silversands Rd ☎0734 747133 or ☎0721 724489, ⓦdriftwoodclub.com. With a deserved and very long-established reputation among the local Anglo-Kenyan community for its excellent food and service, the *Driftwood* is highly recommended – though expensive for non-residents. As well as homely garden rooms with a/c and nets, there are two luxury a/c cottages sharing a private pool. Facilities include a nice pool and a very good restaurant (see opposite). Rates are non-seasonal, except for a Christmas/New Year supplement. BB §249

Kilili Baharini 4km south, on Casuarina Rd ☎0770 206500 or ☎0702 999566, ⓦkililibaharini.com. Rather a classy setup, with rooms organized in small enclaves, each group clustered around its own pool. There's also a bigger main pool. The a/c rooms are fresh, with tasteful Swahili-style furniture. Big on massage treatments and very popular with Italian visitors. BB €190

Osteria Bed and Breakfast 2km south, Casuarina Rd ☎0739 877584, ⓦfacebook.com/osteriabedand breakfast. Small complex of fourteen tidy, comfortable self-catering apartments run by the restaurant chain Osteria, each with one bedroom and modest kitchen facilities. They're around a smallish pool, but one street up from the beach, which is a good 10min walk away. Breakfast is available, but no proper restaurant. Room only Ksh10,000

Sandies Tropical Village and **Diamonds Dream of Africa** 3km south, on Casuarina Rd ☎042 2120444 or ☎0720 607075, ⓦplanhotel.com. Stretched along 300m of shoreline, this is an Italian-slanted holiday complex, encompassing two different hotels: the *Tropical*

Village, which has more than one hundred rooms, and the pricier *Dream of Africa*, offering 35 suites. Both have all the facilities you'd expect at an all-inclusive resort. AI: Sandies **Ksh15,800**, Diamonds **Ksh29,800**

★ **Scorpio Villas** 1km south, on Vasco da Gama Rd, not directly on the beach ☎ 042 2120194 or ☎ 0700 437680, ✉ scorpio-villas.com. Small-scale, Italian-owned "village", in a plot dense with tropical vegetation, rebuilt since a fire in 2007. The 48 a/c rooms with nets, DSTV and fridges are characterful, with Swahili-style four-poster beds. Four pools and its own, semi-private beach area. Remarkably good value. BB **$96**

EATING

Malindi's speciality is **smoked sailfish**, absolutely delicious and often available as a starter. **Malindi Market** is celebrated for fruit and vegetables – second, on the coast, only to Mombasa's.

HOTELIS AND CHEAP RESTAURANTS

Baobab Vasco da Gama Rd, on the seafront next to the Portuguese Chapel ☎ 0722 829867. Moderately priced curries, Italian and African dishes (mostly from Ksh400), and pricey prawns and lobster (from Ksh1200). Popular as much for its food as for the cheap, cold beer (Ksh150) and sweeping views over the beach and fishing boats. Daily 7am–11pm.

★ **Bawaly & Sons Halwa Shop** In the town centre near Uhuru Gardens ☎ 0722 591237. Long-established spot, famous for its fragrant version of the gooey sweet (from Ksh500/kg). The minimum order is 250g, but you can eat a small amount on the spot and have the rest wrapped up to take away. Tiny cups of spiced *kahawa* come free. Daily 8.30am–12.15pm & 3–5.45pm.

Dagama's Inn Vasco da Gama Rd, on the seafront ☎ 0701 864446. Basic *hoteli* menu, plus curries from Ksh250, seafood from Ksh350 and steaks from Ksh450. This can be a lively place to eat when it's busy but it's always best to order in advance. Daily 7am–10pm.

Delicious Café Kenyatta Rd ☎ 0722 804624. A small and friendly diner with a pleasant, shady terrace, serving full breakfasts (Ksh275), snacks and basic cheap meals like *kienyeji na mataha* (Ksh130), plus cold sodas. Mon–Sat 6am–9pm.

Gilani's Vasco da Gama Rd, on the seafront ☎ 0722 646872. Wide-ranging offerings, many of which are available in high season, in an old house filled with an eccentric, rather dusty collection of African art. Dishes include chicken and fish from Ksh400, pizzas from Ksh350, even bruschetta (Ksh100) and salads (from Ksh100). Daily 7am–11pm.

★ **Johari's Garden** Across from Equity Bank ☎ 0722 318170. Cool hideaway that's always busy with upcountry folks enjoying excellent-value, large portions of well-prepared, fresh Kikuyu dishes, including beef stew with *mataha* (Ksh270) and *githeri* (Ksh100). Lovely fresh passionfruit juice. Mon–Sat 6am–9pm.

Malindi Pastry Shop Mama Ngina St, near the market. Not what you'd expect to find here – a decent baker and patisserie, with a big variety of tempting home-made cakes (from Ksh40) and cookies (from Ksh100/pack). Daily 6.30am–noon & 2–7.30pm.

Oasis Gelateria Silversands Rd, 1.8km from Uhuru Gardens ☎ 0719 131691, ✉ oasisgelateria.com. This big snack bar is as good for its delicious omelettes and espresso as for its ice cream (Ksh100/scoop). Daily 11am–10.30pm.

Open View By the Total roundabout. One of Malindi's biggest and best-value *nyama choma* joints (beef Ksh500/kg), with mostly outside seating. No shortage of company, and they never run out of beer, but it can be noisy and fumey until the traffic has died down. Daily 24hr.

People Lamu Rd ☎ 0720 747180. Small and relatively unassuming café that makes for a good lunch stop, serving reasonably priced paninis (from Ksh300), focaccia (from Ksh200), wood-fired oven pizzas (from Ksh400) and home-made pasta dishes. Daily 7am–11pm.

★ **Taheri Fast Food** Fakhri Complex, Tsavo Rd ☎ 0720 482790. A great spot for juices, snacks and cheap meals. Try the chicken tikka (Ksh250), shish kebab (Ksh180) or "*chaana* mix" – vegetable-based snacks in your choice of sauce (Ksh100). Reliably cold sodas, too. Tues–Thurs 7.30am–8.30pm, Fri–Sun 7.30am–11pm.

UPMARKET RESTAURANTS

★ **Baby Marrow** Vasco da Gama Rd, near the Portuguese Chapel ☎ 0700 766704. One of Malindi's best restaurants, *Baby Marrow* aims for Italian bush elegance. Starters include smoked sailfish, and mains feature lots of prawn and lobster dishes (Ksh1000–2300), meat dishes for around Ksh1200, and a wide range of delicious wood-fired oven pizzas. Daily 7–11pm.

Bar Bar Sabaki Centre, Lamu Rd ☎ 042 2120502 or ☎ 0727 636452. Authentic and tasty pizzas and pasta (most from Ksh500), and pricier meat and seafood dishes (most from Ksh800), rounded off with excellent espresso. Daily 7am–10pm.

★ **Driftwood Club** Silversands Beach ☎ 0734 747133 or ☎ 0721 724489, ✉ driftwoodclub.com. Always a good place to eat, with seafood making a very strong showing (oysters, smoked sailfish and excellent sashimi are always available). The BBQ (Fri; from Ksh780/item), curry lunch buffet (Sun; Ksh1600) and Mongolian night (Thurs; all you can eat Ksh1450) are worth planning around. Daily noon–3pm & 7.30–10pm.

I Love Pizza Vasco da Gama Rd, on the seafront ☎ 042

6

2120672 or ☎0734 645567, ⓦbit.ly/ILovePizzaMalindi. Well-established seafront place with a pleasant terrace, though in the daytime the traffic can be offputting. The pizzas (from Ksh423) and pasta dishes (from Ksh550) are fine, though they push their more expensive seafood (seafood platter for two, for example, Ksh1314), which is also good. Prices don't include taxes. Daily 11am–3pm & 6–11pm.

Karen Blixen Galana Shopping Centre ☎0717 775888, ⓦkarenblixen.net. Probably the classiest of the downtown street-side cafes, this cool covered courtyard serves espresso drinks to a largely Italian clientele, with pricey pasta and pizzas on offer, too (from Ksh900) On weekend nights it absorbs the spillover from nearby clubs. Mon & Tues 7.30am–11pm, Wed–Sun 24hr.

★**My Way** Vasco da Gama Rd, on the seafront near the tourist market ☎0708 487927. With a kitchen supervised by its owner-manager, this multipurpose open-air restaurant, sports bar and music venue has locals and tourists gravitating for good chicken and pizzas, Kikuyu dishes, big screens, free wi-fi and the pool table. Pizzas from Ksh500, steaks from Ksh600, *mataha* Ksh150, beers Ksh180. Daily 9am–11pm, or later.

★**The Old Man and The Sea** Vasco da Gama Rd, on the seafront ☎0786 718811. Consistently good, professionally managed Moorish-style restaurant specializing in perfectly prepared seafood – the giant tiger prawns are famous (Ksh1700) – with some vegetarian dishes and steaks (from Ksh650). Great value for such excellent food – expect a bill of around Ksh2000–3000/person, plus drinks. Prices don't include taxes. Daily noon–2.30pm & 5–10.30pm.

Osteria Vasco da Gama Rd and 4km south, on Casuarina Rd ☎0725 525665 (town), ☎0711 480046 (beach). Malindi now boasts two branches of this well-known Nairobi restaurant, one in town and another, *Osteria Beach House*, in a beautiful spot on the shore. Both serve Italian classics with a coastal twist – think black tagliolini with squid and prawns (Ksh1500), or crab linguine (Ksh1000) – with Italian salami and home-made cheese as starters. The attached gelateria at the town branch also has excellent ice cream. Osteria daily 7am–11pm; Osteria Beach House daily 9am–6pm.

★**Rosada** 4.5 km south, on Casuarina Rd ☎0700 501813 or ☎0719 897003. Right on the beach, with breezy terrace seating overlooking rows of lounge chairs on the sand, this popular restaurant attracts hordes of holiday-makers with its cocktails (Ksh750) and pizzas, though it also serves some wonderful, imaginative seafood dishes like spaghetti with sea urchins (Ksh900) and tuna steak with cashews (Ksh1700). Daily 8am–5.30pm, or until 11pm in high season.

DRINKING AND NIGHTLIFE

After dark, especially in high season, Malindi's **clubs** and **bars** throb with action and, regardless of your gender, status or, increasingly, even your age, you're unlikely to avoid being propositioned, and not necessarily by a sex worker. Entry charges are rare unless entertainment has been laid on.

Casino Malindi Lamu Rd ☎042 2130878, ⓦcasinomalindi.com. With free entry to anyone gambling, it's almost worth playing a few hands just to watch the grim-looking Italian bosses tending their novice Kenyan croupiers. Good steaks, too. Daily 9am–5am.

Club 28 Lamu Rd, adjacent to Eden Roc Hotel. This smaller, mostly outdoor club gets busy later, and is usually considered the last place to visit – it can be heaving at 4am. Beer Ksh200. Daily 24hr.

Fermento Galana Shopping Centre. A/c disco-bar with affordable drinks, for those who feel like staying up all night. You take a ticket and pay your bill on departure (beer Ksh200). High season Tues–Sun 10pm–late; low season Wed, Fri & Sat 10pm–late.

★**Pata Pata Beach Club** On the beach, north side of town ☎0720 449561, ⓦfacebook.com/patapatamalindi. Mediterranean-style super club – part-covered, part-outdoors – with a capacity of four thousand, an 18,000-watt sound system, two bars, two dancefloors, comfy sofas and garden seating, foam guns, lights and a freeform dance pool. Entry Ksh300. High season daily 9pm–6am; low season Sat 9pm–6am.

Stars and Garters Lamu Rd, next to Barclays Bank. Brash and busy *makuti*-roofed complex, especially popular for the flatscreen TVs showing English football. Good range of snacks, and fuller meals too, including pasta (from Ksh700), seafood and grills. There's a disco most evenings and live music more often than anywhere else in town. Daily 24hr.

Urafiki Highway Bar Kenyatta Rd. Cheerful, cheap and unpretentious local bar with tables inside and out (warm beers Ksh150) and not another tourist in sight. Daily 24hr.

SHOPPING

There are two main crafts markets to head for when you're in the buying mood. Alternatively, for more expensive crafts and the possibility of browsing unhurriedly, try one of the **upmarket shops** along Lamu Rd, just to the north of Uhuru Gardens. Prices tend to be high, but visits are useful for checking comparative values.

DIANI BEACH (P.431) >

★**A.A. Shakir** Mama Ngina Rd, next to Kenol ☎0721 209244 or ☎0733 744412, ⊛shakirmalindi.com. The best selection of *kikois* in town (Ksh500 each), as well as beautiful printed cottons sold by the metre, scarves and a range of ready-made kanga skirts and trousers. They can also make clothes to order. Mon–Sat 8.30am–1pm & 2.30-6.30pm.

Al-Baity Spice Shop Mama Ngina Rd ☎0720 263962. With a pleasing range of dried goods and spices displayed across the counter, this is the shop to secure those aromatic souvenirs at regular prices. Sat–Thurs 7.30am–12.45pm & 2.30–7.30pm, Fri 7.30am–12.45pm.

The Cheese Shop Utalii Parade ☎0723 411424. More than a dozen cheeses are available here, along with fresh yogurt, honey and mushrooms, much of it made or grown locally on the shop's own farm; they're always happy to give free tastes. Mon–Sat 8am–9pm.

Lalla Spagnol Lamu Rd, just north of the Galana shopping centre ☎0733 802599. High-end interior design and furnishings, including lots of owner-made and owner-commissioned stuff from Lamu and the Far East. Mon–Sat 9am–6.30pm.

Malindi Handicraft Co-operative 2.5km west of the main market and matatu stage on the Mombasa road. Here you can watch and freely photograph the woodcarvers at work, but there's no bargaining at the shop. Daily 8am–6.30pm.

Maridadi Seasons Old Town ☎0723 245186. Sales of nearly all the well-priced sisal baskets, beaded bags, sandals, belts and leatherwork in this shop support crafts makers from the community. Mon–Sat 8.30am–6pm.

Mohawk Lamu Rd, opposite the Sabaki Centre ☎0700 787845. Two shops: on the left, nice beaded designer sandals, bags, cushions, women's clothes, accessories and jewellery; on the right, tableware, furnishings, wall hangings, mirrors and knick-knacks. Mon–Sat 9am–1pm & 3.30–7pm.

★**Mulla Boutique** Lamu Rd ☎0727 644864, ⊛mullaboutique.com. Several floors bursting with old and new objects from Asia and Africa, with some fascinating antique telephones and hurricane lamps from India, carvings, beautiful sisal rugs and antique furniture. Mon–Sat 8.30am–12.30pm & 2.30–6.30pm.

Nafisa and Rasani's At the southern end of Lamu Rd, on the corner near Uhuru Gardens ☎0720 037420 (Nafisa), ☎0770242115 (Rasani's). Lots of top-quality crafts and *objets d'art* in these two shops, and their neighbours, including old Lamu silver and jewellery as well as more familiar items available on the street. Nafisa Mon–Sat 8.30am–12.30pm & 2.30–6pm; Rasani's Mon–Sat 9am–12.30pm & 2.30–6pm.

Tourist Crafts Market On the seashore below the old town. Good selection, but if you stray down here you'll be pounced upon, and leaving without buying anything isn't easy. On the other hand, you can also leave with all sorts of little free gifts if you strike the right bargain. Daily 8am–6pm.

DIRECTORY

Banks Barclays, Equity, KCB and Standard Chartered banks all have 24hr ATMs.

Golf Malindi Golf and Country Club (☎020 2600720, ⊛malindigolfclub.com) features an unusual eleven-hole (fifteen-tee) course behind the dunes on the north side of town.

Honorary consul The Italian honorary consul, the only diplomatic representative in Malindi (Mon–Fri 9am–noon; ☎0722 825392) has an office in the Sabaki Centre, behind *Bar Bar*.

Hospital The efficient Italian-run St Peter's Hospital on Casuarina Rd (☎0706 169125) has an ambulance service.

Immigration Get your visitor's permit extended in the office near the Oilibya roundabout (☎042 2120149).

Internet access BSM's Cyber on Uhuru Rd (daily 9am–12.30pm & 3-6.30pm), opposite *Tana Guest House*.

Kenya Wildlife Service Casuarina Point (daily 6am–6pm). Point of issue and point of sale for National Park Smartcards.

Pharmacy Sabaki Pharmacy (daily 8am–8.30pm), Kenyatta Rd, at the corner of Tsavo Rd.

Supermarkets There are several small places in the shopping arcades up Lamu Rd in the town centre, the best – with the widest range – being Multi-Grocers (Mon–Sat 8am–6.30pm, Sun 8am–1pm). Alternately, try the Italian Supermarket at the Sabaki Centre (Mon–Sat 9am–1pm & 4–7pm, Sun 9am–1pm), or Pappa i Chakula, at the back of Multi-Grocers, a good little Italian deli where you can stock up on fresh pasta, olives and salami (Mon–Sat 8am–5.30pm). The Nakumatt on Lamu Rd (Mon–Sat 8.30am–10pm, Sun 10am–9.30pm) is the biggest place of all.

Travel agents A good scattering along Lamu Rd and the seafront all offer similar services, including safaris to Tsavo East and as far as Maasai Mara. Try Southern Sky Safaris, Malindi Complex (☎042 2130547) or Allamanda Safaris at the airport (☎0721 251461, ⊛allamandasafaris.com).

The Tana Delta

North out of Malindi, the **road to Lamu** sets off as a tarmac highway, crosses the Sabaki (Galana) River and passes one or two resort developments and the anachronistic little seaside town of **MAMBRUI**, with its pretty mosque, semi-ruined

TROUBLE IN THE TANA DELTA

Despite progress at the micro level with initiatives like those of *Delta Dunes* lodge (see p.477) and the Lower Tana Delta Trust, the **threats to the Tana Delta** region seem to be accumulating (see ⓦtanariver delta.org). After the failure of a highly damaging irrigation and rice-growing project in the 1990s, the latest, environmentally disastrous, idea is a gigantic biofuel project that would carpet more than 200 square kilometres of bush and flood land with sugar-cane plantations for cheap ethanol – plans that may not be entirely prevented by the delta being recently put under international protection as Kenya's sixth Ramsar Site, a wetlands area of global importance. Competition for **scarce resources** is also pitching communities against each other: in 2012 and 2013, more than one hundred people from the pastoralist Orma and farming Pokomo communities were killed in alternate raids on each other's villages, sparked by disputes over water and grazing rights. There were fresh attacks in 2014, when gunmen claiming to be part of the Islamist group **Al-Shabaab** attacked a passenger bus and several villages in Tana River and Lamu counties, killing 87 people. Though no foreign visitors were affected, travel advisories were still warning against visiting the region as this book went to print and if you're travelling by private vehicle, the police may require you to travel in convoy anywhere east of Garsen. Wherever you are hoping to visit, it's a good idea to seek local advice before attempting an independent excursion to the area.

pillar tomb and the unusual spectacle of cows on the beach. The idyllic kitesurfing base of *Che Shale* (see p.470) is further up the coast on the south side of the **Ras Ngomeni peninsula**. About 60km north of Malindi, you leave the *shambas* and scattered homesteads behind and enter the bush of the **Tana Delta**, with the road arrowing straight across the flat, gentle landscape, brown and arid or grey-green and swampy depending on the season.

The former ferry-crossing town of **Garsen** has been sidelined by the tarmac **New Garsen Causeway**, which sweeps over the Tana River 7km to the south of the flyblown town before petering out into a dirt track after you reach Witu. Garsen has a KCB bank with an ATM and, in season, some of the best and cheapest mangoes in Kenya.

Between the river and the end of the trip, the scenery can pall, but if you're on the bus, the journey is always enlivened by the other passengers and by stops at various small Tana delta towns and villages. Occasional flashes of colour – the sky-blue cloaks of **Orma** herders or the red, black and white of shawled **Somali** women – break up the journey, along with wonderful **birdlife** and some **big game**, too: especially giraffe and antelope (notably waterbuck), and even the odd elephant if you look hard enough. The road passes right through the **Kipini sanctuary** (see p.477).

Note that parts of this area were severely affected by **ethnic violence** in 2012, 2013 and 2014 (see box above); at the time of writing most government travel advisories were still warning travellers to avoid it.

Tana River National Primate Reserve

40km north of Garsen, straddling the Tana River • $25 • ⓦ cca.kws.go.ke/Tana Primate National Reserve.html • If you're driving, the Mchelelo track to the river is the one to use, though it's not signposted from the road; if you want to try to visit the reserve using public transport, you need to allow time for unforeseen delays: buses heading from Malindi to Garissa occasionally stop in Mnazini village, just outside the southern end of the reserve, or can drop you on the highway at one of the two turnings, Hara village or the KWS signpost, where you could wait for a lift or walk (5–10km) • 170 square kilometres

The **Tana River National Primate Reserve** is a refuge for two of Kenya's rarest and most beautiful monkeys, the **Tana River red colobus** and the **Tana River mangabey**. This is a remote area, with little in the way of supplies, so you'll need to call ahead and bring provisions with you. The forest is magically beautiful, cool and dark, with huge, buttress-rooted trees, and surprisingly restricted in extent, often spreading less than 1km away from the riverbank.

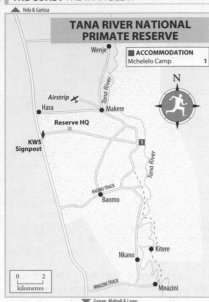

TANA RIVER NATIONAL PRIMATE RESERVE

ACCOMMODATION
Mchelelo Camp 1

▲ Hola & Garissa
Wenje
Airstrip ✈
Hara
Makere
Reserve HQ
KWS Signpost
BAOMO TRACK
Baomo
Nkano ● Kitere
MNAZINI TRACK
Mnazini
0   2
kilometres
▼ Garsen, Malindi & Lamu

MNAZINI is a fine, coastal-style village beneath mango trees. There are no lodgings, but *hotelis* will take you in for the night once you've cleared your stay with the sub-chief and the headman. The shops have basic provisions, as do those in Wenje and Hara.

Nobody in the area knows the Tana River National Primate Reserve by that name. Locals all refer to **Mchelelo**, the site of the primate research headquarters on the west bank of the Tana. There is a basic campsite run by KWS (see below), but few other facilities.

Wildlife

Although little is laid on for the few visitors who come, you may well be given a detail of armed rangers from the anti-poaching force to accompany you as you walk the trails looking for **red colobus** and **crested mangabey monkeys**. Continued human encroachment on the forest, which is increasingly split into small intact zones, threatens both species, and the colobus very rarely leave the trees, limiting them to whichever patch they find themselves in.

Your chances of seeing both kinds of monkey are good, and the other highlights of the reserve are mostly avian: the superb birdlife includes goliath heron, Pel's fishing owl, southern banded snake eagle and the exceedingly rare Tana River cisticola, not to mention vast numbers of Palaearctic migrants in season. **Mammals** in the reserve, apart from the rare primates, include blue monkeys, baboons, Grevy's and Burchell's zebra, oryx, lesser kudu, and even lions, giraffe and buffalo. On the east side of the park you can see elephants, and there's also a small seasonal population of the endangered Hunter's hartebeest, or hirola. If you're interested in making a boat trip on the sluggish river, dodging the large numbers of hippos and crocodiles, you're likely to find local Pokomo boatmen willing to take you.

ACCOMMODATION

TANA RIVER NATIONAL PRIMATE RESERVE

Mchelelo Camp Tana River National Primate Reserve, enquiries through KWS in Nairobi ☏ 0726 610508, ✉ reservations@kws.go.ke (copying ✉ tanaprimate@ kws.go.ke). The thatched forest *bandas* here were under renovation at the time of writing, but if you're equipped with a tent you can still camp on the site – toilets are available, but no showers, and you'll have to bring all your own supplies. Camping **$20**

Kipini and around

If you have a 4WD vehicle and a fair amount of patience, the trip to Lamu can be stretched over several days, with time to explore the fascinating region around the Tana Delta. This area includes the dune-shrouded coast and the village of Kipini, with the Swahili ruins of **Ungwana**, **Shaka** and **Mwana** along the shore to the east, within a few kilometres. If you're interested in exploring down here, try to see the warden of the museum at Fort Jesus in Mombasa (see p.400) for further information. These sites were partially excavated in the 1970s and 1980s, but have since largely returned to bush and jungle. Ungwana is the most impressive, with an unusual mosque with two *mihrabs* and strange tombs with cruciform markings.

As yet almost wholly untouched by tourism, the district around the fishing village of **KIPINI** at the mouth of the Tana and the larger market centre of **WITU**, 21km inland, repays the slight effort of getting here and finding somewhere to stay. Kipini was once the headquarters of Tana River District, before that title was shifted to Hola at the time of independence. Nowadays, its former importance is evident only in a mixed population of Orma, Pokomo, Bajun, Somali and Swahili, who get by on fishing, small-scale farming and some herding.

Kipini Wildlife and Botanical Conservancy

Northeast of Kipini • Daily • No fees; contact the conservancy in advance • ⓦ kenyaforestservice.org

The **Kipini Wildlife and Botanical Conservancy** is a former ranch – the Nairobi Cattle Ranch – that failed, largely because of tsetse fly, and has now been reborn as a sanctuary. The people of the area, traditional hunter-gatherers, the **Boni**, are now mostly subsistence farmers. The conservancy is still in its infancy, but the intention is to create a viable natural resource, modelled on the former ranches of Laikipia. As you'll see if you stop off here, the area is full of **wildlife**, including elephants, giraffe, buffalo, lesser kudu, hirola, lions, the odd dugong in the creeks and, they claim, hunting dogs.

ARRIVAL AND INFORMATION   **KIPINI AND AROUND**

By public transport To get to Kipini by public transport, leave the Lamu bus at Witu, where there's a connecting matatu to the village (most buses heading for Lamu or Malindi pass through Witu). Village *hotelis* serve delicious *dalasini* cinnamon tea.

Security As with elsewhere in the delta, you should seek local advice on the security situation (see p.475) before traveling around here on your own.

ACCOMMODATION

Kipini has no **formal lodgings**, but you should be able to stay with a local family for a few hundred shillings. Alternatively, you could stay in Witu itself (again, no formal lodgings), and rent a bicycle locally for getting around.

Delta Dunes On the bush-covered sand dunes near the ocean, midway across the delta's width, most easily accessible by charter flight ⓞ0718 139359, ⓔ bookings@africanterritories.co.ke. It's possible to stay near the delta mouth at the highly appealing, castaway-style *Delta Dunes*, where there are six s/c *bandas* made from driftwood, mangrove poles and *makuti*. Stays include all meals and drinks, boat trips, fishing, game and bird walks and village visits. *Delta Dunes* works with thirteen thousand local people – Orma herders and Pokomo farmers – through the community's Lower Tana Delta Trust, and a proportion of income from guests goes direct to community bank accounts. Conservancy fee $60. Closed June 1–July 15. Al **$900**

The Lamu archipelago

A cluster of desert islands tucked into Kenya's north coast, the **Lamu archipelago** has long held an irresistible appeal for visitors. Together these islands form a separate spectrum of Swahili culture, a world apart from the beaches of Mombasa and Malindi.

To some extent the archipelago is an anachronism: there are still almost no motor vehicles, and life moves at the pace of a donkey or a dhow. Lamu island itself, however, has seen drastic changes. Because of its special status in the Islamic world as a much-respected centre of **religious teaching**, Saudi aid has poured in: the hospital, schools and religious centres are all supported by it. In recent times too, the tourist economy, and consequent investment, has boomed. The island has outgrown its roots as a 1970s budget travellers' paradise to become something entirely more **commercial**: by the early 2000s guesthouses and boutique hotels were thick on the ground in both Lamu town and Shela, along with satellite dishes, cybercafés and souvenir shops.

Today, islanders are concerned about the future. Western travel advisories (see box, p.475) have hit the **tourism industry** hard over the past few years, with a number of

6

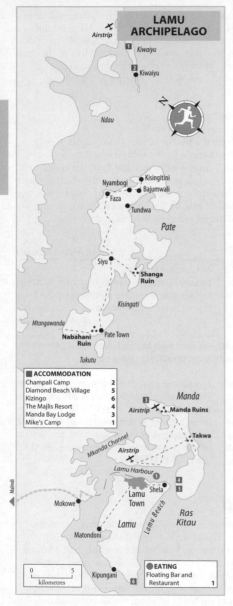

LAMU ARCHIPELAGO

Airstrip

Kiwaiyu

Kiwaiyu

N

Ndau

Kisingitini
Nyambogi   Bajumwali
Faza
Tundwa

Pate

Siyu

Shanga
Ruin

Kisingati

Mtangawanda

Nabahani   Pate Town
Ruin

Tukutu

■ **ACCOMMODATION**
Champali Camp	2
Diamond Beach Village	5
Kizingo	6
The Majlis Resort	4
Manda Bay Lodge	3
Mike's Camp	1

Manda

Airstrip   Manda Ruins

Takwa

Mkanda Channel   Airstrip

Lamu Harbour

Lamu   Shela
Town

Mokowe

Matondoni   Lamu Beach   Ras
Lamu   Kitau

0   5
kilometres

Kipungani

● **EATING**
Floating Bar and Restaurant	1

Malindi

hotels and restaurants forced to close, or at least go into hibernation. A massive new **port** is planned (see p.481), which might provide some jobs, although it will wreak havoc on the livelihoods of Lamu's small fishermen and contribute to the destruction of the islands' historic character.

The damage that would be done goes further than spoiling the tranquillity. The Lamu archipelago is one of the most important sources for knowledge about pre-colonial Africa. **Archeological sites** indicate that towns have existed on these islands for at least 1200 years. The dunes behind Lamu beach, for example, are said to conceal the remains of long-deserted settlements. And somewhere close by on the mainland, perhaps just over the border in Somalia, archeologists expect one day to uncover the ruins of Shungwaya, the town that the nine tribes that comprise the Mijikenda people claim as their ancestral home.

For now, however, **Lamu island** itself, most people's single destination, still has plenty to recommend it. Here you will find the archipelago's best beach and its two main towns, **Lamu** and **Shela**. **Manda island**, directly opposite, is little visited except as Lamu's gateway to the outside world (the airstrip), though its own beach is beautiful and there are a few delightful places to stay. **Pate island**, accessible by dhow or motorboat, but completely off the tourism radar, makes a fascinating excursion if you have a week or more in the area.

Lamu island

Perhaps best left until the end of your stay in Kenya, **Lamu island** may otherwise precipitate a change in your plans as you're lulled into its slow, soothing rhythm and deliciously lazy atmosphere. All the senses get a full workout here, so while there are sights and activities on offer, actually *doing* anything is sometimes a problem. You can spend hours on a roof or veranda just watching life go by, feeling its mood swing effortlessly through its well-worn cycles – from prayer call to prayer call, from tide to tide and from dawn to dusk.

If this doesn't hit the right note for you, you might actually rather hate Lamu: hot, dirty and boring are adjectives that have been applied by sane and pleasant people. You

SECURITY IN THE LAMU ARCHIPELAGO

In 2011, two separate and unprecedented events sparked intense media attention questioning the **safety** of tourism in the Lamu archipelago. In September, bandits raided a British couple's *banda* at *Kiwayu Safari Village* on a remote beach on the mainland facing the northern tip of Kiwaiyu island. The man was shot dead and his wife kidnapped – she was released six months later after a ransom was paid. In October an elderly French expatriate was kidnapped from her home on the island of Manda. She died soon afterwards due to her fragile state of health.

In 2014, the **mainland** of Lamu county was subjected to two major **terrorist attacks** when gunmen stormed the small towns of Mpeketoni and Hindi, killing nearly one hundred people, most of them migrants from central Kenya. The Somali Islamist group Al-Shabaab claimed responsibility for both atrocities.

While tourists have not been targeted and **Lamu island** itself has seen no violence, security measures in the archipelago have been significantly heightened in recent years and foreign governments periodically warn against travel in the area. At the time of writing buses between Lamu and Malindi were still being forced to travel in convoys, and British travel advice was still warning against travel to all of Lamu county, including Lamu island itself – although if you fly in and out of Lamu you shouldn't be in any danger.

6

can certainly improve your chances of liking it by not coming here at the tail end of the dry season, when gutters are blocked with refuse, courtyard gardens wilt under the sun and the heat is sapping.

Lamu town, a UNESCO World Heritage Site, is something of a **myth** factory. Conventionally labelled an "Arab trading town", it is actually one of the last viable remnants of the **Swahili civilization** that was the dominant cultural force along the coast until the arrival of the British. In the 1960s, its unique blend of beaches, gentle Islamic ambience, funky old town and a host population well used to strangers was a recipe which took over where Marrakesh left off, and it acquired a reputation as Kenya's Kathmandu: the end of the African hippie trail and a stopover on the way to India. Shaggy foreigners were only allowed to visit on condition they stayed in lodgings and didn't camp on the beach. Not many people want to camp out these days. The proliferation of guesthouses in the heart of town encourages an ethos that is more interactive than hippie-escapist. The crime rate is low, and the labyrinthine warren of narrow alleyways is safe to wander at all hours; leave your room at midnight for a breath of air and you can stroll around to your heart's content, fearing nothing.

If you want to spend all your time on the **beach**, staying in **Shela** is the obvious solution, and there's an ever-growing range of quite stylish possibilities there, including one hostel where you can also camp.

Fewer people see the **interior** of Lamu island itself, which is a pity, as it's a pretty, if rather inhospitable area. Much of it is patched into *shambas* with the herds of cattle, coconut palms, mango and citrus trees that still provide the bulk of Lamu's wealth. The two villages you might head for here are **Matondoni**, on the north shore of the island, by the creek, and **Kipungani**, on the western side.

Brief history

The undeniably **Arab** flavour of Lamu is not nearly as old as the town itself. It derives from the later nineteenth century when the **Omanis**, and to some extent the **Hadhramis** from what is now Yemen, held sway in the town. The first British representatives in Lamu found themselves among pale-skinned, slave-owning Arab rulers, and the cultural and racial stereotypes that were propagated have never completely disappeared.

Lamu was established on its present site by the fourteenth century, but there have been people living on the island for much longer than that. The fresh-water supplies beneath Shela made the island attractive to refugees from the mainland and people have been escaping here for two thousand years or more. It was also one of the

6

LAMU FESTIVALS

Maulidi, a week-long celebration of Muhammad's birth (see p.69), sees Lamu town involved in processions and dances, and draws in pilgrims from all over East Africa and the Indian Ocean. For faithful participants, the Lamu Maulidi is so laden with *baraka* (blessings) that some say two trips to Lamu are worth one to Mecca in the eyes of God. If you can possibly arrange it, this is the occasion to be in Lamu, but unless you make bookings, you'll need to arrive at least a week in advance to have any hope of getting a room.

The **Lamu Cultural Festival** is held in November to promote Swahili culture and heritage. With donkey and dhow racing, swimming, dancing and traditional craft displays, including carving, dhow-building, embroidery and henna decoration – all of it fairly competitive – the festival engages Lamu town for the best part of a week. A more recent initiative, the **Lamu Yoga Festival** (Ⓦlamuyoga.org) in March brings together several hundred people, and yoga teachers from around the world, for four days of classes in different yoga styles in idyllic settings around Lamu town, Shela and Manda; the event revolves around Shela's two yoga retreats, *Banana House* and *Fatuma's Tower* (see p.490).

earliest places on the coast to attract settlers from the Persian Gulf and there were almost certainly people here from Arabia and southwest Asia even before the foundation of Islam.

In 1505, Lamu was visited by a heavily armed **Portuguese** man-of-war and the king of the town quickly agreed to pay the first of many cash tributes as protection money. For the next 180 years Lamu was nominally under Portuguese rule, though the Portuguese favoured Pate as a place to live. In the 1580s, the **Turkish** fleet of Amir Ali Bey threatened Portuguese dominance, but superior firepower and relentless savagery kept them out, and Lamu, with little in the way of an arsenal, had no choice but to bend with the wind – losing a king now and then to the Portuguese executioners – until the Omanis arrived with fast ships and a serious bid for lasting control.

The Golden Age

By the end of the seventeenth century, Lamu's Portuguese predators were vanquished and for nearly 150 years it had a revitalizing breathing space. This was its **Golden Age**, when Lamu became a republic, ruled over by the *Yumbe*, a council of elders who deliberated in the palace (now a ruined plot in the centre of town), with only the loosest control imposed by their Omani overlords. This was the period when most of the big houses were built and when Lamu's classic architectural style found its greatest expression. Arts and crafts flourished and business along the waterfront made the town a magnet throughout the Indian Ocean. Huge ocean-going dhows rested half the year in the harbour, taking on ivory, rhino horn, mangrove poles and cereals. There was time to compose long poems and argue about language, the Koran and local politics. Lamu became the northern coast's **literary and scholastic focus**, a distinction inherited from Pate.

The Battle of Shela

For a brief time, Lamu's star was in the ascendant in all fields. There was even a famous victory at the **Battle of Shela** in 1812. A combined Pate-Mazrui force landed at Shela with the simple plan of capturing Lamu – not known for its resolve in battle – and finishing the construction of the fort that the Nabahanis from Pate had begun a few years earlier. To everyone's surprise, particularly the Lamu defenders, the tide had gone out and the invaders were massacred as they tried to push their boats off the beach. Appalled at the overkill and expecting a swift response from the Mazruis in Mombasa, Lamu sent to Oman itself for Busaidi protection and threw away independence forever. Had the eventual outcome of this panicky request been foreseen, the Lamu *Yumbe* might have reconsidered. Seyyid Said, Sultan of Oman, was more than happy to send a garrison to complete and occupy Lamu's fort – and from this toehold in Africa, he went on to smash the Mazrui rebels in Mombasa (see p.395), taking the entire coast and moving his own sultanate to Zanzibar.

The decline of Lamu

Lamu gradually sank into economic collapse towards the end of the nineteenth century as Zanzibar and Mombasa grew in importance. In a sense, it has been stagnating ever since. The building of the Uganda railway from Mombasa and the abolition of slavery did nothing to improve matters for Lamu in economic terms, and its decline has kept up with the shrinking population – though the **resettlement programme** on the nearby mainland has led to a revived upcountry commercialism taking root around the market square.

In March 2012, the government announced a massive US$20 billion infrastructure development project – the Lamu Port-South Sudan-Ethiopia Transport Corridor (**LAPSSET**) – at Manda Bay, 16km north of Lamu. This, the continent's largest ever civil engineering project, would see a pipeline built to deliver oil from South Sudan to a new refinery near Lamu island; the building of a giant tanker terminal; more than 1700km of new highways and railways to South Sudan and Ethiopia; and three new airports and tourist resorts in Lamu, Isiolo and Lake Turkana. Unsurprisingly, the plans have met resistance from local groups, and so far little has been achieved but lucrative land sales and huge kickbacks from "feasibility studies". With no financial backer and no credible economic rationale for the project, LAPSSET looks like a classic white elephant.

Lamu town

Perhaps surprisingly for so laidback a corner of Kenya, there's no shortage of things to do in **LAMU TOWN**. A UNESCO World Heritage Site, it's unendingly fascinating to stroll through, with few monuments but hundreds of ancient houses, arresting street scenes and cool corners to sit and rest. And the **museum** outshines all others in Kenya bar the National Museum in Nairobi.

Initially confusing, Lamu town is not the random clutter of houses and alleys it appears. The town is divided into two main parts – long-established Mkomani in the north and still-expanding Langoni in the south. This north–south division is found in

---

TRADITION AND MORALITY IN LAMU

A number of **old photographs** on display in Lamu's museum undermine assumptions about Lamu's "ancient" traditions. The women's cover-all black **buibui**, for example, turns out to be a fashion innovation introduced comparatively recently from southern Arabia. It wasn't worn in Lamu much before the 1930s when, ironically, a degree of emancipation encouraged women of all classes to adopt the high-status styles of purdah. In earlier times, high-born women would appear in public entirely hidden inside a tent-like canopy called a **shiraa**, which had to be supported by slaves; the abolition of slavery at the beginning of the twentieth century marked the demise of this odd fashion.

Outsiders have tended to get the wrong end of the stick about Swahili seclusion. While women are undoubtedly heavily restricted in their public lives, in private they have considerable freedom. The notion of **romantic love** runs deep in Swahili culture. Love affairs, divorces and remarriage are the norm, and the *buibui* is perhaps as useful to women in disguising their liaisons as it is to their husbands in preventing them.

All this comes into focus a little when wandering through the alleys. You may even bump into some of Lamu's **transvestite** community – cross-dressing men whose lifestyle, which derives from Oman, is accepted and long established. In fact, the more you explore, the more you realize that the town's conventional image is like the walls of its houses – a severe facade concealing an unrestrained interior.

6

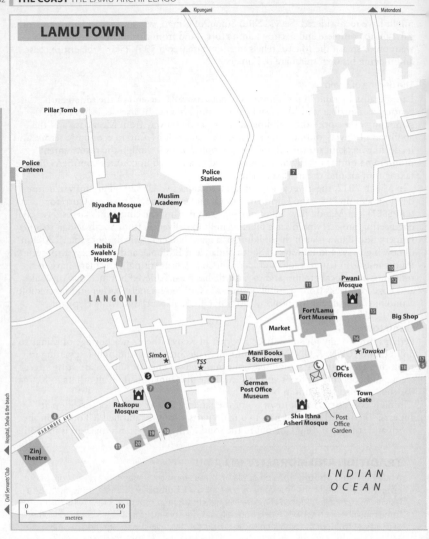

LAMU TOWN

Kipungani

Matondoni

Pillar Tomb

Police Canteen

Police Station

Riyadha Mosque

Muslim Academy

Habib Swaleh's House

LANGONI

Pwani Mosque

Fort/Lamu Fort Museum

Big Shop

Market

Simba

TSS

Mani Books & Stationers

★ Tawakal

DC's Offices

German Post Office Museum

Town Gate

Raskopu Mosque

HARAMBEE AVE

Shia Ithna Asheri Mosque

Post Office Garden

Zinj Theatre

Hospital, Shela & the beach

Civil Servants' Club

INDIAN OCEAN

0   100
metres

most Swahili towns and reflects the importance of Mecca, which is due north of Lamu. The town is divided further into forty *mitaa* or **wards**, roughly corresponding to the blocks in a modern city. The names of these suggest a great deal about how it once looked. Kinooni ("whetstone corner") still boasts a heavy block of stone for sharpening swords, and Utakuni ("main market") ward has a row of shops, even though most of the buildings on this north side of town are now purely residential.

Very few towns in sub-Saharan Africa have kept their original **town plan** so intact. The other main division, apart from Mkomani and Langoni, is between the **waterfront** buildings and the town behind, separated by **Usita wa Mui**, now Harambee Avenue (actually a narrow alley for the most part). Until around 1830, this was the waterfront, but the pile of accumulated rubbish in the harbour had become large enough by the time the fort was finished to consider reclaiming it, and, gradually, those who could

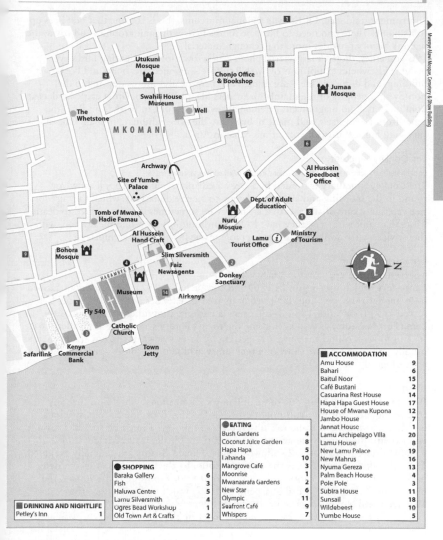

6

ACCOMMODATION
Amu House	9
Bahari	6
Baitul Noor	15
Café Bustani	2
Casuarina Rest House	14
Hapa Hapa Guest House	17
House of Mwana Kupona	12
Jambo House	7
Jannat House	1
Lamu Archipelago Villa	20
Lamu House	8
New Lamu Palace	19
New Mahrus	16
Nyuma Gereza	13
Palm Beach House	4
Pole Pole	3
Subira House	11
Sunsail	18
Wildebeest	10
Yumbe House	5

EATING
Bush Gardens	4
Coconut Juice Garden	8
Hapa Hapa	5
Labanda	10
Mangrove Café	3
Moonrise	1
Mwanaarafa Gardens	2
New Star	6
Olympic	11
Seafront Café	9
Whispers	7

SHOPPING
Baraka Gallery	6
Fish	3
Haluwa Centre	5
Lamu Silversmith	4
Ogres Bead Workshop	1
Old Town Art & Crafts	2

DRINKING AND NIGHTLIFE
Petley's Inn	1

afford to, built on it. The **fort** lost its pre-eminent position and Lamu, from the sea, took on a different aspect, which included Indian styles such as arches, verandas and shuttered windows.

When discovering Lamu for yourself, you shouldn't get lost too easily if you remember that **Harambee Avenue** runs parallel to and 50m behind the waterfront, and that streets leading into town all run slightly uphill.

Lamu Museum

On the waterfront promenade • Daily 8am–6pm • Ksh500 • Ⓦ museums.or.ke • The museum can arrange guided tours to archeological sites on Manda and Pate islands: contact the curator, Galo Galo Ⓣ 0721 660645, or email via the Nairobi headquarters (see p.112)

The one place you should definitely count on devoting an hour or so to is **Lamu Museum**. The house, built in 1891 on the waterfront, once served as a British colonial government residence. Of Kenya's regional museums, this is the one that best lives up to its name. There's no need to fill spare rooms here with game trophies and trivia; the region's history provides more than enough material.

As you enter, there's a large aerial photo of the town for a fascinating bird's-eye insight. Elsewhere, exhibitions of **Swahili culture** – architecture, boats and boat-building, and domestic life – are displayed. There are also rooms devoted to the non-Swahili peoples of the mainland: farmers like the **Pokomo**, **Orma** cattle herders and **Boni** hunters. Two magnificent ceremonial **siwa horns**, one in ivory from Pate, the other from Lamu itself, and made of brass, are the prize exhibits – probably the oldest surviving musical instruments in sub-Saharan Africa.

The Donkey Sanctuary
On the waterfront • Daily; mornings only • Donations accepted • ⓦ thedonkeysanctuary.org.uk

The **Donkey Sanctuary** is funded by a UK-based animal charity. They'll show you round in the morning and are always happy to receive donations, which they use for free veterinary care of animals that are otherwise sometimes literally worked to death. More than animal-lovers, they have had a significant impact economically, too, with their twice-yearly donkey de-worming programme in the Lamu archipelago.

Lamu Fort Museum
Harambee Ave • Daily 8am–6pm • Ksh500 • ⓦ museums.or.ke

Lamu **fort**, which was begun in 1809 and completed in 1821, seems oddly stranded in its modern-day position, deprived of its role as defender of the waterfront. It served as a prison until 1984, but it's now a national monument and open as the **Lamu Fort Museum**, as well as housing the town's **library** and acting as a gallery space. It's fun to walk round the ramparts, getting bird's-eye views of the town, and there's usually an interesting art show or a **temporary exhibition** of photos or local archeological finds on display.

Mosques
When you start checking out some of Lamu's 23 **mosques**, you'll find that any tone of rigid conformity you might expect is lacking. Most are simple, spacious buildings, as much local men's clubs as places of prayer. There's no special reason to enter them; their doors are always open and there's little to see. Male visitors, suitably dressed, are normally allowed inside; female visitors are generally excluded. The oldest-known mosque is the **Pwani Mosque**, by the fort, parts of which date back to the fourteenth century. Lamu's current Friday mosque is the **Jumaa**, the big one in Pangahari ("sword-sharpening place") ward. Unfortunately, the **Mwenye Alawi Mosque**, at the north end of town, which was once Lamu's only exclusively female mosque, has been taken over by the men, leaving the women to pray at home.

The star of Lamu's mosques, as well as being one of the most recent, is the sumptuous **Riyadha Mosque** located well to the back of the town, in Langoni. Built at the beginning of the twentieth century, the mosque has brought about a radical shift in Lamu's style of Islam, and indeed in the status of Lamu in the Islamic world. It was founded by a sharif, a descendant of the prophet, called **Habib Swaleh**, who came from the Hadramaut (present-day Yemen) to settle in Lamu in the mid-nineteenth century. His house, close by the mosque, is acknowledged with a plaque, but is basically a simple wattle-and-daub structure, containing a caretaker's bed and a few old papers. Habib Swaleh and his group introduced a new freedom to the five-times-daily prayers, with singing, tambourines and spontaneous readings from the Koran. They attracted a large following, particularly from the slave and ex-slave community, but gradually from all social spheres, even the aristocratic families with long Lamu pedigrees.

SWAHILI STONE ARCHITECTURE

Lamu's **stone houses** are perfect examples of architecture appropriate to its setting. The basic design is an open box shape enclosing a large courtyard, around the inner walls of which are set inward-facing rooms on two or three floors, the top floor forming an open roof terrace with a *makuti* roof. The rooms are thus long and narrow, their ceilings supported by close-set timbers or mangrove poles (*boriti*). Most had exquisite carved doors at one time, though in all but a few dozen homes these have been sold off to pay for upkeep. Many also had *zidaka*, plasterwork niches in the walls to give an illusion of extended space, which are now just as rare. Bathroom arrangements are ingenious, with fish kept in the large water storage cisterns to eat mosquito larvae. In parts of Lamu these old houses are built so close together you could step over the street from one roof to another.

The private space inside Lamu's houses is barely distinguishable from the public space outside. The noises of the town percolate into the interiors, encouraged by the constant flow of air created by the narrow coolness of the dark streets and the heat that accumulates on upper surfaces exposed to the sun.

Some of the other mosques later adopted the style, but the Riyadha, apart from being Lamu's largest mosque, is still the one most closely associated with this kind of inspirational worship. Non-Muslim men who visit while worship is in session are likely to be invited in and encouraged to sit cross-legged with the rest of the assembly. Any sense of stale ritual is far removed: the atmosphere is light, the music infectious. The Riyadha is also famous as the spiritual home of Lamu's annual **Maulidi** celebration (see p.480).

Next to the Riyadha is the big, square **Muslim Academy** – a major teaching establishment, and, like the Riyadha itself and so much else in Lamu, heavily under Saudi patronage. Both men and women are allowed to have a look around, but there's very little to see. More interesting are some of the students, who come from all over the Islamic world.

Tombs

After the fort, the only other national monument in Lamu (though you may not believe it when you see it) is the fluted **pillar tomb** behind Riyadha Mosque. This may date from as far back as the fourteenth century, and the occasional visit by a tourist might persuade the families in the neighbourhood that it's worth preserving; it can only be a matter of time before it leans too far and collapses on a passing child. In the middle of town, by a betel vine plot, is another tomb, that of **Mwana Hadie Famau**, a local woman of the fifteenth or sixteenth century. This has been walled up and has lost the porcelain-embedded pillars that would once have stood at each corner.

Swahili House Museum

West of Harambee Ave • Daily 8am–6pm • Ksh500 • ⓦ museums.or.ke

The **Swahili House Museum** in Mkomani is an eighteenth-century house that's been restored to an approximation of its original appearance. Unfortunately, the guided tour (included in the entrance fee) is brief and the house is very small, consisting only of a small courtyard, two sleeping galleries, two toilets and an upstairs kitchen and roof.

The cemetery and around

Heading north out of town, through the wards of Tundani ("fruit-picking place") and Weyoni ("donkey racetrack"), you reach the **cemetery**. This is the goal of many religious processions and strolling up there makes an interesting twenty-minute walk. You then come into the former town dump, now a landfill and land reclamation area. In the inlet behind it, several large **dhows** and smaller boats are moored. Many are rotting, but one or two are quite new, even unfitted. If you have dreams of owning a dhow (they make great houseboats), you're looking at around $10,000 for a 12m hull. The price depends largely on the time required to build it – two years isn't unusual.

Shela

SHELA, 2km south of Lamu town, was once a thriving, self-contained community: Shela's people trace their ancestry back to Manda island and speak a dialect of Swahili quite distinct from that of Lamu town. After the demise of slavery, however, and the coming of the Europeans, it was in limbo for decades; then, post-independence, it found itself midway between rural decline and upmarket **tourist boom**. Since the turn of the 21st century that balance has definitively altered: the tourists have won. Most of the fine old houses have been bought by foreigners and converted into ravishing holiday homes, decked in bougainvillea. But, since becoming a UNESCO World Heritage Site in 2001, there has also been a surge in new building, sending multi-floored luxury homes and boutique hotels up above the palms. In global terms, the boom is still small-scale, but intense enough to have already overshadowed the historical buildings in the village centre.

Lamu beach and sand dunes

A usually deserted 12km sickle of white sand, backed by empty sand dunes, **Lamu beach** is the real thing; you half-expect Robinson Crusoe to come striding out of the heat haze. Unprotected by a reef, the sea here has some motion to it, and it is one of the few places on the coast where, at certain times of the year, you can bodysurf (August is probably best). Unfortunately, **security** can be an issue – women may find that wanderers along the beach can be a nuisance, muggings are not unheard of, and there have been incidents of rape. Stay within shouting distance of other sunbathers and preferably go to the beach in company.

All that said, the **sun** is a more likely assailant. There's absolutely no cover and you'll often find that the wind is too strong for erecting a sunshade. Sunscreen cream is available in town – avoid using coconut oil.

Friday Mosque

Behind Peponi Hotel

One of Shela's few historical sights is the strange and much-photographed **Friday Mosque**, built in 1829, which stands out for its unusual, rocket-shaped minaret and once stood high above every other building. Not any more. If you're suitably dressed, you can ask to visit and may even be able to go to the top.

Matondoni

MATONDONI is the most talked-about destination on Lamu apart from Shela and the beach, but in truth, it's not wildly exciting and its fame as the district's principal dhow-building centre seems misplaced. However, the one-hour walk there from Lamu town is a fine one if you start early (the soft sand track isn't fun in blazing sunshine). A sane, enjoyable alternative is to go by **donkey**: fix up a beast through your guesthouse reception, or you can take one of the sand dhows on its trip from Lamu jetty to Matondoni, get some lunch and walk back, following the telephone wires.

Kipungani

If you really want to look around the whole island, proceed from Matondoni to **KIPUNGANI**, one hour's walk from the end of the beach (4hr from Shela). This is the halfway mark on the round-the-island walk; the whole trip takes eight or nine hours at least. It is useful to know the state of the tides for the stretch from Matondoni to Kipungani, as you can take a direct route through the mangroves at low tide (but don't get caught out).

ARRIVAL AND DEPARTURE

LAMU ISLAND

By plane Planes land on Manda island, across the harbour directly opposite Lamu town. The short boat trip from the airstrip (Ksh100) gives you a wonderful introductory panorama of Lamu's nineteenth-century waterfront. There are currently four airlines connecting the islands with Kiwaiyu, Malindi, Mombasa and Nairobi – unfortunately, Kenya Airways has cancelled its Lamu service. SafariLink, next to *Bush Gardens* (☎ 042 4632211, ✆ flysafarilink.com) and Airkenya, next to *Casuarina Rest House* (☎ 042 4633445, ✆ airkenya.com), have daily flights to Nairobi Wilson, Airkenya going via Malindi. Fly540, next to the Catholic church (☎ 042 2130312 or ☎ 0723 573873, ✆ fly540.com) and Jambo Jet, which has an agent in *Hapa Hapa* restaurant (☎ 0728 065560, ✆ jambojet.com), both fly daily to Nairobi JKIA, via Malindi.

By bus Simba, Tahmeed, Tawakal and TSS run daily services to Mombasa. Buses depart from Mokowe jetty on the mainland, starting at 7am, and run every hour; the first *mtaboti* ferries leave Lamu town at 6–6.30am to connect. Buy tickets (about Ksh1000 to Mombasa) the day before or earlier to be sure of a seat – most of the booking offices are on Harambee Ave. Tawakal (☎ 042 4033380) is the fastest, costs a little more than the others (Mombasa Ksh1200) and sells out more quickly. It also runs more services, until late morning or early afternoon (usually 7am, 11am & 1pm).

From the mainland The bus trip or drive to Lamu ends at Mokowe dock, on the mainland, where a chugging *mtaboti* (motorboat taxi, Ksh100) takes you around the creek for the 30min ride to Lamu town. The *mtabotis* are timed to coincide with the buses, though there are other less frequent services throughout the day. Grab your luggage, ignore the touts pulling you every which way and jump on the boat which seems fullest – they all go to Lamu. Don't be misled by anyone trying to sell you a *mtaboti* charter; just wait for the next public *mtaboti* with everyone else. Alternatively, you can take a fast boat for Ksh150, or charter either for Ksh1500–2000. If you drive up, remove all your valuables and leave your vehicle in the car park where it should be safe (tipping the *askari* beforehand may improve security further).

6

DHOW TRIPS

Where the hotel hustlers left off after you settled in, the dhow-ride men take up the challenge. You'll be persistently hassled until you agree to go on a trip and then, as if the word's gone out, you'll be left alone. The fact is your face quickly becomes familiar to anyone whose livelihood depends upon tourists. Dhow trips are usually a lot of fun and, all things considered, very good value. The simplicity of Swahili sailing is delightful, using a single lateen sail that can be set in virtually any position and never seems to obstruct the view. Sloping past the mangroves, with their primeval-looking tangle of roots at eye level, hearing any number of squeaks and splashes from the small animals and birds that live among them, is quite a serene pleasure.

There are limitless possibilities for dhow trips, though only a short menu of excursions is usually offered. The cheapest is a slow sail across Lamu harbour and up Takwa "river", fishing as you go, followed by a barbecue on the beach at **Manda island**, then back to town. This might commence with some squelching around in the mud under the mangroves, digging for huge bait-worms. If the trip is timed properly with the tides, you can include a visit to **Takwa ruins**, or, for rather more money, you can stay the night on the beach behind the ruins and come back the next day. This is usually done around full moon. Takwa has to be approached from the landward side up the creek, and this can only be done at high tide. A further variation has you sailing south through Lamu harbour, past the headland at Shela and out towards the ocean for some **snorkelling** over the reefs on the southwest corner of Manda around **Kinyika rock**. Snorkel and mask are normally provided, but bringing your own is obviously much better. Although all dhows should carry enough useable life jackets, this is particularly essential if you're venturing beyond the reef, where the seas can be very rough and accidents happen all too often.

The **price** you pay will depend on how many are in your party, where you want to go, for how long, and how much work it's going to be for the crew. Agree on the price beforehand (a full day with lunch starts from around Ksh1200/person) and pay up afterwards, although some captains may ask you for a small deposit to buy food. Be clear on who is supplying food and drink, apart from any fish you might catch.

Cameras are easily damaged on dhow trips, so wrap them up well in a plastic bag. And take the clothes and drinks you'd need for a 24-hour spell in the Sahara – you'll burn up and dry out otherwise. The Promise Ahadi Dhow Operators Collective (☎ 0710 519156), on the waterfront in Lamu town, organizes recommended dhow trips.

6

GETTING AROUND

From Lamu town to Shela It's possible to catch a local boat from Lamu to Shela for Ksh100/person (or Ksh200 after dark; 30–40min), or you can charter a water taxi from the Shela jetty or Peponi beach for around Ksh500. Check with *Bush Gardens Restaurant* (see p.491) on Lamu waterfront for departure times and locations of the shared boats.

Speedboat charter Not exactly in keeping with the spirit of Lamu's lifestyle, it certainly gets you from A to B effectively, but drinks diesel fuel and is thus expensive. You can rent a boat via the Promise Ahadi Dhow Operators Collective in Lamu town (☎ 0710 519156). Rates are around Ksh10,000 to Pate, Ksh10,000 to Faza and Ksh18,000 to Kiwaiyu.

INFORMATION

Tourist office At the north end of town on the waterfront, near *Lamu House* (Mon–Fri 7.30am–12.30pm & 2–4.30pm; ☎ 042 4633132).

Beach boy hustlers and guides Once you're at the harbour, you'll inevitably be met by a bevy of beach boy hustlers offering to take your baggage and guide you to a hotel. Some work for hotels or guesthouses and are just trying to fill rooms; some think they may get lucky with a quick tip for helping you, or commission from the hotel owner; others genuinely want to be your guide for the duration of your stay. It's difficult to avoid these characters and they certainly won't allow you to stand around on the quayside looking at your map, so it's best to know in

advance how to get to your preferred destination from the jetty. As usual, firmness, smiles and robust clarity are the best course. If you don't want a guide, be quite clear about that, and if they follow you anyway, explain what has happened to the hotel receptionist. The whole palaver is usually over very quickly as they turn their attentions to the next boatload of arrivals. If you need a guide for any of the islands – and they can be useful and informative – your best bet is to ask other travellers to recommend one, or visit the tourist office and be sure your guide has a proper ID card. You'll need to tell any guide you engage which places you would like to visit and agree a fee: Ksh1000/half-day is about right, for a group of up to three people.

ACCOMMODATION

LAMU TOWN

The better lodgings are generally those on the waterfront or those with a height advantage; places on Harambee Ave tend to be suffocatingly hot. In Dec and Jan, and particularly during Maulidi, room availability can be tight, so book ahead if you can. Between April and June, you may find some places closed. Room prices depend on the season as well as your bargaining skills – haggling is possible at most lodgings, even those places charging eye-watering sums, though if you rely on beach boys to find you a room the price will be marginally higher to account for their commissions. The size of your group, how long you intend to stay and when you will actually pay are all useful bargaining chips. Unless the town is heaving with visitors, you shouldn't have any problem getting a discount. If you like the place, aim to agree a rate for the duration of your stay and then pay daily. As well as hotels and guesthouses, it's often possible to rent private houses by the week or month. The quantity and standard of furnishing varies, but there's always a kitchen and usually a cook and cleaner. Visit ⓦ lamu.org for a wide variety of the options in Lamu, Manda and Shela; if you're already in town, put the word out that you're interested in finding a house, and they'll find you.

Amu House ☎ 0710 580405, ⓦ amuhousekenya.com. Extremely attractive and welcoming, this is a restored, American-owned stone house with newer rooms added on top, built in the same style and offering really good value. The doubles and triples are airy, with large bathrooms, and there's a roof deck with a hammock. BB **Ksh2500**

Bahari ☎ 042 4633172 or ☎ 0724 120600,

ⓔ kitendetini@gmail.com. Basic but spacious rooms on several floors, around a cool, plant-filled courtyard. A little rough around the edges but features include amusingly tokenistic "four-poster" beds, nets and fans, and most rooms have a fridge. The restaurant on the excellent rooftop terrace is a good place to meet travellers. Haggle hard. Wi-fi. BB **Ksh2500**

Baitul Noor ☎ 0723 760296. The only real backpackers in town, in an old, traditional and very vertical house, with small dorms and doubles set around a tiny garden courtyard; the most expensive room is on the roof. Breakfast and other meals available, though they cost extra. Room only: dorms **Ksh1000**, doubles **Ksh2500**

Café Bustani ☎ 0722 859594, ⓔ lamuchonjo@yahoo .com. One very nice top-floor room, with good ventilation, Swahili four-posters with nets and fan and a large bathroom. Terraces close to the room, and they do good coffee, juices and smoothies in the pretty, overgrown courtyard garden. Wi-fi. BB **Ksh2600**

Casuarina Rest House ☎ 0711 257328 or ☎ 0722 915746, ⓔ kaluc36@yahoo.com. A warren of rooms on the seafront, with nets and fans, in a nice position but very basic. Passable if you're prepared to put up with rudimentary comforts and security. Two rooms are s/c, the rest are not. Room only **Ksh500**

Hapa Hapa Guest House ☎ 0712 526215. Behind and above the popular eating place of the same name, this has one big double room at the front, with a balcony and a fan but rather poor ventilation. BB **Ksh3000**

House of Mwana Kupona ☎ 0701 754274. Owned by

Nairobi-based expats, the home of the famous nineteenth-century female poet Mwana Kupona is rented as two apartments with a shared kitchen, each with a large, secure room, plus several other, pleasant, more flexible rooms with double beds. Meals available on request. Room only Ksh3000

★**Jambo House** ✆0713 411714, ⊛jambohouse.com. A homely guesthouse run by an attentive world-traveller. The five bedrooms – three s/c and two non-s/c – are cosy and clean, and there's an airy upstairs terrace where good breakfasts are served. The owner organizes tours and excursions around Lamu, and provides free tea and coffee all day. Wi-fi. BB Ksh1600

Jannat House ✆0714 969831, ⊛jannathouselamu .com. Atmospheric, Swedish-owned boutique hotel with fifteen s/c and non-s/c rooms (nets and fans), a very nice, small pool and a bar-restaurant. Arranged around a heavily planted courtyard with much of its original decoration (*zidaka* stuccowork niches and furniture) still intact, plenty of terraces with comfy chairs and lovely views over the town. Wi-fi. BB $59

Lamu Archipelago Villa ✆0721 108650, ⊜ramamwandi@yahoo.com. The rooms here aren't that great – rather plain, with dowdy decor – but the position, right on the waterfront, is a plus, and the breakfast terrace overlooks the busy harbour. The rooms at the front are by far the best. BB Ksh2500

★**Lamu House** ✆0708 073164, ⊛lamuhouse.com. A stunning conversion, based on two traditional houses, each with five suites with private terrace, comfortable beds and superb bathrooms. Rooms downstairs can be a little dark: ideally get one upstairs at the front. There are also two cool, white courtyards with plunge pools, and a decent swimming pool. Excellent on-site restaurant and bar run by a charming Belgian restaurateur. Wi-fi. BB $174

New Lamu Palace ✆0723 593292. Comfortable, airy and elegant common areas with an attractive bar/restaurant and a spacious front porch, good for sundowners. The rooms themselves, though, are relatively basic and fairly expensive for what you get. Wi-fi. BB Ksh8340

New Mahrus ✆0720 574446. Although not on the waterfront, this rambling old place, with its own creaking, run-down charm, has a great location by the square, looking across to the fort. It's one of the cheapest places in town, especially for non-s/c rooms, but they could be cleaner and security is rather uncertain. The upper rooms, facing the square, are best, and the rooftop restaurant is a good place to get a local meal. Room only Ksh400

★**Nyuma Gereza** ✆0722 721232, ⊛nyumagereza hotel.blogspot.com. Located behind the fort, and personally run by its devoutly Muslim owner (no alcohol or beach boys in rooms), this excellent conversion has nine rooms with fans and nets. Most are non-s/c, but the shared bathrooms are immaculate, and guests have use of a kitchen (but no fridge). BB Ksh1800

Palm Beach House ✆0725 617996, ⊛lamuvilla.com. Decorated in bright colours and hung with batiks, this well-lit, airy house is getting tired, but it still offers spacious rooms with high ceilings. The huge top-floor "suite" opens on all sides, and has great views. Wi-fi. BB Ksh6000

Pole Pole ✆0722 736768. This guesthouse is getting fairly run down, but still pleasant, and very good value, especially if you're used to B&Ls. It has a fantastic roof terrace with a bird's-eye view from the roof, one of the highest in town. Nets and fans in most rooms. Room only Ksh1000

★**Subira House** ✆0726 916686, ⊛subirahouse.com. Built for a governor of the Sultan of Zanzibar, this palace-turned-boutique-hotel behind the fort features breezy lounging galleries throughout its three storeys, decorated in authentic Lamu style. Rooms are clean, private and spacious with strong eco values from the friendly and helpful Swedish owners. The restaurant, which is open to non-guests (book ahead), features light, healthy meals with produce from their organic farm. Wi-fi. BB $123

Sunsail ✆042 4632065, ⊛facebook.com/ lamusunsailhotel. Situated in the old stone "Mackenzie" trader's house on the waterfront, the rooms here have high ceilings, smart bathrooms and a/c, but this doesn't compensate for their small size – and only the two at the front have sea views. Unfortunately the roof terrace is enclosed. Reasonable value. BB Ksh4000

★**Wildebeest** ✆0720 996998 or ✆0712 851499, ⊜wildebeeste@hotmail.com. Fascinating old artists' workshop-cum-apartments, with a hair-raising multiplicity of steep, Escher-like staircases and a multitude of cosy nooks and crannies. Owned by a Nairobi-based American artist and managed by a Lamu artist-caretaker, the place is stuffed with artwork and interesting bric-a-brac, and offers breathtaking views from the topmost rooms. Breakfast and other meals available by prior arrangement. Exceptional value. Room only Ksh1500

Yumbe House ✆042 4633101 or ✆0725 352117. A cut above the average lodging, this has ten, mostly quite spacious rooms, including some good-value singles, all with fans, nets and fridge (a nice touch), above a well-planted courtyard. The top room is easily the best. BB Ksh3000

SHELA

While Shela can be a hedonistic place to pass a few days, it doesn't offer the thrill of staying among the mosques and street life of Lamu town itself. In addition, the price of rooms here can be up to twice what they would be in town, and there are few restaurants aside from those in the hotels. In addition to hotels and guesthouses, though, there are now more than twenty self-catering houses to rent, with prices starting at around $200/night. For more information, contact Lamu Retreats (⊛lamuretreats.com) or Lamu Homes & Safaris (✆020 4446384, ⊛lamuhomes.com).

6

Banana House 200m inland from the waterfront ☎0721 275538, ⊛bananahouse-lamu.com. A wellness centre offering yoga, massage and ayurvedic cuisine. The penthouse rooms have excellent ocean views, while the spacious common areas, garden and pool are great for meeting other travellers. There's also a kitchen for self-catering. Wi-fi. BB €119

Dudu Villas & Lamu Backpackers 500m north of the Shela jetty, behind Talking Trees restaurant ☎0717 081488 or ☎0718 195952, ⊕duduvillasncottages@gmail.com. At the back of this vast expanse of sandy garden sit several blocks of acceptable if unexciting rooms, two of which serve as three- to four-bed dorms, all with fans, nets and porches. There's also a restaurant – just as well since it's a bit of a walk into the village – and space for camping. Camping Ksh500; BB dorms Ksh1000, doubles Ksh3800

Fatuma's Tower Back of the village ☎0722 277138, ⊛fatumastower.com. A truly enchanting garden experience in a spacious, self-contained compound among frangipanis and a restored 200-year-old tower, once a private residence. Rooms are furnished with antiques, and there's a yoga hall, plunge pool and library. The penthouse suite, which has a great view, is the best value. Wi-fi. BB €85

Island Hotel Back of the village, near the sand dunes ☎0721 212786, ⊛islandhotellamu.com. An older-style place, with spacious, attractively furnished rooms, all with nets on frames, and a restful atmosphere. Rooms 16 and 17 are especially appealing – almost open-air, like sleeping on the roof but in privacy and comfort, and with their own private rooftop decks. The *Barracuda* rooftop restaurant is good and reasonably priced, but doesn't have an alcohol licence. BB Ksh3500

Jannatan In the centre of the village ☎0722 698059 or ☎0722 729219. Big place with a deep pool. However, it's essentially just a modern hotel, and not especially attractive. There are 22 rooms on five floors, with good views from the roof deck on top – but no atmosphere. BB Ksh4000

★**Kijani House** On the waterfront north of Shela ☎0202 435700 or ☎0725 545264, ⊛kijani-lamu.com. Comfortable and pretty, environmentally conscious Swiss-owned hotel, with eleven lovely rooms (with solar-heated showers, fans, frame nets and safes) around tropical gardens, and their own fruit farm close by. There are also two small pools, a restaurant serving Italian-style dishes, and a bar with a range of Italian and South African wines. Closed May & June. Wi-fi. BB €175

★**Peponi** On the beach, 100m south of the Shela jetty ☎0703 790411 or ☎0722 203082, ⊛peponi-lamu.com. Shela's main beachfront focus, where everyone stops in for a cold drink, *Peponi* is fabulously situated, and offers probably the best food on Lamu (mains Ksh1500–2500). There's a wide variety of attractive rooms on offer, all facing the sea, some with huge private balconies. Rooms in the main house are more characterful than those in the garden. Good pool. Closed May & June. Wi-fi. BB €235

★**Pwani Guest House** Behind Peponi ☎0712 506778, ⊕shelapwanigap@gmail.com. Stylish, roomy traditional house with the three doubles and two singles, all a good deal by Shela standards, with sea views, old furniture, antique stucco work and soft lighting. Breakfast and dinner are served on the rooftop terrace, which has beautiful sea views. BB Ksh4500

Shella Bahari Guest House On the waterfront, 100m north of Peponi ☎0722 901643, ⊛facebook.com/Shelabahariguesthouse. You pay a premium for the location here, next to the water. The five rooms, all with different rates, are simple but nicely done – the top one comes with a huge private balcony – and there's an excellent restaurant. BB Ksh6000

Shella Royal House 100m inland from the waterfront ☎0722 698059. Bright and breezy, with yellow floors and stairs. The rooms, all with mahogany four-posters, are of varying standards. There's a roof terrace for lounging, with a 360-degree view, and fabulous views from the "honeymoon room" on the top floor. BB Ksh7000

Stopover On the waterfront, south of Kijani House ☎0720 127222. Six simple, but nicely done rooms directly on the seafront near the dhow harbour, all opening out onto balconies with sea views. There's a ground-floor restaurant overlooking the sea, serving great fish curries, and kitchen facilities for those who prefer to self-cater. BB Ksh8000

★**Waridi House** Just in front of Fatuma's Tower ☎0722 994974, ⊛waridihouse.com. Just four elegant, open rooms, two small and two large, with enormous bathrooms and spacious private balconies. The whole place is filled with billowing white curtains, couches and hanging beds perfect for lounging, and with its composting toilets and solar lighting it's eco-friendly, too. All rooms are self-catering, but a chef is on-hand to cook the food you provide. A very good deal considering the standard. Room only Ksh6500

SOUTHWEST LAMU

A good bet if you want to rent a house in this remote part of Lamu, there are several lavish beachfront properties on a 24-acre private stretch north of *Kizingo*. Check out ⊛kizingonibeach.com for more details.

★**Kizingo** On the southwest tip of the island ☎0733 954770 or ☎0722 901544, ⊛kizingo.com. A secluded eco-lodge, created in partnership with nearby Kipungani village. There are eight thatched s/c *bandas* nestled among the sand dunes, each with perfect sea views, and the food served at the restaurant is wonderfully fresh. From Nov to April you can swim with wild bottlenose dolphins, and between Nov and June turtles lay eggs on the beach; the owners will take guests to watch the newborn turtles make their way into the ocean. Closed May & June. FB $400

EATING

There are enough **restaurants** and passable **hotelis** in Lamu town to enable you to eat out twice a day for a week without going back to your first port of call. A fine balance has been achieved between what is demanded and what can be supplied: yoghurt, fruit salad, pancakes, milkshakes and puréed fruit juices have become Lamu specialities. Superb lobster and crab dishes, oysters, snapper and delicious steaks of swordfish, barracuda and shark are also on many menus – it's a nice change to find a fishing town where you can actually eat seafood relatively affordably. Upcountry staples – beans, curries, pilau, steak, chicken, chips, eggs, even *ugali* – are available from a number of ordinary *hotelis* crowded along Harambee Ave, particularly in Langoni. Also along Harambee Ave, you'll find tiny mutton kebabs and cakes on sale at night; they cost next to nothing and are usually delicious. Prices are fairly standard, Ksh80 to Ksh180 for shakes and juices, depending on size, and Ksh500 to Ksh1000 for full meals. Cheaper places that don't go out of their way to attract tourists serve meals for Ksh150 to Ksh250.

6

SNACK BARS AND LOCAL HOTELIS

Coconut Juice Garden Harambee Ave ☎0725 251422. Good juices and shakes, blended as you wish, served on a rooftop terrace – combinations include passionfruit and pawpaw, and a sublime coconut and banana (Ksh50–200). Daily 7am–6pm.

Labanda On the waterfront, Langoni ☎0718 699769, ⓦfacebook.com/LabandaRestaurant. Popular local joint serving cheap Kenyan dishes – beef stew, fried fish and *pilau* – on a fabulous first-floor wooden balcony overlooking the boats, out of reach of the beach boys. Most mains below Ksh200. Daily 7am–10pm.

RESTAURANTS AND TRAVELLERS' CAFÉS

★ **Bush Gardens** On the waterfront, Mkomani ☎0714 934804. Competing for the same business as *Hapa Hapa* (see below) but more upmarket, this seafood and kebab place has a popular following and a charming proprietor. The food varies from average to first-rate (the grilled garlic fish, for Ksh575, is magnificent) and prices are reasonable – shakes Ksh80–180, fish around Ksh600. Daily 7am–10pm.

Floating Bar and Restaurant Lamu harbour, half way between Lamu town and Shela ☎0721 510852. A floating wooden platform with woven mat walls and a *makuti* roof, where you can feast on the catch of the day for around Ksh500 a head, or tuck into more expensive dishes like crab and prawns. This also doubles as a local bar, so the atmosphere's far from refined, but it's still good fun. Local boatmen will take you over for around Ksh500, or the restaurant can arrange transport if you call ahead. Daily 10am–11pm.

Hapa Hapa On the waterfront, Mkomani ☎0712 526215, ⓦbit.ly/HapaHapaRestaurant. Popular, central seafront rendezvous – the food, which includes seafood curry and the like (Ksh400), is generally good, and occasionally excellent. And then there are the famous pint jugs of freshly pressed juices, shakes and smoothies, as well as decent breakfasts. A good place to people-watch, or just daydream. Daily 8am–10pm.

Mangrove Café Next to Petley's ☎0722 471266. Popular travellers' café serving freshly squeezed juices (Ksh50), snacks and the usual range of Kenyan and seafood dishes (Ksh250–1000). Daily 6am–10pm.

★ **Moonrise** Lamu House, on the waterfront, Mkomani ☎0708 073164, ⓦlamuhouse.com. With its terrace cleverly tucked away behind a low wall, eating here is more relaxing than in some of the more exposed restaurants. Although not cheap, it's not as expensive as you might imagine (Ksh2500 for three courses, without drinks), and the seafood dishes are invariably fragrant and well prepared. Daily 7am–10pm.

Mwanaarafa Gardens On the waterfront, Mkomani ☎0722 758659. The food here – mainly curries (from Ksh300), seafood and chicken dishes – is pretty unremarkable. But the peaceful garden setting, with its spreading flamboyant tree, is pleasant on a hot afternoon, and it's always a good place to stop for a cold juice. Daily 11am–9pm.

New Star Harambee Ave, Langoni ☎0722 105033. With its lime-green walls, this Lamu institution (35 years and still going strong) is one of the few restaurants catering equally to travellers and locals, and one of the cheapest in town, with tasty stew and rice for Ksh180. Especially good for breakfast before an early-morning walk to the beach. Daily 5.30am–6pm.

★ **Olympic** On the waterfront, Langoni, behind the old Olympic restaurant ☎0728 667692. Popular, long-established place that's currently operating out of the owner's modest living room, making it a wonderful opportunity to experience real home-cooked rice and fish-based meals (from Ksh500), alongside fresh juices and snacks, with an emphasis on delicious Indian sauces like tamarind and chilli. Daily 7am–9pm.

Seafront Café On the waterfront, Langoni ☎0728 711832, ⓦfacebook.com/seafrontcafeandguesthouse. This travellers' restaurant offers coconut fish or beans, rice, pilau, *karanga* and pancakes, though standards are variable; most mains Ksh500–1000. Daily 7am–10pm.

★ **Whispers** Harambee Ave, Langoni ☎042 4632024. If you need a break from the local joints on the waterfront, try this lovely garden coffee shop for real espressos, wonderful cakes, smoothies, pizzas, pastas and salads that are hard to resist. Unless, that is, you're really counting the pennies – a snack and a coffee can cost Ksh600. There's a deli section and takeaway, though portions tend to be on the small side. Usually closed May & June. Mon–Sat 9am–2pm & 4–6.30pm.

6

DRINKING

Petley's Inn On Lamu town waterfront, above the hotel of the same name. The only stand-alone bar in town is a pleasant rooftop affair with comfy couches and great views, and it's a good spot to catch football games on TV. It's also one of the few places you can order a beer (Ksh220), though it can get loud in the evenings. Daily 4.30pm–midnight.

SHOPPING

The **woodcarving** shops in Lamu town are mostly found in Mkomani, along the waterfront and along Harambee Ave. Model dhows, chests, furniture and *siwa* horns are all attractive, if bulky. Beautifully hand-carved safari chairs are also a hassle to carry, but the prices make them worth acquiring. Wooden trays are lighter and useful but also show off Lamu craftsmanship. If you have something in mind, and a day or two in hand, you can always order a particular piece or design. Some of the shops selling **jewellery** and **trinkets** have genuinely old and interesting pieces: look out especially for tiny lime caskets in silver, earlobe plugs in buffalo horn or silver, and old coins. A number of **tailors** along Harambee Ave will run up shirts, trousers, shorts and skirts very cheaply in a day or so. The easiest way to end up with something that fits is to provide a model garment for them to copy. Langoni is the place to hunt out pairs of printed ladies' *kangas* and men's woven *kikoi* wraps.

Baraka Gallery Harambee Ave, Langoni ☎ 042 4633399. Even if it's expensive, the wares here are so diverse and attractive – from silver and glass jewellery to intricate basketware, leather goods and paper crafts – that it's a must-visit for souvenir hunters. Daily 9am–1pm & 3.30–7.30pm.

Fish Harambee Ave ☎ 0724 697940. A variety of art, jewellery and practical objects made from recycled materials, including old shoes, driftwood and dhow sails – look out for the colourful beaded curtains fashioned from flip-flop foam. Daily 9am–1pm & 2.30–6pm.

Haluwa Centre Harambee Ave, across from Whispers ☎ 0724 937956. Run by the same family for more than a century, this small shop makes sweet, fragrant *halwa* fresh every day; the most basic flavours sell for Ksh100/quarter kilo. Daily 7am–9pm.

Lamu Silversmith Harambee Ave, just up from Lamu Guest House ☎ 0733 789211. Long-established and recommended silver craftsmen who will design to order. Mon–Sat 9am–12.30pm & 2.30–6pm, Sun 9am–12.30pm.

Ogres Bead Workshop Just off Harambee Ave, Mkomani ☎ 0722 261917, ✺ ogresbeads.weebly.com. Run by two brothers from Nairobi, this workshop sells wonderful handmade jewellery. Custom pieces made to order. Mon–Sat 9am–1pm & 3–6pm.

Old Town Art & Crafts Mkomani ☎ 0724 697940. Big shop of carvings, paintings and jewellery – the sort of stuff you don't easily find elsewhere in Lamu. Like an upcountry souvenir emporium, but in a relaxed atmosphere. Daily 9am–1pm & 2–6pm.

DIRECTORY

Bank KCB, on Lamu town's waterfront, has an ATM. There is also an ATM in Shela.

Books and newspapers Mani Books & Stationers (daily 8.30am–12.30pm & 3–9pm; ☎ 042 6432238), near the fort in Lamu town, sells newspapers and magazines. For a selection of books, visit the offices of *Lamu Chonjo* magazine, at *Café Bustani* in Mkomani, near the Swahili House Museum.

Cinema The Zinj Theatre on Harambee Ave in Langoni screens international and Bollywood films. It also occasionally screens live English Premiership or European Champions League football matches.

Henna painting A number of women around town offer henna designs for hands and feet, for which you can expect to pay around Ksh1000 for both hands or both feet. The best women have portfolios of designs to choose from – you'll see them in one or two shop fronts and private doorways. If done properly, your hands or feet will be bound in cloth for twelve hours and the design should stay for several weeks, or six months on nails.

Internet access You can get online at Al-Miftah, in Langoni (Mon–Sat 8am–8pm), or at the *New Mahrus Hotel* (see p.489), first floor (hours vary).

Hospital The Saudi-funded hospital, between Lamu town and Shela (☎ 042 4633012), attracts patients from a huge part of northeastern Kenya. There are several private clinics.

DINNER AT HOME

If you spend any time in Lamu, you'll probably run into someone offering you a "genuine" **Swahili dinner** at home. At its best, this is a great way of seeing how the majority of Lamu's inhabitants live, and the food can be delicious. On the other hand, the price demanded at the end (which, like everything in Lamu, depends mainly on how hard you haggle and your perceived ability to pay) might not necessarily be any cheaper than eating in a decent restaurant. As in a restaurant, you should pay after your meal, not before.

MARKETS AND SELF-CATERING IN LAMU

If you enjoy doing your own cooking (several lodgings have kitchens you can use), a whole new world starts to open up. The **produce market** in front of the fort in Lamu town – run for the most part by upcountry women – has everything you'll need, with separate sections for meat, fish, and fruit and vegetables. For fish and shellfish, get there very early: by 9am all the interesting stock has been sold. Lamu has wonderful fruit and is famous for its enormous, aromatic mangoes, but you should also try the unusually sweet, juicy grapefruit. While you're here, you might also find one of Lamu's traditional exports, betel, the green vine you see trailing out of all the empty plots in town. The sweet, hot-tasting leaves are wrapped around other ingredients, including white lime and betel nut, which stains the teeth red, to make *pan* which you chew (see p.407). For something sweet, try the *halwa* shop on Harambee Avenue in Langoni (see opposite).

Library Lamu town library (Mon–Fri 8am–12.30pm & 2–5.30pm, Sat 10am–noon) is on the top floor of the fort. It has a surprisingly good collection, with lots on Lamu, as well as a sixteenth-century Koranic manuscript.

Supermarkets/general stores Big Shop, Harambee Ave (daily 10am–10pm), can supply basic goods and toiletries.

Swahili lessons Being suffused in Swahili culture, Lamu is a good place to learn the language – the tourist office (see p.488) can put you in touch with a teacher. Alternatively, ask at the Department of Adult Education on Harambee Ave or at Lamu Museum.

Tide tables Check out *Coast Week* (ⓦ coastweek.com).

Visa extensions Immigration office in the District Commissioner's (DC's) offices on the waterfront.

Manda island

Practically within shouting distance of Lamu town, **Manda island** – with next to no fresh water – was only recently almost uninhabited but is now the site of several new luxury homes and a couple of boutique resorts. Aside from the allure of the pristine beach, it is also the site of the main airstrip on the islands, and the location of the old ruined town of **Takwa** (favourite destination of the dhow-trip operators). Significant archeologically for the ruins of Takwa and Manda, the north side of the island is also the location of the fabulous *Manda Bay Lodge* (see p.494).

Manda ruins
Daily 24hr • Free

You can walk from *Manda Bay* to the nearby **Manda ruins**, just fifteen minutes away. The population of this town is estimated to have been around three thousand. It's a fascinating, barely excavated site, with baobabs poking through the old walls. The remnants include the *mihrab*, and most of the walls, of a sizeable mosque. Watch out for **snakes** – the island has a diverse variety.

Takwa ruins
Daily 8am–6pm • Ksh500 • A 30min boat ride from Lamu

Whether you make a flying visit to **Takwa** or sleep out on the beach behind it, the ruins are well worth seeing. A flourishing town in the sixteenth and seventeenth centuries, the site was eventually deserted (as usual, no one knows why), and is in many respects reminiscent of Gedi (see p.456). As at other sites, toilets and bathrooms figure prominently in the architecture. In Islam, cleanliness is so close to godliness as to almost signify it – the Takwans must have been a devout community. The doors of all the houses face north towards Mecca, as does the main street with the **mosque** at the end of it. The mosque is interesting for the pillar at one end, which suggests it was built on a tomb site (that of a founder of the town perhaps), and for the simple lines of its *mihrab*, so different from the ornate curlicues of later designs. Another impressive **pillar tomb** stands alone, just outside the town walls, its date translating to about 1683, and it still occasionally attracts pilgrims from Shela (some of whom claim their ancestry lies in Takwa), who come here to pray for rain.

6

Takwa has been thoroughly cleared but, in order to preserve it for the future, hardly excavated at all. What has been found, however, suggests an industrious and healthy community, living in an easily defensible position with a wall all around the town, the ocean on one side behind the dunes, and mangroves on the other. Despite this, they appear to have left in a panic and, as usual, there's ample room for conjecture about why. Part of the great appeal of Kenya's ruined towns lies in the open debate that still continues about who, precisely, their builders and citizens were, and why they so often left in such evident haste. And there's always the fascinating possibility that old Swahili manuscripts will turn up to explain it all.

ARRIVAL AND DEPARTURE   MANDA ISLAND

By boat Local boats run between Shela jetty on Lamu island and Manda beach for Ksh100, or you can charter one from Lamu town (Ksh500) or Shela (Ksh350).

ACCOMMODATION AND EATING

★**Diamond Beach Village** On the southern arm of Manda, facing Shela ☎0720 915001, ⓦdiamond beachvillage.com. Simple s/c *bandas*, a beach bar/restaurant with wood-fired pizza oven, a treehouse in a baobab, sound environmental principles and a superb beachfront location. Great social setting with weekly pizza and movie nights (Sat) – plus evening electricity, good food and strong Bloody Marys. Closed April 15–June 30. BB **£70**

The Majlis Resort Down the beach from Diamond Beach Village, facing Shela ☎0773 777066, ⓦthemajlisresorts.com. A series of exclusive beachfront luxury villas and suites catering mostly to Kenyan politicians and high rollers. The neo-Roman architecture can be off-putting and locals have complained about the damage the resort has done to the beach and mangroves, but the beach bar and restaurant serves up some good fine dining, and the second-floor bar in the main building is the perfect spot to watch the sunset while sipping an (overpriced) margarita. FB **$420**

★**Manda Bay Lodge** At the northwestern tip of Manda ☎0722 203329 or ☎0722 203109, ⓦmandabay.com. This exclusive beach camp of palm mat, wood and *makuti* s/c *bandas* in an extravagantly beautiful setting is the perfect honeymoon retreat. When you're not participating in every conceivable watersport, or taking a sundowner trip on the lodge's own enormous dhow, you can swing in your hammock and be entertained by a huge variety of birds (there are bird baths outside every *banda*). FB **$850**

Pate island

Just two or three hours by ferry from Lamu, totally unaffected by tourism and rarely visited, **Pate island** has some of the most impressive ruins anywhere on the coast and a clutch of old Swahili settlements which, at different times, have been as important as Lamu – or more so. There are few places on the coast as memorable.

Pate is mostly low-lying and almost surrounded by mangrove swamps; no two maps of it ever agree – ours shows only the permanent dry land, not the ever-changing mangrove forests that surround it (see p.478), so getting on and off the island requires deft awareness of the tides. Its remoteness, coupled with limited transport, deters travellers. In truth, though, Pate is not a difficult destination, and is an easier island to physically walk around than Lamu, with none of that island's exhausting soft sand.

It's wise to take **water** with you, as Pate's supplies are unpredictable and often very briny. Most islanders live on home-produced **food** and staples brought from Lamu and, although there are a few small shops on the island, it's a good idea to have some emergency provisions. **Mosquitoes** and flies are a serious menace, especially during the long rains; carry repellent.

Brief history

According to its own **history**, the *Pate Chronicle*, Pate was founded in the early years of Islam with the arrival of Arabian immigrants. This mini-state is supposed to have lasted until the thirteenth century, when another group of dispossessed Arab rulers – the **Nabahani** – arrived. The story may have been embellished by time, but archeological evidence does support the existence of a flourishing port on the present site of Pate as early as the ninth century. Probably by the fifteenth century the town exerted a considerable influence on most of the quasi-autonomous settlements along the coast, including Lamu.

The first **Portuguese** visitors traded with the Pateans for the multicoloured silk cloth for which the town had become famous, and they also introduced gunpowder, which enabled wells to be easily excavated, a fact which must have played a part in Pate's rising fortunes. During the sixteenth century, a number of Portuguese merchants settled and married in the town, but as Portugal tightened its grip and imposed taxes, relations quickly deteriorated. There were repeated uprisings and reprisals until, by the middle of the seventeenth century, the Portuguese had withdrawn to the security of Fort Jesus in Mombasa. Even today, though, several families in Pate are said to be Wa-reno (from the Portuguese *reino*, "kingdom"), meaning of Portuguese descent.

During the late seventeenth and eighteenth centuries, having thrown out the old rulers, Pate underwent a **cultural rebirth** and experienced a flood of creative activity similar to Lamu's. The two towns had a lively relationship, and were frequently in a state of war; Pate was ruled by a Nabahani king who considered Lamu part of his realm. The disastrous Battle of Shela of 1812 (see p.480) marked the end of Lamu's political allegiance to Pate and the end of Pate as a city-state.

Pate town

From the dock at Mtangawanda there's more than one route to **PATE TOWN**. The old path, a narrow **footpath** through thick bush – the *ndia ya Pate*, or "path to Pate" – is the one people will show you, and once on the trail it's easy to follow. You cross a broad, tidal "desert", then climb a slight rise to drop through thicker bush, and arrive after an hour on the edge of town. However, there's a new **motorable road** to the town as well, from where you might be able to get a lift.

Despite its small size, Pate could hardly be described as a village. Yet with its only link with government an assistant chief and its sole provision a primary school, the town is today a mere shadow of its former self. But at least its inhabitants can depend on a cash crop, **tobacco**, possibly introduced by the Portuguese and certainly grown here longer than anywhere else on the coast.

After Lamu, Pate brings many surprises. There's no electricity, no alcohol and, apart from a handful of matatus and a few motorbikes, very few vehicles. The **town plan** is pretty much the same – a maze of narrow streets and high-walled houses – but here the streets are made of earth, and the houses are built of coral and dried mud. The overall layout is confusing; Pateans refer to the "upper" and "lower" parts of town – Kitokwe and Mitaaguu respectively. The lower part is down near the town dock, which is only briefly underwater at high tide. You're also likely to be struck immediately by the *Wapate* – the **people**, and notably the women. Brilliant, determined, with short, bushy hair and rows of gold earrings, they stare out directly, unhidden by *buibuis*. *Wazungu* are rare and Pate is arrestingly upfront in its dealings with foreigners.

Nabahani ruins

Daily • 24hr • Check with the museum in Lamu town (see p.483) to hire a local guide for Ksh500 (☎ 0721 660645); boys will guide you around the ruins for a small payment, but don't expect anyone to take you at night – although it's very beautiful in a full moon, you'll have to go alone because the locals are afraid of the djinn and ghosts living there

More layers are peeled off Pate's enigmatic exterior when you start to explore the ruins of the **Nabahani** town, just outside the modern one. The walls, roofless buildings, tombs, mosques and unidentifiable structures, stretching across several acres, are fascinating, the more so perhaps because this isn't an "archeological site" in the commonly expected mould. Farmers cultivate tobacco and other crops in the stony fields between the walls. Indeed, many of the walls and buildings have already been demolished to obtain lime for tobacco cultivation. Without weighty financial backing, it's hard to see how the National Museums of Kenya could preserve the remains of old Pate as well as compensate the farmers. Gradually, tragically, it is all returning to the soil.

For now, however, most impressive of the remaining buildings are the **Mosque with Two Mihrabs**, a nearby house that still has a facing of beautiful *zidaka* (niches) on one wall and the remains of a sizeable mansion. This last building, you'll be told, is a **Portuguese house**. Certainly, the worn-down stumps of bottle glass projecting from the top of one of its walls do lend it a curiously European flavour, and in the plaster on another wall are scratched two very obvious galleons. Its ceiling slots are square for timbers rather than round for *boriti*, as elsewhere in the ruins.

Shards of pottery and household objects lie in the rubble everywhere, but many of the interiors of the buildings are so clogged with tangled roots and vegetation that getting in is almost impossible. It is worth persevering, however: the sense of discovery is exciting.

Siyu

The walk from Pate town to **SIYU** is a slightly tricky 8km, or you can take a matatu (Ksh100). Having set off in the correct direction, you will find the first half-hour fairly straightforward; if in doubt, bear right. You come to a crossroads (easily missed unless you look backwards) and turn right. This narrow red-dirt path soon broadens into a track that takes you to a normally dry tidal inlet where you veer left a little before continuing straight on through thick bush for another hour to reach Siyu. Wherever the bush on either side is high enough you may come across gigantic spiders' webs strung across the path. The spiders are brightly coloured and merely waiting for insects, but they are nevertheless intimidating.

Siyu is even less well documented than Pate. Still less accessible by sea, the town was a flourishing and unsuspected centre of Islamic scholarship from the seventeenth to the nineteenth century and apparently something of a **sanctuary** for Muslim intellectuals and craftsmen. While Lamu, Pate and other trading towns were engaged in political rivalry and physical skirmishing, Siyu never had its heart in commerce or maritime activities, and never attracted much Portuguese attention. Instead, there was enormous devotion to **Koran-copying**, **book-making**, **text illumination** and cottage industries like the **woodcarving** and **leatherwork** for which it's still famous locally. Siyu **sandals** are said to be absolutely the best (though plastic flip-flops have forced almost all the makers out of business), and Siyu **carved doors** are among the most beautiful of all Swahili doors, with distinctive guilloche patterns and inlays of ground shell.

The sources of wealth and stability for Siyu's flowering are a little mysterious, but the town's agricultural base obviously supported it well and it was probably the largest settlement on the island in the early nineteenth century, with up to thirty thousand inhabitants. In 1873, the British vice-consul in Zanzibar could still describe Siyu as "the pulse of the whole district". These days you wouldn't know it. Fewer than four thousand people live here, and signs of the old brilliance are hard to find. Siyu lost its independence and presumably much of its artistic flair when the Sultan of Zanzibar's Omani troops first occupied the fort in 1847.

Most of Siyu's houses today conform to the "open-box" plan typical of the Kenyan coast: yellowish mud with a ridged *makuti* roof, open at each end. These houses stand, each on its own, with no real streets to connect them, so that although it's larger than Pate, Siyu feels far more like a village. There are still few *buibuis* here, but there's much less jewellery in evidence and the atmosphere is altogether less severe.

Siyu Fort

Daily 24hr • Free

Built in the early nineteenth century (no one knows for sure by whom), **Siyu Fort** is the town's most striking building and indeed, in purely monumental terms, the most imposing building anywhere in the Lamu archipelago. Substantially renovated, it is one of the few surviving traces of the glory days. It's freely accessible, though watch out for dangers like the well and the unstable walls. Around the outskirts of Siyu on the south side are a number of quite impressive **tombs**. The big domed tomb with porcelain niches dates from 1853.

Shanga ruins

South coast of Pate island, about 1hr walk from Siyu • Daily 24hr • Expect to pay around Ksh1000 for a guide

You'll need the help of a good guide if you hope to visit the ruins of **Shanga**, a large Swahili town at least one thousand years old, which would be almost impossible to find unaided. You literally have to hack your way through the undergrowth when you arrive at the ruins. The most impressive sight is the white pillar tomb, eminently phallic, which you come to first. The very large Friday mosque nearby and a second mosque nearer the sea are only the most obvious of innumerable other remains in every direction.

Excavations at Shanga have revealed a walled site of 12 acres with five access gates and a cemetery outside the walls containing 340 stone tombs. There was even a sea wall. Inside the town, 130 houses were surveyed, together with what looks to have been a palace similar in some respects to the one at Gedi. Shanga is believed to have been occupied from the ninth to the fourteenth centuries and, in a pattern that may sound familiar, no very convincing reasons have been found for its abandonment, nor for why it was never mentioned by travellers and traders of the time.

A limited amount of work has been done to restore some of the plaster in a set of *zidaka* wall niches and on the fluted pillar tomb, but on the whole the excavations only seem to have encouraged the jungle. Getting from one ruin to the next isn't easy. Dangerously camouflaged **wells**, and **snakes**, both of which are common, enliven the Shanga experience. If you walk on down to the sea – and assuming you have a certain capacity for hardship in paradise – there's a beautiful **beach** and some ideal camping spots. Perhaps needless to say, you would need to be completely self-reliant, and preferably in a group.

Faza

The walk from Siyu to **FAZA** is shorter and more interesting than from Pate to Siyu, through waist-high grass, fertile *shambas* and sections of bush. It takes about two hours, but you'll need guidance, at least as far as the airstrip that was inherited from a 1980s oil-prospecting venture. From there it's straightforward. An hour or so out of Siyu, you reach the first *shambas*. You could also travel from Mtangawanda to Faza by matatu (Ksh200).

Faza itself is almost an **island**, surrounded by tidal flats and mangroves, with a secondary school, health centre, police station and post office that have made it the most important settlement on the island. Fishing is the commonest occupation, with much of the catch going to a cold room at Kisingitini, from where it's shipped to Mombasa. As a contemporary Kenyan rural centre, it makes an interesting place to walk around and you're almost certain to have plenty of time to fill before the boat leaves. Due to a recent fire that destroyed most of the homes, however, the village now features rows of tin-roofed houses that lack the charm of its previous historic structures.

A fine evening stroll takes you across the mud on the concrete causeway to the thickets on the "mainland", where the island's expanding secondary school is located. The other villages on the island, all fairly modern and bunched together, lie within a forty-minute walk of Faza: **Kisingitini**, **Bajumwali**, **Tundwa**, and the closest, **Nyambogi**.

Faza's ruins

In terms of **archeological ruins**, Faza has less to offer than its neighbours. It was one of the most defiant Swahili towns over any attempts to usurp its independence, and was

6

6

razed by the Pate army after a dispute over water rights in the fifteenth century, and again by the Portuguese in 1586 after collaborating with the Turkish fleet of Amir Ali Bey. On this occasion, the entire population was massacred and the head of Faza's king was taken to Goa in a barrel of salt to be paraded triumphantly in the streets. Faza's unfortunate history may partly account for its relative lack of ruins, but one success is commemorated in the **tomb** of Seyyid Hamed bin Ahmed al-Busaidy, commander-in-chief of the Sultan of Zanzibar's forces, who met his death in 1844 under a hail of arrows. His grave or *kaburi*, with a long epitaph, lies just outside the village.

There are several ruined mosques around Faza, including the very crumbled **Kunjanja** mosque and ruins of the eighteenth-century **Mbwarashally**, or **Shala Fatani** mosque, which merit a visit. Now theoretically protected by the National Museums of Kenya, most of the mosque is a pile of rubble. Its *mihrab*, however, turns out to incorporate exquisite and unusual heart motifs, including the Islamic creed, or *shahada*, inscribed within an inverted heart shape.

ARRIVAL AND DEPARTURE
PATE ISLAND

By mtaboti water taxi A water taxi (Ksh250) departs from the municipal jetty in Lamu daily except Fri for Pate island's main dock at Mtangawanda, a quiet spot on the island's southwest tip (2–3hr), then Faza (1hr); some, but not all, then continue on to Kisingitini (30min). The boats usually leave about an hour before high tide. Since the dredging of the Mkanda channel between Manda and the mainland, they can reach Mtangawanda at any state of the tide, but getting close enough to Faza and Kisingitini still requires careful timing. Pate town lies in the southeast corner of the island at the head of a creek so shallow that it's difficult to get up there even in a flat-bottomed boat at high tide.

By boat Rather than taking the *mtaboti* water taxi, you could choose to take a dhow to Pate. Alternatively, if you have less time but can afford to spend a lot more, you might look into taking a speedboat (see p.488), which would enable you to reach Pate town direct, at high tide, in less than 30min (Ksh10,000). But timing is critical, only small boats can make it at all, and you have to wait until the next high tide to get out of Pate creek again – unless the speedboat captain goes round to Mtangawanda or Siyu, leaving you to walk. The obvious plan, having walked from Mtangawanda dock to Pate town (allow at least 1hr), is then to walk through Siyu to Faza, returning to Lamu by ferry from there. The walk from Pate town to Faza can be done in a day if the tides force an early start.

ACCOMMODATION

Accommodation is rarely a problem (normally, you'll be invited to stay by someone almost as soon as you arrive in a village), but as there are no proper lodgings, a **tent** is a useful back-up. If you plan on spending several days on Pate, and especially if you're interested in the archeology of the region, you should ask at Lamu Museum (see p.483) and Lamu Fort (see p.484) for **advice**.

Kiwaiyu

From Faza you're within striking distance of the desert island retreat of **Kiwaiyu** (also spelt Kiwayu). The island is a long strip of sand dunes, held in place with low scrub and the odd tree and fronted on the ocean side by a superb beach. The village of **KIWAIYU**, near the southern end of the island, has limited provisions at a couple of shops. Twenty minutes' walk to the south, you reach a private fishing lodge on the high southern tip of the island. From here, the empty, ocean-facing beach, with the reef close offshore, is just a scramble down the sandy hillside. There are one or two first-class **snorkelling** spots off this southern tip of the island, with huge coral heads and a multitude of fish. Ask for precise directions, as it's possible to spend hours looking and still miss them.

Since the tragic events of September 2011 (see box, p.479) and the Kenyan military incursion into Somalia, *Kiwayu Safari Village* (the luxury beach lodge on the mainland facing the northern tip of the island that was the location of the first kidnapping) has been closed and tourism to the island has dropped off – check the **latest security advice** before travelling here.

ARRIVAL AND DEPARTURE

By mtaboti Kiwaiyu is about an hour from Faza by *mtaboti*, if you can find one.

By speedboat A round-trip speedboat (2–3hr each way) from Lamu will cost Ksh18,000–20,000.

By dhow charter A group dhow charter in Lamu is probably the cheapest option: you can charter a small dhow for Ksh10,000 to Ksh12,000 a day. That should include breakfast and dinner for a small group, snorkelling and fishing gear, and plenty of fresh water. Your captain will cook you the most amazing fresh fish, grilled on the

KIWAIYU

back of the dhow over charcoal. You can expect to spend at least 24 hours on the journey in each direction, depending on wind, tides and the skill of the crew. The experience of sailing, the nights under the stars, and the company of the Swahili crew are altogether highly recommended.

By plane SafariLink (ⓦflysafarilink.com) offers charter services to Kiwaiyu. Airkenya flights from Nairobi and SafariLink flights from Nairobi via Lamu were suspended at the time of writing.

6

ACCOMMODATION

Along with the options below, there's a scattering of local **bandas** in this area where you can stay for around Ksh1500 a night; for something a little different, ask your captain on the boat over about a fantastic little hut in a baobab tree.

Champali Camp On a mangrove creek within the Kiunga Marine National Marine Reserve at the southern end of Kiwaiyu ☎0723 487145, ⓦchampali .co.ke. This self-catering camp offers stylish s/c *bandas*. The camp is staffed, but there are no hosts so you have the place to yourselves. It is more affordable than *Mike's* and ideal for groups of up to ten. Closed May–July. Conservation fee $20/person. Whole camp, room only <u>Ksh28,000</u>

★**Mike's Camp** About 2km north of Kiwaiyu village ☎020 2617367 or ☎0718 004920, ⓦmikescampkiwayu.com. Seven spacious, comfortable s/c *bandas* of palm mats and wood, planted on the crest of the island to catch the breeze. The camp, run by the laidback Mike Kennedy, is only accessible up the inside channel between Kiwaiyu and the mainland at high tide. Their little shop sells articles made by local people from recycled odds and ends, and they also have possibly the coldest beers on the coast and brand-new diving equipment: there's fantastic coral right off the beach down on the ocean side. *Mike's* is run entirely on wind power. Closed May & June. FB <u>$300</u>

The north

GIRAFFES, LAIKIPIA

The north

There is one half of Kenya about which the other half knows nothing and seems to care even less.
Negley Farson, *Last Chance in Africa*

You rarely think of deserts in Kenya, but the north – more than half the country – is an arid zone, most of it cinder-dry for ten months of the year. The old "Northern Frontier District" remains one of the most exciting and adventurous parts of Africa: a vast tract of territory, crisscrossed by ancient migration routes, and still tramped by nomadic Samburu, Boran, Rendille, Gabbra, Turkana and Somali herders. Unfortunately, it also has a dangerous reputation, with livestock-rustling and tribal feuding widespread, while banditry, and the spillover from Somalia's civil conflict, make it too risky to visit northeastern Kenya – the whole area east of the Isiolo–Marsabit–Moyale road. By contrast, the vast territories to the north and west of Mount Kenya, including Lake Turkana and the beautiful Laikipia region, are safe – if still adventurous – areas to visit.

7

The most obvious attraction in northern Kenya is the **Laikipia plateau**, a region of hilly savanna to the northwest of Mount Kenya. Second in wildlife density only to the Maasai Mara, Laikipia boasts more endangered species than anywhere else in the country (including Kenya's biggest population of black rhinos) alongside some very successful examples of mixed ranching and conservation, and some very upmarket boutique lodges and camps.

While Laikipia is increasingly popular for high-end fly-in safaris, the classic travel target in the far north is the wonderful jade splash of **Lake Turkana**. The lake's islands, prehistoric sites and, over the past decade or so, the Lake Turkana Festival, are major attractions to add to the strong appeal of the adventurous journey to the lakeshore.

Although **Moyale** is little more than Kenya's border town with Ethiopia, the remote road north to the frontier runs past fascinating **Marsabit National Park**, with its misty, highland forests rising above the desert. Looking east, not many people take the long road to **Garissa** or use this route to reach the coast, but as long as the Tana River route remains relatively safe, it's a recommended alternative to joining the heavy traffic on the Mombasa highway.

In terms of **climate**, although the landscape is parched for most of the year, when the **rains** do come (usually around May) they can have a dramatic effect, bringing torrents of water along the ravines and *luggas* (watercourses) and tearing away bridges and concrete fords with a violence that has to be seen to be believed. Flood waters often sweep over the plains to leave an ooze of mud and, within twenty-four hours, new

LAKE TURKANA FESTIVAL

Highlights

❶ Track wild dogs Extremely rare and elusive wild dogs are making a comeback in Kenya and can be seen quite frequently in the north, especially on some of the Laikipia ranches, where they are carefully monitored. **See box, p.505**

❷ Laikipia eco-lodges Visiting one of the game sanctuaries in this high plains region is one of the best ways to see some of Kenya's surviving black rhinos and other rare wildlife. **See p.510**

❸ Walk with baboons Pay a visit to a habituated baboon troop accompanied by an informative primate researcher. **See p.513**

❹ Central Island National Park Totally untouched volcanic sanctuary in the middle of

Lake Turkana, where Nile crocodiles breed. A memorable boat trip from the lake's western shore. **See p.522**

❺ Maralal The most scruffily picturesque town in Kenya, with a wild atmosphere and an annual camel-racing tournament in August. **See p. 524**

❻ Lake Turkana Festival On the eastern shore of shimmering Lake Turkana, this annual three-day tribal jamboree offers remarkable cross-cultural encounters. **See box, p.533**

❼ Marsabit This remote highland oasis in the northern deserts has a fascinating cultural mix. It's close to Marsabit National Park with its superb crater lakes, elephants and birdlife. **See p.544**

HIGHLIGHTS ARE MARKED ON THE MAP ON P.504

shoots. In these conditions, you can easily get stranded. However, if your plans are flexible, being up north during the rains is an exciting time to explore.

GETTING AROUND   THE NORTH

BY PLANE

With its high-end lodges attracting luxury safari travellers, most parts of Laikipia are commonly accessed by scheduled light aircraft services to the airfields at Nanyuki, Lewa Downs and Loisaba. By the time you read this, Isiolo airstrip should have being upgraded into an international airport – the first in northern Kenya – opening up flight options to the region. If you're heading to Turkana, the flight options are to Lodwar on the western lakeshore and to Lokichokio, near the South Sudanese border, although charter trips to other parts of the Turkana region are available at a price.

BY CAR

Routes If you're travelling by land any further north than Laikipia, the layout of the routes radiating north from the Central Highlands means you'll need to make a decision about which of them to use, since there are few east–west routes linking the north–south arteries. The road network limits you to four main possibilities: the direct route from Kitale to the west shore of Lake Turkana at Kalokol; the

other direct route from Maralal to the east shore at Loiyangalani; the route that passes close to the Mathews Range north of Samburu-land and joins the route to Loiyangalani; and the route via Marsabit and North Horr that also reaches Loiyangalani – eventually.

Practicalities If you're driving in the north, good mechanical know-how and having enough water and fuel should be your priorities, since you'll need to be almost self-sufficient, and always make sure you have two spare tyres. It's best to take a sturdy 4WD, and while you might manage in a Suzuki or something similar in the dry season, in the rains it's absolutely essential to have a very rugged vehicle such as a Land Rover or a Land Cruiser.

BY PUBLIC TRANSPORT

By bus or matatu Bus and matatu services are patchy at best, and while informal rides with trucks can work out they are exhausting and very unpredictable. Where information is available it's included in the "Arrival and departure" sections throughout this chapter.

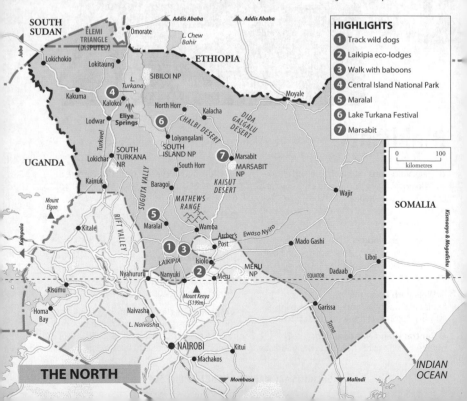

HIGHLIGHTS
1 Track wild dogs
2 Laikipia eco-lodges
3 Walk with baboons
4 Central Island National Park
5 Maralal
6 Lake Turkana Festival
7 Marsabit

> ## WILDLIFE IN LAIKIPIA
>
> Laikipia is increasingly recognized as one of the jewels in Kenya's safari crown. The district contains a wealth of endangered species, including **black rhinos**, whose world population is between three thousand and four thousand, a few hundred of them in Kenya. Of those, half are in Laikipia. As browsers rather than grazers, black rhinos don't interfere with cattle pasture, and do well in the same environment so long as the bush isn't cleared. Apart from the rhinos, more than two thousand **elephants** still undertake a seasonal migration during the long rains from Laikipia northwards into the Samburu rangelands. The district also supports an estimated 80 percent of the world's remaining population of **Grevy's zebra**, a species fast disappearing in its other habitats in Ethiopia. There are also several elusive packs of **African wild dogs**.
>
> In Laikipia, wildlife tends to be more closely managed than in the national parks. Some rhinos, for example, are individually monitored by assigned rangers, while African wild dog packs are fitted with VHF (very high frequency) collars and their movements tracked using GPS. The solutions may seem unnatural, but they're working. For further information, check out the excellent website of the **Laikipia Wildlife Forum** (ⓦ laikipia.org), the body that coordinates the region's various interest groups and visitor facilities. There are a number of informative downloads available on the site, including the *Wildlife Conservation Strategy for Laikipia County 2012–2030*.

7

Laikipia

ⓦ laikipiatourism.com

Northwest of Mount Kenya, **Laikipia District** is a vast plateau of more than 9000 square kilometres encompassing much of the transitional land between the well-watered Central Highlands to the south and the semi-desert grazing steppe of the Samburu in the north. On the face of it, the region is not an obvious destination and the few roads that cross it are mostly poor and sometimes impassable in the rains. In addition, it straddles the increasingly blurred divisions between Samburu and Kalenjin pastoralists and Kikuyu agriculturalists, which has led periodically to **ethnic violence**. The area also remains the focus of a century-old land dispute between the Laikipiak Maasai and white ranchers.

At the same time, while competition with wildlife has increased, there is now widespread cooperation between local people and ranchers, resulting in some of Kenya's most encouraging conservation success stories and making Laikipia one of the best regions in Kenya to see **wildlife**. There are no national parks or reserves here – all the conservation initiatives are undertaken privately or in the voluntary sector – and yet community land is managed in ways that respect traditional lifestyles while meeting the needs of wildlife and producing revenues from tourism. As tourist numbers grow, indigenously owned group ranches are also beginning to work independently to achieve the same ends.

The market town of **Nanyuki** (see p.180) is the main supply hub for Laikipia's remote residents offering everything from groceries and fuel to pharmacies and a few good restaurants. The fringes of southern Laikipia are covered in Chapter 2 (see p.196).

Ol Pejeta Conservancy

Daily 7am–7pm • $95 for 24hr (conservancy fee included in most stays; see exceptions under "Accommodation") • ⓦ olpejetaconservancy
.org • 365 square kilometres

For immersion in the Laikipia ecosystem, **Ol Pejeta Conservancy**, just a few kilometres west of Nanyuki (see p.180), is a good place to start. Formerly a cattle ranch belonging to the Lonrho corporation, it is now owned by Fauna & Flora International (ⓦ fauna-flora .org) and run as a not-for-profit business. Consisting mostly of rolling grasslands and acacia thicket, with boreholes providing ample water, it contains some of Laikipia's greatest concentrations of mammals, including all the big plains game.

The ranch combines wildlife management with running the world's largest herd of Boran cattle – the breed considered to be the best beef producer for Africa. The cattle are kept in mobile *bomas* at night to protect them from predators, and the cattle-wildlife combination is judged to be a model of integrated ranching and conservation: cattle-grazing stimulates new pasture for the wildlife, and the surrounding communities benefit from slaughtering facilities and stock improvement for their own herds.

The Eastern sector of Ol Pejeta is the oldest part of the reserve, formerly the Sweetwaters Rhino Sanctuary (now seamlessly incorporated into the rest of Ol Pejeta), one inhabitant of which, a black rhino bull called **Morani**, was tame enough to be fed by visitors and became an icon for Ol Pejeta's conservation work. Morani died in 2008, and a successor, a blind black rhino called **Baraka** has been introduced to close encounters with tourists in Morani's special square-kilometre paddock. Apart from Baraka, it's hard to see **black rhinos**, of which there are around a hundred

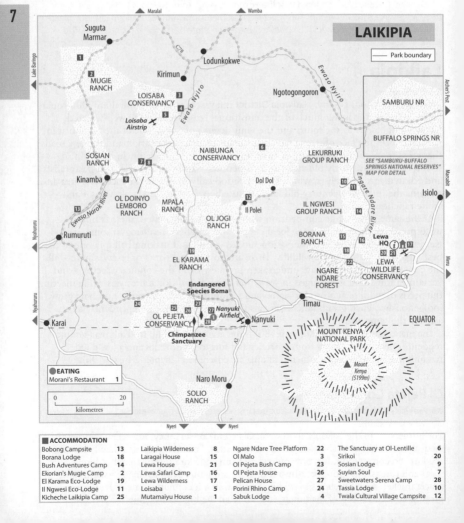

roaming through Ol Pejeta, as they stay well away from the tracks, seeking out good browsing in the thickets.

You will much more easily spot the conservancy's less timid and even larger **southern white rhinos** as they tank their way through the bush in search of pasture. The last **northern white rhinos** of the subspecies were moved to Ol Pejeta from a zoo in the Czech Republic in 2009 after the remaining wild individuals were poached to extinction in northern DRC. They are closely protected in a 30-square-kilometre sanctuary, and although the hope was to breed them with the southern white rhinos and then select for northern white traits and steadily preserve the characteristics of the subspecies, so far attempts have been unsuccessful.

Chimpanzee Sanctuary

Daily 9.30am–4.30pm • Free (with conservancy fee)

Ol Pejeta also contains a **chimpanzee sanctuary**, with chimps from the Jane Goodall Institute in Burundi, and confiscated pets and bushmeat-trade orphans from other parts of Africa. The one-square-kilometre haven, unique in Kenya – a country that has had no wild chimps in historical times – protects 39 of the great apes in two troops: a younger troop on the west side of the Ewaso Nyiro River, and an older troop, that visitors can view, on the east side. This is strictly an animal refuge, supported by a number of charities and individuals at a cost of more than $4000 a year per chimp. The chimps, all of which have suffered varying degrees of psychological trauma, are given contraceptive medication to prevent them from breeding, and fed on a daily supply of fruit and vegetables supplied by the rangers. As the crazier of the chimps smash sticks against the electric fence to the amusement of visitors, it all feels sadly institutionalized, despite the relative space and freedom, and may leave you wondering what connection, if any, it has with the long-term conservation of this highly endangered species.

Endangered Species Boma

Daily 9am–4pm • $40 per person; a maximum of twelve people can visit per day (six in the morning, six in the afternoon)

Ol Pejeta's **Endangered Species Boma** is home to the world's last remaining northern white rhinos, along with a number of other endangered animals including the Grevy's zebra, Jackson's hartebeest and much larger numbers of the southern white rhino. There are no predators in this section of the conservancy, where efforts are focused solely on saving these creatures from extinction.

ARRIVAL AND DEPARTURE	**OL PEJETA CONSERVANCY**

By air There are flights to Nanyuki airport (see p.181) on SafariLink or Airkenya, with onward transfers organized by Ol Pejeta. Private shuttles are also available with Tropic Air, landing right in the conservancy.

By road Approaching by road, turn left just south of the "Equator" signs on the way into Nanyuki (west; signposted "Ol Pejeta House 20km, Sweetwaters 15km") for the 13km dirt track to Rongai Gate, the main park gate.

ACCOMMODATION

Unless otherwise specified, all accommodation rates include Ol Pejeta's $95 nightly conservancy fee.

Camping sites ☎ 0752 325379 or ☎ 0707 187141, ⓦ olpejetaconservancy.org/plan-your-visit. Ol Pejeta offers five camping sites available on an exclusive, pre-booked basis only: *Hippo Hide* and *Ewaso* on the banks of the Ewaso Nyiro River; *Murera Donga* in an area of thick vegetation; and *Olerai* and *Ngobit* on the banks of the Ngobit River. When you add up the costs, this isn't budget camping, but toilets, firewood and water are provided. Conservancy fee extra. Daily fee whole site <u>Ksh7000</u>, camping <u>Ksh1000</u>

★ **Kicheche Laikipia Camp** ☎ 020 2493569, ⓦ kicheche .com; map p.506. Set in a remote stretch of bush, on a gentle slope above a broad, seasonal waterhole, this is the first *Kicheche* camp outside the Mara, offering six very comfortable spacious tents, plus a family tent, with stylish extra touches – plants, rugs, wooden bathroom furniture, excellent food and wine – and warm, enthusiastic and experienced hosts. Lion-tracking drives available, submitting data to predator researchers. Closed April & May. FB <u>$1400</u>

7

Ol Pejeta Bush Camp ☎0721 242361, ⓦinsiders africa.com; map p.506. Five comfortable tents on the banks of the Ewaso Nyiro, with solar lighting, local community guides and lots of game walks. Salt scattered on the opposite bank often brings rhinos at night. Excellent for photographers. Wi-fi. Closed May & Nov. AI **$920**, package **$1020**

Ol Pejeta House ☎0736 515151 or ☎0734 699861, ⓦserenahotels.com; map p.506. Bursting with design novelties, original art and flawed magnificence, this is arms tycoon Adnan Khashoggi's former holiday retreat, comprising the flamboyant and monster-bedded "Mr Khashoggi's Room" and "Mrs Khashoggi's Room", plus two upper guest rooms (1 double, 1 twin), and a cottage with two large suites. Giraffes stalk the gardens and there are two pools. Wi-fi. Conservancy fee extra. FB **$482**

Pelican House ☎0707 187141 or ☎020 2033244, ⓦolpejetaconservancy.org/plan-your-visit/escapes; map p.506. A beautifully renovated traditional highlands thatched farm cottage with views of a nearby dam, sleeping eight people in three double rooms (or up to twelve using four extra single beds). Amenities include a garden and veranda, generator, kitchen (fridge-freezer, gas cooker), all bedding and towels, plus the services of a housekeeper/cook and *askari*. Wi-fi. Conservancy fee extra. Whole house **Ksh35,000**

★**Porini Rhino Camp** ☎020 7123129 or ☎0722 509200, ⓦporini.com; map p.506. A simple and unfussy low-impact bush camp, consisting of seven very spacious tents erected along a *lugga*. Everything here is run on entirely sustainable principles, with safari showers, solar power throughout and all non-biodegradable waste returned to Nairobi. Excellent staff and guides. Closed mid-April to end of May. Eco-Tourism Kenya Silver Award. Package including flights from Nairobi, based on obligatory minimum two nights, **$1220** per night

Sweetwaters Serena Camp ☎0734 699851 or ☎0734 699852, ⓦserenahotels.com; map p.506. The most affordable camp in Ol Pejeta, with 112 beds, a small pool and decent and varied food on a flat but very wheelchair-accessible site. All the tents (some older and simpler, some newer, more spacious and luxurious) face the electric-fence-protected waterhole. Most tents face Mt Kenya (be up by 6.45am for photos), but with its hotel-like public areas and night lights shining from Nanyuki's flower farms, this is not the place if you want to be deep in the bush. Wi-fi. Conservancy fee extra. FB **$382**

EATING

Morani's Restaurant Morani Information Centre enclosure ☎0706 160114, ⓦbit.ly/MoranisRestaurant. Ol Pejeta's first and only restaurant outside the camps and lodges. Grab a snack or drink (shakes and smoothies Ksh350, beers Ksh280, wine Ksh480) or choose from all-day breakfasts, burgers, salads and daily specials from around Ksh850. There are also public toilets and a picnic area. Daily 8am–5pm.

Eastern Laikipia

In the far southeast of Laikipia lies the former cattle ranch of **Lewa Downs**, one of the earliest ranches to convert to wildlife conservation and now largely incorporated into the **Lewa Wildlife Conservancy**. A little to the north of Lewa – and in much wilder country – are the locally owned group ranches of **Il Ngwesi** and **Lekurruki**, while bordering Lewa to the west is an exemplary game-and-cattle ranch, **Borana**.

Lewa Wildlife Conservancy

Entrance via the Matunda gate on the west side of the Timau–Isiolo road, 4km from the Meru junction, from where it's 8km along an earth road to the Wildlife Conservancy headquarters; entry by 4WD only • $105 • ⓦlewa.org • 250 square kilometres

Lewa Wildlife Conservancy is conservation as a business. As well as the high daily fees, the revenue from the café and gift shop (closed Sun) and expensive accommodation all help to support the **Northern Rangelands Trust**, partnering Lewa with local communities. In 2013, Lewa gained UNESCO World Heritage status as part of the Mount Kenya World Heritage Site.

Lewa incorporates the former Ngare Sergoi Rhino Sanctuary, set up by the owners in 1983, and the entire area is now home to thriving communities of black and white rhinos. This grassland environment, a mixture of open plains, scrub bush and woodland in the valleys, is one area in Kenya where sightings of black rhinos are the norm rather than a special event. In addition, there are some 350 Grevy's zebra, accounting for more than a tenth of the world's remaining wild population.

The well-organized annual **Lewa Marathon** (see p.71), each June, has been run on the conservancy since 1999 to raise funds for conservation and development in Kenya, and now attracts more than 1200 international entrants.

Il Ngwesi Group Ranch

Scheduled flights to Lewa Downs, then a 90min transfer; alternatively, the ranch is also reachable by driving via Nanyuki and Lewa HQ • No casual entry (conservancy fees included in overnight stays) • ☎ 020 2033122, ⓦ ilngwesi.com

While parts of Lewa are fenced, the group ranches northwest of Lewa Downs are traditional, unfenced community land, incorporating fixed and transient communities, grazing herds and substantial wildlife. In both areas, you'll get the most out of the experience if you get out into the bush **on foot**, with armed guides.

Foremost among these areas is the six-thousand-strong Laikipiak Maasai community of **Il Ngwesi Group Ranch**, a 145-square-kilometre slab of wilderness, adjoining Lewa to the south, bounded by the Ngare Ndare and Tinga rivers to the east and north, and by the dramatic hills of the **Mukogodo Forest** to the west. Options included in most stays include night drives, bush walks, riverside breakfasts, hikes in the Mukogodo Forest and visits to Il Ngwesi's rhino sanctuary.

Lekurruki Group Ranch

Scheduled flights to Lewa Downs, then a 2hr 30min transfer; alternatively, the ranch is also reachable by driving via Lewa HQ • $60 • ☎ 0724 107998, ⓦ nrt-kenya.org/lekurruki • 240 square kilometres

Like Il Ngwesi, the **Lekurruki Group Ranch** is superb wildlife territory, but even wilder and hillier. Adjoining Il Ngwesi's north side, the ranch assures a migration corridor between the Samburu and Buffalo Springs reserves to the north and the Il Ngwesi and Lewa conservancies to the south, although animals can be hard to spot. The Tusk Trust has trained two-dozen rangers to patrol the no-grazing areas of the ranch where the wildlife has pre-eminence – there's no mixed herding and wildlife conservation model here. The ranch's *Tassia Lodge* is a good two hours' drive from Lewa HQ, although it's better to allow three.

Borana Ranch

Drive through Timau towards Meru and turn left after 500m; Borana Lodge (see p.512) is 20km further, via the small centre of Ethi • $105 • ☎ 020 2115453, ⓦ borana.co.ke • 142 square kilometres

The **Borana Ranch** is a settler farm that has evolved into a model of twenty-first-century holistic land management. Like Ol Pejeta, Borana has successfully integrated farming with conservation by allowing intensive short-term livestock grazing of managed areas, followed by long periods of recovery and game grazing. The ranch mixes beef farming from a two-thousand-strong herd of Boran cattle with organic vegetable production. This combination of rare species conservation and high-end tourism is available to a maximum of 54 visitors at any one time.

Borana works closely with Lewa Conservancy, and in 2014, the fence-line between the two areas was taken down to enable the Lewa rhinos to wander even more freely. Borana currently has around three hundred **elephants** (twelve matriarchs with collars so that tabs can be kept on where they are) and four prides of **lions** (again, with a radio-collared lioness in each pride). They also monitor **wild dogs**, **hyenas** and **cheetahs** and have stable populations of all three. Borana is also home to a small population of **black rhinos**, which were introduced in 2013.

For visitors, apart from the chance to participate in game and wildlife management, the big activity at Borana is **riding**, allowing you to get very close to wildlife that would naturally shy away from vehicles or visitors on foot. Most of the thoroughbreds here are not really for beginners but perfect for experienced equestrians – although, on the eastern side of the ranch, they have a stable of children's and novice mounts too. As well as **walking**, another hugely enjoyable option here is **mountain biking**. Most activities are included in the accommodation packages.

Ngare Ndare Forest

Drive through Timau towards Meru and turn left after 500m; Ngare Ndare Forest gate is 12km further on, via the small centre of Ethi • ⓣ 0722 886456, ⓦ website.ngarendare.org

Wedged between the foothills of Mount Kenya and Lewa Wildlife Conservancy, **Ngare Ndare Forest** is a fine stretch of indigenous forest, with a limited number of trails and a campsite. The forest has been recognized for its outstanding beauty and in 2013 was incorporated into the Mount Kenya World Heritage Site. The tree-level **canopy walkway** looks precarious, but it's proving very popular with local urbanites, especially from Nanyuki, as a way of reconnecting with nature without exposing themselves to mud, thorns or the possibility of meeting large animals at ground level. Rangers ensure the safety of visitors.

ARRIVAL AND DEPARTURE   EASTERN LAIKIPIA

Most people fly up to the Lewa area, either on a scheduled service to Lewa HQ's Lewa Downs airfield (at least daily from Nairobi, 1hr 15min; sometimes also from Maasai Mara, 1hr 45min), or by charter to the airstrips at *Il Ngwesi* or *Tassia Lodge*. If you drive up, Lewa HQ is about four hours from Nairobi. If you're driving beyond Lewa, ensure you leave two hours to get from Lewa HQ to *Il Ngwesi*, and three hours to reach *Tassia Lodge*. It can be quicker to drive via Borana Ranch (see p.509), but check with them first. The tracks are rough in parts and hard to follow: a smart phone, GPS unit or, better still, a guide, is very useful.

ACCOMMODATION

Unless otherwise specified, all accommodation rates include the relevant daily conservancy fees.

LEWA WILDLIFE CONSERVANCY

Lewa House 8km north of Lewa HQ ⓣ 0710 781303, ⓦ lewahouse.com (Nairobi reservations ⓣ 020 6000457, ⓦ bush-and-beyond.com); map p.506. Rustic but elegant, this is Lewa's top residence, with three large cottages (with one double and one twin room) and four single-room cottages. Game-watching includes day and night drives, and game walks. There are also beautiful gardens, a pool overlooking the waterhole and solar power. Mobile network available. Closed April & Nov. Package **$1800**

Lewa Safari Camp On the west side of the conservancy ⓣ 0720 499425, ⓦ lewasafaricamp.com Nairobi reservations ⓣ 0730 127000, ⓦ chelipeacock.com); map p.506. This is the most affordable, relatively speaking, of the Lewa options: eleven well-spaced, homely and very comfortably furnished double and twin tents, some with fine views, plus two family tents for four people. The main lodge building is thatched cedar, with a lounge overlooking a floodlit waterhole where animals come to drink. Service is usually excellent and there's a pool. Eco-Tourism Kenya Gold Award. Slow and patchy wi-fi. Package **$1842**, family tent **$2240**

Lewa Wilderness Eastern side of Lewa ⓣ 0723 273668, ⓦ lewawilderness.com (Nairobi reservations ⓣ 020 6000457, ⓦ bush-and-beyond.com); map p.506. The former home of the Craig family, who came to Lewa in the 1920s, with a pre-war English-country-house atmosphere, congenial hosts and staff, superior cooking (often using ingredients from the organic garden), infinity pool and accommodation in ten rooms. Riding is available at the large

stables. Wi-fi in the main house. Closed April, May & Nov. Package **$1800**

★**Sirikoi** Centre of Lewa, by Sirikoi Swamp, 5km west of Lewa HQ ⓣ 0727 232445, ⓦ sirikoi .com; map p.506. The most upmarket of the Lewa properties, this superb game camp has four huge luxury tents on wooden platforms, plus a cottage sleeping four and a house sleeping six (both for exclusive use), all nestled among acacias near a permanent swamp bursting with wildlife day and night. Most meals are sourced from the organic garden, which guests are encouraged to visit. Day and night game drives, game walks and bush meals are all included. No under-5s in tents. Wi-fi. Package **$1930**

IL NGWESI GROUP RANCH

Bush Adventures Camp ⓣ 0724 301095, ⓦ bush-adventures.com; map p.506. Far from the lavish tented camps of the Mara, *Bush Adventures* offers an experience that is much more integrated into the local environment, and particularly the local Laikipiak Maasai culture. You stay here to experience life in the bush and learn the ways of a warrior, with a full schedule of real training. The camp of comfortable but modest tents, with solar-powered hot water, is set high on the river bank. No sockets for charging and limited mobile network. No under-5s. Three-night minimum stay. Package **$1130**

★**Il Ngwesi Eco-Lodge** Local reservations Laipha House, Nanyuki ⓣ 020 2033122, ⓦ ilngwesi.com; map p.506. A much lauded eco-lodge, owned and managed by the local Maasai community, perched along

FROM TOP BABY BABOON; BREAKFAST AT *SABUK LODGE* (P.515) >

a ridge facing a game-rich valley. Uniquely, *all* the proceeds go to the local community. The six spacious, raised, open-fronted *bandas* incorporate twisting branches and wonderful views, while *bandas* #1 and #5 have star-beds which can be pulled out onto their decks. There's a small infinity pool. Guaranteed wildlife, including elephants, seen daily at the waterhole. Eco-Tourism Kenya Silver Award. Package $770

LEKURRUKI GROUP RANCH

★**Tassia Lodge** Lekurruki Group Ranch ☎0725 972923 or ☎0727 049489, ⓦtassiasafaris.com; map p.506. This beautifully sited lodge overlooks a scenic valley where you have a good chance of spotting elephants. There are just six rooms, emerging seemingly organically from the landscape, a naturally formed swimming pool nestled in the rocks and exceptionally good and varied food, including plenty of salads and vegetarian options. Activities include game walks; overnight, camel-assisted fly-camping; and paragliding with expert guidance (bring your own equipment). No TV, no network, no internet – the whole idea is to completely escape all that. Eco-Tourism Kenya Silver Award. Closed April & Nov. AI $960

BORANA RANCH

Borana Lodge Central Borana Ranch ☎0715 579999, ☎0728 608594 or ☎020 2115453, ⓦborana .co.ke; map p.506. A Responsible Tourism Awards winner, built in 1992 in a hilly area with dramatic views in every direction, *Borana* has eight immaculate,

well-spaced cottages of cedar, thatch and stone, with fireplaces (at 2000m, you'll often need a fire). The lodge overlooks a waterhole-dam where elephants sometimes swim, and close-up views from the hide are possible. The infinity pool is sited high, with awe-inspiring views. Wi-fi. Package $1490

★**Laragai House** Northern Borana, 8km north of Borana Lodge ☎0715 579999 or ☎020 2115453 ⓦborana.co.ke; map p.506. Perched in an extraordinary site on the edge of an escarpment looking north, this house of almost palatial proportions has a large, heated pool, a waterhole-dam 400m down the hillside and stunning views all around. There's a superb sound system in the lounge, and you get excellent meals and service. It's perfect for a luxury house party, which is just as well as you have to take the whole property (minimum six people, maximum 16). Wi-fi. Whole house package $4470

NGARE NDARE FOREST

Ngare Ndare Tree Platform Just south of Borana Ranch in the Ngare Ndare Forest ☎0722 886456; map p.506. The showcase forest campsite for a recently established elephant corridor, allowing elephants to migrate freely between the slopes of Mount Kenya and the plains of Laikipia. Built 7m up a *mugumu* tree, the platform can be used as a lounge and observation point while you camp on the ground, or alternatively free-standing tents can be erected on the platform itself for up to six people. Clean running water and toilets available at ground level. Support rangers and *askaris* are on hand if needed. Camping $30

Central Laikipia

A great chunk of land in central Laikipia, on the east side of the Ewaso Nyiro, is now managed as the **Naibunga Conservancy**, covering more than 170 square kilometres and comprising swathes of conservation land ceded by eight community-owned group ranches in the area: **Il Motiok, Kijabe, Koija, Kuri-Kuri, Morupusi, Nkiloriti, Tiemamut** and **Il Polei**. There is, as yet, a limited range of places to stay, though several of the group ranches are encouraging wild camping with guides (for more on camping see ⓦlaikipiatourism.com/camp-sites).

Privately owned ranches northwest of Nanyuki include El Karama, Ol Jogi and Mpala. **El Karama**, a settler ranch since the early 1960s, covers nearly sixty square kilometres and as well as being a working ranch with a herd of unusual Sahiwal cattle also provides a home for Grevy's zebra, plenty of elephants, reticulated giraffe, leopards, at least one pride of lions and – occasionally – wild dogs, among many other species.

Mpala Ranch and Conservancy, owned by the American Mpala Wildlife Foundation, ranges across two hundred square kilometres and incorporates a state-of-the-art wildlife and environmental research centre. However, there is no accommodation on the ranch for tourist visitors.

Ol Jogi is a 270-square-kilometre ranch owned by the art-dealing and horse-racing Wildenstein family, where KWS staff and US government vets are engaged in a long-term project to extract **gerenuk** semen for captive breeding.

Il Polei Group Ranch: Walking with Baboons

Walks (2hr) and cost $20 per person in a group of up to four • Call Jonathan Rana on ☎ 0724 943948, ⓦ baboonsrus.com

An interesting community activity at Twala Cultural Village, near Il Polei, is **Walking with Baboons**, a chance for visitors to overturn some of the popular myths and prejudices that our species holds for this less cultured, but no less social, primate. In the early morning or at dusk you go out with a guide trained by the Uaso Ngiro Baboon Project to observe a habituated troop at close quarters on their rocky sleeping ledges. You'll learn about the importance of avoiding eye contact and the subtlety of baboon family and social life. It's a fascinating and highly recommended experience, and the money goes to support local community projects.

ARRIVAL AND DEPARTURE   CENTRAL LAIKIPIA

The main central Laikipia road goes northwest from Nanyuki, passing the turning (on the left after 9km) to Rumuruti and Nyahururu, then continues, still paved, via the small centres of **Jua Kali** and **Naibor** and turns into dirt road (25km), where the track to **Il Polei** and **Dol Dol** heads off to the right. Having passed the turnings for El Karama (left, 33km, at the "El K" stone, then a further 9km to reach the headquarters and lodge) and Ol Jogi Ranch (right, 39km), the road crosses the big metal bridge over the Ewaso Nyiro (47km), immediately passing the turning for Mpala Ranch and then, after 77km, reaching Sosian Ranch (see p.514).

ACCOMMODATION

Unless otherwise specified, all accommodation rates include the relevant daily conservancy fees.

★**El Karama Eco-Lodge** 42km northwest of Nanyuki ☎ 0702 996902 (send an SMS first), ⓦ laikipiasafaris .com; map p.506. An exceptionally nice and affordable set-up on the banks of the Ewaso Nyiro River, with four comfy s/c *bandas* and two cottages. You can camp, self-cater or be pampered on a full-board basis (drinks extra). Excellent day and night game drives and game walks with experienced, armed guide-ranger are included in the price, and there are delicious, hearty meals, using ranch produce. Limited mobile network. The whole lodge is exclusively solar-powered. Camping (when available): whole campsite for up to five campers. Conservancy fee ($60 per person) extra. **Ksh10,000**, package **$640**
★**Laikipia Wilderness** Ol Doinyo Lemboro Ranch, 50km north of Nanyuki, past Mpala Ranch ☎ 0727 804926, ⓦ laikipia-wilderness.com; map p.506. Opened in 2012, this tented camp is run by a couple with a great deal of experience. The east-facing tents are perched high above the Ewaso Narok River, and the area teems with wildlife, including elephants, leopards and wild dogs.

Activities include game walks, day and night game drives, river tubing, rock scrambling and fishing. Package **$1200**
The Sanctuary at Ol-Lentille Ol-Lentille Conservancy, Kijabe Group Ranch ☎ 020 2047491, ⓦ ol-lentille.com; map p.506. Spectacular all round, and truly remote, this Maasai-owned lodge (with strong local community links) is Laikipia's most expensive address: four houses, each sleeping two to six and with its own staff, guide and 4WD. Most activities, including riding, quad bikes and game drives (relatively limited wildlife but occasional wild dogs), are included, but simply relaxing and soaking up the peaceful environment – there's a good pool and spa – is a large part of the appeal. Wi-fi. Package **$1990**
Twala Cultural Village Campsite Near Il Polei town, 43km from Nanyuki along the Dol Dol road (no phone); map p.506. Simple if rather expensive campsite with water, firewood, showers and toilets. This is the place to hook up for the "Walking with Baboons" experience (see above). Walking with the Maasai and their cattle and walking with plants are also possible ($10 each walk). Camping **$35**

Northwestern Laikipia

The ranches to the **west of the Ewaso Nyiro** are the most remote of the Laikipia range lands and include large tracts of country that are still not open to the public or easily visited, including some very big private and corporate landholdings such as author Kuki Gallman's **Ol Ari Nyiro Laikipia Wildlife Conservancy** (ⓦ gallmannkenya.org).

Loisaba Community Trust

120km from Nanyuki, 110km from Nyahururu • $90 • ⓦ loisaba.com • 250 square kilometres

The **Loisaba** is a private ranch-cum-game sanctuary with a 2500-strong herd of Boran cattle, stretching from the bush-covered slopes and valleys near the river to high, flat grasslands in the west, bordering Mugie Ranch. There's an array of activities available, arranged through the *Loisaba* (see opposite), including camel rides, mountain biking, balloon trips, helicopter flights, horse-riding, lion-tracking, fishing and river-rafting (in season).

Mugie Ranch and Sanctuary

Based around the junction of the Rumuruti–Maralal road with the road to Lake Baringo • $60 • Minimum 24hr pre-booking required • ☎ 0722 903179, ⓦ mugie.org

Easily accessed direct from the Rumuruti–Maralal road, **Mugie Ranch** covers 186 square kilometres, almost half of which has been set aside as a wildlife sanctuary (formerly the Mugie Rhino Sanctuary). Though the rhinos were relocated in 2012, the sanctuary is still brimming with creatures big and small: expect to be stopped more than once by a passing herd of elephants or shaken by the roar of a lion just a few feet away. Encounters with a number of rare species, including Grevy's zebra and Jackson's hartebeest, are also common.

Ol Malo Wildlife Conservancy

Scheduled flights to Loisaba (or Nanyuki plus charter flight to Ol Malo airstrip), or a 3hr-plus drive from Nanyuki • $90 • ⓦ olmalo.org • 20 square kilometres

At the northernmost ranch in northwestern Laikipia, the privately owned **Ol Malo**, elephants and leopards are seen right below the lodge almost every day. Formerly a cattle ranch, and by all accounts not a very well-managed one, it is now a thriving wildlife sanctuary with a wide range of species.

Sosian Ranch

28km north of Rumuruti (at Kinamba village, bear right under the open boom gate; after 5.5km you reach a sign on a stone; the ranch HQ and *Sosian Lodge* are 1.5km further on) • $105 • ⓦ sosian.com • 100 square kilometres

The **Sosian Ranch** has superb wildlife, with all the large mammals you would expect, bar rhinos, including a resident, breeding pack of wild dogs. The ranch does active work in predator research, collaborating with neighbouring Mpala Ranch, and guests at the lodge can easily go out tracking the dogs, which can be highly rewarding, especially on foot. Sightings aren't guaranteed, but they're frequent enough to make them a likely possibility.

ARRIVAL AND DEPARTURE   NORTHWESTERN LAIKIPIA

By plane There are several airstrips for charter flights, but most visitors use the SafariLink scheduled service to Loisaba airstrip (check if the service is running in their low season, April 1–June 15 & Nov 1–Dec 15). Destinations include Maasai Mara (1 daily; 1hr 45min) and Nairobi (1 daily; 1hr).

By road Some of the ranches are tough to reach by road, especially those down towards the Ewaso Nyiro River, such as Loisaba, Sabuk and Ol Malo. Route coverage is given from Nyahururu via Rumuruti to Maralal (see p.524), from where these ranches and lodges are most easily accessed if you're driving.

ACCOMMODATION

If you're on any kind of budget, *Bobong* at *Ol Maisor Ranch* is a good – in fact your only – choice. Unless otherwise specified, all accommodation rates include the relevant daily conservancy fees.

Bobong Campsite Ol Maisor Ranch, 20km north of Rumuruti, on a bluff just west of the road, 300m after the blue shipping container ☎ 0735 243075, ✉ olmaisor@africaonline.co.ke; map p.506. Deliberately low-key and child-friendly campsite, boasting fantastic views over the Laikipia plains, a small pool and a jungle gym. Activities range from bird walks along the Ewaso Narok River and Turkana cultural village visits to camel rides and longer camel safaris (Ksh3000/day or part-day), while animal orphans are always around and the daily life of the family farm is part of the appeal. As well as camping space there are also fully equipped and furnished self-catering s/c *bandas* (with one double bed and one single). Camping **Ksh500**, *bandas* **Ksh5000**

Ekorian's Mugie Camp Mugie Ranch, just off the Maralal road ☎ 0722 385727, ⓦ ekorian.com; map p.506. A fairly recent addition to the Mugie conservancy, this family-run camp has six spacious tents, plus one for families. Pruned gardens, terrific wildlife in the area and the sundowner pool deck all add to its appeal. Wi-fi in the lounge. Sometimes closed May and Nov – check before arrival. Package $1370

Loisaba Loisaba Community Trust ☏0705 202375, Ⓦ loisaba.com; map p.506. Sadly, a bush fire tore through the original multi-award-winning *Loisaba* in 2013, devastating the property. At the time of writing, work was under way to build a brand-new tented camp with ten rooms, four of them suites and two for families which was set to open in January 2016. Two star-bed sites still remain and make for an enchanting night's stay: *Loisaba Starbeds* above the Kiboko dam and *Koija Starbeds* on the east bank of the river. Wide range of activites available. Patchy wi-fi. Eco-Tourism Kenya Bronze Award. Conservancy fees ($90) extra. Package $900

Mutamaiyu House Mugie conservancy, 10km northwest of the Baringo junction ☏0722 903179, Ⓦ mugie.org; map.506. Expansive and gracious Swiss- and German-owned country house, decorated with tribal art, surrounded by African olives (*mutamaiyu*) and beautifully tended gardens, with a heated pool, in a relatively gentle, hilly landscape. As in most of the lodges in northwestern Laikipia, the wildlife is not just out in the bush, but encountered on the paths, in your outdoor shower or on the way to dinner: warriors always accompany guests when anything dangerous is nearby. Six cottages are also available. Wi-fi throughout. Conservancy fee ($60) extra. Package $930

Ol Malo ☏0721 630686, Ⓦ olmalo.com; map p.506. A Responsible Tourism Award-winning family-owned lodge commanding a vantage point high above the valley of the Ewaso Nyiro. Guest rooms, annexed off the main building, feature window glass (most Laikipia rooms are open-fronted) and are big on polished stone and wood. The more recent *Ol Malo House* (sleeps 12) is similar, but with a kitsch, animal theme in the coloured-cement decor. Wi-fi. Closed April, May & Nov. Package $1700

★**Sabuk Lodge** Sabuk Conservancy, west bank of the Ewaso Nyiro ☏0721 337988, Ⓦ sabuklodge.com; map p.506. Intimate and compellingly sited lodge, bursting with character, built on the edge of a remote gorge through which the Ewaso Nyiro permanently rushes and where elephants frequently cross. There are eight spacious cottages, including a double and a triple cottage with their own plunge pools, while camel-assisted walking safaris (from a few hours to several nights) can be included in your stay at no extra cost. Warmly and intelligently hosted by a highly experienced safari guide, it's great for children and serves superb food. Two-night minimum stay. Wi-fi. Package $1450

★**Sosian Lodge** Near Kinamba ☏0704 909357, Ⓦ sosian.com (reservations ☏0704 909355, Ⓦ offbeat safaris.com); map p.506. Built in 1920, abandoned in the 1990s and completely restored as a riding and ecotourism base in 2002, *Sosian* is peaceful, roomy and supremely relaxing, with well-designed furniture in the seven rooms, charming hosts, excellent guides (all silver-rated) and delicious meals (the chef, with 30 years' experience, relies greatly on the lodge's own garden produce). Patchy mobile network. Closed May & Nov. Conservancy fee $105 extra. Package $1190

Suyian Soul Suyian Ranch, north bank of the Ewaso Narok ☏0720 576 000 or ☏0719 407997 (send an SMS first), Ⓦ suyian.com; map p.506. Just half an hour's drive from the Loisaba airstrip, this simple eco-camp, near a spring and salt lick, on a century-old ranch of more than 170 square kilometres, is unusual in its commitment to the environment. It relies entirely on solar energy and is built exclusively with materials found on the ranch, where the family have reared livestock for nearly a century. Limited wi-fi. Package $880

Turkana

Straddling the Ethiopian border at its northern end, **Lake Turkana** stretches south for 250km, bisecting Kenya's rocky deserts like a turquoise sickle, hemmed in by sandy wastes and black-and-brown volcanic ranges. The water, a glassy, milky blue one minute, can become slate-grey and choppy or a glaring emerald green the next. Turkana's **climate** is extremely hot and dry for ten months of the year, and very humid during the rains. The lake is notorious for its strong easterly winds and the squalls whipped up are the cause of most accidental deaths on the lake, rather than hippos or crocodiles. The lake was discovered for the rest of the world only in 1888 by the Hungarian explorer **Count Samuel Teleki de Szék** and his Austrian co-expeditionary **Ludwig von Höhnel**. They named it Lake Rudolf after their patron, the Crown Prince of Austria. Later, it became eulogized as the "Jade Sea" in travel writer John Hillaby's book (see p.593) about his camel trek. The name "Turkana" only came into being during the wholesale Kenyanization of place names in the 1970s. By then, it had also been dubbed the "Cradle of Mankind", the site of revelatory fossil discoveries in the field of **human**

evolution. Apart from a couple of basic lodges and one or two windy campsites, the tourist infrastructure is nil, while only a single paved road reaches the region, stretching from Kitale to Lodwar (in dire condition) and on to the town of Lokichokio. And although vast reserves of oil continue to be discovered near Lokichokio, sadly this has yet to provide any sort of positive development for the region (Jessica Hatcher's *Exploiting Turkana: Robbing the cradle of mankind* is a useful account on this topic and is available for download from Amazon).

Turkana's **traditional cultures** are still very much a vibrant part of the scene, wherever you travel: the people you're most likely to encounter are **Turkana** (see box, p.520) on the western and southern shores, **Samburu** (see box, p.524) south of Loiyangalani, **Elmolo** (see box, p.537) to the north of Loiyangalani, and **Gabbra** (see p.547) further east. The Turkana and Samburu are pastoralists, who hold their cattle in great reverence; the Gabbra herd camels; while the Elmolo are traditionally property-less hunters and fishers. The best expression of the breadth of this cultural richness is the **Lake Turkana Cultural Festival** (see box, p.533), which has taken place on the eastern shores of the lake every year since 2008, and brings together fourteen different communities from the region for performances and to share cultural traditions.

ARRIVAL AND DEPARTURE   TURKANA

By plane Scheduled air services to Lodwar from Nairobi have increased in recent years (see p.51). Charter flights are also available from Nairobi to Loiyangalani, Lodwar and Kitale through Phoenix Aviation (wphoenixaviation.co.ke) at a considerable cost, as well as to Lokichokio with Fly-SAX (wfly-sax .com).

Overland To get to this remote desert lake overland you have three main options: sign up for one of the limited number of organized camping safaris; take the matatus and lorries that transport goods and people north from the urban hubs in the Kenya highlands; or drive yourself. Relatively few visitors drive, though Turkana is becoming more popular with 4WD fans, especially as the roads gradually improve. There are three road routes to Lake Turkana described below: one to the western shore starting in Kitale, and two to the eastern shore – from Maralal and from Marsabit (the latter very remote). There is no route connecting the east and west shores (the volcanic Suguta Valley forming a blazing hot barrier) and there are no ferries on the lake itself either – Lake Turkana's only shipping is government-owned or private.

Via Kitale and Lodwar The western approach, from Kitale to Lodwar, is the one used by most independent travellers without their own vehicles. For transport,

LAKE TURKANA

ETHIOPIA
Omorate & Addis Ababa

Lokitaung
Ileret
North Island
Koobi Fora **1**
SIBILOI NATIONAL PARK
2
Lake Turkana
KWS HQ
Ferguson's Gulf
Allia Bay **i** **3**
Kalokol
CENTRAL ISLAND NATIONAL PARK
4
Namoratunga
Moiti Hill
Gajos
Lodwar
5
Eliye Springs **6**
Turkwel River
Hurran Hurra
Komote
Elmolo Bay
SOUTH ISLAND NATIONAL PARK
Mount Kulal (2285m)
Layeni
Loiyangalani
OL DOINYO MARA
NYIRU RANGE
Tuum
Kurungu Teiyo Camp **7**
8 South Horr
SUGATA VALLEY
9
10
Ewaso Rongai
Baragoi
Maralal

Lokichokio & Sudan
Kitale
North Horr, Kalacha & Marsabit

N

0   50
kilometres

■ **ACCOMMODATION**
Alia Bay Guesthouse	3
Desert Rose Lodge	9
Eliye Springs Resort	6
Forest Department Camp Site	10
Koobi Fora Bandas	1
KWS Campsites	3
Kurungu Teiyo Camp	7
Lake Turkana Guest House	4
Lobolo Camp	5
Museum Bandas	2
Samburu Sports Camp & Safari	8

7

ECOLOGY AND WILDLIFE OF LAKE TURKANA

Lake Turkana is the biggest permanent desert lake in the world, a UNESCO World Heritage Site with a shoreline longer than the whole of Kenya's sea coast. Yet 10,000 years ago its surface was 150m higher than today. It spread south as far as the now desolate Suguta Valley and fed the headwaters of the Nile. Today it has been reduced to a mere sliver of its former expanse. A gigantic natural sump, with rivers flowing in but no outlets, it loses a staggering 3m of water through **evaporation** from its surface each year (nearly a centimetre every day). As a result, the lake water is quite alkaline – although you can just about drink it, and it's not hostile to all aquatic life.

Turkana's **water level** is subject to wild fluctuations. From the mid-1980s to 1997, the level receded steadily, leaving parts of the former shoreline more than 8km from the lake. But heavy El Niño rains in 1998 led to a 6m rise in the lake level in less than a year. Fish stocks recovered and former fishing communities rediscovered their vocation. Since then, however, the level has fallen again, the lakeshore receding by as much as 1km in some places. The massive Gilgel Gibe III dam under construction on Ethiopia's Omo River – Lake Turkana's biggest source – poses a huge threat to the lake and may lower the water surface by up to 10m with a rise in salinity that would threaten fish stocks and wildlife and the livelihoods of thousands of people. The Friends of Lake Turkana, who work on environmental and community issues in the Turkana region, have a highly recommended website (⊕ friendsoflaketurkana.org).

The prehistoric connection with the Nile accounts for the presence of enormous **Nile perch** (some weighing more than 100kg) and Africa's biggest population of **Nile crocodiles** – some 10,000 to 22,000 of them. Turkana is one of the few places where you can still see great stacks of crocs basking on sand banks. There is a profusion of **birdlife**, too, including European migrants seen most spectacularly on their way home between March and May. **Hippos**, widely hunted and starved out of many of their former lakeshore haunts through lack of grazing, manage to hang on in fairly large numbers, though you won't see many unless you go out of your way.

7

there's a choice of buses or lorries. Whichever way you do it, the road is diabolical, and although there are plans to re-pave it to accommodate traffic to the new oil fields and foster trade opportunities with South Sudan, no date has been set for work to begin. The best part of the journey is the beginning, covered in Chapter 4 (see p.295). The last ATM before you reach Lodwar is at Makutano (see p.295), where it is also a good idea to fill up with fuel, though you should be able to find that further north at Ortum.

Via Maralal and Loiyangalani The journey up to Samburu-land en route to Lake Turkana is a good deal shorter in distance than that to the west shore, but it's still at least a two-day drive from Nairobi, with an overnight stop in Maralal and – since it takes in excess of eight hours from there on to Loiyangalani – you might also consider spending a second night in South Horr as well. If driving,

you'll need a high-clearance 4WD, a couple of spare tyres and extra fuel. During the rainy season you could be held up for a day or more at several points waiting for swollen *luggas* to subside. Travelling north of Maralal without your own vehicle may require patience since there's little public transport and you may have to hitchhike for rides.

Via Marsabit and Loiyangalani It's also possible to travel independently from Isiolo to Loiyangalani via Marsabit and North Horr, but be prepared to wait a long time for lifts, first from Isiolo to Marsabit, and then on to North Horr. If driving yourself on this route, travelling with at least one other vehicle is recommended as you can expect to get stuck several times in the sand. Gametrackers use this route on their northbound Turkana Truck trip via the Chalbi Desert (see box, p.518).

The A1 road to Lodwar

From Kitale, the **A1 road to Lodwar** heads north over the **Cherangani Hills**. After climbing over the **Marich Pass** (see p.295 and map, p.252), you leave the hill country and drop onto the plain, passing from Pokot into Turkana territory when you cross the Turkwel River just before **Kainuk** – an occasional flashpoint for inter-communal violence that lies 130km north of Kitale and 170km south of Lodwar. The change of scenery here is dramatic, but it's hard to extract much of scenic interest from the thorny wilderness of the **Turkana Plains** beyond – although if you're travelling by bus or lorry the regular stops to pick up increasingly wild-looking passengers maintain gently heightening expectations as you head north.

Nasalot National Reserve

20km west of Kainuk off the A1 Kitale–Lodwar road (no public transport) • Daily 6am–6pm • $25

From Kainuk you can detour to the small **Nasalot National Reserve**, which bounds the northern slopes of the mountains and the southern fringes of the south Turkana plains. From the gate, 6km off the Lodwar road (signposted on the left, west), the winding paved route drops several hundred metres into the heat, with plunging precipices and spectacular views all round, to the **Turkwel Gorge** and **hydroelectric dam**.

As the reserve is mostly covered with thick bush, **spotting animals** isn't all that easy, and you'd be unusually fortunate to see any of the reserve's lions and leopards. The elephants here, though larger than their southern cousins, hide themselves pretty well, and your best chance of seeing them is on the paved road at dawn or dusk.

South Turkana National Reserve

20km north of Nasalot, then 10km east off the A1 Kitale–Lodwar road • $30 • ☎ 0724 954745

The **South Turkana National Reserve** lacks Nasalot's scenic grandeur, but is where the elephants migrate to between March and July. The lack of infrastructure (including much in the way of roads) makes it more challenging to explore, particularly since the reserve is over ten times the size of Nasalot. Wildlife includes giraffes, buffaloes and crocodiles, which can sometimes be seen napping on the banks of the Kerio River.

Lodwar

For most Kenyans, mention of **LODWAR** conjures up remote and outlandish images of the badlands, an aberrant place where anything could befall you. The Turkana District capital is, to put it mildly, a wild town, and somewhat unformed and incongruous in this searing wilderness. During the 1980s it became Kenya's desert boomtown, the lake's fishing, the possibility of oil discoveries and the new road from Kitale all encouraging inward migration. While **Turkana people** have always predominated, **Luo** and **Luhya** also arrived in search of opportunities. With the exhaustion of farming country in the south, Lodwar and the area around it became increasingly attractive to pioneers and cowboys of all sorts. The discovery of oil reserves in the region has led to a second influx of prospectors, with an increase in air services, although for now Lodwar remains little more than a dusty frontier town.

Despite the heat and the dust, some people find the rough, frontier atmosphere of Lodwar exhilarating, but there's not a lot to do. If you have the time and energy, you can **hike** up one of the hills behind the town (the guides from *Nawoitorong Guesthouse* are best; see p.520), from where the view stretches for many kilometres. For **handicrafts**, you'll find good woven baskets on sale at the *Nawoitorong Guesthouse*. You might also want to pick up a pair of **5000-mile shoes** – flip-flops (thongs) made from old truck tyres – which are comfortable, virtually unbreakable and can be purchased for around Ksh300 in the streets behind *Salama Hotel*.

ARRIVAL AND DEPARTURE
LODWAR

By plane By far the most comfortable way in and out of Lodwar is by air. Fly540 flies 1–2 times daily between Lodwar and Nairobi JKIA (2hr; Ksh15,350) via Kitale (40min; Ksh6740). Their office is on the main street next to the Eldoret Express office (☎0713 161297; daily 8am–5pm). From Nairobi Wilson (2hr), Safarilink also operates one flight per day Mon–Fri (7am; one-way $175) and Skyward Express operates daily (one-way Ksh12,500).

By bus From Kitale, a couple of buses leave for Lodwar in the morning (the first at around 9am); more leave between 2pm and 6pm, travelling in the evening to beat the heat. Buses generally take 10–12hr to shudder and jolt along the 285km of crumbling asphalt laid in the early 1980s, though the journey will be shortened dramatically once the road improves. From Lodwar, buses to Kitale gather in the main street around *Salama Hotel*, and always leave in the evening, around 5–7pm. The one daily bus to Nairobi, run by Daya Coaches, leaves at 3am from its office next to the *Salama Hotel*.

Destinations Kitale (3 daily; 10–12hr); Lokichokio (1 daily; 4hr); Nairobi (1 daily; 18hr).

By matatu Matatus for Kitale leave from the main stage in the centre of town, near the buses, but vehicles for Lokichokio (4hr) and Kalokol (1hr 30min) have their own stages on the east side of town opposite the Kobil filling station.

Destinations Kalokol (1hr 30min); Lokichokio (4hr).

Hitchhiking To hitchhike from Lodwar to Kitale, head in the morning to the roundabout at the eastern end of the main street, where you can flag down a lorry heading south. This is one of the best ways to travel if you don't want to make the journey at night. Local lads may also offer to help you find a vehicle for a small tip, but it's advisable to find out the going rate in advance if you think the driver will want paying (allow up to Ksh1200 to Kitale). Be aware, however, that Turkana bandits have been known to attack lorries along this road; some drivers choose to hire a guard – often just a local tribesman with a uniform and a gun – which seems to solve the problem. In any case, it's worth checking the security situation before you set out. Heading north from Kitale, there are always a few lorries bound for Lokichokio and the South Sudan border, and finding a vehicle is not too difficult. Make sure you take plenty of water for this trip, as delays and breakdowns are all too common and people are expected to fend for themselves.

DRINKING AND NIGHTLIFE
Beer Garden 1
Lodwar Lodge 2

EATING
Nawoitorong Guesthouse 3
New Gulf Hotel 2
Turkwel Lodge 1

ACCOMMODATION
Ceamo Prestige Lodge 1
Lodwar Lodge 3
Nawoitorong Guesthouse 4
Turkwel Lodge 2

INFORMATION

Services There's a KCB bank with an ATM, and a post office, both in the town centre. For internet access try Purelink (daily 8am–7.30pm; Ksh2/min) or Infolink (daily 7am–9pm; Ksh1/min), both in the town centre.

ACCOMMODATION

With the exception of *Nawoitorong Guesthouse* and *Ceamo Prestige Lodge* most of Lodwar's accommodation is tucked away behind a clutch of popular bars, which can make for a colourful stay. None of the following (apart from *Ceamo Prestige Lodge*) has hot water as such, although the supply is invariably tepid rather than cold, especially by evening time.

★**Ceamo Prestige Lodge** ☎0721 555565, ⌨ceamo lodge.com. Lodwar's newest place to stay, with large, cool rooms (s/c and non-s/c options available) and a modern restaurant serving decent, if expensive, food (mains approximately Ksh1000). The best central option in Lodwar, although pricey. Wi-fi. BB Ksh6500

7

THE TURKANA

Until a few decades ago, the **Turkana**, the main people of the western shore of the lake, had very little contact with the outside world, or even with the Republic of Kenya. Turkana people did not traditionally wear clothing, though the women wear several tiers of beads around their necks and, if married, a metal band too. Turkana men are rarely seen without their *akichalong*, a small wooden headrest, like a stool, on which they recline at any opportunity. Many still wear a wide bracelet on their wrists called an *aberait*, which is in fact a weapon. Although it's usually covered with a leather guard, the edge of the *aberait* is razor-sharp, and can be wielded in a fight like a slashing knife, while leaving the hands free.

Linguistically, the Turkana are related to the Maa-speaking Samburu and Maasai. Indeed, along the northwest shore of the lake, the people are probably an old mixture of Turkana and Samburu, although, like the Luo (also distantly related by language), the Turkana did not traditionally practise circumcision. They moved east from their old homeland around the present-day borders of Sudan and Uganda in the seventeenth century. The desolate region between the lake and the Ugandan border that they now occupy is barely habitable land, and their daily **struggle for existence** has profoundly influenced the shape of their society and, inevitably, helped create the funnel into modern Kenya that Lodwar, with its road, has become.

The Turkana are more individualistic than most Kenyan peoples and they show a disregard for the ties of clan and family that must have emerged through repeated famines and wars. Some anthropologists have suggested that loyalty to particular **cattle brands** is a more important indicator of identity than blood ties or lineage. Although essentially **pastoralists**, always on the move to the next spot of grazing, the Turkana, with characteristic pragmatism, have scorned the taboo against fish so prevalent among herders, and **fishing** is a viable option that is increasingly

Lodwar Lodge ☎0728 007512. This popular hotel offers rows of quiet, spacious *bandas* (both s/c and non-s/c) behind a busy bar area, but be prepared for a bit of local colour; there are also cheaper rooms in an adjacent concrete block. BB **Ksh1500**

★**Nawoitorong Guesthouse** 1km south over the Turkwel bridge, then 1.5km east ☎0704 911947. Part of the Turkana Women's Conference Centre, a cooperative set up in 1984 by four women who began baking bread together, *Nawoitorong* is made of local materials, is partly solar-powered and uses profits to promote Turkana women's education. The non-s/c rooms in the main compound are spotless and have great mosquito nets but lack privacy and can be noisy; the three s/c cottages (Ksh3000) are better but more expensive. There's also excellent food. By far the best place to stay in Lodwar but some way out of town. BB **Ksh800**

Turkwel Lodge ☎0712 689861. A presentable town-centre lodge, with clean rooms with nets and ceiling fans, plus a few tidy cottages at the back (all s/c). The rooms are reasonably quiet, and there's a good bar and restaurant out front. BB **Ksh1500**

EATING

For **food** supplies the two main supermarket/grocery stores, Naipa (Mon–Sat 8.30am–8pm, Sun 11am–7.30pm) and Kakumatt (daily 7am–9pm), will fulfil most of your needs.

Nawoitorong Guesthouse 1km south over the Turkwel bridge, then 1.5km east ☎0704 911947. Probably the best food in Lodwar, with a menu offering everything from local curries to burgers and fries. Food takes forever to arrive, so order in advance or be prepared to wait. Mains from Ksh700. Daily 6am–9.30pm.

New Gulf Hotel Opposite the Oilibya petrol station, near the Loki stage. Cavernous place serving tea, chapattis, *mandaazi* and all the usual staples for around Ksh200. Daily 6am–6pm.

Turkwel Lodge ☎0712 689861. Good, solid meals, with a focus on meats cooked every way you could imagine (Ksh350 for a quarter-chicken). There's also some pleasant outdoor seating for drinkers. Daily 6am–11pm.

DRINKING AND NIGHTLIFE

Beer Garden One of Lodwar's few discos, with DJs spinning a mix of Kenyan music and reggae and determined regulars partying well into the small hours. Fri & Sat 5pm–late.

Lodwar Lodge ☎0728 007512. Large, convivial outdoor bar and terrace that serves as a magnet for local men during football matches; on game days the place gets packed, but at other times it's a nice spot to shoot some pool. Daily 7.30am–11pm.

popular. They also grow crops when they can get seeds and when there's adequate rainfall. Often the rains fail, notably during the prolonged drought of the early 1980s, which took a terrible toll on Turkana children. The situation eased up until 2007, when, again, a prolonged drought set in. Although the rains have been good for the past few years, life here is still very much a matter of day-to-day survival, supplemented here and there by food aid.

Turkana **bellicosity** is infamous in Kenya (Turkana migrants to the towns of the south are frequently employed as *askaris*). Relations with their neighbours – especially the Merille to the north of the lake, the Samburu to the south and the Pokot to the southwest – have often been openly aggressive. In 2015, raids and violent clashes between the Pokot and Samburu left 92 people dead, 400 goats stolen and 350 families displaced.

British forces were engaged in the gradual conquest of the Turkana – the usual killings, livestock raids and property destruction – and they succeeded, at some cost, in eventually disarming them of their guns in the 1920s. But the Merille, meanwhile, were obtaining arms from Abyssinia's imperial government, and they took advantage of the Turkana's defenceless position. When war was declared by Italian-held Abyssinia in 1940, the British rearmed the Turkana, who swiftly exacted a savage revenge on the Merille. They were later disarmed again. Since then, the Turkana have fallen victim to heavily armed Toposa raiders from Sudan, who are thought to have killed as many as ten thousand Turkana in the far north. A tribal peace pact was signed in 2011, which helped matters, and the region is relatively quiet at the moment.

Turkana **directness** is unmistakeable in all their dealings with *wazungu*. They are, for example, resolute and stubborn bargainers, while offers of relatively large sums for photos often leave them stone cold – not necessarily from any mystical fear of the camera, but because of a shrewd estimation of what the market will stand, and hence, presumably, of their own reputation.

The western lakeshore

Fringed by swaying palm trees and teeming with wildlife, the windswept **western lakeshore** feels like an oasis in this sun-baked region, and is certainly the most obvious focus of a trip to Turkana. It is, however, fairly inaccessible – many of the attractions in the area are difficult (if not impossible) to reach by public transport, and roads between them are few. Still, these wild, windswept beaches are hard to beat for their end-of-the-world appeal, and the sense that you've got the vast desert lake all to yourself.

Kalokol

Ferguson's Gulf is the only easily accessible place to head for on the lakeshore, accessed via the village of **KALOKOL**. Kalokol has a surprising amount of hassle for such a small place, although its main appeal is as an especially good place for buying **Turkana crafts**: wonderful (but far too big to transport) baskets, rich-smelling, oiled head stools (*akichalong*), ostrich-shell necklaces and an array of snuff and tobacco horns made of cow horn (traditionally) or pieces of plastic piping.

ARRIVAL AND DEPARTURE   KALOKOL

Several **matatus** make the 60km trip every day from Lodwar. When you've had enough, take a matatu back to Lodwar, but don't leave it till too late in the afternoon; the last one leaves no later than 2pm. Alternatively, you could try **hitchhiking** out of Kalokol – far from guaranteed, though vehicles occasionally go all the way through to Kitale.

ACCOMMODATION AND EATING

Kalokol has only one basic **place to stay**, and while **food** supplies have improved a little with the opening of a few *dukas*, it's not a bad idea to bring at least some fruit with you from Lodwar. Piles of cheap and delicious fried **lake fish** are usually available at least once a day at one of the houses in Kalokol. Ksh100 will pay for more than enough for one person; ask around.

Lake Turkana Guest House ☏ 0713 679687. Cheap, and near the matatu stage, though the non-s/c rooms are spartan and rather cramped and management is fairly non-existent. The restaurant in front serves decent fried meat and pilau (mains around Ksh200). Room only Ksh500

THE DANCING STONES OF NAMORATUNGA

During the journey between Lodwar and Kalokol, look out for the **standing stones of Namoratunga**, 15km southwest of Kalokol some 50m off on the south side of the road. They're easy to miss, being only a small cluster of metre-high cylindrical stones, but the Turkana are in the habit of balancing small rocks on top of them, so you'll know them when you see them. Like a miniature Stonehenge, the pillars are a spiritual focus and the scene of a major annual gathering of Turkana clans, usually in December. The stones pre-date the arrival of the Turkana, but little is known about them, even by the people themselves (the name "namoratunga" is used by Turkana to describe any standing-stone site). One theory is that the stones were aligned with the positions of important stars in Eastern Cushitic astronomy and were used to determine the dates of ritual ceremonies. Some people call them "dancing stones", following a legend that told of a tribe dancing on the site, who were turned to stone by the ridicule of a group of new arrivals, the Turkana. More plausible reasons for their existence might be the concentration of haematite and copper ore around the site, the smelting of which (for making weapons) has historically had ritual significance. Uphill from the stones you'll find several raised rock cairns covering ancient graves, some perfectly delineated with larger regular stones. It's a fascinating site, and all rather mysterious.

7

Ferguson's Gulf

Kalokol is about 3km from the shallow waters of **Ferguson's Gulf**: just follow the river course as it drains east. Hanging out by the lake here is fascinating, with the constantly mutating background of the western shore across the bay, as well as the closer prospect of Turkana fishermen, hundreds of species of birds and the occasional glimpse of crocodile or hippo on the water's surface. From a distance, the activity at the water's edge seems silent since the wind whips all sound away, lending the whole scene a slightly dream-like quality.

Down on the shore you can talk with the children who follow you everywhere, and who often speak good English. If you make friends, you can be taken looking for snakes (be careful), to see *tembo* brewing (always by women) or, if you're lucky, to a dance. Teenagers' and children's dances happen several times a week, but they're best when there's a full moon: the boys tie cans of stones to their ankles and pretend to ignore the girls' flirting.

When you're tired of wandering around, being mobbed by toddlers, watching the fishermen paddling out on their waterlogged rafts and the pied kingfishers hovering and plunging over the shallows, you might consider having a **swim**. People may tell you it's safe, but going in is always a risk because of crocodiles.

Central Island National Park

Accessible from Eliye Springs or Ferguson's Gulf (round trip Ksh15,000–18,000 including petrol) • Daily 6am–6pm • $25 • ⓦ bit.ly/CentralIslandNP • Camp wild on the beach with your own equipment costs $20; toilets only • Five square kilometres

A trip to the **Central Island National Park** is highly recommended, and the park warden or one of his rangers will normally accompany you. Make sure, however, that the boat you go in is thoroughly lake-worthy, equipped with life jackets, and that the crew know what they are doing – vicious squalls can blow up fast and it's more than 9km to the island. This is one of two island national parks in the lake (the other is the less accessible South Island), which, together with Sibiloi National Park on the northeast shore of the lake, are a UNESCO World Heritage Site.

Central Island is a unique triple volcano poking gauntly out of the water. Most of the island is taken up by two crater lakes (a third has dried up) hidden behind its rocky shores. One of the **lakes** is the only known habitat of an ancient species of tilapia, a reminder of the time when Lake Turkana was connected to the Nile. The island is also the nesting ground for big colonies of water birds but, like some African Galapagos, it really belongs to the reptiles, with **crocodiles** found here in large numbers. The vegetation is scant, but some of the sheltered lees are overgrown with thick grass and bushes for a short period each year, and the nests are dug beneath this foliage.

Eliye Springs

Eliye Springs, 66km east of Lodwar, used to be *the* place for travellers on the lakeshore and it still attracts the occasional overland truck and 4WD weekenders. It may be difficult to reach, but Eliye Springs readily compensates for the hassles of the journey – a paradisal place with rustling *doum* palms watered by hot springs, gorgeous views and nothing to do except lounge about and enjoy the lakeside ambience.

ARRIVAL AND DEPARTURE   ELIYE SPRINGS

Getting to the springs and back is the main problem, as there's **no public transport**. You can rent a vehicle with a driver for the day for around Ksh10,000 (4WD advisable as the trail gets very sandy towards the end). Alternatively, it's possible to walk along the lakeshore from Ferguson's Gulf – hire a guide (Ksh3000), load up with water and follow the lake south for 45km. A night walk by moonlight is best, but watch out for crocodiles.

ACCOMMODATION

Eliye Springs Resort 📞0703 891810 or 📞0738 827552, 🌐eliyespringsresort.com; map p.516. The only real place to stay in Eliye Springs, this laidback lakeside resort offers a range of accommodation for all budgets. At the top end are luxurious Turkana *bomas*, but simple *manyattas* (non-s/c) are also available. Alternatively, you can pitch your own tent among the palms or hire a mosquito-net tent (it's see-through) and fall asleep looking at the stars. Boats for tours and fishing trips also available. Camping

(own tent) $10, mosquito-net tent $23, *manyatta* $35 *boma* FB $290

Lobolo Camp About 25km south of Kalokol, on the shore 📞0722 799027 🌐bit.ly/lobolo; map p.516. The first permanent tented camp in Turkana, Lobolo has six spacious tents with spring-water showers and raised beds to catch the breeze. Meals, served at the central mess tent, are the best you'll find in the region. Activities, including overnight fly camping at Central Island National Park, can be arranged. FB $700

Lokichokio and around

The border town of **LOKICHOKIO** (also spelled Lokichoggio and often just called Loki) is an unremittingly dry and rocky place, and even more of a cowboy town than Lodwar. Prior to South Sudan's independence, Loki was something of a supply boomtown for the war as the main UN aid centre, but the UN moved on to Juba in 2011. Today Loki remains a forgotten place, its once-upscale lodges slowly rotting away, and the dusty streets have been reclaimed by Turkana herdsmen and their goats.

Kakuma

The road to Lokichokio passes the huge refugee camp at **Kakuma**, 144km northwest of Lodwar, which follows the banks of the Tarach *lugga* for nearly 10km. Set up for South Sudanese refugees, this sprawl of huts and shacks nearly doubled in size in 2015 to cope with the mass displacement from the continually raging conflict across the border. Kakuma has food and basic lodgings (and usually fuel), but nothing to warrant a stopover.

ARRIVAL AND INFORMATION   LOKICHOKIO AND AROUND

By plane Fly-SAX (📞0707 305305, 🌐fly-sax.com) offers three flights weekly to Loki with prices starting from $225 one-way.

Services There's a KCB bank with an ATM off the Lopiding road, and a post office at the north end of town, off the Juba road opposite the immigration office.

ACCOMMODATION AND EATING

748 Camp Lopiding road, 500m south of town 📞0720 772335. One of the last of Loki's once numerous luxury camps, this landscaped compound is overpriced and reeks of abandonment. But the roomy *bandas* are still in good shape, the garden is attractive and there's even a tiny gym. You can get burgers and steaks at the bar/restaurant for

around Ksh650. FB $60

Ana Hotel Ejokonoi On the Lodwar road, 100m before the Makuti Guesthouse 📞0726 996045 🌐analoki.com. Charming little café run by a local women's group, serving Kenyan staples alongside pasta (Ksh180), pancakes and sandwiches. Order two days in advance and they can even

7

7

THE SAMBURU

The **Samburu** are historically close to the Maasai. Their languages are nearly the same (both Maa) and culturally they are virtually indistinguishable to an outsider. Both came from the region around present-day northwest Turkana in the seventeenth century. The Samburu turned east, establishing themselves in the mountain pastures and spreading across to the plains; the Maasai continued south.

Improvements in health and veterinary care over the last century have swelled the Samburu population and the size of their herds. Many in the driest areas of their range in the northeast have turned to camel herding as a better insurance against drought than cattle. Since livestock is the basis of relations between in-laws (through the giving of "bride wealth" from the husband to his wife's family), having camel herds has disrupted patterns of marriage and initiation into new generations because they increase in number more slowly than cattle herds. Memories, recording every transaction over successive generations, are phenomenal (the Samburu have only begun to acquire writing in the last five decades or so).

The Samburu age-set system, like many others in Africa, is a complicated arrangement to which a number of anthropologists have devoted lifetimes of investigation. Essentially it's a **gerontocracy** (rule by old men), and the polygamous elders are assured, by the system they manipulate, of having the first choice of young women to marry. The promiscuous and jingoistic – but, by Samburu reckoning, still juvenile – warriors are forced to wait, usually until their thirties, before initiation into elderhood and subsequent marriage and fatherhood bring

whip up a pizza. Daily 6.30am–9pm.

Makuti Guesthouse Town centre, on the main Lodwar road opposite the Sunbird ☎ 0735 199217. Clean, good-sized non-s/c rooms with nets and fans, all facing onto a brightly painted courtyard. The main drawback is the raucous bar out front, though it's a good place to grab some *nyama choma* or goat stew (around

Ksh150). Room only **Ksh1000**

Sunbird Town centre, on the main Lodwar road opposite the Makuti ☎ 0708 325173. Run by a Christian family, this quiet guesthouse has clean, non-s/c rooms with fans and nets and doesn't allow alcohol on the premises, which makes it a perfect place to escape the noisy bars across the street. Room only **Ksh900**

Samburu-land

Samburu-land is the vast stretch of country to the southeast of Lake Turkana inhabited for the last three to four hundred years by the traditionally nomadic Samburu people, who are very closely related to the Maasai, and speak the same language, Maa. The easiest way to explore the region is to take an organized safari (see p.123), but if your budget is tight, and you have time, a flexible attitude and don't want a spoon-fed adventure, you'll get the maximum exposure to the area by travelling completely independently and without your own vehicle.

The C77 road to Maralal

Rumuruti (onomatopoeic Maa for "mosquito") is the first town you come to. Though fairly insignificant these days – it merely marks the end of the paved road from Nyahururu and the Central Highlands (see p.197) – this former Maasai stronghold of western Laikipia was settled by British soldiers after World War I and many of their ranches still exist. There's some very good game country in the vicinity, so you might want to stay nearby, for example at *Bobong Campsite* (see p.514).

Suguta Marmar, 15km north of the Baringo junction and 20km south of Kisima, has little more than a livestock auction yard, a basic checkpoint and a few cheap *hotelis*.

Maralal

Some of the Laikipia settlers who ended up around Rumuruti would have dearly liked to set themselves up around the cool, conifer-draped highlands of **MARALAL**. But even before British administrators made this the district capital, Maralal had been a spiritual them a measure of real respect. In turn, they perpetuate the system on their own sons, who have everything to gain by falling in line and much to lose if they withdraw their stake in the tradition – perhaps by going to Nairobi or the coast to look for work.

For **women** the situation is very different. They are married at 15 or 16, immediately after the still widely performed operation of clitoridectomy and before they have much chance to rebel. But they may continue affairs with their *morani* boyfriends, the unmarried juniors of their new, much older husbands. This polygamy in itself seems to be an important motivating force for the whole generation system. For the warriors and their girlfriends, there's a special young people's language – a vocabulary of conspiratorial songs and idioms – which has to be modified with the initiation of every age-set, so that it's kept secret from the elders.

This highly intricate system is now beginning to collapse in many areas, with a widespread disruption of pre-colonial ways; even the circumcision initiation of boys to warriorhood is less of a mass ceremony. While herds are still the principal criterion of wealth, people in some areas are turning to agriculture. There are enormous problems for such initiatives, especially when there's no aid or government support, but they do show that the standard stereotypes don't always fit. As for the *morani* warriors, opportunities for cattle-raiding and lion-killing have diminished with more efficient policing of their territories, although there are still frequent clashes with the Turkana on their northern borders. For some, tourist hunting has taken over: *morani* in full rig, striding past the beach hotels, looking for sales opportunities or liaisons, are no longer an unusual sight.

7

focus for the **Samburu people** and, despite some dithering, the colonial administrators didn't accede to the settlers' demands.

Maralal is a peculiar town, spread with abandon around a depression in the hills. Samburu people trudge its dusty streets – creating a brilliant collage of skins, blankets, beads, brass and iron, and giving the town a special smell, too, of sour milk, fat and cattle. You'll see warriors in full rig on bicycles; warriors with braided hair and bracelets, but wearing jeans and singlets; women decked with flanges of necklaces; old men with sticks; and young men carrying old rifles. The main town-centre watering hole is the *Buffalo House Hotel*: the place sets itself up for Wild West comparisons and the climate is appropriate – unbelievably dusty, almost always windy and, at 2220m, sharp enough at night for log fires. All it needs is coyotes – and even there hyenas fill the role with their nocturnal whooping.

A notable resident of Maralal until 1994 was the travel writer and Arabist **Wilfred Thesiger**, who had made the town his home and had adopted a number of orphaned boys. Thesiger made his name with his accounts of the Shia Arabs of southern Iraq and the Bedu of the Arabian peninsula, and followed up these achievements with several books on Kenya, notably *My Kenya Days*. Among the Samburu he found equally congenial companions for his old age.

Kenyatta House
West of the town centre • Daily 8am–5pm • Free, but donations accepted

If you neglect to visit the liberally signposted **Kenyatta House**, don't fret. The fact that Kenyatta was detained here in 1961 before his final release doesn't really improve the interest of this unexceptional and almost empty bungalow. In a way it seems a pity that it's a slightly unloved national monument and not some family's home.

MARALAL INTERNATIONAL CAMEL DERBY

The Maralal International **Camel Derby** makes for a strange weekend during the second week of August. Anyone can enter, or just watch, as dozens of competitors from East Africa, Europe, China, Australia and South Africa battle it out over 10km amateur and 21km semi-professional stages. There is also an amateur camel triathlon consisting of 2km camel race, 5km bike ride and a 3km run. For more info head to ⓦ samburu.go.ke.

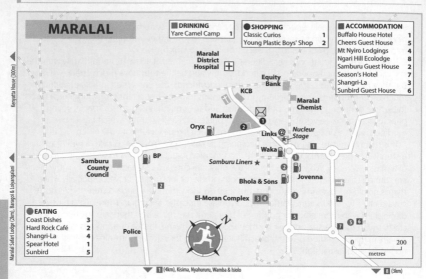

Maralal National Sanctuary

Maralal Safari Lodge, 2km southwest from the town centre • Daily 24hr • Free

Although in theory the **Maralal National Sanctuary** covers more than 200 square kilometres to the west and north of Maralal, in practice almost all of it is now farmed or grazed, leaving just a couple of square kilometres around *Maralal Safari Lodge* (see opposite) where plains wildlife is fairly common. You can sit on the terrace, or in the bar-restaurant, and watch a succession of wildlife from the sanctuary and nearby Yamo Forest, including zebra, baboon, warthog and impala – and, less often, eland, buffalo and hyena – file up the hill to the concrete waterhole a few metres away.

ARRIVAL AND DEPARTURE   MARALAL

Most matatus, and the few larger buses that serve Maralal, congregate in the centre of town between the market and what would be the main roundabout if the traffic observed it. The main bus or matatu companies are Nucleur (sic) and Samburu Liners. They both have ticket kiosks in the area.

GETTING TO MARALAL

From Nyahururu The easiest route to Maralal, the C77 rolls up from Nyahururu via Rumuruti. The road is tarmac as far as Rumuruti, and then poor-quality *murram* to Maralal. Regular buses serve this route from Nyahururu (5 daily; 4hr; Ksh500) with 2–3 connections daily to Nairobi (7hr; Ksh500).

From Isiolo and Wamba A second route to Maralal is the A2 from Isiolo past Archer's Post, then west along the C79 past the turn for Wamba, where it becomes the C78. Buses connect Maralal with both Wamba (2 daily; 3hr; Ksh500) and Isiolo (5 daily; 5hr; Ksh900). Despite some bad corrugations, scenically the C79/78 has everything to recommend it, including some magnificent desert buttes and sweeping views over the valley of the Ewaso Nyiro River, which flows east through the Samburu National Reserve. Some 176km from Isiolo and 86km from Wamba you reach flyblown little Kisima, at the junction with the C77 Rumuruti–Maralal road.

From Lake Baringo A third possible route to Maralal is the lonely but reasonable *murram* road from Lake Baringo, which in its earlier stages has some breathtaking viewpoints back over the lake and fascinating Pokot villages on the way.

NORTH TO LAKE TURKANA

There's a once-daily bus north of Maralal to Baragoi (4hr), but no regular public transport beyond there, so if you're not driving, hitchhiking is usually the only way to Loiyangalani. It's best not to go to Baragoi without a confirmed lift on to Loiyangalani. In Maralal, your best bet for a lift is to spread the word at the petrol stations. Gametrackers' Turkana safari (see box, p.518) reaches Maralal most Friday evenings, and if there's room you might persuade the driver to give you a lift, for a fee. Members of the Plastic Boys, Group (see box opposite) can also be helpful. If you're driving, note that Maralal is the last place where you can rely on supplies of beer, petrol and diesel (around ten percent more expensive here than in the towns to the south).

THE YOUNG PLASTIC BOYS' CO-OPERATIVE SELF-HELP GROUP

Arriving in Maralal, you'll invariably attract a flock of (often annoying) "**guides**" offering evening excursions to see traditional dancing in nearby *manyattas*, or else visits to local Samburu witch doctors and blacksmiths and Turkana villages. Use your judgement before accepting, making it absolutely clear how much you are prepared to pay. Recent visitors have reported relatively non-commercial and very worthwhile excursions.

An attempt to tame the guides by organizing them into disciplined groups is the **Young Plastic Boys' Co-operative Self-Help Group**, named after the street children who used to make dolls and trinkets using plastic bags and cartons. They have now progressed, under the guidance of KWS and various NGOs, to carving and selling woodcrafts, spears and other souvenirs. Their shop is near the market, and sells a decent range of Pokot, Turkana, Rendille and Samburu crafts (or items inspired by those cultures), and they should also be able to sort you out with a reliable guide, should you need one, and advise on onward travel if you're having difficulties. If you want to look further for crafts, seek out a Plastic Boys offshoot, **Classic Curios**, a little crafts shop beside the post office.

7

ACCOMMODATION

At the time of writing, *Lemartis Camp* was being relocated from Koija Group Ranch to a new location in the Karisia Hills near Maralal; for more information see ⓦ lemartiscamp.com. The *Maralal Safari Lodge*, 2km southwest of the centre, had undergone extensive refurbishment and reopened in 2014 after many years sitting idle, but was ransacked by Samburu County officials in 2015 and was closed until further notice.

Buffalo House Hotel Town centre (no phone). Ultra-basic and a shadow of its former self, this centrally located boozer is just the thing if you're counting every penny, with single-bedded rooms around a small courtyard and dubious shared showers and loos. The rooms (all non-s/c) are possibly the cheapest in Kenya, and definitely the cheapest in this book. Room only Ksh300

Cheers Guest House Town centre ☎0722 655877. Deteriorated in recent years, *Cheers* has 45 rooms with bathrooms, TV and nets, all of a fairly low quality. The three second-floor "executive" rooms (Ksh600 extra) are the breeziest and equipped with instant showers. They also have a laundry service and a breakfast room and restaurant on the ground floor (full English Ksh350). Wi-fi. BB Ksh1500

Mt Nyiro Lodgings Town centre (no phone). Very basic, but clean, in a little block of s/c rooms. Go for room #1 at the top, which gets the best breeze. Safe parking. Hot water mornings only. Room only Ksh800

★ Ngari Hill Ecolodge 3km east of Maralal on a hilltop on the road to the Karisia Hills ☎020 2011609 or ☎0735 228649, ⓦ ngarihill.com. Filling a much-needed gap in town, this relatively new guesthouse with cottages and "tented rooms" offers the most comfortable accommodation in Maralal, though it's not convenient if you don't have your own transport. Wi-fi. Camping Ksh1100, BB Ksh6200

★ Samburu Guest House Opposite the police housing on the way into town from the south ☎020 2374919 or ☎0725 363471. One of the best places to stay in town,

with clean rooms (s/c and non-s/c options available), outward-facing windows, flatscreen TVs, bathrooms that work and safe parking in the courtyard. Room #10, at the front, with two big beds, is the best in the house. Downstairs, the restaurant (daily 7am–9pm; no bar) is supplied by enthusiastic kitchen staff. Wi-fi throughout – in theory. BB Ksh3500

Season's Hotel Town centre (no phone). A new kid on the block which looks colourful and appealing from the outside, but sadly isn't much to write home about on the inside. There are twenty clean (s/c and non-s/c) rooms, seventeen of which are doubles, but they're rather dark and poky. On a more positive note, the restaurant is decent, and fitted with a well-stocked drinks fridge and cold beers. Wi-fi (technically). BB Ksh2000

Shangri-La El-Moran complex ☎0717 558883. The most interesting thing about the Samburu-owned *Shangri-La* is that each of the 21 rooms is named after one of the 21 generations of Samburu warriors who have been initiated since 1705. Rooms have instant showers, TV and nets, though they're dull and a bit dark, and fairly worn. You can tear into some roast meat at the *Choma Gardens* at the back, and wash it down in the *Shangri-La Bar*. BB Ksh1200

★ Sunbird Guest House Town centre ☎0722 622947. A lovely retreat from the hustle of town, this has fantastically clean, fresh rooms (s/c and non-s/c), with electricity, all charmingly and reassuringly well managed, with a wholesome *hoteli* attached for the wholesome clients they prefer to welcome. Great value. Wi-fi. Room only Ksh1200

EATING

Coast Dishes Town centre. Friendly local restaurant run by folks from Mombasa ("The neighbourhood will never be the same again" they proclaim in large letters on their facade) with Al Jazeera in English on the TV and tasty, cheap and filling rice-based dishes – *mchele*, pilau and especially *katakata* (only Ksh80), – plus chapattis and *mahamri*. Eat and drink for Ksh200. Daily 6.30am–8.30pm.

Hard Rock Café Town centre. Excellent little place with cheap food including samosas, and meat-and-carb dishes such as pilau (Ksh100), chapatti and stew (Ksh200) and chapatti and beans (Ksh140) and friendly owners, who are generous with advice on travel in the region. Daily 6am–8pm.

★**Shangri-La** El-Moran complex ☎ 0717 558883. This one-time upmarket restaurant in Maralal's first "mall" still maintains a certain style, but at super-competitive prices, with a full English breakfast for Ksh350, continental breakfast Ksh250, masala chips Ksh200 and Spanish omelette Ksh50. Daily 6am–10.30pm.

Spear Hotel Town centre. Reliable and popular *hoteli*, with a great atmosphere, breakfasts and a good list of filling dishes, including beef and rice (Ksh150) and *nyama choma* (half a kilo of beef for Ksh200). Daily 6am–10pm.

★**Sunbird** Town centre. Smart *hoteli* with an outdoor garden area offering the best food in Maralal. Order ahead for meals, which are good value and well prepared, and mostly fried dishes (around Ksh400/plate). They don't have a bar, but beer is available, though it can only be served with food. Daily 6.30am–9pm.

DRINKING

A night spent in the town's numerous **bars** can be exhilarating, infuriating and silly, but rarely dangerous.

Yare Camel Camp 4km down the Isiolo road ☎ 0722 333674, ⊕ yarecamelcamp.co.ke. Until the *Buffalo House Hotel* (the town's former leading watering hole) is sold and reinvented as a flatscreen sports bar (yet to arrive in town), the best bar in the area is at the *Yare Camel Camp*, which we wouldn't recommend staying at, but is highly recommended for a drink and a spot of pool with the locals. Daily 9am–midnight.

DIRECTORY

Banks Maralal is the last place to get cash en route to Lake Turkana – at the KCB or Equity banks (both in the town centre, both with ATMs).

Internet Links Cybercafé, town centre (Mon–Sat 8am–7.30pm, Sun 2–7.30pm; Ksh5/min)

Pharmacy Maralal Chemist, town centre (Mon–Sat 8am–6pm).

The Mathews Range

In the context of the vast spaces of the north, the **Mathews Range** – named after the Welshman General Lloyd Mathews, one-time commander-in-chief of the Sultan of Zanzibar's army – is virtually on Maralal's doorstep. The range, most of which is a forest reserve, is impressively wild hill country, with Mathew Peak (Ol Doinyo Lenkiyo) rising to 2375m. Lower down, the mountains are heavily cloaked in forest and thick bush; unusual vegetation includes "living fossil" cycad plants, giant cedars and podocarpus. Among the plentiful animal life are forest buffalo and outstanding butterflies.

Wamba

Matatus run between Maralal and Wamba (3hr) and between Isiolo and Wamba (3hr)

To visit the Mathews, unless your main aim is to stay at *Sarara Camp* (see opposite), your most promising first target is **WAMBA**, a one-street town 5km off the C78/79 highway, roughly midway between Maralal and Isiolo. Wamba's main focus and chief claim to fame is the large, modern Catholic **hospital** on the way into town, which has the best medical facilities in northern Kenya. Wamba is a great place to restock supplies if you're heading into the Mathews Range or across to Maralal. There's a petrol station, fresh fruit and veg stalls, a post office and a community police station.

The big mountain you can see to the southeast of the town is **Warges** (2688m, 9km from Wamba as the crow flies), a southern outlier of the Mathews. Guides from Wamba will take you up there, though they'll stress how full of wild animals it is and how much their lives (not yours of course) are at risk.

The Kitich area

The main continuation from Wamba is towards the luxury **Kitich Camp** (see p.530), for which a 4WD is essential (there's no public transport, and note that there's no fuel along the way and normally none for sale at *Kitich*). Contact the camp in advance for directions as new road development was taking place at the time of writing. There was once a KWS campsite near here, but this was closed at the time of writing with no clear plans to reopen.

If you want to explore the area, head to the KWS in Wamba to find a guide (essential) before heading into the mountain range. This is first-rate **walking** and exploring country for hardy travellers. It's a very game-rich area with elephants everywhere, buffaloes, hyenas, leopards and many other creatures, and you really have to watch yourself, especially if you go down near the river. It's a lot of fun, but take care.

Namunyak Wildlife Conservation Trust

Accessible by charter flight from Nanyuki to *Sarara*'s airstrip or by road along the A2 to Sereolipi (97km north of Isiolo), then turning left and – *luggas* permitting – heading a further 32km along a bush track • $110 • ⓦ www.nrt-kenya.org/namunyak • 340 square kilometres

The community-managed **Namunyak Wildlife Conservation Trust** forms a great stretch of rugged bush and forest, supported by the Tusk Trust. Here, with Warges rearing behind, is one of the north's best tented camps, *Sarara Camp*, and the only one to be found in the vast wilderness area of Namunyak. While game can be hard to spot – you might see klipspringer, Chandler's mountain reedbuck, elephant and (very rarely) leopard – the conservancy has rich pickings for birders, with Kenya's largest nesting colony of Rüppell's vultures and frequent sightings of Gambaga flycatcher, shining sunbird, tiny cisticola and stone partridge.

ACCOMMODATION AND EATING   THE MATHEWS RANGE

WAMBA

There are a few *dukas*, though they offer little in the way of fresh food beyond basic fruit and vegetables.

Imani Bar & Restaurant Wamba centre. Serves the usual limited range of stews (from Ksh150) and a reasonable *githeri* (Ksh100), plus warm beers, to a grateful local crowd. Daily 7am–late.

Saudia Lodge Wamba centre. One of the few B&Ls in town with clean and pleasant rooms (non-s/c), and pretty good value for the price. Room only Ksh900

NAMUNYAK WILDLIFE CONSERVATION TRUST

★ **Sarara Camp** Between the Isiolo–Marsabit road and Wamba ⓦ sararacamp.com (Nairobi reservations ☎ 020 6000457, ⓦ bush-and-beyond.com). A community-owned tented camp run by an experienced safari-business family, *Sarara*'s six tents – all rustic Africa luxury – have great outdoor loos-with-a-view and open-air showers. Go out with the guides (all bronze, but highly experienced) on drives and walks, or relax in the natural-rock infinity pool

---

CAMEL SAFARIS IN THE NORTH

Samburu camel herders drive their beasts to grazing all over this part of Kenya, and a number of small safari operators can offer the experience of walking with them along routes that depend on your time and budget. You can occasionally ride a camel, too, though the experience is far from comfortable, and most camels are not used to it. You will see a fair amount of wildlife, but the main point is to experience the magnificent desert and mountain landscapes in the area, and to understand something of Samburu culture (see box, p.524) through the stories and background you will learn along the way from the herders who accompany you.

Karisia Walking Safaris Tumaren Ranch, near Kimanjo, 80km southeast of Maralal (Nairobi office ☎ 0721 836792) ⓦ karisia.com. All-inclusive camel-assisted walking safaris in the Karisia Hills and Mathews Range, from $200 per person per day.

Ol Maisor Camels Bobong Campsite, north of Rumuruti (see p.514) ☎ 0735 243075 (send an SMS first), ⓔ olmaisor@africaonline.co.ke. Camel-assisted

walking safaris as far north as Lake Turkana. All-inclusive (including a "modicum" of beer and wine) from $100 per person per day.

Wild Frontiers Office in Naro Moru (see p.174) ☎ +8821 643334603 (satellite), ⓦ wildfrontiers kenya.com. Camel-assisted walking safaris, with one or two riding camels always available. Prices depend on requirements.

overlooking the waterhole and wait for the animals to come to you. Photographers will love the hide – perfect for viewing elephants that often come in droves. They also now offer the fantastically remote and comfortable *Star Camp* with beds covered only by mosquito nets – breathtaking stargazing. Closed April 1–June 1 & Oct 15–Dec 14. Package **$1590**

KITICH CAMP

Kitich Camp Mathews forest ☎ +8821 643330048 (satellite), Nairobi reservations ☎ 020 6006482, 🌐 bit.ly/KitichCamp. Nestled unobtrusively on the river bank beneath towering giant figs, *Kitich* is one of Kenya's most legendary locations, with six generously sized canvas tents and huge open-air, stone showers. The camp is exclusively solar-powered, and it's gold-rated by Ecotourism Kenya. The very personally hosted style, with the main activity being game walks in the forested hills, leaves a lasting impression of a remote and beautiful wilderness, and there are some fine excursions, including short walks up the valley to some deep rock pools where you can swim. Patchy wi-fi. Closed April 1– June 1 & Nov 1–Dec 15. $60 conservancy fee extra. Package **$936**

North to Loiyangalani

Bumpy and rocky in places, the road from Maralal to Loiyangalani is in serious need of upgrade and repair. A decent 4WD and a strong stomach are required to make the eight-hour journey. Security-wise, there are no problems beyond random roadside banditry. Ethnic tensions remain a big issue, however, expressed in livestock rustling and poor or partial policing.

The first stretch of the road north from Maralal climbs higher into the Podocarpus forests of the **Maralal National Sanctuary**, before dropping down across the Lopet Plateau to the Elbarta Plains, 15km east of the scorching Suguta Valley. Settlements from here on are few but evenly scattered. The first two – **Morijo** and, 20km north, **Marti** – each have basic *chai* kiosks, one or two Somali-run stores, a mission and a police station.

Losiolo Escarpment

20km north of Maralal then a 6km detour through Poror, past a large wheat-farming project, to the edge of the escarpment • Ksh400 per person to enter the area • Ksh300–600 to camp, depending on your bargaining skills

The Rift Valley is, by its nature, bordered from end to end by vertiginous escarpments and each one seems more impressive than the last. But the dramatic, scimitar edge of **Losiolo** is not just an escarpment; it's a colossal amphitheatre dropping down to the Suguta Valley, 2000m below. Try to get here very early in the morning while the air is still clear.

BARAGOI lies on the northern fringes of the barren Elbarta Plains, 37km north of Marti. Watered only occasionally by run-off from the Samburu Hills and Ndoto Mountains – the *lugga* that skirts the town is dry for much of the year – this is normally a blistering, unforgiving land, dotted here and there with sun-bleached cattle bones. First settled in the 1930s, Baragoi retains its original function as the region's major livestock market, attracting both Samburu from the southeast and Turkana from the northwest, for whom the town is one marker on the once invisible boundary – now usually considered to be the road – between their much disputed grazing lands.

Baragoi is a good place to stop and check the **security situation** on the roads heading further north. Try the police station on the main road at the far end of town heading north to South Horr. In 2012, a tribal conflict near the town between the Samburu and Turkana people resulted in the deaths of at least 46 people, including police officers trying to stop the violence. While tribal clashes still exist, nothing of this magnitude has taken place since.

On the northwest side of town is the **livestock market**. It's a gentle, unhurried affair where old men with gnarled hands and ostrich plumes in their hair play *ngiles* (or *mbau*) with stones and seeds on "boards" carved out of the bone-dry earth as they wait for business to arrive. Here, Samburu deal with Rendille and Turkana, some of whom spend up to seven days walking their livestock from Lake Turkana. In turn Samburu trek southeast for five or six days to reach Isiolo, where they aim to resell their animals at a profit.

If the herder is a **courting** age warrior (a *moran* in Samburu or a *lmoli* in Turkana), Isiolo is also where he buys the beads and bangles he needs in order to get a bride. Once back home, he presents the girl with the gifts and hosts a dance to mime and sing the attributes of the animals that will form his "bride wealth" (see box, p.524) and provide the future family with their means of survival. The young herder is expected to build the confidence of a bride-to-be by representing his beasts favourably and, to this end, he selects a single castrated bull, camel or goat, which he then mimics, gesturing to indicate its size, colour, the shape of its horns, even its temperament. There's a comical side, too, for even the poorest herder, trying his luck with a billy goat with lopsided horns, has to dance to attract a spouse, raising a few smiles with a self-deprecating parody of his goat.

Courtship dances are held frequently in the *manyattas* on the outskirts of town. They are wild and hugely enjoyable events, where you'll certainly be made welcome – though cameras are generally not acceptable.

ARRIVAL AND DEPARTURE

BARAGOI

One daily **matatu** links Baragoi with Maralal but there are no matatus to Loiyangalani. If you're heading north, you'll have to line up a lift with a supply truck or a mission 4WD – ask at the lodgings and *hotelis*. The police station on the north side of town is helpful in finding likely drivers, but be prepared to wait all day. If you're **driving**, The Star filling station usually has fuel at about twenty percent markup on usual prices, and the *jua kali* repair yard on the south side of the main street has a generator for pumping tyres.

INFORMATION

Services Baragoi has no ATM or forex bureau, although there is a post office on the main street. For internet access, try Digitech Computer Services on the main street (Ksh5/

Mb). There's also a police station at the northern end of the town.

ACCOMMODATION AND EATING

Morning Star Guest House Main street, town centre ☏ 0725 440974. The best place to stay in Baragoi, this B&L, owned by Paramount Chief Letelen Lenatorono, is very basic – no running water – but the non-s/c rooms are reasonably clean and there's a bar-restaurant on the ground floor. Room only __Ksh600__

Promise Bar A two-minute walk west of the town

centre. Nothing out of the ordinary, but with its fridge full of cold Tuskers (Ksh130) and nicely reggae-fied Samburu atmosphere, this is the standout choice among Baragoi's various watering holes. Daily 24hr.

Tawakal Hotel Main street, town centre. The best *hoteli* in town, with *nyama karanga* for Ksh200 and pilau at Ksh150. Daily dawn to mid-evening.

Mount Nyiru

From Baragoi, which marks the end of the forbidding Elbarta Plains, the road climbs into mountain country where the peaks are fantastically green if there's been rain and even the plains can be covered in a blanket of grass and wild flowers. Rising up ahead on the left is **Mount Nyiru** (also known as the Nyiru Range), a sheer stack of rugged mountains, partly swathed in thick forest, from which giant rocks jut; through it water gushes along steep ravines, and near the top perches one of Kenya's most remote and beguiling luxury lodges, **Desert Rose**.

To get here, some 16km north of Baragoi, take a track to the left at a T-junction indicated by a pockmarked gas cylinder – the lodge is signed on a small rock tucked into the grass. Some impressively large **desert monitors** live in this area. This track heads west for 10km then forks (left to Tuum, right to *Desert Rose* and Mount Nyiru). For the lodge, you drive a further 13km, passing through the cool, pretty settlement of **Ewaso Rongai** with its thick covering of huge acacia and fig trees, nestled deep in the valley, then climb a final 2km up a track cut partly through the bed rock and at times so steep and narrow it tests the nerve of even experienced 4WD drivers. The views en route to the track's end, at the high eyrie of *Desert Rose Lodge* – perched on the steep slopes of Mount Nyiru among crags and euphorbias – are magnificent.

ACCOMMODATION AND EATING   MOUNT NYIRU

★ **Desert Rose Lodge** Mount Nyiru, 24km from the Baragoi–South Horr road ☎0716 575942 or ☎0725 320923 ⓦ desertrosekenya.com (Nairobi reservations ☎020 2663397, ⓦ africanterritories.co.ke); map p.516. Exhilarating to reach (by airstrip, helipad or mountain road), amid the towering landscapes of Mount Nyiru, and deeply relaxing once you've arrived, this remote and beautiful lodge has five open-plan cottages and does wholesome meals with a bit of zing (home-grown fruit and veg). Unique in Kenya, it's perfect for children and teens, with its pool, local walks and natural waterslide. Patchy wi-fi. Open all year. Package **S1470**

South Horr

Camel hire from Ksh1000 per camel/day, plus guide (from Ksh1000/day) and guard/porter fees (from Ksh700/day)

There's a positive jungle all year round at the oasis village of **SOUTH HORR** (*horr* means "flowing water"), the largest settlement between Baragoi and Loiyangalani, wedged tightly between the Nyiru and Ol Doinyo Mara mountains. With its pleasantly somnolent atmosphere, ample shade and relaxed Samburu camel herders lounging under the trees with their beasts, this is a great place to bunk down for a night or three, and making friends with local Samburu is easy. It's also a good place from which to set our for a **walk with camels** for a few hours or a few days.

The **mountain forest** around South Horr hides lots of wildlife and bursts with birds and butterflies, though unfortunately, many of the elephants and buffaloes have been poached. You can be guided by Samburu *morani* up the lower slopes of Nyiru and Ol Doinyo Mara, or, more ambitiously, on the stiff hike up to the peak of **Mount Nyiru**, with its stunning views over Lake Turkana. If you're thinking of doing any more daring expeditions in the region, be careful if you're embarking on anything way off the beaten track. Many local men who like to sell themselves as **guides** have led surprisingly sheltered lives and they don't know the desert like the backs of their hands any more than you do. Real knowledge and experience are sought after, and more expensive, so give yourself plenty of time and try to make contacts in advance, contacting a camel safari operator if possible (see box, p.529).

ACCOMMODATION   SOUTH HORR

Forest Department Campsite South side of the village, up a rough trail to the west of the road 1km south of the centre; map p.516. Long-drop toilets, an *askari*, and a river that provides drinking water (once you've purified it), bathing spots and a means to wash the dust out of your clothes. Camping **Ksh300**

Kurungu Teiyo Camp 7.5km north of the sharp left (north) turn on the road through South Horr (on the right, marked by a large concrete sign); map p.516. Community camp on the Teiyo River, well shaded by fine old trees. Camping **Ksh500** per person

Samburu Sports Camp & Safari Lodges North side of the village (marked by a large stone sign on the right), 700m north of where the road through the village turns sharp left ☎0720 334561 or ☎0724 832088, ⓦ safari sportscamp.com; map p.516. Run by a born-again Christian Samburu couple in partnership with US missionaries, this offers a variety of *bandas* (all non-s/c), a range of sports facilities and home-grown produce. It's a bit run down, with crusty walls and a couple of toilets that don't bear thinking about, but the staff are friendly and attentive and it's cheap. No alcohol is sold or allowed. Wi-fi. Room only **Ksh1000**

SAMBURU DANCE PERFORMANCES

Around South Horr, you are likely to have the mixed pleasure of **Samburu dancing**, especially if you're on an organized safari. Payment of around Ksh1000 allows you to take as many pictures of the dancers as you want. Scepticism is briefly swamped by the hour-long jamboree that follows. A troupe of *morani* goes through an informal dance programme, flirtatiously threatening the audience with whoops and pounces. Young women and girls join in – sometimes with the evident disapproval of older Samburu onlookers – to be mock-propositioned with whisks of the men's ochre hairdos. Meanwhile, there's the constant offering of necklaces, trinkets, spears, tobacco pouches and more photo poses, to be negotiated individually with those who are too old or too young to dance. It's best not to worry about the fleeting illusion of "authenticity" on these occasions, but to accept them for what they are: vivid, funny, dynamic entertainment.

LAKE TURKANA FESTIVAL

Visit Loiyangalani in May or June, and you'll find the annual **Lake Turkana Festival** (ⓦ laketurkanaculturalfestival.com) taking place. Initiated in 2008 by the German embassy and coordinated by National Museums of Kenya, members of all the main communities of the northwest – Borana, Burji, Dassanech, Elmolo, Gabbra, Garee, Konso, Rendille, Sakuye, Samburu, Somali, Turkana and Wata – gather in their thousands, in finest traditional garb, to dance and sing.

But the festival is as much about **reconciliation** as it is about partying. It brings together ethnic groups who have frequently fought over grazing rights and have bitter histories of conflict and mutually exclusive world views. It's a memorable experience to wander down Loiyangalani's main street – renamed Festival Avenue for the occasion – and see a group of Samburu warriors in their best beads and hair being appraised by their opposite numbers from the Turkana community, and then see a cluster of Dassanech girls from the far north, being admired by two Borana elders.

The high point of the festival comes on the **third afternoon**, when everyone troops out to the festival grounds (a flat piece of desert, with a useful rocky ridge on one side that gives local kids a good vantage point) and – after a series of suitably verbose speeches by various politicians finally ends – each tribe's festival troupe takes it in turn to present their cultural traditions through performances of music and dance.

It's not a huge event, which means you can get as close to the action as you want. There's a marquee and seating – first come, first served – but it's just as much fun to wander through the crowds of locals and participants, visit the **ethnic houses** at the edge of the arena that each troupe has built and enjoy an atmosphere of unrestrained goodwill. The festival is also a photographer's dream. Everyone takes pictures of everyone (including locals, with their mobiles, of tourists), and for the occasion, nobody minds or dreams of asking for payment.

As the sun goes down on the last day, the performances shift from vivid dance and song to message-driven drama, then a fashion show in traditional costume and finally a disco, capped by a famous local singer.

Festival events (all free) are held at various sites around Loiyangalani. If you want to attend, book accommodation and transport as early as possible: it's a popular annual event and demand tends to outstrip Loiyangalani's limited accommodation options.

From South Horr to the lake

After South Horr, the track winds down between the Nyiru Range to the west and the Ol Doinyo Mara mountains to the east, and for some 40km it stays fast with a sandy surface. Eventually it opens onto a featureless plain of black lava, where the going is much rockier and the gaunt massif of **Mount Kulal** dominates the northern horizon.

Both Samburu and Turkana live in, and move across, this area. The numerous **stone circles** and **cairns** around here are the remains of settlements and burial sites, which you'll come to recognize all over the region. Most distinctive are the low semicircular constructions, which you'll see in use as you approach the lake: these serve as shelters against the viciously hot wind that blows almost incessantly off the flanks of Kulal. The burial cairns are not as ancient as they may appear, as traditionally neither the Turkana nor Samburu buried their dead, but instead simply left the bodies out in the open for wild animals to eat. The more important members of the community, such as blacksmiths and respected elders, were sometimes buried under cairns, or were left in a hut whose door would be walled up. The site would be abandoned and never used again for human habitation. Since independence and the arrival of Christian missions, however, both Turkana and Samburu are now obliged to bury their dead.

As the road drops away in front, **Lake Turkana** suddenly appears, usually as a stunning vista of shot blues and greens, with the black, castellated silhouette of South Island hanging as if suspended between lake and sky. Descending a little further along a rocky stretch of road – known to drivers as The Staircase, part of which has now been concreted – you reach several bays. People have gone swimming here in the past, but crocodiles make this really inadvisable. You pass a few frail and temporary fishing settlements, seemingly stranded among the rocks, and, an hour or so later, reach Loiyangalani.

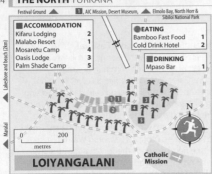

Festival Ground ▲ | 1 AIC Mission, Desert Museum, ▲ Elmolo Bay, North Horr & Sibiloi National Park

■ ACCOMMODATION
Kifaru Lodging	2
Malabo Resort	1
Mosaretu Camp	4
Oasis Lodge	3
Palm Shade Camp	5

● EATING
| Bamboo Fast Food | 1 |
| Cold Drink Hotel | 2 |

■ DRINKING
| Mpaso Bar | 1 |

Lakeshore and beach (2km) ◀
Maralal ◀

0 — 200 metres

N

Catholic Mission

LOIYANGALANI

Loiyangalani

LOIYANGALANI – "the place of the trees" – is a small community far from metropolitan Kenya, a vague agglomeration of grass huts, mud huts, tin shacks, a police station, a school, a few campsites and a handful of simple tourist lodges. The land around is mostly barren and stony, scattered with the bones of livestock, with palm trees and acacias clustered around the settlement's life source, a **warm spring** of fresh water.

The village – it's barely a town – came into being in the early 1960s with the arrival of the Italian mission to the **Elmolo** people and the first incarnation of *Oasis Lodge* (built in 1958). Somali raiders ransacked both establishments in 1965 – incidents reprised in some of the later scenes in Fernando Meirelles' film *The Constant Gardener*, which were shot here and made the town look like Darfur – but since then they have been left alone.

The original people of the area are the Elmolo, a small group who live by hunting and fishing on the southeastern lakeshore, but there has been so much reconciliation of previously warring groups in the area, and intermarriage, that a new ethnic group – the so-called **Elmosaretu**, or Elmolo, Samburu, Rendille and Turkana – is often cited as being the "tribe" of the district, and people proudly remind visitors of the annual Lake Turkana Festival (see box, p.533) and the peaceful progress being made here. The mission, too, is thriving as its net of influence reaches out to most of Loiyangalani's more permanent inhabitants, especially the children who attend the school.

For all its apparent drabness, Loiyangalani is far from dull. When you've had enough of haggling in what passes for the high street for artefacts and fantastic quartz, onyx, amethyst and other semi-precious stones collected from Kulal, as well as the odd fossil fish vertebra, you can stroll around the south side of the village to the mission and school. You'll inevitably pick up a cluster of teenagers eager to practise their English. Swahili has never made much impact in this part of Kenya and English is the usual teaching medium. Education is perhaps the most positive of the major influences, including tourism, state interference and Christianity, that pressurize local customs and traditions.

Desert Museum

4km north of Loiyangalani • Daily 8am–6pm • Ksh500 • ⓦ bit.ly/DesertMuseum

Loiyangalani's **Desert Museum** is a purpose-built, crescent-shaped exhibition space in a fine location overlooking the lake. Although it displays photos of eight different tribes of the north and clearly deserves support, what is on offer – an information centre, essentially – is much too limited in scope for the entry price.

Loiyangalani beach

2km west of Loiyangalani

Loiyangalani's **beach** is a grubby strip of gravel. People do swim here, and during the annual Lake Turkana Festival (see box, p.533) one morning is usually devoted to boat races and other events. Crocodiles rarely venture this close to town, but never say never. The beach has other potential dangers too: many of the loose stones on the shore shelter scorpions and carpet vipers. A scorpion sting isn't too serious but a viper bite can be dangerous if not treated.

ARRIVAL AND INFORMATION

Transport Charter flights are available from Nairobi to Loiyangalani through Phoenix Aviation (ⓦ phoenixaviation .co.ke), though they're costly. There is no regular ground transport into or out of Loiyangalani. You'll need to put the

GOD'S WORK

The **Loiyangalani mission**, while changing the structure of traditional society through conversions to Catholicism (particularly sweeping among the Elmolo), is at the same time helping to make local people sufficiently independent to resist unwanted change and to make choices about their future, by helping establish income-generating schemes such as shops and boats. Some of the Italian missionaries are extremely open and informative and the chance to talk to them may well arise if you're around for a few days. For non-Christians, however, the whole concept of missionaries and their work can be difficult to swallow. For all their schools and clinics, it's difficult to escape the feeling that the local people – for so long "untouched" by the outside world – managed very well with their original beliefs and traditions, which underpinned their society, cosmology and relationships. With Christianity now ascendant, the old structures are breaking down fast and some risk being lost completely. And by preferring to convert children, rather than their more obstinate parents, the deeper morality of the well-meaning missionaries is questionable at best.

7

word around in the village and visit the lodge and the camps to see if any vehicles are going your way. There is no petrol station and you should bring all the fuel you need. In an emergency, supplies are available in small quantities.

Services Loiyangalani has a post office in the town centre and a reasonable mobile network (Safaricom phone credit is available if you have a local SIM card), but there is no ATM or forex bureau.

ACCOMMODATION

Wherever you stay in Loiyangalani, be prepared for **wind and dust**: it just never stops. Campers, in particular, tend to struggle, because pegs get yanked out and everything blows away. Nights can be noisy too, with palm fronds crashing together overhead. Accommodation fills up during the festival, so **book** well in advance.

Kifaru Lodging Loiyangalani centre (no phone). Also known as *Rhino Camp* (*kifaru* meaning rhino), this very basic central camp has no clear signage so ask around in town when you arrive. There are small *bandas* protected by elementary security, with long-drop loos and an erratic water supply. You'll be lucky to get much in the way of bedding for your foam mattress. Room only Ksh600

Malabo Resort North side of town, east of the airstrip 📞0724 705800, 📧malaboresort@gmail.com, 🌐bit.ly/Malabo. Clean, popular and fairly new to town, with spacious round s/c *bandas*. While the infrastructure is sound, the shadeless setting leaves something to be desired and it's quite overpriced. Good sunset views. BB Ksh5000

Mosaretu Camp Loiyangalani centre (no phone). Run by the Mosaretu Women's Group and offering camping as well as traditional *bandas* (all non-s/c) under the palm trees, with mosquito nets and mattresses. Facilities include toilets, showers, a curio shop and a shared kitchen. Camping Ksh300, *bandas* Ksh1000

Oasis Lodge Loiyangalani centre 📞0722 884697, 🌐oasis-lodge.com. German-run lodge of 18 basic, twin-bedded chalet-style rooms, that tries to be exclusive, and

certainly charges as if it were, though is in fact fairly shabby. Although conceived as a fishing lodge, they don't always have a boat available, and their 4WD vehicle hire – another facility – is also barely operational (one Land Cruiser, seating four, Ksh10,000/day). The views from the bar-restaurant and their two pools are the main draws (Ksh500 daily entrance fee to casual visitors allows use of the pools). Meals are largely set menus (breakfast Ksh1500, lunch and dinner Ksh2000). Soda Ksh150, beer Ksh250, wine Ksh1500/bottle. FB $240

★**Palm Shade Camp** Loiyangalani centre 📞0726 714768. This well-kept, shady site with 11 reasonably cool s/c *bandas* with nets – and eight more s/c rooms which should be ready by the time you read this – is worth booking, especially during the festival. The very decent shared European toilets and adequate shared showers are supplied direct from the warm springs. Decent meals (Ksh500) are available, as is water (Ksh100/litre), ice-cold sodas (Ksh100) and beers (Ksh200). There's also a generator (sometimes off during the day) till late evening and a charging point by the dining area. Camp owner Benedict is incredibly helpful and can arrange activities around Loiyangalani. Camping Ksh600, *bandas* BB Ksh4000

EATING

Loiyangalani doesn't have a single establishment you could honestly call a restaurant. During the Lake Turkana Festival, some of the places below turn a faster trade than usual, but for most of the year food that's ready to serve is the exception rather than the rule; order in advance where possible. Most places don't have menus but can offer chapattis, rice, meat and sometimes fish – eventually – but you may find providing extra raw ingredients to the cook (tomatoes, potatoes, garlic and carrots, for example) is the best way to be sure of a good meal. They'll make a vegetable stew or cook them to order for a small fee. During the festival, the camps or lodge can be a better bet for (more expensive) meals and drinks.

Bamboo Fast Food Main street, north side, opposite Cold Drink Hotel. "Fast" is purely relative: they only cook to order and don't have a menu to choose from, but you can certainly eat reasonably well here for Ksh300. And they do boast a large fridge which comes on in the morning and by sunset is providing cold water and sodas (but no beer; it's a Muslim establishment). Daily 6.30am–8pm.

Cold Drink Hotel Main street, south side. There's always food available here (good pancakes, for example, Ksh20 each), but cold drinks can't be guaranteed. Daily early until late.

DRINKING

Mpaso Bar 20m behind Bamboo Fast Food. *Mpaso* ("The Lake") sells pleasingly cold Tuskers and stays open late – although as the evening wears on some of the clientele can become a nuisance, especially to female customers. And the music is terrible. Daily mid-morning to 11pm.

Elmolo Bay

8km north of Loiyangalani • Ksh1500 per person paid to the headman, which includes permission to take photos

The last viable community of Elmolo people (see box opposite) lives at **ELMOLO BAY**. During the week, many children are at school in Loiyangalani; they come home at the weekend, which is the best time to visit. There are two very small villages – **Layeni** 8km north of Loiyangalani, facing an island 500m offshore, and **Komote**, 4km further north, on the other side of the bay, where there is a church. Which of the two villages you visit depends on whom you hook up with in Loiyangalani, and their contacts. It's best to take a local guide with you.

Impromptu dances start and little hands are slipped engagingly into yours for a walk around the low, grass huts. Digital cameras and smart phones are extremely popular with the village children, eager to look at their image on screen. You will also be shown the "market", a stall in the centre of the village displaying beadwork, belts, fertility dolls and gourds, which you're invited to buy. It's a novel, disturbing experience that contrives to be stage-managed and voyeuristic at the same time. Because of their friendliness, their small number and the increased interest shown in them, the Elmolo risk being taken advantage of by tourists. However, the usual rules apply: ask before you take pictures and be generous with your time and your wallet. Incidentally, don't get worried when a mother hands you her child, then asks for money; she's not selling her offspring, but simply wants you to sponsor the child's education with a large wad of cash.

If you're taken over to the island facing Layeni, you should see **crocodiles** if you walk softly and approach the far shore cautiously. On the stern, rocky beaches on the western side, the remains of Elmolo fish picnics and old camps, even the occasional virtually fossilized hippo tusk, can be found everywhere.

South Island National Park

4000Ksh • kws.go.ke • 39 square kilometres

If you want to visit the UNESCO World Heritage Site of **South Island National Park**, you should first ask about a trip at *Oasis Lodge* (see p.535), but spread the word and you may find a much cheaper means of getting there. It's a 30km round trip, so the

LOIYANGALANI DANCES

In the evenings, dances often take place around Loiyangalani – informal, energetic, pogo-style performances for fun, that are always worth checking out. Track them down by the booming sound of collective larynxes. At Loiyangalani it's often the girls who ask the boys to dance, and you're welcome to join in. As usual, no cameras are allowed unless permission is expressly given and paid for (usually Ksh1000/person).

THE ELMOLO

The people of Loiyangalani with the best claim to being its original inhabitants are the **Elmolo**. The Elmolo call themselves *el-Des*, but their usual name comes from the Samburu *loo molo onsikirri*, "the people who eat fish". They once inhabited South Island, but now occupy a few clusters of grass huts on the torrid shores 8km north of Loiyangalani. Most of the six-hundred-strong community lives here, partly by fishing and the occasional heroic crocodile or hippo hunt (officially banned), and partly by cash receipts from tourist visitors.

The Elmolo are enigmatic. At the time of Teleki's discovery of the lake, they spoke a **Cushitic** language, the family of languages to which Somali and Rendille belong. Recent linguistic research on historical migrations points to their having arrived on the shores of Lake Turkana at a very early time – perhaps more than two thousand years ago. They seem to have no tradition of livestock herding, which might have been kept up if they had turned, like the Turkana, to fishing as a supplement. Today they speak the Samburu dialect of Maa (the last Elmolo-speaker died in 1998) and have started to intermarry with the Samburu. This, as well as the mission's influence, has been quite significant in raising their numbers (from fewer than 200 fifty-odd years ago) but also in diluting their cultural identity. Once strictly monogamous, polygamy isn't uncommon now, and they also send many children to the school in Loiyangalani as weekly boarders. On the slope, right behind the village, looms the fairly recent Catholic church.

All this signals the final curtain for a culture and history that has been largely ignored or denied. The conventional wisdom about hunter-gatherers in Kenya is that they are often the descendants of pastoralists who lost their herds. But if the Elmolo are, as some say, pastoral Rendille who took to fishing in order to survive, then it's strange that they have never tried to replace their herds. For without herds, they could never hope to pay bride wealth for wives from their non-fishing neighbours in the traditional way. A better explanation, and one favoured by the Elmolo themselves, is that their people have always been fishermen and hunters and that pressures from other tribes, particularly the Turkana, had pushed them almost to the point of annihilation.

By the end of the twentieth century, the Elmolo fishing culture was rubbing off on other ethnic groups and even the Samburu had started to eat fish. As long ago as 1972, Peter Matthiessen wrote in *The Tree Where Man was Born*:

The Samburu and Turkana may linger for weeks at a time as guests of the Llo-molo, who have plenty of fish and cannot bear to eat with all these strangers hanging around looking so hungry. Other tribes, the Llo-molo say, know how to eat fish better than they know how to catch them . . . "We have to feed them," one Llo-molo says, "so that they will feel strong enough to go away."

The Elmolo are a charming and hospitable people, and how they survive in their chosen environment is hard to imagine. They are slightly smaller than the other peoples of the area, but the bowed legs that are supposed to be the characteristic result of their diet seem to be confined to the older people – you might have thought all that fish would give them strong bones.

7

weather needs to be fair. Although the warden doesn't always grant permission to camp there for the night, if you get the chance, it's one of the weirdest places to stay: its volcanic vents, rising some 300m above lake level, give out a ghostly luminous glow that has long put off local fishermen from venturing there.

Mount Kulal

Expect to pay Ksh30,000/day for vehicle hire with driver – bargain hard – and Ksh2000/day for a guide; both can be arranged with Benedict at *Palm Shade Camp* (☎ 0726 714768)

It's a tough trip, but you could make a stab at climbing **Mount Kulal** (2285m), comprising two summits joined by a narrow and dicey ridge. The climb itself, once you're on the right track, is straightforward enough. But note that, although Kulal seems to tower over Loiyangalani (its summit is more than 1900m above the lake), two days is barely enough to walk to the base and back, and the summit is 25km east of Loiyangalani as the crow flies. Factor in wind, dust and heat and you can see why you'd be well advised to get transport as far up the mountain as possible before you start climbing. The views from the top are fabulous, with the lake on one side and the searing Chalbi Desert on the other, and birdwatchers have the added incentive of a rare species of **white-eye** peculiar to the mountain. Bring all the water you'll need, as there are no supplies on the mountain.

Sibiloi National Park

$15 • ⓦ sibiloi.com • Possibly the best way of visiting the fossil sites is by timing your trip to coincide with a field school organized by the National Museums of Kenya in tandem with George Washington University (ⓦ bit.ly/koobifora) • 1571 square kilometres

Sibiloi National Park, a huge area stretching inland from Lake Turkana's northeast shore, provides, with its spectacular flora (after the rains) and famous **fossil sites**, a powerful incentive to continue further north. The so-called **Camp Turkana**, near the shore just south of Alia Bay, is the administrative centre marking the park's southern boundary and is where you'll find the KWS park headquarters. The National Museums of Kenya research base camp at **Koobi Fora**, the promontory halfway up the park's shore (ⓦkfrp .com), is 30km further north. Koobi Fora is said to be a Gabbra corruption of Commiphora – the thorny bush of the region.

The fossils

Sibiloi was created to protect the sites of numerous remarkable **hominin fossil** finds that have been made since 1968 by Richard Leakey's, and latterly Kamoya Kimeu's, teams from the University of Nairobi. The rock desert and arid bush that make up the park are an exceptional source because many of the fossils are found on the surface, blown clean by the unabating wind. The finds push the dates of intelligent, cooperative, tool-making behaviour among hominins further and further back all the time. Most of the species concerned, however, are assumed to have died out, and the crucial discoveries that will link humankind to our prehuman ancestors have yet to be made. One striking find made at Sibiloi in 1972 was the skull labelled "1470", first thought to be of a *Homo habilis* ("Handy man") and then renamed *Homo rudolfensis* ("Rudolf man"), which is about 1.9 million years old. Although quite different from other species of early human-like primates, with its large brain and big, flat face, Rudolf man may yet be shown to be a direct ancestor of modern *Homo sapiens*. As more and more hominin discoveries are made at Sibiloi and on the other side of Lake Turkana (where excavations have yielded the earliest *australopithecine* yet discovered, *Australopithecus anamensis*, dated to between 4.2 and 3.9 million years), the evolutionary theories continue to flesh out.

Wildlife

Sadly, intense drought and human–wildlife conflict in recent years mean wildlife viewing is pretty limited at Sibiloi National Park (with the exception of birdlife, which is flourishing, particularly at Alia Bay). It wasn't always like this – until the 1930s, there were large numbers of elephant living here, but rainless years, ivory hunters and, especially, increases in the herds of livestock contributed to their demise. Nowadays, you may spot cheetah, hyena, both kinds of zebra (the ordinary Grant's and the finer-striped, taller Grevy's), ostrich, topi, kudu and gerenuk, as well as crocodiles, but they only exist in very low numbers and don't hold your breath. The tree cover is also minimal: the only trees you might see are in the petrified forest of stone trunks, at the beautiful **Sibiloi Fossil Forest**, a few kilometres east of the park headquarters – reminders of the lush vegetation of the lakeshore in prehistoric times.

Koobi Fora Museum

Koobi Fora Base Camp • Daily 8am–6pm • Ksh500 • ⓦ bit.ly/KoobiForaMuseum

A little dusty but still in good shape, the small **Koobi Fora Museum**, where hominin fossils were formerly displayed alongside dioramas of prehistoric life, is well worth a visit while you're in the area. They've moved the valuable remains to Nairobi and less impressive bones now make up most of the exhibits. Nearby, however, are several *in situ* fossil presentations, displayed exactly as they were unearthed, and left in the ground: of a prehistoric crocodile, a two-million-year-old elephant – estimated to have been as much as 6m in height – and a gigantic prehistoric tortoise as big as a small dinghy, that apparently died on its back, unable to right itself.

ARRIVAL AND DEPARTURE   SIBILOI NATIONAL PARK

By local truck or supply vehicle Vehicles heading up from Loiyangalani or Marsabit are rare and you could wait a week or more.

By 4WD A day's drive should get you from Loiyangalani to the park headquarters at Alia Bay. Driving along the Loiyangalani–North Horr road, turn north after some 45km. From here, a desolate track heads more or less due north for 40km to the settlement of Hurran Hurra, where a left turn should bring you to the camel watering-point and settlement of Gajos, another 40km northwest. Another left here (heading west, then northwest) begins the 15km gentle descent to the lake and the national park HQ. Leaving the park northwards, driving to Ileret and the

unmarked Ethiopian border is straightforward. If you want to drive into Ethiopia here, you have to report to immigration at Omorate, just as if you were coming from Lokitaung on the west side of the lake.

By plane or boat Apart from chartering a plane from Nairobi's Wilson airport (see p.118), an alternative way of getting to Sibiloi is by boat from Ferguson's Gulf on the lake's western shore, near Kalokol (p.522). There's an infrequent National Museums supply boat from here. Expect to pay anything from Ksh20,000 to Ksh30,000 for the round trip, and probably no less if you choose not to return to the western shore.

7

ACCOMMODATION

Alia Bay Guesthouse KWS park headquarters, Alia Bay (Nairobi reservations ☎0726 610508), ⌨bit.ly /AliaBayGuesthouse; map p.516. A three-room self-catering cottage sleeping five, with solar electricity, bathroom, lounge and functional kitchen. Whole house $100

Koobi Fora Bandas Research Base Camp, Koobi Fora (Nairobi reservations ☎020 8164134, ⌨bit.ly/ KoobiForaBandas; map p.516. These simple dorms with nets and shared European loos and showers can be used except in June and July when they're full of American research students. Dorm beds Ksh1000

KWS Campsites Near the KWS park HQ, Alia Bay (Nairobi reservations ☎0726 610508, ⌨kws.go.ke); map p.516. There's a choice of three sites, one by the lake and two inland, but there are no facilities – you'll have to be entirely self-sufficient. Camping $15

Museum Bandas 3km southeast of the Research Base Camp, Koobi Fora, 300m from the shore (Nairobi reservations ☎020 8164134, ⌨museums.or.ke); map p.516. Basic *bandas* in a remote spot, with three single beds each, shared showers, toilets and kitchen. Room only Ksh1100

The northeast

Travel in **northeastern Kenya** has a special quality. For much of the time, the normal stimuli – passing scenery, animals, people and fleetingly witnessed events – are replaced with a massive open sky, shimmering greenish-brown earth, and, just occasionally, a speck of movement. It might be some camels, a pair of ostriches, or perhaps a family moving somewhere with their donkeys. It's a sparse, absorbingly simple landscape, and not the least of its attractions is the restful absence of hassle and shove, and a solitude hardly found anywhere else.

GETTING AROUND   THE NORTHEAST

Although the distances are huge, northeastern Kenya has a relatively restricted travel circuit because two-thirds of it is effectively an off-limits "orange zone" (see box, p.118). The region gets little tourism, because what appear to be major roads on the map often turn out to be rough – and at times almost indiscernible – tracks. From **Isiolo** the most popular route simply goes north to **Marsabit** and **Marsabit National Park**. Most people who visit **Moyale** are going on to Ethiopia, or arriving from there. There is also a route along the A3 road towards the coast via **Garissa**, but travel on this road was not advised at the time of writing (see p.541). You can also head northwest from Marsabit to **Lake Turkana**, via North Horr and some of the country's remotest districts; or do the reverse, leaving the more frequented route from Maralal to Lake Turkana and heading east to Marsabit.

Garissa

Some 390km east of Nairobi, on the route to Somalia, **GARISSA** is the capital of Garissa County, sprawling out widely across the plains, east of the bridge across the Tana River. Garissa used to be the furthest east you could safely go towards Somalia, but several terrorist attacks attributed to Al-Shabaab took place in 2015 – including one on Garissa University College in which at least 148 people were killed – and the town now falls into the off-limits "orange zone" (see box opposite). We have not been able to visit the area since 2012, and as a result some of the following information is likely to be out of date.

ARRIVAL AND DEPARTURE   GARISSA

By buses/matatu There are daily services between Garissa and Nairobi, with most Nairobi-bound buses terminating in Eastleigh's busy 12th Street (which also falls into the off-limits "orange zone" (see box opposite). Transport south along the Tana, and on to Malindi and Mombasa, is more intermittent. Taking buses north or east is highly inadvisable.

Destinations Hola (2 daily; 3hr); Malindi (2 daily; 8hr); Mombasa (2 daily; 11hr); Nairobi (10 daily; 7hr).

By car The A3 highway to Nairobi is fast and smooth for much of its length, with just one nasty section of potholed surface about 60km west of Garissa. Driving down the Tana on the B8 is a different matter, and you're best off with a 4WD with good suspension, plenty of fuel and two spare tyres. From the Garissa–Hola T-junction (13km west of the bridge), the road south is badly potholed at irregular intervals, but long good stretches mean a 40km/h average speed is possible. The road is particularly bad south of the Bura junction for 40km, where you'll make better speed off the road, on the sidetracks, than on it. The first 30km south of the Hola junction (where work extending north from Malindi has reached) is good tarmac. Thereafter, it's a mixture of re-surfacing and road-building as you pass the Garsen junction and the junction for Witu and Mokowe (Lamu). You can do Garissa–Malindi in five hours, but six is more comfortable.

INFORMATION

Services The KCB, Barclays and Equity banks have ATMs. There are no chain supermarkets, but Al-Fatah, beneath the *Hiddig Hotel*, is reasonable, while the friendly Garissa mini-market imports goods from the UK and is also a bit cheaper. Pharmacy Amani (daily 6am–10pm; ☎0725 580260) offers a wide range of medical services, including malaria tests (Ksh100).

▶ ACCOMMODATION AND EATING

Almond Resort Signposted on the right, 1km along Lamu Rd ☎020 232 5721 or 0711 829899, ⊛almond-resort.com. With 80 rooms, each with DSTV, decent nets and free wi-fi (but no fans), and a huge, inviting pool (Ksh500 for non-guests), this is currently the best option in Garissa. There's a large a/c gym too, though as usual no bar (the neighbouring police mess substitutes). Wi-fi. BB **Ksh6000**

Hiddig Hotel Opposite the post office ☎0720 963377. Simple but respectable rooms with a/c, fans, nets and DSTV in a convenient, central part of town, very close to shops and restaurants. BB **Ksh2500**

▶ EATING

Finding tasty pilau or pasta is easy enough, although many establishments are dry, and neither sell, nor permit the consumption of, alcohol.

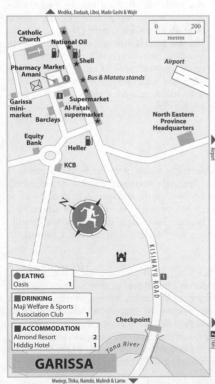

Modika, Dadaab, Liboi, Mado Gashi & Wajir

Catholic Church
National Oil
Shell
Pharmacy Market
Amani
Bus & Matatu stands
Garissa mini-market
Supermarket
Al-Fatah supermarket
Barclays
Equity Bank
Heller
KCB

0   200
metres

Airport

North Eastern Province Headquarters

KISIMAYU ROAD

Checkpoint

Tana River

● EATING
Oasis   1

■ DRINKING
Maji Welfare & Sports
Association Club   1

■ ACCOMMODATION
Almond Resort   2
Hiddig Hotel   1

GARISSA

Mwingi, Thika, Nairobi, Malindi & Lamu

TRAVEL IN THE NORTHEAST: A WARNING

Northeastern Kenya has long had a reputation for lawlessness, but what was sometimes dismissed as the exaggerations and ignorance of "down-country" Kenyans acquired a more brutal reality in the 1990s, which continues to this day. Since the flight of **Somalia**'s dictator Siad Barre in 1991, and that country's anarchic disintegration into warring fiefdoms, northeastern Kenya has borne the full brunt of Somalia's desperate refugee crisis, with increasingly violent bandits targeting commercial vehicles, foreign aid workers and refugee camps.

The northeast is also home to **pastoralist tribes** who frequently engage in livestock rustling and clash over grazing and water rights. You can be sure of one thing: there are more people than ever before with little to their names but guns and ammunition.

We've endeavoured to note the current security situation for all parts of this chapter, but as the lifetime of this guide extends to 2019, and the situation can change quickly, you are strongly advised to seek advice on the ground before travelling anywhere covered in the following pages. If you're driving in this region, ask advice everywhere you go and always stop at police checkpoints and ask them about the road ahead. You may sometimes be asked to travel in convoy, or to take an armed police officer as an escort to your next stop.

The **area to avoid** at the time of writing, according to the UK Foreign and Commonwealth Office's advice (the "orange zone" on their travel map at ⓦ bit.ly/fcoKenya), is a large, thinly populated chunk of northeastern Kenya comprising: all of Garissa and Lamu counties; all the border areas within 60km of the Somalian border; and a thin strip along the coast as far south of the Galana River. The travel advisory does not include Shaba National Reserve or Meru National Park, both of which are safe.

7

Oasis Near the bus stages. This recommended *hoteli* has all the staples: get your fix of *mandaazi*, *chai* and *karanga*

na chapatti (Ksh180). Daily 6.30am–10pm.

DRINKING

Maji Welfare & Sports Association Club Kisimayu Rd. Compared with the average upcountry bar, this is very sedate and not particularly sporty, with outdoor tables and

TVs and sodas at Ksh70, beers at Ksh150. Daily 8am–11pm.

Isiolo

ISIOLO – the northeast's most important town and the hub for travel to Marsabit and Moyale – is a frontier in every respect. The **Somali influence** here is noticeable everywhere in the northeast, and Isiolo is one of their most important towns in Kenya. It was here that many veteran Somali soldiers from World War I were settled: having been recruited in Aden and Kismayu, they gave up their nomadic lifestyle to become livestock dealers and retail traders.

The town is a real **cultural kaleidoscope**, with Boran, Meru, Samburu and some Turkana inhabitants, as well as the Somalis. To someone newly arrived from Nanyuki or Meru, the upland towns seem ordinary in comparison. Women from the irrigated *shambas* around Isiolo sell cabbages, tomatoes and carrots in the busy market; cattle owners, nomadic camel traders and merchants exchange greetings and the latest news from Nairobi and Moyale; in the livestock market, goats scamper through the alleys, while hawkers stroll along the road raising their Somali swords and strings of bangles to the minibuses heading up to reserves. And, in the shade, energetic *miraa*-chewing and hanging around are the major occupations. *Miraa* has a long history in Somali culture; the Nyambeni Hills, where most of the Kenyan crop is grown, are just 30km away (p.186).

Isiolo is lively, welcoming and relatively safe, with new solar-powered streetlights brightening it up at night, though when the tourist season is in full swing, with vehicles driving through to Samburu and the other reserves, it can seem as if you can't take a step here without being approached to buy something. If you're staying the night it's worth getting up early enough to have a chance of seeing the distinctive silhouette of **Mount Kenya** rising directly above the main A2 highway through town, 60km to the south.

ARRIVAL AND DEPARTURE   ISIOLO

By plane Isiolo's airstrip was being upgraded at the time of writing into northern Kenya's first international airport. For more information contact the Kenya Airports Authority (☏ 0722 205061, ⓦ kaa.go.ke).

By bus or matatu For southbound matatus it's best to be at the market stage (at the far end of the town if coming from the north) before sunrise – last departures at 6am are not unheard of for some destinations. For matatus heading north to Wamba, Archer's Post and Merille, the same time applies at their stages around Equity Bank. You can book bus tickets at their stages and offices the evening before.

Destinations Archer's Post (many daily; 20min); Maralal (3 daily; 4hr); Marsabit (daily with Liban and/or Moyale Express: 4hr); Maua, for Meru National Park (several daily;

2hr 30min); Merille (several daily; 2hr); Meru (many daily; 1hr); Moyale (several weekly; 12hr-plus); Nairobi (several daily with Nairobi Express; 4–5hr); Nanyuki (many daily; 2hr); Wamba (6 daily; 3hr).

By truck or hitchhiking There are usually trucks at least daily up to Marsabit and 2–3 times weekly to Moyale. Most take passengers, charging Ksh800 to Marsabit and Ksh1500 to Moyale, with supplements to ride in the cab (journey times unpredictable). For Samburu, Buffalo Springs and Shaba National Reserves (see p.377), Isiolo is the town through which nearly all road safari tourists pass.

By car The fast A2 highway sweeps north through Archer's Post and on to Merille, 137km north of Isiolo, and the gravel road from Merille to Marsabit is now graded, meaning the whole drive can be done in half a day.

INFORMATION

Services There are branches of KCB, Barclays, Consolidated, K-Rep and Equity banks, all with ATMs, as well as Western Union for money transfers. For internet

access try Rehoboth Copy Master (Mon–Fri 8am–6pm, Sat 8.30am–6pm; Ksh1.50/min).

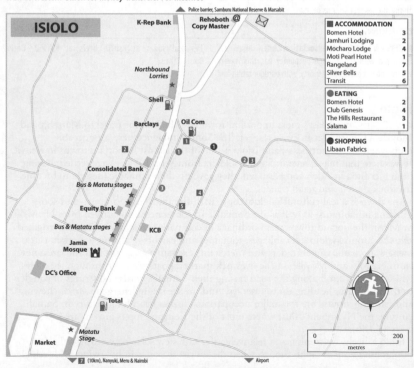

ACCOMMODATION
Bomen Hotel	3
Jamhuri Lodging	2
Mocharo Lodge	4
Moti Pearl Hotel	1
Rangeland	7
Silver Bells	5
Transit	6

EATING
Bomen Hotel	2
Club Genesis	4
The Hills Restaurant	3
Salama	1

SHOPPING
| Libaan Fabrics | 1 |

ACCOMMODATION

Isiolo has some reasonable, mid-range **hotels** and some very cheap basic lodgings. You can **camp** in the gardens of the pleasant *Rangeland Hotel*.

★**Bomen Hotel** Off the A2 highway, central Isiolo ☎0700 858882, ⓦbomenhotel.co.ke. The busiest place in town: clean, polite and serving good food in its restaurant. Rooms lack fans but have nets, TVs and electric showers. The breezy top-floor suites are relatively good value for Ksh1000 extra. Free wi-fi (in theory). BB Ksh3500

★**Jamhuri Lodging** Off the A2 highway, central Isiolo ☎0722 384544. Relatively clean, courteous, mellow (no alcohol or prostitutes allowed) and incredibly cheap, although rooms are non-s/c (there are s/c rooms for Ksh50 more in their building around the corner). Hot water mornings only. The nets are a bit perfunctory and/or badly hung, but the instant showers look safer than usual. Secure parking in the compound. Wi-fi. Room only Ksh500

Mocharo Lodge Off the A2 highway, central Isiolo ☎0700 858676. With excellent security, top-floor "suites", with TV and nets, friendly staff and a good dining room downstairs, this is very good value for money. S/c and non-s/c rooms available. Safe parking in courtyard. BB Ksh1800

Moti Pearl Hotel A2 highway, central Isiolo ☎0725 800820, ⓦmoti.co.ke. Although relatively new, this aspiring "pearl of Isiolo" is too lacking in atmosphere to be really appealing. The balconies are good, but apart from

the functional breakfast room, there's nowhere to eat or hang out and alcohol is neither served nor tolerated. BB Ksh3500

Rangeland 10km south of Isiolo ☎0720 060038 or 0721 434353, ⓦbit.ly/Rangeland. Set in pleasant grounds, around which hyraxes scamper, the rooms in the eight garden cottages are decent value, with nets but no other extras. A little above the average B&L, this is a popular out-of-town drinking spot, and tends to be noisy in the evenings. Camping Ksh500, BB Ksh2500

Silver Bells Off the A2 highway, central Isiolo ☎0702 591757, ⓦsilverbellshotelisiolo.com. The newest place to stay in Isiolo, with clean and comfortable rooms, all with European toilets and hot showers, though not much personality. The nice rooftop area with a couple of wooden tables and chairs is probably the biggest selling point; there's no bar, so if you want a drink ask downstairs and take it up yourself. Wi-fi. BB Ksh3000

Transit Off the A2 highway, central Isiolo ☎0723 362669. Simple, clean rooms with nets and fans but old-style showers (hot water mornings only), and not as good as *Mocharo*, which it competes with. Forty-eight rooms, comfy enough, but overpriced. BB Ksh2500

EATING

Most of the Somali *hotelis* provide excellent **food**, day and night. You'll see pasta (usually spaghetti) appearing quite prominently on menus – one of the better Italian bequests to the Somalis.

Bomen Hotel Off the A2 highway, central Isiolo ☎0700 858882, ⓦbomenhotel.co.ke. Ground-floor bar and restaurant, doing grills (most dishes Ksh300–400) and beer (Ksh180). Popular outdoor *nyama choma* grill. Daily 6am–11pm or later.

Club Genesis Off the A2 highway, central Isiolo. Busy bar and *nyama choma* joint, catering primarily to upcountry clients, and vibrating with deafening reggae by night. Daily 24hr.

The Hills Restaurant A2 highway, central Isiolo ☎0711 502609, ⓦbit.ly/TheHillsIsiolo. Bustling bar, restaurant (pancakes Ksh80, quarter-chicken Ksh250) and *nyama choma* barbecue (beef Ksh500/kg), offering beers at Ksh180 and wine from Ksh800/bottle. Daily 6.30am–11pm.

Salama A2 highway, central Isiolo. Friendly and popular place, recommended for an early breakfast or the very good spaghetti with gravy. Daily 6am–10pm.

SHOPPING

Isiolo is one of the best places to buy copper, brass and aluminium **bracelets**, costing around Ksh50 for simple ones, and from Ksh100 for the heavier, more complicated designs – assuming you bargain effectively (starting prices are much higher). Short **"Somali swords"** in red leather scabbards are also much in evidence. The lads who mob you near the markets will invariably offer to guide you to one of the few blacksmiths in town to watch the fascinating process of twisting the wires for the bangles. Profits come from buying rough bangles, then polishing and selling them. If you go, you're generally expected to make a purchase and tip a few shillings to the young man. For their part, women offer small **wooden dolls** with woven hair, which in the past were given to young girls as both toys and fertility charms.

Libaan Fabrics Between the A2 main road and the Bomen Hotel. A good place to buy local fabrics, offering a well-priced range of two-piece sets and large, ornately

woven *gutina* cloths, with silver thread and tassels. Daily 9am–9pm.

To Marsabit and North Horr

At one time, no matter what speed you travelled, this was a fantastically uncomfortable trip, with rocks, ruts and corrugations that knocked the daylights out of most vehicles and could shake smaller cars almost literally to bits. That picture may return in the future, but as of mid-2015 the road **from Isiolo to Marsabit** was beautifully surfaced nearly the whole way (the tarmac drops out about 50km before you reach Marsabit) and work was under way to finish the remaining stretch – by the time you read this it should have been completed. When complete, the whole journey should be feasible in about three and a half hours in a private 4WD.

Archer's Post

35km north of Isiolo • Fuel is available at the Safaris Oil petrol station • Gate for Samburu National Reserve (see p.377)

Driving north from Isiolo, and passing over the occasionally dry, occasionally flooded Ewaso Nyiro River, you hit the agglomeration of shiny-roofed shacks, rows of *dukas* and a scattering of cheap lodgings and *hotelis* that is **ARCHER'S POST**. This is as far north as you'll easily get by matatu, although the odd vehicle continues to Laisamis.

Ol Olokwe

Climbing the mountain will cost $20 conservancy fee plus whatever you negotiate for your guide – Ksh1000 for the day is about right, or more if you're in a group

North of Archer's Post, the road veers northwest and for thirty minutes the great mesa of **Ol Olokwe Mountain** (also known as Ol Doinyo Sabache) spreads massively across the horizon in front of you. If you're travelling independently with your own vehicle, you'll be in a position to climb it. If you want to have a crack at this, take the Wamba road and stop at the first village, Lerata; find the General Store and start asking for the Namunyak Conservancy manager (see p.529). You can climb Ol Olokwe in a day from Lerata with a crack-of-dawn start, or camp at *Sabrash Camp* (no phone, ask in Lerata) at the bottom of the mountain, which has *bandas* and a decent bar.

Ol Olokwe to Marsabit

For an hour north of Ol Olokwe you speed through a Wild West landscape of rearing mountains and endless bush. At the hamlet of Sereolipi, 62km from Archer's Post, there's a turning left, for *Sarara Camp* (see p.529). Look out for the **Cat and Mouse mesas** to the east of the road, and stay alert for **wildlife** by the road: ostrich, elephant, various antelopes, zebra and giraffe can all be seen.

At the bridge over the **Merille lugga**, you start crossing the flat **Kaisut Desert** and plough through the **Losai National Reserve**– scrubby bush like the rest of the scenery around here. The desert settlement of **Laisamis** isn't much of a break – a windblown strew of tin-roofed huts, offering sodas and *chai* to travellers. The **approach to Marsabit**, however, is unmistakeable. The road begins to climb and suddenly you're on a hilly island in the desert, a region of multiple volcanic craters, lush meadows and forest. The branches of the trees on the steep slopes are disguised by swathes of Spanish moss, looking at first glance like algae-covered rocks in shades of grey and green.

Marsabit

MARSABIT is a surprise. It's hard to prepare yourself, after the flat dust lands, for this fascinating hill oasis – in the desert but not of it. Rising a thousand metres above the surrounding plains, **Mount Marsabit**, or *Saku*, as it is known by locals, is permanently green, well watered by the clouds that form and disperse over it in a daily cycle. The high forest is usually mist-covered until late morning, the trees a characteristic tangle of foliage and lianas.

FROM TOP FOOTHILLS OF MOUNT NYIRU (P.531); KALACHA CATHOLIC CHURCH (P.550) >

The town is the capital of the largest administrative district in the country, as well as a major meat- and livestock-trading centre, its rough roads either dusty or churned with mud. Small and intimate in feel, the lively cultural mix in the main market area is the biggest buzz: transient **Gabbra** herdsmen and **Boran** with their prized short-horn cattle, women in the printed shawls and chiffon wraps of **Somali** costume rubbing elbows with ochre-daubed **Rendille** wearing skins, high stacks of beads and wire, and fantastic braided hairstyles. There are government workers here, too, from other parts of Kenya, and a scattering of **Ethiopian immigrants** (mainly Burji) and refugees. For some Marsabit background, try Mude Dae Mude's novel *The Hills are Falling* (1979), now out of print, but you might still find a copy in Nairobi.

Hill and crater walks

There are several excursions you can do from Marsabit in a few hours. An easy short walk, for example, takes you up to a big, wind-powered **generator** on a hill just west of the town. A slightly longer hike goes up to the **VOK transmitter** behind the town, a route that passes through lush forest and offers magnificent panoramas of the whole district from the top.

The closest sizeable crater to Marsabit town is **Gof Redo**, about 5km north of the centre, in the fork of the roads to Moyale and North Horr. Either drive or walk out along the North Horr road until you see tracks branching off right after about 500m. If you have a vehicle you can drive most of the way to the base of the crater itself: head for the low col about 1.5km ahead: the gentler west side of the crater wall rises up here. There are some *manyattas* on the southwest rim, and you should be able to hire a guide quite easily if you want to scramble down inside Gof in an hour or two. The crater is quite a favoured hideout for greater kudu.

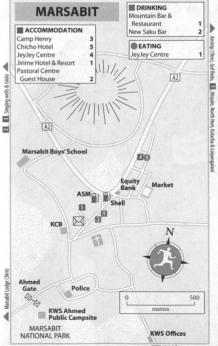

MARSABIT

■ **ACCOMMODATION**
Camp Henry	3
Chicho Hotel	5
JeyJey Centre	4
Jirime Hotel & Resort	1
Pastoral Centre Guest House	2

■ **DRINKING**
Mountain Bar & Restaurant	1
New Saku Bar	2

● **EATING**
JeyJey Centre	1

A2

Marsabit Boys' School

Equity Bank — Market

ASM — Shell

KCB

N

Ahmed Gate — Police

KWS Ahmed Public Campsite

MARSABIT NATIONAL PARK

KWS Offices

Abdul Gate

0 — 500 metres

Airstrip (1km); Gof Redo,

Moyale, North Horr, Kalacha & Loiyangalani

Singing wells & Isiolo

Marsabit Lodge (3km)

The singing wells

Guides will take you to the well for about Ksh500

A popular local walk goes to the "**singing wells**" near Ulanula (also known as Hula-Hula), a conical peak to the west of the Isiolo road, about 6km from town. These are less exotic than they sound, but they're still a good excuse to explore. Leaving Marsabit, you cross two bridges, then turn left and climb 200–300m up a narrow, tangled ravine. A concrete holding-tank, visible from the road, gives the place away. Behind it are two natural wells, the first with a wooden trough in front, the second longer and apparently deeper, containing a fluctuating depth of brown, frog-filled water. A silent pump house stands by.

The **singing** is done not by the wells but by the Boran herders who use them. When the water is low, human chains are formed to get it out with luxuriantly leaking leather buckets, and singing helps the work. At the driest times of the year you may be lucky and witness this, but try to get here early; animals are usually driven to the wells after dawn. without a vehicle it's a brisk 75-minute walk from

PEOPLES OF THE NORTHEAST

Identities in the northeast can be confusing to foreigners. The largest group are the **Boran**, part of the **Oromo peoples** (formerly called Galla, an Amhara term of abuse), whose homeland was near the Bale Mountains in Ethiopia, from where they suddenly exploded out, in all directions, in the sixteenth century. The pastoral Boran developed and flourished in what is now southern Ethiopia, but Menelik's conquest of the area and the oppressive Amhara regime caused some of them to move down to the lowlands of northern Kenya, a much less suitable region for their cattle. The first Boran arrived in Marsabit only in 1921.

Similarly, the **Burji** are recent Ethiopian immigrants to the region between Marsabit and Moyale – an agricultural people who were encouraged to move south by colonial administrators in the 1930s who wanted more crops grown in the district. The Burji took quickly to Western education and trade, and as a result dominated Marsabit politically in the first decade after independence. There's traditionally little love lost between the nomadic Boran and the settled Burji.

At around the time of the Oromo expansion, another group of people – the forefathers of the Gabbra – arrived in northern Kenya, causing havoc in the region, only to be themselves pressured by the ensuing expansion of **Muslim Somalis** from the east. The ancestors of the **Gabbra** became "Boranized" to the extent that they changed their language and adopted Boran customs. Although most Boran and Gabbra, especially those who adopted a more sedentary life, have adopted Somali styles in dress and culture, they eschew Islam, preferring their own religions.

The **Rendille**, whose homeland is to the northwest of Marsabit, look and act like Samburu, with whom they are frequently allied; they speak a language close to Somali but have non-Muslim religious beliefs. They normally herd camels rather than cattle and, to a great extent, continue to roam the deserts, facing the prospect of settling down without any enthusiasm at all and visiting Marsabit only for vital needs or a brief holiday.

In Marsabit itself, distinctions other than superficial ones were becoming increasingly hard to apply by the 1990s, as people intermarried, sent more children to school and absorbed new ideas from Nairobi – and from Christian missionaries. Still, language and religious beliefs remain significant in deciding who does what and with whom. Outside the town individual tribal identities are as strong – and potentially bloody – as ever. Since the massacre in 2005 at Turbi (a remote village 150km north of Marsabit), when Boran warriors attacked Gabbra villagers during a flare-up of customary inter-tribal cattle rustling, and killed sixty people, Marsabit has seen a deep chill in relations between the different peoples.

7

town. Go out there in the late afternoon, though, and you should get a lift back with one of the day's vehicles up from Isiolo. Alternatively, local guides tend to know exactly when the singing will take place, so ask around in town.

ARRIVAL AND DEPARTURE — MARSABIT

By plane MAF (Mission Aviation Fellowship; bookings on ✉ ke-bookings@MAF.org) operates flights from Nairobi Wilson to Marsabit and back, once or twice a week, usually on Tues and/or Fri mornings. When seats are available the going rate is Ksh10,000 one-way.

By bus or truck Buses (the older Liban and more modern Moyale Express) connect Moyale, Marsabit, Isiolo and Nairobi more or less daily, sometimes running more than one service. Marsabit–Nairobi is a 12hr trip (Ksh1500). The Isiolo bus leaves at 6am and the Nairobi one at 9am. If you're moving on from Marsabit by any available means, you'll find that one or two trucks usually spend the night here, en route from Moyale or Isiolo. The best place to wait for a lift south to Isiolo (going rate: Ksh800 in the back, Ksh1400 in the cab) is at the police checkpoint on the Isiolo road 3.5km from the Shell station. For a lift to Moyale

(same prices), ask at the petrol stations or around the *JeyJey Centre*. Transport along the Lake Turkana road (Maikona, Kalacha, North Horr, Loiyangalani, Sibiloi National Park) is rare, with only a few vehicles each day – and sometimes none – and very little in the way of goods vehicles. Ask at the camps and hotels.

By car For servicing and parts, the best store is the ASM petrol station and garage. With the improvement of the A2 highway from 50km south of Marsabit to Isiolo (see p.544), vehicles travel faster and security seems to have improved. Safety may deteriorate again, however, during the lifetime of this edition, so always ask about the road ahead as you pass through police checkpoints. As of mid-2015, private vehicles were travelling freely – unescorted and not in convoys – between Marsabit and Isiolo and Marsabit and Loiyangalani. The route from Marsabit to Loiyangalani via North Horr and

Kalacha is rough in parts, but feasible in all weathers – though you'll need GPS and/or a guide as passenger in one or two places where the route is unclear. When it's dry, most vehicles shoot across the Chalbi desert – not possible after rain when the floodwaters cover huge areas. Allow a full day, or ideally two, and make an early start.

INFORMATION

Services There are KCB and Equity banks, both with ATMs. Marsabit has a post office and there's reasonable mobile network in town, though it's very patchy in the national park.

ACCOMMODATION

There's a fair spread of cheap accommodation in town – plus the tourist lodge in the national park. Wherever you choose, ask about **hot water** before moving in, as nights can get chilly (by some accounts, *Marsabit* means "place of cold") and lukewarm showers are no fun here. Moreover, in recent years, Marsabit has experienced terrible problems with water supplies. To **camp**, most people head for *Camp Henry*, but you can also camp just inside the national park's main gate (though you have to pay park fees); see below.

★**Camp Henry** Signposted off the north side of the Isiolo road, 2km west of the Shell station, then 1.4km north ☎020 8004392, ✉dommann@africaonline.co.ke. Excellent campsite, popular with self-catering overlanders, run by a Swiss former volunteer and Marsabit resident of 38 years and his wife, with shady pitches, clean showers and toilets. There's also a fine turf-roofed dorm bunkhouse (Samburu-hut-meets-Swiss-chalet, non-s/c) with four single beds and two twin bunks, with bedding. The shared rondavel-lounge has a fridge and there's a BBQ with free firewood. Camping **Ksh400**, dorm beds **Ksh500**

Chicho Hotel Behind the post office ☎0706 153827, ⓦchichohotel.com. This is the boutique offering among Marsabit's digs, with five cute, somewhat cramped rooms, fitted out with flatscreen DSTVs, electric showers, plus a pleasant dining room for breakfast and snacks. Wi-fi. BB **Ksh3500**

JeyJey Centre Isiolo–Moyale road ☎0728 808802. Pleasant, if not entirely clean and now shabby in parts, *JeyJey* has 30 rooms, mostly non s/c (Ksh500 extra for s/c

with squat loo). It's owned by former Saku MP Jarso Falana, who sometimes trucks water in from far away to supply guests. Patchy wi-fi. Room only **Ksh1000**

★**Jirime Hotel & Resort** Isiolo–Moyale road ☎0704 232065, ⓦjirimehotel.com. Just north of Marsabit town, this is the most luxurious place to stay in the area. It's set on sixteen acres of farmland with pleasant views of the surrounding scrub. Like many of the accommodation options in the north, the interior is still fairly basic and characterless, but the rooms are clean and spacious and the beds comfortable. Wi-fi. BB **Ksh5000**

Pastoral Centre Guest House Signposted off the north side of the Isiolo road, 1.8km west of the Shell station, then 500m north ☎020 2059329. Clean, quiet and secure accommodation, with a chapel, pleasant grounds and accommodation in s/c single rooms (no doubles), plus dorms with shared showers and toilets. Simple meals are included, and beers or sodas can be obtained if requested. BB **Ksh1500** (single), **Ksh1000 for a dorm.**

EATING

JeyJey Centre Isiolo–Moyale road ☎0728 808802. The best place to eat in Marsabit (spaghetti bolognese Ksh250, beef stew and chapatti Ksh240) though there's no bar. Daily 6am–8.30pm.

DRINKING

Mountain Bar & Restaurant Between the Shell station and post office. Friendly die-hards' drinking den, with sodas at Ksh80 and beers for Ksh150, but no evidence of food. Daily 8am–11pm.

New Saku Bar Next door to Mountain Bar. Similar in most respects to its neighbour, if a little more restrained, this is largely an evening haunt and sometimes fills with drivers en route to Moyale or Isiolo. Daily 9am–10pm.

Marsabit National Park

The main (Ahmed) gate is at the edge of town, past the bank and the District Commissioner's office • $25 • ⓦbit.ly/MarsabitNP • 1554 square kilometres

Having made the long journey to Marsabit, you'll certainly want to get into **Marsabit National Park**. The forest is wild and dense and the two crater lakes idyllically beautiful, although between the nearly impenetrable forests of the peaks and the stony scrub desert at the base of the mountain, you'll need a little luck for wildlife sightings. This is a rewarding park, but one where your animal count will very much depend on the season of your visit. Good rains can encourage the grazers off the mountain and out into the temporarily lush desert, and predators will follow.

Except during the long rains (March to June), you're reasonably likely to see some of the long-tusked Marsabit **elephants** – head to Gof Sokorte Guda (Lake Paradise) at sunset for the best chance. The elephants are relatives of the park's former inhabitant, the famous Ahmed – a particularly huge and well-endowed "big tusker" to whom Kenya's founding president Jomo Kenyatta gave "presidential protection" after seeing him, with elephant guards tracking him day and night – ironically, since Kenyatta's family were implicated in some of Kenya's biggest ivory smuggling scandals. Ahmed is, nonetheless, impressively replicated in fibreglass in the National Museum in Nairobi. His replacement, Mohammed, whose tusks were estimated at a cool 45kg each, has also gone to the elephant's graveyard. Elephants are tremendous wanderers, sometimes strolling into town, causing pandemonium. More problematically, the people of Marsabit have been encouraged to cultivate around the base of the mountain, thus creating a barrier to the elephants' free movement and unintentionally providing them with free lunches.

As well as big tuskers, the park is renowned for its **greater kudu**, and there's a wide range of other wildlife, plus an amazing array of **birds**: almost four hundred species have been recorded, including 52 different birds of prey. Very rare **lammergeiers** (bearded vultures) are thought to nest on the sheer cliffs of Gof Bongole, the largest crater, which has a driveable track around its 10km rim. Marsabit is also something of a **snake** sanctuary, with some very large cobras – this isn't a place to go barefoot or in sandals.

ARRIVAL AND DEPARTURE   MARSABIT NATIONAL PARK

The best way to see the park if you don't have your own vehicle is to hire a **guide** in Marsabit who can arrange transport for about Ksh3000 per day (including guide fee); try Jamal (☎0721 886113). A short trip will take you to the view over the first lake – Gof Sokorte Dika – and its forested rim, or you can venture right to Lake Paradise. You might also be able to convince an **armed ranger** to escort you on foot as far as the first lake (a Ksh1000 payment should be enough). This is a wonderful walk through the

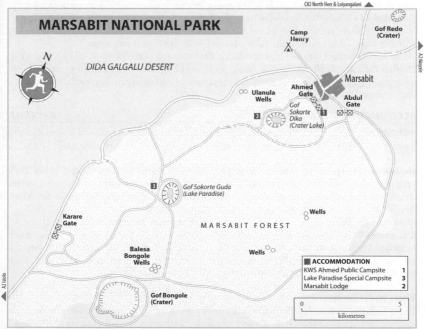

MARSABIT NATIONAL PARK

C82 North Horr & Loiyangalani

A2 Moyale

A2 Isiolo

DIDA GALGALU DESERT

Camp Henry

Gof Redo (Crater)

Marsabit

Ulanula Wells

Ahmed Gate

Abdul Gate

Gof Sokorte Dika (Crater Lake)

Gof Sokorte Guda (Lake Paradise)

Wells

Karare Gate

MARSABIT FOREST

Balesa Bongole Wells

Wells

Gof Bongole (Crater)

■ **ACCOMMODATION**
KWS Ahmed Public Campsite   1
Lake Paradise Special Campsite 3
Marsabit Lodge   2

0   5
kilometres

forest, with clouds of butterflies and the occasional mouth-drying encounter with buffalo or elephant. Don't attempt to **drive in the park** without 4WD, as many of the roads are steep and tend to be ridiculously muddy. If you have your own vehicle, head for the Ahmed Gate (the only one with decent road access into the park) and ask the rangers at the gate to direct you.

ACCOMMODATION

KWS Ahmed Public Campsite Near Ahmed gate, 100m down the hairpin to the left of the ranger's house ☎0722 857233. This is a wonderfully shaded spot, somewhat overrun with baboons. $20

Lake Paradise Special Campsite Lake Paradise (Gof Sokorte Guda) ☎0722 857233 (Nairobi reservations ☎0726 610508, ⓦkws.go.ke). A stunning, dark pool for much of the year, Lake Paradise has a wonderful KWS "special campsite" deep in the forest on its crater rim, where elephant, lion, leopard and the rare and shaggy striped hyena are all seen and heard from time to time. It requires a security vehicle (Ksh300) with someone to keep an eye on you, but you'll be left alone with your campfire for an

evening. No facilities – you need to bring everything. $35

★**Marsabit Lodge** On the shore of Gof Sokorte Dika ☎0722 328394, ⓦmarsabitlodge.com. Outstanding views and the exquisite peace and beauty of its location, with wildlife converging at the lake and eagles swooping through the trees, compensate for the fairly rudimentary comforts (for a tourist-class lodge) and rather spooky emptiness. The lodge was semi-closed for years but had a facelift a few years ago and provides all the essentials, including electric showers and clean sheets, so long as you don't expect luxury or style. There's a bar, veranda and dining room (serving adequate, filling meals), a generator in the mornings and evenings and very nice staff. HB Ksh9500

Maikona

MAIKONA, 90km from Marsabit on the road to North Horr, is a friendly Gabbra settlement on the fringes of the Chalbi Desert, with the last fresh water for 35km and a thriving daily market for goats and cattle. As with all the villages up here, keep your camera out of sight, and ask permission if you want to take **photographs**: belief in the camera's evil eye is prevalent.

Kalacha

The springs of **Kalacha Goda** are the *raison d'être* for the small town of **KALACHA**. You'll find them on the southwest side of the sprawling settlement, usually surrounded by hundreds of camels. While you're here, the **Kalacha Catholic Church** (unmissable in the "centre" of town, on the east side of the road; free entry; Mass 9am Sunday) is well worth a look, its interior beautifully adorned with Ethiopian paintings.

The first **Kalacha Cultural Food and Music Festival** took place in April 2012, on similar lines to the Lake Turkana Festival (see p.533), and has become an annual event, now taking place in December. Contact the organizers, Kivulini Trust, for further details and timings (ⓦkivulinitrust.org).

ACCOMMODATION AND EATING   KALACHA

Tropic Air's *Kalacha Camp*, a community collaboration 2.5km southwest of the AIC (African Inland Church) mission and formerly the area's best accommodation, has sadly closed down indefinitely. Note that there is little to no mobile signal in Kalacha.

Abudo Ganya's Lodge 500m west of the AIC mission. Reasonable non-s/c *banda* camp (run by the twin brother of the local MP Chachu Ganya), with food available to order, though sadly no longer a functioning swimming pool. Whole *banda* Ksh1000

Acacia Camp AIC mission compound (no phone). With its shady pitches, showers and toilets, and the bonus of the inventive "tank" swimming pool supplied by a wind pump from the borehole, this is better than you have any right to

expect out in these northern badlands. They have a full-service garage for emergency repairs, and services in their church, with its stained-glass windows, on Sun at 9am. Camping Ksh500

Chalbi Safari Resort 1km southwest of the AIC mission ☎0727 218556. Women's group project specializing in cultural dances. Small non-s/c *bandas*, a camping area and meals available to order. *Banda* Ksh2500, camping Ksh400

The Chalbi Desert

From Kalacha to North Horr, the track streaks out over the blinding white saltpans and shifting soft sands of the **Chalbi Desert**, ducks behind straggly oasis clusters of half-dead palm trees and finally loses itself in a vast orange expanse rimmed only by the hulks of distant mountains. There are many routes and the best path to take varies annually. In April and May when the rains come, the desert routes are often impassable and drivers use a more northerly, rocky route to avoid the flooded plains.

North Horr

NORTH HORR, when you finally reach it, is a welcome haven (although searingly hot), with a handful of *dukas* and *hotelis*, a busy Catholic mission and a number of NGOs, including the base of VSF Germany, the veterinarian support group working with pastoralists.

From here on down to Loiyangalani, the route – rarely much more than a set of wheel tracks – shifts between sandy *luggas* liable to flood and crunchy, black lava plains, as it skirts the northern flanks of Mount Kulal. The views, when you crest the ridge, looking down over Lake Turkana far away, can be spellbinding.

ACCOMMODATION AND EATING   **NORTH HORR**

Catholic Mission Guest House North Horr centre ☎0720 959708. Simple but not very clean non s/c twin rooms, with shared shower and toilet. Room only __Ksh600__ per person

Midland Entertainment North Horr centre, opposite the New Mandera. When you really need a cold drink, this has one of North Horr's most reliably stocked fridges. Daily 7am–9pm.

New Mandera Tourist Hotel North Horr centre ☎0716 628080 (phone signal is very poor). Rooms available at the back of the compound, with no nets or refinements. *Chai*, chapattis, cold sodas, pilau and spaghetti are always available at rock-bottom prices, as are the genuinely helpful family and friends to guide you on your way. Room only __Ksh300__

To Moyale and Ethiopia

From Marsabit, the **journey to Moyale**, which straddles the Ethiopian border, takes upwards of eight hours depending on the vehicle. For the first three of these you descend from the mountain's greenery past spectacular craters – **Gof Choba** is the whopper on the left – to the forbidding black moonscape of the **Dida Galgalu Desert**. Dida Galgalu means "plains of darkness", according to one old story told by Boran pastoralists. Another account derives it from Galgalu, a woman buried here after she died of thirst trying to cross it. The road arrows north for endless kilometres, then cuts east across watercourses and through bushier country beneath high crags on the Ethiopian frontier. En route, you pass the turning to the small village of **Sololo** on the Ethiopian border, arrestingly sited between soaring peaks that can be climbed for stunning views over the northern plains and Ethiopian highlands.

There are some magnificent, towering **termite mounds** along the northern part of the route. They're a sight that seems quintessentially African, yet one that can quickly be taken for granted, like leafless trees in a northern winter. As the kilometres roll away, the 250km from Marsabit to Moyale is resolved in just a few bends and a couple of minor scenery changes. Over distances that would take days to cover on foot you can see where you have been and where you are going – a still, vast landscape seemingly echoed in the pastoralists' conservatism.

Towards the end of the journey, the road bends south, then doubles north again and winds up through the settlements of Burji farmers – an agricultural people who emigrated from Ethiopia early in the twentieth century (see box, p.547) – past their beautifully sculpted houses and sparse fields, to Moyale.

Moyale

Straddling the Ethiopian border, **MOYALE** makes Marsabit look like a metropolis. Though the town is growing rapidly, the centre is small enough to walk around in fifteen minutes. You'll find several sandy streets, a pretty mosque, a few *dukas*, a bar, a

7

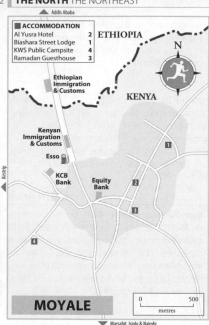

▲ Addis Ababa

■ ACCOMMODATION
Al Yusra Hotel	2
Biashara Street Lodge	1
KWS Public Campsite	4
Ramadan Guesthouse	3

ETHIOPIA

N

Ethiopian Immigration & Customs

KENYA

Kenyan Immigration & Customs

Esso

KCB Bank

Equity Bank

Airstrip

MOYALE

0   500
metres

▼ Marsabit, Isiolo & Nairobi

camel-tethering ground, two petrol stations (one of which occasionally belies its defunct appearance), a big police station, a fairly large market area, two banks with ATMs and an incredibly slow post office. Moyale is not much to write home about in fact, and there's not a lot to do except wander around, perhaps try some camel milk (very rich and creamy) and pass the time of day with everyone else, with or without the aid of *miraa*, universally popular in the northeast (see p.186).

The most interesting aspect of Moyale is its **architecture** – at least, the good number of traditionally built houses that are still standing. The Boran build in several styles, including circular mud-and-thatch huts, but in town the houses are rectangular, made of mud and dung on a wood frame, with a flat or slightly tilted roof projecting 1–2m to form a porch, supported by sturdy posts and tree trunks. The roof is up to 50cm thick, a fantastic accretion of dried mud, sticks, scrap and vegetation. Chickens and goats get up there, improving the roof's fertility, and every time it rains another layer of insulating herbage springs up. As a result, the houses are cool while the outside temperature hovers above 30°C for most of the year.

ARRIVAL AND DEPARTURE   MOYALE

By bus Liban bus and the faster and more comfortable Moyale Express connect Moyale with Marsabit and Isiolo daily (the Moyale Express continues to Nairobi). Moyale to Marsabit is generally a 8hr-plus trip, with the continuation to Isiolo taking another 6hr and Nairobi a further 5hr.

By truck If there's no bus, or the bus is full, goods trucks are usually available to get you as far as Marsabit, where there's more transport. Expect to pay around Ksh300–500 riding on top or in the back, and several hundred shillings more to get a seat in the cab.

By car If you've just crossed the border from Ethiopia, you'll be pleased to know that roads south towards Nairobi are better than they've been for years, though the section as far as Marsabit will still test your vehicle. Depending on inter-ethnic tensions in the Moyale area and banditry incidents on the road, you may have to travel in convoy, but this security measure seems to be on the wane as the improved roads encourage more – and faster – traffic, and regular police checkpoints reduce the need for convoys.

ACCOMMODATION

There's no shortage of **accommodation**, but finding anything above the very low budget category is tricky – and most of the local *hotelis* and bars are equally basic when it comes to **meals and drinks**. *Al Yusra* is by far your best bet. The water in Moyale can be briny at times, and it's worth bringing as much drinking water with you as you can.

★**Al Yusra Hotel** Town centre (it's the unmissable orange building by the hospital) ✆0722 257028, ⓦalyusrahotelmoyale.co.ke. Moyale's only proper hotel, with clean, s/c rooms with hot showers and decent meals

available in the *Maasai Mara Restaurant*. Wi-fi. BB **Ksh3000**

Biashara Street Lodge Out of the town centre (no phone). A very clean and quiet place with showers, but inconveniently located. Room only Ksh500

KWS Public Campsite West side of Moyale. The Kenya Wildlife Service campsite on the west side of town has showers and toilets but no other facilities. You're likely to run into other overland travellers here. Camping Ksh500

Ramadan Guesthouse Near the mosque (no phone). Very clean, and in a relatively quiet area that's usefully close to the town centre. Room only Ksh500

Into Ethiopia

Even if you're not intending to travel in **Ethiopia** (and if you haven't got a visa already, you won't be able to do so), the most interesting prospect in Moyale is to cross the valley into Kenya's neighbouring state and spend a few hours there. For Kenyans and Ethiopians, the border is an open one. It used to be possible for foreigners wanting to have a short look around to be granted entry for a couple of hours without a passport, but heightened security means this is no longer generally permitted. You can still try to persuade the Ethiopian immigration officers that a quick visit to their country would make your day –but you'll certainly have to leave your passport with them for safekeeping.

Ethiopian Moyale is larger than its Kenyan counterpart and somewhat more prosperous, with piped water, and a long-established electricity supply. In town, there are lots of simple stores, and plenty of eating places. You can pay for everything in Kenyan shillings. The market buzzes colourfully with camels and goats, piles of spices, flour and vegetables. Otherwise, life here seems much the same as over the border, but easier. As a back-door view of Ethiopia, however, it is no more representative than the other side of town is of Kenya.

7

GABBRA WOMAN, LOIYANGALANI

Contexts

History

Kenya's pre-colonial past is still the subject of endless conjecture, and it can be difficult for the traveller to make much sense of it – especially since the physical record in ancient architecture is virtually nonexistent upcountry. On the coast, settlement ruins, old documents and the Islamic tradition help to convey the past. What follows, up to the colonial period, is a much condensed overview, intended to pull together the historical accounts of individual peoples that are given throughout the Guide. More emphasis is given here to the history of the last hundred years or so.

The cradle of humankind

Kenya is quite likely to be the place where human beings first evolved. Some of the oldest fossils of **ancestral hominins** have been found in the Tugen Hills, and the remains of what are thought to be our later ancestors were discovered on the shores of Lake Turkana. Even so, concrete evidence of the origins of humanity remains scant, and new finds could easily turn the latest theories upside down.

The East African **Rift Valley** is ideal territory for the search for human origins: volcanic eruptions have repeatedly showered thick layers of ash and cinders over fossil beds, building up strata that can be reliably used to compare ages. The **Leakey** family has been instrumental in much of the work that has been done. Olduvai Gorge in Tanzania was the first major site to disclose evidence of human prehistory, and Louis Leakey and his wife, Mary, worked there from the 1930s. Their son, Richard, went on to explore the Turkana region and found even older fossils, putting Kenya under the scientific spotlight. A suggestion in support of the "cradle of humankind" idea is that the Rift Valley's very formation – a major event on the earth's crust, which began some twenty million years ago – could have been the environmental spark that was the catalyst for human evolution.

In 2000, the Tugen Hills yielded finds from around six million years ago of a hitherto unknown species named *Orrorin tugenensis*. It was possibly the **first hominin** – that is to say, the first known specimen of a creature on our side of the evolutionary divide between humans and the modern-day great apes – although *Sahelanthropus tchadensis*, discovered in Chad in 2002, is another possible contender. The *O. tugenensis* remains were of a creature that was still an ape, but one that walked upright on two legs. Specimens have also been found in Kenya of the hominins known as **australopithecines**, which seem to have appeared around 4.2 million years ago. Samples of *Australopithecus anamensis*, the earliest known australopithecine, were unearthed on the east side of Lake Turkana in 1965. Examples of later australopithecines have also been found in Kenya, but it is no longer thought that these were our direct ancestors. Evidence that they were not comes in the form of **fossil skull 1470** (its catalogue

20 million years ago	6 million years ago	4.2 million years ago
Rift Valley formed	Earliest human ancestors live in Tugen Hills	Australopithecines inhabit Rift Valley

number), discovered by Bernard Ngeneo in 1972 and now in the National Museum in Nairobi (see p.113). Dated at 1.9 million years old, it was first believed to be an example of *Homo habilis* ("Handy man") and later renamed *Homo rudolfensis*. It proved that the earliest members of our genus, *Homo*, had co-existed with the later australopithecines.

Almost as important was the discovery in 1984 of the nearly complete 1.6-million-year-old skeleton of 12-year-old "**Turkana Boy**", a member of the later species *Homo erectus* ("Upright man"), the immediate ancestor of the human species, found at Nariokotome on the western shore of Lake Turkana. It was probably *Homo erectus* who developed **speech** and discovered how to make **fire**, while improving enormously on the **tool-making** efforts of *Homo habilis*. **Olorgasailie** and **Kariandusi** are two "hand-axe" sites, probably belonging to *Homo erectus*, which have been used within the last five hundred thousand years. And it was *Homo erectus* who, if the "cradle" theory is right, spread the humanoid gene pool to Asia, Europe and the rest of Africa, where, over the next few hundred thousand years, *Homo sapiens* emerged on the scene.

Early inhabitants: up to 1600

Real history begins with *Homo sapiens*, living as **hunter-gatherers**. Numbering probably fewer than a hundred thousand, living in small units of several families, and either staying in one place for generations or moving through the country according to the dictates of the seasons, these earliest human inhabitants of Kenya may have been related to the ancestors of present-day Pygmy and Khoisan (Bushmen) peoples, and probably spoke "click" languages similar to those of today's Khoisan peoples of southern Africa and Tanzania.

The earliest distinct migration to Kenya was of **Cushitic**-speaking people from the Ethiopian Highlands who are thought to have arrived some time between 9000 BC and 1000 BC. Occasional hunters and gatherers themselves, they were also livestock herders and farmers. Over the centuries, they filled the areas that were too dry for a purely subsistence way of life. They also absorbed many of the previous inhabitants through intermarriage. Having herds and cultivating land brought up questions of ownership, inheritance and water rights, and an elaboration of social institutions and customs to deal with them. The Cushites had a strong material culture, using stone, particularly obsidian, to make beautiful arrowheads, knives and axes, as well as producing a range of pottery utensils. They also left evidence of their settlements in burial cairns and living sites at places like Hyrax Hill, near Nakuru. The same people may have built the irrigation works still used today along the Elgeyo Escarpment, west of Lake Baringo. For the most part, the earliest Cushites were absorbed by peoples who came later, and whose new languages and customs they adopted. The changes were not all one-sided, however: **circumcision** and **clitoridectomy** (so-called female circumcision), practised by the early Cushites, became important cultural rituals for many of the peoples who succeeded and absorbed them. The **Somali** and **Rendille** of the northeast are the main groups still speaking Cushitic languages, although their arrival in Kenya was more recent. Today, only the Boni speak a language related to the Southern Cushitic of the first farmers and herders, although the Boni themselves are hunter-gatherers.

1.9 million years ago	1.6 million years ago	9000–1000 BC
Direct human ancestor, "Handy man", lives on east shores of Lake Turkana	Direct human ancestor, "Upright man", lives on west shores of Lake Turkana	Cushitic-speaking peoples appear in Kenya

For present-day Kenya, the most important arrivals began to reach the country in the first few centuries AD. From the northwest and the headwaters of the Nile came the **Nilotic**-speaking ancestors of the so-called **Kalenjin** peoples; from the west and south came speakers of **Bantu** languages (see p.605), forebears of today's **Kikuyu, Gusii, Kamba** and **Mijikenda**, among others.

Along with their languages, the new arrivals brought technological innovations, including **iron-working**. Iron had enabled the Bantu to spread from the Nigeria/Cameroon area across central Africa, clearing the virgin forests and hocing the ground for their crops. As they headed eastwards, they encountered new Asian food crops – bananas, yams and rice – some of which arrived in East Africa by way of the Indonesian colonization of Madagascar. This new diversity of foods helped people to settle permanently in their chosen regions. The Kalenjin peoples consolidated in the western highlands. The Bantu were particularly successful and, as their broad economic base took hold across the southern half of Kenya, their languages quickly spread. Herding, hunting, fishing and gathering were important supplements to the agricultural mainstay, while trade conducted with their exclusively pastoral or hunter-gatherer neighbours, especially in iron tools, carried their influence further. By about 1000 AD, Kenya's Stone Age technology had been largely replaced by an Iron Age one and, as human domination of the country increased, the beginnings of real specialization in agriculture and herding set in among the different tribes.

Down on the **coast**, Bantu immigrants mixed, over several hundred years, with the Cushitic-speaking inhabitants and with a continuous trickle of settlers from Arabia and the Persian Gulf. With the advent of Islam, this mélange gradually gave rise to a distinct culture and civilization – **Swahili** – speaking a Bantu language laced with foreign vocabulary. The Swahili (see p.414) were Kenya's link with the rest of the world, trading animal skins, ivory, agricultural produce and slaves in exchange for cloth, metals, ceramics, grain, ghee and sugar, with ships from the Middle East, India and even China. The Swahili were the first Kenyans to acquire firearms. They were also the first to write their language (in the Arabic script) and the first to develop complex, stratified communities based on town and countryside.

Later arrivals: 1600–1885

New **American crops** – corn, cassava and tobacco – spread through Kenya after the Portuguese arrived on the coast in the early sixteenth century. They hugely increased the country's population capacity, while enabling a greater degree of permanent

200 AD	500 AD	1000 AD	1100
Nilotic-speaking ancestors of Kalenjin arrive in Kenya from the north	Bantu-speaking peoples arrive from the west	Iron Age culture replaces Stone Age culture throughout Kenya	Swahili culture established on coast

settlement and providing new trade goods.

At about this time, a pastoral **Nilotic**-speaking people, distantly related to the earlier Kalenjin arrivals, began a migration from the northwest. These were the first **Luo**-speakers who, some generations earlier, had left their homeland (around Wau in southern Sudan) owing to droughts along the Nile. The Luo ancestors were always on the move, herding, planting, hunting or fishing. Several good years might be followed by drought, and population pressure then forced less dominant groups to go off in search of water and pasture. The overall trend was southwards. Groups of migrants picked up other, non-Luo-speakers on the way, gradually assimilating them through intermarriage and language change, always drawing attention with the impressive regalia and social standing of their *ruoth* – the Luo kings.

On the shores of Lake Victoria, where the Luo finally settled, sleeping sickness is thought to have wiped out many of their herds. But they were pragmatic, resourceful people, whose background of mixed farming and herding during the era of migration supported them. They turned to agriculture and, increasingly, to fishing.

Another Nilotic, pastoral people, the **Turkana** appeared in Kenya later in the seventeenth century. Linguistically closer to the Maasai Nilotes, they seem to have shared the Luo resilience to economic hardship and they, too, have more recently turned to fishing. Also like the Luo, and almost unique among Kenyan peoples, they have never practised circumcision.

The arrival of the Maasai

The Maa-speakers – **Maasai** and **Samburu** – were the last major group to arrive in Kenya, and their rise and fall had far-reaching effects on neighbouring peoples. Moving southwards from the upper Nile valley, from the beginning of the seventeenth century, they expanded swiftly thanks to their nomadic pastoral lifestyle, transforming within a few generations from an obscure group into a dominant force in the region. Culturally, they borrowed extensively from their neighbours, especially the Nandi-speaking **Kalenjin** peoples. **Nandi** words and Kalenjin cultural values were adopted, including circumcision, the age-set system and some ancient (originally probably Cushitic) taboos against eating fish and certain wild animals. It's likely that much of the "traditional" Maasai appearance also owes something to these contacts. The Maasai migration was rapid. Their cattle were periodically herded south and other peoples raided en route to enlarge the herds: by 1800, they were widely established in the Rift Valley and on the plains, everywhere between Lake Turkana and Kilimanjaro. In response to Maasai dominance, many of the Bantu peoples adopted their styles and customs. Initiation by genital mutilation, probably already practised by most Bantu-speakers, was imbued with a new significance – especially for the Kikuyu – by intermarriage and close, if not always peaceable, relations with the Maasai.

Severe **droughts** in the nineteenth century pushed the Maasai further and further afield in search of new pastures, bringing them into conflict, and trade, with other peoples. Drought, disease and rinderpest epidemics (which killed off their cattle) were also responsible for a series of **Maasai civil wars** in the second half of the nineteenth century that disrupted the trading networks that had been set up between the coast and the interior. These were mainly controlled by Swahili, Mijikenda, Kamba and Kikuyu traders. Dutch, English and French goods were finding their way upcountry, and

1500	Around 1500	Around 1650	Around 1680
Nilotic-speaking ancestors of Luo arrive from the north	American crops first appear in Kenya	Nilotic-speaking Turkana arrive from the north	Maasai and Samburu arrive from the north

American interests were already being served during this period, as white calico cloth (still called *amerikani* today) became a major item of profit. In the slave trade's last throes, slaves were exported from western Kenya and Uganda to the coast and even to the Persian Gulf.

Largely in response to slavery and widespread fighting, the first **missionaries** installed themselves upcountry (the earliest went inland from Mombasa in 1846). Throughout this period, the Maasai disrupted travel in their territories, attacking Swahili slavers, Bantu traders and explorer-missionaries alike. The Maasai *morani* were specifically trained for raiding – a kind of guerrilla warfare – but, while their reputation lived on, they were bitterly divided among themselves and not organized on anything like a tribal scale.

By the end of the nineteenth century, with the European invasion of Africa in full swing, the Maasai, who could have been the imperialists' most intractable enemies, were unable to retaliate effectively. The **Nandi** of the western highlands, the main people of the Kalenjin group, had begun to take the Maasai's place as Kenya's most feared adversaries, and put up the stiffest resistance. They were organized to the extent of having a single spiritual leader, the *orkoiyot*, who ruled what was in effect a theocracy. Their war of attrition against the British delayed advances for a number of years. But the Nandi did not have the territorial advantage that would have helped the Maasai, and the assassination of their *orkoiyot*, Koitalel, by the British, destroyed their military organization.

On the coast, the **Sultanate of Oman**, which had ousted the Portuguese from Mombasa in 1698, ruled the whole region between Lamu and Mozambique, and made Zanzibar its capital in 1840. Oman was already under British influence, and officially a British protectorate, when the country split in 1856; Zanzibar, including what is now the coast of Kenya, became a sultanate in its own right. Coastal history is covered in more detail in Chapter 6 (see p.394).

The "Scramble for Africa"

All Kenya's peoples resisted colonial domination to some degree. In the first twenty years of British attempts to rule the region, tens of thousands were killed in ugly massacres and manhunts, and many more were made homeless. Administrators – whose memoirs (see p.594) are the most revealing background for that period – all differed in their ideas of the ultimate purpose of their work and the best means of imposing British authority.

British interests in East Africa at the close of the nineteenth century had sprung from the European power struggle and the "Scramble for Africa". The 1885 **Berlin Conference** chopped the continent into arbitrary spheres of influence. Germany was awarded what was to become Tanganyika; Britain got Kenya and Uganda. In 1886, formal agreements were drawn up and Kilimanjaro was ceded to Queen Victoria's grandson, the Kaiser, giving each monarch a snowcapped, equatorial mountain.

Uganda was the focus of British interest, since Kenya – decimated by drought, locusts, rinderpest and civil war – seemed largely a deserted wasteland. And Uganda was strategically important for **control of the Nile** – which had long been a British preoccupation. But rivalry wasn't far beneath the seemingly amicable surface and

1840	1790s–1880s	1846	1870s
Sultanate of Oman rules coast	Thousands of slaves transported from coast to Middle East and Persian Gulf	First European missionaries arrive in Kenya	Maasai civil wars

Germany clearly had Uganda earmarked too. The country needed to be properly garrisoned and supplied, and Kenya was the necessary base from which to do that.

In 1888, the British government granted permission for commercial operations in Uganda to the **Imperial British East Africa Company** (IBEAC), which, for sea access, leased a wide swath of southern Kenya from the Sultan of Zanzibar. The British also authorized the IBEAC to administer Uganda and that section of Kenya on their behalf. The company officers – mostly young and totally inexperienced English clerks – established a series of trading forts at fifty-mile intervals in a line connected by a rough ox-track leading from Mombasa into Uganda. Machakos, Murang'a and Mumias all began as IBEAC stations.

The IBEAC eventually went bankrupt, however, having failed to establish any kind of administration, and in 1895 the British government stepped into the breach, declared a **protectorate** over Uganda and Kenya and decided to build a **railway** from Kenya's coast to its interior. This classic, valedictory piece of Victorian engineering took six years to complete and cost the lives of hundreds of Indian labourers. Financially, the "lunatic line" (as it came to be called) was a commitment that grew out of all proportion to the likely returns and continued to grow long after the last rail was laid. But its completion transformed the future of East Africa. From now on, the supply lines were secure and the interior only a month's journey from Europe by ship and rail. Suddenly, the prospects for developing the cool, fertile Kenya highlands looked much more attractive than the distant unknowns of Uganda and its powerful kingdoms.

More immediately, the railway physically divided the **Maasai** at a time when they were not united, and moreover were moving into alliances with the British. Their grazing lands, together with the regions of the **Kalenjin** peoples and the **Kikuyu** on the lower slopes of the highlands, were to become the heartland of the white settler colony.

The Kenya colony

Many people in Edwardian Britain saw Kenya as a land of opportunity: a new New Zealand, or even a Jewish homeland (a party of Zionists was actually escorted around Kenya but declined the offer). It was Sir Charles Eliot, the Protectorate's second governor, who was the main mover behind the **settlement scheme**. While some colonialists urged consideration for the "rights of natives", the growing clamour of voices claiming the support of British taxpayers – who had met the bill for the railway – outweighed any altruism. Eliot's extravagant reports on the potential of British East Africa were published, and government policy was thereafter directed towards getting the settlers in and making the railway pay. And so a trickle of landless aristocrats, middle-class adventurers, big-game hunters, ex-servicemen and Afrikaners (the farming land was also advertised in South Africa) began travelling up the line. Using ox-wagons to get to the tracts of bush they had leased, they started their farms from scratch. Lord Delamere, governor himself for a time, was their biggest champion. In the years leading up to World War I, the trickle of settlers became a flood, and by 1916 the area "alienated" to **European settlers** had risen to 15,000 square kilometres of the best land. The so-called "**White Highlands**" were mostly on the slopes of Mount Kenya and the Aberdare range, but also in the Rift Valley where the Maasai had been pushed out and Kikuyu labourers – known as squatters – were encouraged to migrate to work on the

1885	1888	1895–1901	1916
Berlin Conference carves up Africa for the European powers	Imperial British East Africa Company founded	"Lunatic line" built from Mombasa to Lake Victoria	European settlers flood into Kenya

European farms. Imported livestock was hybridized with hardy, local breeds; coffee, tea, sisal and pineapples were introduced and thrived; European crops flourished and cereals soon covered vast areas.

Nearly half the land worth farming was now in the hands of settlers, but it had become clear that it was far from empty of local inhabitants. Colonial invasion had occurred at a low point in the fortunes of Kenya's peoples and, unprepared for the scale of the incursion, they had been swiftly pushed aside into "native reserves" or became squatters without rights. As populations recovered, serious land shortages set in. The British appointment of "chiefs" – whose main task was to collect a tax on every hut – had the effect of diverting grievances against colonial policy onto these early collaborators and laying the foundations of a class structure in Kenyan society. Without a money economy, employment was the only means available to pay taxes and, effectively, a system of forced labour had been created. The whole apparatus quickly became entrenched in a series of **land and labour laws**. A poll tax was added to the hut tax; all African men were compelled to register to facilitate labour recruitment; squatters on alienated land were required to pay rent, through labour; and cash cropping on African plots was discouraged or banned (coffee licences, for example, were restricted to white farmers). The highlands were strictly reserved for white settlement, while land not owned by Europeans became Crown Land, its African occupants "tenants at will" of the Crown and liable to summary eviction.

Asians, too, were excluded from the highlands. While the leader of Kenya's Indians, **A.M. Jeevanjee**, had called for the transformation of Kenya into the "America of the Hindu", the proposal never came near consideration by the British. Barred from farming on any scale – except in the far west, where they developed sugar cane as an important crop – Indians concentrated on the middle ground, setting up general stores (*dukas*) across the country, investing in small industries and handling services.

World War I

World War I had a number of profound effects, although there were comparatively few battles in Kenya itself. Some 200,000 African porters and soldiers were conscripted and sent to Tanganyika (German East Africa), where 50,000 of them died. **General von Lettow Vorbeck**, the German commander, waged a dogged campaign against British forces despite the fact that his own were vastly outnumbered. Kenyan troops were deeply influenced by the experience. They had seen Europeans at war with each other and witnessed both European fallibility and the kind of organization used to overcome it.

Sir Edward Northey, governor of Kenya at the time of the armistice, pushed his **Soldier Settlement Scheme** through without difficulty. Its aim, to increase revenue by doubling the settler population in Kenya to nine thousand, seemed promising enough to a government sapped by war. But the Soldier Settlement Scheme was bitterly resented by Africans, particularly those who had fought alongside the soldiers and were now excluded from their gains.

Early nationalism and reaction

Political associations sprang up among ex-servicemen and those with a mission-school education: the Kikuyu Association, the Young Kikuyu Association and the Young Kavirondo Association. **Harry Thuku**, secretary of the Young Kikuyus, realized its

1900s	**Around 1892**	**1914–18**	**1918**
Land and labour laws enacted, including a hut tax	Jomo Kenyatta born in Kiambu, north of Nairobi	200,000 African porters conscripted to serve in World War I	Soldier settlement scheme devised to double settler population to 9000

potential and re-formed it as the East Africa Association in order to recruit on a nationwide basis. The hated registration law by which every African was obliged to carry a pass – the *kipande* – was a prime grievance, but tax reduction, introduction of land title deeds and wage increases were demanded as well. Alliances were built up with associations of embittered Indians and 1921 saw a year of protests and rallies. These culminated in Thuku's detention and the shooting by police of 25 demonstrators at a mass rally calling for his release. He remained in detention for eleven years.

The Indian constituency eventually secured two seats (nominated, not elected) on the Legislative Council. Africans, meanwhile, remained landless, disenfranchised and, like the Indians, racially segregated from the white community. As the settlers became established, they began to contribute appreciably to the income of the colony (which Kenya had officially become in 1920). Most of them seem to have believed that they were the founders of what would be a long and glorious era of white dominion. Indeed settler self-government, along Canadian or South African lines, was a declared aim. African demands were hardly heeded by the authorities, but the Colonial Office was in a difficult position over the **Indians**, who were already British subjects with the rights and privileges of Indians on the subcontinent and whose demands for equal rights they had trouble in refuting. Tentative proposals to give them voting rights, allow unrestricted immigration from India and abolish segregation caused indignation among the settlers. Their **Convention of Associations**, already arguing the case for white home rule, formed a "Vigilance Committee" which worked out detailed military plans for rebellion, including the kidnapping of the governor and the deportation of the Indians. Sensing a crisis, the Colonial Office drew up a white paper and a grudging settlement was reached that allowed five Indians and one Arab to be elected to the Legislative Council (the colony's local government), alongside eleven Europeans.

Although the "paramountcy of native interests" was reiterated in the Colonial Office's 1923 **Devonshire Declaration** (a government green paper designed to forestall the political demands of Indian settlers), Africans were in reality still denied any equality before the law. A system of **de facto apartheid** was being practised, and it was in this climate in the 1920s and 1930s that, floating above their economic troubles, the settlers had their heyday – the **Happy Valley life** so appallingly and fascinatingly depicted in *White Mischief* (see p.597) and other books.

Education, Kenyatta and the Kikuyu

The opportunities available to Africans came almost entirely through **mission schools** at first. Again, there was conflict between government and settlers on the question of **education**. The Colonial Office was committed, on paper at least, to the general development of the country for all its inhabitants, while the white farmers were on the whole adamant that raising educational standards could only lead to trouble. A crude form of Swahili had become the language of communication between Africans and Europeans. But the teaching of English was a controversial issue that hardliners foresaw eventually rebounding on government and settlers alike. In frustration, the Kikuyu set up self-help **independent schools** in the 1930s, primarily in order to teach their own children English.

Whether barring access to English education would ultimately have made any difference is debatable, but by the late 1930s there were already enough educated Africans to pose the beginnings of a serious challenge to white supremacy. One of these

1920	1921	1921	1923–39
Kenya officially becomes a British Colony	Political associations form to protest taxes, lack of land title deeds and low wages	Police shoot dead 25 political protestors	Kenya Colony's "Happy Valley" heyday

was Kamau wa Ngengi, who later adopted the name **Jomo Kenyatta**. Born some time between 1889 and 1895 near Kiambu, just north of Nairobi, and educated at the Scottish Mission Centre in nearby Thogoto, Kenyatta adopted his name from the traditional beaded belt (*kenyatta*) he always wore.

After Thuku's imprisonment and the bloodshed at Nairobi in 1921, the East African Association was dissolved and was succeeded by the **Kikuyu Central Association (KCA)**, which Kenyatta – by now a government employee in Nairobi – joined in 1924. The KCA was the spearhead of nationalism and lobbied hard for tax reductions, a return of alienated land and the election of African representatives to the Legislative Council. It also protested against missionary efforts to outlaw **female circumcision**, on the grounds that the Church was attempting to undermine Kikuyu culture. This last conflict led to a leadership crisis in the KCA and for a number of years threatened to swamp other issues.

Kenya survived the 1929 stock market crash and the resulting global **depression** as the colonial government became increasingly committed to the struggling settlers it was now bailing out. Exports fell catastrophically, coffee planting by non-whites was still prohibited and the tax burden continued to be placed squarely on Africans. Faced with this crisis, even some of the settlers began to accept that large-scale changes were in order. Just as awareness was growing that the economy could not survive indefinitely unless Africans were given more of a chance to participate, Kenya was thrown into World War II.

World War II

Perhaps not surprisingly, soldiers were easily recruited into the **King's African Rifles** when Italian-held Ethiopia (then Abyssinia) declared war on Kenya in 1940. Volunteers wanted money, education and a chance to see the world; conscripts, filling the quotas assigned to their chiefs, faced a life at home or on the native reserve that was no better than enlisting. Propaganda immediately succeeded in casting Hitler's image as the embodiment of all racist evil. Some Africans thought the war, once won, would improve their position in Kenya. They were partly right. Military campaigns in Ethiopia and Burma owed much of their success to African troops, and during the war their efforts were glowingly praised by Allied commanders.

On the soldiers' return, a new awareness, more profound than that felt by those returning from World War I, came upon them. The white tribes of Europe had fought the war on the issue of self-determination; the message wasn't lost on Africans. Yet still, in almost every other sphere of life, they were demeaned and humiliated. The KCA had been banned at the outbreak of war, allegedly for supporting the Italian fascists, and African political life was subdued. Real change, for 99 percent of the population, was still a dream.

Kenya's food-exporting economy had done well out of the war and it was clear the colony could make a major contribution to Britain's recovery. The postwar Labour government encouraged economic expansion without going far enough to include Africans among the beneficiaries. Industrialization gathered momentum and there was a rapid growth of towns. There was also further promotion of **white immigration** – a new influx of European settlers arrived soon after the war – and greater power was given to the settlers on the Legislative and Executive Councils. Population growth and intense pressure on land in the rural areas – especially among the Kikuyu in the Central Highlands – forced people to leave their villages to search for work in the towns, while recently arrived European settlers created farms and plantations on the land from

1928	1929	1939–45	1944
Jomo Kenyatta joins the Kikuyu Central Association	Wall Street crash and global depression leads to catastrophic fall in Kenya's exports	World War II: Kenyans fight for the British in Ethiopia and Burma	Eliud Mathu appointed as first African member of the legislative council

which they had been removed. On the political front, militant **trade unionism**, dominated by ex-servicemen, gradually usurped the positions of those African leaders who had been prepared to work with the government.

Postwar African politics

A single African member, Eliud Mathu, was appointed to the Legislative Council in 1944. More significant, however, was the formation in 1944 of the **Kenya African Union** (**KAU**), a consultative group of leaders and spokesmen, whose first president was Harry Thuku, set up with the governor's approval to liaise with Mathu.

Kenyatta had spent most of the period between 1929 and 1946 in Britain, though there were stays in Russia where he studied revolutionary theory. He initially went to London with a petition from the KCA about land grievances, and continued to work as a KCA campaigner until the organization was banned, while also studying anthropology under Bronisław Malinowski at the London School of Economics, writing his homage to the Kikuyu people, *Facing Mount Kenya*, and participating in the Fifth Pan-African Congress, in Manchester, immediately after the war in 1945. Kenyatta's **return to Kenya** in September 1946 coincided with an escalating uproar about land rights, and the successful, well-travelled and highly networked Kenyatta received an enthusiastic welcome, his arrival signalling the birth of a new current of **nationalism**. The KAU, which Kenyatta joined in 1947, was transformed into an active political party – and ran straight into conflict with itself. The radicals within the party wanted sweeping changes in land ownership, equal voting rights and abolition of the pass law, under which all black Kenyans were restricted in their movements and forced to carry an internal passport and obey the pass law restricting their movements. The moderates were for negotiation, educational improvement, multiracial progress and a gradual shift of power. They were not convinced that their best interests lay in confronting the British head-on; they had all achieved considerable ambitions within the settler economy. Kenyatta, elected KAU president in 1947, was ambitious himself, and the Europeans mistrusted his intentions and rumour-mongered about his personal life and his communist connections.

Despite Kenyatta's efforts to steer a middle course, the KAU became increasingly radical and Kikuyu-dominated. While Kenyatta angled to give the party a multi-tribal profile to appease the settlers, he also managed to sacrifice some moderates in the leadership for the sake of party unity. There were defections as well: several radicals joined an underground movement and took oaths of allegiance against the British. Oath-taking groups emerged secretly all around the Central Highlands and, in 1951, a Central Committee was organized by key KAU members in Nairobi, Fred Kubai and Bildad Kaggia, to coordinate insurgent activities.

The Mau Mau Rebellion

The Central Committee began murdering its opponents and attacking white-owned property in what became known as the **Mau Mau Rebellion**. The origin of the name is obscure (it may derive from *muma*, a traditional Kikuyu oath), but the insurgents never used it, calling themselves the **Land and Freedom Army** (**LFA**). The British accused Kenyatta of involvement, but this seems unlikely, although the insurgents used his name in their propaganda to justify their attacks. The LFA consisted largely of young

1945	**1945–48**	**1947**	**1951**
Jomo Kenyatta attends Pan-African Congress in Manchester	Postwar European immigration encouraged	Jomo Kenyatta becomes leader of Kenya African Union	Mau Mau oath-taking becomes widespread

men from the rural periphery of towns like Nyeri, Fort Hall (Murang'a) and Nairobi, and membership was overwhelmingly Kikuyu.

In August 1952, following arson attacks on the homes of people who had refused to take the Mau Mau oath, the government imposed a curfew on three districts of Nairobi. In October, **Chief Waruhiu wa Kungu**, the government's most senior African official, was murdered in Nairobi after making a speech condemning the Mau Mau; in response the British declared a **State of Emergency** and arrested any suspected insurgents. Within ten days, they had detained nearly four thousand people.

Kenyatta had played a delicate political game, condemning strikes and even oath-taking, but he was ready to seize any chance to exploit the situation. Now, in October 1952, he and other KAU leaders were arrested and interned for their supposed part in the uprising. The governor arranged for the bribing of a witness to give false evidence against Kenyatta. Meanwhile, tens of thousands of squatters in the Rift Valley were sacked by the white farmers and drifted home, where many took Mau Mau oaths. Thousands of **British troops** were sent to Kenya and a **Kikuyu Home Guard** formed to combat the Mau Mau, but the hardcore guerrillas fled from their villages and lived off the jungle for months on end, launching surprise attacks at night. They also relied on considerable support from Kikuyu homesteads for supplies, intelligence reports and stolen weapons.

By early 1953, the rebels were becoming more daring. In January they murdered a settler family, the Rucks, including their 6-year-old son, and in March, a party of 83 insurgents raided **Naivasha police station**, releasing 173 detainees and seizing a large quantity of weaponry. Almost simultaneously, a force of around a thousand insurgents attacked the village of **Lari**, northwest of Nairobi, whose residents were largely Kikuyus loyal to the colonial regime, many of them Home Guard members. The insurgents burnt down their homes and hacked to death more than eighty people. The following day, Home Guard reprisal killings of Mau Mau sympathizers in the district topped one hundred, killed in a series of mass shootings.

The British now declared "**Special Areas**" in which anyone who failed to stop when challenged would be shot, and "**Prohibited Areas**" – including the Aberdare range and Mount Kenya – in which all Africans would be shot on sight. In April 1954 they put Nairobi under military control, rounding up all the city's Kikuyu residents and detaining seventeen thousand of them, before extending the operation to other Kikuyu areas. By the end of the year, there were 77,000 prisoners, held in more than fifty British **concentration camps** throughout the country, where they were subject to arbitrary acts of brutality and murder at the hands of British troops. At one point, a third of the entire male adult Kikuyu population was being held in detention. Under emergency powers, a policy of "**villagization**" was also enforced: by the end of 1955, more than a million people – almost the entire Kikuyu population – had been forcibly resettled in villages policed by guards and fenced with barbed wire.

British atrocities

At its height, in 1953–54, the insurgency consisted of some fifteen thousand guerrillas, but little by little the British hunted them down. By September 1956, only around five thousand remained. The **end of the revolt** came in October 1956 with the capture and execution of **Dedan Kimathi**, the LFA's commander-in-chief. The State of Emergency nonetheless continued until 1960, when it was abandoned after news emerged in the

August 1952	October 1952	March 1953
Curfew imposed in parts of Nairobi	State of Emergency declared and Kenyatta arrested	Homes burnt and more than eighty Kikuyu loyal to the British massacred by insurgents at Lari

press that British troops had bludgeoned detainees at **Hola** detention camp in March 1959, killing eleven and injuring sixty, sparking outrage in Britain.

During the Mau Mau uprising, insurgents murdered 32 white settlers and around 2000 Kenyan civilians, while fifty British troops lost their lives. In response, the British hanged 1090 rebels – more than in any other colonial uprising – and claimed to have killed around 11,000 guerrillas, destroying much of the documentation about the detention camps before independence. Evidence that has come to light since the turn of the century, however (see p.597), suggests that British forces killed more than 50,000 people, and perhaps as many as 100,000. The evidence also shows that torture was a widespread tool of interrogation: being screened and questioned, thousands of detainees and villagers were subjected to gross human rights abuses ranging from mutilation to rape, many of which resulted in death.

No British officials, nor any of the settlers who were also involved, have yet been prosecuted for atrocities committed during the Emergency. Nor has Britain yet paid any compensation or made any formal apology. Finally, in 2012, after years of representations, three elderly victims of torture during the Mau Mau period won the right to sue the UK government for reparations.

Independence: Uhuru

With the Emergency over, the KAU leaders still at liberty set about exploiting the European fear of a repeat episode. Anything that now delayed the fulfilment of African nationalist aspirations could be seen as fuel for another revolt. There was no longer any question of a South African-style, white-dominated independence. Settlers, mindful of the preparations for independence taking place in other African countries, began rallying to the cry of multiracialism in a vain attempt to secure what looked like a very shaky future.

At the 1960 Lancaster House Conference in London, called to discuss Kenya's future, African representatives won a convincing victory by pushing through measures to give them majorities in the Legislative Council and the Council of Ministers. The members of these bodies, all nominated by the colonial authorities, included **Tom Mboya**, the prominent and charismatic Luo trade unionist, and the radical politician **Oginga Odinga** (another Luo), as well as **Daniel Arap Moi** and the Mijikenda leader **Ronald Ngala**. A new constitution was drawn up and the right of access for all races to the "White Highlands" was confirmed. The declaration promised that "Kenya was to be an African country": the path to independence was guaranteed; British Prime Minister Harold Macmillan said as much in his "**Wind of Change**" speech to the South African parliament at the time when the Lancaster House Conference was meeting. The settlers perceived a "calamitous betrayal", with universal franchise and African-dominated independence expected within a few years.

Minority tribal associations, meanwhile, foresaw troubles ahead if the Kikuyu/Luo elite achieved independence for Kenya at the cost of the smaller constituencies. In 1960, the **Kenya African National Union** (**KANU**) was formed, dominated by the Kikuyu and Luo politicians who had campaigned most prominently against British colonial rule. Soon after, a second, more moderate party, the **Kenya African Democratic Union** (**KADU**), was created, with Britain's help, to federate the minority, largely rural-based political associations in a broad defensive alliance against Kikuyu/Luo domination. One of KADU's leading members was Daniel Arap Moi.

1953	**1954**	**1955**
Aberdare range and Mount Kenya declared "Probited Areas" in which any Africans were shot on sight	77,000 prisoners held by the British in concentration camps	Most Kikuyu forced out of homes and interned in camps

In the elections of 1963 KANU emerged with a a mandate for a non-federal structure. On June 1 – **Madaraka Day** – Kenyatta became Kenya's first prime minister. And on December 12, 1963, control of foreign affairs was handed over and Kenya became formally **independent**.

The Kenyatta years: harambee

It was barely sixty years since the pioneer settlers had arrived. Many of them had panicked, sold up and left before independence, but others decided to stay under an **African government**. Despite his years in detention, Kenyatta turned out to have more consideration for their interests than could have been foreseen. He held successful meetings with settlers in his home village; his bearded, genial image and conciliatory speeches assuring them of their rights and security quickly earned him wide international support and the respected title Mzee (Elder). Many Europeans retained important positions in the administration and judiciary.

Milton Obote and Julius Nyerere, leaders of newly independent Uganda and Tanzania, held talks with Kenyatta on setting up an **East African Community** to share railways, aviation, telecommunications and customs. The union was formally inaugurated in 1967. There was a mood of optimism: it looked very much as if Kenya had succeeded against all the odds.

But there were urgent issues to contend with, among which **land reform** and the rehabilitation of freedom fighters and detainees were the most pressing. Large tracts of European land were bought up by the government and a programme to provide small plots to landless peasants was rapidly instigated. Political questions loomed large as well. On December 12, 1964, Kenya became a republic, its head of state no longer the Queen, but rather President Kenyatta. KADU was dissolved "in the interests of national unity" and its leaders absorbed into the ruling KANU party, making Kenya a de facto one-party state. For the sake of "national security", British troops were kept on, initially to quell a revolt of ethnic Somalis in the northeast and an army mutiny in Nairobi. A defence treaty has kept a British force at Nanyuki ever since.

There was heavy emphasis on **harambee** (pulling together), endorsed by Kenyatta at all his public appearances. *Harambee* meetings became a unique national institution: fund-raising events at which – in a not untraditional way – donations were made by local notables and politicians towards self-help education and health programmes. During the 1960s and 1970s, hundreds of *harambee* schools were built and equipped in this way. But the ostentatious gifts, and particularly the guaranteed press coverage the next day with donors listed in order of value, sometimes reduced the *harambee* vision of community development to an exercise in patronage and competitive status-seeking.

On the **economic front**, the first decade of independence saw remarkable changes and rapid growth. The settlers' fairly broad-based crop-exporting economy was a powerful springboard for development, and not difficult to transfer to African control. While many large landholdings were sold *en bloc* to African investors, smaller farmers began to contribute significantly to export earnings through coffee, tea, pyrethrum and fruit. Industrialization proceeded at a slower pace: Kenya's mineral resources are limited and the country relies heavily on oil imports. **Foreign investment** wasn't especially beneficial, as investors were given wide freedoms to import equipment and technical skills and to re-export much of the profit.

October 1956	March 3 1959	July–Dec 1959	January 1960
Mau Mau leader Dedan Kimathi captured and executed	Hola massacre: eleven detainees bludgeoned to death by British troops	All "villagization" and detention camps closed and prisoners released	Harold Macmillan gives "Wind of Change" speech

The resettlement programme was abandoned in 1966, its objectives "largely attained". But many peasants, having been squatters on European farms, were now "illegal squatters" on private African land. Thousands migrated to the towns where unemployment was already a serious problem. Kenya was becoming a class-divided society. **Growth**, rather than a radical redistribution of wealth, was the government's main concern. Although by 1970 more than two-thirds of the European mixed farming lands were occupied by some fifty thousand Africans, and the overall standard of living had improved considerably, income disparities were greater than ever. **Kikuyu domination** was strongly resented by other groups, although it was perhaps inevitable that the people who had lost most and suffered most under British rule should expect to receive the most benefits from independence.

Political opposition

It was in this climate that KANU's leadership split. **Oginga Odinga**, the party vice president, resigned in 1966 to form the socialist **Kenya People's Union (KPU)** and 29 MPs joined him. The ex-guerrilla Bildad Kaggia became deputy head of the KPU and a vocal agitator for poorer Kikuyu. Kenyatta and Mboya closed ranks in KANU and prepared for political conflict. KPU was anti-capitalist and in favour of non-alignment, while KANU – led in this respect by Tom Mboya – stressed the need for close ties with the West and for economic conditions that would attract foreign investment. It was the last time in independent Kenya that clearly contrasting party policies were to be given a proper airing, although the KPU's stand was denounced as divisive, and the party was barely tolerated for three years, its members harassed and detained by the security forces, its activities obstructed by new legislation and constitutional amendments.

In KANU, Odinga's post of vice president was taken, briefly, by Joseph Murumbi and then, with behind-the-scenes encouragement from the British (keen to avoid a radical in the job), by Daniel Arap Moi. Odinga had strong, grassroots support in the Luo and Gusii districts of western Kenya. But Tom Mboya's supporters came from an even broader base, including many poor Kikuyu. By the end of the 1960s, speculation was mounting about whether he would be able to take over the presidency on Kenyatta's death. As the Mzee's right-hand man he was widely tipped to succeed – a possibility that alarmed Kenyatta's more high-profile Kikuyu supporters. In July 1969, Mboya was gunned down by a Kikuyu assassin in central Nairobi. No high-level complicity in the murder was ever brought to light, but Mboya's death was a devastating blow to Kenya's fragile stability, setting off shock waves along both class and tribal divisions. There was widespread fighting and rioting between Kikuyu and Luo, fuelled by years of rivalry and growing feelings of Luo exclusion from government. During a visit by Kenyatta to Kisumu – where he attended a public meeting at which Odinga and his supporters were present – hostility against his entourage was so great that police opened fire, killing at least ten demonstrators.

The KPU was immediately banned and Odinga detained without trial. Although the constitution continued to guarantee the right to form opposition parties, non-KANU nominations to parliament were, in practice, forbidden. There was a resurgence of oath-taking among Kikuyu, Meru and Embu, pledging to maintain the Kikuyu hold on power. The Kikuyu contingent in the army was strengthened and a new force of shock troops, the **General Service Unit (GSU)**, was recruited under Kikuyu officers; independent of police and army, it was to act as an internal security force. In the early

1960	1961	June 1 1963
The Kenya African National Union, a political party dominated by the Kikuyu and Luo elite, is formed	Jomo Kenyatta freed from house arrest	Kenya achieves self-government (Madaraka Day) under Prime Minister Jomo Kenyatta

RELIGION IN KENYA

Indigenous religion (mostly based around the idea of a supreme god and intercession between the living and the spirit worlds by deceased ancestors) survives as an inclusive belief system only in remote areas of northern Kenya, among the remaining Okiek (or Ndorobo) hunter-gatherers in a few forests and to some extent among pastoralists like the Maasai. While it is continually under threat from Christian missionaries, its influence over the lives of many nominally Christian or Muslim Kenyans remains powerful.

Varieties of **Catholicism** and **Protestantism** are dominant in the Highlands and westwards, and are increasingly pervasive elsewhere. In the Rift Valley and the far west, especially towards Lake Victoria, there are many minor Christian sects and churches – more than a thousand denominations in all – often based around the teachings of local prophets and preachers.

The moderate **Ismaili Muslim** sect is an influential Asian constituency with powerful business interests, led by the Aga Khan, whose Aga Khan Foundation is a major development agency in Kenya, investing in schools, hospitals and the tourist industry – it owns Serena Hotels.

Otherwise, broad-based, non-fundamentalist **Sunni Islam** dominates the coast and northeast, and is the fastest-growing religion in the country. Many towns have several mosques, of which one usually serves as the focal Friday mosque for the whole community. Most Kenyan Muslims are moderate, but the government blames a small number of home-grown extremists for sporadic, usually unattributed terror attacks on non-Muslims in parts of the coast, the northeast and Nairobi.

Hindu and **Sikh** temples are found in most large towns, and there are also adherents of **Jainism** and the **Baha'i** faith.

1970s, Kikuyu control – of the government, the administration, business interests and land – gripped tighter and tighter.

Kenyatta's closing years

Internationally, Kenya was seen as one of the safest **African investments** – a model of stability only too happy to allow the multinational corporations access to its resources and markets. The development of the tourist industry helped give the country a positive profile, and, in comparison with most other African countries, some still fighting for independence and others beset by civil war or paralysed by drought, Kenya's future looked healthy enough. But in achieving record economic growth, foreign interests often seemed to crush indigenous ones. An elite of profiteers – nicknamed the **wabenzi** after the Mercedes-Benzes they favoured – extracted enormous bribes out of transactions with foreign companies. Nepotism was blatant and Kenyatta himself was rumoured to be one of the richest men in the world. For the majority of Kenyan people, life was hardly any better than before independence.

In 1975, in the first ever explicit public attack on the Kikuyu monopoly of power, the radical populist MP **J.M. Kariuki** warned that Kenya could become a country of "ten millionaires and ten million beggars". He was arrested for his pains then released and, some weeks later, found murdered in the Ngong Hills. A massive turnout at his funeral was followed by angry **student demonstrations**. "Kariuki's death", wrote the then outspoken *Weekly Review*, "instils in the minds of the public the fear of dissidence, the fear to criticize, the fear to stand out and take an unconventional public stance." In the following years, a number of other MPs were detained, and the issue of landlessness ceased to be one that many people were prepared to shout about.

Dec 12 1964	**1965**	**1966**
Kenya becomes a republic (Jamhuri Day) in the British Commonwealth, its head of state now President Jomo Kenyatta	KADU party dissolved and Kenya becomes a de facto one-party state	KANU splits, with Vice President Oginga Odinga resigning to form the socialist, non-aligned Kenya People's Union

Kenyatta retreated into dictatorial seclusion, propped up by close Kikuyu cronies. As parliament, and even the cabinet, took an increasingly passive role in decision-making, the pronouncements from the Mzee's "court" began to be accompanied by vague suggestions that threats to his government were being made by unspecified foreign powers. By 1977, the **East African Community** had ceased to function. Delayed elections, hostility towards socialist Tanzania, further detentions and growing allegations of corruption formed the sullen backdrop to **Kenyatta's death**, in bed, on August 28, 1978.

Kenya under Moi: nyayo

The passing of the Mzee took Kenya by surprise. There was a nationwide outpouring of grief and shock, but for many, also a sense of relief, and anticipation that the future might better reflect the ideals of twenty years earlier. Vice President Daniel Arap Moi smoothly assumed power and gathered popular support with moves against corruption in the civil service, his stand against tribal nepotism (he himself was from the minority Kalenjin) and the release of all Kenyatta's political prisoners.

But the honeymoon was short. In the first year or two of his presidency, Moi's **nyayo** (footsteps) philosophy of "peace, love and unity" in the wake of Kenyatta found wide appeal, and his apparent honesty and outspoken attacks against tribalism impressed many, making him friends abroad. But economic management was weak, and the failure to make any adjustments in economic policy in favour of the rural and urban poor caused growing resentment at home. Oginga Odinga and other ex-KPU MPs were prevented from standing in the 1979 elections. Student protests began again and the closing of the university became an annual event. On the international scene, the whole Indian Ocean region became strategically important with the fall of the Shah of Iran and the Soviet invasion of Afghanistan, and Kenya developed close ties with the US.

On Sunday August 1, 1982 – three months after constitutional amendments were pushed through to make Kenya officially a one-party state (to prevent Oginga Odinga registering the new Kenya Socialist Alliance party) – sections of the Kenya Air Force attempted a **military coup**. Without support in the other armed forces, however, the coup was easily put down by the army and the GSU, who killed scores of perceived coup supporters. The coup attempt heralded a new clampdown on students and "dissidents", such as Oginga Odinga, who was placed under house arrest.

Despite Moi's efforts to throttle all dissent, the groundswell of resentment continued to grow. An opposition group, **Mwakenya** (a Swahili acronym for Union of Nationalists to Liberate Kenya), attracted attention through its pamphlets calling for the replacement of the Moi government, new democratic freedoms and an end to corruption and Western influence. Hundreds of people, and sometimes their defence lawyers, were arrested. A 1987 **Amnesty International** report condemned Kenya's human rights record, as detainees died in custody and prisoners were routinely tortured and kept in waterlogged cells beneath Nyayo House in Nairobi. Public meetings of more than five people were banned, and all dissent, even within KANU, was crushed.

The path to multiparty democracy

In February 1990 **Robert Ouko**, the Luo foreign minister favoured by the West and widely viewed as a potential successor to the presidency, was murdered, sparking off a

July 1969	July 1969	March 2 1975
KANU party leader-in-waiting, Jomo Kenyatta's charismatic right-hand man and Luo trade unionist, Tom Mboya, is assassinated	The KPU is banned and Oginga Odinga detained without trial	Outspoken Kikuyu commentator J.M. Kariuki is murdered after criticizing the nepotism and corruption of the ruling elite

RICHARD LEAKEY AND THE KENYA WILDLIFE SERVICE

Although now internationally renowned as a wildlife conservationist, **Richard Leakey** rose to prominence as a paleontologist from the shadows of his eminent parents Mary and Louis Leakey, publishing several books and eventually becoming head of the National Museums of Kenya in Nairobi.

In 1989, facing an international outcry over the poaching of elephants and the serious impact that was having on the tourist industry, President Moi hired Leakey to take charge of the newly formed **Kenya Wildlife Service** (KWS). Leakey's first move was a characteristically bold one: he invited the world's press to watch Moi ignite Kenya's US$3 million stockpile of confiscated **ivory** – producing the most memorable photo opportunity of the Moi presidency. He went on, with Moi's support, to create anti-poaching units and briefed them to shoot to kill any poachers in the parks. The World Bank and other donors were so impressed that they gave more than US$140 million in grants. The poaching stopped, elephants and rhinos were saved from the brink of extinction, and Kenya's international image was partially restored.

But Leakey's success went too far for some local politicians, particularly in Maasai-land. His confrontational approach to the balance of human and animal needs in the parks – all humans out – infuriated many. And he seemed incorruptible: the KWS had dried up completely as a source of patronage.

In June 1993, on a routine flight at the controls of his Cessna plane, Leakey crashed, losing both legs in the accident. Foul play was suspected, but not proven. Within months he was walking on artificial limbs, anxious to get back to work. But there had been a mood change in his employers. Noah Ngala, tourism minister at the time, announced that evidence of corruption and mismanagement had been unearthed at the KWS. No more bitter irony could be imagined. Leakey resigned and was replaced by the less trenchant David Western, an advocate of human–animal coexistence. Western was sacked in 1998 after falling out with government over their corrupt interference at Lake Nakuru and Tsavo West national parks and Leakey was reinstated, only to leave again to join the government itself.

Since the turn of the century, the increasingly militarized KWS has been run by a succession of appointees, each one determined to be seen as hard on poachers, but caught between government interference, the global conservation lobby and the needs of the tourist industry.

week of nationwide **rioting**, most violent in Ouko's home town of Kisumu. Public opposition to the government mounted, and a Nairobi pro-democracy rally on July 7 (**Saba Saba** – Swahili for 7/7, as the event came to be known) degenerated into a riot, leading to dozens of deaths in street battles with armed police.

Moi blamed "hooligans and drug addicts" for the Saba Saba riots, and the government came down hard on journalists, stifling local newspapers and accusing the foreign press, particularly the BBC, of mischief-making. Relations with the international community plummeted. Against the prevailing, post-Cold War trend in Africa, Moi's stubborn resistance to multiparty democracy riled his overseas backers. He seemed barely aware of the new global consensus and the hard reassessment of aid distribution taking place among the rich countries.

In 1991, the steady build-up of an opposition lobby became so powerful it could no longer be dismantled. Oginga Odinga – effectively Kenya's elder statesman – set up the **Forum for the Restoration of Democracy (FORD)** in association with his son **Raila Odinga**

1978	1979	May 1982
Vice President Daniel Arap Moi succeeds as president and releases all political prisoners	Oginga Odinga and other opposition activists prevented from standing in elections	Constitutional amendments make Kenya officially a one-party state

and the influential Law Society chairman, **Paul Muite**. FORD quickly attracted government opponents from all quarters. Meanwhile, **John Troon**, the ex-Scotland Yard policeman hired by Moi to investigate Ouko's murder, revealed that the greatest suspicion fell on the president's closest adviser Nicholas Biwott, and his internal security chief, Hezekiah Oyugi, both of whom were sacked, arrested and later released "for lack of evidence", but not reinstated. Major donor nations subsequently suspended balance-of-payment support to Kenya, pending economic and political reforms. Moi got the message. Within days he announced there would be multiparty elections for the next parliament and a free vote for the presidency at the end of 1992. At the same time, the **Goldenberg scandal** began, a massive scheme to defraud Kenya's treasury of up to $600m worth of export compensation credits for gold "exported" from Kenya (which has almost no gold mines) that had in fact been smuggled from DRC. It is presumed that much of this money was used in the election campaigns.

The 1992 elections

FORD found the transformation from opposition lobby group to **political party** hard to manage. It extended a welcome to every ex-KANU minister who made the leap, and with elections approaching, the party promptly split into three ethnic factions, each with its own presidential candidate, and none with any clear party ideology. Dozens were killed and thousands made homeless in tribal violence in the Rift Valley, mainly between indigenous Kalenjin people who supported Moi, and migrant farmers and traders from central Kenya.

Using a combination of fraud, ballot-stuffing, manipulation of electoral rules, physical prevention of opposition candidates from presenting nomination papers, printing money to buy off the voters and changing the polling date at the last minute, Moi made sure that he and his party won the **1992 election**. But for the first time there was also an elected multiparty opposition (even though there were few declared policies in the air), including the three FORD factions, and the Democratic Party (DP) under former Vice President Mwai Kibaki, who came third in the presidential poll behind Moi and Odinga. KANU had almost no MPs from Kikuyu or Luo areas.

The 1997 elections and the US embassy bombing

Several years of economic slowdown followed, with strikes by teachers and nurses, mass demonstrations for constitutional reform and the breakdown of relations with the International Monetary Fund (IMF). Senior figures in the main opposition parties agreed to work together, with a single presidential candidate for the **1997 elections**, the economist and career politician Mwai Kibaki. **Richard Leakey** (see box, p.571) coordinated the alliance and raised funds. By June 1997, the opposition, and particularly students, were howling for reforms in advance of the elections. Police stormed Nairobi University to stop a rally commemorating the 1990 Saba Saba demonstrations and left more than a dozen dead, while brutally putting down protests that had broken out around the country.

For the rest of the year, repression alternated with promises of reform, punctuated by a series of national strikes. Mombasa erupted in violence in August 1997, when two police stations were attacked, six policemen killed, weapons stolen and dozens of upcountry people later killed and thousands more expelled by armed gangs who terrorized the district of **Likoni**. Notices circulated "reclaiming" the coast for its indigenous inhabitants, and demanding that the largely Kikuyu newcomers return to

Aug 1 1982	**February 1984**	**1987**	**1989**
Attempted coup by Kenya Air Force violently suppressed by army and GSU	Massacre of up to 3000 Degodia Somalis at Wagalla Airstrip in Wajir	Amnesty International report condemns Kenya's human rights record	Kenya's stockpile of ivory is burned in a PR stunt organized by KWS director Richard Leakey

their home districts. In November 1997, parliament finally removed some of the legislation restricting freedom of movement and speech.

Elections were held in December, and the vote, predictably, split along ethnic lines. Mwai Kibaki's DP did well in the Kikuyu areas; Raila Odinga's National Development Party (NDP) took most of Luo-land; and Moi's KANU was widely endorsed on the coast and in the Rift Valley and north, securing Moi the presidency against second-placed Kibaki.

On the morning of August 7, 1998, a van containing 800kg of TNT exploded in the parking area behind the **US embassy in Nairobi**. In the embassy itself – the terrorists' intended target – some forty people, twelve of them Americans, perished; but the brunt of the blast was borne by the adjacent four-storey Ufundi Cooperative House. The resulting carnage led to 218 deaths and more than five thousand people injured, nearly all of them Kenyans, and property damage estimated at around $500 million. It is widely suspected that local **Al-Qaeda** operatives were responsible for the attack, as well as the bombing of the US embassy in Dar es Salaam, just a few minutes later.

Moi's final term

The aftermath of the elections saw discussion on constitutional reform getting under way, with Moi bringing opposition figures on side. Raila Odinga was made chair of the constitutional reform committee and Richard Leakey was appointed as cabinet secretary with special responsibility for combating corruption. In June 2001, KANU and Odinga's NDP joined together in a formal coalition, Odinga joining the cabinet as energy minister.

Before the 2002 elections, Kenya's tourist industry was shaken by an **Al-Qaeda suicide bomb attack** on the Israeli-owned *Paradise Hotel* at Kikambala that killed sixteen people, simultaneous with a failed attempt to shoot down an Israel-bound charter flight leaving Mombasa. With the elections approaching Odinga dissolved the NDP, which merged into KANU, a move that Moi hoped would bring Luo voters over to the party. The opposition also did some merging, when twelve groups joined to form the **National Alliance Party of Kenya (NAK)**. Meanwhile the elderly Moi decided to back Uhuru Kenyatta as KANU's presidential candidate. Kenyatta was widely seen as a figurehead who would front a new regime on Moi's behalf, and Moi's backing of him particularly annoyed Raila Odinga, who had hoped to be the party's candidate. He and a number of other KANU grandees resigned their ministerial posts and set up a "Rainbow Alliance" within the party, opposed to Kenyatta's candidacy. In October they left KANU and formed the Liberal Democratic Party (LDP), which joined with the NAK to form the **National Rainbow Coalition (NARC)**, with a single presidential candidate, Mwai Kibaki. NARC won a landslide victory in the December **2002 elections**, and KANU was turfed out of government for the first time since independence.

Kenya under Kibaki

Kibaki took up the presidency with an empty promise: **constitutional reform** within one hundred days. The biggest wrangle involved the proposed post of prime minister, which Odinga, apparently following a secret deal, saw as his. Part of the problem was that NARC was a loose alliance of politicians and ethnic blocs, and it soon began to fragment without Moi as a common opponent to unite it.

Feb 1990	Dec 1992	July 7 1997
Murder of Luo foreign minister Robert Ouko sparks widespread rioting	Ethnic violence precedes first multiparty elections, and President Moi is re-elected	Police kill dozens of students during rally commemorating Saba Saba killings

POLITICAL VIOLENCE AND THE RISE OF DEMOCRACY

For decades, the Rift Valley and other relatively unproductive areas had been the destination for migrants from the Kikuyu, Kamba and Gusii tribes, who bought up marginal farmlands and tried to apply their farming techniques among the local Kalenjin and Maa-speakers while benefiting from local aid and subsistence initiatives.

From independence to the late 1980s any reference to **multiparty politics** by KANU leaders was accompanied by dire warnings of the bloody consequences for tribal harmony of such a system. With the end of the Cold War, and rapid signs of democracy across Africa, foreign aid donors forced the Moi government into a corner on the issue, and the prophecy was quickly realized. Ethnic allegiances swamped the new political order before it had even consolidated, so that the opposition parties were unable to formulate policies and election strategies that were free of ethnic considerations.

In the 1990s, at least three thousand people were killed in violence between different language groups in the Rift Valley, western Kenya and on the coast, and at least three hundred thousand were displaced in **ethnic cleansing**. The violence would build up in the run-up to the elections and, in late 1992 and 1997 (and to a lesser extent in 2002), tensions ran high in traditional flashpoints.

Victims of **attacks in the Rift Valley** described organized gangs of youths terrorizing non-Kalenjin homesteads and villages, while local police arrived too late to do anything or just stood by. The violence included looting, livestock rustling, arson attacks and beating up or killing anyone who got in the way. The message was "Get off our land", and thousands of victims moved to refugee camps outside Eldoret, Nanyuki and other towns.

In **electioneering** terms, the violence usually proved counterproductive, as the government lost more votes from disgust with their inaction than it gained from forcing opposition voters out of marginal KANU constituencies. Probably the aim was simply to demonstrate to the world at large that multipartyism in Africa leads to tribal violence. In this – to the Moi government's lasting shame – it succeeded.

As the results came in after the **2007 presidential election**, both the Luo leader Raila Odinga and the incumbent Kikuyu president Mwai Kibaki declared victory, but it was Kibaki's swearing in on December 30 that sparked an instant, violent reaction across the country. Gangs of Odinga supporters rampaged in the Rift Valley, in Kisumu and on the coast, attacking Kikuyu homes and businesses, and in one notorious incident burning a church sheltering fleeing Kikuyus, killing 35 people. There were running battles in Nairobi's slums between club and machete-wielding youths of different tribes. By the end of January 2008, more than 1300 people had been killed and more than half a million displaced. The majority of the victims were Kikuyu, but other tribes were the targets of Kikuyu reprisal attacks and the police shot dead more than 100 demonstrators and looters. Unlike the largely rural violence of the 1990s, much of the carnage took place in towns, often relayed in real time on social media.

Despite serious concerns that Kenya's **2013 general election** would also spark widespread violence and chaos, they passed off largely peacefully.

A constitutional convention was set up at the **Bomas of Kenya** conference centre in April 2003, but in a **draft constitution** passed in June 2005 the original Bomas proposals were shot through with amendments tabled in parliament, most notable among them the provision that the post of prime minister be in the president's gift. While the amendments also included a radical shake-up of Kenya's **land laws**, including proposals that women should have the right to inherit land and that foreigners should

Dec 1997	August 7 1998	Dec 2002
Second multiparty elections result in another victory for Moi, to a backdrop of ethnic violence in the Rift Valley	Al-Qaeda bomb attack on US Embassy in Nairobi kills 218 and injures 5000	Opposition removes KANU from power, winning a landslide election victory with Mwai Kibaki

not be able to own land, Odinga and several other cabinet ministers campaigned for a "no" vote (represented by an orange) to the proposed constitution, which went to the country in a **referendum** in November 2005, resulting in a two-to-one rejection of the proposed constitution. His plans thwarted, Kibaki dismissed his entire cabinet, and then reappointed them all, with the exception of Odinga and his senior followers, the Orange Team, who moved over to join KANU in opposition, marking the death of the NARC coalition. Constitutional reform was left in the air.

In other fields, Kibaki's reform ideas fared better. In 2003, his administration introduced **free primary education** for all, bringing schooling to 1.5 million more children, although the move was beset by teacher shortages, and a fall in state schools' performance in league tables. Post-Moi, the **press** was largely freer, although in an infamous raid in 2006, masked policemen stormed the offices of the Standard media group (which includes KTN TV, owned by the Moi family), burning papers, smashing equipment and seizing tapes, allegedly at the behest of President Kibaki's outspoken wife, who was being linked to drug-trafficking, among other scandals.

The IMF and the World Bank resumed lending to Kenya in 2003 after the new government set up a five-year **Economic Recovery Strategy**, with a commitment to fighting corruption while opening up to privatization. The anti-corruption campaigner **John Githongo** was appointed Permanent Secretary for Government and Ethics, reporting directly to Kibaki. But high-level **corruption** continued virtually unabated. In 2005, the then British High Commissioner Sir Edward Clay memorably accused "gluttonous" officials of "vomiting on the shoes of donors" in a "looting spree" that had cost Kenya hundreds of millions of dollars. The scandal, which largely focused on the security industry, came to be known as **Anglo-Leasing** (the name of one of the companies involved) – a web of scams in which government money was paid to non-existent companies or for bogus or massively inflated contracts. Githongo took his job seriously and uncovered so much sleaze that when he presented his findings to the president, they were met with indignation rather than approval. He received death threats and had to flee into exile in the UK.

Public support for Kibaki's new **Party of National Unity** (**PNU**) government was wearing very thin as the country prepared for the 2007 elections, in which Kibaki was the PNU's candidate and Odinga, representing the Orange Democratic Movement (the successor party to the constitutional referendum's "no" vote), his rival. Throughout the Rift Valley, western Kenya and on the coast there was outright hostility to what was perceived to be a "Mount Kenya Mafia" running the country. The violent response to the elections, rigged by a government bent on staying in power, almost led to the break-up of Kenya itself in the **tribal clashes** of 2007 to 2008 (see box opposite).

The Grand Coalition: 2008–2013

Brokered by an international team headed by Kofi Annan, a bloated **Grand Coalition** government emerged from the wreckage of the post-election violence. Led by **Mwai Kibaki**, who retained the presidency, and his ODM opponent, **Raila Odinga**, who became prime minister, it gave almost every senior politician in the country a cabinet job. Part of the settlement was the establishment of the **Commission of Inquiry on Post-Election Violence**, headed by Justice Philip Waki.

2003	Nov 2005	2005
Free primary education introduced for all	Proposed new constitution put to the country in a referendum and rejected in protest at powers vested in the president	Government-appointed "anti-corruption czar" John Githongo flees Kenya after pointing the finger at President Kibaki

The report of the **Waki Commission** was presented to Kibaki and Odinga in October 2008 and a secret list of names of alleged perpetrators of crimes against humanity was handed to Kofi Annan. Waki proposed that a post-election violence tribunal should be set up in Kenya, but as parliament endlessly kicked the matter down the road, the clamour grew to hand the cases over to the International Criminal Court. "Don't be vague, let's go to The Hague" ran the popular slogan of the time. In the end, the ICC announced in 2010 that four key figures, two from the Kalenjin community, and two Kikuyu, were to be charged for their close links to the violence. They included **William Ruto**, the Kalenjin leader and political heir to Daniel Arap Moi, radio presenter **Joshua Sang**, and **Uhuru Kenyatta**, the country's richest man and son of Kenya's founding president Jomo Kenyatta. As this book goes to press, only the cases against Ruto and Sang continue, with the murmur of frustration among Ruto's supporters that he has been stitched up growing in volume.

As Kenyans struggled to apportion blame for the post-election violence, the **police** and their paramilitary wing, the GSU, continued to behave as if answerable to no one, shooting hundreds of alleged "Mungiki thugs" (see p.161), and launching a local war in the Mount Elgon region (see p.299).

Extra-judicial executions are one of many government excesses that Kenya's **new constitution** was supposed to curb. Driven through as a result of Kofi Annan's post-election mediation work, the new constitution was finally enacted in 2010 after a 67 percent "yes" vote in a final referendum. Among its many progressive features, the constitution makes a clear **separation of powers** between the executive, the legislature and the judiciary, devolves powers to 47 new **counties**, provides for a **bill of rights** and guarantees **freedom of expression**. The constitution also includes an **integrity chapter** for leaders, which should have ruled out of running for office in the 2013 election anyone charged with a crime against humanity. But such legal niceties depend on Kenya's independent judiciary making clear rulings, and on the **Commission for the Implementation of the Constitution** making faster progress. It has been sitting since 2010.

WOMEN'S RIGHTS AND FGM

Women's groups flourish across the country, but tend to be concerned more with improvement of incomes, education, health and nutrition than social or political emancipation. The government-sponsored **Maendeleo ya Wanawake Organization** (**MYWO**) started to help women at a very basic level in the 1950s. It now encourages economic independence and, with a nominal annual membership fee, almost every woman in Kenya can belong. The umbrella group teaches basic literacy, family planning and nutrition, and is also working hard to abolish the practice of ritual **female genital mutilation** (FGM). This is carried out as a rite of passage on a significant proportion of Kenyan girls, and is more prevalent in some ethnic groups (the Gusii and the Maasai, for example, where it may still affect up to fifty percent) than others. Unsurprisingly, it is more common in rural areas and among uneducated communities. Kenya is a signatory to the UN's Human Rights Convention, which proscribes FGM, and the government promised in 1990 to ban the practice, but it was finally outlawed only in 2011. Women's groups are trying to persuade rural communities to accept a mutilation-free "alternative rite of passage", with some success.

Dec 2007–Feb 2008	April 2008	2009
Rigged elections spark widespread violence, with more than 1300 people killed and half a million displaced	"Grand Coalition" government formed after months of negotiation, initially brokered by Kofi Annan	United Nations representative Philip Alston lambasts government for extra-judicial killings

AL-SHABAAB AND TROUBLE ON THE COAST

With the emergence of the **Al-Shabaab** jihadist organization in Somalia and their alliance with Al-Qaeda in 2010, Kenya continues to face serious threats across the porous Somali border and potentially at home, too, with a predictable effect on the country's tourist industry.

The first series of incidents began in 2011 with **kidnappings** of aid workers and tourists, including a British couple, abducted from a beach lodge close to the Somalian border, the husband murdered in the process and the wife released after a ransom was paid, and a French woman, taken from her winter home on Manda island who died from lack of medication while being held. Security in the Lamu archipelago was quickly reinforced with the help of local hoteliers and the US air force. Despite being carried out by profit-motivated criminals rather than well-organized militants, the kidnappings precipitated a major **military intervention** by Kenya's army, navy and air force, the Kenya Defence Forces, or KDF, into Somalia.

In reprisal, Al-Shabaab, uprooted from its former bases in southern Somalia, staged a series of ad hoc **gun and grenade attacks**. There were however three, far more devastating episodes. In September 2013, gunmen attacked the Israeli-owned **Westgate** shopping mall in Nairobi, killing 67 people in a four-day siege notable for the slow and incoherent response of the security services. In June 2014 there were two attacks in the district of **Mpeketoni** (a remote, largely Kikuyu migrant area on the mainland of Lamu County), which left more than seventy dead. Security forces stationed nearby only arrived on the scene long after the assailants had left. Al-Shabaab claimed responsibility for the second attack, while President Kenyatta puzzled observers by his claim that local politicians were to blame for the first. In May 2015, a brazen attack by Al-Shabaab gunmen on **Garissa University**, on the outskirts of Garissa town in the northeast, left 142 students, mostly non-Muslims, dead.

In May 2014, footage of the **departure of tourists** from the beaches, when charter airlines cancelled their flights, led to the virtual shutdown of tourism. The London *Daily Mail* made much of the suspected involvement with Al-Shabaab of the wife of one of the 7/7 London bombers, Samantha Lewthwaite, the so-called **"White Widow"**. The Al-Jazeera news channel's more serious investigation found evidence that radical Muslim leaders on the coast have been systematically eliminated in a string of **extra-judicial executions** by Kenya's security services, with assistance from Israeli and British intelligence. A radical Muslim preacher, **Aboud Rogo**, implicated in fundraising for Al-Shabaab and murdered in a drive-by shooting in August 2012, was the most high-profile victim.

The Kenyan government's public response to Al-Shabaab terrorism was **internment** – the mass detention of thousands of men from the Somali community, imprisoned and questioned for weeks at Nairobi's **Kasarani sports stadium**. The treatment of the Somalis, reminiscent of the tactics used by the British on the Kikuyu community in the 1950s during the Emergency (see p.566), caused an outcry in the media and only fuelled the resentment it was supposed to quash. Domestically, Al-Shabaab's attacks have also been mixed up with the separatist group, the **Mombasa Republican Council**, or MRC, which campaigns under the slogan "Pwani si Kenya" ("The Coast is not Kenya"). The ban on the MRC was lifted by the High Court in Mombasa in July 2012, though the Kenya government continues to treat the MRC as outlaws.

On the coast, where the tourism-based economy flounders, and a climate of suspicion and state-sanctioned murder persists, there is mounting evidence that unemployed young men are vulnerable to **radicalization**, easy prey to offers of money, a warped purpose and a new life in an echo of tactics used by Islamic State in the Middle East and Europe.

Meanwhile, the **war in Somalia** between Al-Shabaab and the KDF (now acting as part of AMISOM, the African Union Mission in Somalia) was showing no sign of coming to an early conclusion as this book went to press in early 2016.

2010	Aug 2010	April 2011
Widespread floods follow 2009's crippling droughts and bring death and destruction	New constitution approved in referendum after long consultative process	Six key figures, including two presidential candidates, named by ICC in The Hague in connection with 2008 post-election violence

The 2013 general election

Despite there being eight presidential candidates in 2013's general election, only **Uhuru Kenyatta**, the son of Kenya's founding president, and **Raila Odinga**, the son of the founding president's arch-rival, had a chance of achieving a majority. Just weeks before the election, the avowed political rivals Kenyatta and **William Ruto**, leaders in all but name of the Kikuyu and Kalenjin communities respectively, joined their parties to form the strategic **Jubilee Alliance**. With both men facing high-profile war crimes trials in The Hague, Kenyatta ran for president with Ruto as his running mate, employing British PR firm BTP Advisers to mount a well-funded campaign around a nationalism and self-determination ticket, accusing Britain and the US of interference in Kenyan affairs.

Many voters appeared willing to swallow the message that only by looking to the future and not dwelling on the past could Kenya thrive and prosper. Even at the likely cost of ushering in another government of kleptocrats, an alliance of erstwhile enemies with each others' blood on their hands, there was a widespread commitment to peace and above all to an avoidance of any repeat of the electoral violence of 2007/8. *Chagua Amani*, or "Choose Peace", was the most resonant slogan of the election.

Kenya's notorious propensity for **ethnic-block voting** meant that Ruto was able to deliver the vast majority of his Kalenjin ethnic followers' vote for Jubilee. Kenyatta secured the presidency in the first round, with no need for a run off, gaining a wafer-thin overall majority of 50.07 per cent of the vote, and Ruto became vice president. To more sceptical Kenyans, especially the many who rely on social media, it felt like the outcome was determined not by the voters, but by the vote counters, or in this case the **Independent Electoral and Boundaries Commission** (IEBC) that had been placed in charge of US$100 million-worth of electronic voting equipment at 33,000 polling stations.

Voter turnout was extraordinarily high, around 80–90 per cent, and **regional voting patterns** showed marked contrasts across the country. Of Kenya's eight regions, Kenyatta won the vote in Central, Rift Valley and Northeastern, while Odinga came out on top in Nairobi, Coast, Eastern, Western and Nyanza.

Kenya under the Jubilee Alliance

There was little jubilation as Kenya celebrated **50 years of independence** from Britain in December 2013. Kenyans were unanimously relieved to have avoided the bloodbath that some had predicted, but hopes for security, a better life and the rule of law remained dreams for most. The changes to the **land laws** enshrined in the new constitution were rarely tested in the courts or were applied corruptly by partisan lawyers. In a high-profile example that received international attention, the police tear-gassed primary school children who tried to reclaim their playground in **Langata**, Nairobi from a Jubilee politician who had grabbed the land in January 2015.

Apart from land grabbing, **corruption scandals** continue unabated. To flag only the most egregious: a $3.2 billion contract was speedily awarded to two related Chinese companies to supervise and build the new **standard-gauge rail line** between Mombasa and Nairobi, in partnership with a pair of Kenyan companies neither of

Sep 2011	Oct 2011	Aug 2012	Oct 2012
Two tourists kidnapped and one killed in two incidents in the Lamu archipelago	Kenya Defence Force (KDF) enters Somalia to combat Al-Shabaab terrorists	Assassination of Muslim preacher in Mombasa sparks three days of rioting in city centre	Elderly victims of torture during Mau Mau period win right to sue the UK government; KDF capture southern Somali city of Kismayo

which has any experience in supervision or construction of massive civil engineering works; $1.7 billion was unaccounted for in the **Eurobond scandal**, in which a $2 billion loan was raised from private foreign finance, with capital repayment and compound interest totalling more than $3.2 billion due to be repaid out of Kenya's public purse by 2024; a total of $550 million was spent by the government-owned **Geothermal Generation Company** on "drilling" at Menengai Crater, without producing one watt of electricity; and in the **Ministry of Devolution**, one of the worst culprits, tens of millions of dollars was revealed to have been "spent" on pens, wall partitions, condom dispensers and other items, at prices consistently ten times more than the market cost.

In response to the media outcry, a **Parliamentary Powers and Privileges Bill** was passed into legislation in October 2015, seeking to muzzle the press by requiring journalists to seek approval before reporting on parliament or any of its committees.

Into the future

Kenya's prospects would look doubtful even if the country had a healthy environment and a sustainable economy. In fact, parts of the **private sector** are making profits, driving growth and essentially keeping the country alive: Safaricom's mobile money service **M-Pesa** and the innovative tech sector are the envy of many countries in the region. But the underlying issues are huge: crippling cycles of drought and flooding caused by **climate change** have seen millions of people in the north and east needing food aid. And instead of sustainable economic growth, the government touts major infrastructure projects that create huge excitement but come to nothing: for example the long dreamed-of oil boom in the north, which seemed within grasp in 2012 when potentially viable **oil reserves** were located in Turkana but for which there has been no interested investor; and the grandiose plans hatched in 2006 for a high-speed rail line and oil pipeline between South Sudan and Lamu (the **Lamu Port–South Sudan–Ethiopia Transport Corridor** or LAPSSET), which has so far delivered nothing but an empty HQ building on the mainland near Manda island, and kickbacks to government ministers from grotesquely expensive "feasibility studies".

Kenya's **poverty gap** increases every year – it's especially pronounced in the populous Central Highlands – and steep price rises for essential commodities such as flour, milk and sugar have seen many urban Kenyans struggling to meet basic daily needs. Meanwhile politicians and civil servants continue to mouth platitudes about Rome not being built in a day, while stealing public funds and public lands on a scale beyond anything previously dared under the governments of Kibaki, Moi or Jomo Kenyatta.

Although Kenyans are anticipating the **next general election**, scheduled for August 2017, with some nervousness, many argue that things must improve, eventually, as they have been arguing for half a century. But this endearing, ingrained optimism is not borne out by experience. The super-rich elite, and even many middle-class professionals, may bolt their security gates and thrive in their bubble – at least for now – but life for the majority of Kenyans has never been so hard. This socio-economic climate would be a free-for-all, were it not for the huge costs paid by the poor on whose backs the whole edifice is ultimately carried.

Sep 2013	Dec 2014	July 2015
Al-Shabaab terrorists attack the Westgate shopping mall in Nairobi, shooting dead 67 people and wounding more than 170	The ICC drops charges against President Kenyatta, as most of the witnesses against him withdraw their testimonies, die or disappear	Barack Obama captivates Kenya during his first visit as president, calling for gay equality, equal rights for women and an end to tribalism and corruption

Music

The music of Kenya is less well known abroad than that of a number of other African countries, but its home-grown vitality is there if you listen, and Nairobi's audiences and recording facilities have long been a draw for musicians from all over east and central Africa, bringing a Pan-African musical flavour to the city.

All the people of Kenya have traditional musical cultures, some of which have survived more intact than others – with the majority of Kenyans nowadays being Christian, **gospel music** has all but obliterated traditional music in many areas. Among the Kikuyu and the Kalenjin, for example, traditional music is almost extinct, and elsewhere, to hear anything at all, you need time, patience and local people's trust before being allowed to witness what can still be very sacred events. Kenyan gospel itself has been going through a transformation. On the one hand it's not the uplifting soulful version associated with African American churches in the US, but neither is it any longer simply the tinny, synthesized, homogeneous beats of a few years ago. It still includes the choirs of the churches, both urban and rural, but modern gospel now mirrors every kind of pop music within Kenya..

As for **popular music**, there is no single identifiable genre of "Kenyan pop", but rather a number of styles that borrow freely and cross-fertilize one another. Within Kenya's widespread **benga** style, many musicians perform most of their songs in one of Kenya's indigenous languages. Other musicians, especially those playing rumba styles, aim at a broad national audience and thus perform in **Swahili**; the big-name bands can usually muster large crowds in sprawling, ethnically diverse towns like Nairobi, Nakuru or Mombasa. Others offer a local variant of the **Congolese** sound, with lyrics in **Lingala**, a Congolese language understood by few people in Kenya. Meanwhile, **international pop sounds** such as R&B, hip-hop, reggae, ragga and dancehall have taken a more prominent role in Kenya's pop music sound, especially among the younger Kenyans.

A good complement to this music overview can be found at ⓦeastafricanmusic.com, a website put together by the author of this article, that features biographies of several musicians, articles on the Kenyan scene over the years and lists of recommended albums.

Traditional music

Music has traditionally been used to accompany ceremonies, events and **rites of passage**, from celebrations at a baby's birth to songs of adolescence and warriorhood, and from marriage, harvests and solar and lunar cycles to festivities, religious events and death. The oldest of Kenya's musical traditions is **ngoma**, a term which, in most Bantu languages of Kenya, refers to a specific kind of drum and a related dance; *ngoma* is nowadays used generally to describe all the facets of a musical performance, including the accompanying dances.

Although an inter-ethnic *ngoma* called *beni* ("band") emerged on the coast at the beginning of the twentieth century and spread inland (you can still witness this anachronistic, marching-band form on special occasions in Lamu), *ngoma* music today is essentially ethnic, related to a specific language group and using the respective vernacular and local dance rhythms. *Ngoma* also provides most of the music used during the life-cycle festivities (birth, initiation and circumcision, marriage and death), whether in the town or the country. Look out for recordings by Luhya *sukuti* groups, the *sukuti* being the central drum of these ensembles.

The following is a brief tribe-by-tribe rundown of more easily encountered traditional music and instruments. Obviously, there's much more available if you know where to search and what to ask for: essential **reading** for this is George Senoga-Zake's *Folk Music of Kenya* (Uzima Press, Nairobi). Other books about Kenyan music are thin on the ground, though most bookshops stock some school textbooks on music, some of which provide a handy introduction to the subject. You can usually find a few CDs of traditional music locally – and even the odd cassette – though it may take a little perseverance. Another source of background on traditional music, with audio clips, is ⓦbluegecko.org.

Kamba and Chuka

The **Kamba** are best known for their skill at drumming, but this tradition has sadly now all but disappeared. To find any musicians, you'll have to go well off the beaten track in Ukambani. Start in the big town of Machakos and then move on to Kitui. Like the music of the Kamba, Chuka music from the east side of Mount Kenya is drumming genius and, sadly, equally near-extinct.

Bajuni

The **Bajuni** are a small ethnic group living in the Lamu archipelago and on the nearby mainland, and are known musically for a recording of an epic women's work song called *Mashindano Ni Matezo*. One of only a very few easily available recordings of women singing traditionally in Kenya, it features counterpoint singing that gradually becomes hypnotic, punctuated by metallic rattles and supported by subdued drumming. You can find it in Lamu, Kilifi or Mombasa.

Boran

The **Boran**, who live between Marsabit and the Ethiopian border, have a rich musical tradition. Some Arab influence is readily discernible, as are more typically North African rhythms; most distinctive is their use of the *chamonge* calabash guitar, nowadays a large cooking pot loosely strung with metal wires. Recordings are difficult to obtain; ask in Isiolo or Marsabit.

Gusii

Gusii music is perhaps Kenya's oddest. The favoured instrument is the *obokano*, an enormous, deep-voiced version of the Luo *nyatiti* lyre, which at times can sound like roaring thunder. They also use the ground bow, essentially a large hole dug in the ground over which an animal skin is tightly pegged. The skin has a small hole cut in the centre, into which a single-stringed bow is placed and plucked: the sound defies description. Ask around in Kisii and you should be able to pick up recordings easily enough.

Luhya

Luhya music has a clear Bantu flavour, easily discernible in the pre-eminence of drums. Of these, the *sukuti* is best known, sometimes played in ensembles, and still used in rites of passage such as circumcision. Recordings are easily available in Kakamega and Kitale, and in some of the shops around River Road in Nairobi.

Luo

The **Luo** are best known as the originators of *benga* (see p.584). Their most distinctive musical instrument is the *nyatiti*, a double-necked eight-string lyre with a skin resonator which is also struck on one neck with a metal ring tied to the toe. It produces a tight, resonant sound, and is used to generate hypnotic, sometimes remarkably complex, rhythms. The instrument was used in the fields to relieve workers' tiredness, the music typically beginning at a moderate pace and quickening progressively, the musician singing over the sound. Look out also for recordings of *onand* (accordion) and *orutu* (single-stringed fiddle).

Maasai

The traditional nomadic lifestyle of the **Maasai** tended to preclude the carrying of large instruments, and as a result their music is one of the most distinctive in Kenya, characterized by a total lack of instruments and by some astonishing polyphonic multipart singing. This can be call-and-response, and sometimes women are included in the chorus, but the most famous form is the songs of the warriors or *morani*, where each man sings part of a rhythm, more often than not from his throat (rather like a grunt), which together with the calls of his companions creates a pattern of rhythms. The songs are usually competitive (expressed through the singers alternately leaping as high as they can) or bragging – about how the singer killed a lion, or rustled cattle from a neighbouring community. The Maasai have retained much of their traditional culture, so singing is still very much used in traditional ceremonies, most spectacularly in the *eunoto* circumcision ceremony in which boys are initiated into manhood to begin their ten- to fifteen-year stint as *morani*.

Most tourists staying in big coastal hotels or in game park lodges in Amboseli and Maasai Mara will have a chance to sample Maasai music in the form of groups of *morani* playing at the behest of hotel management. Recordings can be difficult to find, though.

Mijikenda

The **Mijikenda** of the coast have a prolific musical tradition which has survived Christian conversion, and is readily available on tape throughout the coastal region. Performances can occasionally be seen in the larger hotels. Most of the music available is from the Giriama section of the Mijikenda, who live inland of Malindi. Like the Kamba, the Mijikenda are superb drummers and athletic dancers. The music is generally light and overlaid with complex rhythms, impossible not to dance to. Look out also for the *kiringongo* music of the Chonyi people, which features the xylophone (an instrument otherwise unknown in Kenya).

Samburu

Despite having been discovered by tourists and authors of coffee-table books, the only recordings of **Samburu** music are tracks on occasional compilations. Like their Maasai cousins, whose singing it closely resembles, Samburu music includes no instruments – at least in theory. In practice, they do play small pipes, and also a kind of guitar with a box resonator and loose metal strings – which seems to be related to the *chamonge* of the Boran. But these are played purely for pleasure, or to soothe a crying baby, and are thus not deemed "music" by Samburu. Listen out also for the sinuously erotic rain songs sung by women in times of drought. For recordings, ask around in Maralal.

Turkana

Until the 1970s, the **Turkana** were one of Kenya's remotest tribes, and in large part they're still untouched by Christian missionaries. Their traditional music is based loosely on a call-and-response pattern. The main instrument is a kudu antelope horn with or without finger holes, but most of their music is entirely vocal. A rarity to listen out for are the women's rain songs, sung to the god Akuj during times of drought. Traditional music is still played on ceremonial occasions but finding cassettes is extremely difficult; it's a question of asking around in Loiyangalani. You're usually welcome to join performances in Loiyangalani for a small fee.

Popular music

Until the mid-1990s, the defining elements of Kenyan popular music had always been the interplay of guitars, with prominent solos, and the **cavacha** rhythm – a kind of *clavé* beat, popularized in the mid-1970s by Congolese groups such as Zaiko Langa Langa and Orchestra Shama Shama. While rapid-fire percussion, usually on the snare or high hat, continues to underlie a great sweep of Kenyan music, it's worth noting that the scene is very different from that of the 1970s and 1980s; the ranks of the older generation of pop musicians have thinned quickly in recent years, with a huge number of experienced younger musicians having died from AIDS-related illnesses. The effects have been devastating, not only in the loss of creative talent, but because with these musicians goes the living memory of the evolution of Kenyan music in its historical context.

The arrival of the guitar

From the early 1950s on, with the coming of recording and broadcasting, the introduction of new instruments and the more widespread use of the **guitar**, an acoustic guitar-based music developed as accompaniment to songs sung in **Swahili**.

TAARAB MUSIC

Taarab (or *tarab/tarabu*), the main popular music of the coastal Swahili people, has a long tradition in the festive life of the Swahili, especially at weddings. Many of the lead singers and bandleaders of *taarab* groups are women, a phenomenon almost unique in Kenyan traditional music. Furthermore, the music has strong Arabic/Islamic overtones in instrumentation, especially in the haunting vocals. While the Indian harmonium was (and still is) the main *taarab* instrument in the Lamu archipelago, earlier *taarab* groups in Mombasa used the full Arabian orchestra, including the lute-like *oud* and violins. Today, the main instruments tend to be guitar and electronic organ or synthesizer, and either an Indian harmonium or a small electronic organ/piano, plus a variety of local, Arabian or Indian drums. Indian movies, with their strong musical component, are very popular on the coast, and this has led to many of the features of Indian music being absorbed into *taarab*.

On Lamu island, the old centre of Swahili culture, most weddings today are served by a few amateur *taarab* groups, with professional groups bussed up from Mombasa only for more well-to-do marriages. The **Zein Musical Party**, now based in Mombasa, is the heir of Lamu's *taarab* tradition. Zein l'Abdin was born in Lamu and hails from a family in which the Swahili arts were highly valued. Together with the Swahili poet Sheikh Nabhany, Zein has unearthed a number of poems, dating back to the nineteenth century, which he includes in his repertoire. But Zein isn't just a fabulous singer and composer; he also ranks as the finest *oud* player in East Africa and is well known throughout the Islamic world.

Maulidi Musical Party, **Juma Bhalo** and **Zuhura & Party** were for more than three decades Mombasa's main wedding favourites. Singers Maulidi Juma and Juma Bhalo are at ease both with traditional Swahili wedding songs and the Hindi-style songs so characteristic of Mombasa *taarab*, with Swahili words set to tunes from the latest Bollywood movies. Maulidi Musical Party are the archetypal Mombasa ensemble, their sound being based on a keyboard, with fills by accordion, guitar, bass and percussion, and many rhythms rooted in local *ngoma* (drum and dance) traditions. In Maulidi's group, Mohamed Shigoo's keyboard work stands out as especially original, with a strong flavour of harmonium (which he used to play earlier in his career) and *nzumari* (a local double-reed horn). He was also backed by the distinctive voice of female singer **Malika** until her emigration to the US. Mombasa's main remaining female star is the enchanting **Zuhura Swaleh**, whose energetic songs have a firm base in the local *chakacha* rhythms and lyrics.

With Zein, Maulidi and Zuhura now into their seventies, their voices having suffered from the strain of non-stop singing for six hours at countless weddings, they are mostly heard on local radio stations or on CDs bought in street markets. **Diamond Star**, led by **Mbarak Ali Haj**, now caters for local wedding audiences with a style closer to modern Tanzanian *taarab*. Another more recent appearance on the scene is **Yusuf Mohamed "Tenge"**, who follows in the steps of Maulidi and Juma Bhalo. More recently **Prince Adio**, son of Mohamed Shigoo, has created some waves in linking *taarab* musical sensibilities and poetry with modern sequencing techniques, arriving at a mix of styles that is close to Tanzanian bongo flava and Swahili hip-hop. . Female pop singer **Nyota Ndogo** (real name Mwanaisha Abdalla) although she doesn't identify as a *taarab* singer, also sometimes features songs inspired by the style.

A basis for Swahili-language popular music had already been laid by the *beni* groups flourishing in East African towns during the first half of the twentieth century. *Beni* songs, as well as the new guitar songs, featured the strong and critical social commentary so beloved of Kenyans. The songs were usually in the form of a short story and sometimes commented on an actual political or social topic, or perhaps recounted a personal experience of the musician. Romantic lyrics from this time are almost non-existent, even in songs dealing with men and women.

The guitar styles themselves developed out of different instrumental techniques and musical perceptions, but they were influenced by the records available at the time, mainly from other parts of Africa. Kenyan musicians of the period cite as important inspirations the finger-picking style of **Jean Bosco Mwenda** and **Losta Abelo**, both from Katanga Province in the Democratic Republic of Congo, and **George Sibanda**, from Bulawayo in Zimbabwe. From this period, the notables of Kenya's acoustic guitar styles were **John Mwale**, **George Mukabi** (directly out of the Luhya *sukuti* tradition) and **Ben Blastus O'Bulawayo** (Ben Obolla).

The 1960s saw the introduction of **electric guitars** as well as larger groups of three to four guitars. Finger-picking guitarists from western Kenya and the smoother, driving, electric-guitar sound of groups like **Equator Sound Band** (Equator was a leading record label of the time), featuring the songs of **Daudi Kabaka**, **Fadhili William**, **Nashil Pichen** and **Peter Tsotsi**, dominated the airwaves and the record stores. Daudi Kabaka reigned as the "King of Twist", the twist being essentially a fast version of the South African rhythm found in songs such as "The Lion Sleeps Tonight". Into the 1970s, while Kabaka's African Eagles and others continued to play their brands of Swahili music, many top Kenyan groups, such as the Ashantis, Air Fiesta and the Hodi Boys, were playing Congolese covers and international pop, especially soul music, in the Nairobi clubs.

Benga and other modern styles

In the 1970s, a number of musicians began to define the direction of an emerging form, **benga**, which more than any other Kenyan music became Kenya's most characteristic pop sound. Although it originated with the Luo people of western Kenya, practically all the Kenyan guitar bands play variants of it, and today most of the regional or ethnic pop groups refer generally to their music as *benga*.

As a pop style, *benga* actually dates back to the 1950s, when musicians began adapting traditional dance rhythms and the sounds of the *nyatiti* and *orutu* to the acoustic guitar and later to electric instruments. During its heyday in the 1970s and up to the 1990s, *benga* music dominated Kenya's recording industry and was very popular even in west and southern Africa.

By any standard, the most famous *benga* group is **Shirati Jazz**, led by singer, songwriter, and guitarist D.O. (Daniel Owino) Misiani. Born in Shirati, Tanzania, just south of the Kenyan border, Misiani gained experience early in his career performing with Daudi Kabaka in the Equator Sound Band up to 1967. After that, he formed the band that refined and ultimately defined the sound that became the *benga* juggernaut of the 1970s and beyond. His style is characterized by soft, flowing and melodic two-part vocal harmonies, a very active, pulsating bass line that derives at least in part from traditional *nyatiti* and drum rhythms, and stacks of invigorating guitar work, the lead alternating with the vocal. Misiani and Shirati Jazz continued to lead the Luo *benga* universe up to his death in a road accident in 2006.

Other historically important *benga* artists include the pioneering **Colella Mazee** and **Ochieng Nelly** – either together or separately in various incarnations of **Victoria Jazz** and the **Victoria Kings**, Kawere Boys Band, as well as George Ramogi and his Continental Luo Sweet Band. *benga* is alive and well today with such practitioners as Linet Aluoch Pamba and her Karapul Jazz Band and Dr Osito Kale and Orchestra Nabi Kings..

One Luo name which doesn't fit neatly under the *benga* banner is **Ochieng Kabaselleh** with his Luna Kidi Band. Kabaselleh's songs were mostly in Luo, but sometimes with a liberal seasoning of Swahili and English. Likewise, the melodies and harmonies are from the *benga* realm, but the rhythm, guitar work and horns suggest influences from the Congolese/Swahili-dominated sound. Kabaselleh, who languished in prison for several years for "subversion" in the 1980s, returned to the music world with a flood of new releases in the 1990s and died in 1998.

A related group, set up by Kabaselleh in the late 1970s with several of his brothers, continues today as **Bana Kadori**. Originally brought together as a recording group, they are now an active performing band, their music running from Kabaselleh's hybrid *benga*-rumba style to mainstream *benga*. This *benga*-rumba style became increasingly popular in the 2000s with **Musa Juma** and his Limpopo International Band. Still rooted in Luo melodies and harmonies, the syncopated *benga* bass lines have given way to smoother, flowing rumba, with great commercial success in the pop music wars. After the release of his sixth CD in 2010, Musa Juma toured the US, but died on his return to Kenya in 2011, pneumonia the suspected cause. The uniquely Kenyan fusion of *benga* with Congolese rumba, originating with Ochieng Kabaselleh and institutionalized by Musa Juma, continues to be played today by popular practitioners such as Igwe Prezda Bandasonn and his Patrons Musica, Johnny Junior with B-V Band and Musa's own sister Milly Fedha and Super Limpopo International.

Luhya

Many of Kenya's famous guitarists and vocalists come from the Luhya highlands just to the north of Lake Victoria and Luo-land. This was the ancestral home of early finger-picking guitarists like **John Mwale** and **George Mukabi**, as well as **Daudi Kabaka** and another twist proponent still active in the music business, **John Nzenze**. While these musicians cultivated broad appeal through the use of Swahili lyrics, other Luhya musicians stayed closer to their home areas linguistically as well as musically. In *benga* style, **Sukuma bin Ongaro** is famous for his humorous social commentaries. Even if you can't understand the language, his music is great to dance to and, of course, has some super guitar licks.

Shem Tube is a Luhya vocalist/guitarist whose music straddles both past and present – though it's his past that brought him a following in Europe, thanks to a vintage compilation in the *omutibo* style featuring his group **Abana ba Nasery** (The Nursery Boys). Coming together as a trio in the early 1960s, Abana ba Nasery used traditional Luhya rhythms and melody lines, but their two-guitar line-up and three-part vocal harmonies, with rhythms scraped from the neck ridges of an old Fanta bottle, presaged elements of modern Kenyan pop. Although they've never earned enough money to buy their own electric guitars and amps, Abana ba Nasery has had a string of local hits as an electric band under the stage names Mwilonje Jazz and Super Bunyore Band.

Kikuyu

As Kenya's largest ethnic group, the Kikuyu-speaking people of the Central Highlands and Nairobi are a major market force in Kenya's music industry. Perhaps because of this large "built-in" audience, few Kikuyu *benga* musicians have tried to cross over into the national Swahili or English-language markets.

Kikuyu pop has a traditional melodic structure, quite distinct from the Luo and Luhya traditions of western Kenya. Most often the songs incorporate elements of *benga* and *cavacha*, but it's not unusual for there to be a dose of country and western, reggae or Congolese *soukous*. From the 1970s into the 1990s the indisputable king of Kikuyu pop was **Joseph Kamaru**, who, over the course of his career, carved out something of a musical empire, including a large band and dancers, two music stores and a recording studio. Still going strong in 1993, Kamaru shocked his fans by announcing that he had been "born again" and retired from music performance to devote his efforts to evangelism and gospel music promotion – a precursor to a much larger shift to gospel music in Kenyan society and the music business.

At least a part of the void left by Kamaru was filled by Jane Nyambura, one of very few female headliners in Kikuyu pop. Known simply as **Queen Jane**, she was a staunch advocate of the inclusion of traditional folk forms and local languages within contemporary pop, an approach which limited her radio exposure, but didn't stop her and four of her brothers and sisters from making their living from her band. Her death in 2010, while only in her mid-40s, was a huge blow for Kikuyu music fans and *benga* fans generally. It remains to be seen if one of the newer *benga* stars can fill the void: **Joyce wa Mamaa** (Joyce Wanjiku Njoki) is off to a solid start with her "Menya Wari Wakwa" album. Meanwhile, Kikuyu stalwarts **John De'Mathew**, **Musaimo**, and **Mike Rua** continue to perform every weekend in bars in and around Nairobi.

Kamba

Kamba pop music is firmly entrenched in the *benga/cavacha* camp, though it has distinctive features of its own. One is the delicate, flowing rhythm guitar, often reminiscent of the old carousel calliope that underlies many arrangements. While the primary guitar plays chords in the lower range, the second guitar, often in a high register, plays a fast pattern of fills. This is discernible in many of the recordings of the three most famous Kamba groups; the **Kalambya Boys** and **Kalambya Sisters**, **Peter Mwambi and his Kyanganga Boys** and **Les Kilimambogo Brothers Band**. With socially relevant lyrics, intricate guitar weaves and a solid dance-beat backing, Les Kilimambogo Brothers Band began recording in Swahili and achieved widespread popularity in Kenya, though its career was brought to an end by the death of leader **Kakai Kilonzo** in 1987. These days, a new generation of musicians is drawing the limelight away from the old guard, with the likes of **Ken wa Maria** and **Ben Mbatha** dominating the Kamba market.

Congolese

Congolese musicians have been making musical waves in Kenya since the late 1950s, but it wasn't until the mid-1970s, after the passing of the American soul craze, that music from Congo began to dominate the city nightclubs. One of the first Congolese musicians to settle in Kenya during this period was **Baba Gaston**, who had already been in the business for twenty years when he arrived in Nairobi with his group Baba National in 1975. A prolific musician, he stole the scene until his retirement in 1989. Following Gaston, such groups as **Super Mazembe** and **Les Mangelepa** (some of Gaston's own musicians), as well as **Samba Mapangala** and an early version of his **Orchestra Virunga**, took hold in the city. This period is still regarded as the golden age of Lingala music in Kenya and it flourishes locally with plenty of CD reissues in the shops.

Congolese music remains popular in various clubs in Nairobi and Kenya's big towns. In fact, some of the musicians of this golden period can be found performing today in successor bands to Mazembe and Mangelepa. But it's the more recent Congolese outfits who have regular gigs around Nairobi; groups like **Rhumba Japan**, **Bilenge Musica** and **Sultani Skassy Kasambula** and **Mitwango ya Jiji Orchestra**.

In both Congolese and Swahili popular music, **rumba** has always been a major ingredient. Songs typically open with a slow-to-medium rumba that ambles through the verses, backed by a light percussion of gentle congas, snare and high hat. Then, three or four minutes into the song there's a transition – or more often a hiatus. It's goodbye to verses and rolling rumba as a much faster rhythm, known as the *sebene* in Congo, highlighting the instrumental parts, especially solo guitar and brass, takes over with a vengeance. Swahili music over the last thirty years has been particularly faithful to this two-part structure, although today, both Swahili and Congolese musicians often dispense with the slow portion altogether.

Swahili bands: the Tanzanian influence

Kenya's own brand of **Swahili pop** music has its origin in the Tanzanian pop styles of the 1970s, though the Kenyan variety has followed a separate evolutionary path from the

Tanzanian mainstream. In addition to the stylistic features it shares with the Congolese sound (light, high-hat-and-conga percussion and a delicate two/three-guitar interweave), the Kenyan Swahili sound is instrumentally sparse, allowing the bass to fill in gaps, often in syncopated rhythms. While the Congolese musicians are famous for their vocals and their intricate harmonies, Swahili groups are renowned for their demon guitarists and crisp, clear guitar interplay. Trumpets and saxes are common in recorded arrangements but usually omitted in club performances because of the extra expense.

SWAHILI POP LYRICS

These are two songs you're almost certain to hear, sooner of later, regardless of where you stay or how you travel.

JAMBO BWANA

by Teddy Kalanda Harrison

Jambo, jambo Bwana	Greetings, greetings Bwana
Habari gani?	How are you doing?
Nzuri sana	Very well
Wageni, mwakaribishwa	Visitors, you are all welcomed
Kenya yetu	In our Kenya
Hakuna matata	There are no problems
Kenya ni nchi nzuri	Kenya's a beautiful country
Hakuna matata	There are no problems
Nchi ya kupendeza	A pleasing country
Hakuna matata	There are no problems
Nchi ya maajabu	A country of wonders
Hakuna matata	There are no problems
Nchi yenye amani	A country of peace
Hakuna matata	There are no problems

MALAIKA

Authorship disputed, first popularized by Fadhili William

Malaika, nakupenda malaika	Angel, I love you angel
Malaika, nakupenda malaika	Angel, I love you angel
Nami nifanyeje, kijana mwenzio?	And me, what shall I, your boyfriend, do?
Nashindwa na mali sina wee	If I weren't struggling for money
Ningekuoa malaika	I would marry you angel
Nashindwa na mali sina wee	If I weren't struggling for money
Ningekuoa malaika	I would marry you angel
Pesa zasumbuwa roho yangu	Money is the source of my heartache
Pesa zasumbuwa roho yangu	Money is the source of my heartache
Nami nifanyeje, kijana mwenzio?	And me, what shall I, your boyfriend, do?
Nashindwa na mali sina wee	If I weren't struggling for money
Ningekuoa malaika	I would marry you angel
Nashindwa na mali sina wee	If I weren't struggling for money
Ningekuoa malaika	I would marry you angel
Kidege, hukuwaza kidege	Little bird, I'm always dreaming of you, little bird
Kidege, hukuwaza kidege	Little bird, I'm always dreaming of you, little bird
Nami nifanyeje, kijana mwenzio?	And me, what shall I, your boyfriend, do?
Nashindwa na mali sina wee	If I weren't struggling for money
Ningekuoa malaika	I would marry you angel
Nashindwa na mali sina wee	If I weren't struggling for money
Ningekuoa malaika	I would marry you angel

One of the first Tanzanian groups to migrate to Kenya was **Arusha Jazz**, the predecessor of what is now the legendary **Simba Wanyika Original** ("Simba Wanyika" means "Lion of the Savanna"). Founded by Wilson Peter Kinyonga and his brothers George and William, the group began performing in Mombasa in 1971. In 1975, with Tanzanian recruit Omar Shabani on rhythm and Kenyan Tom Malanga on bass, the brothers shifted to Nairobi where, over a twenty-year period, they were favourites of the city's club scene and made scores of recordings. They broke up in the 1990s after the deaths of George and Wilson Kinyonga.

The **Wanyika** name is also famous in East Africa for several bands that emerged from Simba Wanyika Original. The group's first big split occurred in 1978 when the core of supporting musicians around the Kinyonga brothers left to form **Les Wanyika**. Under the leadership of Tanzanian lead guitarist John Ngereza, they remained one of Nairobi's top bands – distinguished by imaginative compositions and arrangements, a lean sound and the delicious blend of Professor Omari's rhythm guitar with John Ngereza's lead and Tom Malanga's bass – right up to Ngereza's death in 2000 (Omari had died in 1998) when the group broke up.

Another important figure in the Wanyika story is Tanzania-born **Issa Juma**, who quickly established a name for himself in Kenya as a premier vocalist in the early days of Les Wanyika. Issa formed Super Wanyika in 1981 and over the next few years had a series of hits featuring half a dozen other variations on the Wanyika names. One of the most prolific artists of the 1980s, he was perhaps the most versatile and creative of the Swahili artists in his willingness to take his music in different directions. His recorded output features many numbers that were a kind of fusion of Swahili rumba and *benga,* but isn't limited to this.

Foremost among other Tanzanians and Kenyans performing in the Swahili style are the **Maroon Commandos**. Members of the Kenyan Army, the Commandos are one of the oldest performing groups in the country. They first came together in 1970 and were initially mainly a covers band playing Congolese hits, but by 1977 they had become a strong force in the Swahili style with the huge Taita-language hit "Charonyi Ni Wasi". The Commandos have proven themselves quite experimental at times, mingling Swahili and *benga* styles and occasionally adding a keyboard and innovative guitar effects. Most recently, the Commandos have updated their sound to match the intensity of the *sebenes* of the Congolese groups; that fast-moving instrumental climax that builds over the last half of the song. At present, the Swahili rumba sound in Kenya is threatened with extinction. There are no established groups focused on this style, yet many bands of diverse styles will, in performance, cover the cherished songs of the Swahili rumba era.

Tourist and international pop

Where Kenyan pop meets the tourist industry, at the coastal resorts around Mombasa, bands can make a living just playing hotel gigs. These bands typically feature highly competent musicians, relatively good equipment and a fairly polished sound. The best of them are worth catching, typically playing an eclectic selection of old Congolese rumba tunes as warm-ups, popular international covers, a few Congolese favourites of the day, greatest hits from Kenya's past and some original material that leans heavily towards the American/Euro pop sound, but with lyrics relating to local topics.

The most successful Kenyan group in this field has been the oddly named **Them Mushrooms**, sometimes working under the name **Uyoga**, Swahili for "mushroom". The band managed to graduate from the coastal hotel circuit when they moved to Nairobi in 1987, but their music lives on at the coast, in particular their crowning achievement, the tourist anthem "Jambo Bwana". While the Mushrooms are proud to take credit for this insidiously infectious bit of fluff, they have shown over their long career that they have serious musical intentions, having been involved in a series of highly successful and diverse collaborations, including with one of the earliest of Kenyan guitar pioneers, **Fundi Konde**, *taarab* star Malika and the Kikuyu singer Queen Jane. Since 1993, the band have returned to their reggae roots.

Them Mushrooms' long-time counterpart in the hotel circuit, **Safari Sound**, have the distinction of having made Kenya's bestselling album ever in *The Best of African Songs*, a veritable greatest hits of hotel classics with songs such as "Malaika", a beautiful composition about ill-starred love (see box, p.587), that has been covered by everyone from Harry Belafonte and Miriam Makeba to Angelique Kidjo.

The evolving scene

In the early 1990s, the Kenyan music business was at a low point. Piracy and diminishing sales meant that, as a business, recorded music was hardly worth the effort – and the music that was being produced at the time hardly seemed worth buying anyway. By the mid-1990s, however, a number of factors had set the stage for a radical departure from the styles of previous generations. For one thing, Kenya experienced the rise of commercial **FM radio**, which helped acquaint Kenyans with reggae, ragga, house, dancehall, hip-hop and R&B from abroad. Also around this time, **new technology** made recording much more affordable, and a new breed of independent Kenyan producer began to emerge. New groups were formed, performing in styles inspired largely by music from abroad, but adding local elements in language, subject matter and sometimes melody and instrumentation. **Tedd Joslah**, **Bruce Odhiambo** and **Suzanne and Gido Kibukosya** were among the producers who were instrumental in shepherding along these new artists, often with quite different musical intentions, from hip-hop covers of African pop classics to gospel balladry.

Eric Wainaina, who brought together an innovative mix of Kenyan pop sounds with American soft-rock influences, was one of the stars of this new generation of Kenyan musicians, especially in the turbulent early years of multiparty democracy, when his lyrics about corruption and poverty resonated across the country. Some of the best material of the late 1990s was showcased on two CDs put together by Tedd Josiah, *Kenyan: The First Chapter* and *Kenyan: The Second Chapter*. Notable from the first of these is **Kalamashaka's** "Tafsiri Hii", the trio's trendsetting Swahili hip-hop song addressing the reality of street life. *The Second Chapter* introduced the duo **Gidigidi Majimaji**, perhaps the most innovative and successful of Kenya's new breed of music stars, blending clever lyrics, African rhythms and instruments and contemporary hip-hop.

In much the same way that Josiah's *Chapters* CDs introduced a host of new artists to radio and the public, the production house known as **Ogopa Deejays** released three compilations featuring acts who have become fixtures of the Kenyan pop charts, including **Redsan**, **Kleptomaniax**, **Wahu**, **Big Pin**, **Mr Lenny** and the late **E-Sir**. Much of the early Ogopa sound was characterized as **kapuka**, a style built on a mixture of Kenyan hip-hop, ragga and house. It was a commercial sound that got plenty of airplay, and *kapuka* artists were often featured at corporate-sponsored events and festivals. As all this was playing out several years back, Kenyan **hip-hop** artists were quick to make a distinction between their music and *kapuka*, criticizing the latter for its shallowness and lack of meaningful social content. They argued that a great many *kapuka* practitioners never experienced the hardships of the poor in the urban slums, and their love songs and party music represented the rich boys and girls of the middle class. And indeed, one of the biggest of today's stars is the wealthy rapper **CMB Prezzo**, who likes to brag about his good fortune. Always the showman, Prezzo makes a point of arriving at concerts with a well-dressed entourage in flashy cars. He even hired a helicopter to airdrop him into a music awards ceremony, scoring points for brazen style – but no awards. However, his 2012 runner-up finish on the **Big Brother Africa StarGame** TV show has done him well in keeping his stock high.

Similar in sound to *kapuka* but lyrically deeper, the hip-hop genre known as **genge**, promoted by production house Calif Records, aims to be music for the masses, and indeed Calif artistes **Jua Cali** and **Nonini** have scored some massive hits in recent years. While the *genge/kapuka* rivalry didn't quite match the East Coast–West Coast hip-hop wars of the 1990s in the US, it does parallel the outcome in that, today, hip-hop is firmly established as one of the dominant commercial genres of Kenyan pop, and you don't have to look far to find some entertaining rivalries among artists – for example the ongoing dialogue in the media between Prezzo and Jaguar.

On the contemporary Kenyan scene, there is still no single genre that could represent a "Kenyan sound". There are multiple sounds, some of them quite engaging and well developed but having nothing particularly Kenyan about them. **Camp Mulla**, for example, is a Nairobi-based hip-hop group topping the charts with English rap, packaged in R&B and dance beats: very much a soulful, international, urban "bubblegum" hip-hop sound. There is nothing really local about it except that the younger Kenyan audience loves it. Similarly, in a pop-rock vein, there are some really excellent bands, perhaps a little more closely tied to African pop genres, but essentially competing on the international market with indie bands of all genres. A few of the recent standouts have been groups like **Sauti Sol**, **H_art the Band**, and **Eric Wainaina and the Best Band in Africa**. Each of these groups features soulful, vocally rich melodies and harmonies and a clean, light, often finger-picking, acoustic guitar sound – occasionally with some African guitar embellishments – and usually delivered with a mix of Swahili and English lyrics.

Just a Band also have another polished international sound – this time, a fusion of house, electronica and R&B. They won the 2008 Kisima award for Best Urban Fusion category. Fusion is the operative word for a great many of the current pop headliners. **Daddy Owen**, one the top gospel stars, has made a name for himself doing *kapungala*, the combination of *kapuka* and Congolese Lingala. **Dan "Chizi" Aceda** bills himself as the Crown Prince of Benga, putting a *benga* take on R&B, house, reggae and other genres, while James Jozee and Susan Wanjiru, as **Gogosimo**, bring a contemporary coastal sound merging international pop with local sounds like the *chakacha* rhythm or the easy-listening so-called *bango* style, with mellow sax, popularized by Joseph Ngala.

Traditional instruments have returned in several pop forms. Drawing on Luo traditions, the group **Kenge Kenge** combines *orutu* fiddle, flute, horn, vocal harmonies and lively percussion on traditional Luo drums. Their high-energy music guarantees a packed house any night of the week. Taking these Luo musical elements in a different direction, *ohangla* musicians such as **Tony Nyadundo** and **Osogo Winyo** combine traditional percussion with keyboard, harmonica and drum kit for an updated version of the music formerly reserved for funerals, country beer parties and celebrations such as for the birth of twins. This is must-see entertainment when live in its full social context, though it's less compelling for non-Luo-speakers listening on CD.

Another segment of Kenya's new music scene includes musicians looking to their roots for ways to reshape contemporary pop. **Yunasi**, **Kayamba Afrika** (and their offshoots) and US-based **Jabali Afrika** emphasize rich vocal harmonies blended with traditional African percussion and stringed instruments, along with guitar, bass and keyboards. **Makadem** is another Afro-fusion performer who brings together several styles including *benga* and *ohangla*, hip-hop and dance beats. Singer-songwriter and guitarist **Suzzana Owiyo** deserves special mention for her innovative approach to bringing the melodies and instruments of her traditional Luo culture into modern pop. All these efforts attract great critical interest and, despite being largely ignored by Kenyan radio and most under-30s, have resulted in financial support from cultural exchange organizations like the Alliance Française and the Goethe-Institut, and invitations to the artists to perform in music festivals across Africa and overseas.

Finally, **gospel** is probably be the most popular music in Kenya today. While not a music genre in itself but more a category – songs with a religious message – gospel reflects and borrows from most of today's popular music styles. **Juliani**, for example, was once part of the **Ukoo Flani** hip-hop collective but has branched out on his own with soulful rap to become one of Kenya's major gospel stars, with a message that is not only religious but also touches on social and environmental causes. Others, like best-seller **Emmy Kosgei**, have a choral flavour and South African sound, while **Daddy Owen** has built on Congolese rumba.

Kenya's ever-expanding musical universe is ripe for exploration – or even participation if you're a musician. If you want to learn more, most of the artists mentioned can be heard on YouTube, Reverbnation, SoundCloud and Spotify.

Discography

Music shops throughout Kenya will have CDs or, more likely, DVDs by many of the artists mentioned above. You can usually find a few CDs of **traditional music** locally, though you may have to persevere a little to find someone who sells them. The local download market is served by ⓦkentunes.com and ⓦmdundo.com.

★**Golden Sounds Band** Swahili Rumba (Naxos World, US). Led by the brilliant saxophonist/arranger Twahir Mohamed, Golden Sounds played rumba music in the tradition of the Wanyika bands and Maroon Commandos. Repeated hearings are required before you really begin to appreciate everything this album offers in the evolutionary development of musical motifs over tracks lasting around eight minutes apiece.

★**Issa Juma and Super Wanyika Stars** World Defeats the Grandfathers: Swinging Swahili Rumba 1982–1986 (Stern's Africa, UK). With his big voice, accompanied by great guitar solos, the deep-voiced Tanzanian led the third, more rockin', incarnation of the "Wanyika" groups to a string of hits. If this one brings you back demanding more, you're in luck: there's a follow-up online-only album, World Defeats the Grandfathers, Vol. 2.

H.N. Ochieng Kabaselleh & the Lunna Kidi Band Sanduku ya Mapendo and Achi Maria (Equator Heritage Sounds, US). From the area around Lake Victoria, Kabaselleh was one Kenyan bandleader whose music always stood apart – an interesting mix of Luo benga, Swahili rumba and Congolese influences, exemplified by these two collections of Kabaselleh's double-A-sided singles from the 1980s.

Kakai Kilonzo Best of Kakai Vols 1 & 2 (Shava Musik, Germany). From the mid-1970s until his death in 1987, Kakai was at the top of the Kamba music scene in Kenya, with catchy Swahili lyrics and a tight benga sound. This is a fine compilation of vinyl singles from the 1980s which usually featured one song split between the A- and B-sides, but which here have been neatly stitched back together.

Fundi Konde Fundi Konde Retrospective Vol 1, 1947–56 (RetroAfric, UK). Full of enticing, vintage Kenyan pop. Imagine a vocal line like a mellow, two-part "Chattanooga Choo Choo", add a smooth, jazzy electric guitar, bass and clarinet, and you have the ingredients for the typical Konde track. Konde's heyday was the 1950s, but he was rediscovered in the 1990s through his collaboration with Them Mushrooms.

★**Les Wanyika** Paulina: The Best of Professor Omari Shabani and John Ngereza (Tamasha, Kenya). Les Wanyika was the last of the great Swahili rumba bands in the "Wanyika" lineage, dating back to the early 1970s, and this

album is a gem, bringing together some of their finest material. The eloquent interplay of the guitars of John Ngereza and Professor Omari is stunning.

★**Samba Mapangala & Virunga** African Classics (Sheer Sound). From the mid-1970s to the early 1990s, Virunga was one of Kenya's most exciting groups, while Samba Mapangala is still a favourite in East Africa despite having relocated to the US. Each song is like a ten-minute story, exploring different combinations of rhythm, melody and harmony. This collection pulls together some of the best tracks of Samba's thirty-years-plus under the Virunga name, with classics such as "Malako", "Yembele" and "Sungura". For those who'd like to hear Samba's present-day sound, his 2011 release, Maisha Ni Matumu (Virunga Records), provides some first-rate dance numbers in a rumba sampler.

Maroon Commandos Shika Kamba (Sound Africa, Kenya). Tilting a little more towards the Congolese rumba sound in this release, Maroon Commandos is still a great sound as Kenya's longest-running rumba group.

Collela Mazee and Victoria B Kings Band Jessica (Equator Heritage Sounds). Classic Luo benga music of the late 1970s and early 1980s: a pounding beat, pulsing bass and brilliant guitars, each track ending with a luscious guitar solo.

D.O. Misiani & Shirati Band The King of History (Stern's Africa, UK), Benga Blast! (Earthworks/Stern's, UK) and Piny Ose Mer/The World Upside Down (GlobeStyle, UK). Daniel Owino Misiani was one of the founding fathers of benga music and these are three fine examples of his work, the first two in glorious mono; the last is a special recording for the GlobeStyle label in 1989.

John Amutabi Nzenze & Friends Angelike Twist (Equator Heritage Sounds). A pioneering figure in Kenyan music, Nzenze started his recording career as a teen back in the 1950s. This compilation beautifully highlights his contribution to the acoustic finger-picking guitar styles of the 1950s and the electric "twist" style that followed in the 1960s.

★**Ayub Ogada** En Mana Kuoyo (Real World, UK). Sounding every bit as fresh and engaging as when first released in 1993, Ayub Ogada takes traditional Luo instruments and melodies in a new direction. This enthralling, low-key, largely acoustic album has beautiful melodies and captivating rhythms, featuring Ogada on the eight-stringed *nyatiti* lyre.

★**Orchestra Super Mazembe** *Giants of East Africa* (Earthworks/Stern's, UK). Congolese group Super Mazembe played the dance halls and bars of Kenya for nearly thirty years before its demise. In songs such as "Kasongo" and "Shauri Yako", they exemplified the definitive sound of Congolese rumba in East Africa. Mazembe's early 1980s LP, *Kaivaska*, kindled much of the early enthusiasm for African music in the UK and Europe. This collection includes five of the best songs off *Kaivaska*, including "Kasongo" and "Shauri Yako". Eighteen Mazembe singles, never released on LP or CD, have been recently collected together on the superb *Mazembe @ 45RPM Volumes 1 & 2* (Stern's, UK)

Suzzana Owiyo *Mama Africa* (ARC Music, UK). This debut from a talented singer-songwriter is a delightful mix of traditional instruments, Owiyo's acoustic guitar and electric sounds with a few rough edges. *Yamo Kudho* (Blu Zebra, Kenya) picks up where *Mama Africa* left off, in a more polished, tighter package, delivering sublime melodies with a bright acoustic sound and mixing in traditional Luo

orutu, oporo (horn) and percussion. Her third CD, *My Roots* (Kirkelig kulturverksted), is a superb production with plenty of Luo "roots" from traditional to innovative fusion numbers.

Eric Wainaina *Sawa Sawa* (Wainaina/Kaufmann Prod, US/Kenya). Originally part of the Five Alive singing group of the mid-1990s, Wainaina went off to the US to study music. Spanning a broad range of styles, from up-tempo African dance rhythms to ballads and smooth jazz, and including "Nchi ya Kitu Kidogo" (Nation of a Little Something), decrying, with great humour, the way bribery has permeated Kenyan society. For Swahili-speakers, there were comic interludes from the Kenyan stand-up troupe Redykyulass. Wainaina followed up with the meticulously produced modern pop album, *Twende Twende* (Enkare, Kenya), and, from 2011, Eric's *Love + Protest* with The Best Band in Africa.

Zuhura Swaleh with Maulidi Musical Party *Jino la Pembe* (GlobeStyle, UK). Beautiful *taarab* songs from the Kenyan coast's biggest female star of this ocean-going, traditionally rooted Swahili style, supported by one of the region's top ensembles. Once heard, never forgotten.

COMPILATIONS

★**Kenya Dance Mania** (Earthworks/Stern's, UK). An excellent introduction to Kenya's various styles. *Dance Mania* includes some classics of the 1970s and 1980s, such as Les Wanyika's "Sina Makosa" and Maroon Commandos' evergreen hit "Charonyi Ni Wasi".

The Nairobi Beat: Kenyan Pop Music Today (Rounder, USA). A cross-section of mid-1980s Kenyan pop put together by Doug Paterson, showcasing some of the best examples of regional *benga* styles: Luo, Kikuyu, Kamba and Luhya, plus a couple of Swahili and Congolese dance tunes for good measure.

★**The Rough Guide to the Music of Kenya** (World Music Network, UK). A sampling of the many styles of Kenyan popular music, including the guitar-centric *benga* and Swahili rumba styles, *taarab* from the coastal region, current "traditional" sounds and the shifting sounds of the younger generation (including Gidigidi Majimaji's "Ting Badi Malo").

Zanzibara 2: 1965–1975 (Buda Musique, France). A delightful collection of *taarab* music recorded by Mombasa's Mzuri Records. Features songs by the likes of Zuhura Swaleh, Zein l'Abdin and Maulidi Juma.

Written and researched by Doug Paterson (**W** eastafricanmusic.com), with contributions from Jens Finke on traditional music (**W** bluegecko.org) and Werner Graebner on *taarab* (**W** jahazi-media.com).

Books

Literacy has massively improved in Kenya in recent decades and more than ninety percent of Kenyans can now read. Although a number of Kenyan authors have written in indigenous languages, English still predominates: check out the excellent blogs and websites (see p.26 and p.68). Locally printed books are sometimes very cheap, and offer insights into Kenyan life you wouldn't otherwise find. The Africa Book Centre (ⓦafricabookcentre .com) is a good source of print editions, and Kwani? (ⓦkwani.org) is Kenya's best literary website. Titles marked ★ are particularly recommended.

COFFEE-TABLE BOOKS

Mohamed Amin *Cradle of Mankind and Portrait of Kenya*. Stunning photographs of the Lake Turkana region by the award-winning maverick photo-journalist, killed in the Comoros plane hijack in 1997.

Yann Arthus-Bertrand *Kenya from the Air*. Superb images of the country from the eagle's viewpoint.

★Mitsuaki Iwago *Serengeti: Natural Order on the African Plain*. Simply the best volume of wildlife photography ever assembled, this makes most glossies look feeble. If you're trying to persuade someone to visit East Africa – or if any aesthetic argument were needed to preserve the parks and animals – this is the book to use.

Brian Jackman and Jonathan Scott *The Marsh Lions*. Painstakingly researched and devotedly written study of the big cats and other animals around the Musiara Marsh in the Maasai Mara Reserve.

★David Keith Jones *Shepherds of the Desert*. Brilliant photos, many in black and white, with a text more lucid and less superficial than most glossies, although the book concerns itself only with northern Kenya.

Nigel Pavitt *Kenya: A Country in the Making 1880–1940*. A much-admired production in Kenya itself, where many people – particularly Euro-Kenyan settler families – feel a connection to one or more of the 720 digitally restored photos in this sumptuous tome.

Jonathan Scott and Angela Scott *Stars of Big Cat Diary*. Valedictory volume for fans of the hit BBC series.

Tepilit Ole Saitoti and Carol Beckwith *Maasai*. The Maasai coffee-table book, with exquisite staged portraits of Maasai culture (and even Beckwith's camera can't disguise the tourist souvenirs in the background). Variably interesting, chauvinistic text, which plays the cult value of the Maasai for all it's worth.

TRAVEL AND GENERAL ACCOUNTS

★David Bennum *Tick Bite Fever*. Full of acid wit, this memoir by a British newspaper journalist about growing up in an expat household in the 1970s offers an amusingly dry alternative to more cloying accounts.

Bill Bryson *Bill Bryson's Africa Diary*. A very brief but typically engaging little book recounting Bryson's travels around Kenya learning about the work of Care International. All profits go to the charity.

Bartle Bull *Safari: A Chronicle of Adventure*. A great, macho slab of a book, chronicling the history of the hunting safari, jammed with photos – grotesque but utterly compelling.

Adharanand Finn *Running with the Kenyans: Discovering the Secrets of the Fastest People on Earth*. The journalist and runner spent several months living in Iten with his young family – an inspiring work for aspiring world-beaters.

John Hillaby *Journey to the Jade Sea*. An obvious one to read before a trip to Lake Turkana, Hillaby's account of his walk in the early 1960s was an adventure "for the hell of it",

as he wrote, complete with tall stories and madcap incompetence.

★Corinne Hofmann *The White Masai*. Ridiculed and revered in equal measure, a Swiss woman's account of her extended love affair with a Samburu man, and her life in Barsaloi in the early 1990s.

J. Ludwig Krapf *Travel, Researches and Missionary Labours during an Eighteen Years Residence in Eastern Africa*. Fascinating account of travels to "Mombaz" and "Tzawo" among other localities: Krapf was the first missionary in Kenya, and the first European to set eyes on Mount Kenya.

★Peter Matthiessen *The Tree Where Man Was Born*. Wanderings and musings in Kenya and northern Tanzania, first published in 1972. Enthralling for its detail on nature, society, culture and prehistory, and beautifully written, this is a gentle, appetizing introduction to the land and its people.

George Monbiot *No Man's Land*. A journey through Kenya and Tanzania, providing a shocking exposé of Maasai dispossession and trenchant criticism of the wildlife conservation movement.

Cynthia Moss *Elephant Memories: Thirteen Years in the Life of an Elephant Family*. A fascinating, moving account of her work in Amboseli by one of the world's leading authorities on the social life of the elephant.

Dervla Murphy *The Ukimwi Road*. Murphy's early 1990s bike ride from Kenya to Zimbabwe becomes – for her – a trip through lands lost to AIDS and neo-colonialism.

★**Shiva Naipaul** *North of South*. First published in 1978, this classic account of Naipaul's life and travels in East Africa is caustic but always readable and sometimes hilarious.

Barack Obama *Dreams from My Father: A Story of Race and Inheritance*. Describing a 1988 journey during which the future 44th president of the US spent five weeks visiting his father's family in Kenya – hanging out in Nairobi, going to the Mara and visiting his father's grave in Kogelo.

Joyce Poole *Coming of Age with Elephants*. Deeply sympathetic account of studying the social and sexual behaviour of elephants in Amboseli alongside Cynthia Moss.

Keith B. Richburg *Out of America: A Black Man Confronts Africa*. Nairobi bureau chief for the *Washington Times* from 1991–94, Richburg discovered that he was American, not African, and preferred it that way.

Rick Ridgeway *The Shadow of Kilimanjaro*. The American adventurer and film-maker took a walk in 1997 through the bush from Kilimanjaro to Mombasa – mostly through Tsavo West and East, along the Tsavo-Galana River. Robust, readable and full of passionate enthusiasm for the wild country and the wildlife.

★**Stephen Spawls and Glenn Mathews** *Kenya: a Natural History*. This recently published, profusely illustrated heavyweight treasure trove of fact and anecdote about Kenya's land, people, animals and plants – and the people who have researched them – is a delight for naturalists and Kenya-lovers. Well worth every penny of the hefty price tag.

Wilfred Thesiger *My Kenya Days*. The account of thirty years in northern Kenya by a very strange man indeed – an old Etonian noble savage, wedded to his own ego and a reactionary, glamour-laden view of his tribal companions.

Joseph Thomson *Through Masai Land: A Journey Of Exploration Among The Snow-Clad Volcanic Mountains And Strange Tribes Of Eastern Equatorial Africa*. First published in 1885, these two volumes detail Thomson's African journeys of exploration and demonstrate his early eco-consciousness and sensitivity to the peoples he visited.

COLONIAL WRITERS AND BIOGRAPHIES

★**Isak Dinesen (Karen Blixen)** *Out of Africa*. First published in 1937, this book describes Blixen's (Dinesen was a nom de plume) life on her Ngong Hills coffee farm between the wars. It's an intense read – lyrical, introspective, sometimes obnoxiously and intricately racist, but worth pursuing and never superficial, unlike Sydney Pollack's film. Blixen's *Letters from Africa 1914– 1931*, translated by Anne Born, gives posthumous insights.

Elspeth Huxley *The Flame Trees of Thika: Memories of an African Childhood* and *The Mottled Lizard*. Based on her own childhood, from a prolific author who also wrote numerous works on colonial history and society, including *White Man's Country*, a biography of the settlers' doyen, Lord Delamere, and *Out in the Midday Sun: My Kenya* – both as readable, and, to be fair, as predictable, as any. Her last book, *Nine Faces of Kenya*, is a somewhat dewy-eyed anthology of colonial East African ephemera. More interesting is the collection of her mother's letters, *Nellie: Letters from Africa*, which includes compelling coverage of the Mau Mau years from the pen of a likeably eccentric settler.

Beryl Markham *West with the Night*. Markham made the first east–west solo flight across the Atlantic. This is her only book about her life in the interwar Kenya colony, drawing together adventures, landscapes and contemporary figures.

★**Richard Meinertzhagen** *Kenya Diary 1902–1906*.

The haunting day-to-day narrative of a young British officer in the protectorate. Meinertzhagen's brutal descriptions of "punitive expeditions" are chillingly matter-of-fact and make the endless tally of his wildlife slaughter pale inoffensively by comparison. As a reminder of the savagery that accompanied the British intrusion (Meinertzhagen is notorious as the murderer of the Nandi chief, Koitalel), and a stark insight into the complex mind of one of its perpetrators, this is disturbing, but highly recommended. Good photos, too.

Edward Paice *Lost Lion of Empire: The Life of Ewart Grogan DSO, 1876–1976*. Fascinating biography of one of the Kenya colony's most rumbustious movers and shakers.

Paul Sullivan *Kikuyu District: The Edited Letters of Francis Hall 1892–1901*. The fascinating monthly letters home of one of the earliest officers in the East Africa Protectorate, stationed at what is now Murang'a, in the Central Highlands, are an easier read than Meinertzhagen's diary.

Judith Thurman *Isak Dinesen: The Life of a Storyteller*. A revisionist biography that was much used as a source for Sydney Pollack's *Out of Africa* film.

Sarah Wheeler *Too Close to the Sun: The Life and Times of Denys Finch Hatton*. Stylishly written biography of the colony's coolest dude, the enigmatic lover of Karen Blixen, who died at the controls of his plane in 1931.

KENYAN FICTION IN ENGLISH

Chinua Achebe and C.L. Innes (eds) *African Short Stories*. A collection that treats its material geographically, including Kenyan stories from Jomo Kenyatta, Grace Ogot, Ngugi and a spooky offering (*The Spider's Web*) from Leonard Kibera.

Thomas Akare *The Slums*. A bleaker read than Meja Mwangi (see below), but also more humane. The dialogue melds seamlessly into the narrative; there are no doubts about the authentic rhythms of Kenyan English here, but much is assumed to be understood and there's much that won't be, unless perhaps you're sitting under a 25-watt light bulb in a River Road B&L.

Charlotte H. Bruner (ed) *Unwinding Threads: Writing by Women in Africa*. The East Africa contributions feature Kenyan writers Charity Waciuma and the excellent Grace Ogot, whose *The Rain Came* is a bewitching mystery myth, combining traditional Luo tales with her own fiction in a perplexingly Western form.

John Kiriamiti *My Life in Crime*. This racy autobiographical account, penned in prison by a professional robber, was so successful that the author went on to write two novels (*Son of Fate* and *The Sinister Trophy*) plus an account of his time as a villain told from his fiancée's point of view (*My Life with a Criminal: Millie's Story*).

Charles Mangua *Son of Woman*. Mangua tells the tale of a son of a prostitute and his misadventures: hard-bitten and cynical, but still engaging.

Ali Mazrui *The Trial of Christopher Okigbo*. A clever novel of ideas from the US-based political scientist, now in his 80s, who always infuriates both critics and supporters of Kenya.

★**Meja Mwangi** *Going Down River Road*; *Carcass for Hounds*; *Kill Me Quick*. Popular author Meja Mwangi is lighter and more accessible than Ngugi, his fiction infused with the absurdities of urban Nairobi slum life. *Going Down River Road* is his best-known work – perfect for reading *in situ*, with convincing scenes, chaotic action and sharp dialogue. Mwangi was shortlisted for the Commonwealth Writers' Prize with *Striving for the Wind* (1992), which is set in a rural rather than urban location.

★**Ngugi wa Thiong'o** *Decolonising the Mind: The Politics of Language in African Literature*. Ngugi, who writes in Kikuyu as well as English, has long been closely associated with attempts to move Kenyan literature and African literature in general towards expression in the readers' mother tongues (see box below).

M.G. Vassanji *The In-between World of Vikram Lall*. Remarkable epic of multiple alienations and the power of corruption in a world of competing moralities. Lall is the chief protagonist, a Ugandan Asian exiled to Canada having been named Kenya's most corrupt man.

★**Binyavanga Wainaina** *Discovering Home*. A collection of short stories, including the title piece that won him the 2002 Caine Prize for African Writing. Wainaina takes Kenyan humour, tragedy, and especially the meaning of home for diaspora Kenyans, and mounts them in a beautiful frame. His latest, *One Day I Will Write About This Place*, is a superbly written coming-of-age tale.

NGUGI WA THIONG'O

Ngugi wa Thiong'o, the dominant figure of modern Kenyan literature, currently lives in the USA: although his books in English are no longer banned in Kenya, his political sympathies are unwelcome. Ngugi's work is art serving the revolution – didactic, brusque, graphic and unsentimental. He writes in Kikuyu, then translates his work into English. Powerful themes – exploitation, betrayal, cultural oppression, the imposition of Christianity, loss of and search for identity drive the stories urgently along

Disillusioned with English, Ngugi's first work in Kikuyu, in collaboration with Ngugi wa Mirii, was the play *Ngahiika Ndeenda* (*I Will Marry When I Want*), and its public performance by illiterate peasants at the Kamiriithu Cultural Centre in Limuru got him detained for a year.

For a first dip into Ngugi, try *Secret Lives* for short stories, *Weep Not, Child* for a brief but glowing early novel, or, for the mature Ngugi, *Petals of Blood* – a richly satisfying detective story that is at the same time a saga of wretchedness and struggle. Other novels include *The River Between*, on the old Kikuyu society and the coming of the Europeans; *A Grain of Wheat*, about the eve of independence; *Devil on the Cross* (originally written in detention on scraps of toilet paper); and *Matigari* ("The Patriots"). *Matigari*, first published in Kikuyu in 1986, had a remarkable effect in the Central Highlands. Rumours circulated that a man was spreading militant propaganda against the government of Daniel Arap Moi. The police even tried to track him down, before realizing he was a fictional character and confiscating all copies of the book.

His epic, satirical novel, *The Wizard of the Crow*, was his last work of fiction, published in 2006 to huge acclaim, before he started to write autobiographically about his childhood: *Dreams in a Time of War* (2010) and *In the House of the Intepreter* (2012). Ngugi's contribution to Kenyan literature is enormous, and delving in is rewarding, if not always easy.

KENYAN POETRY

The oldest form of written poetry in Kenya is from the coast. **Swahili poetry** reads beautifully even if you don't understand the words. Written for at least 300 years, and sung for a good deal longer, it's one of Kenya's most enduring art forms. An *Anthology of Swahili Poetry* has been compiled and rather woodenly translated by **Ali A. Jahadmy**, but some of Swahili's best-known classical compositions from the Lamu archipelago are included, with pertinent background. There's a more enjoyable anthology of romantic and erotic verse, *A Choice of Flowers*, with **Jan Knappert**'s idiosyncratic translations and interpretations, and the same linguist's *Four Centuries of Swahili Verse*, which expounds and creatively interprets at much greater length. Upcountry poetry in the sense of written verse is a recent form (though oral folk literature was often relayed in the context of music, rhythm and dance). *The Penguin Book of Modern African Poetry*, edited by Gerald Moore, is hefty and diverse, with a good selection of Kenyan contributions.

FOREIGN FICTION

★**Justin Cartwright** *Masai Dreaming*. A compelling novel that juxtaposes a film-maker's vision of Maasai-land with the barbarities of the Holocaust, linked by the tapes of a Jewish anthropologist.

★**Richard Crompton** *The Honey Guide*. The first in a series of Kenya-based detective stories by a former BBC Nairobi correspondent featuring Maasai loner sleuth, DC Mollel, this well-crafted and beautifully described – if implausibly honourable – chase through the alleys and alliances of Nairobi crime and politics finishes on the eve of the post-election violence in 2007. Follow-up case *Hell's Gate* (a national park pleading for a crime novel if ever there was one) is just as good.

Nicholas Drayson *A Guide to the Birds of East Africa*. Somewhat after the style of McCall Smith's *The No.1 Ladies' Detective Agency* – but with more substance – Drayson's gently satirical lark among Nairobi's Asian community is a readable introduction to the lighter side of contemporary life in the capital – and a delight for birders.

★**Adam Foulds** *The Broken Word*. Moving, gripping and beautifully crafted novella-length prose poem about a young recruit swept up in the hunt for Mau Mau guerrillas.

Jeremy Gavron *Moon*. Vivid short novel about a white boy growing up on a farm during the Mau Mau uprising.

Martha Gellhorn *The Weather in Africa*. Three absorbing novellas, each dealing with aspects of the Europe–Africa relationship, set on the slopes of Kilimanjaro, in the "White Highlands" of Kenya and on the tourist coast north of Mombasa.

David Lambkin *The Hanging Tree*. A human-nature-through-the-ages saga which makes a good yarn – in fact, several yarns.

★**John Le Carré** *The Constant Gardener*. The spymaster turns his hand to a whodunit set in Kenya, in which a campaigner against the misdeeds of Big Pharma is murdered. A brilliantly crafted story (though oddly unconvincing in its portrayal of expat society), turned into a multi-Oscar-winning movie by Fernando Meirelles.

Barbara Wood *Green City in the Sun*. A sprawling saga, in which, among a slew of fizzing plot lines, a settler family comes into conflict with a Kikuyu medicine woman. One of the few credible novels about the realities of colonial Kenya by a *mzungu* writer.

HISTORY

GENERAL HISTORY

Guy Arnold *Africa: a Modern History*. A huge reference history of the continent, from 1960 up until 2000, that places Kenya in context and succinctly ticks all the boxes linking present conditions with past causes.

★**Richard Dowden** *Africa: Altered States, Ordinary Miracles*. The wealth of experience and engagement of Dowden – respected journalist and director of the Royal African Society – come through in this collection of extended essays, including a brilliant encapsulation of Kenya's downward spiral of greed and corruption.

★**G.S.P. Freeman-Grenville** *The East African Coast*. Fascinating, vivid and often extraordinary – a series of accounts from the first century to the nineteenth.

Christopher Hibbert *Africa Explored: Europeans in the Dark Continent 1769–1889*. Entertaining read, devoted in large part to the "discovery" of East and Central Africa.

Terry Hirst *The Struggle for Nairobi*. A sort of "Nairobi for

Beginners" that manages to make town planning (or the lack of it) fascinating, bringing together a mass of otherwise hard-to-get information about the city's growth.

Robert M. Maxon and Thomas P. Ofcansky *Historical Dictionary of Kenya*. An A to Z of Kenya's history (including an extensive bibliography) from a reliable series that covers nearly every African country.

★**Alan Moorehead** *The White Nile*. A riveting account of the search for the source and European rivalries for control in the region.

Roland Oliver and J.D. Fage *A Short History of Africa*. Dated, but still a good introduction.

Thomas Pakenham *The Scramble for Africa*. The story of the European rush to exploit Africa in the name of commerce, Christianity and civilization in the last two decades of the nineteenth century.

COLONIAL KENYA

Chloe Campbell *Race and Empire: Eugenics in Colonial Kenya*. Disconcertingly readable, scholarly work that shows how deeply the possibilities raised by eugenics were part of the pre-1939 colonial project in Kenya and how quickly they were shelved after the horrors of World War II.

★ **James Fox** *White Mischief*. Investigative romp through the events surrounding the notorious unsolved murder of Lord Errol, one of Kenya's most aristocratic settlers, at Karen in 1941. Well told and highly revealing of British Kenyan society of the time. Michael Radford's 1987 film version is equally enjoyable.

Charles Miller *The Lunatic Express: An Entertainment in Imperialism*. The story of the Uganda Railway. Miller narrates the drama of one of the great feats of Victorian engineering – as bizarre and as madly magnificent as any Wild West epic – adding weight with a broad historical background of East Africa from the year dot. The same author's very readable *The Battle for the Bundu* follows a little-known corner of World War I as fought out on the plains of Tsavo between British Kenya and German Tanganyika.

THE MAU MAU REBELLION

★ **David Anderson** *Histories of the Hanged: Testimonies from the Mau Mau Rebellion in Kenya*. Previously published as *Britain's Dirty War in Kenya*, this deeply researched study concludes that the British response to Mau Mau was unnecessarily harsh and of doubtful legality, and that many Mau Mau trials were flawed.

Caroline Elkins *Britain's Gulag: The Brutal End of Empire in Kenya*. Pulitzer prize-winning study of Britain's network of Mau Mau detention camps. Less dispassionate and more one-sided than *Histories of the Hanged* (Elkins spends little time discussing Mau Mau atrocities), Elkins has been accused of exaggeration. But this book is nevertheless a shocking indictment of British methods, and provides strong support for the legal cases that some survivors have lodged.

Tabitha Kanogo *Squatters and the Roots of Mau Mau 1905–63*. Delves into the early years of the "White Highlands" to show how resistance, and the conditions for revolt, were built into the relations between the settler land-grabbers and the peasant farmers and herders ("squatters") they usurped. Strong on the role of women in the Mau Mau movement.

J.M. Kariuki *Mau Mau Detainee: The Account by a Kenya African of His Experience in Detention Camps*. A remarkably

forbearing account of life and death in the detention camps, Kariuki's vision for the future of Kenya and his loyalty to Kenyatta have a special irony after his assassination in 1975.

★ **David Throup** *Economic and Social Origins of Mau Mau*. An examination of the story from the end of World War II, covering the colonial mentality and differences in efficiency between peasant cash-cropping and more wasteful plantation agriculture.

POST INDEPENDENCE

Jean Davison *Voices from Mutira: Change in the Lives of Rural Gikuyu Women 1910–1995*. Moving and particularly interesting for the attitudes it documents on bride price and FGM.

Charles Hornsby *Kenya: A History Since Independence*. A detailed survey of Kenya's first half-century of nationhood that balances cold analysis of contemporary failures against the unpromising historical context out of which they emerged.

Joseph Karimi and Philip Ochieng *The Kenyatta Succession*. Worth tracking down and a good read about how the clique surrounding Kenyatta planned to seize power when he died, murdering Moi in the process. By good fortune, Kenyatta died in the wrong place: the Mzee's cronies would have been far worse than Moi.

Ambreena Manji *Whose Land Is It Anyway? The Failure of Land Law Reform in Kenya*. What it says – a brief, and admirably clear pamphlet from the independent Africa Research Institute think-tank outlining the failures and challenges of land reform in Kenya. Available at ⊛ bit.ly/KenyaLandLaw.

Tom Mboya *The Challenge of Nationhood*. The vision of Kenya's best-loved statesman – and a Luo – assassinated in 1969 for looking like a popular successor to Kenyatta.

Miguna Miguna *Peeling Back the Mask: A Quest for Justice in Kenya*. This book by the former prime minister's senior adviser, sacked in 2011, dishes the dirt about Raila Odinga and the Grand Coalition and caused a storm in Kenya when it was launched in Nairobi in 2012.

★ **Michaela Wrong** *It's Our Turn to Eat: The Story of a Kenyan Whistle Blower*. "To eat" is a Kenyan euphemism for helping yourself to what doesn't belong to you – what those in power have been doing since independence. British journalist Michaela Wrong's jaw-dropping account narrates the story of what happened when anti-corruption czar John Githongo tried to do his job.

ANTHROPOLOGY AND KENYAN LIFE

★ **James de Vere Allen** *Swahili Origins: Swahili Culture and the Shungwaya Phenomenon*. The life work of a challenging and readable scholar.

Jeffrey A. Fadiman *When We Began There Were*

Witchmen. Recounts the story of the Meru people from their mythical origins in Shungwaya in northeastern Kenya to the decimation of Meru culture by a tiny handful of missionaries and colonial administrators.

Jomo Kenyatta *Facing Mount Kenya*. A traditional, anthropological monograph, written from the rather conservative functionalist perspective, but, uniquely for its era, by a member of the society in question – in this case, the Kikuyu. This is one of the few scholarly works ever written on traditional Kikuyu culture, and as interesting for the insights it offers on Kenyatta as for its quite readable content.

Renato Kizito Sesana *Father Kizito's Notebook*. Kenyan life from the Catholic perspective of Father Kizito's weekly columns in the *Sunday Nation*. Full of insights into the struggle to survive that Kenyans call life, infused with humour and compassion.

Sarah Mirza *Three Swahili Women: Life Histories from Mombasa, Kenya*. Three histories of ritual, three women's lives. Born between 1890 and 1920 into different social backgrounds, these biographies document enormous changes from the most important of neglected viewpoints.

Wahome Mutahi *How to be a Kenyan*. A satirical view of Kenyan life by one of the country's most popular newspaper columnists. Painfully funny, and close to the bone.

Thomas Spear and Richard Waller (eds) *Being Maasai*. Articles about Maasai identity – a subtle and interesting field, and vital reading for anyone concerned with the ethnic politics of modern Kenya.

SPECIALIST GUIDES

ARTS

Susan Denyer *African Traditional Architecture*. Useful and interesting, with hundreds of photos (most of them old) and detailed line drawings.

Frank Willett *African Art*. An accessible volume; good value, with a generous ratio of illustrations to text.

Geoffrey Williams *African Designs from Traditional Sources*. A designer's and enthusiast's sourcebook.

WILDLIFE

Ann Birnie & Tim Noad *Trees of Kenya: An Illustrated Field Guide*. A very useful handbook, covering 300 of Kenya's most common native and exotic species.

Michael Blundell *Field Guide to the Wild Flowers of East Africa*. Botanical companion in the Collins series.

Adam Scott Kennedy *Birds of the Masai Mara* and *Animals of the Masai Mara*. Outstandingly photographed field guides to more than 200 species of birds, 65 mammals and 17 reptiles by a naturalist who has spent years hunting images.

★**Jonathan Kingdon** *The Kingdon Pocket Guide to African Mammals*. The definitive handbook, abridged to this game-viewing format, with identification illustrations and distribution maps.

Cynthia Moss, Harvey Croze and Phyllis C Lee (eds) *The Amboseli Elephants: A Long-term Perspective on a Long-lived Mammal*. Beautifully produced, moving and highly readable round-up of the Amboseli Elephant Research

Project's three decades of work.

Dave Richards *A Photographic Guide to the Birds of East Africa*. Ideal if you're a holiday birder, with more than 300 photos.

Chris Stuart and Tilde Stuart *Field Guide to the Larger Mammals of Africa*. Beautifully illustrated and well-edited field guide published in 2006.

Nigel Wheatley *Where to Watch Birds in Africa*. Tight structure and plenty of useful detail make this a must-have for serious birdwatchers. Includes 25 pages on Kenya.

D.A. Zimmerman, D.A. Turner and D.J. Pearson *Birds of Kenya & Northern Tanzania*. Weighty and comprehensive coverage for the serious birder; also available in a more portable paperback edition.

CLIMBING AND DIVING GUIDES

Iain Allan *The Mountain Club of Kenya Guide to Mount Kenya and Kilimanjaro*. For fully equipped alpinism, this is indispensable.

Helmut Debelius *Indian Ocean Reef Guide*. Field guide to all the main species of fish and invertebrates, with excellent identification photos.

Anton Koornhof *The Dive Sites of Kenya and Tanzania*. Highly recommended, with detailed, beautifully illustrated text on every major site.

Andrew Wielochowski *Mount Kenya 1:50,000 Map and Guide*. Covers just the mountain itself, and includes technical information if you're scaling Nelion and Batian.

Language

Surprisingly, perhaps, Swahili is one of the easiest languages to learn. It's pronounced exactly as it's written, with the stress nearly always on the penultimate syllable. And it's satisfyingly regular, so even with limited knowledge you can make yourself understood and construct simple sentences.

In Kenya, you'd rarely be stuck without Swahili, but it makes a huge difference to your perceptions if you try to speak it. People are delighted if you make the effort (though they'll also tend to assume you understand more than you do) and for travels further afield in East Africa, and especially in Tanzania, some knowledge of Swahili is a very useful backup. Don't forget that for many Kenyans Swahili is another foreign language they get by in, like English.

The language has spread widely from its coastal origins to become the lingua franca of East Africa and it has tended to lose its richness and complexity as a result. Upcountry, it is often spoken as a second language with a minimum of grammar. On the coast, you'll hear it spoken with tremendous panache: oratorical skills and punning (to which it lends itself with great facility) are much appreciated. Swahili is a Bantu language, and in fact one of the more mainstream of the family, but it has incorporated thousands of foreign words, the majority of them Arabic, but including Portuguese and English. Far more of this Arabic inheritance and borrowing is preserved on the coast. The "standard" dialect is derived from Zanzibar Swahili, the dialect the early missionaries learned and first transcribed into the Roman alphabet. **Written Swahili** is still not completely uniform, and you'll come across slight variations in spelling, particularly on menus.

Swahili language books and courses

There are several published language **courses** around. *Teach Yourself Swahili* by Joan Russell is an excellent book and CD, with practical Swahili that you can use from the beginning. *Kiswahili kwa Kitendo* ("Swahili by Action", by Sharifa Zawawi) is the best bet if you find ordinary grammars indigestible. The free online resource Mwana Simba (◍bit.ly/MwanaSimba) includes grammar as well as an extensive dictionary. As for **phrasebooks**, try the pocket-sized *Rough Guide Swahili Dictionary Phrasebook*, which includes links to MP3 files to practise your pronunciation at ◍tinyurl.com/yhwqwyn.

Swahili pronunciation

Once you get the hang of voicing every syllable and remember that each vowel is a syllable and that nothing is silent, **pronunciation** is easy. However, odd-looking combinations of consonants are often pronounced as one, double-length syllable. **Mzee**, for example, is pronounced "mz-ay-ay" (rhyming with "hey") and **shauri** (troubles, problem) is pronounced "sha-oo-ri" while **mgonjwa** (ill) has just two syllables "mgo-njwa".

You'll often come across an "m" where it looks out of place: this letter can precede any other. That is because it's a noun prefix (usually replaced in the plural with "wa-" or "mi-"), as in **mtoto** (child; plural **watoto**) or **mti** (tree; plural **miti**). Just add a bit of an "m" sound at the beginning; "mm-toto". If you say "um-toto" or "ma-toto" you'll be misunderstood. "Ng" followed by an apostrophe makes a sound like the "ng" in banger, not Bangor (try saying "banger" without the "ba", and then use it in a word like ng'ombe – cow or beef). Without the apostrophe, the ng is like two separate letters as in "finger" (as in nguo – garment, clothes).

For memorizing, it often helps to ignore the first letter or syllable. Thousands of nouns, for example, start with "ki" (singular) and "vi" (plural), and they're all in the same noun class.

A as in Arthur	M as in Martian
B as in bed	N as in nonsense
C doesn't exist on its own	NG as in finger or hunger, with a clear "g" sound
CH as in church, but often sounds like a "t", a "dj" or a "ky"	NG' as in wrong or banger, with no "g" sound
D as in donkey	O as in orange, never as in "open" or "do"
DJ like the "j" in pyjamas	P as in penguin
DH like a cross between dhow and thou	Q doesn't exist (except in early Romanized texts; now "k")
E between the "e" in Edward and "ai" in ailing	R as in rapid
F as in fan	S as in Samson
G as in good	T as in tiny
GH at the back of the throat, like a gargle or a French "r"	TH as in thanks, never as in "them"
H as in harmless	U as in lute
I like the "e" in evil	V as in victory
J as in jug	W as in wobble
K as in kiosk, sometimes like soft "t" or "ch"	X doesn't exist
KH like the "ch" in loch	Y as in you
L as in lullaby, but often pronounced like an "r"	Z as in zero

Swahili words and phrases

The words and phrases listed here are all in common usage, but Swahili (like English) is far from being a homogeneous language, so don't be surprised if you sometimes get some funny looks. And, for lack of space for explanation, there are a number of apparent inconsistencies; just ignore them unless you intend to learn the language seriously. These phrases should at least make you understood.

GREETINGS AND TERMS OF ADDRESS

Tourists are greeted with **Jambo?** or more correctly **Hujambo?** (a multipurpose greeting, meaning "Things?" or "Problems?"). If you don't speak any Swahili, replying **Jambo** is fine, but if you want to make an effort, say **Sijambo** ("No problems") and continue with one of the following:

News?	Habari?	Very (a common emphasis)	Sana
Your news?	Habari yako?		
What news?	Habari gani?	Mister	Bwana (pl. mabwana)
Good, thanks	Nzuri	Addressing an adult woman	Mama
How goes?	Mambo?		
Well, thanks	Nzuri	Addressing an old lady	Bibi
What's up?	Vipi?		
Cool, sweet	Safi, poa	Addressing an old man	Babu
Cool, excellent	Fiti		
Hello? Anyone in?	Hodi!	Youth, teenager	Kijana (pl. vijana)
Come in! Welcome! (also said on offering something)	Karibu	Child	Mtoto (pl. watoto)
		What's your name?	Jina lako nani?
Goodbye to one/many	Kwaheri/ni	White, European	-zungu (eg mzungu white person; wazungu white people)
Thank you to one/many	Asante/ni		

BASICS

My name is/ I am called	Jina langu/Nina itwa	soon	sasa hivi
Where are you from?	Unatoka wapi?	why?	kwa nini?
Where are you staying?	Unakaa wapi?	because	kwa sababu
I am from ...	Ninatoka	but	lakini
I am staying (at/in)	Ninakaa	who?	nani?
See you!	Tutaonana!	what?	nini?
Yes, that's right	ndiyo	which?	gani?
No	hapana; siyo; la (Arabic, heard mostly on the coast)	true	kweli
		and/with	na
		or	au
		isn't it?	siyo?
I don't understand	Sifahamu/Sielewi	I'm English (or	Mimi ni mwingereza/
I don't speak Swahili, but	Sisemi kiswahili, lakini ...	British)/Scottish/ Welsh/Irish/	mskochi/mwelsh/ muairish
How do you say ... in Swahili ...	Unasemaje kwa kiswahili ...?	American/ Canadian/	/mwamerika/ mkanada/
Could you repeat that?	Sema tena	Australian/	mwaustralia/
Speak slowly	Sema pole pole	a New Zealander/	mnyuziland/
I don't know	Sijui	Kenyan	mkenya
where (is)?	wapi?		
here	hapa	The plurals for nationalities begin with "**Wa-**" instead	
when?	lini?	of "**M-**".	
now	sasa		

SIGNS AND COMMON PHRASES

Danger	Hatari!	And two phrases you're more likely to hear than to ever say	
Warning	Angalia!/Onyo!		
Fierce dog!	Mbwa mkali!	Take a picture of me!	Piga picha mimi!
No entry!	Hakuna njia	Help the poor!	Saidia maskini!

ADJECTIVES AND IDIOMS

good (with a prefix at the front)	-zuri	problems, hassles	wasiwasi, matata
		friend	rafiki
bad (ditto)	-baya	sorry, pardon	samahani
big	-kubwa	It's nothing	Si kitu
small	-dogo	Excuse me, let me through	Hebu
a lot of	-ingi		
other/another	-ingine	What's up?	Namna gani?
not bad	si mbaya	If God wills it	Inshallah
OK, right, fine	sawa	(heard often on	
fine, cool	safi	the coast)	
completely	kabisa	please	tafadhali (rare
thing(s)	kitu (vitu)		upcountry and not
No problem	Hakuna wasiwasi/ Hakuna matata		heard much on the coast either)

DAILY NEEDS

Where can I sleep?	Naweza kulala wapi?	table(s)	meza
Can I stay here?	Naweza kulala hapa?	toilet, bathroom	choo, bafu
		men, women	wanaume, wanawakea
room(s)	chumba (vyumba)	washing water	maji ya kuosha
bed(s)	kitanda (vitanda)	hot/cold water	maji moto/baridi
chair(s)	kiti (viti)	I'm hungry	Nina njaa

I'm thirsty	Nina kiu	cheap (also "easy")	rahisi
Is there any ...?	Iko ...? or Kuna ...?	fifty cents	sumni
Yes there is ...	Iko ... or Kuna ...	Reduce the price,	Punguza kidogo!
No there isn't any	Haiko ... or Hakuna ...	come down a little!	
How much?	Ngapi?	shop	duka
money	pesa	bank	benki
What price ...?	Bei gani ...?	post office	posta
How much is ...?	Pesa ngapi ...?	café, restaurant	hoteli
I want...	Nataka ...	telephone	simu
I don't want ...	Sitaki ...	cigarettes	sigara
Give me/Bring	Nipe/Niletee	I'm ill	Mimi mgonjwa
me (can I have?)		doctor	daktari
again/more	tena	hospital	hospitali
enough	tosha/basi	police	polisi
expensive	ghali sana	tip, bribe	chai

TRAVEL AND DIRECTIONS

travel	kusafiri	Where are you going?	Unaenda wapi?
journey	safari	To where?	Mpaka wapi?
bus(es)	bas, basi/mabasi	From where?	Kutoka wapi?
car(s), vehicle/s	gari (magari)	How many	Kilometa ngapi?
taxi	teksi	kilometres?	
bicycle	baiskeli	This road, it goes	Barabara hii, ni njia
train	treni	to ...?	ya ...?
plane	ndege	I'm going to...	Nenda ...
boat/ship	chombo/meli	Move along, squeeze	Songa!/Songa kidogo
petrol	petroli	up a little	
road, path	njia/ndia	Let's go, carry on	Twende, endelea
highway	barabara	straight ahead	moja kwa moja
on foot/walking	kwa miguu	right	kulia
When does it leave?	Inaondoka lini?	left	kushoto
When will we arrive?	Tutafika lini?	up	juu
slowly	pole pole	down	chini
fast, quickly	haraka	I want to get	Nataka kushuka hapa
Wait!/Hang on	Ngoja!/Ngoja kidogo!	off here	
a moment!		The car has	Gari imevunjika
Stop!	Simama!	broken down	

TIME, CALENDAR AND NUMBERS

What time is it?	Saa ngapi?	today	leo
four o'clock	saa nne (ie 4hr	tomorrow	kesho
	past dawn or dusk, in	last week/this	wiki iliopita/wiki hii/
	other words 10am or	week/next week	wiki ijayo
	10pm)	this year	mwaka huu
quarter past	na robo	this month	mwezi huu
half past	na nusu	Monday	jumatatu
quarter to	kasa robo	Tuesday	jumanne
minutes	dakika	Wednesday	jumatano
daytime	mchana	Thursday	alhamisi
night-time	usiku	Friday	ijumaa
dawn	alfajiri	Saturday	jumamosi
morning	asubuhi	Sunday	jumapili
early	mapema	1	moja
yesterday	jana	2	mbili

3	tatu	21	ishirini na moja
4	nne	30	thelathini
5	tano	40	arobaini
6	sita	50	hamsini
7	saba	60	sitini
8	nane	70	sabini
9	tisa	80	themanini
10	kumi	90	tisini
11	kumi na moja	100	mia moja
12	kumi na mbili	121	mia moja na ishirini na moja
20	ishirini	1000	elfu

Menu and food terms

The lists below should be adequate for translating most Swahili menus and explaining what you want, though bear in mind that spelling may vary.

BASICS

barafu	ice	mboga	vegetables
baridi	cold	mchuzi	sauce
chakula	food	meza	table
chemka	boiled	mkate	bread
choma	roast	moto	hot
chumvi	salt	nusu	half
chupa	bottle	nyama	meat
hesabu	bill	piripiri	pepper
ingine	more, another	sahani	plate
kaanga	fried	samaki	fish
kijiko	spoon	siagi	butter, margarine
kisu	knife	sukari	sugar
maji	water, juice	uma	fork
matunda	fruit	yai (mayai)	egg(s)
maziwa	milk		

SNACKS

"bitings"	pre-dinner snacks		flavoured with spices,
chapatti	unleavened, flat wheat		known as *mahamri*
	bread, baked on a		on the coast
	hot plate or in an	maziwalala	yoghurt (literally "milk
	oven (tandoor)		asleep")
halwa	gelatinous sweetmeat,	mkate mayai	"egg-bread"; soft
	like Turkish delight		thin dough wrapped
keki	cake		around fried egg and
kachumbari	tomato, onion and		minced meat
	coriander relish	samosa	deep-fried triangular
kitumbuo	deep-fried rice bread		case of chopped
mandaazi	deep-fried sweet		meat and vegetables
	dough, sometimes	tosti/slice	slice of bread

DISHES

frigisi	chicken giblets	irio/kienyeji/mataha	potato, cabbage and
githeri	Kikuyu dish of beans		beans mashed together
	and corn, sometimes		
	with meat		

kata-kata	("half-half") a mix of whatever is available, usually including spaghetti, beans, rice, goat meat and shredded cabbage and carrot	michicha	spinach cooked with onions and tomatoes
kima	mince	mukimo	pumpkin leaf and potato mash, with corn
koroga	(literally "to stir" or "cook" in Swahili) a meal style, rather than a dish: you buy the ingredients at a *koroga* restaurant and cook them in the garden with the equipment provided	pilau	rice with spices and meat
		sukuma wiki	boiled green leaves, usually a kind of spinach
		ugali/sima	cornmeal boiled to a solid porridge with water, occasionally milk; yellow ugali is considered inferior to white but is more nutritious
matoke	green banana, usually boiled and mashed		
mboga	vegetables usually potatoes, carrots and onions in meaty gravy	uji	porridge or gruel made of millet; good for chilly mornings
mchele	plain white rice	wali	rice with added fat and spices (almost pilau)

MEAT

kondo	lamb	ng'ombe	beef
kuku	chicken	nguruwe	pork
mbuzi	goat	nyama choma	roast meat
mushkaki	kebab; small pieces of grilled, marinated meat on or off the skewer	steki	steak, grilled meat

FRUIT

limau	lime	nazi	coconuts
machungwa	oranges	ndimu	lemon
madafu	green coconuts	ndizi	bananas
maembe	mangos	papai	papaya/pawpaw
mastafeli	soursops	parachichi	avocado
matopetope	custard apples	pera	guava
nanasi	pineapple	sandara	mandarins

VEGETABLES

maharagwe	red kidney beans, often cooked with coconut	muhogo	cassava
		ndizi	bananas or plantains
		nyanya	tomatoes (also means "grandmother")
mahindi	maize		
mbaazi	pigeon peas, small beans	viazi	potatoes
mtama	millet	vitunguu	onions

DRINKS

busaa	maize beer		and millet beer
chai, chai kavu, chai strungi	tea, black tea, strongly spiced tea	mabziwalala	fermented milk/almost yoghurt
changa'a	hooch, illegal spirits	kahawa	coffee
mnazi	coconut palm wine	bia, tembo	beer
muratina	porridgey Kikuyu honey	pombe	booze

Swahili animal names

Animal is **mnyama** (plural **wanyama**) but the names of most species are the same in singular and plural.

Aardvark	Muhanga	Kudu	Tandala
Baboon	Nyani	Leopard	Chui
Bat-eared fox	Bweha masigio	Lion	Simba
Bird (also	Ndege	Lizard	Mjusi
means plane)		Mongoose	Nguchiro
Buffalo	Nyati	Monkey (usually	Kima
Bushbaby	Komba	Sykes' monkey)	
Cane rat	Ndeze	Oribi	Taya
Caracal	Simbamangu	Oryx	Choroa
Cat	Paka	Ostrich	Mbuni
Cheetah	Duma	Otter	Fisi maji
Chimpanzee	Soko	Pangolin	Kakukuona
Civet	Fungo	Pig, hog	Nguruwe
Colobus monkey	Mbega	Porcupine	Nungu
Crocodile	Mamba	Ratel	Nyegere
De Brazza's monkey	Kalasinga	Reedbuck	Tohe
Dog	Mbwa	Rhinoceros	Faru
Duiker	Nsya	Roan antelope	Korongo
Eland	Pofu	Rock hyrax	Pimbi
Elephant	Ndovu	Sable antelope	Pala hala
Elephant shrew	Sange	Serval	Mondo
Genet	Kanu	Shark	Papa
Gerenuk	Swala twiga	Snake	Nyoka
Giraffe	Twiga	Springhare	Kamandegere
Grant's gazelle	Swala granti	Steinbok, grysbok	Dondoo
Ground squirrel	Kindi	Suni antelope	Paa
Hare, rabbit	Sunguru	Thomson's gazelle	Swala tomi
Hartebeest	Kongoni	Topi	Nyamera
Hedgehog	Kalunguyeye	Tortoise	Kobe
Hippopotamus	Kiboko	Tree hyrax	Pembere
Horse, ass	Punda	Vervet monkey	Tumbili
Hunting dog	Mbwa mwitu	Warthog	Ngiri
Hyena	Fisi	Waterbuck	Kuru
Impala	Swala pala	Wild cat	Paka pori
Insect, bug	Mdudu	Wildebeest	Nyumbu
Jackal	Bweha	Zebra	Punda milia
Klipspringer	Mbuzi mawe		

Regional languages

Kenya's many languages are grouped into related clusters, comparable to Romance and Germanic languages in Europe. "Bantu", a word coined by twentieth-century linguists, derives from the common stem for "person" – ntu – and the plural prefix – ba – found in most of the six hundred contemporary Bantu languages across Africa. Look out for the way names vary with context: Mkamba, for example, refers to a Kamba person, Wakamba to Kamba people and Kikamba to the Kamba language. The following brief word lists are intended only for introductions and as a springboard for communication. If you'll be spending time in a particular linguistic region, you may be surprised at how difficult it is to track down usable primers and phrasebooks for these languages.

KALENJIN (RIFT VALLEY)

Hi, hello	Chamgei	1	Akenge
Sleep well	Rui komie	2	Aena
Goodbye	Sai sere	3	Somok
Thank you	Kongoe	4	Angwan
Good	Kararan	5	Mut
Yes	Uoi	6	Lo
No	Adja	7	Tisap
How are you?	I amu ne?	8	Sisit
Fine	Misi	9	Sokol
I am hungry	Ama rubet!	10	Taman

KAMBA (UKAMBANI, EAST OF NAIROBI)

How are you (sing.)?	Wimuseo?	Goodbye/go well (staying, pl.)	Endai noseo
Fine (sing.)	Nikuseo		
How are you (pl.)?	Mwiaseo?	1	Imwe
Fine (pl.)	Twiaseo	2	Ile
How are things?	Maundu mailye ata?	3	Itatu
Things are well	Maundu ni maseo	4	Inya
No problem /nothing wrong	Aiyie	5	Itano
		6	Thanthatu
Goodbye (leaving, sing.)	Tiwa noseo	7	Muonza
Goodbye (leaving, pl.)	Tiwai na useo	8	Nyanya
Goodbye/go well (staying, sing.)	Enda noseo	9	Kenda
		10	Ikumi

KIKUYU (CENTRAL HIGHLANDS)

How are things?	Kweruo atia?	3	Ithatu
Fine!	Ni kuega!	4	Inya
Are you well? (pl.)	Wi mwega/Muri ega?	5	Ithano
Response ("Nothing wrong")	Asha, ndi mwega	6	Ithathatu
		7	Mugwanja
Goodbye	Tigwo na wega	8	Inyanya
Goodbye (staying)	Thii na wega	9	Kenda
1	Imwe	10	Ikumi
2	Igiri		

LUHYA (KAKAMEGA & WESTERN KENYA)

Good morning	Vushele (boo-sher-ae)	1	Indala
Hello, Good afternoon	Mulembe (moo-rem-bae)	2	Zivili
Good evening	Vwakhila (wah-hee-ra)	3	Vizaka
Responses	Vushele muno,	4	Zinee
	Mulembe muno,	5	Ziranu
	Vwakhila muno	6	Zisasava
How are you?	Karina?	7	Saba
Well, very well	Malahi (ma-lay-ee),	8	Munane
	Malahi sana	9	Tisa
Thank you	Urio muno (or-e-om-ono)	10	Likhomi
Goodbye	Vulahi (vu-lay-ee)		

LUO (LAKE VICTORIA)

How do you do?	Iriyo nade?	1	Achiel
Response	Ariyo maber!	2	Ariyo
Thank you	Erokamano	3	Adek

KENYA'S MAIN LANGUAGE GROUPS

Bantu-speaking
Western Bantu: Luhya, Gusii, Kuria
Central Bantu: Kamba, Kikuyu, Embu, Meru, Mbere, Tharaka
Coastal Bantu: Swahili, Mijikenda, Segeju, Pokomo, Taita, Taveta

Cushitic-speaking
Southern Cushitic: Boni
Eastern Cushitic: Somali, Rendille, Orma, Boran, Gabbra ("Oromo" is often used collectively for all four languages)

Nilotic-speaking
Lake-River Nilotic: Luo
Plains Nilotic: Maasai and Samburu (Maa-speakers), Turkana, Teso, Njemps, Elmolo
Highland Nilotic: Kalenjin (Nandi and its dialects), Marakwet, Pokot, Tugen, Kipsigis, Elkony

4	Angwen	8		Aboro	
5	Abich	9		Ochiko	
6	Auchiely	10		Apar	
7	Abiriyo				

MAA (MAASAI)

Greetings to a man	Lo murrani! Supa!	3		Okuni
Response	Ipa!	4		Oonguan
Greetings to a woman	Na kitok! Takuenya!	5		Imiet
Response	Iko!	6		Ile
Thank you (very much!)	Ashe (naleng!)	7		Oopishana
Goodbye!	Sere!	8		Isiet
1	Obo	9		Ooudo
2	Aare	10		Tomon

Glossary

These words – not all of them Swahili – are all in common usage. Remember, however, that plural forms often have different beginnings.

Administration Police (AP) Paramilitary police force, often stationed in areas of ethnic conflict

Age-set/age grade Generation who have passed through rites of passage together, often including people of widely differing chronological ages

ASK Agricultural Society of Kenya

Askari Policeman, security guard, soldier

Banda Any kind of hut, usually round and thatched

Bangi, Bhang Marijuana

Baobab Species of tree whose trunk retains water

Barabara Main road

Bau Traditional calculation game of pebbles and holes

Boarding & lodging (B&L) Cheap guesthouse

Boda-boda Bicycle taxi

Boma A fort or defensive stockade, often used to mean a small village or cluster of huts

Boriti Mangrove poles, used on the coast for building and exported to the Gulf states for the same purpose

Buibui The black cover-all cloak and scarf of Swahili women

Bwana Mister, a polite form of address

Chai Not just tea, but also the common term for a tip, or more often a small bribe or persuasion

Choo Toilet (pronounced "cho")

Conservancy Private or communally owned land given over to conservation and controlled tourism

CORD Coalition for Reform and Democracy, the main opposition grouping after the March 2013 elections (see "Jubilee")

Day & Night Club Low-budget, 24-hour bar and occasional music club

Duka Shop, store

Duka la dawa Chemist

Enkang Maasai village

Fundi Mechanic, craftsman, expert

Gari Car

Gema The ethnic grouping of Gikuyu (Kikuyu), Embu and Meru

General Service Unit (GSU) Paramilitary security unit reporting directly to the president

GK or GOK Government of Kenya

Group ranch Community-owned grazing area with title deeds, rather than traditional rights

Harambee "Pull together" – the ideology of peaceable community development espoused by Jomo Kenyatta. *Harambee* meetings are local fund-raising gatherings for schools, clinics, etc.

Hoteli Small restaurant, tea shop or café

Jamhuri Republic

Jiko Kitchen or cooker

Jua kali "Hot sun" – open-air car repairer's yard or small workshop

Jubilee The coalition of parties in power after the March 2013 elections (see "CORD")

Kanga Printed cotton sheet used as a wrap, often incorporating a motto

Kanisa Church

KBC Kenya Broadcasting Corporation

Kikoi Brightly coloured woven cloth

KPSGA Kenya Professional Safari Guides Association

Kopje A small, isolated hill

KWS Kenya Wildlife Service

Laibon Maasai spiritual leader, with the status of regional headman

Lugga/Laga Dry river valley (usually in the north)

Mabati Corrugated-iron roofing sheets

Maendeleo Progress, development

Madaraka Independence

Magendo Corruption, bribery, abuse of power

Majimboism The creation of federal blocks in formerly heterogeneous regions – these days associated with ethnic cleansing

Makonde Beautifully worked Tanzanian woodcarving, typically in ebony and representing entwined spirit families

Makutano Junction

Makuti Palm-leaf roof common on the coast

Malaika Angel

Malaya Prostitute

Mama Common term of address for married women

Manamba Matatu tout, "turnboy"

Manyatta Temporary cattle camp, often loosely used for a village (Maasai)

Maskini The poor, beggars (*Saidia maskini!* "Help the poor!")

Matatu Shared minibus

Mbenzi Member of the rich elite (presumed to have a Mercedes; plural *wabenzi*)

Mbuyu Baobab (Swahili)

Mgeni Guest, tourist (pl. *wageni*)

Mgunga Acacia or gum arabic tree (Swahili)

Miraa Qat or khat, a natural stimulant

Mitumba Second-hand clothes, imported in bulk from Europe and sold at the roadside and in markets around the country

Mkenya Kenyan (pl. *wakenya*)

Mkoko Mangrove

Moran Man in the warrior age group of Maasai or Samburu (pl. *morani*)

Msikiti Mosque

Mtalii Tourist (pl. *watalii*)

Mtoto Child (pl. *watoto*)

Mungiki Anti-establishment Kikuyu youth cult that violently rejects Western values

Mungu God

Murram Red or black clay soil, usually referring to a road

Mwananchi Person, peasant, worker (pl. *wananchi*)

Mzee Old man – "the Mzee" is Kenyatta

Mzungu White person (pl. *wazungu*)

NCCK National Christian Council of Kenya

Ngai Supreme god of the Kikuyu and other groups

NGO Non-governmental organization

Ngoma Dancing, drumming, party, celebration

Njia Road, path

Nyama Animal, game, meat

Nyayo "Footsteps" – the follow-in-his-footsteps philosophy of post-Kenyatta Kenya propounded by President Moi

PEV The post-election violence of 2007–2008

Panga Multipurpose short machete carried everywhere in the countryside

Pesa Money, cash

Pombe Booze

Rondavel Round hut or small house (see *banda*)

SACCO Savings and credit co-operative (or credit union) – popular in rural areas for providing a shared-ownership matatu for transport, income and credit

Safari Journey of any kind, but in the modern sense a trip of one or more days to see animals

Shamba Small farm, plot

Sista Informal term of address to young woman

Slum Any area of poor housing (no pejorative connotation)

Soda Fizzy drink, but also a euphemism for a tip

Soja Soldier, watchman, guard

Stage Matatu stand

Syce Groom or stable hand

Uhuru Freedom, independence

Ukimwi AIDS

Ulaya Europe

Upcountry The lands and culture of the interior, notably the highlands, as distinct from the coast

Wageni See *mgeni*

Wananchi See *mwananchi*

Watu Literally "people", but often used slightly disparagingly by expats and Anglo-Kenyans, especially when referring to their staff

Wazungu See *mzungu*

Small print and index

A ROUGH GUIDE TO ROUGH GUIDES

Published in 1982, the first Rough Guide – to Greece – was a student scheme that became a publishing phenomenon. Mark Ellingham, a recent graduate in English from Bristol University, had been travelling in Greece the previous summer and couldn't find the right guidebook. With a small group of friends he wrote his own guide, combining a highly contemporary, journalistic style with a thoroughly practical approach to travellers' needs.

The immediate success of the book spawned a series that rapidly covered dozens of destinations. And, in addition to impecunious backpackers, Rough Guides soon acquired a much broader readership that relished the guides' wit and inquisitiveness as much as their enthusiastic, critical approach and value-for-money ethos.

These days, Rough Guides include recommendations from budget to luxury and cover more than 120 destinations around the globe, as well as producing an ever-growing range of ebooks.

Visit **roughguides.com** to find all our latest books, read articles, get inspired and share travel tips with the Rough Guides community.

Rough Guide credits

Editors: Edward Aves, Samantha Cook and Tim Locke
Layout: Ankur Guha and Pradeep Thapliyal
Cartography: Rajesh Chhibber and Swati Handoo
Picture editor: Marta Bescos
Proofreader: Jennifer Speake
Managing editor: Andy Turner
Assistant editor: Divya Grace Mathew

Production: Jimmy Lao
Cover photo research: Nicole Newman
Editorial assistant: Freya Godfrey
Senior pre-press designer: Dan May
Programme manager: Gareth Lowe
Publisher: Keith Drew
Publishing director: Georgina Dee

Publishing information

This eleventh edition published May 2016 by
Rough Guides Ltd,
80 Strand, London WC2R 0RL
11, Community Centre, Panchsheel Park,
New Delhi 110017, India
Distributed by Penguin Random House
Penguin Books Ltd, 80 Strand, London WC2R 0RL
Penguin Group (USA), 345 Hudson Street, NY 10014, USA
Penguin Group (Australia), 250 Camberwell Road,
Camberwell, Victoria 3124, Australia
Penguin Group (NZ), 67 Apollo Drive, Mairangi Bay,
Auckland 1310, New Zealand
Penguin Group (South Africa), Block D, Rosebank Office
Park, 181 Jan Smuts Avenue, Parktown North, Gauteng,
South Africa 2193
Rough Guides is represented in Canada by DK Canada, 320
Front Street West, Suite 1400,Toronto, Ontario M5V 3B6
Printed in Singapore
© Rough Guides, 2016
Maps © Rough Guides

632pp includes index
A catalogue record for this book is available from the
British Library
ISBN: 978-0-24124-148-6
1 3 5 7 9 8 6 4 2

MIX
Paper from
responsible sources
FSC™ C018179

Help us update

We've gone to a lot of effort to ensure that the eleventh
edition of **The Rough Guide to Kenya** is accurate and up-
to-date. However, things change – places get "discovered",
opening hours are notoriously fickle, restaurants and
rooms raise prices or lower standards. If you feel we've got
it wrong or left something out, we'd like to know, and if
you can remember the address, the price, the hours, the
phone number, so much the better.

Please send your comments with the subject line
"**Rough Guide Kenya Update**" to mail@uk.roughguides
.com. We'll credit all contributions and send a copy of the
next edition (or any other Rough Guide if you prefer) for
the very best emails.

Find more travel information, connect with fellow
travellers and plan your trip on Ⓦroughguides.com.

ABOUT THE AUTHORS

Richard Trillo (@richardtrillo.com) is the Kenya Programme Manager at Expert Africa, a UK tour operator specializing in tailor-made trips to East and southern Africa. For many years he was Director of Communications at Rough Guides, and as well as *The Rough Guide to Kenya* he is the author of *the Rough Guide to West Africa* and co-author of *The Rough Guide to First-Time Africa*. He has travelled widely in Africa on every kind of budget and, since first visiting Kenya in 1981, has covered the length and breadth of the country many times. He has a master's degree in anthropology and African linguistics from the School of Oriental and African Studies, London University, but his first passion was wildlife – his childhood ambition to be a zoologist was thwarted by a total impatience with chemistry. He lives in remote suburbia with his wife, Teresa Driver, and their transient offspring.

Harriet Constable is a freelance journalist and blogger based between London and Nairobi. She specializes in travel, food and lifestyle and her work is mostly feature-length pieces for online and print. She writes for the *Financial Times, SUITCASE Magazine, Wanderlust* and more. She has stepped foot on every continent.

Hilary Heuler is a freelance journalist, researcher and travel writer who has spent the last decade or so exploring and writing about Europe, Asia and nearly half the countries in Africa. When not braving potholes and cramped matatus, she can be found at home in Nairobi with her husband and three dogs.

Lizzie Williams Originally from the UK, Lizzie has been travelling in Africa for more than twenty years, first as a tour guide on overland trucks and now as a guidebook writer. She has authored and contributed to more than fifty titles for various publishers. When not on the road, Lizzie lives in beautiful Cape Town.

Acknowledgements

Richard Trillo My eternal gratitude goes to Jeremy Torr for his English Cycles mountain bike that got me around Kenya on the first edition, and for assistance from Jackie Switzer, Rosie Mercer and the Khans in Kisii. For work on previous editions, my continuing thanks to Daniel Jacobs, Emma Gregg, Jens Finke, Nana Luckham, Okigbo Ojukwu, Matt Brown, Ayako Bertolli and Hilary Heuler.

For their much tested support, all my love and boundless thanks to Teresa and to our children, for whom Kenya and the Rough Guide were part of growing up. On this edition, very grateful thanks go to researcher-updaters Hilary Heuler (once again) and to Lizzie Williams and Harriet Constable for all the graft on the ground. Many thanks as ever to Doug Paterson and Werner Graebner for musical input. At Rough Guides, huge thanks to my patient and perceptive editor Ed Aves, magnificently supported by Sam Cook and Tim Locke; to Rajesh Chibber and Swati Handoo for all their work on the maps; to Ankur Guha and Pradeep Thapliyal for layout; Marta Bescos for picture research; Nicole Newman for a memorable new cover; and Lottie Gross, Tom Waller, Duncan Campbell and Rebecca Hallett for connections.

At Expert Africa, many thanks to Chris McIntyre, Ellie Dunkels and my other colleagues for their unstinting support for our Kenya programme and their contributions to this edition and the last. My grateful thanks too, to the many Expert Africa travellers whose experiences in Kenya are posted in our reports on camps and lodges on the @expertafrica.com website.

For kind help and information, many thanks to Jake Grieves-Cook and Mohanjeet Brar at Gamewatchers; journalists Wolfgang Thome, Brian Jackman and John Aglionby; Monika Solanki at Lofty Tours; Mohammed Hersi at Heritage; Matthew Wilkinson at @safaritalk.com; Romain Mari at Distant Relatives; Alan Dixson at Uniglobe Let's Go Travel; Kate Kenward at AITO; Daniela Resentera, Josie Self and Sophie Banna at the Kenya Tourist Board in London; Ndolo Kaleli; and Robert Gordon and family.

Harriet Constable Many thanks to Olive Group (@olivegroup.com), who provided handy tracking equipment during my trip.

Lizzie Williams would like to thank: Perrie Hennessy at *Island Camp* and Chala at *Roberts' Camp*, Lake Baringo; the Carnelley family at Camp Carnelley's at Lake Naivasha; Cathy at KWS in Nairobi and Grace and Johan at KWS at Lake Nakuru National Park; Job and Nicholas at *Flamingo Hill Camp* in Lake Nakuru National Park and Carol at African Connections; Betty Olwenyi at Mada Hotels; Manja Seifert at *Severin Safari Camp*, Tsavo West National Park. Valerie at *The Sleeping Warrior* at Lake Elmenteita; Menno Bartlema and Virginia at *Tawi Lodge* and Doris and Irene at *Kibo Safari Camp*, Amboseli National Park; and Basil Criticos and Patrick at *Grogan's Castle*. Finally, many thanks for the wheels to Mohez Karmali, Cathy, Aimee and Michael at Concorde Car Hire & Safaris in Nairobi.

Readers' updates

Many thanks to the following readers for their letters, comments and emails. Apologies to anyone whose name we have left out.

Ben Anderson; Liliane Barbier; Ann Baudewyn; Debbie Brown; Neil Carrier, Chris Coe; Sandra Cook; Dany Cuyt; Hartmut Fischer; Bee Friedmann; Yuri Horowitz; Suzie Horsley; Bjørn O Isachsen; Otto Kele; Colin & Kay Kenning; Gerda Kuiper; Romuald & Sabine Lambrigts; Jennifer MacLeod; Rupert McCammon; Annick Martineau;

Massimiliano Masa; Rosey Mitchell; Stefan Moosleitner; Neil Morrison; Dorian & Sue Neill; Michael O'Hanlon; Radek Okienczuk; Gavin Parnaby; Scott Patterson; Toby Perry; Margaret Pomfret; Tara Scarfe; Kendra Sutherland; Suzanne Swift; Kim Waruhiu; Judy Wiles; Cathy Winder; Jan Van Wolvelaer.

Photo credits

All photos © Rough Guides except the following:
(Key: a-above, t-top; b-bottom/below; l-left; c-centre; r-right)

p.1 Alamy Images: robertharding
p.2 Alamy Images: Rolf Nussbaumer Photography
p.4 Alamy Images: Matan Golan
p.5 Corbis: Masterfile/Alberto Biscaro
p.9 Getty Images: Nigel Pavitt
p.11 Getty Images: AFP (t); Alamy Images: robertharding (c); Richard Trillo (b)
p.12 Alamy Images: John Warburton-Lee
p.13 Alamy Images: Milesy (t); Getty Images: Panoramic Images (c); Alamy Images: blickwinkel (b)
p.14 Richard Trillo (t); Corbis: Denis-Huot (b)
p.15 Getty Images: Danita Delimont (t); Corbis: David Mbiyu (br)
p.16 Richard Trillo (t); Getty Images: Nigel Pavitt (bl); Getty Images: Steve J. Benbow (br)
p.17 Alamy Images: Lee Dalton (t); Getty Images: Nigel Pavitt (b)
p.18 Getty Images: Nigel Pavitt (t)
p.19 Richard Trillo (t, b); Alamy Images: Ariadne Van Zandbergen (c)
p.20 Getty Images: Nigel Pavitt (l, r); Getty Images: Joseph Van Os (c)
p.25 NaturePL: Anup Shah (tl, c, br); NaturePL: Andy Rouse (tr); NaturePL: Ole Jorgen Liodden (bl)
p.27 NaturePL: Laurent Geslin (t); NaturePL: Nick Garbutt (cl); Corbis: Suzi Eszterhas (cr); Getty Images: Joe McDonald (b)
p.29 Getty Images: Visuals Unlimited, Inc/Joe McDonald (tl); NaturePL: Charlie Summers (tr, cl); NaturePL: Anup Shah (cr); Corbis: NaturePL: Christophe Courteau (bl); Joe Petersburger (br)
p.31 NaturePL: Andy Rouse (t); NaturePL: Anup Shah (b)
p.33 NaturePL: Anup Shah (tl, cl); NaturePL: Mark Carwardine (tr); NaturePL: Tony Heald (cr); NaturePL: Roland Seitre (bl); Getty Images: Roger de la Harpe (br)
p.35 NaturePL: Andy Rouse (tl); Getty Images: Sue Flood (tr); NaturePL: Tony Heald (cl); NaturePL: T.J. Rich (cr); NaturePL: Jeff Vanuga (bl); NaturePL: Suzi Eszterhas (br)
p.37 NaturePL: Anup Shah (tl, bc, bl); NaturePL: Visuals Unlimited (tr); Getty Images: (acl); NaturePL: Bernard Castelein (acr); NaturePL: Tony Heald (bcl); Anup Shah (bcr); NaturePL: Ann & Steve Toon (br)
p.39 NaturePL: Visuals Unlimited (tl); NaturePL: David Noton (tc); NaturePL: Tony Heald (tr, bl); NaturePL: Peter Blackwell (cl); NaturePL: Richard Du Toit (cr, br)
p.41 NaturePL: Anup Shah (tl, cl); NaturePL: Rod Williams (tr); NaturePL: Jabruson (cr); NaturePL: Charlie Summers (bl); NaturePL: Paul Hobson (bc); NaturePL: Philippe Clement (br)

p.43 Getty Images: Martin Harvey (tl); NaturePL: Bernard Castelein (tr, cl); NaturePL: Ann & Steve Toon (bl); NaturePL: Anup Shah (br)
p.45 NaturePL: Peter Blackwell (tl); NaturePL: Rod Williams (tr); Alamy Images: Ivan Kuzmin (acl); NaturePL: Pete Oxford (bcl); NaturePL: Anup Shah (cr); NaturePL: Doug Perrine (b)
pp.96–97 Corbis: Keith Levit
p.99 Alamy Images: Barbara von Hoffmann
p.121 Alamy Images: Greenshoots Communications (t); Alamy Images: Xavi Herrero (b)
p.135 Alamy Images: Zute Lightfoot (t); Corbis: Xinhua Press/Ding Haitao (b)
p.145 Alamy Images: Mark Pearson (t); Getty Images: Nigel Pavitt (b)
pp.156–157 Alamy Images: Michele Burgess
p.159 Getty Images: Pat Parsons
p.177 Alamy Images: Bill Gozansky
pp.200–201 Corbis: Denis-Huot
p.203 Corbis: William Gray
p.229 Corbis: Juan-Carlos Muñoz (t); Getty Images: Nigel Pavitt (b)
pp.248–249 Getty Images: Nigel Pavitt
p.251 Getty Images: Nigel Pavitt
p.269 Getty Images: Nigel Pavitt
p.293 Alamy Images: Ariadne Van Zandbergen (t, b)
pp.310–311 Getty Images: Nico Tondini
p.313 Getty Images: Nigel Pavitt
p.343 Getty Images: Nigel Pavitt (t); Alamy Images: sonnenklang-photo (b)
p.365 Getty Images: Keith Lewis (t); Richard Trillo: (b)
pp.386–387 Getty Images: Nigel Pavitt
p.389 Getty Images: John Warburton-Lee
p.417 Alamy Images: Julio Etchart (t); Getty Images: Nigel Pavitt (b)
p.443 Alamy Images: dbimages (t); Alamy Images: Ian Wood (b)
p.473 Getty Images: Nigel Pavitt
pp.500–501 Richard Trillo
p.503 Corbis: David Mbiyu
p.511 William Manning (t); Getty Images: John Warburton-Lee (b)
p.545 Getty Images: Nigel Pavitt (t, b)
p.554 Alamy Images: Eric Lafforgue

Front cover and spine A mother cheetah and cub, Maasai Mara © AWL Images: JAS
Back cover African elephant © Alamy Images: Design Pics Inc (t); canoes off Diani Beach © AWL Images: Nigel Pavitt (bl); giant lobelia rosette, Mount Kenya © AWL Images: Danita Delimont Stock (br)

Index

Maps are marked in grey

E

Map symbols

The symbols below are used on maps throughout the book

	Major road (mostly paved)		Park HQ		Post office
	Minor road (mostly unpaved)		Gate		Parking
	Unpaved road		Campsite		Monastery
	Mountain or hill range		Monument		Synagogue
	Mountain peak		Airport		Mosque
	Escarpment		Airstrip		Temple
	Cliff		Ruin		Church
	Viewpoint		Bus or matatu stop		Building
	Crater		Petrol station		Stadium
	Cave		Hospital		Christian cemetery
	Waterfall		Internet access		Muslim cemetery
	Marshland		Information office		Park/reserve
	Spring		Telephone		Beach
	Point of interest		Arch		Forest
	Lighthouse		Forest		Mangrove
	Picnic area		Baobabs		Coral reef
	Golf course		Palms		
	Lodge		Rainforest		

Listings key

- Accommodation
- Eating
- Drinking and nightlife
- Shopping

Talk to an expert: call the author...

I first went to Kenya in 1981 at the end of an independent overland trip through Africa. We spent six months there, taking buses, matatus and the train (which still ran twice daily) grabbing lifts and cycling all over the country. On our very first safari – camping in the Maasai Mara – we watched in awe as hordes of wildebeest surged up the riverbank towards us, and huge crocs thrashed around in the brown waters.

I went back a few years later to research this Rough Guide – the first practical guide to Kenya – and I've since been back countless times to update the guide, write newspaper and magazine articles and go on family safaris. Our first trip with the children – Alex aged 4 and David aged 5 months – started with a Christmas eve drive from Nairobi to the Maasai Mara, in heavy rain. Our latest family trip featured Maasai warrior training, a safari in the shadow of Kilimanjaro and the perfect family house on Tiwi Beach.

Although I've been all over Kenya, there is always a host of new discoveries each time I return. My most recent experiences have been hiking in the cloud forest of the Chyulu Hills, exploring the wild dog country of Laikipia and – to my delight – seeing rhinos in the Maasai Mara for the first time in 30 years.

I'm happy to admit it – I'm a Kenya travel addict. And since 2012 I have been part of the team at the award-winning tour operator **Expert Africa**, passing on my knowledge and experience through the safari programme I've created.

I'm on hand to discuss Expert Africa's unusually diverse range of camps and lodges in Kenya, and help you plan the perfect trip.

Chat through your ideas with me or one of my expert colleagues on the numbers below. Or email me at richard.trillo@expertafrica.com and I'll get straight back to you.

Richard Trillo